A SELECT LIBRARY

OF THE

NICENE AND POST-NICENE FATHERS

OF

THE CHRISTIAN CHURCH

EDITED BY

PHILIP SCHAFF, D.D., LL.D.,

PROFESSOR IN THE UNION THEOLOGICAL SEMINARY, NEW YORK,

IN CONNECTION WITH A NUMBER OF PATRISTIC SCHOLARS OF EUROPE AND AMERICA

VOLUME VI

SAINT AUGUSTIN:

SERMON ON THE MOUNT   HARMONY OF THE GOSPELS

HOMILIES ON THE GOSPELS

T&T CLARK
EDINBURGH

WM. B. EERDMANS PUBLISHING COMPANY
GRAND RAPIDS, MICHIGAN

British Library Cataloguing in Publication Data

Nicene & Post-Nicene Fathers. — 1st series
1. Fathers of the church
I. Title   II. Schaff, Philip
230′.11   BR60.A62

T&T Clark ISBN 0 567 09395 6

Eerdmans ISBN 0-8028-8103-3

Reprinted, January 1991

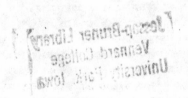

CONTENTS.

PREFACE.

THIS volume contains the exegetical and homiletical writings of St. Augustin on the Gospels.

The seventh volume will be devoted to his Commentary on the Gospel and First Epistle of John, and the Soliloquies. It will be finished by the 1st of next April.

The eighth and last volume is reserved for his Commentary on the Psalms, and will appear in July, 1888.

These eight volumes will form the most complete edition of St. Augustin's Works in the English language, embracing the Edinburgh and Oxford translations, and several treatises never before translated, with introductions and explanatory notes.

Arrangements have been made for the regular issue of the Works of St. Chrysostom according to the terms of the Publisher's Prospectus, which so far has been promptly carried out. The favourable reception of the preceding volumes by the public and the press, including some leading theological journals of Europe (such as *The Church Quarterly Review*, and Harnack's *Theologische Literaturzeitung*), will encourage the editor and publisher to carry on this Patristic Library with undiminished energy and zeal.

PHILIP SCHAFF.

NEW YORK, December, 1887.

INTRODUCTORY ESSAY.

ST. AUGUSTIN AS AN EXEGETE.

BY THE REV. DAVID SCHLEY SCHAFF.

THE exegetical writings of Augustin are commentaries on Genesis (first three chapters), the Psalms, the Gospel and First Epistle of John, the Sermon on the Mount, the Epistles to the Romans and Galatians, and a *Harmony of the Gospels*. Many of his commentaries, like those of Chrysostom, are expository homilies preached to his congregation at Hippo; all are practical rather than grammatical and critical. He only covered the first five verses of the first chapter of Romans, and found his comments so elaborate, that, from fear of the immense proportions a commentary on the whole Epistle would assume, he drew back from the task. Augustin's other writings abound in quotations from Scripture, and pertinent expositions. His controversies with the Manichæans and Donatists were particularly adapted to render him thorough in the knowledge of the Bible, and skilled in its use.

The opinions of Augustin's ability as an exegete, and the worth of his labors in the department of connected Biblical exposition, have greatly differed. Some not only represent him at his weakest in this capacity, but disparage his exegesis as of inferior merit. Others have given him, and some at the present time still give him, a very high rank among the chief commentators of the early Church. Père Simon, as quoted by Archbishop Trench (*Sermon on the Mount*, p. 65), says, "One must needs read a vast deal in the exegetical writings of Augustin to light on any thing which is good." Reuss expresses himself thus: "The fact is, that his exegesis was the weak side of the great man" (*Gesch. d. heil. Schriften N. T.* p. 263). Farrar, in his *History of Interpretation* (p. 24), declares his comments to be "sometimes painfully beside the mark," and in general depreciates the value of Augustin's expository writings.

On the other hand, the student is struck with the profound esteem in which Augustin was held as an interpreter of Scripture during the Middle Ages. His exposition was looked upon as the highest authority; and a saying was current, that, if one had Augustin on his side, it was sufficient (*Si Augustinus adest, sufficit ipse tibi*). So powerful was his influence, that Rupert of Deutz, in the preface to his Commentary on St. John, deemed it necessary to state, in part in vindication of his own effort, that, though the eagle wings of the Bishop of Hippo overshadowed the Gospel, he did not exhaust the right of all Christians to handle the Gospel. The Reformers quote Augustin more frequently than any Father, and were greatly indebted to his writings, especially for their views on sin and grace. Among modern opinions according to him a high rank in this department may be mentioned two. The Rev. H. Browne, in the preface to the translation of Augustin's *Homilies on St. John*, in the Oxford Library of the Fathers (I. vi.), is somewhat extravagant in his praise, when he says, that, "as an interpreter of the Word of God, St. Augustin is acknowledged to stand at an elevation which few have reached, none surpassed." Archbishop Trench, in the essay on Augustin as an interpreter of Scripture, prefixed to his edition of the

Sermon on the Mount, accords equal praise, and speaks specifically of the "tact and skill with which he unfolded to others the riches which the Word contains" (p. 133).

The truth certainly is not with those who minimize Augustin's services in the department of exposition. Whether we compare him with ancient or modern commentators, he will fall behind the greatest in some particulars; but in profundity of insight into the meaning of the text, in comprehensive knowledge of the whole Scriptures, in simplicity of spiritual aim, he stands in the first rank. It is as a contributor to theological and religious thought that he asserts his eminence. Exposition is something more than bald textual and lexicographical comment: it aims also at a spiritual perception of the truth as it is in Christ, and requires a capacity to extract, for the spiritual nutriment of the reader, the vital forces of the Scriptures. In this sense Augustin is eminently worthy of study. Of textual details, he gives only the barest minimum of any value. His mistakes, arising out of his slender philological apparatus and his reverence for the LXX., are numerous and glaring. He often wanders far away from the plain meaning of the text, into allegorical and typical fancies, like the other Fathers, and many of the older Protestant commentators. He was not prepared for, nor did he aim at, grammatico-historical exegesis in the modern sense of the word; but he possessed extraordinary acumen and depth, spiritual insight, an uncommon knowledge of Scripture as a whole, and a pious intention to bring the truth to the convictions of men, and to extend the kingdom of Christ.

As to Augustin's special equipment for the work of an exegete and on his exegetical principles, the following may be added: —

EXEGETICAL EQUIPMENT.

1. Augustin had no knowledge of Hebrew (*Confessions*, xi. 3; in this ed. vol. i. p. 164). His knowledge of Greek was only superficial, and far inferior to that of Jerome (vol. i. p. 9). He depended almost entirely on the imperfect old Latin version before its revision by Jerome, and was at first even prejudiced against this revision, the so-called Vulgate. But it should be remembered that only two of the great expositors of the ancient Church were familiar with Hebrew, — Origen and Jerome. Augustin knew only a few Hebrew words. In the treatise on *Christian Doctrine* (ii. 11, 16; this ed. vol. ii. p. 540) he adduces the words *Amen* and *Hallelujah* as being left untranslated on account of the sacredness of the original forms, and the words *Racha* and *Hosanna* as being untranslatable by any single Latin equivalents. In the *Sermon on the Mount* (i. 9, 23) he refers again to *Racha*, and defends its Hebrew origin as against those who derived it from the Greek term ῥάκος (a rag).

Augustin's linguistic attainments seem to have included familiarity with Punic (*Sermon on the Mount*, ii. 14, 47). The Phoenician origin of the North African people, the location of his birthplace and his episcopal diocese, furnish an explanation of this.

2. For the Old Testament, Augustin used, besides the Latin version, occasionally the Septuagint, and had at hand the versions of Symmachus, Theodotion, and Aquila (*Quæst. in Num.* 52). He had profound reverence for the LXX., and was inclined to give credit to the Jewish tradition that each of the translators was confined in a separate cell, and on comparing their work, which they had accomplished without communication with each other, found their several versions to agree, word for word. He held that the original was given through them in Greek by the special direction of the Holy Spirit, and in such a way as to be most suitable for the Gentiles (*Christian Doctrine*, ii. 15, 22; this ed. p. 542). He declared that the Latin copies were to be corrected from the LXX., which was as authoritative as the Hebrew. Such a claim for the authority of the Greek translation would make a knowledge of the Hebrew almost unnecessary.

This excessive reverence for the LXX. has led Augustin to uphold, in his exegesis of the Old Testament, all its errors of translation, which a different view, coupled with a knowledge of Hebrew, would in most cases have prevented him from accepting. Even at its plain and palpable mistakes he takes no offence. He accepts the translation, "Yet three days and Nineveh shall be overthrown," as of equal authority with the "forty days" of the original, claiming a special symbolic meaning for both.

3. For the New Testament, Augustin used some Latin translation or translations older than the Vulgate. He declares the Latin translations to be without number (*Christian Doctr.* ii. 11, 16; this ed. vol. ii. p. 540). There was already in his day " an endless diversity " of readings in the Latin manuscripts. He vindicated for the Greek original the claim of final authority, to which the Latin copies were to yield. As there was likewise diversity of text among the Greek copies, he laid down the rule, that those manuscripts were to be chosen for comparison by the Latin student which were preserved in the churches of greater learning and research (*Christian Doctr.* ii. 15, 22; in this ed. ii. p. 543). Not infrequently does Augustin cite the readings of the Greek. In some cases he makes references to passages where there is a conflict of text in the Latin authorities. He differs quite largely from Jerome's Vulgate, to which he offered opposition, on the ground that a new translation might unsettle the faith of some. In these variations of construction and language he was sometimes nearer the original than Jerome. Sometimes he does not approximate so closely. As a matter of interest, and for the convenience of the reader, the differences of Augustin's text and the Vulgate will be found, in all important cases, noted down in this edition of the *Sermon on the Mount*.

Examples of Augustin's improvement upon the Vulgate are the omission of the clause, "and despitefully use you " (*et calumniantibus vos*, Matt. v. 44), the use of *quotidianum panem* ("daily bread ") instead of *supersubstantialem*, and of *inferas* ("bring ") instead of *inducas* ("lead "), in the fourth and sixth petitions of the Lord's Prayer (Matt. vi. 11, 12). In reference to the last passage, it must be said, however, that he notes a difference in the Latin MSS., some using *infero*, some *induco*; and while he adopts the former verb, he finds the terms equivalent in meaning (*Serm. on the Mt.* ii. 9, 30).

4. Augustin's textual and grammatical comments are few in number, but they cannot be said to be wanting in all value. A few instances will suffice for a judgment of their merit : —

In the *Harmony of the Gospels* (ii. 29, 67), writing of the daughter of Jairus (Matt. ix. 29), he mentions that some codices contain the reading "woman " (*mulier*) for "damsel." Commenting on Matt. v. 22, "Whosoever is angry with his brother without a cause," he includes the expression "without a cause " (εἰκῇ) without even a hint of its spuriousness (*Serm. on the Mt.* i. 9, 25); but in his *Retractations* (i. 19. 4) he makes the correction, "The Greek manuscripts do not contain *sine causa*." Tischendorf, Westcott and Hort, the Vulgate and the Revised English Version, in agreement with the oldest MSS., omit the clause. He refers to a conflict of the Greek and Latin text of Matt. v. 39 ("Whosoever shall smite thee on thy right cheek "), and follows the authority of the Greek in omitting the adjective "right " (*Serm. on the Mt.* i. 19, 58). At Matt. vi. 4 he casts out, on the authority of the Greek, the adverb *palam* ("openly "), which was found in many Latin translations (as it is also found in the *Textus Receptus*, but not in the Vulgate, and the Sinaitic, B, D, and other MSS.). Commenting on Matt. vii. 12, " Wherefore all things whatsoever ye would that men," etc., he refers to the addition of " good" before " things " by the Latins, and insists upon its erasure on the basis of the Greek text (*Serm. on the Mt.* ii. 22, 74).

On occasion, though very rarely, he quotes the Greek, as in the *Sermon on the Mount* (νὴ τὴν καύχησιν, i. 17, 51; ἱμάτιον, i. 19, 60), in confirmation of his opinions of the text.

At other times he compares Greek and Latin terms of synonymous or kindred meanings. One of the most important of these is the passage (*City of God*, x. 1; this ed. vol. ii. p. 181) where he draws a clear distinction between λατρεία, θρησκεία, εὐσέβεια, θεοσέβεια. Other examples of the kind under review are given by Trench (p. 20 sqq.).

It is evident that Augustin's equipment was defective from the stand-point of the modern critical exegete. It would be wrong, however, to say that he shows no concern about textual questions. But his exegetical power shows itself in other ways than minute textual investigation,

— in comprehensive comparison of Scripture with Scripture, and penetrating spiritual vision. To these qualities he adds a purpose to be exhaustive, sparing no pains to develop the full meaning of the passage under review. More exhaustive discussions can hardly be found, to take a single example, than that on Matt. v. 25, "Agree with thine adversary quickly" (*Serm. on the Mt.* xi. 31, where, however, the view least reasonable is taken), or spiritually satisfactory ones than the discussion of the gradation of sin and its punishment (Matt. v. 21, 22 ; *Serm. on the Mt.* ix. 22), and "Judge not, that ye be not judged " (Matt. vii. 1), or pungently suggestive than the handling of the words of our Lord at the marriage feast at Cana : " Woman, what have I to do with thee ? " (John ii. 4 ; Homily VIII.), or more indicative of great principles underlying the vindication to the evangelists of a true historical character and of independence of each other (at least in minor details) than discussions like that about the differences in the details of the miracle of the five loaves and two fishes, alone common of the miracles to the fourfold Gospel (a sort of prelude to works like Blunt's *Undesigned Coincidences*), and the relation of this miracle to the miracle of the seven loaves (*Harmony*, xlvi.–l.).

EXEGETICAL PRINCIPLES.

Augustin has laid down in a separate treatise a code of exegetical principles. His *Christian Doctrine* (vol. ii. of this series) is the earliest manual of Biblical hermeneutics. In spite of irrelevant and lengthy digressions, it contains many suggestions of value, which have not been improved upon in modern treatises on the subject.

1. He emphasizes Hebrew and Greek scholarship as an important aid to the expositor, and an essential condition of the interpretation of the figurative language of Scripture (ii. 11, 16 ; 16, 23, this ed., pp. 539, 543).

2. He will have his interpreter acquainted with sacred geography (ii. 29, 45, p. 549), natural history (ii. 16, 24, p. 543 ; 29, 45, p. 549), music (ii. 16, 26, p. 544), chronology (ii. 28, 42, p. 549) and the science of numbers (ii. 16, 25, p. 543), natural science generally (ii. 29, 45 sqq., p. 549 sqq.), history (ii. 28, 43, p. 549), dialectics (ii. 31, 48, p. 550), and the writings of the ancient philosophers (ii. 40, 60, p. 554). He was the first to suggest a work which has been realized in our dictionaries of the Bible. Pertinent to the subject he says, " What some men have done in regard to all words and names found in Scripture, in the Hebrew and Syriac and Egyptian and other tongues, taking up and interpreting separately such as were left in Scripture without interpretation ; and what Eusebius has done in regard to the history of the past . . . I think might be done in regard to other matters. . . . For the advantage of his brethren a competent man might arrange in their several classes, and give an account of, the unknown places, and animals and plants, and trees and stones and metals, and other species of things mentioned in Scripture " (ii. 39, 59, p. 554). It is, in view of this sage suggestion, almost incomprehensible that Augustin pays no attention to these subjects in his commentaries. Jerome, on the other hand, is quite rich in these departments.

3. He presses the view that the Scripture is designed to have more interpretations than one (*Christ. Doctr.* iii. 27, 38 sq. ; this ed. p. 567). Augustin constantly applies this canon (e.g., on the petition, " Thy will be done," *Sermon on the Mount*, ii. 7, 21–23). He adopted the seven rules of the Donatist Tichonius as assisting to a deep understanding of the Word. These rules relate (1) to the Lord and His body, (2) to the twofold division of the Lord's body, (3) to the promises and the Law, (4) to species and genus, (5) to times, (6) to recapitulation, (7) to the devil and his body (*Christ. Doctr.* iii. 30, 42, pp. 568–573). He explains and illustrates these laws at length, but denies that they exhaust the rules for discovering the hidden truth of Scripture.

4. He commends the method of interpreting obscure passages by the light of passages that are understood, and prefers it before the interpretation by reason (*Christ. Doctr.* iii. 29, 39, p. 567).

5. The spirit and intent of the interpreter are of more importance than verbal accuracy and critical acumen (a qualification not always too strictly insisted upon in these modern days of commentators and critical Biblical study). One must be in sympathy with the Gospel of Christ to interpret its records.[1] Even the mistakes of an exegete, properly disposed, may confirm religious faith and character; and so far forth are his labors to be commended, though he himself is to be corrected, that he err not again after the same manner. "If the mistaken interpretation," he says, "tends to build up love, which is the end of the commandment, the interpreter goes astray in much the same way as a man who, by mistake, quits the highroad, but yet reaches, through the fields, the same place to which the road leads" (*Christ. Doctr.* i. 36, 41 sq.; ii. p. 533).

That Augustin followed his own canons of interpretation, his writings show. He does not hesitate to put more than one interpretation upon a text (as especially in the Psalms), and none has been more elaborate in comparing Scripture with Scripture than he. If he had possessed the familiarity with the Hebrew that he recommends so strongly to others, he would have been preserved from the misinterpretations with which his commentaries on the Old Testament abound.

USE OF ALLEGORY.

Augustin's use of allegory has exposed him to much harsh criticism. What was the practice of all, ought not to be considered a mortal fault in one. None of the ancient expositors were free from it. Some of the modern expositors, except as their works are designed only as a critical arsenal for the student, are defective because of all absence of the allegorical element.

Where Scripture itself has led the way, as in the case of the allegory of Hagar and Sarah (Gal. iv.) and other cases, the uninspired penman will be pardoned if he follow. The use of the allegorical method, however, was carried to the most unreasonable excess, reaching its culmination in Gregory's Commentary on Job. That writer finds that the patriarch of Uz represents Christ, his sons the clergy, his three daughters the three classes of the laity who are to worship the Trinity, his friends the heretics, the oxen and she-asses the heathen, etc. The frequent extravagance of Augustin, proceeding out of his intellectual and Scriptural exuberance, cannot be commended; but it will be found that his allegory is seldom commonplace, and mingled with it, where it is most vicious, are comments of rare aptness and common sense. In the Old Testament he looks upon almost every character and event as symbolic of Christ and Christian institutions. But, as Trench well says, "it is indeed far better to find Christ everywhere in the Old Testament than to find Him nowhere" (p. 54).

In his effort to display the unity and harmony of all Scripture (to which he was forced by the controversy with the Manichæans) he often strains after comparisons; and this came to be so much of a habit with him, that, where he had no special purpose to gain, he is guilty of the same excess. An instance among many is furnished in the opening chapters of the *Sermon on the Mount* (iv. 11), where a close comparison is instituted between the Beatitudes and the seven Spiritual operations of Isa. xi. 2, 3. The historical element is nowhere denied, but something else is constantly being superinduced upon it, especially in the Old Testament.

A single illustration of Augustin's allegorical interpretation will suffice. Turning away from the Psalms, where his imagination is particularly fertile along this line, I extract one on the parable of the five loaves and two fishes, as found in the XXIV. Homily on John. The five loaves mean the five Books of Moses. They are not wheaten, but barley, because they belong to the Old Testament. The nature of barley is such that it is hard to be got at, as the kernel is set in a coating of husk which is tenacious and hard to be stripped off. Such is the letter of the Old Testa-

---

[1] On the principle that *Davidica intelligit, qui Davidica patitur;* or, as the German couplet runs, —
"*Wer den Dichter will verstehen*
Muss in Dichters Lande gehen."

ment, enveloped in a covering of carnal sacraments. The little lad represents the people of Israel, which, in its childishness of mind, carried but did not eat. The two fishes signify the persons of the Priest and King, which therefore point to Christ. The multiplication of the loaves signifies the exposition into many volumes of the five Books of Moses. There were five thousand people fed, because they were under the Law, which is unfolded in five books. "They sat upon the grass;" that is, they were carnally minded, and rested in carnal things. The "fragments" are the truths of hidden import which the people cannot receive, and which were therefore entrusted to the twelve apostles.

The excessive taste for this style of interpretation, in which the homilists and Biblical writers of a thousand years had revelled, was sternly rebuked by the Reformers. Especially did Luther utter his protest, on the ground that the fancies into which this method was apt to lead had a tendency to shake confidence in the literal truth of the sacred volume. He remarks, "Augustin said beautifully that a figure proves nothing;" but, probably from the high regard he had for the great theologian, he did not condemn his allegorizing exegesis.[1]

However much the great African bishop may have laid himself open to the rebuke of a more critical and mechanical age in this regard and others, his exegesis will continue to be admired for the diligence with which the sacred text is scanned, the reverent frame of heart with which it is approached, and the rich treasures of spiritual truth which it brings forth to the willing and devout reader.

---

[1] The passage is quoted in full by Trench (p. 64). His work, *St. Augustin on the Sermon on the Mount*, 4th ed., London, 1881, contains an elaborate introductory essay on *Augustin as an Interpreter of Scripture*. His use of allegory is considered in a separate chapter (iv). An older work is by CLAUSEN: *Augustinus, Sac. Script. Interpres*, pp. 267, Berol. 1828.

ST. AUGUSTIN:

OUR LORD'S SERMON ON THE MOUNT,

ACCORDING TO MATTHEW.

[*De Sermone Domini in Monte secundum Matthaeum.*]

TRANSLATED BY

THE REV. WILLIAM FINDLAY, M.A.,

LARKHALL.

REVISED AND ANNOTATED BY

THE REV. D. S. SCHAFF,

KANSAS CITY.

CONTENTS.

OUR LORD'S SERMON ON THE MOUNT.

OUR LORD'S SERMON ON THE MOUNT.

BOOK I.

EXPLANATION OF THE FIRST PART OF THE SERMON DELIVERED BY OUR LORD ON THE MOUNT, AS CONTAINED IN THE FIFTH CHAPTER OF MATTHEW.

CHAP. I. — I. If any one will piously and soberly consider the sermon which our Lord Jesus Christ spoke on the mount, as we read it in the Gospel according to Matthew, I think that he will find in it, so far as regards the highest morals, a perfect standard of the Christian life : and this we do not rashly venture to promise, but gather it from the very words of the Lord Himself. For the sermon itself is brought to a close in such a way, that it is clear there are in it all the precepts which go to mould the life. For thus He speaks : "Therefore, whosoever heareth these words of mine, and doeth them, I will liken [1] him unto a wise man, which built his house upon a rock : and the rain descended, and the floods came, and the winds blew, and beat [2] upon that house ; and it fell not : for it was founded upon a rock. And every one that heareth these words of mine, and doeth them not, I will liken [3] unto a foolish man, which built his house upon the sand : and the rain descended, and the floods came, and the winds blew, and beat upon that house ; and it fell : and great was the fall of it." Since, therefore, He has not simply said, "Whosoever heareth my words," but has made an addition, saying, "Whosoever heareth *these* words of mine," He has sufficiently indicated, as I think, that these sayings which He uttered on the mount so perfectly guide the life of those who may be willing to live according to them, that they may justly be compared to one building upon a rock. I have said this merely that it may be clear that the sermon before us is perfect in all the precepts by which the Christian life is moulded ; for as regards this particular section

a more careful treatment will be given in its own place.[4]

[4] The main purpose of the Sermon on the Mount has been variously stated. Augustin regards it as a perfect code of morals. Tholuck (*Die Bergpredigt*) calls it "the Magna Charta of the kingdom of heaven." Lange says, "The grand fundamental idea is to present the righteousness of the kingdom of heaven in its relation to that of the Old Testament theocracy." Geikie declares it to be the "formal inauguration of the kingdom of God and the Magna Charta of our faith." Edersheim regards it as presenting "the full delineation of the ideal man of God, of prayer, and of righteousness ; in short, of the inward and outward manifestation of discipleship." Meyer (*Com.* 6th ed. p. 210) says that the aim of Jesus is, as the One who fulfils the Law and the Prophets, to present the moral conditions of participation in the Messianic kingdom. Weiss (*Leben Jesu*) speaks of it as being "as little an ethical discourse as a new proclamation of law. It is nothing else than an announcement of the kingdom of God, in which is visible everywhere the purpose of Jesus to distinguish between its righteousness and the righteousness revealed in the Old Testament as well as that taught by the teachers of his day."

The Sermon on the Mount is a practical discourse, containing little of what, in the strict sense, may be termed the *credenda* of Christianity. It is the fullest statement of the nature and obligations of citizenship in God's kingdom. It is noteworthy for its omissions as well as for its contents. No reference is made to a priesthood, a ritual, sacred places, or offerings. There is almost a total absence of all that is sensuous and external. It deals with the motives and affections of the inner man, and so comes into comparison and contrast with the Mosaic law as well as with the Pharisaic ceremonialism of the Lord's Day. The moral grandeur of the precepts of the Sermon on the Mount has been acknowledged by believers and sceptics alike. Renan (*Life of Jesus*) says, "The Sermon on the Mount will never be surpassed." On the 15th of October, 1852, two weeks before he died, Daniel Webster wrote and signed his name to the following words, containing a testimony to this portion of Scripture, which he also ordered placed upon his tombstone: "Lord, I believe; help thou mine unbelief. . . . My heart has assured me and reassured me, that the gospel of Jesus Christ must be a divine reality. The Sermon on the Mount cannot be a merely human production. This belief enters into the very depth of my conscience. The whole history of man proves it" (Curtis, *Life of Webster*, ii. p. 684).

The relation which the reports of Matthew and Luke (vi. 20-49) sustain to each other is ignored by Augustin here (who, except in rare cases, omits all critical discussion), but is discussed in his *Harmony of the Gospels*, ii. 19. The agreements are numerous. The differences are striking, and concern the matter, the arrangement, the language, and the setting of the sermon. Matthew has a hundred and seven verses, Luke thirty. Matthew has seven (or eight) beatitudes, Luke but four, and adds four woes which Matthew omits. According to the first evangelist Jesus spoke sitting on a mountain: according to the third evangelist He spoke standing, and in the plain. The views are, (1) Matthew and Luke give accounts of the same discourse (Origen, Chrysostom, Calvin, Tholuck, Meyer, Keil, Schaff, Weiss). (2) They report different sermons spoken at different times (Augustin not positively, Storr, Plumptre). This is not probable, as so much of the matter in both is identical; both begin with the same beatitude, and close with the same parable; and both accounts are followed with the report of the healing of the centurion's servant. (3) The two sermons were delivered in close succession on the summit of the mountain to the disciples, and on the plain to the multitude (Lange). Alford confesses inability to reconcile the discrepancy.

---

[1] *Similabo.* The Vulgate, conforming more closely to the Greek, has *assimilabitur*, "shall be likened."

[2] *Offenderunt ;* the Vulgate has *irruerunt.*

[3] The Vulgate, more closely conforming to the Greek, has *similis erit.*

2. The beginning, then, of this sermon is introduced as follows: "And when He saw the great [1] multitudes, He went up into a mountain: [2] and when He was set, His disciples came unto Him: and He opened His mouth, and taught them, saying." If it is asked what the "mountain" means, it may well be understood as meaning the greater precepts of righteousness; for there were lesser ones which were given to the Jews. Yet it is one God who, through His holy prophets and servants, according to a thoroughly arranged distribution of times, gave the lesser precepts to a people who as yet required to be bound by fear; and who, through His Son, gave the greater ones to a people whom it had now become suitable to set free by love. Moreover, when the lesser are given to the lesser, and the greater to the greater, they are given by Him who alone knows how to present to the human race the medicine suited to the occasion. Nor is it surprising that the greater precepts are given for the kingdom of heaven, and the lesser for an earthly kingdom, by that one and the same God who made heaven and earth. With respect, therefore, to that righteousness which is the greater, it is said through the prophet, "Thy righteousness is like the mountains of God:" [3] and this may well mean that the one Master alone fit to teach matters of so great importance teaches on a mountain. Then He teaches sitting, as behooves the dignity of the instructor's office; and His disciples come to Him, in order that they might be nearer in body for hearing His words, as they also approached in spirit to fulfil His precepts. "And He opened His mouth, and taught them, saying." The circumlocution before us, which runs, "And He opened His mouth," perhaps gracefully intimates by the mere pause that the sermon will be somewhat longer than usual, unless, perchance, it should not be without meaning, that now He is said to have opened His own mouth, whereas under the old law He was accustomed to open the mouths of the prophets. [4]

3. What, then, does He say? "Blessed are the poor in spirit, for theirs is the kingdom of heaven." We read in Scripture concerning the striving after temporal things, "All is vanity and presumption of spirit;" [5] but presumption of spirit means audacity and pride: usually also the proud are said to have great spirits; and rightly, inasmuch as the wind also is called spirit. And hence it is written, "Fire, hail, snow, ice, spirit of tempest." [6] But, indeed, who does not know that the proud are spoken of as puffed up, as if swelled out with wind? And hence also that expression of the apostle, "Knowledge puffeth up, but charity edifieth." [7] And "the poor in spirit" are rightly understood here, as meaning the humble and God-fearing, i.e. those who have not the spirit which puffeth up. Nor ought blessedness to begin at any other point whatever, if indeed it is to attain unto the highest wisdom; "but the fear of the Lord is the beginning of wisdom;" [8] for, on the other hand also, "pride" is entitled "the beginning of all sin." [9] Let the proud, therefore, seek after and love the kingdoms of the earth; but "blessed are the poor in spirit, for theirs is the kingdom of heaven." [10]

CHAP. II. — 4. "Blessed are the meek, for they shall by inheritance possess [11] the earth:" that earth, I suppose, of which it is said in the Psalm, "Thou art my refuge, my portion in the land of the living." [12] For it signifies a certain firmness and stability of the perpetual inheritance, where the soul, by means of a good disposition, rests, as it were, in its own place, just as the body rests on the earth, and is nourished from it with its own food, as the body from the earth. This is the very rest and life of the saints. Then, the meek are those who yield to acts of wickedness, and do not resist evil, but overcome evil with good. [13] Let those, then, who are not meek quarrel and fight for earthly and temporal things; but "blessed are the meek, for they

---

[1] Multas turbas. The Vulgate omits multas.
[2] The Greek has the definite article (τὸ ὄρος). Some, on this ground, explain the expression to mean "mountain region." According to the Latin tradition of the time of the Crusaders, the exact spot is the Horns of Hattin, which Dean Stanley (Sinai and Palestine, Am. ed. p. 436) and most others adopt. The hill, which is horned like a saddle, is south-west of Capernaum, and commands a good view of the Lake of Galilee. It seems to meet the requirements of the text. Robinson says there are a dozen other hills as eligible as this one. Tholuck enlarges upon the "beautiful temple of nature in which the Lord delivered the sermon." Matthew Henry says, "When the law was given, the Lord came down upon the mountain, now the Lord went up; then He spake in thunder and lightning, now in a still, small voice; then the people were ordered to keep their distance, now they are invited to draw near, — a blessed change!"
[3] Ps. xxxvi. 6.
[4] Chrysostom, Euthymius, etc., see in the expression the implication that Christ also taught by works. Tholuck, with many modern commentators, finds in it a reference to "loud and solemn utterance."

[5] Eccles. i. 14.　　[6] Ps. cxlviii. 8.　　[7] 1 Cor. viii. 1.
[8] Ps. cxi. 10.　　[9] Ecclus. x. 13.
[10] Not the intellectually poor (Fritzsche), nor the poor in worldly goods, as we might gather from Luke (vi. 20). Roman-Catholic commentators have found here support for the doctrine of voluntary poverty (Cornelius à Lapide, Maldonatus, etc.). The Emperor Julian, in allusion to this passage and others like it, said he would only confiscate the goods of Christians, that they might enter as the poor into the kingdom of heaven (Lett. xliii.). Some (Olearius, Michaelis, Paulus) have joined "in spirit" with "blessed." Augustin explains the passage of those who are not elated or proud, taking "spirit" in an evil sense. In another place he says, "Blessed are the poor in their own spirit, rich in God's Spirit; for every man who follows his own spirit is proud." He then compares him who subdues his own spirit to one living in a valley which is filled with water from the hills (En. in Ps. cxli. 4). The most explain of those who are conscious of spiritual need (Matt. xi. 28), and are ready to be filled with the gospel riches, as opposed to the spiritually proud, the just who need no repentance (Tholuck, Meyer, Lange, etc.). "Many are poor in the world, but high in spirit: poor and proud, murmuring and complaining, and blaming their lot. Laodicea was poor in spirituals, and yet rich in spirit; so well increased with goods as to have need of nothing. Paul was rich in spirituals, excelling most in gifts and graces, and yet poor in spirit; the least of the apostles, and less than the least of all saints" (M. Henry).
[11] Hereditate possidebunt. Vulgate omits hereditate. The passage is quoted almost literally in the Teaching of the Twelve Apostles, iii. 7.
[12] Ps. cxlii. 5.　　　　　　[13] Rom. xii. 21.

shall by inheritance possess the earth," from which they cannot be driven out.[1]

5. "Blessed are they that mourn:[2] for they shall be comforted." Mourning is sorrow arising from the loss of things held dear; but those who are converted to God lose those things which they were accustomed to embrace as dear in this world: for they do not rejoice in those things in which they formerly rejoiced; and until the love of eternal things be in them, they are wounded by some measure of grief. Therefore they will be comforted by the Holy Spirit, who on this account chiefly is called the Paraclete, i.e. the Comforter, in order that, while losing the temporal joy, they may enjoy to the full that which is eternal.[3]

6. "Blessed are they which do hunger and thirst after righteousness: for they shall be filled." Now He calls those parties, lovers of a true and indestructible good. They will therefore be filled with that food of which the Lord Himself says, "My meat is to do the will of my Father," which is righteousness; and with that water, of which whosoever "drinketh," as he also says, it "shall be in him a well of water, springing up into everlasting life."[4]

7. "Blessed are the merciful: for they shall obtain mercy."[5] He says that they are blessed who relieve the miserable, for it is paid back to them in such a way that they are freed from misery.

8. "Blessed are the pure in heart:[6] for they shall see God." How foolish, therefore, are those who seek God with these outward eyes, since He is seen with the heart! as it is written elsewhere, "And in singleness of heart seek Him."[7] For that is a pure heart which is a single heart: and just as this light cannot be seen, except with pure eyes; so neither is God seen, unless that is pure by which He can be seen.[8]

9. "Blessed are the peacemakers: for they shall be called the children of God." It is the perfection of peace, where nothing offers opposition; and the children of God are peacemakers, because nothing resists God, and surely children ought to have the likeness of their father. Now, they are peacemakers in themselves who, by bringing in order all the motions of their soul, and subjecting them to reason — i.e. to the mind and spirit — and by having their carnal lusts thoroughly subdued, become a kingdom of God: in which all things are so arranged, that that which is chief and pre-eminent in man rules without resistance over the other elements, which are common to us with the beasts; and that very element which is pre-eminent in man, i.e. mind and reason, is brought under subjection to something better still, which is the truth itself, the only-begotten Son of God. For a man is not able to rule over things which are inferior, unless he subjects himself to what is superior. And this is the peace which is given on earth to men of goodwill;[9] this the life of the fully developed and perfect wise man. From a kingdom of this sort brought to a condition of thorough peace and order, the prince of this world is cast out, who rules where there is perversity and disorder.[10] When this peace has been inwardly established and confirmed, whatever persecutions he who has been cast out shall stir up from without, he only increases the glory which is according to God; being unable to shake anything in that edifice, but by the failure of his machinations making it to be known with how great strength it has been built from within outwardly. Hence there follows: "Blessed are they which are persecuted for righteousness' sake: for theirs is the kingdom of heaven."

CHAP. III. — 10. There are in all, then, these eight sentences. For now in what remains He speaks in the way of direct address to those who were present, saying: "Blessed shall ye be when men shall revile you and persecute you." But the former sentences He addressed in a general way: for He did not say, Blessed are ye poor in spirit, for yours is the kingdom of heaven; but He says, "Blessed are the poor in spirit, for

---

[1] The order in which Augustin places this Beatitude is followed in *Cod.* D, and approved by Lachmann, Tischendorf, Neander, and others (not Westcott and Hort). The meek not only bear provocation, but quietly submit to God's dealings, and comply with His designs. The temporal possession promised is one of the few temporal promises in the New Testament. The inheritance of the earth is referred to "earthly good and possessions," by Chrysostom, Euthymius, Luther, etc.; to conquest of the world by the kingdom of God, by Neander; to the actual kingdom on this earth, first in its millennial then in its blessed state, by Alford; typically to the Messiah's kingdom, by Meyer; to the land of the living beyond the heavens, by Gregory of Nyssa. "Humility and meekness have been proved to be a conquering principle in the world's history" (Tholuck).

[2] *Lugentes.* Greek, πενθοῦντες. The Vulgate, *qui lugent*, which Augustin follows, p. 7.

[3] The mourning is a mourning over sins of their own and others (Chrysostom, etc.); too restricted, as is also Augustin's explanation. Spiritual mourning in general (Ambrose, Jerome, Tholuck, etc.), sorrow according to God (2 Cor. vii. 10). We are helped to the meaning by comparing the woe on those that laugh (Luke vi. 22); that is, upon those who are satisfied with earthly things, and avoid the seriousness of repentance.

[4] John iv. 34, 14.

[5] *Ipsorum miserabitur;* closer to the Greek than the Vulgate *ipsi misericordiam consequentur.* The same thought that underlies the fifth petition of the Lord's Prayer, as Augustin also says, *Retract.* I. xix. 3.

[6] *Mundi corde;* the Vulgate, *mundo corde.*

[7] Wisd. i. 1.

[8] "Pure in heart." "Ceremonial purity does not suffice" (Bengel). The singleness of heart which has God's will for its aim, and

follows integrity with our fellow-men (Tholuck). "Shall see God:" the most infinite communion with God (Tholuck). The promise is fulfilled even here (Lange, Alford, Schaff, etc.). It concerns only the beatific vision in the spiritual body (Meyer). Not a felicity to the impure to see God (Henry). Comp. 1 John iii. 2, Rev. xxii. 4, etc. Augustin has a brilliant description of the future vision of God in *City of God* (this series, vol. ii. pp. 507-509).

[9] Luke ii. 14.

[10] The "peacemakers" not only establish peace within themselves, as Augustin, encouraged by the Latin word, explains, but diffuse peace around about them, — heal the alienations and discords of others, and bring about reconciliations in the world; not merely peaceful, but peacemakers. "In most kingdoms those stand highest who make war: in the Messiah's kingdom the crowning beatitude respects those who make peace." The expressions will be remembered, "peace of God" (Phil. iv. 7); "peace of Christ" (Col. iii. 15); "God of peace" (Rom. xv. 33), etc. "If the peacemakers are blessed, woe to the peacebreakers!" (M. Henry).

theirs is the kingdom of heaven : " nor, Blessed are ye meek, for ye shall inherit the earth ; but, "Blessed are the meek, for they shall inherit the earth." And so the others up to the eighth sentence, where He says : "Blessed are they which are persecuted for righteousness' sake, for theirs is the kingdom of heaven." After that He now begins to speak in the way of direct address to those present, although what has been said before referred also to His present audience ; and that which follows, and which seems to be spoken specially to those present, refers also to those who were absent, or who would afterwards come into existence.

For this reason the number of sentences before us is to be carefully considered. For the beatitudes begin with humility : "Blessed are the poor in spirit," *i.e.* those not puffed up, while the soul submits itself to divine authority, fearing lest after this life it go away to punishment, although perhaps in this life it might seem to itself to be happy. Then it (the soul) comes to the knowledge of the divine Scriptures, where it must show itself meek in its piety, lest it should venture to condemn that which seems absurd to the unlearned, and should itself be rendered unteachable by obstinate disputations. After that, it now begins to know in what entanglements of this world it is held by reason of carnal custom and sins : and so in this third stage, in which there is knowledge, the loss of the highest good is mourned over, because it sticks fast in what is lowest. Then, in the fourth stage there is labour, where vehement exertion is put forth, in order that the mind may wrench itself away from those things in which, by reason of their pestilential sweetness, it is entangled : here therefore righteousness is hungered and thirsted after, and fortitude is very necessary ; because what is retained with delight is not abandoned without pain. Then, at the fifth stage, to those persevering in labour, counsel for getting rid of it is given ; for unless each one is assisted by a superior, in no way is he fit in his own case to extricate himself from so great entanglements of miseries. But it is a just counsel, that he who wishes to be assisted by a stronger should assist him who is weaker in that in which he himself is stronger : therefore "blessed are the merciful, for they shall obtain mercy." At the sixth stage there is purity of heart, able from a good conscience of good works to contemplate that highest good, which can be discerned by the pure and tranquil intellect alone. Lastly is the seventh, wisdom itself — *i.e.* the contemplation of the truth, tranquillizing the whole man, and assuming the likeness of God, which is thus summed up : "Blessed are the peacemakers, for they shall be called the children of God." The eighth, as it were, returns to the starting-point,

because it shows and commends what is complete and perfect : [1] therefore in the first and in the eighth the kingdom of heaven is named, "Blessed are the poor in spirit, for theirs is the kingdom of heaven ; " and, "Blessed are they which are persecuted for righteousness' sake, for theirs is the kingdom of heaven : " as it is now said, "Who shall separate us from the love of Christ? shall tribulation, or distress, or persecution, or famine, or nakedness, or peril, or sword?"[2] Seven in number, therefore, are the things which bring perfection : for the eighth brings into light and shows what is perfect, so that starting, as it were, from the beginning again, the others also are perfected by means of these stages.

Chap. IV. — 11. Hence also the sevenfold operation of the Holy Ghost, of which Isaiah speaks,[3] seems to me to correspond to these stages and sentences. But there is a difference of order : for there the enumeration begins with the more excellent, but here with the inferior. For there it begins with wisdom, and closes with the fear of God : but "the fear of the Lord is the beginning of wisdom." And therefore, if we reckon as it were in a gradually ascending series, there the fear of God is first, piety second, knowledge third, fortitude fourth, counsel fifth, understanding sixth, wisdom seventh. The fear of God corresponds to the humble, of whom it is here said, "Blessed are the poor in spirit," *i.e.* those not puffed up, not proud : to whom the apostle says, "Be not high-minded, but fear ; "[4] *i.e.* be not lifted up. Piety[5] corresponds to the meek : for he who inquires piously honours Holy Scripture, and does not censure what he does not yet understand, and on this account does not offer resistance ; and this is to be meek : whence it is here said, "Blessed are the meek." Knowledge corresponds to those that mourn who already have found out in the Scriptures by what evils they are held chained which they ignorantly have coveted as though they were good and useful. Fortitude corresponds to those hungering and thirsting : for they labour in earnestly desiring joy from things that are truly good, and in eagerly seeking to turn away their love from earthly and corporeal things : and of them it is here said, "Blessed are they which do hunger and thirst after righteousness." Counsel corresponds to the merciful : for this is the one remedy for escaping from so great evils, that we forgive, as we wish to be

---

[1] "In the eighth beatitude the other seven are only summed up under the idea of the righteousness of the kingdom in its relation to those who persecute it ; while the ninth is a description of the eighth, with reference to the relation in which these righteous persons stand to Christ" (Lange).
[2] Rom. viii. 35.   [3] Isa. xi. 2, 3.   [4] Rom. xi. 20.
[5] Augustin follows the Septuagint, which has "piety" instead of "the fear of the Lord" in the last clause of Isa. xi. 2.

ourselves forgiven; and that we assist others so far as we are able, as we ourselves desire to be assisted where we are not able: and of them it is here said, "Blessed are the merciful." Understanding corresponds to the pure in heart, the eye being as it were purged, by which that may be beheld which eye hath not seen, nor ear heard, and what hath not entered into the heart of man:[1] and of them it is here said, "Blessed are the pure in heart." Wisdom corresponds to the peacemakers, in whom all things are now brought into order, and no passion is in a state of rebellion against reason, but all things together obey the spirit of man, while he himself also obeys God: and of them it is here said, "Blessed are the peacemakers."[2]

12. Moreover, the one reward, which is the kingdom of heaven, is variously named according to these stages. In the first, just as ought to be the case, is placed the kingdom of heaven, which is the perfect and highest wisdom of the rational soul. Thus, therefore, it is said, "Blessed are the poor in spirit, for theirs is the kingdom of heaven:" as if it were said, "The fear of the Lord is the beginning of wisdom." To the meek an inheritance is given, as it were the testament of a father to those dutifully seeking it: "Blessed are the meek, for they shall inherit the earth." To the mourners comfort, as to those who know what they have lost, and in what evils they are sunk: "Blessed are they that mourn, for they shall be comforted." To those hungering and thirsting, a full supply, as it were a refreshment to those labouring and bravely contending for salvation: "Blessed are they which do hunger and thirst after righteousness, for they shall be filled." To the merciful mercy, as to those following a true and excellent counsel, so that this same treatment is extended toward them by one who is stronger, which they extend toward the weaker: "Blessed are the merciful, for they shall obtain mercy." To the pure in heart is given the power of seeing God, as to those bearing about with them a pure eye for discerning eternal things: "Blessed are the pure in heart, for they shall see God." To the peacemakers the likeness of God is given, as being perfectly wise, and formed after the image of God by means of the regeneration of the renewed man: "Blessed are the peacemakers, for they shall be called the children of God." And those promises can indeed be fulfilled in this life, as we believe them to have been fulfilled in the case of the apostles. For that all-embracing change into the angelic form, which is promised after this life, cannot be explained in any words. "Blessed," therefore, "are they which are persecuted for righteousness' sake,

for theirs is the kingdom of heaven." This eighth sentence, which goes back to the starting-point, and makes manifest the perfect man, is perhaps set forth in its meaning both by the circumcision on the eighth day in the Old Testament, and by the resurrection of the Lord after the Sabbath, the day which is certainly the eighth, and at the same time the first day; and by the celebration of the eight festival days which we celebrate in the case of the regeneration of the new man; and by the very number of Pentecost. For to the number seven, seven times multiplied, by which we make forty-nine, as it were an eighth is added, so that fifty may be made up, and we, as it were, return to the starting-point: on which day the Holy Spirit was sent, by whom we are led into the kingdom of heaven, and receive the inheritance, and are comforted; and are fed, and obtain mercy, and are purified, and are made peacemakers; and being thus perfect, we bear all troubles brought upon us from without for the sake of truth and righteousness.

CHAP. v. — 13. "Blessed are ye," says He, "when men shall revile you, and persecute you, and shall say all manner of evil against you falsely for my sake. Rejoice and be exceeding glad: for great[3] is your reward in heaven." Let any one who is seeking after the delights of this world and the riches of temporal things under the Christian name, consider that our blessedness is within; as it is said of the soul of the Church[4] by the mouth of the prophet, "All the beauty of the king's daughter is within;"[5] for outwardly revilings, and persecutions, and disparagements are promised; and yet, from these things there is a great reward in heaven, which is felt in the heart of those who endure, those who can now say, "We glory in tribulations: knowing that tribulation worketh patience; and patience, experience; and experience, hope: and hope maketh not ashamed; because the love of God is shed abroad in our hearts by the Holy Ghost which is given unto us."[6] For it is not simply the enduring of such things that is advantageous, but the bearing of such things for the name of Christ not only with tranquil mind, but even with exultation. For many heretics, deceiving souls under the Christian name, endure many such things; but they are excluded from that reward on this account, that it is not said merely, "Blessed are they which endure persecution;" but it is added, "for righteousness' sake." Now, where there is no sound faith, there can be no righteousness, for the just [righteous] man lives by faith.[7] Neither let schismatics promise themselves anything of that reward; for similarly,

---

[1] Isa. lxiv. 4 and 1 Cor. ii. 9.
[2] This is guarded against misconstruction in the *Retract.* I. xix. 1.

[3] *Multa;* Vulgate, *copiosa.*   [4] *Anima ecclesiastica.*
[5] Ps. xlv. 13.   [6] Rom. v. 3–5.   [7] Hab. ii. 4 and Rom. i. 17.

where there is no love, there cannot be righteousness, for "love worketh no ill to his neighbour;"[1] and if they had it, they would not tear in pieces Christ's body, which is the Church.[2]

14. But it may be asked, What is the difference when He says, "when men shall revile you," and "when they shall say all manner of evil against you," since to revile[3] is just this, to say evil against?[4] But it is one thing when the reviling word is hurled with contumely in presence of him who is reviled, as it was said to our Lord, "Say we not the truth[5] that thou art a Samaritan, and hast a devil?"[6] and another thing, when our reputation is injured in our absence, as it is also written of Him, "Some said, He is a prophet;[7] others said, Nay, but He deceiveth the people."[8] Then, further, to persecute is to inflict violence, or to assail with snares, as was done by him who betrayed Him, and by them who crucified Him. Certainly, as for the fact that this also is not put in a bare form, so that it should be said, "and shall say all manner of evil against you," but there is added the word "falsely," and also the expression "for my sake;" I think that the addition is made for the sake of those who wish to glory in persecutions, and in the baseness of their reputation; and to say that Christ belongs to them for this reason, that many bad things are said about them; while, on the one hand, the things said are true, when they are said respecting their error; and, on the other hand, if sometimes also some false charges are thrown out, which frequently happens from the rashness of men, yet they do not suffer such things for Christ's sake.[9] For he is not a follower of Christ who is not called a Christian according to the true faith and the catholic discipline.

15. "Rejoice," says He, "and be exceeding glad: for great is your reward in heaven." I do not think that it is the higher parts of this visible world that are here called heaven. For our reward, which ought to be immoveable and eternal, is not to be placed in things fleeting and temporal. But I think the expression "in heaven" means in the spiritual firmament, where dwells everlasting righteousness: in comparison with which a wicked soul is called earth, to which it is said when it sins, "Earth thou art, and unto earth thou shalt return."[10] Of this heaven the apostle says, "For our conversation is in heaven."[11] Hence they who rejoice in spiritual

good are conscious of that reward now; but then it will be perfected in every part, when this mortal also shall have put on immortality. "For," says He, "so persecuted they the prophets also which were before you." In the present case He has used "persecution" in a general sense, as applying alike to abusive words and to the tearing in pieces of one's reputation; and has well encouraged them by an example, because they who speak true things are wont to suffer persecution: nevertheless did not the ancient prophets on this account, through fear of persecution, give over the preaching of the truth.

Chap. VI. — 16. Hence there follows most justly the statement, "Ye are the salt of the earth;" showing that those parties are to be judged insipid, who, either in the eager pursuit after abundance of earthly blessings, or through the dread of want, lose the eternal things which can neither be given nor taken away by men. "But[12] if the salt have lost[13] its savour, wherewith shall it be salted?" i.e., If ye, by means of whom the nations in a measure are to be preserved [from corruption], through the dread of temporal persecutions shall lose the kingdom of heaven, where will be the men through whom error may be removed from you, since God has chosen you, in order that through you He might remove the error of others? Hence the savourless salt is "good for nothing, but to be cast out, and trodden under foot of men." It is not therefore he who suffers persecution, but he who is rendered savourless by the fear of persecution, that is trodden under foot of men. For it is only one who is undermost that can be trodden under foot; but he is not undermost, who, however many things he may suffer in his body on the earth, yet has his heart fixed in heaven.[14]

17. "Ye are the light[15] of the world." In the same way as He said above, "the salt of the

---

[1] Rom. xiii. 10. [2] Col. i. 24. [3] *Maledicere.*
[4] *Malum dicere.*
[5] *Verum.* The Vulgate more literally has *bene.*
[6] John viii. 48.
[7] The Vulgate, following the Greek, has *bonus,*—good man.
[8] Chap. vii. 12.
[9] "It is not the suffering, but the cause, that makes men martyrs." For, says Augustin in another place (*En. in Ps.* xxxiv. 23), if the suffering made the martyr, every mine would be full of martyrs, every chain drag them, every one beheaded with the sword be crowned. They who suffer for righteousness' sake, suffer for Christ's sake.
[10] Gen. iii. 19. [11] Phil. iii. 20.

[12] "A warning against pride" (Schaff).
[13] *Infatuatum fuerit;* Vulgate, *evanuerit.*
[14] Others follow Augustin in regarding the connection of this verse and the next with the preceding one as very close. All the more must they refuse to yield to persecution, as they have a function in the world which is well represented by salt and light (Weizsäcker, Meyer, etc.). The function of salt is to preserve and to season. With it Elisha healed the unwholesome water (2 Kings ii. 21). The use of salt in the sacrifices is, no doubt, alluded to (Tholuck). It becomes savourless. Dr. Thomson says (*Land and Book,* ii. 43), "It is a well-known fact that the salt in this country (gathered from the marshes in dry weather), when in contact with the ground, or exposed to air and sun, does become insipid and useless." The disciples are appointed to communicate the truth and moral grace, before spoken of in the Beatitudes, to counteract the error and corruption in the earth. "Earth" not to be confined to "society as then existing, the definite form the world then presented" (Lange), but to mankind in general, as Augustin below. "Wherewith shall it be salted?" does not imply that those who have once fallen cannot be reclaimed (Alford). The comment of Grotius is good: "*Ipsi emendare alios debebent, non autem exsspectare ut ab aliis ipsi emendarentur*" ("They ought to improve others, not expect to be themselves improved by others").
[15] *Lumen,* also used for a *luminary;* Vulgate, *lux.* In a lower and derivative sense are the disciples "the light," etc. (Alford), deriving their light-giving quality from Him who is the "Light of the world" (John viii. 12), so that they become "lights in the world" (Phil. ii. 15). Augustin (*Sermon,* ccclxxx.): *Johannes lumen illuminatum, Christus lumen illuminans.*

earth," so now He says, "the light of the world." For in the former case that earth is not to be understood which we tread with our bodily feet, but the men who dwell upon the earth, or even the sinners, for the preserving of whom and for the extinguishing of whose corruptions the Lord sent the apostolic salt. And here, by the world must be understood not the heavens and the earth, but the men who are in the world or love the world, for the enlightening of whom the apostles were sent.[1] "A city that is set on[2] an hill cannot be hid," *i.e.* [a city] founded upon great and distinguished righteousness, which is also the meaning of the mountain itself on which our Lord is discoursing. "Neither do men light a candle[3] and put it under a bushel measure."[4] What view are we to take? That the expression "under a bushel measure" is so used that only the concealment of the candle is to be understood, as if He were saying, No one lights a candle and conceals it? Or does the bushel measure also mean something, so that to place a candle under a bushel is this, to place the comforts of the body higher than the preaching of the truth; so that one does not preach the truth so long as he is afraid of suffering any annoyance in corporeal and temporal things? And it is well said a bushel measure, whether on account of the recompense of measure, for each one receives the things done in his body, — "that every one," says the apostle, "may there receive[5] the things done in his body;" and it is said in another place, as if of this bushel measure of the body, "For with what measure ye mete, it shall be measured to you again:"[6] — or because temporal good things, which are carried to completion in the body, are both begun and come to an end in a certain definite number of days, which is perhaps meant by the "bushel measure;" while eternal and spiritual things are confined within no such limit, "for God giveth not the Spirit by measure."[7] Every one, therefore, who obscures and covers up the light of good doctrine by means of temporal comforts, places his candle under a bushel measure. "But on a candlestick."[8] Now it is placed on a candlestick by him who subordinates his body to the service of God, so that the preaching of the truth is the higher, and the serving of the body the lower; yet by means even of the service of the body

the doctrine shines more conspicuously, inasmuch as it is insinuated into those who learn by means of bodily functions, *i.e.* by means of the voice and tongue, and the other movements of the body in good works. The apostle therefore puts his candle on a candlestick, when he says, "So fight I, not as one that beateth[9] the air; but I keep under my body, and bring it into subjection, lest that by any means, when I preach to others, I myself should be found a castaway."[10] When He says, however, "that it may give light to all who are in the house," I am of opinion that it is the abode of men which is called a house, *i.e.* the world itself, on account of what He says before, "Ye are the light of the world;" or if any one chooses to understand the house as being the Church, this, too, is not out of place.

CHAP. VII. — 18. "Let your light,"[11] says He, "so shine before men, that they may see your good works, and glorify your Father which is in heaven." If He had merely said, "Let your light so shine before men, that they may see your good works," He would seem to have fixed an end in the praises of men, which hypocrites seek, and those who canvass for honours and covet glory of the emptiest kind. Against such parties it is said, "If I yet pleased men, I should not be the servant of Christ;"[12] and by the prophet, "They who please men are put to shame, because God hath despised them;" and again, "God hath broken the bones of those who please men;"[13] and again the apostle, "Let us not be desirous of vainglory;"[14] and still another time, "But let every man prove his own work, and then shall he have rejoicing in himself alone, and not in another."[15] Hence our Lord has not said merely, "that they may see your good works," but has added, "and glorify your Father who is in heaven:" so that the mere fact that a man by means of good works pleases men, does not there set it up as an end that he should please men; but let him subordinate this to the praise of God, and for this reason please men, that God may be glorified in him. For this is expedient for them who offer praise, that they should honour, not man, but God; as our Lord showed in the case of the man who was carried, where, on the paralytic being healed, the multitude, marvelling at His powers, as it is written in the Gospel, "feared and glorified God, which had given such power unto men."[16] And His imitator, the Apostle Paul, says, "But they

---

[1] "The influence of salt is internal, of light external: hence the element in which they work, the *earth* and the *world*, both referring to mankind: the latter more to its organized external form" (Schaff).

[2] *Constituta*; Vulgate, *posita*. The city was probably visible. Some have thought of the village on Mount Tabor, others of an ancient fortress, predecessor of the present Safed (Dean Stanley, Thomson); certainly not Jerusalem (Weizsäcker).

[3] *Lucerna*.

[4] The Greek has the definite article τὸν μόδιον.

[5] 2 Cor. v. 10. *Recipiat unusquisque quæ gessit in corpore.* Vulgate, *referat unusquisque propria corporis, prout gessit*, etc.

[6] Matt. vii. 2.

[7] John iii. 34; which words, however, are, as Augustin subsequently observed (*Retract.* I. xix. 3), applicable only to Christ.

[8] *Candelabrum.*

[9] *Cædens*; Vulgate, *verberans*.

[10] 1 Cor. ix. 26, 27. *Ne forte aliis prædicans . . . invenir.* Vulgate, *Ne forte cum aliis prædicaverim . . . efficir.*

[11] *Lumen*; Vulgate, *lux.* Christ presupposes His righteousness to have become the principle of their life. "They were to stand forth openly and boldly with the message of the New Testament" (Lange).

[12] Gal. i. 10.   [13] Ps. liii. 5.   [14] Gal. v. 26.

[15] Chap. vi. 4.   [16] Matt. ix. 8.

had heard only, that he which persecuted us in times past now preacheth the faith which once he destroyed ; and they glorified [1] God in me."

19. And therefore, after He has exhorted His hearers that they should prepare themselves to bear all things for truth and righteousness, and that they should not hide the good which they were about to receive, but should learn with such benevolence as to teach others, aiming in their good works not at their own praise, but at the glory of God, He begins now to inform and to teach them what they are to teach ; as if they were asking Him, saying : Lo, we are willing both to bear all things for Thy name, and not to hide Thy doctrine ; but what precisely is this which Thou forbiddest us to hide, and for which Thou commandest us to bear all things? Art Thou about to mention other things contrary to those which are written in the law? "No," says He ; "for think not that I am come to destroy the law, or the prophets : I am not come to destroy, but to fulfil."

CHAP. VIII. — 20. In this sentence the meaning is twofold.[2] We must deal with it in both ways. For He who says, "I am not come [3] to destroy the law, but to fulfil," means it either in the way of adding what is wanting, or of doing what is in it. Let us then consider that first which I have put first : for he who adds what is wanting does not surely destroy what he finds, but rather confirms it by perfecting it ; and accordingly He follows up with the statement, "Verily I say unto you,[4] Till heaven and earth pass, one iota or one tittle shall in nowise pass from the law, till all be fulfilled." For, if even those things which are added for completion are fulfilled, much more are those things fulfilled which are sent in advance as a commencement. Then, as to what He says, "One iota or one tittle shall in nowise pass from the law," nothing else can be understood but a strong expression of perfection, since it is pointed out by means of single letters, among which letters "iota" is smaller than the others, for it is made by a single stroke ; while a "tittle" is but a particle of some sort at the top of even that. And by these words He shows that in the law all the smallest particulars even are to be carried into effect.[5]

After that He subjoins : "Whosoever, therefore, shall break one of these least commandments, and shall teach men so, he shall be called the least in the kingdom of heaven." Hence it is the least commandments that are meant by "one iota" and "one tittle." And therefore, "whosoever shall break and shall teach [men] so," — i.e. in accordance with what he breaks, not in accordance with what he finds and reads, — "shall be called the least in the kingdom of heaven ; " and therefore, perhaps, he will not be in the kingdom of heaven at all, where only the great can be. "But whosoever shall do and teach [men] so,"[6] — i.e. who shall not break, and shall teach men so, in accordance with what he does not break, — "shall be called great in the kingdom of heaven." But in regard to him who shall be called great in the kingdom of heaven, it follows that he is also in the kingdom of heaven, into which the great are admitted : for to this what follows refers.

CHAP. IX. — 21. "For I say unto you, that except your righteousness shall exceed the righteousness of the scribes and Pharisees, ye shall in no case enter into the kingdom of heaven ; "[7] i.e., unless ye shall fulfil not only those least precepts of the law which begin the man, but also those which are added by me, who am not come to destroy the law, but to fulfil it, ye shall not enter into the kingdom of heaven. But you say to me : If, when He was speaking above of those least commandments, He said that whosoever shall break one of them, and shall teach in accordance with his transgression, is called the least in the kingdom of heaven ; but that whosoever shall do them, and shall teach [men] so, is called great, and hence will be already in the kingdom of heaven, because he is great : what need is there for additions to the least precepts of the law, if he can be already in the kingdom of heaven, because whosoever shall do them, and shall so teach, is great? For this reason that sentence is to be understood thus : "But whosoever shall do and teach men so, the same shall be called great in the kingdom of heaven," — i.e. not in accordance with those least commandments, but in accordance with those which I am about to mention. Now what are they? "That your righteousness," says He, "may exceed that of the scribes and Pharisees ; " for unless it shall exceed theirs, ye shall not enter into the kingdom of heaven. Whosoever, there-

---

[1] Gal. i. 23, 24. *Vastabat . . . glorificabant ;* Vulgate, *expugnabat . . . clarificabant.*

[2] Here begins the second part of the Sermon. In it our Lord sets forth His relation as a lawgiver to the Mosaic law, especially as currently interpreted according to the letter only (Meyer, Alford, etc.).

[3] *Veni ;* Greek, ἦλθον.

[4] A decisive assertion of authority. *Asseveratio gravissima, ei propria, qui per se ipsum et per suam veritatem asseverat* (Bengel). The prophet's most emphatic statement was, "Thus saith the Lord." Christ speaks in His own name, as the fount of authority (v. 20 and often: John iii. 3, xiv. 12, etc.).

[5] "Christ's words are decisive against all those who would set aside the Old Testament as without significance, or inconsistent with the New Testament" (Alford). Christ declares the New to be rooted in the Old ; its consummation, not its destruction. The essence and

purport of the law, the "whole law," was fulfilled by Him (Meyer). Theophylact well compares the law to a sketch, which Christ (like the painter) does not destroy, but fills out.

[6] *Sic :* Greek, οὗτος; Vulgate, *hic.*

[7] "With all their care, they had not understood the true spirit of the law" (Schaff). The rest of the Sermon is largely a comment on this verse, Christ giving His interpretation of the law, and the righteousness following upon its observance ; showing that the purport goes beyond the external act of obedience to the purpose of the heart, and that in the external act of obedience the real purport might be ignored.

fore, shall break those least commandments, and shall teach men so, shall be called the least ; but whosoever shall do those least commandments, and shall teach men so, is not necessarily to be reckoned great and meet for the kingdom of heaven ; but yet he is not so much the least as the man who breaks them. But in order that he may be great and fit for that kingdom, he ought to do and teach as Christ now teaches, *i.e.* in order that his righteousness may exceed that of the scribes and Pharisees. The righteousness of the Pharisees is, that they shall not kill ; the righteousness of those who are destined to enter into the kingdom of God, that they be not angry without a cause. The least commandment, therefore, is not to kill ; and whosoever shall break that, shall be called least in the kingdom of heaven ; but whosoever shall fulfil that commandment not to kill, will not, as a necessary consequence, be great and meet for the kingdom of heaven, but yet he ascends a certain step. He will be perfected, however, if he be not angry without a cause ; and if he shall do this, he will be much further removed from murder. For this reason he who teaches that we should not be angry, does not break the law not to kill, but rather fulfils it ; so that we preserve our innocence both outwardly when we do not kill, and in heart when we are not angry.

22. "Ye have heard" therefore, says He, "that it was said to them of old time, Thou shalt not kill ; and whosoever shall kill shall be in danger of the judgment. But I say unto you, that whosoever is angry with his brother without a cause [1] shall be in danger of the judgment : and whosoever shall say to his brother, Raca, shall be in danger of the council : but whosoever shall say, Thou fool, shall be in danger of the gehenna of fire." What is the difference between being in danger of the judgment, and being in danger of the council, and being in danger of the gehenna of fire?[2] For this last sounds most weighty, and reminds us that certain stages were passed over from lighter to more weighty, until the gehenna of fire was reached. And, therefore, if it is a lighter thing to be in danger of the judgment than to be in danger of the council, and if it is also a lighter thing to be in danger of the council than to be in danger of the gehenna of fire, we must understand it to be a lighter thing to be angry with a brother without a cause than to say "Raca ; " and again, to be a lighter thing to say "Raca"

than to say "Thou fool." For the danger would not have gradations, unless the sins also were mentioned in gradation.

23. But here one obscure word has found a place, for "Raca" is neither Latin nor Greek. The others, however, are current in our language. Now, some have wished to derive the interpretation of this expression from the Greek, supposing that a ragged person is called "Raca," because a rag is called in Greek ῥάκος ; yet, when one asks them what a ragged person is called in Greek, they do not answer "Raca ; " and further, the Latin translator might have put the word *ragged* where he has placed "Raca," and not have used a word which, on the one hand, has no existence in the Latin language, and, on the other, is rare in the Greek. Hence the view is more probable which I heard from a certain Hebrew whom I had asked about it ; for he said that the word does not mean anything, but merely expresses the emotion of an angry mind. Grammarians call those particles of speech which express an affection of an agitated mind *interjections ;* as when it is said by one who is grieved, "Alas," or by one who is angry, "Hah." And these words in all languages are proper names, and are not easily translated into another language ; and this cause certainly compelled alike the Greek and the Latin translators to put the word itself, inasmuch as they could find no way of translating it.[3]

24. There is therefore a gradation in the sins referred to, so that first one is angry, and keeps that feeling as a conception in his heart ; but if now that emotion shall draw forth an expression of anger not having any definite meaning, but giving evidence of that feeling of the mind by the very fact of the outbreak wherewith he is assailed with whom one is angry, this is certainly more than if the rising anger were restrained by silence ; but if there is heard not merely an expression of anger, but also a word by which the party using it now indicates and signifies a distinct censure of him against whom it is directed, who doubts but that this is something more than if merely an exclamation of anger were uttered? Hence in the first there is one thing, *i.e.* anger alone ; in the second two things, both anger and a word that expresses anger ; in the third three things, anger and a word that expresses anger, and in that word the utterance of distinct censure. Look now also at the three degrees of liability, — the judgment, the council, the gehenna of fire. For in the judgment an opportunity is still given for defence ; in the council, however, although there is also wont to be a judgment, yet because the very distinction

---

[1] *Sine causa.* The weight of critical evidence is against this clause, which is omitted by Tischendorf, Westcott, and Hort, the Vulgate and the Revised Version.
[2] The "judgment" (κρίσις) was the local court of seven, which every community was enjoined to have (Deut. xvi. 18). The "council" was the Sanhedrin, consisting of seventy-two members, sitting in Jerusalem. The "gehenna" was the vale of Hinnom, on the confines of Jerusalem, where sacrifices were offered to Moloch, and which became the place for refuse and the burning of dead bodies. In the New Testament it is equivalent to "hell."

[3] *Raca* is from the Chald. רֵיקָא, and is a term of contempt equivalent to *empty-headed* (Thayer's *Lexicon*). Trench translates, "Oh, vain man!"

compels us to acknowledge that there is a certain difference in this place, the production of the sentence seems to belong to the council, inasmuch as it is not now the case of the accused himself that is in question, whether he is to be condemned or not, but they who judge confer with one another to what punishment they ought to condemn him, who, it is clear, is to be condemned; but the gehenna of fire does not treat as a doubtful matter either the condemnation, like the judgment, or the punishment of him who is condemned, like the council; for in the gehenna of fire both the condemnation and the punishment of him who is condemned are certain. Thus there are seen certain degrees in the sins and in the liability to punishment;[1] but who can tell in what ways they are invisibly shown in the punishments of souls? We are therefore to learn how great the difference is between the righteousness of the Pharisees and that greater righteousness which introduces into the kingdom of heaven, because while it is a more serious crime to kill than to inflict reproach by means of a word, in the one case killing exposes one to the judgment, but in the other anger exposes one to the judgment, which is the least of those three sins; for in the former case they were discussing the question of murder among men, but in the latter all things are disposed of by means of a divine judgment, where the end of the condemned is the gehenna of fire. But whoever shall say that murder is punished by a more severe penalty under the greater righteousness if a reproach is punished by the gehenna of fire, compels us to understand that there are differences of gehennas.

25. Indeed, in the three statements before us, we must observe that some words are understood. For the first statement has all the words that are necessary. "Whosoever," says He, "is angry with his brother without a cause, shall be in danger of the judgment." But in the second, when He says, "and whosoever shall say to his brother, Raca," there is understood the expression *without cause*,[2] and thus there is subjoined, "shall be in danger of the council." In the third, now, where He says, "but whosoever shall say, Thou fool," two things are understood, both *to his brother* and *without cause*. And in this way we defend the apostle when he calls the Galatians fools,[3] to whom he also gives

the name of brethren; for he does not do it without cause. And here the word *brother* is to be understood for this reason, that the case of an enemy is spoken of afterwards, and how he also is to be treated under the greater righteousness.

CHAP. X. — 26. Next there follows here: "Therefore, if thou hast brought[4] thy gift to the altar, and there rememberest that thy brother hath ought against thee; leave there thy gift before the altar, and go thy way; first be reconciled to thy brother, and then come and offer thy gift." From this surely it is clear that what is said above is said of a brother: inasmuch as the sentence which follows is connected by such a conjunction that it confirms the preceding one; for He does not say, But if thou bring thy gift to the altar; but He says, "Therefore, if thou bring thy gift to the altar." For if it is not lawful to be angry with one's brother without a cause, or to say "Raca," or to say "Thou fool," much less is it lawful so to retain anything in one's mind, as that indignation may be turned into hatred. And to this belongs also what is said in another passage: "Let not the sun go down upon your wrath."[5] We are therefore commanded, when about to bring our gift to the altar, if we remember that our brother hath ought against us, to leave the gift before the altar, and to go and be reconciled to our brother, and then to come and offer the gift.[6] But if this is to be understood literally, one might perhaps suppose that such a thing ought to be done if the brother is present; for it cannot be delayed too long, since you are commanded to leave your gift before the altar. If, therefore, such a thing should come into your mind respecting one who is absent, and, as may happen, even settled down beyond the sea, it is absurd to suppose that your gift is to be left before the altar until you may offer it to God after having traversed both lands and seas. And therefore we are compelled to have recourse to an altogether internal and spiritual interpretation, in order that what has been said may be understood without absurdity.

27. And so we may interpret the altar spiritually, as being faith itself in the inner temple of God, whose emblem is the visible altar. For whatever offering we present to God, whether prophecy, or teaching, or prayer, or a psalm, or a hymn, and whatever other such like spiritual gift occurs to the mind, it cannot be acceptable to God, unless it be sustained by sincerity of

---

[1] It is important "to keep in mind that there is no distinction in *kind* between these punishments, only of *degree*. The 'judgment' (κρίσις) inflicted death by the sword, the Sanhedrin death by stoning, and the disgrace of the gehenna followed as an intensification of death; but the punishment is one and the same, — *death*. So also in the subject of the similitude. All the punishments are *spiritual*; all result in *eternal death*, but with *various degrees*, as the degrees of guilt have been" (Alford).

[2] Augustin helps us to understand how the word εἰκῆ (*without cause*) in the preceding clause crept into some of the MSS. In *Retract.* I. xix. 4 he makes the critical note and correction: "*Codices græci non habent sine causa.*"

[3] Gal. iii. 1.

[4] *Obtuleris;* Vulgate, *offers.*   [5] Eph iv. 26.

[6] The performance of an act of worship does not atone for an offence against a fellow-man. The duties toward God never absolve from man's duties to his neighbour. *Inter rem sacram magis subit recordatio offensarum, quam in strepitu negotiorum* (Bengel).

faith, and, as it were, placed on that fixedly and immoveably, so that what we utter may remain whole and uninjured. For many heretics, not having the altar, *i.e.* true faith, have spoken blasphemies for praise ; being weighed down, to wit, with earthly opinions, and thus, as it were, throwing down their offering on the ground. But there ought also to be purity of intention on the part of the offerer. And therefore, when we are about to present any such offering in our heart, *i.e.* in the inner temple of God (" For," as it is said, " the temple of God is holy, which temple ye are ; "[1] and, " That Christ may dwell in the inner man[2] by faith in your hearts ") if it occur to our mind that a brother hath ought against us, *i.e.* if we have injured him in anything (for then he has something against us ; whereas we have something against him if he has injured us, and in that case it is not necessary to proceed to reconciliation : for you will not ask pardon of one who has done you an injury, but merely forgive him, as you desire to be forgiven by the Lord what you have committed against Him), we are therefore to proceed to reconciliation, when it has occurred to our mind that we have perhaps injured our brother in something ; but this is to be done not with the bodily feet, but with the emotions of the mind, so that you are to prostrate yourself with humble disposition before your brother, to whom you have hastened in affectionate thought, in the presence of Him to whom you are about to present your offering. For thus, even if he should be present, you will be able to soften him by a mind free from dissimulation, and to recall him to goodwill by asking pardon, if first you have done this before God, going to him not with the slow movement of the body, but with the very swift impulse of love ; and then coming, *i.e.* recalling your attention to that which you were beginning to do, you will offer your gift.[3]

28. But who acts in a way that he is neither angry with his brother without a cause, nor says " Raca " without a cause, nor calls him a fool without a cause, all of which are most proudly committed ; or so, that, if perchance he has fallen into any of these, he asks pardon with suppliant mind, which is the only remedy ; who but just the man that is not puffed up with the spirit of empty boasting ? " Blessed " therefore " are the poor in spirit : for theirs is the kingdom of heaven." Let us look now at what follows.

CHAP. XI. — 29. " Be kindly disposed,"[4] says he, " toward thine adversary quickly, whiles thou art in the way with him ; lest at any time the adversary deliver thee to the judge, and the judge deliver thee to the officer, and thou be cast into prison. Verily I say unto thee, thou shalt by no means come out thence, till thou hast paid the uttermost farthing." I understand who the judge is : " For the Father judgeth no man, but hath committed all judgment unto the Son."[5] I understand who the officer is : " And angels," it is said, " ministered unto Him : "[6] and we believe that He will come with His angels to judge the quick and the dead. I understand what is meant by the prison : evidently the punishments of darkness, which He calls in another passage the outer darkness :[7] for this reason, I believe, that the joy of the divine rewards is something internal in the mind itself, or even if anything more hidden can be thought of, that joy of which it is said to the servant who deserved well, " Enter thou into the joy of thy Lord ; "[8] just as also, under this republican government, one who is thrust into prison is sent out from the council chamber, or from the palace of the judge.

30. But now, with respect to paying the uttermost farthing,[9] it may be understood without absurdity either as standing for this, that nothing is left unpunished ; just as in common speech we also say " to the very dregs," when we wish to express that something is so drained out that nothing is left : or by the expression " the uttermost farthing " earthly sins may be meant. For as a fourth part of the separate component parts of this world, and in fact as the last, the earth is found ; so that you begin with the heavens, you reckon the air the second, water the third, the earth the fourth. It may therefore seem to be suitably said, " till thou hast paid the last fourth," in the sense of " till thou hast expiated thy earthly sins : " for this the sinner also heard, " Earth thou art, and unto earth shalt thou return."[10] Then, as to the expression " till thou hast paid," I wonder if it does not mean that punishment which is called eternal.[11] For whence is that debt paid where there is now no opportunity given of repenting and of leading a more

---

[1] 1 Cor. iii. 17.
[2] Eph. iii. 17. *In interiore homine*, a different construction from the Greek, which has εἰς with the accusative. So Vulgate, *in interiorem hominem*.
[3] " Discharge of duty to men does not absolve from duty to God." The passage has strong bearing upon the relation of morality and religion.

[4] *Benevolus;* Vulgate, *consentiens*. What is matter of prudence in a civil case, becomes matter of life and death in spiritual things. The Lord does not intend to inculcate simply a law of worldly prudence, as asserted by a few modern commentators.
[5] John v. 22.　[6] Matt. iv. 11.　[7] Matt. viii. 12.
[8] Matt. xxv. 23.
[9] The word translated " farthing " means literally " a fourth part; " and on this original sense Augustin's second interpretation is based.
[10] Gen. iii. 19.
[11] Universalists have quoted the passage to prove the doctrine that punishment will not be endless, others in favor of purgatory. The main idea is the inexorable rigor of the divine justice against the impenitent. " The whole tone of the passage is that of one who seeks to deepen the sense of danger, not to make light of it; to make men feel that they cannot pay their debt, though God may forgive it freely " (Plumptre).

correct life? For perhaps the expression "till thou hast paid" stands here in the same sense as in that passage where it is said, "Sit Thou at my right hand, until I make Thine enemies Thy footstool;"[1] for not even when the enemies have been put under His feet, will He cease to sit at the right hand: or that statement of the apostle, "For He must reign, till He hath put all enemies under His feet;"[2] for not even when they have been put under His feet, will He cease to reign. Hence, as it is there understood of Him respecting whom it is said, "He must reign, till He hath put His enemies under His feet," that He will reign for ever, inasmuch as they will be for ever under His feet: so here it may be understood of him respecting whom it is said, "Thou shalt by no means come out thence, till thou hast paid the uttermost farthing," that he will never come out; for he is always paying the uttermost farthing, so long as he is suffering the everlasting punishment of his earthly sins. Nor would I say this in such a way as that I should seem to prevent a more careful discussion respecting the punishment of sins, as to how in the Scriptures it is called eternal; although in all possible ways it is to be avoided rather than known.

31. But let us now see who the adversary himself is, with whom we are enjoined to agree quickly, whiles we are in the way with him. For he is either the devil, or a man, or the flesh, or God, or His commandment.[3] But I do not see how we should be enjoined to be on terms of goodwill, i.e. to be of one heart or of one mind, with the devil. For some have rendered the Greek word which is found here "of one heart," others "of one mind:" but neither are we enjoined to show goodwill to the devil (for where there is goodwill there is friendship: and no one would say that we are to make friends with the devil); nor is it expedient to come to an agreement with him, against whom we have declared war by once for all renouncing him, and on conquering whom we shall be crowned; nor ought we now to yield to him, for if we had never yielded to him, we should never have fallen into such miseries. Again, as to the adversary being a man, although we are enjoined to live peaceably with all men, as far as lieth in us, where certainly goodwill, and concord, and consent may be understood; yet I do not see how I can accept the view, that we are delivered to the judge by a man, in a case where I understand Christ to be the judge, "before" whose "judgment-seat we must all appear,"[4] as the apostle says: how then is he to deliver me to

the judge, who will appear equally with me before the judge? Or if any one is delivered to the judge because he has injured a man, although the party who has been injured does not deliver him, it is a much more suitable view, that the guilty party is delivered to the judge by that law against which he acted when he injured the man. And this for the additional reason, that if any one has injured a man by killing him, there will be no time now in which to agree with him; for he is not now in the way with him, i.e. in this life: and yet a remedy will not on that account be excluded, if one repents and flees for refuge with the sacrifice of a broken heart to the mercy of Him who forgives the sins of those who turn to Him, and who rejoices more over one penitent than over ninety-nine just persons.[5] But much less do I see how we are enjoined to bear goodwill towards, or to agree with, or to yield to, the flesh. For it is sinners rather who love their flesh, and agree with it, and yield to it; but those who bring it into subjection are not the parties who yield to it, but rather they compel it to yield to them.

32. Perhaps, therefore, we are enjoined to yield to God, and to be well-disposed towards Him, in order that we may be reconciled to Him, from whom by sinning we have turned away, so that He can be called our adversary. For He is rightly called the adversary of those whom He resists, for "God resisteth the proud, but giveth grace to the humble;"[6] and "pride is the beginning of all sin, but the beginning of man's pride is to become apostate from God;"[7] and the apostle says, "For if, when we were enemies, we were reconciled to God by the death of His Son, much more, being reconciled, we shall be saved by His life."[8] And from this it may be perceived that no nature [as being] bad is an enemy to God, inasmuch as the very parties who were enemies are being reconciled. Whoever, therefore, while in this way, i.e. in this life, shall not have been reconciled to God by the death of His Son, will be delivered to the judge by Him, for "the Father judgeth no man, but hath delivered all judgment to the Son;" and so the other things which are described in this section follow, which we have already discussed. There is only one thing which creates a difficulty as regards this interpretation, viz. how it can be rightly said that we are in the way with God, if in this passage He Himself is to be understood as the adversary of the wicked, with whom we are enjoined to be reconciled quickly; unless, perchance, because He is everywhere, we also, while we are in this way, are certainly with Him. For as it is said, "If I ascend up into heaven, Thou art

---

[1] Ps. cx. 1.   [2] 1 Cor. xv. 25.
[3] "The devil" (Clemens Alex.); "conscience" (Euthymius, Zig.); "the man who has done the injury" (Meyer, Tholuck, Lange, Trench, etc.).
[4] 2 Cor. v. 10. *Exhiberi;* Vulgate, *manifestari.*

[5] Luke xv. 7.   [6] Jas. iv. 6.   [7] Ecclus. x. 13, 12.
[8] Rom. v. 10.

there ; if I make my bed in hell, behold, Thou art there. If I take the wings of the morning, and dwell in the uttermost parts of the sea ; even there shall Thy hand lead me, and Thy right hand shall hold me." [1] Or if the view is not accepted, that the wicked are said to be with God, although there is nowhere where God is not present, — just as we do not say that the blind are with the light, although the light surrounds their eyes, — there is one resource remaining : that we should understand the adversary here as being the commandment of God. For what is so much an adversary to those who wish to sin as the commandment of God, i.e. His law and divine Scripture, which has been given us for this life, that it may be with us in the way, which we must not contradict, lest it deliver us to the judge, but which we ought to submit to quickly? For no one knows when he may depart out of this life. Now, who is it that submits to divine Scripture, save he who reads or hears it piously, deferring to it as of supreme authority ; so that what he understands he does not hate on this account, that he feels it to be opposed to his sins, but rather loves being reproved by it, and rejoices that his maladies are not spared until they are healed ; and so that even in respect to what seems to him obscure or absurd, he does not therefore raise contentious contradictions, but prays that he may understand, yet remembering that goodwill and reverence are to be manifested towards so great an authority? But who does this, unless just the man who has come, not harshly threatening, but in the meekness of piety, for the purpose of opening and ascertaining the contents of his father's will? " Blessed," therefore, " are the meek : for they shall inherit the earth." Let us see what follows.

Chap. XII. — 33. " Ye have heard that it was said to them of old time, Thou shalt not commit adultery : but I say unto you, that whosoever looketh on a woman to lust after her, hath committed adultery with her already in his heart." The lesser righteousness, therefore, is not to commit adultery by carnal connection ; but the greater righteousness of the kingdom of God is not to commit adultery in the heart. Now, the man who does not commit adultery in the heart, much more easily guards against committing adultery in actual fact. Hence He who gave the later precept confirmed the earlier ; for He came not to destroy the law, but to fulfil it. It is well worthy of consideration that He did not say, Whosoever lusteth after a woman, but, " Whosoever looketh on a woman to lust after her," [2] i.e.

turneth toward her with this aim and this intent, that he may lust after her ; which, in fact, is not merely to be tickled [3] by fleshly delight, but fully to consent to lust ; so that the forbidden appetite is not restrained, but satisfied if opportunity should be given.

34. For there are three things which go to complete sin : the suggestion of, the taking pleasure in, and the consenting to. Suggestion takes place either by means of memory, or by means of the bodily senses, when we see, or hear, or smell, or taste, or touch anything. And if it give us pleasure to enjoy this, this pleasure, if illicit, must be restrained. Just as when we are fasting, and on seeing food the appetite of the palate is stirred up, this does not happen without pleasure ; but we do not consent to this liking, and [4] we repress it by the right of reason, which has the supremacy. But if consent shall take place, the sin will be complete, known to God in our heart, although it may not become known to men by deed. There are, then, these steps : the suggestion is made, as it were, by a serpent, that is to say, by a fleeting and rapid, i.e. a temporary, movement of bodies : for if there are also any such images moving about in the soul, they have been derived from without from the body ; and if any hidden sensation of the body besides those five senses touches the soul, that also is temporary and fleeting ; and therefore the more clandestinely it glides in, so as to affect the process of thinking, the more aptly is it compared to a serpent. Hence these three stages, as I was beginning to say, resemble that transaction which is described in Genesis, so that the suggestion and a certain measure of suasion is put forth, as it were, by the serpent ; but the taking pleasure in it lies in the carnal appetite, as it were in Eve ; and the consent lies in the reason, as it were in the man : and these things having been acted through, the man is driven forth, as it were, from paradise, i.e. from the most blessed light of righteousness, into death [5] — in all respects most righteously. For he who puts forth suasion does not compel. And all natures are beautiful in their order, according to their gradations ; but we must not descend from the higher, among which the rational mind has its place assigned, to the lower. Nor is any one compelled to do this ; and therefore, if he does it, he is punished by the just law of God, for he is not guilty of this unwillingly. But yet, previous to habit, either there is no pleasure, or it is so slight that there is hardly any ; and to yield to it is a great sin, as such pleasure is unlawful. Now, when any one does yield, he commits sin in the heart. If, however, he also proceeds to action, the desire seems to be satis-

---

[1] Ps. cxxxix. 8-10.
[2] The Greek πρὸς τὸ ἐπιθυμῆσαι refers to sin of intent. " The particle πρός indicates the mental aim " (Tholuck, Meyer, etc.). So Augustin, rightly : " Qui *hoc fine et hoc animo* attenderit."

[3] *titillari.*
[4] The reading " if " has been proposed by some.   [5] Gen. iii.

fied and extinguished; but afterwards, when the suggestion is repeated, a greater pleasure is kindled, which, however, is as yet much less than that which by continuous practice is converted into habit. For it is very difficult to overcome this; and yet even habit itself, if one does not prove untrue to himself, and does not shrink back in dread from the Christian warfare, he will get the better of under His (*i.e.* Christ's) leadership and assistance; and thus, in accordance with primitive peace and order, both the man is subject to Christ, and the woman is subject to the man.[1]

35. Hence, just as we arrive at sin by three steps, — suggestion, pleasure, consent, — so of sin itself there are three varieties, — in heart, in deed, in habit, — as it were, three deaths: one, as it were, in the house, *i.e.* when we consent to lust in the heart; a second now, as it were, brought forth outside the gate, when assent goes forward into action; a third, when the mind is pressed down by the force of bad habit, as if by a mound of earth, and is now, as it were, rotting in the sepulchre. And whoever reads the Gospel perceives that our Lord raised to life these three varieties of the dead. And perhaps he reflects what differences may be found in the very word of Him who raises them, when He says on one occasion, "Damsel, arise;"[2] on another, "Young man,[3] I say unto thee, Arise;"[4] and when on another occasion He groaned in the spirit, and wept, and again groaned, and then afterwards "cried with a loud voice, Lazarus, come forth."[5]

36. And therefore, under the category of the adultery mentioned in this section, we must understand all fleshly and sensual lust. For when Scripture so constantly speaks of idolatry as fornication, and the Apostle Paul calls avarice by the name of idolatry,[6] who doubts but that every evil lust is rightly called fornication, since the soul, neglecting the higher law by which it is ruled, and prostituting itself for the base pleasure of the lower nature as its reward (so to speak), is thereby corrupted? And therefore let every one who feels carnal pleasure rebelling against right inclination in his own case through the habit of sinning, by whose unsubdued violence he is dragged into captivity, recall to mind as much as he can what kind of peace he has lost by sinning, and let him cry out, "O wretched man that I am! who shall deliver me from the body of this death? I thank God through Jesus Christ."[7] For in this way, when he cries out that he is wretched, in the act of bewailing he implores the help of a comforter. Nor is it a small approach to blessedness, when he has come to know his wretchedness; and therefore "blessed" also "are they that mourn,[8] for they shall be comforted."

Chap. XIII. — 37. In the next place, He goes on to say: "And if thy right eye offend thee, pluck it out, and cast it from thee: for it is profitable for thee that one of thy members should perish, and not that thy whole body should go[9] into hell." Here, certainly, there is need of great courage in order to cut off one's members.[10] For whatever it is that is meant by the "eye," undoubtedly it is such a thing as is ardently loved. For those who wish to express their affection strongly are wont to speak thus: I love him as my own eyes, or even more than my own eyes. Then, when the word "right" is added, it is meant perhaps to intensify the strength of the affection.[11] For although these bodily eyes of ours are turned in a common direction for the purpose of seeing, and if both are turned they have equal power, yet men are more afraid of losing the right one. So that the sense in this case is: Whatever it is which thou so lovest that thou reckonest it as a right eye, if it offends thee, *i.e.* if it proves a hindrance to thee on the way to true happiness, pluck it out and cast it from thee. For it is profitable for thee, that one of these which thou so lovest that they cleave to thee as if they were members, should perish, rather than that thy whole body should be cast into hell.

38. But since He follows it up with a similar statement respecting the right hand, "If thy right hand offend thee, cut it off, and cast it from thee: for it is profitable for thee that one of thy members should perish, and not that thy whole body should go[12] into hell," He compels us to inquire more carefully what He has spoken of as an eye. And as regards this inquiry, nothing occurs to me as a more suitable explanation than a greatly beloved friend: for this, certainly, is something which we may rightly call a member which we ardently love; and this friend a counsellor, for it is an eye, as it were, pointing out the road; and that in divine things, for it is the right eye: so that the left is indeed a beloved counsellor, but in earthly matters, pertaining to

---

[1] 1 Cor. xi. 3 and Eph. v. 23. [2] Mark v. 41.
[3] *Juvenis;* Vulgate, *adolescens.* [4] Luke vii. 14.
[5] John xi. 33-44. [6] Col. iii. 5 and Eph. v. 5.
[7] Rom. vii. 24, 25.

[8] *Lugentes;* Vulgate, *qui lugent.*
[9] *Eat;* Vulgate, *mittatur.*
[10] Not literally (Fritzsche). Excision of the members would not of itself destroy the lust of the heart.
[11] So Meyer *et al.* What Robert South says (*Sermon* on John vii. 17) of the Sermon on the Mount as a whole, can certainly be applied here: "All the particulars of Matt. v.-vii. are wrapt up in the doctrine of self-denial, prescribing to the world the most inward purity of heart, and a constant conflict with all our sensual appetites and worldly interests," etc. Augustin's interpretation is correct as far as it goes, but it is too restricted. Christ does not here insist upon the renunciation of sinful lusts, but upon the evasion of occasions of sin. What is harmless and innocent of itself, when through any temperament or condition it becomes an occasion of sinning, is to be relinquished.
[12] *Eat.* So Vulgate.

the necessities of the body; concerning which as a cause of stumbling it was superfluous to speak, inasmuch as not even the right was to be spared. Now, a counsellor in divine things is a cause of stumbling, if he endeavours to lead one into any dangerous heresy under the guise of religion and doctrine. Hence also let the right hand be taken in the sense of a beloved helper and assistant in divine works: for in like manner as contemplation is rightly understood as having its seat in the eye, so action in the right hand; so that the left hand may be understood in reference to works which are necessary for this life, and for the body.

CHAP. XIV. — 39. "It hath been said, Whosoever shall put away his wife, let him give her a writing of divorcement." This is the lesser righteousness of the Pharisees, which is not opposed by what our Lord says: "But I say unto you, That whosoever shall put away his wife, saving for the cause of fornication, causeth her to commit adultery:[1] and whosoever shall marry her that is loosed from her husband committeth adultery."[2] For He who gave the commandment that a writing of divorcement should be given, did not give the commandment that a wife should be put away; but "whosoever shall put away," says He, "let him give her a writing of divorcement," in order that the thought of such a writing might moderate the rash anger of him who was getting rid of his wife. And, therefore, He who sought to interpose a delay in putting away, indicated as far as He could to hard-hearted men that He did not wish separation. And accordingly the Lord Himself in another passage, when a question was asked Him as to this matter, gave this reply: "Moses did so because of the hardness of your hearts."[3] For however hard-hearted a man may be who wishes to put away his wife, when he reflects that, on a writing of divorcement being given her, she could then without risk marry another, he would be easily appeased. Our Lord, therefore, in order to confirm that principle, that a wife should not lightly be put away, made the single exception of fornication; but enjoins that all other annoyances, if any such should happen to spring up, be borne with fortitude for the sake of conjugal fidelity and for the sake of chastity; and he also calls that man an adulterer who should marry her that has been divorced by her husband. And the Apostle Paul shows the limit of this state of affairs, for he says it is to be observed as long as her husband liveth; but on

the husband's death he gives permission to marry.[4] For he himself also held by this rule, and therein brings forward not his own advice, as in the case of some of his admonitions, but a command enjoined by the Lord when he says: "And unto the married [5] I command, yet not I, but the Lord, Let not the wife [5] depart from her husband: but and if she depart, let her remain unmarried, or be reconciled to her husband: and let not the husband put away his wife."[6] I believe that, according to a similar rule, if he shall put her away, he is to remain unmarried, or be reconciled to his wife. For it may happen that he puts away his wife for the cause of fornication, which our Lord wished to make an exception of. But now, if she is not allowed to marry while the husband is living from whom she has departed, nor he to take another while the wife is living whom he has put away, much less is it right to commit unlawful acts of fornication with any parties whomsoever. More blessed indeed are those marriages to be reckoned, where the parties concerned, whether after the procreation of children, or even through contempt of such an earthly progeny, have been able with common consent to practise self-restraint toward each other: both because nothing is done contrary to that precept whereby the Lord forbids a spouse to be put away (for he does not put her away who lives with her not carnally, but spiritually), and because that principle is observed to which the apostle gives expression, "It remaineth, that they that have wives be as though they had none."[7]

CHAP. XV. — 40. But it is rather that statement which the Lord Himself makes in another passage which is wont to disturb the minds of the little ones, who nevertheless earnestly desire to live now according to the precepts of Christ: "If any man come to me, and hate not his father, and mother, and wife, and children, and brethren, and sisters, yea, and his own life also, he cannot be my disciple."[8] For it may seem a contradiction to the less intelligent, that here He forbids the putting away of a wife saving for the cause of fornication, but that elsewhere He affirms that no one can be a disciple of His who does not hate his wife. But if He were speaking with reference to sexual intercourse, He would not place father, and mother, and brothers in the same category. But how true it is, that "the kingdom of heaven suffereth violence, and they that use violence take it by force!"[9] For how great violence is necessary, in order that

---

[1] *Per alias nuptias, quarum potestatem dat divortium* ("by another marriage, power of which divorce gives." — Bengel). So also Meyer, Alford, etc.
[2] *Solutam a viro . . . moechatur;* Vulgate, *dimissam . . . adulterat.*
[3] Matt. xix. 8.

[4] Rom. vii. 2, 3.
[5] *In conjugio . . . mulierem;* Vulgate, *matrimonio . . . uxorem.*
[6] 1 Cor. vii. 10, 11.   [7] 1 Cor. vii. 29.   [8] Luke xiv. 26.
[9] Matt. xi. 12. *Qui vim faciunt diripiunt illud;* Vulgate, *violenti rapiunt illud.*

a man may love his enemies, and hate his father, and mother, and wife, and children, and brothers! For He commands both things who calls us to the kingdom of heaven. And how these things do not contradict each other, it is easy to show under His guidance; but after they have been understood, it is difficult to carry them out, although this too is very easy when He Himself assists us. For in that eternal kingdom to which He has vouchsafed to call His disciples, to whom He also gives the name of brothers, there are no temporal relationships of this sort. For " there is neither Jew nor Greek, there is neither bond nor free, there is neither male nor female; " " but Christ is all, and in all." [1] And the Lord Himself says : " For in the resurrection they neither marry, nor are given in marriage,[2] but are as the angels of God in heaven." [3] Hence it is necessary that whoever wishes here and now to aim after the life of that kingdom, should hate not the persons themselves, but those temporal relationships by which this life of ours, which is transitory and is comprised in being born and dying, is upheld ; because he who does not hate them, does not yet love that life where there is no condition of being born and dying, which unites parties in earthly wedlock.

41. Therefore, if I were to ask any good Christian who has a wife, and even though he may still be having children by her, whether he would like to have his wife in that kingdom ; mindful in any case of the promises of God, and of that life where this incorruptible shall put on incorruption, and this mortal shall put on immortality ;[4] though at present hesitating from the greatness, or at least from a certain degree of love, he would reply with execration that he is strongly averse to it. Were I to ask him again, whether he would like his wife to live with him there, after the resurrection, when she had undergone that angelic change which is promised to the saints, he would reply that he desired this as strongly as he reprobated the other. Thus a good Christian is found in one and the same woman to love the creature of God, whom he desires to be transformed and renewed ; but to hate the corruptible and mortal conjugal connection and sexual intercourse: i.e. to love in her what is characteristic of a human being, to hate what belongs to her as a wife. So also he loves his enemy, not in as far as he is an enemy, but in as far as he is a man ; so that he wishes the same prosperity to come to him as to himself, viz. that he may reach the kingdom of heaven rectified and renewed. This is to be understood both of father and mother and

the other ties of blood, that we hate in them what has fallen to the lot of the human race in being born and dying, but that we love what can be carried along with us to those realms where no one says, My Father; but all say to the one God, " Our Father : " and no one says, My mother ; but all say to that other Jerusalem, Our mother : and no one says, My brother ; but each says respecting every other, Our brother. But in fact there will be a marriage on our part as of one spouse (when we have been brought together into unity), with Him who hath delivered us from the pollution of this world by the shedding of His own blood. It is necessary, therefore, that the disciple of Christ should hate these things which pass away, in those whom he desires along with himself to reach those things which shall for ever remain ; and that he should the more hate these things in them, the more he loves themselves.

42. A Christian may therefore live in concord with his wife, whether with her providing for a fleshly craving, a thing which the apostle speaks by permission, not by commandment ; or providing for the procreation of children, which may be at present in some degree praiseworthy ; or providing for a brotherly and sisterly fellowship, without any corporeal connection, having his wife as though he had her not, as is most excellent and sublime in the marriage of Christians : yet so that in her he hates the name of temporal relationship, and loves the hope of everlasting blessedness. For we hate, without doubt, that respecting which we wish at least, that at some time hereafter it should' not exist ; as, for instance, this same life of ours in the present world, which if we were not to hate as being temporal, we would not long for the future life, which is not conditioned by time. For as a substitute for this life the soul is put, respecting which it is said in that passage, " If a man hate not his own soul [5] also, he cannot be my disciple." For that corruptible meat is necessary for this life, of which the Lord Himself says, " Is not the soul [6] more than meat? " i.e. this life to which meat is necessary. And when He says that He would lay down His soul [7] for His sheep, He undoubtedly means this life, as He is declaring that He is going to die for us.

CHAP. XVI. — 43. Here there arises a second question, when the Lord allows a wife to be put away for the cause of fornication, in what latitude of meaning fornication is to be understood in this passage, — whether in the sense understood by all, viz. that we are to understand that fornication to be meant which is committed in acts of uncleanness ; or whether, in accordance

---

[1] Gal. iii. 28 and Col. iii. 11.
[2] *Uxores ducent;* Vulgate, *nubentur.*
[3] Matt. xxii. 30.   [4] 1 Cor. xv. 53, 54.

[5] Luke xiv. 26.   [6] Matt. vi. 25.   [7] John x. 15.

with the usage of Scripture in speaking of fornication (as has been mentioned above), as meaning all unlawful corruption, such as idolatry or covetousness, and therefore, of course, every transgression of the law on account of the unlawful lust [involved in it].[1] But let us consult the apostle, that we may not say rashly. "And unto the married I command," says he, "yet not I, but the Lord, Let not the wife depart from her husband: but and if she depart, let her remain unmarried, or be reconciled to her husband." For it may happen that she departs for that cause for which the Lord gives permission to do so. Or, if a woman is at liberty to put away her husband for other causes besides that of fornication, and the husband is not at liberty, what answer shall we give respecting this statement which he has made afterwards, "And let not the husband put away his wife"? Wherefore did he not add, saving for the cause of fornication, which the Lord permits, unless because he wishes a similar rule to be understood, that if he shall put away his wife (which he is permitted to do for the cause of fornication), he is to remain without a wife, or be reconciled to his wife? For it would not be a bad thing for a husband to be reconciled to such a woman as that to whom, when nobody had dared to stone her, the Lord said, "Go, and sin no more."[2] And for this reason also, because He who says, It is not lawful to put away one's wife saving for the cause of fornication, forces him to retain his wife, if there should be no cause of fornication: but if there should be, He does not force him to put her away, but permits him, just as when it is said, Let it not be lawful for a woman to marry another, unless her husband be dead; if she shall marry before the death of her husband, she is guilty; if she shall not marry after the death of her husband, she is not guilty, for she is not commanded to marry, but merely permitted. If, therefore, there is a like rule in the said law of marriage between man and woman, to such an extent that not merely of the woman has the same apostle said, "The wife hath not power of her own body, but the husband;" but he has not been silent respecting him, saying, "And likewise also the husband hath not power of his own body, but the wife;"— if, then, the rule is

similar, there is no necessity for understanding that it is lawful for a woman to put away her husband, saving for the cause of fornication, as is the case also with the husband.

44. It is therefore to be considered in what latitude of meaning we ought to understand the word fornication, and the apostle is to be consulted, as we were beginning to do. For he goes on to say, "But to the rest speak I, not the Lord." Here, first, we must see who are "the rest," for he was speaking before on the part of the Lord to those who are married, but now, as from himself, he speaks to "the rest:" hence perhaps to the unmarried, but this does not follow. For thus he continues: "If any brother hath a wife that believeth not, and she be pleased to dwell with him, let him not put her away." Hence, even now he is speaking to those who are married. What, then, is his object in saying "to the rest," unless that he was speaking before to those who were so united, that they were alike as to their faith in Christ; but that now he is speaking to "the rest," i.e. to those who are so united, that they are not both believers? But what does he say to them? "If any brother hath a wife that believeth not, and she be pleased to dwell with him, let him not put her away. And the woman which hath an husband that believeth not, and if he be pleased to dwell with her, let her not put him away." If, therefore, he does not give a command as from the Lord, but advises as from himself, then this good result springs from it, that if any one act otherwise, he is not a transgressor of a command, just as he says a little after respecting virgins, that he has no command of the Lord, but that he gives his advice; and he so praises virginity, that whoever will may avail himself of it; yet if he shall not do so, he may not be judged to have acted contrary to a command. For there is one thing which is commanded, another respecting which advice is given, another still which is allowed.[3] A wife is commanded not to depart from her husband; and if she depart, to remain unmarried, or to be reconciled to her husband: therefore it is not allowable for her to act otherwise. But a believing husband is advised, if he has an unbelieving wife who is pleased to dwell with him, not to put her away: therefore it is allowable also to put her away, because it is no command of the Lord that he should not put her away, but an advice of the apostle: just as a virgin is advised not to marry; but if she shall marry, she will not indeed adhere to the advice, but she will not act in opposition to a command. Allowance is given[4] when it is said, "But I speak this by permission, and not of commandment." And there-

---

[1] Augustin expresses himself (*Retract.* I. xix. 6) as having misgivings about his own explanation of this matter here. He advises readers to go to his other writings on the subject of marriage and divorce, or to the works of other writers. He says all sin is not fornication (*omne peccatum fornicatio non est*); and to determine which sins are fornication, and when a wife may be dismissed, is a most broad (*latebrosissima*) question. He calls the question a most difficult (*difficillimam*) one, and says, "But verily I feel that I have not come to the perfect conclusion of this matter (*imo non me pervenisse ad hujus rei perfectionem sentio. Retract.* ii. 57). Some of his treatises on the marriage relation: *De Bono Conjugali; De Conjugiis Adulterinis; De Nuptiis et Concupiscientia.*

[2] John viii. 11. *Vide deinceps ne pecces;* Vulgate, *jam amplius noli peccare.*

[3] *Ignoscitur,* lit. "is pardoned." [4] Lit. "it is pardoned."

fore, if it is allowable that an unbelieving wife should be put away, although it is better not to put her away, and yet not allowable, according to the commandment of the Lord, that a wife should be put away, saving for the cause of fornication, [then] unbelief itself also is fornication.

45. For what sayest thou, O apostle? Surely, that a believing husband who has an unbelieving wife pleased to dwell with him is not to put her away? Just so, says he. When, therefore, the Lord also gives this command, that a man should not put away his wife, saving for the cause of fornication, why dost thou say here, "I speak, not the Lord"? For this reason, viz. that the idolatry which unbelievers follow, and every other noxious superstition, is fornication. Now, the Lord permitted a wife to be put away for the cause of fornication; but in permitting, He did not command it: He gave opportunity to the apostle for advising that whoever wished should not put away an unbelieving wife, in order that, perchance, in this way she might become a believer. "For," says he, "the unbelieving husband is sanctified in the wife, and the unbelieving wife is sanctified in the brother."[1] I suppose it had already occurred that some wives were embracing the faith by means of their believing husbands, and husbands by means of their believing wives; and although not mentioning names, he yet urged his case by examples, in order to strengthen his counsel. Then he goes on to say, "Else were your children unclean; but now are they holy." For now the children were Christians, who were sanctified at the instance of one of the parents, or with the consent of both; which would not take place unless the marriage were broken up by one of the parties becoming a believer, and unless the unbelief of the spouse were borne with so far as to give an opportunity of believing. This, therefore, is the counsel of Him whom I regard as having spoken the words, "Whatsoever thou spendest more, when I come again, I will repay thee."[2]

46. Moreover, if unbelief is fornication, and idolatry unbelief, and covetousness idolatry, it is not to be doubted that covetousness also is fornication. Who, then, in that case can rightly separate any unlawful lust whatever from the category of fornication, if covetousness is fornication? And from this we perceive, that because of unlawful lusts, not only those of which one is guilty in acts of uncleanness with another's husband or wife, but any unlawful lusts whatever, which cause the soul making a bad use of the body to wander from the law of God, and to be ruinously and basely corrupted, a man may,

without crime, put away his wife, and a wife her husband, because the Lord makes the cause of fornication an exception; which fornication, in accordance with the above considerations, we are compelled to understand as being general and universal.

47. But when He says, "saving for the cause of fornication," He has not said of which of them, whether the man or the woman.[3] For not only is it allowed to put away a wife who commits fornication; but whoever puts away that wife even by whom he is himself compelled to commit fornication, puts her away undoubtedly for the cause of fornication. As, for instance, if a wife should compel one to sacrifice to idols, the man who puts away such an one puts her away for the cause of fornication, not only on her part, but on his own also: on her part, because she commits fornication; on his own, that he may not commit fornication. Nothing, however, is more unjust than for a man to put away his wife because of fornication, if he himself also is convicted of committing fornication. For that passage occurs to one: "For wherein thou judgest another, thou condemnest thyself; for thou that judgest doest the same things."[4] And for this reason, whosoever wishes to put away his wife because of fornication, ought first to be cleared of fornication; and a like remark I would make respecting the woman also.

48. But in reference to what He says, "Whosoever shall marry her that is divorced[5] committeth adultery," it may be asked whether she also who is married commits adultery in the same way as he does who marries her. For she also is commanded to remain unmarried, or be reconciled to her husband; but this in the case of her departing from her husband. There is, however, a great difference whether she put away or be put away. For if she put away her husband, and marry another, she seems to have left her former husband from a desire of changing her marriage connection, which is, without doubt, an adulterous thought. But if she be put away by the husband, with whom she desired to be, he indeed who marries her commits adultery, according to the Lord's declaration; but whether she also be involved in a like crime is uncertain, — although it is much less easy to discover how, when a man and woman have in-

---

[1] 1 Cor. vii. 14. Augustin conforms to the approved reading in the Greek text: *in uxore . . . in fratre.* Vulgate, *per mulierem, . . . per virum.* (See Revised Version.)

[2] Luke x. 35.

[3] Modern commentators do not spring this question, agreeing that the fornication referred to is of the wife. Paulus, Döllinger (in *Christ. u. Kirche*, to which Professor Conington replied in *Cont. Rev.*, May, 1869) think the fornication of the woman was committed before her marriage. Plumptre also prefers the reference to antenuptial sin.

[4] Rom. ii. 1.

[5] ἀπολελυμένην; that is, one divorced unlawfully, who has not been guilty of fornication (so Meyer very positively, Stier *et. al.*, Alford hesitatingly). This explanation might seem to limit re-marriage to such an one, inasmuch as the essence of the marriage bond has not been touched (So Alford *et. al.*).

tercourse one with another with equal consent, one of them should be an adulterer, and the other not. To this is to be added the consideration, that if he commits adultery by marrying her who is divorced from her husband (although she does not put away, but is put away), she causes him to commit adultery, which nevertheless the Lord forbids. And hence we infer that, whether she has been put away, or has put away her husband, it is necessary for her to remain unmarried, or be reconciled to her husband.[1]

49. Again, it is asked whether, if, with a wife's permission, either a barren one, or one who does not wish to submit to intercourse, a man shall take to himself another woman, not another man's wife, nor one separated from her husband, he can do so without being chargeable with fornication? And an example is found in the Old Testament history;[2] but now there are greater precepts which the human race has reached after having passed that stage; and those matters are to be investigated for the purpose of distinguishing the ages of the dispensation of that divine providence which assists the human race in the most orderly way; but not for the purpose of making use of the rules of living. But yet it may be asked whether what the apostle says, "The wife hath not power of her own body, but the husband; and likewise also the husband hath not power of his own body, but the wife," can be carried so far, that, with the permission of a wife, who possesses the power over her husband's body, a man can have intercourse with another woman, who is neither another man's wife nor divorced from her husband; but such an opinion is not to be entertained, lest it should seem that a woman also, with her husband's permission, could do such a thing, which the instinctive feeling of every one prevents.

50. And yet some occasions may arise, where a wife also, with the consent of her husband, may seem under obligation to do this for the sake of that husband himself; as, for instance, is said to have happened at Antioch about fifty years ago,[3] in the times of Constantius. For Acyndinus, at that time prefect and at one time also consul, when he demanded of a certain public debtor the payment of a poundweight of gold, impelled by I know not what motive, did a thing which is often dangerous in the case of those magistrates to whom anything whatever is lawful, or rather is thought to be lawful, viz. threatened with an oath and with a vehement affirmation, that if he did not pay the foresaid gold on a certain day which he had fixed, he would be put to death. Accordingly, while he was being kept in cruel confinement, and was unable to rid himself of that debt, the dread day began to impend and to draw near. He happened, however, to have a very beautiful wife, but one who had no money wherewith to come to the relief of her husband; and when a certain rich man had had his desires inflamed by the beauty of this woman, and had learned that her husband was placed in that critical situation, he sent to her, promising in return for a single night, if she would consent to hold intercourse with him, that he would give her the pound of gold. Then she, knowing that she herself had not power over her body, but her husband, conveyed the intelligence to him, telling him that she was prepared to do it for the sake of her husband, but only if he himself, the lord by marriage of her body, to whom all that chastity was due, should wish it to be done, as if disposing of his own property for the sake of his life. He thanked her, and commanded that it should be done, in no wise judging that it was an adulterous embrace, because it was no lust, but great love for her husband, that demanded it, at his own bidding and will. The woman came to the villa of that rich man, did what the lewd man wished; but she gave her body only to her husband, who desir d not, as was usual, his marriage rights, but life. She received the gold; but he who gave it took away stealthily what he had given, and substituted a similar bag with earth in it. When the woman, however, on reaching her home, discovered it, she rushed forth in public in order to proclaim the deed she had done, animated by the same tender affection for her husband by which she had been forced to do it; she goes to the prefect, confesses everything, shows the fraud that had been practised upon her. Then indeed the prefect first pronounces himself guilty, because the matter had come to this by means of his threats, and, as if pronouncing sentence upon another, decided that a pound of gold should be brought into the treasury from the property of Acyndinus; but that she (the woman) be installed as mistress of that piece of land whence she had received the earth instead of the gold. I offer no opinion either way from this story: let each one form a judgment as he pleases, for the history is not drawn from divinely authoritative sources; but yet, when the story is related, man's instinctive sense does not so revolt against what was done in the case of this woman, at her husband's bidding, as we formerly shuddered when the thing itself was set forth without any example. But in this section of the Gospel nothing is to be more steadily kept in view, than that so great is the evil of fornication, that, while married people are bound to one another by so strong a

---

[1] That is, innocent or guilty, she cannot marry without committing adultery The Roman-Catholic Church forbids divorces, but permits an indefinite separation *a mensa et toro* ("from table and bed").

[2] Abraham taking Hagar with Sarah's consent.

[3] About the year 343; for Augustin wrote this treatise about the year 393

bond, this one cause of divorce is excepted; but as to what fornication is, that we have already discussed.[1]

CHAP. XVII.—51. "Again," says He, "ye have heard that it hath been said to them of old time, Thou shalt not forswear thyself, but shalt perform unto the Lord thine oath:[2] But I say unto you, Swear not at all; neither by heaven, for it is God's throne; nor by the earth, for it is His footstool; neither by Jerusalem, for it is the city of the great King. Neither shalt thou swear by thy head, because thou canst not make one hair white or black. But let your communication be Yea, yea; Nay, nay: for whatsoever is more[3] than these cometh of evil." The righteousness of the Pharisees is not to forswear oneself; and this is confirmed by Him who gives the command not to swear, so far as relates to the righteousness of the kingdom of heaven. For just as he who does not speak at all cannot speak falsely, so he who does not swear at all cannot swear falsely. But yet, since he who takes God to witness swears, this section must be carefully considered, lest the apostle should seem to have acted contrary to the Lord's precept, who often swore in this way, when he says, "Now the things which I write unto you, be-

hold, before God I lie not;"[4] and again, "The God and Father of our Lord Jesus Christ, which is blessed for evermore, knoweth that I lie not."[5] Of like nature also is that asseveration, "For God is my witness, whom I serve with my spirit in the gospel of His Son, that without ceasing I make mention of you always in my prayers."[6] Unless, perchance, one were to say that it is to be reckoned swearing only when something is spoken of by which one swears; so that he has not used an oath, because he has not said, by God; but has said, "God is witness." It is ridiculous to think so; yet because of the contentious, or those very slow of apprehension, lest any one should think there is a difference, let him know that the apostle has used an oath in this way also, saying, "By your rejoicing, I die daily."[7] And let no one think that this is so expressed as if it were said, Your rejoicing makes me die daily; just as it is said, By his teaching he became learned, i.e. by his teaching it came about that he was perfectly instructed: the Greek copies decide the matter, where we find it written, Νὴ τὴν καύχησιν ὑμετέραν, an expression which is used only by one taking an oath. Thus, then, it is understood that the Lord gave the command not to swear in this sense, lest any one should eagerly seek after an oath as a good thing, and by the constant use of oaths sink down through force of habit into perjury. And therefore let him who understands that swearing is to be reckoned not among things that are good, but among things that are necessary, refrain as far as he can from indulging in it, unless by necessity, when he sees men slow to believe what it is useful for them to believe, except they be assured by an oath. To this, accordingly, reference is made when it is said, "Let your speech be, Yea, yea; Nay, nay;" this is good, and what is to be desired. "For whatsoever is more than these cometh of evil;" i.e., if you are compelled to swear, know that it comes of a necessity arising from the infirmity of those whom you are trying to persuade of something; which infirmity is certainly an evil, from which we daily pray to be delivered, when we say, "Deliver us from evil."[8] Hence He has not said, Whatsoever is more than these is evil; for you are not doing what is evil when you make a good use of an oath, which, although not in itself good, is yet necessary in order to persuade another that you are trying to move him for some useful end; but it "cometh of evil" on his part by whose infirmity you are compelled to swear.[9] But no one learns, unless

---

[1] The law permitted divorce for "some uncleanness" (Deut. xxiv. 1). In the time of Christ divorce was allowed on trivial grounds. While Schammai interpreted the Deuteronomic prescription of *moral* uncleanness or adultery, Hillel interpreted it to include *physical* uncleanness or unattractiveness. A wife's cooking her husband's food unpalatably he declared to be a legitimate cause for a dissolution of the marriage bond. Opposing the loose views current, Christ declared that it was on account of the "hardness of their hearts" that Moses had *suffered* them to put away their wives, and asserted adultery to be the only allowable reason for divorce. The question whether the innocent party may marry, is beset with great difficulties in view of this passage and Matt. xix. 9. The answer turns somewhat upon the construction of the passage. Augustin here, the Council of Trent (and so the Roman-Catholic Church), Weiss, Mansel, and others hold that all marriage of a divorced person is declared illegal. In another place (*De Conj. Adult.* i. 9) Augustin says, "Why, I say, did the Lord interject 'the cause of fornication,' and not say rather, in a general way, 'Whosoever shall put away his wife and marry another commits adultery'? . . . I think, because the Lord wishes to mention that which is greater. For who will deny that it is a greater adultery to marry another when the divorced wife has not committed fornication than when any one divorces his wife and then marries another? Not because this is not adultery, but because it is a lesser sort." The *Apost. Constitutions* (vii. 2) say, "Thou shalt not commit adultery, for thou dividest one flesh into two," etc. Weiss: "Jesus everywhere takes it for granted that in the sight of God there is no such thing as a dissolution of the marriage bond (*Leben Jesu*, i 529). President Woolsey, on the other hand, unhesitatingly declares, that, by Christ's precepts, marriage is dissolved by adultery, so that the innocent party may marry again. According to this passage, the woman divorced on other grounds than adultery seems to be declared adulterous if she marry. According to Matt. xix. 9 the man who puts away his wife for adultery, seems to be permitted to marry without becoming adulterous himself. According to Mark x. 12 the woman had the privilege in that day of putting away her husband, but "there is no evidence in the Hebrew Scriptures that the woman could get herself divorced from her husband." To the able treatment of Augustin, which might seem either exceedingly fearless or mawkish at the present day, according to the stand-point of the critic, the reader would do well to read Alford and Lange on this passage: Stanley on 1 Cor. vii. 11; and Woolsey, art. "Divorce" in *Schaff-Herzog Encycl.* Whatever may be the exact meaning of our Lord concerning the marriage of the innocent party, it is evident that He regards the marriage bond as profoundly sacred, and warrants the celebrant in binding the parties to marriage to be faithful one to the other "till death do you part." He Himself said, "What, therefore, God hath joined together, let not man put asunder" (Mark x. 9).

[2] *Jusjurandum;* Vulgate, *juramenta;* Greek, τοὺς ὅρκους.

[3] *Amplius;* Vulgate, *abundantius.*

[4] Gal. i. 20.   [5] 2 Cor. xi. 31.   [6] Rom. i. 9.

[7] 1 Cor. xv. 31.   [8] Matt. vi. 13.

[9] Revised Version, *Evil One.* So Euthymius, Zig. (*auctorem habet diabolum*), Chrysostom, Theophylact, Fritzsche, Keim, Meyer, Plumptre, etc. The interpretation of Augustin is shared by Luther, Bengel, De Wette, Tholuck, Ewald, etc.

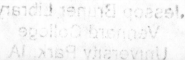

he has had experience, how difficult it is both to get rid of a habit of swearing, and never to do rashly what necessity sometimes compels him to do.[1]

52. But it may be asked why, when it was said, "But I say unto you, Swear not at all," it was added, "neither by heaven, for it is God's throne," etc., up to "neither by thy head." I suppose it was for this reason, that the Jews did not think they were bound by the oath, if they had sworn by such things: and since they had heard it said, "Thou shalt perform unto the Lord thine oath," they did not think an oath brought them under obligation to the Lord, if they swore by heaven, or earth, or by Jerusalem, or by their head; and this happened not from the fault of Him who gave the command, but because they did not rightly understand it. Hence the Lord teaches that there is nothing so worthless among the creatures of God, as that any one should think that he may swear falsely by it; since created things, from the highest down to the lowest, beginning with the throne of God and going down to a white or black hair, are ruled by divine providence. "Neither by heaven," says He, "for it is God's throne; nor by the earth, for it is His footstool:" i.e., when you swear by heaven or the earth, do not imagine that your oath does not bring you under obligation to the Lord; for you are convicted of swearing by Him who has heaven for His throne, and the earth for His footstool. "Neither by Jerusalem, for it is the city of the great King;" a better expression than if He had said, "My [city]; although, however, we understand Him to have meant this. And, because He is undoubtedly the Lord, the man who swears by Jerusalem is bound by his oath to the Lord. "Neither shalt thou swear by thy head." Now, what could any one suppose to belong more to himself than his own head? But how is it ours, when we have not the power of making one hair white or black? Hence, whoever should wish to swear even by his own head, is bound by his oath to God, who in an ineffable way keeps all things in His power, and is everywhere present. And here also all other things are understood, which could not of course be enumerated; just as that saying of the apostle we have mentioned, "By your rejoicing, I die daily." And to show that he was bound by this oath to the Lord, he has added, "which I have in Christ Jesus."

53. But yet (I make the remark for the sake of the carnal) we must not think that heaven is called God's throne, and the earth His footstool, because God has members placed in heaven and in earth, in some such way as we have when we sit down; but that seat means judgment. And since, in this organic whole of the universe, heaven has the greatest appearance, and earth the least, — as if the divine power were more present where the beauty excels, but still were regulating the least degree of it in the most distant and in the lowest regions, — He is said to sit in heaven, and to tread upon the earth. But spiritually the expression heaven means holy souls, and earth sinful ones: and since the spiritual man judges all things, yet he himself is judged of no man,[2] he is suitably spoken of as the seat of God; but the sinner to whom it is said, "Earth thou art, and unto earth shalt thou return," [3] because, in accordance with that justice which assigns what is suitable to men's deserts, he is placed among things that are lowest, and he who would not remain in the law is punished under the law, is suitably taken as His footstool.

CHAP. XVIII. — 54. But now, to conclude by summing up this passage, what can be named or thought of more laborious and toilsome, where the believing soul is straining every nerve of its industry, than the subduing of vicious habit? Let such an one cut off the members which obstruct the kingdom of heaven, and not be overwhelmed by the pain: in conjugal fidelity let him bear with everything which, however grievously annoying it may be, is still free from the

---

[1] Augustin is somewhat perplexed about the meaning, but decides the injunction to be directed against the abuse of the oath, not to forbid it wholly. The oath was permitted by the law (Lev. xxii. 11), was to be held sacred (Num. xxx. 2), and to be made in God's name (Deut. vi. 13). It was customary under the Old Testament to swear (Gen. xxiv. 37, Josh. ix. 15; perhaps only a solemn affirmation), and in the name of the Lord (1 Sam. xx. 42: Irenæus, Clement, Origen, Chrysostom, etc.). The Anabaptists, Mennonites, and Quakers understand the precept to forbid all oaths, even in the civil court. "Christendom, if it were fully conformed to Christ's will, as it should be, would tolerate no oaths whatever" (Meyer). "The proper state of Christians is to require no oaths" (Alford). If interpreted as a definite prohibition of all swearing, the passage comes into conflict with Christ's own example (Matt. xxvi. 63), and the apostle's conduct in the passages quoted by Augustin. The meaning has been restricted to rash and frivolous oaths on the street and in the market (Keim); in daily conversation (Carr, Camb. Bible for Schools). In the ideal Christian community, where truth and honesty prevail, oaths will be superfluous: the simple asseverations, "Yea, nay," will be sufficient. To this, Christ's precept ultimately looks. But He, no doubt, had in mind the widespread profanity of His day, and the current opinion that only oaths containing the name of God were binding (Lightfoot cites from the Rabbinical books to this effect). All unnecessary appeals to God, as well as careless and profane swearing, are forbidden, as coming either from bad passions within or a want of reverence. "Prohibition would be repeal of the Mosaic law" (Plumptre). "All strengthening of the simple 'Yea and nay' is occasioned by the presence of sin and Satan in the world. There is no more striking proof of the existence of evil than the prevalence of the foolish, low, useless habit of swearing. It could never have arisen if men did not believe each other to be liars," etc. (Schaff). "Men use their protestations because they are distrustful one of another. An oath is physic, which supposes disease" (M. Henry). When the oath is performed for the "sake of ethical interests, as when the civil authority demands it," as seems to be necessary and safe for society in its present unsanctified condition, the precept does not interfere (Köstlin, art. "Oath," Schaff-Herzog Encycl., Meyer, Wuttke, Alford, Tholuck, etc.). An interesting imitation of the Rabbinical casuistry above referred to was practised by the crafty and subtle Louis XI. Scott says (Introd. to Quentin Durward), "He admitted to one or two peculiar oaths the force of a binding obligation which he denied to all others, strictly preserving the secret; which mode of swearing he really accounted obligatory, as one of the most valuable of State secrets."

[2] 1 Cor. ii. 15.   [3] Gen. iii. 19.

guilt of unlawful corruption, *i.e.* of fornication : as, for instance, if any one should have a wife either barren, or misshapen in body, or faulty in her members, — either blind, or deaf, or lame, or having any other defect, — or worn out by diseases and' pains and weaknesses, and whatever else may be thought of exceeding horrible, fornication excepted, let him endure it for the sake of his plighted love and conjugal union ; [1] and let him not only not put away such a wife, but even if he have her not, let him not marry one who has been divorced by her husband, though beautiful, healthy, rich, fruitful. And if it is not lawful to do such things, much less is it to be deemed lawful for him to come near any other unlawful embrace ; and let him so flee from fornication, as to withdraw himself from base corruption of every sort. Let him speak the truth, and let him commend it not by frequent oaths, but by the probity of his morals ; and with respect to the innumerable crowds of all bad habits rising up in rebellion against him, of which, in order that all may be understood, a few have been mentioned, let him betake himself to the citadel of Christian warfare, and let him lay them prostrate, as if from a higher ground. But who would venture to enter upon labours so great, unless one who is so inflamed with the love of righteousness, that, as it were utterly consumed with hunger and thirst, and thinking there is no life for him till that is satisfied, he puts forth violence to obtain the kingdom of heaven? For otherwise he will not be able bravely to endure all those things which the lovers of this world reckon toilsome and arduous, and altogether difficult in getting rid of bad habits. " Blessed," therefore, " are they which do hunger and thirst after righteousness : for they shall be filled."

55. But yet, when any one encounters difficulty in these toils, and advancing through hardships and roughnesses surrounded with various temptations, and perceiving the troubles of his past life rise up on this side and on that, becomes afraid lest he should not be able to carry through what he has undertaken, let him eagerly avail himself of the counsel that he may obtain assistance. But what other counsel is there than this, that he who desires to have divine help for his own infirmity should bear that of others, and should assist it as much as possible? And so, therefore, let us look at the precepts of mercy. The meek and the merciful man, however, seem to be one and the same : but there is this difference, that the meek man, of whom we have spoken above, from piety does not gainsay the divine sentences which are brought forward against his sins, nor those statements of God which he does not yet understand ; but he confers no benefit on him whom he does not gainsay or resist. But the merciful man in such a way offers no resistance, that he does it for the purpose of correcting him whom he would render worse by resisting.

CHAP. XIX. — 56. Hence the Lord goes on to say : " Ye have heard that it hath been said, An eye for an eye, and a tooth for a tooth : but I say unto you, that ye resist not evil ; [2] but whosoever shall smite thee on thy right cheek, turn to him the other also. And if any man will sue thee at the law, and take away thy coat [tunic, undergarment], let him have thy cloak [3] also. And whosoever shall compel thee to go a mile, go with him twain. Give to him that asketh thee,[4] and from him that would borrow of thee turn not thou away." It is the lesser righteousness of the Pharisees not to go beyond measure in revenge, that no one should give back more than he has received : and this is a great step. For it is not easy to find any one who, when he has received a blow, wishes merely to return the blow ; and who, on hearing one word from a man who reviles him, is content to return only one, and that just an equivalent ; but he avenges it more immoderately, either under the disturbing influence of anger, or because he thinks it just, that he who first inflicted injury should suffer more severe injury than he suffered who had not inflicted injury. Such a spirit was in great measure restrained by the law, where it was written, " An eye for an eye, and a tooth for a tooth ; " by which expressions a certain measure is intended, so that the vengeance should not exceed the injury. And this is the beginning of peace : but perfect peace is to have no wish at all for such vengeance.

57. Hence, between that first course which goes beyond the law, that a greater evil should be inflicted in return for a lesser, and this to which the Lord has given expression for the purpose of perfecting the disciples, that no evil at all should be inflicted in return for evil, a middle course holds a certain place, viz. that as much be paid back as has been received ; by means of which enactment the transition is made from the highest discord to the highest concord, according to the distribution of times. See, therefore, at how great a distance any one who is the first to do harm to another, with the desire of injuring and hurting him, stands from him who, even when injured, does not pay back the injury. That man, however, who is not the first to do harm to any one, but who yet, when injured, inflicts a greater injury in return, either

<hr />

[1] *Pro fide et societate.*

[2] *Adversus malum;* Vulgate, *malo.*
[3] *Vestimentum;* Vulgate, *pallium.*
[4] *Omni petenti te, da;* Vulgate, *qui petit a te,* etc.

in will or in deed, has so far withdrawn himself from the highest injustice, and made so far an advance to the highest righteousness; but still he does not yet hold by what the law given by Moses commanded. And therefore he who pays back just as much as he has received already forgives something: for the party who injures does not deserve merely as much punishment as the man who was injured by him has innocently suffered. And accordingly this incomplete, by no means severe, but [rather] merciful justice, is carried to perfection by Him who came to fulfil the law, not to destroy it. Hence there are still two intervening steps which He has left to be understood, while He has chosen rather to speak of the very highest development of mercy. For there is still what one may do who does not come fully up to that magnitude of the precept which belongs to the kingdom of heaven; acting in such a way that he does not pay back as much, but less; as, for instance, one blow instead of two, or that he cuts off an ear for an eye that has been plucked out. He who, rising above this, pays back nothing at all, approaches the Lord's precept, but yet he does not reach it. For still it seems to the Lord not enough, if, for the evil which you may have received, you should inflict no evil in return, unless you be prepared to receive even more. And therefore He does not say, "But I say unto you," that you are not to return evil for evil; although even this would be a great precept: but He says, "that ye resist not evil;"[1] so that not only are you not to pay back what may have been inflicted on you, but you are not even to resist other inflictions. For this is what He also goes on to explain: "But whosoever shall smite thee on thy right cheek, turn to him the other also:" for He does not say, If any man smite thee, do not wish to smite him; but, Offer thyself further to him if he should go on to smite thee. As regards compassion, they feel it most who minister to those whom they greatly love as if they were their children, or some very dear friends in sickness, or little children, or insane persons, at whose hands they often endure many things; and if their welfare demand it, they even show themselves ready to endure more, until the weakness either of age or of disease pass away. And so, as regards those whom the Lord, the Physician of souls, was instructing to take care of their neighbours, what else could He teach them, than that they endure quietly the infirmities of those whose welfare they wish to consult?

For all wickedness arises from infirmity[2] of mind: because nothing is more harmless than the man who is perfect in virtue.

58. But it may be asked what the right cheek means. For this is the reading we find in the Greek copies, which are most worthy of confidence; though many Latin ones have only the word "cheek," without the addition of "right." Now the face is that by which any one is recognised; and we read in the apostle's writings, "For ye suffer,[3] if a man bring you into bondage, if a man devour you, if a man take of you, if a man exalt himself, if a man smite you on the face:" then immediately he adds, "I speak as concerning reproach;"[4] so that he explains what striking on the face is, viz. to be contemned and despised. Nor is this indeed said by the apostle for this reason, that they should not bear with those parties; but that they should bear with himself rather, who so loved them, that he was willing that he himself should be spent for them.[5] But since the face cannot be called right and left, and yet there may be a worth according to the estimate of God and according to the estimate of this world, it is so distributed as it were into the right and left cheek, that whatever disciple of Christ might have to bear reproach for being a Christian, he should be much more ready to bear reproach in himself, if he possesses any of the honours of this world. Thus this same apostle, if he had kept silence respecting the dignity which he had in the world, when men were persecuting in him the Christian name, would not have presented the other cheek to those that were smiting the right one. For when he said, I am a Roman citizen,[6] he was not unprepared to submit to be despised, in that which he reckoned as least, by those who had despised in him so precious and life-giving a name. For did he at all the less on that account afterwards submit to the chains, which it was not lawful to put on Roman citizens, or did he wish to accuse any one of this injury? And if any spared him on account of the name of Roman citizenship, yet he did not on that account refrain from offering an object they might strike at, since he wished by his patience to cure of so great perversity those whom he saw honouring in him what belonged to the left members rather than the right. For that point only is to be attended to, in what spirit he did everything, how benevolently and mildly he acted toward those from whom he was suffering such things. For when he was smitten with the hand by order of the high priest, what he seemed to say contumeliously when he affirms, "God shall smite thee, thou whited wall,"

---

[1] With Augustin, Calvin, Tholuck, Ewald, Lange, construe this as neuter, *evil*; Chrysostom, Theophylact, *the devil*; De Wette, Meyer, Alford, Plumptre, as also the Revised Version, *the man who does evil*. Renan says the practice of this doctrine put down slavery: "It was not Spartacus who suppressed slavery, but rather was it Blandina" ("*Ce n'est pas Spartacus qui a supprimé l'esclavage, c'est bien plûtôt Blandine*").

[2] *Imbecillitate.*   [3] *Toleratis;* Vulgate, *sustinetis.*
[4] 2 Cor. xi. 20, 21.   [5] 2 Cor. xii. 15.
[6] Acts xxii. 25.

sounds like an insult to those who do not understand it ; but to those who do, it is a prophecy. For a whited wall is hypocrisy, *i.e.* pretence holding forth the sacerdotal dignity before itself, and under this name, as under a white covering, concealing an inner and as it were sordid baseness. For what belonged to humility he wonderfully preserved, when, on its being said to him, " Revilest thou the high priest? " [1] he replied, " I wist not, brethren, that he was the high priest ; for it is written, Thou shalt not speak evil of the ruler of thy people." [2] And here he showed with what calmness he had spoken that which he seemed to have spoken in anger, because he answered so quickly and so mildly, which cannot be done by those who are indignant and thrown into confusion. And in that very statement he spoke the truth to those who understood him, " I wist not that he was the high priest : " [3] as if he said, I know another High Priest, for whose name I bear such things, whom it is not lawful to revile, and whom ye revile, since in me it is nothing else but His name that ye hate. Thus, therefore, it is necessary for one not to boast of such things in a hypocritical way, but to be prepared in the heart itself for all things, so that he can sing that prophetic word, " My heart is prepared,[4] O God, my heart is prepared." For many have learned how to offer the other cheek, but do not know how to love him by whom they are struck. But in truth, the Lord Himself, who certainly was the first to fulfil the precepts which He taught, did not offer the other cheek to the servant of the high priest when smiting Him thereon ; but, so far from that, said, " If I have spoken evil, bear witness of the evil ; [5] but if well, why smitest thou me ? " [6] Yet was He not on that account unprepared in heart, for the salvation of all, not merely to be smitten on the other cheek, but even to have His whole body crucified.

59. Hence also what follows, " And if any man will sue thee at the law, and take away thy coat, let him have thy cloak [7] also," is rightly understood as a precept having reference to the preparation of heart, not to a vain show of outward deed. But what is said with respect to the coat and cloak is to be carried out not merely in such things, but in the case of everything which on any ground of right we speak of as being ours for time. For if this command is given with respect to what is necessary, how much more does it become us to contemn what

is superfluous ! But still, those things which I have called ours are to be included in that category under which the Lord Himself gives the precept, when He says, " If any man will sue thee at the law, and take away thy coat." Let all these things therefore be understood for which we may be sued at the law, so that the right to them may pass from us to him who sues, or for whom he sues ; such, for instance, as clothing, a house, an estate, a beast of burden, and in general all kinds of property. But whether it is to be understood of slaves also is a great question. For a Christian ought not to possess a slave in the same way as a horse or money : although it may happen that a horse is valued at a greater price than a slave, and some article of gold or silver at much more. But with respect to that slave, if he is being educated and ruled by thee as his master, in a way more upright, and more honourable, and more conducing to the fear of God, than can be done by him who desires to take him away, I do not know whether any one would dare to say that he ought to be despised like a garment. For a man ought to love a fellow-man as himself, inasmuch as he is commanded by the Lord of all (as is shown by what follows) even to love his enemies.

60. It is carefully to be observed that every tunic [8] is a garment,[9] but that every garment is not a tunic. Hence the word garment means more than the word tunic. And therefore I think it is so expressed, " And if any one will sue thee at the law, and take away thy tunic, let him have thy garment also," as if He had said, Whoever wishes to take away thy tunic, give over to him whatever other clothing thou hast. And so some have interpreted the word *pallium*, which in the Greek as used here is ἱμάτιον.

61. " And whosoever," says He, " shall compel [10] thee to go a mile, go with him other two." And this, certainly, not so much in the sense that thou shouldest do it on foot, as that thou shouldest be prepared in mind to do it. For in the Christian history itself, which is authoritative, you will find no such thing done by the saints, or by the Lord Himself when in His human nature, which He condescended to assume, He was showing us an example of how to live ; while at the same time, in almost all places, you will find them prepared to bear with equanimity whatever may have been wickedly forced upon them. But are we to suppose it is said for the sake of the mere expression, " Go with him other two ; " or did He rather wish that three should be completed, — the number which has the meaning of perfection ; so that

---

[1] *Principi sacerdotum ;* Vulgate, *summum sacerdotem.*
[2] Acts xxiii. 3-5.
[3] Interpreted by modern commentators usually of temporary forgetfulness, or, what is much better, failure to recognise through infirmity of vision.
[4] English version, " fixed " — Ps. lvii. 7.
[5] *Exprobra de malo ;* Vulgate, *testimonium perhibe de malo.*
[6] John xviii. 23.
[7] The coat or tunic was the *under-garment.* The cloak, or pallium, was the *outer-garment,* and the more precious.

[8] English version, " coat." [9] English version, " cloak."
[10] The Greek word ἀγγαρεύω is derived from the Persian, to press one into service, as a courier to bear despatches. (See Thayer, *Lexicon.*)

every one should remember when he does this, that he is fulfilling perfect righteousness by compassionately bearing the infirmities of those whom he wishes to be made whole? It may seem for this reason also that He has recommended these precepts by three examples: of which the first is, if any one shall smite thee on the cheek; the second, if any one shall wish to take away thy coat; the third, if any one shall compel thee to go a mile: in which third example twice as much is added to the original unit, so that in this way the triplet is completed. And if this number in the passage before us does not, as has been said, mean perfection, let this be understood, that in laying down His precepts, as it were beginning with what is more tolerable, He has gradually gone on, until He has reached as far as the enduring of twice as much more. For, in the first place, He wished the other cheek to be presented when the right had been smitten, so that you may be prepared to bear less than you have borne. For whatever the right means, it is at least something more dear than that which is meant by the left; and if one who has borne with something in what is more dear, bears with it in what is less dear, it is something less. Then, secondly, in the case of one who wishes to take away a coat, He enjoins that the garment also should be given up to him: which is either just as much, or not much more; not, however, twice as much. In the third place, with respect to the mile, to which He says that two miles are to be added, He enjoins that you should bear with even twice as much more: thus signifying that whether it be somewhat less than the original demand, or just as much, or more, that any wicked man shall wish to take from thee, it is to be borne with tranquil mind.

Chap. xx. — 62. And, indeed, in these three classes of examples, I see that no class of injury is passed over.[1] For all matters in which we suffer any injustice are divided into two classes: of which the one is, where restitution cannot be made; the other, where it can. But in that case where restitution cannot be made, a compensation in revenge is usually sought. For what does it profit, that on being struck you strike in return? Is that part of the body which was injured for that reason restored to its original condition? But an excited mind desires such alleviations. Things of that sort, however, afford no pleasure to a healthy and firm one; nay, such an one judges rather that the other's infirmity is to be compassionately borne with, than that his own (which has no existence) should be soothed by the punishment of another.

63. Nor are we thus precluded from inflicting such punishment [requital][2] as avails for correction, and as compassion itself dictates; nor does it stand in the way of that course proposed, where one is prepared to endure more at the hand of him whom he wishes to set right. But no one is fit for inflicting this punishment except the man who, by the greatness of his love, has overcome that hatred wherewith those are wont to be inflamed who wish to avenge themselves. For it is not to be feared that parents would seem to hate a little son when, on committing an offence, he is beaten by them that he may not go on offending. And certainly the perfection of love is set before us by the imitation of God the Father Himself when it is said in what follows: "Love your enemies, do good to them that hate you, and pray for them[3] which persecute you;" and yet it is said of Him by the prophet, "For whom the Lord loveth He correcteth; yea, He scourgeth every son whom He receiveth."[4] The Lord also says, "The servant that knows not[5] his lord's will, and does things worthy of stripes, shall be beaten with few stripes; but the servant that knows his lord's will, and does things worthy of stripes, shall be beaten with many stripes."[6] No more, therefore, is sought for, except that he should punish to whom, in the natural order of things, the power is given; and that he should punish with the same goodwill which a father has towards his little son, whom by reason of his youth he cannot yet hate. For from this source the most suitable example is drawn, in order that it may be sufficiently manifest that sin can be punished in love rather than be left unpunished; so that one may wish him on whom he inflicts it not to be miserable by means of punishment, but to be happy by means of correction, yet be prepared, if need be, to endure with equanimity more injuries inflicted by him whom he wishes to be corrected, whether he may have the power of putting restraint upon him or not.

64. But great and holy men, although they at the time knew excellently well that that death which separates the soul from the body is not to be dreaded, yet, in accordance with the sentiment of those who might fear it, punished some sins with death, both because the living were struck with a salutary fear, and because it was not death itself that would injure those who were being punished with death, but sin, which might be increased if they continued to live. They did not judge rashly on whom God had bestowed such a power of judging. Hence it is

---

[1] *Exemplum citatur injuriæ privatæ, forensis, curialis* (Bengel).

[2] *Vindicta.*
[3] *Pro eis qui vos persequuntur;* Vulgate, *pro persequentibus.*
[4] Prov. iii. 12. So the LXX. English version: "even as a father the son in whom he delighteth," following the Hebrew.
[5] *Nescit;* Vulgate, *non cognovit.*
[6] Luke xii. 48, 47.

that Elijah inflicted death on many, both with his own hand [1] and by calling down fire from heaven; [2] as was done also without rashness by many other great and godlike men, in the same spirit of concern for the good of humanity. And when the disciples had quoted an example from this Elias, mentioning to the Lord what had been done by him, in order that He might give to themselves also the power of calling down fire from heaven to consume those who would not show Him hospitality, the Lord reproved in them, not the example of the holy prophet, but their ignorance in respect to taking vengeance, their knowledge being as yet elementary; [3] perceiving that they did not in love desire correction, but in hated desired revenge. Accordingly, after He had taught them what it was to love one's neighbour as oneself, and when the Holy Spirit had been poured out, whom, at the end of ten days after His ascension, He sent from above, as He had promised, [4] there were not wanting such acts of vengeance, although much more rarely than in the Old Testament. For there, for the most part, as servants they were kept down by fear; but here mostly as free they were nourished by love. For at the words of the Apostle Peter also, Ananias and his wife, as we read in the Acts of the Apostles, fell down dead, and were not raised to life again, but buried.

65. But if the heretics who are opposed to the Old Testament [5] will not credit this book, let them contemplate the Apostle Paul, whose writings they read along with us, saying with respect to a certain sinner whom he delivered over to Satan for the destruction of the flesh, "that the spirit may be saved." [6] And if they will not here understand death (for perhaps it is uncertain), let them acknowledge that punishment [requital] of some kind or other was inflicted by the apostle through the instrumentality of Satan; and that he did this not in hatred, but in love, is made plain by that addition, "that the spirit may be saved." Or let them notice what we say in those books to which they themselves attribute great authority, where it is written that the Apostle Thomas imprecated on a certain man, by whom he had been struck with the palm of the hand, the punishment of death in a very cruel form, while yet commending his soul to God, that it might be spared in the world to come,—whose hand, torn from the rest of his body after he had been killed by a lion, a dog brought to the table at which the apostle was feasting. It is allowable for us not to credit this writing, for it is not in the catholic canon; yet they both read it, and honour it as being thoroughly uncorrupted and thoroughly

truthful, who rage very fiercely (with I know not what blindness) against the corporeal punishments which are in the Old Testament, being altogether ignorant in what spirit and at what stage in the orderly distribution of times they were inflicted.

66. Hence, in this class of injuries which is atoned for by punishment, such a measure will be preserved by Christians, that, on an injury being received, the mind will not mount up into hatred, but will be ready, in compassion for the infirmity, to endure even more; nor will it neglect the correction, which it can employ either by advice, or by authority, or by [the exercise of] power. There is another class of injuries, where complete restitution is possible, of which there are two species: the one referring to money, the other to labour. And therefore examples are subjoined: of the former in the case of the coat and cloak, of the latter in the case of the compulsory service of one and two miles; for a garment may be given back, and he whom you have assisted by labour may also assist you, if it should be necessary. Unless, perhaps, the distinction should rather be drawn in this way: that the first case which is supposed, in reference to the cheek being struck, means all injuries that are inflicted by the wicked in such a way that restitution cannot be made except by punishment; and that the second case which is supposed, in reference to the garment, means all injuries where restitution can be made without punishment; and therefore, perhaps, it is added, "if any man will sue thee at the law," because what is taken away by means of a judicial sentence is not supposed to be taken away with such a degree of violence as that punishment is due; but that the third case is composed of both, so that restitution may be made both without punishment and with it. For the man who violently exacts labour to which he has no claim, without any judicial process, as he does who wickedly compels a man to go with him, and forces in an unlawful way assistance to be rendered to himself by one who is unwilling, is able both to pay the penalty of his wickedness and to repay the labour, if he who endured the wrong should ask it again. In all these classes of injuries, therefore, the Lord teaches that the disposition of a Christian ought to be most patient and compassionate, and thoroughly prepared to endure more.

67. But since it is a small matter merely to abstain from injuring, unless you also confer a benefit as far as you can, He therefore goes on to say, "Give to every one that asketh thee, and from him that would borrow of thee turn not thou away." "To every one that asketh," says He; not, Everything to him that asketh: so that you are to give that which you can honestly and

---

[1] 1 Kings xviii. 40. [2] 2 Kings i. 10. [3] Luke ix. 52–56.
[4] Acts ii. 1–4. [5] i.e., The Manicheans. [6] 1 Cor. v. 5.

justly give. For what if he should ask money, wherewith he may endeavour to oppress an innocent man? what if, in short, he should ask something unchaste?[1] But not to recount many examples, which are in fact innumerable, that certainly is to be given which may hurt neither thyself nor the other party, as far as can be known or supposed by man; and in the case of him to whom you have justly denied what he asks, justice itself is to be made known, so that you may not send him away empty. Thus you will give to every one that asketh you, although you will not always give what he asks; and you will sometimes give something better, when you have set him right who was making unjust requests.

68. Then, as to what He says, "From him that would borrow of thee turn not thou away," it is to be referred to the mind; for God loveth a cheerful giver.[2] Moreover, every one who accepts anything borrows, even if he himself is not going to pay it; for inasmuch as God pays back more to the merciful, whosoever does a kindness lends at interest. Or if it does not seem good to understand the borrower in any other sense than of him who accepts of anything with the intention of repaying it, we must understand the Lord to have included those two methods of doing a favour. For we either give in a present what we give in the exercise of benevolence, or we lend to one who will repay us. And frequently men who, setting before them the divine reward, are prepared to give away in a present, become slow to give what is asked in loan, as if they were destined to get nothing in return from God, inasmuch as he who receives pays back the thing which is given him. Rightly, therefore, does the divine authority exhort us to this mode of bestowing a favour, saying, "And from him that would borrow of thee turn not thou away:" *i.e.*, do not alienate your goodwill from him who asks it, both because your money will be useless, and because God will not pay you back, inasmuch as the man has done so; but when you do that from a regard to God's precept, it cannot be unfruitful with Him who gives these commands.[3]

CHAP. XXI. — 69. In the next place, He goes on to say, "Ye have heard that it hath been said, Thou shalt love thy neighbour, and hate thine enemy: But I say unto you, Love your enemies, do good to them that hate you, and pray for them

which persecute you;[4] that ye may be the children of your Father which is in heaven: for He commandeth[5] His sun to rise on the evil and on the good, and sendeth rain on the just and on the unjust. For if ye love[6] them which love you, what reward have ye? Do not even the publicans the same? And if ye salute your brethren only, what do ye more than others? Do not even the Gentiles the very same?[7] Be ye therefore perfect, even as your Father who is in heaven[8] is perfect." For without this love, wherewith we are commanded to love even our enemies and persecutors, who can fully carry out those things which are mentioned above? Moreover, the perfection of that mercy, wherewith most of all the soul that is in distress is cared for, cannot be stretched beyond the love of an enemy; and therefore the closing words are: "Be ye therefore perfect, even as your Father who is in heaven is perfect." Yet in such a way that God is understood to be perfect as God, and the soul to be perfect as a soul.

70. That there is, however, a certain step [in advance] in the righteousness of the Pharisees, which belongs to the old law, is perceived from this consideration, that many men hate even those by whom they are loved; as, for instance, luxurious children hate their parents for restraining them in their luxury. That man therefore rises a certain step, who loves his neighbour, although as yet he hates his enemy. But in the kingdom of Him who came to fulfil the law, not to destroy it, he will bring benevolence and kindness to perfection, when he has carried it out so far as to love an enemy. For the former stage, although it is something, is yet so little that it may be reached even by the publicans as well. And as to what is said in the law, "Thou shalt hate thine enemy,"[9] it is not to be understood

---

[1] "To give everything to every one — the sword to the madman, the alms to the impostor, the criminal request to the temptress — would be to act as the enemy of others and ourselves" (Alford). Paul's *willingness* to spend and be spent illustrates a proper conformity to the precept.

[2] 2 Cor. ix. 7.

[3] This section, which concerns the *law of retaliation*, grew out of a rule of every-day life which the Pharisees constructed upon a principle of judicature laid down, Exod. xxi. 24 (Tholuck). The spirit, not the exact letter, of the illustrations is to be observed, and,

when the spirit of the precept would demand it, the exact letter. Christians are taught to bear witness by enduring, yielding, and giving. "Sin is to be conquered by being made to feel the power of goodness." Christ gave a good example at His trial, without following the letter of His precept here; and Paul followed Him (1 Cor. iv. 12, 13).

[4] Augustin, with the best Greek text, omits *et calumniantibus vos* ("and despitefully use you") of the Vulgate.

[5] *Jubet*; Vulgate, *facit* (with the Greek).

[6] *Dilexeritis*; Vulgate, *diligitis.*

[7] *Hoc ipsum*; Vulgate, *hoc*; Greek, τὸ αὐτό.

[8] *Qui est in cælis*; Vulgate, *cœlestis* (see Revised Version).

[9] The first part of the Lord's quotation is found in Lev. xix. 18; these words, whatever may be said about the sanction, real or apparent, of revenge and triumph over an enemy's fall in the Old Testament, are not found there. Bengel well says, "*pessima glossa*" ("wretched gloss"), — a gloss of the Pharisees, "bearing plainly enough the character of post-exilic Judaism in its exclusiveness toward all surrounding nations" (Weiss). Centuries after Christ spoke these words, Maimonides gives utterance to this narrow feeling of hate: "If a Jew see a Gentile fall into the sea, let him by no means take him out; for it is written, 'Thou shalt love thy neighbour's blood,' but this is not thy neighbour." The separation of the Jews, demanded by their theocratic position, was the explanation in part — not an excuse — for such feeling towards people of other nationalities. Heathen peoples had the same feeling towards enemies. "It was the celebrated felicity of Sulla; and this was the crown of Xenophon's panegyric of Cyrus the Younger, that no one had done more good to his friends, or more mischief to his enemies." Plautus said, "Man is a wolf to the stranger" ("*homo homini ignoto lupus est*"). The term "stranger" in Greek means "enemy." But common as this philosophy was to the pre-Christian world, the Jew was specially known for his hatred of

as the voice of command addressed to a righteous man, but rather as the voice of permission to a weak man.

71. Here indeed arises a question in no way to be blinked, that to this precept of the Lord, wherein He exhorts us to love our enemies, and to do good to those who hate us, and to pray for those who persecute us, many other parts of Scripture seem to those who consider them less diligently and soberly to stand opposed; for in the prophets there are found many imprecations against enemies, which are thought to be curses: as, for instance, that one, "Let their table become a snare,"[1] and the other things which are said there; and that one, "Let his children be fatherless, and his wife a widow,"[2] and the other statements which are made either before or afterwards in the same Psalm by the prophet, as bearing on the case of Judas. Many other statements are found in all parts of Scripture, which may seem contrary both to this precept of the Lord, and to that apostolic one, where it is said, "Bless, and curse not;"[3] while it is both written of the Lord, that He cursed the cities which received not His word;[4] and the above-mentioned apostle thus spoke respecting a certain man, "The Lord will reward him according to his works."[5]

72. But these difficulties are easily solved, for the prophet predicted by means of imprecation what was about to happen, not as praying for what he wished, but in the spirit of one who saw it beforehand. So also the Lord, so also the apostle; although even in the words of these we do not find what they have wished, but what they have foretold. For when the Lord says, "Woe unto thee, Capernaum," He does not utter anything else than that some evil will happen to her as a punishment of her unbelief; and that this would happen the Lord did not malevolently wish, but saw by means of His divinity. And the apostle does not say, May [the Lord] reward; but, "The Lord will reward him according to his work;" which is the word of one who foretells, not of one uttering an imprecation. Just as also, in regard to that hypocrisy of the Jews of which we have already spoken, whose destruction he saw to be impending, he said, "God shall smite thee, thou whited wall."[6] But the prophets especially are accustomed to predict future events under the figure of one uttering an imprecation, just as they have often foretold those things which were to come

under the figure of past time: as is the case, for example, in that passage, "Why have the nations raged, and the peoples imagined vain things?"[7] For he has not said, Why will the heathen rage, and the people imagine vain things? although he was not mentioning those things as if they were already past, but was looking forward to them as yet to come. Such also is that passage, "They have parted my garments among them, and have cast lots upon my vesture:"[8] for here also he has not said, They will part my garments among them, and will cast lots upon my vesture. And yet no one finds fault with these words, except the man who does not perceive that variety of figures in speaking in no degree lessens the truth of facts, and adds very much to the impressions on our minds.

CHAP. XXII. — 73. But the question before us is rendered more urgent by what the Apostle John says: "If any man see his brother sin a sin which is not unto death, he shall ask, and the Lord shall give him life for him who sinneth not unto death. There is a sin unto death: I do not say that he shall pray for it."[9] For he manifestly shows that there are certain brethren for whom we are not commanded to pray, although the Lord bids us pray even for our persecutors. Nor can the question in hand be solved, unless we acknowledge that there are certain sins in brethren which are more heinous than the persecution of enemies. Moreover, that brethren mean Christians can be proved by many examples from the divine Scriptures. Yet that one is plainest which the apostle thus states: "For the unbelieving husband is sanctified in the wife, and the unbelieving wife is sanctified in the brother."[10] For he has not added the word our; but has thought it plain, as he wished a Christian who had an unbelieving wife to be understood by the expression brother. And therefore he says a little after, "But if the unbelieving depart, let him depart: a brother or a sister is not under bondage in such cases."[11] Hence I am of opinion that the sin of a brother is unto death, when any one, after coming to the knowledge of God through the grace of our Lord Jesus Christ, makes an assault on the brotherhood, and is impelled by the fires of envy to oppose that grace itself by which he is reconciled to God. But the sin is not unto death, if any one has not withdrawn his love from a brother, but through some infirmity of disposition has failed to perform the incumbent duties of brotherhood. And on this account our Lord also on the cross says, "Father, forgive[12] them; for they know not what they do:"[13]

---

all not of his own nationality (Juvenal, Sat. xiv. 104, etc.). The "enemy" referred to in the passage is not a national enemy (Keim), but a personal one (Weiss, Meyer, etc.). Our Lord subsequently defined who was to be understood by the term "neighbour" in the parable of the Good Samaritan (Luke x. 36).

[1] Ps. lxix. 22.　　[2] Ps. cix. 9.　　[3] Rom. xii. 14.
[4] Matt xi. 20-24 and Luke x. 13-15.
[5] 2 Tim. iv. 14. Augustin here again follows the better text than the Textus Receptus; so also Vulgate, reddet. See Revised Version.
[6] See above, chap. xix. 58.

[7] Ps. ii. 1.　　The English version employs the present tense.
[8] Ps. xxii. 18.
[9] 1 John v. 16.　　[10] See note p.　　[11] 1 Cor. vii. 14, 15.
[12] Ignosce; Vulgate, dimitte.　　[13] Luke xxiii. 34.

for, not yet having become partakers of the grace of the Holy Spirit, they had not yet entered the fellowship of the holy brotherhood. And the blessed Stephen in the Acts of the Apostles prays for those by whom he is being stoned,[1] because they had not yet believed on Christ, and were not fighting against that common grace. And the Apostle Paul on this account, I believe, does not pray for Alexander, because he was already a brother, and had sinned unto death, viz. by making an assault on the brotherhood through envy. But for those who had not broken off their love, but had given way through fear, he prays that they may be pardoned. For thus he expresses it: "Alexander the coppersmith did me much evil: the Lord will reward him according to his works. Of whom be thou ware also; for he hath greatly withstood our words."[2] Then he adds for whom he prays, thus expressing it: "At my first defence no man stood with me, but all men forsook me: I pray God that it may not be laid to their charge."[3]

74. It is this difference in their sins which separates Judas the betrayer from Peter the denier: not that a penitent is not to be pardoned, for we must not come into collision with that declaration of our Lord, where He enjoins that a brother is to be pardoned, when he asks his brother to pardon him;[4] but that the ruin connected with that sin is so great, that he cannot endure the humiliation of asking for it, even if he should be compelled by a bad conscience both to acknowledge and divulge his sin. For when Judas had said, "I have sinned, in that I have betrayed the innocent blood," yet it was easier for him in despair to run and hang himself,[5] than in humility to ask for pardon. And therefore it is of much consequence to know what sort of repentance God pardons. For many much more readily confess that they have sinned, and are so angry with themselves that they vehemently wish they had not sinned; but yet they do not condescend to humble the heart and to make it contrite, and to implore pardon: and this disposition of mind we must suppose them to have, as feeling themselves already condemned because of the greatness of their sin.

75. And this is perhaps the sin against the Holy Ghost, i.e. through malice and envy to act in opposition to brotherly love after receiving the grace of the Holy Ghost, — a sin which our Lord says is not forgiven either in this world or in the world to come. And hence it may be asked whether the Jews sinned against the Holy Ghost, when they said that our Lord was casting out devils by Beelzebub, the prince of the devils:

whether we are to understand this as said against our Lord Himself, because He says of Himself in another passage, "If they have called the Master of the house Beelzebub, how much more shall they call them of His household!"[6] or whether, inasmuch as they had spoken from great envy, being ungrateful for so manifest benefits, although they were not yet Christians, they are, from the very greatness of their envy, to be supposed to have sinned against the Holy Ghost? This latter is certainly not to be gathered from our Lord's words. For although He has said in the same passage, "And whosoever speaketh a word against the Son of man, it shall be forgiven him; but whosoever speaketh a word against the Holy Ghost, it shall not be forgiven him, neither in this world, neither in the world to come;" yet it may seem that He admonished them for this purpose, that they should come to His grace, and after accepting of it should not so sin as they have now sinned. For now they have spoken a word against the Son of man, and it may be forgiven them, if they be converted, and believe on Him, and receive the Holy Ghost; but if, after receiving Him, they should choose to envy the brotherhood, and to assail the grace they have received, it cannot be forgiven them, neither in this world nor in the world to come. For if He reckoned them so condemned, that there was no hope left for them, He would not judge that they ought still to be admonished, as He did by adding the statement, "Either make the tree good, and his fruit good; or else make the tree corrupt, and his fruit corrupt."[7]

76. Let it be understood, therefore, that we are to love our enemies, and to do good to those who hate us, and to pray for those who persecute us, in such a way, that it is at the same time understood that there are certain sins of brethren for which we are not commanded to pray; lest, through unskilfulness on our part, divine Scripture should seem to contradict itself (a thing which cannot happen). But whether, as we are not to pray for certain parties, so we are also to pray against some, has not yet become sufficiently evident. For it is said in general, "Bless, and curse not;" and again, "Recompense to no man evil for evil."[8] Moreover, while you do not pray for one, you do not therefore pray against him: for you may see that his punishment is certain, and his salvation altogether hopeless; and you do not pray for him, not because you hate him, but because you feel you can profit him nothing, and you do not wish your prayer to be rejected by the most righteous Judge. But what are we to think respecting those parties against whom we have it revealed

---

[1] Acts vii. 60.   [2] *Sermonibus;* Vulgate, *verbis.*
[3] 2 Tim. iv. 14-16.   [4] Matt. xviii. 21. Luke xvii. 3.
[5] Matt. xxvii. 4, 5.

[6] Matt. x. 25.   [7] Matt. xii. 24-33.   [8] Rom. xii. 14, 17.

that prayers were offered by the saints, not that they might be turned from their error (for in this way prayer is offered rather for them), but that final condemnation might come upon them : not as it was offered against the betrayer of our Lord by the prophet ; for that, as has been said, was a prediction of things to come, not a wish for punishment : nor as it was offered by the apostle against Alexander ; for respecting that also enough has been already said : but as we read in the Apocalypse of John of the martyrs praying that they may be avenged ; [1] while the well-known first martyr prayed that those who stoned him should be pardoned.

77. But we need not be moved by this circumstance. For who would venture to affirm, in regard to those white-robed saints, when they pleaded that they should be avenged, whether they pleaded against the men themselves or against the dominion of sin? For of itself it is a genuine avenging of the martyrs, and one full of righteousness and mercy, that the dominion of sin should be overthrown, under which dominion they were subjected to so great sufferings. And for its overthrow the apostle strives, saying, " Let not sin therefore reign in your mortal body." [2] But the dominion of sin is destroyed and overthrown, partly by the amendment of men, so that the flesh is brought under subjection to the spirit ; partly by the condemnation of those who persevere in sin, so that they are righteously disposed of in such a way that they cannot be troublesome to the righteous who reign with Christ. Look at the Apostle Paul ; does it not seem to you that he avenges the martyr Stephen in his own person, when he says : " So fight I, not as one that beateth the air : but I keep under my body, and bring it into subjection "? [3] For he was certainly laying prostrate, and weakening, and bringing into subjection, and regulating that principle in himself whence he had persecuted Stephen and the other Christians. Who then can demonstrate that the holy martyrs were not asking from the Lord such an avenging of themselves, when at the same time, in order to their being avenged, they might lawfully wish for the end of this world, in which they had endured such martyrdoms? And they who pray for this, on the one hand pray for their enemies who are curable, and on the other hand do not pray against those who have chosen to be incurable : because God also, in punishing them, is not a malevolent Torturer, but a most righteous Disposer. Without any hesitation, therefore, let us love our enemies, let us do good to those that hate us, and let us pray for those who persecute us.

CHAP. XXIII. — 78. Then, as to the statement which follows, " that ye may be the children of your Father which is in heaven," [4] it is to be understood according to that rule in virtue of which John also says, " He gave them power to become the sons of God." [5] For one is a Son by nature, who knows nothing at all of sin ; but we, by receiving power, are made sons, in as far as we perform those things which are commanded us by Him. And hence the apostolic teaching gives the name of adoption to that by which we are called to an eternal inheritance, that we may be joint-heirs with Christ. [6] We are therefore made sons by a spiritual regeneration, and we are adopted into the kingdom of God, not as aliens, but as being made and created by Him : so that it is one benefit, His having brought us into being through His omnipotence, when before we were nothing ; another, His having adopted us, so that, as being sons, we might enjoy along with Him eternal life for our participation. Therefore He does not say, Do those things, because ye are sons ; but, Do those things, that ye may be sons.

79. But when He calls us to this by the Only-begotten Himself, He calls us to His own likeness. For He, as is said in what follows, " maketh [7] His sun to rise on the evil and on the good, and sendeth rain on the just and on the unjust." Whether you are to understand His sun as being not that which is visible to the fleshly eyes, but that wisdom of which it is said, " She is the brightness of the everlasting light ; " [8] of which it is also said, " The Sun of righteousness has arisen upon me ; " and again, " But unto you that fear the name of the Lord shall the Sun of righteousness arise : " [9] so that you would also understand the rain as being the watering with the doctrine of truth, because Christ hath appeared to the good and the evil, and is preached to the good and the evil. Or whether you choose rather to understand that sun which is set forth before the bodily eyes not only of men, but also of cattle ; and that rain by which the fruits are brought forth, which have been given for the refreshment of the body, which I think is the more probable interpretation : so that that spiritual sun does not rise except on the good and holy ; for it is this very thing which the wicked bewail in that book which is called the Wisdom of Solomon, " And the sun rose not upon us : " [10] and that spiritual rain does not water any except the good ; for the wicked were meant by the vineyard of which

---

[1] Rev. vi. 10.   [2] Rom. vi. 12.
[3] 1 Cor. ix. 26, 27.   *Sevituti subjicio;* Vulgate, *in servitutem redigo.*

[4] " Not in power or wisdom, — which was the cause of man's fall, and leads evermore to the same, — but in love" (Plumptre).
[5] John i. 12.   [6] Rom. viii. 17 and Gal. iv. 5.
[7] *Facit* (above, *jubet*). Bengel's comment is good: "*Magnifica appellatio. Ipse et fecit solem et gubernat et habet in sua unius potestate* (" Splendid designation. He made the sun, governs it, and has it in His own power").
[8] Wisd. vii. 26.   [9] Mal. iv. 2.   [10] Wisd. v. 6.

it is said, " I will also command my clouds that they rain no rain upon it." [1]   But whether you understand the one or the other, it takes place by the great goodness of God, which we are commanded to imitate, if we wish to be the children of God.   For who is there so ungrateful as not to feel how great the comfort, so far as this life is concerned, which that visible light and the material rain bring?   And this comfort we see bestowed in this life alike upon the righteous and upon sinners in common.   But He does not say, " who maketh the sun to rise on the evil and on the good ; " but He has added the word " His," *i.e.* which He Himself made and established, and for the making of which He took nothing from any one, as it is written in Genesis respecting all the luminaries ; [2] and He can properly say that all the things which He has created out of nothing are His own : so that we are hence admonished with how great liberality we ought, according to His precept, to give to our enemies those things which we have not created, but have received from His gifts.

80. But who can either be prepared to bear injuries from the weak, in as far as it is profitable for their salvation ; and to choose rather to suffer more injustice from another than to repay what he has suffered ; to give to every one that asketh anything from him, either what he asks, if it is in his possession, and if it can rightly be given,

or good advice, or to manifest a benevolent disposition, and not to turn away from him who desires to borrow ; to love his enemies, to do good to those who hate him, to pray for those who persecute him ; — who, I say, does these things, but the man who is fully and perfectly merciful? [3]   And with that counsel misery is avoided, by the assistance of Him who says, " I desire mercy, and not sacrifice." [4]   " Blessed," therefore, " are the merciful : for they shall obtain mercy."   But now I think it will be more convenient, that at this point the reader, fatigued with so long a volume, should breathe a little, and recruit himself for considering what remains in another book.

---

[3] " Be ye therefore perfect, as your heavenly Father is perfect." The Greek text has here the future: εσεσθε τελειοι, " Ye therefore shall be perfect" (Revised Version).   Meyer gives the verb the imperative sense; Alford, Lange, and others include the imperative sense.   The imperative force adds not a little to the plausibility of deriving the doctrine of perfectibility on earth, or complete " sanctification," from the passage, as the Pelagians (whom Augustin elsewhere combats) and some Methodist commentators (Whedon, etc.).   Alford, Trench, etc., deny that the verse gives any countenance to the doctrine.   As regards the nature of the perfection, Bengel sententiously says, " *in amore, erga omnes* " (" in love, toward all."   See Col. iii. 14).   It seems " to refer chiefly to the perfection of the divine love" (Mansel); so also Bleek, Meyer.   Weiss (whose *Leben Jesu*, i. 532-534, see) finds an allusion to the fundamental command of the Old Testament, " Be ye holy," etc.   In the place of the divine holiness, or God's elevation above all uncleanness of the creature, is substituted the divine perfection, whose essence is all-comprehensive and unselfish love; and in the place of the God separated from the sinful people, appears He who in love condescends to them and brings them into likeness with Himself as His children.   The last verse of the Sermon as reported by Luke (vi. 36) confirms the idea that the perfection is of love: " Be ye merciful, as your Father which is in heaven is merciful."   Commenting on this verse, Dr. Schaff says, " Instruction in morality cannot rise above this.   Having thus led us up to our heavenly Father as the true standard, our Lord, by a natural transition, passes to our religious duties, *i.e.* duties to our heavenly Father."

---

[1] Isa. v. 6.   [2] Gen. i. 16.   [4] Hos. vi. 6.

BOOK II.

ON THE LATTER PART OF OUR LORD'S SERMON ON THE MOUNT, CONTAINED IN THE SIXTH AND SEVENTH CHAPTERS OF MATTHEW.

CHAP. I. — 1. The subject of mercy, with the treatment of which the first book came to a close, is followed by that of the cleansing of the heart, with which the present one begins.[1] The cleansing of the heart, then, is as it were the cleansing of the eye by which God is seen; and in keeping that single, there ought to be as great care as the dignity of the object demands, which can be beheld by such an eye. But even when this eye is in great part cleansed, it is difficult to prevent certain defilements from creeping insensibly over it, from those things which are wont to accompany even our good actions, — as, for instance, the praise of men. If, indeed, not to live uprightly is hurtful; yet to live uprightly, and not to wish to be praised, what else is this than to be an enemy to the affairs of men, which are certainly so much the more miserable, the less an upright life on the part of men gives pleasure? If, therefore, those among whom you live shall not praise you when living uprightly, they are in error: but if they shall praise you, you are in danger; unless you have a heart so single and pure, that in those things in which you act uprightly you do not so act because of the praises of men; and that you rather congratulate those who praise what is right, as having pleasure in what is good, than yourself; because you would live uprightly even if no one were to praise you: and that you understand this very praise of you to be useful to those who praise you, only when it is not yourself whom they honour in your good life, but God, whose most holy temple every man is who lives well; so that what David says finds its fulfilment, " In the Lord shall my soul be praised; the humble shall hear thereof, and be glad." [2] It belongs therefore to the pure eye not to look at the praises of men in acting rightly, nor to have reference to these while you are acting rightly, i.e. to do anything rightly with the very design of pleasing men. For thus you will be disposed also to counterfeit what is good, if nothing is

kept in view except the praise of man; who, inasmuch as he cannot see the heart, may also praise things that are false. And they who do this, i.e. who counterfeit goodness, are of a double heart. No one therefore has a single, i.e. a pure heart, except the man who rises above the praises of men; and when he lives well, looks at Him only, and strives to please Him who is the only Searcher of the conscience. And whatever proceeds from the purity of that conscience is so much the more praiseworthy, the less it desires the praises of men.

2. "Take heed,[3] therefore," says He, "that ye do not your righteousness [4] before men, to be seen of them:" i.e., take heed that ye do not live righteously with this intent, and that ye do not place your happiness in this, that men may see you. "Otherwise ye have no reward of your Father who is in heaven:" not if ye should be seen by men; but if ye should live righteously with the intent of being seen by men. For, [were it the former], what would become of the statement made in the beginning of this sermon, "Ye are the light of the world. A city that is set on an hill cannot be hid. Neither do men light a candle, and put it under a bushel, but on a candlestick; and it giveth light unto all that are in the house. Let your light so shine before men, that they may see your good works"? But He did not set up this as the end; for He has added, "and glorify your Father who is in heaven." [5] But here, because he is finding fault with this, if the end of our right actions is there, i.e. if we act rightly with this design, only of being seen of men; after He has said, "Take heed that ye do not your righteousness before men," He has added nothing. And hereby it is evident that He has said this, not to prevent us from acting rightly before men, but lest perchance we should act rightly before men for the purpose of being seen by them, i.e. should fix our eye on this, and

---

[1] Jesus passes from the precepts of the genuine righteousness to the actual practice of the same (Meyer, Weiss), from moral to religious duties (Lange), from actions to motives: having spoken to the heart before by inference, he now speaks directly (Alford).
[2] Ps. xxxiv. 2.

[3] Cavete facere : Vulgate, attendite ne faciatis.
[4] In agreement with the best Greek text. (See Revised Version.) This verse is a general proposition. The three leading manifestations of righteousness and practical piety among the Jews follow, — almsgiving, prayer, fasting.
[5] Matt. v. 14-16.

make it the end of what we have set before us.

3. For the apostle also says, "If I yet pleased men, I should not be the servant of Christ;"[1] while he says in another place, "Please all men in all things, even as I also please all men in all things."[2] And they who do not understand this think it a contradiction; while the explanation is, that he has said he does not please men, because he was accustomed to act rightly, not with the express design of pleasing men, but of pleasing God, to the love of whom he wished to turn men's hearts by that very thing in which he was pleasing men. Therefore he was both right in saying that he did not please men, because in that very thing he aimed at pleasing God: and right in authoritatively teaching that we ought to please men, not in order that this should be sought for as the reward of our good deeds; but because the man who would not offer himself for imitation to those whom he wished to be saved, could not please God; but no man possibly can imitate one who has not pleased him. As, therefore, that man would not speak absurdly who should say, In this work of seeking a ship, it is not a ship, but my native country, that I seek: so the apostle also might fitly say, In this work of pleasing men, it is not men, but God, that I please; because I do not aim at pleasing men, but have it as my object, that those whom I wish to be saved may imitate me. Just as he says of an offering that is made for the saints, "Not because I desire a gift, but I desire fruit;"[3] i.e., In seeking your gift, I seek not it, but your fruit. For by this proof it could appear how far they had advanced Godward, when they offered that willingly which was sought from them not for the sake of his own joy over their gifts, but for the sake of the fellowship of love.

4. Although when He also goes on to say, "Otherwise ye have no reward of your Father who is in heaven,"[4] He points out nothing else but that we ought to be on our guard against seeking man's praise as the reward of our deeds, i.e. against thinking we thereby attain to blessedness.

CHAP. II. — 5. "Therefore, when thou doest thine alms," says He, "do not sound a trumpet before thee, as the hypocrites do in the synagogues and in the streets, that they may have glory[5] of men." Do not, says He, desire to become known in the same way as the hypocrites.

Now it is manifest that hypocrites have not that in their heart also which they hold forth before the eyes of men. For hypocrites are pretenders, as it were setters forth of other characters, just as in the plays of the theatre. For he who acts the part of Agamemnon in tragedy, for example, or of any other person belonging to the history or legend which is acted, is not really the person himself, but personates him, and is called a hypocrite. In like manner, in the Church, or in any phase of human life, whoever wishes to seem what he is not is a hypocrite. For he pretends, but does not show himself, to be a righteous man; because he places the whole fruit [of his acting] in the praise of men, which even pretenders may receive, while they deceive those to whom they seem good, and are praised by them. But such do not receive a reward from God the Searcher of the heart, unless it be the punishment of their deceit: from men, however, says He, "They have received their reward;" and most righteously will it be said to them, Depart from me, ye workers of deceit; ye had my name, but ye did not my works. Hence they have received their reward, who do their alms for no other reason than that they may have glory of men; not if they have glory of men, but if they do them for the express purpose of having this glory, as has been discussed above. For the praise of men ought not to be sought by him who acts rightly, but ought to follow him who acts rightly, so that they may profit who can also imitate what they praise, not that he whom they praise may think that they are profiting him anything.

6. "But when thou doest alms, let not thy left hand know what thy right hand doeth." If you should understand unbelievers to be meant by the left hand, then it will seem to be no fault to wish to please believers; while nevertheless we are altogether prohibited from placing the fruit and end of our good deed in the praise of any men whatever. But as regards this point, that those who have been pleased with your good deeds should imitate you, we are to act before the eyes not only of believers, but also of unbelievers, so that by our good works, which are to be praised, they may honour God, and may come to salvation. But if you should be of opinion that the left hand means an enemy, so that your enemy is not to know when you do alms, why did the Lord Himself, when His enemies the Jews were standing round, mercifully heal men? why did the Apostle Peter, by healing the lame man whom he pitied at the gate Beautiful, bring also the wrath of the enemy upon himself, and upon the other disciples of Christ?[6] Then, further, if it is necessary that

---

[1] Gal. i. 10.	[2] 1 Cor. x. 32, 33.	[3] Phil. iv. 17.
[4] Acts otherwise noble and praiseworthy become sin when done to make an appearance before men, and get honour from them. Bad intentions vitiate pious observances.
[5] Glorificantur; Vulgate, honorificentur. The sounding of a trumpet is referred by some to an alleged custom of the parties themselves calling the poor together by a trumpet, or even to the noise of the coins on the trumpet-shaped chests in the temple. Better, it is figurative of "self-laudation and display" (Meyer, Alford, Lange, etc.).

[6] Acts iii., iv.

the enemy should not know when we do our alms, how shall we do with the enemy himself so as to fulfil that precept, "If thine enemy be hungry, give him bread to eat; and if he be thirsty, give him water to drink"?[1]

7. A third opinion is wont to be held by carnal people, so absurd and ridiculous, that I would not mention it had I not found that not a few are entangled in that error, who say that by the expression *left hand* a wife is meant; so that, inasmuch as in family affairs women are wont to be more tenacious of money, it is to be kept hid from them when their husbands compassionately spend anything upon the needy, for fear of domestic quarrels. As if, forsooth, men alone were Christians, and this precept were not addressed to women also! From what left hand, then, is a woman enjoined to conceal her deed of mercy? Is a husband also the left hand of his wife? A statement most absurd. Or if any one thinks that they are left hands to each other; if any part of the family property be expended by the one party in such a way as to be contrary to the will of the other party, such a marriage will not be a Christian one; but whichever of them should choose to do alms according to the command of God, whomsoever he should find opposed, would inevitably be an enemy to the command of God, and therefore reckoned among unbelievers, — the command with respect to such parties being, that a believing husband should win his wife, and a believing wife her husband, by their good conversation and conduct; and therefore they ought not to conceal their good works from each other, by which they are to be mutually attracted, so that the one may be able to attract the other to communion in the Christian faith. Nor are thefts to be perpetrated in order that God may be rendered propitious. But if anything is to be concealed as long as the infirmity of the other party is unable to bear with equanimity what nevertheless is not done unjustly and unlawfully; yet, that the left hand is not meant in such a sense on the present occasion, readily appears from a consideration of the whole section, whereby it will at the same time be discovered what He calls the left hand.

8. "Take heed," says He, "that ye do not your righteousness before men, to be seen of them; otherwise ye have no reward of your Father which is in heaven." Here He has mentioned righteousness generally, then He follows it up in detail. For a deed which is done in the way of alms is a certain part of righteousness, and therefore He connects the two by saying, "Therefore, when thou doest thine alms, do not sound a trumpet before thee, as the hypocrites do in the synagogues and in the streets, that they may have glory of men." In this there is a reference to what He says before, "Take heed that ye do not your righteousness before men, to be seen of them." But what follows, "Verily I say unto you, They have received their reward," refers to that other statement which He has made above, "Otherwise ye have no reward of your Father which is in heaven." Then follows, "But when thou doest alms." When He says, "But thou," what else does He mean but, Not in the same manner as they? What, then, does He bid me do? "But when thou doest alms," says He, "let not thy left hand know what thy right hand doeth." Hence those other parties so act, that their left hand knoweth what their right hand doeth. What, therefore, is blamed in them, this thou art forbidden to do. But this is what is blamed in them, that they act in such a way as to seek the praises of men. And therefore the left hand seems to have no more suitable meaning than just this delight in praise. But the right hand means the intention of fulfilling the divine commands. When, therefore, with the consciousness of him who does alms is mixed up the desire of man's praise, the left hand becomes conscious of the work of the right hand: "Let not, therefore, thy left hand know what thy right hand doeth;"[2] *i.e.* Let there not be mixed up in thy consciousness the desire of man's praise, when in doing alms thou art striving to fulfil a divine command.

9. "That thine alms may be in secret."[3] What else is meant by "in secret," but just in a good conscience, which cannot be shown to human eyes, nor revealed by words? since, indeed, the mass of men tell many lies. And therefore, if the right hand acts inwardly in secret, all outward things, which are visible and temporal, belong to the left hand. Let thine alms, therefore, be in thine own consciousness, where many do alms by their good intention, even if they have no money or anything else which is to be bestowed on one who is needy. But many give alms outwardly, and not inwardly, who either from ambition, or for the sake of some temporal object, wish to appear merciful, in whom the left hand only is to be reckoned as working. Others again hold, as it were, a middle place between the two; so that, with a design which is directed Godward, they do their alms, and yet there insinuates itself into this

---

[1] Prov. xxv. 21.

[2] "With complete modesty; secret, noiseless giving" (Chrysostom). No reference to a counting of the money by the left hand (Paulus, De Wette). Luther's comment is quaint and characteristic: "When thou givest alms with thy right hand, take heed that thou dost not seek with the left to take more, but put it behind thy back." Trench pronounces this discussion concerning the meaning of the *left hand* "laborious, and, as I cannot but think, unnecessary;" but it is ingenious and interesting.

[3] *Pii lucent et tamen latent* (Bengel).

excellent wish also some desire after praise, or after a perishable and temporal object of some sort or other. But our Lord much more strongly prohibits the left hand alone being at work in us, when He even forbids its being mixed up with the works of the right hand : that is to say, that we are not only to beware of doing alms from the desire of temporal objects alone ; but that in this work we are not even to have regard to God in such a way as that there should be mingled up or united therewith the grasping after outward advantages. For the question under discussion is the cleansing of the heart, which, unless it be single, will not be clean. But how will it be single, if it serves two masters, and does not purge its vision by the striving after eternal things alone, but clouds it by the love of mortal and perishable things as well? " Let thine alms," therefore, " be in secret ; and thy [1] Father, who seeth in secret, shall reward thee." Altogether most righteously and most truly. For if you expect a reward from Him who is the only Searcher of the conscience, let conscience itself suffice thee for meriting a reward. Many Latin copies have it thus, " And thy Father who seeth in secret shall reward thee openly ; " but because we have not found the word " openly " in the Greek copies, which are earlier,[2] we have not thought that anything was to be said about it.

CHAP. III.— 10. " And when ye pray," says He, " ye shall not be as the hypocrites are ; for they love to pray standing [3] in the synagogues and in the corners of the streets, that they may be seen of men." And here also it is not the being seen of men that is wrong, but doing these things for the purpose of being seen of men ; and it is superfluous to make the same remark so often, since there is just one rule to be kept, from which we learn that what we should dread and avoid is not that men know these things, but that they be done with this intent, that the fruit of pleasing men should be sought after in them. Our Lord Himself, too, preserves the same words, when He adds similarly, " Verily I say unto you, They have received their reward ; " hereby showing that He forbids this, — the striving after that reward in which fools delight when they are praised by men.

11. " But when ye [4] pray," says He, " enter into your bed-chambers." What are those bed-chambers but just our hearts themselves, as is meant also in the Psalm, when it is said, " What ye say in your hearts, have remorse for even in your beds " ? [5] " And when ye have shut [6] the doors," says He, " pray to your Father who is in secret." [7] It is a small matter to enter into our bed-chambers if the door stand open to the unmannerly, through which the things that are outside profanely rush in and assail our inner man. Now we have said that outside are all temporal and visible things, which make their way through the door, i.e. through the fleshly sense into our thoughts, and clamorously interrupt those who are praying by a crowd of vain phantoms. Hence the door is to be shut, i.e. the fleshly sense is to be resisted, so that spiritual prayer may be directed to the Father, which is done in the inmost heart, where prayer is offered to the Father which is in secret. " And your Father," says He, " who seeth in secret, shall reward you." And this had to be wound up with a closing statement of such a kind ; for here at the present stage the admonition is not that we should pray, but as to how we should pray. Nor is what goes before an admonition that we should give alms, but as to the spirit in which we should do so, inasmuch as He is giving instructions with regard to the cleansing of the heart, which nothing cleanses but the undivided and single-minded striving after eternal life from the pure love of wisdom alone.

12. " But when ye pray," says He, " do not speak much,[8] as the heathen do ; for they think [9] that they shall be heard for their much speaking." As it is characteristic of the hypocrites to exhibit themselves to be gazed at when praying, and their fruit is to please men, so it is characteristic of the heathen, i.e. of the Gentiles, to think they are heard for their much speaking. And in reality, every kind of much speaking comes from the Gentiles, who make it their endeavour to exercise the tongue rather than to cleanse the heart. And this kind of useless exertion they endeavour to transfer even to the influencing of God by prayer, supposing that the Judge, just like man, is brought over by words to a certain way of thinking. " Be not ye, therefore,

---

[1] Not *our* Father

[2] It is wanting in the Sinaitic, B, D, etc., MSS., as also in the Vulgate copies.

[3] They love to *stand* praying, more than they love to pray Like the Mohammedans of to-day, they took delight in airing their piety. Our Lord mentions the most conspicuous localities. The usual posture of the Jews in prayer was standing (1 Sam. i. 26, Luke xviii. 11, etc.).

[4] *Vos ;* Vulgate, *tu* (Revised Version).

[5] Ps. iv. 4. The English version renders, " Commune with your own heart upon your bed, and be still."

[6] *Claudentes ostia ;* Vulgate, *clauso ostio.*

[7] Our Lord on occasion followed this habit (Matt. xiv. 23 and in Gethsemane).

[8] Greek, βαττολογεω " Use not vain repetitions," Revised Version (or *stammer*). Some derive the word from Battus, king of Cyrene, who stuttered, or from Battus, author of wordy poems. The word is probably only an imitation of the sound of the stammerer (Thayer, *Lexicon*, who spells βαττολογεω). The Jews were only doing as well as the Gentiles when they placed virtue in the length of the prayer, and no better. " Who makes his prayer long, shall not return home empty " (Rabbi Chasima, quoted by Hausrath, 73). The Rabbins took up at great length the question how many and what kind of petitions should be offered up at the table spread on different occasions with different viands, whether salutations should be acknowledged in the course of prayer, etc. (see Schürer, pp. 498, 499) Examples of repetitious prayer in Scripture : 1 Kings xviii. 26, Acts xix. 34. The warning is not against frequent prayer (Luke xviii. 1).

[9] *Arbitrantur ;* Vulgate, *putant.*

like unto them," says the only true Master. "For your Father knoweth what things are necessary [1] for you, before ye ask Him." For if many words are made use of with the intent that one who is ignorant may be instructed and taught, what need is there of them for Him who knows all things, to whom all things which exist, by the very fact of their existence, speak, and show themselves as having been brought into existence ; and those things which are future do not remain concealed from His knowledge and wisdom, in which both those things which are past, and those things which will yet come to pass, are all present and cannot pass away?

13. But since, however few they may be, yet there are words which He Himself also is about to speak, by which He would teach us to pray ; it may be asked why even these few words are necessary for Him who knows all things before they take place, and is acquainted, as has been said, with what is necessary for us before we ask Him? Here, in the first place, the answer is, that we ought to urge our case with God, in order to obtain what we wish, not by words, but by the ideas which we cherish in our mind, and by the direction of our thought, with pure love and sincere desire ; but that our Lord has taught us the very ideas in words, that by committing them to memory we may recollect those ideas at the time we pray.

14. But again, it may be asked (whether we are to pray in ideas or in words) what need there is for prayer itself, if God already knows what is necessary for us ; unless it be that the very effort involved in prayer calms and purifies our heart, and makes it more capacious for receiving the divine gifts, which are poured into us spiritually.[2] For it is not on account of the urgency of our prayers that God hears us, who is always ready to give us His light, not of a material kind, but that which is intellectual and spiritual : but we are not always ready to receive, since we are inclined towards other things, and are involved in darkness through our desire for temporal things. Hence there is brought about in prayer a turning of the heart to Him, who is ever ready to give, if we will but take what He has given ; and in the very act of turning there is effected a purging of the inner eye, inasmuch as those things of a temporal kind which were desired are excluded, so that the vision of the pure heart may be able to bear the pure light, divinely shining, without any setting or change : and not only to bear it, but also to remain in it ;

not merely without annoyance, but also with ineffable joy, in which a life truly and sincerely blessed is perfected.

CHAP. IV. — 15. But now we have to consider what things we are taught to pray for by Him through whom we both learn what we are to pray for, and obtain what we pray for. "After this manner, therefore, pray ye," [3] says He: "Our Father who art in heaven, Hallowed be Thy name. Thy kingdom come. Thy will be done on earth, as it is in heaven. Give us this day our daily [4] bread. And forgive us our debts, as we forgive our debtors. And bring [5] us not into temptation, but deliver us from evil." [6] Seeing that in all prayer we have to conciliate the goodwill of him to whom we pray, then to say what we pray for ; goodwill is usually conciliated by our offering praise to him to whom the prayer is directed, and this is usually put in the beginning of the prayer : and in this particular our Lord has bidden us say nothing else but " Our Father who art in heaven." For many things are said in praise of God, which, being scattered variously and widely over all the Holy Scriptures, every one will be able to consider when he reads

---

[3] *Orate ;* Vulgate, *Orabitis.*
[4] *Quotidianum ;* Vulgate, *supersubstantialem.*
[5] *Inferas (Rev. Vers.):* Vulgate, *inducas.*
[6] This prayer is called the Lord's Prayer because our Lord is its author. He did not and could not have used it Himself, on account of (1) the special meaning of the pronoun " our" in the address, (2) the confession of sins in the fifth petition. Luke's account (xi. 1) agrees in the subject of the petitions as in the address, but differs (1) in the omission of the third petition (Crit text) ; (2) in the addition to the fifth petition (which, however, Matthew gives at the close of the prayer in a more elaborate form) ; (3) in adducing a request of the disciples as the occasion of the prayer. Some have thought the prayer was given on two occasions (Meyer in earlier edd., Tholuck). Others hold that Matthew has inserted it out of its proper historical place (Neander, Olshausen, De Wette, Ebrard, Meyer in ed. vi., Weiss, etc.). This question of priority and accuracy as between the forms of Matthew and Luke may be regarded as set at rest by the *Teaching of the Twelve Apostles,* which (viii. 2) gives the exact form of Matthew, with three unimportant differences: viz. (1) *heaven,* οὐρανῷ, instead of *heavens ;* (2) the omission of the article before *earth ;* (3) *debt* instead of *debts.* This document contains the doxology (with the omission of *kingdom*), and supports the *Textus Receptus* in giving the present, *we forgive,* ἀφίεμεν, instead of the perfect, *we have forgiven,* ἀφήκαμεν. — The *division* of the prayer is usually made into (1) address, (2) petitions, (3) doxology (omitted from the approved critical Greek text and the Revised Version). — The petitions are seven according to Augustin, Luther, Bengel, Tholuck, etc. ; six (the two last being combined as one) according to Chrysostom, Reformed catechisms. Calvin, Schaff, etc. The petitions are divided into two groups (Tertullian) or tables (Calvin). — The *contents* of the first three petitions concern the glory of God ; of the last four, the wants of men. In the first group the pronoun is *thy,* and the direction of the thought is from heaven downwards to earth ; in the second group it is *us,* and the direction of the thought is from earth upwards to God. — The numbers, in view of their significance in the Old Testament, 3, 4, 7, are not an uninteresting item Tholuck says: "The attention of the student who has otherwise heard of the doctrine of the Trinity will find a distinct reference to it in the arrangement of this prayer. In the first petition of each group, God is referred to as Creator and Preserver ; in the second as Redeemer ; in the third as the Holy Spirit. — The Lord's Prayer is more than a specimen of prayer : it is a pattern. Different views are held concerning its liturgical use, which can be traced back to Cyprian and Tertullian, and now farther still, to the *Teaching of the Apostles,* which, after giving the prayer, says, "Thrice a day pray thus." It also gives (ix.) a form of prayer to be used after the Eucharist. Of its abuse Luther says, " It is the greatest martyr." — It is not a *compilation,* although similar or the same, petitions may have been in use among the Jews. The simplicity, symmetry of arrangement, depth and progress of thought, reverence of feeling, make it, indeed, the model prayer, — the Lord's Prayer. Tertullian calls it *breviarium totius evangelii* (so Meyer).

---

[1] *Vobis necessarium ;* Vulgate, *opus.*
[2] The illustration is frequently used (M. Henry: after him F. W. Robertson), to represent the position of some, that prayer only has an influence on the petitioner, of a boatman in his boat, taking hold of the wharf with his grappling hook. While prayer does not " inform or persuade God," it is the condition of receiving. The sanctifying influence is secondary and incidental.

them : yet nowhere is there found a precept for the people of Israel, that they should say "Our Father," or that they should pray to God as a Father ; but as Lord He was made known to them, as being yet servants, *i.e.* still living according to the flesh. I say this, however, inasmuch as they received the commands of the law, which they were ordered to observe : for the prophets often show that this same Lord of ours might have been their Father also, if they had not strayed from His commandments : as, for instance, we have that statement, "I have nourished and brought up children, and they have rebelled against me ; "[1] and that other, "I have said, Ye are gods ; and all of you are children of the Most High ; "[2] and this again, "If then I be a Father, where is mine honour? and if I be a Master, where is my fear?"[3] and very many other statements, where the Jews are accused of showing by their sin that they did not wish to become sons : those things being left out of account which are said in prophecy of a future Christian people, that they would have God as a Father, according to that gospel statement, "To them gave He power to become the sons of God."[4] The Apostle Paul, again, says, "The heir, as long as he is a child, differeth nothing from a servant ; " and mentions that we have received the Spirit of adoption, "whereby we cry, Abba, Father."[5]

16. And since the fact that we are called to an eternal inheritance, that we might be fellowheirs with Christ and attain to the adoption of sons, is not of our deserts, but of God's grace ; we put this very same grace in the beginning of our prayer, when we say "Our Father." And by that appellation both love is stirred up — for what ought to be dearer to sons than a father? — and a suppliant disposition, when men say to God, "Our Father : " and a certain presumption of obtaining what we are about to ask ; since, before we ask anything, we have received so great a gift as to be allowed to call God "Our Father."[6] For what would He not now give to sons when they ask, when He has already granted this very thing, namely, that they might be sons? Lastly, how great solicitude takes hold of the mind, that he who says "Our Father," should not prove unworthy of so great a Father ! For if any plebeian should be permitted by the party himself to call a senator of more advanced age father ; without doubt he would tremble, and would not readily venture to do it, reflecting on the humbleness of his origin, and the scantiness of his resources, and the worthlessness of his plebeian person : how much more, therefore,

ought we to tremble to call God Father, if there is so great a stain and so much baseness in our character, that God might much more justly drive forth these from contact with Himself, than that senator might the poverty of any beggar whatever ! Since, indeed, he (the senator) despises that in the beggar to which even he himself may be reduced by the vicissitude of human affairs : but God never falls into baseness of character. And thanks be to the mercy of Him who requires this of us, that He should be our Father, — a relationship which can be brought about by no expenditure of ours, but solely by God's goodwill. Here also there is an admonition to the rich and to those of noble birth, so far as this world is concerned, that when they have become Christians they should not comport themselves proudly towards the poor and the low of birth ; since together with them they call God "Our Father," — an expression which they cannot truly and piously use, unless they recognise that they themselves are brethren.

CHAP. V. — 17. Let the new people, therefore, who are called to an eternal inheritance, use the word of the New Testament, and say, "Our Father who art in heaven,"[7] *i.e.* in the holy and the just. For God is not contained in space. For the heavens are indeed the higher material bodies of the world, but yet material, and therefore cannot exist except in some definite place ; but if God's place is believed to be in the heavens, as meaning the higher parts of the world, the birds are of greater value than we, for their life is nearer to God. But it is not written, The Lord is nigh unto tall men, or unto those who dwell on mountains ; but it is written, "The Lord is nigh unto them that are of a broken heart,"[8] which refers rather to humility. But as a sinner is called earth, when it is said to him, "Earth thou art, and unto earth shalt thou return ; "[9] so, on the other hand, a righteous man may be called heaven. For it is said to the righteous, "For the temple of God is holy, which temple ye are."[10] And therefore, if God dwells in His temple, and the saints are His temple, the expression "which art in heaven" is rightly used in the sense, which art in the saints. And most suitable is such a similitude, so that spiritually there may be seen to be as great a difference between the righteous and sinners, as there is materially between heaven and earth.

18. And for the purpose of showing this, when we stand at prayer, we turn to the east, whence the heaven rises : not as if God also

---

[1] Isa. i. 2.　　[2] Ps. lxxxii. 6.　　[3] Mal. i. 6.
[4] John i. 12.　　[5] Rom. viii. 15–23 and Gal. iv. 1–6.
[6] *Patrem quisquis appellare potest, omnia orare potest* (Bengel).

[7] "The address puts us into the proper attitude of prayer- It indicates our filial relation to God as 'Father' (word of faith), fraternal relation to our fellow-men ('our,' word of love), and our destination of 'heaven' (word of hope)."
[8] Ps. xxxiv. 18.　　[9] Gen. iii. 19.　　[10] 1 Cor. iii. 17.

were dwelling there, in the sense that He who is everywhere present, not as occupying space, but by the power of His majesty, had forsaken the other parts of the world ; but in order that the mind may be admonished to turn to a more excellent nature, *i.e.* to God, when its own body, which is earthly, is turned to a more excellent body, *i.e.* to a heavenly one. It is also suitable for the different stages of religion, and expedient in the highest degree, that in the minds of all, both small and great, there should be cherished worthy conceptions of God. And therefore, as regards those who as yet are taken up with the beauties that are seen, and cannot think of anything incorporeal, inasmuch as they must necessarily prefer heaven to earth, their opinion is more tolerable, if they believe God, whom as yet they think of after a corporeal fashion, to be in heaven rather than upon earth : so that when at any future time they have learned that the dignity of the soul exceeds even a celestial body, they may seek Him in the soul rather than in a celestial body even ; and when they have learned how great a distance there is between the souls of sinners and of the righteous, just as they did not venture, when as yet they were wise only after a carnal fashion, to place Him on earth, but in heaven, so afterwards with better faith or intelligence they may seek Him again in the souls of the righteous rather than in those of sinners. Hence, when it is said, " Our Father which art in heaven," it is rightly understood to mean in the hearts of the righteous, as it were in His holy temple. And at the same time, in such a way that he who prays wishes Him whom he invokes to dwell in himself also ; and when he strives after this, practises righteousness, — a kind of service by which God is attracted to dwell in the soul.

19. Let us see now what things are to be prayed for. For it has been stated who it is that is prayed to, and where He dwells. First of all, then, of those things which are prayed for comes this petition, " Hallowed be Thy name." And this is prayed for, not as if the name of God were not holy already, but that it may be held holy by men ; *i.e.*, that God may so become known to them, that they shall reckon nothing more holy, and which they are more afraid of offending. For, because it is said, " In Judah is God known ; His name is great in Israel," [1] we are not to understand the statement in this way, as if God were less in one place, greater in another ; but there His name is great, where He is named according to the greatness of His majesty. And so there His name is said to be holy, where He is named with veneration and the fear of offending Him. And this is what is

now going on, while the gospel, by becoming known everywhere throughout the different nations, commends the name of the one God by means of the administration of His Son.

CHAP. VI. — 20. In the next place there follows, " Thy kingdom come." Just as the Lord Himself teaches in the Gospel that the day of judgment will take place at the very time when the gospel shall have been preached among all nations : [2] a thing which belongs to the hallowing of God's name. For here also the expression " Thy kingdom come " is not used in such a way as if God were not now reigning. But some one perhaps might say the expression " come " meant *upon earth;* as if, indeed, He were not even now really reigning upon earth, and had not always reigned upon it from the foundation of the world. " Come," therefore, is to be understood in the sense of " manifested to men." For in the same way also as a light which is present is absent to the blind, and to those who shut their eyes ; so the kingdom of God, though it never departs from the earth, is yet absent to those who are ignorant of it. But no one will be allowed to be ignorant of the kingdom of God, when His Only-begotten shall come from heaven, not only in a way to be apprehended by the understanding, but also visibly in the person of the Divine Man, in order to judge the quick and the dead. And after that judgment, *i.e.* when the process of distinguishing and separating the righteous from the unrighteous has taken place, God will so dwell in the righteous, that there will be no need for any one being taught by man, but all will be, as it is written, " taught of God." [3] Then will the blessed life in all its parts be perfected in the saints unto eternity, just as now the most holy and blessed heavenly angels are wise and blessed, from the fact that God alone is their light ; because the Lord hath promised this also to His own : " In the resurrection," says He, " they will be as the angels in heaven." [4]

21. And therefore, after that petition where we say, " Thy kingdom come," there follows, " Thy will be done, as in heaven so in earth :" *i.e.*, just as Thy will is in the angels who are in heaven, so that they wholly cleave to Thee, and thoroughly enjoy Thee, no error beclouding their wisdom, no misery hindering their blessedness ; so let it be done in Thy saints who are on earth, and made from the earth, so far as the body is concerned, and who, although it is into a heavenly habitation and exchange, are yet to be taken from the earth. To this there is a reference also in that doxology of the angels, " Glory to God in the highest,[5] and on earth peace to men of

---

[1] Ps. lxxvi. 1.

[2] Matt. xxiv. 14.   [3] Isa. liv. 13; John vi. 45.
[4] Matt. xxii. 30.   [5] *In excelsis ;* Vulgate, *in altissimis.*

goodwill : " [1] so that when our goodwill has gone before, which follows Him that calleth, the will of God is perfected in us, as it is in the heavenly angels ; so that no antagonism stands in the way of our blessedness : and this is peace. "Thy will be done" is also rightly understood in the sense of, Let obedience be rendered to Thy precepts : "as in heaven so on earth," *i.e.* as by the angels so by men. For, that the will of God is done when His precepts are obeyed, the Lord Himself says, when He affirms, " My meat is to do the will of Him that sent me ; " [2] and often, " I came, not to do mine own will, but the will of Him that sent me ; " [3] and when He says, " Behold my mother and my brethren ! For whosoever shall do the will of God,[4] the same is my brother, and sister, and mother." [5] And therefore, in those at least who do the will of God, the will of God is accomplished ; not because they cause God to will, but because they do what He wills, *i.e.* they do according to His will.

22. There is also that other interpretation, " Thy will be done as in heaven so on earth," — as in the holy and just, so also in sinners. And this, besides, may be understood in two ways : either that we should pray even for our enemies (for what else are they to be reckoned, in spite of whose will the Christian and Catholic name still spreads?), so that it is said, " Thy will be done as in heaven so on earth," — as if the meaning were, As the righteous do Thy will, in like manner let sinners also do it, so that they may be converted unto Thee ; or in this sense, " Let Thy will be done as in heaven so on earth," so that every one may get his own ; which will take place at the last judgment, the righteous being requited with a reward, sinners with con-demnation — when the sheep shall be separated from the goats.[6]

23. That other interpretation also is not ab-surd, nay, it is thoroughly accordant with both our faith and hope, that we are to take heaven and earth in the sense of spirit and flesh. And since the apostle says, " With the mind I myself serve the law of God, but with the flesh the law of sin," [7] we see that the will of God is done in the mind, *i.e.* in the spirit. But when death shall have been swallowed up in victory, and this mortal shall have put on immortality, which will happen at the resurrection of the flesh, and at that change which is promised to the righteous, according to the prediction of the same apostle,[8] let the will of God be done on earth, as it is in heaven ; *i.e.*, in such a way that, in like manner as the spirit does not resist God, but follows and

does His will, so the body also may not resist the spirit or soul, which at present is harassed by the weakness of the body, and is prone to fleshly habit : and this will be an element of the per-fect peace in the life eternal, that not only will the will be present with us, but also the perform-ance of that which is good. " For to will," says he, " is present with me ; but how to perform that which is good I find not : " for not yet in earth as in heaven, *i.e.* not yet in the flesh as in the spirit, is the will of God done. For even in our misery the will of God is done, when we suffer those things through the flesh which are due to us in virtue of our mortality, which our nature has deserved because of its sin. But we are to pray for this, that the will of God may be done as in heaven so in earth ; that in like man-ner as with the heart we delight in the law after the inward man,[9] so also, when the change in our body has taken place, no part of us may, on account of earthly griefs or pleasures, stand opposed to this our delight.

24. Nor is that view inconsistent with truth, that we are to understand the words, " Thy will be done as in heaven so in earth," as in our Lord Jesus Christ Himself, so also in the Church : as if one were to say, As in the man who fulfilled the will of the Father, so also in the woman who is betrothed to him. For heaven and earth are suitably understood as if they were man and wife ; since the earth is fruitful from the heaven fertilizing it.

CHAP. VII. — 25. The fourth petition is, " Give us this day our daily bread." Daily bread is put either for all those things which meet the wants of this life, in reference to which He says in His teaching, " Take no thought for the morrow : " so that on this account there is added, " Give us this day : " or, it is put for the sacrament of the body of Christ, which we daily receive : or, for the spiritual food, of which the same Lord says, " Labour for the meat which perisheth not ; " [10] and again, " I am the bread of life,[11] which came down from heaven." [12] But which of these three views is the more probable, is a question for consideration. For perhaps some one may won-der why we should pray that we may obtain the things which are necessary for this life, — such, for instance, as food and clothing, — when the Lord Himself says, " Be not anxious what ye shall eat, or what ye shall put on." Can any one not be anxious for a thing which he prays that he may obtain ; when prayer is to be offered with so great earnestness of mind, that to this refers all that has been said about shutting our

---

[1] Luke ii. 14.   [2] John iv. 34.   [3] John vi. 38.
[4] Vulgate, *Patris qui in cælis* (" Father who is in heaven"). So the Greek.
[5] Matt. xxii. 49, 50.   [6] Matt. xxv. 33, 46.
[7] Rom. vii. 25.   [8] 1 Cor. xv. 42, 55.

[9] Rom. vii. 18, 22.
[10] *Escam quæ non corrumpitur ;* Vulgate, *non cibum qui perit.*
[11] *Panis vitæ ;* Vulgate, *panis vivus.*   [12] John vi. 27, 41.

closets, and also the command, "Seek ye first the kingdom of God, and His righteousness; and all these things shall be added[1] unto you"? Certainly He does not say, Seek ye first the kingdom of God, and then seek those other things; but "all these things," says He, "shall be added unto you," that is to say, even though ye are not seeking them. But I know not whether it can be found out, how one is rightly said not to seek what he most earnestly pleads with God that he may receive.

26. But with respect to the sacrament of the Lord's body (in order that they may not start a question, who, the most of them being in Eastern parts, do not partake of the Lord's supper daily, while this bread is called daily bread: in order, therefore, that they may be silent, and not defend their way of thinking about this matter even by the very authority of the Church, because they do such things without scandal, and are not prevented from doing them by those who preside over their churches, and when they do not obey are not condemned; whence it is proved that this is not understood as daily bread in these parts: for, if this were the case, they would be charged with the commission of a great sin, who do not on that account receive it daily; but, as has been said, not to argue at all to any extent from the case of such parties), this consideration at least ought to occur to those who reflect, that we have received a rule for prayer from the Lord, which we ought not to transgress, either by adding or omitting anything. And since this is the case, who is there who would venture to say that we ought only once to use the Lord's Prayer, or at least that, even if we have used it a second or a third time before the hour at which we partake of the Lord's body, afterwards we are assuredly not so to pray during the remaining hours of the day? For we shall no longer be able to say, "Give us this day," respecting what we have already received; or every one will be able to compel us to celebrate that sacrament at the very last hour of the day.

27. It remains, therefore, that we should understand the daily bread as spiritual, that is to say, divine precepts, which we ought daily to meditate and to labour after. For just with respect to these the Lord says, "Labour for the meat which perisheth not." That food, moreover, is called daily food at present, so long as this temporal life is measured off by means of days that depart and return. And, in truth, so long as the desire of the soul is directed by turns, now to what is higher, now to what is lower, i.e. now to spiritual things, now to carnal, as is the case with him who at one time is nourished with food, at another time suffers hunger; bread is

daily necessary, in order that the hungry man may be recruited, and he who is falling down may be raised up. As, therefore, our body in this life, that is to say, before that great change, is recruited with food, because it feels loss; so may the soul also, since by means of temporal desires it sustains as it were a loss in its striving after God, be reinvigorated by the food of the precepts. Moreover, it is said, "Give us this day," as long as it is called to-day, i.e. in this temporal life. For we shall be so abundantly provided with spiritual food after this life unto eternity, that it will not then be called daily bread; because there the flight of time, which causes days to succeed days, whence it may be called to-day, will not exist. But as it is said, "To-day, if ye will hear His voice,"[2] which the apostle interprets in the Epistle to the Hebrews, As long as it is called to-day;[3] so here also the expression is to be understood, "Give us this day." But if any one wishes to understand the sentence before us also of food necessary for the body, or of the sacrament of the Lord's body, we must take all three meanings conjointly; that is to say, that we are to ask for all at once as daily bread, both the bread necessary for the body, and the visible hallowed bread, and the invisible bread of the word of God.[4]

CHAP. VIII. — 28. The fifth petition follows: "And forgive us our debts, as we also forgive[5] our debtors." It is manifest that by debts are meant sins, either from that statement which the Lord Himself makes, "Thou shalt by no means come out thence, till thou hast paid the uttermost farthing;"[6] or from the fact that He called those men debtors who were reported to Him as having been killed, either those on whom the tower fell, or those whose blood Herod had mingled with the sacrifice. For He said that men supposed it was because they were debtors above measure, i.e. sinners, and added, "I tell you, Nay: but, except ye repent, ye shall all likewise die."[7] Here, therefore, it is not a money claim that one is pressed to remit, but whatever sins another may have committed against him.

---

[2] Ps. xcv. 7.   [3] Heb. iii. 13.

[4] The Greek ἐπιούσιος, translated *daily* (see margin of Revised Version, with alternate rendering of American Committee), is found only here and in Luke (xi. 3). Its meaning does not seem to come under the review of Augustin, but has troubled modern commentators. It has been taken to mean (1) *needful*, hence sufficient, as opposed to superfluity or want (Chrysostom, Tholuck, Ewald, Ebrard, Weiss, etc.); (2) *daily* (Luther, English version, etc.); (3) *for the coming day* (Grotius, Meyer, Thayer, Lightfoot, who has an elaborate treatment in *Revision of English New Testament*, Append. pp. 195-245). The direct reference of the bread to spiritual food is given by the Vulgate, and generally accepted in the Roman-Catholic Church. Olshausen, Delitzsch, Alford, etc., regard the spiritual nourishment involved by implication in the term.

[5] The present with the Vulgate, *Textus Receptus*, *Teaching of Twelve Apostles*. The perfect is found in א, B, Z, etc., and adopted by Tischendorf, Westcott and Hort, and Revised Version.

[6] Matt. v. 26.

[7] Luke xiii. 1-5. *Moriemini*; Vulgate, *peribitis*. Augustin has written "Herod" instead of "Pilate."

---

[1] *Apponentur;* Vulgate, *adjicientur.*

For we are enjoined to remit a money claim by that precept rather which has been given above, "If any man will sue thee at the law, and take away thy coat, let him have thy cloak also ;"[1] nor is it necessary to remit a debt to every money debtor, but only to him who is unwilling to pay, to such an extent that he wishes even to go to law. "Now the servant of the Lord," as says the apostle, "must not go to law."[2] And therefore to him who shall be unwilling, either spontaneously or when requested, to pay the money which he owes, it is to be remitted. For his unwillingness to pay will arise from one of two causes, either that he has it not, or that he is avaricious and covetous of the property of another ; and both of these belong to a state of poverty : for the former is poverty of substance, the latter poverty of disposition. Whoever, therefore, remits a debt to such an one, remits it to one who is poor, and performs a Christian work ; while that rule remains in force, that he should be prepared in mind to lose what is owing to him. For if he has used exertion in every way, quietly and gently, to have it restored to him, not so much aiming at a money profit, as that he may bring the man round to what is right, to whom without doubt it is hurtful to have the means of paying, and yet not to pay ; not only will he not sin, but he will even do a very great service, in trying to prevent that other, who is wishing to make gain of another's money, from making shipwreck of the faith ; which is so much more serious a thing, that there is no comparison. And hence it is understood that in this fifth petition also, where we say, " Forgive us our debts," the words are spoken not indeed in reference to money, but in reference to all ways in which any one sins against us, and by consequence in reference to money also. For the man who refuses to pay you the money which he owes, when he has the means of doing so, sins against you. And if you do not forgive this sin, you will not be able to say, " Forgive us, as we also forgive ;" but if you pardon it, you see how he who is enjoined to offer such a prayer is admonished also with respect to forgiving a money debt.

29. That may indeed be construed in this way, that when we say, " Forgive us our debts, as[3] we also forgive," then only are we convicted of having acted contrary to this rule, if we do not forgive them who ask pardon, because we also

wish to be forgiven by our most gracious Father when we ask His pardon. But, on the other hand, by that precept whereby we are enjoined to pray for our enemies, it is not for those who ask pardon that we are enjoined to pray. For those who are already in such a state of mind are no longer enemies. By no possibility, however, could one truthfully say that he prays for one whom he has not pardoned. And therefore we must confess that all sins which are committed against us are to be forgiven, if we wish those to be forgiven by our Father which we commit against Him. For the subject of revenge has been sufficiently dicsussed already, as I think.[4]

CHAP. IX. — 30. The sixth petition is, " And bring[5] us not into temptation." Some manuscripts have the word " lead,"[5] which is, I judge, equivalent in meaning : for both translations have arisen from the one Greek word which is used. But many parties in prayer express themselves thus, " Suffer us not to be led into temptation ; " that is to say, explaining in what sense the word " lead " is used. For God does not Himself lead, but suffers that man to be led into temptation whom He has deprived of His assistance, in accordance with a most hidden arrangement, and with his deserts. Often, also, for manifest reasons, He judges him worthy of being so deprived, and allowed to be led into temptation. But it is one thing to be led into temptation, another to be tempted. For without temptation no one can be proved, whether to himself, as it is written, " He that hath not been tempted, what manner of things doth he know?"[6] or to another, as the apostle says, "And your temptation in my flesh ye despised not : "[7] for from this circumstance he learnt that they were stedfast, because they were not turned aside from charity by those tribulations which had happened to the apostle according to the flesh. For even before all temptations we are known to God, who knows all things before they happen.

31. When, therefore, it is said, " The Lord your God tempteth (proveth) you, that He may know if ye love Him,"[8] the words " that He may know " are employed for what is the real state of the case, that He may make you know : just as we speak of a joyful day, because it makes us joyful ; of a sluggish frost, because it makes us sluggish ; and of innumerable things of the same sort, which are found either in ordinary speech, or in the discourse of learned men, or in the Holy Scriptures. And the heretics who

---

[1] Matt. v. 40.　　　[2] 2 Tim. ii. 24.
[3] Not " because," nor " to the same extent as," but " in the same manner as." It is interesting to note the contrast between the spirit of Christianity and Islam as indicated by a comparison of this petition with the prayer offered every night by the ten thousand students at the Mahometan college in Cairo: " I seek refuge with Allah from Satan the accursed. In the name of Allah the compassionate, the merciful, O Lord of all the creatures! O Allah! destroy the infidels and polytheists, thine enemies, the enemies of the religion. O Allah! make their children orphans, and defile their abodes. Cause their feet to slip," etc.

[4] See Book i. chaps. 19, 20.
[5] *Inferas . . . inducas,* as the Vulgate.
[6] Ecclus. xxxiv. 9, 11.
[7] Gal. iv. 13, 14. The English version renders "*my* temptation," but "*your* temptation " is the reading of the oldest MSS.
[8] Deut. xiii. 3.

are opposed to the Old Testament, not under-standing this, think that the brand of ignorance, as it were, is to be placed upon Him of whom it is said, "The Lord your God tempteth you:" as if in the Gospel it were not written of the Lord, "And this He said to tempt (prove) him, for He Himself knew what He would do."[1] For if He knew the heart of him whom He was tempting, what is it that He wished to see by tempting him? But in reality, that was done in order that he who was tempted might become known to himself, and that he might condemn his own despair, on the multitudes being filled with the Lord's bread, while he had thought they had not enough to eat.

32. Here, therefore, the prayer is not, that we should not be tempted, but that we should not be brought into temptation: as if, were it neces-sary that any one should be examined by fire, he should pray, not that he should not be touched by the fire, but that he should not be consumed. For "the furnace proveth the potter's vessels, and the trial of tribulation righteous men."[2] Joseph therefore was tempted with the allure-ment of debauchery, but he was not brought into temptation.[3] Susanna was tempted, but she was not led or brought into temptation;[4] and many others of both sexes: but Job most of all, in regard to whose admirable stedfastness in the Lord his God, those heretical enemies of the Old Testament, when they wish to mock at it with sacrilegious mouth, brandish this above other weapons, that Satan begged that he should be tempted.[5] For they put the question to unskil-ful men by no means able to understand such things, how Satan could speak with God: not understanding (for they cannot, inasmuch as they are blinded by superstition and contro-versy) that God does not occupy space by the mass of His corporeity; and thus exist in one place, and not in another, or at least have one part here, and another elsewhere: but that He is everywhere present in His majesty, not divided by parts, but everywhere complete. But if they take a fleshly view of what is said, "The heaven is my throne, and the earth is my footstool,"[6] — to which passage our Lord also bears testi-mony, when He says, "Swear not at all: neither by heaven, for it is God's throne; nor by the earth, for it is His footstool,"[7] — what wonder if the devil, being placed on earth, stood before the feet of God, and spoke something in His presence? For when will they be able to under-stand that there is no soul, however wicked, which can yet reason in any way, in whose con-science God does not speak? For who but God has written the law of nature in the hearts of

men?—that law concerning which the apostle says: "For when the Gentiles, which have not the law, do by nature the things contained in the law, these, having not the law, are a law unto themselves: which show the work of the law writ-ten in their hearts, their conscience also bearing them witness,[8] and their thoughts[9] the meanwhile accusing or else excusing one another, in the day when the Lord[10] shall judge the secrets of men."[11] And therefore, as in the case of every rational soul, which thinks and reasons, even though blinded by passion, we attribute whatever in its reasoning is true, not to itself but to the very light of truth by which, however faintly, it is according to its capacity illuminated, so as to perceive some measure of truth by its reasoning; what wonder if the depraved spirit of the devil, perverted though it be by lust, should be repre-sented as having heard from the voice of God Himself, *i.e.* from the voice of the very Truth, whatever true thought it has entertained about a righteous man whom it was proposing to tempt? But whatever is false is to be attributed to that lust from which he has received the name of devil. Although it is also the case that God has often spoken by means of a corporeal and visible creature whether to good or bad, as being Lord and Governor of all, and Disposer according to the merits of every deed: as, for instance, by means of angels, who appeared also under the aspect of men; and by means of the prophets, saying, Thus saith the Lord. What wonder then, if, though not in mere thought, at least by means of some creature fitted for such a work, God is said to have spoken with the devil?

33. And let them not imagine it unworthy of His dignity, and as it were of His righteousness, that God spoke with him: inasmuch as He spoke with an angelic spirit, although one foolish and lustful, just as if He were speaking with a foolish and lustful human spirit. Or let such parties themselves tell us how He spoke with that rich man, whose most foolish covetousness He wished to censure, saying: "Thou fool, this night thy soul shall be required[12] of thee: then whose shall those things be which thou hast provided?"[13] Certainly the Lord Himself says so in the Gos-pel, to which those heretics, whether they will or no, bend their necks. But if they are puzzled by this circumstance, that Satan asks from God that a righteous man should be tempted; I do not explain how it happened, but I compel them to explain why it is said in the Gospel by the Lord Himself to the disciples, "Behold, Satan hath desired to have you, that he may sift you

---

[8] *Contestante;* Vulgate, *testimonium reddente.*
[9] *Cogitationum accusantium;* Vulgate, *cogitationibus accu-santibus.*
[10] *Dominus;* Vulgate, *Deus.*   [11] Rom. ii. 14-16.
[12] *Anima expostulatur;* Vulgate, *animam repetunt.*
[13] Luke xii. 20.

[1] John vi. 6.   [2] Ecclus. xxvii. 5.   [3] Gen. xxxix. 7-12.
[4] Hist. of Sus. i. 19-22.   [5] Job i. 11.
[6] Isa. lxvi. 1.   [7] Matt. v. 34, 35.

as wheat;"[1] and He says to Peter, "But I have prayed for thee, that thy faith fail not."[2]　And when they explain this to me, they explain to themselves at the same time that which they question me about.　But if they should not be able to explain this, let them not dare with rashness to blame in any book what they read in the Gospel without offence.

34.　Temptations, therefore, take place by means of Satan not by his power, but by the Lord's permission, either for the purpose of punishing men for their sins, or of proving and exercising them in accordance with the Lord's compassion.　And there is a very great difference in the nature of the temptations into which each one may fall.　For Judas, who sold his Lord, did not fall into one of the same nature as Peter fell into, when, under the influence of terror, he denied his Lord.　There are also temptations common to man, I believe, when every one, though well disposed, yet yielding to human frailty, falls into error in some plan, or is irritated against a brother, in the earnest endeavour to bring him round to what is right, yet a little more than Christian calmness demands: concerning which temptations the apostle says, "There hath no temptation taken you but such as is common to man;" while he says at the same time, "But God is faithful, who will not suffer[3] you to be tempted above that ye are able; but will with the temptation also make a way to escape, that ye may be able to bear[4] it."[5]　And in that sentence he makes it sufficiently evident that we are not to pray that we may not be tempted, but that we may not be led into temptation.　For we are led into temptation, if such temptations have happened to us as we are not able to bear.　But when dangerous temptations, into which it is ruinous for us to be brought and led, arise either from prosperous or adverse temporal circumstances, no one is broken down by the irksomeness of adversity, who is not led captive by the delight of prosperity.[6]

35.　The seventh and last petition is, "But deliver us from evil."[7]　For we are to pray not only that we may not be led into the evil from which we are free, which is asked in the sixth place; but that we may also be delivered from that into which we have been already led.　And when this has been done, nothing will remain

terrible, nor will any temptation at all have to be feared.　And yet in this life, so long as we carry about our present mortality, into which we were led by the persuasion of the serpent, it is not to be hoped that this can be the case; but yet we are to hope that at some future time it will take place: and this is the hope which is not seen, of which the apostle, when speaking, said, "But hope which is seen is not hope."[8] But yet the wisdom which is granted in this life also, is not to be despaired of by the faithful servants of God.　And it is this, that we should with the most wary vigilance shun what we have understood, from the Lord's revealing it, is to be shunned; and that we should with the most ardent love seek after what we have understood, from the Lord's revealing it, is to be sought after.　For thus, after the remaining burden of this mortality has been laid down in the act of dying, there shall be perfected in every part of man at the fit time, the blessedness which has been begun in this life, and which we have from time to time strained every nerve to lay hold of and secure.

CHAP. X. — 36.　But the distinction among these seven petitions is to be considered and commended.　For inasmuch as our temporal life is being spent now, and that which is eternal hoped for, and inasmuch as eternal things are superior in point of dignity, albeit it is only when we have done with temporal things that we pass to the other; although the three first petitions begin to be answered in this life, which is being spent in the present world (for both the hallowing of God's name begins to be carried on just with the coming of the lord of humility; and the coming of His kingdom, to which He will come in splendour, will be manifested, not after the end of the world, but in the end of the world; and the perfect doing of His will in earth as in heaven, whether you understand by heaven and earth the righteous and sinners, or spirit and flesh, or the Lord and the Church, or all these things together, will be brought to completion just with the perfecting of our blessedness, and therefore at the close of the world), yet all three will remain to eternity.　For both the hallowing of God's name will go on for ever, and there is no end of His kingdom, and eternal life is promised to our perfected blessedness. Hence those three things will remain consummated and thoroughly completed in that life which is promised us.

37.　But the other four things which we ask seem to me to belong to this temporal life.[9] And the first of them is, "Give us this day our

---

[1] *Petit vos vexare quomodo triticum;* Vulgate, *expetivit vos ut cribraret sicut triticum.*
[2] Luke xxii. 31, 32.　　[3] *Sinat;* Vulgate, *patietur.*
[4] *Tolerare;* Vulgate, *sustinere.*　　[5] 1 Cor. x. 13.
[6] Trench, giving the essence of Augustin's discussion, says, "God does tempt quite as truly as the devil tempts; all the difference lies in the end and aim with which they severally do it, — the one tempting to deceive, the other to approve: Satan, to their ruin; God, to their everlasting gain."
[7] Alford and other modern commentators agree with Augustin in explaining ἀπὸ τοῦ πονηροοῦ, "of evil;" Bengel, Meyer, Schaff, and others (see Revised Version) make the form masculine, — "the Evil One."

[8] Rom. viii. 24.
[9] Or, as he expresses it in another place (*Sermon* lvii. 7), ' to this life of our pilgrimage" (" *ista vita peregrinationis nostræ* ").

daily bread." For whether by this same thing which is called daily bread be meant spiritual bread, or that which is visible in the sacrament or in this sustenance of ours, it belongs to the present time, which He has called "to-day," not because spiritual food is not everlasting, but because that which is called daily food in the Scriptures is represented to the soul either by the sound of the expression or by temporal signs of any kind : things all of which will certainly no more have existence when all shall be taught of God,[1] and thus shall no longer be making known to others by movement of their bodies, but drinking in each one for himself by the purity of his mind the ineffable light of truth itself. For perhaps for this reason also it is called bread, not drink, because bread is converted into aliment by breaking and masticating it, just as the Scriptures feed the soul by being opened up and made the subject of discourse ; but drink, when prepared, passes as it is into the body : so that at present the truth is bread, when it is called daily bread ; but then it will be drink, when there will be no need of the labour of discussing and discoursing, as it were of breaking and masticating, but merely of drinking unmingled and transparent truth. And sins are at present forgiven us, and at present we forgive them ; which is the second petition of these four that remain : but then there will be no pardon of sins, because there will be no sins. And temptations molest this temporal life ; but they will have no existence when these words shall be fully realized, " Thou shalt hide them in the secret of Thy presence." [2] And the evil from which we wish to be delivered, and the deliverance from evil itself, belong certainly to this life, which as being mortal we have deserved at the hand of God's justice, and from which we are delivered by His mercy.

Chap. XI. — 38. The sevenfold number of these petitions also seems to me to correspond to that sevenfold number out of which the whole sermon before us has had its rise.[3] For if it is the fear of God through which the poor in spirit are blessed, inasmuch as theirs is the kingdom of heaven ; let us ask that the name of God may be hallowed among men through that "fear which is clean, enduring for ever." [4] If it is piety through which the meek are blessed, inasmuch as they shall inherit the earth ; let us ask that His kingdom may come, whether it be over ourselves, that we may become meek, and not resist Him, or whether it be from heaven to earth in the splendour of the Lord's advent, in

which we shall rejoice, and shall be praised, when He says, " Come, ye blessed of my Father, inherit[5] the kingdom prepared for you from the foundation[6] of the world." [7] For "in the Lord," says the prophet, " shall my soul be praised ; the meek shall hear thereof, and be glad." [8] If it is knowledge through which those who mourn are blessed, inasmuch as they shall be comforted ; let us pray that His will may be done as in heaven so in earth, because when the body, which is as it were the earth, shall agree in a final and complete peace with the soul, which is as it were heaven, we shall not mourn : for there is no other mourning belonging to this present time, except when these contend against each other, and compel us to say, " I see another law in my members, warring against the law of my mind ;" and to testify our grief with tearful voice, " O wretched[9] man that I am ! who shall deliver me from the body of this death ? " [10] If it is fortitude through which those are blessed who hunger and thirst after righteousness, inasmuch as they shall be filled ; let us pray that our daily bread may be given to us to-day, by which, supported and sustained, we may be able to reach that most abundant fulness. If it is prudence through which the merciful are blessed, inasmuch as they shall obtain mercy ; let us forgive their debts to our debtors, and let us pray that ours may be forgiven to us. If it is understanding through which the pure in heart are blessed, inasmuch as they shall see God ; let us pray not to be led into temptation, lest we should have a double heart, in not seeking after a single good, to which we may refer all our actings, but at the same time pursuing things temporal and earthly. For temptations arising from those things which seem to men burdensome and calamitous, have no power over us, if those other temptations have no power which befall us through the enticements of such things as men count good and cause for rejoicing. If it is wisdom through which the peacemakers are blessed, inasmuch as they shall be called the children of God ; [11] let us pray that we may be freed from evil, for that very freedom will make us free, *i.e.* sons of God, so that we may cry in the spirit of adoption, " Abba, Father." [12]

39. Nor are we indeed carelessly to pass by the circumstance, that of all those sentences in which the Lord has taught us to pray, He has judged that that one is chiefly to be commended which has reference to the forgiveness of sins : in which He would have us to be merciful, because it is the only wisdom for escaping misery. For in no other sentence do we pray in such a way

---

[1] Isa. liv. 13: John vi. 45.
[2] Ps. xxxi. 20.
[3] Lange draws a comparison between the petitions and the Beatitudes, similar to that which follows.
[4] Ps. xix. 9.

[5] *Accipite ;* Vulgate, *possidete.*
[6] *Origine ;* Vulgate, *constitutione.*   [7] Matt. xxv. 34.
[8] Ps. xxxiv. 2.   [9] *Miser ;* Vulgate, *infelix.*
[10] Rom. vii. 23, 24.
[11] Matt. v. 3-9.   [12] Rom. viii. 15 and Gal. iv. 6.

that we, as it were, enter into a compact with God : for we say, "Forgive us, as we also forgive." And if we lie in that compact, the whole prayer is fruitless. For He speaks thus : "For if ye forgive men their trespasses, your heavenly Father will also forgive you : But if ye forgive not men their trespasses, neither will your Father forgive your trespasses."

CHAP. XII. — 40. There follows a precept concerning fasting, having reference to that same purification of heart which is at present under discussion. For in this work also we must be on our guard, lest there should creep in a certain ostentation and hankering after the praise of man, which would make the heart double, and not allow it to be pure and single for apprehending God. "Moreover, when ye fast," says He, "be not, as the hypocrites, of a sad countenance : for they disfigure their faces,[1] that they may appear[1] unto men to fast. Verily I say unto you, they have their reward. But ye,[2] when ye fast, anoint your head, and wash your face ; that ye appear not unto men to fast, but unto your Father which is in secret : and your Father, which seeth in secret, shall reward you." It is manifest from these precepts that all our effort is to be directed towards inward joys, lest, seeking a reward from without, we should be conformed to this world, and should lose the promise of a blessedness so much the more solid and firm, as it is inward, in which God has chosen that we should become conformed to the image of His Son.[3]

41. But in this section it is chiefly to be noticed, that there may be ostentatious display not merely in the splendour and pomp of things pertaining to the body, but also in doleful squalor itself ; and the more dangerous on this account, that it deceives under the name of serving God. And therefore he who is very conspicuous by immoderate attention to the body, and by the splendour of his clothing or other things, is easily convicted by the things themselves of being a follower of the pomps of the world, and misleads no one by a cunning semblance of sanctity ; but in regard to him who, under a profession of Christianity, fixes the eyes of men upon himself by unusual squalor and filth, when he does it voluntarily, and not under the pressure of necessity, it may be conjectured from the rest of his actings whether he does this from contempt of

superfluous attention to the body, or from a certain ambition : for the Lord has enjoined us to beware of wolves under a sheep's skin ; but "by their fruits," says He, "shall ye know them." For when by temptations of any kind those very things begin to be withdrawn from them or refused to them, which under that veil they either have obtained or desire to obtain, then of necessity it appears whether it is a wolf in a sheep's skin or a sheep in its own. For a Christian ought not to delight the eyes of men by superfluous ornament on this account, because pretenders also too often assume that frugal and merely necessary dress, that they may deceive those who are not on their guard : for those sheep also ought not to lay aside their own skins, if at any time wolves cover themselves there with.

42. It is usual, therefore, to ask what He means, when He says : "But ye, when ye fast, anoint your head, and wash your faces, that ye appear not unto men to fast." For it would not be right in any one to teach (although we may wash our face according to daily custom) that we ought also to have our heads anointed when we fast. If, then, all admit this to be most unseemly, we must understand this precept with respect to anointing the head and washing the face as referring to the inner man.[4] Hence, to anoint the head refers to joy ; to wash the face, on the other hand, refers to purity : and therefore that man anoints his head who rejoices inwardly in his mind and reason. For we rightly understand that as being the head which has the pre-eminence in the soul, and by which it is evident that the other parts of man are ruled and governed. And this is done by him who does not seek his joy from without, so as to draw his delight in a fleshly way from the praises of men. For the flesh, which ought to be subject, is in no way the head of the whole nature of man. "No man," indeed, "ever yet hated his own flesh," as the apostle says, when giving the precept as to loving one's wife ;[5] but the man is the head of the woman, and Christ is the head of the man.[6] Let him, therefore, rejoice inwardly in his fasting[7] in this very circumstance, that by his fasting he so turns away from the pleasure of the world as to be subject to Christ, who according to this precept desires to have the head anointed. For thus also he will wash his face, i.e. cleanse his heart, with which he shall see God, no veil being interposed on account of the infirmity contracted from squalor ; but being firm and stedfast, inasmuch as he is pure and guileless. "Wash you," says He, "make

[1] *Vultum . . . videantur ;* Vulgate, *facies . . . appareant.* The Greek has a play on words, ἀφανίζουσι . . . φανῶσι ("they mar their appearance, that they may make an appearance").

[2] Vulgate has the singular as the Greek. The Pharisees were scrupulous in keeping fast-days. Monday and Thursday were observed by the strict with different degrees of scrupulosity, — the lowest admitting of washing and anointing the head. (See Schürer, *N. Zeitgesch.* p. 505 sqq.). The early practice of fasting in the sub-apostolic Church is evident from the *Teaching of the Twelve Apostles,* which enjoins it before baptism, and on the "fourth day and the Preparation Day" (vii., viii.).

[3] Rom. viii. 29.

[4] So modern exegetes (Meyer, etc.).   [5] Eph. v. 25-33.

[6] 1 Cor. xi. 3.

[7] "It hardly needs to add," says Trench, "that Augustin everywhere interprets '*when ye fast*' as a command."

you clean; put away the evil of your doings from before mine eyes."[1] From the squalor, therefore, by which the eye of God is offended, our face is to be washed. For we, with open face beholding as in a glass the glory of the Lord, are changed into the same image.[2]

43. Often also the thought of things necessary belonging to this life wounds and defiles our inner eye; and frequently it makes the heart double, so that in regard to those things in which we seem to act rightly with our fellow-men, we do not act with that heart wherewith the Lord enjoins us; i.e., it is not because we love them, but because we wish to obtain some advantage from them for the necessity of the present life. But we ought to do them good for their eternal salvation, not for our own temporal advantage. May God, therefore, incline our heart to His testimonies, and not to covetousness.[3] For "the end of the commandment is charity out of a pure heart, and of a good conscience, and of faith unfeigned."[4] But he who looks after his brother from a regard to his own necessities in this life, does not certainly do so from love, because he does not look after him whom he ought to love as himself, but after himself; or rather not even after himself, seeing that in this way he makes his own heart double, by which he is hindered from seeing God, in the vision of whom alone there is certain and lasting blessedness.

CHAP. XIII. — 44. Rightly, therefore, does he who is intent on cleansing our heart follow up[5] what He has said with a precept, where He says: "Lay not up[6] for yourselves treasures upon earth, where moth and rust[7] doth corrupt,[6] and where thieves break through and steal: but lay up for yourselves treasures in heaven, where neither moth nor rust doth corrupt, and where thieves do not break through nor steal. For where your treasure is, there will your heart be[8] also." If, therefore, the heart be on earth, i.e. if one perform anything with a heart bent on obtaining earthly advantage, how will that heart be clean which wallows on earth? But if it be in heaven, it will be clean, because whatever things are heavenly are clean. For anything becomes polluted when it is mixed with a nature that is inferior, although not polluted of its kind; for gold is polluted even by pure silver, if it be mixed with it: so also our mind becomes polluted by the desire after earthly things, although the earth itself be pure of its

kind and order. But we would not understand heaven in this passage as anything corporeal, because everything corporeal is to be reckoned as earth. For he who lays up treasure for himself in heaven ought to despise the whole world. Hence it is in that heaven of which it is said, "The heaven of heavens is the Lord's,[9] i.e. in the spiritual firmament: for it is not in that which is to pass away that we ought to fix and place our treasure and our heart, but in that which ever abideth; but heaven and earth shall pass away.[10]

45. And here He makes it manifest that He gives all these precepts with a view to the cleansing of the heart, when He says: "The candle[11] of the body is the eye: if therefore thine eye be single, thy whole body shall be full of light. But if thine eye be evil, thy whole body shall be full of darkness. If, therefore, the light [lamp][11] that is in thee be darkness, how great is that darkness!" And this passage we are to understand in such a way as to learn from it that all our works are pure and well-pleasing in the sight of God, when they are done with a single heart, i.e. with a heavenly intent, having that end of love in view; for love is also the fulfilling of the law.[12] Hence we ought to take the eye here in the sense of the intent itself, wherewith we do whatever we are doing; and if this be pure and right, and looking at that which ought to be looked at, all our works which we perform in accordance therewith are necessarily good. And all those works He has called the whole body; for the apostle also speaks of certain works of which he disapproves as our members, and teaches that they are to be mortified, saying, "Mortify therefore your members which are upon the earth; fornication, uncleanness, covetousness,"[13] and all other such things.[14]

46. It is not, therefore, what one does, but the intent with which he does it, that is to be considered. For this is the light in us, because it is a thing manifest to ourselves that we do with a good intent what we are doing; for everything which is made manifest is light.[15] For the deeds themselves which go forth from us to human society, have an uncertain issue; and therefore He has called them darkness. For I do not know, when I present money to a poor man who asks it, either what he is to do with it, or what he is to suffer from it; and it may happen that he does some evil with it, or suffers some

---

[1] Isa. i. 16.   [2] 2 Cor. iii. 18.
[3] Ps. cxix. 36.   [4] 1 Tim. i. 5.
[5] Having uttered warnings against formalists, the Lord now passes to the complete dedication of the heart.
[6] Condere . . . tinea et comestura exterminant; Vulgate, thesaurizare . . . ærugo et tinea demolitur.
[7] Not the specific rust of metals; wider sense of wear and tear.
[8] Erit; Vulgate, est.

[9] Ps. cxv. 16.
[10] Matt. xxiv. 35. Robert South gives his sermon on this passage the heading, "No man ever went to heaven whose heart was not there before." It has been remarked, as regards an earthly Church, one does not take abiding interest in it unless one gives toward it.
[11] Lucerna . . . lumen.   [12] Rom. xiii. 10.
[13] Col. iii. 5.
[14] "Singleness of intention will preserve us from the snare of having a double treasure, and therefore a divided heart" (Plumptre).
[15] Eph. v. 13. Augustin's rendering here is the true sense of the original.

evil on account of it, a thing I did not wish to happen when I gave it to him, nor would I have given it with such an intention. If, therefore, I did it with a good intention, — a thing which was known to me when I was doing it, and is therefore called light, — my deed also is lighted up, whatever issue it shall have ; but that issue, inasmuch as it is uncertain and unknown, is called darkness. But if I have done it with a bad intent, the light itself even is darkness. For it is spoken of as light, because every one knows with what intent he acts, even when he acts with a bad intent ; but the light itself is darkness, because the aim is not directed singly to things above, but is turned downwards to things beneath, and makes, as it were, a shadow by means of a double heart. " If, therefore, the light that is in thee be darkness, how great is that darkness ! " *i.e.*, if the very intent of the heart with which you do what you are doing (which is known to you) is polluted by the hunger after earthly and temporal things, and blinded, how much more is the deed itself, whose issue is uncertain, polluted and full of darkness ! Because, although what you do with an intent which is neither upright nor pure, may turn out for some one's good, it is the way in which you have done it, not how it has turned out for him, that is reckoned to you.[1]

CHAP. XIV. — 47. Then, further, the statement which follows, " No man can serve two masters," is to be referred to this very intent, as He goes on to explain, saying : " For either he will hate the one, and love the other ; or else he will[2] submit to the one, and despise the other." And these words are to be carefully considered ; for who the two masters are he forthwith shows, when He says, " Ye cannot serve God and mammon." Riches are said to be called mammon among the Hebrews. The Punic name also corresponds : for gain is called mammon in Punic.[3] But he who serves mammon certainly serves him who, as being set over those earthly things in virtue of his perversity, is called by our Lord the prince of this world.[4] A man will therefore " either hate " this one, " and love the other," *i.e.* God ; " or he will submit to the one, and despise the other. For whoever serves mammon submits to a hard and ruinous master : for, being entangled by his own lust, he becomes a subject of the devil, and he does not love him ; for who is there who loves the devil ? But yet he submits to him ; as in any large house he who is connected with another man's maid servant submits to hard bondage on account of his passion, even though he does not love him whose maid-servant he loves.

48. But " he will despise the other," He has said ; not, he will hate. For almost no one's conscience can hate God ; but he despises, *i.e.* he does not fear Him, as if feeling himself secure in consideration of His goodness. From this carelessness and ruinous security the Holy Spirit recalls us, when He says by the prophet, " My son, do not add sin upon sin, and say, The mercy of God is great ; "[5] and, " Knowest thou not that the patience[6] of God inviteth[6] thee to repentance ? "[7] For whose mercy can be mentioned as being so great as His, who pardons all the sins of those who return, and makes the wild olive a partaker of the fatness of the olive ? and whose severity as being so great as His, who spared not the natural branches, but broke them off because of unbelief ?[8] But let not any one who wishes to love God, and to beware of offending Him, suppose that he can serve two masters ;[9] and let him disentangle the upright intention of his heart from all doubleness : for thus he will think of the Lord with a good heart, and in simplicity of heart will seek Him.[10]

CHAP. XV. — 49. " Therefore," says He, " I say unto you, Have not anxiety[11] for your life, what ye shall eat ;[12] nor yet for your body, what ye shall put on." Lest perchance, although it is not now superfluities that are sought after, the heart should be made double by reason of necessaries themselves, and the aim should be wrenched aside to seek after those things of our own, when we are doing something as it were from compassion ; *i.e.* so that when we wish to appear to be consulting for some one's good, we are in that matter looking after our own profit rather than his advantage : and we do not seem to ourselves to be sinning for this reason, that it is not superfluities, but necessaries, which we wish

---

[1] The eye is as the *lamp* (Revised Version) through which the body gets light, — the organ whose power work it is to transmit light. The blind have no light, because their lamp is out or destroyed. The light within us is " the reason, especially the practical reason " (Meyer) ; that which is left of the divine image in man (Tholuck) ; the reason that was left after the fall of Adam (Calvin) ; the Old-Testament revelation perverted (Lange) ; the conscience (Alford). " The spirit of man is the candle (*lamp*, Revised Version) of the Lord " (Prov. xx. 27) : it guides the faculties of the soul. But if it be in darkness, how great is that darkness ; *i.e.* the darkness which already existed ! What a terrible condition those are in who do not receive the Spirit of enlightenment (who becomes the " inner light "), and feel no need of Him ! " He whose affections are on heavenly things, has his whole soul lighted : he whose affections are depraved, has his understanding and his whole soul darkened also " (Mansel).

[2] *Alterum patietur ;* Vulgate, *unum sustinebit.*

[3] Augustin is the only one to give this derivation. His residence in North Africa is the explanation of his knowledge of the Punic. The word probably comes from the Chaldee and through the Hebrew word *aman*, " what is trusted in." (See Thayer, *Lexicon.*)

[4] John xii. 31 and xiv. 30.   [5] Ecclus. v. 5, 6.
[6] *Patientia . . . invitat ;* Vulgate, *benignitas . . . adducit.*
[7] Rom. ii. 4.   [8] Rom. xi. 17-24.
[9] Luther says the world can do it in a masterly way, and carry the tree (or " water " according to the English figure) on both shoulders. This verse is a rebuke to those who think they can combine a supreme affection for heavenly and for earthly things at the same time, and pursue both with equal zeal.
[10] Wisd. i. 1.
[11] *Habere sollicitudinem ;* Vulgate, *sollicitæ sitis.*
[12] *Edatis ;* Vulgate, *manducetis.*

to obtain. But the Lord admonishes us that we should remember that God, when He made and compounded us of body and soul, gave us much more than food and clothing, through care for which He would not have us make our hearts double. "Is not," says He, "the soul more than the meat?" So that you are to understand that He who gave the soul will much more easily give meat. "And the body than the raiment," *i.e.* is more than raiment: so that similarly you are to understand, that He who gave the body will much more easily give raiment.

50. And in this passage the question is wont to be raised, whether the food spoken of has reference to the soul, since the soul is incorporeal, and the food in question is corporeal food. But let us admit that the soul in this passage stands for the present life, whose support is that corporeal nourishment. In accordance with this signification we have also that statement: "He that loveth his soul shall lose it."[1] And here, unless we understand the expression of this present life, which we ought to lose for the kingdom of God, as it is clear the martyrs were able to do, this precept will be in contradiction to that sentence where it is said: "What is a man profited, if he shall gain the whole world, and lose[2] his own soul?"[3]

51. "Behold," says He, "the fowls of the air: for they sow not, neither do they reap, nor gather into barns; yet your heavenly Father feedeth them: are ye not much better than they?" *i.e.* ye are of more value. For surely a rational being such as man has a higher rank in the nature of things than irrational ones, such as birds. "Which of you, by taking thought,[4] can add one cubit unto his stature?[5] And why take ye thought for raiment?" That is to say, the providence of Him by whose power and sovereignty it has come about that your body was brought up to its present stature, can also clothe you; but that it is not by your care that it has come about that your body should arrive at this stature, may be understood from this circumstance, that if you should take thought, and should wish to add one cubit to this stature, you cannot. Leave, therefore, the care of protecting the body to Him by whose care you see it has come about that you have a body of such a stature.

52. But an example was to be given for the clothing too, just as one is given for the food.

Hence He goes on to say, "Consider the lilies of the field, how they grow; they toil not, neither do they spin: and yet I say unto you, that even Solomon[6] in all his glory was not arrayed[7] like one of these. Wherefore, if God so clothe the grass of the field, which to-day is, and to-morrow is cast into the oven; shall He not much more clothe you, O ye of little faith?" But these examples are not to be treated as allegories, so that we should inquire what the fowls of heaven or the lilies of the field mean: for they stand here, in order that from smaller matters we may be persuaded respecting greater ones;[8] just as is the case in regard to the judge who neither feared God nor regarded man, and yet yielded to the widow who often importuned him to consider her case, not from piety or humanity, but that he might be saved annoyance. For that unjust judge does not in any way allegorically represent the person of God; but yet as to how far God, who is good and just, cares for those who supplicate Him, our Lord wished the inference to be drawn from this circumstance, that not even an unjust man can despise those who assail him with unceasing petitions, even were his motive merely to avoid annoyance.[9]

CHAP. XVI. — 53. "Therefore be not anxious," says He, "saying, What shall we eat?[10] or, What shall we drink? or, Wherewithal shall we be clothed?[10] (For after all these things do the Gentiles seek:) for your Father knoweth that ye have need of all these things. But seek ye first the kingdom of God and His righteousness; and all these things shall be added[11] unto you." Here He shows most manifestly that these things are not to be sought as if they were our blessings in such sort, that on account of them we ought to do well in all our actings, but yet that they are necessary. For what the difference is between a blessing which is to be sought, and a necessary which is to be taken for use, He has made plain by this sentence, when He says, "Seek ye first the kingdom of God and His righteousness, and all these things shall be added unto you."[12] The kingdom and the righteousness of God therefore are our good; and this is to be sought, and there the end is to be set up, on account of which we are to do everything which we do. But because we serve as soldiers in this life, in order that we may be able to

---

[1] John xii. 25.
[2] *Detrimentum faciat;* Vulgate, *detrimentum patiatur.*
[3] Matt. xvi. 26.   [4] *Curans;* Vulgate, *cogitans.*
[5] The term ἡλικία, translated by Augustin and the Vulgate *statura*, and by the English version *stature*, more probably means the *measure of life*, or *age* (American notes to Revised Version, Tholuck, De Wette, Trench, Alford, Meyer, Schaff, Plumptre, Weiss, etc.). A cubit was equal to the length of the forearm. The force of the Lord's words would be greatly diminished if such a measure was conceived of as possible to be added to the stature. The idea is, that human ingenuity and labor cannot add the least measure.

[6] To the Jew the highest representative of splendour and pomp.
[7] *Vestitutus;* Vulgate, *coopertus.* "As the beauties of the flower are unfolded by the divine Creator Spirit from *within*, from the laws and capacities of its own individual life, so must all true adornment of man be unfolded from *within* by the same Spirit. This hidden meaning must not be overlooked" (Alford). The law of spiritual growth is mysterious and spontaneous.
[8] The argument, so called, *a minore ad majus.*
[9] Luke xviii. 2-8.
[10] *Edemus . . . vestiemur;* Vulgate, *manducabimus . . . operiemur.*
[11] *Apponentur;* Vulgate, *adjicientur.*   [12] Matt. vi. 33.

reach that kingdom, and because our life cannot be spent without these necessaries, "These things shall be added unto you," says He; "but seek ye first the kingdom of God and His righteousness." For in using that word "first," He has indicated that this is to be sought later, not in point of time, but in point of importance: the one as being our good, the other as being something necessary for us; but the necessary on account of that good.

54. For neither ought we, for example, to preach the gospel with this object, that we may eat; but to eat with this object, that we may preach the gospel: for if we preach the gospel for this cause, that we may eat, we reckon the gospel of less value than food; and in that case our good will be in eating, but that which is necessary for us in preaching the gospel. And this the apostle also forbids, when he says it is lawful for himself even, and permitted by the Lord, that they who preach the gospel should live of the gospel, i.e. should have from the gospel the necessaries of this life; but yet that he has not made use of this power. For there were many who were desirous of having an occasion for getting and selling the gospel, from whom the apostle wished to cut off this occasion, and therefore he submitted to a way of living by his own hands.[1] For concerning these parties he says in another passage, "That I may cut off occasion from them which seek[2] occasion."[3] Although even if, like the rest of the good apostles, by the permission of the Lord he should live of the gospel, he would not on that account place the end of preaching the gospel in that living, but would rather make the gospel the end of his living; i.e., as I have said above, he would not preach the gospel with this object, that he might get his food and all other necessaries; but he would take such things for this purpose, in order that he might carry out that other object, viz. that willingly, and not of necessity, he should preach the gospel. For this he disapproves of when he says, "Do ye not know, that they which minister in the temple[4] eat the things which are of the temple? and they which wait at the altar are partakers with the altar? Even so hath the Lord ordained that they which preach the gospel should live of the gospel. But I have used none of these things." Hence he shows that it was permitted, not commanded; otherwise he will be held to have acted contrary to the precept of the Lord. Then he goes on to say: "Neither have I written these things, that it should be so done unto me: for it were better for me to die, than that any man should make my glorying void."[5] This

he said, as he had already resolved, because of some who were seeking occasion, to gain a living by his own hands. "For if I preach the gospel," says he, "I have nothing to glory of:" i.e., if I preach the gospel in order that such things may be done in my case, or, if I preach with this object, in order that I may obtain those things, and if I thus place the end of the gospel in meat and drink and clothing. But wherefore has he nothing to glory of? "Necessity," says he, "is laid upon me;" i.e. so that I should preach the gospel for this reason, because I have not the means of living, or so that I should acquire temporal fruit from the preaching of eternal things; for thus, consequently, the preaching of the gospel will be a matter of necessity, not of free choice. "For woe is unto me," says he, "if I preach not the gospel!" But how ought he to preach the gospel? Evidently in such a way as to place the reward in the gospel itself, and in the kingdom of God: for thus he can preach the gospel, not of constraint, but willingly. "For if I do this thing willingly," says he, "I have a reward: but if against my will, a dispensation of the gospel is committed unto me;"[6] if, constrained by the want of those things which are necessary for temporal life, I preach the gospel, others will have through me the reward of the gospel, who love the gospel itself when I preach it; but I shall not have it, because it is not the gospel itself I love, but its price lying in those temporal things. And this is something sinful, that any one should minister the gospel not as a son, but as a servant to whom a stewardship of it has been committed; that he should, as it were, pay out what belongs to another, but should himself receive nothing from it except victuals, which are given not in consideration of his sharing in the kingdom, but from without, for the support of a miserable bondage. Although in another passage he calls himself also a steward. For a servant also, when adopted into the number of the children, is able faithfully to dispense to those who share with him that property in which he has acquired the lot of a fellow-heir. But in the present case, where he says, "But if against my will, a dispensation (stewardship) is committed unto me," he wished such a steward to be understood as dispenses what belongs to another, and from it gets nothing himself.

55. Hence anything whatever that is sought for the sake of something else, is doubtless inferior to that for the sake of which it is sought; and therefore that is first for the sake of which you seek such a thing, not the thing which you seek for the sake of that other. And for this reason, if we seek the gospel and the kingdom

---

[1] Acts xx. 34.　　　[2] Quærunt; Vulgate, volunt.
[3] 2 Cor. xi. 12.　[4] Templo; Vulgate, sacrario.
[5] Inanem faciat; Vulgate, evacuet.

[6] 1 Cor. ix. 13-17.

of God for the sake of food, we place food first, and the kingdom of God last; so that if food were not to fail us, we would not seek the kingdom of God: this is to seek food first, and then the kingdom of God. But if we seek food for this end, that we may gain the kingdom of God, we do what is said, "Seek ye first the kingdom of God and His righteousness; and all these things shall be added unto you."[1]

CHAP. XVII. — 56. For in the case of those who are seeking first the kingdom of God and His righteousness, *i.e.* who are preferring this to all other things, so that for its sake they are seeking the other things, there ought not to remain behind the anxiety lest those things should fail which are necessary to this life for the sake of the kingdom of God. For He has said above, "Your Father knoweth that ye have need of all these things." And therefore, when He had said, "Seek ye first the kingdom of God and His righteousness," He did not say, Then seek such things (although they are necessary), but He affirms "all these things shall be added unto you,"[1] *i.e.* will follow, if ye seek the former, without any hindrance on your part: lest while ye seek such things, ye should be turned away from the other; or lest ye should set up two things to be aimed at, so as to seek both the kingdom of God for its own sake, and such necessaries: but these rather for the sake of that other; so shall they not be wanting to you. For ye cannot serve two masters. But the man is attempting to serve two masters, who seeks both the kingdom of God as a great good, and these temporal things. He will not, however, be able to have a single eye, and to serve the Lord God alone, unless he take all other things, so far as they are necessary, for the sake of this one thing, *i.e.* for the sake of the kingdom of God. But as all who serve as soldiers receive provisions and pay, so all who preach the gospel receive food and clothing. But all do not serve as soldiers for the welfare of the republic, but some do so for what they get: so also all do not minister to God for the welfare of the Church, but some do so for the sake of these temporal things, which they are to obtain in the shape as it were of provisions and pay; or both for the one thing and for the other. But it has been already said above, "Ye cannot serve two masters." Hence it is with a single heart and only for the sake of the kingdom of God that we ought to do good

to all; and we ought not in doing so to think either of the temporal reward alone, or of that along with the kingdom of God: all which temporal things He has placed under the category of to-morrow, saying, "Take no thought for to-morrow."[2] For to-morrow is not spoken of except in time, where the future succeeds the past. Therefore, when we do anything good, let us not think of what is temporal, but of what is eternal; then will that be a good and perfect work. "For the morrow," says He, "will be anxious for the things of itself;"[3] *i.e.*, so that, when you ought, you will take food, or drink, or clothing, that is to say, when necessity itself begins to urge you. For these things will be within reach, because our Father knoweth that we have need of all these things. For "sufficient unto the day," says He, "is the evil thereof;"[4] *i.e.* it is sufficient that necessity itself will urge us to take such things. And for this reason, I suppose, it is called evil, because for us it is penal: for it belongs to this frailty and mortality which we have earned by sinning. Do not add, therefore, to this punishment of temporal necessity anything more burdensome, so that you should not only suffer the want of such things, but should also for the purpose of satisfying this want enlist as a soldier for God.

57. In the use of this passage, however, we must be very specially on our guard, lest perchance, when we see any servant of God making provision that such necessaries shall not be wanting either to himself or to those with whose care he has been entrusted, we should decide that he is acting contrary to the Lord's precept, and is anxious for the morrow.[5] For the Lord Himself also, although angels ministered to Him,[6] yet for the sake of example, that no one might afterwards be scandalized when he observed any of His servants procuring such necessaries, condescended to have money bags, out of which whatever might be required for necessary uses might be provided; of which bags, as it is written, Judas, who betrayed Him, was the keeper and the thief.[7] In like manner, the Apostle Paul also may seem to have taken

---

[1] Nor is it said, "Seek . . . in *order that* all these things may be added;" simply, "*and all*," etc., yet largely inclusive, — sanctity *and* comfort. The comfort follows naturally. The passage is a rebuke to those who condemn the amenities of life and art, and a caution to those who place these things before themselves as a chief end. The passage justifies the statement that religion (or godliness) is profitable for the life that now is. The Psalmist never saw the *righteous* forsaken. A traditional saying of Jesus, quoted by Clement, Origen, and Eusebius, runs, "Ask great things, and little things shall be added; ask heavenly things, and earthly things shall be added."

[2] *Cogitare in crastino;* Vulgate, *solliciti esse in crastinum.* There is no uniformity in Augustin's or the Vulgate's translation of the Greek μεριμνάω ("take anxious thought") in this passage.
[3] The morrow will bring its own vexations and anxieties. The English version entirely misleads as to the meaning of the special clause, "will take care of itself." The Revised Version is a literal translation, and at least gives the true sense by implication. But with each day's temptations and troubles, it is implied, special enablement and deliverance will be provided.
[4] Wiclif, following the Vulgate, translates *malice;* Tyndale, *trouble;* the Genevan Bible, *grief.*
[5] Our Lord's precept is not against provident forethought, — of which Augustin goes on to give examples, — but against anxious thought which implies distrust of God's providence. Anxious, fretful, distrustful care for the future, unreliant upon God's bounty, wisdom, and love (as implied in the address, *your heavenly Father*), is declared to be unnecessary (25, 26), foolish (27–30), and heathenish (32, "After these things do the Gentiles seek"). The passages teach trust in God, who is more interested in His children than in the fowls of the air, and will certainly take care of them.
[6] Matt. iv. 11.   [7] John xii. 6.

thought for the morrow, when he said : " Now concerning the collection for the saints, as I have given order to the saints of Galatia, even so do ye : upon the first day of the week let every one of you lay by him in store [1] what shall seem good unto him, that there be no gatherings when I come. And when I come,[2] whomsoever ye shall approve by your letters, them will I send to bring your liberality unto Jerusalem. And if it be meet that I go also, they shall go with me. Now I will come unto you when I shall pass through Macedonia : for I shall pass through Macedonia. And it may be that I will abide, yea, and winter with you, that ye may bring me on my journey whithersoever I go. For I will not see you now by the way ; but I trust to tarry a while with you, if the Lord permit. But I will tarry at Ephesus until Pentecost."[3]   In the Acts of the Apostles also it is written, that such things as are necessary for food were provided for the future, on account of an impending famine. For we thus read : " And in these days came prophets down from Jerusalem to Antioch,[4] and there was great rejoicing. And when we were gathered together,[4] there stood up one of them named Agabus, and signified by the Spirit that there should be great dearth throughout all the world : which came to pass in the days of Claudius Cæsar. Then the disciples, every one according to his ability, determined to send relief to the elders for the brethren which dwelt in Judæa, which also they did by the hands of Barnabas and Saul."[5]   And in the case of the necessaries presented to him, wherewith the same Apostle Paul when setting sail was laden,[6] food seems to have been furnished for more than a single day. And when the same apostle writes, " Let him that stole steal no more : but rather let him labour, working[7] with his hands the thing which is good, that he may have to give to him that needeth ; "[8] to those who misunderstand him he does not seem to keep the Lord's precept, which runs, " Behold the fowls of the air ; for they sow not, neither do they reap, nor gather into barns ; " and, " Consider the lilies of the field, how they grow ; they toil not, neither do they spin ; " while he enjoins the parties in question to labour, working with their hands, that they may have something which they may be able to give to others also. And in what he often says of himself, that he wrought with his hands that he might not be burdensome ;[9] and in what is written of him,

that he joined himself to Aquila on account of the similarity of their occupation, in order that they might work together at that from which they might make a living ;[10] he does not seem to have imitated the birds of the air and the lilies of the field. From these and such like passages of Scripture, it is sufficiently apparent that our Lord does not disapprove of it, when one looks after such things in the ordinary way that men do ; but only when one enlists as a soldier of God for the sake of such things, so that in what he does he fixes his eye not on the kingdom of God, but on the acquisition of such things.

58. Hence this whole precept is reduced to the following rule, that even in looking after such things we should think of the kingdom of God, but in the service of the kingdom of God we should not think of such things. For in this way, although they should sometimes be wanting (a thing which God often permits for the purpose of exercising us), they not only do not weaken our proposition, but even strengthen it, when it is examined and tested. For, says He, " we glory in tribulations also ; knowing that tribulation worketh patience, and patience experience, and experience hope : And hope maketh not ashamed, because the love of God is shed abroad in our hearts by the Holy Ghost which is given unto us."[11]   Now, in the mention of his tribulations and labours, the same apostle mentions that he has had to endure not only prisons and shipwrecks and many such like annoyances, but also hunger and thirst, cold and nakedness.[12]   But when we read this, let us not imagine that the promises of God have wavered, so that the apostle suffered hunger and thirst and nakedness while seeking the kingdom and righteousness of God, although it is said to us, " Seek ye first the kingdom of God and His righteousness ; and all these things shall be added unto you : " since that Physician to whom we have once for all entrusted ourselves wholly, and from whom we have the promise of life present and future, knows such things just as helps, when He sets them before us, when He takes them away, just as He judges it expedient for us ; whom He rules and directs as parties who require both to be comforted and exercised in this life, and after this life to be established and confirmed in perpetual rest. For man also, when he frequently takes away the fodder from his beast of burden, is not depriving it of his care, but rather does what he is doing in the exercise of care.

CHAP. XVIII. — 59. And inasmuch as when such things are either provided against the time

---

[1] *Thesaurizans ;* Vulgate, *recondens.*
[2] *Advenero ;* Vulgate, *præsens fuero.*   [3] 1 Cor. xvi. 1-8.
[4] Not in the original Greek or Vulgate, but implied in the preceding context.
[5] Acts xi. 27-30. The clause shows much divergence from the Vulgate in construction.
[6] Acts xxviii. 10.   [7] *Operans ;* Vulgate, *operando.*
[8] Eph. iv. 28. *Unde tribuere cui opus est ; Vulgate, unde tribuat necessitatem patienti.*
[9] 1 Thess. ii. 9 ; 2 Thess. iii. 8.

[10] Acts xviii. 2, 3.   [11] Rom. v. 3-5.
[12] 2 Cor. xi. 23-27.

to come, or reserved, if there is no cause wherefore you should expend them, it is uncertain with what intention it is done, since it may be done with a single heart, and also with a double one, He has seasonably added in this passage: "Judge not,[1] that ye be not judged.[2] For with what judgment ye judge, ye shall be judged,[2] and with what measure ye mete, it shall be measured to you again." In this passage, I am of opinion that we are taught nothing else, but that in the case of those actions respecting which it is doubtful with what intention they are done, we are to put the better construction on them. For when it is written, "By their fruits ye shall know them," the statement has reference to things which manifestly cannot be done with a good intention; such as debaucheries, or blasphemies, or thefts, or drunkenness, and all such things, of which we are permitted to judge, according to the apostle's statement: "For what have I to do to judge them also that are without? do not ye judge them that are within?"[3] But concerning the kind of food, because every kind of human food can be taken indiscriminately with a good intention and a single heart, without the vice of concupiscence, the same apostle forbids that they who ate flesh and drank wine be judged by those who abstained from such kinds of sustenance: "Let not him that eateth," says he, "despise him that eateth not; and let not him which eateth not, judge him that eateth." There also he says: "Who art thou that judgest another man's servant? to his own master he standeth or falleth."[4] For in reference to such matters as can be done with a good and single and noble intention, although they may also be done with an intention the reverse of good, those parties wished, howbeit they were [mere] men, to pronounce judgment upon the secrets of the heart, of which God alone is Judge.

60. To this category belongs also what he says in another passage: "Therefore judge nothing before the time, until the Lord come, who both will bring to light the hidden things of darkness, and will make manifest the thoughts[5] of the hearts: and then shall every man have praise of God."[6] There are therefore certain ambiguous actions, respecting which we are ignorant with what intention they are performed, because they may be done both with a good or with an evil one, of which it is rash to judge, especially for the purpose of condemning. Now the time will come for these to be judged, when the Lord

"will bring to light the hidden things of darkness, and will make manifest the counsels of the hearts." In another passage also the same apostle says: "Some men's aims are manifest beforehand, going before to judgment; and some men they follow after." He calls those sins manifest, with regard to which it is clear with what intention they are done; these go before to judgment, because if a judgment shall follow, it is not rash. But those which are concealed follow, because neither shall they remain hid in their own time. So we must understand with respect to good works also. For he adds to this effect: "Likewise also the good works of some are manifest beforehand; and they that are otherwise cannot be hid."[7] Let us judge, therefore, with respect to those which are manifest; but respecting those which are concealed, let us leave the judgment to God: for they also cannot be hid, whether they be good or evil, when the time shall come for them to be manifested.

61. There are two things, moreover, in which we ought to beware of rash judgment; when it is uncertain with what intention any thing is done; or when it is uncertain what sort of a person he is going to be, who at preset is manifestly either good or bad. If, therefore, any one, for example, complaining of his stomach, would not fast, and you, not believing this, were to attribute it to the vice of gluttony, you would judge rashly. Likewise, if you were to come to know the gluttony and drunkenness as being manifest, and were so to administer reproof as if the man could never be amended and changed, you would nevertheless judge rashly. Let us not therefore reprove those things about which we do not know with what intention they are done; nor let us so reprove those things which are manifest, as that we should despair of a return to a right state of mind; and thus we shall avoid the judgment of which in the present instance it is said, "Judge not, that ye be not judged."

62. But what He says may cause perplexity: "For with what judgment ye judge, ye shall be judged; and with what measure ye mete, it shall be measured to you again." Is it the case, then, that if we shall judge any thing with a rash judgment, God will also judge rashly with respect to us? or if we shall measure any thing with an unjust measure, is there with God also an unjust measure, according to which it shall be measured to us again? (for by the expression measure also, I suppose the judgment itself is meant.) By no means does God either judge rashly, or recompense to any one with an unjust measure; but it is so expressed, inasmuch as

---

[1] *Sine scientia, amore, necessitate* ("without knowledge, love, necessity." — Bengel). The discussion is one of the most thorough and satisfactory sections of Augustin's commentary.
[2] *Judicetur de vobis . . . judicabitur;* Vulgate, *judicemini . . . judicabimini.*
[3] 1 Cor. v 12.
[4] Rom. xiv. 3, 4.
[5] *Cogitationes;* Vulgate, *consilia.*
[6] 1 Cor. iv. 5.
[7] 1 Tim. v. 24, 25.

that very same rashness wherewith you punish another must necessarily punish yourself. Unless, perchance, it is to be imagined that injustice does harm in some way to him against whom it goes forth, but in no way to him from whom it goes forth ; but nay, it often does no harm to him who suffers the injury, but it must necessarily do harm to him who inflicts it. For what harm did the injustice of the persecutors do to the martyrs? None ; but very much to the persecutors themselves. For although some of them were turned from the error of their ways, yet at the time at which they were acting as persecutors, their wickedness was blinding them. So also a rash judgment frequently does no harm to him who is the object of the rash judgment ; but to him who judges rashly, the rashness itself must necessarily do harm. According to such a rule, I judge of that saying also : " Every one that strikes[1] with the sword shall perish with the sword." [2] For how many take the sword, and yet do not perish with the sword, Peter himself being an instance ! But lest any should think that he escaped such punishment by the pardon of his sins (although nothing could be more absurd than to think that the punishment of the sword, which did not befall Peter, could have been greater than that of the cross, which actually befell him), yet what would they say of the malefactors who were crucified with our Lord ; for both he who got pardon, got it after he was crucified, and the other did not get it at all? [3] Or had they perhaps crucified all whom they had slain ; and did they therefore themselves too deserve to suffer the same thing? It is ridiculous to think so. For what else is meant by the statement, " For all they that take the sword shall perish with the sword," but that the soul dies by that very sin, whatever it may be, which it has committed?

CHAP. XIX. — 63. And inasmuch as the Lord is admonishing us in this passage with respect to rash and unjust judgment, — for He wishes that whatever we do, we should do it with a heart that is single and directed toward God alone ; and inasmuch as, with respect to many things, it is uncertain with what intention they are done, regarding which it is rash to judge ; inasmuch, moreover, as those parties especially judge rashly respecting things that are uncertain, and readily find fault, who love rather to censure and to condemn than to amend and to improve, which is a fault arising either from pride or from envy ; therefore He has subjoined the statement : " And why beholdest thou the mote that is in thy brother's eye, but considerest not the beam that is in thine own eye?"

So that if perchance, for example, he has transgressed in anger, you should find fault in hatred ; there being, as it were, as much difference between anger and hatred as between a mote and a beam. For hatred is inveterate anger, which, as it were simply by its long duration, has acquired so great strength as to be justly called a beam. Now, it may happen that, though you are angry with a man, you wish him to be turned from his error ; but if you hate a man, you cannot wish to convert him.

64. " Or how wilt[4] thou say to thy brother, Let me pull out the mote out of thine eye ; and, behold, a beam is in thine own eye? Thou hypocrite, first cast out the beam out of thine own eye ; and then shalt thou see clearly to cast out the mote out of thy brother's eye ; " i.e., first cast the hatred away from thee, and then, but not before, shalt thou be able to amend him whom thou lovest.[5] And He well says, " Thou hypocrite." For to make complaint against vices is the duty of good and benevolent men ; and when bad men do it, they are acting a part which does not belong to them ; just like hypocrites, who conceal under a mask what they are, and show themselves off in a mask what they are not. Under the designation hypocrites, therefore, you are to understand pretenders. And there is, in fact, a class of pretenders much to be guarded against, and troublesome, who, while they take up complaints against all kinds of faults from hatred and spite, also wish to appear counsellors. And therefore we must piously and cautiously watch, so that when necessity shall compel us to find fault with or rebuke any one, we may reflect first whether the fault is such as we have never had, or one from which we have now become free ; and if we have never had it, let us reflect that we are men, and might have had it ; but if we have had it, and are now free from it, let the common infirmity touch the memory, that not hatred but pity may go before that fault-finding or administering of rebuke : so that whether it shall serve for the conversion of him on whose account we do it, or for his perversion (for the issue is uncertain), we at least from the singleness of our eye may be free from care. If, however, on reflection, we find ourselves involved in the same fault as he is whom we were preparing to censure, let us not censure nor rebuke ; but yet let us mourn deeply over the case, and let us invite him not to obey us, but to join us in a common effort.

65. For in regard also to what the apostle says, — " Unto the Jews I became as a Jew, that

---

[1] Omnis qui percusserit ; Vulgate, omnes qui acceperint.
[2] Matt. xxvi. 52.   [3] Luke xxiii. 33-43.

[4] The meaning is, how wilt thou have the effrontery to say, dare to say. The precept forbids all meddling, censoriousness, and captious faultfinding, and the spirit of slander, backbiting, calumny, etc.
[5] " Ere you remark another's sin,
Bid your own conscience look within." — Cowper.

I might gain the Jews; to them that are under the law, as under the law (not being under the law), that I might gain them that are under the law; to them that are without law, as without law (being not without law to God, but under the law to Christ), that I might gain them that are without law. To the weak became I as weak, that I might gain the weak: I am made all things to all men, that I might gain all," — he did not certainly so act in the way of pretence, as some wish it to be understood, in order that their detestable pretence may be fortified by the authority of so great an example; but he did so from love, under the influence of which he thought of the infirmity of him whom he wished to help as if it were his own. For this he also lays as the foundation beforehand, when he says: "For although I be free from all men, yet have I made myself servant unto all, that I might gain [1] the more." [2] And that you may understand this as being done not in pretence, but in love, under the influence of which we have compassion for men who are weak as if we were they, he thus admonishes us in another passage, saying, "Brethren, ye have been called unto liberty; only use not liberty for an occasion to the flesh, but by love serve one another." [3] And this cannot be done, unless each one reckon the infirmity of another as his own, so as to bear it with equanimity, until the party for whose welfare he is solicitous is freed from it.

66. Rarely, therefore, and in a case of great necessity, are rebukes to be administered; yet in such a way that even in these very rebukes we may make it our earnest endeavour, not that we, but that God, should be served. For He, and none else, is the end: so that we are to do nothing with a double heart, removing from our own eye the beam of envy, or malice, or pretence, in order that we may see to cast the mote out of a brother's eye. For we shall see it with the dove's eyes, — such eyes as are declared to belong to the spouse of Christ,[4] whom God hath chosen for Himself a glorious Church, not having spot or wrinkle,[5] i.e. pure and guileless.

CHAP. XX. — 67. But inasmuch as the word "guileless" may mislead some who are desirous of obeying God's precepts, so that they may think it wrong, at times, to conceal the truth, just as it is wrong at times to speak a falsehood, and inasmuch as in this way, — by disclosing things which the parties to whom they are disclosed are unable to bear, — they may do more harm than if they were to conceal them altogether and always, He very rightly adds: "Give not that which is holy to the dogs, neither cast ye your pearls before swine, lest they trample them under their feet, and turn again and rend you." For the Lord Himself, although He never told a lie, yet showed that He was concealing certain truths, when He said, "I have yet many things to say unto you, but ye cannot bear them now." [6] And the Apostle Paul, too, says: "And I, brethren, could not speak unto you as unto spiritual, but as unto carnal, even as unto babes in Christ. I have fed you with milk, and not with meat: for hitherto ye were not able to bear it, neither yet now are ye able. For ye are yet carnal." [7]

68. Now, in this precept by which we are forbidden to give what is holy to the dogs, and to cast our pearls before swine, we must carefully inquire what is meant by holy, what by pearls, what by dogs, what by swine. A holy thing is something which it is impious to violate and to corrupt; and the very attempt and wish to commit that crime is held to be criminal, although that holy thing should remain in its nature inviolable and incorruptible. By pearls, again, are meant whatever spiritual things we ought to set a high value upon, both because they lie hid in a secret place, are as it were brought up out of the deep, and are found in wrappings of allegory, as it were in shells that have been opened. We may therefore legitimately understand that one and the same thing may be called both holy and a pearl: but it gets the name of holy for this reason, that it ought not to be corrupted; of a pearl for this reason, that it ought not to be despised. Every one, however, endeavours to corrupt what he does not wish to remain uninjured: but he despises what he thinks worthless, and reckons to be as it were beneath himself; and therefore whatever is despised is said to be trampled on. And hence, inasmuch as dogs spring at a thing in order to tear it in pieces, and do not allow what they are tearing in pieces to remain in its original condition, "Give not," says He, "that which is holy unto the dogs:" for although it cannot be torn in pieces and corrupted, and remains unharmed and inviolable, yet we must think of what is the wish of those parties who bitterly and in a most unfriendly spirit resist, and, as far as in them lies, endeavour, if it were possible, to destroy the truth. But swine, although they do not, like dogs, fall upon an object with their teeth, yet by recklessly trampling on it defile it: "Do not *therefore* cast your pearls before swine, lest they trample them under their feet, and turn again and rend you." We may therefore not unsuitably understand dogs as used to designate the assailants of the truth, swine the despisers of it.

69. But when He says, "they turn again and rend you," He does not say, they rend the pearls

---

[1] *Lucrifacerem;* Vulgate, *facerem salvos.*
[2] 1 Cor. ix. 19-22.   [3] Gal. v. 13.
[4] Cant. iv. 1.   [5] Eph. v. 27.

[6] John xvi. 12.   [7] 1 Cor. iii. 1, 2.

themselves. For by trampling on them, just when they turn in order that they may hear something more, they yet rend him by whom the pearls have just been cast before them which they have trampled on. For you would not easily find out what pleasure the man could have who has trampled pearls under foot, *i.e.* has despised divine things whose discovery is the result of great labour. But in regard to him who teaches such parties, I do not see how he would escape being rent in pieces through their anger and wrathfulness. Moreover, both animals are unclean, the dog as well as the swine. We must therefore be on our guard, lest anything should be opened up to him who does not receive it: for it is better that he should seek for what is hidden, than that he should either attack or slight what is open. Neither, in fact, is any other cause found why they do not receive those things which are manifest and of importance, except hatred and contempt, the one of which gets them the name of dogs, the other that of swine. And all this impurity is generated by the love of temporal things, *i.e.* by the love of this world, which we are commanded to renounce, in order that we may be able to be pure. The man, therefore, who desires to have a pure and single heart, ought not to appear to himself blameworthy, if he conceals anything from him who is unable to receive it. Nor is it to be supposed from this that it is allowable to lie: for it does not follow that when truth is concealed, falsehood is uttered. Hence, steps are to be taken first, that the hindrances which prevent his receiving it may be removed; for certainly if pollution is the reason he does not receive it, he is to be cleansed either by word or by deed, as far as we can possibly do it.

70. Then, further, when our Lord is found to have made certain statements which many who were present did not accept, but either resisted or despised, He is not to be thought to have given that which. is holy to the dogs, or to have cast pearls before swine: for He did not give such things to those who were not able to receive them, but to those who were able, and were at the same time present; whom it was not meet that He should neglect on account of the impurity of others. And when tempters put questions to Him, and He answered them, so that they might have nothing to gainsay, although they might pine away from the effects of their own poisons, rather than be filled with His food, yet others, who were able to receive His teaching, heard to their profit many things in consequence of the opportunity created by these parties. I have said this, lest any one, perhaps, when he is not able to reply to one who puts a question to him, should seem to himself excused, if he should say that he is unwilling to give that

which is holy to the dogs, or to cast pearls before swine. For he who knows what to answer ought to do it, even for the sake of others, in whose minds despair arises, if they believe that the question proposed cannot be answered: and this in reference to matters that are useful, and that belong to saving instruction. For many things which may be the subject of inquiry on the part of idle people are needless and vain, and often hurtful, respecting which, however, something must be said; but this very point is to be opened up and explained, viz. why such things ought not to form the subject of inquiry. In reference, therefore, to things that are useful, we ought sometimes to give a reply to what is asked of us: just as the Lord did, when the Sadducees had asked Him about the woman who had seven husbands, to which of them she would belong in the resurrection. For He answered that in the resurrection they will neither marry, nor be given in marriage, but will be as the angels in heaven. But sometimes, he who asks is to be asked something else, by telling which he would answer himself as to the matter he asked about; but if he should refuse to make a statement, it would not seem to those who are present unfair, if he himself should not hear anything as to the matter he inquired about. For those who put the question, tempting Him, whether tribute was to be paid, were asked another question, viz. whose image the money bore which was brought forward by themselves; and because they told what they had been asked, *i.e.* that the money bore the image of Cæsar, they gave a kind of answer to themselves in reference to the question they had asked the Lord: and accordingly from their answer He drew this inference, " Render therefore unto Cæsar the things which are Cæsar's, and unto God the things that are God's." [1] When, however, the chief priests and elders of the people had asked by what authority He was doing those things, He asked them about the baptism of John: and when they would not make a statement which they saw to be against themselves, and yet would not venture to say anything bad about John, on account of the bystanders, " Neither tell I you," says He, " by what authority I do these things; " [2] a refusal which appeared most just to the bystanders. For they said they were ignorant of that which they really knew, but did not wish to tell. And, in truth, it was right that they who wished to have an answer to what they asked, should themselves first do what they required to be done toward them; and if they had done this, they would certainly have answered themselves. For they themselves had sent to John, asking who he was; or rather they themselves, being priests and Levites, had been

---

[1] Matt. xxii. 15–34.   [2] Chap. xxi. 23–27.

sent, supposing that he was the very Christ, but he said that he was not, and gave forth a testimony concerning the Lord : [1] a testimony respecting which if they chose to make a confession, they would teach themselves by what authority as the Christ He was doing those things ; which as if ignorant of they had asked, in order that they might find an avenue for calumny.

CHAP. XXI. — 71. Since, therefore, a command had been given that what is holy should not be given to dogs, and pearls should not be cast before swine, a hearer might object and say, conscious of his own ignorance and weakness, and hearing a command addressed to him, that he should not give what he felt that he himself had not yet received, — might (I say) object and say, What holy thing do you forbid me to give to the dogs, and what pearls do you forbid me to cast before swine, while as yet I do not see that I possess such things? Most opportunely He has added the statement : "Ask, and it shall be given you ; seek, and ye shall find ; knock, and it shall be opened unto you. For every one that asketh receiveth ; and he that seeketh findeth ; and to him that knocketh it shall be opened." The asking refers to the obtaining by request soundness and strength of mind, so that we may be able to discharge those duties which are commanded ; the seeking, on the other hand, refers to the finding of the truth. For inasmuch as the blessed life is summed up in action and knowledge, action wishes for itself a supply of strength, contemplation desiderates that matters should be made clear : of these therefore the first is to be asked, the second is to be sought ; so that the one may be given, the other found. But knowledge in this life belongs rather to the way than to the possession itself : but whoever has found the true way, will arrive at the possession itself, which, however, is opened to him that knocks.

72. In order, therefore, that these three things — viz. asking, seeking, knocking — may be made clear, let us suppose, for example, the case of one weak in his limbs, who cannot walk : in the first place, he is to be healed and strengthened so as to be able to walk ; and to this refers the expression He has used, " Ask." But what advantage is it that he is now able to walk, or even run, if he should go astray by devious paths? A second thing therefore is, that he should find the road that leads to the place at which he wishes to arrive ; and when he has kept that road, and arrived at the very place where he wishes to dwell, if he find it closed, it will be of no use either that he has been able to walk, or that he has walked and arrived, unless it be opened to him : to this, therefore, the expression refers which has been used, " Knock."

73. Moreover, great hope has been given, and is given, by Him who does not deceive when He promises : for He says, " Every one that asketh, receiveth ; and he that seeketh, findeth ; and to him that knocketh, it shall be opened." Hence there is need of perseverance, in order that we may receive what we ask, and find what we seek, and that what we knock at may be opened.[2] Now, just as He talked of the fowls of heaven and of the lilies of the field, that we might not despair of food and clothing being provided for us, so that our hopes might rise from lesser things to greater ; so also in this passage, " Or what man is there of you," says He, " whom if his son ask bread, will he give him a stone? Or if he ask a fish, will he give him a serpent? If ye then, being evil, know how to give good gifts unto your children, how much more shall your Father which is in heaven give good things to them that ask Him?" How do the evil give good things? Now, He has called those evil [3] who are as yet the lovers of this world and sinners. And, in fact, the good things are to be called good according to their feeling, because they reckon these to be good things. Although in the nature of things also such things are good, but temporal, and pertaining to this feeble life : and whoever that is evil gives them, does not give of his own ; for the earth is the Lord's, and the fulness thereof,[4] who made heaven, and earth, the sea, and all that therein is.[5] How much reason, therefore, there is for the hope that God will give us good things when we ask Him, and that we cannot be deceived, so that we should get one thing instead of another, when we ask Him ; since we even, although we are evil, know how to give that for which we are asked? For we do not deceive our children ; and whatever good things we give are not given of our own, but of what is His.

CHAP. XXII. — 74. Moreover, a certain strength and vigour in walking along the path of wisdom lies in good morals, which are made to extend as far as to purification and singleness of heart, — a subject on which He has now been speaking long, and thus concludes : " Therefore all good [6] things whatsoever ye would that men should do to you, do ye even so to them : for this is the law and the prophets." In the Greek copies we find the passage runs thus : " Therefore all things whatsoever ye would that men

---

[1] John i. 19-27.

[2] The conditions of effective prayer are, that it should be made in the name of Christ (John xv. 16), with faith, and according to God's will (1 John v. 14).
[3] This has been regarded as a strong proof-text for the doctrine of original sin. Bengel calls it " a shining testimony for original sin." Stier says it is " the strongest proof-text for original sin in the whole of the Holy Scriptures." Meyer says the reference is to actual sin ; while Plumptre declares that " the words at once recognise the fact of man's depravity, and assert that it is not total."
[4] Ps. xxiv. 1.   [5] Ps. cxlvi. 6.
[6] Bona; the Vulgate does not contain it.

should do to you, do ye even so to them." But I think the word "good" has been added by the Latins to make the sentence clear. For the thought occurred, that if any one should wish something wicked to be done to him, and should refer this clause to that, — as, for instance, if one should wish to be challenged to drink immoderately, and to get drunk over his cups, and should first do this to the party by whom he wishes it to be done to himself, — it would be ridiculous to imagine that he had fulfilled this clause. Inasmuch, therefore, as they were influenced by this consideration, as I suppose, one word was added to make the matter clear; so that in the statement, "Therefore all things whatsoever ye would that men should do to you," there was inserted the word "good." But if this is wanting in the Greek copies, they also ought to be corrected: but who would venture to do this? It is to be understood, therefore, that the clause is complete and altogether perfect, even if this word be not added. For the expression used, "whatsoever ye would," ought to be understood as used not in a customary and random, but in a strict sense. For there is no will except in the good: for in the case of bad and wicked deeds, desire is strictly spoken of, not will. Not that the Scriptures always speak in a strict sense; but where it is necessary, they so keep a word to its perfectly strict meaning, that they do not allow anything else to be understood.

75. Moreover, this precept seems to refer to the love of our neighbour, and not to the love of God also, seeing that in another passage He says that there are two precepts on which "hang all the law and the prophets." For if He had said, All things whatsoever ye would should be done to you, do ye even so; in this one sentence He would have embraced both those precepts: for it would soon be said that every one wishes that he himself should be loved both by God and by men; and so, when this precept was given to him, that what he wished done to himself he should himself do, that certainly would be equivalent to the precept that he should love God and men. But when it is said more expressly of men, "Therefore all things whatsoever ye would that men should do to you, do ye even so to them," nothing else seems to be meant than, "Thou shalt love thy neighbour as thyself."[1] But we must carefully attend to what He has

added here: "for this is the law and the prophets." Now, in the case of these two precepts, He not merely says, The law and the prophets hang; but He has also added, "all the law and the prophets,"[2] which is the same as the whole of prophecy: and in not making the same addition here, He has kept a place for the other precept, which refers to the love of God. Here, then, inasmuch as He is following out the precepts with respect to a single heart, and it is to be dreaded lest any one should have a double heart toward those from whom the heart can be hid, i.e. toward men, a precept with respect to that very thing was to be given. For there is almost nobody that would wish that any one of double heart should have dealings with himself. But no one can bestow anything upon a fellowman with a single heart, unless he so bestow it that he expects no temporal advantage from him, and does it with the intention which we have sufficiently discussed above, when we were speaking of the single eye.

76. The eye, therefore, being cleansed and rendered single, will be adapted and suited to behold and contemplate its own inner light. For the eye in question is the eye of the heart. Now, such an eye is possessed by him who, in order that his works may be truly good, does not make the aim of his good works that he should please men; but even if it should turn out that he pleases them, he makes this tend rather to their salvation and to the glory of God, not to his own empty boasting; nor does he do anything that is good tending to his neighbour's salvation for the purpose of gaining by it those things that are necessary for getting through this present life; nor does he rashly condemn a man's intention and wish in that action in which it is not apparent with what intention and wish it has been done; and whatever kindnesses he shows to a man, he shows them with the same intention with which he wishes them shown to himself, viz. as not expecting any temporal advantage from him: thus will the heart be single and pure in which God is sought. "Blessed," therefore, "are the pure in heart: for they shall see God."[3]

CHAP. XXIII. — 77. But because this belongs to few, He now begins to speak of searching for and possessing wisdom, which is a tree of life; and certainly, in searching for and possessing, i.e. contemplating this wisdom, such an eye is led through all that precedes to a point where there may now be seen the narrow way and the strait gate. When, therefore, He says in continuation, "Enter ye[4] in at the strait gate: for wide is the gate, and broad is the way, that leadeth to destruction, and many there be which

---

[1] The nearest approach that any uninspired Jewish teacher came to the Golden Rule — the designation by which these words are known — was the saying of Hillel, "What is unpleasant to thyself, do not to thy neighbour. This is the whole law, and all the rest is commentary upon it." Beautiful as the saying is, it falls behind Christ's words, because it is merely negative, while they are a positive requirement. The Stoics and the Chinese ethics also have a similar negative precept. It is strange that the *Teaching of the Twelve Apostles* (i. 2) gives the negative form, and not the positive precept. Augustin says we ought to be glad when writers before Christ spoke things in the Gospel (*En. in Ps.* cxl. 6).

[2] Matt. xxii. 37-40.   [3] Matt. v. 8.
[4] *Introite;* Vulgate, *intrate.*

go in thereat : because strait is the gate, and narrow is the way, which leadeth unto life, and few there be that find it ; [1] He does not say so for this reason, that the Lord's yoke is rough, or His burden heavy ; but because few are willing to bring their labours to an end, giving too little credit to Him who cries, " Come unto me, all ye that labour, and I will give you rest. Take my yoke upon you, and learn of me ; for I am meek and lowly in heart : for my yoke is easy,[2] and my burden [2] is light " [3] (hence, moreover, the sermon before us took as its starting-point the lowly and meek in heart) : and this easy yoke and light burden which many spurn, few submit to ; and on that account the way becomes narrow which leadeth unto life, and the gate strait by which it is entered.

CHAP. XXIV. — 78. Here, therefore, those who promise a wisdom and a knowledge of the truth which they do not possess, are especially to be guarded against ; as, for instance, heretics, who frequently commend themselves on account of their fewness. And hence, when He had said that there are few who find the strait gate and the narrow way, lest they [the heretics] should falsely substitute themselves under the pretext of their fewness, He immediately added, " Beware of false prophets,[4] which come to you in sheep's clothing, but inwardly they are ravening wolves." But such parties do not deceive the single eye, which knows how to distinguish a tree by its fruits. For He says : " Ye shall know them by their fruits." Then He adds the similitudes : " Do men gather grapes of thorns, or figs of thistles ? Even so, every good tree bringeth forth good fruit ; but a corrupt tree bringeth forth evil fruit. A good tree cannot bring forth evil fruit, neither can a corrupt tree bring forth good fruit. Every tree that bringeth not forth good fruit [5] is hewn down, and cast into the fire. Wherefore by their fruits ye shall know them."

79. And in [the interpretation of] this passage we must be very much on our guard against the error of those who judge from these same two trees that there are two original natures, the one of which belongs to God, but the other neither belongs to God nor springs from Him. And this error has both been already discussed

in other books [of ours] [6] very copiously, and if that is still too little, will be discussed again ; but at present we have merely to show that the two trees before us do not help them. In the first place, because it is so clear that He is speaking of men, that whoever reads what goes before and what follows will wonder at their blindness. Secondly, they fix their attention on what is said, " A good tree cannot bring forth evil fruit, neither can a corrupt tree bring forth good fruit," and therefore think that neither can it happen that an evil soul should be changed into something better, nor a good one into something worse ; as if it were said, A good tree cannot become evil, nor an evil tree good. But it is said, " A good tree cannot bring forth evil fruit, neither can a corrupt tree bring forth good fruit." For the tree is certainly the soul itself, i.e. the man himself, but the fruits are the works of the man ; an evil man, therefore, cannot perform good works, nor a good man evil works. If an evil man, therefore, wishes to perform good works, let him first become good. So the Lord Himself says in another passage more plainly : " Either make the tree good, or make the tree bad." But if He were figuratively representing the two natures of such parties by these two trees, He would not say, " Make : " for who of the sons of men can make a nature ? Then also in that passage, when He had made mention of these two trees, He added, " Ye hypocrites, how can ye, being evil, speak good things ? " [7] As long, therefore, as any one is evil, he cannot bring forth good fruits ; for if he were to bring forth good fruits, he would no longer be evil. So it might most truly have been said, snow cannot be warm ; for when it begins to be warm, we no longer call it snow, but water. It may therefore come about, that what was snow is no longer so ; but it cannot happen that snow should be warm. So it may come about, that he who was evil is no longer evil ; it cannot, however, happen that an evil man should do good. And although he is sometimes useful, this is not the man's own doing ; but it is done through him, in virtue of the arrangements of divine providence : as, for instance, it is said of the Pharisees, " What they bid you, do ; but what they do, do not consent to do." This very circumstance, that they spoke things that were good, and that the things which they spoke were usefully listened to and done, was not a matter belonging to them : for, says He, " they sit in Moses' seat." [8] It was, therefore, when engaged through divine providence in preaching the law of God, that they were able to be useful to their

---

[1] The narrowness of the way is taken to represent the self-denial and hardships of disciples (Meyer, Mansel, etc.), or righteousness (Bengel, Schaff, etc.). " The picture is a dark one, and yet it represents but too faithfully the impression made, I do not say on Calvinist or true Christian, but on any ethical teacher, by the actual state of mankind around us. If there is any wider hope, it is found in hints and suggestions of the possibilities of the future (1 Pet. iii. 19, iv. 6)," etc. (Plumptre).

[2] Lene . . . sarcina ; Vulgate, suave . . . onus.

[3] Matt. xi. 28-30.

[4] Cavete a pseudoprophetis ; Vulgate, attendite a falsis prophetis.

[5] Excellency of fruitage is sanctity of life (Bonitas fructuum est sanctitas vitæ (Bengel).

[6] More particularly his works against the Manichæans, Contra Faustum Manichæum, etc. Augustin also made much use of this passage against the Pelagians, to show that the will must be aided to produce good thoughts and deeds ; that the unregenerate man is incapable of restoring himself.

[7] Matt. xii. 33, 34.   [8] Matt. xxiii. 3, 2.

hearers, although they were not so to themselves. Respecting such it is said in another place by the prophet, "They have sown wheat, but shall reap thorns;"[1] because they teach what is good, and do what is evil. Those, therefore, who listened to them, and did what was said by them, did not gather grapes of thorns, but through the thorns gathered grapes of the vine: just as, were any one to thrust his hand through a hedge, or were at least to gather a grape from a vine which was entangled in a hedge, that would not be the fruit of the thorns, but of the vine.

80. The question, indeed, is most rightly put, What are the fruits He would wish us to attend to, whereby we might know the tree? For many reckon among the fruits certain things which belong to the sheep's clothing, and in this way are deceived by wolves: as, for instance, either fastings, or prayers, or almsgivings; but unless all of these things could be done even by hypocrites, He would not say above, "Take heed that ye do not your righteousness before men, to be seen of them." And after prefixing this sentence, He goes on to speak of those very three things, almsgiving, prayer, fasting. For many give largely to the poor, not from compassion, but from vanity; and many pray, or rather seem to pray, while not keeping God in view, but desiring to please men; and many fast, and make a wonderful show of abstinence before those to whom such things appear difficult, and by whom they are reckoned worthy of honour: and catch them with artifices of this sort, while they hold up to view one thing for the purpose of deceiving, and put forth another for the purpose of preying upon or killing those who cannot see the wolves under that sheep's clothing. These, therefore, are not the fruits by which He admonishes us that the tree is known. For such things, when they are done with a good intention in sincerity, are the appropriate clothing of sheep; but when they are done in wicked deception, they cover nothing else but wolves. But the sheep ought not on this account to hate their own clothing, because the wolves often conceal themselves therein.

81. What the fruits are by the finding of which we may know an evil tree, the apostle tells us: "Now the works of the flesh are manifest, which are these; adulteries, fornications, uncleanness, lasciviousness, idolatry, witchcraft, hatreds, variances, emulations, wrath, strife, seditions, heresies, envyings, murders, drunkenness, revellings, and such like: of the which I tell you before, as I have also told you in time past, that they which do such things shall not inherit the kingdom of God." And what the fruits are by which we may know a good tree,

the very same apostle goes on to tell us: "But the fruit of the Spirit is love, joy, peace, longsuffering, gentleness, goodness, faith, meekness, temperance."[2] It must be known, indeed, that "joy" stands here in a strict and proper sense; for bad men are, strictly speaking, not said to rejoice, but to make extravagant demonstrations of joy: just as we have said above, that "will" which the wicked do not possess, stands in a strict sense where it is said, "All things whatsoever ye would that men should do to you, do ye even so to them." In accordance with that strict sense of the word, in virtue of which joy is spoken of only in the good, the prophet also speaks, saying: "Rejoicing is not for the wicked, saith the Lord."[3] So also "faith" stands, not certainly as meaning any kind of it, but true faith: and the other things which find a place here have certain resemblances of their own in bad men and deceivers; so that they entirely mislead, unless one has the pure and single eye by which he may know such things. It is accordingly the best arrangement, that the cleansing of the eye is first discussed, and then mention is made of what things were to be guarded against.

CHAP. XXV. — 82. But seeing that, however pure an eye one may have, i.e. with however single and sincere a heart one may live, he yet cannot look into the heart of another: whatever things could not have become apparent in deeds or words, are disclosed by trials. Now trial is twofold; either in the hope of obtaining some temporal advantage, or in the terror of losing it. And especially must we be on our guard, lest, when striving after wisdom, which can be found in Christ alone, in whom are hid all the treasures of wisdom and knowledge;[4] — we must be on our guard, I say, lest, under the very name of Christ, we be deceived by heretics, or by any parties whatever defective in intelligence, and lovers of this world. For on this account He adds a warning, saying, "Not every one that saith unto Me, Lord, Lord,[5] shall enter into the kingdom of heaven; but he that doeth the will of My Father which is in heaven, he shall enter into the kingdom of heaven:" lest we should think that the mere fact of one saying to our Lord, "Lord, Lord," belongs to those fruits; and from that he should seem to us to be a good tree. But those are the fruits, to do the will of the Father who is in heaven, in the doing of which He has condescended to exhibit Himself as an example.

83. But the question may fairly be started, how with this sentence the statement of the

[1] Jer. xii. 13.

[2] Gal. v. 19-23.   [3] Isa. lvii. 21, according to the Septuagint.
[4] Col. ii. 3.
[5] Many called Him Lord, but He never called any one Lord (ipsum multi, etiam amplissimi viri, — ipse neminem ne Pilatum quidem, dominum vocavit. — Bengel).

apostle is to be reconciled, where he says, " No man speaking by the Spirit of God calleth Jesus accursed ; and no man can say that Jesus is the Lord, but by the Holy Ghost : " [1] for neither can we say that any who have the Holy Spirit will not enter into the kingdom of heaven, if they persevere onwards to the end ; nor can we affirm that those who say, " Lord, Lord," and yet do not enter into the kingdom of heaven, have the Holy Spirit. How then does no one say "that Jesus is the Lord, but by the Holy Ghost," unless it is because the apostle has used the word "say" here in a strict and proper sense, so that it implies the will and understanding of him who says? But the Lord has used the word which He employs in a general sense : " Not every one that saith unto Me, Lord, Lord, shall enter into the kingdom of heaven." For he also who neither wishes nor understands what he says, seems to say it ; but he properly says it, who gives expression to his will and mind by the sound of his voice : just as, a little before, what is called "joy" among the fruits of the Spirit is called so in a strict and proper sense, not in the way in which the same apostle elsewhere uses the expression, " Rejoiceth not in iniquity : " [2] as if any one could rejoice in iniquity : for that transport of a mind making confused and boisterous demonstrations of joy is not joy ; for this latter is possessed by the good alone. Hence those also seem to say it, who neither perceive with the understanding nor engage with the deliberate consent of the will in this which they utter, but utter it with the voice merely ; and after this manner the Lord says, " Not every one that saith unto Me, Lord, Lord, shall enter into the kingdom of heaven." But truly and properly those parties say it whose utterance in speech really represents their will and intention ; and it is in accordance with this signification that the apostle has said, " No one can say that Jesus is the Lord, but by the Holy Ghost."

84. And besides, it belongs especially to the matter in hand, that, in striving after the contemplation of the truth, we should not only not be deceived by the name of Christ, by means of those who have the name and have not the deeds ; but also not by certain deeds and miracles, for when the Lord performed of the same kind for the sake of unbelievers, He has warned us not to be deceived by such things, thinking that an invisible wisdom is present where we see a visible miracle. Hence He annexes the statement : " Many will say to Me on that day, Lord, Lord, have we not prophesied in Thy name, and in Thy name have cast out devils, and in Thy name done many wonderful works? And

then will I say [3] unto them, I never knew you : depart from Me, ye that work iniquity." He will not, therefore, recognise any but the man that worketh righteousness. For He forbade also His own disciples themselves to rejoice in such things, viz. that the spirits were subject unto them : " But rejoice," says He, " because your names are written in heaven ; " [4] I suppose, in that city of Jerusalem which is in heaven, in which only the righteous and holy shall reign. " Know ye not," says the apostle, " that the unrighteous shall not inherit the kingdom of God ? " [5]

85. But perhaps some one may say that the unrighteous cannot perform those visible miracles, and may believe rather that those parties are telling a lie, who will be found saying, " We have prophesied in Thy name, and have cast out devils in Thy name, and have done many wonderful works." Let him therefore read what great things the magi of the Egyptians did who resisted Moses, the servant of God ; [6] or if he will not read this, because they did not do them in the name of Christ, let him read what the Lord Himself says of the false prophets, speaking thus : " Then, if any man shall say unto you, Lo, here is Christ, or there ; believe it not. For there shall arise false Christs, and false prophets, and shall show great signs and wonders, insomuch that the very elect shall be deceived.[7] Behold, I have told you before." [8]

86. How much need, therefore, is there of the pure and single eye, in order that the way of wisdom may be found, against which there is the clamour of so great deceptions and errors on the part of wicked and perverse men, to escape from all of which is indeed to arrive at the most certain peace, and the immoveable stability of wisdom ! For it is greatly to be feared, lest, by eagerness in quarrelling and controversy, one should not see what can be seen by few, that small is the disturbance of gainsayers, unless one also disturbs himself. And in this direction, too, runs that statement of the apostle : " And the servant of the Lord must not strive ; but be gentle [9] unto all men, apt to teach, patient, in meekness instructing those that think differently ; [9] if God peradventure will give them repentance to the acknowledging of the truth." [10] " Blessed," therefore, " are the peacemakers : for they shall be called the children of God." [11]

---

[1] 1 Cor. xii. 3. [2] 1 Cor. xiii. 6.

[3] *Dicam* : Vulgate, *confitebor ;* Greek, ὁμολογήσω. Meyer says, " It is the conscious dignity of the future Judge of the world." Bengel calls attention to the great power of the word (*magna potestas hujus dicti*). In this action Christ lays the most confident claim to functions not imparted to any human being.
[4] Luke x. 20. [5] 1 Cor. vi. 9. [6] Exod. vii. and viii.
[7] *Inducantur etiam elècti ;* Vulgate, *inducantur, si fieri potest, etiam electi.*
[8] Matt. xxiv. 23-25.
[9] *Mitem . . . diversa sentientes ;* Vulgate, *mansuetum . . . resistunt veritati.*
[10] 2 Tim. ii. 24, 25. [11] Matt. v. 9.

87. Hence we must take special notice how terribly the conclusion of the whole sermon is introduced : " Therefore, whosoever heareth these sayings of Mine, and doeth them, is like [1] unto a wise man, which built his house upon the rock." For no one confirms what he hears or understands, unless by doing. And if Christ is the rock, as many Scripture testimonies proclaim,[2] that man builds in Christ who does what he hears from Him. "The rain descended, and the floods came, and the winds blew, and beat [3] upon that house ; and it fell not : for it was founded upon a rock." Such an one, therefore, is not afraid of any gloomy superstitions (for what else is understood by rain, when it is put in the sense of anything bad?), or of rumours of men, which I think are compared to winds ; or of the river of this life, as it were flowing over the earth in carnal lusts. For it is the man who is seduced by the prosperity that is broken down by the adversities arising from these three things ; none of which is feared by him who has his house founded upon a rock, i.e. who not only hears, but also does, the Lord's commands. And the man who hears and does them not is in dangerous proximity to all these, for he has no stable foundation ; but by hearing and not doing, he builds a ruin. For He goes on to say : "And every one that heareth these sayings of Mine,

and doeth them not, shall be like unto a foolish man, which built his house upon the sand : [4] and the rain descended, and the floods came, and the winds blew, and beat [3] upon that house ; and it fell : and great was [5] the fall of it. And it came to pass, when Jesus had ended these sayings, the people were astonished at His doctrine : for He taught them as one having authority, and not as their scribes." [6] This is what I said before was meant by the prophet in the Psalms, when he says : "I will act confidently in regard of him. The words of the Lord are pure words : as silver tried and proved in a furnace of earth, purified seven times." [7] And from this number, I am admonished to trace back those precepts also to the seven sentences which He has placed in the beginning of this sermon, when He was speaking of those who are blessed ; and to those seven operations of the Holy Spirit, which the prophet Isaiah mentions ; [8] but whether the order before us, or some other, is to be considered in these, the things we have heard from the Lord are to be done, if we wish to build upon a rock.

---

[1] Similis est . . .; Vulgate, assimilabitur. Meyer, Tholuck, etc., refer this to the future judgment, "I will make him like," etc., when Christ will establish those who keep His sayings for ever (opposed by Alford, etc.).

[2] 1 Cor. x. 4. So Alford, who thinks this signification too plain to be overlooked.

[3] Offenderunt ; Vulgate, irruerunt.

[4] The transitory teachings and institutions of men as opposed to Christ's own word.

[5] Facta est ; Vulgate, fuit.

[6] Vulgate adds et Pharisæi. The people were astonished, not merely at His teachings, but the dignity and self-consciousness with which Christ uttered them, quod nova quædam majestas et insueta hominum mentes ad se raperet (Calvin). The Scribes spoke as expounders of the law, and referred back to Moses for their authority : Christ spoke in His own name, and as an independent legislator, vested with greater authority than Moses and a higher dignity. The Scribes by elaborate sophistry often drew many meanings from a single precept, and burdened the people with an intricate and endless variety of precepts for the details of conduct, laying painful stress upon their observance : Christ directed attention from outward acts to the motive and intent of the heart. "He opposed a genuine righteousness to the mock righteousness of the Scribes and Pharisees."

[7] Ps. xii. 5, 6.   [8] Isa. xi. 2, 3.

ST. AUGUSTIN:

THE HARMONY OF THE GOSPELS

TRANSLATED BY

THE REV. S. D. F. SALMOND, D.D.,

FREE COLLEGE, ABERDEEN

EDITED, WITH NOTES AND INTRODUCTION, BY

THE REV. M. B. RIDDLE, D.D.,

PROFESSOR OF NEW-TESTAMENT EXEGESIS, WESTERN THEOLOGICAL SEMINARY, ALLEGHENY, PA.

65

INTRODUCTORY ESSAY.

BY PROFESSOR M. B. RIDDLE, D.D.

THE treatise of Augustin ON THE HARMONY OF THE EVANGELISTS (*De Consensu Evangelistarum*) is regarded as the most laborious task undertaken by the great African Father. But its influence has been much less obvious than that of his strictly exegetical and doctrinal works. Dr. Salmond, in his Introductory Notice, gives a discriminating and just estimate of it. Jerome was, in some respects, far better equipped for such a task than Augustin; yet one cannot study this work, bearing in mind the hermeneutical tendencies of the fourth century, without having an increased respect for the ability, candour, and insight of the great theologian when engaged in labours requiring linguistic knowledge, which he did not possess. Despite his ignorance of the correct text in many difficult passages, his lack of familiarity with the Greek original, many of his explanations have stood the test of time, finding acceptance even among the exegetes of this age.

Most modern Harmonies give indications of the abiding influence of the work. Yet the treatise itself has not called forth extended comments. From its character it directs attention to the problems it discusses rather than to its own solutions of them. Hence the difficulty of presenting an adequate Bibliographical List in connection with this work. All Gospel Harmonies, all Lives of Christ, all discussions of the apparent discrepancies of the Gospels, stand related to it. As a complete list was out of the question, it seemed fitting to preface this edition of the work with a few general statements in regard to Harmonies of the Gospels.

The early date of the oldest work of this character, before A.D. 170 (see below), attests the genuineness of our four canonical Gospels, by proving that they, and they only, were generally accepted at that time. But it also shows that the existence of four Gospels, recognised as genuine and authoritative, naturally calls forth harmonistic efforts. Two questions confront every intelligent reader of these four Gospels: (1) In view of the variation in the *order* of events as narrated by the different evangelists, what is the more probable chronological order? (2) In view of the variation in *details*, what is, in each case, the correct explanation of such variations? These problems are largely exegetical; but those of the former class soon lead to the historical method of treatment, while those of the latter class lead to apologetic discussions, when apparent discrepancies are discovered. The work of Augustin deals more largely with the latter; more recent Harmonies lay greater stress upon the historical and chronological questions. The methods represent the tendencies of the age to which they respectively belong. The historical method is doubtless the more correct one; but, when it assumes the extreme form of destructive criticism, it denies the possibility of harmony. On the other hand, the apologetic method, when linked with a mechanical view of inspiration, too often adopts interpretations that are ungrammatical, in order to ignore the necessity of harmonizing differences. The true position lies between these extremes: the grammatico-historical sense must be accepted; the correct text of each Gospel must be determined, independently of verbal variations; the truthfulness of each evangelist must be assumed, until positive error is proven; the more definite statements are to be used in explaining the less definite; the characteristics of each evangelist must be given their proper weight in determining the probabilities of greater or less accuracy of detail.

But the necessary limitations of harmonistic methods should be fully recognised.   Absolute certainty is often impossible : there will always be room for difference of judgment.   For example, there is to-day as little agreement as ever in regard to the length of our Lord's ministry ; *i.e.*, whether the Evangelist John refers to three or four passovers.   The Tripaschal and Quadripaschal theories still divide scholars, as in past ages of the Church.

Still, the progress made in textual criticism has, by indicating more positively the exact words of all four accounts, laid the foundation for better results in harmonistic labours.

One great advantage of a Harmony, as now constructed, with the text of the evangelists in parallel columns, or in independent sections when the matter is peculiar to one of them, is the emphasis it gives to the historical sequence.   The movement of the evangelical narrative is made more apparent ; the relations of the events shed light upon the entire story ; the purpose of discourses and journeys appears ; the training of the Twelve can be better studied ; the emphasis placed upon the closing events of our Lord's life on earth is made more obvious.   A comparison of the several accounts gives to the events new significance, often reveals minute and undesigned coincidences which attest the truthfulness of all the narrators.   Now that the attempt to secure mechanical uniformity in the narratives has been universally rejected by scholars, another advantage of a Harmony is seen to be this : that it sets forth most strikingly the verbal differences and correspondences of the parallel passages.   Only by a minute comparison of these can we discover the data for a settlement of the problem respecting the origin and relation of the Synoptic Gospels.[1].

The dangers attending harmonistic methods are obvious enough, and appeared very early. The tendency has been to create a rigid verbal uniformity.   Hence the peculiarities of the several evangelists are obscured ; the text of one is, consciously or unconsciously, conformed to that of another.   The Gospel of Mark, the most individual and striking of the Synoptics, probably the oldest, has been repeatedly altered to correspond with that of Matthew.   When uniformity could not be secured by this process, false exegesis was often resorted to, and hermeneutical principles avowed which injured the cause of truth.   Evangelical truth cannot be defended with the weapons of error.   This vicious method was usually the result of mechanical views of inspiration.   That view of inspiration which rightly recognises language as vital, and which therefore seeks to know the meaning of every word, has no worse foe than the hermeneutical principle which ignores the historical sense of any word of Scripture.

The tendency just referred to brought harmonistic labours into disrepute.   The immense activity of the present century in exegetical theology has not taken this direction.   Moreover, the historical method received its greatest impulse from the tendency-theory of the Tübingen school, which presupposes the impossibility of constructing a Harmony of the four Gospels. Hence the reaction, in Germany especially, has been excessive.

Yet Harmonies are still prepared, and are still useful.   Harmonistic labours have their rightful, though limited, place in the field of Exegetical Theology.

A very brief sketch of the leading works of this character will serve to illustrate the above statements.

The earliest attempt at constructing a Harmony was that of TATIAN[2] (died A.D. 172).   The date of its appearance was between A.D. 153 and 170 ; and its title, *Diatessaron*, furnishes abundant evidence of the early acceptance of our four canonical Gospels.   Our knowledge of this work was, until recently, very slight.   But the discovery of an Armenian translation of a commentary upon it,

---

[1] The writer may be pardoned for alluding to his own experience in connection with this point. In the exegetical labours of some years, he found himself accepting the theory that the three Synoptists wrote independently of each other. Afterwards, when the task of editing Dr. Robinson's Greek Harmony compelled him to compare again and again every word of each account, the evidences of independence seemed to him to be overwhelming.

[2] See SCHAFF, *History of the Christian Church*, vol. ii. rev. ed., pp. 493 sqq., 726 sqq.; also SCHAFF-HERZOG, *Encyclopædia*, article " Diatessaron." For the literature, see as above, and the supplementary volume of the *Ante-Nicene Fathers*, pp. 33-35. Tatian's *Address to the Greeks* may be found in vol. ii. *Ante-Nicene Fathers*, pp. 65-83.

by Ephraem the Syrian, has enabled ZAHN to reconstruct a large part of the text. The commentary was translated into Latin in 1841, but little attention was paid to it until an edition by MOESIN-GER appeared in 1876.[1] The influence of Tatian's *Diatessaron* upon the Greek text seems to have been unfortunate. Many of the corruptions in the received text of the Gospel of Mark are probably due to the confusion of the separate narratives occasioned by this work. Tregelles (in the new edition of HORNE's *Introduction*, vol. iv. p. 40) says that it "had more effect apparently in the text of the Gospels in use throughout the Church than all the designed falsifications of Marcion and every scion of the Gnostic blood." It seems to have contained nothing indicating heretical bias or intentional alteration.

The next Harmony was that of AMMONIUS of Alexandria, the teacher of Origen, the first work bearing this title ('Αρμονία). It appeared about A.D. 220, but has been lost. Until recently it was supposed that the sections into which some early MSS. divide the Gospels were those of Ammonius himself; but, while he did make such divisions, those bearing his name are to be attributed to Eusebius (see below). Ammonius made Matthew the basis of his work, and by his arrangement destroyed the continuity of the separate narratives. Every Harmony based upon the order of Matthew must be a failure.

EUSEBIUS of Cæsarea (died A.D. 340) adopted a similar set of divisions, adding to them numbers from 1 to 10, called "Canons," which indicate the parallelisms of the sections. These sections and canons are printed in Tischendorf's critical editions of the Greek Testament, and in some other editions.[2] The influence of this system seems to have been great, but Eusebius often accepts a parallelism where there is really none whatever. Some of the sections are very brief, containing only part of a verse. Hence the tables of sections furnish no basis for estimating the matter common to two or more evangelists.

The work of Augustin comes next in order; it deals little with chronological questions, and shows no trace of such complete textual labour as that of Eusebius.

The Reformation gave a new impulse to this department of Biblical study. In the sixteenth century many Harmonies appeared. Among the authors are the well-known names of Osiander, Jansen, Robert Stephens, John Calvin, Du Moulin, Chemnitz. These works were written in Latin, as a rule; and they are worthy of the age which produced them. Lack of sufficient critical material prevented complete accuracy, but the exegetical methods of the sixteenth century obtain in the Harmonies also.

The seventeenth and eighteenth centuries present little in this field of labour that deserves favourable notice. The undisputed reign of the *Textus Receptus* impeded investigation; the super-naturalism of the dominant theology was not favourable to historical investigation; the mechanical theory of inspiration led to arbitrary and forced interpretations. Even the older rationalism, which explained away the supernatural, was scarcely more faulty in its exegesis than many an orthodox commentator. The labours of J. LIGHTFOOT deserve grateful recognition. This great Hebrew scholar did not finish his Harmony of the Gospels, but shed great light upon many of the problems involved, by his knowledge of Jewish customs. J. A. BENGEL, the pioneer of modern textual criticism of the New Testament, published a valuable Harmony in German. W. NEWCOME published a Harmony of the Gospels in Greek (Dublin, 1778). He follows LE CLERC (Amsterdam, 1779), and his Harmony is the basis of the more modern work by EDWARD ROBINSON (see below).

---

[1] For full titles of these volumes, see SCHAFF, as above.

[2] The letter of Eusebius to Caprianus is given by C. R. GREGORY (*Prolegomena* to Tischendorf's eighth edition, part i. pp. 143-153), together with a full list of the sections arranged under the separate canons. The numbers signify as follows: —

1. In all four Gospels, 71.	6. In Matthew, Mark, 47.
2. In Matthew, Mark, Luke, 111.	7. In Matthew, John, 7.
3. In Matthew, Luke, John, 22.	8. In Luke, Mark, 14.
4. In Matthew, Mark, John, 26.	9. In Luke, John, 21.
5. In Matthew, Luke, 82.	10. In one Gospel: Matthew, 62; Mark, 21; Luke, 71; John, 97.

While the Tübingen school, by its tendency-theory, virtually denied the possibility of constructing a Harmony, it compelled the conservative theologians to adopt the historical method. Thus there has been gathered much material for harmonistic labours. But in Germany, as in England and America, Lives of Christ have been more numerous than Harmonies.

K. WIESELER and C. TISCHENDORF, among recent German scholars, have published valuable Harmonies. In England the work most in use is that of E. GRESWELL. The Archbishop of York, WILLIAM THOMSON, presents in Smith's Bible Dictionary a valuable table of the Harmony of the Four Gospels (article "Gospels," Am. ed. vol. ii. p. 751).

An interesting edition of the Synoptic Gospels is that of W. G. RUSHBROOKE (*Synopticon*, Cambridge, 1880–81). It is designed to show, by different type and colour, the divergences and correspondences of the three Gospels. The Greek text is that of Tischendorf, corrected from that of Westcott and Hort. It presents in the readiest form the material for harmonistic comparisons ; but the editor has prepared it with a purpose diametrically opposed to that of the Harmonist, namely, to construct from the matter common to the Synoptists a "triple tradition," which will, in the author's judgment, approximately present the "source" from which all have drawn. The work has great value apart from its theory of the origin of the Synoptic Gospels.

In America EDWARD ROBINSON published, in repeated editions, a Harmony of the Gospels in Greek and also in English. He had previously reprinted that of Newcome.

S. J. ANDREWS (*Life of our Lord ;* New York, 1863), has sought "to arrange the events of the Lord's life, as given us by the evangelists, so far as possible, in a chronological order, and to state the grounds of this order." It is virtually a Harmony, with the full text of the Gospels omitted. Few works of the kind equal it in value, though it needs revision in the light of the more recent results of textual criticism.

FREDERIC GARDINER has published a *Harmony of the Four Gospels in Greek* (Andover, 1871, 1876). It gives the text of Tischendorf (eighth edition), with a collation of the *Textus Receptus*, and of the texts of Griesbach, Lachmann, and Tregelles. The authorities are cited in the case of important variations. Another valuable feature is a comparative table, presenting in parallel columns the arrangement adopted by Greswell, Stroud, Robinson, Thomson, Tischendorf, and Gardiner.

A number of works, aiming to consolidate into one narrative the four accounts, have been passed over.

The Harmony of Dr. Robinson, which has held its ground for more than forty years, has been recently revised by the present writer. The text of Tischendorf has been substituted for that of Hahn ; all the various readings materially affecting the sense which are found in Tregelles, Westcott and Hort, and in the Revised English version of 1881, have been given in footnotes, with a selection of the leading authorities (MSS. and versions) for or against each reading cited. The Appendix has been enlarged to meet the new phases of discussion ; but the whole volume is what it purports to be, — a revision of the standard work of Dr. Robinson. In the matter of the Greek text, the author would probably have done what has now been done by the editor. A similar but less extensive revision of the English Harmony of Dr. Robinson has been published.[1]

---

[1] For lists of Harmonies, see SCHAFF, *History of the Christian Church*, rev. ed. vol. i. pp. 575, 576 ; GARDINER, *Harmony*, pp. xxxiv.-xxxvii.; ROBINSON, *Harmony*, revised by RIDDLE, pp. ix., x. Each of these lists contains references to older authors and their lists. See also SMITH, *Bible Dictionary*, Am. ed. (HACKETT and ABBOT) ii. pp. 950, 960.

ALLEGHENY, PA., Nov. 14, 1887.

TRANSLATOR'S INTRODUCTORY NOTICE.

IN the remarkable work known as his *Retractations*, Augustin makes a brief statement on the subject of this treatise on the *Harmony of the Evangelists*. The sixteenth chapter of the second book of that memorable review of his literary career, contains corrections of certain points on which he believed that he had not been sufficiently accurate in these discussions. In the same passage he informs us that this treatise was undertaken during the years in which he was occupied with his great work on the *Trinity*, and that, breaking in upon the task which had been making gradual progress under his hand, he wrought continuously at this new venture until it was finished. Its composition is assigned to about the year 400 A.D. The date is determined in the following manner: In the first book there is a sentence (§ 27) which appears to indicate that, by the time when Augustin engaged himself with this effort, the destruction of the idols of the old religion was being carried out under express imperial authority. No law of that kind, however, affecting Africa, seems to be found expressed previous to those to which he refers at the close of the eighteenth book of the *City of God*. There he gives us to understand that such measures were put in force in Carthage, under Gaudentius and Jovius, the associates of the Emperor Honorius, and states that for the space of nearly thirty years from that time the Christian religion made advances large enough to arrest general attention. Before that period, which must have been about the year 399, the idols could not be destroyed, as Augustin elsewhere indicates (*Serm.* lxii. 11, n. 17), but with the consent of the parties to whom they belonged. These considerations are taken to fix the composition of this work to a date not earlier than the close of 399 A.D.

Among Augustin's numerous theological productions, this one takes rank with the most toilsome and exhaustive. We find him expressing himself to that effect now and again, when he has occasion to allude to it. Thus, in the 112th *Tractate* on John (n. 1), he calls it a laborious piece of literature; and in the 117th *Tractate* on the same evangelist, he speaks of the themes here dealt with as matters which were discussed with the utmost painstaking.

Its great object is to vindicate the Gospel against the critical assaults of the heathen. Paganism, having tried persecution as its first weapon, and seen it fail, attempted next to discredit the new faith by slandering its doctrine, impeaching its history, and attacking with special persistency the veracity of the Gospel writers. In this it was aided by some of Augustin's heretical antagonists, who endeavoured at times to establish a conspicuous inconsistency between the Jewish Scriptures and the Christian, and at times to prove the several sections of the New Testament to be at variance with each other. Many alleged that the original Gospels had received considerable additions of a spurious character. And it was a favorite method of argumentation, adopted both by heathen and by Manichæan adversaries, to urge that the evangelical historians contradicted each other. Thus, in the present treatise (i. 7), Augustin speaks of this matter of the discrepancies between the Evangelists as the *palmary* argument wielded by his opponents. Hence, as elsewhere he sought to demonstrate the congruity of the Old Testament with the New, he set himself here to exonerate Christianity from the charge of any defect of harmony, whether in the facts recorded or in the order of their narration, between its four fundamental historical documents.

The plan of the work is laid out in four great divisions. In the first book, he refutes those who asserted that Christ was only the wisest among men, and who aimed at detracting from the authority of the Gospels, by insisting on the absence of any written compositions proceeding from the hand of Christ Himself, and by affirming that the disciples went beyond what had been His own teaching both on the subject of His divinity, and on the duty of abandoning the worship of the gods. In the second, he enters upon a careful examination of Matthew's Gospel, on to the record of the supper, comparing it with Mark, Luke, and John, and exhibiting the perfect harmony subsisting between them. In the third, he demonstrates the same consistency between the four Evangelists, from the account of the supper on to the end. And in the fourth, he subjects to a similar investigation those passages in Mark, Luke, and John, which have no proper parallels in Matthew.

For the discharge of a task like this, Augustin was gifted with much, but he also lacked much. The resources of a noble and penetrating intellect, profound spiritual insight, and reverent love for Scripture, formed high qualifications at his command. But he was deficient in exact scholarship. Thoroughly versed in Latin literature, as is evinced here by the happy notices of Ennius, Cicero, Lucan, and others of its great writers, he knew little Greek, and no Hebrew. He refers more than once in the present treatise to his ignorance of the original language of the Old Testament; and while his knowledge of that of the New was probably not so unserviceable as has often been supposed, instances like that in which he solves the apparent difficulty in the two *burdens*, mentioned in Gal. vi., without alluding to the distinction between the Greek words, make it sufficiently plain that it was not at least his invariable habit to prosecute these studies with the original in his view. Hence we find him missing many explanations which would at once have suggested themselves, had he not so implicitly followed the imperfect versions of the sacred text.

An analysis of the contents of the work might show much that is of interest to the Biblical critic. Principles elsewhere theoretically enunciated are seen here in their free application. In some respects, this effort is one of a more severely scientific character than is often the case with Augustin. It displays much less digression than is customary with him. The tendency to extravagant allegorizing is also less frequently indulged in, although it does come to the surface at times, as in the notable example of the interpretation of the names *Leah* and *Rachel*. His inordinate dependence upon the Septuagint, however, is as broadly marked here as anywhere. As he sometimes indicates an inclination to accept the story of Aristeas, in this composition he almost goes the length of claiming a special inspiration for these translators. On the other hand, in many passages we have the privilege of seeing his resolve to be no uncritical expositor. He pauses often to chronicle varieties of reading, sometimes in the Latin text and sometimes in the Greek. Thus he notices the occurrence of *Lebbæus* for *Thaddæus*, of *Dalmanutha* for *Magedan*, and the like, and mentions how some codices read *woman* for *maid*, in the sentence, *The maid is not dead, but sleepeth* (Matt. ix. 24).

His principles of harmonizing are ordinarily characterized by simplicity and good sense. In general, he surmounts the difficulty of what may seem at first sight discordant versions of one incident, by supposing different instances of the same circumstances, or repeated utterances of the same words. He holds emphatically by the position, that wherever it is possible to believe two similar incidents to have taken place, no contradiction can legitimately be alleged, although no Evangelist may relate them both together. All merely verbal variations in the records of the same occurrence he regards as matters of too little consequence to create any serious perplexity to the student whose aim is honestly to reach the sense intended. Such narratives as those of the storm upon the lake, the healing of the centurion's servant, and the denials of Peter, furnish good examples of his method, and of the fair and fearless spirit of his inquiry. And however unsuccessful we may now judge some of his endeavours, when we consider the comparative poverty of his materials, and the untrodden field which he essayed to search, we shall not deny to this treatise the merit of grandeur in original conception, and exemplary faithfulness in actual execution.

S. D. F. S.

CONTENTS OF THE TREATISE ON "THE HARMONY OF THE GOSPELS."

BOOK I.

BOOK II.

BOOK III.

BOOK IV.

THE HARMONY OF THE GOSPELS.

BOOK I.

THE TREATISE OPENS WITH A SHORT STATEMENT ON THE SUBJECT OF THE AUTHORITY OF THE EVANGELISTS, THEIR NUMBER, THEIR ORDER, AND THE DIFFERENT PLANS OF THEIR NARRATIVES. AUGUSTIN THEN PREPARES FOR THE DISCUSSION OF THE QUESTIONS RELATING TO THEIR HARMONY, BY JOINING ISSUE IN THIS BOOK WITH THOSE WHO RAISE A DIFFICULTY IN THE CIRCUMSTANCE THAT CHRIST HAS LEFT NO WRITING OF HIS OWN, OR WHO FALSELY ALLEGE THAT CERTAIN BOOKS WERE COMPOSED BY HIM ON THE ARTS OF MAGIC. HE ALSO MEETS THE OBJECTIONS OF THOSE WHO, IN OPPOSITION TO THE EVANGELICAL TEACHING, ASSERT THAT THE DISCIPLES OF CHRIST AT ONCE ASCRIBED MORE TO THEIR MASTER THAN HE REALLY WAS, WHEN THEY AFFIRMED THAT HE WAS GOD, AND INCULCATED WHAT THEY HAD NOT BEEN INSTRUCTED IN BY HIM, WHEN THEY INTERDICTED THE WORSHIP OF THE GODS. AGAINST THESE ANTAGONISTS HE VINDICATES THE TEACHING OF THE APOSTLES, BY APPEALING TO THE UTTERANCES OF THE PROPHETS, AND BY SHOWING THAT THE GOD OF ISRAEL WAS TO BE THE SOLE OBJECT OF WORSHIP, WHO ALSO, ALTHOUGH HE WAS THE ONLY DEITY TO WHOM ACCEPTANCE WAS DENIED IN FORMER TIMES BY THE ROMANS, AND THAT FOR THE VERY REASON THAT HE PROHIBITED THEM FROM WORSHIPPING OTHER GODS ALONG WITH HIMSELF, HAS NOW IN THE END MADE THE EMPIRE OF ROME SUBJECT TO HIS NAME, AND AMONG ALL NATIONS HAS BROKEN THEIR IDOLS IN PIECES THROUGH THE PREACHING OF THE GOSPEL, AS HE HAD PROMISED BY HIS PROPHETS THAT THE EVENT SHOULD BE.

CHAP. I. — ON THE AUTHORITY OF THE GOSPELS.

1. IN the entire number of those divine records which are contained in the sacred writings, the gospel deservedly stands pre-eminent. For what the law and the prophets aforetime announced as destined to come to pass, is exhibited in the gospel in its realization [1] and fulfilment. The first preachers of this gospel were the apostles, who beheld our Lord and Saviour Jesus Christ in person when He was yet present in the flesh. And not only did these [2] men keep in remembrance the words heard from His lips, and the deeds wrought by Him beneath their eyes; but they were also careful, when the duty of preaching the gospel was laid upon them, to make mankind acquainted with those divine and memorable occurrences which took place at a period antecedent to the formation of their own connection with Him in the way of discipleship, which belonged also to the time of His nativity, His infancy, or His youth, and with regard to which they were able to institute exact inquiry and to obtain information, either at His own hand or at the hands of His parents or other parties, on the ground of the most reliable intimations and the most trustworthy testimonies. Certain of them also — namely, Matthew and John — gave to the world, in their respective books, a written account of all those matters which it seemed needful to commit to writing concerning Him.

2. And to preclude the supposition that, in what concerns the apprehension and proclamation of the gospel, it is a matter of any consequence whether the enunciation comes by men who were actual followers of this same Lord here

---

[1] Reading *redditum*. Four MSS. give *revelatum* = as brought to light. — MIGNE.
[2] Instead of *Qui non solum,* as above, many MSS. read *Cujus,* etc. — MIGNE.

when He manifested Himself in the flesh and had the company of His disciples attendant on Him, or by persons who with due credit received facts with which they became acquainted in a trustworthy manner through the instrumentality of these former, divine providence, through the agency of the Holy Spirit, has taken care that certain of those also who were nothing more than followers of the first apostles should have authority given them not only to preach the gospel, but also to compose an account of it in writing. I refer to Mark and Luke. All those other individuals, however, who have attempted or dared to offer a written record of the acts of the Lord or of the apostles, failed to commend themselves in their own times as men of the character which would induce the Church to yield them its confidence, and to admit their compositions to the canonical authority of the Holy Books. And this was the case not merely because they were persons who could make no rightful claim to have credit given them in their narrations, but also because in a deceitful manner they introduced into their writings certain matters which are condemned at once by the catholic and apostolic rule of faith, and by sound doctrine.[1]

CHAP. II. — ON THE ORDER OF THE EVANGELISTS, AND THE PRINCIPLES ON WHICH THEY WROTE.

3. Now, those four evangelists whose names have gained the most remarkable circulation[2] over the whole world, and whose number has been fixed as four, — it may be for the simple reason that there are four divisions of that world through the universal length of which they, by their number as by a kind of mystical sign, indicated the advancing extension of the Church of Christ, — are believed to have written in the order which follows: first Matthew, then Mark, thirdly Luke, lastly John. Hence, too, [it would appear that] these had one order determined among them with regard to the matters of their personal knowledge and their preaching [of the gospel], but a different order in reference to the task of giving the written narrative. As far, indeed, as concerns the acquisition of their own knowledge and the charge of preaching, those unquestionably came first in order who were actually followers of the Lord when He was present in the flesh, and who heard Him speak and saw Him act; and [with a commission received] from His lips they were despatched to preach the gospel. But as respects the task of composing that record of the gospel which is to be accepted as ordained by divine authority, there

were (only) two, belonging to the number of those whom the Lord chose before the passover, that obtained places, — namely, the first place and the last. For the first place in order was held by Matthew, and the last by John. And thus the remaining two, who did not belong to the number referred to, but who at the same time had become followers of the Christ who spoke in these others, were supported on either side by the same, like sons who were to be embraced, and who in this way were set in the midst between these twain.

4. Of these four, it is true, only Matthew is reckoned to have written in the Hebrew language; the others in Greek. And however they may appear to have kept each of them a certain order of narration proper to himself, this certainly is not to be taken as if each individual writer chose to write in ignorance of what his predecessor had done, or left out as matters about which there was no information things which another nevertheless is discovered to have recorded. But the fact is, that just as they received each of them the gift of inspiration, they abstained from adding to their several labours any superfluous conjoint compositions. For Matthew is understood to have taken it in hand to construct the record of the incarnation of the Lord according to the royal lineage, and to give an account of most part of His deeds and words as they stood in relation to this present life of men. Mark follows him closely, and looks like his attendant and epitomizer.[3] For in his narrative he gives nothing in concert with John apart from the others: by himself separately, he has little to record; in conjunction with Luke, as distinguished from the rest, he has still less; but in concord with Matthew, he has a very large number of passages. Much, too, he narrates in words almost numerically and identically the same as those 'used by Matthew, where the agreement is either with that evangelist alone, or with him in connection with the rest. On the other hand, Luke appears to have occupied himself rather with the priestly lineage and character[4] of the Lord. For although in his own way he carries the descent back to David, what he has followed is not the royal pedigree, but the line of those who were not kings. That genealogy, too, he has brought to a point in Nathan the son of David,[5] which person likewise was no king. It is not thus, however, with Matthew. For in tracing the lineage along through Solomon the king,[6] he has pursued with strict regularity the succession of the other kings; and in enumerating these,

---

[1] [The character of the Apocryphal Gospels is obvious. The reference of Luke (i. 1) is probably to fragmentary records, now lost. Comp. below Book iv. chap. 8. — R.]
[2] *Notissimi.*

[3] [This opinion is not only unwarranted, since Mark shows greater signs of originality, but it has been prejudicial to the correct appreciation of the Gospel of Mark. The verbal identity of Matthew and Mark in parallel passages is far less than commonly supposed. — R.]
[4] *Personam.*   [5] Luke iii. 31.   [6] Matt. i. 6.

he has also conserved that mystical number of which we shall speak hereafter.

CHAP. III. — OF THE FACT THAT MATTHEW, TOGETHER WITH MARK, HAD SPECIALLY IN VIEW THE KINGLY CHARACTER OF CHRIST, WHEREAS LUKE DEALT WITH THE PRIESTLY.

5. For the Lord Jesus Christ, who is the one true King and the one true Priest, the former to rule us, and the latter to make expiation for us, has shown us how His own figure bore these two parts together, which were only separately commended [to notice] among the Fathers.[1] This becomes apparent if (for example) we look to that inscription which was affixed to His cross — "King of the Jews: " in connection also with which, and by a secret instinct, Pilate replied, "What I have written, I have written."[2] For it had been said aforetime in the Psalms, "Destroy not the writing of the title."[3] The same becomes evident, so far as the part of priest is concerned, if we have regard to what He has taught us concerning offering and receiving. For thus it is that He sent us beforehand a prophecy[4] respecting Himself, which runs thus, "Thou art a priest for ever, after the order of Melchisedek."[5] And in many other testimonies of the divine Scriptures, Christ appears both as King and as Priest. Hence, also, even David himself, whose son He is, not without good reason, more frequently declared to be than he is said to be Abraham's son, and whom Matthew and Luke have both alike held by, — the one viewing him as the person from whom, through Solomon, His lineage can be traced down, and the other taking him for the person to whom, through Nathan, His genealogy can be carried up, — did represent the part of a priest, although he was patently a king, when he ate the shew-bread. For it was not lawful for any one to eat that, save the priests only.[6] To this it must be added that Luke is the only one who mentions how Mary was discovered by the angel, and how she was related to Elisabeth,[7] who was the wife of Zacharias the priest. And of this Zacharias the same evangelist has recorded the fact, that the woman whom he had for wife was one of the daughters of Aaron, which is to say she belonged to the tribe of the priests.[8]

6. Whereas, then, Matthew had in view the kingly character, and Luke the priestly, they have at the same time both set forth pre-eminently the humanity of Christ: for it was according to His humanity that Christ was made both King and Priest. To Him, too, God gave the throne of His father David, in order that of His kingdom there should be none end.[9] And this was done with the purpose that there might be a mediator between God and men, the man Christ Jesus,[10] to make intercession for us. Luke, on the other hand, had no one connected with him to act as his summarist in the way that Mark was attached to Matthew. And it may be that this is not without a certain solemn significance.[11] For it is the right of kings not to miss the obedient following of attendants; and hence the evangelist, who had taken it in hand to give an account of the kingly character of Christ, had a person attached to him as his associate who was in some fashion to follow in his steps. But inasmuch as it was the priest's wont to enter all alone into the holy of holies, in accordance with that principle, Luke, whose object contemplated the priestly office of Christ, did not have any one to come after him as a confederate, who was meant in some way to serve as an epitomizer of his narrative.[12]

CHAP. IV. — OF THE FACT THAT JOHN UNDERTOOK THE EXPOSITION OF CHRIST'S DIVINITY.

7. These three evangelists, however, were for the most part engaged with those things which Christ did through the vehicle of the flesh of man, and after the temporal fashion.[13] But John, on the other hand, had in view that true divinity of the Lord in which He is the Father's equal, and directed his efforts above all to the setting forth of the divine nature in his Gospel in such a way as he believed to be adequate to men's needs and notions.[14] Therefore he is borne to loftier heights, in which he leaves the other three far behind him; so that, while in them you see men who have their conversation in a certain manner with the man Christ on earth, in him you perceive one who has passed beyond the cloud in which the whole earth is wrapped, and who has reached the liquid heaven from which, with clearest and steadiest mental eye, he is able to look upon God the Word, who was in the beginning with God, and by whom all things were made.[15] And there, too, he can recognise Him who was made flesh in order that He might dwell amongst us;[16] [that Word of whom we say,] that He assumed the flesh, not that He was changed into the flesh. For had not this assumption of the

---

[1] Some editions insert *antiquos*, the *ancient* Fathers; but the MSS. omit it. — MIGNE.
[2] John xix. 19-22.   [3] Ps. lxxv. 1.
[4] Two MSS. give *prophetam* (" prophet ") instead of *prophetiam* (" prophecy "). — MIGNE.
[5] Ps. cx. 4.   [6] 1 Sam. xxi. 6; Matt. xii. 3.
[7] The reading supported by the manuscripts is: *Mariam commemorat ab Angelo manifestatam cognatam fuisse Elisabeth.* It is sometimes given thus: *Mariam commemorat manifeste cognatam*, etc = mentions that Mary was clearly related to Elizabeth.
[8] Luke i. 36, 5.

[9] Luke i. 32.   [10] 1 Tim. ii. 5.
[11] *Sine aliquo sacramento.*
[12] [Here we have a mystical meaning attached to an opinion unwarranted by facts. Yet Augustin's mystical treatment of the " Synoptic problem " is, with all its faults, not more fanciful and extravagant than some of the modern " critical " solutions of the same problem. — R.]
[13] *Temporaliter.*
[14] *Quantum inter homines sufficere credidit.*
[15] John i. 1, 3.   [16] John i. 14.

flesh been effected in such a manner as at the same time to conserve the unchangeable Divinity, such a word as this could never have been spoken,—namely, " I and the Father are one."[1] For surely the Father and the flesh are not one. And the same John is also the only one who has recorded that witness which the Lord gave concerning Himself, when He said : " He that hath seen me, hath seen the Father also ;" and, " I am in the Father, and the Father is in me ;"[2] "that they may be one, even as we are one ;"[3] and, "Whatsoever the Father doeth, these same things doeth the Son likewise."[4] And whatever other statements there may be to the same effect, calculated to betoken, to those who are possessed of right understanding, that divinity of Christ in which He is the Father's equal, of all these we might almost say that we are indebted for their introduction into the Gospel narrative to John alone. For he is like one who has drunk in the secret of His divinity more richly and somehow more familiarly than others, as if he drew it from the very bosom of his Lord on which it was his wont to recline when He sat at meat.[5]

CHAP. V. — CONCERNING THE TWO VIRTUES, OF WHICH JOHN IS CONVERSANT WITH THE CONTEMPLATIVE, THE OTHER EVANGELISTS WITH THE ACTIVE.

8. Moreover, there are two several virtues (or talents) which have been proposed to the mind of man. Of these, the one is the active, and the other the contemplative : the one being that whereby the way is taken, and the other that whereby the goal is reached ;[6] the one that by which men labour in order that the heart may be purified to see God, and the other that by which men are disengaged[7] and God is seen. Thus the former of these two virtues is occupied with the precepts for the right exercise of the temporal life, whereas the latter deals with the doctrine of that life which is everlasting. In this way, also, the one operates, the other rests ; for the former finds its sphere in the purging of sins, the latter moves in the light[8] of the purged. And thus, again, in this mortal life the one is engaged with the work of a good conversation ; while the other subsists rather on faith, and is seen only in the person of the very few, and through the glass darkly, and only in part in a kind of vision of the unchangeable truth.[9] Now these two virtues are understood to be presented emblematically in the instance of the two wives of Jacob. Of these I have discoursed already up to the measure of my ability, and as fully as seemed to be appropriate

to my task, (in what I have written) in opposition to Faustus the Manichæan.[10] For Lia, indeed, by interpretation means " labouring,"[11] whereas Rachel signifies " the first principle seen."[12] And by this it is given us to understand, if one will only attend carefully to the matter, that those three evangelists who, with pre-eminent fulness, have handled the account of the Lord's temporal doings and those of His sayings which were meant to bear chiefly upon the moulding of the manners of the present life, were conversant with that active virtue ; and that John, on the other hand, who narrates fewer by far of the Lord's doings, but records with greater carefulness and with larger wealth of detail the words which He spoke, and most especially those discourses which were intended to introduce us to the knowledge of the unity of the Trinity and the blessedness of the life eternal, formed his plan and framed his statemnent with a view to commend the contemplative virtue to our regard.

CHAP. VI. — OF THE FOUR LIVING CREATURES IN THE APOCALYPSE, WHICH HAVE BEEN TAKEN BY SOME IN ONE APPLICATION, AND BY OTHERS IN ANOTHER, AS APT FIGURES OF THE FOUR EVANGELISTS.

9. For these reasons, it also appears to me, that of the various parties who have interpreted the living creatures in the Apocalypse as significant of the four evangelists, those who have taken the lion to point to Matthew, the man to Mark, the calf to Luke, and the eagle to John, have made a more reasonable application of the figures than those who have assigned the man to Matthew, the eagle to Mark, and the lion to John.[13] For, in forming their particular idea of

---

[1] John x. 30.   [2] John xiv. 9, 10.   [3] John xvii. 22.
[4] John v. 19.   [5] John xiii. 23.
[6] Illa qua itur, ista qua pervenitur.   [7] Qua vacatur.
[8] Reading lumine ; but one of the Vatican MSS. gives in illuminatione, in the enlightenment of the purged.
[9] 1 Cor. xiii. 12.

[10] Book xxii. 52.   [11] Laborans.
[12] Visum principium. In various editions it is given as visus principium. The MSS. have visum principium. In the passage referred to in the treatise against Faustus the Manichæan, Augustin appends the explanation, sive verbum ex quo videtur principium, = the first principle seen, or the word by which the first principle is seen. The etymologies on which Augustin proceeds may perhaps be these: for Leah, the Hebrew verb Laah, to be wearied (לָאָה) ; and for Rachel the Hebrew forms Raah = see, and Chalal = begin (רָאָה, חָלַל). For another example of extravagant allegorizing on the two wives of Jacob, see Justin Martyr's Dialogue with Trypho, chap. cxl. — Tr.
[13] [The latter application is that of Irenæus (Adv. Hær. iii.) ; but the prevalent application is that of Jerome, which is accepted in mediæval art. It differs from that of Augustin (see table below). As a curious illustration of the fanciful character of such interpretations, the reader may consult the following table, which gives the order of the following living creatures in Rev. iv. 7, with some of the leading " applications."

Rev. iv. 7.	Irenæus.	Augustin.	Jerome.	Lange, Stier.
1. Lion . . .	John.	Matthew.	Mark.	Mark.
2. Calf . . .	Luke.	Luke.	Luke.	Matthew.
3. Man . . .	Matthew.	Mark.	Matthew.	Luke.
4. Eagle . . .	Mark.	John.	John.	John.

No doubt further variations could be discovered. Comp. Schaff's Church History, rev. ed. vol. i. 585–589. — R.]

the matter, these latter have chosen to keep in view simply the beginnings of the books, and not the full design of the several evangelists in its completeness, which was the matter that should, above all, have been thoroughly examined. For surely it is with much greater propriety that the one who has brought under our notice most largely the kingly character of Christ, should be taken to be represented by the lion. Thus is it also that we find the lion mentioned in conjunction with the royal tribe itself, in that passage of the Apocalypse where it is said, "The lion of the tribe of Judah hath prevailed."[1] For in Matthew's narrative the magi are recorded to have come from the east to inquire after the King, and to worship Him whose birth was notified to them by the star. Thus, too, Herod, who himself also was a king, is [said there to be] afraid of the royal child, and to put so many little children to death in order to make sure that the one might be slain.[2] Again, that Luke is intended under the figure of the calf, in reference to the pre-eminent sacrifice made by the priest, has been doubted by neither of the two [sets of interpreters]. For in that Gospel the narrator's account commences with Zacharias the priest. In it mention is also made of the relationship between Mary and Elisabeth.[3] In it, too, it is recorded that the ceremonies proper to the earliest priestly service were attended to in the case of the infant Christ ;[4] and a careful examination brings a variety of other matters under our notice in this Gospel, by which it is made apparent that Luke's object was to deal with the part of the priest. In this way it follows further, that Mark, who has set himself neither to give an account of the kingly lineage, nor to expound anything distinctive of the priesthood, whether on the subject of the relationship or on that of the consecration, and who at the same time comes before us as one who handles the things which the man Christ did, appears to be indicated simply under the figure of the man among those four living creatures. But again, those three living creatures, whether lion, man, or calf, have their course upon this earth ; and in like manner, those three evangelists occupy themselves chiefly with the things which Christ did in the flesh, and with the precepts which He delivered to men, who also bear the burden of the flesh, for their instruction in the rightful exercise of this mortal life. Whereas John, on the other hand, soars like an eagle above the clouds of human infirmity, and gazes upon the light of the unchangeable truth with those keenest and steadiest eyes of the heart.[5]

CHAP. VII. — A STATEMENT OF AUGUSTIN'S REASON FOR UNDERTAKING THIS WORK ON THE HARMONY OF THE EVANGELISTS, AND AN EXAMPLE OF THE METHOD IN WHICH HE MEETS THOSE WHO ALLEGE THAT CHRIST WROTE NOTHING HIMSELF, AND THAT HIS DISCIPLES MADE AN UNWARRANTED AFFIRMATION IN PROCLAIMING HIM TO BE GOD.

10. Those sacred chariots of the Lord,[6] however, in which He is borne throughout the earth and brings the peoples under His easy yoke and His light burden, are assailed with calumnious charges by certain persons who, in impious vanity or in ignorant temerity, think to rob of their credit as veracious historians those teachers by whose instrumentality the Christian religion has been disseminated all the world over, and through whose efforts it has yielded fruits so plentiful that unbelievers now scarcely dare so much as to mutter their slanders in private among themselves, kept in check by the faith of the Gentiles and by the devotion of all the peoples. Nevertheless, inasmuch as they still strive by their calumnious disputations to keep some from making themselves acquainted with the faith, and thus prevent them from becoming believers, while they also endeavour to the utmost of their power to excite agitations among others who have already attained to belief, and thereby give them trouble ; and further, as there are some brethren who, without detriment to their own faith, have a desire to ascertain what answer can be given to such questions, either for the advantage of their own knowledge or for the purpose of refuting the vain utterances of their enemies, with the inspiration and help of the Lord our God (and would that it might prove profitable for the salvation of such men), we have undertaken in this work to demonstrate the errors or the rashness of those who deem themselves able to prefer charges, the subtilty of which is at least sufficiently observable, against those four different books of the gospel which have been written by these four several evangelists. And in order to carry out this design to a successful conclusion, we must prove that the writers in question do not stand in any antagonism to each other. For those adversaries are in the habit of adducing this as the palmary[7] allegation in all their vain objections, namely, that the evangelists are not in harmony with each other.

11. But we must first discuss a matter which is apt to present a difficulty to the minds of some. I refer to the question why the Lord has written nothing Himself, and why He has thus

---

[1] Rev. v. 5.   [2] Matt. ii. 1-18.
[3] Luke i. 5, 36.   [4] Luke ii. 22-24.
[5] See also *Tract.* 36, on John i. 5. [This figure of Augustin has controlled all the subsequent symbolism respecting the Evangelist John, and has been constantly cited by commentators. — R.]

[6] *Has Domini sanctas quadrigas.*
[7] Reading either *palmam suæ vanitatis objicere*, or with several MSS. *palmare*, etc.

left us to the necessity of accepting the testimony of other persons who have prepared records of His history. For this is what those parties — the pagans more than any [1] — allege when they lack boldness enough to impeach or blaspheme the Lord Jesus Christ Himself, and when they allow Him — only as a man, however — to have been possessed of the most distinguished wisdom. In making that admission, they at the same time assert that the disciples claimed more for their Master than He really was; so much more indeed that they even called Him the Son of God, and the Word of God, by whom all things were made, and affirmed that He and God are one. And in the same way they dispose of all other kindred passages in the epistles of the apostles, in the light of which we have been taught that He is to be worshipped as one God with the Father. For they are of opinion that He is certainly to be honoured as the wisest of men; but they deny that He is to be worshipped as God.

12. Wherefore, when they put the question why He has not written in His own person, it would seem as if they were prepared to believe regarding Him whatever He might have written concerning Himself, but not what others may have given the world to know with respect to His life, according to the measure of their own judgment. Well, I ask them in turn why, in the case of certain of the noblest of their own philosophers, they have accepted the statements which their disciples left in the records they have composed, while these sages themselves have given us no written accounts of their own lives? For Pythagoras, than whom Greece in those days [2] did not possess any more illustrious personage in the sphere of that contemplative virtue, is believed to have written absolutely nothing, whether on the subject of his own personal history or on any other theme whatsoever. And as to Socrates, to whom, on the other hand, they have adjudged a position of supremacy above all others in that active virtue by which the moral life is trained, so that they do not hesitate also to aver that he was even pronounced to be the wisest of men by the testimony of their deity Apollo, — it is indeed true that he handled the fables of Æsop in some few short verses, and thus made use of words and numbers of his own in the task of rendering the themes of another. But this was all. And so far was he from having the desire to write anything himself, that he declared that he had done even so much only because he was constrained by the imperial will of his demon, as Plato, the noblest of all his disciples, tells us. That was a work, also, in which he sought to set forth in fair form not so much his

own thoughts, as rather the ideas of another. What reasonable ground, therefore, have they for believing, with regard to those sages, all that their disciples have committed to record in respect of their history, while at the same time they refuse to credit in the case of Christ what His disciples have written on the subject of His life? And all the more may we thus argue, when we see how they admit that all other men have been excelled by Him in the matter of wisdom, although they decline to acknowledge Him to be God. Is it, indeed, the case that those persons whom they do not hesitate to allow to have been by far His inferiors, have had the faculty of making disciples who can be trusted in all that concerns the narrative of their careers, and that He failed in that capacity? But if that is a most absurd statement to venture upon, then in all that belongs to the history of that Person to whom they grant the honour of wisdom, they ought to believe not merely what suits their own notions, but what they read in the narratives of those who learned from this sage Himself those various facts which they have left on record on the subject of His life.

CHAP. VIII. — OF THE QUESTION WHY, IF CHRIST IS BELIEVED TO HAVE BEEN THE WISEST OF MEN ON THE TESTIMONY OF COMMON NARRATIVE REPORT, HE SHOULD NOT BE BELIEVED TO BE GOD ON THE TESTIMONY OF THE SUPERIOR REPORT OF PREACHING.

13. Besides this, they ought to tell us by what means they have succeeded in acquiring their knowledge of this fact that He was the wisest of men, or how it has had the opportunity of reaching their ears. If they have been made acquainted with it simply by current report, then is it the case that common report forms a more trustworthy informant [3] on the subject of His history than those disciples of His who, as they have gone and preached of Him, have disseminated the same report like a penetrating savour throughout the whole world? [4] In fine, they ought to prefer the one kind of report to the other, and believe that account of His life which is the superior of the two. For this report, [5] indeed, which is spread abroad with a wonderful clearness from that Church catholic [6] at whose extension through the whole world those persons are so astonished, prevails in an incomparable fashion over the unsubstantial rumours with which men like them occupy themselves. This report, furthermore, which carries with it such weight and such currency, [7] that in dread of it they can

---

[1] Vel maxime pagani.
[2] Six MSS. omit the tunc, at that time. — MIGNE.

[3] Instead of de illo nuntia fama est, fourteen MSS. give de illo fama nuntiata est = is it a more trustworthy report that has been announced. — MIGNE.
[4] Quibus eum prædicantibus ipsa per totum mundum fama fragravit?
[5] Fama.   [6] De catholica ecclesia.   [7] Celebris.

only mutter their anxious and feeble snatches of paltry objections within their own breasts, as if they were more afraid now of being heard than wishful to receive credit, proclaims Christ to be the only-begotten Son of God, and Himself God,[1] by whom all things were made. If, therefore, they choose report as their witness, why does not their choice fix on this special report, which is so pre-eminently lustrous in its remarkable definiteness? And if they desire the evidence of writings, why do they not take those evangelical writings which excel all others in their commanding authority? On our side, indeed, we accept those statements about their deities which are offered at once in their most ancient writings and by most current report. But if these deities are to be considered proper objects for reverence, why then do they make them the subject of laughter in the theatres? And if, on the other hand, they are proper objects for laughter, the occasion for such laughter must be all the greater when they are made the objects of worship in the theatres. It remains for us to look upon those persons as themselves minded to be witnesses concerning Christ, who, by speaking what they know not, divest themselves of the merit of knowing what they speak about. Or if, again, they assert that they are possessed of any books which they can maintain to have been written by Him, they ought to produce them for our inspection. For assuredly those books (if there are such) must be most profitable and most wholesome, seeing they are the productions of one whom they acknowledge to have been the wisest of men. If, however, they are afraid to produce them, it must be because they are of evil tendency; but if they are evil, then the wisest of men cannot have written them. They acknowledge Christ, however, to be the wisest of men, and consequently Christ cannot have written any such thing.

CHAP. IX. — OF CERTAIN PERSONS WHO PRETEND THAT CHRIST WROTE BOOKS ON THE ARTS OF MAGIC.

14. But, indeed, these persons rise to such a pitch of folly as to allege that the books which they consider to have been written by Him contain the arts by which they think He wrought those miracles, the fame of which has become prevalent in all quarters. And this fancy of theirs betrays what they really love, and what

their aims really are. For thus, indeed, they show us how they entertain this opinion that Christ was the wisest of men only for the reason that He possessed the knowledge of I know not what illicit arts, which are justly condemned, not merely by Christian discipline, but even by the administration of earthly government itself. And, in good sooth, if there are people who affirm that they have read books of this nature composed by Christ, then why do they not perform with their own hand some such works as those which so greatly excite their wonder when wrought by Him, by taking advantage of the information which they have derived from these books?

CHAP. X. — OF SOME WHO ARE MAD ENOUGH TO SUPPOSE THAT THE BOOKS WERE INSCRIBED WITH THE NAMES OF PETER AND PAUL.

15. Nay more, as by divine judgment, some of those who either believe, or wish to have it believed, that Christ wrote matter of that description, have even wandered so far into error as to allege that these same books bore on their front, in the form of epistolary superscription, a designation addressed to Peter and Paul. And it is quite possible that either the enemies of the name of Christ, or certain parties who thought that they might impart to this kind of execrable arts the weight of authority drawn from so glorious a name, may have written things of that nature under the name of Christ and the apostles. But in such most deceitful audacity they have been so utterly blinded as simply to have made themselves fitting objects for laughter, even with young people who as yet know Christian literature only in boyish fashion, and rank merely in the grade of readers.

16. For when they made up their minds to represent Christ to have written in such strain as that to His disciples, they bethought themselves of those of His followers who might best be taken for the persons to whom Christ might most readily be believed to have written, as the individuals who had kept by Him on the most familiar terms of friendship. And so Peter and Paul occurred to them, I believe, just because in many places they chanced to see these two apostles represented in pictures as both in company with Him.[2] For Rome, in a specially honourable and solemn manner,[3] commends the merits of Peter and of Paul, for this reason among others, namely, that they suffered [martyrdom] on the same day. Thus to fall most completely into error was the due desert of men who sought for Christ and His apostles not in the holy writings, but on painted walls. Neither

---

[1] The words stand, as above, in the great majority of MSS.: *tam celebris, ut eam timendo isti trepidas et tepidas contradictiunculas in sinu suo rodant, jam plus metuentes audiri quam volentes credi, Filium Dei Unigenitum et Deum prædicat Christum?* In some MSS. and editions the sense is altered by inserting *est* after *celebris*, and substituting *nolentes* for *volentes*, and *prædicari* for *prædicat;* so that it becomes = that report is of such distinguished currency, that in dread of it they can only mutter, etc. . . . as now rather fearing to be heard than refusing to admit the belief that Christ is proclaimed to be the only-begotten Son of God, etc. See Migne. — TR.

[2] *Simul eos cum illo pictos viderent.*

[3] The text gives *diem celebrius solemniter*, etc.; others give *diem celebrius et solemniter;* and three MSS. have *diem celeberrimum solemniter*. — MIGNE.

is it to be wondered at, that these fiction-limners were misled by the painters.[1] For throughout the whole period during which Christ lived in our mortal flesh in fellowship with His disciples, Paul had never become His disciple. Only after His passion, after His resurrection, after His ascension, after the mission of the Holy Spirit from heaven, after many Jews had been converted and had shown marvellous faith, after the stoning of Stephen the deacon and martyr, and when Paul still bore the name Saul, and was grievously persecuting those who had become believers in Christ, did Christ call that man [by a voice] from heaven, and made him His disciple and apostle.[2] How, then, is it possible that Christ could have written those books which they wish to have it believed that He did write before His death, and which were addressed to Peter and Paul, as those among His disciples who had been most intimate with Him, seeing that up to that date Paul had not yet become a disciple of His at all?

CHAP. XI. — IN OPPOSITION TO THOSE WHO FOOLISHLY IMAGINE THAT CHRIST CONVERTED THE PEOPLE TO HIMSELF BY MAGICAL ARTS.

17. Moreover, let those who madly fancy that it was by the use of magical arts that He was able to do the great things which He did, and that it was by the practice of such rites that He made His name a sacred thing to the peoples who were to be converted to Him, give their attention to this question, — namely, whether by the exercise of magical arts, and before He was born on this earth, He could also have filled with the Holy Spirit those mighty prophets who aforetime declared those very things concerning Him as things destined to come to pass, which we can now read in their accomplishment in the gospel, and which we can see in their present realization in the world. For surely, even if it was by magical arts that He secured worship for Himself, and that, too, after His death, it is not the case that He was a magician before He was born. Nay, for the office of prophesying on the subject of His coming, one nation had been most specially deputed; and the entire administration of that commonwealth was ordained to be a prophecy of this King who was to come, and who was to found a heavenly state[3] drawn out of all nations.

CHAP. XII. — OF THE FACT THAT THE GOD OF THE JEWS, AFTER THE SUBJUGATION OF THAT PEOPLE, WAS STILL NOT ACCEPTED BY THE ROMANS, BECAUSE HIS COMMANDMENT WAS THAT HE ALONE SHOULD BE WORSHIPPED, AND IMAGES DESTROYED.

18. Furthermore, that Hebrew nation, which,

as I have said, was commissioned to prophesy of Christ, had no other God but one God, the true God, who made heaven and earth, and all that therein is. Under His displeasure they were ofttimes given into the power of their enemies. And now, indeed, on account of their most heinous sin in putting Christ to death, they have been thoroughly rooted out of Jerusalem itself, which was the capital of their kingdom, and have been made subject to the Roman empire. Now the Romans were in the habit of propitiating[4] the deities of those nations whom they conquered by worshipping these themselves, and they were accustomed to undertake the charge of their sacred rites. But they declined to act on that principle with regard to the God of the Hebrew nation, either when they made their attack or when they reduced the people. I believe that they perceived that, if they admitted the worship of this Deity, whose commandment was that He only should be worshipped, and that images should be destroyed, they would have to put away from them all those objects to which formerly they had undertaken to do religious service, and by the worship of which they believed their empire had grown. But in this the falseness of their demons mightily deceived them. For surely they ought to have apprehended the fact that it is only by the hidden will of the true God, in whose hand resides the supreme power in all things, that the kingdom was given them and has been made to increase, and that their position was not due to the favour of those deities who, if they could have wielded any influence whatever in that matter, would rather have protected their own people from being over-mastered by the Romans, or would have brought the Romans themselves into complete subjection to them.

19. Certainly they cannot possibly affirm that the kind of piety and manners exemplified by them became objects of love and choice on the part of the gods of the nations which they conquered. They will never make such an assertion, if they only recall their own early beginnings, the asylum for abandoned criminals and the fratricide of Romulus. For when Remus and Romulus established their asylum, with the intention that whoever took refuge there, be the crime what it might be with which he stood charged, should enjoy impunity in his deed, they did not promulgate any precepts of penitence for bringing the minds of such wretched men back to a right condition. By this bribe of impunity did they not rather arm the gathered band of fearful fugitives against the states to which they properly belonged, and the laws of which they dreaded? Or when Romulus slew his brother, who had perpetrated no evil against

---

[1] A pingentibus fingentes decepti sunt.
[2] Acts ix. 1–30.   [3] Civitatem.

[4] The text gives deos . . . colendos propitiare. Five MSS. give deos . . . colendo propitiare. — MIGNE.

him, is it the case that his mind was bent on the vindication of justice, and not on the acquisition of absolute power? And is it true that the deities did take their delight in manners like these, as if they were themselves enemies to their own states, in so far as they favoured those who were the enemies of these communities? Nay rather, neither did they by deserting them harm the one class, nor did they by passing over to their side in any sense help the other. For they have it not in their power to give kingship or to remove it. But that is done by the one true God, according to His hidden counsel. And it is not His mind to make those necessarily blessed to whom He may have given an earthly kingdom, or to make those necessarily unhappy whom He has deprived of that position. But He makes men blessed or wretched for other reasons and by other means, and either by permission or by actual gift distributes temporal and earthly kingdoms to whomsoever He pleases, and for whatsoever period He chooses, according to the fore-ordained order of the ages.

CHAP. XIII. — OF THE QUESTION WHY GOD SUFFERED THE JEWS TO BE REDUCED TO SUBJECTION.

20. Hence also they cannot meet us fairly with this question: Why, then, did the God of the Hebrews, whom you declare to be the supreme and true God, not only not subdue the Romans under their power, but even fail to secure those Hebrews themselves against subjugation by the Romans? For there were open sins of theirs that went before them, and on account of which the prophets so long time ago predicted that this very thing would overtake them; and above all, the reason lay in the fact, that in their impious fury they put Christ to death, in the commission of which sin they were made blind [to the guilt of their crime] through the deserts of other hidden transgressions. That His sufferings also would be for the benefit of the Gentiles, was foretold by the same prophetic testimony. Nor, in another point of view, did the fact appear clearer, that the kingdom of that nation, and its temple, and its priesthood, and its sacrificial system, and that mystical unction which is called χρῖσμα[1] in Greek, from which the name of *Christ* takes its evident application, and on account of which that nation was accustomed to speak of its kings as *anointed ones*,[2] were ordained with the express object of prefiguring Christ, than has the kindred fact become apparent, that after the resurrection of the Christ who was put to death began to be preached unto the believing Gentiles, all those

things came to their end, all unrecognised as the circumstance was, whether by the Romans, through whose victory, or by the Jews, through whose subjugation, it was brought about that they did thus reach their conclusion.

CHAP. XIV. — OF THE FACT THAT THE GOD OF THE HEBREWS, ALTHOUGH THE PEOPLE WERE CONQUERED, PROVED HIMSELF TO BE UNCONQUERED, BY OVERTHROWING THE IDOLS, AND BY TURNING ALL THE GENTILES TO HIS OWN SERVICE.

21. Here indeed we have a wonderful fact, which is not remarked by those few pagans who have remained such, — namely, that this God of the Hebrews who was offended by the conquered, and who was also denied acceptance by the conquerors, is now preached and worshipped among all nations. This is that God of Israel of whom the prophet spake so long time since, when he thus addressed the people of God: "And He who brought thee out, the God of Israel, shall be called (the God) of the whole earth."[3] What was thus prophesied has been brought to pass through the name of the Christ, who comes to men in the form of a descendant of that very Israel who was the grandson of Abraham, with whom the race of the Hebrews began.[4] For it was to this Israel also that it was said, "In thy seed shall all the tribes of the earth be blessed."[5] Thus it is shown that the God of Israel, the true God who made heaven and earth, and who administers human affairs justly and mercifully in such wise that neither does justice exclude mercy with Him, nor does mercy hinder justice, was not overcome Himself when His Hebrew people suffered their overthrow, in virtue of His permitting the kingdom and priesthood of that nation to be seized and subverted by the Romans. For now, indeed, by the might of this gospel of Christ, the true King and Priest, the advent of which was prefigured by that kingdom and priesthood, the God of Israel Himself is everywhere destroying the idols of the nations. And, in truth, it was to prevent that destruction that the Romans refused to admit the sacred rites of this God in the way that they admitted those of the gods of the other nations whom they conquered. Thus did He remove both kingdom and priesthood from the prophetic nation, because He who was promised to men through the agency of that people had already come. And by Christ the King He has brought into

---

[3] *Et qui eruit te, Deus Israel, universæ terræ vocabitur.* Isa. liv. 5. [Compare the Hebrew, from which the Latin citation varies. — R.]
[4] In his *Retractations* (ii. 16) Augustin alludes to this sentence, and says that the word *Hebrews* (*Hebræi*) may be derived from *Abraham*, as if the original form had been *Abrahæi*, but that it is more correct to take it from *Heber*, so that *Hebræi* is for Heberæi. He refers us also to his discussion in the *City of God*, xvi. 11.
[5] Gen. xxviii. 14.

---

[1] *Chrism.*   [2] *Christos.*

subjection to His own name that Roman empire by which the said nation was overcome ; and by the strength and devotion of Christian faith, He has converted it so as to effect a subversion of those idols, the honour ascribed to which precluded His worship from obtaining entrance.

22. I am of opinion that it was not by means of magical arts that Christ, previous to His birth among men, brought it about that those things which were destined to come to pass in the course of His history, were pre-announced by so many prophets, and prefigured also by the kingdom and priesthood established in a certain nation. For the people who are connected with that now abolished kingdom, and who in the wonderful providence of God are scattered throughout all lands, have indeed remained without any unction from the true King and Priest ; in which anointing [1] the import of the name of Christ is plainly discovered. But notwithstanding this, they still retain remnants of some of their observances ; while, on the other hand, not even in their state of overthrow and subjugation have they accepted those Roman rites which are connected with the worship of idols. Thus they still keep the prophetic books as the witness of Christ ; and in this way in the documents of His enemies we find proof presented [2] of the truth of this Christ who is the subject of prophecy. What, then, do these unhappy men disclose themselves to be, by the unworthy method in which they laud [3] the name of Christ ? If anything relating to the practice of magic has been written under His name, while the doctrine of Christ is so vehemently antagonistic to such arts, these men ought rather in the light of this fact to gather some idea of the greatness of that name, by the addition of which even persons who live in opposition to His precepts endeavour to dignify their nefarious practices. For just as, in the course of the diverse errors of men, many persons have set up their varied heresies against the truth under the cover of His name, so the very enemies of Christ think that, for the purposes of gaining acceptance for opinions which they propound in opposition to the doctrine of Christ, they have no weight of authority at their service unless they have the name of Christ.

CHAP. XV. — OF THE FACT THAT THE PAGANS, WHEN CONSTRAINED TO LAUD CHRIST, HAVE LAUNCHED THEIR INSULTS AGAINST HIS DISCIPLES.

23. But what shall be said to this, if those vain eulogizers of Christ, and those crooked slanderers of the Christian religion, lack the daring to blaspheme Christ, for this particular reason that some of their philosophers, as Porphyry of Sicily [4] has given us to understand in his books, consulted their gods as to their response on the subject of [the claims of] Christ, and were constrained by their own oracles to laud Christ ? Nor should that seem incredible. For we also read in the Gospel that the demons confessed Him ; [5] and in our prophets it is written in this wise : " For the gods of the nations are demons." [6] Thus it happens, then, that in order to avoid attempting aught in opposition to the responses of their own deities, they turn their blasphemies aside from Christ, and pour them forth against His disciples. It seems to me, however, that these gods of the Gentiles, whom the philosophers of the pagans may have consulted, if they were asked to give their judgment on the disciples of Christ, as well as on Christ Himself, would be constrained to praise them in like manner.

CHAP. XVI. — OF THE FACT THAT, ON THE SUBJECT OF THE DESTRUCTION OF IDOLS, THE APOSTLES TAUGHT NOTHING DIFFERENT FROM WHAT WAS TAUGHT BY CHRIST OR BY THE PROPHETS.

24. Nevertheless these persons argue still to the effect that this demolition of temples, and this condemnation of sacrifices, and this shattering of all images, are brought about, not in virtue of the doctrine of Christ Himself, but only by the hand of His apostles, who, as they contend, taught something different from what He taught. They think by this device, while honouring and lauding Christ, to tear the Christian faith in pieces. For it is at least true, that it is by the disciples of Christ that at once the works and the words of Christ have been made known, on which this Christian religion is established, with which a very few people of this character are still in antagonism, who do not now indeed openly assail it, but yet continue even in these days to utter their mutterings against it. But if they refuse to believe that Christ taught in the way indicated, let them read the prophets, who not only enjoined the complete destruction of the superstitions of idols, but also predicted that this subversion would come to pass in Christian times. And if these spoke falsely, why is their word fulfilled with so mighty a demonstration ? But if they spoke truly, why is resistance offered to such divine power ? [7]

---

[1] Chrism.
[2] The text gives *probetur veritas Christi*, etc.; six MSS. give *profertur veritas*, etc. — MIGNE.
[3] Or *adduce — male laudando.*

[4] The philosopher of the Neo-Platonic school, better known as one of the earliest and most learned antagonists of Christianity. Though a native either of Tyre or Batanea, he is called here, as also again in the *Retractations*, ii. 31, a Sicilian, because, according to Jerome and Eusebius (*Hist. Eccles.* vi. 19), it was in Sicily that he wrote his treatise in fifteen books against the Christian religion. — TR.
[5] Luke iv. 41.
[6] Ps. xcvi. 5. [Comp 1 Cor. x. 20, where " demons " is the more correct rendering (so Revised Version margin and American revisers' text). — R.]
[7] Or, to such power in interpreting the divine mind — *tantæ divinitati resistatur.*

CHAP. XVII. — IN OPPOSITION TO THE ROMANS, WHO REJECTED THE GOD OF ISRAEL ALONE.

25. However, here is a matter which should meet with more careful consideration at their hands, — namely, what they take the God of Israel to be, and why they have not admitted Him to the honours of worship among them, in the way that they have done with the gods of other nations that have been made subject to the imperial power of Rome? This question demands an answer all the more, when we see that they are of the mind that all the gods ought to be worshipped by the man of wisdom. Why, then, has He been excluded from the number of these others? If He is very mighty, why is He the only deity that is not worshipped by them? If He has little or no might, why are the images of other gods broken in pieces by all the nations, while He is now almost the only God that is worshipped among these peoples? From the grasp of this question these men shall never be able to extricate themselves, who worship both the greater and the lesser deities, whom they hold to be gods, and at the same time refuse to worship this God, who has proved Himself stronger than all those to whom they do service. If He is [a God] of great virtue,[1] why has He been deemed worthy only of rejection? And if He is [a God] of little or no power, why has He been able to accomplish so much, although rejected? If He is good, why is He the only one separated from the other good deities? And if He is evil, why is He, who stands thus alone, not subjugated by so many good deities? If He is truthful, why are His precepts scorned? And if He is a liar, why are His predictions fulfilled?

CHAP. XVIII. — OF THE FACT THAT THE GOD OF THE HEBREWS IS NOT RECEIVED BY THE ROMANS, BECAUSE HIS WILL IS THAT HE ALONE SHOULD BE WORSHIPPED.

26. In fine, they may think of Him as they please. Still, we may ask whether it is the case that the Romans refuse to consider evil deities as also proper objects of worship, — those Romans who have erected fanes to Pallor and Fever, and who enjoin both that the good demons are to been treated,[2] and that the evil demons are to be propitiated. Whatever their opinion, then, of Him may be, the question still is, Why is He the only Deity whom they have judged worthy neither of being called upon for help, nor of being propitiated? What God is this, who is either one so unknown, that He is the only one not discovered as yet among so many gods, or who is one so well known that He is now the only one worshipped by so many men? There remains, then, nothing which they can possibly allege in explanation of their refusal to admit the worship of this God, except that His will was that He alone should be worshipped; and His command was, that those gods of the Gentiles that they were worshipping at the time should cease to be worshipped. But an answer to this other question is rather to be required of them, namely, what or what manner of deity they consider this God to be, who has forbidden the worship of those other gods for whom they erected temples and images, — this God, who has also been possessed of might so vast that His will has prevailed more in effecting the destruction of their images than theirs has availed to secure the non-admittance of His worship. And, indeed, the opinion of that philosopher of theirs is given in plain terms, whom, even on the authority of their own oracle, they have maintained to have been the wisest of all men. For the opinion of Socrates is, that every deity whatsoever ought to be worshipped just in the manner in which he may have ordained that he should be worshipped. Consequently it became a matter of the supremest necessity with them to refuse to worship the God of the Hebrews. For if they were minded to worship Him in a method different from the way in which He had declared that He ought to be worshipped, then assuredly they would have been worshipping not this God as He is, but some figment of their own. And, on the other hand, if they were willing to worship Him in the manner which He had indicated, then they could not but perceive that they were not at liberty to worship those other deities whom He interdicted them from worshipping. Thus was it, therefore, that they rejected the service of the one true God, because they were afraid that they might offend the many false gods. For they thought that the anger of those deities would be more to their injury, than the goodwill of this God would be to their profit.

CHAP. XIX. — THE PROOF THAT THIS GOD IS THE TRUE GOD.

27. But that must have been a vain necessity and a ridiculous timidity.[3] We ask now what opinion regarding this God is formed by those men whose pleasure it is that all gods ought to be worshipped. For if He ought not to be worshipped, how are all worshipped when He is not worshipped? And if He ought to be worshipped, it cannot be that all others are to be worshipped along with Him. For unless He is worshipped alone, He is really not worshipped

---

[1] Or, power — *virtutis*.
[2] The text gives *invitandos;* others read *imitandos*, to be imitated.

[3] Or, Away with that vain necessity and ridiculous timidity — *Sed fuerit ista vana necessitas*, etc.

at all. Or may it perhaps be the case, that they will allege Him to be no God at all, while they call those gods who, as we believe, have no power to do anything except so far as permission is given them by His judgment, — have not merely no power to do good to any one, but no power even to do harm to any, except to those who are judged by Him, who possesses all power, to merit so to be harmed? But, as they themselves are compelled to admit, those deities have shown less power than He has done. For if those are held to be gods whose prophets, when consulted by men, have returned responses which, that I may not call them false, were at least most convenient for their private interests, how is not He to be regarded as God whose prophets have not only given the congruous answer on subjects regarding which they were consulted at the special time, but who also, in the case of subjects respecting which they were not consulted, and which related to the universal race of man and all nations, have announced prophetically so long time before the event those very things of which we now read, and which indeed we now behold? If they gave the name of god to that being under whose inspiration the Sibyl sung of the fates [1] of the Romans, how is not He (to be called) God, who, in accordance with the announcement aforetime given, has shown us how the Romans and all nations are coming to believe in Himself through the gospel of Christ, as the one God, and to demolish all the images of their fathers? Finally, if they designate those as gods who have never dared through their prophets to say anything against this God, how is not He (to be designated) God, who not only commanded by the mouth of His prophets the destruction of their images, but who also predicted that among all the Gentiles they would be destroyed by those who should be enjoined to abandon their idols and to worship Him alone, and who, on receiving these injunctions, should be His servants? [2]

CHAP. XX. — OF THE FACT THAT NOTHING IS DISCOVERED TO HAVE BEEN PREDICTED BY THE PROPHETS OF THE PAGANS IN OPPOSITION TO THE GOD OF THE HEBREWS.

28. Or let them aver, if they are able, that some Sibyl of theirs, or any one whatever among their other prophets, announced long ago that it would come to pass that the God of the Hebrews, the God of Israel, would be worshipped by all nations, declaring, at the same time, that the worshippers of other gods before that time had rightly rejected Him; and again, that the

compositions of His prophets would be in such exalted authority,[3] that in obedience to them the Roman government itself would command the destruction of images, the said seers at the same time giving warning against acting upon such ordinances ; — let them, I say, read out any utterances like these, if they can, from any of the books of their prophets. For I stop not to state that those things which we can read in their books repeat a testimony on behalf of our religion, that is, the Christian religon, which they might have heard from the holy angels and from our prophets themselves ; just as the very devils were compelled to confess Christ when He was present in the flesh. But I pass by these matters, regarding which, when we bring them forward, their contention is that they were invented by our party. Most certainly, however, they may themselves be pressed to adduce anything which has been prophesied by the seers of their own gods against the God of the Hebrews ; as, on our side, we can point to declarations so remarkable at once for number and for weight recorded in the books of our prophets against their gods, in which also we can both note the command and recite the prediction and demonstrate the event. And over the realization of these things, that comparatively small number of heathens who have remained such are more inclined to grieve than they are ready to acknowledge that God who has had the power to foretell these things as events destined to be made good ; whereas in their dealings with their own false gods, who are genuine demons, they prize nothing else so highly as to be informed by their responses of something which is to take place with them.[4]

CHAP. XXI. — AN ARGUMENT FOR THE EXCLUSIVE WORSHIP OF THIS GOD, WHO, WHILE HE PROHIBITS OTHER DEITIES FROM BEING WORSHIPPED, IS NOT HIMSELF INTERDICTED BY OTHER DIVINITIES FROM BEING WORSHIPPED.

29. Seeing, then, that these things are so, why do not these unhappy men rather apprehend the fact that this God is the true God, whom they perceive to be placed in a position so thoroughly separated from the company of their own deities, that, although they are compelled to acknowledge Him to be God, those very persons who profess that all gods ought to be worshipped are nevertheless not permitted to worship Him along with the rest? Now, since these deities and this God cannot be worshipped together, why is not He selected who forbids those others to be worshipped ; and why are not

[1] Reading *fata*. Seven mss. give *facta* = deeds.
[2] [This reference to the destruction of idols has been used to fix the date of the *Harmony*: see Introductory Notice of translator. The polemic character of the larger part of Book i. seems due to the circumstances of that particular period in North Africa. — R.]
[3] Reading *futuras etiam litteras . . . in auctoritate ita sublimi*. Six mss. give *futurum . . . sublimari*, but with substantially the same sense.
[4] *Nihil aliud pro magno appetant quam cum aliquid eorum responsis sibi futurum esse didicerint.*

those deities abandoned, who do not interdict Him from being worshipped? Or if they do indeed forbid His worship, let the interdict be read. For what has greater claims to be recited to their people in their temples, in which the sound of no such thing has ever been heard? And, in good sooth, the prohibition directed by so many against one ought to be more notable [1] and more potent than the prohibition launched by one against so many. For if the worship of this God is impious, then those gods are profitless, who do not interdict men from that impiety; but if the worship of this God is pious, then, as in that worship the commandment is given that these others are not to be worshipped, their worship is impious. If, again, those deities forbid His worship, but only so diffidently that they rather fear to be heard [2] than dare to prohibit, who is so unwise as not to draw his own inference from the fact, who fails to perceive that this God ought to be chosen, who in so public a manner prohibits their worship, who commanded that their images should be destroyed, who foretold that demolition, who Himself effected it, in preference to those deities of whom we know not that they ordained abstinence from His worship, of whom we do not read that they foretold such an event, and in whom we do not see power sufficient to have it brought about? I put the question, let them give the answer: Who is this God, who thus harasses all the gods of the Gentiles, who thus betrays all their sacred rites, who thus renders them extinct?

CHAP. XXII. — OF THE OPINION ENTERTAINED BY THE GENTILES REGARDING OUR GOD.

30. But why do I interrogate men whose native wit has deserted them in answering the question as to who this God is? Some say that He is Saturn. I fancy the reason of that is found in the sanctification of the Sabbath; for those men assign that day to Saturn. But their own Varro, than whom they can point to no man of greater learning among them, thought that the God of the Jews was Jupiter, and he judged that it mattered not what name was employed, provided the same subject was understood under it; in which, I believe, we see how he was subdued by His supremacy. For, inasmuch as the Romans are not accustomed to worship any more exalted object than Jupiter, of which fact their Capitol is the open and sufficient attestation, and deem him to be the king of all gods; when he observed that the Jews worshipped the supreme

God, he could not think of any object under that title other than Jupiter himself. But whether men call the God of the Hebrews Saturn, or declare Him to be Jupiter, let them tell us when Saturn dared to prohibit the worship of a second deity. He did not venture to interdict the worship even of this very Jupiter, who is said to have expelled him from his kingdom, — the son thus expelling the father. And if Jupiter, as the more powerful deity and the conqueror, has been accepted by his worshippers, then they ought not to worship Saturn, the conquered and expelled. But neither, on the other hand, did Jove put his worship under the ban. Nay, that deity whom he had power to overcome, he nevertheless suffered to continue a god.

CHAP. XXIII. — OF THE FOLLIES WHICH THE PAGANS HAVE INDULGED IN REGARDING JUPITER AND SATURN.

31. These narratives of yours, say they, are but fables which have to be interpreted by the wise, or else they are fit only to be laughed at; but we revere that Jupiter of whom Maro says that

"All things are full of Jove,"
— VIRGIL'S *Eclogues*, iii. v. 60;

that is to say, the spirit of life [3] that vivifies all things. It is not without some reason, therefore, that Varro thought that Jove was worshipped by the Jews; for the God of the Jews says by His prophet, "I fill heaven and earth." [4] But what is meant by that which the same poet names Ether? How do they take the term? For he speaks thus:

"Then the omnipotent father Ether, with fertilizing showers,
Came down into the bosom of his fruitful spouse."
— VIRGIL'S *Georgics*, ii. 325.

They say, indeed, that this Ether is not spirit, [5] but a lofty body in which the heaven is stretched above the air. [6] Is liberty conceded to the poet to speak at one time in the language of the followers of Plato, as if God was not body, but spirit, and at another time in the language of the Stoics, as if God was a body? What is it, then, that they worship in their Capitol? If it is a spirit, or if again it is, in short, the corporeal heaven itself, then what does that shield of Jupiter there which they style the Ægis? The origin of that name, indeed, is explained by the circumstance that a goat [7] nourished Jupiter when he was concealed by his mother. Or is this a fiction of the poets? But are the capitols of the Romans, then, also the mere creations of the poets? And what is the meaning of that, cer-

---

[1] Reading *notior*; others give *potior* = preferable. [The text of Migne reads *notior et potentior*, but five MSS. read *notior et potior*. The argument favours the former reading, and the latter can readily be accounted for. — R.]

[2] Some read *audere timeant* = fear to dare. But the MSS. give more correctly *audiri timeant* = fear to be heard; *i.e.*, the demons were afraid that, if they interdicted His worship, the true God might be made known by their own hand. — MIGNE.

[3] Or, the breathed air — *spiritum*.   [4] Jer. xxiii. 24.
[5] *Spiritum*, breath.   [6] *Aerem*.
[7] Alluding to the derivation of the word *Ægis* = αἰγίς, a goatskin, from the Greek αἴξ = goat.

tainly not poetical, but unmistakeably farcical, variability of yours, in seeking your gods according to the ideas of philosophers in books, and revering them according to the notions of poets in your temples?

32. But was that Euhemerus also a poet, who declares both Jupiter himself, and his father Saturn, and Pluto and Neptune his brothers, to have been men, in terms so exceedingly plain that their worshippers ought all the more to render thanks to the poets, because their inventions have not been intended so much to disparage them as rather to dress them up? Albeit Cicero [1] mentions that this same Euhemerus was translated into Latin by the poet Ennius.[2] Or was Cicero himself a poet, who, in counselling the person with whom he debates in his *Tusculan Disputations*, addresses him as one possessing knowledge of things secret, in the following terms: "If, indeed, I were to attempt to search into antiquity, and produce from thence the subjects which the writers of Greece have given to the world, it would be found that even those deities who are reckoned gods of the higher orders have gone from us into heaven. Ask whose sepulchres are pointed out in Greece: call to mind, since you have been initiated, the things which are delivered in the mysteries: then, doubtless, you will comprehend how widely extended this belief is."[3] This author certainly makes ample acknowledgment of the doctrine that those gods of theirs were originally men. He does, indeed, benevolently surmise that they made their way into heaven. But he did not hesitate to say in public, that even the honour thus given them in general repute[4] was conferred upon them by men, when he spoke of Romulus in these words: "By good will and repute we have raised to the immortal gods that Romulus who founded this city."[5] How should it be such a wonderful thing, therefore, to suppose that the more ancient men did with respect to Jupiter and Saturn and the others what the Romans have done with respect to Romulus, and what, in good truth, they have thought of doing even in these more recent times also in the case of Cæsar? And to these same Virgil has addressed the additional flattery of song, saying:

"Lo, the star of Cæsar, descendant of Dione, arose."
— *Eclogue*, ix. ver. 47.

Let them see to it, then, that the truth of history do not turn out to exhibit to our view sepulchres erected for their false gods here upon the earth! and let them take heed lest the vanity of poetry, instead of fixing, may be but feigning[6] stars for their deities there in heaven. For, in reality, that one is not the star of Jupiter, neither is this one the star of Saturn; but the simple fact is, that upon these stars, which were set from the foundation of the world, the names of those persons were imposed after their death by men who were minded to honour them as gods on their departure from this life. And with respect to these we may, indeed, ask how there should be such ill desert in chastity, or such good desert in voluptuousness, that Venus should have a star, and Minerva be denied one among those luminaries which revolve along with the sun and moon?

33. But it may be said that Cicero, the Academic sage, who has been bold enough to make mention of the sepulchres of their gods, and to commit the statement to writing, is a more doubtful authority than the poets; although he did not presume to offer that assertion simply as his own personal opinion, but put it on record as a statement contained among the traditions of their own sacred rites. Well, then, can it also be maintained that Varro either gives expression merely to an invention of his own, as a poet might do, or puts the matter only dubiously, as might be the case with an Academician, because he declares that, in the instance of all such gods, the matters of their worship had their origin either in the life which they lived, or in the death which they died, among men? Or was that Egyptian priest, Leon,[7] either a poet or an Academician, who expounded the origin of those gods of theirs to Alexander of Macedon, in a way somewhat different indeed from the opinion advanced by the Greeks, but nevertheless so far accordant therewith as to make out their deities to have been originally men?

34. But what is all this to us?[8] Let them assert that they worship Jupiter, and not a dead man; let them maintain that they have dedicated their Capitol not to a dead man, but to the Spirit that vivifies all things and fills the world. And as to that shield of his, which was made of the skin of a she-goat in honour of his nurse, let them put upon it whatever interpretation they please. What do they say, however, about Saturn?[9] What is it that they worship

---

[1] See the first book of his *De Natura Deorum*, c. 42. Compare also Lactantius, *De Falsa Religione*, i. 11; and Varro, *De Re Rustica*, i. 48.

[2] The father of Roman literature, born B.C. 239 at Rudiæ in Calabria, both a poet and a man of learning, and well versed, among other things, in Oscan, Latin, and Greek — linguistic accomplishments beyond his day. Of his writings we now possess only fragments, preserved by Cicero, Macrobius, Aulus Gellius, and others.

[3] *Tusculan Disputations*, Book i. 13. [4] *Honorem opinionis*.

[5] From the *Third Oration against Catiline*, § 1.

[6] *Non figat sed fingat.*

[7] On this Leo or Leon, see also Augustin's *City of God*, viii. 5. Reference is often made to him by early Christian writers as a thinker agreeing so far with the principles of Euhemerus (in whose time, or perhaps somewhat before it, he flourished) as to teach that the gods of the old heathen world were originally men. He is mentioned by Arnobius, *Adversus Gentes*, iv. 29; Clement of Alexandria, *Stromata*, i. 23; Tertullian, *De Corona*, c. 7; Tatian, etc.

[8] Reading, with Migne, *Sed quid ad nos? Dicant se Jovem*, etc. Others give, *Sed quid ad nos si decant*, etc. = But what is it to us although they say that they worship, etc. The *si*, however, is wanting in the MSS.

[9] Reading, with Migne, *Quid dicunt de Saturno? Quem*, etc. Others give, *Quid dicunt de Saturno qui* = What do those say about Saturn who worship Saturn? The MSS. have *quem*.

under the name of Saturn? Is not this the deity that was the first to come down to us from Olympus (of whom the poet sings) :

> "Then from Olympus' height came down
> Good Saturn, exiled from his crown
> By Jove, his mightier heir :
> He brought the race to union first
> Erewhile on mountain-tops dispersed,
> And gave them statutes to obey,
> And willed the land wherein he lay
> Should Latium's title bear."

—VIRGIL'S *Æneid*, viii. 320–324, Conington's trans.

Does not his very image, made as it is with the head covered, present him as one under conceal-ment?[1] Was it not he that made the practice of agriculture known to the people of Italy,—a fact which is expressed by the reaping-hook?[2] No, say they; for you may see whether the being of whom such things are recorded was a man,[3] and indeed one particular king : we, however, in-terpret Saturn to be *universal Time*, as is signi-fied also by his name in Greek : for he is called *Chronus*,[4] which word, with the aspiration thus given it, is also the vocable for *time:* whence, too, in Latin he gets the name of *Saturn*, as if it meant that he is *sated*[5] with years. But now, what we are to make of people like these I know not, who, in their very effort to put a more favourable meaning upon the names and the images of their gods, make the confession that the very god who is their major deity, and the father of the rest, is Time. For what else do they thus betray but, in fact, that all those gods of theirs are only temporal, seeing that the very parent of them all is made out to be Time?

35. Accordingly, their more recent philoso-phers of the Platonic school, who have flourished in Christian times, have been ashamed of such fancies, and have endeavoured to interpret Saturn in another way, affirming that he received the name Χρόνος[6] in order to signify, as it were, the fulness of intellect ; their explanation being, that in Greek *fulness*[7] is expressed by the term χόρος,[8] and *intellect* or *mind* by the term νοῦς ;[9] which etymology seems to be favoured also by the Latin name, on the supposition that the first part of the word (Saturnus) came from the Latin, and the second part from the Greek : so that he got the title Saturnus as an equivalent to *satur, νοῦς*.[10] For they saw how absurd it was to have that Jupiter regarded as a son of Time,

whom they either considered, or wished to have considered, eternal deity. Furthermore, how-ever, according to this novel interpretation, which it is marvellous that Cicero and Varro should have suffered to escape their notice, if their ancient authorities really had it, they call Jupiter the son of Saturn, thus denoting him, it may be, as the spirit that proceedeth forth from that supreme mind — the spirit which they choose to look upon as the soul of this world, so to speak, filling alike all heavenly and all earthly bodies. Whence comes also that saying of Maro, which I have cited a little ago, namely, "All things are full of Jove"? Should they not, then, if they are possessed of the ability, alter the superstitions indulged in by men, just as they alter their inter-pretation ; and either erect no images at all, or at least build capitols to Saturn rather than to Jupiter? For they also maintain that no rational soul can be produced gifted with wisdom, except by participation in that supreme and unchange-able wisdom of his ; and this affirmation they advance not only with respect to the soul of a man, but even with respect to that same soul of the world which they also designate Jove. Now we not only concede, but even very particularly proclaim, that there is a certain supreme wisdom of God, by participation in which every soul what-soever that is constituted truly wise acquires its wisdom. But whether that universal corporeal mass, which is called the world, has a kind of soul, or, so to speak, its own soul, that is to say, a rational life by which it can govern its own movements, as is the case with every sort of ani-mal, is a question both vast and obscure. That is an opinion which ought not to be affirmed, unless its truth is clearly ascertained ; neither ought it to be rejected, unless its falsehood is as clearly ascertained. And what will it matter to man, even should this question remain for ever unsolved, since, in any case, no soul becomes wise or blessed by drawing from any other soul but from that one supreme and immutable wis-dom of God?

36. The Romans, however, who have founded a Capitol in honour of Jupiter, but none in hon-our of Saturn, as also these other nations whose opinion it has been that Jupiter ought to be worshipped pre-eminently and above the rest of the gods, have certainly not agreed in sentiment with the persons referred to ; who, in accordance with that mad view of theirs, would dedicate their loftiest citadels[11] rather to Saturn, if they had any power in these things, and who most particularly would annihilate those mathema-ticians and nativity-spinners[12] by whom this Saturn, whom their opponents would designate the maker of the wise, has been placed with the

---

[1] *Quasi latentem indicat*, in reference to the story introduced in the Virgilian passage, that the country got its name, *Latium*, from the disappearance of the god.
[2] The statue of Saturn represented him with a sickle or pruning-knife in his hand.
[3] Migne's text gives, on the authority of MSS., the reading, *Nam videris si fuit ille homo*, etc. Others edit, *Nam tametsi fuerit ille*, etc. = For although he may have been a man . . . yet we inter-pret, etc.
[4] For Kronos.
[5] *Satureur* — saturated, abundantly furnished.
[6] Chronos, Kronos.　　[7] Or satiety.　　[8] Choros.
[9] *Nous*.　　[10] Full, mind.

[11] Reading *arces*. Some editions give *artes* = arts.
[12] *Genethliacos*.

character of a deity of evil among the other stars. But this opinion, nevertheless, has prevailed so mightily against them in the mind of humanity, that men decline even to name that god, and call him *Ancient* [1] rather than Saturn ; and that in so fearful a spirit of superstition, that the Carthaginians have now gone very near to change the designation of their town, and call it the town of the Ancient [2] more frequently than the town of Saturn. [3]

CHAP. XXIV. — OF THE FACT THAT THOSE PERSONS WHO REJECT THE GOD OF ISRAEL, IN CONSEQUENCE FAIL TO WORSHIP ALL THE GODS ; AND, ON THE OTHER HAND, THAT THOSE WHO WORSHIP OTHER GODS, FAIL TO WORSHIP HIM.

37. It is well understood, therefore, what these worshippers of images are convicted in reality of revering, and what they attempt to colour over. [4] But even these new interpreters of Saturn must be required to tell us what they think of the God of the Hebrews. For to them also it seemed right to worship all the gods, as is done by the heathen nations, because their pride made them ashamed to humble themselves under Christ for the remission of their sins. What opinion, therefore, do they entertain regarding the God of Israel ? For if they do not worship Him, then they do not worship all gods ; and if they do worship Him, they do not worship Him in the way that He has ordained for His own worship, because they worship others also whose worship He has interdicted. Against such practices He issued His prohibition by the mouth of those same prophets by whom He also announced beforehand the destined occurrence of those very things which their images are now sustaining at the hands of the Christians. For whatever the explanation may be, whether it be that the angels were sent to those prophets to show them figuratively, and by the congruous forms of visible objects, the one true God, the Creator of all things, to whom the whole universe is made subject, and to indicate the method in which He enjoined His own worship to proceed ; or whether it was that the minds of some among them were so mightily elevated by the Holy Spirit, as to enable them to see those things in that kind of vision in which the angels themselves behold objects : in either case it is the incontestable fact, that they did serve that God who has prohibited the worship of other gods ; and, moreover, it is equally certain, that with the faithfulness of piety, in the kingly and in the priestly office, they ministered at once for the good of their country, and in the interest of those sacred ordinances which were significant

of the coming of Christ as the true King and Priest.

CHAP. XXV. — OF THE FACT THAT THE FALSE GODS DO NOT FORBID OTHERS TO BE WORSHIPPED ALONG WITH THEMSELVES. THAT THE GOD OF ISRAEL IS THE TRUE GOD, IS PROVED BY HIS WORKS, BOTH IN PROPHECY AND IN FULFILMENT.

38. But further, in the case of the gods of the Gentiles (in their willingness to worship whom they exhibit their unwillingness to worship that God who cannot be worshipped together with them), let them tell us the reason why no one is found in the number of their deities who thinks of interdicting the worship of another ; while they institute them in different offices and functions, and hold them to preside each one over objects which pertain properly to his own special province. For if Jupiter does not prohibit the worship of Saturn, because he is not to be taken merely for a man, who drove another man, namely his father, out of his kingdom, but either for the body of the heavens, or for the spirit that fills both heaven and earth, and because thus he cannot prevent that supernal mind from being worshipped, from which he is said to have emanated : if, on the same principle also, Saturn cannot interdict the worship of Jupiter, because he is not [to be supposed to be merely] one who was conquered by that other in rebellion, — as was the case with a person of the same name, by the hand of some one or other called Jupiter, from whose arms he was fleeing when he came into Italy, — and because the primal mind favours the mind that springs from it : yet Vulcan at least might [be expected to] put under the ban the worship of Mars, the paramour of his wife, and Hercules [might be thought likely to interdict] the worship of Juno, his persecutor. What kind of foul consent must subsist among them, if even Diana, the chaste virgin, fails to interdict the worship, I do not say merely of Venus, but even of Priapus ? For if the same individual decides to be at once a hunter and a farmer, he must be the servant of both these deities ; and yet he will be ashamed to do even so much as erect temples for them side by side. But they may aver, that by interpretation Diana means a certain virtue, be it what they please ; and they may tell us that Priapus really denotes the deity of fecundity, [5] — to such an effect, at any rate, that Juno may well be ashamed to have such a coadjutor in the task of making females fruitful. They may say what they please ; they may put any explanation upon these things which in their wisdom they think fit : only, in spite of all that, the God of Israel will confound all their argumentations. For in prohibiting all those

---

[1] Senex.   [2] Vicus Senis.   [3] Vicus Saturni.
[4] Reading *colorare*, as in the MSS. Some editions give *colere* = revere.

[5] Reading *fecunditatis*. *Fœditatis*, foulness, also occurs.

deities from being worshipped, while His own worship is hindered by none of them, and in at once commanding, foretelling, and effecting destruction for their images and sacred rites, He has shown with sufficient clearness that they are false and lying deities, and that He Himself is the one true and truthful God.

39. Moreover, to whom should it not seem strange that those worshippers, now become few in number, of deities both numerous and false, should refuse to do homage to Him of whom, when the question is put to them as to what deity He is, they dare not at least assert, whatever answer they may think to give, that He is no God at all? For if they deny His deity, they are very easily refuted by His works, both in prophecy and in fulfilment. I do not speak of those works which they deem themselves at liberty not to credit, such as His work in the beginning, when He made heaven and earth, and all that is in them.[1] Neither do I specify here those events which carry us back into the remotest antiquity, such as the translation of Enoch,[2] the destruction of the impious by the flood, and the saving of righteous Noah and his house from the deluge, by means of the [ark of] wood.[3] I begin the statement of His doings among men with Abraham. To this man, indeed, was given by an angelic oracle an intelligible promise, which we now see in its realization. For to him it was said, " In thy seed shall all nations be blessed." [4] Of his seed, then, sprang the people of Israel, whence came the Virgin Mary, who was the mother of Christ; and that in Him all the nations are blessed, let them now be bold enough to deny if they can. This same promise was made also to Isaac the son of Abraham.[5] It was given again to Jacob the grandson of Abraham. This Jacob was also called Israel, from whom that whole people derived both its descent and its name so that indeed the God of this people was called the God of Israel: not that He is not also the God of the Gentiles, whether they are ignorant of Him or now know Him; but that in this people He willed that the power of His promises should be made more conspicuously apparent. For that people, which at first was multiplied in Egypt, and after a time was delivered from a state of slavery there by the hand of Moses, with many signs and portents, saw most of the Gentile nations subdued under it, and obtained possession also of the land of promise, in which it reigned in the person of kings of its own, who sprang from the tribe of Judah. This Judah, also, was one of the twelve sons of Israel, the grandson of Abraham. And from him were descended the people called the Jews, who, with the help of God Himself,

did great achievements, and who also, when He chastised them, endured many sufferings on account of their sins, until the coming of that Seed to whom the promise was given, in whom all the nations were to be blessed, and [for whose sake] they were willingly to break in pieces the idols of their fathers.

CHAP. XXVI. — OF THE FACT THAT IDOLATRY HAS BEEN SUBVERTED BY THE NAME OF CHRIST, AND BY THE FAITH OF CHRISTIANS ACCORDING TO THE PROPHECIES.

40. For truly what is thus effected by Christians is not a thing which belongs only to Christian times, but one which was predicted very long ago. Those very Jews who have remained enemies to the name of Christ, and regarding whose destined perfidy these prophetic writings have not been silent, do themselves possess and peruse the prophet who says : " O Lord my God, and my refuge in the day of evil, the Gentiles shall come unto Thee from the ends of the earth, and shall say, Surely our fathers have worshipped mendacious idols, and there is no profit in them." [6] Behold, that is now being done ; behold, now the Gentiles are coming from the ends of the earth to Christ, uttering things like these, and breaking their idols ! Of signal consequence, too, is this which God has done for His Church in its world-wide extension, in that the Jewish nation, which has been deservedly overthrown and scattered abroad throughout the lands, has been made to carry about with it everywhere the records of our prophecies, so that it might not be possible to look upon these predictions as concocted by ourselves ; and thus the enemy of our faith has been made a witness to our truth. How, then, can it be possible that the disciples of Christ have taught what they have not learned from Christ, as those foolish men in their silly fancies object, with the view of getting the superstitious worship of heathen gods and idols subverted? Can it be said also that those prophecies which are still read in these days, in the books of the enemies of Christ, were the inventions of the disciples of Christ?

41. Who, then, has effected the demolition of these systems but the God of Israel? For to this people was the announcement made by those divine voices which were addressed to Moses : " Hear, O Israel ; the Lord thy God is one God." [7] " Thou shalt not make unto thee any graven image, or any likeness of anything that is in heaven above or that is in the earth beneath." [8] And again, in order that this peo-

---

[1] Gen. i. 1.   [2] Gen. v. 24.   [3] Gen vii.
[4] Gen. xxii. 18.   [5] Gen. xxvi. 4.
[6] Jer. xvi. 19.
[7] Deut. vi. 4. [See Revised Version, text and margin, for the variations in the rendering of the Hebrew. Comp. Mark xii. 29 for similar variations in the passage as cited in the New Testament. — R.]
[8] Exod. xx. 4.

ple might put an end to these things wherever it received power to do so, this commandment was also laid upon the nation : " Thou shalt not bow down to their gods, nor serve them ; thou shalt not do after their works, but thou shalt utterly overthrow them, and quite break down their images." [1]   But who shall say that Christ and Christians have no connection with Israel, seeing that Israel was the grandson of Abraham, to whom first, as afterwards to his son Isaac, and then to his grandson Israel himself, that promise was given, which I have already mentioned, namely : " In thy seed shall all nations be blessed " ? That prediction we see now in its fulfilment in Christ. For it was of this line that the Virgin was born, concerning whom a prophet of the people of Israel and of the God of Israel sang in these terms : " Behold, a virgin shall conceive, and bear a son ; and they shall call [2] His name Emmanuel." For by interpretation, Emmanuel means, " God with us." [3] This God of Israel, therefore, who has interdicted the worship of other gods, who has interdicted the making of idols, who has commanded their destruction, who by His prophet has predicted that the Gentiles from the ends of the earth would say, " Surely our fathers have worshipped mendacious idols, in which there is no profit ; " this same God is He who, by the name of Christ and by the faith of Christians, has ordered, promised, and exhibited the overthrow of all these superstitions. In vain, therefore, do these unhappy men, knowing that they have been prohibited from blaspheming the name of Christ, even by their own gods, that is to say, by the demons who fear the name of Christ, seek to make it out, that this kind of doctrine is something strange to Him, in the power of which the Christians dispute against idols, and root out all those false religions, wherever they have the opportunity.

CHAP. XXVII. — AN ARGUMENT URGING IT UPON THE REMNANT OF IDOLATERS THAT THEY SHOULD AT LENGTH BECOME SERVANTS OF THIS TRUE GOD, WHO EVERYWHERE IS SUBVERTING IDOLS.

42. Let them now give their answer with respect to the God of Israel, to whom, as teaching and enjoining such things, witness is borne not only by the books of the Christians, but also by those of the Jews. Regarding Him, let them ask the counsel of their own deities, who have prevented the blaspheming of Christ. Concerning the God of Israel, let them give a contumelious response if they dare. But whom are they to consult? or where are they to ask counsel now? Let them peruse the books of

their own authorities. If they consider the God of Israel to be Jupiter, as Varro has written (that I may speak for the time being in accordance with their own way of thinking), why then do they not believe that the idols are to be destroyed by Jupiter? If they deem Him to be Saturn,[4] why do they not worship Him? Or why do they not worship Him in that manner in which, by the voice of those prophets through whom He has made good the things which He has foretold, He has ordained His worship to be conducted? Why do they not believe that images are to be destroyed by Him, and the worship of other gods forbidden? If He is neither Jove nor Saturn (and surely, if He were one of these, He would not speak out so mightily against the sacred rites of their Jove and Saturn), who then is this God, who, with all their consideration for other gods, is the only Deity not worshipped by them, and who, nevertheless, so manifestly brings it about that He shall Himself be the sole object of worship, to the overthrow of all other gods, and to the humiliation of everything proud and highly exalted, which has lifted itself up against Christ in behalf of idols, persecuting and slaying Christians? But, in good truth, men are now asking into what secret recesses these worshippers withdraw, when they are minded to offer sacrifice ; or into what regions of obscurity they thrust back these same gods of theirs, to prevent their being discovered and broken in pieces by the Christians. Whence comes this mode of dealing, if not from the fear of those laws and those rulers by whose instrumentality the God of Israel discovers His power, and who are now made subject to the name of Christ. And that it should be so He promised long ago, when He said by the prophet : " Yea, all kings of the earth shall worship Him : all nations shall serve Him." [5]

CHAP. XXVIII. — OF THE PREDICTED REJECTION OF IDOLS.

43. It cannot be questioned that what was predicted at sundry times by His prophets is now being realized, — namely, the announcement that He would disclaim His impious people (not, indeed, the people as a whole, because even of the Israelites many have believed in Christ ; for His apostles themselves belonged to that nation), and would humble every proud and injurious person, so that He should Himself alone be exalted, that is to say, alone be manifested to men as lofty and mighty ; until idols should be cast away by those who believe, and be concealed by those who believe not ; when the earth is broken by His fear, that is to say, when the men of

---

[1] Exod. xxiii. 24. [*Simulacra eorum.* The Revised Version renders " their pillars," with " obelisks " in the margin. — R.]
[2] *Vocabunt.*   [3] Isa. vii. 14; Matt. i. 23.

[4] Reading *Si Saturnum putant.* Others read, *Si Saturnum Deum putant* = if they deem Saturn to be God, etc.
[5] Ps. lxxii. 11.

earth are subdued by fear, to wit, by fearing His law, or the law of those who, being at once believers in His name and rulers among the nations, shall interdict such sacrilegious practices.

44. For these things, which I have thus briefly stated in the way of introduction, and with a view to their readier apprehension, are thus expressed by the prophet: And now, O house of Jacob, come ye, and let us walk in the light of the Lord. For He has disclaimed His people the house of Israel, because the country was replenished, as from the beginning, with their soothsayings as with those of strangers, and many strange children were born to them. For their country was replenished with silver and gold, neither was there any numbering of their treasures; their land also is full of horses, neither was there any numbering of their chariots: their land also is full of the abominations of the works of their own hands, and they have worshipped that which their own fingers have made. And the mean. man [1] has bowed himself, and the great man [2] has humbled himself, and I will not forgive it them. And now enter ye into the rocks, and hide yourselves in the earth from before the fear of the Lord, and from the majesty of His power, when He arises to crush the earth: for the eyes of the Lord are lofty, and man is low; and the haughtiness of men shall be humbled, and the Lord alone shall be exalted in that day. For the day of the Lord of Hosts shall be upon every one that is injurious and proud, and upon every one that is lifted up and humbled,[3] and they shall be brought low; and upon every cedar of Lebanon of the high ones and the lifted up,[4] and upon every tree of the Lebanon of Bashan,[5] and upon every mountain, and upon every high hill,[6] and upon every ship of the sea, and upon every spectacle of the beauty of ships. And the contumely of men shall be humbled and shall fall, and the Lord alone shall be exalted in that day;[7] and all things made by hands they shall hide in dens, and in holes of the rocks, and in caves of the earth, from before the fear of the Lord, and from the majesty of His power, when He arises to crush the earth: for in that day a man shall cast away the abominations of gold and silver, the vain and evil things which they made for worship, in order to go into the clefts of the solid rock, and into the holes of the rocks, from before the fear of the Lord, and from the majesty of His power, when He arises to break the earth in pieces.[8]

CHAP. XXIX. — OF THE QUESTION WHY THE HEATHEN SHOULD REFUSE TO WORSHIP THE GOD OF ISRAEL, EVEN ALTHOUGH THEY DEEM HIM TO BE ONLY THE PRESIDING DIVINITY OF THE ELEMENTS?

45. What do they say of this God of Sabaoth, which term, by interpretation, means the God of powers or of armies, inasmuch as the powers and the armies of the angels serve Him? What do they say of this God of Israel; for He is the God of that people from whom came the seed wherein all the nations were to be blessed? Why is He the only deity excluded from worship by those very persons who contend that all the gods ought to be worshipped? Why do they refuse their belief to Him who both proves other gods to be false gods, and also overthrows them? I have heard one of them declare that he had read, in some philosopher or other, the statement that, from what the Jews did in their sacred observances, he had come to know what God they worshipped. "He is the deity," said he, "that presides over those elements of which this visible and material universe is constructed;" when in the Holy Scriptures of His prophets it is plainly shown that the people of Israel were commanded to worship that God who made heaven and earth, and from whom comes all true wisdom. But what need is there for further disputation on this subject, seeing that it is quite sufficient for my present purpose to point out how they entertain any kind of presumptuous opinions regarding that God whom yet they cannot deny to be a God? If, indeed, He is the deity that presides over the elements of which this world consists, why is He not worshipped in preference to Neptune, who presides over the sea only? Why not, again, in preference to Silvanus, who presides over the fields and woods only? Why not in preference to the Sun, who presides over the day only, or who also rules over the entire heat of heaven? Why not in preference to the Moon, who presides over the night only, or who also shines pre-eminent for power over moisture? Why not in preference to Juno, who is supposed to hold possession of the air only? For certainly those deities, whoever they may be, who preside over the parts, must necessarily be under that Deity who wields the presidency over all the elements, and over the entire universe. But this Deity prohibits the worship of all those deities. Why, then, is it that these men, in opposition to the injunction of One greater than those deities, not only choose to worship them, but also decline, for

---

[1] *Homo.*　　[2] *Vir.*

[3] The text gives *humiliatum;* but *elatum* seems to be required, corresponding with the LXX. μετέωρον.

[4] Reading *cedrum Libani excelsorum et elatorum*, which is given by the MSS., and is accordant with the LXX. ὑψηλῶν καὶ μετεώρων. Some editions give *cedrum Libani excelsam et elatam* = Every high and elevated cedar of Lebanon.

[5] The LXX. here has καὶ επι παν δενδρον βαλάνου Βασάν = And upon every tree of the acorn of Bashan. For the βαλάνου Augustin adopts *Libani*, as if he read in the Greek Λιβάνου.

[6] The fifteenth verse of our version is wholly omitted.

[7] [Ver. 18, though very relevant, is omitted: "And the idols shall utterly pass away." — R.]

[8] Isa. ii. 5–21. [The variations from the Hebrew are quite numerous; compare the English versions. — R.]

their sakes, to worship Him? Not yet have they discovered any constant and intelligible judgment to pronounce on this God of Israel; neither will they ever discover any such judgment, until they find out that He alone is the true God, by whom all things were created.

CHAP. XXX. — OF THE FACT THAT, AS THE PROPHECIES HAVE BEEN FULFILLED, THE GOD OF ISRAEL HAS NOW BEEN MADE KNOWN EVERYWHERE.

46. Thus it was with a certain person named Lucan, one of their great declaimers in verse. For a long time, as I believe, he endeavored to find out, by his own cogitations, or by the perusal of the books of his own fellow-countrymen,[1] who the God of the Jews was; and failing to prosecute his inquiry in the way of piety, he did not succeed. Yet he chose rather to speak of Him as the uncertain God whom he did not find out, than absolutely to deny the title of God to that Deity of whose existence he perceived proofs so great. For he says:

" And Judæa, devoted to the worship
   Of an uncertain God."[2]
          — LUCAN, Book ii. towards the end.

And as yet this God, the holy and true God of Israel, had not done by the name of Christ among all nations works so great as those which have been wrought after Lucan's times up to our own day. But now who is so obdurate as not to be moved, who so dull[3] as not to be inflamed, seeing that the saying of Scripture is fulfilled, " For there is not one that is hid from the heat thereof;"[4] and seeing also that those other things which were predicted so long time ago in this same Psalm from which I have cited one little verse, are now set forth in their accomplishment in the clearest light? For under this term of the " heavens" the apostles of Jesus Christ were denoted, because God was to preside in them with a view to the publishing of the gospel. Now, therefore, the heavens have declared the glory of God, and the firmament has proclaimed the works of His hands. Day unto day has given forth speech, and night unto night has shown knowledge. Now there is no speech or language where their voices are not heard. Their sound has gone out into all the earth, and their words to the end of the world. Now hath He set His tabernacle in the sun, that is, in manifestation; which tabernacle is His Church. For in order to do so (as the words proceed in the passage) He came forth from His chamber like a bridegroom; that is to say, the Word,

wedded with the flesh of man, came forth from the Virgin's womb. Now has He rejoiced as a strong man, and has run His race. Now has His going forth been made from the height of heaven, and His return even to the height of heaven.[5] And accordingly, with the completest propriety, there follows upon this the verse which I have already mentioned : "And there is not one that is hid from the heat thereof [or, His heat]." And still these men make choice of their little, weak, prating objections, which are like stubble to be reduced to ashes in that fire, rather than like gold to be purged of its dross by it; while at once the fallacious monuments of their false gods have been brought to nought, and the veracious promises of that uncertain God have been proved to be sure.

CHAP. XXXI. — THE FULFILMENT OF THE PROPHECIES CONCERNING CHRIST.

47. Wherefore let those evil applauders of Christ, who refuse to become Christians, desist from making the allegation that Christ did not teach that their gods were to be abandoned, and their images broken in pieces. For the God of Israel, regarding whom it was declared aforetime that He should be called the God of the whole earth, is now indeed actually called the God of the whole earth. By the mouth of His prophets He predicted that this would come to pass, and by Christ He did bring it eventually to pass at the fit time. Assuredly, if the God of Israel is now named the God of the whole earth, what He has commanded must needs be made good; for He who has given the commandment is now well known. But, further, that He is made known by Christ and in Christ, in order that His Church may be extended throughout the world, and that by its instrumentality the God of Israel may be named the God of the whole earth, those who please may read a little earlier in the same prophet. That paragraph may also be cited by me. It is not so long as to make it requisite for us to pass it by. Here there is much said about the presence, the humility, and the passion of Christ, and about the body of which He is the Head, that is, His Church, where it is called barren, like one that did not bear. For during many years the Church, which was destined to subsist among all the nations with its children, that is, with its saints, was not apparent, as Christ remained yet unannounced by the evangelists to those to whom He had not been declared by the prophets. Again, it is said that there shall be more children for her who is forsaken than for her who has a husband, under which name of a husband the Law was signified, or the King whom the people of Israel

---

[1] Per suorum libros.
[2]   [. . . Et dedita sacris
         Incerti Judæa Dei. — R]
[3] Reading torpidus ; for which others give tepidus, cool.
[4] Ps. xix. 6.

[5] [Ps. xix. 1-6, partly in citation, partly in allegorizing paraphrase. — R.]

first received. For neither had the Gentiles received the Law at the period at which the prophet spake; nor had the King of Christians yet appeared to the nations, although from these Gentile nations a much more fruitful and numerous multitude of saints has now proceeded. It is in this manner, therefore, that Isaiah speaks, commencing with the humility [1] of Christ, and turning afterwards to an address to the Church, on to that verse which we have already instanced, where he says: And He who brought thee out, the same God of Israel, shall be called the God of the whole earth.[2] Behold, says he, my Servant shall deal prudently, and shall be exalted and honoured exceedingly. As many shall be astonied at Thee; so shall Thy marred visage, nevertheless, be seen by all, and Thine honour by men. For so shall many nations be astonied at Him, and the kings shall shut their mouths. For they shall see to whom it has not been told of Him; and those who have not heard shall understand. O Lord, who hath believed our report, and to whom is the arm of the Lord revealed? We have proclaimed before Him as a servant,[3] as a root in a thirsty soil; He hath no form nor comeliness. And we have seen Him, and He had neither beauty nor seemliness; but His countenance is despised, and His state rejected by all men: a man stricken, and acquainted with the bearing of infirmities; on account of which His face is turned aside, injured, and little esteemed. He bears our infirmities, and is in sorrows for us. And we did esteem Him to be in sorrows, and to be stricken and in punishment. But He was wounded for our transgressions, and He was enfeebled for our iniquities; the chastisement of our peace was upon Him, and with His stripes we are healed. All we, like sheep, have gone astray, and the Lord hath given Him up for our sins. And whereas He was evil entreated, He opened not His mouth; He was brought as a sheep to the slaughter; and as a lamb before him who shears it is dumb, so He opened not His mouth. In humility was His judgment taken. Who shall declare His generation? For His life shall be cut off out of the land; by the iniquities of my people is He led to death. Therefore shall I give the wicked for His sepulture, and the rich on account of His death; because He did no iniquity, neither was any deceit in His mouth. The Lord is pleased to clear Him in regard to His stroke.[4] If ye shall give your soul for your offences, ye shall see the seed of the longest life. And the Lord is pleased to take away His soul from sorrows, to show Him the light, and to set Him forth in sight,[5] and to justify the righteous One who serves many well; and He shall bear their sins. Therefore shall He have many for His inheritance, and shall divide the spoils of the strong; for which reason His soul was delivered over to death, and He was numbered with the transgressors, and He bare the sins of many, and was delivered for their iniquities. Rejoice, O barren, thou that dost not bear: exult, and cry aloud, thou that dost not travail with child; for more are the children of the desolate than those of her who has a husband. For the Lord hath said, Enlarge the place of thy tent, and fix thy courts;[6] there is no reason why thou shouldst spare: lengthen thy cords, and strengthen Thy stakes firmly. Yea, again and again break thou forth on the right hand and on the left. For thy seed shall inherit the Gentiles, and thou shalt inhabit the cities which were desolate. There is nothing for thee to fear. For thou shalt prevail, and be not thou confounded as if thou shalt be put to shame. For thou shalt forget thy confusion for ever: thou shalt not remember the shame of thy widowhood, since I who made thee am the Lord; the Lord is His name: and He who brought thee out, the very God of Israel, shall be called the God of the whole earth.[7]

48. What can be said in opposition to this evidence, and this expression of things both foretold and fulfilled? If they suppose that His disciples have given a false testimony on the subject of the divinity of Christ, will they also doubt the passion of Christ? No: they are not accustomed to believe that He rose from the dead; but, at the same time, they are quite ready to believe that He suffered all that men are wont to suffer, because they wish Him to be held to be a man and nothing more. According to this, then, He was led like a sheep to the slaughter; He was numbered with the transgressors; He was wounded for our sins; by His stripes were we healed; His face was marred, and little esteemed, and smitten with the palms, and defiled with the spittle; His position was disfigured on the cross; He was led to death by the iniquities of the people Israel; He is the man who had no form nor comeliness when He was buffeted with the fists, when He was crowned with the thorns, when He was derided as He hung (upon the tree); He is the man who, as the lamb is dumb before its shearer, opened not His mouth, when it was said to Him by those who mocked Him, "Prophesy to us, thou Christ."[8] Now, however, He is exalted

---

[1] Reading *humilitate;* some editions give *humanitate,* the humanity.
[2] Isa. liv. 5.　　　　　　　　[3] *Puer.*
[4] *Purgare deus illum de plaga.*

[5] *Figurare per sensum* = set forth in sensible figure.
[6] Reading *aulas tuas confige;* others give *caulas* = thy folds.
[7] Isa. lii. 13–liv. 5 [The variations from the Hebrew, especially in some of the more obscure passages, are worthy of notice. Compare the Revised Version, text and margin, *in loco.* — R.]
[8] Matt. xxvi., xxvii.; Mark xiv., xv.; Luke xxii., xxiii.; John xviii., xix.

verily, now He is honoured exceedingly; truly many nations are now astonied at Him.[1]   Now the kings have shut their mouth, by which they were wont to promulgate the most ruthless laws against the Christians.   Truly those now see to whom it was not told of Him, and those who have not heard understand.[2]   For those Gentile nations to whom the prophets made no announcement, do now rather see for themselves how true these things are which were of old reported by the prophets;[3] and those who have not heard Isaiah speak in his own proper person, now understand from his writings the things which he spoke concerning Him.   For even in the said nation of the Jews, who believed the report of the prophets, or to whom was that arm of the Lord revealed, which is this very Christ who was announced by them,[4] seeing that by their own hands they perpetrated those crimes against Christ, the commission of which had been predicted by the prophets whom they possessed?   But now, indeed, He possesses many by inheritance; and He divides the spoils of the strong, since the devil and the demons have now been cast out and given up, and the possessions once held by them have been distributed by Him among the fabrics of His churches and for other necessary services.

CHAP. XXXII. — A STATEMENT IN VINDICATION OF THE DOCTRINE OF THE APOSTLES AS OPPOSED TO IDOLATRY, IN THE WORDS OF THE PROPHECIES.

49. What, then, do these men, who are at once the perverse applauders of Christ and the slanderers of Christians, say to these facts?   Can it be that Christ, by the use of magical arts, caused those predictions to be uttered so long ago by the prophets? or have His disciples invented them?   Is it thus that the Church, in her extension among the Gentile nations, though once barren, has been made to rejoice now in the possession of more children than that synagogue had which, in its Law or its King, had received, as it were, a husband? or is it thus that this Church has been led to enlarge the place of her tent, and to occupy all nations and tongues, so that now she lengthens her cords beyond the limits to which the rights of the empire of Rome extend, yea, even on to the territories of the Persians and the Indians and other barbarous nations? or that, on the right hand by means of true Christians, and on the left hand by means of pretended Christians, His name is being made known among such a multitude of peoples? or that His seed is made to inherit the Gentiles,

so as now to inhabit cities which had been left desolate of the true worship of God and the true religion? or that His Church has been so little daunted by the threats and furies of men, even at times when she has been covered with the blood of martyrs, like one clad in purple array, that she has prevailed over persecutors at once so numerous, so violent, and so powerful? or that she has not been confounded, like one put to shame, when it was a great crime to be or to become a Christian? or that she is made to forget her confusion for ever, because, where sin had abounded, grace did much more abound?[5] or that she is taught not to remember the shame of her widowhood, because only for a little was she forsaken and subjected to opprobrium, while now she shines forth once more with such eminent glory? or, in fine, is it only a fiction concocted by Christ's disciples, that the Lord who made her, and brought her forth from the denomination of the devil and the demons, the very God of Israel is now called the God of the whole earth; all which, nevertheless, the prophets, whose books are now in the hands of the enemies of Christ, foretold so long before Christ became the Son of man?

50. From this, therefore, let them understand that the matter is not left obscure or doubtful even to the slowest and dullest minds: from this, I say, let these perverse applauders of Christ and execrators of the Christian religion understand that the disciples of Christ have learned and taught, in opposition to their gods, precisely what the doctrine of Christ contains.   For the God of Israel is found to have enjoined in the books of the prophets that all these objects which those men are minded to worship should be held in abomination and be destroyed, while He Himself is now named the God of the whole earth, through the instrumentality of Christ and the Church of Christ, exactly as He promised so long time ago.   For if, indeed, in their marvellous folly, they fancy that Christ worshipped their gods, and that it was only through them that He had power to do things so great as these, we may well ask whether the God of Israel also worshipped their gods, who has now fulfilled by Christ what He promised with respect to the extension of His own worship through all the nations, and with respect to the detestation and subversion of those other deities?[6]   Where are their gods?   Where are the vaticinations of their fanatics, and the divinations of their prophets?[7]   Where are the auguries, or the auspices, or the soothsayings,[8] or the oracles of demons?   Why is it that, out of the ancient books which constitute the records of this type of religion, nothing in the form

---

[1] [Isa. lii. 15 (in the Revised Version): "So shall He sprinkle many nations," with margin, "Or, startle." — R.]
[2] Rom. xv. 16, 21.
[3] Magis ipsæ vident quam vera nuntiata sint per prophetas.
[4] John xii. 37, 38; Rom. x. 16.

[5] Rom. v. 20.
[6] Deut. vii. 5.   [7] Pythonum.   [8] Aruspicia.

either of admonition or of prediction is advanced to oppose the Christian faith, or to controvert the truth of those prophets of ours, who have now come to be so well understood among all nations? "We have offended our gods," they say in reply, "and they have deserted us for that reason : that explains it also why the Christians have prevailed against us, and why the bliss of human life, exhausted [1] and impaired, goes to wreck among us." We challenge them, however, to take the books of their own seers, and read out to us any statement purporting that the kind of issue which has come upon them would be brought on them by the Christians : nay, we challenge them to recite any passages in which, if not Christ (for they wish to make Him out to have been a worshipper of their own gods), at least this God of Israel, who is allowed to be the subverter of other deities, is held up as a deity destined to be rejected and worthy of detestation. But never will they produce any such passage, unless, perchance, it be some fabrication of their own. And if ever they do cite any such statement, the fact that it is but a fiction of their own will betray itself in the unnoticeable manner in which a matter of so grave importance is found adduced ; whereas, in good truth, before what has been predicted should have come to pass, it behoved to have been proclaimed in the temples of the gods of all nations, with a view to the timeous preparation and warning of all who are now minded [2] to be Christians.

CHAP. XXXIII.—A STATEMENT IN OPPOSITION TO THOSE WHO MAKE THE COMPLAINT THAT THE BLISS OF HUMAN LIFE HAS BEEN IMPAIRED BY THE ENTRANCE OF CHRISTIAN TIMES.

51. Finally, as to the complaint which they make with respect to the impairing of the bliss of human life by the entrance of Christian times, if they only peruse the books of their own philosophers, who reprehend those very things which are now being taken out of their way in spite of all their unwillingness and murmuring, they will indeed find that great praise is due to the times of Christ. For what diminution is made in their happiness, unless it be in what they most basely and luxuriously abused, to the great injury of their Creator? or unless, perchance, it be the case that evil times originate in such circumstances as these, in which throughout almost all states the theatres are falling, and with them, too, the dens of vice and the public profession of iniquity : yea, altogether the forums and cities in which the demons used to be worshipped are falling. How comes it, then, that they are falling, unless it be in consequence of the failure of those very things, in the lustful and sacrilegious

use of which they were constructed? Did not their own Cicero, when commending a certain actor of the name of Roscius, call him a man so clever as to be the only one worthy enough to make it due for him to come upon the stage ; and yet, again, so good a man as to be the only one so worthy as to make it due for him not to approach it? [3] What else did he disclose with such remarkable clearness by this saying, but the fact that the stage was so base there, that a person was under the greater obligation not to connect himself with it, in proportion as he was a better man than most? And yet their gods were pleased with such things of shame as he deemed fit only to be removed to a distance from good men. But we have also an open confession of the same Cicero, where he says that he had to appease Flora, the mother of sports, by frequent celebration ; [4] in which sports such an excess of vice is wont to be exhibited, that, in comparison with them, others are respectable, from engaging in which, nevertheless, good men are prohibited. Who is this mother Flora, and what manner of goddess is she, who is thus conciliated and propitiated by a practice of vice indulged in with more than usual frequency and with looser reins? How much more honourable now was it for a Roscius to step upon the stage, than for a Cicero to worship a goddess of this kind ! If the gods of the Gentile nations are offended because the supplies are lessened which are instituted for the purpose of such celebrations, it is apparent of what character those must be who are delighted with such things. But if, on the other hand, the gods themselves in their wrath diminish these supplies, their anger yields us better services than their placability. Wherefore let these men either confute their own philosophers, who have reprehended the same practices on the side of wanton men ; or else let them break in pieces those gods of theirs who have made such demands upon their worshippers, if indeed they still find any such deities either to break in pieces or to conceal. But let them cease from their blasphemous habit of charging Christian times with the failure of their true prosperity, — a prosperity, indeed, so used by them that they were sinking into all that is base and hurtful, — lest thereby they be only putting us all the more emphatically in mind of reasons for the ampler praise of the power of Christ.

CHAP. XXXIV. — EPILOGUE TO THE PRECEDING.

52. Much more might I say on this subject, were it not that the requirements of the task which I have undertaken compel me to conclude this book, and revert to the object originally proposed. When, indeed, I took it in hand to solve

---

[1] Reading *defessa ;* others give *depressa*, crushed.
[2] Others read *nolunt*, who refuse.

[3] See Cicero's *Oration in behalf of Roscius.*
[4] See Cicero, *Against Verres*, 5.

those problems of the Gospels which meet us where the four evangelists, as it seems to certain critics, fail to harmonize with each other, by setting forth to the best of my ability the particular designs which they severally have in view, I was met first by the necessity of discussing a question which some are accustomed to bring before us, — the question, namely, as to the reason why we cannot produce any writings composed by Christ Himself. For their aim is to get Him credited with the writing of some other composition, I know not of what sort, which may be suitable to their inclinations, and with having indulged in no sentiments of antagonism to their gods, but rather with having paid respect to them in a kind of magical worship ; and their wish is also to get it believed that His disciples not only gave a false account of Him when they declared Him to be the God by whom all things were made, while He was really nothing more than a man, although certainly a man of the most exalted wisdom, but also that they taught with regard to these gods of theirs something different from what they had themselves learned from Him. This is how it happens that we have been engaged preferentially in pressing them with arguments concerning the God of Israel, who is now worshipped by all nations through the medium of the Church of the Christians, who is also subverting their sacrilegious vanities the whole world over, exactly as He announced by the mouth of the prophets so long ago, and who has now fulfilled those predictions by the name of Christ, in whom He had promised that all nations should be blessed. And from all this they ought to understand that Christ could neither have known nor taught anything else with regard to their gods than what was enjoined and foretold by the God of Israel through the agency of these prophets of His by whom He promised, and ultimately sent, this very Christ, in whose name, according to the promise given to the fathers, when all nations were pronounced blessed, it has come to pass that this same God of Israel should be called the God of the whole earth. By this, too, they ought to see that His disciples did not depart from the doctrine of their Master when they forbade the worship of the gods of the Gentiles, with the view of preventing us from addressing our supplications to insensate images, or from having fellowship with demons, or from serving the creature rather than the Creator with the homage of religious worship.

CHAP. XXXV. — OF THE FACT THAT THE MYSTERY OF A MEDIATOR WAS MADE KNOWN TO THOSE WHO LIVED IN ANCIENT TIMES BY THE AGENCY OF PROPHECY, AS IT IS NOW DECLARED TO US IN THE GOSPEL.

53. Wherefore, seeing that Christ Himself is that Wisdom of God by whom all things were created, and considering that no rational intelligences, whether of angels or of men, receive wisdom except by participation in this Wisdom wherewith we are united by that Holy Spirit through whom charity is shed abroad in our hearts [1] (which Trinity at the same time constitutes one God), Divine Providence, having respect to the interests of mortal men whose time-bound life was held engaged in things which rise into being and die,[2] decreed that this same Wisdom of God, assuming into the unity of His person the (nature of) man, in which He might be born according to the conditions of time, and live and die and rise again, should utter and perform and bear and sustain things congruous to our salvation ; and thus, in exemplary fashion, show at once to men on earth the way for a return to heaven, and to those angels who are above us, the way to retain their position in heaven.[3] For unless, also, in the nature of the reasonable soul, and under the conditions of an existence in time, something came newly into being, — that is to say, unless that began to be which previously was not, — there could never be any passing from a life of utter corruption and folly into one of wisdom and true goodness. And thus, as truth in the contemplative lives in the enjoyment of things eternal, while faith in the believing is what is due to things which are made, man is purified through that faith which is conversant with temporal things, in order to his being made capable of receiving the truth of things eternal. For one of their noblest intellects, the philosopher Plato, in the treatise which is named the *Timæus*, speaks also to this effect : " As eternity is to that which is made, so truth to faith." Those two belong to the things above, — namely, eternity and truth ; these two belong to the things below, — namely, that which is made and faith. In order, therefore, that we may be called off from the lowest objects, and led up again to the highest, and in order also that what is made may attain to the eternal, we must come through faith to truth. And because all contraries are reduced to unity by some middle factor, and because also the iniquity of time alienated us from the righteousness of eternity, there was need of some mediatorial righteousness of a temporal nature ; which mediatizing factor might be temporal on the side of those lowest objects, but also righteous on the side of these highest,[4] and thus, by

[1] Rom. v. 5.
[2] *In rebus orientibus et occidentibus occupata tenebatur.*
[3] *Fieret et deorsum hominibus exemplum redeundi et eis qui sursum sunt angelis exemplum manendi.*
[4] Reading *quæ medietas temporalis esset de imis, justa de summis.* Another version gives *quæ medietas temporalis esset de imis mixta et summis* = which temporal mediatizing factor might be made up of the lowest and the highest objects together, or = which might be a temporal mediatizing factor made up, etc.

adapting itself to the former without cutting itself off from the latter, might bring back those lowest objects to the highest. Accordingly, Christ was named the Mediator between God and men, who stood between the immortal God and mortal man, as being Himself both God and man,[1] who reconciled mån to God, who continued to be what He (formerly) was, but was made also what He (formerly) was not. And the same Person is for us at once the (centre of the) said faith in things that are made, and the truth in things eternal.

54. This great and unutterable mystery, this kingdom and priesthood, was revealed by prophecy to the men of ancient time, and is now preached by the gospel to their descendants. For it behoved that, at some period or other, that should be made good among all nations which for a long time had been promised through the medium of a single nation. Accordingly, He who sent the prophets before His own descent also despatched the apostles after His ascension. Moreover, in virtue of the man[2] assumed by Him, He stands to all His disciples in the relation of the head to the members of His body. Therefore, when those disciples have written matters which He declared and spake to them, it ought not by any means to be said that He has written nothing Himself; since the truth is, that His members have accomplished only what they became acquainted with by the repeated statements of the Head. For all that He was minded to give for our perusal on the subject of His own doings and sayings, He commanded to be written by those disciples, whom He thus used as if they were His own hands. Whoever apprehends this correspondence of unity and this concordant service of the members, all in harmony in the discharge of diverse offices under the Head, will receive the account which he gets in the Gospel through the narratives constructed by the disciples, in the same kind of spirit in which he might look upon the actual hand of the Lord Himself, which He bore in that body which was made His own, were he to see it engaged in the act of writing. For this reason let us now rather proceed to examine into the real character of those passages in which these critics suppose the evangelists to have given contradictory accounts (a thing which only those who fail to understand the matter aright can fancy to be the case) ; so that, when these problems are solved, it may also be made apparent that the members in that body have preserved a befitting harmony in the unity of the body itself, not only by identity in sentiment, but also by constructing records consonant with that identity.

---

[1] 1 Tim. ii. 5.　　　　　[2] *Hominem.*

BOOK II.

IN THIS BOOK AUGUSTIN UNDERTAKES AN ORDERLY EXAMINATION OF THE GOSPEL ACCORDING TO MATTHEW, ON TO THE NARRATIVE OF THE SUPPER, AND INSTITUTES A COMPARISON BETWEEN IT AND THE OTHER GOSPELS BY MARK, LUKE, AND JOHN, WITH THE VIEW OF DEMONSTRATING A COMPLETE HARMONY BETWEEN THE FOUR EVANGELISTS THROUGHOUT ALL THESE SECTIONS.

THE PROLOGUE.

1. WHEREAS, in a discourse of no small length and of imperative importance, which we have finished within the compass of one book, we have refuted the folly of those who think that the disciples who have given us these Gospel histories deserve only to be disparagingly handled, for the express reason that no writings are produced by us with the claim of being compositions which have proceeded immediately from the hand of that Christ whom they refuse indeed to worship as God, but whom, nevertheless, they do not hesitate to pronounce worthy to be honoured as a man far surpassing all other men in wisdom ; and as, further, we have confuted those who strive to make Him out to have written in a strain suiting their perverted inclinations, but not in terms calculated, by their perusal and acceptance, to set men right, or to turn them from their perverse ways, let us now look into the accounts which the four evangelists have given us of Christ, with the view of seeing how self-consistent they are, and how truly in harmony with each other. And let us do so in the hope that no offence, even of the smallest order, may be felt in this line of things in the Christian faith by those who exhibit more curiosity than capacity, in so far as they think that a study of the evangelical books, conducted not in the way of a merely cursory perusal, but in the form of a more than ordinarily careful investigation, has disclosed to them certain matters of an inapposite and contradictory nature, and in so far as their notion is, that these things are to be held up as objections in the spirit of contention, rather than pondered in the spirit of consideration.

CHAP. I. — A STATEMENT OF THE REASON WHY THE ENUMERATION OF THE ANCESTORS OF CHRIST IS CARRIED DOWN TO JOSEPH, WHILE CHRIST WAS NOT BORN OF THAT MAN'S SEED, BUT OF THE VIRGIN MARY.

2. The evangelist Matthew has commenced his narrative in these terms : "The book of the generation of Jesus Christ, the son of David, the son of Abraham." [1] By this exordium he shows with sufficient clearness that his undertaking is to give an account of the generation of Christ according to the flesh. For, according to this, Christ is the Son of man, — a title which He also gives very frequently to Himself, [2] thereby commending to our notice what in His compassion He has condescended to be on our behalf. For that heavenly and eternal generation, in virtue of which He is the only-begotten Son of God, before every creature, because all things were made by Him, is so ineffable, that it is of it that the word of the prophet must be understood when he says, "Who shall declare His generation?" [3] Matthew therefore traces out the human generation of Christ, mentioning His ancestors from Abraham downwards, and carrying them on to Joseph the husband of Mary, of whom Jesus was born. For it was not held allowable to consider him dissociated from the married estate which was entered into with Mary, on the ground that she gave birth to Christ, not as the wedded wife of Joseph, but as a virgin. For by this example an illustrious recommendation is made to faithful married persons of the principle, that even when by common consent they maintain their continence, the relation can still remain, and can still be called one of wedlock, inasmuch as, although there is no connection between the sexes of the body, there is the keeping of the affections of the mind ; particularly so for this reason, that in their case we see how the birth of a son was a possibility apart from anything of that carnal intercourse which is to be practised with the purpose of the procreation of children only. Moreover, the mere fact that he had not begotten Him by act of his own, was no sufficient reason why Joseph should not be called the father of Christ ; for indeed he could be in all propriety the father of one whom he had not

---

[1] Matt. i. 1.   [2] Matt. viii. 20, ix. 6.   [3] Isa. liii. 8.

begotten by his own wife, but had adopted from some other person.

3. Christ, it is true, was also supposed to be the son of Joseph in another way, as if He had been born simply of that man's seed. But this supposition was entertained by persons whose notice the virginity of Mary escaped. For Luke says : "And Jesus Himself began to be about thirty years of age, being (as was supposed) the son of Joseph." [1] This Luke, however, instead of naming Mary His only parent, had not the slightest hesitation in also speaking of both parties as His parents, when he says : "And the boy grew and waxed strong, filled with wisdom, and the grace of God was in Him : and His parents went to Jerusalem every year at the feast of the passover." [2] But lest any one may fancy that by the "parents" here are rather to be understood the blood relations of Mary along with the mother herself, what shall be said to that preceding word of the same Luke, namely, "And His father [3] and mother marvelled at those things which were spoken of Him"? [4] Since, then, he also makes the statement that Christ was born, not in consequence of Joseph's connection with the mother, but simply of Mary the virgin, how can he call him His father, unless it be that we are to understand him to have been truly the husband of Mary, without the intercourse of the flesh indeed, but in virtue of the real union of marriage ; and thus also to have been in a much closer relation the father of Christ, in so far as He was born of his wife, than would have been the case had He been only adopted from some other party? And this makes it clear that the clause, "as was supposed," [5] is inserted with a view to those who are of opinion that He was begotten by Joseph in the same way as other men are begotten.

CHAP. II. — AN EXPLANATION OF THE SENSE IN WHICH CHRIST IS THE SON OF DAVID, ALTHOUGH HE WAS NOT BEGOTTEN IN THE WAY OF ORDINARY GENERATION BY JOSEPH THE SON OF DAVID.

4. Thus, too, even if one were able to demonstrate that no descent, according to the laws of blood, could be claimed from David for Mary, we should have warrant enough to hold Christ to be the son of David, on the ground of that same mode of reckoning by which also Joseph is called His father. But seeing that the Apostle Paul unmistakably tells us that "Christ was of the seed of David according to the flesh," [6] how much more ought we to accept without any hesitation the position that Mary herself also was descended in some way, according to the laws of blood, from the lineage of David? Moreover, since this woman's connection with the priestly family also is a matter not left in absolute obscurity, inasmuch as Luke inserts the statement that Elisabeth, whom he records to be of the daughters of Aaron, [7] was her cousin, [8] we ought most firmly to hold by the fact that the flesh of Christ sprang from both lines ; to wit, from the line of the kings, and from that of the priests, in the case of which persons there was also instituted a certain mystical unction which was symbolically expressive among this people of the Hebrews. In other words, there was a *chrism ;* which term makes the import of the name of *Christ* patent, and presents it as something indicated so long time ago by an intimation so very intelligible.

CHAP. III. — A STATEMENT OF THE REASON WHY MATTHEW ENUMERATES ONE SUCCESSION OF ANCESTORS FOR CHRIST, AND LUKE ANOTHER.

5. Furthermore, as to those critics who find a difficulty in the circumstance that Matthew enumerates one series of ancestors, beginning with David and travelling downwards to Joseph, [9] while Luke specifies a different succession, tracing it from Joseph upwards as far as to David, [10] they might easily perceive that Joseph may have had two fathers, — namely, one by whom he was begotten, and a second by whom he may have been adopted. [11] For it was an ancient custom also among that people to adopt children with the view of making sons for themselves of those whom they had not begotten. For, leaving out of sight the fact that Pharaoh's daughter [12] adopted Moses (as she was a foreigner), Jacob himself adopted his own grandsons, the sons of Joseph, in these very intelligible terms : "Now, therefore, thy two sons which were born unto thee before I came unto thee, are mine : Ephraim and Manasseh shall be mine, as Reuben and Simeon : and

---

[1] Luke iii. 23. [Revised Version, "And Jesus Himself, when He began *to teach,* was about," etc. The Latin, *erat incipiens,* conveys the same sense. — R.]

[2] Luke ii. 40, 41.]

[3] *Et erat pater ejus,* etc., instead of *Joseph,* etc. [The correct text in Luke ii. 33 is undoubtedly that given by Augustin. Compare critical editions of the Greek text. So Revised Version, "And His father and His mother," etc. — R.]

[4] Luke ii. 33.]

[5] [Compare Revised Version, where the parenthesis is correctly given. — R.]

[6] Rom. i. 3.　　　[7] Luke i. 5.　　　[8] Luke i. 36.
[9] Matt. i. 1-16.　　[10] Luke iii. 23-38.
[11] In the *Retractations* (ii. 16), Augustin alludes to this passage with the view of correcting his statement regarding the adoption. He tells us that, in speaking of the two several fathers whom Joseph may have had, he should not have said that there "was one by whom Joseph was begotten, and another by whom he may have been adopted," but should rather have put it thus: "one by whom he was begotten, and another *unto* whom he was adopted" (*alteri* instead of *ab altero adoptatus*). And the reason indicated for the correction is the probability that the father who begat Joseph was the mother's second husband, who, according to the Levirate law, had married her on the death of his brother without issue. [That Luke gives the lineage of Mary, who was the daughter of Heli, has been held by many scholars. Weiss, in his edition of Meyer's Commentary, claims that this is the only grammatical view; see Robinson's Greek Harmony, rev. ed. pp. 207, 208. Augustin passes over this solution apparently because he was more concerned to press the priestly lineage of Mary. — R.]
[12] Ex. ii. 10.

thy issue which thou begettest after them shall be thine."[1] Whence also it came to pass that there were twelve tribes of Israel, although the tribe of Levi was omitted, which did service in the temple; for along with that one the whole number was thirteen, the sons of Jacob themselves being twelve. Thus, too, we can understand how Luke, in the genealogy contained in his Gospel, has named a father for Joseph, not in the person of the father by whom he was begotten, but in that of the father by whom he was adopted, tracing the list of the progenitors upwards until David is reached. For, seeing that there is a necessity, as both evangelists give a true narrative, — to wit, both Matthew and Luke, — that one of them should hold by the line of the father who begat Joseph, and the other by the line of the father who adopted him, whom should we suppose more likely to have preserved the lineage of the adopting father, than that evangelist who has declined to speak of Joseph as begotten by the person whose son he has nevertheless reported him to be? For it is more appropriate that one should have been called the son of the man by whom he was adopted, than that he should be said to have been begotten by the man of whose flesh he was not descended. Now when Matthew, accordingly, used the phrases, "Abraham begat Isaac," "Isaac begat Jacob," and so on, keeping steadily by the term "begat," until he said at the close, "and Jacob begat Joseph," he gave us to know with sufficient clearness, that he had traced out the order[2] of ancestors on to that father by whom Joseph was not adopted, but begotten.

6. But even although Luke had said that Joseph was begotten by Heli, that expression ought not to disturb us to such an extent as to lead us to believe anything else than that by the one evangelist the father begetting was mentioned, and by the other the father adopting. For there is nothing absurd in saying that a person has begotten, not after the flesh, it may be, but in love, one whom he has adopted as a son. Those of us, to wit, to whom God has given power to become His sons, He did not beget of His own nature and substance, as was the case with His only Son; but He did indeed adopt us in His love. And this phrase the apostle is seen repeatedly to employ just in order to distinguish from us the only-begotten Son who is before every creature, by whom all things were made, who alone is begotten of the substance of the Father; who, in accordance with the equality of divinity, is absolutely what the Father is, and who is declared to have been sent with the view of assuming to Himself the flesh proper to that race to which we too belong according to our nature, in order that by His participation in our mortality, through His love for us, He might make us partakers of His own divinity in the way of adoption. For the apostle speaks thus: "But when the fulness of time was come, God sent forth His Son, made of a woman, made under the law, to redeem them that were under the law, that we might receive[3] the adoption of sons."[4] And yet we are also said to be born of God, — that is to say, in so far as we, who already were men, have received power to be made the sons of God, — to be made such, moreover, by grace, and not by nature. For if we were sons by nature, we never could have been aught else. But when John said, "To them gave He power to become the sons of God, even to them that believe on His name," he proceeded at once to add these words, "which were born not of blood, nor of the will of the flesh, nor of the will of man, but of God."[5] Thus, of the same persons he said, first, that having received power they became the sons of God, which is what is meant by that adoption which Paul mentions; and secondly, that they were born of God. And in order the more plainly to show by what grace this is effected, he continued thus: "And the Word was made flesh, and dwelt among us,"[6] — as if he meant to say, What wonder is it that those should have been made sons of God, although they were flesh, on whose behalf the only Son was made flesh, although He was the Word? Howbeit there is this vast difference between the two cases, that when we are made the sons of God we are changed for the better; but when the Son of God was made the son of man, He was not indeed changed into the worse, but He did certainly assume to Himself what was below Him. James also speaks to this effect: "Of His own will begat He us by the word of truth, that we should be a kind of first fruits[7] of His creatures."[8] And to preclude our supposing, as it might appear from the use of this term "begat," that we are made what He is Himself, he here points out very plainly, that what is conceded to us in virtue of this adoption, is a kind of headship[9] among the creatures.

7. It would be no departure from the truth, therefore, even had Luke said that Joseph was begotten by the person by whom he was really adopted. Even in that way he did in fact beget him, not indeed to be a man, but certainly to be a son; just as God has begotten us to be His sons, whom He had previously made to the effect of being men. But He begat only one to be not simply the Son, which the Father is not, but also God, which the Father in like manner is. At

---

[1] Gen. xlviii. 5, 6.
[2] Reading *ordinem*; others have *originem*, descent.

[3] *Reciperemus.* Most of the older MSS. give *recipiamus*, may receive.
[4] Gal. iv. 4, 5.   [5] John i. 12, 13.   [6] John i. 14.
[7] *Initium*, beginning.   [8] Jas. i. 18.   [9] *Principatum.*

the same time, it is evident that if Luke had employed that phraseology, it would be altogether a matter of dubiety as to which of the two writers mentioned the father adopting, and which the father begetting of his own flesh ; just as, on the other hand, although neither of them had used the word "begat," and although the former evangelist had called him the son of the one person, and the latter the son of the other, it would nevertheless be doubtful which of them named the father by whom he was begotten, and which the father by whom he was adopted. As the case stands now, however, — the one evangelist saying that "Jacob begat Joseph," and the other speaking of "Joseph who was the son of Heli," — by the very distinction which they have made between the expressions, they have elegantly indicated the different objects which they have taken in hand. But surely it might easily suggest itself, as I have said, to a man of piety decided enough to make him consider it right to seek some worthier explanation than that of simply crediting the evangelist with stating what is false ; it might, I repeat, readily suggest itself to such a person to examine what reasons there might be for one man being (supposed) capable of having two fathers. This, indeed, might have suggested itself even to those detractors, were it not that they preferred contention to consideration.

CHAP. IV. — OF THE REASON WHY FORTY GENERATIONS (NOT INCLUDING CHRIST HIMSELF) ARE FOUND IN MATTHEW, ALTHOUGH HE DIVIDES THEM INTO THREE SUCCESSIONS OF FOURTEEN EACH.

8. The matter next to be introduced, moreover, is one requiring, in order to its right apprehension and contemplation, a reader of the greatest attention and carefulness. For it has been acutely observed that Matthew, who had proposed to himself the task of commending the kingly character in Christ, named, exclusive of Christ Himself, forty men in the series of generations. Now this number denotes the period in which, in this age and on this earth, it behoves us to be ruled by Christ in accordance with that painful discipline whereby "God scourgeth," as it is written, "every son that He receiveth ;"[1] and of which also an apostle says that "we must through much tribulation enter into the kingdom of God."[2] This discipline is also signified by that rod of iron, concerning which we read this statement in a Psalm : "Thou shalt rule them with a rod of iron ;"[3] which words occur after the saying, "Yet I am set king by Him upon His holy hill of Zion !"[4] For the good, too, are ruled with a rod of iron, as it is said of them : "The time is come that judgment should begin at the house

of God ; and if it first begin at us, what shall the end be to them that obey not the gospel of God? and if the righteous scarcely be saved, where shall the ungodly and the sinner appear?"[5] To the same persons the sentence that follows also applies : "Thou shalt dash them in pieces like a potter's vessel." For the good, indeed, are ruled by this discipline, while the wicked are crushed by it. And these two different classes of persons are mentioned here as if they were the same, on account of the identity of the signs[6] employed in reference to the wicked in common with the good.

9. That this number, then, is a sign of that laborious period in which, under the discipline of Christ the King, we have to fight against the devil, is also indicated by the fact that both the law and the prophets solemnized a fast of forty days, — that is to say, a humbling of the soul, — in the person of Moses and Elias, who fasted each for a space of forty days.[7] And what else does the Gospel narrative shadow forth under the fast of the Lord Himself, during which forty days He was also tempted of the devil,[8] than that condition of temptation which appertains to us through all the space of this age, and which He bore in the flesh which He condescended to take to Himself from our mortality? After the resurrection also, it was His will to remain with His disciples on the earth not longer than forty days,[9] continuing to mingle for that space of time with this life of theirs in the way of human intercourse, and partaking along with them of the food needful for mortal men, although He Himself was to die no more ; and all this was done with the view of signifying to them through these forty days, that although His presence should be hidden from their eyes, He would yet fulfil what He promised when He said, "Lo, I am with you, even to the end of the world."[10] And in explanation of the circumstance that this particular number should denote this temporal and earthly life, what suggests itself most immediately in the meantime, although there may be another and subtler method of accounting for it, is the consideration that the seasons of the years also revolve in four successive alternations, and that the world itself has its bounds determined by four divisions, which Scripture sometimes designates by the names of the winds, — East and West, Aquilo [or North] and Meridian [or South].[11] But the number forty is equivalent to four times ten. Furthermore, the number ten itself is made up by adding the several numbers in succession from one up to four together.

---

[1] Heb. xii. 6. [2] Acts xiv. 22. [3] Ps. ii. 9.
[4] Ps. ii. 6.

[5] 1 Pet. iv. 17, 18. [6] *Sacramenta.*
[7] Exod. xxxiv. 28; 1 Kings xix. 8. [8] Matt. iv. 1, 2.
[9] Acts i. 3. [10] Matt. xxviii. 20.
[11] Zech. xiv. 4.

10. In this way, then, as Matthew undertook the task of presenting the record of Christ as the King who came into this world, and into this earthly and mortal life of men, for the purpose of exercising rule over us who have to struggle with temptation, he began with Abraham, and enumerated forty men. For Christ came in the flesh from that very nation of the Hebrews, with a view to the keeping of which as a people distinct from the other nations, God separated Abraham from his own country and his own kindred.[1] And the circumstance that the promise contained an intimation of the race from which He was destined to come, served very specially to make the prediction and announcement concerning Him something all the clearer. Thus the evangelist did indeed mark out fourteen generations in each of three several members, stating that from Abraham until David there were fourteen generations, and from David until the carrying away into Babylon other fourteen generations, and another fourteen from that period on to the nativity of Christ.[2] But he did not then reckon them all up in one sum, counting them one by one, and saying that thus they make up forty-two in all. For among these progenitors there is one who is enumerated twice, namely Jechonias, with whom a kind of deflection was made in the direction of extraneous nations at the time when the transmigration into Babylon took place.[3] When the enumeration, moreover, is thus bent from the direct order of progression, and is made to form, if we may so say, a kind of corner for the purpose of taking a different course, what meets us at that corner is mentioned twice over, — namely, at the close of the preceding series, and at the head of the deflection specified. And this, too, was a figure of Christ as the one who was, in a certain sense, to pass from the circumcision to the uncircumcision, or, so to speak, from Jerusalem to Babylon, and to be, as it were, the corner-stone to all who believe on Him, whether on the one side or on the other. Thus was God making preparations then in a figurative manner for things which were to come in truth. For Jechonias himself, with whose name the kind of corner which I have in view was prefigured, is by interpretation the "preparation of God."[4] In this way, therefore, there are really not forty-two distinct generations named here, which would be the proper sum of three times fourteen; but, as there is a double enumeration of one of the names, we have here forty generations in all, taking into

account the fact that Christ Himself is reckoned in the number, who, like the kingly president over this [significant] number forty, superintends the administration of this temporal and earthly life of ours.

11. And inasmuch as it was Matthew's intention to set forth Christ as descending with the object of sharing this mortal state with us, he has mentioned those same generations from Abraham on to Joseph, and on to the birth of Christ Himself, in the form of a descending scale, and at the very beginning of his Gospel. Luke, on the other hand, details those generations not at the commencement of his Gospel, but at the point of Christ's baptism, and gives them not in the descending, but in the ascending order, ascribing to Him preferentially the character of a priest in the expiation of sins, as where the voice from heaven declared Him, and where John himself delivered his testimony in these terms: "Behold the Lamb of God, that taketh away the sin of the world!"[5] Besides, in the process by which he traces the genealogy upwards, he passes Abraham and carries us back to God, to whom, purified and atoned for, we are reconciled. Of merit, too, He has sustained in Himself the origination of our adoption; for we are made the sons of God through adoption, by believing on the Son of God. Moreover, on our account the Son of God was pleased to be made the son of man by the generation which is proper to the flesh. And the evangelist has shown clearly enough that he did not name Joseph the son of Heli on the ground that he was begotten of him, but only on the ground that he was adopted by him. For he has spoken of Adam also as the son of God, who, strictly speaking, was made by God, but was also, as it may be said, constituted a son in paradise by the grace which afterwards he lost through his transgression.

12. In this way, it is the taking of our sins upon Himself by the Lord Christ that is signified in the genealogy of Matthew, while in the genealogy of Luke it is the abolition of our sins by the Lord Christ that is expressed. In accordance with these ideas, the one details the names in the descending scale, and the other in the ascending. For when the apostle says, "God sent His Son in the likeness of the flesh of sin,"[6] he refers to the taking of our sins upon Himself by Christ. But when he adds, "for sin, to condemn sin in the flesh,"[7] he expresses the expiation of sins. Consequently Matthew traces the succession downwards from David through Solomon, in connection with whose mother it was that he sinned; while Luke carries the gene-

---

[1] Gen. xii. 1, 2. [2] Matt. i. 17.
[3] [It is more probable that David should be reckoned twice, in making out the series. Augustin passes over the more serious difficulty arising from the omissions in the genealogy given by Matthew. These omissions, however, show that the evangelist had some purpose in his use of the number "fourteen." Of any design to emphasize the number "forty" there is no evidence. — R.]
[4] Præparatio Dei.

[5] John i. 29.
[6] Rom. viii. 3. [Comp. Revised Version margin. — R.]
[7] Ut de peccato damnaret peccatum in carne. [Revised Version, "And as an offering for sin," etc. — R.]

alogy upwards to the same David through Nathan,[1] by which prophet God took away[2] his sin.[3] The number, also, which Luke follows does most certainly best indicate the taking away of sins. For inasmuch as in Christ, who Himself had no sin, there is assuredly no iniquity allied to the iniquities of men which He bore in His flesh, the number adopted by Matthew makes forty when Christ is excepted. On the contrary, inasmuch as, by clearing us of all sin and purging us, He places us in a right relation to His own and His Father's righteousness (so that the apostle's word is made good: "But he that is joined to the Lord is one spirit"[4]), in the number used by Luke we find included both Christ Himself, with whom the enumeration begins, and God, with whom it closes; and the sum becomes thus seventy-seven, which denotes the thorough remission and abolition of all sins. This perfect removal of sins the Lord Himself also clearly represented under the mystery of this number, when He said that the person sinning ought to be forgiven not only seven times, but even unto seventy times seven.[5]

13. A careful inquiry will make it plain that it is not without some reason that this latter number is made to refer to the purging of all sins. For the number ten is shown to be, as one may say, the number of justice [righteousness] in the instance of the ten precepts of the law. Moreover, sin is the transgression of the law. And the transgression[6] of the number ten is expressed suitably in the eleven; whence also we find instructions to have been given to the effect that there should be eleven curtains of haircloth constructed in the tabernacle;[7] for who can doubt that the haircloth has a bearing upon the expression of sin? Thus, too, inasmuch as all time in its revolution runs in spaces of days designated by the number seven, we find that when the number eleven is multiplied by the number seven, we are brought with all due propriety to the number seventy-seven as the sign of sin in its totality. In this enumeration, therefore, we come upon the symbol for the full remission of sins, as expiation is made for us by the flesh of our Priest, with whose name the calculation of this number starts here; and as reconciliation is also effected for us with God, with whose name the reckoning of this number

is here brought to its conclusion by the Holy Spirit, who appeared in the form of a dove on the occasion of that baptism in connection with which the number in question is mentioned.[8]

CHAP. V. — A STATEMENT OF THE MANNER IN WHICH LUKE'S PROCEDURE IS PROVED TO BE IN HARMONY WITH MATTHEW'S IN THOSE MATTERS CONCERNING THE CONCEPTION AND THE INFANCY OR BOYHOOD OF CHRIST, WHICH ARE OMITTED BY THE ONE AND RECORDED BY THE OTHER.

14. After the enumeration of the generations, Matthew proceeds thus: Now the birth of Christ[9] was on this wise. Whereas His mother Mary was espoused to Joseph, before they came together, she was found with child of the Holy Ghost.[10] What Matthew has omitted to state here regarding the way in which that came to pass, has been set forth by Luke after his account of the conception of John. His narrative is to the following effect: And in the sixth month the angel Gabriel was sent from God unto a city of Galilee named Nazareth, to a virgin espoused to a man whose name was Joseph, of the house of David: and the virgin's name was Mary. And the angel came in unto her, and said, Hail, thou that art full of grace,[11] the Lord is with thee: blessed art thou among women. And when she saw[12] these things, she was troubled at his saying, and cast in her mind what manner of salutation this should be. And the angel said unto her: Fear not, Mary; for thou hast found favour with God. Behold, thou shalt conceive in thy womb, and bring forth a son, and shalt call His name Jesus. He shall be great, and shall be called the Son of the Highest; and the Lord God shall give unto Him the throne of His father David: and He shall reign in the house of Jacob for ever; and of His kingdom there shall be no end. Then said Mary unto the angel, How shall this be, seeing I know not a man? And the angel answered and said unto her, The Holy Ghost shall come upon thee, and the power of the Highest shall overshadow thee: therefore also that holy thing which shall be born[13] shall be called the Son of God;[14] and then follow matters not belonging to the question at present in hand. Now all this Matthew has recorded [summarily], when he tells us of Mary that "she was found with child of the Holy Ghost." Neither

---

[1] 2 Sam. xii. 1-14.   [2] *Expiavit.*
[3] In his *Retractations* (ii. 16) Augustin refers to this sentence in order to chronicle a correction. He tells us that, instead of saying that "Luke carries the genealogy upwards to the same David through Nathan, by which prophet God took away his sin," he should have said "by a prophet of which name," etc., because although the name was the same, the progenitor was a different person from the prophet Nathan.
[4] 1 Cor. vi. 17.
[5] Matt. xviii. 22. [Augustin apparently follows the rendering: "seventy times and seven" (see Revised Version margin), accepted by Meyer and many others. His whole argument turns upon the presence of the number "eleven" as a factor. — R.]
[6] *Transgressio,* overstepping.   [7] Exod. xxvi. 7.

[8] Luke iii. 22.
[9] [The omission of "Jesus" is an early variation of the Latin text of the Gospel. — R.]
[10] Matt. i. 18.
[11] *Gratia plena.* [Comp. Revised Version margin. — R.]
[12] *Quæ cum vidisset.* Others read *audisset,* heard. [The better Greek MSS. omit the clause. The variation in the Latin text here was probably due to the later gloss of the scribes. — R.]
[13] Various editions insert *ex te,* of thee: but the words are omitted in three Vatican MSS., and most of the Gallican. See Migne's note. [Omitted in the Greek text, according to the best authorities. — R.]
[14] Luke i. 26-34. [Ver. 34 is differently rendered in the text of the Revised Version. The Latin of Augustin would perhaps admit of the same sense, but is more naturally explained as above. — R.]

is there any contradiction between the two evangelists, in so far as Luke has set forth in detail what Matthew has omitted to notice; for both bear witness that Mary conceived by the Holy Ghost. And in the same way there is no want of concord between them, when Matthew, in his turn, connects with the narrative something which Luke leaves out. For Matthew proceeds to give us the following statement: Then Joseph, her husband, being a just man, and not willing to make her a public example, was minded to put her away privily. But while he thought on these things, behold, the angel of the Lord appeared unto him in a dream, saying, Joseph, thou son of David, fear not to take unto thee Mary thy wife, for that which is conceived in her is of the Holy Ghost. And she shall bring forth a son, and thou shalt call His name Jesus; for He shall save His people from their sins. Now all this was done that it might be fulfilled which was spoken of the Lord by the prophet, saying, Behold, a virgin shall be with child, and shall bring forth a son; and His name shall be called [1] Emmanuel, which, being interpreted, is, God with us. Then Joseph, being raised from sleep, did as the angel of the Lord had bidden him, and took unto him his wife; and knew her not till she had brought forth her first-born son; [2] and he called His name Jesus. Now when Jesus was born in Bethlehem of Judæa, in the days of Herod the king, and so forth.[3]

15. With respect to the city of Bethlehem, Matthew and Luke are at one. But Luke explains in what way and for what reason Joseph and Mary came to it; whereas Matthew gives no such explanation. On the other hand, while Luke is silent on the subject of the journey of the magi from the east, Matthew furnishes an account of it. That narrative he constructs as follows, in immediate connection with what he has already offered: Behold, there came wise men from the east to Jerusalem, saying, Where is He that is born King of the Jews? for we have seen His star in the east, and are come to worship Him. Now, when Herod the king had heard these things, he was troubled.[4] And in this manner the account goes on, down to the passage where of these magi it is written that, "being warned of God in a dream that they should not return to Herod, they departed into their own country another way."[5] This entire section is omitted by Luke, just as Matthew fails to mention some other circumstances which are mentioned by Luke: as, for example, that the Lord was laid

in a manger; and that an angel announced His birth to the shepherds; and that there was with the angel a multitude of the heavenly host praising God; and that the shepherds came and saw that that was true which the angel had announced to them; and that on the day of His circumcision He received His name; as also the incidents reported by the same Luke to have occurred after the days of the purification of Mary were fulfilled, — namely, their taking Him to Jerusalem, and the words spoken in the temple by Simeon or Anna concerning Him, when, filled with the Holy Ghost, they recognized Him. Of all these things Matthew says nothing.

16. Hence, a subject which deserves inquiry is the question concerning the precise time when these events took place which are omitted by Matthew and given by Luke, and those, on the other hand, which have been omitted by Luke and given by Matthew. For after his account of the return of the magi who had come from the east to their own country, Matthew proceeds to tell us how Joseph was warned by an angel to flee into Egypt with the young child, to prevent His being put to death by Herod; and then how Herod failed to find Him, but slew the children from two years old and under; thereafter, how, when Herod was dead, Joseph returned from Egypt, and, on hearing that Archelaus reigned in Judæa instead of his father Herod, went to reside with the boy in Galilee, at the city Nazareth. All these facts, again, are passed over by Luke. Nothing, however, like a want of harmony can be made out between the two writers merely on the ground that the latter states what the former omits, or that the former mentions what the latter leaves unnoticed. But the real question is as to the exact period at which these things could have taken place which Matthew has linked on to his narrative; to wit, the departure of the family into Egypt, and their return from it after Herod's death, and their residence at that time in the town of Nazareth, the very place to which Luke tells us that they went back after they had performed in the temple all things regarding the boy according to the law of the Lord. Here, accordingly, we have to take notice of a fact which will also hold good for other like cases, and which will secure our minds against similar agitation or disturbance in subsequent instances. I refer to the circumstance that each evangelist constructs his own particular narrative on a kind of plan which gives it the appearance of being the complete and orderly record of the events in their succession. For, preserving a simple silence on the subject of those incidents of which he intends to give no account, he then connects those which he does wish to relate with what he has been immediately recounting, in such a manner

[1] *Vocabitur.* The MSS. give *vocabunt*, they shall call; one MS. gives *vocabis*, thou shalt call. [The proper reading is probably *vocabitur*; at all events, this accords with the Greek text. The variations can be accounted for by the presence of *vocabitur* and *vocabis* in previous part of the paragraph. — R.]
[2] [The best Greek MSS. read "a son" in Matt. i. 23. In Luke ii. 7 "first-born" occurs. — R.]
[3] Matt. i. 19–21.   [4] Matt. ii. 1–3.   [5] Matt. ii. 12.

as to make the recital seem continuous. At the same time, when one of them mentions facts of which the other has given no notice, the order of narrative, if carefully considered, will be found to indicate the point at which the writer by whom the omissions are made has taken the leap in his account, and thus has attached the facts, which it was his purpose to introduce, in such a manner to the preceding context as to give the appearance of a connected series, in which the one incident follows immediately on the other, without the interposition of anything else. On this principle, therefore, we understand that where he tells us how the wise men were warned in a dream not to return to Herod, and how they went back to their own country by another way, Matthew has simply omitted all that Luke has related respecting all that happened to the Lord in the temple, and all that was said by Simeon and Anna; while, on the other hand, Luke has omitted in the same place all notice of the journey into Egypt, which is given by Matthew, and has introduced the return to the city of Nazareth as if it were immediately consecutive.

17. If any one wishes, however, to make up one complete narrative out of all that is said or left unsaid by these two evangelists respectively, on the subject of Christ's nativity and infancy or boyhood, he may arrange the different statements in the following order: — Now the birth of Christ was on this wise.[1] There was, in the days of Herod the king of Judæa, a certain priest named Zacharias, of the course of Abia; and his wife was of the daughters of Aaron, and her name was Elisabeth. And they were both righteous before God, walking in all the commandments and ordinances of the Lord blameless. And they had no child, because that Elisabeth was barren, and they both were well stricken in years. And it came to pass, that while he executed the priest's office before God, in the order of his course, according to the custom of the priest's office, his lot was to burn incense when he went into the temple of the Lord: and the whole multitude of the people were praying without at the time of incense. And there appeared unto him an angel of the Lord standing on the right side of the altar of incense. And when Zacharias saw him he was troubled, and fear fell upon him. But the angel said unto him, Fear not, Zacharias: for thy prayer is heard; and thy wife Elisabeth shall bear thee a son, and thou shalt call his name John. And thou shalt have joy and gladness; and many shall rejoice at his birth. For he

shall be great in the sight of the Lord: and he shall drink neither wine nor strong drink; and he shall be filled with the Holy Ghost, even from his mother's womb. And many of the children of Israel shall he turn to the Lord their God. And he shall go before him in the spirit and power of Elias, to turn the hearts of the fathers to the children, and the disobedient to the wisdom of the just; to make ready a people perfect[2] for the Lord. And Zacharias said unto the angel, Whereby shall I know this? for I am an old man, and my wife well stricken in years. And the angel, answering, said unto him, I am Gabriel, that stand in the presence of God; and am sent to speak unto thee, and to show thee these glad tidings. And, behold, thou shalt be dumb,[3] and not able to speak, until the day that these things shall be performed, because thou hast not believed my words, which shall be fulfilled in their season. And the people waited for Zacharias, and marvelled that he tarried in the temple. And when he came out, he could not speak unto them: and they perceived that he had seen a vision in the temple: and he beckoned unto them, and remained speechless. And it came to pass that, as soon as the days of his ministration were accomplished, he departed to his own house. And after those days his wife Elisabeth conceived, and hid herself five months, saying, Thus hath the Lord dealt with me in the days wherein He looked upon me, to take away my reproach among men. And in the sixth month the angel Gabriel was sent from God unto a city of Galilee, named Nazareth, to a virgin espoused to a man whose name was Joseph, of the house of David; and the virgin's name was Mary. And the angel came in unto her, and said, Hail, thou that art full of grace,[4] the Lord is with thee; blessed art thou among women. And when she saw him, she was troubled at his saying, and cast in her mind what manner of salutation this should be. And the angel said unto her, Fear not, Mary: for thou hast found favour with God. Behold, thou shalt conceive in thy womb, and bring forth a son, and shalt call His name Jesus. He shall be great, and shall be called the Son of the Highest; and the Lord God shall give unto Him the throne of His father David: and He shall reign in the house of Jacob for ever; and of His kingdom there shall be no end. Then said Mary unto the angel, How shall this be, seeing I know not a man? And the angel answered and said unto her, The Holy Ghost shall come upon thee, and the power of the Highest shall overshadow thee: therefore also that holy

---

[1] Matt. i. 18; Luke i. 5. [In this extended citation from the Gospels of Matthew and Luke, the Latin text given by Augustin is, in many cases, more closely reproduced in the Revised Version than in the Authorized. The translator has, as usual, taken the language of the latter, except in a few places, where the difference seemed more important and striking. — R.]

[2] *Perfectum.*
[3] [*Tacens;* the fair equivalent of the original Greek phrase, properly rendered "silent" in the Revised Version. — R.]
[4] *Gratia plena.*

thing which shall be born of thee shall be called the Son of God.[1] And, behold, thy cousin Elisabeth, she hath also conceived a son in her old age : and this is the sixth month with her, who is called[2] barren. For with God nothing shall be impossible. And Mary said, Behold the handmaid of the Lord ; be it unto me according to thy word. And the angel departed from her. And Mary arose in those days, and went into the hill country with haste, into a city of Juda ; and entered into the house of Zacharias, and saluted Elisabeth. And it came to pass, that when Elisabeth heard the salutation of Mary, the babe leaped in her womb ; and Elisabeth was filled with the Holy Ghost : and she spake out with a loud voice, and said, Blessed art thou among women, and blessed is the fruit of thy womb. And whence is this to me, that the mother of my Lord should come to me ? for, lo, as soon as the voice of thy salutation sounded in mine ears, the babe leaped in my womb for joy. And blessed art thou that didst believe,[3] for there shall be a performance of those things which were told thee from the Lord. And Mary said, My soul doth magnify the Lord, and my spirit hath rejoiced in God my Saviour. For He hath regarded the low estate of His handmaiden : for, behold, from henceforth all generations shall call me blessed. For He that is mighty hath done to me great things, and holy is His name. And His mercy is on them that fear Him, from generation to generation. He hath made[4] strength with His arm ; He hath scattered the proud in the imagination of their heart. He hath put down the mighty from their seat, and exalted them of low degree. He hath filled the hungry with good things, and the rich He hath sent empty away. He hath holpen[5] His servant Israel, in remembrance of his mercy : as He spake to our fathers, to Abraham, and to his seed for ever. And Mary abode with her about three months, and returned to her own house.[6] Then it proceeds thus : — She was found with child of the Holy Ghost.[7] Then Joseph her husband, being a just man, and not willing to make her a public example, was minded to put her away privily. But while he thought on these things, behold, the angel of the Lord appeared unto him in a dream, saying, Joseph, thou son of David, fear not to take unto thee Mary thy wife : for that which is conceived in her is of the Holy Ghost. And she shall bring forth a son, and thou shalt call His name Jesus : for He shall save His people from their sins. Now all this was done,

that it might be fulfilled which was spoken of the Lord by the prophet, saying, Behold, a virgin shall be with child, and shall bring forth a son, and they shall call His name Emmanuel ; which, being interpreted, is, God with us. Then Joseph, being raised from sleep, did as the angel of the Lord had bidden him, and took unto him his wife, and knew her not.[8] Now[9] Elisabeth's full time came that she should be delivered, and she brought forth a son. And her neighbours and her relatives[10] heard that the Lord magnified His mercy with her ; and they congratulated her. And it came to pass, that on the eighth day they came to circumcise the child ; and they called[11] him Zacharias, after the name of his father. And his mother answered and said, Not so ; but he shall be called John. And they said unto her, There is none of thy kindred that is called by this name. And they made signs to his father, how he would have him called. And he asked for a writing table, and wrote, saying, His name is John. And they marvelled all. And his mouth was opened immediately, and his tongue, and he spake and praised God. And fear came on all them that dwelt round about them : and all these sayings were noised abroad throughout all the hill country of Judæa. And all they that had heard them laid them up in their heart, saying, What manner of child, thinkest thou, shall this be ? For the hand of the Lord was with him. And his father Zacharias was filled with the Holy Ghost, and prophesied, saying, Blessed be the Lord God of Israel ; for He hath visited and redeemed His people, and hath raised up an horn of salvation for us in the house of His servant David ; as He spake by the mouth of His holy prophets, which have been since the world began ; (to give) salvation from our enemies, and from the hand of all that hate us : to perform mercy with our fathers, and to remember His holy covenant, the oath which He sware to Abraham our father that He would give to us ; in order that, being saved out of the hand of our enemies, we might serve Him without fear, in holiness and righteousness before Him, all our days. And thou, child, shalt be called the Prophet of the Highest : for thou shalt go before the face of the Lord to prepare His ways ; to give knowledge of salvation unto His people, for the remission[12] of their sins, through the tender mercy of our God ; whereby the dayspring from on high hath visited us, to give light to them that sit in darkness and in the shadow of death, to guide our feet into the way of peace. And the child grew, and waxed

---

[1] [Compare above on § 14. — R.]   [2] Vocatur.
[3] Beata quæ credidisti.   [4] Fecit.
[5] Undertaken — suscepit.   [6] Luke i. 5–36.
[7] Matt. i. 18. [The discovery of Mary's condition probably occurred, as the order of Augustin implies, after the return of Mary from the visit to Elisabeth. But it is altogether uncertain whether it preceded the birth of John the Baptist. — R.]

[8] Matt. i. 18–25. [The last clause of ver. 25 is omitted here, but given in § 14. Possibly the variation was intentional. — R.]
[9] Luke i. 57.   [10] Cognati.
[11] [Vocabunt, "would have called," answering to the Greek imperfect of arrested action. — R.]
[12] In remissionem.

strong in spirit, and was in the deserts until the day of his showing unto Israel. And it came to pass in those days, that there went out a decree from Cæsar Augustus, that all the world should be taxed.[1] This first taxing[2] was made when Syrinus[3] was governor of Syria. And all went to be taxed,[4] every one into his own city. And Joseph also went up from Galilee, out of the city of Nazareth, into Judæa, unto the city of David, which is called Bethlehem, because he was of the house and lineage of David, to be taxed[5] with Mary his espoused wife, being great with child. And so it was, that while they were there, the days were accomplished that she should be delivered. And she brought forth her first-born son, and wrapped Him in swaddling-clothes, and laid Him in a manger; because there was no room for them in the inn. And there were in the same country shepherds watching and keeping the virgils of the night over their flock. And, lo, the angel of the Lord stood by them, and the glory of the Lord shone round about them; and they were sore afraid. And the angel said unto them, Fear not: for, behold, I bring you good tidings of great joy, which shall be to all people. For unto you is born this day, in the city of David, a Saviour, which is Christ the Lord. And this shall be a sign unto you: Ye shall find the babe wrapped in swaddling-clothes, lying in a manger. And suddenly there was with the angel a multitude of the heavenly host praising God, and saying, Glory to God in the highest, and on earth peace to men of goodwill.[6] And it came to pass, as the angels were gone away from them into heaven, the shepherds said one to another, Let us now go even unto Bethlehem, and see this thing which is come to pass, which the Lord hath made known unto us. And they came with haste, and found Mary and Joseph, and the babe lying in a manger. And when they had seen it, they understood[7] the saying which had been told them concerning this child. And all they that heard it, wondered also at those things which were told them by the shepherds. But Mary kept all these things, and pondered them in her heart. And the shepherds returned, glorifying and praising God for all the things that they had heard and seen, as it was told unto them. And when eight days were accomplished for the circumcising of the child, His name was called Jesus, which was so named of the angel before He was conceived in the womb.[8] And

then it proceeds thus:[9] Behold, there came wise men from the east to Jerusalem, saying, Where is He that is born King of the Jews? for we have seen His star in the east, and are come to worship Him. Now when Herod the king had heard these things, he was troubled, and all Jerusalem with him. And when he had gathered all the chief priests and scribes of the people together, he demanded of them where Christ should be born. And they said unto him, In Bethlehem of Judæa; for thus it is written by the prophet, And thou, Bethlehem, in the land of Juda, art not the least among the princes of Juda: for out of thee shall come a Governor that shall rule my people Israel. Then Herod, when he had privily called the wise men, inquired of them diligently the time of the star which appeared unto them. And he sent them to Bethlehem, and said, Go and search diligently for the young child; and when ye have found him, bring me word again, that I may come and worship him also. When they had heard the king, they departed; and, lo, the star which they had seen in the east went before them, until it came and stood over where the young child was. And when they saw the star, they rejoiced with exceeding great joy. And when they were come into the house, they found[10] the child with Mary His mother, and fell down and worshipped Him: and when they had opened their treasures, they presented unto Him gifts, gold, frankincense, and myrrh. And being warned of God in a dream that they should not return unto Herod, they departed into their own country another way.[11] Then, after this account of their return, the narrative goes on thus:[12] When the days of her (His mother's) purification, according to the law of Moses, were accomplished, they brought Him to Jerusalem, to present Him to the Lord (as it is written in the law of the Lord, Every male that openeth the womb shall be called holy to the Lord), and to offer a sacrifice according to that which is said in the law of the Lord, A pair of turtle-doves, or two young pigeons. And, behold, there was a man in Jerusalem whose name was Simeon; and the same man was just and devout, waiting for the consolation of Israel: and the Holy Ghost was in him. And it had been revealed unto him[13] by the Holy Ghost, that he should not see death before he had seen the Lord's Christ. And he came by the Spirit into the temple. And when His parents brought in the child Jesus, to do for Him after the cus-

---

[1] *Describeretur*, registered. [Revised Version, "should be enrolled." — R.]
[2] *Descriptio prima* [This is now the accepted sense of the phrase in Luke ii. 2; Comp. Revised Version. — R.]
[3] Reading *præside Syriæ Syrino*; in some MSS. it is *a præside*, etc., and *sub præside* also occurs.
[4] *Profiterentur*, to make their declaration.
[5] *Profiteretur*, make his declaration.
[6] *Hominibus bonæ voluntatis*. [Comp. Revised Version. — R.]
[7] *Cognoverunt*.   [8] Luke i. 57–ii. 21.

[9] Matt. ii. 1. [It is here assumed that the visit of the Magi preceded the presentation in the temple. But this order cannot be positively established. The two events must be placed near together. In chap. xi. Augustin implies that there was an interval of some length. The traditional date of the Epiphany (Jan. 6) is clearly too early, since it assumes an interval of twenty-seven days. — R.]
[10] *Invenerunt*.   [11] Matt. ii. 1–12.
[12] Luke ii. 22.   [13] *Responsum acceperat*.

tom of the law, then took he Him up in his arms, and said, Lord, now lettest Thou Thy servant depart in peace, according to Thy word: for mine eyes have seen Thy salvation, which Thou hast prepared before the face of all people; a light to lighten the Gentiles, and the glory of Thy people Israel. And His father and mother[1] marvelled at those things which were spoken of Him. And Simeon blessed them, and said unto Mary His mother, Behold, this child is set for the fall and rising again of many in Israel, and for a sign that shall be spoken against; and a sword shall pierce through thy own soul also, that the thoughts of many hearts may be revealed. And there was one Anna, a prophetess, the daughter of Phanuel, of the tribe of Aser: she was of a great age, and had lived with her husband seven years from her virginity; and she was a widow of about fourscore and four years, which departed not from the temple, but served God with fastings and prayers day and night. And she, coming in that instant, gave thanks[2] also unto the Lord, and spake of Him to all them that looked for the redemption of Jerusalem.[3] And when they had performed all things according to the law of the Lord,[4] behold,[5] the angel of the Lord appeared to Joseph in a dream, saying, Arise, and take the young child and His mother, and flee into Egypt, and be thou there until I bring thee word; for Herod will seek the young child to destroy Him. When he arose, he took the young child and His mother by night, and departed into Egypt, and was there until the death of Herod; that it might be fulfilled which was spoken of the Lord by the prophet, saying, Out of Egypt have I called my Son. Then Herod, when he saw that he was mocked of the wise men, was exceeding wroth, and sent forth, and slew all the children that were in Bethlehem, and in all the coasts thereof, from two years old and under, according to the time which he had diligently inquired of the wise men. Then was fulfilled that which was spoken by Jeremy the prophet, saying, In Rama was there a voice heard, lamentation and great mourning,[6] Rachel weeping for her children, and would not be comforted, because they are not. But when Herod was dead, behold, an angel of the Lord appeared in a dream to Joseph in Egypt, saying, Arise, and take the young child and His mother, and go into the land of Israel; for they are dead which sought the young child's life. And he arose,

and took the young child and His mother, and came into the land of Israel. But when he heard that Archelaus did reign in Judæa, in the room of his father Herod, he was afraid to go thither; and being warned of God in a dream, he turned aside into the parts of Galilee; and he came and dwelt in a city called Nazareth, that it might be fulfilled which was spoken by the prophets, He shall be called a Nazarene.[7] And[8] the child grew, and waxed strong, filled with wisdom; and the grace of God was in Him. And His parents went to Jerusalem every year, at the feast of the passover. And when He was twelve years old, they went up to Jerusalem, after the custom of the feast. And when they had fulfilled the days, as they returned, the child Jesus tarried behind in Jerusalem; and His parents[9] knew not of it. But they, supposing Him to have been in the company, went a day's journey; and they sought Him among their kinsfolk and acquaintance. And when they found Him not, they turned back again to Jerusalem, seeking Him. And it came to pass, that after three days they found Him in the temple, sitting in the midst of the doctors, both hearing them and asking them questions. And all that heard Him were astonished at His understanding and answers. And when they saw Him, they were amazed. And His mother said to Him, Son, why hast thou thus dealt with us? behold, thy father and I sought thee sorrowing. And He said unto them, How is it that ye sought me? Wist ye not that I must be about my Father's business?[10] And they understood not the saying which He spake unto them. And He went down with them, and came to Nazareth, and was subject unto them; and His mother kept all these sayings in her heart.[11] And Jesus increased in wisdom and age,[12] and in favour with God and men.[13]

CHAP. VI. — ON THE POSITION GIVEN TO THE PREACHING OF JOHN THE BAPTIST IN ALL THE FOUR EVANGELISTS.

18. Now at this point commences the account of the preaching of John, which is presented by all the four. For after the words which I have placed last in the order of his narrative thus far, — the words with which he introduces the testimony from the prophet, namely, He shall be called a Nazarene, — Matthew proceeds immediately to give us this recital: " In those days came John the Baptist, preaching in the wilder-

---

[1] *Pater ejus et mater.* ["Joseph" was early substituted. Augustin follows the text now accepted on the authority of the best Greek mss. — R.]
[2] *Confitebatur*, made acknowledgment.
[3] Reading *redemptionem Jerusalem;* for which some editions gave *redemptionem Israel.*
[4] Luke ii. 22–39.   [5] Matt. ii. 13.
[6] [The briefer reading, here accepted, is more correctly rendered in the Revised Version. — R.]

[7] Matt. ii. 13–23.   [8] Luke ii. 40.
[9] *Parentes ejus.* ["Joseph and His mother" is the later reading, followed in the Authorized Version. — R.]
[10] *In his quæ Patris mei sunt.* [Comp. Revised Version. — R.]
[11] Reading, with the mss., *conservabat omnia verba hæc in corde suo.* Some editions insert *conferens*, pondering them.
[12] *Ætate.* [So Revised Version margin. — R.]
[13] Luke ii. 40–52.

ness of Judæa," [1] etc. And Mark, who has told us nothing of the nativity or infancy or youth of the Lord, has made his Gospel begin with the same event, — that is to say, with the preaching of John. For it is thus that he sets out : The beginning of the Gospel of Jesus Christ, the Son of God ; as it is written in the prophet Isaiah,[2] Behold, I send a messenger [3] before Thy face, which shall prepare Thy way before Thee. The voice of one crying in the wilderness, Prepare ye the way of the Lord, make His paths straight. John was in the wilderness baptizing, and preaching the baptism of repentance for the remission of sins,[4] etc. Luke, again, follows up the passage in which he says, " And Jesus increased in wisdom and age,[5] and in favour with God and man," by a section in which he speaks of the preaching of John in these terms : Now in the fifteenth year of the reign of Tiberius Cæsar, Pontius Pilate being governor of Judæa, and Herod being tetrarch of Galilee, and his brother Philip tetrarch of Ituræa and of the region of Trachonitis, and Lysanias the tetrarch of Abilene, Annas and Caiaphas being the high priests, the word of God came unto John, the son of Zacharias, in the wilderness,[6] etc. The Apostle John, too, the most eminent of the four evangelists, after discoursing of the Word of God, who is also the Son, antecedent to all the ages of creaturely existence, inasmuch as all things were made by Him, has introduced in the immediate context his account of the preaching and testimony of John, and proceeds thus : There was a man sent from God, whose name was John.[7] This will be enough at once to make it plain that the narratives concerning John the Baptist given by the four evangelists are not at variance with one another. And there will be no occasion for requiring or demanding that to be done in all detail in this instance which we have already done in the case of the genealogies of the Christ who was born of Mary, to the effect of proving how Matthew and Luke are in harmony with each other, of showing how we might construct one consistent narrative out of the two, and of demonstrating on behoof of those of less acute perception, that although one of these evangelists may mention what the other omits, or omit what the other mentions, he does not thereby make it in any sense difficult to accept the veracity of the account given by the other. For when a single example [of this method of harmonizing] has been set before us, whether in the way in which it has been presented by me, or in some other method in which it may more satisfactorily be exhibited, every man can understand

that, in all other similar passages, what he has seen done here may be done again.

19. Accordingly, let us now study, as I have said, the harmony of the four evangelists in the narratives regarding John the Baptist. Matthew proceeds in these terms : In those days came John the Baptist, preaching in the wilderness of Judæa.[1] Mark has not used the phrase " In those days," because he has given no recital of any series of events at the head of his Gospel immediately before this narrative, so that he might be understood to speak in reference to the dates of such events under the terms, " In those days." [8] Luke, on the other hand, with greater precision has defined those times of the preaching or baptism of John, by means of the notes of the temporal power. For he says : Now, in the fifteenth year of the reign of Tiberius Cæsar, Pontius Pilate being governor of Judæa, and Herod being tetrarch of Galilee, and his brother Philip tetrarch of Ituræa and of the region of Trachonitis, and Lysanias the tetrarch of Abilene, Annas and Caiaphas being the high priests, the word of God came unto John, the son of Zacharias, in the wilderness.[9] We ought not, however, to understand that what was actually meant by Matthew when He said, " In those days," was simply the space of days literally limited to the specified period of these powers. On the contrary, it is apparent that he intended the note of time which was conveyed in the phrase " In those days," to be taken to refer to a much longer period. For he first gives us the account of the return of Christ from Egypt after the death of Herod, — an incident, indeed, which took place at the time of His infancy or childhood, and with which, consequently, Luke's statement of what befell Him in the temple when He was twelve years of age is quite consistent.[10] Then, immediately after this narrative of the recall of the infant or boy out of Egypt, Matthew continues thus in due order : " Now, in those days came John the Baptist." And thus under that phrase he certainly covers not merely the days of His childhood, but all the days intervening between His nativity and this period at which John began to preach and to baptize. At this period, moreover, Christ is found already to have attained to man's estate ; [11] for John and he were of the same age ; [12] and it is stated that He was about [13] thirty years of age when He was baptized by the former.

CHAP. VII. — OF THE TWO HERODS.

20. But with respect to the mention of Herod, it is well understood that some are apt to be in-

---

[1] Matt. iii. 1.
[2] *In Isaia propheta.* [So the Greek text, according to the best MSS. Comp. Revised Version. — R.]
[3] *Angelum.*　　[4] Mark i. 1-4.　　[5] *Ætate.*
[6] Luke iii. 1, 2.　　[7] John i. 6.

[8] Mark i. 4.　　[9] Luke iii. 1-3.　　[10] Luke ii. 42-50.
[11] *Juvenilis ætas.* For *juvenilis ætas*, the MSS. give regularly *juvenalis ætas.*
[12] *Coævi.*　　[13] *Ferme.*

fluenced by the circumstance that Luke has told us how, in the days of John's baptizing, and at the time when the Lord, being then a grown man, was also baptized, Herod was tetrarch of Galilee ;[1] whereas Matthew tells us that the boy[2] Jesus returned from Egypt after the death of Herod. Now these two accounts cannot both be true, unless we may also suppose that there were two different Herods. But as no one can fail to be aware that this is a perfectly possible case, what must be the blindness in which those persons pursue their mad follies, who are so quick to launch false charges against the truth of the Gospels ; and how miserably inconsiderate must they be, not to reflect that two men may have been called by the same name? Yet this is a thing of which examples abound on all sides. For this latter Herod is understood to have been the son of the former Herod : just as Archelaus also was, whom Matthew states to have succeeded to the throne of Judæa on the death of his father; and as Philip was, who is introduced by Luke as the brother of Herod the tetrarch, and as himself tetrarch of Ituræa. For the Herod who sought the life of the child Christ was king ; whereas this other Herod, his son, was not called king, but tetrarch, which is a Greek word, signifying etymologically one set over the fourth part of a kingdom.

CHAP. VIII. — AN EXPLANATION OF THE STATE-MENT MADE BY MATTHEW, TO THE EFFECT THAT JOSEPH WAS AFRAID TO GO WITH THE INFANT CHRIST INTO JERUSALEM ON ACCOUNT OF ARCHELAUS, AND YET WAS NOT AFRAID TO GO INTO GALILEE, WHERE HEROD, THAT PRINCE'S BROTHER, WAS TETRARCH.

21. Here again, however, it may happen that a difficulty will be found, and that some, seeing that Matthew has told us how Joseph was afraid to go into Judæa with the child on his return, expressly for the reason that Archelaus the son reigned there in place of his father Herod, may be led to ask how he could have gone into Galilee, where, as Luke bears witness, there was another son of that Herod, namely, Herod the tetrarch. But such a difficulty can only be founded on the fancy that the times indicated as those in which there was such apprehension on the child's account were identical with the times dealt with now by Luke : whereas it is conspicuously evident that there is a change in the periods, because we no longer find Archelaus represented as king in Judæa ; but in place of him we have Pontius Pilate, who also was not the king of the Jews, but only their governor, in whose times the sons of the elder Herod,

acting under Tiberius Cæsar, held not the kingdom, but the tetrarchy. And all this certainly had not come to pass at the time when Joseph, in fear of the Archelaus who was then reigning in Judæa, betook himself, together with the child, into Galilee, where was also his city Nazareth.

CHAP. IX. — AN EXPLANATION OF THE CIRCUM-STANCE THAT MATTHEW STATES THAT JOSEPH'S REASON FOR GOING INTO GALILEE WITH THE CHILD CHRIST WAS HIS FEAR OF ARCHELAUS, WHO WAS REIGNING AT THAT TIME IN JERUSA-LEM IN PLACE OF HIS FATHER, WHILE LUKE TELLS US THAT THE REASON FOR GOING INTO GALILEE WAS THE FACT THAT THEIR CITY NAZARETH WAS THERE.

22. Or may a question perchance be raised as to how Matthew tells us that His parents went with the boy Jesus into Galilee, because they were unwilling to go into Judæa in consequence of their fear of Archelaus ; whereas it would rather appear that the reason for their go-ing into Galilee was, as Luke has not failed to indicate, the consideration that their city was Nazareth of Galilee? Well, but we must observe, that when the angel said to Joseph in his dreams in Egypt, " Arise, and take the young child and His mother, and go into the land of Israel,"[3] the words were understood at first by Joseph in a way that made him consider himself commanded to journey into Judæa. For that was the first in-terpretation that could have been put upon the phrase, " the land of Israel." But again, after ascertaining that Archelaus, the son of Herod, was reigning there, he declined to expose him-self to such danger, inasmuch as this phrase, " the land of Israel," was capable also of being so understood as to cover Galilee too, because the people of Israel were occupants of that ter-ritory as well as the other. At the same time, this question also admits of being solved in another manner. For it might have appeared to the parents of Christ that they were called to take up their residence along with the boy, concerning whom such information had been conveyed to them through the responses of angels, just in Jerusalem itself, where was the temple of the Lord : and it may thus be, that when they came back out of Egypt, they would have gone directly thither in that belief, and have taken up their abode there, had it not been that they were terrified at the presence of Archelaus. And certainly they did not receive any such instructions from heaven to take up their residence there as would have made it their imperative duty to set at nought the fears they entertained of Archelaus.

---

[1] Luke iii. 1-21.   [2] *Puerum.*   [3] Matt. ii. 19, 20.

CHAP. X. — A STATEMENT OF THE REASON WHY LUKE TELLS US THAT "HIS PARENTS WENT TO JERUSALEM EVERY YEAR AT THE FEAST OF THE PASSOVER" ALONG WITH THE BOY; WHILE MATTHEW INTIMATES THAT THEIR DREAD OF ARCHELAUS MADE THEM AFRAID TO GO THERE ON THEIR RETURN FROM EGYPT.

23. Or does any one put to us this question, How was it, then, that His parents went up to Jerusalem every year during the boyhood of Christ, as Luke's narrative bears, if they were prevented from going there by the fear of Archelaus? Well, I should not deem it any very difficult task to solve this question, even although none of the evangelists has given us to understand how long Archelaus reigned there. For it might have been the case that, simply for that one day, and with the intention of returning forthwith, they went up on the day of the feast, without attracting any notice among the vast multitudes then assembled, to the city where, nevertheless, they were afraid to make their residence on other days. And thus they might at once have saved themselves from the appearance of being so irreligious as to neglect the observance of the feast, and have avoided drawing attention upon themselves by a continued sojourn. But further, although all the evangelists have omitted to tell us what was the length of the reign of Archelaus, we have still open to us this obvious method of explaining the matter, namely, to understand the custom to which Luke refers, when he says that they were in the habit of going to Jerusalem every year,[1] as one prosecuted at a time when Archelaus was no more an object of fear. But if the reign of Archelaus should be made out to have lasted for a somewhat longer period on the authority of any extra-evangelical history which appears to deserve credit, the consideration which I have indicated above should still prove quite sufficient, —namely, the supposition that the fear which the parents of the child entertained of a residence in Jerusalem was, nevertheless, not of such a nature as to lead them to neglect the observance of the sacred festival to which they were under obligation in the fear of God, and which they might very easily go about in a manner that would not attract public attention to them. For surely it is nothing incredible that, by taking advantage of favourable opportunities, whether by day or by hour, men may (safely venture to) approach places in which they nevertheless are afraid to be found tarrying.

CHAP. XI. — AN EXAMINATION OF THE QUESTION AS TO HOW IT WAS POSSIBLE FOR THEM TO GO UP, ACCORDING TO LUKE'S STATEMENT, WITH HIM TO JERUSALEM TO THE TEMPLE, WHEN THE DAYS OF THE PURIFICATION OF THE MOTHER OF CHRIST WERE ACCOMPLISHED, IN ORDER TO PERFORM THE USUAL RITES, IF IT IS CORRECTLY RECORDED BY MATTHEW, THAT HEROD HAD ALREADY LEARNED FROM THE WISE MEN THAT THE CHILD WAS BORN IN WHOSE STEAD, WHEN HE SOUGHT FOR HIM, HE SLEW SO MANY CHILDREN.

24. Hereby also we see how another question is solved, if any one indeed finds a difficulty in it. I allude to the question as to how it was possible, on the supposition that the elder Herod was already anxious (to obtain information regarding Him), and agitated by the intelligence received from the wise men concerning the birth of the King of the Jews, for them, when the days of the purification of His mother were accomplished, to go up in any safety with Him to the temple, in order to see to the performance of those things which were according to the law of the Lord, and which are specified by Luke.[2] For who can fail to perceive that this solitary day might very easily have escaped the notice of a king, whose attention was engaged with a multitude of affairs? Or if it does not appear probable that Herod, who was waiting in the extremest anxiety to see what report the wise men would bring back to him concerning the child, should have been so long in finding out how he had been mocked, that, only after the mother's purification was already past, and the solemnities proper to the first-born were performed with respect to the child in the temple, nay more, only after their departure into Egypt, did it come into his mind to seek the life of the child, and to slay so many little ones; — if, I say, any one finds a difficulty in this, I shall not pause to state the numerous and important occupations by which the king's attention may have been engaged, and for the space of many days either wholly diverted from such thoughts, or prevented from following them out. For it is not possible to enumerate all the cases which might have made that perfectly possible. No one, however, is so ignorant of human affairs as either to deny or to question that there may very easily have been many such matters of importance (to preoccupy the king). For to whom will not the thought occur, that reports, whether true or false, of many other more terrible things may possibly have been brought to the king, so that the person who had been apprehensive of a certain royal child, who after a number of years might prove an adversary to himself or to his sons, might be so agitated with the terrors of certain more immediate dangers, as to have his attention forcibly removed from that earlier

---

[1] Luke ii. 4.

[2] [Compare note on the relative position of the visit of the Magi and the presentation in the temple, § 17. — R.]

anxiety, and engaged rather with the devising of measures to ward off other more instantly threatening perils? Wherefore, leaving all such considerations unspecified, I simply venture on the assertion that, when the wise men failed to bring back any report to him, Herod may have believed that they had been misled by a deceptive vision of a star, and that, after their want of success in discovering Him whom they had supposed to have been born, they had been ashamed to return to him; and that in this way the king, having his fears allayed, had given up the idea of asking after and persecuting the child. Consequently, when they had gone with Him to Jerusalem after the purification of His mother, and when those things had been performed in the temple which are recounted by Luke,[1] inasmuch as the words which were spoken by Simeon and Anna in their prophesyings regarding Him, when publicity began to be given to them by the persons who had heard them, were like to call back the king's mind then to its original design, Joseph obeyed the warning conveyed to him in the dream, and fled with the child and His mother into Egypt. Afterwards, when the things which had been done and said in the temple were made quite public, Herod perceived that he had been mocked; and then, in his desire to get at the death of Christ, he slew the multitude of children, as Matthew records.[2]

CHAP. XII. — CONCERNING THE WORDS ASCRIBED TO JOHN BY ALL THE FOUR EVANGELISTS RESPECTIVELY.

25. Moreover, Matthew makes up his account of John in the following manner : — Now in those days came John the Baptist, preaching in the wilderness of Judæa, and saying, Repent ye, for the kingdom of heaven is at hand. For this is He that is spoken of by the prophet Esaias, saying, The voice of one crying in the wilderness, Prepare ye the way of the Lord, make His paths straight.[3] Mark also and Luke agree in presenting this testimony of Isaiah as one referring to John.[4] Luke, indeed, has likewise recorded some other words from the same prophet, which follow those already cited, when he gives his narrative of John the Baptist. The evangelist John, again, mentions that John the Baptist did also personally advance this same testimony of Isaiah regarding himself.[5] And, to a similar effect, Matthew here has given us certain words of John which are unrecorded by the other evangelists. For he speaks of him as " preaching in the wilderness of Judæa, and saying, Repent ye, for the kingdom of heaven is at hand ; " which words of John have been omitted by the others. In

what follows, however, in immediate connection with that passage in Matthew's Gospel, — namely, the sentence, " The voice of one crying in the wilderness, Prepare ye the way of the Lord, make His paths straight," — the position is ambiguous ; and it does not clearly appear whether this is something recited by Matthew in his own person, or rather a continuance of the words spoken by John himself, so as to lead us to understand the whole passage to be the reproduction of John's own utterance, in this way : " Repent ye, for the kingdom of heaven is at hand ; for this is He that was spoken of by the prophet Isaiah," and so on. For it ought to create no difficulty against this latter view, that he does not say, " For I am He that was spoken of by the prophet Isaiah," but employs the phraseology, " For this is He that was spoken of." For that, indeed, is a mode of speech [6] which the evangelists Matthew and John are in the habit of using in reference to themselves. Thus Matthew has adopted the phrase, " He found [7] a man sitting at the receipt of custom," [8] instead of " He found me." John, too, says, " This is the disciple which testifieth of these things, and wrote these things, and we know that his testimony is true," [9] instead of " I am," etc., or, " My testimony is true." Yea, our Lord Himself very frequently uses the words, " The Son of man, [10] or, " The Son of God," [11] instead of saying, " I." So, again, He tells us that " it behoved Christ to suffer, and to rise from the dead the third day," [12] instead of saying, " It behoved me to suffer." Consequently it is perfectly possible that the clause, " For this is He that was spoken of by the prophet Isaiah," which immediately follows the saying, " Repent ye, for the kingdom of heaven is at hand," may be but a continuation of what John the Baptist said of himself ; so that only after these words cited from the speaker himself will Matthew's own narrative proceed, being thus resumed : " And the same John had his raiment of camel's hair," and so forth. But if this is the case, then it need not seem wonderful that, when asked what he had to say regarding himself, he should reply, according to the narrative of the evangelist John, " I am the voice of one crying in the wilderness," [5] as he had already spoken in the same terms when enjoining on them the duty of repentance. Accordingly, Matthew goes on to tell us about his attire and his mode of living, and continues his account thus : And the same John had his raiment of camel's hair, and a leathern girdle about his loins, and his meat was

---

[6] Reading *solet quippe esse talis locutio*, etc. Some codices give *solet quippe esse quasi de aliis locutio* = a mode of speech as if other persons were meant.
[7] *Invenit.*   [8] Matt. ix. 9.   [9] John xxi. 24.
[10] Matt. ix. 6, xvi. 27.   [11] John v. 25.   [12] Luke xxiv. 46.

---

[1] Luke ii. 22-39.   [2] Matt. ii. 3-16.   [3] Matt. iii. 1-3.
[4] Mark i. 3; Luke iii. 4.   [5] John i. 23.

locusts and wild honey. Mark also gives us this same statement almost in so many words. But the other two evangelists omit it.

26. Matthew then proceeds with his narrative, and says: Then went out to him Jerusalem and all Judæa, and all the region round about Jordan, and were baptized by him in Jordan, confessing their sins. But when he saw many of the Pharisees and Sadducees come to his baptism, he said unto them, O generation of vipers, who hath warned you to flee from the wrath to come? Bring forth therefore fruits meet for repentance; and think not to say within yourselves, We have Abraham to our father: for I say unto you, that God is able of these stones to raise up children unto Abraham. For now the axe is laid unto the root of the trees: therefore every tree which bringeth not forth good fruit, shall be hewn down and cast into the fire. I indeed baptize you with water unto repentance; but He that is to come after me is mightier than I, whose shoes I am not worthy to bear: He shall baptize you in the Holy Spirit and fire: whose fan is in His hand, and He will thoroughly purge His floor, and gather His wheat into the garner; but He will burn up the chaff with unquenchable fire.[1] This whole passage is also given by Luke, who ascribes almost the same words to John. And where there is any variation in the words, there is nevertheless no real departure from the sense. Thus, for example, Matthew tells us that John said, "And think not to say within yourselves, We have Abraham to our father," where Luke puts it thus: "And begin not to say, We have Abraham to our father." Again, in the former we have the words, "I indeed baptize you with water unto repentance;" whereas the latter brings in the questions put by the multitudes as to what they should do, and represents John to have replied to them with a statement of good works as the fruits of repentance, — all which is omitted by Matthew. So, when Luke tells us what reply the Baptist made to the people when they were musing in their hearts concerning Him, and thinking whether He were the Christ, he gives us simply the words, "I indeed baptize you with water," and does not add the phrase, "unto repentance." Further, in Matthew the Baptist says, "But he that is to come after me is mightier than I;" while in Luke he is exhibited as saying, "But one mightier than I cometh." In like manner, according to Matthew, he says, "whose shoes I am not worthy to bear;" but according to the other, his words are, "the latchet of whose shoes I am not worthy to unloose." The latter sayings are recorded also by Mark, although he makes no mention of those other matters. For,

after noticing his attire and his mode of living, he goes on thus: "And preached, saying, There cometh one mightier than I after me, the latchet of whose shoes I am not worthy to stoop down and unloose: I have baptized you with water, but He shall baptize you in the Holy Spirit." In the notice of the shoes, therefore, he differs from Luke in so far as he has added the words, "to stoop down;" and in the account of the baptism he differs from both these others in so far as he does not say, "and in fire," but only, "in the Holy Spirit." For as in Matthew, so also in Luke, the words are the same, and they are given in the same order, "He shall baptize you in the Spirit and in fire," — with this single exception, that Luke has not added the adjective "Holy,"[2] while Matthew has given it thus: "in the Holy Spirit and in fire."[3] The statements made by these three are attested by the evangelist John, when he says: "John bears witness[4] of Him, and cries, saying, This was He of whom I spake, He that cometh after me is preferred before me; for He was before me."[5] For thus he indicates that the thing was spoken by John at the time at which those other evangelists record him to have uttered the words. Thus, too, he gives us to understand that John was repeating and calling into notice again something which he had already spoken, when he said, "This was He of whom I spake, He that cometh after me."

27. If now the question is asked, as to which of the words we are to suppose the most likely to have been the precise words used by John the Baptist, whether those recorded as spoken by him in Matthew's Gospel, or those in Luke's, or those which Mark has introduced, among the few sentences which he mentions to have been uttered by him, while he omits notice of all the rest, it will not be deemed worth while creating any difficulty for oneself in a matter of that kind, by any one who wisely understands that the real requisite in order to get at the knowledge of the truth is just to make sure of the things really meant, whatever may be the precise words in which they happen to be expressed. For although one writer may retain a certain order in the words, and another present a different one, there is surely no real contradiction in that. Nor, again, need there be any antagonism between the two, although one may state what another omits. For it is evident that the evangelists have set forth these matters just in accordance with the recollection each retained of them, and just according as their several predilections prompted them to employ greater brevity or richer detail

---

[1] Matt. iii. 4-12.

[2] Greek and Latin Bibles now, however, add the word *Holy* in Luke. [The variation does not occur in early Greek mss. — R.]
[3] Matt. iii. 3-12; Mark i. 6-8; Luke iii. 7-17.
[4] *Perhibet.*   [5] John i. 15.

on certain points, while giving, nevertheless, the same account of the subjects themselves.

28. Thus, too, in what more pertinently concerns the matter in hand, it is sufficiently obvious that, since the truth of the Gospel, conveyed in that word of God which abides eternal and unchangeable above all that is created, but which at the same time has been disseminated[1] throughout the world by the instrumentality of temporal symbols, and by the tongues of men, has possessed itself of the most exalted height of authority, we ought not to suppose that any one of the writers is giving an unreliable account, if, when several persons are recalling some matter either heard or seen by them, they fail to follow the very same plan, or to use the very same words, while describing, nevertheless, the self-same fact. Neither should we indulge such a supposition, although the order of the words may be varied ; or although some words may be substituted in place of others, which nevertheless have the same meaning ; or although something may be left unsaid, either because it has not occurred to the mind of the recorder, or because it becomes readily intelligible from other statements which are given ; or although, among other matters which (may not bear directly on his immediate purpose, but which) he decides on mentioning rather for the sake of the narrative, and in order to preserve the proper order of time, one of them may introduce something which he does not feel called upon to expound as a whole at length, but only to touch upon in part ; or although, with the view of illustrating his meaning, and making it thoroughly clear, the person to whom authority is given to compose the narrative makes some additions of his own, not indeed in the subject-matter itself, but in the words by which it is expressed ; or although, while retaining a perfectly reliable comprehension of the fact itself, he may not be entirely successful, however he may make that his aim, in calling to mind and reciting anew with the most literal accuracy the very words which he heard on the occasion. Moreover, if any one affirms that the evangelists ought certainly to have had that kind of capacity imparted to them by the power of the Holy Spirit, which would secure them against all variation the one from the other, either in the kind of words, or in their order, or in their number, that person fails to perceive, that just in proportion as the authority of the evangelists [under their existing conditions] is made pre-eminent, the credit of all other men who offer true statements of events ought to have been established on a stronger basis by their instrumentality : so that when several parties happen to narrate the same circumstance, none of them can by any means be rightly charged with untruthfulness if he differs from the other only in such a way as can be defended on the ground of the antecedent example of the evangelists themselves. For as we are not at liberty either to suppose or to say that any one of the evangelists has stated what is false, so it will be apparent that any other writer is as little chargeable with untruth, with whom, in the process of recalling anything for narration, it has fared only in a way similar to that in which it is shown to have fared with those evangelists. And just as it belongs to the highest morality to guard against all that is false, so ought we all the more to be ruled by an authority so eminent, to the effect that we should not suppose ourselves to come upon what must be false, when we find the narratives of any writers differ from each other in the manner in which the records of the evangelists are proved to contain variations. At the same time, in what most seriously concerns the faithfulness of doctrinal teaching, we should also understand that it is not so much in mere words, as rather truth in the facts themselves, that is to be sought and embraced ; for as to writers who do not employ precisely the same modes of statement, if they only do not present discrepancies with respect to the facts and the sentiments themselves, we accept them as holding the same position in veracity.[2]

29. With respect, then, to those comparisons which I have instituted between the several narratives of the evangelists, what do these present that must be considered to be of a contradictory order? Are we to regard in this light the circumstance that one of them has given us the words, "whose shoes I am not worthy to bear," whereas the others speak of the "unloosing of the latchet of the shoe"? For here, indeed, the difference seems to be neither in the mere words, nor in the order of the words, nor in any matter of simple phraseology, but in the actual matter of fact, when in the one case the "bearing of the shoe" is mentioned, and in the other the "unloosing of the shoe's latchet." Quite fairly, therefore, may the question be put, as to what it was that John declared himself unworthy to do — whether to bear the shoes, or to unloose the shoe's latchet. For if only the one of these two sentences was uttered by him, then that evangelist will appear to have given the correct narrative who was in a position to record what was said ; while the writer who has given the saying in another form, although he may not indeed have offered an [intentionally] false account of it, may at any rate be taken to have made a slip of memory, and will be reckoned thus to have stated one thing instead of another. It is only seemly, however, that no charge of absolute unveracity should be laid

---

[1] Dispensato.

[2] Or, as abiding by the same truth — in eadem veritate constitisse approbamus.

against the evangelists, and that, too, not only with regard to that kind of unveracity which comes by the positive telling of what is false, but also with regard to that which arises through forgetfulness. Therefore, if it is pertinent to the matter to deduce one sense from the words " to bear the shoes," and another sense from the words " to unloose the shoe's latchet," what should one suppose the correct interpretation to be put on the facts, but that John did give utterance to both these sentences, either on two different occasions or in one and the same connection? For he might very well have expressed himself thus, " whose shoe's latchet I am not worthy to unloose, and whose shoes I am not worthy to bear : " and then one of the evangelists may have reproduced the one portion of the saying, and the rest of them the other ; while, notwithstanding this, all of them have really given a veracious narrative. But further, if, when he spoke of the shoes of the Lord, John meant nothing more than to convey the idea of His supremacy and his own lowliness, then, whichever of the two sayings may have actually been uttered by him, whether that regarding the unloosing of the latchet of the shoes, or that respecting the bearing of the shoes, the self-same sense is still correctly preserved by any writer who, while making mention of the shoes in words of his own, has expressed at the same time the same idea of lowliness, and thus has not made any departure from the real mind [of the person of whom he writes]. It is therefore a useful principle, and one particularly worthy of being borne in mind, when we are speaking of the concord of the evangelists, that there is no divergence [to be supposed] from truth, even when they introduce some saying different from what was actually uttered by the person concerning whom the narrative is given, provided that, notwithstanding this, they set forth as his mind precisely what is also so conveyed by that one among them who reproduces the words as they were literally spoken. For thus we learn the salutary lesson, that our aim should be nothing else than to ascertain what is the mind and intention of the person who speaks.

CHAP. XIII. — OF THE BAPTISM OF JESUS.

30. Matthew then continues his narrative in the following terms : " Then cometh Jesus from Galilee to Jordan unto John, to be baptized of him. But John forbade Him, saying, I have need to be baptized of Thee, and comest Thou to me? And Jesus answering, said unto him, Suffer it to be so now ; for thus it becometh us to fulfil all righteousness. Then he suffered Him." [1] The others also attest the fact that Jesus came to John. The three also mention that He was baptized. But they omit all mention of one circumstance recorded by Matthew, namely, that John addressed the Lord, or that the Lord made answer to John.[2]

CHAP. XIV. — OF THE WORDS OF THE VOICE THAT CAME FROM HEAVEN UPON HIM WHEN HE HAD BEEN BAPTIZED.

31. Thereafter Matthew proceeds thus : " And Jesus, when He was baptized, went up straightway out of the water ; and, lo, the heavens were opened unto Him, and He saw the Spirit of God descending like a dove, and lighting upon Him ; and, lo, a voice from heaven saying, This is my beloved Son, in whom I am well pleased." This incident is also recorded in a similar manner by two of the others, namely Mark and Luke. But at the same time, while preserving the sense intact, they use different modes of expression in reproducing the terms of the voice which came from heaven. For although Matthew tells us that the words were, " This is my beloved Son," while the other two put them in this form, " Thou art my beloved Son," these different methods of speech serve but to convey the same sense, according to the principle which has been discussed above. For the heavenly voice gave utterance only to one of these sentences ; but by the form of words thus adopted, namely, " This is my beloved Son," it was the evangelist's intention to show that the saying was meant to intimate specially to the hearers there [and not to Jesus] the fact that He was the Son of God. With this view, he chose to give the sentence, " Thou art my beloved Son," this turn, " This is my beloved Son," as if it were addressed directly to the people. For it was not meant to intimate to Christ a fact which He knew already ; but the object was to let the people who were present hear it, for whose sakes indeed the voice itself was given. But furthermore now, with regard to the circumstance that the first of them puts the saying thus, " In whom I am well pleased," [3] the second thus, " In Thee I am well pleased ; " [4] and the third thus, " In Thee it has pleased me ; " [5] — if you ask which of these different modes represents what was actually expressed by the voice, you may fix on whichever you will, provided only that you understand that those of the writers who have not reproduced the self-same form of speech have still reproduced the identical sense intended to be conveyed. And these variations in the modes of expression are also useful in this way, that they make it possible for us to

---

[1] *Dimisit eum.*

[2] Matt. iii. 13-15; Mark i. 9; Luke iii. 21; John i. 32-34.
[3] *In quo mihi complacui* — well pleased with myself.
[4] *In te complacui.*
[5] *In te complacuit mihi.* Matt. iii. 16, 17; Mark i. 10, 11; Luke iii. 22. [The Greek MSS., of most weight, show no variation between Mark and Luke in the last clause. — R.]

reach a more adequate conception of the saying than might have been the case with only one form, and that they also secure it against being interpreted in a sense not consonant with the real state of the case. For as to the sentence, " In whom I am well pleased," [1] if any one thinks of taking it as if it meant that God is pleased with Himself in the Son, he is taught a lesson of prudence by the other turn which is given to the saying, " In Thee I am well pleased." [2] And on the other hand, if, looking at this last by itself, any one supposes the meaning to be, that in the Son the Father had favour with men, he learns something from the third form of the utterance, " In Thee it has pleased me." [3] From this it becomes sufficiently apparent, that whichever of the evangelists may have preserved for us the words as they were literally uttered by the heavenly voice, the others have varied the terms only with the object of setting forth the same sense more familiarly ; so that what is thus given by all of them might be understood as if the expression were : In Thee I have set my good pleasure ; that is to say, by Thee to do what is my pleasure. [4] But once more, with respect to that rendering which is contained in some codices of the Gospel according to Luke, and which bears that the words heard in the heavenly voice were those that are written in the Psalm, " Thou art my Son, this day have I begotten Thee ; " [5] although it is said not to be found in the more ancient Greek codices, yet if it can be established by any copies worthy of credit, what results but that we suppose both voices to have been heard from heaven, in one or other verbal order ?

CHAP. XV. — AN EXPLANATION OF THE CIRCUMSTANCE THAT, ACCORDING TO THE EVANGELIST JOHN, JOHN THE BAPTIST SAYS, " I KNEW HIM NOT ; " WHILE, ACCORDING TO THE OTHERS, IT IS FOUND THAT HE DID ALREADY KNOW HIM.

32. Again, the account of the dove given in the Gospel according to John does not mention the time at which the incident happened, but contains a statement of the words of John the Baptist as reporting what he saw. In this section, the question rises as to how it is said, " And I knew Him not : but He that sent me to baptize with water, the same said unto me, Upon whom thou shalt see the Spirit descending and remaining on Him, the same is He which baptizeth with the Holy Spirit." [6] For if he came to know Him only at the time when he saw the

dove descending upon Him, the inquiry is raised as to how he could have said to Him, as He came to be baptized, " I ought rather to be baptized of Thee." [7] For the Baptist addressed Him thus before the dove descended. From this, however, it is evident that, although he did know Him [in a certain sense] before this time, — for he even leaped in his mother's womb when Mary visited Elisabeth, [8] — there was yet something which was not known to him up to this time, and which he learned by the descending of the dove, — namely, the fact that He baptized in the Holy Spirit by a certain divine power proper to Himself ; so that no man who received this baptism from God, even although he baptized some, should be able to say that that which he imparted was his own, or that the Holy Spirit was given by him.

CHAP. XVI. — OF THE TEMPTATION OF JESUS.

33. Matthew proceeds with his narrative in these terms : " Then was Jesus led up of the Spirit into the wilderness, to be tempted of the devil. And when He had fasted forty days and forty nights, he was afterward an hungered. And when the tempter came to Him, he said, If thou be the Son of God, command that these stones be made bread. But He answered and said, It is written, Man shall not live by bread alone, but by every word that proceedeth out of the mouth of God. And so the account continues, until we come to the words, Then the devil left [9] him : and, behold, angels came and ministered unto Him." [10] This whole narrative is given also in a similar manner by Luke, although not in the same order. And this makes it uncertain which of the two latter temptations took place first : whether it was that the kingdoms of the world were shown Him first, and then that He Himself was taken up to the pinnacle of the temple thereafter ; or whether it was that this latter act occurred first, and that the other scene followed it. It is, however, a matter of no real consequence, provided it be clear that all these incidents did take place. And as Luke sets forth the same events and ideas in different words, attention need not ever be called to the fact that no loss results thereby to truth. Mark, again, does indeed attest the fact that He was tempted of the devil in the wilderness for forty days and forty nights ; but he gives no statement of what was said to Him, or of the replies He made. At the same time, he does not fail to notice the circumstance which is omitted by Luke, namely, that the angels ministered unto Him. [11] John, however, has left out this whole passage.

---

[1] In quo mihi complacui — as it = in whom I am well pleased with myself.
[2] In te complacui.   [3] In te complacuit mihi.
[4] In te placitum meum constitui, hoc est, per te gerere quod mihi placet. [The Greek aorist points to a past act; hence " set my good pleasure" is a better rendering of the verb, in all three accounts, than " am well pleased." — R.]
[5] Ps. ii. 7.   [6] John i. 33.

[7] Matt. iii. 14.   [8] Luke i. 41.   [9] Reliquit.
[10] Matt. iv. 1-11.   [11] Mark i. 12, 13; Luke iv. 1-13.

CHAP. XVII. — OF THE CALLING OF THE APOSTLES
AS THEY WERE FISHING.

34. Matthew's narrative is continued thus: "Now when Jesus had heard that John was cast into prison, He departed into Galilee." [1] Mark states the same fact, as also does Luke,[2] only Luke says nothing in the present section as to John being cast into prison. The evangelist John, again, tells us that, before Jesus went into Galilee, Peter and Andrew were with Him one day, and that on that occasion the former had this name, Peter, given him, while before that period he was called Simon. Likewise John tells us, that on the day following, when Jesus was now desirous of going forth unto Galilee, He found Philip, and said to him that he should follow Him. Thus, too, the evangelist comes to give the narrative about Nathanael.[3] Further, he informs us that on the third day, when He was yet in Galilee, Jesus wrought the miracle of the turning of the water into wine at Cana.[4] All these incidents are left unrecorded by the other evangelists, who continue their narratives at once with the statement of the return of Jesus into Galilee. Hence we are to understand that there was an interval here of several days, during which those incidents took place in the history of the disciples which are inserted at this point by John.[5] Neither is there anything contradictory here to that other passage where Matthew tells us how the Lord said to Peter, "Thou art Peter, and upon this rock will I build my Church." [6] But we are not to understand that that was the time when he first received this name; but we are rather to suppose that this took place on the occasion when it was said to him, as John mentions, "Thou shalt be called Cephas, which is, by interpretation, A stone." [7] Thus the Lord could address him at that later period by this very name, when He said, "Thou art Peter." For He does not say then, "Thou shalt be called Peter," but, "Thou art Peter;" because on a previous occasion he had already been spoken to in this manner, "Thou shalt be called."

35. After this, Matthew goes on with his narrative in these terms: "And leaving the city of Nazareth, He came and dwelt in Capharnaum, which is upon the sea-coast, in the borders of Zabulon and Nephthalim;" and so forth, until we come to the conclusion of the sermon which He delivered on the mount. In this section of the narrative, Mark agrees with him in attesting the calling of the disciples Peter and Andrew, and a little after that, the calling of James and

John. But whereas Matthew introduces in this immediate context his account of that lengthened sermon which He delivered on the mount, after He cured a multitude, and when great crowds followed Him, Mark has inserted other matters at this point, touching His teaching in the synagogue, and the people's amazement at His doctrine. Then, too, he has stated what Matthew also states, although not till after that lengthened sermon has been given, namely, that "He taught them as one that had authority, and not as the scribes." He has likewise given us the account of the man out of whom the unclean spirit was cast; and after that the story of Peter's mother-in-law. In these things, moreover, Luke is in accord with him.[8] But Matthew has given us no notice of the evil spirit here. The story of Peter's mother-in-law, however, he has not omitted, only he brings it in at a later stage.[9]

36. In this paragraph, moreover, which we are at present considering, the same Matthew follows up his account of the calling of those disciples to whom, when they were engaged in fishing, He gave the command to follow Him, by a narrative to the effect that He went about Galilee, teaching in the synagogues, and preaching the gospel, and healing all manner of sickness; and that when multitudes had gathered about Him, He went up into a mountain, and delivered that lengthened sermon [already alluded to]. Thus the evangelist gives us ground for understanding that those incidents which are recorded by Mark after the election of those same disciples, took place at the period when He was going about Galilee, and teaching in their synagogues. We are at liberty also to suppose that what happened to Peter's mother-in-law came in at this point; and that he has mentioned at a later stage what he has passed over here, although he has not indeed brought up at that later point, for direct recital, everything else which is omitted at the earlier.[10]

37. The question may indeed be raised as to how John gives us this account of the calling of the disciples, which is to the effect that, certainly not in Galilee, but in the vicinity of the Jordan, Andrew first of all became a follower of the Lord, together with another disciple whose name is not declared; that, in the second place, Peter got that name from Him; and thirdly, that Philip was called to follow Him; whereas the other three evangelists, in a satisfactory concord with each other, Matthew and Mark in particular being remarkably at one here, tell us that the men were called when they were engaged in fishing. Luke, it is true, does not mention An-

---

[1] Matt. iv. 12.   [2] Mark i. 14; Luke iv. 14.
[3] John i. 39, etc.   [4] John ii. 1-11.
[5] [The interval between the temptation and the return to Galilee, referred to by the Synoptists, was at least nine months; possibly more than a year. Augustin implies, in § 42, that this journey was a different one. — R.]
[6] Matt. xvi. 18.   [7] John i. 42.

[8] Matt. iv. 13, vii. 29; Mark i. 16-31; Luke iv. 31-39.
[9] Matt. viii. 14, 15.
[10] [There is here a partial recognition of the fact, now widely received, that the order of Mark is the most exact. No harmony can be successfully constructed on the order of Matthew. — R.]

drew by name. Nevertheless, we can gather that he was in that same vessel, from the narrative of Matthew and Mark, who furnish a concise history of the manner in which the affair was gone about. Luke, however, presents us with a fuller and clearer exposition of the circumstances, and gives us also an account of the miracle which was performed there in the haul of fishes, and of the fact that previous to that the Lord spake to the multitudes when He was seated in the boat. There may also seem to be a discrepancy in this respect, that Luke records the saying, "From henceforth thou shalt catch men,"[1] as if it had been addressed by the Lord to Peter alone, while the others have exhibited it as spoken to both the brothers.[2] But it may very well be the case that these words were spoken first to Peter himself, when he was seized with amazement at the immense multitude of fishes which were caught, and this will then be the incident introduced by Luke; and that they were addressed to the two together somewhat later, which [second utterance] will be the one noticed by the other two evangelists. Therefore the circumstance which we have mentioned with regard to John's narrative deserves to be carefully considered; for it may indeed be supposed to bring before us a contradiction of no slight importance. For if it be the case that in the vicinity of the Jordan, and before Jesus went into Galilee, two men, on hearing the testimony of John the Baptist, followed Jesus; that of these two disciples the one was Andrew, who at once went and brought his own brother Simon to Jesus; and that on this occasion that brother received the name Peter, by which he was thereafter to be called,—how can it be said by the other evangelists that He found them engaged in fishing in Galilee, and called them there to be His disciples?[3] How can these diverse accounts be reconciled, unless it be that we are to understand that those men did not gain such a view of Jesus on the occasion connected with the vicinity of the Jordan as would lead them to attach themselves to Him for ever, but that they simply came to know who He was, and, after their first wonder at His Person, returned to their former engagements?

38. For [it is noticeable that] again in Cana of Galilee, after He had turned the water into wine, this same John tells us how His disciples believed on Him. The narrative of that miracle proceeds thus: "And the third day there was a marriage in Cana of Galilee; and the mother of Jesus was there. And both Jesus was called and His disciples to the marriage."[4] Now, surely, if it was on this occasion that they be-

lieved on Him, as the evangelist tells us a little further on, they were not yet His disciples at the time when they were called to the marriage. This, however, is a mode of speech of the same kind with what is intended when we say that the Apostle Paul was born in Tarsus of Cilicia;[5] for certainly he was not an apostle at that period. In like manner are we told here that the disciples of Christ were invited to the marriage, by which we are to understand, not that they were already disciples, but only that they were to be His disciples. For, at the time when this narrative was prepared and committed to writing, they were the disciples of Christ in fact; and that is the reason why the evangelist, as the historian of past times, has thus spoken of them.

39. But further, as to John's statement, that "after this He went down to Capharnaum, He and His mother, and His brethren and His disciples; and they continued there not many days;"[6] it is uncertain whether by this period these men had already attached themselves to Him, in particular Peter and Andrew, and the sons of Zebedee. For Matthew first of all tells us that He came and dwelt in Capharnaum,[7] and then that He called them from their boats as they were engaged in fishing. On the other hand, John says that His disciples came with Him to Capharnaum. Now it may be the case that Matthew has but gone over here something he had omitted in its proper order. For he does not say, "After this, walking by the sea of Galilee, He saw two brethren," but, without any indication of the strict consecution of time, simply, "And walking by the sea of Galilee, He saw two brethren,"[8] and so forth: consequently it is quite possible that he has recorded at this later period not something which took place actually at that later time, but only something which he had omitted to introduce before; so that the men may be understood in this way to have come along with Him to Capharnaum, to which place John states that He did come, He and His mother and His disciples: or should we rather suppose that these were a different body of disciples, as He [may already have] had a follower in Philip, whom He called in this particular manner, by saying to him, "Follow me"? For in what order all the twelve apostles were called is not apparent from the narratives of the evangelists. Indeed, not only is the succession of the various callings left unrecorded; but even the fact of the calling is not mentioned in the case of all of them, the only vocations specified being those of Philip, and Peter and Andrew, and the sons of Zebedee, and Matthew the publican, who was also called Levi.[9] The first and

1 Luke v. 10.   2 Matt. iv. 10; Mark i. 17.
3 Matt. iv. 13-23; Mark i. 16-20; Luke v. 1-11; John i. 35-44.
4 John ii. 1, 2.
5 Acts xxii. 3.
6 John ii. 12.   7 Matt. iv. 13.   8 Matt. iv. 18.
9 Matt. iv. 18-22, ix. 9; Mark i. 16-20, ii. 14; Luke v. 1-11; John i. 35-44.

only person, however, who received a separate name from Him was Peter.[1] For He did not give the sons of Zebedee their names individually, but He called them both together the sons of thunder.[2]

40. Besides, we ought certainly to note the fact that the evangelical and apostolical Scriptures do not confine this designation of His "disciples" to those twelve alone, but give the same appellation to all those who believed on Him, and were educated under His instruction for the kingdom of heaven. Out of the whole number of such He chose twelve, whom He also named apostles, as Luke mentions. For a little further on he says : And He came down with them, and stood in the plain, and the concourse[3] of His disciples and a great multitude of people.[4] And surely he would not speak of a "concourse" [or "crowd"] of disciples if he referred only to twelve men. In other passages of the Scriptures also the fact is plainly apparent, that all those were called His disciples who were instructed by Him in what pertained to eternal life.

41. But the question may be asked, how He called the fishermen from their boats two by two, namely, calling Peter and Andrew first, and then going forward a little and calling other two, namely the sons of Zebedee, according to the narratives of Matthew and Mark ; whereas Luke's version of the matter is, that both their boats were filled with the immense haul of fishes. And his statement bears further, that Peter's partners, to wit, James and John, the sons of Zebedee, were summoned to the men's help when they were unable to drag out their crowded nets, and that all who were there were astonished at the enormous draught of fishes which had been taken ; and that when Jesus said to Peter, "Fear not, from henceforth thou shalt catch men," although the words had been addressed to Peter alone, they all nevertheless followed Him when they had brought their ships to land.[5] Well, we are to understand by this, that what Luke introduces here was what took place first, and that these men were not called by the Lord on this occasion, but only that the prediction was uttered to Peter by himself, that he would be a fisher of men. That saying, moreover, was not intended to convey that they would never thereafter be catchers of fish. For we read that even after the Lord's resurrection they were engaged again in fishing.[6] The words, therefore, imported simply that thereafter he would catch men, and they did not bear that henceforth he would not catch fish. And in this way we are at perfect liberty to suppose that they returned to the catching of fish, according to their habit ; so that those incidents which are related by Matthew

and Mark might easily take place at a period subsequent to this. I refer to what occurred at the time when He called the disciples two by two, and Himself gave them the command to follow Him, at first addressing Peter and Andrew, and then the others, namely, the two sons of Zebedee. For on that occasion they did not follow Him only after they had drawn up their ships on shore, as with the intention of returning to them, but they went after Him immediately, as after one who summoned and commanded them to follow Him.

CHAP. XVIII. — OF THE DATE OF HIS DEPARTURE INTO GALILEE.

42. Furthermore, we must consider the question how the evangelist John, before there is any mention of the casting of John the Baptist into prison, tells us that Jesus went into Galilee. For, after relating how He turned the water into wine at Cana of Galilee, and how He came down to Capernaum with His mother and His disciples, and how they abode there not many days, he tells us that He went up then to Jerusalem on account of the passover ; that after this He came into the land of Judæa along with His disciples, and tarried there with them, and baptized ; and then in what follows at this point the evangelist says : "And John also was baptizing in Ænon, near to Salim, because there was much water there ; and they came, and were baptized : for John was not yet cast into prison."[7] On the other hand, Matthew says : "Now when He had heard that John was cast into prison, Jesus departed into Galilee."[8] In like manner, Mark's words are : "Now, after that John was put in prison, Jesus came into Galilee."[9] Luke, again, says nothing indeed about the imprisonment of John ; but notwithstanding this, after his account of the baptism and temptation of Christ, he also makes a statement to the same effect with that of these other two, namely, that Jesus went into Galilee. For he has connected the several parts of his narrative here in this way : "And when all the temptation was ended, the devil departed from Him for a season ; and Jesus returned in the power of the Spirit into Galilee, and there went out a fame of Him through all the region round about."[10] From all this, however, we may gather, not that these three evangelists have made any statement opposed to the evangelist John, but only that they have left unrecorded the Lord's first advent in Galilee after His baptism ; on which occasion also He turned the water into wine there. For at that period John had not yet been cast into prison. And we are also to understand that these three evangelists have introduced into the context of these narratives an account of another journey of His into

[1] John i. 42.   [2] Mark iii. 17.   [3] Turba.
[4] Luke vi. 17.   [5] Luke v. 1-11.   [6] John xxi. 3.
[7] John ii. 13, iii. 22-24.   [8] Matt. iv. 12.   [9] Mark i. 14.
[10] Luke iv. 13, 14.

Galilee, which took place after John's imprisonment, regarding which return into Galilee the evangelist John himself furnishes the following notice : "When, therefore, Jesus knew how the Pharisees had heard that Jesus makes and baptizes more disciples than John (though Jesus Himself baptized not, but His disciples), he left Judæa, and departed again into Galilee." [1] So, then, we perceive that by that time John had been already cast into prison ; and further, that the Jews had heard that He was making and baptizing more disciples than John had made and baptized.

CHAP. XIX. — OF THE LENGTHENED SERMON WHICH, ACCORDING TO MATTHEW, HE DELIVERED ON THE MOUNT.

43. Now, regarding that lengthened sermon which, according to Matthew, the Lord delivered on the mount, let us at present see whether it appears that the rest of the evangelists stand in no manner of antagonism to it. Mark, it is true, has not recorded it at all, neither has he preserved any utterances of Christ's in any way resembling it, with the exception of certain sentences which are not given connectedly, but occur here and there, and which the Lord repeated in other places. Nevertheless, he has left a space in the text of his narrative indicating the point at which we may understand this sermon to have been spoken, although it has been left unrecited. That is the place where he says : "And He was preaching in their synagogues, and in all Galilee, and was casting out devils." [2] Under the head of this preaching, in which he says Jesus engaged in all Galilee, we may also understand that discourse to be comprehended which was delivered on the mount, and which is detailed by Matthew. For the same Mark continues his account thus : "And there came a leper to Him, beseeching Him ; and kneeling down to Him, said, If Thou wilt, Thou canst make me clean." [3] And he goes on with the rest of the story of the cleansing of this leper, in such a manner as to make it intelligible to us that the person in question is the very man who is mentioned by Matthew as having been healed at the time when the Lord came down from the mount after the delivery of His discourse. For this is how Matthew gives the history there : "Now, when He was come down from the mountain, great multitudes followed Him ; and, behold, there came a leper, and worshipped Him, saying, Lord, if Thou wilt, Thou canst make me clean ; " [4] and so on.

44. This leper is also referred to by Luke,[5]

not indeed in this order, but after the manner in which the writers are accustomed to act, recording at a subsequent point things which have been omitted at a previous stage, or bringing in at an earlier point occurrences which took place at a later period, according as they had incidents suggested to their minds by the heavenly influence, with which indeed they had become acquainted before, but which they were afterwards prompted to commit to writing as they came up to their recollection. This same Luke, however, has also left us a version of his own of that copious discourse of the Lord, in a passage which he commences just as the section in Matthew begins. For in the latter the words run thus : "Blessed are the poor in spirit : for theirs is the kingdom of heaven ; " [6] while in the former they are put thus : "Blessed be ye poor : for yours is the kingdom of God." [7] Then, too, much of what follows in Luke's narrative is similar to what we have in the other. And finally, the conclusion given to the sermon is repeated in both Gospels in its entire identity, — namely, the story of the wise man who builds upon the rock, and the foolish man who builds upon the sand ; the only difference being, that Luke speaks only of the stream beating against the house, and does not mention also the rain and the wind, as they occur in Matthew. Accordingly, it might very readily be believed that he has there introduced the self-same discourse of the Lord, but that at the same time he has omitted certain sentences which Matthew has inserted ; that he has also brought in other sayings which Matthew has not mentioned ; and that, in a similar manner, he has expressed certain of these utterances in somewhat different terms, but without detriment to the integrity of the truth.

45. This we might very well suppose to have been the case, as I have said, were it not that a difficulty is felt to attach to the circumstance that Matthew tells us how this discourse was delivered on a mount by the Lord in a sitting posture ; while Luke says that it was spoken on a plain by the Lord in a standing posture. This difference, accordingly, makes it seem as if the former referred to one discourse, and the latter to another. And what should there be, indeed, to hinder [us from supposing] Christ to have repeated elsewhere some words which He had already spoken, or from doing a second time certain things which He had already done on some previous occasion? However, that these two discourses, of which the one is inserted by Matthew and the other by Luke, are not separated by a long space of time, is with much probability inferred from the fact that, at once in what precedes and in what follows

---

[1] John iv. 1–3.   [2] Mark i. 39.
[3] Mark i. 40.   [4] Matt. viii. 1, 2.
[5] Luke v. 12, 13. [It seems altogether more probable that the healing of the leper occurred, before the Sermon on the Mount, at the time indicated by Luke. — R.]

[6] Matt. v. 3.   [7] Luke vi. 20.

them, both the evangelists have related certain incidents either similar or perfectly identical, so that it is not unreasonably felt that the narrations of the writers who introduce these things are occupied with the same localities and days. For Matthew's recital proceeds in the following terms : " And there followed Him great multitudes of people from Galilee, and from Decapolis, and from Jerusalem, and from Judæa, and from beyond Jordan. And seeing the multitudes, He went up into a mountain ; and when He was set, His disciples came unto Him : and He opened His mouth, and taught them, saying, Blessed are the poor in spirit : for theirs is the kingdom of heaven ;"[1] and so forth. Here it may appear that His desire was to free Himself from the great crowds of people, and that for this reason He went up into the mountain, as if He meant to withdraw Himself from the multitudes, and seek an opportunity of speaking with His disciples alone. And this seems to be certified also by Luke, whose account is to the following effect : " And it came to pass in those days, that He went out into a mountain to pray, and continued all night in prayer to God. And when it was day, He called unto Him His disciples : and of them He chose twelve, whom also He named apostles ; Simon, whom He also named Peter, and Andrew his brother, James and John, Philip and Bartholomew, Matthew and Thomas, James the son of Alpheus, and Simon, who is called Zelotes, Judas the brother of James, and Judas Scarioth, which was the traitor. And He came down with them, and stood in the plain, and the company of His disciples, and a great multitude of people out of all Judæa and Jerusalem, and from the sea-coast of Tyre[2] and Sidon, which had come to hear Him, and to be healed of their diseases ; and they that were vexed with unclean spirits were healed.[3] And the whole multitude sought to touch Him : for there went virtue out of Him, and healed them all. And He lifted up His eyes on His disciples, and said, Blessed be ye poor : for yours is the kingdom of heaven ;"[4] and so on. Here the relation permits us to understand that, after selecting on the mountain twelve disciples out of the larger body, whom He also named apostles (which incident Matthew has omitted), He then delivered that discourse which Matthew has introduced, and which Luke has left unnoticed, — that is to say, the one on the mount ; and that thereafter, when He had now come down, He spoke in the plain a second discourse similar to the first, on which Matthew is silent, but which is detailed by Luke ; and further, that

both these sermons were concluded in the same manner.[5]

46. But, again, as regards what Matthew proceeds to state after the termination of that discourse — namely this, " And it came to pass, when Jesus had ended these sayings, the people[6] were astonished at His doctrine,"[7] — it may appear that the speakers there were those multitudes of disciples out of whom He had chosen the twelve. Moreover, when the evangelist goes on immediately in these terms, "And when He was come down from the mountain, great multitudes followed Him ; and, behold, there came a leper and worshipped Him,"[8] we are at liberty to suppose that that incident took place subsequently to both discourses, — not only after the one which Matthew records, but also after the one which Luke inserts. For it is not made apparent what length of time elapsed after the descent from the mountain. But Matthew's intention was simply to indicate the fact itself, that after that descent there were great multitudes of people with the Lord on the occasion when He cleansed the leper, and not to specify what period of time had intervened. And this supposition may all the more readily be entertained, since [we find that] Luke tells us how the same leper was cleansed at a time when the Lord was now in a certain city, — a circumstance which Matthew has not cared to mention.

47. After all, however, this explanation may also be suggested, — namely, that in the first instance the Lord, along with His disciples and no others, was on some more elevated portion of the mountain, and that during the period of His stay there He chose out of the number of His followers those twelve ; that then He came down in company with them, not indeed from the mountain itself, but from that said altitude on the mountain, into the plain — that is to say, into some level spot which was found on the slope of the mountain, and which was capable of accommodating great multitudes ; and that thereafter, when He had seated Himself, His disciples took up their position next Him, and in these circumstances He delivered both to them and to the other multitudes who were present one discourse, which Matthew and Luke have both recorded, their modes of narrating it being indeed different, but the truth being given with equal fidelity by the two writers in all that concerns the facts and sayings which both of them have recounted. For we have already prefaced our inquiry with the position, which indeed ought of itself to have been obvious to all without the need of any one to give them counsel to that effect beforehand,

---

[1] Matt. iv. 25, etc.
[2] Various MSS. and editions insert *et* before the *Tyri* = both of Tyre, although it is wanting in the Greek.
[3] *Qui vexabantur a spiritibus immundis curabantur.*
[4] Luke vi. 12-20.

[5] [The explanation suggested in § 47 is altogether more probable. — R.]
[6] *Turbæ*, multitudes.   [7] Matt. vii. 28.
[8] Matt. viii. 1, 2.

that there is not [necessarily] any antagonism between writers, although one may omit something which another mentions; nor, again, although one states a fact in one way, and another in a different method, provided that the same truth is set forth in regard to the objects and sayings themselves.   In this way, therefore, Matthew's sentence, "Now when He was come down from the mountain," may at the same time be understood to refer also to the plain, which there might very well have been on the slope of the mountain.   And thereafter Matthew tells the story of the cleansing of the leper, which is also given in a similar manner by Mark and Luke.

CHAP. XX. — AN EXPLANATION OF THE CIRCUM-
STANCE THAT MATTHEW TELLS US HOW THE
CENTURION CAME TO JESUS ON BEHALF OF HIS
SERVANT, WHILE LUKE'S STATEMENT IS THAT
THE CENTURION DESPATCHED FRIENDS TO HIM.

48. After these things, Matthew proceeds with his narrative in the following terms: "And when Jesus was entered into Capharnaum, there came unto Him a centurion, beseeching Him, and saying, Lord, my servant lieth at home sick of the palsy, and he is grievously tormented;" and so forth, on to the place where it is said, "And his servant was healed in the self-same hour."[1] This case of the centurion's servant is related also by Luke; only Luke does not bring it in, as Matthew does, after the cleansing of the leper, whose story he has recorded as something suggested to his recollection at a later stage, but introduces it after the conclusion of that lengthened sermon already discussed.   For he connects the two sections in this way: "Now when He had ended all His sayings in the audience of the people, He entered into Capharnaum; and a certain centurion's servant, who was dear unto him, was sick and ready to die;" and so forth, until we come to the verse where it is said that he was healed.[2]   Here, then, we notice that it was not till after He had ended all His words in the hearing of the people that Christ entered Capharnaum; by which we are to understand simply that He did not make that entrance before He had brought these sayings to their conclusion; and we are not to take it as intimating the length of that period of time which intervened between the delivery of these discourses and the entrance into Capharnaum.   In this interval that leper was cleansed, whose case is recorded by Matthew in its own proper place, but is given by Luke only at a later point.[3]

49. Accordingly, let us proceed to consider whether Matthew and Luke are at one in the account of this servant.   Matthew's words, then, are these: "There came unto Him a centurion, beseeching Him, and saying, My servant lieth at home sick of the palsy."[4]   Now this seems to be inconsistent with the version presented by Luke, which runs thus: "And when he heard of Jesus, he sent unto Him the elders of the Jews, beseeching Him that He would come and heal his servant.   And when they came to Jesus, they besought Him instantly, saying, That he was worthy for whom He should do this: for he loveth our nation, and he hath built us a synagogue.   Then Jesus went with them.   And when He was now not far from the house, the centurion sent friends to Him, saying unto Him, Lord, trouble not Thyself; for I am not worthy that Thou shouldest enter under my roof: wherefore neither thought I myself worthy to come unto Thee: but say in a word, and my servant shall be healed."[5]   For if this was the manner in which the incident took place, how can Matthew's statement, that there "came to Him a certain centurion," be correct, seeing that the man did not come in person, but sent his friends?   The apparent discrepancy, however, will disappear if we look carefully into the matter, and observe that Matthew has simply held by a very familiar mode of expression.   For not only are we accustomed to speak of one as coming[6] even before he actually reaches the place he is said to have approached,[7] whence, too, we speak of one as making small approach or making great approach[8] to what he is desirous of reaching; but we also not unfrequently speak of that access,[9] for the sake of getting at which the approach is made, as reached even although the person who is said to reach another may not himself see the individual whom he reaches, inasmuch as it may be through a friend that he reaches the person whose favour is necessary to him.   This, indeed, is a custom which has so thoroughly established itself, that even in the language of every-day life now those men are called *Perventores*[10] who, in the practice of canvassing,[11] get at the inaccessible ears, as one may say, of any of the men of influence, by the intervention of suitable personages.   If, therefore, access[12] itself is thus familiarly said to be gained by the means of other parties, how much more may an approach[13] be said to take place, although it be by means of others, which always remains something short of actual access!   For it is surely the case, that a person may be able to do very much in the way of approach, but yet may have failed to succeed in actually reaching what he sought to get at.   Consequently it is nothing out of the way for Matthew, — a fact, indeed, which may be understood by any intelligence, — when thus dealing

---

[1] Matt. viii. 5-13.
[2] Luke vii. 1-10.
[3] [But see note on § 44. — R.]

[4] Matt. viii. 5, 6.
[5] Luke vii. 3-7.
[6] *Accessisse*, approaching.
[7] *Accessisse*, come to.
[8] *Parum accessit vel multum accessit.*   [9] *Perventio*, arrival.
[10] Reachers, comers at.   [11] *Ambitionis arte.*
[12] *Perventio.*   [13] Coming at — *accessus.*

with an approach on the part of the centurion to the Lord, which was effected in the person of others, to have chosen to express the matter in this compendious method, "There came a centurion to Him."

50. At the same time, however, we must be careful enough to discern a certain mystical depth in the phraseology adopted by the evangelist, which is in accordance with these words of the Psalm, "Come ye to Him, and be ye lightened." [1]   For in this way, inasmuch as the Lord Himself commended the faith of the centurion, in which indeed his approach was really made to Jesus, in such terms that He declared, " I have not found so great faith in Israel," the evangelist wisely chose to speak of the man himself as coming to Jesus, rather than to bring in the persons through whom he had conveyed his words.   And furthermore, Luke has unfolded the whole incident to us just as it occurred, in a form constraining us to understand from his narrative in what manner another writer, who was also incapable of making any false statement, might have spoken of the man himself as coming.   It is in this way, too, that the woman who suffered from the issue of blood, although she took hold merely of the hem of His garment, did yet touch the Lord more effectually than those multitudes did by whom He was thronged.[2]   For just as she touched the Lord the more effectually, in so far as she believed the more earnestly, so the centurion also came the more really to the Lord, inasmuch as he believed the more thoroughly.   And now, as regards the rest of this paragraph, it would be a superfluous task to go over in detail the various matters which are recounted by the one and omitted by the other.   For, according to the principle brought under notice at the outset, there is not to be found in these peculiarities any actual antagonism between the writers.

CHAP. XXI.—OF THE ORDER IN WHICH THE NAR-
RATIVE CONCERNING PETER'S MOTHER-IN-LAW IS
INTRODUCED.

51. Matthew proceeds in the following terms : " And when Jesus was come into Peter's house, He saw his wife's mother laid, and sick of a fever. And He touched her hand, and the fever left her : and she arose, and ministered unto them." [3] Matthew has not indicated the date of this incident ; that is to say, he has specified neither before what event nor after what occurrence it took place.   For we are certainly under no necessity of supposing that, because it is recorded after a certain event, it must also have happened in actual matter of fact after that event.   And unquestionably, in this case, we are to under-

stand that he has introduced for record here something which he had omitted to notice previously.   For Mark brings in this narrative before his account of that cleansing of the leper which he would appear to have placed after the delivery of the sermon on the mount ; [4] which discourse, however, he has left unrelated.   And thus, too, Luke [5] inserts this story of Peter's mother-in-law after an occurrence [6] which it follows likewise in Mark's version, but also before that lengthened discourse, which has been reproduced by him, and which may appear to be one with the sermon which Matthew states to have been delivered on the mount.   For of what consequence is it in what place any of them may give his account ; or what difference does it make whether he inserts the matter in its proper order, or brings in at a particular point what was previously omitted, or mentions at an earlier stage what really happened at a later, provided only that he contradicts neither himself nor a second writer in the narrative of the same facts or of others ?   For as it is not in one's own power, however admirable and trustworthy may be the knowledge he has once obtained of the facts, to determine the order in which he will recall them to memory (for the way in which one thing comes into a person's mind before or after another is something which proceeds not as we will, but simply as it is given to us), it is reasonable enough to suppose that each of the evangelists believed it to have been his duty to relate what he had to relate in that order in which it had pleased God to suggest to his recollection the matters he was engaged in recording.   At least this might hold good in the case of those incidents with regard to which the question of order, whether it were this or that, detracted nothing from evangelical authority and truth.

52. But as to the reason why the Holy Spirit, who divideth to every man severally as He will,[7] and who therefore undoubtedly, with a view to the establishing of their books on so distinguished an eminence of authority, also governs and rules the minds of the holy men themselves in the matter of suggesting the things they were to commit to writing, has left one historian at liberty to construct his narrative in one way, and another in a different fashion, that is a question which any one may look into with pious consideration, and for which, by divine help, the answer also may possibly be found.   That, however, is not the object of the work which we have taken in hand at present.   The task we have

---

[1] *Accedite ad eum et illuminamini.* Ps. xxxiv. 5.
[2] Luke vii. 42–48.   [3] Matt. viii. 14, 15.

[4] Cf. what is said above (chap. xix. 43) as to the note of time implied in the statement (Mark i. 39), that He preached in their synagogues throughout all Galilee, and cast out devils. [The order of Mark is probably correct. — R.]
[5] Luke iv. 38, 39.
[6] Referring, apparently, to the casting out of the unclean spirit (Mark i. 23, etc.; Luke iv. 33, etc.).
[7] 1 Cor. xii. 11.

proposed to ourselves is simply to demonstrate that not one of the evangelists contradicts either himself or his fellow-historians, whatever be the precise order in which he may have had the ability or may have preferred to compose his account of matters belonging to the doings and sayings of Christ; and that, too, at once in the case of subjects identical with those recorded by others, and in the case of subjects different from these. For this reason, therefore, when the order of times is not apparent, we ought not to feel it a matter of any consequence what order any of them may have adopted in relating the events. But wherever the order is apparent, if the evangelist then presents anything which seems to be inconsistent with his own statements, or with those of another, we must certainly take the passage into consideration, and endeavour to clear up the difficulty.

CHAP. XXII. — OF THE ORDER OF THE INCIDENTS WHICH ARE RECORDED AFTER THIS SECTION, AND OF THE QUESTION WHETHER MATTHEW, MARK, AND LUKE ARE CONSISTENT WITH EACH OTHER IN THESE.

53. Matthew, accordingly, continues his narration thus: " Now when the even was come, they brought unto Him many that were possessed with devils; and He cast out the spirits with His word, and healed all that were sick: that it might be fulfilled which was spoken by Esaias the prophet, saying, Himself took our infirmities, and bare our sicknesses." [1] That this belongs in date to the same day, he indicates with sufficient clearness by these words which he subjoins, " Now when the even was come." In a similar manner, after concluding his account of the healing of Peter's mother-in-law with the sentence, " And she ministered unto them," Mark has appended the following statement: " And at even, when the sun did set, they brought unto Him all that were diseased, and them that were possessed of the devils. And all the city was gathered together at the door. And He healed many that were sick of divers diseases, and cast out many devils; and suffered not the devils to speak, because they knew Him. And in the morning, rising up a great while before day, He went out, and departed into a solitary place." [2] Here Mark appears to have preserved the order in such wise, that after the statement conveyed in the words " And at even," he gives this note of time: " And in the morning, rising up a great while before day." And although there is no absolute necessity for supposing either that, when we have the words " And at even," the reference must be to the evening of the very same day, or that when the phrase

" In the morning" meets us, it must mean the morning [3] after the self-same night; still, however that may be, this order in the occurrences may fairly appear to have been preserved with a view to an orderly arrangement of the times. Moreover, Luke, too, after relating the story of Peter's mother-in-law, while he does not indeed say expressly, " And at even," has at least used a phrase which conveys the same sense. For he proceeds thus: " Now when the sun had set, [4] all they that had any sick with divers diseases brought them unto Him; and He laid His hands on every one of them, and healed them. And devils also came out of many, crying out, and saying, Thou art Christ the Son of God. And He, rebuking them, suffered them not to speak: for they knew that He was Christ. And when it was day, He departed and went into a desert place." [5] Here, again, we see precisely the same order of times preserved as we discovered in Mark. But Matthew, who appears to have introduced the story of Peter's mother-in-law not according to the order in which the incident itself took place, but simply in the succession in which he had it suggested to his mind after previous omission, has first recorded what happened on that same day, to wit, when even was come; and thereafter, instead of subjoining the notice of the *morning*, goes on with his account in these terms: " Now when Jesus saw great multitudes about Him, He gave commandment to depart unto the other side of the lake." [6] This, then, is something new, differing from what is given in the context by Mark and Luke, who, after the notice of the *even*, bring in the mention of the *morning*. Consequently, as regards this verse in Matthew, " Now when Jesus saw great multitudes about Him, He gave commandment to depart unto the other side of the lake," we ought simply to understand that he has introduced here another fact which he has had brought to mind at this point, — namely, the fact that on a certain day, when Jesus had seen great multitudes about Him, He gave instructions to cross to the other side of the lake.

CHAP. XXIII. — OF THE PERSON WHO SAID TO THE LORD, " I WILL FOLLOW THEE WHITHERSOEVER THOU GOEST;" AND OF OTHER THINGS CONNECTED THEREWITH, AND OF THE ORDER IN WHICH THEY ARE RECORDED BY MATTHEW AND LUKE.

54. He next appends the following statement: " And a certain scribe came and said unto Him, Master, I will follow Thee whithersoever thou goest;" and so on, down to the words, " Let the dead bury their dead." [7] We have a narrative in similar terms also in Luke. But he

---

[1] Matt. viii. 16-18.   [2] Mark i. 31-35.

[3] *Diluculum*, dawn.   [4] *Occidisset*.   [5] Luke iv. 40-42.
[6] Matt. viii. 18.   [7] Matt. viii. 19-22.

inserts it only after a variety of other matters, and without any explicit note of the order of time, but after the fashion of one only bethinking himself of the incident at that point. He leaves us also uncertain whether he brings it in there as something previously omitted, or as an anticipatory notice of something which in actual fact took place subsequently to those incidents by which it is followed in the history. For he proceeds thus : "And it came to pass, that as they went in the way, a certain man said unto Him, I will follow Thee whithersoever Thou goest."[1] And the Lord's answer is given here in precisely the same terms as we find recited in Matthew. Now, although Matthew tells us that this took place at the time when He gave commandment to depart unto the other side of the lake, and Luke, on the other hand, speaks of an occasion when they "went in the way," there is no necessary contradiction in that. For it may be the case that they went in the way just in order to come to the lake. Again, in what is said about the person who begged to be allowed first to bury his father, Matthew and Luke are thoroughly at one. For the mere fact that Matthew has introduced first the words of the man who made the request regarding his father, and that he has put after that the saying of the Lord, "Follow me," whereas Luke puts the Lord's command, "Follow me," first, and the declaration of the petitioner second, is a matter of no consequence to the sense itself. Luke has also made mention of yet another person, who said, "Lord, I will follow Thee, but let me first bid them farewell which are at home at my house ;"[2] of which individual Matthew says nothing. And thereafter Luke proceeds to another subject altogether, and not to what followed in the actual order of time. The passage runs : "*And after these things*, the Lord appointed other seventy-two also."[3] That this occurred "after these things" is indeed manifest ; but at what length of time after these things the Lord did so is not apparent. Nevertheless, in this interval that took place which Matthew subjoins next in succession. For the same Matthew still keeps up the order of time, and continues his narrative, as we shall now see.

CHAP. XXIV. — OF THE LORD'S CROSSING THE LAKE ON THAT OCCASION ON WHICH HE SLEPT IN THE VESSEL, AND OF THE CASTING OUT OF THOSE DEVILS WHOM HE SUFFERED TO GO INTO THE SWINE ; AND OF THE CONSISTENCY OF THE ACCOUNTS GIVEN BY MATTHEW, MARK, AND LUKE OF ALL THAT WAS DONE AND SAID ON THESE OCCASIONS.

55. "And when He was entered into a ship,

His disciples followed Him. And, behold, there arose a great tempest in the sea." And so the story goes on, until we come to the words, "And He came into His own city."[4] Those two narratives which are told by Matthew in continuous succession, — namely, that regarding the calm upon the sea after Jesus was roused from His sleep and had commanded the winds, and that concerning the persons who were possessed with the fierce devil, and who brake their bands and were driven into the wilderness, — are given also in like manner by Mark and Luke.[5] Some parts of these stories are expressed, indeed, in different terms by the different writers, but the sense remains the same. This is the case, for example, when Matthew represents the Lord to have said, "Why are ye fearful, O ye of little faith?"[6] while Mark's version is, "Why are ye fearful? Is it that ye have no faith?"[7] For Mark's word refers to that perfect faith which is like a grain of mustard seed ; and so he, too, speaks in effect of the "little faith." Luke, again, puts it thus : "Where is your faith?"[8] Accordingly, the whole utterance may perhaps have gone thus : "Why are ye fearful? Where is your faith, O ye of little faith?" And so one of them records one part, and another another part, of the entire saying. The same may be the case with the words spoken by the disciples when they awoke Him. Matthew gives us : "Lord, save us : we perish."[9] Mark has : "Master, carest Thou not that we perish?"[10] And Luke says simply, "Master, we perish."[11] These different expressions, however, convey one and the same meaning on the part of those who were awaking the Lord, and who were wishful to secure their safety. Neither need we inquire which of these several forms is to be preferred as the one actually addressed to Christ. For whether they really used the one or the other of these three phraseologies, or expressed themselves in different words, which are unrecorded by any one of the evangelists, but which were equally well adapted to give the like representation of what was meant, what difference does it make in the fact itself? At the same time, it may also possibly have been the case that, when several parties in concert were trying to awake Him, all these various modes of expression had been used, one by one person, and another by another. In the same way, too, we may deal with the exclamation on the stilling of the tempest, which, according to Matthew, was, "What manner of man is this, that the winds and the sea obey Him?"[12] according to Mark, "What man, thinkest thou, is this,[13] that both the wind

---

[1] Luke ix. 57.   [2] Luke ix. 61.
[3] *Septuaginta duo* Luke x. 1. [An early variation in the Greek text; comp. Revised Version margin. — R.]

[4] Matt. viii. 23–ix. 1.   [5] Mark iv. 36; Luke viii. 22–37.
[6] Matt. viii. 16.
[7] Mark iv. 40. [The variations in the Greek text are numerous. Augustin gives *necdum*, which represents the reading followed in the Revised Version. — R.]
[8] Luke viii. 25.   [9] Matt. viii. 25.   [10] Mark iv. 38.
[11] Luke viii. 24.   [12] Matt. viii. 27.   [13] *Quis putas est iste.*

and the sea obey Him?"[1] and according to Luke, "What man, thinkest thou, is this?"[2] for He commandeth both the winds and the sea,[3] and they obey Him." Who can fail to see that the sense in all these forms is quite identical? For the expression, "What man, thinkest thou, is this?" has precisely the same import with the other, "What manner of man is this?"[4] And where the words "He commandeth" are omitted, it can at least be understood as a matter of course that the obedience is rendered to the person commanding.

56. Moreover, with respect to the circumstance that Matthew states that there were two men who were afflicted with the legion of devils which received permission to go into the swine, whereas Mark and Luke instance only a single individual, we may suppose that one of these parties was a person of some kind of superior notability and repute, whose case was particularly lamented by that district, and for whose deliverance there was special anxiety. With the intention of indicating that fact, two of the evangelists have judged it proper to make mention only of the one person, in connection with whom the fame of this deed had been spread abroad the more extensively and remarkably. Neither should any scruple be excited by the different forms in which the words uttered by the possessed[5] have been reproduced by the various evangelists. For we may either resolve them all into one and the same thing, or suppose them all to have been actually spoken. Nor, again, should we find any difficulty in the circumstance that with Matthew the address is couched in the plural number, but with Mark and Luke in the singular. For these latter two tell us at the same time, that when the man was asked what was his name, he answered that he was Legion, because the devils were many. Nor, once more, is there any discrepancy between Mark's statement that the herd of swine was round about the mountain,[6] and Luke's, that they were on the mountain.[7] For the herd of swine was so great that one portion of it might be on the mountain, and another only round about it. For, as Mark has expressly informed us, there were about two thousand swine.

CHAP. XXV. — OF THE MAN SICK OF THE PALSY TO WHOM THE LORD SAID, "THY SINS ARE FORGIVEN THEE," AND "TAKE UP THY BED;" AND IN ESPECIAL, OF THE QUESTION WHETHER MATTHEW AND MARK ARE CONSISTENT WITH EACH OTHER IN THEIR NOTICE OF THE PLACE WHERE THIS INCIDENT TOOK PLACE, IN SO FAR AS MATTHEW SAYS IT HAPPENED "IN HIS OWN CITY," WHILE MARK SAYS IT WAS IN CAPHARNAUM.

57. Hereupon Matthew proceeds with his recital, still preserving the order of time, and connects his narrative in the following manner: — "And He entered into a ship, and passed over, and came into His own city. And, behold, they brought to Him a man sick of the palsy, lying on a bed;" and so on, down to where it is said, "But when the multitude saw it, they marvelled, and glorified God, which had given such power unto men."[8] Mark and Luke have also told the story of this paralytic. Now, as regards Matthew's stating that the Lord said, "Son, be of good cheer, thy sins are forgiven thee;" while Luke makes the address run, not as "son," but as "man,"—this only helps to bring out the Lord's meaning more explicitly. For these sins were [thus said to be] forgiven to the "man," inasmuch as the very fact that he was a man would make it impossible for him to say, "I have not sinned;" and at the same time, that mode of address served to indicate that He who forgave sins to man was Himself God. Mark, again, has given the same form of words as Matthew, but he has left out the terms, "Be of good cheer." It is also possible, indeed, that the whole saying ran thus: "Man, be of good cheer: son, thy sins are forgiven thee;" or thus: "Son, be of good cheer: man, thy sins are forgiven thee;" or the words may have been spoken in some other congruous order.

58. A difficulty, however, may certainly arise when we observe how Matthew tells the story of the paralytic after this fashion: "And He entered into a ship, and passed over, and came into His own city. And, behold, they brought to Him a man sick of the palsy, lying on a bed;" whereas Mark speaks of the incident as taking place not in His own city, which indeed is called Nazareth, but in Capharnaum. His narrative is to the following effect: — "And again He entered into Capharnaum after some days; and it was noised that He was in the house. And straightway many were gathered together, insomuch that there was no room to receive them, no, not so much as about the door: and He spake a word[9] unto them. And they came unto Him, bringing one sick of the palsy, which was borne of four. And when they could not come nigh unto Him for the press, they uncovered the roof where He was: and when they had broken it up, they let down the bed wherein the sick of the palsy lay. And when Jesus saw their faith;"

---

[1] Mark iv. 41. [The Greek text in Mark and Luke has nothing corresponding to "thinkest thou." The Authorized Version, given above, has an unnecessary variation; "that," "that," "for." The Greek particle is the same, and Augustin gives *quia* three times. — R.]

[2] *Quis putas hic est.*   [3] *Mari.*   [4] *Qualis est hic.*

[5] Or, the devils — *dæmonum.*

[6] *Circa montem.* [The correct Greek text is rendered "on the mountain side" in the Revised Version. — R.]

[7] *In monte.*

[8] Matt. ix. 1-8.

[9] *Loquebatur verbum.* ["Was speaking the word" is probably the meaning. — R.]

and so forth.[1] Luke, on the other hand, does not mention the place in which the incident happened, but gives the tale thus : "And it came to pass on a certain day that He was sitting teaching,[2] and there were Pharisees and doctors of the law also sitting by, which were come out of every town of Galilee, and Judæa, and Jerusalem : and the power of the Lord was present to heal them. And, behold, men brought in a bed a man which was taken with a palsy : and they sought means to bring him in, and to lay him before Him. And when they could not find by what way they might bring him in because of the multitude, they went upon the house-top, and let him down through the tiling with his couch into the midst before Jesus. And when He saw their faith, He said, Man, thy sins are forgiven thee ; " and so forth.[3] The question, therefore, remains one between Mark and Matthew, in so far as Matthew writes of the incident as taking place in the Lord's city ;[4] while Mark locates it in Capharnaum. This question would be more difficult to solve if Matthew mentioned Nazareth by name. But, as the case stands, when we reflect that the state of Galilee itself might have been called Christ's city,[5] because Nazareth was in Galilee, just as the whole region which was made up of so many cities[6] is yet called a Roman state ;[7] when, further, it is considered that so many nations are comprehended in that city, of which it is written, "Glorious things are spoken of thee, O city of God ;"[8] and also that God's ancient people, though dwelling in so many cities, have yet been spoken of as one house, the house of Israel,[9]— who can doubt that [it may be fairly said that] Jesus wrought this work in His own city [or, *state*], inasmuch as He did it in the city of Capharnaum, which was a city of that Galilee to which He had returned when He crossed over again from the country of the Gerasenes, so that when He came into Galilee He might correctly be said to have come into His own city [or, *state*], in whichever town of Galilee He might happen to be? This explanation may be vindicated more particularly on the ground that Capharnaum itself held a position of such eminence in Galilee that it was reckoned to be a kind of metropolis. But even were it altogether illegitimate to take the city of Christ in the sense either of Galilee itself, in which Nazareth was situated, or of Capharnaum, which was distinguished as in a certain sense the capital of Galilee, we might still affirm that Matthew has simply passed over all that happened after Jesus came into His own city until He reached Capharnaum, and that he has simply

tacked on the narrative of the healing of the paralytic at this point ; just as the writers do in many instances, leaving unnoticed much that intervenes, and, without any express indication of the omissions they are making, proceeding precisely as if what they subjoin, followed actually in literal succession.[10]

CHAP. XXVI. — OF THE CALLING OF MATTHEW, AND OF THE QUESTION WHETHER MATTHEW'S OWN ACCOUNT IS IN HARMONY WITH THOSE OF MARK AND LUKE WHEN THEY SPEAK OF LEVI THE SON OF ALPHÆUS.

59. Matthew next continues his narrative in the following terms : — "And as Jesus passed forth from thence, He saw a man named Matthew, sitting at the receipt of custom : and He saith unto him, Follow me. And he arose and followed Him." [11] Mark gives this story also, and keeps the same order, bringing it in after the notice of the healing of the man who was sick of the palsy. His version runs thus : "And He went forth again by the sea-side ; and all the multitude resorted unto Him, and He taught them. And as He passed by, He saw Levi the son of Alphæus sitting at the receipt of custom, and said unto him, Follow me. And he arose, and followed Him." [12] There is no contradiction here ; for Matthew is the same person with Levi. Luke also introduces this after the story of the healing of the same man who was sick of the palsy. He writes in these terms : "And after these things He went forth, and saw a publican, named Levi, sitting at the receipt of custom : and He said unto him, Follow me. And he left all, rose up, and followed Him." [13] Now, from this it will appear to be the most reasonable explanation to say that Matthew records these things here in the form of things previously passed over, and now brought to mind. For certainly we must believe that Matthew's calling took place before the delivery of the sermon on the mount. For Luke tells us that on this mountain on that occasion the election was made of all these twelve, whom Jesus also named apostles, out of the larger body of the disciples.[14]

CHAP. XXVII. — OF THE FEAST AT WHICH IT WAS OBJECTED AT ONCE THAT CHRIST ATE WITH SINNERS, AND THAT HIS DISCIPLES DID NOT FAST ; OF THE CIRCUMSTANCE THAT THE EVANGELISTS SEEM TO GIVE DIFFERENT ACCOUNTS OF THE PARTIES BY WHOM THESE OBJECTIONS WERE ALLEGED ; AND OF THE QUESTION WHETHER

---

[1] Mark ii. 1-12.   [2] *Et ipse sedebat docens.*
[3] Luke v. 17-26.   [4] Or, state — *civitate.*
[5] Or, state — *civitas.*   [6] *Civitatibus.*
[7] *Civitas*, city.   [8] Ps. lxxxvii. 3.
[9] Isa. v. 7 ; Jer. iii. 20 ; Ezek. iii. 4.

[10] [The true solution of the difficulty is simple. Our Lord had already left Nazareth, and made Capernaum His headquarters (comp. Luke iv. 30, 31). But Augustin identifies that incident with a subsequent visit to Nazareth (see ch. xlii.). — R.]
[11] Matt. ix. 9.   [12] Mark ii. 13, 14.   [13] Luke v. 27, 28.
[14] Luke vi. 13. [This fact shows that the order of Matthew is not chronological. Indeed, as Augustin goes on, he is led more and more to accept the order of the other evangelists. — R.]

MATTHEW AND MARK AND LUKE ARE ALSO IN HARMONY WITH EACH OTHER IN THE REPORTS GIVEN OF THE WORDS OF THESE PERSONS, AND OF THE REPLIES RETURNED BY THE LORD.

60. Matthew, accordingly, goes on to say: "And it came to pass, as He sat at meat in the house, behold, many publicans and sinners came and sat down with Jesus and His disciples;" and so on, down to where we read, "But they put new wine into new bottles, and both are preserved." [1] Here Matthew has not told us particularly in whose house it was that Jesus was sitting at meat along with the publicans and sinners. This might make it appear as if he had not appended this notice in its strict order here, but had introduced at this point, in the way of reminiscence, something which actually took place on a different occasion, were it not that Mark and Luke, who repeat the account in terms thoroughly similar, have made it plain that it was in the house of Levi — that is to say, Matthew — that Jesus sat at meat, and all these sayings were uttered which follow. For Mark states the same fact, keeping also the same order, in the following manner: "And it came to pass, as He sat at meat in his house, many publicans and sinners sat also together with Jesus." [2] Accordingly, when he says, "in his house," he certainly refers to the person of whom he was speaking directly before, and that was Levi. To the same effect, after the words, "He saith unto him, Follow me; and he left all, rose up, and followed Him," [3] Luke has appended immediately this statement: "And Levi made Him a great feast in his own house: and there was a great company of publicans and of others that sat down with them." And thus it is manifest in whose house it was that these things took place.

61. Let us next look into the words which these three evangelists have all brought in as having been addressed to the Lord, and also into the replies which were made by Him. Matthew says: "And when the Pharisees saw it, they said unto His disciples, Why eateth your Master with publicans and sinners?" [4] This reappears very nearly in the same words in Mark: "How is it that He eateth and drinketh with publicans and sinners?" [5] Only we find thus that Matthew has omitted one thing which Mark inserts — namely, the addition "and drinketh." But of what consequence can that be, since the sense is fully given, the idea suggested being that they were partaking of a repast in company? Luke, on the other hand, seems to have recorded this scene somewhat differently. For his version proceeds thus: "But their scribes and Phari-

sees murmured against His disciples, saying, Why do ye eat and drink with publicans and sinners?" [6] But his intention in this certainly is not [7] to indicate that their Master was not referred to on that occasion, but to intimate that the objection was levelled against all of them together, both Himself and His disciples; the charge, however, which was to be taken to be meant both of Him and of them, being addressed directly not to Him, but to them. For the fact is that Luke himself, no less than the others, represents the Lord as making the reply, and saying, "I came not to call the righteous, but sinners to repentance." [8] And He would not have returned that answer to them, had not their words, "Why do ye eat and drink?" been directed very specially to Himself. For the same reason, Matthew and Mark have told us that the objection which was brought against Him was stated immediately to His disciples, because, when the allegation was addressed to the disciples, the charge was thereby laid all the more seriously against the Master whom these disciples were imitating and following. One and the same sense, therefore, is conveyed; and it is expressed all the better in consequence of these variations employed in some of the terms, while the matter of fact itself is left intact. In like manner we may deal with the accounts of the Lord's reply. Matthew's runs thus: "They that be whole need not a physician, but they that are sick; but go ye and learn what this meaneth, I will have mercy, and not sacrifice: for I am not come to call the righteous, but sinners." [9] Mark and Luke have also preserved for us the same sense in almost the same words, with this exception, that they both fail to introduce that quotation from the prophet, "I will have mercy, and not sacrifice." Luke, again, after the words, "I came not to call the righteous, but sinners," has added the term, "unto repentance." This addition serves to bring out the sense more fully, so as to preclude any one from supposing that sinners are loved by Christ, purely for the very reason that they are sinners. For this similitude also of the *sick* indicates clearly what God means by the calling of sinners, — that it is like the physician with the sick, — and that its object verily is that men should be saved from their iniquity as from disease; which healing is effected by repentance.

62. In the same way, we may subject what is said about the disciples of John to examination. Matthew's words are these: "Then came to

---

[6] Luke v. 30.
[7] *Non utique magistrum eorum nolens illic intelligi*, with most MSS. The reading *volens* occurs in some = not meaning their Master to be referred to, he intimates, etc.
[8] Luke v. 32.
[9] Omitting *in pœnitentiam* = unto repentance. [These words should be omitted in Matthew and Mark, according to the Greek MSS. Comp. Revised Version. — R.]

Him the disciples of John, saying, Why do we and the Pharisees fast oft?"[1] The purport of Mark's version is similar: "And the disciples of John and the Pharisees[2] used to fast.[3] And they come and say unto Him, Why do the disciples of John and the Pharisees[4] fast, but thy disciples fast not?"[5] The only semblance of a discrepancy that can be found here, is in the possibility of supposing that the mention of the Pharisees as having spoken along with the disciples of John is an addition of Mark's, while Matthew states only that the disciples of John expressed themselves to the above effect. But the words which were actually uttered by the parties, according to Mark's version, rather indicate that the speakers and the persons spoken of were not the same individuals. I mean, that the persons who came to Jesus were the guests who were then present, that they came because the disciples of John and the Pharisees were fasting, and that they uttered the above words with respect to these parties. In this way, the evangelist's phrase, "they come," would not refer to the persons regarding whom he had just thrown in the remark, "And the disciples of John and the Pharisees were fasting." But the case would be, that as those parties were fasting, some others here, who are moved by that fact, come to Him, and put this question to Him, "Why do the disciples of John and of the Pharisees fast, but thy disciples fast not?" This is more clearly expressed by Luke. For, evidently with the same idea in his mind, after stating what answer the Lord returned in the words in which He spoke about the calling of sinners under the similitude of those who are sick, he proceeds thus: "And they said unto Him, Why do the disciples of John fast often, and make prayers, and likewise the disciples of the Pharisees, but thine eat and drink?"[6] Here, then, we see that, as was the case with Mark, Luke has mentioned one party as speaking to this intent in relation to other parties. How comes it, therefore, that Matthew says, "Then came to Him the disciples of John, saying, Why do we and the Pharisees fast?" The explanation may be, that those individuals were also present, and that all these various parties were eager to advance this charge, as they severally found opportunity. And the sentiments which sought expression on this occasion have been conveyed by the three evangelists under varied terms, but yet without any divergence from a true statement of the fact itself.

63. Once more, we find that Matthew and Mark have given similar accounts of what was said about the children of the bridegroom not fasting as long as the bridegroom is with them, with this exception, that Mark has named them the children of the bridals,[7] while Matthew has designated them the children of the bridegroom.[8] That, however, is a matter of no moment. For by the children of the bridals we understand at once those connected with the bridegroom, and those connected with the bride. The sense, therefore, is obvious and identical, and neither different nor contradictory. Luke, again, does not say, "Can the children of the bridegroom fast?" but, "Can ye make the children of the bridegroom fast, while the bridegroom is with them?" By expressing it in this method, the evangelist has elegantly opened up the self-same sense in a way calculated to suggest something else. For thus the idea is conveyed, that those very persons who were speaking would try to make the children of the bridegroom mourn and fast, inasmuch as they would [seek to] put the bridegroom to death. Moreover, Matthew's phrase, "mourn," is of the same import as that used by Mark and Luke, namely, "fast." For Matthew also says further on, "Then shall they fast," and not, "Then shall they mourn." But by the use of this phrase, he has indicated that the Lord spoke of that kind of fasting which pertains to the lowliness of tribulation. In the same way, too, the Lord may be understood to have pictured out a different kind of fasting, which stands related to the rapture of a mind dwelling in the heights of things spiritual, and for that reason estranged in a certain measure from the meats that are for the body, when He made use of those subsequent similitudes touching the new cloth and the new wine, by which He showed that this kind of fasting is an incongruity for sensual[9] and carnal people, who are taken up with the cares of the body, and who consequently still remain in the old mind. These similitudes are also embodied in similar terms by the other two evangelists. And it should be sufficiently evident that there need be no real discrepancy, although one may introduce something, whether belonging to the subject-matter itself, or merely to the terms in which that subject is expressed, which another leaves out; provided only that there be neither any departure from a genuine identity in sense, nor any contradiction created between the different forms which may be adopted for expressing the same thing.

CHAP. XXVIII. — OF THE RAISING OF THE DAUGHTER OF THE RULER OF THE SYNAGOGUE, AND OF THE WOMAN WHO TOUCHED THE HEM OF HIS GARMENT; OF THE QUESTION, ALSO, AS TO

---

[1] Matt. ix. 14.
[2] *Pharisæi*, not *Pharisæorum*. [So the Greek text. — R.]
[3] Or, as Augustin's reasoning implies that he understood it, *were fasting—erant jejunantes*. [So Revised Version. — R.]
[4] *Pharisæorum*.   [5] Mark ii. 18.
[6] Luke v. 33.

[7] *Filios nuptiarum*.   [8] *Filios sponsi*.
[9] *Animalibus*.

WHETHER THE ORDER IN WHICH THESE INCI-
DENTS ARE NARRATED EXHIBITS ANY CONTRA-
DICTION IN ANY OF THE WRITERS BY WHOM
THEY ARE REPORTED ; AND IN PARTICULAR, OF
THE WORDS IN WHICH THE RULER OF THE
SYNAGOGUE ADDRESSED HIS REQUEST TO THE
LORD.

64. Still keeping by the order of time, Matthew
next continues to the following effect : " While
He spake these things unto them, behold, there
came a certain ruler, and worshipped Him, saying, My daughter is even now dead ; but come
and lay Thy hand upon her, and she shall live ;"
and so on, until we come to the words, "and the
maid arose. And the fame hereof went abroad
into all that land."[1] The other two, namely,
Mark and Luke, in like manner give this same
account, only they do not keep by the same
order now. For they bring up this narrative in
a different place, and insert it in another connection ; to wit, at the point where He crosses
the lake and returns from the country of the
Gerasenes, after casting out the devils and permitting them to go into the swine. Thus Mark
introduces it, after he has related what took place
among the Gerasenes, in the following manner :
" And when Jesus was passed over again by ship
unto the other side, much people gathered unto
Him : and He was nigh unto the sea. And
there cometh one of the rulers of the synagogue,
Jairus by name ; and when he saw Him, he fell
at His feet," etc.[2] By this, then, we are certainly to understand that the occurrence in connection with the daughter of the ruler of the
synagogue did take place after Jesus had passed
across the lake again in the ship.[3] It does not,
however, appear from the words themselves how
long after that passage this thing happened. But
that some time did elapse is clear. For had
there not been an interval, no period would be
left within which those circumstances might fall
which Matthew has just related in the matter of
the feast in his house. These, indeed, he has
told after the fashion of the evangelists, as if
they were the story of another person's doings.
But they are the story really of what took place
in his own case, and at his own house. And after
that narrative, what follows in the immediate
context is nothing else than this notice of the
daughter of the ruler of the synagogue. For he
has constructed the whole recital in such a manner, that the mode of transition from one thing to
the other has itself indicated with sufficient clearness that the words immediately, following give
the narrative of what actually took place in
immediate consecution. For after mentioning,

in connection with the former incident, those
words which Jesus spake with respect to the new
cloth and the new wine, he has subjoined these
other words, without any interruption in the narrative, namely, " While He spake these things unto
them, behold, there came a certain ruler." And
this shows that, if the person approached Him
while He was speaking these things, nothing else
either done or said by Him could have intervened. In Mark's account, on the other hand,
the place is quite apparent, as we have already
pointed out, where other things [left unrecorded
by him] might very well have come in. The
case is much the same also with Luke, who,
when he proceeds to follow up his version of
the story of the miracle wrought among the
Gerasenes, by giving his account of the daughter
of the ruler of the synagogue, does not pass on
to that in any such way as to place it in antagonism with Matthew's version, who, by his words,
" While He yet spake these things," gives us
plainly to understand that the occurrence took
place after those parables about the cloth and
the wine. For when he has concluded his statement of what happened among the Gerasenes,
Luke passes to the next subject in the following
manner ; " And it came to pass that, when Jesus
was returned, the people gladly received Him ;
for they were all waiting for Him. And, behold,
there came a man named Jairus, and he was a
ruler of the synagogue, and he fell down at
Jesus' feet," and so on.[4] Thus we are given to
understand that the crowd did indeed receive
Jesus forthwith on the said occasion : for He
was the person for whose return they were waiting. But what is conveyed in the words which
are directly added, " And, behold, there came a
man whose name was Jairus," is not to be taken
to have occurred literally in immediate succession. On the contrary, the feast with the publicans, as Matthew records it, took place before
that. For Matthew connects this present incident with that feast in such a way as to make it
impossible for us to suppose that any other
sequence of events can be the correct order.[5]

65. In this narrative, then, which we have
undertaken to consider at present, all these three
evangelists indeed are unquestionably at one in
the account which they give of the woman who
was afflicted with the issue of blood. Nor is it
a matter of any real consequence, that something
which is passed by in silence by one of them is
related by another ; or that Mark says, " Who
touched my clothes ? " while Luke says, " Who
touched me ? " For the one has only adopted
the phrase in use and wont, whereas the other has

---

[1] Matt. ix. 18–26.   [2] Mark v. 21–43.
[3] [The events can be arranged in the order of Mark, with the
exception of the passage, chap. ii. 15–22. This must be placed, as
Augustin says, after the return from " the country of the Gerasenes."
Comp. § 89.—R.]

[4] Luke viii. 40–56.
[5] [This is one of the rare cases where the order of Matthew is
more exact than that of Mark and Luke. But the former evangelist
has dislocated a long series of events in the same connection. See
above.—R.]

given the stricter expression. But for all that, both of them convey the same meaning. For it is more usual with us to say, "You are tearing me,"[1] than to say, "You are tearing my clothes;" as, notwithstanding the term, the sense we wish to convey is obvious enough.

66. At the same time, however, there remains the fact that Matthew represents the ruler of the synagogue to have spoken to the Lord of his daughter, not merely as one likely to die, or as dying, or as on the very point of expiring, but as even then dead; while these other two evangelists report her as now nigh unto death, but not yet really dead, and keep so strictly to that version of the circumstances, that they tell us how the persons came at a later stage with the intelligence of her actual death, and with the message that for this reason the Master ought not now to trouble Himself by coming, with the purpose of laying His hand upon her, and so preventing her from dying, — the matter not being put as if He was one possessed of ability to raise the once dead to life. It becomes necessary for us, therefore, to investigate this fact, lest it may seem to exhibit any contradiction between the accounts. And the way to explain it is to suppose that, by reason of brevity in the narrative, Matthew has preferred to express it as if the Lord had been really asked to do what it is clear He did actually do, namely, raise the dead to life. For what Matthew directs our attention to, is not the mere words spoken by the father about his daughter, but what is of more importance, his mind and purpose. Thus he has given words calculated to represent the father's real thoughts. For he had so thoroughly despaired of his child's case, that not believing that she whom he had just left dying, could possibly now be found yet in life, his thought rather was that she might be made alive again. Accordingly two of the evangelists have introduced the words which were literally spoken by Jairus. But Matthew has exhibited rather what the man secretly wished and thought. Thus both petitions were really addressed to the Lord; namely, either that He should restore the dying damsel, or that, if she was already dead, He might raise her to life again. But as it was Matthew's object to tell the whole story in short compass, he has represented the father as directly expressing in his request what, it is certain, had been his own real wish, and what Christ actually did. It is true, indeed, that if those two evangelists, or one of them, had told us that the father himself spake the words which the parties who came from his house uttered, — namely, that Jesus should not now trouble Himself, because the damsel had died, — then the words which Matthew has put

into his mouth would not be in harmony with his thoughts. But, as the case really stands, it is not said that he gave his consent to the parties who brought that report, and who bade the Master no more think of coming now. And together with this, we have to observe, that when the Lord addressed him in these terms, "Fear not: believe only, and she shall be made whole,"[2] He did not find fault with him on the ground of his want of belief, but really encouraged him to a yet stronger faith. For this ruler had faith like that which was exhibited by the person who said, "Lord, I believe; help Thou mine unbelief."[3]

67. Seeing, then, that the case stands thus, from these varied and yet not inconsistent modes of statement adopted by the evangelists, we evidently learn a lesson of the utmost utility, and of great necessity, — namely, that in any man's words the thing which we ought narrowly to regard is only the writer's thought which was meant to be expressed, and to which the words ought to be subservient; and further, that we should not suppose one to be giving an incorrect statement, if he happens to convey in different words what the person really meant whose words he fails to reproduce literally. And we ought not to let the wretched cavillers at words fancy that truth must be tied somehow or other to the jots and tittles of letters; whereas the fact is, that not in the matter of words only, but equally in all other methods by which sentiments are indicated, the sentiment itself, and nothing else, is what ought to be looked at.

68. Moreover, as to the circumstance that some codices of Matthew's Gospel contain the reading, "For the woman[4] is not dead, but sleepeth," while Mark and Luke certify that she was a damsel of the age of twelve years, we may suppose that Matthew has followed the Hebrew mode of speech here. For in other passages of Scripture, as well as here, it is found that not only those who had already known a man, but all females in general, including untouched virgins, are called women.[5] That is the case, for instance, where it is written of Eve, "He made it[6] into a woman;"[7] and again, in the book of Numbers, where the women[5] who have not known a man by lying with him, that is to say, the virgins, are ordered to be saved from being put to death.[8] Adopting the same phraseology, Paul, too, says of Christ Himself, that He was "made of a woman."[9] And it is better, therefore, to understand the matter according to these analogies, than to suppose that

---

[1] *Conscindis.*

[2] Luke viii. 50.
[3] Mark ix. 24.
[6] *Eam,* her.
[9] Gal. ii. 4.

[4] *Mulier.*
[7] Gen. ii. 22.

[5] *Mulieres.*
[8] Num. xxxi. 18.

this damsel of twelve years of age was already married, or had known a man.[1]

CHAP. XXIX. — OF THE TWO BLIND MEN AND THE DUMB DEMONIAC WHOSE STORIES ARE RELATED ONLY BY MATTHEW.

69. Matthew proceeds with his narrative in the following terms: "And when Jesus departed thence, two blind men followed Him, crying and saying, Thou son of David, have mercy on us;" and so on, down to the verse where we read, "But the Pharisees said, He casteth out devils through the prince of the devils."[2] Matthew is the only one who introduces this account of the two blind men and the dumb demoniac. For those two blind men, whose story is given also by the others,[3] are not the two before us here. Nevertheless there is such similarity in the occurrences, that if Matthew himself had not recorded the latter incident as well as the former, it might have been thought that the one which he relates at present has also been given by these other two evangelists. There is this fact, therefore, which we ought to bear carefully in mind, — namely, that there are some occurrences which resemble each other. For we have a proof of this in the circumstance that the very same evangelist mentions both incidents here. And thus, if at any time we find any such occurrences narrated individually by the several evangelists, and discover some contradiction in the accounts, which seems not to admit of being solved [on the principle of harmonizing], it may occur to us that the explanation simply is, that this [apparently contradictory] circumstance did not take place [on that particular occasion], but that what did happen then was only something resembling it, or something which was gone about in a similar manner.

CHAP. XXX. — OF THE SECTION WHERE IT IS RE-CORDED, THAT BEING MOVED WITH COMPASSION FOR THE MULTITUDES, HE SENT HIS DISCIPLES, GIVING THEM POWER TO WORK CURES, AND CHARGED THEM WITH MANY INSTRUCTIONS, DI-RECTING THEM HOW TO LIVE; AND OF THE QUESTION CONCERNING THE PROOF OF MAT-THEW'S HARMONY HERE WITH MARK AND LUKE, ESPECIALLY ON THE SUBJECT OF THE STAFF, WHICH MATTHEW SAYS THE LORD TOLD THEM THEY WERE NOT TO CARRY, WHILE ACCORDING TO MARK IT IS THE ONLY THING THEY WERE TO CARRY; AND ALSO OF THE WEARING OF THE SHOES AND COATS.

70. As to the events next related, it is true that their exact order is not made apparent by Matthew's narrative. For after the notices of the two incidents in connection with the blind men and the dumb demoniac, he continues in the following manner: "And Jesus went about all the cities and villages, teaching in their synagogues, and preaching the kingdom of the gospel,[4] and healing every sickness and every disease. But when He saw the multitudes, He was moved with compassion on them, because they were troubled and prostrate,[5] as sheep having no shepherd. Then saith He unto His disciples, The harvest truly is plenteous, but the labourers are few: pray ye therefore the Lord of the harvest, that He will send forth[6] labourers into His harvest. And when He had called unto Him His twelve disciples, He gave them power against unclean spirits;" and so forth, down to the words, "Verily I say unto you, he shall not lose his reward."[7] This whole passage which we have now mentioned shows how He gave many counsels to His disciples. But whether Matthew has subjoined this section in its historical order, or has made its order dependent only on the succession in which it came up to his own mind, as has already been said, is not made apparent. Mark appears to have handled this paragraph in a succinct method, and to have entered upon its recital in the following terms: "And He went round about the villages, teaching in their circuit:[8] and He called unto Him the twelve, and began to send them by two and two, and gave them power over unclean spirits;" and so on, down to where we read, "Shake off the dust from your feet for a testimony against them."[9] But before narrating this incident, Mark has inserted, immediately after the story of the raising of the daughter of the ruler of the synagogue, an account of what took place on that occasion on which, in His own country, the people were astonished at the Lord, and asked from whence He had such wisdom and such capabilities,[10] when they perceived His judgment: which account is given by Matthew after these counsels to the disciples, and after a number of other matters.[11] It is uncertain, therefore, whether what thus happened in His own country has been recorded by Matthew in the succession in which it came to mind, after having been omitted at first, or whether it has been introduced by Mark in the way of an anticipation; and which of them, in short, has kept the order of actual occurrence, and which of them the order of his own recollection. Luke, again, in immediate succession to the mention of the raising of the daughter of Jaïrus to life, subjoins this paragraph, bearing on the

---

[1] [The curious variation in text noted above was probably due to the scribe's confounding the "damsel" with the "woman" who had just been spoken of. — R.]
[2] Matt. ix. 27-34. [The view of Augustin is that now generally accepted by harmonists. — R.]
[3] Mark x. 46-52; Luke xviii. 35-43.

[4] *Regnum evangelii.*   [5] *Vexati et jacentes.*
[6] The MSS. read *ejicias:* some editions have *mittat*, send.
[7] Matt. ix. 35-x. 42.   [8] *In circuitu docens.*
[9] Mark vi. 6-11.   [10] *Virtutes.*   [11] Matt. xiii. 54.

power and the counsels given to the disciples, and that indeed with as great brevity as Mark.[1] This evangelist, however, does not, any more than the others, introduce the subject in such a way as to produce the impression that it comes in also in the strictly historical order. Moreover, with regard to the names of the disciples, Luke, who gives their names in another place,[2] — that is to say, in the earlier passage, where they are [represented as being] chosen on the mountain, — is not at variance in any respect with Matthew, with the exception of the single instance of the name of Judas the brother of James, whom Matthew designates Thaddæus, although some codices also read Lebbæus.[3] But who would ever think of denying that one man may be known under two or three names?

71. Another question which it is also usual to put is this: How comes it that Matthew and Luke have stated that the Lord said to His disciples that they were not to take a staff with them, whereas Mark puts the matter in this way: "And He commanded them that they should take nothing for their journey, save a staff only;"[4] and proceeds further in this strain, "no scrip, no bread, no money in their purse:" thereby making it quite evident that his narrative belongs to the same place and circumstances with which the narratives of those others deal who have mentioned that the staff was not to be taken? Now this question admits of being solved on the principle of understanding that the staff which, according to Mark, was to be taken, bears one sense, and that the staff which, according to Matthew and Luke, was not to be taken with them, is to be interpreted in a different sense; just in the same way as we find the term "temptation" used in one meaning, when it is said, "God tempteth no man,"[5] and in a different meaning where it is said, "The Lord your God tempteth [proveth] you, to know whether ye love Him."[6] For in the former case the temptation of seduction is intended; but in the latter the temptation of probation. Another parallel occurs in the case of the term "judgment," which must be taken in one way, where it is said, "They that have done good unto the resurrection of life, and they that have done evil unto the resurrection of judgment;"[7] and in another way, where it is said, "Judge

me, O God, and discern[8] my cause, in respect of an ungodly nation."[9] For the former refers to the judgment of damnation, and the latter to the judgment of discrimination.

72. And there are many other words which do not retain one uniform signification, but are introduced so as to suit a variety of connections, and thus are understood in a variety of ways, and sometimes, indeed, are adopted along with an explanation. We have an example in the saying, "Be not children[10] in understanding; howbeit in malice be ye little children, that in understanding ye may be perfect."[11] For here is a sentence which, in a brief and pregnant form, might have been expressed thus: "Be ye not children; howbeit be ye children." The same is the case with the words, "If any man among you thinketh himself to be wise in this world, let him become a fool that he may be wise."[12] For what else is the statement there but this: "Let him not be wise, that he may be wise"? Moreover, the sentences are sometimes so put as to exercise the judgment of the inquirer. An instance of this kind occurs in what is said in the Epistle to the Galatians: "Bear ye one another's burdens, and so ye will fulfil the law of Christ. For if a man thinketh himself to be something, when he is nothing, he deceiveth himself. But it is meet that every man should prove his own work; and then shall he have rejoicing in himself, and not in another. For every man shall bear his own burden."[13] Now, unless the word "burden" can be taken in different senses, without doubt one would suppose that the same writer contradicts himself in what he says here, and that, too, when the words are placed in such close neighbourhood in one paragraph.[14] For when he has just said, "One shall bear another's burdens," after the lapse of a very brief interval he says, "Every man shall bear his own burden." But the one refers to the burdens which are to be borne in sharing in one's infirmity, the other to the burdens borne in the rendering of an account of our own actions to God: the former are burdens to be borne in our [duties of] fellowship with brethren; the latter are those peculiar to ourselves, and borne by every man for himself. And in the same way, once more, the "rod" of which the apostle spoke in the words, "Shall I come unto you with a rod?"[15] is meant in a spiritual sense; while the same term bears the literal meaning when it occurs of the rod applied to a horse, or used for some other purpose of the

---

[1] Luke ix. 1-6.
[2] The Ratisbon edition and nineteen MSS. read *alio nomine*, by another name, instead of *alio loco.* — MIGNE.
[3] In five MSS. *Lebdæum*, Lebdeus, is given instead of Lebbeus, but wrongly, as appears from the Greek text of Matt. x. 3. — MIGNE. [The Vulgate (Matt. x. 3) reads *Thaddæus*, now accepted by critical editors; so Revised Version. The Authorized Version follows a composite reading (with two early uncials and Syriac versions): "Lebbæus, whose surname was Thaddæus." A harmonistic gloss. — R.]
[4] Mark vi. 8. [In Matt. x. 10, Luke ix. 3, the later authorities substitute the plural "staves," probably to avoid the seeming discrepancy. The better sustained reading in both passages is "staff." — R.]
[5] Jas. i. 13.   [6] Deut. xiii. 3.   [7] *Judicii.* John v. 29.

[8] *Discerne.*   [9] Ps. xliii. 1.   [10] *Pueri.*
[11] *Parvuli estote ut sensibus perfecti sitis.* 1 Cor. xiv. 20.
[12] 1 Cor. iii. 18.
[13] Gal. vi. 2-5.
[14] [Augustin fails to notice that the word "burden" represents different Greek words in Gal. vi. 2-5. His argument here resembles the method of modern expositors who explain the discrepancies of the Authorized Version without consulting the original. — R.]
[15] 1 Cor. iv. 21.

kind, not to mention, in the meantime, also other metaphorical significations of this phrase.

73. Both these counsels, therefore, must be accepted as having been spoken by the Lord to the apostles; namely, at once that they should not take a staff, and that they should take nothing save a staff only. For when He said to them, according to Matthew, "Provide neither gold nor silver, nor money in your purses, nor scrip for your journey, neither two coats, neither shoes, nor yet a staff," He added immediately, "for the workman is worthy of his meat." And by this He makes it sufficiently obvious why it is that He would have them provide and carry none of these things. He shows that His reason was, not that these things are not necessary for the sustenance of this life, but because He was sending them in such a manner as to declare plainly that these things were due to them by those very persons who were to hear believingly the gospel preached by them; just as wages are the soldier's due, and as the fruit of the vine is the right of the planters, and the milk of the flock the right of the shepherds. For which reason Paul also speaks in this wise: "Who goeth a warfare any time at his own charges? who planteth a vineyard, and eateth not of the fruit thereof? who feedeth a flock, and eateth not of the milk of the flock?"[1] For under these figures he was speaking of those things which are necessary to the preachers of the gospel. And so, a little further on, he says: "If we have sown unto you spiritual things, is it a great thing if we shall reap your carnal things? If others are partakers of this power over you, are not we rather? Nevertheless we have not used this power."[2] This makes it apparent that by these instructions the Lord did not mean that the evangelists should not seek their support in any other way than by depending on what was offered them by those to whom they preached the gospel (otherwise this very apostle acted contrary to this precept when he acquired a livelihood for himself by the labours of his own hands, because he would not be chargeable to any of them[3]), but that He gave them a power in the exercise of which they should know such things to be their due. Now, when any commandment is given by the Lord, there is the guilt of non-obedience if it is not observed; but when any power is given, any one is at liberty to abstain from its use, and, as it were, to recede from his right. Accordingly, when the Lord spake these things to the disciples, He did what that apostle expounds more clearly a little further on, when he says, "Do ye not know that they who minister in the temple[4] live of the things of the temple? and they which wait at the

altar are partakers with the altar? Even so hath the Lord ordained, that they which preach the gospel should live of the gospel. But I have used none of these things."[5] When he says, therefore, that the Lord ordained it thus, but that he did not use the ordinance, he certainly indicates that it was a power to use that was given him, and not a necessity of service that was imposed upon him.

74. Accordingly, as our Lord ordained what the apostle declares Him to have ordained, — namely, that those who preach the gospel should live of the gospel, — He gave these counsels to the apostles in order that they might be without the care of providing[6] or of carrying with them things necessary for this life, whether great or the very smallest; consequently He introduced this term, "neither a staff," with the view of showing that, on the part of those who were faithful to Him, all things were due to His ministers, who themselves, too, required nothing superfluous. And thus, when He added the words, "For the workman is worthy of his meat," He indicated quite clearly, and made it thoroughly plain, how and for what reason it was that He spake all these things. It is this kind of power, therefore, that the Lord denoted under the term "staff," when He said that they should "take nothing" for their journey, save a staff only. For the sentence might also have been briefly expressed in this way: "Take with you none of the necessaries of life, neither a staff, save a staff only." So that the phrase "neither a staff" may be taken to be equivalent to "not even the smallest things;" while the addition, "save a staff only," may be understood to mean that, in virtue of that power which they received from the Lord, and which was signified by the name "staff" [or, "rod"], even those things which were not carried with them would not be wanting to them. Our Lord therefore used both phrases. But inasmuch as one and the same evangelist has not recorded them both, the writer who has told us that the rod, as introduced in the one sense, was to be taken, is supposed to be in antagonism to him who has told us that the rod, as occurring again in the other sense, was not to be taken. After this explanation of the matter, however, no such supposition ought to be entertained.

75. In like manner, also, when Matthew tells us that the shoes were not to be carried with them on the journey, what is intended is the checking of that care which thinks that such things must be carried with them, because otherwise they might be unprovided. Thus, too, the import of what is said regarding the two coats is, that none of them should think of taking with him another coat in addition to the one in

---

which he was clad, as if he was afraid that he might come to be in want, while all the time the power (which was received from the Lord) made him sure of getting what was needful. To the same effect, when Mark says that they were to be shod with sandals or soles, he gives us to understand that this matter of the shoe has some sort of mystical significance, the point being that the foot is to be neither covered, nor yet left bare to the ground; by which the idea may be conveyed that the gospel was neither to be concealed, nor yet made to depend on the good things of earth. And as to the fact that what is forbidden is neither the carrying nor the possessing of two coats, but more distinctly the putting of them on, — the words being, "and not put on two coats," — what counsel is conveyed to them therein but this, that they ought to walk not in duplicity, but in simplicity?

76. Thus it is not by any means to be made a matter of doubt that the Lord Himself spake all these words, some of them with a literal import, and others of them with a figurative, although the evangelists may have introduced them only in part into their writings, — one inserting one section, and another giving a different portion. Certain passages, at the same time, have been recorded in identical terms either by some two of them, or by some three, or even by all the four together. And yet not even when this is the case can we take it for granted that everything has been committed to writing which was either uttered or done by Him. Moreover, if any one fancies that the Lord could not in the course of the same discourse have used some expressions with a figurative application and others with a literal, let him but examine His other addresses, and he will see how rash and inconsiderate such a notion is. For, then (to mention but a single instance which occurs meantime to my mind), when Christ gives the counsel not to let the left hand know what the right hand doeth,[1] he may suppose himself under the necessity of accepting in the same figurative sense at once the almsgivings themselves referred to, and the other instructions offered on that occasion.

77. In good truth, I must repeat here once more an admonition which it behoves the reader to keep in mind, so as not to be requiring that kind of advice so very frequently, namely, that in various passages of His discourses, the Lord has reiterated much which He had uttered already on other occasions. It is needful, indeed, to call this fact to mind, lest, when it happens that the order of such passages does not appear to fit in with the narrative of another of the evangelists, the reader should fancy that this

establishes some contradiction between them; whereas he ought really to understand it to be due to the fact that something is repeated a second time in that connection which had been already expressed elsewhere. And this is a remark that should be held applicable not only to His words, but also to His deeds. For there is nothing to hinder us from believing that the same thing may have taken place more than once. But for a man to impeach the gospel simply because he does not believe in the repeated occurrence of some incident, which no one [at least] can prove to be an impossible event, betrays mere sacrilegious vanity.

CHAP. XXXI. — OF THE ACCOUNT GIVEN BY MATTHEW AND LUKE OF THE OCCASION WHEN JOHN THE BAPTIST WAS IN PRISON, AND DESPATCHED HIS DISCIPLES ON A MISSION TO THE LORD.

78. Matthew proceeds with his narrative in the following terms: "And it came to pass, when Jesus had made an end of commanding His twelve disciples, He departed thence to teach and to preach in their cities. Now, when John had heard in the prison the works of Christ, he sent two of his disciples, and said unto Him, Art thou He that should come, or do we look for another?" and so on, until we come to the words, "And Wisdom is justified of her children."[2] This whole section relating to John the Baptist, touching the message which he sent to Jesus, and the tenor of the reply which those whom he despatched received, and the terms in which the Lord spoke of John after the departure of these persons, is introduced also by Luke.[3] The order, however, is not the same. But it is not made clear which of them gives the order of his own recollections, and which keeps by the historical succession of the things themselves.[4]

CHAP. XXXII. — OF THE OCCASION ON WHICH HE UPBRAIDED THE CITIES BECAUSE THEY REPENTED NOT, WHICH INCIDENT IS RECORDED BY LUKE AS WELL AS BY MATTHEW; AND OF THE QUESTION REGARDING MATTHEW'S HARMONY WITH LUKE IN THE MATTER OF THE ORDER.

79. Thereafter Matthew goes on as follows: "Then began He to upbraid the cities wherein most of His mighty works were done, because they repented not;" and so on, down to where we read, "It shall be more tolerable for the land of Sodom at the day of judgment, than for you."[5] This section likewise is given by Luke, who reports it also as an utterance from the lips of the Lord in connection with a certain continuous

---

[1] Matt. vi. 3.

[2] Matt. xi. 1-19.　　　[3] Luke vii. 18-35.
[4] [The order of Luke seems to be more exact. Matt. xii., xiii., must be distributed through an earlier part of the history. — R.]
[5] Matt. xi. 20-24.

discourse which He delivered. This circumstance makes it the rather appear that Luke has recorded these words in the strict consecution in which they were spoken by the Lord, while Matthew has kept by the order of his own recollections. Or if it is supposed that Matthew's words, "Then began He to upbraid the cities," must be taken in such a way as to imply that the intention was to express, by the term "then," the precise point of time at which the saying was uttered, and not to signify in a somewhat broader way the period at which many of these things were done and spoken, then I say that any one entertaining that idea may equally well believe these sentences to have been pronounced on two different occasions. For if it is the fact that even in one and the same evangelist some things are found which the Lord utters twice over, as is the case with this very Luke in the instance of the counsel not to take a scrip for the journey, and so with other things in like manner which we find to have been spoken by the Lord in two different places,[1] — why should it seem strange if some other word of the Lord, which was originally uttered on two separate occasions, may happen also to be recorded by two several evangelists, each of whom gives it in the order in which it was actually spoken, and if thus the order seems to be different in the two, simply because the sentences were uttered both on the occasion noticed by the one, and on that referred to by the other?

CHAP. XXXIII. — OF THE OCCASION ON WHICH HE CALLS THEM TO TAKE HIS YOKE AND BURDEN UPON THEM, AND OF THE QUESTION AS TO THE ABSENCE OF ANY DISCREPANCY BETWEEN MATTHEW AND LUKE IN THE ORDER OF NARRATION.

80. Matthew proceeds thus: "At that time Jesus answered and said, I make my acknowledgment to Thee,[2] O Father, Lord of heaven and earth, that Thou hast hid these things from the wise and prudent," and so on, down to where we read, "For my yoke is easy, and my burden is light."[3] This passage is also noticed by Luke, but only in part. For he does not give us the words, "Come unto me, all ye that labour," and the rest. It is, however, quite legitimate to suppose that all this may have been said on one occasion by the Lord, and yet that Luke has not recorded the whole of what was said on that occasion. For Matthew's phrase is, that "at that time Jesus answered and said," by which is meant the time after His upbraiding of the cities. Luke, on the other hand, interposes some mat-

ters, although they are not many, after that upbraiding of the cities; and then he subjoins this sentence: "In that hour He rejoiced in the Holy Spirit,[4] and said."[5] Thus, too, we see that even if Matthew's expression had been, not "at that time," but "in that very hour," still what Luke inserts in the interval is so little that it would not appear an unreasonable thing to give it as all spoken in the same hour.

CHAP. XXXIV. — OF THE PASSAGE IN WHICH IT IS SAID THAT THE DISCIPLES PLUCKED THE EARS OF CORN AND ATE THEM; AND OF THE QUESTION AS TO HOW MATTHEW, MARK, AND LUKE ARE IN HARMONY WITH EACH OTHER WITH RESPECT TO THE ORDER OF NARRATION THERE.

81. Matthew continues his history in the following terms: "At that time Jesus went on the Sabbath-day through the corn; and His disciples were an hungered, and began to pluck the ears of corn, and to eat;" and so forth, on to the words, "For the Son of man is Lord even of the Sabbath-day."[6] This is also given both by Mark and by Luke, in a way precluding any idea of antagonism.[7] At the same time, these latter do not employ the definition "at that time." That fact, consequently, may perhaps make it the more probable that Matthew has retained the order of actual occurrence here, and that the others have kept by the order of their own recollections; unless, indeed, this phrase "at that time" is to be taken in a broader sense, that is to say, as indicating the period at which these many and various incidents took place.[8]

CHAP. XXXV. — OF THE MAN WITH THE WITHERED HAND, WHO WAS RESTORED ON THE SABBATH-DAY; AND OF THE QUESTION AS TO HOW MATTHEW'S NARRATIVE OF THIS INCIDENT CAN BE HARMONIZED WITH THOSE OF MARK AND LUKE, EITHER IN THE MATTER OF THE ORDER OF EVENTS, OR IN THE REPORT OF THE WORDS SPOKEN BY THE LORD AND BY THE JEWS.

82. Matthew continues his account thus: "And when He was departed thence, He went into their synagogue: and, behold, there was a man which had his hand withered;" and so on, down to the words, "And it was restored whole, like as the other."[9] The restoring of this man who had the withered hand is also not passed over in silence by Mark and Luke.[10] Now, the circumstance that this day is also designated a Sabbath might possibly lead us to suppose that both the plucking of the ears of corn and the healing of this man took place on the same day, were it not

1 Luke ix. 3, x. 4. [The view of Augustin is now generally accepted. The occasions when the sayings were uttered are distinguished in the accounts of Matthew and Luke. — R.]
2 *Confiteor tibi.* [Comp. Revised Version. — R.]
3 Matt. xi. 25-30.

4 *Spiritu sancto.*   5 Luke x. 21.
6 Matt. xii. 1-8.   7 Mark ii. 23-28; Luke vi. 1-5.
8 [Clearly the Sabbath controversies must be placed before the Sermon on the Mount, as indicated by the order of Mark and Luke. — R.]
9 Matt. xii. 9-13.   10 Mark iii. 1-5; Luke vi. 6-10.

that Luke has made it plain that it was on a different Sabbath that the cure of the withered hand was wrought. Accordingly, when Matthew says, "And when He was departed thence, He came into their synagogue," the words do indeed import that the said coming did not take place until after He had departed from the previously mentioned locality; but, at the same time, they leave the question undecided as to the number of days which may have elapsed between His passing from the aforesaid corn-field and His coming into their synagogue; and they express nothing as to His going there in direct and immediate succession. And thus space is offered us for getting in the narrative of Luke, who tells us that it was on another Sabbath that this man's hand was restored. But it is possible that a difficulty may be felt in the circumstance that Matthew has told us how the people put this question to the Lord, " Is it lawful to heal on the Sabbath-day?" wishing thereby to find an occasion for accusing Him; and that in reply He set before them the parable of the sheep in these terms: "What man shall there be among you that shall have one sheep, and if it fall into a pit on the Sabbath-day, will he not lay hold on it and lift it out? How much, then, is a man better than a sheep? Wherefore it is lawful to do well on the Sabbath-days;"[1] whereas Mark and Luke rather represent the people to have had this question put to them by the Lord, " Is it lawful to do good on the Sabbath-day, or to do evil? to save life, or to kill?"[2] We solve this difficulty, however, by the supposition that the people in the first instance asked the Lord, " Is it lawful to heal on the Sabbath-day?" that thereupon, knowing the thoughts of the men who were thus seeking an occasion for accusing Him, He set the man whom He had been on the point of healing in their midst, and addressed to them the interrogations which Mark and Luke mention to have been put; that, as they remained silent, He next put before them the parable of the sheep, and drew the conclusion that it was lawful to do good on the Sabbath-day; and that, finally, when He had looked round about on them with anger, as Mark tells us, being grieved for the hardness of their hearts, He said to the man, " Stretch forth thine hand."

CHAP. XXXVI. — OF ANOTHER QUESTION WHICH DEMANDS OUR CONSIDERATION, NAMELY, WHETHER, IN PASSING FROM THE ACCOUNT OF THE MAN WHOSE WITHERED HAND WAS RESTORED, THESE THREE EVANGELISTS PROCEED TO THEIR NEXT SUBJECTS IN SUCH A WAY AS TO CREATE NO CONTRADICTIONS IN REGARD TO THE ORDER OF THEIR NARRATIONS.

83. Matthew continues his narrative, connecting it in the following manner with what precedes: " But the Pharisees went out and held a council against Him, how they might destroy Him. But when Jesus knew it, He withdrew Himself from thence : and great multitudes followed Him, and He healed them all ; and charged them that they should not make Him known : that it might be fulfilled which was spoken by the prophet Esaias, saying ; " and so forth, down to where it is said, " And in His name shall the Gentiles trust."[3] He is the only one that records these facts. The other two have advanced to other themes. Mark, it is true, seems to some extent to have kept by the historical order : for he tells us how Jesus, on discovering the malignant disposition which was entertained toward Him by the Jews, withdrew to the sea along with His disciples, and that then vast multitudes flocked to Him, and He healed great numbers of them.[4] But, at the same time, it is not quite clear at what precise point He begins to pass to a new subject, different from what would have followed in strict succession. He leaves it uncertain whether such a transition is made at the point where he tells us how the multitudes gathered about Him (for if that was the case now, it might equally well have been the case at some other time), or at the point where He says that " He goeth up into a mountain." It is this latter circumstance that Luke also appears to notice when he says, " And it came to pass in those days, that He went out into a mountain to pray."[5] For by the expression " in those days," he makes it plain enough that the incident referred to did not occur in immediate succession upon what precedes.[6]

CHAP. XXXVII. — OF THE CONSISTENCY OF THE ACCOUNTS GIVEN BY MATTHEW AND LUKE REGARDING THE DUMB AND BLIND MAN WHO WAS POSSESSED WITH A DEVIL.

84. Matthew then goes on with his recital in the following fashion : " Then was brought unto Him one possessed with a devil, blind and dumb ; and He healed him, insomuch that he both spake and saw."[7] Luke introduces this narrative, not in the same order, but after a number of other matters. He also speaks of the man only as dumb, and not as blind in addition.[8] But it is not to be inferred, from the mere circumstance of his silence as to some portion or other of the account, that he speaks of an entirely different person. For he has likewise recorded what followed [immediately after that cure], as it stands also in Matthew.

---

[1] Matt. xii. 10–12.   [2] Mark iii. 4; Luke vi. 9.

[3] Matt. xii. 14–21. [Sperabunt, "hope," as in Revised Version. — R.]
[4] Mark iii. 7–12.
[5] Luke vi. 12.
[6] [The Sermon on the Mount was delivered during the withdrawal here referred to. — R.]
[7] Matt. xii. 22.   [8] Luke xi. 14.

CHAP. XXXVIII. — OF THE OCCASION ON WHICH IT WAS SAID TO HIM THAT HE CAST OUT DEVILS IN THE POWER OF BEELZEBUB, AND OF THE DECLARATIONS DRAWN FORTH FROM HIM BY THAT CIRCUMSTANCE IN REGARD TO THE BLASPHEMY AGAINST THE HOLY SPIRIT, AND WITH RESPECT TO THE TWO TREES; AND OF THE QUESTION WHETHER THERE IS NOT SOME DISCREPANCY IN THESE SECTIONS BETWEEN MATTHEW AND THE OTHER TWO EVANGELISTS, AND PARTICULARLY BETWEEN MATTHEW AND LUKE.

85. Matthew proceeds with his narrative in the following terms : " And all the people were amazed, and said, Is not this the son of David? But when the Pharisees heard it, they said, This fellow doth not cast out devils but in Beelzebub, the prince of the devils. And Jesus knew their thoughts, and said unto them, Every kingdom divided against itself shall be brought to desolation ; " and so on, down to the words, " By thy words thou shalt be justified, and by thy words thou shalt be condemned." [1] Mark does not bring in this allegation against Jesus, that He cast out devils in [the power of] Beelzebub, in immediate sequence on the story of the dumb man ; but after certain other matters, recorded by himself alone, he introduces this incident also, either because he recalled it to mind in a different connection, and so appended it there, or because he had at first made certain omissions in his history, and after noticing these, took up this order of narration again.[2] On the other hand, Luke gives an account of these things almost in the same language as Matthew has employed.[3] And the circumstance that Luke here designates the Spirit of God as the finger of God, does not betray any departure from a genuine identity in sense ; but it rather teaches us an additional lesson, giving us to know in what manner we are to interpret the phrase " the finger of God" wherever it occurs in the Scriptures. Moreover, with regard to other matters which are left unmentioned in this section both by Mark and by Luke, no difficulty can be raised by these. Neither can that be the case with some other circumstances which are related by them in somewhat different terms, for the sense still remains the same.

CHAP. XXXIX. — OF THE QUESTION AS TO THE MANNER OF MATTHEW'S AGREEMENT WITH LUKE IN THE ACCOUNTS WHICH ARE GIVEN OF THE LORD'S REPLY TO CERTAIN PERSONS WHO SOUGHT A SIGN, WHEN HE SPOKE OF JONAS THE PROPHET, AND OF THE NINEVITES, AND OF THE QUEEN OF THE SOUTH, AND OF THE UNCLEAN SPIRIT WHICH, WHEN IT HAS GONE OUT OF THE MAN, RETURNS AND FINDS THE HOUSE GARNISHED.

86. Matthew goes on and relates what fol-lowed thus : " Then certain of the scribes and of the Pharisees answered, saying, Master, we would see a sign of thee ; " and so on, down to where we read, " Even so shall it be also unto this wicked generation." [4] These words are recorded also by Luke in this connection, although in a somewhat different order.[5] For he has mentioned the fact that they sought of the Lord a sign from heaven at an earlier point in his narrative, which makes it follow immediately on his version of the miracle wrought on the dumb man. He has not, however, recorded there the reply which was given to them by the Lord. But further on, after [telling us how] the people were gathered together, he states that this answer was returned to the persons who, as he gives us to understand, were mentioned by him in those earlier verses as seeking of Him a sign from heaven. And that reply he also subjoins, only after introducing the passage regarding the woman who said to the Lord, " Blessed is the womb that bare thee." [6] This notice of the woman, moreover, he inserts after relating the Lord's discourse concerning the unclean spirit that goes out of the man, and then returns and finds the house garnished. In this way, then, after the notice of the woman, and after his statement of the reply which was made to the multitudes on the subject of the sign which they sought from heaven, he brings in the similitude of the prophet Jonas ; and then, directly continuing the Lord's discourse, he next instances what was said concerning the Queen of the South and the Ninevites. Thus he has rather related something which Matthew has passed over in silence, than omitted any of the facts which that evangelist has narrated in this place. And furthermore, who can fail to perceive that the question as to the precise order in which these words were uttered by the Lord is a superfluous one? For this lesson also we ought to learn, on the unimpeachable authority of the evangelists, — namely, that no offence against truth need be supposed on the part of a writer, although he may not reproduce the discourse of some speaker in the precise order in which the person from whose lips it proceeded might have given it ; the fact being, that the mere item of the order, whether it be this or that, does not affect the subject-matter itself. And by his present version Luke indicates that this discourse of the Lord was of greater length than we might otherwise have supposed ; and he records certain topics handled in it, which resemble those which are mentioned by Matthew in his recital of the sermon which was delivered on the mount.[7] So that we take these words to have been spoken twice over, to wit, on that previous occasion, and

---

[1] Matt. xii. 23–37.   [2] Mark iii. 22–30.   [3] Luke xi. 14–26.

[4] Matt. xii. 38.
[5] Luke xi. 16–37.   [6] Luke xi. 27.   [7] Matt. v.–vii.

again on this one.   But on the conclusion of this discourse Luke proceeds to another subject, as to which it is uncertain whether, in the account which he gives of it, he has kept by the order of actual occurrence.   For he connects it in this way : " And as He spake, a certain Pharisee besought Him to dine with him." [1]   He does not say, however, " as He spake these words," but only " as He spake."   For if he had said, " as He spake these words," the expression would of course have compelled us to suppose that the incidents referred to, besides being recorded by him in this order, also took place on the Lord's part in that same order.

CHAP. XL. — OF THE QUESTION AS TO WHETHER THERE IS ANY DISCREPANCY BETWEEN MATTHEW ON THE ONE HAND, AND MARK AND LUKE ON THE OTHER, IN REGARD TO THE ORDER IN WHICH THE NOTICE IS GIVEN OF THE OCCASION ON WHICH HIS MOTHER AND HIS BRETHREN WERE ANNOUNCED TO HIM.

87. Matthew then proceeds with his narrative in the following terms : " While He yet talked to the people, behold, His mother and His brethren stood without, desiring to speak to Him ; " and so on, down to the words, " For whosoever shall do the will of my Father which is in heaven, the same is my brother, and sister, and mother." [2]   Without doubt, we ought to understand this to have occurred in immediate sequence on the preceding incidents.   For he has prefaced his transition to this narrative by the words, " While He yet talked to the people ; " and what does this term " yet " refer to, but to the very matter of which He was speaking on that occasion?   For the expression is not, " When He talked to the people, behold, His mother and His brethren ; " but, " While He was yet speaking," etc.   And that phraseology compels us to suppose that it was at the very time when He was still engaged in speaking of those things which were mentioned immediately above.   For Mark has also related what our Lord said after His declaration on the subject of the blasphemy against the Holy Spirit.   He gives it thus : " And there came His mother and His brethren," [3] omitting certain matters which meet us in the context connected with that discourse of the Lord, and which Matthew has introduced there with greater fulness than Mark, and Luke, again, with greater fulness than Matthew.   On the other hand, Luke has not kept the historical order in the report which he offers of this incident, but has given it by anticipation, and has narrated it as he recalled it to memory, at a point antecedent to the date of its literal occurrence.   But furthermore, he has brought it in in

such a manner that it appears dissociated from any close connection either with what precedes it or with what follows it.   For, after reporting certain of the Lord's parables, he has introduced his notice of what took place with His mother and His brethren in the following manner : " Then came to Him His mother and His brethren, and could not come at Him for the press." [4]   Thus he has not explained at what precise time it was that they came to Him.   And again, when he passes off from this subject, he proceeds in these terms : " Now it came to pass on one of the days, that He went into a ship with His disciples." [5]   And certainly, when he employs this expression, " it came to pass on one of the days," he indicates clearly enough that we are under no necessity of supposing that the day meant was the very day on which this incident took place, or the one following in immediate succession.   Consequently, neither in the matter of the Lord's words, nor in that of the historical order of the occurrences related, does Matthew's account of the incident which occurred in connection with the mother and the brethren of the Lord, exhibit any want of harmony with the versions given of the same by the other two evangelists.

CHAP. XLI. — OF THE WORDS WHICH WERE SPOKEN OUT OF THE SHIP ON THE SUBJECT OF THE SOWER, WHOSE SEED, AS HE SOWED IT, FELL PARTLY ON THE WAYSIDE, ETC. ; AND CONCERNING THE MAN WHO HAD TARES SOWED OVER AND ABOVE HIS WHEAT ; AND CONCERNING THE GRAIN OF MUSTARD SEED AND THE LEAVEN ; AS ALSO OF WHAT HE SAID IN THE HOUSE REGARDING THE TREASURE HID IN THE FIELD, AND THE PEARL, AND THE NET CAST INTO THE SEA, AND THE MAN THAT BRINGS OUT OF HIS TREASURE THINGS NEW AND OLD ; AND OF THE METHOD IN WHICH MATTHEW'S HARMONY WITH MARK AND LUKE IS PROVED BOTH WITH RESPECT TO THE THINGS WHICH THEY HAVE REPORTED IN COMMON WITH HIM, AND IN THE MATTER OF THE ORDER OF NARRATION.

88. Matthew continues thus : " In that day went Jesus out of the house, and sat by the seaside : and great multitudes were gathered together unto Him, so that He went into a ship and sat, and the whole multitude stood on the shore.   And He spake many things unto them in parables, saying ; " and so on, down to the words, " Therefore every scribe which is instructed in the kingdom of heaven is like unto a man that is an householder, which bringeth forth out of his treasure things new and old." [6]   That the things narrated in this passage took place immediately after the incident touching the mother and the

---

brethren of the Lord, and that Matthew has also retained that historical order in his version. of these events, is indicated by the circumstance that, in passing from the one subject to the other, he has expressed the connection by this mode of speech : " In that day went Jesus out of the house, and sat by the sea-side ; and great multitudes were gathered together unto Him." For by adopting this phrase, " in that day " (unless perchance the word "day," in accordance with a use and wont of the Scriptures, may signify simply " time "), he intimates clearly enough either that the thing now related took place in immediate succession on what precedes, or that much at least could not have intervened. This inference is confirmed by the fact that Mark keeps by the same order.[1] Luke, on the other hand, after his account of what happened with the mother and the brethren of the Lord, passes to a different subject. But at the same time, in making that transition, he does not institute any such connection as bears the appearance of a want of consistency with this order.[2] Consequently, in all those passages in which Mark and Luke have reported in common with Matthew the words which were spoken by the Lord, there is no questioning their harmony with one another. Moreover, the sections which are given by Matthew only are even much more beyond the range of controversy. And in the matter of the order of narration, although it is presented somewhat differently by the various evangelists, according as they have proceeded severally along the line of historical succession, or along that of the succession of recollection, I see as little reason for alleging any discrepancy of statement or any contradiction between any of the writers.[3]

CHAP. XLII. — OF HIS COMING INTO HIS OWN COUNTRY, AND OF THE ASTONISHMENT OF THE PEOPLE AT HIS DOCTRINE, AS THEY LOOKED WITH CONTEMPT UPON HIS LINEAGE ; OF MATTHEW'S HARMONY WITH MARK AND LUKE IN THIS SECTION ; AND IN PARTICULAR, OF THE QUESTION WHETHER THE ORDER OF NARRATION WHICH IS PRESENTED BY THE FIRST OF THESE EVANGELISTS DOES NOT EXHIBIT SOME WANT OF CONSISTENCY WITH THAT OF THE OTHER TWO.

89. Matthew thence proceeds as follows : " And it came to pass that, when Jesus had finished these parables, He departed thence : and when He was come into His own country, He taught them in their synagogues ; "[4] and so on, down to the words, " And He did not many mighty works there because of their unbelief." [5]

Thus he passes from the above discourse containing the parables, on to this passage, in such a way as not to make it absolutely necessary for us to take the one to have followed in immediate historical succession upon the other. All the more may we suppose this to be the case, when we see how Mark passes on from these parables to a subject which is not identical with Matthew's directly succeeding theme, but quite different from that, and agreeing rather with what Luke introduces ; and how he has constructed his narrative in such a manner as to make the balance of credibility rest on the side of the supposition, that what followed in immediate historical sequence was rather the occurrences which these two latter evangelists both insert in near connection [with the parables], — namely, the incidents of the ship in which Jesus was asleep, and the miracle performed in the expulsion of the devils in the country of the Gerasenes,[6] — two events which Matthew has already recalled and introduced at an earlier stage of his record.[7] At present, therefore, we have to consider whether [Matthew's report of] what the Lord spoke, and what was said to Him in His own country, is in concord with the accounts given by the other two, namely, Mark and Luke. For, in widely different and dissimilar sections of his history, John mentions words, either spoken to the Lord or spoken by Him,[8] which resemble those recorded in this passage by the other three evangelists.

90. Now Mark, indeed, gives this passage in terms almost precisely identical with those which meet us in Matthew ; with the one exception, that what he says the Lord was called by His fellow-townsmen is, " the carpenter, and the son of Mary," [9] and not, as Matthew tells us, the "carpenter's son." Neither is there anything to marvel at in this, since He might quite fairly have been designated by both these names. For in taking Him to be the son of a carpenter, they naturally also took Him to be a carpenter. Luke, on the other hand, sets forth the same incident on a wider scale, and records a variety of other matters which took place in that connection. And this account he brings in at a point not long subsequent to His baptism and temptation, thus unquestionably introducing by anticipation what really happened only after the occurrence of a number of intervening circumstances. In this, therefore, every one may see an illustration of a principle of prime consequence in relation to this most weighty question concerning the harmony of the evangelists, which we have undertaken to solve by the help of God,

---

[1] Mark iv. 1-34.   [2] Luke viii. 22.
[3] [The discourse in parables must be placed before the voyage to the country of the Gadarenes; comp. Mark iv. 36, and Augustin's remark in § 89. — R.]
[4] Three MSS., however, give *in synagoga eorum* — in their synagogue — as in our version.
[5] Matt. xiii. 53-58.

[6] Mark iv. 35, v. 17; Luke viii. 22-37. [On the variations in the name, see critical editions of Greek text. Comp. Revised Version. The Latin versions generally read " Gerasenes " in all three accounts. — R.]
[7] Matt. viii. 23-34.   [8] John vi. 42.   [9] Mark vi. 1-6.

— the principle, namely, that it is not by mere ignorance that these writers have been led to make certain omissions, and that it is as little through simple ignorance of the actual historical order of events that they have [at times] preferred to keep by the order in which these events were recalled to their own memory. The correctness of this principle may be gathered most clearly from the fact that, at a point antecedent to any account given by him of anything done by the Lord at Capharnaum, Luke has anticipated the literal date, and has inserted this passage which we have at present under consideration, and in which we are told how His fellow-citizens at once were astonished at the might of the authority which was in Him, and expressed their contempt for the meanness of His family. For he tells us that He addressed them in these terms: "Ye will surely say unto me, Physician, heal thyself: whatsoever we have heard done in Capharnaum, do also here in thy country;"[1] while, so far as the narrative of this same Luke is concerned, we have not yet read of Him as having done anything at Capharnaum. Furthermore, as it will not take up much time, and as, besides, it is both a very simple and a highly needful matter to do so, we insert here the whole context, showing the subject from which and the method in which the writer has come to give the contents of this section. After his statement regarding the Lord's baptism and temptation, he proceeds in these terms: "And when the devil had ended all the temptation, he departed from Him for a season. And Jesus returned in the power of the Spirit into Galilee: and there went out a fame of Him through all the region round about. And He taught in their synagogues, and was magnified of all. And He came to Nazareth, where He had been brought up: and, as his custom was, He went into the synagogue on the Sabbath-day, and stood up for to read. And there was delivered unto Him the book of the prophet Esaias: and when He had opened the book, He found the place where it was written, The Spirit of the Lord is upon me, because He hath anointed me. He hath sent me to preach the gospel to the poor, to proclaim deliverance to the captives, and sight to the blind; to set at liberty them that are bruised, to proclaim the accepted year of the Lord, and the day of retribution. And when He had closed the book, He gave it again to the minister, and sat down: and the eyes of all them that were in the synagogue were fastened on Him. And He began to say unto them, This day is this scripture fulfilled in your ears. And all bare Him witness, and wondered at the gracious words which proceeded out of His mouth.

And they said, Is not this Joseph's son? And He said unto them, Ye will surely say unto me this proverb, Physician, heal thyself: whatsoever we have heard done in Capharnaum, do also here in thy country."[2] And so he continues with the rest, until this entire section in his narrative is gone over. What, therefore, can be more manifest, than that he has knowingly introduced this notice at a point antecedent to its historical date, seeing it admits of no question that he knows and refers to certain mighty deeds done by Him before this period in Capharnaum, which, at the same time, he is aware he has not as yet narrated in detail? For certainly he has not made such an advance with his history from his notice of the Lord's baptism, as that he should be supposed to have forgotten the fact that up to this point he has not mentioned any of the things which took place in Capharnaum; the truth being, that he has just begun here, after the baptism, to give us his narrative concerning the Lord personally.[3]

CHAP. XLIII. — OF THE MUTUAL CONSISTENCY OF THE ACCOUNTS WHICH ARE GIVEN BY MATTHEW, MARK, AND LUKE OF WHAT WAS SAID BY HEROD ON HEARING ABOUT THE WONDERFUL WORKS OF THE LORD, AND OF THEIR CONCORD IN REGARD TO THE ORDER OF NARRATION.

91. Matthew continues: "At that time Herod the tetrarch heard of the fame of Jesus, and said unto his servants, This is John the Baptist: he is risen from the dead; and therefore mighty works do show forth themselves in him."[4] Mark gives the same passage, and in the same manner, but not in the same order.[5] For, after relating how the Lord sent forth the disciples with the charge to take nothing with them on the journey save a staff only, and after bringing to its close so much of the discourse which was then delivered as has been recorded by him, he has subjoined this section. He does not, however, connect it in such a way as to compel us to suppose that what it narrates took place actually in immediate sequence on what precedes it in the history. And in this, indeed, Matthew is at one with him. For Matthew's expression is, "at that time," not "on that day," or "at that hour." Only there is this difference between them, that Mark refers not to Herod himself as the utterer of the words in question, but to the people, his statement being this: "They said[6] that John the Baptist was risen from the dead;" whereas Matthew makes Herod himself the

---

[1] Luke iv. 23.

[2] Luke iv. 13–23.
[3] [The question of the identity of the visits to Nazareth is still an open one. But there are some points ignored by Augustin which indicate that Luke refers to an earlier visit. — R.]
[4] Matt. xiv. 1, 2.   [5] Mark vi. 14–16.
[6] *Dicebant;* so that the reading ἔλεγον is followed instead of ἔλεγεν in Mark vi. 14. [Westcott and Hort give the plural in their text, following the Vatican codex and some other authorities. — R.]

speaker, the phrase being: "He said unto his servants." Luke, again, keeping the same order of narration as Mark, and introducing it also indeed, like Mark, in no such way as to compel us to suppose that his order must have been the order of actual occurrence, presents his version of the same passage in the following terms: "Herod the tetrarch heard of all that was done by Him: and he was perplexed, because that it was said of some, that John was risen from the dead; and of some, that Elias had appeared; and of others, that one of the old prophets was risen again. And Herod said, John have I beheaded: but who is this of whom I hear such things? And he desired to see Him."[1] In these words Luke also attests Mark's statement, at least, so far as concerns the affirmation that it was not Herod himself, but other parties, who said that John was risen from the dead. But as regards his mentioning how Herod was perplexed, and his bringing in thereafter those words of the same prince: "John have I beheaded: but who is this of whom I hear such things?" we must either understand that after the said perplexity he became persuaded in his own mind of the truth of what was asserted by others, when he spoke to his servants, in accordance with the version given by Matthew, which runs thus: "And he said to his servants, This is John the Baptist: he is risen from the dead; and therefore mighty works do show forth themselves in him;" or we must suppose that these words were uttered in a manner betraying that he was still in a state of perplexity. For had he said, "Can this be John the Baptist?" or, "Can it chance that this is John the Baptist?" there would have been no need of saying anything about a mode of utterance by which he might have revealed his dubiety and perplexity. But seeing that these forms of expression are not before us, his words may be taken to have been pronounced in either of two ways: so that we may either suppose him to have been convinced by what was said by others, and so to have spoken the words in question with a real belief [in John's reappearance]; or we may imagine him to have been still in that state of hesitancy of which mention is made by Luke. Our explanation is favoured by the fact that Mark, who had already told us how it was by others that the statement was made as to John having risen from the dead, does not fail to let us know also that in the end Herod himself spoke to this effect: "It is John whom I beheaded: he is risen from the dead."[2] For these words may also be taken to have been pronounced in either of two ways,—namely, as the utterances either of one corroborating a fact,

or of one in doubt. Moreover, while Luke passes on to a new subject after the notice which he gives of this incident, those other two, Matthew and Mark, take occasion to tell us at this point in what way John was put to death by Herod.

CHAP. XLIV. — OF THE ORDER IN WHICH THE ACCOUNTS OF JOHN'S IMPRISONMENT AND DEATH ARE GIVEN BY THESE THREE EVANGELISTS.

92. Matthew then proceeds with his narrative in the following terms: "For Herod laid hold on John, and bound him, and put him in prison for Herodias' sake, his brother's wife;" and so on, down to the words, "And his disciples came and took up the body, and buried it, and went and told Jesus."[3] Mark gives this narrative in similar terms.[4] Luke, on the other hand, does not relate it in the same succession, but introduces it in connection with his statement of the baptism wherewith the Lord was baptized. Hence we are to understand him to have acted by anticipation here, and to have taken the opportunity of recording at this point an event which took place actually a considerable period later. For he has first reported those words which John spake with regard to the Lord — namely, that "His fan is in His hand, and that He will thoroughly purge His floor, and will gather the wheat into His garner; but the chaff He will burn up with fire unquenchable;" and immediately thereafter he has appended his statement of an incident which the evangelist John demonstrates not to have taken place in direct historical sequence. For this latter writer mentions that, after Jesus had been baptized, He went into Galilee at the period when He turned the water into wine; and that, after a sojourn of a few days in Capharnaum, He left that district and returned to the land of Judæa, and there baptized a multitude about the Jordan, previous to the time when John was imprisoned.[5] Now what reader, unless he were all the better versed[6] in these writings, would not take it to be implied here that it was after the utterance of the words with regard to the fan and the purged floor that Herod became incensed against John, and cast him into prison? Yet, that the incident referred to here did not, as matter of fact, occur in the order in which it is here recorded, we have already shown elsewhere; and, indeed, Luke himself puts the proof into our hands.[7] For if [he had meant that] John's incarceration took place immediately after the utterance of those words, then what are we to make of the fact

---

[1] Luke ix. 7-9.
[2] [Augustin gives the reading followed in the Revised Version ("John whom I beheaded, he is risen"). The translator gives the words of the Authorized Version. — R.]

[3] Matt. xiv. 3-12.   [4] Mark vi. 17-29.   [5] John ii. 1, 12, iii. 22-24.
[6] The reading in the mss. and in Migne's text is, *quis autem non putet qui minus in his litteris eruditus est;* for which some give, *quis autem non putet nisi qui minus,* etc.
[7] Luke iii. 15-21.

that in Luke's own narrative the baptism of Jesus is introduced subsequently to his notice of the imprisonment of John? Consequently it is manifest that, recalling the circumstance in connection with the present occasion, he has brought it in here by anticipation, and has thus inserted it in his history at a point antecedent to a number of incidents, of which it was his purpose to leave us some record, and which, in point of time, were antecedent to this mishap that befell John. But it is as little the case that the other two evangelists, Matthew and Mark, have placed the fact of John's imprisonment in that position in their narratives which, as is apparent also from their own writings, belonged to it in the actual order of events. For they, too, have told us how it was on John's being cast into prison that the Lord went into Galilee; [1] and then, after [relating] a number of things which He did in Galilee, they come to Herod's admonition or doubt as to the rising again from the dead of that John whom he beheaded; [2] and in connection with this latter occasion, they give us the story of all that occurred in the matter of John's incarceration and death.

CHAP. XLV. — OF THE ORDER AND THE METHOD IN WHICH ALL THE FOUR EVANGELISTS COME TO THE NARRATION OF THE MIRACLE OF THE FIVE LOAVES.

93. After stating how the report of John's death was brought to Christ, Matthew continues his account, and introduces it in the following connection: "When Jesus heard of it, He departed thence by ship into a desert place apart: and when the people had heard thereof, they followed Him on foot out of the cities. And He went forth, and saw a great multitude, and was moved with compassion toward them, and He healed their sick." [3] He mentions, therefore, that this took place immediately after John had suffered. Consequently it was after this that those things took place which have been previously recorded — namely, the circumstances which alarmed Herod, and induced him to say, "John have I beheaded." [4] For it must surely be understood that these incidents occurred subsequently which report carried to the ears of Herod, so that he became anxious, and was in perplexity as to who that person possibly could be of whom he heard things so remarkable, when he had himself put John to death. Mark, again, after relating how John suffered, mentions that the disciples who had been sent forth returned to Jesus, and told Him all that they had done and taught; and that the Lord (a fact which he alone records) directed them to rest for a little while in a desert place, and that He went on board a vessel with them, and departed; and that the crowds of people, when they perceived that movement, went before them to that place; and that the Lord had compassion on them, and taught them many things; and that, when the hour was now advancing, it came to pass that all who were present were made to eat of the five loaves and the two fishes. [5] This miracle has been recorded by all the four evangelists. For in like manner, Luke, who has given an account of the death of John at a much earlier stage in his narrative, [6] in connection with the occasion of which we have spoken, in the present context tells us first of Herod's perplexity as to who the Lord could be, and immediately thereafter appends statements to the same effect with those in Mark, — namely, that the apostles returned to Him, and reported to Him all that they had done; and that then He took them with Him and departed into a desert place, and that the multitudes followed Him thither, and that He spake to them concerning the kingdom of God, and restored those who stood in need of healing. Then, too, he mentions that, when the day was declining, the miracle of the five loaves was wrought. [7]

94. But John, again, who differs greatly from those three in this respect, that he deals more with the discourses which the Lord delivered than with the works which He so marvellously wrought, after recording how He left Judæa and departed the second time into Galilee, which departure is understood to have taken place at the time to which the other evangelists also refer when they tell us that on John's imprisonment He went into Galilee, — after recording this, I say, John inserts in the immediate context of his narrative the considerable discourse which He spake as He was passing through Samaria, on the occasion of His meeting with the Samaritan woman whom He found at the well; and then he states that two days after this He departed thence and went into Galilee, and that thereupon He came to Cana of Galilee, where He had turned the water into wine, and that there He healed the son of a certain nobleman. [8] But as to other things which the rest have told us He did and said in Galilee, John is silent. At the same time, however, he mentions something which the others have left unnoticed, — namely, the fact that He went up to Jerusalem on the day of the feast, and there wrought the miracle on the man who had the infirmity of thirty-eight years' standing, and who found no one by whose help he might be carried down to the pool in which people afflicted with various diseases were

---

[1] Matt. iv. 12; Mark i. 14.
[2] Matt. xiv. 1, 2; Mark vi. 14–16.
[3] Matt. xiv. 13, 14.　　　　[4] Luke ix. 9.
[5] Mark vi. 30–44.　　　　[6] Luke iii. 20.
[7] Luke ix. 10–17.　　　　[8] John iv. 3, 5, 43–54.

healed.[1] In connection with this, John also relates how He spake many things on that occasion. He tells us, further, that after these events He departed across the sea of Galilee, which is also the sea of Tiberias, and that a great multitude followed Him; that thereupon He went away to a mountain, and there sat with His disciples, — the passover, a feast of the Jews, being then nigh; that then, on lifting up His eyes and seeing a very great company, He fed them with the five loaves and the two fishes;[2] which notice is given us also by the other evangelists. And this makes it certain that he has passed by those incidents which form the course along which these others have come to introduce the notice of this miracle into their narratives. Nevertheless, while different methods of narration, as it appears, are prosecuted, and while the first three evangelists have thus left unnoticed certain matters which the fourth has recorded, we see how those three, on the one hand, who have been keeping nearly the same course, have found a direct meeting-point with each other at this miracle of the five loaves; and how this fourth writer, on the other hand, who is conversant above all with the profound teachings of the Lord's discourses, in relating some other matters on which the rest are silent, has sped round in a certain method upon their track, and, while about to soar off from their pathway after a brief space again into the region of loftier subjects, has found a meeting-point with them in the view of presenting this narrative of the miracle of the five loaves, which is common to them all.

CHAP. XLVI. — OF THE QUESTION AS TO HOW THE FOUR EVANGELISTS HARMONIZE WITH EACH OTHER ON THIS SAME SUBJECT OF THE MIRACLE OF THE FIVE LOAVES.

95. Matthew then proceeds and carries on his narrative in due consecution to the said incident connected with the five loaves in the following manner: "And when it was evening, His disciples came to Him, saying, This is a desert place, and the time is now past; send the multitude away, that they may go into the villages, and buy themselves victuals. But Jesus said unto them, They need not depart; give ye them to eat;" and so forth, down to where we read, "And the number of those who ate was five thousand men, besides women and children."[3] This miracle, therefore, which all the four evangelists record,[4] and in which they are supposed

to betray certain discrepancies with each other, must be examined and subjected to discussion, in order that we may also learn from this instance some rules which will be applicable to all other similar cases in the form of principles regulating modes of statement in which, however diverse they may be, the same sense is nevertheless retained, and the same veracity in the expression of matters of fact is preserved. And, indeed, this investigation ought to begin not with Matthew, although that would be in accordance with the order in which the evangelists stand, but rather with John, by whom the narrative in question is told with such particularity as to record even the names of the disciples with whom the Lord conversed on this subject. For he gives the history in the following terms: "When Jesus than lifted up His eyes, and saw a very great company come unto Him, He saith unto Philip, Whence shall we buy bread, that these may eat? And this He said to prove him; for He Himself knew what He would do. Philip answered Him, Two hundred pennyworth of bread is not sufficient for them, that every one of them may take a little. One of His disciples, Andrew, Simon Peter's brother, saith unto Him, There is a lad here, which hath five barley loaves, and two fishes; but what are they among so many? Jesus said therefore, Make the men sit down. Now there was much grass in the place. So the men sat down, in number about five thousand. Jesus then took the loaves; and when He had given thanks, He distributed to the disciples, and the disciples to them that were set down; and likewise of the fishes as much as they would. And when they were filled, He said unto His disciples, Gather up the fragments that remain, that they be not lost. Therefore they gathered them together, and filled twelve baskets with the fragments of the five barley loaves, which remained over and above unto them that had eaten."[5]

96. The inquiry which we have here to handle does not concern itself with a statement given by this evangelist, in which he specifies the kind of loaves; for he has not omitted to mention, what has been omitted by the others, that they were barley loaves. Neither does the question deal with what he has left unnoticed, — namely, the fact that, in addition to the five thousand men, there were also women and children, as Matthew tells us. And it ought now by all means to be a settled matter, and one kept regularly in view in all such investigations, that no one should find any difficulty in the mere circumstance that something which is unrecorded by one writer is related by another. But the question here is as to how the several matters narrated by these writers may be [shown to be]

---

[1] [Augustin here passes over one of the most difficult questions in connection with the Gospel history. The length of our Lord's ministry turns upon the feast referred to in John v. If it was a passover, then John refers to four passovers; and our Lord's ministry extended over three years and a few weeks. If some other feast is meant, the ministry covered but two years and a few weeks. — R.]

[2] John v.-vi. 13.

[3] Matt. xiv. 15-21.   [4] Mark vi. 34-44; Luke ix. 12-17.

[5] John vi. 5-13.

all true, so that the one of them, in giving his own peculiar version, does not put out of court the account offered by the other. For if the Lord, according to the narrative of John, on seeing the multitudes before Him, asked Philip, with the view of proving him, whence bread might be got to be given to them, a difficulty may be raised as to the truth of the statement which is made by the others, — namely, that the disciples first said to the Lord that He should send the multitudes away, in order that they might go and purchase food for themselves in the neighbouring localities, and that He made this reply to them, according to Matthew: "They need not depart; give ye them to eat." [1] With this last Mark and Luke also agree, only that they leave out the words, "They need not depart." We are to suppose, therefore, that after these words the Lord looked at the multitude, and spoke to Philip in the terms which John records, but which those others have omitted. Then the reply which, according to John, was made by Philip, is mentioned by Mark as having been given by the disciples, — the intention being, that we should understand Philip to have returned this answer as the mouthpiece of the rest; although they may also have put the plural number in place of the singular, according to very frequent usage. The words here actually ascribed to Philip — namely, "Two hundred pennyworth of bread is not sufficient for them, that every one of them may take a little" [2] — have their counterpart in this version by Mark, "Shall we go and buy two hundred pennyworth of bread, and give them to eat?" [3] The expression, again, which the same Mark relates to have been used by the Lord, namely, "How many loaves have ye?" has been passed by without notice by the rest. On the other hand, the statement occurring in John, to the effect that Andrew made the suggestion about the five loaves and the two fishes, appears in the others, who use here the plural number instead of the singular, as a notice referring the suggestion to the disciples generally. And, indeed, Luke has coupled Philip's reply together with Andrew's answer in one sentence. For when he says, "We have no more but five loaves and two fishes," he reports Andrew's response; but when he adds, "except we should go and buy meat for all this people," he seems to carry us back to Philip's reply, only that he has left unnoticed the "two hundred pennyworth." At the same time, that [sentence about the going and buying meat] may also be understood to be implied in Andrew's own words. For after saying, "There is a lad here which hath five barley loaves and two fishes," he likewise subjoined, "But what are they among so many?" And this last clause

really means the same as the expression in question, namely, "except we should go and buy meat for all this people."

97. From all this variety of statement which is found in connection with a genuine harmony in regard to the matters of fact and the ideas conveyed, it becomes sufficiently clear that we have the wholesome lesson inculcated upon us, that what we have to look to in studying a person's words is nothing else than the intention of the speakers; in setting forth which intention all truthful narrators ought to take the utmost pains when they record anything, whether it may relate to man, or to angels, or to God. For the subjects' mind and intention admit of being expressed in words which should leave no appearance of any discrepancies as regards the matter of fact.

98. In this connection, it is true, we ought not to omit to direct the reader's attention to certain other matters which may turn out to be of a kindred nature with those already considered. One of these is found in the circumstance that Luke has stated that they were ordered to sit down by fifties, whereas Mark's version is that it was by hundreds and by fifties. This difference, however, creates no real difficulty. The truth is, that the one has reported simply a part, and the other has given the whole. For the evangelist who has introduced the notice of the hundreds as well as the fifties has just mentioned something which the other has left unmentioned. But there is no contradiction between them on that account. If, indeed, the one had noticed only the fifties, and the other only the hundreds, they might certainly have seemed to be in some antagonism with each other, and it might not have been easy to make it plain that both instructions were actually uttered, although only the one has been specified by the former writer, and the other by the latter. And yet, even in such a case, who will not acknowledge that when the matter was subjected to more careful consideration, the solution should have been discovered? This I have instanced now for this reason, that matters of that kind do often present themselves, which, while they really contain no discrepancies, appear to do so to persons who pay insufficient attention to them, and pronounce upon them inconsiderately.

CHAP. XLVII. — OF HIS WALKING UPON THE WATER, AND OF THE QUESTIONS REGARDING THE HARMONY OF THE EVANGELISTS WHO HAVE NARRATED THAT SCENE, AND REGARDING THE MANNER IN WHICH THEY PASS OFF FROM THE SECTION RECORDING THE OCCASION ON WHICH HE FED THE MULTITUDES WITH THE FIVE LOAVES.

99. Matthew goes on with his account in the

---

[1] Matt. xiv. 16.   [2] John vi. 7.   [3] Mark vi. 37.

following terms: "And when He had sent the multitudes away, He went up into a mountain apart to pray: and when the evening was come, He was there alone. But the ship was now in the midst of the sea, tossed with waves: for the wind was contrary. And in the fourth watch of the night He came unto them, walking on the sea. And when the disciples saw Him walking on the sea, they were troubled, saying, It is a spirit;" and so on, down to the words, "They came and worshipped Him, saying, Of a truth Thou art the Son of God." [1] In like manner, Mark, after narrating the miracle of the five loaves, gives his account of this same incident in the following terms: "And when it was late, the ship was in the midst of the sea, and He alone on the land. And He saw them toiling in rowing: for the wind was contrary to them," and so on. [2] This is similar to Matthew's version, except that nothing is said as to Peter's walking upon the waters. But here we must see to it, that no difficulty be found in what Mark has stated regarding the Lord, namely, that, when He walked upon the waters, He would also have passed by them. For in what way could they have understood this, were it not that He was really proceeding in a different direction from them, as if minded to pass those persons by like strangers, who were so far from recognizing Him that they took Him to be a spirit? Who, however, is so obtuse as not to perceive that this bears a mystical significance? At the same time, too, He came to the help of the men in their perturbation and outcry, and said to them, "Be of good cheer, it is I; be not afraid." What is the explanation, therefore, of His wish to pass by those persons whom nevertheless He thus encouraged when they were in terror, but that that intention to pass them by was made to serve the purpose of drawing forth those cries to which it was meet to bear succour?

100. Furthermore, John still tarries for a little space with these others. For, after his recital of the miracle of the five loaves, he also gives us some account of the vessel that laboured, and of the Lord's act in walking upon the sea. This notice he connects with his preceding narrative in the following manner: "When Jesus therefore perceived that they would come and take Him by force and make Him a king, He departed again into a mountain Himself alone. And when it became late, His disciples went down unto the sea; and when they had entered into a ship, they came over the sea to Capharnaum: and it was now dark, and Jesus was not come to them. And the sea arose by reason of a great wind that blew," and so on. [3] In this there cannot appear to be anything contrary to the records preserved in the other Gospels, unless it be the circumstance that Matthew tells us how, when the multitudes were sent away, He went up into a mountain, in order that there He might pray alone; while John states that He was on a mountain with those same multitudes whom He fed with the five loaves. [4] But seeing that John also informs us how He departed into a mountain after the said miracle, to preclude His being taken possession of by the multitudes, who wished to make Him a king, it is surely evident that they had come down from the mountain to more level ground when those loaves were provided for the crowds. And consequently there is no contradiction between the statements made by Matthew and John as to His going up again to the mountain. The only difference is, that Matthew uses the phrase "He went up," while John's term is "He departed." And there would be an antagonism between these two, only if in departing He had not gone up. Nor, again, is any want of harmony betrayed by the fact that Matthew's words are, "He went up into a mountain apart to pray;" whereas John puts it thus: "When He perceived that they would come to make Him a king, He departed again into a mountain Himself alone." Surely the matter of the departure is in no way a thing antagonistic to the matter of prayer. For, indeed, the Lord, who in His own person transformed the body of our humiliation in order that He might make it like unto the body of His own glory, [5] hereby taught us also the truth that the matter of departure should be to us in like manner grave matter for prayer. Neither, again, is there any defect of consistency proved by the circumstance that Matthew has told us first how He commanded His disciples to embark in the little ship, and to go before Him unto the other side of the lake until He sent the multitudes away, and then informs us that, after the multitudes were sent away, He Himself went up into a mountain alone to pray; while John mentions first that He departed unto a mountain alone, and then proceeds thus: "And when it became late, His disciples came down unto the sea; and when they had entered into a ship," etc. For who will not perceive that, in recapitulating the facts, John has spoken of something as actually done at a later point by the disciples, which Jesus had already charged them to do before His own departure unto the mountain; just as it is a familiar procedure in discourse, to revert in some fashion or other to any matter

---

1 Matt. xiv. 23-33.
2 Mark vi. 47-54.   3 John vi. 15-21.

4 Reading *in monte fuisse cum eisdem turbis quas de quinque panibus pavit.* According to Migne, this is the reading of several MSS. of the better class; some twelve other MSS. give *in monte fuisse cum eisdem turbas,* etc. = "He was on a mountain when He fed," etc. Some editions have also *in montem fugisse cum eisdem,* etc. = "He departed to a mountain when He fed," etc.
5 Phil. iii. 21.

which otherwise would have been passed over? But inasmuch as it may not be specifically noted that a reversion, especially when done briefly and instantaneously, is made to something omitted, the auditors are sometimes led to suppose that the occurrence which is mentioned at the later stage also took place literally at the later period. In this way the evangelist's statement really is, that to those persons whom he had described as embarking in the ship and coming across the sea to Capharnaum, the Lord came, walking toward them upon the waters, as they were toiling in the deep; which approach of the Lord of course took place at the earlier point, during the said voyage in which they were making their way to Capharnaum.[1]

101. On the other hand, Luke, after the record of the miracle of the five loaves, passes to another subject, and diverges from this order of narration. For he makes no mention of that little ship, and of the Lord's pathway over the waters. But after the statement conveyed in these words, "And they did all eat, and were filled, and there was taken up of fragments that remained to them twelve baskets," he has subjoined the following notice: "And it came to pass, as He was alone praying, His disciples were with Him; and He asked them, saying, Who say the people that I am?"[2] Thus he relates in this succession something new, which is not given by those three who have left us the account of the manner in which the Lord walked upon the waters, and came to the disciples when they were on the voyage. It ought not, however, on this account, to be supposed that it was on that same mountain to which Matthew has told us He went up in order to pray alone, that He said to His disciples, "Who say the people that I am?" For Luke, too, seems to harmonize with Matthew in this, because his words are, "as He was alone praying;" while Matthew's were, "He went up unto a mountain alone to pray." But it must by all means be held to have been on a different occasion that He put this question, since [it is said here, both that] He prayed alone, and [that] the disciples were with Him. Thus Luke, indeed, has mentioned only the fact of His being alone, but has said nothing of His being without His disciples, as is the case with Matthew and John, since [according to these latter] they left Him in order to go before Him to the other side of the sea. For with unmistakeable plainness Luke has added

the statement that "His disciples also were with Him." Consequently, in saying that He was alone, he meant his statement to refer to the multitudes, who did not abide with Him.

CHAP. XLVIII. — OF THE ABSENCE OF ANY DISCREPANCY BETWEEN MATTHEW AND MARK ON THE ONE HAND, AND JOHN ON THE OTHER, IN THE ACCOUNTS WHICH THE THREE GIVE TOGETHER OF WHAT TOOK PLACE AFTER THE OTHER SIDE OF THE LAKE WAS REACHED.

102. Matthew proceeds as follows: "And when they were gone over, they came into the land of Genesar. And when the men of that place had knowledge of Him, they sent out unto all that country round about, and brought unto Him all that were diseased, and besought Him that they might only touch the hem of His garment: and as many as touched were made perfectly whole. Then came to Him scribes and Pharisees from Jerusalem, saying, Why do thy disciples transgress the tradition of the elders? for they wash not their hands when they eat bread," and so on, down to the words, "But to eat with unwashen hands defileth not a man."[3] This is also related by Mark, in a way which precludes the raising of any question about discrepancies. For anything expressed here by the one in a form differing from that used by the other, involves at least no departure from identity in sense. John, on the other hand, fixing his attention, as his wont is, upon the Lord's discourses, passes on from the notice of the ship, which the Lord reached by walking upon the waters, to what took place after they disembarked upon the land, and mentions that He took occasion from the eating of the bread to deliver many lessons, dealing pre-eminently with divine things. After this address, too, his narrative is again borne on to one subject after another, in a sublime strain.[4] At the same time, this transition which he thus makes to different themes does not involve any real want of harmony, although he exhibits certain divergencies from these others, with the order of events presented by the rest of the evangelists. For what is there to hinder us from supposing at once that those persons, whose story is given by Matthew and Mark, were healed by the Lord, and that He delivered this discourse which John recounts to the people who followed Him across the sea? Such a supposition is made all the more reasonable by the fact that Capharnaum, to which place they are said, according to John, to have crossed, is near the lake of Genesar; and that, again, is the district into which they came, according to Matthew, on landing.

---

[1] [The difficulty in regard to the course of the ship did not suggest itself to Augustin, nor does he allude to the position of Bethsaida. Luke ix. 10 seems to place it on one side of the lake, and Mark vi. 45 on the other. A contrary wind would blow them across the lake, unless they were trying to get to some point on the eastern shore; from which shore they certainly started, after the feeding of the five thousand. — R.]

[2] Luke ix. 17, 18.

[3] Matt. xiv. 34–xv. 20.

[4] John vi. 22–72.

CHAP. XLIX. — OF THE WOMAN OF CANAAN WHO SAID, "YET THE DOGS EAT OF THE CRUMBS WHICH FALL FROM THEIR MASTERS' TABLES," AND OF THE HARMONY BETWEEN THE ACCOUNT GIVEN BY MATTHEW AND THAT BY LUKE.

103. Matthew, accordingly, proceeds with his narrative, after the notice of that discourse which the Lord delivered in the presence of the Pharisees on the subject of the unwashed hands. Preserving also the order of the succeeding events, as far as it is indicated by the transitions from the one to the other, he introduces this account into the context in the following manner: "And Jesus went thence, and departed into the coasts of Tyre and Sidon. And, behold, a woman of Canaan came out of the same coasts, and cried unto Him, saying, Have mercy on me, O Lord, Thou son of David; my daughter is grievously vexed with a devil. But He answered her not a word," and so on, down to the words, "O woman, great is thy faith: be it unto thee even as thou wilt. And her daughter was made whole from that very hour."[1] This story of the woman of Canaan is recorded also by Mark, who keeps the same order of events, and gives no occasion to raise any question as to a want of harmony, unless it be found in the circumstance that he tells us how the Lord was in the house at the time when the said woman came to Him with the petition on behalf of her daughter.[2] Now we might readily suppose that Matthew has simply omitted mention of the house, while nevertheless relating the same occurrence. But inasmuch as he states that the disciples made the suggestion to Him in these terms, "Send her away, for she crieth after us," he seems to imply distinctly that the woman gave utterance to these cries of entreaty behind the Lord as He walked on. In what sense, then, could it have been "in the house," unless we are to take Mark to have intimated the fact, that she had gone into the place where Jesus then was, when he mentioned at the beginning of the narrative that He was in the house? But when Matthew says that "He answered her not a word," he has given us also to understand what neither of the two evangelists has related explicitly, — namely, the fact that during that silence which He maintained Jesus went out of the house. And in this manner all the other particulars are brought into a connection which from this point onwards presents no kind of appearance of discrepancy. For as to what Mark records with respect to the answer which the Lord gave her, to the effect that it was not meet to take the children's bread and cast it unto the dogs, that reply was returned only after the interposition of certain sayings which Matthew has not left unrecorded. That is to say, [we are to suppose that] there came in first the request which the disciples addressed to Him in regard to the woman's case, and the answer He gave them, to the effect that He was not sent but unto the lost sheep of the house of Israel; that next there was her own approach, or, in other words, her coming after Him, and worshipping Him, saying, "Lord, help me;" and that then, after all these incidents, those words were spoken which have been recorded by both the evangelists.

CHAP. L. — OF THE OCCASION ON WHICH HE FED THE MULTITUDES WITH THE SEVEN LOAVES, AND OF THE QUESTION AS TO THE HARMONY BETWEEN MATTHEW AND MARK IN THEIR ACCOUNTS OF THAT MIRACLE.

104. Matthew proceeds with his narrative in the following terms: "And when Jesus had departed from thence, He came nigh unto the sea of Galilee; and went up into a mountain, and sat down there. And great multitudes came unto Him, having with them those that were lame, blind, dumb, maimed, and many others, and cast them down at Jesus' feet, and He healed them; insomuch that the multitudes wondered, when they saw the dumb to speak, the maimed to be whole, the lame to walk, and the blind to see: and they glorified the God of Israel. Then Jesus called His disciples unto Him, and said, I have compassion on the multitude, because they continue with me now three days, and have nothing to eat," and so on, down to the words, "And they that did eat were four thousand men, besides women and children."[3] This other miracle of the seven loaves and the few little fishes is recorded also by Mark, and that too in almost the same order; the exception being that he inserts before it a narrative given by no other, — namely, that relating to the deaf man whose ears the Lord opened, when He spat and said, "Effeta," that is, Be opened.[4]

105. In the case of this miracle of the seven loaves, it is certainly not a superfluous task to call attention to the fact that these two evangelists, Matthew and Mark, have thus introduced it into their narrative. For if one of them had recorded this miracle, who at the same time had taken no notice of the instance of the five loaves, he would have been judged to stand opposed to the rest. For in such circumstances, who would not have supposed that there was only the one miracle wrought in actual fact, and that an incomplete and unveracious version of it had been given by the writer referred to,

---

[1] Matt. xv. 21-28. [2] Mark vii. 24-30. [3] Matt. xv. 29-38. [4] Mark vii. 31-viii. 9.

or by the others, or by all of them together; so [that we must have imagined] either that the one evangelist, by a mistake on his own part, had been led to mention seven loaves instead of five; or that the other two, whether as having both presented an incorrect statement, or as having been misled through a slip of memory, had put the number five for the number seven. In like manner, it might have been supposed that there was a contradiction between the twelve baskets[1] and the seven baskets,[2] and again, between the five thousand and the four thousand, expressing the numbers of those who were fed. But now, since those evangelists who have given us the account of the miracle of the seven loaves have also not failed to mention the other miracle of the five loaves, no difficulty can be felt by any one, and all can see that both works were really wrought. This, accordingly, we have instanced, in order that, if in any other passage we come upon some similar deed of the Lord's, which, as told by one evangelist, seems so utterly contrary to the version of it given by another that no method of solving the difficulty can possibly be found, we may understand the explanation to be simply this, that both incidents really took place, and that they were recorded separately by the two several writers. This is precisely what we have already recommended to attention in the matter of the seating of the multitudes by hundreds and by fifties. For were it not for the circumstance that both these numbers are found noted by the one historian, we might have supposed that the different writers had made contradictory statements.[3]

CHAP. LI. — OF MATTHEW'S DECLARATION THAT, ON LEAVING THESE PARTS, HE CAME INTO THE COASTS OF MAGEDAN; AND OF THE QUESTION AS TO HIS AGREEMENT WITH MARK IN THAT INTIMATION, AS WELL AS IN THE NOTICE OF THE SAYING ABOUT JONAH, WHICH WAS RETURNED AGAIN AS AN ANSWER TO THOSE WHO SOUGHT A SIGN.

106. Matthew continues as follows: "And He sent away the multitude, and took ship, and came into the coasts of Magedan;" and so on, down to the words, "A wicked and adulterous generation seeketh after a sign; and there shall no sign be given unto it but the sign of the prophet Jonas."[4] This has already been recorded in another connection by the same Matthew.[5] Hence again and again we must hold by the position that the Lord spake the same words on repeated occasions; so that when any completely irreconcilable difference appears between statements of His utterances, we are to

understand the words to have been spoken twice over. In this case, indeed, Mark also keeps the same order; and after his account of the miracle of the seven loaves, subjoins the same intimation as is given us in Matthew, only with this difference, that Matthew's expression for the locality is not Dalmanutha, as is read in certain codices, but Magedan.[6] There is no reason, however, for questioning the fact that it is the same place that is intended under both names. For most codices, even of Mark's Gospel, give no other reading than that of Magedan.[7] Neither should any difficulty be felt in the fact that Mark does not say, as Matthew does, that in the answer which the Lord returned to those who sought after a sign, He referred to Jonah, but mentions simply that He replied in these terms: "There shall no sign be given unto it." For we are given to understand what kind of sign they asked — namely, one from heaven. And he has simply omitted to specify the words which Matthew has introduced regarding Jonas.

CHAP. LII. — OF MATTHEW'S AGREEMENT WITH MARK IN THE STATEMENT ABOUT THE LEAVEN OF THE PHARISEES, AS REGARDS BOTH THE SUBJECT ITSELF AND THE ORDER OF NARRATIVE.

107. Matthew proceeds: "And He left them, and departed. And when His disciples were come to the other side, they forgot to take bread. Then Jesus said unto them, Take heed, and beware of the leaven of the Pharisees and of the Sadducees;" and so forth, down to where we read, "Then understood they that He bade them not beware of the leaven of bread, but of the doctrine of the Pharisees and of the Sadducees."[8] These words are recorded also by Mark, and that likewise in the same order.[9]

CHAP. LIII. — OF THE OCCASION ON WHICH HE ASKED THE DISCIPLES WHOM MEN SAID THAT HE WAS; AND OF THE QUESTION WHETHER, WITH REGARD EITHER TO THE SUBJECT-MATTER OR THE ORDER, THERE ARE ANY DISCREPANCIES BETWEEN MATTHEW, MARK, AND LUKE.

108. Matthew continues thus: "And Jesus came into the coasts of Cæsarea Philippi; and He asked His disciples, saying, Whom do men say that I,[10] the Son of man, am? And they said, Some say that Thou art John the Baptist; some, Elias; and others, Jeremias, or one of the prophets;" and so on, down to the words, "And

---

[1] *Cophinis.*　　[2] *Sportis.*　　[3] See above, chap. xlvi.
[4] Matt. xv. 39–xvi. 4.　　[5] Matt. xii. 38.

[6] Mark viii. 10–12.
[7] ["Magdala," as the Authorized Version reads in Matthew, is poorly supported, and was probably substituted by some ignorant scribe for "Magadan" (comp. Revised Version). In Mark viii. 10, however, the reading "Dalmanutha" is well attested. Augustin refers to Latin codices. — R.]
[8] Matt. xvi. 5–12.　　　　[9] Mark viii. 13–21.
[10] Some editions omit the *me* in *quem me dicunt*, etc., and make it = Whom do men say that the Son of man is?

whatsoever thou shalt loose on earth shall be loosed in heaven." [1]   Mark relates this nearly in the same order.   But he has brought in before it a narrative which is given by him alone, — namely, that regarding the giving of sight to that blind man who said to the Lord, "I see men as trees walking." [2]   Luke, again, also records this incident, inserting it after his account of the miracle of the five loaves ; [3] and, as we have already shown above, the order of recollection which is followed in his case is not antagonistic to the order adopted by these others. Some difficulty, however, may be imagined in the circumstance that Luke's representation bears that the Lord put this question, as to whom men held Him to be, to His disciples at a time when He was alone praying, and when His disciples were also with Him ; whereas Mark, on the other hand, tells us that the question was put by Him to the disciples when they were on the way.   But this will be a difficulty only to the man who has never prayed on the way. [4]

109. I recollect having already stated that no one should suppose that Peter received that name for the first time on the occasion when He said to Him, "Thou art Peter, and upon this rock I will build my Church."   For the time at which he did obtain this name was that referred to by John, when he mentions that he was addressed in these terms : "Thou shalt be called Cephas, which is, by interpretation, Peter." [5] Hence, too, we are as little to think that Peter got this designation on the occasion to which Mark alludes, when he recounts the twelve apostles individually by name, and tells us how James and John were called the sons of thunder, merely on the ground that in that passage he has recorded the fact that He surnamed him Peter. [6] For that circumstance is noticed there simply because it was suggested to the writer's recollection at that particular point, and not because it took place in actual fact at that specific time.

CHAP. LIV. — OF THE OCCASION ON WHICH HE ANNOUNCED HIS COMING PASSION TO THE DISCIPLES, AND OF THE MEASURE OF CONCORD BETWEEN MATTHEW, MARK, AND LUKE IN THE ACCOUNTS WHICH THEY GIVE OF THE SAME.

110. Matthew proceeds in the following strain : "Then charged He His disciples that they should tell no man that He was Jesus the Christ. From that time forth began Jesus to show unto His disciples how that He must go into Jerusalem, and suffer many things of the elders, and chief priests, and scribes ; " and so on, down to where we read, "Thou savourest not the things

that be of God, but those that be of men." [7] Mark and Luke add these passages in the same order.   Only Luke says nothing about the opposition which Peter expressed to the passion of Christ.

CHAP. LV. — OF THE HARMONY BETWEEN THE THREE EVANGELISTS IN THE NOTICES WHICH THEY SUBJOIN OF THE MANNER IN WHICH THE LORD CHARGED THE MAN TO FOLLOW HIM WHO WISHED TO COME AFTER HIM.

111. Matthew continues thus : "Then said Jesus unto His disciples, If any man will come after me, let him deny himself, and take up his cross, and follow me ; " and so on, down to the words, "And then He shall reward every man according to his work." [8]   This is appended also by Mark, who keeps the same order.   But he does not say of the Son of man, who was to come with His angels, that He is to reward every man according to his work.   Nevertheless, he mentions at the same time that the Lord spoke to this effect : "Whosoever shall be ashamed of me and my words in this adulterous and sinful generation, of him also shall the Son of man be ashamed when He comes in the glory of His Father with the holy angels." [9]   And this may be taken to bear the same sense as is expressed by Matthew, when he says, that "He shall reward every man according to his work."   Luke [10] also adds the same statements in the same order, slightly varying the terms indeed in which they are conveyed, but still showing a complete parallel with the others in regard to the truthful reproduction of the self-same ideas. [11]

CHAP. LVI. — OF THE MANIFESTATION WHICH THE LORD MADE OF HIMSELF, IN COMPANY WITH MOSES AND ELIAS, TO HIS DISCIPLES ON THE MOUNTAIN ; AND OF THE QUESTION CONCERNING THE HARMONY BETWEEN THE FIRST THREE EVANGELISTS WITH REGARD TO THE ORDER AND THE CIRCUMSTANCES OF THAT EVENT ; AND IN ESPECIAL, THE NUMBER OF THE DAYS, IN SO FAR AS MATTHEW AND MARK STATE THAT IT TOOK PLACE AFTER SIX DAYS, WHILE LUKE SAYS THAT IT WAS AFTER EIGHT DAYS.

112. Matthew proceeds thus : "Verily I say unto you, There be some standing here which shall not taste of death till they see the Son of man coming in His kingdom.   And after six days, Jesus taketh Peter, James, and John his brother, and brought them up into an high mountain ; " and so on, down to where we read, "Tell the vision to no man until the Son of man be risen again from the dead."   This vision of the Lord upon the mount in the presence of the

---

[1] Matt. xvi. 13-19.   [2] Mark viii. 22-29.   [3] Luke ix. 18-20.
[4] Adopting, with the Ratisbon MSS., *eum movet qui nunquam oravit in via.*   Another reading is, *eum movet qui putat nunquam,* etc. = a difficulty to the man who thinks He never prayed on the way.
[5] John i. 42.   [6] Mark iii. 16-19.

[7] Matt. xvi. 20-23.
[8] Matt. xvi. 24-27.   [9] Mark viii. 34-38.   [10] Luke ix. 25, 26.
[11] The text gives, *eadem tamen sententiarum veritate simillimus.*   Another reading is, *sententiam veritate simillimo.*

three disciples, Peter, James, and John, on which occasion also the testimony of the Father's voice was borne Him from heaven, is related by the three evangelists in the same order, and in a manner expressing the same sense completely.[1] And as regards other matters, they may be seen by the readers to be in accordance with those modes of narration of which we have given examples in many passages already, and in which there are diversities in expression without any consequent diversity in meaning.

113. But with respect to the circumstance that Mark, along with Matthew, tells us how the event took place after six days, while Luke states that it was after eight days, those who find a difficulty here do not deserve to be set aside with contempt, but should be enlightened by the offering of explanations. For when we announce a space of days in these terms, "after so many days," sometimes we do not include in the number the day on which we speak, or the day on which the thing itself which we intimate beforehand or promise is declared to take place, but reckon only the intervening days, on the real and full and final expiry of which the incident in question is to occur. This is what Matthew and Mark have done. Leaving out of their calculation the day on which Jesus spoke these words, and the day on which He exhibited that memorable spectacle on the mount, they have regarded simply the intermediate days, and thus have used the expression, "after six days." But Luke, reckoning in the extreme day at either end, that is to say, the first day and the last day, has made it "after eight days," in accordance with that mode of speech in which the part is put for the whole.

114. Moreover, the statement which Luke makes with regard to Moses and Elias in these terms, "And it came to pass, as they departed[2] from Him, Peter said unto Jesus, Master, it is good for us to be here," and so forth, ought not to be considered antagonistic to what Matthew and Mark have subjoined to the same effect, as if they made Peter offer this suggestion while Moses and Elias were still talking with the Lord. For they have not expressly said that it was at that time, but rather they have simply left unnoticed the fact which Luke has added, — namely, that it was as they went away that Peter made the suggestion to the Lord with respect to the making of three tabernacles. At the same time, Luke has appended the intimation that it was as they were entering the cloud that the voice came from heaven, — a circumstance which is not affirmed, but which is as little contradicted, by the others.

CHAP. LVII. — OF THE HARMONY BETWEEN MATTHEW AND MARK IN THE ACCOUNTS GIVEN OF THE OCCASION ON WHICH HE SPOKE TO THE DISCIPLES CONCERNING THE COMING OF ELIAS.

115. Matthew goes on thus: "And His disciples asked Him, saying, Why then say the scribes that Elias must first come? And Jesus answered and said unto them, Elias truly shall first come and restore all things. But I say unto you, that Elias is come already, and they knew him not, but have done unto him whatsoever they listed. Likewise shall also the Son of man suffer of them. Then the disciples understood that He spake unto them of John the Baptist."[3] This same passage is given also by Mark, who keeps also the same order; and although he exhibits some diversity of expression, he makes no departure from a truthful representation of the same sense.[4] He has not, however, added the statement, that the disciples understood that the Lord had referred to John the Baptist in saying that Elias was come already.

CHAP. LVIII. — OF THE MAN WHO BROUGHT BEFORE HIM HIS SON, WHOM THE DISCIPLES WERE UNABLE TO HEAL; AND OF THE QUESTION CONCERNING THE AGREEMENT BETWEEN THESE THREE EVANGELISTS ALSO IN THE MATTER OF THE ORDER OF NARRATION HERE.

116. Matthew goes on in the following terms: "And when He was come[5] to the multitude, there came to Him a certain man, kneeling down before Him, and saying, Lord, have mercy on my son; for he is lunatic, and sore vexed;" and so on, down to the words, "Howbeit this kind is not cast out but by prayer and fasting."[6] Both Mark and Luke record this incident, and that, too, in the same order, without any suspicion of a want of harmony.[7]

CHAP. LIX. — OF THE OCCASION ON WHICH THE DISCIPLES WERE EXCEEDING SORRY WHEN HE SPOKE TO THEM OF HIS PASSION, AS IT IS RELATED IN THE SAME ORDER BY THE THREE EVANGELISTS.

117. Matthew continues thus: "And while they abode in Galilee, Jesus said unto them, The Son of man shall be betrayed into the hands of men; and they shall kill Him, and the third day He shall rise again. And they were exceeding sorry."[8] Mark and Luke record this passage in the same order.[9]

CHAP. LX. — OF HIS PAYING THE TRIBUTE MONEY OUT OF THE MOUTH OF THE FISH, AN INCIDENT WHICH MATTHEW ALONE MENTIONS.

118. Matthew continues in these terms:

---

[1] Matt. xvi. 28–xvii. 9; Mark viii. 39–ix. 9; Luke ix. 27–36.
[2] [Dum discederent. The Revised Version correctly renders the Greek: "as they were parting." — R.]

[3] Matt. xvii. 10–13.　　[4] Mark ix. 10–12.　　[5] Venisset.
[6] Matt. xvii. 14–20.　　[7] Mark ix. 16–28; Luke ix. 38–45.
[8] Matt. xvii. 21, 22.　　[9] Mark ix. 29–31; Luke ix. 44, 45.

"And when they were come to Capharnaum, they that received tribute money came to Peter, and said to him, Doth not your master pay tribute? He saith, Yes;" and so on, down to where we read: "Thou shalt find a piece of money: that take, and give unto them for me and thee." [1] He is the only one who relates this occurrence, after the interposition of which he follows again the order which is pursued also by Mark and Luke in company with him.

CHAP. LXI. — OF THE LITTLE CHILD WHOM HE SET BEFORE THEM FOR THEIR IMITATION, AND OF THE OFFENCES OF THE WORLD; OF THE MEMBERS OF THE BODY CAUSING OFFENCES; OF THE ANGELS OF THE LITTLE ONES, WHO BEHOLD THE FACE OF THE FATHER; OF THE ONE SHEEP OUT OF THE HUNDRED SHEEP; OF THE REPROVING OF A BROTHER IN PRIVATE; OF THE LOOSING AND THE BINDING OF SINS; OF THE AGREEMENT OF TWO, AND THE GATHERING TOGETHER OF THREE; OF THE FORGIVING OF SINS EVEN UNTO SEVENTY TIMES SEVEN; OF THE SERVANT WHO HAD HIS OWN LARGE DEBT REMITTED, AND YET REFUSED TO REMIT THE SMALL DEBT WHICH HIS FELLOW-SERVANT OWED TO HIM; AND OF THE QUESTION AS TO MATTHEW'S HARMONY WITH THE OTHER EVANGELISTS ON ALL THESE SUBJECTS.

119. The same Matthew then proceeds with his narrative in the following terms: "In that hour came the disciples unto Jesus, saying, Who, thinkest Thou, is the greater in the kingdom of heaven? And Jesus called a little child unto Him, and set him in the midst of them, and said, Verily I say unto you, Except ye be converted, and become as little children, ye shall not enter into the kingdom of heaven;" and so on, down to the words, "So likewise shall my heavenly Father do also unto you, if ye from your hearts forgive not every one his brother their trespasses." [2] Of this somewhat lengthened discourse which was spoken by the Lord, Mark, instead of giving the whole, has presented only certain portions, in dealing with which he follows meantime the same order. He has also introduced some matters which Matthew does not mention. [3] Moreover, in this complete discourse, so far as we have taken it under consideration, the only interruption is that which is made by Peter, when he inquires how often a brother ought to be forgiven. The Lord, however, was speaking in a strain which makes it quite clear that even the question which Peter thus proposed, and the answer which was returned to him, belong really to the same address. Luke, again, records none of these things in the order here observed, with the ex-

ception of the incident with the little child whom He set before His disciples, for their imitation when they were thinking of their own greatness. [4] For if he has also narrated some other matters of a tenor resembling those which are inserted in this discourse, these are sayings which he has recalled for notice in other connections, and on occasions different from the present: just as John [5] introduces the Lord's words on the subject of the forgiveness of sins, — namely, those to the effect that they should be remitted to him to whom the apostles remitted them, and that they should be retained to him to whom they retained them, as spoken by the Lord after His resurrection; while Matthew mentions that in the discourse now under notice the Lord made this declaration, which, however, the self-same evangelist at the same time affirms to have been given on a previous occasion to Peter. [6] Therefore, to preclude the necessity of having always to inculcate the same rule, we ought to bear in mind the fact that Jesus uttered the same word repeatedly, and in a number of different places, — a principle which we have pressed so often upon your attention already; and this consideration should save us from feeling any perplexity, even although the order of the sayings may be thought to create some difficulty.

CHAP. LXII. — OF THE HARMONY SUBSISTING BETWEEN MATTHEW AND MARK IN THE ACCOUNTS WHICH THEY OFFER OF THE TIME WHEN HE WAS ASKED WHETHER IT WAS LAWFUL TO PUT AWAY ONE'S WIFE, AND ESPECIALLY IN REGARD TO THE SPECIFIC QUESTIONS AND REPLIES WHICH PASSED BETWEEN THE LORD AND THE JEWS, AND IN WHICH THE EVANGELISTS SEEM TO BE, TO SOME SMALL EXTENT, AT VARIANCE.

120. Matthew continues giving his narrative in the following manner: "And it came to pass, that when Jesus had finished these sayings, He departed from Galilee, and came into the coasts of Judæa beyond Jordan; and great multitudes followed Him; and He healed them there. [7] The Pharisees also came unto Him, tempting Him, and saying, Is it lawful for a man to put away his wife for every cause?" And so on, down to the words, "He that is able to receive it, let him receive it." [8] Mark also records this, and observes the same order. At the same time, we must certainly see to it that no appearance

---

[1] Matt. xvii. 23–27.   [2] Matt. xviii.   [3] Mark ix. 33–49.

[4] Luke ix. 46–48.   [5] John xx. 23.   [6] Matt. xvi. 19.
[7] [Augustin entirely ignores the most perplexing problem in the Gospel history, namely, the proper distribution of the matter peculiar to Luke and John, at this point in the narrative. The passages are: Luke ix. 51–xviii. 14 and John vii. 2–xi. 54. These events cover about six months, but Matthew and Mark omit all reference to them. The difficulty is all the greater, since Luke inserts in his narrative many things that evidently belong to an earlier period (e.g., chaps. xi. 14–xiii. 19). There are also peculiar difficulties connected with the chronology of John x. and xi. — R.]
[8] Matt. xix. 1–12.

of contradiction be supposed to arise from the circumstance that the same Mark tells us how the Pharisees were asked by the Lord as to what Moses commanded them, and that on His questioning them to that effect they returned the answer regarding the bill of divorcement which Moses suffered them to write; whereas, according to Matthew's version, it was after the Lord had spoken those words in which He had shown them, out of the law, how God made male and female to be one flesh, and how, therefore, those [thus joined together of Him] ought not to be put asunder by man, that they gave the reply, "Why did Moses then command to give a writing of divorcement, and to put her away?" To this interrogation, also [as Matthew puts it], He says again in reply, "Moses, because of the hardness of your hearts, suffered you to put away your wives: but from the beginning it was not so." There is no difficulty, I repeat, in this; for it is not the case that Mark makes no kind of mention of the reply which was thus given by the Lord, but he brings it in after the answer which was returned by them to His question relating to the bill of divorcement.

121. As far as the order or method of statement here adopted is concerned, we ought to understand that it in no way affects the truth of the subject itself, whether the question regarding the permission to write a bill of divorcement given by the said Moses, by whom also it is recorded that God made male and female to be one flesh,[1] was addressed by these Pharisees to the Lord at the time when He was forbidding the separation of husband and wife, and confirming His declaration on that subject by the authority of the law; or whether the said question was conveyed in the reply which the same persons returned to the Lord, at the time when He asked them about what Moses had commanded them. For His intention was not to offer them any reason for the permission which Moses thus granted them until they had first mentioned the matter themselves; which intention on His part is what is indicated by the inquiry which Mark has introduced. On the other hand, their desire was to use the authority of Moses in commanding the giving of a bill of divorcement, for the purpose of stopping His mouth, so to speak, in the matter of forbidding, as they believed He undoubtedly would do, a man to put away his wife. For they had approached Him with the view of saying what would tempt Him. And this desire of theirs is what is indicated by Matthew, when, instead of stating how they were interrogated first themselves, he represents them as having of their own accord put the question about the precept of Moses, in order that they

might thereby, as it were, convict the Lord of doing what was wrong in prohibiting the putting away of wives. Wherefore, since the mind of the speakers, in the service of which the words ought to stand, has been exhibited by both evangelists, it is no matter how the modes of narration adopted by the two may differ, provided neither of them fails to give a correct representation of the subject itself.

122. Another view of the matter may also be taken, namely, that, in accordance with Mark's statement, when these persons began by questioning the Lord on the subject of the putting away of a wife, He questioned them in turn as to what Moses commanded them; and that, on their replying that Moses suffered them to write a bill of divorcement and put the wife away, He made His answer to them regarding the said law which was given by Moses, reminding them how God instituted the union of male and female, and addressing them in the words which are inserted by Matthew, namely, "Have ye not read that He which made them at the beginning made them male and female?" and so on. On hearing these words, they repeated in the form of an inquiry what they had already given utterance to when replying to His first interrogation, namely the expression, "Why did Moses then command to give a writing of divorcement, and to put her away?" Then Jesus showed that the reason was the hardness of their heart; which explanation Mark brings in, with a view to brevity, at an earlier point, as if it had been given in reply to that former response of theirs, which Matthew has passed over. And this he does as judging that no injury could be done to the truth at whichever point the explanation might be introduced, seeing that the words, with a view to which it was returned, had been uttered twice in the same form; and seeing also that the Lord, in any case, had offered the said explanation in reply to such words.

CHAP. LXIII. — OF THE LITTLE CHILDREN ON WHOM HE LAID HIS HANDS; OF THE RICH MAN TO WHOM HE SAID, "SELL ALL THAT THOU HAST;" OF THE VINEYARD IN WHICH THE LABOURERS WERE HIRED AT DIFFERENT HOURS; AND OF THE QUESTION AS TO THE ABSENCE OF ANY DISCREPANCY BETWEEN MATTHEW AND THE OTHER TWO EVANGELISTS ON THESE SUBJECTS.

123. Matthew proceeds thus: "Then were there brought unto Him little children, that He should put His hands on them, and pray; and the disciples rebuked them;" and so on, down to where we read, "For many are called, but few are chosen."[2] Mark has followed the same order here as Matthew.[3] But Matthew is the only one

---

[1] Gen. ii. 24.

[2] Matt. xix. 13-xx. 16.   [3] Mark x. 13-31.

who introduces the section relating to the labourers who were hired for the vineyard. Luke,
on the other hand, first mentions what He said
to those who were asking each other who should
be the greatest, and next subjoins at once the
passage concerning the man whom they had seen
casting out devils, although he did not follow
Him ; then he parts company with the other two
at the point where he tells us how He stedfastly
set His face to go to ·Jerusalem ;¹ and after the
interposition of a number of subjects,² he joins
them again in giving the story of the rich man,
to whom the word is addressed, "Sell all that
thou hast," ³ which individual's case is related
here by the other two evangelists, but still in the
succession which is followed by all the narratives
alike. For in the passage referred to in Luke,
that writer does not fail to bring in the story of
the little children, just as the other two do immediately before the mention of the rich man.
With regard, then, to the accounts which are
given us of this rich person, who asks what good
thing he should do in order to obtain eternal
life, there may appear to be some discrepancy
between them, because the words were, according to Matthew, "Why askest thou me about the
good?" while according to the others they were,
"Why callest thou me good?" The sentence,
"Why askest thou me about the good?" may
then be referred more particularly to what was
expressed by the man when he put the question,
"What good thing shall I do?" For there we
have both the name "good" applied to Christ,
and the question put.⁴ But the address "Good
Master" does not of itself convey the question.
Accordingly, the best method of disposing of it
is to understand both these sentences to have
been uttered, "Why callest thou me good?"
and, "Why askest thou me about the good?"

CHAP. LXIV.— OF THE OCCASIONS ON WHICH HE
  FORETOLD HIS PASSION IN PRIVATE TO HIS
  DISCIPLES ; AND OF THE TIME WHEN THE
  MOTHER OF ZEBEDEE'S CHILDREN CAME WITH
  HER SONS, REQUESTING THAT ONE OF THEM
  SHOULD SIT ON HIS RIGHT HAND, AND THE
  OTHER ON HIS LEFT HAND ; AND OF THE
  ABSENCE OF ANY DISCREPANCY BETWEEN MAT-
  THEW AND THE OTHER TWO EVANGELISTS ON
  THESE SUBJECTS.

124. Matthew continues his narrative in the
following terms : "And Jesus, going up to Jerusalem, took the twelve disciples apart, and said

unto them, Behold, we go up to Jerusalem ; and
the Son of man shall be betrayed unto the chief
priests and unto the scribes, and they shall condemn Him to death, and shall deliver Him to
the Gentiles to mock, and to scourge, and to
crucify Him ; and the third day He shall rise
again. Then came to Him the mother of Zebedee's children with her sons, worshipping Him,
and desiring a certain thing of Him ;" and so
on, down to the words, "Even as the Son of man
came not to be ministered unto, but to minister,
and to give His life a ransom for many." ⁵ Here
again Mark keeps the same order as Matthew,
only he represents the sons of Zebedee to have
made the request themselves ; while Matthew
has stated that it was preferred on their behalf
not by their own personal application, but by
their mother, as she had laid what was their wish
before the Lord. Hence Mark has briefly intimated what was said on that occasion as spoken
by them, rather than by her [in their name].
And to conclude with the matter, it is to them
rather than to her, according to Matthew no less
than according to Mark, that the Lord returned
His reply. Luke, on the other hand, after narrating in the same order our Lord's predictions
to the twelve disciples on the subject of His
passion and resurrection, leaves unnoticed what
the other two evangelists immediately go on to
record ; and after the interposition of these passages, he is joined by his fellow-writers again
[at the point where they report the incident] at
Jericho.⁶ Moreover, as to what Matthew and
Mark have stated with respect to the princes of
the Gentiles exercising dominion over those who
are subject to them, — namely, that it should not
be so with them [the disciples], but that he
who was greatest among them should even be
a servant to the others, — Luke also gives us
something of the same tenor, although not in
that connection ;⁷ and the order itself indicates
that the same sentiment was expressed by the
Lord on a second occasion.

CHAP. LXV. — OF THE ABSENCE OF ANY ANTAGO-
  NISM BETWEEN MATTHEW AND MARK, OR BE-
  TWEEN MATTHEW AND LUKE, IN THE ACCOUNT
  OFFERED OF THE GIVING OF SIGHT TO THE
  BLIND MEN OF JERICHO.

125. Matthew continues thus : "And as they
departed from Jericho, a great multitude followed Him. And, behold, two blind men sitting
by the wayside heard that Jesus passed by, and
cried out, saying, Have mercy on us, O Lord,
thou Son of David ;" and so on, down to the
words, "And immediately their eyes received
sight, and they followed Him." ⁸ Mark also records this incident, but mentions only one blind

---

¹ Luke ix. 46-51.   ² [Compare note on § 120. — R.]
³ Luke xviii. 18-30
⁴ The Latin version is followed here. In Matt. xix. 17, where
the English version gives, "Why callest thou me good?" the Vulgate
has, *Quid me interrogas de bono ?* [The Revised Version text agrees
with the Vulgate (in Matthew), following the most ancient Greek MSS.
But the same authorities read "Master" instead of "good Master,"
differing from the Vulgate Augustin accepts the latter reading. —
R.]

⁵ Matt. xx. 17-28.   ⁶ Luke xviii. 31-35.
⁷ Luke xxii. 24-27.   ⁸ Matt. xx. 29-34.

man.[1] This difficulty is solved in the way in which a former difficulty was explained which met us in the case of the two persons who were tormented by the legion of devils in the territory of the Gerasenes.[2] For, that in this instance also of the two blind men whom he [Matthew] alone has introduced here, one of them was of pre-eminent note and repute in that city, is a fact made clear enough by the single consideration, that Mark has recorded both his own name and his father's ; a circumstance which scarcely comes across us in all the many cases of healing which had been already performed by the Lord, unless that miracle be an exception, in the recital of which the evangelist has mentioned by name Jairus, the ruler of the synagogue, whose daughter Jesus restored to life.[3] And in this latter instance this intention becomes the more apparent, from the fact that the said ruler of the synagogue was certainly a man of rank in the place. Consequently there can be little doubt that this Bartimæus, the son of Timæus, had fallen from some position of great prosperity, and was now regarded as an object of the most notorious and the most remarkable wretchedness, because, in addition to being blind, he had also to sit begging. And this is also the reason, then, why Mark has chosen to mention only the one whose restoration to sight acquired for the miracle a fame as widespread as was the notoriety which the man's misfortune itself had gained.

126. But Luke, although he mentions an incident altogether of the same tenor, is nevertheless to be understood as really narrating only a similar miracle which was wrought in the case of another blind man, and as putting on record its similarity to the said miracle in the method of performance. For he states that it was performed when He was coming nigh unto Jericho ;[4] while the others say that it took place when He was departing from Jericho. Now the name of the city, and the resemblance in the deed, favour the supposition that there was but one such occurrence. But still, the idea that the evangelists really contradict each other here, in so far as the one says, "As He was come nigh unto Jericho," while the others put it thus, "As He came out of Jericho," is one which no one surely will be prevailed on to accept, unless those who would have it more readily credited that the gospel is unveracious, than that He wrought two miracles of a similar nature and in similar circumstances.[5] But every faithful son of the gospel will most readily perceive which of these two alternatives is the more credible, and which the rather to be accepted as true ; and, indeed, every gainsayer

too, when he is advised concerning the real state of the case, will answer himself either by the silence which he will have to observe, or at least by the tenor of his reflections should he decline to be silent.

CHAP. LXVI. — OF THE COLT OF THE ASS WHICH IS MENTIONED BY MATTHEW, AND OF THE CONSISTENCY OF HIS ACCOUNT WITH THAT OF THE OTHER EVANGELISTS, WHO SPEAK ONLY OF THE ASS.

127. Matthew goes on with his narrative in the following terms : "And when they drew nigh unto Jerusalem, and were come to Bethphage, unto the Mount of Olives, then sent Jesus two disciples, saying unto them, Go into the village over against you, and straightway ye shall find an ass tied, and a colt with her ; " and so on, down to the words, " Blessed is He that cometh in the name of the Lord : Hosanna in the highest."[6] Mark also records this occurrence, and inserts it in the same order.[7] Luke, on the other hand, tarries a space by Jericho, recounting certain matters which these others have omitted, — namely, the story of Zacchæus, the chief of the publicans, and some sayings which are couched in parabolic form. After instancing these things, however, this evangelist again joins company with the others in the narrative relating to the ass on which Jesus sat.[8] And let not the circumstance stagger us, that Matthew speaks both of an ass and of the colt of an ass, while the others say nothing of the ass. For here again we must bear in mind the rule which we have already introduced in dealing with the statements about the seating of the people by fifties and by hundreds on the occasion on which the multitudes were fed with the five loaves.[9] Now, after this principle has been brought into application, the reader should not feel any serious difficulty in the present case. Indeed, even had Matthew said nothing about the colt, just as his fellow-historians have taken no notice of the ass, the fact should not have created any such perplexity as to induce the idea of an insuperable contradiction between the two statements, when the one writer speaks only of the ass, and the others only of the colt of the ass. But how much less cause then for any disquietude ought there to be, when we see that the one writer has mentioned the ass to which the others have omitted to refer, in such a manner as at the same time not to leave unnoticed also the colt of which the rest have spoken ! In fine, where it is possible to suppose both objects to have been included in the occurrence, there is no real antagonism, although the one writer may specify only the one thing, and another only the other. How much less need

---

[1] Mark x. 46–52.　　　　　[2] See chap. xxiv. § 56.
[3] Mark v. 22–43.　　　　　[4] Luke xviii. 35–43.
[5] [Various other solutions are suggested. Comp. Robinson's Greek Harmony, rev. ed. pp. 234, 235. — R.]

[6] Matt. xxi. 1–9.　　　　　[7] Mark xi. 1–10.
[8] Luke xix. 1–38.　　　　　[9] See above, chap. xlvi. § 98.

there be any contradiction, when the one writer particularizes the one object, and another instances both !

128. Again, although John tells us nothing as to the way in which the Lord despatched His disciples to fetch these animals to Him, nevertheless he inserts a brief allusion to this colt, and cites also the word of the prophet which Matthew makes use of.[1] In the case also of this testimony from the prophet, the terms in which it is reproduced by the evangelists, although they exhibit certain differences, do not fail to express a sense identical in intention. Some difficulty, however, may be felt in the fact that Matthew adduces this passage in a form which represents the prophet to have made mention of the ass ; whereas this is not the case, either with the quotation as introduced by John, or with the version given in the ecclesiastical codices of the translation in common use. An explanation of this variation seems to me to be found in the fact that Matthew is understood to have written his Gospel in the Hebrew language. Moreover, it is manifest that the translation which bears the name of the Septuagint differs in some particulars from the text which is found in the Hebrew by those who know that tongue, and by the several scholars who have given us renderings of the same Hebrew books. And if an explanation is asked for this discrepancy, or for the circumstance that the weighty authority of the Septuagint translation diverges in many passages from the rendering of the truth which is discovered in the Hebrew codices, I am of opinion that no more probable account of the matter will suggest itself, than the supposition that the Seventy composed their version under the influence of the very Spirit by whose inspiration the things which they were engaged in translating had been originally spoken. This is an idea which receives confirmation also from the marvellous consent which is asserted to have characterized them.[2] Consequently, when these translators, while not departing from the real mind of God from which these sayings proceeded, and to the expression of which the words ought to be subservient, gave a different form to some matters in their reproduction of the text, they had no intention of exemplifying anything else than the very thing which we now admiringly contemplate in that kind of harmonious diversity which marks the four evangelists, and in the light of which it is made clear that there is no failure from strict truth, although one historian may give an account of some theme in a manner different indeed from another, and yet not so different as to involve an actual departure from the sense intended by the person with whom he is bound to be in concord and agreement. To understand this is of advantage to character, with a view at once to guard against what is false, and to pronounce correctly upon it ; and it is of no less consequence to faith itself, in the way of precluding the supposition that, as it were with consecrated sounds, truth has a kind of defence provided for it which might imply God's handing over to us not only the thing itself, but likewise the very words which are required for its enunciation ; whereas the fact rather is, that the theme itself which is to be expressed is so decidedly deemed of superior importance to the words in which it has to be expressed,[3] that we would be under no obligation to ask about them at all, if it were possible for us to know the truth without the terms, as God knows it, and as His angels also know it in Him.

CHAP. LXVII. — OF THE EXPULSION OF THE SELLERS AND BUYERS FROM THE TEMPLE, AND OF THE QUESTION AS TO THE HARMONY BETWEEN THE FIRST THREE EVANGELISTS AND JOHN, WHO RELATES THE SAME INCIDENT IN A WIDELY DIFFERENT CONNECTION.

129. Matthew goes on with his narrative in the following terms : " And when He was come into Jerusalem, all the city was moved, saying, Who is this? And the multitude said, This is Jesus, the prophet of Nazareth of Galilee. And Jesus went into the temple of God, and cast out all them that sold and bought in the temple ; " and so on, down to where we read, " But ye have made it a den of thieves." This account of the multitude of sellers who were cast out of the temple is given by all the evangelists ; but John introduces it in a remarkably different order.[4] For, after recording the testimony borne by John the Baptist to Jesus, and mentioning that He went into Galilee at the time when He turned the water into wine, and after he has also noticed the sojourn of a few days in Capharnaum, John proceeds to tell us that He went up to Jerusalem at the season of the Jews' passover, and when He had made a scourge of small cords, drove out of the temple those who were selling in it. This makes it evident that this act was performed by the Lord not on a single occasion, but twice over ; but that only the first instance is put on record by John, and the last by the other three.

CHAP. LXVIII. — OF THE WITHERING OF THE FIG-TREE, AND OF THE QUESTION AS TO THE ABSENCE OF ANY CONTRADICTION BETWEEN MAT-

---

[1] John xii. 14, 15.
[2] [The reference here is to the story of Aristeas, to the effect that the translators, though separated, produced identical versions. Compare translator's remark in Introductory Notice. — R.]

[3] Reading quæ dicenda est, sermonibus per quos dicenda. The Ratisbon edition and twelve MSS. give in both instances dicenda = to be learned, instead of dicenda = to be expressed. See Migne.
[4] Matt. xxi. 10-13; Mark xi. 15-17; Luke xix. 45, 46; John ii. 1-17.

THEW AND THE OTHER EVANGELISTS IN THE ACCOUNTS GIVEN OF THAT INCIDENT, AS WELL AS THE OTHER MATTERS RELATED IN CONNECTION WITH IT ; AND VERY SPECIALLY AS TO THE CONSISTENCY BETWEEN MATTHEW AND MARK IN THE MATTER OF THE ORDER OF NARRATION.

130. Matthew continues thus : " And the blind and the lame came to Him in the temple, and He healed them.   And when the chief priests and scribes saw the wonderful things that He did, and the children crying in the temple, and saying, Hosanna to the Son of David, they were sore displeased, and said unto Him, Hearest thou what these say ?   And Jesus saith unto them, Yea ; have ye never read, Out of the mouth of babes and sucklings Thou hast perfected praise ?   And He left them, and went out of the city into Bethany ; and He lodged there. Now in the morning, as He returned into the city, He hungered.   And when He saw a single [1] fig-tree in the way, He came to it, and found nothing thereon but leaves only, and said unto it, Let no fruit grow on thee henceforward for ever. And presently the fig-tree withered away.   And when the disciples saw it, they marvelled, saying, How soon is the fig-tree withered away !   But Jesus answered and said unto them, Verily I say unto you, If ye have faith, and doubt not, ye shall not only do this which is done to the fig-tree ; but also, if ye shall say unto this mountain, Be thou removed, and be thou cast into the sea, it shall be done.   And all things, whatsoever ye shall ask in prayer, believing, ye shall receive." [2]

131. Mark also records this occurrence in due succession.[3]   He does not, however, follow the same order in his narrative.   For first of all, the fact which is related by Matthew, namely, that Jesus went into the temple, and cast out those who sold and bought there, is not mentioned at that point by Mark.   On the other hand, Mark tells us that He looked round about upon all things, and, when the eventide was now come, went out into Bethany with the twelve.   Next he informs us that on another day,[4] when they were coming from Bethany, He was hungry, and cursed the fig-tree, as Matthew also intimates. Then the said Mark subjoins the statement that He came into Jerusalem, and that, on going into the temple, He cast out those who sold and bought there, as if that incident took place not on the first day specified, but on a different day.[5]   But inasmuch as Matthew puts the connection in these terms, " And He left them, and went out of the city into Bethany," [6] and tells us that it was when returning in the morning into the city that He cursed the tree, it is more reasonable to suppose that he, rather than Mark,

has preserved the strict order of time so far as regards the incident of the expulsion of the sellers and buyers from the temple.   For when he uses the phrase, " And He left them, and went out," who can be understood by those parties whom He is thus said to have left, but those with whom He was previously speaking, — namely, the persons who were so sore displeased because the children cried out, " Hosanna to the Son of David " ?   It follows, then, that Mark has omitted what took place on the first day, when He went into the temple ; and in mentioning that He found nothing on the fig-tree but leaves, he has introduced what He called to mind only there, but what really occurred on the second day, as both evangelists testify.   Then, further, his account bears that the astonishment which the disciples expressed at finding how the fig-tree had withered away, and the reply which the Lord made to them on the subject of faith, and the casting of the mountain into the sea, belonged not to this same second day on which He said to the tree, " No man eat fruit of thee hereafter for ever," but to a third day.   For in connection with the second day, the said Mark has recorded the incident of the casting of the sellers out of the temple, which he had omitted to notice as belonging to the first day.   Accordingly, it is in connection with this second day that he tells us how Jesus went out of the city, when even was come, and how, when they passed by in the morning, the disciples saw the fig-tree dried up from the roots, and how Peter, calling to remembrance, said unto Him, " Master, behold the fig-tree which Thou cursedst is withered away." [7]   Then, too, he informs us that He gave the answer relating to the power of faith.   On the other hand, Matthew recounts these matters in a manner importing that they all took place on this second day ; that is to say, both the word addressed to the tree, " Let no fruit grow on thee from henceforward for ever," and the withering that ensued so speedily in the tree, and the reply which He made on the subject of the power of faith to His disciples when they observed that withering and marvelled at it.   From this we are to understand that Mark, on his side, has recorded in connection with the second day what he had omitted to notice as occurring really on the first, — namely, the incident of the expulsion of the sellers and buyers from the temple.   On the other hand, Matthew, after mentioning what was done on the second day, — namely, the cursing of the fig-tree as He was returning in the morning from Bethany into the city, — has omitted certain facts which Mark has inserted, namely, His coming into the city, and His going out of it in the evening, and the aston-

---

[1] *Unam.*   [2] Matt. xxi. 14-22.   [3] *Consequenter.*
[4] *Alia die.*   [5] Mark xi. 11-17.   [6] Matt. xxi. 17.

[7] Mark xi. 20, 21.

ishment which the disciples expressed at finding the tree dried up as they passed by in the morning; and then to what had taken place on the second day, which was the day on which the tree was cursed, he has attached what really took place on the third day, — namely, the amazement of the disciples at seeing the tree's withered condition, and the declaration which they heard from the Lord on the subject of the power of faith.[1] These several facts Matthew has connected together in such a manner that, were we not compelled to turn our attention to the matter by Mark's narrative, we should be unable to recognise either at what point or with regard to what circumstances the former writer has left anything unrecorded in his narrative. The case therefore stands thus: Matthew first presents the facts conveyed in these words, "And He left them, and went out of the city into Bethany; and He lodged there. Now in the morning, as He returned into the city, He hungered; and when He saw a single fig-tree in the way, He came to it, and found nothing thereon but leaves only, and said unto it, Let no fruit grow on thee henceforward for ever; and presently the fig-tree withered away." Then, omitting the other matters which belonged to that same day, he has immediately subjoined this statement, "And when the disciples saw it, they marvelled, saying, How soon is it withered away!" although it was on another day that they saw this sight, and on another day that they thus marvelled. But it is understood that the tree did not wither at the precise time when they saw it, but presently when it was cursed. For what they saw was not the tree in the process of drying up, but the tree already dried completely up; and thus they learned that it had withered away immediately on the Lord's sentence.

CHAP. LXIX. — OF THE HARMONY BETWEEN THE FIRST THREE EVANGELISTS IN THEIR ACCOUNTS OF THE OCCASION ON WHICH THE JEWS ASKED THE LORD BY WHAT AUTHORITY HE DID THESE THINGS.

132. Matthew continues his narrative in the following terms: "And when He was come into the temple, the chief priests and the elders of the people came unto Him as He was teaching, and said, By what authority doest thou these things? and who gave thee this authority? And Jesus answered and said unto them, I also will ask you one thing, which if ye tell me, I in like wise will tell you by what authority I do these things. The baptism of John, whence was it?" and so on, down to the words, "Neither tell I you by what authority I do these things."[2] The other two, Mark and Luke, have also set forth this whole passage, and that, too, in almost as many words.[3] Neither does there appear to be any discrepancy between them in regard to the order, the only exception being found in the circumstance of which I have spoken above, — namely, that Matthew omits certain matters belonging to a different day, and has constructed his narrative with a connection which, were our attention not called [otherwise] to the fact, might lead to the supposition that he was still treating of the second day, where Mark deals with the third. Moreover, Luke has not appended his notice of this incident, as if he meant to go over the days in orderly succession; but after recording the expulsion of the sellers and buyers from the temple, he has passed by without notice all that is contained in the statements above — His going out into Bethany, and His returning to the city, and what was done to the fig-tree, and the reply touching the power of faith which was made to the disciples when they marvelled. And then, after all these omissions, he has introduced the next section of his narrative in these terms: "And He taught daily in the temple. But the chief priests, and the scribes, and the chief of the people sought to destroy Him; and could not find what they might do: for all the people were very attentive to hear Him. And it came to pass, that on one of these days, as He taught the people in the temple, and preached the gospel, the chief priests and the scribes came upon Him with the elders, and spake unto Him, saying, Tell us, by what authority doest thou these things?" and so on; all which the other two evangelists record in like manner. From this it is apparent that he is in no antagonism with the others, even with regard to the order; since what he states to have taken place "on one of those days," may be understood to belong to that particular day on which they also have reported it to have occurred.[4]

CHAP. LXX. — OF THE TWO SONS WHO WERE COMMANDED BY THEIR FATHER TO GO INTO HIS VINEYARD, AND OF THE VINEYARD WHICH WAS LET OUT TO OTHER HUSBANDMEN; OF THE QUESTION CONCERNING THE CONSISTENCY OF MATTHEW'S VERSION OF THESE PASSAGES WITH THOSE GIVEN BY THE OTHER TWO EVANGELISTS, WITH WHOM HE RETAINS THE SAME ORDER; AS ALSO, IN PARTICULAR, CONCERNING THE HARMONY OF HIS VERSION OF THE PARABLE, WHICH IS RECORDED BY ALL THE THREE, REGARDING THE VINEYARD THAT WAS LET OUT; AND IN

---

[1] [The explanation of Augustin is still accepted by many. But the order of Mark may be followed without any difficulty. The long discourses occurred on the third day, and the blasted condition of the fig-tree was first noticed on the morning of that day: these are the main points. — R.]

[2] Matt. xxi. 23-27.　　[3] Mark xi. 27-33; Luke xix. 47-xx. 8.
[4] [The order of occurrences during this day of public controversy in the temple presents few difficulties. It was probably the Tuesday of Passion Week. The day of the month is in dispute because of the still mooted question, whether our Lord ate the last passover at the regular time or one day earlier. — R.]

REFERENCE SPECIALLY TO THE REPLY MADE BY THE PERSONS TO WHOM THAT PARABLE WAS SPOKEN, IN RELATING WHICH MATTHEW SEEMS TO DIFFER SOMEWHAT FROM THE OTHERS.

133. Matthew goes on thus : " But what think ye ? A certain man had two sons ; and he came to the first, and said, Son, go work to-day in my vineyard. But he answered and said, I will not ; but afterward he repented, and went. And he came to the second, and said likewise. And he answered and said, I go, sir ; and went not ; " and so on, down to the words, " And whosoever shall fall upon this stone shall be broken ; but on whomsoever it shall fall, it will grind him to powder." [1] Mark and Luke do not mention the parable of the two sons to whom the order was given to go and labour in the vineyard. But what is narrated by Matthew subsequently to that, — namely, the parable of the vineyard which was let out to the husbandmen, who persecuted the servants that were sent to them, and afterwards put to death the beloved son, and thrust him out of the vineyard, — is not left unrecorded also by those two. And in detailing it they likewise both retain the same order, that is to say, they bring it in after that declaration of their inability to tell which was made by the Jews when interrogated regarding the baptism of John, and after the reply which He returned to them in these words : " Neither do I tell you by what authority I do these things." [2]

134. Now no question implying any contradiction between these accounts rises here, unless it be raised by the circumstance that Matthew, after telling us how the Lord addressed to the Jews this interrogation, " When the lord, therefore, of the vineyard cometh, what will he do unto those husbandmen ? " adds, that they answered and said, " He will miserably destroy those wicked men, and will let out his vineyard unto other husbandmen, which shall render him the fruits in their seasons." For Mark does not record these last words as if they constituted the reply returned by the men ; but he introduces them as if they were really spoken by the Lord immediately after the question which was put by Him, so that in a certain way He answered Himself. For [in this Gospel] He speaks thus : " What shall therefore the lord of the vineyard do ? he will come and destroy the husbandmen, and will give the vineyard unto others." But it is quite easy for us to suppose, either that the men's words are subjoined here without the insertion of the explanatory clause " they said," or " they replied," that being left to be understood ; or else that the said response is ascribed to the Lord Himself rather than to

these men, because when they answered with such truth, He also, who is Himself the Truth, really gave the same reply in reference to the persons in question.

135. More serious difficulty, however, may be created by the fact that Luke not only does not speak of them as the parties who made that answer (for he, as well as Mark, attributes these words to the Lord), but even represents them to have given a contrary reply, and to have said, " God forbid." For his narrative proceeds in these terms : " What therefore shall the lord of the vineyard do unto them ? He shall come and destroy these husbandmen, and shall give the vineyard to others. And when they heard it, they said, God forbid. And He beheld them, and said, What is this then that is written, The stone which the builders rejected, the same is become the head of the corner ? " [3] How then is it that, according to Matthew's version, the men to whom He spake these words said, " He will miserably destroy those wicked men, and will let out this vineyard unto other husbandmen, which shall render him the fruits in their seasons ; " whereas, according to Luke, they gave a reply inconsistent with any terms like these, when they said, " God forbid " ? And, in truth, what the Lord proceeds immediately to say regarding the stone which was rejected by the builders, and yet was made the head of the corner, is introduced in a manner implying that by this testimony those were confuted who were gainsaying the real meaning of the parable. For Matthew, no less than Luke, records that passage as if it were intended to meet the gainsayers, when he says, " Did ye never read in the scriptures, The stone which the builders rejected, the same is become the head of the corner ? " For what is implied by this question, " Did ye never read," but that the answer which they had given was opposed to the real intention [of the parable] ? This is also indicated by Mark, who gives these same words in the following manner : " And have ye not read this scripture, The stone which the builders rejected is become the head of the corner ? " This sentence, therefore, appears to occupy in Luke, rather than the others, the place which is properly assignable to it as originally uttered. For it is brought in by him directly after the contradiction expressed by those men when they said, " God forbid." And the form in which it is cast by him, — namely, " What is this then that is written, The stone which the builders rejected, the same is become the head of the corner ? " — is equivalent in sense to the other modes of statement. For the real meaning of the sentence is indicated equally well, whichever of the three phrases is used,

---

[1] Matt. xxi. 28-44.   [2] Mark xii. 1-11; Luke xx. 9-18.   [3] Luke xx. 15-17.

"Did ye never read?" or, "And have ye not read?" or, "What is this, then, that is written?"

136. It remains, therefore, for us to understand that among the people who were listening on that occasion, there were some who replied in the terms related by Matthew, when he writes thus: "They say unto Him, He will miserably destroy those wicked men, and will let out his vineyard unto other husbandmen;" and that there were also some who answered in the way indicated by Luke, that is to say, with the words, "God forbid." Accordingly, those persons who had replied to the Lord to the former effect, were replied to by these other individuals in the crowd with the explanation, "God forbid." But the answer which was really given by the first of these two parties, to whom the second said in return, "God forbid," has been ascribed both by Mark and by Luke to the Lord Himself, on the ground that, as I have already intimated, the Truth Himself spake by these men, whether as by persons who knew not that they were wicked, in the same way that He spake also by Caiaphas, who when he was high priest prophesied without realizing what he said,[1] or as by persons who did understand, and who had come by this time both to knowledge and to belief. For there was also present on this occasion that multitude of people at whose hand the prophecy had already received a fulfilment, when they met Him in a mighty concourse on His approach, and hailed Him with the acclaim, "Blessed is He that cometh in the name of the Lord."[2]

137. Neither should we stumble at the circumstance that the same Matthew has stated that the chief priests and the elders of the people came to the Lord, and asked Him by what authority He did these things, and who gave Him this authority, on the occasion when He to, in turn, interrogated them concerning the baptism of John, inquiring whence it was, whether from heaven or of men; to whom also, on their replying that they did not know, He said, "Neither do I tell you by what authority I do those things." For he has followed up this with the words introduced in the immediate context, "But what think ye? A certain man had two sons," and so forth. Thus this discourse is brought into a connection which is continued, uninterrupted by the interposition either of any thing or of any person, down to what is related regarding the vineyard which was let out to the husbandmen. It may, indeed, be supposed that He spake all these words to the chief priests and the elders of the people, by whom He had been interrogated with regard to His authority. But then, if these persons had indeed questioned Him with a view to tempt Him, and with a hostile intention, they could not be taken for men who had believed, and who cited the remarkable testimony in favour of the Lord which was taken from a prophet; and surely it is only if they had the character of those who believed, and not of those who were ignorant, that they could have given a reply like this: "He will miserably destroy those wicked men, and will let out his vineyard to other husbandmen." This peculiarity [of Matthew's account], however, should not by any means so perplex us as to lead us to imagine that there were none who believed among the multitudes who listened at this time to the Lord's parables. For it is only for the sake of brevity that the same Matthew has passed over in silence what Luke does not fail to mention, — namely, the fact that the said parable was not spoken only to the parties who had interrogated Him on the subject of His authority, but to the people. For the latter evangelist puts it thus: "Then began He to speak to the people this parable; A certain man planted a vineyard," and so on. Accordingly, we may well understand that among the people then assembled there might also have been persons who could listen to Him as those did who before this had said, "Blessed is He that cometh in the name of the Lord;" and that either these, or some of them, were the individuals who replied in the words, "He will miserably destroy these wicked men, and will let out his vineyard to other husbandmen." The answer actually returned by these men, moreover, has been attributed to the Lord Himself by Mark and Luke, not only because their words were really His words, inasmuch[3] as He is the Truth that ofttimes speaks even by the wicked and the ignorant, moving the mind of man by a certain hidden instinct, not in the merit of man's holiness, but by the right of His own proper power; but also because the men may have been of a character admitting of their being reckoned, not without reason, as already members in the true body of Christ, so that what was said by them might quite warrantably be ascribed to Him whose members they were. For by this time He had baptized more than John,[4] and had multitudes of disciples, as the same evangelists repeatedly testify; and from among these followers He also drew those five hundred brethren, to whom the Apostle Paul tells us that He showed Himself after His resurrection.[5] And this explanation of the matter is supported by the fact that the phrase which occurs in the version by this same Matthew, — namely, "They say unto Him,[6] He will miserably destroy those wicked men," — is not put in a form necessitating us to take the pronoun *illi* in the plural number, as

---

[1] John xi. 49-51. [2] Ps. cxviii. 26; Matt. xxi. 9.

[3] Keeping *quia veritas est*, for which the reading *qui veritas est* = "who is the truth," also occurs.
[4] John iv. 1.   [5] 1 Cor. xv. 6.   [6] *Aiunt illi.*

if it was intended to mark out the words expressly as the reply made by the persons who had
craftily questioned Him on the subject of His
authority; but the clause, "They say unto Him,"[1]
is so expressed that the term *illi* should be
taken for the singular pronoun, and not the
plural, and should be held to signify "unto
Him," that is to say, unto the Lord Himself, as
is made clear in the Greek codices,[2] without a
single atom of ambiguity.

138. There is a certain discourse of the Lord
which is given by the evangelist John, and which
may help us more readily to understand the
statement I thus make. It is to this effect:
"Then said Jesus to those Jews which believed
on Him, If ye continue in my word, then ye shall
be my disciples indeed; and ye shall know the
truth, and the truth shall make you free. And
they answered Him, We be Abraham's seed, and
were never in bondage to any man: how sayest
thou, Ye shall be free?[3] Jesus answered them,
Verily, verily, I say unto you, Whosoever committeth sin is the servant of sin. And the servant abideth not in the house for ever; but
the Son abideth for ever. If the Son, therefore, shall make you free, ye shall be free
indeed. I know that ye are Abraham's seed;
but ye seek to kill me, because my word hath
no place in you."[4] Now surely it is not to be
supposed that He spake these words, "Ye seek
to kill me," to those persons who had already
believed on Him, and to whom He had said,
"If ye abide in my word, then shall ye be
my disciples indeed." But inasmuch as He had
spoken in these latter terms to the men who had
already believed on Him, and as, moreover,
there was present on that occasion a multitude
of people, among whom there were many who
were hostile to Him, even although the evangelist does not tell us explicitly who those parties
were who made the reply referred to, the very
nature of the answer which they gave, and the
tenor of the words which thereupon were rightly
directed to them by Him, make it sufficiently
clear what specific persons were then addressed,
and what words were spoken to them in particular. Precisely, therefore, as in the multitude
thus alluded to by John there were some who
had already believed on Jesus, and also some
who sought to kill Him, in that other concourse
which we are discussing at present there were
some who had craftily questioned the Lord on
the subject of the authority by which He did
these things; and there were also others who had
hailed Him, not in deceit, but in faith, with
the acclaim, "Blessed is He that cometh in the
name of the Lord." And thus, too, there were

persons present who could say, "He will destroy
those men, and will give his vineyard to others."
This saying, furthermore, may be rightly understood to have been the voice of the Lord Himself, either in virtue of that Truth which in His
own Person He is Himself, or on the ground of
the unity which subsists between the members
of His body and the head. There were also
certain individuals present who, when these
other parties gave that kind of answer, said to
them, "God forbid," because they understood
the parable to be directed against themselves.

CHAP. LXXI. — OF THE MARRIAGE OF THE KING'S
SON, TO WHICH THE MULTITUDES WERE INVITED;
AND OF THE ORDER IN WHICH MATTHEW IN-
TRODUCES THAT SECTION AS COMPARED WITH
LUKE, WHO GIVES US A SOMEWHAT SIMILAR
NARRATIVE IN ANOTHER CONNECTION.

139. Matthew goes on as follows: "And when
the chief priests and Pharisees had heard His
parables, they perceived that He spake of them:
and when they sought to lay hands on Him, they
feared the multitude, because they took Him for
a prophet. And Jesus answered and spake unto
them again by parables, and said, The kingdom
of heaven is like unto a certain king which made
a marriage for his son, and sent forth his servants
to call them that were bidden to the wedding,
and they would not come;" and so on, down to
the words, "For many are called, but few are
chosen."[5] This parable concerning the guests
who were invited to the wedding is related only
by Matthew. Luke also records something
which resembles it. But that is really a different
passage, as the order itself sufficiently indicates,
although there is some similarity between the
two.[6] The matters introduced, however, by
Matthew immediately after the parable concerning the vineyard, and the killing of the son of
the head of the house, — namely, the Jews' perception that this whole discourse was directed
against them, and their beginning to contrive
treacherous schemes against Him, — are attested
likewise by Mark and Luke, who also keep the
same order in inserting them.[7] But after this
paragraph they proceed to another subject, and
immediately subjoin a passage which Matthew
has also indeed introduced in due order, but
only subsequently to this parable of the marriage,
which he alone has put on record here.

CHAP. LXXII. — OF THE HARMONY CHARACTERIZ-
ING THE NARRATIVES GIVEN BY THESE THREE
EVANGELISTS REGARDING THE DUTY OF RENDER-
ING TO CÆSAR THE COIN BEARING HIS IMAGE,
AND REGARDING THE WOMAN WHO HAD BEEN
MARRIED TO THE SEVEN BROTHERS.

140. Matthew then continues in these terms:

---

[1] *Aiunt illi.*
[2] That is to say, the *aiunt illi* is the rendering for λέγουσιν
αὐτῷ. [This reading of the Greek text is abundantly attested. — R.]
[3] *Liberi eritis.*   [4] John viii. 31-37.

[5] Matt. xxi. 45–xxii. 14.   [6] Luke xiv. 16-24.
[7] Mark xii. 12; Luke xx. 19.

"Then went the Pharisees, and took counsel how they might entangle Him in His talk. And they send out unto Him their disciples, with the Herodians, saying, Master, we know that thou art true, and teachest the way of God in truth, neither carest thou for any man; for thou regardest not the person of men: tell us therefore, What thinkest thou? Is it lawful to give tribute to Cæsar, or not?" and so on, down to the words, "And when the multitude heard this, they were astonished at His doctrine."[1] Mark and Luke give a similar account of these two replies made by the Lord, — namely, the one on the subject of the coin, which was prompted by the question as to the duty of giving tribute to Cæsar; and the other on the subject of the resurrection, which was suggested by the case of the woman who had married the seven brothers in succession. Neither do these two evangelists differ in the matter of the order.[2] For after the parable which told of the men to whom the vineyard was let out, and which also dealt with the Jews (against whom it was directed), and the evil counsel they were devising (which sections are given by all three evangelists together), these two, Mark and Luke, pass over the parable of the guests who were invited to the wedding (which only Matthew has introduced), and thereafter they join company again with the first evangelist, when they record these two passages which deal with Cæsar's tribute, and the woman who was the wife of seven different husbands, inserting them in precisely the same order, with a consistency which admits of no question.

CHAP. LXXIII. — OF THE PERSON TO WHOM THE TWO PRECEPTS CONCERNING THE LOVE OF GOD AND THE LOVE OF OUR NEIGHBOUR WERE COMMENDED; AND OF THE QUESTION AS TO THE ORDER OF NARRATION WHICH IS OBSERVED BY MATTHEW AND MARK, AND THE ABSENCE OF ANY DISCREPANCY BETWEEN THEM AND LUKE.

141. Matthew then proceeds with his narrative in the following terms: "But when the Pharisees had heard that He had put the Sadducees to silence, they were gathered together. And one of them, which was a lawyer, asked Him a question, tempting Him, and saying, Master, which is the great commandment in the law? Jesus said unto him, Thou shalt love the Lord thy God with all thy heart, and with all thy soul, and with all thy mind. This is the first and great commandment. And the second is like unto it, Thou shalt love thy neighbour as thyself. On these two commandments hang all the law and the prophets."[3] This is recorded also by Mark, and that too in the same order. Neither should there be any difficulty in the statement made by Matthew, to the effect that the person by whom the question was put to the Lord tempted Him; whereas Mark[4] says nothing about that, but tells us at the end of the paragraph how the Lord said to the man, as to one who answered discreetly, "Thou art not far from the kingdom of God." For it is quite possible that, although the man approached Him with the view of tempting Him, he may have been set right by the Lord's response. Or we need not at any rate take the tempting referred to in a bad sense, as if it were the device of one who sought to deceive an adversary; but we may rather suppose it to have been the result of caution, as if it were the act of one who wished to have further trial of a person who was unknown to him. For it is not without a good purpose that this sentence has been written, "He that is hasty to give credit is light-minded, and shall be impaired."[5]

142. Luke, on the other hand, not indeed in this order, but in a widely different connection, introduces something which resembles this.[6] But whether in that passage he is actually recording this same incident, or whether the person with whom the Lord [is represented to have] dealt in a similar manner there on the subject of those two commandments is quite another individual, is altogether uncertain. At the same time, it may appear right to regard the person who is introduced by Luke as a different individual from the one before us here, not only on the ground of the remarkable divergence in the order of narration, but also because he is there reported to have replied to a question which was addressed to him by the Lord, and in that reply to have himself mentioned those two precepts. The same opinion is further confirmed by the fact that, after telling us how the Lord said to him, "This do, and thou shalt live," — thus instructing him to do that great thing which, according to his own answer, was contained in the law, — the evangelist follows up what had passed with the statement, "But he, willing to justify himself, said unto Jesus, And who is my neighbour?"[7] Thereupon, too [according to Luke], the Lord told the story of the man who was going down from Jerusalem to Jericho, and fell among robbers. Consequently, considering that this individual is described at the outset as tempting Christ, and is represented to have repeated the two commandments in his reply; and considering, further, that after the counsel which was given by the Lord in the words, "This do, and thou shalt live," he is not commended as good, but, on the contrary, has this said of him, "But he, willing to justify himself," etc., whereas the

---

[1] Matt. xxii. 15-33.
[2] Mark xii. 13-27; Luke xx. 20-40. [3] Matt. xxii. 34-40.

[4] Another but evidently faulty reading is sometimes found here, — namely, *Lucas autem hoc tacet et in fine Marcus*, etc. = whereas Luke says nothing about that, and Mark tells us, etc.
[5] *Minorabitur.* Ecclus. xix. 4. [6] Luke x. 25-37.
[7] Luke x. 29.

person who is mentioned in parallel order both by Mark and by Luke received a commendation so marked, that the Lord spake to him in these terms, " Thou art not far from the kingdom of God," — the more probable view is that which takes the person who appears on that occasion to be a different individual from the man who comes before us here.

CHAP. LXXIV. — OF THE PASSAGE IN WHICH THE JEWS ARE ASKED TO SAY WHOSE SON THEY SUP- POSE CHRIST TO BE ; AND OF THE QUESTION WHETHER THERE IS NOT A DISCREPANCY BE- TWEEN MATTHEW AND THE OTHER TWO EVAN- GELISTS, IN SO FAR AS HE STATES THE INQUIRY TO HAVE BEEN, " WHAT THINK YE OF CHRIST ? WHOSE SON IS HE ? " AND TELLS US THAT TO THIS THEY REPLIED, " THE SON OF DAVID ; " WHEREAS THE OTHERS PUT IT THUS, " HOW SAY THE SCRIBES THAT CHRIST IS DAVID'S SON ? "

143. Matthew goes on thus : " Now when the Pharisees were gathered together, Jesus asked them, saying, What think ye of Christ? Whose son is He? They say unto Him, The son of David. He saith unto them, How then doth David in Spirit call Him Lord, saying, The Lord said unto my Lord, Sit Thou on my right hand, till I make Thine enemies Thy footstool? If David then call Him Lord, how is He his son? And no man was able to answer Him a word, neither durst any man from that day forth ask Him any more questions." [1]   This is given also by Mark in due course, and in the same order. [2] Luke, again, only omits mention of the person who asked the Lord which was the first com- mandment in the law, and, after passing over that incident in silence, observes the same order once more as the others, narrating just as these do this question which the Lord put to the Jews concerning Christ, as to how He was David's son. [3]   Neither is the sense at all affected by the circumstance that, as Matthew puts it, when Jesus had asked them what they thought of Christ, and whose son He was, they [the Phari- sees] replied, " The son of David," and then He proposed the further query as to how David then called Him Lord ; whereas, according to the version presented by the other two, Mark and Luke, we do not find either that these persons were directly interrogated, or that they made any answer.   For we ought to take this view of the matter, namely, that these two evangelists have introduced the sentiments which were expressed by the Lord Himself after the reply made by those parties, and have recorded the terms in which He spoke in the hearing of those whom He wished profitably to instruct in His authority, and to turn away from the teaching of the scribes,

and whose knowledge of Christ amounted then only to this, that He was made of the seed of David according to the flesh, while they did not understand that He was God, and on that ground also the Lord even of David.   It is in this way, therefore, that in the accounts given by these two evangelists, the Lord is mentioned in a manner which makes it appear as if He was discoursing on the subject of these erroneous teachers to men whom He desired to see delivered from the errors in which these scribes were involved. Thus, too, the question, which is presented by Matthew in the form, " What say ye ? " is to be taken not as addressed directly to these [Phari- sees], but rather as expressed only with refer- ence to those parties, and directed really to the persons whom He was desirous of instructing.

CHAP. LXXV. — OF THE PHARISEES WHO SIT IN THE SEAT OF MOSES, AND ENJOIN THINGS WHICH THEY DO NOT, AND OF THE OTHER WORDS SPOKEN BY THE LORD AGAINST THESE SAME PHARISEES ; OF THE QUESTION WHETHER MAT- THEW'S NARRATIVE AGREES HERE WITH THOSE WHICH ARE GIVEN BY THE OTHER TWO EVANGEL- ISTS, AND IN PARTICULAR WITH THAT OF LUKE, WHO INTRODUCES A PASSAGE RESEMBLING THIS ONE, ALTHOUGH IT IS BROUGHT IN NOT IN THIS ORDER, BUT IN ANOTHER CONNECTION.

144. Matthew proceeds with his account, ob- serving the following order of narration : " Then spake Jesus to the multitude, and to His dis- ciples, saying, The scribes and the Pharisees sit in Moses' seat : all, therefore, whatsoever they bid you observe, that observe and do ; but do not ye after their works : for they say, and do not ; " and so on, down to the words, " Ye shall not see me henceforth, till ye shall say, Blessed is He that cometh in the name of the Lord." [4] Luke also mentions a similar discourse which was spoken by the Lord in opposition to the Pharisees and the scribes and the doctors of the law, but reports it as delivered in the house of a certain Pharisee, who had invited Him to a feast.   In order to relate that passage, he has made a digression from the order which is fol- lowed by Matthew, about the point at which they have both put on record the Lord's sayings respecting the sign of the three days and nights in the history of Jonas, and the queen of the south, and the unclean spirit that returns and finds the house swept. [5]   And that paragraph is followed up by Matthew with these words : " While He yet talked to the people, behold, His mother and His brethren stood without, desiring to speak with Him."   But in the version which the third Gospel presents of the discourse then spoken by the Lord, after the recital of certain

---

[1] Matt. xxii. 41–46.   [2] Mark xii. 35–37.
[3] Luke xx. 41–44.

[4] Matt. xxiii.   [5] Matt. xii. 39–46.

sayings of the Lord which Matthew has omitted to notice, Luke turns off from the order which he had been observing in concert with Matthew, so that his immediately subsequent narrative runs thus : "And as He spake, a certain Pharisee besought Him to dine with him : and He went in, and sat down to meat. And when the Pharisee saw it, he marvelled that He had not first washed before dinner. And the Lord said unto him, Now do ye Pharisees make clean the outside of the cup and platter." ¹ And after this, Luke reports other utterances which were directed against the said Pharisees and scribes and teachers of the law, which are of a similar tenor to those which Matthew also recounts in this passage which we have taken in hand at present to consider.² Wherefore, although Matthew records these things in a manner which, while it is true indeed that the house of that Pharisee is not mentioned by name, yet does not specify as the scene where the words were spoken any place entirely inconsistent with the idea of His having been in the house referred to ; still the facts that the Lord by this time [*i.e.* according to Matthew's Gospel] had left Galilee and come into Jerusalem, and that the incidents alluded to above, on to the discourse which is now under review,³ are so arranged in the context after His arrival as to make it only reasonable to understand them to have taken place in Jerusalem, whereas Luke's narrative deals with what occurred at the time when the Lord as yet was only journeying towards Jerusalem, are considerations which lead me to the conclusion that these are not the same, but only two similar discourses, of which the former evangelist has reported the one, and the latter the other.

145. This is also a matter which requires some consideration, — namely, the question how it is said here, "Ye shall not see me henceforth, till ye shall say, Blessed is He that cometh in the name of the Lord," ⁴ when, according to this same Matthew, they had already expressed themselves to this effect.⁵ Besides, Luke likewise tells us that a reply containing these very words had previously been returned by the Lord to the persons who had counselled Him to leave their locality, because Herod sought to kill Him. That evangelist represents these self-same terms, which Matthew records here, to have been employed by Him in the declaration which He directed on that occasion against Jerusalem itself. For Luke's narrative proceeds in the following manner : "The same day there came certain of the Pharisees, saying unto Him, Get thee out, and depart hence : for Herod will kill thee. And He said unto them, Go ye and tell that fox, Behold, I cast out devils,

and I do cures to-day and to-morrow, and the third day I am perfected. Nevertheless, I must walk to-day, and to-morrow, and the day following ; for it cannot be that a prophet perish out of Jerusalem. O Jerusalem, Jerusalem, which killest the prophets, and stonest them that are sent unto thee ; how often would I have gathered thy children together, as a hen doth gather her brood under her wings, and ye would not ! Behold, your house shall be left unto you desolate : and I say unto you, that ye shall not see me until the time come when ye shall say, Blessed is He that cometh in the name of the Lord." ⁶ There does not seem, however, to be anything contradictory to the narration thus given by Luke in the circumstance that the multitudes said, when the Lord was approaching Jerusalem, "Blessed is He that cometh in the name of the Lord." For, according to the order which is followed by Luke, He had not yet come to the scene in question, and the words had not been uttered. But since he does not tell us that He did actually leave the place at that time, not to return to it until the period came when such words would be spoken by them (for He continues on His journey until he arrives at Jerusalem ; and the saying, "Behold, I cast out devils, and I do cures to-day and to-morrow, and the third day I am perfected," is to be taken to have been uttered by Him in a mystical and figurative sense : for certainly He did not suffer at a time answering literally to the third day after the present occasion ; nay, He immediately goes on to say, "Nevertheless, I must walk to-day, and to-morrow, and the day following"), we are indeed constrained also to put a mystical interpretation upon the sentence, "Ye shall not see me henceforth, until the time come when ye shall say, Blessed is He that cometh in the name of the Lord," and to understand it to refer to that advent of His in which He is to come in His effulgent brightness ;⁷ it being thereby also implied, that what He expressed in the declaration, "I cast out devils, and I do cures to-day and to-morrow, and the third day I am perfected," bears upon His body, which is the Church. For devils are cast out when the nations abandon their ancestral superstitions and believe on Him ; and cures are wrought when men renounce the devil and this world, and live in accordance with His commandments, even unto the consummation of the resurrection, in which there shall, as it were, be realized that perfecting on the third day ; that is to say, the Church shall be perfected up to the measure of the angelic fulness through the realized immortality of the body as well as the soul. Therefore the order followed by Matthew is by no means

¹ Luke xi. 29-39.   ² Luke xi. 40-52.   ³ In Matt. xxiii.
⁴ Matt. xxiii. 39.   ⁵ Matt. xxi. 9.   ⁶ Luke xiii 31-35.   ⁷ *In claritate.*

to be understood to involve a digression to another connection. But we are rather to suppose, either that Luke has antedated the events which took place in Jerusalem, and has introduced them at this point simply as they were here suggested to his recollection, before his narrative really brings the Lord to Jerusalem; or that the Lord, when drawing near the same city on that occasion, did actually reply to the persons who counselled Him to be on His guard against Herod, in terms resembling those in which Matthew represents Him to have spoken also to the multitudes at a period when He had already arrived in Jerusalem, and when all these events had taken place which have been detailed above.

CHAP. LXXVI. — OF THE HARMONY IN RESPECT OF THE ORDER OF NARRATION SUBSISTING BETWEEN MATTHEW AND THE OTHER TWO EVANGELISTS IN THE ACCOUNTS GIVEN OF THE OCCASION ON WHICH HE FORETOLD THE DESTRUCTION OF THE TEMPLE.

146. Matthew proceeds with his history in the following terms: "And Jesus went out and departed from the temple; and His disciples came to Him for to show Him the buildings of the temple. And Jesus said unto them, See ye all these things? Verily I say unto you, There shall not be left here one stone upon another which shall not be thrown down."[1] This incident is related also by Mark, and nearly in the same order. But he brings it in after a digression of some small extent, which is made with a view to mention the case of the widow who put the two mites into the treasury,[2] which occurrence is recorded only by Mark and Luke. For [in proof that Mark's order is essentially the same as Matthew's, we need only notice that] in Mark's version also, after the account of the Lord's discussion with the Jews on the occasion when He asked them how they held Christ to be David's son, we have a narrative of what He said in warning them against the Pharisees and their hypocrisy, — a section which Matthew has presented on the amplest scale, introducing into it a larger number of the Lord's sayings on that occasion. Then after this paragraph, which has been handled briefly by Mark, and treated with great fulness by Matthew, Mark, as I have said, introduces the passage about the widow who was at once so extremely poor, and yet abounded so remarkably. And finally, without interpolating anything else, he subjoins a section in which he comes again into unison with Matthew, — namely, that relating to the

destruction of the temple. In like manner, Luke first states the question which was propounded regarding Christ, as to how He was the son of David, and then mentions a few of the words which were spoken in cautioning them against the hypocrisy of the Pharisees. Thereafter he proceeds, as Mark does, to tell the story of the widow who cast the two mites into the treasury. And finally he appends the statement,[3] which appears also in Matthew and Mark, on the subject of the destined overthrow of the temple.[4]

CHAP. LXXVII. — OF THE HARMONY SUBSISTING BETWEEN THE THREE EVANGELISTS IN THEIR NARRATIVES OF THE DISCOURSE WHICH HE DELIVERED ON THE MOUNT OF OLIVES, WHEN THE DISCIPLES ASKED WHEN THE CONSUMMATION SHOULD HAPPEN.

147. Matthew continues in the following strain: "And as He sat upon the mount of Olives, the disciples came unto Him privately, saying, Tell us, when shall these things be? and what shall be the sign of Thy coming, and of the end of the world? And Jesus answered, and said unto them, Take heed that no man deceive you: for many shall come in my name, saying, I am Christ; and shall deceive many;" and so on, down to where we read, "And these shall go away into everlasting punishment, but the righteous into life eternal." We have now, therefore, to examine this lengthened discourse as it meets us in the three evangelists, Matthew, Mark, and Luke. For they all introduce it in their narratives, and that, too, in the same order.[5] Here, as elsewhere, each of these writers gives some matters which are peculiar to himself, in which, nevertheless, we have not to apprehend any suspicion of inconsistency. But what we have to make sure of is the proof that, in those passages which are exact parallels, they are nowhere to be regarded as in antagonism with each other. For if anything bearing the appearance of a contradiction meets us here, the simple affirmation that it is something wholly distinct, and uttered by the Lord in similar terms indeed, but on a totally different occasion, cannot be deemed a legitimate mode of explanation in a case like this, where the narrative, as given by all the three evangelists, moves in the same connection at once of subjects and of dates. Moreover, the mere fact that the writers do not all observe the same order in the reports which they give of the same sentiments expressed by the Lord, certainly does not in any way affect either the understanding or the communication

---

[1] Matt. xxiv. 1, 2. According to Migne, certain codices add here the clause, "when the disciples were asking the Lord privately what was the sign of His coming."
[2] Mark xii. 41–xiii. 2.

[3] Luke xx. 16–xxi. 6.
[4] [Many harmonists insert at this point the events narrated in John xii. 20–50. Augustin does not express an opinion in regard to this passage. — R.]
[5] Matt. xxiv. 3–xxv. 46; Mark xiii. 4–37; Luke xxi. 7–36.

of the subject itself, provided the matters which are represented by them to have been spoken by Him are not inconsistent the one with the other.

148. Again, what Matthew states in this form, "And this gospel of the kingdom shall be preached in all the world for a witness unto all nations, and then shall the end come,"[1] is given also in the same connection by Mark in the following manner: "And the gospel must first be published among all nations."[2] Mark has not added the words, "and then shall the end come;" but he indicates what they express, when he uses the phrase "first" in the sentence, "And the gospel must first be published among all nations." For they had asked Him about the end. And therefore, when He addresses them thus, "The gospel must first be published among all nations," the term "first" clearly suggests the idea of something to be done before the consummation should come.

149. In like manner, what Matthew states thus, "When ye therefore shall see the abomination of desolation, spoken of by Daniel the prophet, stand in the holy place, whoso readeth, let him understand,"[3] is put in the following form by Mark: "But when ye shall see the abomination of desolation standing where it ought not, let him that readeth understand."[4] But though the phrase is thus altered, the sense conveyed is the same. For the point of the clause "where it ought not," is that the abomination of desolation ought not to be in the holy place. Luke's method of putting it, again, is neither, "And when ye shall see the abomination of desolation stand in the holy place," nor, "where it ought not," but, "And when ye shall see Jerusalem compassed with an army, then know that the desolation thereof is nigh."[5] At that time, therefore, will the abomination of desolation be in the holy place.

150. Again, what is given by Matthew in the following terms: "Then let them which be in Judæa flee into the mountains; and let him which is on the house-top not come down to take anything out of his house; neither let him which is in the field return back to take his clothes,"[6] is reported also by Mark almost in so many words. On the other hand, Luke's version proceeds thus: "Then let them which are in Judæa flee to the mountains."[7] Thus far he agrees with the other two. But he presents what is subsequent to that in a different form. For he goes on to say, "And let them which

are in the midst of it depart out; and let not them that are in the countries enter thereinto: for these be the days of vengeance, that all things which are written may be fulfilled." Now these statements seem to present differences enough between each other. For the one, as it occurs in the first two evangelists, runs thus: "Let him which is on the house-top not come down to take anything out of his house;" whereas what is given by the third evangelist is to this effect: "And let them which are in the midst of it depart out." The import, however, may be, that in the great agitation which will arise in the face of so mighty an impending peril, those shut up in the state of siege (which is expressed by the phrase, "they which are in the midst of it") will appear upon the house-top [or "wall"], amazed and anxious to see what terror hangs over them, or what method of escape may open. Still the question rises, How does this third evangelist say here, "let them depart out," when he has already used these terms: "And when ye shall see Jerusalem compassed with an army"? For what is brought in after this—namely, the sentence, "And let not them that are in the countries enter thereinto"—appears to form part of one consistent admonition; and we can perceive how those who are outside the city are not to enter into it; but the difficulty is to see how those who are in the midst of it are to depart out, when the city is already compassed with an army. Well, may not this expression, "in the midst of it," indicate a time when the danger will be so urgent as to leave no opportunity open, so far as temporal means are concerned, for the preservation of this present life in the body, and that the fact that this will be a time when the soul ought to be ready and free, and neither taken up with, nor burdened by, carnal desires, is imported by the phrase employed by the first two writers—namely, "on the house-top," or, "on the wall"? In this way the third evangelist's phraseology, "let them depart out" (which really means, let them no more be engrossed with the desire of this life, but let them be prepared to pass into another life), is equivalent in sense to the terms used by the other two, "let him not come down to take anything out of his house" (which really means, "let not his affections turn towards the flesh, as if it could yield him anything to his advantage then"). And in like manner the phrase adopted by the one, "And let not them that are in the countries enter thereunto" (which is to say, "Let not those who, with good purpose of heart, have already placed themselves outside it, indulge again in any carnal lust or longing after it"), denotes precisely what the other two evangelists embody in the sentence, "Neither let him which is in the field return

[1] Matt. xxiv. 14.   [2] Mark xiii. 10.
[3] Matt. xxiv. 15.
[4] Mark xiii 14. [The Greek text of Mark, according to the best authorities, does not contain the phrase "spoken of by Daniel the prophet." Augustin also omits the clause, but the Edinburgh edition inserts it, following the Authorized Version. It has therefore been stricken out in this edition.—R.]
[5] Luke xxi. 20.   [6] Matt. xxiv. 16–18.   [7] Luke xxi. 21.

back to take his clothes," which is much the same as to state that he should not again involve himself in cares of which he had been unburdened.

151. Moreover, Matthew proceeds thus : "But pray ye that your flight be not in the winter, neither on the Sabbath-day." Part of this is given and part omitted by Mark, when he says, "And pray ye that your flight be not in the winter." Luke, on the other hand, leaves this out entirely, and instead of it introduces something which is peculiar to himself, and by which he appears to me to have cast light upon this very clause which has been set before us somewhat obscurely by these others. For his version runs thus : "And take heed to yourselves, lest at any time your hearts be overcharged with surfeiting, and drunkenness, and cares of this life, and so that day come upon you unawares. For as a snare shall it come on all them that dwell on the face of the whole earth. Watch ye therefore, and pray always, that ye may be accounted worthy to escape all these things that shall come to pass." [1] This is to be understood to be the same flight as is mentioned by Matthew, which should not be taken in the winter or on the Sabbath-day. That "winter," moreover, refers to these "cares of this life" which Luke has specified directly ; and the "Sabbath-day" refers in like manner to the "surfeiting and drunkenness." For sad cares are like a winter ; and surfeiting and drunkenness drown and bury the heart in carnal delights and luxury — an evil which is expressed under the term "Sabbath-day," because of old, as is the case with them still, the Jews had the very pernicious custom of revelling in pleasure on that day, when they were ignorant of the spiritual Sabbath. Or, if something else is intended by the words which thus appear in Matthew and Mark, Luke's terms may also be taken to bear on something else, while no question implying any antagonism between them need be raised for all that. At present, however, we have not undertaken the task of expounding the Gospels, but only that of defending them against groundless charges of falsehood and deceit. Furthermore, other matters which Matthew has inserted in this discourse, and which are common to him and Mark, present no difficulty. On the other hand, with respect to those sections which are common to him and Luke, [it is to be remarked that] these are not introduced into the present discourse by Luke, although in regard to the order of narration here they are at one. But he records sentences of like tenor in other connections, either reproducing them as they suggested themselves to his memory, and thus bringing them

in by anticipation so as to relate at an earlier point words which, as spoken by the Lord, belong really to a later ; or else, giving us to understand that they were uttered twice over by the Lord, once on the occasion referred to by Matthew, and on a second occasion, with which Luke himself deals.

CHAP. LXXVIII. — OF THE QUESTION WHETHER THERE IS ANY CONTRADICTION BETWEEN MATTHEW AND MARK ON THE ONE HAND, AND JOHN ON THE OTHER, IN SO FAR AS THE FORMER STATE THAT AFTER TWO DAYS WAS TO BE THE FEAST OF THE PASSOVER, AND AFTERWARDS TELLS US THAT HE WAS IN BETHANY, WHILE THE LATTER GIVES A PARALLEL NARRATIVE OF WHAT TOOK PLACE AT BETHANY, BUT MENTIONS THAT IT WAS SIX DAYS BEFORE THE PASSOVER.

152. Matthew continues thus : "And it came to pass, when Jesus had finished all these sayings, He said unto His disciples, Ye know that after two days will be the feast of the passover, and the Son of man shall be betrayed to be crucified." [2] This is attested in like manner by the other two, — namely, Mark and Luke, — and that, too, with a thorough harmony on the subject of the order of narration.[3] They do not, however, introduce the sentence as one spoken by the Lord Himself. They make no statement to that effect. At the same time, Mark, speaking in his own person, does tell us that "after two days was the feast of the passover and of unleavened bread." And Luke likewise gives this as his own affirmation : "Now the feast of unleavened bread drew nigh, which is called the passover ; " that is to say, it "drew nigh" in this sense, that it was to take place after two days' space, as the other two are more apparently at one in expressing it. John, on the other hand, has mentioned in three several places the nearness of this same feast-day. In the two earlier instances the intimation is made when he is engaged in recording certain matters of another tenor. But on the third occasion his narrative appears clearly to deal with those very times, in connection with which the other three evangelists also notice the subject, — that is to say, the times when the Lord's passion was actually imminent.[4]

153. But to those who look into the matter without sufficient care, there may seem to be a contradiction involved in the fact that Matthew and Mark, after stating that the passover was to be after two days, have at once informed us how Jesus was in Bethany on that occasion, on which the account of the precious ointment

---

[1] Luke xxi. 34–36.

[2] Matt. xxvi. 1, 2. [It cannot be determined with certainty how much time is to be included in the phrase "after two days." Moreover, the difficulty in regard to the time of the Last Supper affects this question, to some extent at least. — R.]

[3] Mark xiv. 1 ; Luke xxii. 1.   [4] John xi. 55, xii. 1, xiii. 1.

comes before us; whereas John, when he is about to give us the same narrative concerning the ointment, begins by telling us that Jesus came to Bethany six days before the passover.[1] Now, the question is, how the passover could be spoken of by those two evangelists as about to be celebrated two days after, seeing that we find them, immediately after they have made this statement, in company with John, giving us an account of the scene with the ointment in Bethany; while in that connection the last-named writer informs us, that the feast of the passover was to take place six days after. Nevertheless, those who are perplexed by this difficulty simply fail to perceive that Matthew and Mark have brought in their account of the scene which was enacted in Bethany really in the form of a recapitulation, not as if the time of its occurrence was actually subsequent to the [time indicated in the] announcement made by them on the subject of the two days' space, but as an event which had already taken place at a date when there was still a period of six days preceding the passover. For neither of them has appended his account of what took place at Bethany to his statement regarding the celebration of the passover after two days' space in any such terms as these: "After these things, when He was in Bethany." But Matthew's phrase is this: "Now when Jesus was in Bethany." And Mark's version is simply this: "And being in Bethany," etc.; which is a method of expression that may certainly be taken to refer to a period antecedent to the utterance of what was said two days before the passover. The case, therefore, stands thus: As we gather from the narrative of John, Jesus came to Bethany six days before the passover; there the supper took place, in connection with which we get the account of the precious ointment; leaving this place, He came next to Jerusalem, sitting upon an ass; and thereafter happened those things which they relate to have occurred after this arrival of His in Jerusalem. Consequently, even although the evangelists do not mention the fact, we understand that between the day on which He came to Bethany, and which witnessed the scene with the ointment, and the day to which all these deeds and words which are at present before us belonged, there elapsed a period of four days, so that at this point might come in the day which the two evangelists have defined by their statement as to the celebration of the passover two days after. Further, when Luke says, "Now the feast of unleavened bread drew nigh," he does not indeed make any express mention of a two days' space; but still, the nearness which he has instanced ought to be accepted as made

good by this very space of two days. Again, when John makes the statement that "the Jews' passover was nigh at hand,"[2] he does not intend a two days' space to be understood thereby, but means that there was a period of six days before the passover. Thus it is that, on recording certain matters immediately after this affirmation, with the intention of specifying what measure of nearness he had in view when he spoke of the passover as nigh at hand, he next proceeds in the following strain: "Then Jesus, six days before the passover, came to Bethany, where Lazarus had died, whom Jesus raised from the dead;[3] and there they made Him a supper."[4] This is the incident which Matthew and Mark introduce in the form of a recapitulation, after the statement that after two days would be the passover. In their recapitulation they thus come back upon the day in Bethany, which was yet a six days' space off from the passover, and give us the account which John also gives of the supper and the ointment. Subsequently to that scene, we are to suppose Him to come to Jerusalem, and then, after the occurrence of the other things recorded, to reach this day, which was still a two days' space from the passover, and from which these evangelists have made this digression, with the object of giving a recapitulatory notice of the incident with the ointment in Bethany. And after the completion of that narrative, they return once more to the point from which they made the digression; that is to say, they now proceed to record the words spoken by the Lord two days before the passover. For if we remove the notice of the incident at Bethany, which they have introduced as a digression from the literal order, and have given in the form of a recollection and recapitulation inserted at a point subsequent to its actual historical position, and if we then set the narrative in its regular connection, the recital will go on as follows;—according to Matthew, the Lord's words coming in thus: "Ye know that after two days shall be the feast of the passover, and the Son of man shall be betrayed to be crucified. Then assembled together the chief priests and the elders of the people unto the palace of the high priest, who was called Caiaphas, and consulted that they might take Jesus by subtilty, and kill Him. But they said, Not on the feast-day, lest there be an uproar among the people. Then one of the twelve, called Judas Scarioth, went unto the chief priests,"[5] etc. For between the place where it is said, "lest there be an uproar among the people," and the passage where we read, "then one of the disciples, called Judas, went," etc., that notice of the scene at Bethany

---

[1] John xii. 1.

[2] John xi. 55.
[3] *Ubi fuerat Lazarus mortuus quem suscitavit Jesus.*
[4] John xii. 1, 2.   [5] Matt. xxvi. 2-5, 14, etc.

intervenes, which they have introduced by way of recapitulation. Consequently, by leaving it out, we have established such a connection in the narrative as may make our conclusion satisfactory, that there is no contradiction here in the matter of the order of times. Again, if we deal with Mark's Gospel in like manner, and omit the account of the same supper at Bethany, which he also has brought in as a recapitulation, his narrative will proceed in the following order : " Now after two days was the feast of the passover, and of unleavened bread : and the chief priests and the scribes sought how they might take Him by craft, and put Him to death. For they said,[1] Not on the feast-day, lest there be an uproar of the people. And Judas Scariothes, one of the twelve, went unto the chief priests, to betray Him." [2] Here, again, the incident at Bethany which these evangelists have inserted, by way of recapitulation, is placed between the clause, " lest there be an uproar of the people," and the verse which we have attached immediately to that, namely, " And Judas Scariothes, one of the twelve." Luke, on the other hand, has simply omitted the said occurrence at Bethany. This is the explanation which we give in reference to the six days before the passover, which is the space mentioned by John when narrating what took place at Bethany, and in reference to the two days before the passover, which is the period specified by Matthew and Mark when presenting their account, in direct sequence upon the statement thus made, of that same scene in Bethany which has been recorded also by John. [3]

CHAP. LXXIX. — OF THE CONCORD BETWEEN MATTHEW, MARK, AND JOHN IN THEIR NOTICES OF THE SUPPER AT BETHANY, AT WHICH THE WOMAN POURED THE PRECIOUS OINTMENT ON THE LORD, AND OF THE METHOD IN WHICH THESE ACCOUNTS ARE TO BE HARMONIZED WITH THAT OF LUKE, WHEN HE RECORDS AN INCIDENT OF A SIMILAR NATURE AT A DIFFERENT PERIOD.

154. Matthew, then, continuing his narrative from the point up to which we had concluded its examination, proceeds in the following terms : " Then assembled together the chief priests and the elders of the people unto the palace of the high priest, who was called Caiaphas, and consulted that they might take Jesus by subtilty and kill Him : but they said, Not on the feast-day, lest there be an uproar among the people. Now when Jesus was in Bethany, in the house of Simon the leper, there came unto Him a woman having an alabaster box of precious ointment, and poured it on His head as He sat at meat ; " and so on down to the words, " there shall also this that this woman hath done be told for a memorial of her." [4] The scene with the woman and the costly ointment at Bethany we have now to consider, as it is thus detailed. For although Luke records an incident resembling this, and although the name which he assigns to the person in whose house the Lord was supping might also suggest an identity between the two narratives (for Luke likewise names the host "Simon"), still, since there is nothing either in nature or in the customs of men to make the case an incredible one, that as one man may have two names, two men may with all the greater likelihood have one and the same name, it is more reasonable to believe that the Simon in whose house [it is thus supposed, according to Luke's version, that] this scene at Bethany took place, was a different person from the Simon [named by Matthew]. For Luke, again, does not specify Bethany as the place where the incident which he records happened. And although it is true that he in no way particularizes the town or village in which that occurrence took place, still his narrative does not seem to deal with the same locality. Consequently, my opinion is, that there is but one interpretation to be put upon the matter. That is not, however, to suppose that the woman who appears in Matthew was an entirely different person from the woman who approached the feet of Jesus on that occasion in the character of a sinner, and kissed them, and washed them with her tears, and wiped them with her hair, and anointed them with ointment, in reference to whose case Jesus also made use of the parable of the two debtors, and said that her sins, which were many, were forgiven her because she loved much. But my theory is, that it was the same Mary who did this deed on two separate occasions, the one being that which Luke has put on record, when she approached Him first of all in that remarkable humility, and with those tears, and obtained the forgiveness of her sins.[5] For John, too, although he has not given the kind of recital which Luke has left us of the circumstances connected with that incident, has at least mentioned the fact, in commending the same Mary to our notice, when he has just begun to tell the story of the raising of Lazarus, and before his narrative brings the Lord to Bethany itself. The history which he offers us of that transaction proceeds thus : " Now a certain man was sick, named Lazarus, of Bethany, the town of Mary, and her sister

---

[1] *Dicebant enim.*　　[2] Mark xiv. 1, 2, 10.
[3] [This view is rejected by Dr. Robinson in his Harmony, but accepted by many commentators. See Robinson's Greek Harmony, rev. ed. pp. 236-238. — R.]

[4] Matt. xxvi. 3-13.
[5] Luke vii. 36-50. [This identification of Mary of Bethany with the woman spoken of by Luke is part of the process by which the latter is assumed to be Mary Magdalene. The occasions were different, and it is far more likely that there were two women, neither of them Mary Magdalene. — R.]

Martha. It was that Mary which anointed the Lord with ointment, and wiped His feet with her hair, whose brother Lazarus was sick." [1] By this statement John attests what Luke has told us when he records a scene of this nature in the house of a certain Pharisee, whose name was Simon. Here, then, we see that Mary had acted in this way before that time. And what she did a second time in Bethany is a different matter, which does not belong to Luke's narrative, but is related by three of the evangelists in concert, namely, John, Matthew, and Mark.[2]

155. Let us therefore notice how harmony is maintained here between these three evangelists, Matthew, Mark, and John, regarding whom there is no doubt that they record the self-same occurrence at Bethany, on occasion of which the disciples also, as all three mention, murmured against the woman, ostensibly on the ground of the waste of the very precious ointment. Now the further fact that Matthew and Mark tell us that it was the Lord's head on which the ointment was poured, while John says it was His feet, can be shown to involve no contradiction, if we apply the principle which we have already expounded in dealing with the scene of the feeding of the multitudes with the five loaves. For as there was one writer who, in giving his account of that incident, did not fail to specify that the people sat down at once by fifties and by hundreds, although another spoke only of the fifties, no contradiction could be supposed to emerge. There might indeed have seemed to be some difficulty, if the one evangelist had referred only to the hundreds, and the other only to the fifties ; and yet, even in that case, the correct finding should have been to the effect that they were seated both by fifties and by hundreds. And this example ought to have made it plain to us, as I pressed it upon my readers in discussing that section, that even where the several evangelists introduce only the one fact each, we should take the case to have been really, that both things were elements in the actual occurrence.[3] In the same way, our conclusion with regard to the passage now before us should be, that the woman poured the ointment not only upon the Lord's head, but also on His feet. It is true that some person may possibly be found absurd and artful enough to argue, that because Mark states that the ointment was poured out only after the alabaster vase was broken, there could not have remained in the shattered vessel anything with which she could anoint His feet. But while a person of that character, in his endeavours to disprove the veracity of the

Gospel, may contend that the vase was broken, in a manner making it impossible that any portion of the contents could have been left in it, how much better and more accordant with piety must the position of a very different individual appear, whose aim will be to uphold the truthfulness of the Gospel, and who may therefore contend that the vessel was not broken in a manner involving the total outpouring of the ointment ! Moreover, if that calumniator is so persistently blinded as to attempt to shatter the harmony of the evangelists on this subject of the shattering of the vase,[4] he should rather accept the alternative, that the [Lord's] feet were anointed before the vessel itself was broken, and that it thus remained whole, and filled with ointment sufficient for the anointing also of the head, when, by the breakage referred to, the entire contents were discharged. For we allow that there is a due regard to the several parts of our nature when the act commences with the head, but [we may also say that] an equally natural order is preserved when we ascend from the feet to the head.

156. The other matters belonging to this incident do not seem to me to raise any question really involving a difficulty. There is the circumstance that the other evangelists mention how the disciples murmured about the [wasteful] outpouring of the precious ointment, whereas John states that Judas was the person who thus expressed himself, and tells us, in explanation of the fact, that "he was a thief." But I think it is evident that this same Judas was the person referred to under the [general] name of the disciples, the plural number being used here instead of the singular, in accordance with that mode of speech of which we have already introduced an explanation in the case of Philip and the miracle of the five loaves.[5] It may also be understood in this way, that the other disciples either felt as Judas felt, or spoke as he did, or were brought over to that view of the matter by what Judas said, and that Matthew and Mark consequently have expressed in word what was really the mind of the whole company ; but that Judas spoke as he did just because he was a thief, whereas what prompted the rest was their care for the poor ; and further, that John has chosen to record the utterance of such sentiments only in the instance of that one [among the disciples] whose habit of acting the thief he believed it right to bring out in connection with this occasion.

CHAP. LXXX. — OF THE HARMONY CHARACTERIZING THE ACCOUNTS WHICH ARE GIVEN BY MATTHEW, MARK, AND LUKE, OF THE OCCASION ON WHICH

---

[1] John xi. 1, 2. [John's language is more properly referred to what was well known among Christians when he wrote, than to what had occurred before the sickness of Lazarus. — R.]

[2] John xii. 1-8; Matt. xxvi. 3-13; Mark xiv. 3-9.

[3] See above, chap. xlvi. § 98.

[4] De alabastro fracto frangere conetur.   [5] See above, § 96.

HE SENT HIS DISCIPLES TO MAKE PREPARATIONS FOR HIS EATING THE PASSOVER.

157. Matthew proceeds thus : " Then one of the twelve, who is called Judas [of] Scarioth, went unto the chief priests, and said unto them, What will ye give me, and I will deliver Him unto you? And they covenanted with him for thirty pieces of silver ; " and so on down to the words, " And the disciples did as Jesus had appointed them, and they made ready the passover." [1] Nothing in this section can be supposed to stand in any contradiction with the versions of Mark and Luke, who record this same passage in a similar manner.[2] For as regards the statement given by Matthew in these terms, " Go into the city to such a man, and say unto him, The Master saith, My time is at hand : I will keep the passover at thy house with my disciples," [3] it just indicates the person whom Mark and Luke name the " goodman of the house," [4] or the " master of the house," [5] in which the dining-room was shown them where they were to make ready the passover. And Matthew has expressed this by simply bringing in the phrase, " to such a man," as a brief explanation introduced by himself with the view of succinctly giving us to understand who the person referred to was. For if he had said that the Lord addressed them in words like these : " Go into the city, and say unto him [or " it "],[6] The Master saith, My time is at hand, I will keep the passover at thy house," it might have been supposed that the terms were intended to be directed to the city itself. For this reason, therefore, Matthew has inserted the statement, that the Lord bade them go " to such a man," not, however, as a statement made by the Lord, whose instructions he was recording, but simply as one volunteered by himself, with the view of avoiding the necessity of narrating the whole at length, when it seemed to him that this was all that required to be mentioned in order to bring out with sufficient accuracy what was really meant by the person who gave the order. For who can fail to see that no one naturally speaks to others in such an indefinite fashion as this, " Go ye to such a man "? If, again, the words had been, " Go ye to any one whatsoever," or " to any one you please," [7] the mode of expression might have been correct enough, but the person to whom the disciples were sent would have been left uncertain : whereas Mark and Luke present him as a certain definitely indicated individual, although they pass over his

name in silence. The Lord Himself, we may be sure, knew to what person it was that He despatched them. And in order that those also whom He was thus sending might be able to discover the individual meant, He gave them, before they set out, a particular sign which they were to follow, — namely, the appearance of a man bearing a pitcher or a vessel of water, — and told them, that if they went after him, they would reach the house which He intended. Hence, seeing that it was not competent here to employ the phraseology, " Go to any one you please," which is indeed legitimate enough, so far as the demands of linguistic propriety are concerned, but which an accurate statement of the matter dealt with here renders inadmissible in this passage, with how much less warrant could an expression like this have been used here (by the speaker Himself), " Go to such a man," which the usage of correct language can never admit at all? But it is manifest that the disciples were sent by the Lord, plainly, not to any man they pleased, but to " such a man," that is to say, to a certain definite individual. And that is a thing which the evangelist, speaking in his own person, could quite rightly have related to us, by putting it in this way : " He sent them to such a man,[8] in order to say to him, I will keep the passover at thy house." He might also have expressed it thus : " He sent them to such a man, saying, Go, say to him, I will keep the passover at thy house." And thus it is that, after giving us the words actually spoken by the Lord Himself, namely, " Go into the city," he has introduced this addition of his own, " to such a man," which he does, however, not as if the Lord had thus expressed Himself, but simply with the view of giving us to understand, although the name is left unrecorded, that there was a particular person in the city to whom the Lord's disciples were sent, in order to make ready the passover. Thus, too, after the two [or three] words brought in in that manner as an explanation of his own, he takes up again the order of the words as they were uttered by the Lord Himself, namely, " And say unto him, The Master saith." And if you ask now " to whom " they were to say this, the correct reply is given [at once] in these terms, To that particular man to whom the evangelist has given us to understand that the Lord sent them, when, speaking in His own person, he introduced the clause, " to such a man." The clause thus inserted may indeed contain a rather unusual mode of expression, but still it is a perfectly legitimate phraseology when it is thus understood. Or it may be, that in the Hebrew language, in which Matthew is reported to have written, there is

---

[1] Matt. xxvi. 14-19.   [2] Mark xiv. 10-16; Luke xxii. 3-13.
[3] Matt. xxvi. 18.   [4] Patrem familias.   [5] Dominum domus.
[6] Ite in civitatem et dicite ei. Turning on the identity of form retained by the Latin pronoun in all the genders of the dative case, this, of course, cannot be precisely represented in English.
[7] Ad quemcunque aut ad quemlibet.

[8] Ad quendam.

some peculiar usage which might make it entirely accordant with the laws of correct expression, even were the whole taken to have been spoken by the Lord Himself. Whether that is the case, those who understand that tongue may decide. Even in the Latin language itself, indeed, this kind of expression might also be used, in terms like these : " Go into the city to such a man as may be indicated by a person who shall meet you carrying a pitcher of water." If the instructions were conveyed in such words as these, they could be acted upon without any ambiguity. Or again, if the terms were anything like these, " Go into the city to such a man, who resides in this or the other place, in such and such a house," then the note thus given of the place and the designation of the house would make it quite possible to understand the commission delivered, and to execute it. But when these instructions, and all others of a similar order, are left entirely untold, the person who in such circumstances uses this kind of address, " Go to such a man, and say unto him," cannot possibly be listened to intelligently for this obvious reason, that when he employs the terms, " to such a man," he intends a certain particular individual to be understood by them, and yet offers us no hint by which he may be identified. But if we are to suppose that the clause referred to is one introduced as an explanation by the evangelist himself, [we may find that] the requirements of brevity will ren-der the expression somewhat obscure, without, however, making it incorrect. Moreover, as to the fact, that where Mark speaks of a pitcher [1] of water, Luke mentions a vessel,[2] the simple explanation is, that the one has used a word indicative of the kind of vessel, and the other a term indicative of its capacity, while both evangelists have nevertheless preserved the real meaning actually intended.

158. Matthew proceeds thus : " Now when the even was come, He sat down with the twelve disciples ; and as they did eat, He said, Verily I say unto you, that one of you shall betray me. And they were exceeding sorrowful, and began every one of them to say, Lord, is it I?" and so on, down to where we read, " Then Judas, which betrayed Him, answered and said, Master, is it I?   He said unto him, Thou hast said."[3] In what we have now presented for consideration here, the other three evangelists,[4] who also record such matters, offer nothing calculated to raise any question of serious difficulty.[5]

---

[1] *Lagenam*, bottle.
[2] *Amphoram*, large measure.   [3] Matt. xxvi. 20–25.
[4] Mark xiv. 17–21; Luke xxii. 14–23; John xiii. 21–27.
[5] [No notice is taken by Augustin, in this treatise, of the most serious difficulty connected with the narratives of the Lord's Supper; namely, that of the day of the month on which it was instituted. The Synoptists distinctly declare that our Lord ate the passover supper with His disciples at the regular time (Matt. xxvi. 17; Mark xiv. 12; Luke xxii. 7), but some passages in John (xiii. 1, 27–30; xviii. 28; xix. 31) seem to indicate that the proper time of its observance had not yet come. Hence many commentators think that the Lord's Supper was instituted on the evening of the 13th of Nisan, one day before the regular time of the paschal supper. — R.]

BOOK III

THIS BOOK CONTAINS A DEMONSTRATION OF THE HARMONY OF THE EVANGELISTS FROM THE ACCOUNTS OF THE SUPPER ON TO THE END OF THE GOSPEL, THE NARRATIVES GIVEN BY THE SEVERAL WRITERS BEING COLLATED, AND THE WHOLE ARRANGED IN ONE ORDERLY CONNECTION.

PROLOGUE.

1. INASMUCH as we have now reached that point in the history at which all the four evangelists necessarily hold their course in company on to the conclusion, without presenting any serious divergence the one from the other, if it happens anywhere that one of them makes mention of something which another leaves unnoticed, it appears to me that we may demonstrate the consistency maintained by the various evangelists with greater expedition, if from this point onwards we now bring all the statements given by all the writers together into one connection, and arrange the whole in a single narration, and under one view.[1] I consider that in this way the task which we have undertaken may be discharged with greater convenience and facility than otherwise might be the case. What we have now before us, therefore, is to attempt the construction of a single narrative, in which we shall include all the particulars, and for which we shall possess the attestation of those evangelists who, (each selecting for recital out of the whole number of facts those which he had either the ability or the desire to relate,) have prepared these records for us:[2] this being done in such a manner, moreover, that all these statements, in regard to which we have to prove an entire freedom from contradictions, are taken as made by all the evangelists together.

CHAP. I. — OF THE METHOD IN WHICH THE FOUR EVANGELISTS ARE SHOWN TO BE AT ONE IN THE ACCOUNTS GIVEN OF THE LORD'S SUPPER AND THE INDICATION OF HIS BETRAYER.

2. Let us commence here, accordingly, with the notice presented by Matthew, [which runs thus]: "And as they were eating, Jesus took bread, and blessed it, and brake it, and gave it to His disciples, and said, Take, eat; this is my body."[3] Both Mark and Luke also gave this section.[4] It is true that Luke has made mention of the cup twice over: first before He gave the bread; and, secondly, after the bread has been given. But the fact is, that what is stated in that earlier connection has been introduced, according to this writer's habit, by anticipation, while the words which he has inserted here in their proper order are left unrecorded in those previous verses, and the two passages when put together make up exactly what stands expressed by those other evangelists.[5] John, on the other hand, has said nothing about the body and blood of the Lord in this context; but he plainly certifies that the Lord spake to that effect on another occasion,[6] with much greater fulness than here. At present, however, after recording how the Lord rose from supper and washed the disciples' feet, and after telling us also the reason why the Lord dealt thus with them, in expressing which He had intimated, although still obscurely, and by the use of a testimony of Scripture, the fact that He was being betrayed by the man who was to eat of His bread, at this point John comes to the section in question, which the other three evangelists also unite in introducing. He presents it thus: "When Jesus had thus said, He was troubled in spirit, and testified, and said, Verily, verily, I say unto you, That one of you shall betray me. Then the disciples looked (as the same John subjoins) one on another, doubting of whom He spake."[7] "And (as Matthew and Mark tell us) they were exceeding sorrowful, and began every one of them to say unto Him, Is it I? And He answered and said (as Matthew proceeds to state), He that dippeth his hand with me in the dish, the same shall betray me." Matthew also goes on to make the following addition to the preceding: "The Son of man

---

[1] The text gives: *et in unam narrationem faciemque digeramus.* For *faciem* the reading *seriem*, series, also occurs.
[2] The text gives: *ut aggrediamur narrationem omnia commemorantes, cum eorum evangelistarum attestatione qui ex his omnibus,* etc. Some editions have *cum eorundem evangelistarum attestatione quid ex his,* etc. = the attestation of the same evangelists as to what, etc.

[3] Matt. xxvi. 26.   [4] Mark xiv. 22; Luke xxii 49.
[5] [Luke's first reference to the cup belongs to the passover celebration, in distinction from the Lord's Supper. — R.]
[6] John vi. 32–64.   [7] John xiii. 21, 22.

indeed goeth, as it is written of Him ; but woe
unto that man by whom the Son of man shall
be betrayed ! it had been good for that man
if he had not been born." [1] Mark, too, is at
one with him here as regards both the words
themselves and the order of narration.[2] Then
Matthew continues thus : "Then Judas, which
betrayed Him, answered and said, Master, is it
I? He said unto him, Thou hast said." Even
these words did not say explicitly whether he
was himself the man. For the sentence still
admits of being understood as if its point was
this, " I am not the person who has said so." [3]
All this, too, may quite easily have been uttered
by Judas and answered by the Lord without its
being noticed by all the others.

3. After this, Matthew proceeds to insert the
mystery of His body and blood, as it was committed then by the Lord to the disciples. Here
Mark and Luke act correspondingly. But after
He had handed the cup to them, [we find that]
He spoke again concerning His betrayer, in
terms which Luke recounts, when he says, " But,
behold, the hand of him that betrayeth me is
with me on the table. And truly the Son of
man goeth as it was determined : but woe unto
that man by whom He shall be betrayed." [4] At
this point we must now suppose that to come in
which is narrated by John while these others
omit it, just as John has also passed by certain
matters which they have detailed. In accordance with this, after the giving of the cup, and
after the Lord's subsequent saying which has
been brought in by Luke, — namely, " But, behold, the hand of him that betrayeth me is with
me on the table," etc., — the statement made
by John is [to be taken as immediately] subjoined. It is to the following effect : " Now
there was leaning on Jesus' bosom one of His
disciples, whom Jesus loved. Simon Peter therefore beckoned to him, and said unto him,[5] Who
is he of whom He speaketh? He then, when
he had laid himself on Jesus' breast, saith unto
Him, Lord, who is it? Jesus answered, He it
is to whom I shall give a sop, when I have
dipped it. And when He had dipped the sop,
He gave it to Judas, the son of Simon [of]
Scarioth. And after the sop Satan then entered
into him." [6]

4. Here we must take care not to let John
underlie the appearance not only of standing in
antagonism to Luke, who had stated before this,
that Satan entered into the heart of Judas at
the time when he made his bargain with the
Jews to betray Him on receipt of a sum of

money, but also of contradicting himself. For,
at an earlier point, and previous to [his notice
of] the receiving of this sop, he had made use
of these terms : "And supper being ended, the
devil having now put into the heart of Judas
to betray Him." [7] And how does he enter into
the heart, but by putting unrighteous persuasions
into the thoughts of unrighteous men? The
explanation, however, is this. We ought to
suppose Judas to have been more fully taken
possession of by the devil now, just as on the
other hand, in the instance of the good, those
who had already received the Holy Spirit on
that occasion, subsequently to His resurrection,
when He breathed upon them and said, " Receive ye the Holy Ghost," [8] also obtained a
fuller gift of that Spirit at a later time, namely,
when He was sent down from above on the day
of Pentecost. In like manner, Satan then entered into this man after the sop. And (as John
himself mentions in the immediate context)
"Jesus saith unto him, What thou doest, do
quickly. Now no man at the table knew for
what intent He spake this unto him ; for some
of them thought, because Judas had the bag,
that Jesus said unto him, Buy those things that
we have need of against the feast ; or, that he
should give something to the poor. He then,
having received the sop, went immediately out ;
and it was night. Therefore, when he was gone
out, Jesus saith, Now is the Son of man glorified,
and God is glorified in Him : and if God be
glorified in Him, God shall also glorify Him in
Himself, and shall straightway glorify Him." [9]

CHAP. II. — OF THE PROOF OF THEIR FREEDOM
FROM ANY DISCREPANCIES IN THE NOTICES
GIVEN OF THE PREDICTIONS OF PETER'S DENI-
ALS.

5. " Little children, yet a little while I am
with you. Ye shall seek me : and, as I said
unto the Jews, Whither I go, ye cannot come ;
so now I say unto you. A new commandment
I give unto you, That ye love one another ; as I
have loved you, that ye also love one another.
By this shall all men know that ye are my disciples, if ye have love one to another. Simon
Peter saith unto Him, Lord, whither goest thou?
Jesus answered him, Whither I go, thou canst
not follow me now, but thou shalt follow me
afterwards. Peter saith unto Him, Lord, why
cannot I follow Thee now? I will lay down
my life for Thy sake. Jesus answered him,
Wilt thou lay down thy life for my sake? Verily,
verily, I say unto thee, The cock shall not crow,
until thou deniest me thrice." [10] John, from
whose Gospel I have taken the passage introduced above, is not the only evangelist who

---

[1] Matt. xxvi. 22–25.   [2] Mark xiv. 19–21.
[3] [This explanation seems altogether inadmissible, and is equally
unnecessary. — R.]
[4] Luke xxii. 21, 22.
[5] *Innuit ergo huic Simon Petrus et dixit ei.*
[6] John xiii. 23–27. [Whether this preceded or followed the giving
of the cup is still in dispute. — R.]

[7] John xiii. 2.   [8] John xx. 22.   [9] John xiii. 28–32.
[10] John xiii. 33–38.

details this incident of the prophetic announcement of his own denial to Peter. The other three also record the same thing.[1] They do not, however, take one and the same particular point in the discourses [of Christ] as their occasion for proceeding to this narration. For Matthew and Mark both introduce it in a completely parallel order, and at the same stage of their narrative, namely, after the Lord left the house in which they had eaten the passover; while Luke and John, on the other hand, bring it in before He left that scene. Still we might easily suppose, either that it has been inserted in the way of a recapitulation by the one couple of evangelists, or that it has been inserted in the way of an anticipation by the other; only such a supposition may be made more doubtful by the circumstance that there is so remarkable a diversity, not only in the Lord's words, but even in those sentiments of His by which the incident in question is introduced, and by which Peter was moved to venture his presumptuous asseveration that he would die with the Lord or for the Lord. These considerations may constrain us rather to understand the narratives really to import that the man uttered his presumptuous declaration thrice over, as it was called forth by different occasions in the series of Christ's discourses, and that also three several times the answer was returned him by the Lord, which intimated that before the cock crew he would deny Him thrice.

6. And surely there is nothing incredible in supposing that Peter was moved to such an act of presumption on several occasions, separated from each other by certain intervals of time, as he was actually instigated to deny Him repeatedly. Neither should it seem unreasonable to fancy that the Lord gave him a reply in similar terms at three successive periods, especially when [we see that] in immediate connection with each other, and without the interposition of anything else either in fact or word, Christ addressed the question to him three several times whether he loved Him, and that, when Peter returned the same answer thrice over, He also gave him thrice over the self-same charge to feed His sheep.[2] That it is the more reasonable thing to suppose that Peter displayed his presumption on three different occasions, and that thrice over he received from the Lord a warning with respect to his triple denial, is further proved, as we may see, by the very terms employed by the evangelists, which record sayings uttered by the Lord in diverse form and of diverse import. Let us here call attention again to that passage which I introduced a little ago from the Gospel of John. There we certainly

find that He had expressed Himself in this way: "Little children, yet a little while I am with you. Ye shall seek me: and as I said unto the Jews, Whither I go, ye cannot come; so now I say to you. A new commandment I give unto you, That ye love one another; as I have loved you, that ye love one another. By this shall all men know that ye are my disciples, if ye have love one to another. Simon Peter saith unto Him, Lord, whither goest Thou?"[3] Now, surely it is evident here that what moved Peter to utter this question, "Lord, whither goest Thou?" was the words which the Lord Himself had spoken. For he had heard Him say, "Whither I go, ye cannot come." Then Jesus made this reply to the said Peter: "Whither I go, thou canst not follow me now, but thou shalt follow me afterwards." Thereupon Peter expressed himself thus: "Lord, why cannot I follow Thee now? I will lay down my life for Thy sake."[4] And to this presumptuous declaration the Lord responded by predicting his denial. Luke, again, first mentions how the Lord said, "Simon, behold Satan hath desired to have you, that he may sift you as wheat; but I have prayed for thee, that thy faith fail not; and, when thou art converted, strengthen thy brethren:" next he proceeds immediately to tell us how Peter replied to this effect: "Lord, I am ready to go with Thee, both unto prison and to death;" and then he continues thus: "And He said, I tell thee, Peter, the cock shall not crow this day, before that thou shalt thrice deny that thou knowest me."[5] Now, who can fail to perceive that this is an occasion by itself, and that the incident in connection with which Peter was incited to make the presumptuous declaration already referred to is an entirely different one? But, once more, Matthew presents us with the following passage: "And when they had sung an hymn," he says, "they went out into the Mount of Olives. Then saith Jesus unto them, All ye shall be offended because of me this night: for it is written, I will smite the shepherd, and the sheep of the flock shall be scattered abroad. But after I am risen again, I will go before you into Galilee."[6] The same passage is given in precisely the same form by Mark.[7] What similarity is there, however, in these words, or in the ideas expressed by them, either to the terms in which John represents Peter to have made his presumptuous declaration, or to those in which Luke exhibits him as uttering such an asseveration? And so we find that in Matthew's narrative the connection proceeds immediately thus: "Peter answered and said unto Him, Though all men shall be offended because of Thee, yet will I never be offended.

---

[1] Matt. xxvi. 30-35; Mark xiv. 26-31; Luke xxii. 31-34.
[2] John xxi. 15-17.

[3] John xiii. 33-36.   [4] John xiii. 37.
[5] Luke xxii. 31-33.   [6] Matt. xxvi. 30-32.   [7] Mark xiv. 26-28.

Jesus saith unto him, Verily, I say unto thee, that this night, before the cock crow, thou shalt deny me thrice. Peter saith unto him, Though I should die with Thee, yet will I not deny Thee. Likewise also said all His disciples." [1]

7. All this is recorded almost in the same language also by Mark, only that he has not put in so general a form what the Lord said with regard to the manner in which the event [of Peter's failure] was to be brought about, but has given it a more particular turn. For his version is this: "Verily I say unto thee, That this day, even in this night, before the cock crow twice, thou shalt deny me thrice." [2] Thus it appears that all of them tell us how the Lord foretold that Peter would deny Him before the cock crew, but that they do not all mention how often the cock was to crow, and that Mark is the only one who has presented a more explicit notice of this incident in the narrative. Hence some are of opinion that Mark's statement is not in harmony with those of the others. But this is simply because they do not give sufficient attention to the facts of the case, and, above all, because they approach the question under the cloud of a prejudiced mind, in consequence of their being possessed by a hostile disposition towards the gospel. The fact is, that Peter's denial, when taken as a whole, is a threefold denial. For he remained in the same state of mental agitation, and harboured the same mendacious intention, until what had been foretold regarding him was brought to his mind, and healing came to him by bitter weeping and sorrow of heart. It is evident, however, that if this complete denial — that is to say, the threefold denial — is taken to have commenced only after the first crowing of the cock, three of the evangelists will appear to have given an incorrect account of the matter. For Matthew's version is this: "Verily I say unto thee, That this night, before the cock crow, thou shalt deny me thrice;" and Luke puts it thus: "I tell thee, Peter, the cock shall not crow this day, before that thou shalt thrice deny that thou knowest me;" and John presents it in this form: "Verily, verily, I say unto thee, the cock shall not crow till thou hast denied me thrice." And thus, in different terms and with words introduced in diverse successions, these three evangelists have expressed one and the same sense as conveyed by the words which the Lord spake — namely, the fact that, before the cock should crow, Peter was to deny

Him thrice. On the other hand, if [we suppose that] he went through the whole triple denial before the cock began to crow at all, then Mark will be made to underlie the charge of having given a superfluous statement when he puts these words into the Lord's mouth: "Verily I say unto thee, That this day, before the cock crow twice, thou shalt deny me thrice." For to what purpose would it be to say, "before the cock crow twice," when, on the supposition that this entire threefold denial was gone through previous to the first crowing of the cock, it is self-evident that a negation, which would thus be proved to have been completed before the first cockcrow, must also, as matter of course, be understood to have been fully uttered before the second cockcrow and before the third, and, in short, before all the cockcrowings which took place on that same night? But, inasmuch as this threefold denial was begun previous to the first crowing of the cock, those three evangelists concerned themselves with noticing, not the time at which Peter was to complete it, but the extent [3] to which it was to be carried, and the period at which it was to commence; that is to say, their object was to bring out the facts that it was to be thrice repeated, and that it was to begin previous to the cockcrowing. At the same time, so far as the man's own mind is concerned, we might also quite well understand it to have been engaged in, as a whole, previous to the first cockcrow. For although it is true that, so far as regards the actual utterance of the individual who was guilty of the denial, that threefold negation was only entered upon previous to the first cockcrow, and really finished before the second cockcrow, still it is equally true that, in so far as the disposition of mind and the apprehensions indulged by Peter were concerned, it was conceived, [4] as a whole, before the first cockcrow. Neither is it a matter of any consequence of what duration those intervals of delay were which elapsed between the several utterances of that thrice-recurring voice, if it is the case that the denial completely possessed his heart even previous to the first cockcrow, — in consequence, indeed, of his having imbibed a spirit of terror so abject as to make him capable of denying the Lord when he was questioned regarding Him, not only once, but a second time, and even a third time. Thus, a more correct and careful consideration of the matter might show us [5] that, precisely as it is declared that the man who looketh on a woman to lust after her has committed

---

[1] Matt. xxvi. 33-35. [It is very probable that the prediction of Peter's denial was repeated, being first spoken in the upper room (Luke, John), and afterwards on the way to Gethsemane (Matthew, Mark) — R.]

[2] Mark xiv. 30. [The Latin reproduces the emphatic form of the Greek text: "That thou to-day, *even* this night, before the cock crow twice, shalt deny me thrice" (Revised Version). It seems probable that this is the most accurate report, derived from Peter himself. — R.]

[3] Reading *quanta futura esset*. *Quando* also occurs for *quanta*, in which case the sense would be = the period at which it was to take place.

[4] Adopting *concepta est*. There is another reading, *coepta est* = it was commenced.

[5] The text gives simply: *ut rectius diligentiusque attendentibus*. Migne states that in six MSS. *videtur* is added = it seems to those who consider the matter more correctly, etc.

adultery with her already in his heart,[1] so, in the present instance, inasmuch as in the words which he spoke, Peter merely expressed the apprehension which he had already conceived with such intensity in his mind as to make it capable of enduring even on to a third repetition of his denial of the Lord, this threefold negation is to be assigned as a whole to that particular period at which the fear that sufficed thus to carry him on to a threefold denial took possession of him. In this way, too, it may be made apparent that, even if the words in which the denial was couched began to break forth from him only after the first cockcrow, when his heart was smitten by the inquiries addressed to him, it would involve neither any absurdity nor any untruthfulness, although it were said that before the cock crew he denied Him thrice, seeing that, in any case, previous to the crowing of the cock, his mind had been assailed by an apprehension violent enough to be able to draw him [2] on even to a third denial. All the less, therefore, ought we to feel any difficulty in the matter, if it appears that the threefold denial, as expressed also in the thrice-recurring utterances of the person who made the denial, was entered upon previous to the crowing of the cock, although it was not completed before the first cockcrow. We may take a parallel case, and suppose an intimation to be made to the following effect to a person : " This night, before the cock crow, you will write a letter to me, in which you will revile me thrice." Well, surely in this instance, if the man began to write the letter before the cock had crowed at all, and finished it after the cock had crowed for the first time, that would be no reason for alleging that the intimation previously made was false. The fact, therefore, is that, in putting these words into the Lord's lips, " Before the cock crow twice, thou shalt deny me thrice," Mark has given us a plainer indication of the intervals of time which separated the utterances themselves. And when we come to the said section of the evangelical narrative, we shall see that the circumstances are presented in a manner which exhibits, in that connection also, the harmony subsisting among the evangelists.

8. If, however, the demand is to get at the very words, literally and completely, which the Lord addressed to Peter, we answer that it is impossible to discover these ; and further, that it is simply superfluous to ask them, inasmuch as the speaker's meaning — to intimate which was the object He had in view in uttering the words — admits of being understood with the utmost plainness, even under the diverse terms employed by the evangelists. And whether, then, it be the case that Peter, instigated at different occasions in the course of the Lord's sayings, made his presumptuous declaration three several times, and had his denial foretold him thrice over by the Lord, as is the more probable result to which our investigation points us ; or whether it may appear that the accounts given by all the evangelists are capable of being reduced to a single statement, when a certain order of narration is adopted, so that it could be proved that it was only on one occasion that the Lord predicted to Peter, on the exhibition of his presumptuous spirit, the fact that he would deny Him ; — in either case, any contradiction between the evangelists will fail to be detected, as nothing of that nature really exists.

CHAP. III. — OF THE MANNER IN WHICH IT CAN BE SHOWN THAT NO DISCREPANCIES EXIST BETWEEN THEM IN THE ACCOUNTS WHICH THEY GIVE OF THE WORDS WHICH WERE SPOKEN BY THE LORD, ON TO THE TIME OF HIS LEAVING THE HOUSE IN WHICH THEY HAD SUPPED.

9. At this point, therefore, we may now follow, as far as we can, the order of the narrative, as gathered from all the evangelists together. Thus, then, after the prediction in question had been made to Peter, according to John's version, the same John proceeds with his statement, and introduces in this connection the Lord's discourse, which was to the following effect : " Let not your heart be troubled : ye believe in God, believe also in me. In my Father's house are many mansions ; "[3] and so forth. He narrates at length the sayings, so memorable and so pre-eminently sublime, of which He delivered Himself in the course of that address, until, in due connection, he comes to the passage where the Lord speaks as follows : " O righteous Father, the world hath not known Thee : but I have known Thee, and these have known that Thou hast sent me. And I have declared unto them Thy name, and will declare it ; that the love wherewith Thou hast loved me may be in them, and I in them."[4] Again we find, according to the narrative given by Luke, that there arose " a strife among them which of them should be accounted the greatest. And He said unto them, The kings of the Gentiles exercise lordship over them ; and they that exercise authority upon them are called benefactors. But ye shall not be so : but he that is greatest among you, let him be as the younger ;[5] and he that is chief, as he that doth serve. For whether is greater, he that sitteth at meat, or he that serveth ? is not he that sitteth at meat ? but I am among you as he that serveth. And ye are

---

[1] Matt. v. 28.
[2] The text gives *eum*. Another common reading is *eam* = it, *i.e.* his mind.

[3] John xiv. 1, 2.
[4] John xvii. 25, 26.
[5] Another reading is *minor* = as the less.

they which have continued with me in my temptations: and I appoint unto you a kingdom, as my Father hath appointed unto me; that ye may eat and drink at my table in my kingdom, and sit on thrones, judging the twelve tribes of Israel."[1]   The said Luke also immediately subjoins to these words the following passage: "And the Lord said to Simon: Simon, behold, Satan hath desired to have you, that he may sift you as wheat: but I have prayed for thee, that thy faith fail not: and when thou art converted, strengthen thy brethren. And he said unto Him: Lord, I am ready to go with Thee, both into prison, and to death. And He said, I tell thee, Peter, the cock shall not crow this day, before that thou shalt thrice deny that thou knowest me. And He said unto them, When I sent you without purse, and scrip, and shoes, lacked ye anything? And they said, Nothing. Then said He unto them, But now, he that hath a purse, let him take it, and likewise his scrip: and he that hath no sword, let him sell his garment, and buy one. For I say unto you, this that is written must yet be accomplished in me, And He was reckoned among the transgressors: for the things concerning me have an end. And they said, Lord, behold, here are two swords. And He said unto them, It is enough."[2]   Next comes the passage, given both by Matthew and by Mark: "And when they had sung an hymn, they went out into the Mount of Olives. Then saith Jesus unto them, All ye shall be offended because of me this night: for it is written, I will smite the Shepherd, and the sheep of the flock shall be scattered abroad. But after I am risen again, I will go before you into Galilee. Peter answered and said unto Him, Though all men shall be offended because of Thee, yet will I never be offended. Jesus saith unto him, Verily I say unto thee, That this night, before the cock crow, thou shalt deny me thrice. Peter saith unto Him, Though I should die with Thee, yet will I not deny Thee. Likewise also said all the disciples."[3]   We have introduced the preceding section as it is presented by Matthew. But Mark also records it almost in so many and the same words, with the exception of the apparent discrepancy, which we have already cleared up above, on the subject of the crowing of the cock.

CHAP. IV. — OF WHAT TOOK PLACE IN THE PIECE OF GROUND OR GARDEN TO WHICH THEY CAME ON LEAVING THE HOUSE AFTER THE SUPPER; AND OF THE METHOD IN WHICH, IN JOHN'S SILENCE ON THE SUBJECT, A REAL HARMONY CAN BE DEMONSTRATED BETWEEN THE OTHER THREE EVANGELISTS — NAMELY, MATTHEW, MARK, AND LUKE.

10. Matthew then proceeds with his narrative in the same connection as follows: "Then cometh Jesus with them unto a place called Gethsemane."[4]   This is mentioned also by Mark.[5] Luke, too, refers to it, although he does not notice the piece of ground by name. For he says: "And He came out, and went, as was His wont, to the Mount of Olives; and His disciples also followed Him. And when He was at the place, He said unto them, Pray that ye enter not into temptation."[6]   That is the place which the other two have instanced under the name of Gethsemane. There, we understand, was the garden which John brings into notice when he gives the following narration: "When Jesus had spoken these words, He went forth with His disciples over the brook Cedron, where was a garden, into the which He entered, and His disciples."[7]   Then taking Matthew's record, we get this statement next in order: "He said unto His disciples, Sit ye here, while I go and pray yonder.[8]   And He took with Him Peter and the two sons of Zebedee, and began to be sorrowful and very heavy. Then saith He unto them, My soul is exceeding sorrowful, even unto death: tarry ye here, and watch with me. And He went a little farther, and fell on His face, and prayed, saying, O my Father, if it be possible, let this cup pass from me: nevertheless not as I will, but as Thou wilt. And He cometh unto the disciples, and findeth them asleep, and saith unto Peter, What! could ye not watch with me one hour? Watch and pray, that ye enter not into temptation: the spirit indeed is willing, but the flesh is weak. He went away again the second time, and prayed, saying, O my Father, if this cup may not pass away from me except I drink it, Thy will be done. And He came and found them asleep again: for their eyes were heavy. And He left them, and went away again, and prayed the third time, saying the same words. Then cometh He to His disciples, and saith unto them, Sleep on now, and take your rest: behold, the hour is at hand, and the Son of man shall be betrayed into the hands of sinners. Rise, let us be going: behold, he is at hand that shall betray me."[4]

11. Mark also records these passages, introducing them quite in the same method and succession. Some of the sentences, however, are given with greater brevity by him, and others are somewhat more fully explained. These sayings

---

[1] Luke xxii. 24-30. [This incident may with more propriety be placed before the washing of the disciples' feet. — R.]
[2] Luke xxii. 31-38. [The conversation in regard to the swords (vers. 35-38) probably preceded the discourse reported by John (xiv.-xvii.). — R.]
[3] Matt. xxvi. 30-35.

[4] Matt. xxvi. 36-46.   [5] Mark xiv. 32-42.
[6] Luke xxii. 39-46.   [7] John xviii. 1.
[8] ["Go yonder and pray;" so the Latin, as well as the Greek text. Comp. Revised Version, which in some other instances, in the passage here cited, agrees more closely with Augustin's text than does the Authorized Version. — R.]

of our Lord, indeed, may seem in one portion to stand in some manner of contradiction to each other as they are presented in Matthew's version. I refer to the fact that [it is stated there that] He came to His disciples after His third prayer, and said to them, "Sleep on now, and take your rest : behold, the hour is at hand, and the Son of man shall be betrayed into the hands of sinners. Rise, let us be going : behold, he is at hand that shall betray me." For what are we to make of the direction thus given above, "Sleep on now, and take your rest," when there is immediately subjoined this other declaration, "Behold, the hour is at hand," and thereafter also the instruction, "Arise, let us be going"? Those readers who perceive something like a contradiction here, seek to pronounce these words, "Sleep on now, and take your rest," in a way betokening that they were spoken in reproach, and not in permission. And this is an expedient which might quite fairly be adopted were there any necessity for it. Mark, however, has reproduced these sayings in a manner which implies that after He had expressed himself in the terms, "Sleep on now, and take your rest," He added the words, "It is enough," and then appended to these the further statement, "The hour is come ; behold, the Son of man shall be betrayed." [1] Hence we may conclude that the case really stood thus : namely, that after addressing these words to them, "Sleep on now, and take your rest," the Lord was silent for a space, so that what He had thus given them permission to do might be [seen to be] really acted upon ; and that thereafter He made the other declaration, "Behold, the hour is come." Thus it is that in Mark's Gospel we find those words [regarding the sleeping] followed immediately by the phrase, "It is enough ; " that is to say, "the rest which you have had is enough now." But as no distinct notice is introduced of this silence on the Lord's part which intervened then, the passage comes to be understood in a forced manner, and it is supposed that a peculiar pronunciation must be given to these words.

12. Luke, on the other hand, has omitted to mention the number of times that He prayed. He has told us, however, a fact which is not recorded by the others — namely, that when He prayed He was strengthened by an angel, and that, as He prayed more earnestly, He had a bloody sweat, with drops falling down to the ground. Thus it appears that when he makes the statement, "And when He rose up from prayer, and was come to His disciples," he does not indicate how often He had prayed by that time. But still, in so doing, he does not stand in any kind of antagonism to the other two.

Moreover, John does indeed mention how He entered into the garden along with His disciples. But he does not relate how He was occupied there up to the period when His betrayer came in along with the Jews to apprehend Him.

13. These three evangelists, therefore, have in this manner narrated the same incident, just as, on the other hand, one man might give three several accounts of a single occurrence, with a certain measure of diversity in his statements, and yet without any real contradiction. Luke, for example, has specified the distance to which He went forward from the disciples — that is to say, when He withdrew from them in order to pray — more definitely than the others. For he tells us that it was "about a stone's cast." Mark, again, states first of all in his own words how the Lord prayed that, "If it were possible, the hour might pass from Him," referring to the hour of His Passion, which he also expresses presently by the term "cup." He then reproduces the Lord's own words, in the following manner : "Abba, Father, all things are possible to Thee : take away this cup from me." And if we connect with these terms the clause which is given by the other two evangelists, and for which Mark himself has also already introduced a clear parallel, presented as a statement made in his own person instead of the Lord's, the whole sentence will be exhibited in this form : "Father, if it be possible, (for) all things are possible unto Thee, take away this cup from me." And it will be so put just to prevent any one from supposing that He made the Father's power less than it is when He said, "If it be possible." For thus His words were not, "If Thou canst do it ; " but, "If it be possible." And anything is possible which He wills. Therefore, the expression, "If it be possible," has here just the same force as, "If Thou wilt." For Mark has made the sense in which the phrase, "If it be possible," is to be taken quite plain, when he says, "All things are possible unto Thee." And further, the fact that these writers have recorded how He said, "Nevertheless, not what I will, but what Thou wilt " (an expression which means precisely the same as this other form, "Nevertheless, not my will but Thine be done "), shows us clearly enough that it was with reference not to any absolute impossibility on the Father's side, but only to His will, that these words, "If it be possible," were spoken. This is made the more apparent by the plainer statement which Luke has presented to the same effect. For his version is not, "If it be possible," but, "If Thou be willing." And to this clearer declaration of what was really meant we may add, with the effect of still greater clearness, the clause which Mark has inserted, so that the whole will proceed thus : "If Thou be willing, (for) all things are

[1] Mark xiv. 41. [On the various explanations of this difficult passage, see commentaries." — R.]

possible unto Thee, take away this cup from me."

14. Again, as to Mark's mentioning that the Lord said not only "Father," but "Abba, Father," the explanation simply is, that "Abba" is in Hebrew exactly what "Pater" is in Latin. And perhaps the Lord may have used both words with some kind of symbolical significance, intending to indicate thereby, that in sustaining this sorrow He bore the part of His body, which is the Church, of which He has been made the corner-stone, and which comes to Him [in the person of disciples gathered] partly out of the Hebrews, to whom He refers when He says "Abba," and partly out of the Gentiles, to whom He refers when He says "Pater" [Father].[1] The Apostle Paul also makes use of the same significant expression. For he says, "In whom we cry, Abba, Father;"[2] and, in another passage, "God sent His Spirit into your hearts, crying, Abba, Father."[3] For it was meet that the good Master and true Saviour, by sharing in the sufferings of the more infirm,[4] should in His own person illustrate the truth that His witnesses ought not to despair, although it might perchance happen that, through human frailty, sorrow might steal in upon their hearts at the time of suffering; seeing that they would overcome it if, mindful that God knows what is best for those whose well-being He regards, they gave His will the preference over their own. On this subject, however, as a whole, the present is not the time for entering on any more detailed discussion. For we have to deal simply with the question concerning the harmony of the evangelists, from whose varied modes of narration we gather the wholesome lesson that, in order to get at the truth, the one essential thing to aim at in dealing with the terms is simply the intention which the speaker had in view in using them. For the word "Father" means just the same as the phrase "Abba, Father." But with a view to bring out the mystic significance, the expression, "Abba, Father," is the clearer form; while, for indicating the unity, the word "Father" is sufficient. And that the Lord did indeed employ this method of address, "Abba, Father," must be accepted as matter of fact. But still His intention would not appear very obvious were there not the means (since others use simply the term "Father") to show that under such a form of expression those two Churches, which are constituted, the one out of the Jews, and the other out of the Gentiles, are presented as also really one. In this way, then, [we may suppose that] the phrase, "Abba, Father," was adopted in order to convey the same idea as was indicated by the Lord on another occasion, when He said, "Other sheep I have which are not of this fold."[5] In these words He certainly referred to the Gentiles, since He had sheep also among the people of Israel. But in that passage He goes on immediately to add the declaration, "Them also I must bring, that there may be one fold and one Shepherd." And so we may say that, just as the phrase, "Abba, Father," contains the idea of [the two races,] the Israelites and the Gentiles, the word "Father," used alone, points to the one flock which these two constitute.

CHAP. V. — OF THE ACCOUNTS WHICH ARE GIVEN BY ALL THE FOUR EVANGELISTS IN REGARD TO WHAT WAS DONE AND SAID ON THE OCCASION OF HIS APPREHENSION, AND OF THE PROOF THAT THESE DIFFERENT NARRATIVES EXHIBIT NO REAL DISCREPANCIES.

15. When we follow the versions presented by Matthew and Mark, we find that the history now proceeds thus : " And while He yet spake, lo, Judas, one of the twelve, came, and with him a great multitude, with swords and staves, from the chief priests and elders of the people. Now he that betrayed Him, gave them a sign, saying, Whomsoever I shall kiss, that same is He ; hold Him fast. And forthwith he came to Jesus, and said, Hail, Master; and kissed Him."[6] First of all, however, as we gather from Luke's statement, He said to the traitor, " Judas, betrayest thou the Son of man with a kiss?"[7] Next, as we learn from Matthew, He spoke thus : " Friend, wherefore art thou come?" Thereafter He added certain words which are found in John's narrative, which runs in the following strain : " Whom seek ye? They answered Him, Jesus of Nazareth. Jesus saith unto them, I am He. And Judas also, which betrayed Him, stood with them. As soon then as He had said unto them, I am He, they went backward, and fell to the ground. Then asked He them again, Whom seek ye? And they said, Jesus of Nazareth. Jesus answered, I have told you that I am He : if therefore ye seek me, let these go their way; that the saying might be fulfilled which He spake, Of them which thou gavest me have I lost none."[8]

16. Next comes in a passage, which is given by Luke as follows : "When they which were about Him saw what would follow, they said unto Him, Lord, shall we smite with the sword? And one of them smote the servant of the high priest," as is noticed by all the four historians, " and cut off his ear," which, as we are informed by Luke and John, was his "right ear." More-

---

[1] See Eph. ii. 11-22.   [2] Rom. viii. 15.   [3] Gal. iv. 6.
[4] Or = having compassion on the more infirm; *infirmioribus compatiens.*

[5] John x. 16.   [6] Matt. xxvi. 47-56; Mark xiv. 43-50.
[7] Luke xii. 48.
[8] John xviii. 4-9. [This passage is more naturally placed before the kissing by Judas. — R.]

over, we gather also from John that the person who smote the servant was Peter, and that the name of the man whom he thus struck was Malchus. Next we take what Luke mentions, namely, "Jesus answered and said, Suffer ye thus far;"[1] with which we must connect the words appended by Matthew, namely, "Put up thy sword into his place: for all they that take the sword shall perish with the sword. Thinkest thou that I cannot now pray to my Father, and He shall presently give me more than twelve legions of angels? But how then shall the Scriptures be fulfilled, that thus it must be?"[2] Along with these words we may also place the question to which John tells us He gave utterance on the same occasion, namely, "The cup which my Father hath given me, shall I not drink it?"[3] And then, as is recorded by Luke, He touched the ear of the person who had been struck, and healed him.

17. Neither should we let the idea disturb us, that some contradiction may be found in the circumstance that Luke tells us how, when the disciples asked Him whether they should smite with the sword, the Lord replied in these words, "Suffer ye thus far," in a manner which might seem to imply that He thus expressed Himself, after the blow had been struck, in terms bearing that He was satisfied with what had been done so far, but desired nothing further to be done; whereas the language which is employed by Matthew might give us rather to understand that this whole incident of the use which Peter made of the sword was displeasing to the Lord. For it is more correct to suppose that when they put the question to Him, "Lord, shall we smite with the sword?" He replied then, "Suffer ye thus far;" His meaning being this: "Let not what is about to take place agitate you. These men are to be suffered to go thus far; that is to say, so far as to apprehend me, and thus to effect the fulfilment of those things which are written of me." We have further to suppose, however, that during the time which passed in the interchange of the question addressed by them to the Lord, and the reply returned by Him to them, Peter was borne on by his intense desire to appear as defender, and by his stronger excitement in the Lord's behalf, to deal the blow. But while these two things might easily have happened at the same time, two different statements could not have been uttered by the same person in one breath.[4] For the writer would not have used the expression, "And Jesus answered and said," unless the words were a reply to the question which had been addressed by those who were about

Him, and not a statement directed to Peter's act. For Matthew is the only one who has recorded the judgment passed by Jesus on Peter's act. And in that passage the phrase which Matthew has employed is also not in the form, "Jesus answered Peter thus, Put up thy sword;" but it runs in these terms: "Then said Jesus unto him, Put up thy sword;" from which it appears that it was after the deed that Jesus thus declared Himself. What is contained, again, in the phraseology used by Luke, namely, "And Jesus answered and said, Suffer ye thus far," must be taken to have been the reply which was returned to the parties who had put the question to Him. But inasmuch as, according to our previous explanation, the single blow with which the servant was struck was delivered just during the time when the terms of the said question and answer were passing between these persons and the Lord, the writer has considered it right to record that act in the same particular order, so that it stands inserted between the words of the interrogation and those in which the response was couched. Consequently, there is nothing here in antagonism to the statement introduced by Matthew, namely, "For all they that take the sword shall perish with the sword," — that is to say, those who may have used the sword. But there might appear to be some inconsistency here if the Lord's answer were taken in a sense which would show Him to have expressed approval on this occasion of the voluntary use of the sword, even although it was only to the effect of a single wound, and that, too, not a fatal one. The words, however, which were addressed to Peter may be understood, as a whole, in an application quite in harmony with the rest; so that, bringing in also what Luke and Matthew have reported, as I have stated above, we obtain the following connection: "Suffer ye thus far. Put up thy sword into its place; for all they that take the sword shall perish with the sword," etc. In what way, moreover, this sentence, "Suffer ye thus far," is to be understood, I have explained already. And if there is any better method of interpreting it, be it so. Only let the veracity of the evangelists be maintained in any case.

18. After this, Matthew continues the narrative, and mentions that in that hour He addressed the multitude as follows: "Are ye come out as against a thief with swords and staves for to take me? I sat daily with you teaching in the temple, and ye laid no hold on me."[5] Then He added also certain words, which Luke introduces thus: "But this is your hour, and the power of darkness."[6] Next comes the sentence given by Matthew: "But all this was done that the Scriptures of the prophets might be fulfilled. Then

---

[1] Luke xxii. 51.   [2] Matt. xxvi. 52–55.   [3] John xviii. 11.
[4] That is to say, while Christ's answer to the disciples and Peter's act might easily have been synchronous, the Lord could not have addressed Himself in different senses to two distinct parties at the same time, namely, to the persons who put the question, and to Peter.

[5] Matt. xxvi. 53.   [6] Luke xxii. 53.

all the disciples forsook Him and fled." This last fact is recorded also by Mark. The same evangelist makes also the following addition: "And there followed Him a certain young man, having a linen cloth cast about his naked body; and when they laid hold on him, he left the linen cloth, and fled from them naked."[1]

CHAP. VI.—OF THE HARMONY CHARACTERIZING THE ACCOUNTS WHICH THESE EVANGELISTS GIVE OF WHAT HAPPENED WHEN THE LORD WAS LED AWAY TO THE HOUSE OF THE HIGH PRIEST, AS ALSO OF THE OCCURRENCES WHICH TOOK PLACE WITHIN THE SAID HOUSE AFTER HE WAS CONDUCTED THERE IN THE NIGHT-TIME, AND IN PARTICULAR OF THE INCIDENT OF PETER'S DENIAL.

19. In the line of Matthew's narrative we come next upon this statement: "And they that laid hold on Jesus led Him away to Caiaphas the high priest, where the scribes and the elders were assembled."[2] We learn, however, from John that He was conducted first to Annas, the father-in-law of Caiaphas.[3] On the other hand, Mark and Luke omit all mention of the name of the high priest.[4] Moreover [we find that] He was led away bound. For, as John informs us, there were at hand there, in the multitude, a tribune and a cohort, and the servants of the Jews.[5] Then in Matthew we have these words: "But Peter followed Him afar off unto the high priest's palace, and went in and sat with the servants to see the end."[6] To this passage in the narrative Mark makes this addition: "And he warmed himself at the fire."[7] Luke also makes a statement which amounts to the same, thus: "Peter followed afar off: and when they had kindled a fire in the midst of the hall, and were sat down together, Peter sat down among them."[8] And John proceeds in these terms: "And Simon Peter followed Jesus, and so did another disciple. That disciple (namely, that other) was known unto the high priest, and went in (as John also tells us) with Jesus into the palace of the high priest. But Peter (as the same John adds) stood at the door without. Then went out that other disciple, which was known unto the high priest, and spake unto her that kept the door, and brought in Peter."[9] For the last fact we are thus indebted to John's narrative. And in this way we see how it came about that Peter also got inside, and was within the hall, as the other evangelists mention.[10]

20. Then Matthew's report goes on thus:

"Now the chief priests and elders and all the council sought false witness against Jesus, to put Him to death, but found none: yea, though many false witnesses came, yet found they none."[11] Mark comes in here with the explanation, that "their witness agreed not together."[12] But, as Matthew continues, "At the last came two false witnesses, and said, This fellow said, I am able to destroy the temple of God, and to build it in three days."[13] Mark states that there were also others who said, "We have heard him say, I will destroy this temple that is made with hands, and within three days I will build another made without hands. And therefore (as Mark also observes in the same passage) their witness did not agree together."[14] Then Matthew gives us the following relation: "And the high priest arose and said unto Him, Answerest thou nothing? What is it which these witness against thee? But Jesus held His peace. And the high priest answered and said unto Him, I adjure thee by the living God, that thou tell us whether thou be the Christ, the Son of God. Jesus saith unto him, Thou hast said."[15] Mark reports the same passage in different terms, only he omits to mention the fact that the high priest adjured Him. He makes it plain, however, that the two expressions ascribed to Jesus as the reply to the high priest,—namely, "Thou hast said," and, "I am,"[16]—really amount to the same. For, as the said Mark puts it, the narrative goes on thus: "And Jesus said, I am; and ye shall see the Son of man sitting on the right hand of power, and coming with the clouds of heaven."[16] This is just as Matthew also presents the passage, with the solitary exception that he does not say that Jesus replied in the phrase "I am." Again, Matthew goes on further in this strain: "Then the high priest rent his clothes, saying, He hath spoken blasphemy; what further need have we of witnesses? Behold, now ye have heard his blasphemy. What think ye? And they answered and said, He is guilty of death."[17] Mark's version of this is entirely to the same effect. So Matthew continues, "Then did they spit in His face, and buffeted Him, and others smote Him with the palms of their hands, saying, Prophesy unto us, thou Christ, Who is he that smote thee?"[18] Mark reports these things in like manner. He also mentions a further fact, namely, that they covered His face.[19] On these incidents we have likewise the testimony of Luke.

21. These things the Lord is understood to have passed through on to the early morning in the high priest's house, to which He was first conducted, and in which Peter was also tempted.

---

[1] Mark xiv. 52.
[2] Matt. xxvi. 57.   [3] John xviii. 13.
[4] Mark xiv. 53; Luke xxii. 54.   [5] John xviii. 12.
[6] Matt. xxvi. 58.   [7] Mark xiv. 54.
[8] Luke xxii. 54, 55.   [9] John xviii. 15-18.
[10] [It is implied here that the denials of Peter took place in the house of Annas, and also that Matthew and Mark, in their account of the night examination, refer to the same event described by John (xviii. 19-23). The objection to this is found in the explicit statement of Matthew (xxvi. 57) in regard to Caiaphas. — R.]

[11] Matt. xxvi. 59, 60.   [12] Mark xiv. 56.
[13] Matt. xxvi. 61.   [14] Mark xiv. 57-59.
[15] Matt. xxvi. 62-64.   [16] Mark xiv. 62.
[17] Matt. xxvi. 65, 66.   [18] Matt. xxvi. 67, 68.
[19] Mark xiv. 65.

With respect, however, to this temptation of Peter, which took place during the time that the Lord was enduring these injuries, the several evangelists do not present the same order in the recital of the circumstances. For Matthew and Mark first narrate the injuries offered to the Lord, and then this temptation of Peter. Luke, again, first describes Peter's temptation, and only after that the reproaches borne by the Lord; while John, on the other hand, first recounts part of Peter's temptation, then introduces some verses recording what the Lord had to bear, next appends a statement to the effect that the Lord was sent away thence (*i.e.* from Annas) to Caiaphas the high priest, and then at this point resumes and sums up the relation which he had commenced of Peter's temptation in the house to which he was first conducted, giving a full account of that incident, thereafter reverting to the succession of things befalling the Lord, and telling us how He was brought to Caiaphas.[1]

22. Accordingly, Matthew proceeds as follows: "Now Peter sat without in the palace; and a damsel came unto him, saying, Thou also wast with Jesus of Galilee. But he denied before them all, saying, I know not what thou sayest. And as he went out into the porch, another maid saw him, and said unto them that were there, This fellow was also with Jesus of Nazareth. And again he denied with an oath, I do not know the man. And after a while came unto him they that stood by, and said to Peter, Surely thou also art one of them, for thy speech bewrayeth thee. Then began he to curse and to swear, saying that he knew not the man. And immediately the cock crew."[2] Such is Matthew's version. But we are also given to understand that after he had gone outside, and when he had now denied the Lord once, the first cock crew, —a fact which Matthew does not specify, but which is intimated by Mark.

23. But it was not when he was outside at the gate that he denied the Lord the second time. That took place after he had come back to the fire-place. There was no need, however, to mention the precise time at which he did thus return. Consequently Mark goes on with his narrative of the incident in these terms: "And he went out into the porch, and the cock crew. And a maid saw him again, and began to say to them that stood by, This is one of them. And he denied it again."[3] This is not the same maid, however, as the former one, but another, as Matthew tells us. Nay, we gather further that on the occasion of the second denial he

was addressed by two parties, namely, by the maid who is mentioned by Matthew and Mark, and also by another person who is noticed by Luke. For Luke's account runs in this style: "And Peter followed afar off. And when they had kindled a fire in the midst of the hall, and were sat down together, Peter sat down among them. But a certain maid beheld him as he sat by the fire, and earnestly looked upon him, and said, This man was also with him. And he denied Him, saying, Woman, I know Him not. And after a little while, another saw him, and said, "Thou art also of them."[4] Now the clause, "And after a little while," which Luke introduces, covers the period during which [we may suppose that] Peter went out and the first cock crew. By this time, however, he had come in again; and thus we can understand the consistency of John's narrative, which informs us that he denied the Lord the second time as he stood by the fire. For in his version of Peter's first denial, John not only says nothing about the first crowing of the cock (which holds good of the other evangelists, too, with the exception of Mark), but also leaves unnoticed the fact that it was as he sat by the fire that the maid recognised him. For all that John says there is this, "Then saith the damsel that kept the door unto Peter, Art not thou also one of this man's disciples? He saith, I am not."[5] Then he brings in the statement which he deemed it right to make on the subject of what took place with Jesus in that same house. His record of this is to the following effect: "And the servants and officers stood there, who had made a fire of coals, for it was cold. And they warmed themselves; and Peter stood with them, and warmed himself."[6] Here, therefore, we may suppose Peter to have gone out, and by this time to have come in again. For at first he was sitting by the fire; and after a space, as we gather, he had returned, and commenced to stand [by the hearth].

24. It may be, however, that some one will say to us: Peter had not actually gone out as yet, but had only risen with the purpose of going out. This may be the allegation of one who is of opinion that the second interrogation and denial took place when Peter was outside at the door. Let us therefore look at what follows in John's narrative. It is to this effect: "The high priest then asked Jesus of His disciples, and of His doctrine. Jesus answered him, I spake openly to the world; I ever taught in the synagogue, and in the temple, whither the Jews always resort; and in secret have I said nothing. Why askest thou me? ask them which heard me what I have said unto them: behold, they know what I said. And when He had

---

[1] [The evangelists indicate three distinct episodes of recognition and denial, but do not refer to the same facts in detail. This Augustin seems to apprehend — R.]

[2] Matt. xxvi. 69–74.   [3] Mark xiv. 68–70.

[4] Luke xxii. 54–58.   [5] John xviii. 17.   [6] John xviii. 18.

thus spoken, one of the officers which stood by struck Jesus with the palm of his hand, saying, Answerest thou the high priest so? Jesus answered him, If I have spoken evil, bear witness of the evil; but if well, why smitest thou me? And Annas sent Him bound to Caiaphas the high priest." [1] This certainly shows us that Annas was high priest. For Jesus had not been sent to Caiaphas as yet, when the question was thus put to Him, "Answerest thou the high priest so?" Mention is also made of Annas and Caiaphas as high priests by Luke at the beginning of his Gospel. [2] After these statements, John reverts to the account which he had previously begun of Peter's denial. Thus he brings us back to the house in which the incidents took place which he has recorded, and from which Jesus was sent away to Caiaphas, to whom He was being conducted at the commencement of this scene, as Matthew has informed us. [3] Moreover, it is in the way of a recapitulation that John records the matters regarding Peter which he has introduced at this point. Falling back upon his narration of that incident with the view of making up a complete account of the threefold denial, he proceeds thus: "And Simon stood and warmed himself. They said therefore unto him, Art not thou also one of his disciples? He denied it, and said, I am not." [4] Here, therefore, we find that Peter's second denial occurred, not when he was at the door, but as he was standing by the fire. This, however, could not have been the case, had he not returned by this time after having gone outside. For it is not that by this second occasion he had actually gone out, and that the other maid who is referred to saw him there outside; but the matter is put as if it was on his going out that she saw him; or, in other words, it was when he rose to go out that she observed him, and said to those who were there, — that is, to those who were gathered by the fire inside, within the court, — "This fellow was also with Jesus of Nazareth." Then we are to suppose that the man who had thus gone outside, on hearing this assertion, came in again, and swore to those who were now inimically disposed, "I do not know the man." [5] In like manner, Mark also says of this same maid, that "she began to say to them that stood by, This is one of them." [6] For this damsel was speaking not to Peter, but to those who had remained there when he went out. At the same time, she spoke in such a manner that

he heard her words; whereupon he came back and stood again by the fire, and met their words with a negative. Then we have the statement made by John in these terms: "They said, Art not thou also one of his disciples?" We understand this question to have been addressed to him on his return as he stood there; and we also recognise the harmony in which this stands with the position that on this occasion Peter had to do not only with that other maid who is mentioned by Matthew and Mark in connection with this second denial, but also with that other person who is introduced by Luke. This is the reason why John uses the plural, "They said." The explanation then may be, that when the maid said to those who were with her in the court as he went out, "This is one of them," he heard her words and returned with the purpose of clearing himself, as it were, by a denial. Or, in accordance with the more probable theory, we may suppose that he did not catch what was said about him as he went out, and that on his return the maid and the other person who is introduced by Luke addressed him thus, "Art not thou also one of his disciples?" that he met them with a denial, "and said, I am not;" and further, that when this other person of whom Luke speaks insisted more pertinaciously, and said, "Surely thou art one of them," Peter answered thus, "Man, I am not." Still, when we compare together all the statements made by the several evangelists on this subject, we come clearly to the conclusion, that Peter's second denial took place, not when he was at the door, but when he was within, by the fire in the court. It becomes evident, therefore, that Matthew and Mark, who have told us how he went without, have left the fact of his return unnoticed simply with a view to brevity.

25. Accordingly, let us next examine into the consistency of the evangelists so far as the third denial is concerned, which we have previously instanced in the statement given by Matthew only. Mark then goes on with his version in these terms: "And a little after, they that stood by said again to Peter, Surely thou art one of them; for thou art a Galilæan. But he began to curse and to swear, saying, I know not this man of whom ye speak. And immediately the second time the cock crew." [7] Luke, again, continues his narrative, relating the same incident in this fashion: "And about the space of one hour after, another confidently affirmed, Of a truth this fellow also was with him; for he is a Galilæan. And Peter said, Man, I know not what thou sayest. And immediately while he yet spake the cock crew." [8] John follows with his account of Peter's third denial, which is thus

[1] John xviii. 19-24.   [2] Luke iii. 2.
[3] Matt. xxviii. 57. [See note on § 19. Augustin's Latin text in John xviii. 24, *et misit eum*, etc., agrees in tense with the Greek. The Authorized Version incorrectly renders, "Now Annas had sent," etc. The Revised Version has, "Annas therefore sent." The theory of two distinct night examinations (before Annas first, and then before Caiaphas) agrees best with the literal sense. Both may have occupied parts of the same house. — R.]
[4] John xviii. 25.   [5] Matt. xxviii. 71.   [6] Mark xiv. 69.
[7] Mark xiv. 70-72.   [8] Luke xxii. 59, 60.

given : " One of the servants of the high priest, being his kinsman whose ear Peter cut off, saith, Did not I see thee in the garden with him? Peter then denied again ; and immediately the cock crew." [1]   Now what precise period of time is meant under the phrase, " a little after," which is employed by Matthew and Mark, is made clear by Luke, when he says, " And about the space of one hour after." John, however, conveys no intimation of this space of time. Again, with respect to the circumstance that Matthew and Mark use the plural number instead of the singular, and speak of the persons who were engaged with Peter, while Luke mentions only a single individual, and John, too, specifies but one, particularizing him further as kinsman to him whose ear Peter cut off ; we may easily explain it either by understanding Matthew and Mark to have adopted a familiar method of speech here in employing the plural number simply instead of the singular, or by supposing that one of the persons present — one who knew Peter and had seen him — took the lead in making the declaration, and that the rest, imitating his confidence, joined him in pressing the assertion upon Peter. If this is the case, then two of the evangelists have given the general statement, using simply the plural number ; while the other two have preferred to particularize only the one special individual who played the chief part in the transaction. But, once more, Matthew affirms that the words, " Surely thou also art one of them, for thy speech bewrayeth thee," were spoken to Peter himself. In like manner, John tells us that the question, " Did not I see thee in the garden with him? " was addressed directly to Peter. But Mark, on the other hand, gives us to understand that the sentence, " Surely he is one of them, for he is also a Galilæan," was what those who stood by said to each other about Peter. And, in the same way, Luke indicates that the declaration uttered by the other person, who said, " Of a truth, this fellow also was with him, for he is a Galilæan," was not addressed to Peter, but was made regarding Peter. These variations, however, may be explained either by understanding the evangelists, who speak of Peter as the person directly addressed, to have fairly reproduced the general sense, inasmuch as what was spoken about the man in his own presence was much the same as if it had been spoken immediately to him ; or by supposing that both these methods of address were actually practised, and that the one has been noticed by the former evangelists, and the other by the latter. Moreover, we take the second cockcrowing to have occurred after the third denial, as Mark has expressly informed us.

26. Matthew then proceeds with his narrative in these terms : " And Peter remembered the word of Jesus which He had said unto him, Before the cock crow thou shalt deny me thrice. And he went out and wept bitterly." [2]   Mark, again, gives it thus : " And Peter called to mind the word that Jesus had said unto him, Before the cock crow twice thou shalt deny me thrice. And he began to weep." [3]   Luke's version is as follows : " And the Lord turned and looked upon Peter. And Peter remembered the word of the Lord, how He had said unto him, Before the cock crow thou shalt deny me thrice. And Peter went out and wept bitterly." [4]   John says nothing about Peter's recollection and weeping. Now, the statement made here by Luke, to the effect that " the Lord turned and looked upon Peter," is one which requires more careful consideration, with a view to its correct acceptance. For although there are also inner halls (or courts), so named, it was in the outer court (or hall) that Peter appeared on this occasion among the servants, who were warming themselves along with him at the fire. And it is not a credible supposition that Jesus was heard by the Jews in this place, so that we might also understand the *look* referred to to have been a look with the bodily eye. For Matthew presents us first with this narrative : " Then did they spit in His face and buffeted Him ; and others smote Him with the palms of their hands, saying, Prophesy unto us, thou Christ, who is he that smote thee ? " [5]   And then he follows this up immediately with the paragraph about Peter : " Now Peter sat without in the palace." [6]   He would not, however, have used this latter expression, had it not been the case that the things previously alluded to were done to the Lord inside the house. And, indeed, as we gather from Mark's version, these things took place not simply in the interior, but also in the upper parts of the house. For, after recording the said circumstances, Mark goes on thus : " And as Peter was beneath in the palace." [7]   Thus, as Matthew's words, " Now Peter sat without in the palace," show us that the things previously mentioned took place inside the house, so Mark's words, " And as Peter was beneath in the palace," indicate that they were done not only in the interior, but in the upper parts of the house. But if this is the case, how could the Lord have looked on Peter with the actual glance of the bodily eye? These considerations bring

---

[1] John xviii. 26, 27.

[2] Matt. xxvi. 75.
[3] Mark xiv. 72: the words, "when he thought thereon," being omitted. [There is nothing omitted. The difficult Greek term (ἐπιβαλών) is explained by "when he thought thereon " in the Authorized Version. Augustin's view is given in Revised Version margin, " And he began to weep." — R.]
[4] Luke xxii. 61, 62.   [5] Matt. xxvi. 67, 68.
[6] *Atrio*, court. [The Revised Version properly renders the terms referring to the " court," etc. " Palace " (Authorized Version) is misleading. — R.]
[7] Mark xiv. 66.

me to the conclusion, that the look in question was one cast upon Peter from Heaven, the effect of which was to bring up before his mind the number of times he had now denied [his Master], and the declaration which the Lord had made to him prophetically, and in this way (the Lord thus looking mercifully upon him [1]), to lead him to repent, and to weep salutary tears. The expression, therefore, will be a parallel to other modes of speech which we employ daily, as when we thus pray, "Lord, look upon me ; " or as when, in reference to one who has been delivered by the divine mercy from some danger or trouble, we say that the " Lord looked upon him." In the Scriptures, also, we find such words as these : " Look upon me and hear me ; " [2] and " Return,[3] O Lord, and deliver my soul." [4] And, according to my judgment, a similar view is to be taken of the expression adopted here, when it is said that " the Lord turned and looked upon Peter ; and Peter remembered the word of the Lord." Finally, we have to notice how, while it is the more usual practice with the evangelists to employ the name " Jesus " in preference to the word " Lord " in their narratives, Luke has used the latter term exclusively in the said sentence, saying expressly, " The ' Lord ' turned and looked upon Peter ; and Peter remembered the word of the ' Lord : ' " whereas Matthew and Mark have passed over this " look " in silence, and consequently have said that Peter remembered not the word of the " Lord, " but the word of " Jesus." From this, therefore, we may gather that the " look " thus proceeding from Jesus was not one with the eyes of the human body, but a look cast from Heaven.[5]

CHAP. VII. — OF THE THOROUGH HARMONY OF THE EVANGELISTS IN THE DIFFERENT ACCOUNTS OF WHAT TOOK PLACE IN THE EARLY MORNING, PREVIOUS TO THE DELIVERY OF JESUS TO PILATE ; AND OF THE QUESTION TOUCHING THE PASSAGE WHICH IS QUOTED ON THE SUBJECT OF THE PRICE SET UPON THE LORD, AND WHICH IS ASCRIBED TO JEREMIAH BY MATTHEW, ALTHOUGH NO SUCH PARAGRAPH IS FOUND IN THE WRITINGS OF THAT PROPHET.

27. Matthew next proceeds as follows : " When the morning was come, all the chief priests and elders of the people took counsel against Jesus, to put Him to death ; and when they had bound Him, they led Him away, and delivered Him to Pontius Pilate the governor." [6] Mark's version is to the like effect : " And straightway in the morning, the chief priests held a consultation with the elders and scribes, and the whole council, and bound Jesus, and carried Him away,

and delivered Him to Pilate." [7] Luke, again, after completing his account of Peter's denial, recapitulates what Jesus had to endure when it was now about daybreak, as it appears, and continues his narrative in the following connection : " And the men that held Jesus mocked Him, and smote Him ; and when they had blindfolded Him, they struck Him on the face, and asked Him, saying, Prophesy, who is it that smote thee ? And many other things blasphemously spake they against Him. And as soon as it was day, the elders of the people, and the chief priests, and the scribes came together, and led Him into their council, saying, Art thou the Christ? tell us. And He said unto them, If I tell you, ye will not believe ; and if I also ask you, ye will not answer me, nor let me go. Hereafter shall the Son of man sit on the right hand of the power of God. Then said they all, Art thou then the Son of God ? And He said unto them, Ye say that I am. And they said, What need we further witness? For we ourselves have heard of His own mouth. And the whole multitude of them arose, and led Him unto Pilate." [8] Luke has thus recorded all these things. His statement contains certain facts which are also related by Matthew and Mark ; namely, that the Lord was asked whether He was the Son of God, and that He made this reply, " I say unto you, hereafter shall ye see the Son of man sitting on the right hand of power, and coming in the clouds of heaven." And we gather that these things took place when the day was now breaking, because Luke's expression is, " And as soon as it was day." Thus Luke's narrative is similar to those of the others, although he also introduces something which these others have left unnoticed. We gather further, that when it was yet night, the Lord faced the ordeal of the false witnesses,— a fact which is recorded briefly by Matthew and Mark, and which is passed over in silence by Luke, who, however, has told the story of what was done when the dawn was coming in. The former two — namely, Matthew and Mark — have given connected narratives of all that the Lord passed through until early morning. After that, however, they have reverted to the story of Peter's denial ; on the conclusion of which they have come back upon the events of the early morning, and have introduced the other circumstances which remained for recital with a view to the completion of their account of what befell the Lord.[9] But up to this point they have given no account of the occurrences belonging specifically to the morning.[10] In like manner

[1] Or, regarding him, respiciente.
[2] Ps. xiii. 3.   [3] Converte.   [4] Ps. vi. 4.
[5] [This fanciful interpretation is unnecessary. The inner court of the large Jewish house, with rooms looking upon it, would allow place for all the incidents, without any departure from the simple historical sense. — R.]
[6] Matt. xxvii. 1, 2.

[7] Mark xv. 1, 2.
[8] Luke xxii. 63–xxiii. 1. [That Luke's account gives in detail the formal meeting of the Sanhedrin at daybreak is altogether probable, since Matthew and Mark distinguish this assembly from the night examination. — R.]
[9] The text gives: ut inde cætera contexerent quousque perducerent, etc. Seven MSS. read perduxerant, = as far as they had drawn out their account, etc.
[10] Matt. xxvi. 59–xxvii. 1, 2; Mark xiv. 55–xv. 1, 2.

John, after recording what was done with the Lord as fully as he deemed requisite, and after telling also the whole story of Peter's denial, continues his narrative in these terms: "Then lead they Jesus to Caiaphas,[1] unto the hall of judgment. And it was early."[2] Here we might suppose either that there had been something imperatively requiring Caiaphas' presence in the hall of judgment, and that he was absent on the occasion when the other chief priests held an inquiry on the Lord; or else that the hall of judgment was in his house; and that yet from the beginning of this scene they had thus only been leading Jesus away to the personage in whose presence He was at last actually conducted. But as they brought the accused person in the character of one already convicted, and as it had previously approved itself to Caiaphas' judgment that Jesus should die, there was no further delay in delivering Him over to Pilate, with a view to His being put to death.[3] And thus it is that Matthew here relates what took place between Pilate and the Lord.

28. First, however, he makes a digression with the purpose of telling the story of Judas' end, which is related only by him. His account is in these terms: "Then Judas, which had betrayed Him, when he saw that He was condemned, repented himself, and brought again the thirty pieces of silver to the chief priests and elders, saying, I have sinned, in that I have betrayed the innocent blood. And they said, What is that to us? See thou to that. And he cast down the pieces of silver in the temple, and departed, and went and hanged himself. And the chief priests took the silver pieces, and said, It is not lawful for to put them into the treasury, because it is the price of blood. And they took counsel, and bought with them the potter's field, to bury strangers in. Wherefore that field was called, The field of blood, unto this day. Then was fulfilled that which was spoken by Jeremy the prophet, saying, And they took the thirty pieces of silver, the price of Him that was valued, whom the children of Israel[4] did value, and gave them for the potter's field, as the Lord appointed me."[5]

29. Now, if any one finds a difficulty in the circumstance that this passage is not found in the writings of the prophet Jeremiah, and thinks that damage is thus done to the veracity of the evangelist, let him first take notice of the fact that this ascription of the passage to Jeremiah is not contained in all the codices of the Gospels, and that some of them state simply that it was spoken "*by the prophet.*" It is possible, therefore, to affirm that those codices deserve rather to be followed which do not contain the name of Jeremiah. For these words were certainly spoken by a prophet, only that prophet was Zechariah. In this way the supposition is, that those codices are faulty which contain the name of Jeremiah, because they ought either to have given the name of Zechariah or to have mentioned no name at all, as is the case with a certain copy, merely stating that it was spoken "*by the prophet, saying,*" which prophet would assuredly be understood to be Zechariah. However, let others adopt this method of defence, if they are so minded. For my part, I am not satisfied with it; and the reason is, that a majority of codices contain the name of Jeremiah, and that those critics who have studied the Gospel with more than usual care in the Greek copies, report that they have found it stand so in the more ancient Greek exemplars. I look also to this further consideration, namely, that there was no reason why this name should have been added [subsequently to the true text], and a corruption thus created; whereas there was certainly an intelligible reason for erasing the name from so many of the codices. For venturesome inexperience might readily have done that, when perplexed with the problem presented by the fact that this passage could not be found in Jeremiah.[6]

30. How, then, is the matter to be explained, but by supposing that this has been done in accordance with the more secret counsel of that providence of God by which the minds of the evangelists were governed? For it may have been the case, that when Matthew was engaged in composing his Gospel, the word Jeremiah occurred to his mind, in accordance with a familiar experience, instead of Zechariah. Such an inaccuracy, however, he would most undoubtedly have corrected (having his attention called to it, as surely would have been the case, by some who might have read it while he was still alive in the flesh), had he not reflected that [perhaps] it was not without a purpose that the name of the one prophet had been suggested instead of the other in the process of recalling the circumstances (which process of recollection was also directed by the Holy Spirit), and that this might not have occurred to him had it not been the Lord's purpose to have it so written. If it is asked, however, why the Lord should have so determined it, there is this first and most serviceable reason, which deserves our most immediate

[1] Adducunt ergo Jesum *ad* Caiapham.   [2] John xviii. 28.
[3] In his 114 *Tractate* on John, Augustin again attempts to grapple with the difficulty created here by the reading which was before him, namely, *to* Caiaphas, instead of *from* Caiaphas. [The Greek text is "from Caiaphas." The other reading is probably a harmonistic error, of early origin. — R.]
[4] The text gives *filii Israel,* instead of *a filiis Israel* = they of the children of Israel.
[5] Matt. xxvii. 3-10.

[6] [It is refreshing to find this exhibition of critical judgment and candour. The critical canon respecting the *lectio difficilior* is virtually accepted. The easier reading was suggested by Origen. — R.]

consideration, namely, that some idea was thus conveyed of the marvellous manner in which all the holy prophets, speaking in one spirit, continued in perfect unison with each other in their utterances,—a circumstance certainly much more calculated to impress the mind than would have been the case had all the words of all these prophets been spoken by the mouth of a single individual. The same consideration might also fitly suggest the duty of accepting unhesitatingly whatever the Holy Spirit has given expression to through the agency of these prophets, and of looking upon their individual communications as also those of the whole body, and on their collective communications as also those of each separately. If, then, it is the case that words spoken by Jeremiah are really as much Zechariah's as Jeremiah's, and, on the other hand, that words spoken by Zechariah are really as much Jeremiah's as they are Zechariah's, what necessity was there for Matthew to correct his text when he read over what he had written, and found that the one name had occurred to him instead of the other? Was it not rather the proper course for him to bow to the authority of the Holy Spirit, under whose guidance he certainly felt his mind to be placed in a more decided sense than is the case with us, and consequently to leave untouched what he had thus written, in accordance with the Lord's counsel and appointment, with the intent to give us to understand that the prophets maintain so complete a harmony with each other in the matter of their utterances that it becomes nothing absurd, but, in fact, a most consistent thing for us to credit Jeremiah with a sentence originally spoken by Zechariah?[1] For if, in these days of ours, a person, desiring to bring under our notice the words of a certain individual, happens to mention the name of another by whom the words were not actually uttered,[2] but who at the same time is the most intimate friend and associate of the man by whom they were really spoken; and if forthwith recollecting that he has given the one name instead of the other, he recovers himself and corrects the mistake, but does it nevertheless in some such way as this, "After all, what I said was not amiss;" what would we take to be meant by this, but just that there subsists so perfect a unison of sentiment between the two parties — that is to say, the man whose words the individual in question intended to repeat, and the second person whose name occurred to him at the time instead of that of the other — that it comes much to the same thing to represent the words to have been spoken by

the former as to say that they were uttered by the latter? How much more, then, is this a usage which might well be understood and most particularly commended to our attention in the case of the holy prophets, so that we might accept the books composed by the whole series of them, as if they formed but a single book written by one author, in which no discrepancy with regard to the subjects dealt with should be supposed to exist, as none would be found, and in which there would be a more remarkable example of consistency and veracity than would have been the case had a single individual, even the most learned, been the enunciator of all these sayings? Therefore, while there are those, whether unbelievers or merely ignorant men, who endeavour to find an argument here to help them in demonstrating a want of harmony between the holy evangelists, men of faith and learning, on the other hand, ought rather to bring this into the service of proving the unity which characterizes the holy prophets.[3]

31. I have also another reason (the fuller discussion of which must be reserved, I think, for another opportunity, in order to prevent the present discourse from extending to larger limits than may be allowed by the necessity which rests upon us to bring this work to a conclusion) to offer in explanation of the fact that the name of Jeremiah has been permitted, or rather directed, by the authority of the Holy Spirit, to stand in this passage instead of that of Zechariah. It is stated in Jeremiah that he bought a field from the son of his brother, and paid him money for it. That sum of money is not given, indeed, under the name of the particular price which is found in Zechariah, namely, thirty pieces of silver; but, on the other hand, there is no mention of the buying of the field in Zechariah. Now, it is evident that the evangelist has interpreted the prophecy which speaks of the thirty pieces of silver as something which has received its fulfilment only in the Lord's case, so that it is made to stand for the price set upon Him. But again, that the words which were uttered by Jeremiah on the subject of the purchase of the field have also a bearing upon the same matter, may have been mystically signified by the selection thus made in introducing [into the evangelical narrative] the name of Jeremiah, who spoke of the purchase of the field, instead of that of Zechariah, to whom we are indebted for the notice of the thirty pieces of silver. In this way, on perusing first the Gospel, and finding the name of Jeremiah there, and then, again, on perusing Jeremiah, and failing there to discover the passage about the thirty pieces of silver, but seeing at the same

---

[1] [The simplest explanation is, that the name "Jeremiah" was applied to the collection of prophetical books, in which it was placed first by the Jews. — R.]

[2] Reading *a quo non dicta sint.* Most of the mss. omit the *non.*

[3] [This explanation is at variance with many of the healthy expressions regarding inspiration which abound in Augustin's expository writings. — R.]

time the section about the purchase of the field, the reader would be taught to compare the two paragraphs together, and get at the real meaning of the prophecy, and learn how it also stands in relation to this fulfilment of prophecy which was exhibited in the instance of our Lord. For [it is also to be remarked that] Matthew makes the following addition to the passage cited, namely, " Whom the children of Israel did value ; and gave them the potter's field, as the Lord appointed me." Now, these words are not to be found either in Zechariah or in Jeremiah. Hence we must rather take them to have been inserted with a nice and mystical meaning by the evangelist, on his own responsibility, — the Lord having given him to understand, by revelation, that a prophecy of the said tenor had a real reference to this occurrence, which took place in connection with the price set upon Christ. Moreover, in Jeremiah, the evidence of the purchase of the field is ordered to be cast into an earthen vessel. In like manner, we find in the Gospel that the money paid for the Lord was used for the purchase of a potter's field, which field also was to be employed as a burying-place for strangers. And it may be that all this was significant of the permanence of the repose of those who sojourn like strangers in this present world, and are buried with Christ by baptism. For the Lord also declared to Jeremiah, that the said purchase of the field was expressive of the fact that in that land [of Judæa] there would be a remnant of the people delivered from their captivity.[1] I judged it proper to give some sort of sketch[2] of these things, as I was calling attention to the kind of significance which a really careful and painstaking study should look for in these testimonies of the prophets, when they are reduced to a unity and compared with the evangelical narrative. These, then, are the statements which Matthew has introduced with reference to the traitor Judas.

CHAP. VIII. — OF THE ABSENCE OF ANY DISCREPANCIES IN THE ACCOUNTS WHICH THE EVANGELISTS GIVE OF WHAT TOOK PLACE IN PILATE'S PRESENCE.

32. He next proceeds as follows : "And Jesus stood before the governor : and the governor asked Him, saying, Art thou the King of the Jews? Jesus saith unto him, Thou sayest. And when He was accused of the chief priests and elders, He answered nothing. Then saith Pilate unto Him, Hearest thou not how many things they witness against thee? And He answered him to never a word ; insomuch that the governor marvelled greatly. Now at that feast the governor was wont to release unto the people a prisoner, whom they would. And they had then a notable prisoner, called Barabbas. Therefore when they were gathered together, Pilate said unto them, Whom will ye that I release unto you? Barabbas, or Jesus which is called Christ? For he knew that for envy they had delivered Him. But when he was set down on the judgment-seat, his wife sent unto him, saying, Have thou nothing to do with that just man : for I have suffered many things this day in a dream because of him. But the chief priests and elders persuaded the multitude that they should ask Barabbas, and destroy Jesus. But the governor answered and said unto them, Whether of the twain will ye that I release unto you? And they said, Barabbas. Pilate saith unto them, What shall I do then with Jesus which is called Christ? They all say, Let him be crucified. The governor said to them, Why, what evil hath he done? But they cried out the more, saying, Let him be crucified. When Pilate saw that he could prevail nothing, but that rather a tumult was made, he took water and washed his hands before the multitude, saying, I am innocent of the blood of this just person ; see ye to it. Then answered all the people, and said, His blood be on us, and on our children. Then released he Barabbas unto them ; and when he had scourged Jesus, he delivered Him to them to be crucified."[3] These are the things which Matthew has reported to have been done to the Lord by Pilate.

33. Mark also presents an almost entire identity with the above, both in language and in subject. The words, however, in which Pilate replied to the people when they asked him to release one prisoner according to the custom of the feast, are reported by this evangelist as follows : " But Pilate answered them, saying, Will ye that I release unto you the King of the Jews?"[4] On the other hand, Matthew gives them thus : "Therefore when they were gathered together, Pilate said unto them, Whom will ye that I release unto you? Barabbas, or Jesus which is called Christ?" There need be no difficulty in the circumstance that Matthew says nothing about the people having requested that one should be released unto them. But it may fairly be asked, what were the words which Pilate actually uttered, whether these reported by Matthew, or those recited by Mark. For there seems to be some difference between these two forms of expression, namely, "Whom will ye that I release unto you? Barabbas, or Jesus which is called Christ?" and, "Will ye that I release unto you the King of the Jews?" Nevertheless, as they were in the habit of calling

---

[1] See Jer. xxxii.
[2] Reading *delineanda*. Four MSS. give *delibanda* = proper to touch upon.

[3] Matt. xxvii. 11-26.　　　[4] Mark xv. 9.

their kings "anointed ones," [1] and one might use the one term or the other, [2] it is evident that what Pilate asked them was whether they would have the King of the Jews, that is, the Christ, released unto them. And it matters nothing to the real identity in meaning that Mark, desiring simply to relate what concerned the Lord Himself, has not mentioned Barabbas here. For, in the report which he gives of their reply, he indicates with sufficient clearness who the person was whom they asked to have released unto them. His version is this: "But the chief priests moved the people, that he should rather release Barabbas unto them." Then he proceeds to add the sentence, "And Pilate answered and said again unto them, What will ye then that I should do unto him whom ye call the King of the Jews?" This makes it plain enough now, that in speaking of the King of the Jews, Mark meant to express the very sense which Matthew intended to convey by using the term "Christ." For kings were not called "anointed ones" [1] except among the Jews; and the form which Matthew gives to the words in question is this, "Pilate saith unto them, What shall I do then with Jesus which is called Christ?" So Mark continues, "And they cried out again, Crucify him:" which appears thus in Matthew, "They all say unto him, Let him be crucified." Again Mark goes on, "Then Pilate said unto them, Why, what evil hath he done? And they cried out the more exceedingly, Crucify him." Matthew has not recorded this passage; but he has introduced the statement, "When Pilate saw that he could prevail nothing, but that rather a tumult was made," and has also informed us how he washed his hands before the people with the view of declaring himself innocent of the blood of that just person (a circumstance not reported by Mark and the others). And thus he has also shown us with all due plainness how the governor dealt with the people with the intention of securing His release. This has been briefly referred to by Mark, when he tells us that Pilate said, "Why, what evil hath he done?" And thereupon Mark also concludes his account of what took place between Pilate and the Lord in these terms: "And so Pilate, willing to content the people, released Barabbas unto them, and delivered Jesus, when he had scourged Him, to be crucified." The above is Mark's recital of what occurred in presence of the governor. [3]

34. Luke gives the following version of what took place in presence of Pilate: "And they began to accuse Him, saying, We found this fellow perverting the nation, and forbidding to give tribute to Cæsar, and saying that he himself is Christ a king." [4] The previous two evangelists have not recorded these words, although they do mention the fact that these parties accused Him. Luke is thus the one who has specified the terms of the false accusations which were brought against Him. On the other hand, he does not state that Pilate said to Him, "Answerest thou nothing? behold, how many things they witness against thee." Instead of introducing these sentences, Luke goes on to relate other matters which are also reported by these two. Thus he continues: "And Pilate asked Him, saying, Art thou the King of the Jews? And He answered him and said, Thou sayest." Matthew and Mark have likewise inserted this fact, previous to the statement that Jesus was taken to task for not answering His accusers. The truth, however, is not at all affected by the order in which Luke has narrated these things; and as little is it affected by the mere circumstance that one writer passes over some incident without notice, which another expressly specifies. We have an instance in what follows; namely, "Then said Pilate to the chief priests and to the people, I find no fault in this man. And they were the more fierce, saying, He stirreth up the people, teaching throughout all Jewry, beginning from Galilee to this place. But when Pilate heard of Galilee, he asked whether the man were a Galilean. And as soon as he knew that He belonged unto Herod's jurisdiction, he sent Him to Herod, who himself also was at Jerusalem at that time. And when Herod saw Jesus, he was exceeding glad; for he was desirous to see Him of a long season, because he had heard many things of Him, and he hoped to see some miracle done by Him. Then he questioned with Him in many words; but He answered him nothing. And the chief priests and scribes stood and vehemently accused Him. And Herod with his men of war set Him at nought, and mocked Him, and arrayed Him in a gorgeous robe, and sent Him again to Pilate. And the same day Herod and Pilate were made friends together: for before they were at enmity between themselves." [5] All these things are related by Luke alone, namely, the fact that the Lord was sent by Pilate to Herod, and the account of what took place on that occasion. At the same time, among the statements which he makes in this passage, there are some bearing a resemblance to matters which may be found reported by the other evangelists in connection with different portions of their narrations. But the immediate object of these others, however, was to recount simply the various things which were done in Pilate's presence on to the time when the Lord was delivered over to be crucified.

[1] Or, *Christs*, Christos.
[2] The text gives: *et qui dixit illum an illum.*
[3] Mark xv. 2–15.

[4] Luke xxiii. 2, 3.   [5] Luke xxii. 4–12.

In accordance with his own plan, however, Luke makes the above digression with the view of telling what occurred with Herod; and after that he reverts to the history of what took place in the governor's presence. Thus he now continues as follows: "And Pilate, when he had called together the chief priests and the rulers and the people, said unto them, Ye have brought this man unto me as one that perverteth the people: and, behold, I having examined him before you, have found no fault in this man touching those things whereof ye accuse him." [1] Here we notice that he has omitted to mention how Pilate asked the Lord what answer He had to make to His accusers. Thereafter he proceeds in these terms: "No, nor yet Herod: for I sent you to him: and, lo, nothing worthy of death is done unto him. I will therefore chastise him and release him. For of necessity he must release one unto them at the feast. And they cried out all at once, saying, Away with this man, and release unto us Barabbas; who for a certain sedition made in the city, and for murder, was cast into prison. Pilate, therefore, willing to release Jesus, spake again to them. But they cried, saying, Crucify him, crucify him. And he said unto them the third time, Why, what evil hath he done? I have found no cause of death in him: I will therefore chastise him and let him go. And they were instant with loud voices, requiring that He might be crucified; and the voices of them [2] prevailed." [3] The repeated effort which Pilate, in his desire to accomplish the release of Jesus, thus made to gain the people's consent, is satisfactorily attested by Matthew, although in a very few words, when he says, "But when Pilate saw that he could prevail nothing, but that rather a tumult was made." For he would not have made such a statement at all, had not Pilate exerted himself earnestly in that direction, although at the same time he has not told us how often he made such attempts to rescue Jesus from their fury. Accordingly, Luke concludes his report of what took place in the governor's presence in this fashion: "And Pilate gave sentence that it should be as they required. And he released unto them him that for sedition and murder was cast into prison, whom they desired; but he delivered Jesus to their will." [4]

35. Let us next take the account of these same incidents — that is to say, those in which Pilate was engaged — as it is presented by John. He proceeds thus: "And they themselves went not into the judgment-hall, lest they should be defiled; but that they might eat the passover. Pilate then went out unto them, and said, What accusation bring ye against this man? They answered and said unto him, If he were not a malefactor, we would not have delivered him up unto thee." [5] We must look into this passage in order to show that it contains nothing inconsistent with Luke's version, which states that certain charges were brought against Him, and also specifies their terms. For Luke's words are these: "And they began to accuse Him, saying, We found this fellow perverting the nation, and forbidding to give tribute to Cæsar, saying that he himself is Christ a king." On the other hand, according to the paragraph which I have now cited from John, the Jews seem to have been unwilling to state any specific accusations, when Pilate asked them, "What accusation bring ye against this man?" For their reply was, "If he were not a malefactor, we would not have delivered him up unto thee;" the purport of which was, that he should accept their authority, cease to inquire what fault was alleged against Him, and believe Him guilty for the simple reason that He had been [reckoned] worthy of being delivered up by them to him. This being the case, then, we ought to suppose that both these versions report words which were actually said, both the one before us at present, and the one given by Luke. For among the multitude of sayings and replies which passed between the parties, these writers have made their own selections as far as their judgment allowed them to go, and each of them has introduced into his narrative just what he considered sufficient. It is also true that John himself mentions certain charges which were alleged against Him, and which we shall find in their proper connections. Here, then, he proceeds thus: "Then said Pilate unto them, Take y° him, and judge him according to your law. The Jews, therefore, said unto him, It is not lawful for us to put any man to death; that the saying of Jesus might be fulfilled, which He spake, signifying what death He should die. Then Pilate entered into the judgment-hall again, and called Jesus, and said unto Him, Art thou the King of the Jews? And Jesus answered, Sayest thou this thing of thyself, or did others tell it thee of me?" [6] This again may seem not to harmonize with what is recorded by the others, — namely, "Jesus answered, Thou sayest," — unless it is made clear in what follows that the one thing was said as well as the other. Hence he gives us to understand that the matters which he records next are [not to be regarded as] things never actually uttered by the Lord, but are rather to be considered things which have been passed

[1] Luke xxiii. 13, 14.
[2] The words, *and of the chief priests*, are omitted in the text. [So the Greek text, according to the best authorities. Comp. Revised Version. — R.]
[3] Luke xxiii. 15-23.   [4] Luke xxiii. 24, 25.   [5] John xviii. 28-30.   [6] John xviii. 31-34.

over in silence by the other evangelists. Mark, therefore, what remains of his narrative. It proceeds thus: "Pilate answered, Am I a Jew? Thine own nation, and the chief priests, have delivered thee unto me: what hast thou done? Jesus answered, My kingdom is not of this world: if my kingdom were of this world, then would my servants fight, that I should not be delivered to the Jews; but now is my kingdom not from hence. Pilate therefore said unto Him, Art thou a king then? Jesus answered, Thou sayest that I am a king."[1] Behold, here is the point at which he comes to that which the other evangelists have reported. And then he goes on, the Lord being still the speaker, to recite other matters which the rest have not recorded. His terms are these: "To this end was I born, and for this cause came I into the world, that I should bear witness unto the truth. Every one that is of the truth heareth my voice. Pilate saith unto him, What is truth? And when he had said this, he went out again unto the Jews, and saith unto them, I find no fault in him. But ye have a custom, that I should release unto you one at the passover: will ye, therefore, that I release unto you the King of the Jews? Then cried they all again, Not this man, but Barabbas. Now Barabbas was a robber. Then Pilate, therefore, took Jesus, and scourged Him. And the soldiers platted a crown of thorns, and put it on His head, and they put on Him a purple robe; and they came to Him and said, Hail, King of the Jews! and they smote Him with their hands. Pilate went forth again, and saith unto them, Behold, I bring him forth to you, that ye may know that I find no fault in him. Then came Jesus forth, wearing the crown of thorns and the purple robe. And Pilate saith unto them, Behold the man! When the chief priests therefore and officers saw Him, they cried out, saying, Crucify him, crucify him. Pilate saith unto them, Take ye him, and crucify him; for I find no fault in him. The Jews answered him, We have a law, and by our law he ought to die, because he made himself the Son of God."[2] This may fit in with what Luke reports to have been stated in the accusation brought by the Jews,—namely, "We found this fellow perverting our nation,"—so that we might append here the reason given for it, "Because he made himself the Son of God." John then goes on in the following strain: "When Pilate, therefore, heard that saying, he was the more afraid, and went again into the judgment-hall, and saith unto Jesus, Whence art thou? But Jesus gave him no answer. Then saith Pilate unto Him, Speakest thou not unto me? knowest thou not that I have power to crucify thee, and have power to release thee? Jesus

answered, Thou couldest have no power at all against me, except it were given thee from above: therefore he that delivered me unto thee hath the greater sin. From thenceforth Pilate sought to release Him: but the Jews cried out, saying, If thou let this man go, thou art not Cæsar's friend: whosoever maketh himself a king, speaketh against Cæsar."[3] This may very well agree with what Luke records in connection with the said accusation brought by the Jews. For after the words, "We found this fellow perverting our nation," he has added the clause, "And forbidding to give tribute to Cæsar, and saying that he himself is Christ a king." This will also offer a solution for the difficulty previously referred to, namely, the occasion which might seem to be given for supposing John to have indicated that no specific charge was laid by the Jews against the Lord, when they answered and said unto him, "If he were not a malefactor, we would not have delivered him up unto thee." John then continues in the following strain: "When Pilate therefore heard that saying, he brought Jesus forth, and sat down in the judgment-seat, in a place that is called the Pavement, but in the Hebrew, Gabbatha. And it was the preparation of the passover, and about the sixth hour; and he saith unto the Jews, Behold your King? But they cried out, Away with him, crucify him. Pilate saith unto them, Shall I crucify your king? The chief priests answered, We have no king but Cæsar. Then delivered he Him therefore unto them to be crucified."[4] The above is John's version of what was done by Pilate.[5]

CHAP. IX.—OF THE MOCKERY WHICH HE SUSTAINED AT THE HANDS OF PILATE'S COHORT, AND OF THE HARMONY SUBSISTING AMONG THE THREE EVANGELISTS WHO REPORT THAT SCENE, NAMELY, MATTHEW, MARK, AND JOHN.

36. We have now reached the point at which we may study the Lord's passion, strictly so called, as it is presented in the narrative of these four evangelists. Matthew commences his account as follows: "Then the soldiers of the governor took Jesus into the common hall, and gathered unto Him the whole band of soldiers. And they stripped Him, and put on Him a scarlet robe. And when they had platted a crown of thorns, they put it upon His head, and a reed in His right hand: and they bowed the knee before Him, and mocked Him, saying, Hail, King of the Jews!"[6] At the same stage in the narrative, Mark delivers himself thus: "And the soldiers led Him away into the hall

---

[1] John xviii. 35–37.   [2] John xviii. 37–xix. 7.

[3] John xix. 8–12.   [4] John xix. 13–16.
[5] [Many harmonists, in view of the fact that Jesus had been scourged before the events narrated in John xix. 2–16, place these occurrences after the delivery of Jesus to be crucified. In § 36 Augustin defends the view that Matthew and Mark have varied from the order. See also chap. xiii.—R.]
[6] Matt. xxvii. 27–31.

called Prætorium; and they called together the whole band. And they clothed Him with purple, and platted a crown of thorns, and put it on His head, and began to salute Him, saying, Hail, King of the Jews! And they smote Him on the head with a reed, and did spit upon Him, and, bowing their knees, worshipped Him." [1] Here, therefore, we perceive that while Matthew tells us how they "put on Him a scarlet robe," Mark speaks of purple, with which He was clothed. The explanation may be that the said scarlet robe was employed instead of the royal purple by these scoffers. There is also a certain red-coloured purple which resembles scarlet very closely. And it may also be the case that Mark has noticed the purple which the robe contained, although it was properly scarlet. Luke has left this without mention. On the other hand, previous to stating how Pilate delivered Him up to be crucified, John has introduced the following passage: "Then Pilate therefore took Jesus, and scourged Him. And the soldiers platted a crown of thorns, and put it on His head, and they put on Him a purple robe, and said, Hail, King of the Jews! And they smote Him with their hands." [2] This makes it evident that Matthew and Mark have reported this incident in the way of a recapitulation, and that it did not actually take place after Pilate had delivered Him up to be crucified. For John informs us distinctly enough that these things took place when He yet was with Pilate. Hence we conclude that the other evangelists have introduced the occurrence at that particular point, just because, having previously passed it by, they recollected it there. This is also borne out by what Matthew proceeds next to relate. He continues thus: "And they spit upon Him, and took the reed, and smote Him on the head. And after that they had mocked Him, they took the robe off from Him, and put His own raiment on Him, and led Him away to crucify Him." [3] Here we are given to understand that the taking the robe off Him and the clothing Him with His own raiment were done at the close, when He was being led away. This is given by Mark, as follows: "And when they had mocked Him, they took off the purple from Him, and put His own clothes on Him." [4]

CHAP. X. — OF THE METHOD IN WHICH WE CAN RECONCILE THE STATEMENT WHICH IS MADE BY MATTHEW, MARK, AND LUKE, TO THE EFFECT THAT ANOTHER PERSON WAS PRESSED INTO THE SERVICE OF CARRYING THE CROSS OF JESUS, WITH THAT GIVEN BY JOHN, WHO SAYS THAT JESUS BORE IT HIMSELF.

37. Matthew, accordingly, goes on with his narrative in these terms: "And as they came out, they found a man of Cyrene, Simon by name: him they compelled to bear His cross." [5] In like manner, Mark says: "And they led Him out to be crucified. And they compelled one Simon, a Cyrenian, who passed by, coming out of the country, the father of Alexander and Rufus, to bear His cross." [6] Luke's version is also to this effect: "And as they led Him away, they laid hold upon one Simon a Cyrenian, coming out of the country; and on him they laid the cross, that he might bear it after Jesus." [7] On the other hand, John records the matter as follows: "And they took Jesus, and led Him away. And He bearing His cross went forth into a place called the place of a skull, which is called in the Hebrew, Golgotha; where they crucified Him." [8] From all this we understand that Jesus was carrying the cross Himself as He went forth into the place mentioned. But on the way the said Simon, who is named by the other three evangelists, was pressed into the service, and got the cross to carry for the rest of the course until the spot was reached. Thus we find that both circumstances really took place; namely, first the one noticed by John, and thereafter the one instanced by the other three.

CHAP. XI. — OF THE CONSISTENCY OF MATTHEW'S VERSION WITH THAT OF MARK IN THE ACCOUNT OF THE POTION OFFERED HIM TO DRINK, WHICH IS INTRODUCED BEFORE THE NARRATIVE OF HIS CRUCIFIXION.

38. Matthew then proceeds in these terms: "And they came unto a place called Golgotha; that is to say, a place of a skull." [9] So far as the place is concerned, they are most unmistakeably at one. The same Matthew next adds, "and they gave Him wine [10] to drink, mingled with gall; and when He had tasted thereof, He would not drink." [11] This is given by Mark as follows: "And they gave Him to drink wine mingled with myrrh; and He received it not." [12] Here we may understand Matthew to have conveyed the same sense as Mark, when he speaks of the wine being "mingled with gall." For the gall is mentioned with a view to express the bitterness of the potion. And wine mingled with myrrh is remarkable for its bitterness. The fact may also be that gall and myrrh together made the wine exceedingly bitter. Again, when Mark says that "He received it not," we understand the phrase to denote that He did not receive it so as actually to drink it. He did taste

---

[1] Mark xv. 16-20.   [2] John xix. 1-3.   [3] Matt. xxvii. 30, 31.
[4] Mark xv. 20

[5] Matt. xxvii. 32.   [6] Mark xv. 20, 21.
[7] Luke xxiii. 26. [This probably implies that the afterpart of the cross was laid upon Simon, not the whole of it. This obviates the necessity for the explanation given by Augustin. — R.]
[8] John xix. 16-18.
[9] Matt. xxvii. 33.
[10] *Vinum.* [So the correct Greek text. Comp. Revised Version. — R.]
[11] Matt. xxvii. 34.   [12] Mark xv. 23.

it, however, as Matthew certifies. Thus Mark's words, " He received it not," convey the same meaning as Matthew's version, " He would not drink." The former, however, has said nothing about His tasting the potion.

CHAP. XII. — OF THE CONCORD PRESERVED AMONG ALL THE FOUR EVANGELISTS ON THE SUBJECT OF THE PARTING OF HIS RAIMENT.

39. Matthew goes on thus : " And after they crucified Him, they parted His garments, casting lots : and sitting down, they watched Him."[1] Mark reports the same incident, as follows : " And crucifying Him, they parted His garments, casting lots upon them, what every man should take."[2]   In like manner Luke says : " And they parted His raiment, and cast lots. And the people stood beholding."[3]   The occurrence is thus recorded briefly by the first three. But John gives us a more detailed narrative of the method in which the act was gone about. His version runs thus : " Then the soldiers, when they had crucified Jesus, took His garments, and made four parts, to every soldier a part ; and also His coat : now the coat was without seam, woven from the top throughout. They said therefore among themselves, Let us not rend it, but cast lots for it, whose it shall be : that the Scripture might be fulfilled, which saith, They parted my garments, and for my vesture they did cast lots."[4]

CHAP. XIII. — OF THE HOUR OF THE LORD'S PASSION, AND OF THE QUESTION CONCERNING THE ABSENCE OF ANY DISCREPANCY BETWEEN MARK AND JOHN IN THE ARTICLE OF THE " THIRD " HOUR AND THE " SIXTH."

40. Matthew continues thus : " And they set up over His head His accusation written, ' This is Jesus the King of the Jews.' "[5] Mark, on the other hand, before making any such statement, inserts these words : " And it was the third hour, and they crucified Him."[6] For he subjoins these terms immediately after he has told us about the parting of the garments. This, then, is a matter which we must consider with special care, lest any serious error emerge. For there are some who entertain the idea that the Lord was certainly crucified at the third hour ; and that thereafter, from the sixth hour on to the ninth, the darkness covered the land. According to this theory, we should have to understand three hours to have passed between the time when He was crucified and the time when

the darkness occurred. And this view might certainly be held with all due warrant, were it not that John has stated that it was about the sixth hour when Pilate sat down on the judgment-seat, in a place that is called the Pavement, but in Hebrew, Gabbatha. For his version goes on in this manner : " And as it was the preparation of the passover, and about the sixth hour : and he saith unto the Jews, Behold your King ! But they cried out, Away with him, away with him ! crucify him ! Pilate said unto them, Shall I crucify your king ? The chief priests answered, We have no king but Cæsar. Then delivered he Him therefore unto them to be crucified."[7] If Jesus, therefore, was delivered up to the Jews to be crucified when it was about the sixth hour, and when Pilate was then sitting upon the judgment-seat, how could He have been crucified at the third hour, as some have been led to suppose, in consequence of a misinterpretation of the words of Mark ?

41. First, then, let us consider what the hour really is at which He can have been crucified ; and then we shall see how it happens that Mark has reported Him to have been crucified at the third hour. Now it was about the sixth hour when Pilate, who was sitting, as has been stated, at the time upon the judgment-seat, delivered Him up to be crucified. The expression is not that it was the sixth hour fully, but only that it was *about* the sixth hour ; that is to say, the fifth hour was entirely gone, and so much of the sixth hour had also been entered upon. These writers, however, could not naturally use such phraseologies as the fifth hour and a quarter, or the fifth hour and a third, or the fifth hour and a half, or anything of that kind. For the Scriptures have the well-known habit of dealing simply with the round numbers, without mention of fractions, especially in matters of time. We have an example of this in the case of the " eight days," after which, as they tell us, He went up into a mountain,[8] — a space which is given by Matthew and Mark as " six days after,"[9] because they look simply at the days between the one from which the reckoning commences and the one with which it closes. This is particularly to be kept in view when we notice how measured the terms are which John employs here. For he says not " the sixth hour," but " about the sixth hour." And yet, even had he not expressed himself in that way, but had stated merely that it was the sixth hour, it would still be competent for us to interpret the phrase in accordance with the method of speech with which we are, as I said, familiar in Scripture, namely, the use of the round numbers. And thus we could still take the sense quite fairly to be that, on the comple-

1 Matt. xxvii. 35, 36. The words, "that it might be fulfilled which was spoken by the prophet, They parted my garments among them, and upon my vesture did they cast lots," are omitted. [So the Greek text, according to the best authorities. Comp. Revised Version. — R.]
2 Mark xv. 24.   3 Luke xxiii. 34, 35.   4 John xix. 23, 24.
5 Matt. xxvii. 37. [No notice is taken of the different forms of the " title " on the cross, recorded by the evangelists. — R.]
6 Mark xv. 25.
7 John xix. 13-16.   8 Luke ix. 28.
9 Matt. xvii. 1; Mark ix. 1.

tion of the fifth hour and the commencement of the sixth, those matters were going on which are recorded in connection with the Lord's crucifixion, until, on the close of the sixth hour, and when He was hanging on the cross, the darkness occurred which is attested by three of the evangelists, namely, Matthew, Mark, and Luke.[1]

42. In due order, let us now inquire how it is that Mark, after telling us that they parted His garments when they were crucifying Him, casting lots upon them what every man should take, has appended this statement, "And it was the third hour, and they crucified Him."[2]   Now here he had already made the declaration, "And crucifying Him, they parted His garments;" and the other evangelists also certify that, when He was crucified, they parted His garments. If, therefore, it was Mark's design to specify the time at which the incident took place, it would have been enough for him to say simply, "And it was the third hour." What reason, then, can be assigned for his having added these words, "And they crucified Him," but that, under the summary statement thus inserted, he intended significantly to suggest something which might be found a subject for consideration, when the Scripture in question was read in times in which the whole Church knew perfectly well what hour it was at which the Lord was hanged upon the tree, and the means were possessed for either correcting the writer's error or confuting his want of truth? But, inasmuch as he was quite aware of the fact that the Lord was suspended [on the cross] by the soldiers, and not by the Jews, as John most plainly affirms,[3] his hidden object [in bringing in the said clause] was to convey the idea that those parties who cried out that He should be crucified were the Lord's real crucifiers, rather than the men who simply discharged their service to their chief in accordance with their duty. We understand, accordingly, that it was the third hour when the Jews cried out that the Lord should be crucified. And thus it is intimated most truly that these persons did really crucify Christ at the time when they cried out. All the more, too, did this merit notice, because they were unwilling to have the appearance of having done the deed themselves, and with that view delivered Him up unto Pilate, as their words indicate clearly enough in the report given by John. For, after stating how Pilate said to them, "What accusation bring ye against this man?" his version proceeds thus: "They answered and said unto him, If he were not a malefactor, we would not have delivered him up unto thee. Then said Pilate unto them, Take ye him, and judge him according to your law. The Jews therefore said unto him, It is not lawful for us to put any man to death."[4]   Consequently, what they were especially unwilling to have the appearance of doing, that Mark here shows that they actually did do at the third hour. For he judged most truly that the Lord's murderer was rather the tongue of the Jews than the hand of the soldiers.

43. Moreover, if any one alleges that it was not the third hour when the Jews cried out for the first time in the terms referred to, he simply displays himself most insanely to be an enemy to the Gospel; unless perchance he can prove himself able to produce some new solution of the problem. For he cannot possibly establish the position that it was not the third hour at the period alluded to. And, consequently, we surely ought rather to credit a veracious evangelist than the contentious suspicions of men. But you may ask, How can you prove that it was the third hour? I answer, Because I believe the evangelists; and if you also believe them, show me how the Lord can have been crucified both at the sixth hour and at the third. For, to make a frank acknowledgment, we cannot get over the statement of the sixth hour in John's narrative; and Mark records the third hour: and, therefore, if both of us accept the testimony of these writers, show me any other way in which both these notes of time can be taken as literally correct. If you can do so, I shall most cheerfully acquiesce. For what I prize is not my own opinion, but the truth of the Gospel. And I could wish, indeed, that more methods of clearing up this problem might be discovered by others. Until that be done, however, join me, if it please you, in taking advantage of the solution which I have propounded. For if no explanation can be found, this one will suffice of itself. But if another can be devised, when it is unfolded, we shall make our choice. Only don't consider it an inevitable conclusion that any one of all the four evangelists has stated what is false, or has fallen into error in a position of authority at once so elevated and so holy.

44. Again, if any one affirms his ability to prove it not to have been the third hour when the Jews cried out in the terms in question, because, after Mark's statement to this effect, "And Pilate answered, and said again unto them, What will ye then that I shall do unto him whom ye call the King of the Jews? And they cried out again, Crucify him," we find no further details introduced into the narrative of the same evangelist, but are led on at once to the statement, that the Lord was delivered up by Pilate to be crucified — an act which John mentions

---

[1] Matt. xxvii. 45; Mark xv. 33; Luke xxiii. 44.
[2] Mark xv. 25.   [3] John xix. 23.

[4] John xviii. 29-31.

to have taken place about the sixth hour ; — I repeat, if any one adduces such an argument, let him understand that many things have been passed by without record here, which occurred in the interval when Pilate was engaged in looking out for some means by which he could rescue Jesus from the Jews, and was exerting himself most strenuously by every means in his power to withstand their maddened desires. For Matthew says, " Pilate saith unto them, What shall I do, then, with Jesus, which is called Christ? They all say, Let him be crucified." Then we affirm it to have been the third hour. And when the same Matthew goes on to add the sentence, " But when Pilate saw that he could prevail nothing, but that rather a tumult was made," we understand that a period of two hours had passed, during the attempts made by Pilate to effect the release of Jesus, and the tumults raised by the Jews in their efforts to defeat him, and that the sixth hour had then commenced, previous to the close of which those things took place which are related as happening between the time when Pilate delivered up the Lord and the oncoming of the darkness. Once more, as regards what Matthew records above, — namely, " And when he was set down on the judgment-seat, his wife sent unto him, saying, Have thou nothing to do with that just man ; for I have suffered many things this day in a dream because of him," [1] — we remark, that Pilate really took his seat upon the tribunal at a later point, but that, among the earlier incidents which Matthew was recounting, the account given of Pilate's wife came into his mind, and he decided on inserting it in this particular connection, with the view of preparing us for understanding how Pilate had an especially urgent reason for wishing, even on to the last, not to deliver Him up to the Jews.

45. Luke, again, after mentioning how Pilate said, " I will therefore chastise him and let him go," tells us that the whole multitude then cried out, " Away with this man, and release unto us Barabbas." [2] But perhaps they had not yet exclaimed, " Crucify him ! " For Luke next proceeds thus : " Pilate therefore, willing to release Jesus, spake again to them. But they cried, saying, Crucify him, crucify him ! " [3] This is understood to have been at the third hour. Luke then continues in these terms : " And he said unto them the third time, Why, what evil hath he done ? I have found no cause of death in him : I will therefore chastise him and let him go. And they were instant with loud voices requiring that He might be crucified. And the voices of them prevailed." [4] Here, then, this evangelist also makes it quite evident that there was a great tumult. With sufficient accuracy

for the purposes of my inquiry into the truth, we can further gather how long the interval was after which he spoke to them in these terms, " Why, what evil hath he done ? " And when he adds thereafter, " They were instant with loud voices, requiring that He might be crucified, and the voices of them prevailed," who can fail to perceive that this clamour was made just because they saw that Pilate was unwilling to deliver the Lord up to them ? And, inasmuch as he was exceedingly reluctant to give Him up, he did not certainly yield at present in a moment, but in reality two hours and something more were passed by him in that state of hesitancy.

46. Interrogate John in like manner, and see how strong this hesitancy was on Pilate's part, and how he shrank from so shameful a service. For this evangelist records these incidents much more fully, although even he certainly does not mention all the occurrences which took up these two hours and part of the sixth hour. After telling us how Pilate scourged Jesus, and allowed the robe to be put on Him in derision by the soldiers, and suffered Him to be subjected to ill-treatment and many acts of mockery (all of which was permitted by Pilate, as I believe, really with the view of mitigating their fury and keeping them from persevering in their maddened desire for His death), John continues his account in the following manner : " Pilate went forth again, and saith unto them, Behold, I bring him forth to you, that ye may know that I find no fault in him. Then came Jesus forth, wearing the crown of thorns, and the purple robe. And Pilate saith unto them, Behold the man ! " [5] The object of this was, that they might gaze upon that spectacle of ignominy and be appeased. But the evangelist proceeds again : " When the chief priests therefore and officers saw Him, they cried out, saying, Crucify him, crucify him ! " [6] It was then the third hour, as we maintain. Mark also what follows : " Pilate saith unto them, Take ye him, and crucify him ; for I find no fault in him. The Jews answered him, We have a law, and by our law he ought to die, because he made himself the Son of God. When Pilate therefore heard that saying, he was the more afraid ; and went again into the judgment-hall, and saith unto Jesus, Whence art thou ? But Jesus gave him no answer. Then saith Pilate unto Him, Speakest thou not unto me ? knowest thou not that I have power to crucify thee, and have power to release thee ? Jesus answered, Thou couldest have no power at all against me, except it were given thee from above : therefore he that delivered me unto thee hath the greater sin. From thenceforth Pilate sought to release Him." [7] Now, when it is said here

---

[1] Matt. xxvii. 19.   [2] Luke xxiii. 16, 18.
[3] Luke xxiii. 20, 21.   [4] Luke xxiii. 22, 23.

[5] John xix. 4, 5.   [6] John xix. 6.   [7] John xix. 6-12.

that " Pilate sought to release Him," how long a space of time may we suppose to have been spent in that effort, and how many things may have been omitted here among the sayings which were uttered by Pilate, or the contradictions which were raised by the Jews, until these Jews gave expression to the words which moved him, and made him yield? For the writer goes on thus :. " But the Jews cried out, saying, If thou let this man go, thou art not Cæsar's friend : whosoever maketh himself a king speaketh against Cæsar. When Pilate therefore heard that saying, he brought Jesus forth, and sat down in the judgment-seat, in a place that is called the Pavement, but in the Hebrew, Gabbatha. And it was the preparation of the passover, about the sixth hour." [1] Thus, then, between that exclamation of the Jews when they first cried out, " Crucify him," at which period it was the third hour, and this moment when he sat down on the judgment-seat, two hours had passed, which had been taken up with Pilate's attempts to delay matters and the tumults raised by the Jews ; and by this time the fifth hour was quite spent, and so much of the sixth hour had been entered. Then the narrative goes on thus : " He saith unto the Jews, Behold your King ! But they cried out, Away with him, away with him ! crucify him ! " [2] But not even now was Pilate so overcome by the apprehension of their bringing a charge against himself as to be very ready to yield. For his wife had sent to him when he was sitting at this time upon the judgment-seat, — an incident which Matthew, who is the only one that records it, has given by anticipation, introducing it before he comes to its proper place (according to the order of time) in his narrative, and bringing it in at another point which he judged opportune. In this way, Pilate, still continuing his efforts to prevent further advances, said then to them, " Shall I crucify your king ? " Thereupon " the chief priests answered, We have no king but Cæsar. Then delivered he Him therefore unto them to be crucified." [3] And in the time that passed when He was on the way, and when He was crucified along with the two robbers, and when His garments were parted and the possession of His coat was decided by lot, and the various deeds of contumely were done to Him (for, while these different things were going on, gibes were also cast at Him), the sixth hour was fully spent, and the darkness came on, which is mentioned by Matthew, Mark, and Luke.[4]

47. Let such impious pertinacity therefore perish, and let it be believed that the Lord Jesus Christ was crucified at once at the third hour by the voice of the Jews, and at the sixth by the hands of the soldiers. For during these tumults on the part of the Jews, and these agitations on the side of Pilate, upwards of two hours elapsed from the time when they burst out with the cry, " Crucify Him." But again, even Mark, who studies brevity above all the other evangelists, has been pleased to give a concise indication of Pilate's desire and of his efforts to save the Lord's life. For, after giving us this statement, " And they cried again, Crucify him " (in which he gives us to understand that they had cried out before this, when they asked that Barabbas might be released to them), he has appended these words : " Then Pilate continued to say unto them, Why, what evil hath he done? " [5] Thus by one short sentence he has given us an idea of matters which took a long time for their transaction. At the same time, however, keeping in view the correct apprehension of his meaning, he does not say, " Then Pilate *said* unto them," but expresses himself thus : " Then Pilate *continued to say* unto them, Why, what evil hath he done? " For, if his phrase had been " *said*," [6] we might have understood him to mean that such words were uttered only once. But, by adopting the terms, " *continued to say*," [7] he has made it clear enough to the intelligent that Pilate spoke repeatedly, and in a number of ways. Let us therefore consider how briefly Mark has expressed this as compared with Matthew, how briefly Matthew as compared with Luke, how briefly Luke as compared with John, while at the same time each of these writers has introduced now one thing and now another peculiar to himself. In fine, let us also consider how brief is even the narrative given by John himself, as compared with the number of things which took place, and the space of time occupied by their occurrence. And let us give up the madness of opposition, and believe that two hours, and something more, may quite well have passed in the interval referred to.

48. If any one, however, asserts that if this was the real state of the case, Mark might have mentioned the third hour explicitly at the point at which it really was the third hour, namely, when the voices of the Jews were lifted up demanding that the Lord should be crucified ; and, further, that he might have told us plainly there that those vociferators did really crucify Him at that time, — such a reasoner is simply imposing laws upon the historians of truth in his own overweening pride. For he might as well

---

[1] John xix. 12–14.   [2] John xix. 15.   [3] John xix. 15, 16.
[4] [The arrangement of the various details is open to discussion; but the probability is, that the virtual surrender of Pilate to the demand of the Jews took place about the third hour (9 A.M.), and that it was nearly two hours before the crucifixion took place. — R.]

[5] Mark xv. 13, 14.   [6] *Dixit*.
[7] *Dicebat*. [The Greek also has the imperfect, ἔλεγεν. But in the use of this verb in the New Testament the continuous force of the imperfect cannot be insisted upon, as many examples will show. The conclusion of Augustin is correct, despite the insufficiency of this argument. — R.]

maintain that if he were himself to be a narrator of these occurrences, they ought all to be recorded just in the same way and the same order by all other writers as they have been recorded by himself. Let him therefore be content to reckon his own notion inferior to that of Mark the evangelist, who has judged it right to insert the statement just at the point at which it was suggested to him by divine inspiration. For the recollections of those historians have been ruled by the hand of Him who rules the waters, as it is written, according to His own good pleasure. For the human memory moves [1] through a variety of thoughts, and it is not in any man's power to regulate either the subject which comes into his mind or the time of its suggestion. Seeing, then, that those holy and truthful men, in this matter of the order of their narrations, committed the casualties of their recollections (if such a phrase may be used) to the direction of the hidden power of God, to whom nothing is casual, it does not become any mere man, in his low estate, removed far from the vision of God, and sojourning distantly from Him, to say, "This ought to have been introduced here;" for he is utterly ignorant of the reason which led God to will its being inserted in the place it occupies. The word of an apostle is to this effect: "But if our gospel be hid, it is hid to them that are lost." [2]   And again he says: "To the one indeed we are the savour of life unto life; to the other, the savour of death unto death;" and adds immediately, "And who is sufficient for these things?" [3] — that is to say, who is sufficient to comprehend how righteously that is done? The Lord Himself expresses the same when He says, "I am come that they which see not might see, and that they which see might be made blind." [4]   For it is in the depth of the riches of the knowledge and wisdom of God that it comes to pass that of the same lump one vessel is made unto honour, and another unto dishonour. [5]   And to flesh and blood it is said, "O man, who art thou that repliest against God?" [6] Who, then, knows the mind of the Lord in the matter now under consideration? or who hath been His counsellor, [7] where He has in such wise ruled the hearts of these evangelists in their recollections, and has raised them to so commanding a position of authority in the sublime edifice of His Church, that those very things which are capable of presenting the appearance of contradictions in them become the means by which many are made blind, deservedly given over to the lusts of their own heart, and to a reprobate mind; [8] and by which also many are exercised in the thorough cultivation of a pious

understanding, in accordance with the hidden righteousness of the Almighty? For the language of a prophet in speaking to the Lord is this: "Thy thoughts are exceeding deep. An inconsiderate man will not know, and a foolish man will not understand these things." [9]

49. Moreover, I request and admonish those who read the statement which, with the help of the Lord, has thus been elaborated by us, to bear in mind this discourse, which I have thought it needful to introduce in the present connection, in every similar difficulty which may be raised in such inquiries, so that there may be no necessity for repeating the same thing over and over again. Besides, any one who is willing to clear himself of the hardness of impiety, and to give his attention to the subject, will easily perceive how opportune the place is in which Mark has inserted this notice of the third hour, so that every one may there be led to bethink himself of an hour at which the Jews really crucified the Lord, although they sought to transfer the burden of the crime to the Romans, whether to the leaders among them or to the soldiers, [as we see] when we come here upon the record of what was done by the soldiers in the discharge of their duty. For this writer says here, "And crucifying Him, they parted His garments, casting lots upon them, what every man should take." [10]   And to whom can this refer but to the soldiers, as is made manifest in John's narrative? Thus, lest any one should leave the Jews out of account, and make the conception of so great a crime lie against those soldiers, Mark gives us here the statement, "And it was the third hour, and they crucified Him," — his object being to have those Jews rather discovered to be the real crucifiers, who will be found by the careful investigator in a position making it quite possible for them to have cried out for the Lord's crucifixion at the third hour, while he observes that what was done by the soldiers took place at the sixth hour. [11]

50. At the same time, however, there are not wanting persons who would have the time of the preparation — which is referred to by John, when he says, "And it was the preparation of the passover, about the sixth hour" — understood under this third hour of the day, which was also the period at which Pilate sat down upon the judgment-seat. In this way the completion of the said third hour would appear to be the time when He was crucified, and when He was now hanging on the tree. Other three hours must then be supposed to have passed, at the end

---

[9] Ps. xcii. 5, 6.   [10] Mark xv. 24.
[11] [There is so much force in the positions of Augustin in regard to the time of day, that one may overlook the irrelevant arguments he introduces. He at least candidly accepts the readings before him. The supposition of an early confusion of the numbers has no support, and such an alteration is altogether unlikely. — R.]

[1] *Fluitat* = floats.   [2] 2 Cor. iv. 3.   [3] 2 Cor. ii. 16.
[4] John ix 39.   [5] Rom. ix, 21.   [6] Rom. ix. 20.
[7] Rom. xi. 34.   [8] Rom. i. 24-28.

of which He gave up the ghost. According to this idea, too, the darkness would have commenced with the hour at which He died — that is to say, the sixth hour of the day — and have lasted until the ninth. For these persons affirm that the preparation of the passover of the Jews was indeed on the day which was followed by the day of the Sabbath, because the days of unleavened bread began with the said Sabbath; but that, nevertheless, the true passover, which was being realized in the Lord's passion, the passover not of the Jews, but of the Christians, began to be prepared — that is, to have its *parasceue* — from the ninth hour of the night onwards, inasmuch as the Lord was then being prepared for being put to death by the Jews. For the term *parasceue* means by interpretation "preparation." Between the said ninth hour of the night, therefore, and His crucifixion, the period occurs which is called by John the sixth hour of the *parasceue*, and by Mark the third hour of the day; so that, according to this view, Mark has not introduced by way of recapitulation into his record the hour at which the Jews cried out, "Crucify him, crucify him," but has expressly mentioned the third hour as the hour at which the Lord was nailed to the tree. What believer would not receive this solution of the problem with favour, were it only possible to find some point [in the narrative of incidents] in connection with the said ninth hour, at which we could suppose, in due consistency with other circumstances, the *parasceue* of our passover — that is to say, the preparation of the death of Christ — to have commenced. For, if we say that it began at the time when the Lord was apprehended by the Jews, it was still but the first parts of the night. If we hold that it was at the time when He was conducted to the house of Caiaphas' father-in-law, where He was also heard by the chief priests, the cock had not crowed at all as yet, as we gather from Peter's denial, which took place only when the cock was heard. Again, if we suppose it was at the time when He was delivered up to Pilate, we have in the plainest terms the statement of Scripture, to the effect that by this time it was morning. Consequently, it only remains for us to understand that this *parasceue* of the passover — that is to say, the preparation for the death of the Lord — commenced at the period when all the chief priests, in whose presence He was first heard, answered and said, "He is guilty of death," an utterance which we find reported both by Matthew and by Mark:[1] so that they are taken to have introduced, in the form of a recapitulation, at a later stage, facts relating to the denial of Peter, which in point of historical order had taken place at an earlier point. And it is nothing unreasonable to conjecture, that the time at which, as I have said, they pronounced Him guilty of death, may very well have been the ninth hour of the night, between which time and the hour at which Pilate sat down on the judgment-seat there came in this sixth hour, as it is called — not, however, the sixth hour of the day, but that of the *parasceue* — that is to say, the preparation for the sacrifice of the Lord, which is the true passover. And, on this theory, the Lord was suspended on the tree when the sixth hour of the same *parasceue* was completed, which occurred at the completion of the third hour of the day.[2] We may make our choice, therefore, between this view and the other, which supposes Mark to have introduced the third hour by way of reminiscence, and to have had it especially in view, in mentioning the hour there, to suggest the fact of the condemnation brought upon the Jews in the matter of the Lord's crucifixion, in so far as they are understood to have been in a position to raise the clamour for His crucifixion to such an effect that we may hold them to have been the persons who actually crucified Him, rather than the men by whose hands He was suspended on the tree; just as the centurion, already referred to, approached the Lord in a more genuine sense than could be said of those friends whom He sent [on the matter-of-fact mission].[3] But whichever of these two views we adopt, unquestionably a solution is found for this problem on the subject of the hour of the Lord's passion, which is most remarkably apt at once to excite the impudence of the contentious and to agitate the inexperience of the weak.

CHAP. XIV. — OF THE HARMONY PRESERVED AMONG ALL THE EVANGELISTS ON THE SUBJECT OF THE TWO ROBBERS WHO WERE CRUCIFIED ALONG WITH HIM.

51. Matthew continues his narrative in the following terms: "Then were there two robbers crucified with Him, one on the right hand, and another on the left."[4] Mark and Luke give it also in a similar form.[5] Neither does John raise any question of difficulty, although he has made no mention of those robbers. For he says, "And two other with Him, on either side one, and Jesus in the midst."[6] But there would have been a contradiction if John had spoken of these others as innocent, while the former evangelists called them robbers.

---

[1] Matt. xxvi. 66; Mark xiv. 64.

[2] [This view is extremely fanciful. "Preparation" was a Jewish term, with a distinct meaning. In early Christian times it meant Friday. To modify the sense is impossible. — R.]
[3] See above, Book ii. ch. 20.   [4] Matt. xxvii. 38.
[5] Mark xv. 27; Luke xxiii. 33.
[6] John xix. 18.

CHAP. XV. — OF THE CONSISTENCY OF THE AC-
COUNTS GIVEN BY MATTHEW, MARK, AND LUKE
ON THE SUBJECT OF THE PARTIES WHO IN-
SULTED THE LORD.

52. Matthew goes on in the following strain:
"And they that passed by reviled Him, wagging
their heads, and saying, Thou that destroyest
the temple, and buildest it in three days, save
thyself: if thou be the Son of God, come down
from the cross."[1] Mark's statement agrees with
this almost to the letter. Then Matthew continues thus: "Likewise also the chief priests,
mocking Him, with the scribes and elders, said,
He saved others; himself he cannot save: if
he be the King of Israel, let him now come
down from the cross, and we will believe him.
He trusted in God; let Him deliver him now,
if He will: for he said, I am the Son of God."[2]
Mark and Luke, although they report the words
differently, nevertheless agree in conveying the
same meaning, although the one passes without
notice something which the other mentions.[3]
For they are both really at one on the subject
of the chief priests, giving us to understand
that they insulted the Lord when He was crucified. The only difference is, that Mark does
not specify the elders, while Luke, who has
instanced the rulers, has not added the designation "of the priests," and thus has rather
comprehended the whole body of the leading
men under the general designation; so that we
may fairly take both the scribes and the elders
to be included in his description.

CHAP. XVI. — OF THE DERISION ASCRIBED TO THE
ROBBERS, AND OF THE QUESTION REGARDING
THE ABSENCE OF ANY DISCREPANCY BETWEEN
MATTHEW AND MARK ON THE ONE HAND, AND
LUKE ON THE OTHER, WHEN THE LAST-NAMED
EVANGELIST STATES THAT ONE OF THE TWO
MOCKED HIM, AND THAT THE OTHER BELIEVED
ON HIM.

53. Matthew continues his narrative in these
terms: "The robbers also, which were crucified
with Him, cast the same in His teeth."[4] Mark
is quite in harmony with Matthew here, giving
the same statement in different words.[5] On the
other hand, Luke may be thought to contradict
this, unless we be careful not to forget a certain
mode of speech which is sufficiently familiar.
For Luke's narrative runs thus: "And one of
the malefactors which were hanged railed on
Him, saying, If thou be Christ, save thyself and
us."[6] And then the same writer proceeds to
introduce into the same context the following
recital: "But the other answering, rebuked him,
saying, Dost not thou fear God, seeing thou art
in the same condemnation? And we indeed

justly; for we receive the due reward of our
deeds: but this man hath done nothing amiss.
And he said unto Jesus, Lord, remember me
when Thou comest into Thy kingdom. And
Jesus said unto him, Verily, I say unto thee,
To-day thou shalt be with me in paradise."[7]
The question then is, how we can reconcile
either Matthew's report, "The robbers also,
which were crucified with Him, cast the same
in His teeth," or Mark's, namely, "And they
that were crucified with Him reviled Him,"
with Luke's testimony, which is to the effect
that one of them reviled Christ, but that the
other arrested him and believed on the Lord.
The explanation will be, that Matthew and Mark,
presenting a concise version of the passage
under review, have employed the plural number
instead of the singular; as is the case in the
Epistle to the Hebrews, where we find the
statement given in the plural form, that "they
stopped the mouths of lions,"[8] while Daniel
alone is understood to be referred to. Again,
the plural number is adopted where it is said
that they "were sawn asunder,"[9] while that
manner of death is reported only of Isaiah. In
the same way, when it is said in the Psalm,
"The kings of the earth set themselves, and the
rulers took counsel together," etc.,[10] the plural
number is employed instead of the singular,
according to the exposition given of the passage
in the Acts of the Apostles. For those who
have made use of the testimony of the said
Psalm in that book take the kings to refer to
Herod, and the princes to Pilate.[11] But further,
inasmuch as the pagans are in the habit of bringing such slanderous charges against the Gospel,
I would ask them to consider how their own
writers have spoken of Phaedras and Medeas
and Clytemnestras, when there really was but a
single individual reputed under each of these
names. And what is more common, for example, than for a person to say, "The rustics also
behave insolently to me," even although it
should only be one that acted rudely? In
short, no real discrepancy would be created by
the restriction of Luke's report to one of the two
robbers, unless the other evangelists had declared expressly that "both" the malefactors
reviled the Lord; for in that case it would not
be possible for us to suppose only one individual
intended under the plural number. Seeing,
however, that the phrase employed is "the robbers," or "those who were crucified with Him,"
and the term "both" is not added, the expression is one which might have been used if both
these men had been engaged in the thing, but
which might equally well be adopted if one of
the two had been implicated in it, — that fact

---

[1] Matt. xxvii. 39, 40.
[2] Matt. xxvii. 41-43.
[3] Mark xv. 29-32; Luke xxiii. 35-37.
[4] Matt. xxvii. 44.
[5] Mark xv. 32.
[6] Luke xxiii. 39.
[7] Luke xxiii. 40-43.
[8] Heb. xi. 33.
[9] Heb. xi. 37.
[10] Ps. ii. 2.
[11] Acts iv. 26, 27.

being then conveyed by the use of the plural number, according to a familiar method of speech.

CHAP. XVII.— OF THE HARMONY OF THE FOUR EVANGELISTS IN THEIR NOTICES OF THE DRAUGHT OF VINEGAR.

54. Matthew proceeds in the following terms : "Now from the sixth hour there was darkness over all the land unto the ninth hour." [1] The same fact is attested by two others of the evangelists.[2] Luke adds, however, a statement of the cause of the darkness, namely, that " the sun was darkened." Again, Matthew continues thus : "And about the ninth hour Jesus cried with a loud voice, saying, Eli, Eli, lama sabachthani ! that is to say, My God, my God, why hast Thou forsaken me ? And some of them that stood there, when they heard that, said, This man calleth for Elias." [3] Mark's agreement with this is almost complete, so far as regards the words, and not only almost, but altogether complete, so far as the sense is concerned. Matthew next makes this statement : "And straightway one of them ran, and took a sponge, and filled it with vinegar, and put it on a reed, and gave Him to drink." [4] Mark presents it in a similar form : "And one ran, and filled a sponge full of vinegar, and put it on a reed, and gave Him to drink, saying, Let alone ; let us see whether Elias will come to take Him down." [5] Matthew, however, has represented these words about Elias to have been spoken, not by the person who offered the sponge with the vinegar, but by the rest. For his version runs thus : "But the rest said, Let be ; let us see whether Elias will come to save Him ; " [6] — from which, therefore, we infer that both the man specially referred to and the others who were there expressed themselves in these terms. Luke, again, has introduced this notice of the vinegar previous to his report of the robber's insolence. He gives it thus : "And the soldiers also mocked Him, coming to Him, and offering Him vinegar, and saying, If thou be the King of the Jews, save thyself." [7] It has been Luke's purpose to embrace in one statement what was done and what was said by the soldiers. And we ought to feel no difficulty in the circumstance that he has not said explicitly that it was " one " of them who offered the vinegar. For, adopting a method of expression which we have discussed above,[8] he has simply put the plural number for the singular.[9] Moreover, John has also given us an account of the vinegar, where he says : "After this, Jesus, knowing that all

things were now accomplished, that the Scripture might be fulfilled, said, I thirst. Now there was set a vessel full of vinegar : and they filled a sponge with vinegar, and put it upon hyssop, and put it to His mouth." [10] But although the said John thus informs us that Jesus said " I thirst," and also mentions that there was a vessel full of vinegar there, while the other evangelists leave these things unspecified, there is nothing to marvel at in this.

CHAP. XVIII.— OF THE LORD'S SUCCESSIVE UTTERANCES WHEN HE WAS ABOUT TO DIE; AND OF THE QUESTION WHETHER MATTHEW AND MARK ARE IN HARMONY WITH LUKE IN THEIR REPORTS OF THESE SAYINGS, AND ALSO WHETHER THESE THREE EVANGELISTS ARE IN HARMONY WITH JOHN.

55. Matthew proceeds as follows : "And Jesus, crying again with a loud voice, yielded up the ghost." [11] In like manner, Mark says, "And Jesus cried with a loud voice, and gave up the ghost." [12] Luke, again, has told us what He said when that loud voice was uttered. For his version is thus : "And Jesus, crying with a loud voice, said, Father, into Thy hands I commend my spirit : and saying this, He gave up the ghost." [13] John, on the other hand, as he has left unnoticed the first voice, which Matthew and Mark have reported — namely, " Eli, Eli " — has also passed over in silence the one which has been recited only by Luke, while the other two have referred to it under the designation of the " loud voice." I allude to the cry, " Father, into Thy hands I commend my spirit." Luke has also attested the fact that this exclamation was uttered with a loud voice ; and hence we may understand this particular cry to be identified with the loud voice which Matthew and Mark have specified. But John has stated a fact which is noticed by none of the other three, namely, that He said " It is finished," after He had received the vinegar. This cry we take to have been uttered previous to the loud voice referred to. For these are John's words : "When Jesus, therefore, had received the vinegar, He said, It is finished ; and He bowed His head, and gave up the ghost." [14] In the interval elapsing between this cry, " It is finished," and what is referred to in the subsequent sentence, "and He bowed His head and gave up the ghost," the voice was uttered which John himself has passed over without record, but which the other three have noticed. For the precise succession appears to be this, namely, that He said first " It is finished," when what had been prophesied regarding Him was fulfilled in Him, and that thereafter — as if He had been waiting for this, like one, indeed, who died when He willed it to be so — He commended His

---

[1] Matt. xxvii. 45.
[2] Mark xv. 33-36; Luke xxiii. 44, 45.   [3] Matt. xxvii. 46, 47.
[4] Matt. xxvii. 48.   [5] Mark xv. 36.   [6] Matt xxvii. 49.
[7] Luke xxiii. 36, 37.   [8] See chap. xvi.
[9] [This act of the soldiers was probably distinct from the giving of the vinegar referred to by the other evangelists; it belongs to the time when all were mocking the Crucified One. — R.]

[10] John xix. 28, 29.   [11] Matt. xxvii. 50.   [12] Mark xv. 37.
[13] Luke xxiii. 46.   [14] John xix. 30.

spirit [to His Father], and resigned it.[1] But, whatever the order may be in which a person may consider it likely that these words were spoken, he ought above all things to guard against entertaining the notion that any one of the evangelists is in antagonism with another, when one leaves unmentioned something which another has repeated, or particularizes something which another has passed by in silence.

56. Matthew proceeds thus : "And, behold, the veil of the temple was rent in twain from the top to the bottom."[2] Mark's version is also as follows : "And the veil of the temple was rent in twain from the top to the bottom."[3] Luke likewise gives a statement in similar terms : "And the veil of the temple was rent in the midst."[4] He does not introduce it, however, in the same order. For, with the intention of attaching miracle to miracle, he has told us first how "the sun was darkened," and then has deemed it right to subjoin the said sentence in immediate succession, namely, "And the veil of the temple was rent in the midst." Thus it would appear that he has introduced at an earlier point this incident, which really took place when the Lord expired, so as to give us there a summary description of the circumstances relating to the drinking of the vinegar, and the loud voice, and the death itself, which are understood to have taken place previous to the rending of the veil, and after the darkness had come in. For Matthew has inserted this sentence, "And, behold, the veil of the temple was rent," in immediate succession to the statement, "And Jesus, crying again with a loud voice, yielded up the ghost ;" and has thus given us clearly to understand that the time when the veil was rent was after Jesus had given up His spirit. If, however, he had not added the words, "And behold," but had said simply, "And the veil of the temple was rent," it would have been uncertain whether Mark and he had narrated the incident in the form of a recapitulation, while Luke had kept the exact order, or whether Luke had given the summary account of what these others had introduced in the correct historical succession.

57. Matthew proceeds thus : "And the earth did quake, and the rocks rent ; and the graves were opened ; and many bodies of the saints which slept arose, and came out of the graves after the resurrection, and went into the holy city, and appeared unto many."[5] There is no reason to fear that these facts, which have been related only by Matthew, may appear to be inconsistent with the narratives presented by any one of the rest. The same evangelist then continues as follows : "Now when the centurion, and they that were with him watching Jesus, saw the earthquake, and those things that were done, they feared greatly, saying, Truly this was the Son of God."[6] Mark offers this version : "And when the centurion which stood over against Him saw that He so cried out, and gave up the ghost, he said, Truly this was the Son of God."[7] Luke's report runs thus : "Now when the centurion saw what was done, he glorified God, saying, Certainly this was a righteous man."[8] Here Matthew says that it was when they saw the earthquake that the centurion and those who were with him were thus astonished, whereas Luke represents the man's amazement to have been drawn forth by the fact that Jesus uttered such a cry, and then gave up the ghost ; thus making it clear how He had it in His own power to determine the time for His dying. But this involves no discrepancy. For as the said Matthew not only tells us how the centurion "saw the earthquake," but also appends the words, "and those that were done," he has indicated that there was room enough for Luke to represent the Lord's death as itself the thing which called forth the centurion's wonder. For that event is also one of the things which were done in so marvellous a manner then. At the same time, even although Matthew had not added any such statement, it would still have been perfectly legitimate to suppose, that as many astonishing things did take place at that time, and as the centurion and those who were with him may well have looked upon them all with amazement, the historians were at liberty to select for narration any particular incident which they were severally disposed to instance as the subject of the man's wonder. And it would not be fair to impeach them with inconsistency, simply because one of them may have specified one occurrence as the immediate cause of the centurion's amazement, while another introduces a different incident. For all these events together had really been matters for the man's astonishment. Again, the mere fact that one evangelist tells us that the centurion said, "Truly this was the Son of God," while another informs us that the words were, "Truly this man was the Son of God," will create no difficulty to

---

[1] [This view of the order is altogether the more probable one. See commentaries. — R.]
[2] Matt. xxvii. 51.   [3] Mark xv. 38.   [4] Luke xxiii. 45.

[5] Matt. xxvii. 51-53.   [6] Matt. xxvii. 54.   [7] Mark xv. 39.
[8] Luke xxiii. 47.

any one who has retained some recollection of the numerous statements and discussions bearing upon similar cases, which have already been given above. For these different versions of the words both convey precisely the same sense; and although one writer introduces the word " man " while another does not, that implies no kind of contradiction. A greater appearance of discrepancy may be supposed to be created by the circumstance, that the words which Luke reports the centurion to have uttered are not "This was the Son of God," but "This was a righteous man." But we ought to suppose either that both things were actually said by the centurion, and that two of the evangelists have recorded the one expression, and the third the other; or else perhaps that it was Luke's intention to bring out the exact idea which the centurion had in view when he said that Jesus was the Son of God. For it may be the case that the centurion did not really understand Him to be the Only-begotten, equal with the Father; but that he called Him the Son of God simply because he believed Him to be a righteous man, as many righteous men have been named sons of God. Moreover, when Luke says, "Now when the centurion saw what was done," he has really used terms which cover all the marvellous things which occurred on that occasion, commemorating a single deed of wonder, so to speak, of which all those miraculous incidents were, as we may say, members and parts. But, once more, as regards the circumstance that Matthew has also referred to those who were with the centurion, while the others have left these parties unnoticed, to whom will this not explain itself on the well-understood principle that there is no contradiction necessarily involved in the mere fact that one writer records what another passes by without mention? And, finally, as to Matthew's having told us that " they feared greatly," while Luke has said nothing about the man being afraid, but has informed us that " he glorified God," who can fail to understand that he glorified [God] just by the fear which he exhibited?

CHAP. XXI. — OF THE WOMEN WHO WERE STANDING THERE, AND OF THE QUESTION WHETHER MATTHEW, MARK, AND LUKE, WHO HAVE STATED THAT THEY STOOD AFAR OFF, ARE IN ANTAGONISM WITH JOHN, WHO HAS MENTIONED THAT ONE OF THEM STOOD BY THE CROSS.

58. Matthew proceeds thus: " And many women were there beholding afar off, which followed Jesus from Galilee: among which was Mary Magdalene, and Mary the mother of James and Joseph, and the mother of Zebedee's children." [1] Mark gives it in this form: " There were also women looking on afar off: among whom was Mary Magdalene, and Mary the mother of James the Less and of Joseph, and Salome (who also, when He was in Galilee, followed Him, and ministered unto Him); and many other women which came up with Him unto Jerusalem." [2] I see nothing which can be supposed to constitute a discrepancy between these writers here. For in what way can the truth be affected by the fact that some of these women are named in both lists, while others are referred to only in the one? Luke has likewise connected his narrations as follows: " And all the people that came together to that sight, beholding the things which were done, smote their breasts, and returned. And all His acquaintance and the women that followed Him from Galilee stood afar off beholding these things." [3] Here we perceive that he is quite in harmony with the former two as far as regards the presence of the women, although he does not mention any of them by name. On the subject of the multitude of people who were also present, and who, as they beheld the things which were done, smote their breasts and returned, he is in like manner at one with Matthew, although that evangelist has introduced into the context this distinct statement: " Now the centurion and they that were with him." Thus it simply appears that Luke is the only one who has spoken expressly of His " acquaintance " who stood afar off. For John has also noticed the presence of the women before the Lord gave up the ghost. His narrative runs thus: " Now there stood by the cross of Jesus His mother, and His mother's sister, Mary the wife of Cleophas, and Mary Magdalene. When Jesus therefore saw His mother, and the disciple standing by whom He loved, He saith unto His mother, Woman, behold thy son! Then saith He to the disciple, Behold thy mother! And from that hour that disciple took her unto his own home." [4] Now, as regards this statement, had not Matthew and Mark at the same time mentioned Mary Magdalene most explicitly by name, it might have been possible for us to say that there was one company of women afar off, and another near the cross. For none of these writers has mentioned the Lord's mother here but John himself. The question, therefore, which rises now is this, How can we understand the same Mary Magdalene both to have stood afar off along with other women, as the accounts of Matthew and Mark bear, and to have been by the cross, as John tells us, unless it be the case that these women were at such a distance as made it quite legitimate to say at once that they were near, because they were at hand there in the sight of Him, and also afar off in comparison with the crowd of people who were

---

[1] Matt. xxvii. 55, 56.
[2] Mark xv. 40, 41.
[3] Luke xxiii. 48, 49.
[4] John xix. 25-27.

standing round about in closer vicinity along with the centurion and the soldiers? It is open for us, then, to suppose that those women who were present at the scene along with the Lord's mother, after He commended her to the disciple, began then to retire with the view of extricating themselves from the dense mass of people, and of looking on at what remained to be done from a greater distance. And in this way the rest of the evangelists, who have introduced their notices of these women only after the Lord's death, have properly reported them to be standing by that time afar off.

CHAP. XXII. — OF THE QUESTION WHETHER THE EVANGELISTS ARE ALL AT ONE ON THE SUBJECT OF THE NARRATIVE REGARDING JOSEPH, WHO BEGGED THE LORD'S BODY FROM PILATE, AND WHETHER JOHN'S VERSION CONTAINS ANY STATEMENTS AT VARIANCE WITH EACH OTHER.

59. Matthew proceeds as follows : " Now when the even was come, there came a rich man of Arimathea, named Joseph, who also himself was Jesus' disciple : he went to Pilate, and begged the body of Jesus. Then Pilate commanded the body to be delivered." [1] Mark presents it in this form : " And now when the even was come, because it was the preparation, that is, the day before the Sabbath, Joseph of Arimathea, an honourable councillor, which also waited for the kingdom of God, came, and went in boldly unto Pilate, and craved the body of Jesus. And Pilate marvelled if He were already dead : and, calling unto him the centurion, he asked him whether He had been any while [2] dead. And when he knew it of the centurion, he gave the body to Joseph." [3] Luke's report runs in these terms : " And, behold, there was a man named Joseph, a councillor; and he was a good man, and a just (the same had not consented to the counsel and deed of them) : he was of Arimathea, a city of the Jews : who also himself waited for the kingdom of God. This man went unto Pilate, and begged the body of Jesus." [4] John, on the other hand, first narrates the breaking of the legs of those who had been crucified with the Lord, and the piercing of the Lord's side with the lance (which whole passage has been recorded by him alone), and then subjoins a statement which is of the same tenor with what is given by the other evangelists. It proceeds in these terms : " And after this, Joseph of Arimathea, being a disciple of Jesus, but secretly for fear of the Jews, besought Pilate that he might take away the body of Jesus : and Pilate gave him leave. He came therefore, and took the body of Jesus." [5] There is nothing here to give any

one of them the appearance of being in antagonism with another. But some one may perhaps ask whether John is not inconsistent with himself, when he at once unites with the rest in telling us how Joseph begged the body of Jesus, and comes forward as the only one who states here that Joseph had been a disciple of Jesus secretly for fear of the Jews. For the question may reasonably be raised as to how it happened that the man who had been a disciple secretly for fear had the courage to beg His body — a thing which not one of those who were His open followers was bold enough to do. We must understand, however, that this man did so in the confidence which his dignified position gave him, the possession of which rendered it possible for him to make his way on familiar terms into Pilate's presence. And we must suppose, further, that in the performance of that last service relating to the interment, he cared less for the Jews, however he tried in ordinary circumstances, when hearing the Lord, to avoid exposing himself to their enmity.

CHAP. XXIII. — OF THE QUESTION WHETHER THE FIRST THREE EVANGELISTS ARE QUITE IN HARMONY WITH JOHN IN THE ACCOUNTS GIVEN OF HIS BURIAL.

60. Matthew proceeds thus : " And when Joseph had taken the body, he wrapped it in a clean linen cloth, and laid it in his own new tomb, which he had hewn out in the rock : and he rolled a great stone to the door of the sepulchre, and departed." [6] Mark's version is as follows : " And he bought fine linen, [7] and took Him down, and wrapped Him in the linen, and laid Him in a sepulchre which was hewn out of a rock, and rolled a stone unto the door of the sepulchre." [8] Luke reports it in those terms : " And he took it down, and wrapped it in linen, and laid it in a sepulchre that was hewn in stone, wherein never man before was laid." [9] So far as these three narratives are concerned, no allegation of a want of harmony can possibly be raised. John, however, tells us that the burial of the Lord was attended to not only by Joseph, but also by Nicodemus. For he begins with Nicodemus in due connection with what precedes, and goes on with his narrative as follows : " And there came also Nicodemus (which at the first came to Jesus by night), and brought a mixture of myrrh and aloes, about an hundred pound weight." [10] Then, introducing Joseph again at this point, he continues in these terms : " Then took they the body of Jesus, and wound it in linen clothes with the

---

[1] Matt. xxvii. 57, 58.
[2] [Augustin's text has *jam* a second time, agreeing with some early Greek MSS. Comp. Revised Version margin, " were already dead." — R.]
[3] Mark xv. 42–45.   [4] Luke xxiii. 50–52.   [5] John xix. 38.

[6] Matt. xxvii. 59, 60.
[7] [All three evangelists use the same term in referring to " the linen cloth;" so the Latin text. The Authorized Version makes an unnecessary variation. John uses another word: see below. — R.]
[8] Mark xv. 46.   [9] Luke xxiii. 53.
[10] John xix. 39.

spices, as the manner of the Jews is to bury. Now in the place where He was crucified there was a garden; and in the garden a new sepulchre, wherein was never man yet laid. There laid they Jesus, therefore, because of the Jews' preparation day; for the sepulchre was nigh at hand."[1] But there is really as little ground for supposing any discrepancy here as there was in the former case, if we take a correct view of the statement. For those evangelists who have left Nicodemus unnoticed have not affirmed that the Lord was buried by Joseph alone, although he is the only one introduced into their records. Neither does the fact, that these three are all at one in informing us how the Lord was wrapped in the linen cloth by Joseph, preclude us from entertaining the idea that other linen stuffs may have been brought by Nicodemus, and added to what was given by Joseph, so that John may be perfectly correct in his narrative, especially as what he tells us is that the Lord was wrapped not in a linen cloth, but in linen clothes.[2] At the same time, when we take into account the handkerchief which was used for the head, and the bandages with which the whole body was swathed, and consider that all these were made of linen, we can see how, even although there was really but a single linen cloth [of the kind referred to by the first three evangelists] there, it could still have been stated with the most perfect truth that "they wound Him in linen clothes." For the phrase, linen clothes, is one applied generally to all textures made of flax.

CHAP. XXIV. — OF THE ABSENCE OF ALL DISCREP-
ANCIES IN THE NARRATIVES CONSTRUCTED BY
THE FOUR EVANGELISTS ON THE SUBJECT OF
THE EVENTS WHICH TOOK PLACE ABOUT THE
TIME OF THE LORD'S RESURRECTION.

61. Matthew proceeds thus: "And there was there Mary Magdalene, and the other Mary, sitting over against the sepulchre."[3] This is given by Mark as follows: "And Mary Magdalene, and Mary the mother of Joseph, beheld where He was laid."[4] So far it is evident that there is no kind of inconsistency between the accounts.

62. Matthew continues in these terms: "Now the next day, that followed the day of the preparation, the chief priests and Pharisees came together unto Pilate, saying, Sir, we have remembered that that deceiver said, while he was yet alive, After three days I will rise again. Command therefore that the sepulchre be made sure until the third day, lest his disciples come by night and steal him away, and say unto the people, He is risen from the dead: so the last error shall be worse than the first. Pilate said unto them, Ye have

a watch; go your way, make it as sure as ye can. So they went, and made the sepulchre sure, sealing the stone, and setting a watch."[5] This narrative is given only by Matthew. Nothing, however, is stated by any of the others which can have the appearance of contrariety.

63. Again, the same Matthew carries on his recital as follows: "Now, in the evening of the Sabbath,[6] when it began to dawn towards the first day of the week,[7] came Mary Magdalene, and the other Mary, to see the sepulchre. And, behold, there was a great earthquake: for the angel of the Lord descended from heaven, and came and rolled back the stone from the door, and sat upon it. And his countenance was like lightning, and his raiment white as snow: and for fear of him the keepers did shake, and became as dead men. And the angel answered and said unto the women, Fear not ye: for I know that ye seek Jesus, which was crucified. He is not here; for He is risen, as He said. Come, see the place where the Lord lay: And go quickly, and tell His disciples that He is risen from the dead; and, behold, He goeth before you into Galilee; there shall ye see Him: lo, I have told you."[8] Mark is in harmony with this. It is possible, however, that some difficulty may be felt in the circumstance that, according to Matthew's version, the stone was already rolled away from the sepulchre, and the angel was sitting upon it. For Mark tells us that tne women entered into the sepulchre, and there saw a young man sitting on the right side, covered with a long white garment, and that they were affrighted.[9] But the explanation may be, that Matthew has simply said nothing about the angel whom they saw when they entered into the sepulchre, and that Mark has said nothing about the one whom they saw sitting outside upon the stone. In this way they would have seen two angels, and have got two separate angelic reports relating to Jesus, — namely, first one from the angel whom they saw sitting outside upon the stone, and then another from the angel whom they saw sitting on the right side when they entered into the sepulchre. Thus, too, the injunction given them by the angel who was sitting outside, and which was conveyed in the words, "Come, and see the place where the Lord lay," would have served to encourage them to go within the tomb; on coming to which, as has been said, and venturing within it, we may suppose them to have seen the angel concerning whom Matthew tells us nothing, but of whom Mark discourses, sitting on the right

---

[1] John xix. 40–42.
[2] [John uses the term ὀθονίοις, which the Latin renders linteis. Augustin's discussion is not intelligible unles s this variation is recognised. — R]
[3] Matt. xxvii. 61.　　　　　　　[4] Mark xv. 47.

[5] Matt. xxvii. 62–66.
[6] Vespere autem Sabbati. [The Greek does not present the difficulty which is found in the Latin text, and discussed by Augustin in § 65 (latter part). The phrase is properly rendered in the Revised Version, "Now late on the Sabbath-day."— R.]
[7] The editions often give, in prima Sabbati = on the first day of the week. The best MSS. read, as above, in primam, etc.
[8] Matt. xxviii. 1–7.　　　　　　[9] Mark xvi. 5.

side, from whom also they heard things of like tenor to those they had previously listened to. Or if this explanation is not satisfactory, we ought certainly to accept the theory that, as they entered into the sepulchre, they came within a section of the ground where, it is reasonable to suppose, a certain space had been by that time securely enclosed, extending a little distance in front of the rock which had been cut out in order to construct the place of sepulture; so that, according to this view, what they really beheld was the one angel sitting on the right side, in the space thus referred to, which same angel Matthew also represents to have been sitting upon the stone which he had rolled away from the mouth of the tomb when the earthquake took place, that is to say, from the place which had been dug out in the rock for a sepulchre.

64. It may also be asked how it is that Mark says: "And they went out quickly, and fled from the sepulchre; for they trembled and were amazed: neither said they anything to any man; for they were afraid;"[1] whereas Matthew's statement is in these terms: "And they departed quickly from the sepulchre with fear and great joy, and did run to bring His disciples word."[2] The explanation, however, may be that the women did not venture to tell either of the angels themselves, — that is, they had not courage enough to say anything in reply to what they had heard from the angels. Or, indeed, it may be that they were not bold enough to speak to the guards whom they saw lying there; for the joy which Matthew mentions is not inconsistent with the fear of which Mark takes notice. Indeed, we ought to have supposed that both feelings had possession of their minds, even although Matthew himself had said nothing about the fear. But now, when this evangelist also particularizes it, saying, "They departed quickly from the sepulchre with fear and great joy," he allows nothing to remain which can occasion any question of difficulty on this subject.

65. At the same time, a question, which is not to be dealt with lightly, does arise here with respect to the exact hour at which the women came to the sepulchre. For when Matthew says, "Now, on the evening of the Sabbath, when it was dawning toward the first day of the week, came Mary Magdalene, and the other Mary, to see the sepulchre," what are we to make of Mark's statement, which runs thus: "And very early in the morning, the first day of the week, they came unto the sepulchre at the rising of the sun"?[3] It is to be observed

that in this Mark states nothing inconsistent with the reports given by other two of the evangelists, namely, Luke and John. For when Luke says, "Very early in the morning," and when John puts it thus, "Early, when it was yet dark," they convey the same sense which Mark is understood to express when he says, "Very early, at the rising of the sun;" that is to say, they all refer to the period when the heavens were now beginning to brighten in the east, which, of course, does not take place but when the sunrise is at hand. For it is the brightness which is diffused by the rising sun that is familiarly designated by the name of the dawn.[4] Consequently, Mark does not contradict the other evangelist who uses the phrase, "When it was yet dark;" for as the day breaks, what remains of the darkness [of the night] passes away just in proportion as the sun continues to rise. And this phrase, "Very early in the morning," need not be taken to mean that the sun itself was actually seen by this time [blazing] over the lands; but it is rather to be taken as like the kind of expression which we are in the habit of employing when speaking to people to whom we wish to intimate that something should be done more betimes than usual. For when we have used the term, "Early in the morning,"[5] if we wish to keep the persons addressed from supposing that we refer directly to the time when the sun is already conspicuously visible over earth, we usually add the word "very," and say, "very early in the morning," in order that they may clearly understand that we allude to the time which is also called the daybreak.[6] At the same time, it is also customary for men, after the cockcrow has been repeatedly heard, and when they begin to surmise that the day is now approaching, to say, "It is now early in the morning;"[5] and when after this they weigh their words and observe that, as the sun now rises, — that is to say, as it now makes its immediate advent into these parts, — the sky is just beginning to redden, or to brighten, those who said, "It is early in the morning," then amplify their expression and say, "It is very early in the morning." But what does it matter, provided only that, whichever method of explanation be preferred, we understand that what is meant by Mark, when he uses the terms "early in the morning,"[5] is just the same as is intended by Luke when he adopts the phrase, "in the morning;"[7] and that the whole expression employed by the former — namely, "very early in the morning"[8] — amounts to the same as that which we find in Luke — namely, "very early in the dawn,"[9] — and as that which is chosen by John

---

[1] Mark xvi. 8.   [2] Matt. xxviii. 8.
[3] Mark xvi. 2. [Mark's expression, according to the Greek text, is more explicit: "when the sun was risen." But this is to be explained by the context, as Augustin indicates. — R.]

[4] Aurorœ.   [5] Mane.   [6] Albescente.
[7] Diluculo.   [8] Valde mane.
[9] Valde diluculo.

when he says, "early, when it was yet dark"?[1] Moreover, when Mark speaks of the "rising of the sun," he just means that by its rising the sun was now beginning to bring the light in upon the sky. But the question now is this: how can Matthew be in harmony with these three when he says neither "in the early morning" nor "early in the morning," but "in the evening of the Sabbath, when it was beginning to dawn toward the first day of the week"? This is a matter which must be carefully investigated.[2] Now, under that first part of the night, which is [here called] the evening, Matthew intended to refer to this particular night, at the close of which the women came to the sepulchre. And we understand his reason for so referring to the said night to have been this: that by the time of the evening it was lawful for them to bring the spices, because the Sabbath was then indeed over. Consequently, as they were hindered by the Sabbath from doing so previously, he has given a designation of the night, taken from the time at which it began to be a lawful thing for them to do what they did at any period of the same night which pleased them. Thus, therefore, the phrase "in the evening of the Sabbath" is used, as if what was said had been "in the night of the Sabbath," or in other words, "in the night which follows the day of the Sabbath. The express words which he employs thus indicate this with sufficient clearness. For his terms are these: "Now, in the evening of the Sabbath, when it began to dawn toward the first day of the week;" and that could not be the case if what we had to understand to be denoted by the mention of the "evening" was simply the first short space of the night, or in other words, only the beginning of the night. For what can be said "to begin to dawn toward the first day of the week" is not explicitly the beginning [of the night], but the night itself, as it commences to be brought to its close by the advance of the light. For the *terminus* of the first part of the night is just the beginning of the second part, but the *terminus* of the whole night is the light. Hence we could not speak of the evening as dawning toward the first day of the week unless under the term "evening" we should understand the night itself to be meant, which, as a whole, is brought to its close by the light. It is also a familiar method of speech in divine Scripture to express the whole under the part; and thus, under the word "evening" here, the evangelist has denoted the whole night, which finds its extreme point in the dawn.[3] For it was in the dawn that those women came to the sepulchre; and in this way they really came on the night, which is here indicated by the term "evening." For, as I have said, the night as a whole is denoted by that word; consequently, at whatever period of that night they might have come, they certainly did come in the said night. And, accordingly, if they came at the latest point in that night, it is still unquestionably the case that they did come in the said night. But it could not be said to be on "the evening, when it began to dawn toward the first day of the week," unless the night as a whole can be understood under that expression. Accordingly, the women who came in the night referred to, came in the evening specified. And if they came at any period, even the latest during that night, they surely came in the night itself.

66. For the space of three days, which elapsed between the Lord's death and resurrection, cannot be correctly understood except in the light of that form of expression according to which the part is dealt with as the whole.[4] For He said Himself, "For as Jonas was three days and three nights in the whale's belly, so shall the Son of man be three days and three nights in the heart of the earth."[5] Now, in whichever way we reckon the times, whether from the point when He yielded up the ghost, or from the date of his burial, the sum does not come out clearly, unless we take the intermediate day, that is to say, the Sabbath, as a complete day—in other words, a full day along with its night,—and, on the other hand, understand those days between which that one intervenes—that is to say, the day of the preparation and the first day of the week, which we designate the Lord's day—to be dealt with on the principle of the part standing for the whole. For of what avail is it that some, hard pressed by these difficulties, and not knowing the very large part which the mode of expression referred to—namely, that which takes the part as the whole—plays in the matter of solving the problems presented in the Holy Scriptures, have struck out the idea of reckoning as a distinct night those three hours, namely, from the sixth hour to the ninth, during which the sun was darkened, and as a distinct day the other three hours, during which the sun was restored again to the lands, that is to say, from the ninth hour on to its setting? For the night connected with the coming Sabbath follows, and if we compute it along with its day, there will then be two days and two nights. But, further, after the Sabbath there comes in the night connected with the first day of the week, that is to say, with the

---

[1] *Mane cum adhuc tenebræ essent.*
[2] [The difficulty arises from taking *vespere* in its technical sense, as referring to the previous evening As already intimated (see note on § 63), the Greek does not necessarily imply this. — R.]
[3] *Diluculo.*
[4] A sentence is sometimes added here in the editions, namely, *Hinc magna redditur ratio verbi Domini* = hence a large account is given of the Lord's word. It is omitted in the MSS.
[5] Matt. xii. 40.

dawning of the Lord's day, which was the time when the Lord arose. Consequently, the result to which this mode of calculation leads us will be just two days and two nights, and one night, even supposing it possible to take the last as a complete night, and taking it for granted that we were not to show that the said dawn was in reality the ultimate portion of the same. Thus it would appear that, even although we were to compute these six hours in that fashion, during three of which the sun was darkened, and during the other three of which it shone forth again, we would not establish a satisfactory reckoning of three days and three nights. In accordance, therefore, with the usage which meets us so frequently in the language of the Scriptures, and which deals with the part as the whole, it remains for us to hold the time of the preparation to constitute the day at the one extremity,[1] on which the Lord was crucified and buried, and, from that limit, to find one whole day along with its night which was fully spent. In this way, too, we must take the intermediate member, that is to say the day of the Sabbath, not as calculated simply from the part, but as a really complete day. The third day, again, must be computed from its first part; that is to say, calculating from the night, we must look upon it as making up a whole day when its day-portion is connected with it. Thus we shall get a space of three days, on the analogy of a case already considered, namely, those eight days after which the Lord went up into a mountain; with respect to which period we find that Matthew and Mark, fixing their attention simply on the complete days intervening, have put it thus, "After six days," whereas Luke's representation of the same is this, "An eight days after."[2]

67. Let us now proceed, therefore, to look into the rest of this passage, and see how in other respects these statements are quite consistent with what is given by Matthew. For Luke tells us, with the utmost plainness, that two angels were seen by those women who came to the sepulchre. One of these angels we have understood to be referred to by each of the first two evangelists; that is to say, one of them is noticed by Matthew, namely, the one who was sitting outside upon the stone, and a second by Mark, namely, the one who was sitting within the sepulchre on the right side. But Luke's version of the scene is to the following effect : "And that day was the preparation, and the Sabbath drew on. And the women which had come with Him from Galilee beheld the sepulchre, and how His body was laid. And they returned, and prepared spices and ointments; and rested the Sabbath-day, according to the commandment.[3] Now upon the first day of the week, very early in the morning, they came unto the sepulchre, bringing the spices which they had prepared.[4] And they found the stone rolled away from the sepulchre. And they entered in, and found not the body of the Lord Jesus. And it came to pass, as they were much perplexed thereabout, behold, two men stood by them in shining garments ; and as they were afraid, and bowed down their faces to the earth, they said unto them, Why seek ye the living among the dead? He is not here, but is risen : remember how He spake unto you when He was yet in Galilee, saying, The Son of man must be delivered into the hands of sinful men, and be crucified, and the third day rise again. And they remembered His words. And they returned from the sepulchre, and told all these things unto the eleven, and to all the rest."[5] The question, therefore, is this, how can these angels have been seen sitting each one separately,— namely, one outside upon the stone, according to Matthew, and another within upon the right side, according to Mark,—if Luke's report of the same bears that the two stood beside those women, although the words ascribed to them are similar? Well, it is still possible for us to suppose that one angel was seen by the women in the position assigned by Matthew, and in the circumstances indicated by Mark, as we have already explained. In this way, we may understand the said women to have entered into the sepulchre, that is to say, into a certain space which had been fenced off within a kind of enclosure, in such a manner that an entrance might be said to be made when they came in front of the rocky place in which the sepulchre was constructed ; and there we may take them to have beheld the angel sitting upon the stone which had been rolled away from the tomb, as Matthew tells us, or in other words, the angel sitting on the right side, as Mark expresses it.[6] And then we may further surmise that the said women, after they had gone within, and when they were looking at the place where the body of the Lord lay, saw other two angels standing, as Luke informs us, by whom they were addressed in similar terms, with a view to animate their minds and edify their faith.[7]

68. But let us also examine John's version, and see whether or in what manner its consistency with these others is apparent. John, then,

---

[1] The text gives, *extremum diem tempus parasceues.* One of the Vatican MSS. reads *primum diem,* etc. = the first day.

[2] See above, Book ii. chap. 56, § 113.

[3] [The Greek text connects closely this clause with the following one. Comp. Revised Version. — R.]

[4] The words, "*and certain others with them,*" are omitted here. [So the Greek text, according to the best authorities. Comp. Revised Version. — R.]

[5] Luke xxiii. 54–xxiv. 12.

[6] [Matthew tells nothing of their entering the tomb; but Mark distinctly affirms this, as does Luke. — R.]

[7] [The view that there were two parties of women is not noticed by Augustin. His explanations are in the main pertinent, though harmonists and commentators still disagree in regard to the details. — R.]

narrates these incidents as follows : " Now the first day of the week cometh Mary Magdalene early, when it was yet dark, unto the sepulchre, and saw the stone taken away from the sepulchre. Then she runneth, and cometh to Simon Peter, and to the other disciples whom Jesus loved, and saith unto them, They have taken away the Lord out of the sepulchre, and we know not where they have laid Him.   Peter therefore went forth, and that other disciple, and they came to the sepulchre.   So they ran both together : and the other disciple did outrun Peter, and came first to the sepulchre.   And he, stooping down, saw the linen clothes lying ; yet went he not in. Then cometh Simon Peter following him, and went into the sepulchre, and seeth the linen clothes lie, and the napkin, that was about His head, not lying with the linen clothes, but wrapped together in a place by itself.   Then went in also that other disciple, which came first to the sepulchre, and he saw, and believed.   For as yet they knew not the Scripture, that He must rise again from the dead.   Then the disciples went away again unto their own home.   But Mary stood without at the sepulchre weeping : and, as she wept, she stooped down, and looked into the sepulchre, and seeth two angels in white sitting, the one at the head, and the other at the feet, where the body of Jesus had lain.   They say unto her, Woman, why weepest thou ?   She saith unto them, Because they have taken away my Lord, and I know not where they have laid Him. And when she had thus said, she turned herself back, and saw Jesus standing, and knew not that it was Jesus.   Jesus saith unto her, Woman, why weepest thou ? whom seekest thou ?   She, suppos- ing Him to be the gardener, saith unto Him, Sir, if thou have borne Him hence, tell me where thou hast laid Him, and I will take Him away.   Jesus saith unto her, Mary.   She turned herself, and saith unto Him, Rabboni ; which is to say, Master.   Jesus saith unto her, Touch me not ; for I am not yet ascended to my Father : but go to my brethren, and say unto them, I ascend unto my Father, and your Father ; and to my God, and your God.   Mary Magdalene came and told the disciples that she had seen the Lord, and that He had spoken these things unto her." [1] In the narrative thus given by John, the state- ment of the day or time when the sepulchre was come to agrees with the accounts presented by the rest.   Again, in the report of two angels who were seen, he is also at one with Luke.   But when we observe how the one evangelist tells us that these angels were seen standing, while the other says that they were sitting ; when we notice, also, that there are certain other things which are left unrecorded by these two writers ;

and, further, when we consider how questions are thus raised regarding the possibility of proving the consistency of the one set of historians with the other on these subjects, and of fixing the order in which those said things took place, — we see that, unless we submit the whole to a careful examination, there may easily appear to be contradictions here between the several nar- ratives.

69. This being the case, therefore, let us, so far as the Lord may help us, take all these inci- dents, which took place about the time of the Lord's resurrection, as they are brought before us in the statements of all the evangelists to- gether, and let us arrange them in one connected narrative, which will exhibit them precisely as they may have actually occurred.   It was in the early morning of the first day of the week, as all the evangelists are at one in attesting, that the women came to the sepulchre.   By that time, all that is recorded by Matthew alone had already taken place ; that is to say, in regard to the quaking of the earth, and the rolling away of the stone, and the terror of the guards, with which they were so stricken, that in some part they lay like dead men.   Then, as John informs us, came Mary Magdalene, who unquestionably was surpassingly more ardent in her love than these other women [2] who had ministered to the Lord ; so that it was not unreasonable in John to make mention of her alone, leaving those others unnamed, who, however, were along with her, as we gather from the reports given by others of the evangelists.   She came accordingly ; and when she saw the stone taken away from the sepulchre, without pausing to make any more minute investigation, and never doubting but that the body of Jesus had been removed from the tomb, she ran, as the same John states, and told the state of matters to Peter and to John himself.   For John is himself that disciple whom Jesus loved.   They then set out running to the sepulchre ; and John, reaching the spot first, stooped down and saw the linen clothes lying, but he did not go within.   But Peter followed up, and went into the sepulchre, and saw the linen clothes lie, and the napkin, which had been about His head, not lying with the linen clothes, but wrapped together in a place by itself. Then John entered also, and saw in like manner, and believed what Mary had told him, namely, that the Lord had been taken away from the sepulchre.   " For as yet they knew not the Scrip- ture, that He must rise again from the dead. Then the disciples went away again unto their own home.   But Mary stood without at the

---

[1] John xx. 1-18.

[2] The text follows the MSS. in reading *sine dubio cæteris mulie-ribus . . . plurimum dilectione ferventior.*   Some editions insert *cum* before *cæteris mulieribus ;* in which case the sense would be = Mary Magdalene, unquestionably accompanied by the other women who had ministered to the Lord, but herself more ardent, etc.

sepulchre weeping," [1] — that is to say, before the place in the rock in which the sepulchre was constructed, but at the same time within that space into which they had now entered; for there was a garden there, as the same John mentions. [2] Then they saw the angel sitting on the right side, upon the stone which was rolled away from the sepulchre; of which angel both Matthew and Mark discourse. "Then he said unto them, Fear not ye; for I know that ye seek Jesus, which was crucified. He is not here; for He is risen, as He said. Come, see the place where the Lord lay: and go quickly, and tell His disciples that He is risen from the dead; and, behold, He goeth before you into Galilee; there shall ye see Him: lo, I have told you." [3] In Mark we also find a passage similar in tenor to the above. At these words, Mary, still weeping, bent down and looked forwards into the sepulchre, and beheld the two angels, who are introduced to us in John's narrative, sitting in white raiment, one at the head, and the other at the feet, where the body of Jesus had been deposited. "They say unto her, Woman, why weepest thou? She saith unto them, Because they have taken away my Lord, and I know not where they have laid Him." [4] Here we are to suppose the angels to have risen up, so that they could be seen standing, as Luke states that they were seen, and then, according to the narrative of the same Luke, to have addressed the women, as they were afraid and bowed down their faces to the earth. The terms were these: "Why seek ye the living among the dead? He is not here, but is risen: remember how He spake unto you when He was yet in Galilee, saying, The Son of man must be delivered into the hands of sinful men, and be crucified, and the third day rise. And they remembered His words." [5] It was after this that, as we learn from John, "Mary turned herself back, and saw Jesus standing, and knew not that it was Jesus. Jesus saith unto her, Woman, why weepest thou? whom seekest thou? She, supposing Him to be the gardener, saith unto Him, Sir, if thou have borne Him hence, tell me where thou hast laid Him, and I will take Him away. Jesus saith unto her, Mary. She turned herself, and saith unto Him, Rabboni; which is to say, Master. Jesus saith unto her, Touch me not; for I am not yet ascended to my Father: but go to my brethren, and say unto them, I ascend unto my Father, and your Father; and to my God, and your God." [6] Then she departed from the sepulchre, that is to say, from the ground where there was space for the garden in front of the stone which had been dug out. Along with her there were also those other women, who, as Mark tells us, were surprised with fear and trembling. And they told nothing to any one. At this point we next take up what Matthew has recorded in the following passage: "Behold, Jesus met them, saying, All hail! And they came and held Him by the feet, and worshipped Him." [7] For thus we gather that, on coming to the sepulchre, they were twice addressed by the angels; and, again, that they were also twice addressed by the Lord Himself, namely, at the point at which Mary took Him to be the gardener, and a second time at present, when He meets them on the way, with a view to strengthen them by such a repetition, and to bring them out of their state of fear. "Then, accordingly, said He unto them, Be not afraid: go, tell my brethren that they go into Galilee, and there shall they see me." [8] "Then came Mary Magdalene, and told the disciples that she had seen the Lord, and that He had spoken these things unto her;" [9] — not herself alone, however, but with her also those other women to whom Luke alludes when he says, "Which told these things unto the eleven disciples, and all the rest. And their words seemed to them like madness, and they believed them not." [10] Mark also attests these facts; for, after telling us how the women went out from the sepulchre, trembling and amazed, and said nothing to any man, he subjoins the statement, that the Lord rose early the first day of the week, and appeared first to Mary Magdalene, out of whom He had cast seven devils, and that she went and told them who had been with Him, as they mourned and wept, and that they, when they heard that He was alive, and had been seen of her, believed not. [11] It is further to be observed, that Matthew has also introduced a notice to the effect that, as the women who had seen and heard all these things were going away, there came likewise into the city some of the guards who had been lying like dead men, and that these persons reported to the chief priests all the things that were done, that is to say, those of them which they were themselves also in a position to observe. He tells us, moreover, that when they were assembled with the elders and had taken counsel, they gave large money unto the soldiers, and bade them say that His disciples came and stole Him away while they slept, promising at the same time to secure them against the governor, who had given those guards. Finally, he adds that they took the money, and did as they had been taught, and that this saying is commonly reported among the Jews until this day. [12]

---

[1] John xx. 9, 10.   [2] John xix. 41.
[3] Matt. xxviii. 5-7.   [4] John xx. 13.
[5] Luke xxiv. 5-8.   [6] John xx. 13-18.

[7] Matt. xxviii. 9.   [8] Matt. xxviii. 10.
[9] John xx. 18.   [10] Luke xxiv. 10, 11.
[11] [Augustin makes no allusion to the doubtful genuineness of Mark xvi. 9-20. The passage appears in nearly all early Latin codices. — R.]
[12] Matt. xxviii. 11-15.

CHAP. XXV. — OF CHRIST'S SUBSEQUENT MANI-
FESTATIONS OF HIMSELF TO THE DISCIPLES,
AND OF THE QUESTION WHETHER A THOROUGH
HARMONY CAN BE ESTABLISHED BETWEEN THE
DIFFERENT NARRATIVES WHEN THE NOTICES
GIVEN BY THE FOUR SEVERAL EVANGELISTS, AS
WELL AS THOSE PRESENTED BY THE APOSTLE
PAUL AND IN THE ACTS OF THE APOSTLES, ARE
COMPARED TOGETHER.

70. We must take up the consideration of the
manner in which the Lord showed Himself to
the disciples after His resurrection, and that with
the view not only of bringing out clearly the consistency of the four evangelists with each other
on these subjects, but also of exhibiting their
agreement with the Apostle Paul, who discourses
of the theme in his First Epistle to the Corinthians. The statement by the latter runs in the
following terms : " For I delivered unto you first
of all that which I also received, how that Christ
died for our sins according to the Scriptures ;
and that He was buried, and that He rose again
the third day according to the Scriptures ; and
that He was seen of Cephas, then of the twelve : [1]
after that He was seen of above five hundred
brethren at once ; of whom the greater part remain unto this day, but some are fallen asleep.
After that, He was seen of James ; then of all
the apostles. And last of all He was seen of
me also, as of one born out of due time." [2]
Now this succession of the appearances is one
which has been given by none of the evangelists. Hence we must examine whether the order
which they have put on record does not stand in
antagonism to this. For neither has Paul related
all, nor have the evangelists included everything
in their reports. And the real subject for our
investigation, therefore, is the question, whether,
among the incidents which do come under our
notice in these various narratives, there is anything fitted to establish a discrepancy between
the writers. Now Luke is the only one among
the four evangelists who omits to tell us how the
Lord was seen by the women, and confines his
statement to the appearance of the angels.
Matthew, again, informs us that He met them as
they were returning from the sepulchre. Mark
likewise mentions that He appeared first to Mary
Magdalene ; as also does John. Only Mark does
not state how He manifested Himself to her,
while John does give us an explanation of that.
Moreover, Luke not only passes by in silence
the fact that He showed Himself to the women,
as I have already remarked, but also reports that
two disciples, one of whom was Cleophas, talked
with Him, before they recognised Him, in a
strain which seems to imply that the women
had related no other appearance seen by them
than that of the angels who told them that He

was alive. For Luke's narrative proceeds thus :
" And, behold, two of them went that same day
to a village called Emmaus, which was from
Jerusalem about threescore furlongs. And they
talked together of all these things which had
happened. And it came to pass that, while
they communed together and reasoned, Jesus
Himself drew near, and went with them. But
their eyes were holden, that they should not
know Him. And He said unto them, What
manner of communications are these that ye have
one to another, as ye walk, and are sad ? And the
one of them, whose name was Cleophas, answering, said unto Him, Art thou only a stranger [3] in
Jerusalem, and hast not known the things which
are come to pass there in these days ? And He
said unto them, What things ? And they said
unto Him, Concerning Jesus of Nazareth, which
was a prophet mighty in deed and word before
God and all the people ; and how the chief
priests and our rulers delivered Him to be condemned to death, and have crucified Him. But
we trusted that it had been He that should have
redeemed Israel : and besides all this, to-day
is the third day since these things were done.
Yea, and certain women also of our company
made us astonished, which were early at the
sepulchre ; and when they found not His body,
they came, saying, that they had also seen a
vision of angels, which said that He was alive.
And certain of them which were with us went
to the sepulchre, and found it even so as the
women said ; but Him they saw [4] not." [5] All
these things they relate, according to Luke's
narrative, just as they were able to command
their recollections and bethink themselves of
what had been reported to them by the women,
or by the disciples who had run to the sepulchre
when the intelligence was conveyed to them that
His body had been removed from the place. It
is at the same time true that Luke himself reports only Peter to have run to the tomb, and
there to have stooped down and seen the linen
clothes laid by themselves, and then to have departed, wondering in himself at that which was
come to pass. This notice about Peter, moreover, is introduced previous to the narrative of
these two disciples whom He found on the way,
and subsequently to the story of the women who
had seen the angels, and who had heard from
them that Jesus had risen again ; so that this
position might seem to mark the period at which
Peter ran to the sepulchre. But still we must
suppose that Luke has inserted the passage about
Peter here in the form of a recapitulation. For
the time when Peter ran to the sepulchre was

---

[1] Some editions read *undecim* = the eleven.
[2] 1 Cor. xv. 3-8.

[3] [*Tu solus peregrinus es*, agreeing with the Greek text: " Art
thou the only sojourner," etc. But comp. Revised Version — R.]
[4] Another reading occurs here, *non invenerunt* = Him they
found not.
[5] Luke xxiv. 13-24.

also the time when John ran to it; and at that point all that they had heard was simply the statement conveyed to them by the women, and in particular by Mary Magdalene, to the effect that the body had been carried away. Furthermore, the period at which the said woman brought such tidings was just the occasion when she saw the stone rolled away from the sepulchre. And it was at a later point that these other things occurred, connected with the vision of the angels, and the appearance of the Lord Himself, who showed Himself twice over to the women, namely, once at the sepulchre, and a second time when He met them as they were returning from the tomb. This, however, took place previous to His being seen by those two upon the journey, one of whom was Cleophas. For, when this Cleophas was talking with the Lord, before he recognized who He was, he did not say expressly that Peter had gone to the sepulchre. But his words were these: "Certain of them which were with us went to the sepulchre, and found it even so as the women said;" which last statement is also to be understood as introduced in the form of a recapitulation. For the reference is to the report brought first of all by the women to Peter and John about the removal of the body. And thus, when Luke here informs us that Peter ran to the sepulchre, and also states how Cleophas mentioned that some of those who were with them went to the tomb, he is to be taken as attesting John's account, which bears that two persons proceeded to the sepulchre. But Luke has specified Peter alone in the first instance, just because it was to him that Mary had brought the earliest tidings. A difficulty, however, may also be felt in the circumstance that the same Luke does not say that Peter entered, but only that he stooped down and saw the linen clothes laid by themselves, and that thereupon he departed, wondering in himself; whereas John intimates that it was rather himself (for he is the disciple whom Jesus loved) that looked at the scene in this fashion, not going within the sepulchre, which he was the first to reach, but simply bending down and beholding the linen clothes laid in their place; although he also adds that he did enter the tomb afterwards. The explanation, therefore, is simply this, that Peter at first did stoop down and look in after the fashion which Luke specifies, but to which John makes no allusion; and that he went actually in somewhat later, but still before John entered. And in this way we shall find that all these writers have given a true account of what occurred in terms which betray no discrepancies.[1]

71. Taking, then, not only the reports present-

ed by the four evangelists, but also the statement given by the Apostle Paul, we shall endeavour to bring the whole into a single connected narrative, and exhibit the order in which all these incidents may have taken place, comprehending all the Lord's appearances to the male disciples, and leaving out His earlier declarations to the women. Now, in the entire number of the men, Peter is understood to be the one to whom Christ showed Himself first. At least, this holds good so far as regards all the individuals who are actually mentioned by the four evangelists, and by the Apostle Paul. But, at the same time, who would be bold enough either to affirm or to deny that He may have appeared to some one among them before He showed Himself to Peter, although all these writers pass the matter over in silence? For the statement which Paul also gives is not in the form, "He was seen first of Cephas." But it runs thus: "He was seen of Cephas, then of the twelve: after that He was seen of above five hundred brethren at once." And thus it is not made clear who these twelve were, just as we are not informed who these five hundred were. It is quite possible, indeed, that the twelve here instanced were some unknown twelve belonging to the multitude of the disciples. For now the apostle might speak of those whom the Lord designated apostles, not as the twelve, but as the eleven. Some codices, indeed, contain this very reading. I take that, however, to be an emendation introduced by men who were perplexed by the text, supposing it to refer to those twelve apostles who, by the time when Judas disappeared, were really only eleven. It may be the case, then, that those are the more correct codices which contain the reading "eleven;" or it may be that Paul intended some other twelve disciples to be understood by that phrase;[2] or, once more, the fact may be that he meant that consecrated number[3] to remain as before, although the circle had been reduced to eleven: for this number twelve, as it was used of the apostles, had so mystical an importance, that, in order to keep the spiritual symbol of the same number, there could be but a single individual, namely, Matthias, elected to fill the place of Judas.[4] But whichever of these several views may be adopted, nothing necessarily results which can appear to be inconsistent with truth, or at variance with any one most trustworthy historian among them. Still, it remains the probable supposition, that, after He was seen of Peter, He appeared next to those two, of whom Cleophas was one, and regarding whom Luke

[1] [Luke xxiv. 12 is omitted by Tischendorf, on the authority of codices allied to the text of the Vulgate. The omission was probably occasioned by the difficulties discussed above. — R.]

[2] The text has, Sive alios quosdam duodecim discipulos Paulus, etc. In the MSS. another reading is found: Sive alios quosdam duodecim apostolus, etc. = it may be that the Apostle Paul intended some other twelve to be understood, etc.

[3] For sacratum illum numerum, five MSS. give sacramentum illius numeri = the mystical symbol of that number.

[4] Acts i. 26.

presents us with a complete narrative, while Mark gives us only a very brief notice. The latter evangelist [1] reports the same incident in these concise terms : " And after that He appeared in another form unto two of them, as they walked and went to a country-seat." [2]   For it is not un-reasonable for us to suppose that the place of residence [3] referred to may also have been styled a country-seat ; [4] just as Bethlehem itself, which formerly was called a city, is even at the present time also named a village, although its honour has now been made so much the greater since the name of this Lord, who was born in it, has been proclaimed so extensively throughout the Churches of all nations.   In the Greek codices, indeed, the reading which we discover is rather " estate " [5] than " country-seat."   But that term was employed not only of residences,[6] but also of free towns [7] and colonies beyond the city, which is the head and mother of the rest, and is therefore called the metropolis.

72. Again, if Mark tells us that the Lord appeared to these persons in another form, Luke refers to the same when he says that their eyes were holden, that they should not know Him. For something had come upon their eyes which was suffered to remain until the breaking of the bread, in reference to a well-known mystery, so that only then was the different form in Him made visible to them, and they did not recognise Him, as is shown by Luke's narrative, until the breaking of the bread took place.   And thus, in apt accordance with the state of their minds, which were still ignorant of the truth, that it behoved Christ to die and rise again, their eyes sustained something of a similar order ; not, in-deed, that the truth itself proved misleading, but that they were themselves incompetent to per-ceive the truth, and thought of the matter as something else than it was.   The deeper signifi-cance of all which is this, that no one should consider himself to have attained the knowledge of Christ, if he is not a member in His body — that is to say, in His Church — the unity of which is commended to our notice under the sacra-mental symbol of the bread by an apostle, when he says : " We being many are one bread and one body." [8]   So was it that, when He handed to them the bread which He had blessed, their eyes were opened, and they recognised Him, that is to say, their eyes were opened for such knowl-edge of Him, in so far as the impediment was now removed which had prevented them from recognising Him.   For certainly they were not walking with closed eyes.   But there was some-thing in them which debarred them from seeing

correctly what was in their view, — a state of matters, indeed, which is the familiar result of darkness, or of a certain kind of humour.   It is not meant by this, however, that the Lord could not alter the form of His flesh, so that His figure might be literally and actually different, and not the one which they were in the habit of be-holding.   For, indeed, even before His passion, He was transfigured on the mount so that His countenance " did shine as the sun." [9]   And He who made genuine wine out of genuine water can also transform any body whatsoever in all un-questionable reality into any other kind of body which may please Him.   But what is meant is, that He had not acted so when He appeared in another form unto those two individuals.   For He did not appear to be what He was [10] to these men, because their eyes were holden, so that they should not know Him.   Moreover, not unsuita-bly may we suppose that this impediment in their eyes came from Satan, with the view of preclud-ing their recognition of Jesus.   But, neverthe-less, permission that it should be so was given by Christ on to the point at which the mystery of the bread was taken up.   And thus the lesson might be, that it is when we become participants in the unity of His body, that we are to understand the impediment of the adversary to be removed, and liberty to be given us to know Christ.

73. Besides, it is necessary to believe that these were the same persons to whom Mark also refers.   For he informs us, that they went and told these things to the rest : just as Luke states, that the persons in question rose up the same hour and returned to Jerusalem, and found the eleven gathered together, and them that were with them, saying, " The Lord is risen in-deed, and hath appeared to Simon." [11]   And then he adds that these two also told what things were done on the way, and how He was known of them in breaking of bread.[12]   By this time, therefore, a report of the resurrection of Jesus had been conveyed by those women, and also by Simon Peter, to whom He had already shown Himself.   For these two disciples found those to whom they came in Jerusalem talking of that very subject.   Consequently, it may be the case that fear made them decline mentioning for-merly, when they were on the way, that they had heard that He had risen again, so that they con-fined themselves to stating how the angels had been seen by the women.   For, not knowing with whom they were conversing, they might reasonably be anxious not to let any word drop from them on the subject of Christ's resurrec-

---

[1] Mark xvi. 12.   [2] *In villam.*   [3] *Castellum.*
[4] *Villam.*
[5] *Agrum* = field, domain, as the equivalent for ἀγρόν.
[6] *Castella.*   [7] *Municipia.*   [8] 1 Cor. x. 17.

[9] Matt. xvii. 2.
[10] The text gives, *Non enim sicut erat, apparuit,* etc.   Some editions make it *non enim aliter quam erat, sed sicut erat appa-ruit* = for He did not really assume another form, but appeared in that which He had.
[11] Luke xxiv. 33, 34.   [12] Luke xxiv. 35.

tion, lest they should fall into the hands of the Jews. But again, we must remark that Mark states that "they went and told it unto the residue: neither believed they them:"[1] whereas Luke tells us that these others were already saying that the Lord was risen indeed, and had appeared unto Simon. Is not the explanation, however, simply this, that there were some of them there who refused to credit what was related? Moreover, to whom can it fail to be clear that Mark has just omitted certain matters which are fully set forth in Luke's narrative,— that is to say, the subjects of the conversation which Jesus had with them before He recognised them, and the manner in which they came to know Him in the breaking of the bread? For, after recording how He appeared to them in another form, as they went towards a countryseat, Mark has immediately appended the sentence, "And they went and told it unto the residue: neither believed they them;" as if men could tell of a person whom they had not recognised, or as if those to whom He had appeared only in another form could know Him! Without doubt, therefore, Mark has simply given us no explanation of the way in which they came to know Him, so as to be able to report the same to others. And this, then, is a thing which deserves to be imprinted on our memory, in order that we may accustom ourselves to keep in view the habit which these evangelists have of passing over those matters which they do not put on record, and of connecting the facts which they do relate in such a manner that, among those who fail to give due consideration to the usage referred to, nothing proves itself a more fruitful source of misapprehension than this, leading them to imagine the existence of discrepancies in the sacred writers.

74. Luke next proceeds with his narrative in the following terms: "And as they thus spake, Jesus Himself stood in the midst of them, and saith unto them, Peace be unto you: it is I; be not afraid.[2] But they were terrified and affrighted, and supposed that they had seen a spirit. And He said unto them, Why are ye troubled? and why do thoughts arise in your hearts? Behold my hands and my feet, that it is I myself: handle me and see; for a spirit hath not flesh and bones, as ye see me have. And when He had thus spoken, He showed them His hands and His feet."[3] It is to this act, by which the Lord showed Himself after His resurrection, that John is also understood to refer when he discourses as follows: "Then, when it was late on the first day of the week, and when the doors were shut where the dis-

ciples were assembled for fear of the Jews, came Jesus, and stood in the midst, and saith unto them, Peace be unto you. And when He had so said, He showed unto them His hands and His side."[4] Thus, too, we may connect with these words of John certain matters which Luke reports, but which John Himself omits. For Luke continues in these terms: "And while they yet believed not for joy, and wondered, He said unto them, Have ye here any meat? And they gave Him a piece of a broiled fish, and of an honeycomb. And when He had eaten before them, He took what remained,[5] and gave it unto them."[6] Again, a passage which Luke omits, but which John presents, may next be connected with these words. It is to the following effect: "Then were the disciples glad when they saw the Lord. Then said Jesus to them again, Peace be unto you: as my Father hath sent me, even so send I you. And when He had said this, He breathed on them, and saith unto them, Receive ye the Holy Ghost: Whose soever sins ye remit, they are remittted unto them; and whose soever sins ye retain, they are retained."[7] Once more, we may attach to the above section another which John has left out, but which Luke inserts. It runs thus: "And He said unto them, These are the words which I spake unto you while I was yet with you, that all things must be fulfilled which were written in the law of Moses, and in the prophets, and in the Psalms, concerning me. Then opened He their understanding, that they might understand the Scriptures, and said unto them, Thus it is written, and thus it behoved Christ to suffer, and to rise from the dead the third day: and that repentance and remission of sins should be preached in His name among all nations, beginning at Jerusalem. And ye are witnesses of these things. And I send the promise of my Father upon you: but tarry ye in the city, until ye be endued with power from on high."[8] Observe, then, how Luke has here referred to that promise of the Holy Spirit which we do not elsewhere find made by the Lord, save in John's Gospel.[9] And this deserves something more than a passing notice, in order that we may bear in mind how the evangelists attest each other's truth, even on subjects which some of them may not themselves record, but which they nevertheless know to have been reported. After these matters, Luke passes over in silence all else that happened, and introduces nothing into his nar-

---

[1] Mark xvi. 13.
[2] The words *Ego sum, nolite timere*, are thus inserted.
[3] Luke xxiv. 36-40.

[4] John xx. 19, 20.
[5] *Et cum manducasset coram eis, sumens reliquias dedit eis.*
[6] Luke xxiv. 41-43.   [7] John xx. 20-23.
[8] Luke xxiv. 44-49. [Many harmonists place this passage in connection with this appearance (evening of the Resurrection day); but part of it may belong to the final appearance, or be a summary of the teaching during the forty days. — R.]
[9] John xiv. 26, xv. 26.

rative beyond the occasion when Jesus ascended into heaven. And at the same time he appends this [statement of the ascension], just as if it followed immediately upon these words which the Lord spake, at the same time with those other transactions on the first day of the week, that is to say, on the day on which the Lord rose again; whereas, in the Acts of the Apostles,[1] the self-same Luke tells us that the event really took place on the fortieth day after His resurrection. Finally, as regards the fact that John states that the Apostle Thomas was not present with these others on the occasion under review, whereas, according to Luke, the two disciples, of whom Cleophas was one, returned to Jerusalem, and found the eleven assembled and those who were with them, it admits of little doubt that we must suppose Thomas simply to have left the company before the Lord showed Himself to the brethren when they were talking in the terms noticed above.

75. This being the case, John now records a second manifestation of Himself, which was vouchsafed by the Lord to the disciples eight days after, on which occasion Thomas also was present, who had not seen Him up to that time. The narrative proceeds thus: "And after eight days again His disciples were within, and Thomas with them. Then came Jesus, the doors being shut, and stood in the midst, and said, Peace be unto you. Then saith He to Thomas, Reach hither thy finger, and behold my hands; and reach hither thy hand, and thrust it into my side: and be not faithless, but believing. Thomas answered and said unto Him, My Lord and my God. Jesus saith unto Him, Thomas, because thou hast seen me, thou hast believed: blessed are they that have not seen, and yet have believed."[2] This second appearance of the Lord among the disciples — that is to say, the appearance which John records in the second instance — we might also recognise as alluded to by Mark in a section concisely disposing of it, according to that evangelist's habit. A difficulty, however, is created by the circumstance that his terms are these: "Lastly,[3] He appeared unto those eleven as they sat at meat."[4] The difficulty does not lie in the mere fact that John says nothing about their sitting at meat, for he might well have omitted that; but it does rest in the use of the word "lastly," for that makes it seem as if He did not show Himself to them after that occasion, whereas John still proceeds to record a third appearance of the Lord by the sea of Tiberias. And then we have to keep in view the fact that the same Mark tells us how Jesus

"upbraided them with their unbelief and hardness of heart, because they believed not them which had seen Him after He was risen." In these words he refers to the two disciples to whom He appeared after He was risen, as they went toward a country-seat, and to Peter, to whom the examination of Luke's narrative has shown us that He manifested Himself first of all [among the apostles], — perhaps also to Mary Magdalene, and those other women who were along with her on the occasion when He was seen by them at the sepulchre, and again when He met them as they were returning on the way. For the said Mark has constructed his record in a manner which leads him first to insert his brief notice of the two disciples to whom He appeared as they went toward the country-seat, and of their giving a report to the residue and obtaining no credit, and then to subjoin in the immediate connection this statement: "Lastly, He appeared unto the eleven as they sat at meat, and upbraided them with their unbelief and hardness of heart, because they believed not them which had seen Him after He was risen." How, then, is this phrase "*lastly*" used, as if they did not see Him subsequently to this occasion? For the last time that the apostles saw the Lord upon the earth was really the time when He ascended into heaven, and that event took place on the fortieth day after His resurrection. Now, is it likely that He would upbraid them at that period on the ground that they had not believed those who had seen Him after He was risen, when by that time they had seen Him themselves so often after His resurrection, and especially when they had seen Him on the very day of His resurrection, — that is to say, on the first day of the week, when it was now about night, as Luke and John record? It remains for us, therefore, to suppose that, in the passage under review, it was Mark's intention to give a statement, in his own concise fashion, simply on the subject of the said day of the Lord's resurrection; that is to say, that first day of the week on which Mary and the other women who were along with her saw Him after daybreak, on which also Peter beheld Him, on which likewise He appeared to the two disciples, of whom Cleophas was one, and to whom Mark himself also seems to refer; on which, further, when it was now about night, He showed Himself to the eleven (Thomas, however, being excepted) and those who were with them; and on which, finally, the persons already instanced reported to the disciples the things which they had seen. Hence it is that he has employed the term "*lastly*," because the incident mentioned was the last that took place on this same day. For the night was now coming on by the time that the two disciples had re-

1 Acts i 2-9.   2 John xx. 26-29.
3 *Novissime.* [The Greek is ὕστερον, "afterwards," not necessarily "lastly." — R.]
4 Mark xvi. 14.

turned from the place where they had recognised Him in the breaking of bread, and had made their way into Jerusalem and found the eleven, as Luke tells us, and those who were with them, speaking to each other about the Lord's resurrection and about His having appeared to Peter; to whom these two also related what had occurred on the way, and how they came to know Him in the breaking of bread. But, assuredly, there were also there some who did not believe. Hence we see the truth of Mark's words, "Neither believed they them." When these, therefore, were now sitting at meat, as Mark informs us, and when they were talking of these subjects, as Luke tells us, the Lord stood in their midst, and said unto them, "Peace be unto you," as Luke and John both record. Moreover, the doors were shut when He entered among them, as John alone mentions. And thus, among the words which, as Luke and John have reported, the Lord spoke to the disciples on that occasion, this expostulation also comes in, which is instanced by Mark, and in which He upbraided them for not believing those who had seen Him after He was risen.

76. But, again, a difficulty may also be felt in understanding how Mark says that the Lord appeared to the eleven as they sat at meat, if the time referred to is really the beginning of the night of that Lord's day, as is indicated by Luke and John. For John, indeed, tells us plainly that the Apostle Thomas was not with them on that occasion; and we believe that he left them before the Lord entered among them, but after the two disciples who returned from the village had been conversing with the eleven, as we discover from Luke. Luke, it is true, presents a point in his narrative, at which we may fairly suppose, first, that Thomas went out while they were talking of these subjects, and then that the Lord came in. Mark, however, who says, "Lastly, He appeared unto the eleven as they sat at meat," compels us to admit that Thomas also was there. But it may be the case, perhaps, that he chose to style them the eleven, although one of the company was absent, because the same apostolic society was designated by this number at the time previous to the election of Matthias in the place of Judas. Or, if there is a difficulty in accepting this explanation, we may still suppose that, after the many manifestations in which He vouchsafed His presence to the disciples during the forty days, He also showed Himself on one final occasion to the eleven as they sat at meat, — that is to say, on the fortieth day itself; and that, as He was now on the point of leaving them and ascending into heaven, He was minded on that memorable day specially to upbraid them with their refusal to believe those who had

seen Him after He had risen until they should first have seen Him themselves; and this particularly because it was the case that, when they preached the gospel subsequently to His ascension, the very Gentiles would be ready to believe what they did not see. For, after mentioning this upbraiding, Mark at once proceeds to subjoin this passage: "And He said unto them, Go ye into all the world, and preach the gospel to every creature. He that believeth and is baptized shall be saved; but he that believeth not shall be damned."[1] If, therefore, they were charged to preach that he who believes not shall be condemned, when that indeed which he believes not is just what he has not seen, was it not meet that they should themselves first of all be thus reproved for their own refusal to believe those to whom the Lord had shown Himself at an earlier stage until they should have seen Him with their own eyes?

77. In what follows we have a further recommendation to take this to have been the last manifestation of Himself in bodily fashion which the Lord gave to the apostles. For the same Mark continues in these terms: "And these signs shall follow them that believe: In my name shall they cast out devils; they shall speak with new tongues; they shall take up serpents; and if they drink any deadly thing, it shall not hurt them; they shall lay hands on the sick, and they shall recover."[2] Then he appends this statement: "So then, after the Lord had spoken unto them, He was received up into heaven, and sat on the right hand of God. And they went forth, and preached everywhere, the Lord working with them, and confirming the word by signs following."[3] Now, when he says, "So then, after the Lord had spoken unto them, He was received up into heaven," he appears probably enough to indicate that this was the last discourse He held with them upon the earth. At the same time, the words do not seem to shut us up to that idea absolutely. For what he says is not, "after He had spoken *these things* unto them," but simply, "after He had spoken unto them;" and hence it would be quite admissible, were there any necessity for such a theory, to suppose that this was not the last discourse, and that that was not the last day on which He was present with them upon the earth, but that all the matters regarding which He spake with them in all these days may be referred to in the sentence, "After He had spoken unto them, He was received up into heaven." But, inasmuch as the considerations which we have detailed above lead us rather to conclude that this was the last day, than to suppose that the allusion is specifically to the eleven at a time

<hr>

[1] Mark xvi. 15, 16.   [2] Mark xvi. 17, 18.
[3] Mark xvi. 19, 20.

when, in consequence of the absence of Thomas, they were only ten, we are of opinion that after this discourse which Mark mentions, and with which we have to connect in their proper order those other words, whether of the disciples or of the Lord Himself, which are recorded in the Acts of the Apostles,[1] we must believe the Lord to have been received up into heaven, to wit, on the fortieth day after the day of His resurrection.

78. John, again, although he tells us plainly that he has passed over many of the things which Jesus did, has been pleased, nevertheless, to give us a narrative of a third manifestation of Himself, which the Lord granted to the disciples after the resurrection, namely, by the sea of Tiberias, and before seven of the disciples, — that is to say, Peter, Thomas, Nathanael, the sons of Zebedee, and two others who are not mentioned by name. That is the occasion when they were engaged in fishing; when, in obedience to His command, they cast the nets on the right side, and drew to land great fishes, a hundred and fifty and three: when He also asked Peter three times whether He was loved by him, and charged him to feed His sheep, and delivered a prophecy regarding what he would suffer, and said also, with reference to John, "Thus[2] I will that he tarry till I come." And with this John has brought his Gospel to its conclusion.

79. We have next to consider now what was the occasion of His first appearance to the disciples in Galilee. For this incident, which John narrates as the third in order, took place in Galilee by the sea of Tiberias. And one may perceive that the scene was in that district, if he calls to mind the miracle of the five loaves, the narrative of which the same John commences in these terms: "After these things Jesus went over the sea of Galilee, which is the sea of Tiberias."[3] And what should naturally be supposed to be the proper locality for His first manifestation to the disciples after His resurrection but Galilee? This seems to be the conclusion to which we should be led when we recollect the words of the angel who, according to Matthew's Gospel, addressed the women as they came to the sepulchre. The words were these: "Fear not ye; for I know that ye seek Jesus of Nazareth, which was crucified. He is not here; for He is risen, as He said. Come, see the place where the Lord lay: and go quickly, and tell His disciples that He is risen from the dead; and, behold, He goeth before you into Galilee; there shall ye see Him: lo, I have told you."[4] Mark presents a similar report, whether the angel of whom he

speaks be the same one or a different. His version runs thus: "Be not affrighted: ye seek Jesus of Nazareth which was crucified; He is risen; He is not here: behold the place where they laid Him. But go your way, tell His disciples and Peter that He goeth before you into Galilee: there shall ye see Him, as He said unto you."[5] Now the impression which these words seem to produce is, that Jesus was not to show Himself to His disciples after His resurrection, but in Galilee. The appearance thus referred to, however, is not recorded even by Mark himself, who has informed us how He showed Himself first to Mary Magdalene in the early morning of the first day of the week; how she went and told them that had been with Him as they mourned and wept; how these persons refused to believe her; how, after this, He was next seen by the two disciples who were going to the residence in the country; how these twain reported what had occurred to them to the residue, which, as Luke and John agree in certifying, took place in Jerusalem on the very day of the Lord's resurrection, and when night was now coming on. Thereafter the same evangelist comes next to that appearance which he calls His last, and which was vouchsafed to the eleven as they sat at meat; and when he has given us his account of that scene, he tells us how He was received up into heaven, which event took place, as we know, on the Mount Olivet, at no great distance from Jerusalem. Thus Mark nowhere relates the actual fulfilment of that which he declares to have been announced beforehand by the angel. Matthew, on the other hand, confines his statement to a single cccurrence, and refers to no other locality whatsoever, whether earlier or later, where the disciples saw the Lord after He was risen, but the Galilee which was specified in the angel's prediction. This evangelist, in short, first introduces his notice of the terms in which the women were addressed by the angel; then he subjoins an account of what happened as they were going, and how the members of the watch were bribed to give a false report; and then he inserts his statement [of the appearance in Galilee], just as if that were the very event which followed immediately on what he has been relating. For, indeed, the angel's words, "He is risen; and behold, He goeth before you into Galilee," were really such as might make it seem reasonable to suppose that nothing would intervene [before that manifestation in Galilee]. Matthew's version, accordingly, proceeds as follows: "Then the eleven disciples went away into Galilee, into a mountain where Jesus had appointed them. And when they saw Him, they worshipped Him: but some doubted. And

---

[1] Acts i. 4-8.
[2] Some editions read *si* = if I will, etc. But the best editions and MSS. give *sic*, as above. And that Augustin read it so, is clear also from what occurs further on in Book iv. 20.
[3] John vi. 1.   [4] Matt. xxviii. 5-7.

[5] Mark xvi. 6, 7.

Jesus came and spake unto them, saying, All power is given unto me in heaven and in earth. Go ye therefore, and teach all nations, baptizing them in the name of the Father, and of the Son, and of the Holy Ghost; teaching them to observe all things whatsoever I have commanded you: and, lo, I am with you alway, even unto the end of the world."[1]   In these terms has Matthew closed his Gospel.

80. Thus, then, were it not that the consideration of the narratives given by others of the evangelists led us inevitably to examine the whole subject with greater care, we might entertain the idea that the scene of the Lord's first manifestation of Himself to the disciples after His resurrection, could be nowhere else but in Galilee. In like manner, had Mark passed over the angel's announcement without notice, any one might have supposed that Matthew was induced to tell us how the disciples went away to a mountain in Galilee, and there worshipped the Lord, by his desire to show the actual fulfilment of the charge, and of the prediction which he had also recorded to have been conveyed by the angel. As the case now stands, however, Luke and John both certify with sufficient clearness, that on the very day of His resurrection the Lord was seen by His disciples in Jerusalem, which is at such a distance from Galilee as makes it impossible for Him to have been seen by these same individuals in both places in the course of a single day.   In like manner, Mark, while he does report in similar terms the announcement made by the angel, nowhere mentions that the Lord actually was seen in Galilee by His disciples after He was risen.   These, therefore, are considerations which strongly force upon us an inquiry into the real import of this saying, "Behold, He goeth before you into Galilee! there shall ye see Him."   For if Matthew himself, too, had not stated that the eleven disciples went away into Galilee into a mountain, where Jesus had appointed them, and that they saw Him there and worshipped Him, we might have supposed that there was no literal fulfilment of the prediction in question, but that the whole announcement was intended to convey a figurative meaning.   And a parallel to that we should then find in the words recorded by Luke, namely, "Behold I cast out devils, and I do cures to-day and to-morrow, and the third day I shall be perfected;"[2] which prediction certainly was not accomplished in the letter.   In like manner, if the angel had said, "He goeth before you into Galilee, there shall ye see Him first;" or, "Only there shall ye see Him;" or, "Nowhere else but there shall ye see Him;" unquestionably, in that case, Matthew would have been in an-

tagonism with the rest of the evangelists. As the matter stands, however, the words are simply these: "Behold, He goeth before you into Galilee; there shall ye see Him;" and there is no statement of the precise time at which that meeting was to take place — whether at the earliest opportunity, and before He was seen by them elsewhere, or at a later period, and after they had seen Him also in other places besides Galilee; and, further, although Matthew relates that the disciples went away into Galilee into a mountain, he neither specifies the day of that departure, nor constructs his narrative in an order which would force upon us the necessity of supposing that this particular event must have been actually the first appearance.   Consequently, we may conclude that Matthew stands in no antagonism with the narratives of the other evangelists, but that he makes it quite competent for us, in due consistency with his own report, to understand the meaning and accept the truth of these other accounts.   At the same time, as the Lord thus pointed, not to the place where He intended first to manifest Himself, but to the locality of Galilee, where undoubtedly He appeared afterwards; and as He conveyed these instructions about beholding Himself at once through the angel, who said, "Behold, He goeth before you into Galilee: there shall ye see Him;" and by His own words, "Go, tell my brethren, that they go into Galilee, and there shall ye see me;" — in these facts we find considerations which make every believer anxious to inquire with what mystical significance all this may be understood to have been stated.

81. In the first place, however, we must also consider the question of the time at which He may thus have shown Himself in bodily form in Galilee, according to the statement given by Matthew in these terms: "Then the eleven disciples went away into Galilee into a mountain where Jesus had appointed them; and when they saw Him, they worshipped Him; but some doubted."   That it was not on the day of His resurrection is manifest.   For Luke and John agree in telling us most plainly that He was seen in Jerusalem that very day, when the night was coming on; while Mark is not so clear on the subject.   When was it, then, that they saw the Lord in Galilee?   I do not refer to the appearance mentioned by John, by the sea of Tiberias; for on that occasion there were only seven of them present, and they were found fishing.   But I mean the appearance detailed by Matthew, when the eleven were on the mountain, to which Jesus had gone before them, according to the announcement made by the angel.   For the import of Matthew's statement appears to be this, that they found Him there just because He had gone before them according to appointment.

[1] Matt. xxviii. 16-20.
[2] Luke xiii. 32.   See above, Book ii. chap. 75, § 145.

It did not take place, then, either on the day on which He rose, or in the eight days that followed, after which space John states that the Lord showed Himself to the disciples, when Thomas, who had not seen Him on the day of His resurrection, saw Him for the first time. For, surely, on the supposition that the eleven had really seen Him on the mountain in Galilee within the period of these eight days, it may well be asked how Thomas, who had been of the number of these eleven, could be said to have seen Him for the first time at the end of these eight days. To that question there is no answer, unless, indeed, one could say that they were not the eleven, who by that time bore the specific designation of Apostles, but some other eleven disciples singled out of the numerous body of His followers. For those eleven were, indeed, the only persons who were yet called by the name of Apostles, but they were not the only disciples. It may perhaps be the case, therefore, that the apostles are really referred to ; that not all but only some of them were there ; that there were also other disciples with them, so that the number of persons present was made up to eleven ; and that Thomas, who saw the Lord for the first time at the end of those eight days, was absent on this occasion. For when Mark mentions the said eleven, he does not use the general expression " eleven," but says explicitly, " He appeared unto *the* eleven." [1] Luke, likewise, puts it thus : " They returned to Jerusalem, and found the eleven gathered together, and them that were with them." There he gives us to understand that these were *the* eleven — that is to say, the apostles. For when he adds, " and those who were with them," he has surely indicated plainly enough, that those with whom these others were, were styled " the eleven " in some eminent sense ; and this leads us to understand those to be meant who were now called distinctively Apostles. Consequently, it is quite possible that, out of the body of apostles and other disciples, the number of eleven disciples was made up who saw Jesus upon the mountain in Galilee, within the space of these eight days.

82. But another difficulty in the way of this settlement arises here. For, when John has recorded how the Lord was seen, not by the eleven on the mountain, but by seven of them when they were fishing in the sea of Tiberias, he appends the following statement : " This is now the third time that Jesus showed Himself to His disciples, after that He was risen from the dead." [2] Now, if we accept the theory that the Lord was seen by the company of the eleven disciples within the period of these eight days,

and previous to His being seen by Thomas, this scene by the sea of Tiberias will not be the third but the fourth time that He showed Himself. Here, indeed, we must take care not to let any one suppose that, in speaking of the third time, John meant that there were in all only three appearances of the Lord. On the contrary, we must understand him to refer to the number of the days, and not to the number of the manifestations themselves ; and, further, it is to be observed that these days are not presented as coming in immediate succession after each other, but as separated by intervals in accordance with intimations given by the evangelist himself. For, keeping out of view His appearance to the women, it is made perfectly plain in the Gospel that He showed Himself three several times on the first day after He was risen ; namely, once to Peter ; again to those two disciples, of whom Cleophas was one ; and a third time to the larger body, while they were conversing with each other as the night came on. But all these John, looking to the fact that they took place on a single day, reckons as one appearance. Then he identifies a second — that is to say, an appearance on another day — with the occasion on which Thomas also saw Him ; and he particularizes a third by the sea of Tiberias, that is to say, not literally His third appearance, but the third day of His self-manifestations. Thus the result is, that after all these incidents, we are constrained to suppose this other occasion to have occurred on which, according to Matthew, the eleven disciples saw Him on the mountain in Galilee, to which He had gone before them according to appointment, so that all that had been foretold, both by the angel and by Himself, should be fulfilled even to the letter.

83. Consequently, in the four evangelists we find mention made of ten distinct appearances of the Lord to different persons after His resurrection. First, to the women near the sepulchre.[3] Secondly, to the same women as they were on the way returning from the sepulchre.[4] Thirdly, to Peter.[5] Fourthly, to the two who were going to the place in the country.[6] Fifthly, to the larger number in Jerusalem, when Thomas was not present.[7] Sixthly, on the occasion when Thomas saw Him.[8] Seventhly, by the sea of Tiberias.[9] Eighthly, on the mountain in Galilee, of which Matthew speaks.[10] Ninthly, at the time to which Mark refers in the words, " Lastly, as they sat at meat," thereby intimating that now they were no more to eat with Him upon the earth.[11] Tenthly, on the same day, not now indeed upon the earth, but lifted up in the

---

[1] *Illis undecim* = those eleven.   [2] John xxi. 14.

[3] John xx. 14.   [4] Matt. xxviii. 9.   [5] Luke xxiv. 35.
[6] Luke xxiv. 15.   [7] John xx. 19–24.   [8] John xx. 26.
[9] John xxi. 1.   [10] Matt. xxviii. 16, 17.   [11] Mark xvi. 14.

cloud, as He ascended into heaven, as Mark and Luke record. This last appearance, indeed, is introduced by Mark, directly after he has told us how the Lord showed Himself to them as they sat at meat. For his narrative goes on connectedly as follows: "So then, after the Lord had spoken unto them, He was received up into heaven." [1] Luke, on the other hand, omits all that may have passed between Him and His disciples during the forty days, and, after giving the history of the first day of His resurrection-life, when He showed Himself to the larger number in Jerusalem, he silently connects therewith the closing day on which He ascended up into heaven. His statement proceeds in this form: "And He led them out as far as to Bethany; and He lifted up His hands, and blessed them; and it came to pass, that while He blessed them, He was parted from them, and carried up into heaven." [2] Thus, therefore, besides seeing Him upon the earth, they beheld Him also as He was borne up into heaven. So many times, then, is He reported in the evangelical books to have been seen by different individuals, previous to His completed ascension into heaven, namely, nine times upon the earth, and once in the air as He was ascending.

84. At the same time, all is not recorded, as John plainly declares.[3] For He had frequent intercourse with His disciples during the forty days which preceded His ascension into heaven.[4] He had not, however, showed Himself to them throughout all these forty days without interruption. For John tells us, that after the first day of His resurrection-life, there elapsed other eight days, at the end of which space He appeared to them again. The appearance which is identified [in John] as the third — namely, the one by the sea of Tiberias — may perhaps have taken place on an immediately succeeding day; for there is nothing antagonistic to that. And then He showed Himself when it seemed the proper time to Him, as He had appointed with them (which appointment had also been conveyed in the previous prophetic announcement) to go before them into Galilee. And all throughout these forty days, He appeared on occasions, and to individuals, and in modes, just as He was minded. To these appearances Peter alludes when, in the discourse which he delivered before Cornelius and those who were with him, he says, "Even to us who did eat and drink with Him after He rose from the dead, for the space of forty days." [5] It is not meant, however, that they had eaten and drunk with Him daily throughout these forty days. For that would be contrary to John's statement, who has interposed the space of eight days, during which He was not seen, and makes His third appearance take place by the sea of Tiberias. At the same time, even although He [should be supposed to have] manifested Himself to them and lived with them every day after that period, that would not come into antagonism with anything in the narrative. And, perhaps, this expression, "for the space of forty days," which is equivalent to four times ten, and may thus sustain a mystical reference to the whole world or the whole temporal age, has been used just because those first ten days, within which the said eight fall, may not incongruously be reckoned, in accordance with the practice of the Scriptures, on the principle of dealing with the part in general terms as the whole.

85. Let us therefore compare what is said by the Apostle Paul with the view of deciding whether it raises any question of difficulty. His statement proceeds thus: "That He rose again the third day according to the Scriptures, and that He was seen of Cephas." [6] He does not say, "He was seen *first* of Cephas." For this would be inconsistent with the fact that it is recorded in the Gospel that He appeared first to the women. He continues thus: "then of the twelve;" and whoever the individuals may have been to whom He then showed Himself, and whatever the precise hour, this was at least on the very day of His resurrection. Again he goes on: "After that He was seen of above five hundred brethren at once." And whether these were gathered together with the eleven when the doors were shut for fear of the Jews, and when Jesus came to them after Thomas had gone out from the company, or whether the reference is to some other appearance subsequent to these eight days, no discrepancy is created. Again he says, "after that He was seen of James." We ought not, however, to suppose this to mean that this was the first occasion on which He was seen of James; but we may take it to allude to some special appearance to that apostle by himself. Next he adds, "then of all the apostles," which does not imply that this was the first time that He showed Himself to them, but that from this period He lived in more familiar intercourse with them on to the day of His ascension. Finally he says, "And last of all He was seen of me also, as of one born out of due time." But that was a revelation of Himself from heaven some considerable time after His ascension.

86. Consequently, let us now take up the subject which we had postponed, and inquire what mystical meaning may underlie the report given by Matthew and Mark, namely, that on rising

---

[1] Mark xvi. 19.　　[2] Luke xxiv. 50, 51.　　[3] John xxi. 25.
[4] Acts i. 3.
[5] Acts x. 41 — the words, *per quadraginta dies*, being added.

[6] 1 Cor. xv. 4, 5.

He made this statement, "I will go before you into Galilee: there shall ye see me." For this announcement, if it was fulfilled at all, was certainly not fulfilled till a considerable interval had elapsed; whereas it is couched in terms which seem to lead us (although such a conclusion is not an absolute necessity) most naturally to expect that the appearance referred to would be either the only one or the first that would ensue. We observe, however, that the words in question are not given as the words of the evangelist himself, in the form of a narrative of a past occurrence, but as the words of the angel, who spoke according to the Lord's commission, and subsequently also as the words of the Lord Himself; that is to say, the words are used by the evangelist in his narrative, but they are presented by him as a direct statement of what was spoken by the angel and by the Lord. This, therefore, unquestionably compels us to accept them as uttered prophetically.[1] Now Galilee may be interpreted to mean either "Transmigration" or "Revelation." Consequently, if we adopt the idea of "Transmigration," what other sense occurs to us to put upon the sentence, "He goeth before you into Galilee, there shall you see Him," but just this, that the grace of Christ was to be transferred from the people of Israel to the Gentiles? That in preaching the gospel to these Gentiles, the apostles would meet with no acceptance unless the Lord prepared a way for them in the hearts of men, — this may be what is to be understood by the sentence, "He goeth before you into Galilee." And, again, that they would look with joy and wonder at the breaking down and removing of difficulties, and at the opening of a door for them in the Lord through the enlightenment of the believing, — this is what is to be understood by the words, "there shall ye see Him;" that is to say, there shall ye find His members, there shall ye recognise His living body in the person of those who shall receive you. Or, if we follow the second view, which takes Galilee to signify "Revelation," the idea may be, that He was now no more to be in the form of a servant, but in that form in which He is equal with the Father;[2] as He promised to those who loved Him when He said, according to the testimony of John, "And I will love him, and will manifest myself to him."[3] That is to say, He was afterwards to manifest Himself, not merely as they saw Him before, nor merely in the way in which, rising as He did with His wounds upon Him, He was to give Himself to be touched as well as seen by them, but in the character of that ineffable light, wherewith He enlightens every man that cometh into this world, and in virtue of which He shineth in darkness, and the darkness comprehends Him not.[4] Thus has He gone before us to something from which He withdraws not, although He comes to us, and which does not involve His leaving us, although He has preceded us thither. That will be a revelation which may be spoken of as a true Galilee, when we shall be like Him; there shall we see Him as He is.[5] Then, also, will there be for us the more blessed transmigration, from this world into that eternity, if we embrace His precepts so as to be counted worthy of being set apart on His right hand. For there, those on the left hand shall go away into eternal burning, but the righteous into life eternal.[6] Hence they shall pass thither, and there shall they see Him, as the wicked do not see Him. For the wicked shall be taken away, so that he shall not see the brightness of the Lord;[7] and the unrighteousness shall not see the light. For He says, "And this is life eternal, that they might know Thee, the only true God, and Jesus Christ, whom Thou hast sent;"[8] even as He shall be known in that eternity to which He will bring His servants by the form of a servant, in order that in liberty they may contemplate the form of the Lord.

---

[1] [The discussion of the appearances of the Risen Lord is so clear and candid, that one must regret that it finds its conclusion in the allegorizing exegesis of this section. — R.]

[2] Phil. ii. 6, 7.　[3] John xiv. 21.　[4] John i. 5–9.
[5] 1 John iii. 2.　[6] Matt. xxv. 33–46.　[7] Isa. xxvi. 10.
[8] John xviii. 3.

BOOK IV.

THIS BOOK EMBRACES A DISCUSSION OF THOSE PASSAGES WHICH ARE PECULIAR TO MARK, LUKE, OR JOHN.

PROLOGUE.

1. As we have examined Matthew's narrative in its complete connection, and as the comparison which we have carried out between it and the other three on to its conclusion has established the fact, that not one of these evangelists contains anything either at variance with other statements in his own Gospel, or inconsistent with the accounts presented by his fellow-historians, let us now subject Mark to a similar scrutiny. Our plan will be to omit those sections which he has in common with Matthew, which we have already investigated as far as seemed requisite and are now done with, and to take up those paragraphs which remain, with the view of submitting them to discussion and comparison, and of demonstrating their thorough harmony with what is related by the other evangelists on to the notice of the Lord's Supper. For we have already dealt with all the incidents which are reported in all the four Gospels from that point on to the end, and have considered the subject of their mutual consistency.

CHAP. I. — OF THE QUESTION REGARDING THE PROOF THAT MARK'S GOSPEL IS IN HARMONY WITH THE REST IN WHAT IS NARRATED (THOSE PASSAGES WHICH HE HAS IN COMMON WITH MATTHEW BEING LEFT OUT OF ACCOUNT), FROM ITS BEGINNING DOWN TO THE SECTION WHERE IT IS SAID, "AND THEY GO INTO CAPHARNAUM, AND STRAIGHTWAY ON THE SABBATH-DAY HE TAUGHT THEM:" WHICH INCIDENT IS REPORTED ALSO BY LUKE.

2. Mark, then, commences as follows: "The beginning of the gospel of Jesus Christ, the Son of God: as it is written in the prophet Isaiah;" and so on, down to where it is said, "And they go into Capharnaum; and straightway on the Sabbath-day He entered into the synagogue and taught them."[1] In this entire context, everything has been examined above in connection with Matthew. This particular statement, however, about His going into the synagogue at Capharnaum and teaching them on the Sabbath-day, is one which Mark has in common with Luke.[2] But it raises no question of difficulty.

CHAP. II. — OF THE MAN OUT OF WHOM THE UNCLEAN SPIRIT THAT WAS TORMENTING HIM WAS CAST, AND OF THE QUESTION WHETHER MARK'S VERSION IS QUITE CONSISTENT WITH THAT OF LUKE, WHO IS AT ONE WITH HIM IN REPORTING THE INCIDENT.

3. Mark proceeds with his narrative in the following terms: "And they were astonished at His doctrine: for He taught them as one that had authority, and not as the scribes. And there was in their synagogue a man with an unclean spirit: and he cried out, saying,[3] What have we to do with thee, thou Jesus of Nazareth? Art thou come to destroy us?" and so on, down to the passage where we read, "And He preached in the synagogues throughout all Galilee, and cast out devils."[4] Although there are some points here which are common only to Mark and Luke, the entire contents of this section have also been already dealt with when we were going over Matthew's narrative in its continuity. For all these matters came into the order of narration in such a manner that I thought they could not be passed over. But Luke says that this unclean spirit went out of the man in such a way as not to hurt him: whereas Mark's statement is to this effect: "And the unclean spirit cometh out of him, tearing him, and crying with a loud voice." There may seem, therefore, to be some discrepancy here. For how could the unclean spirit have been "tearing him," or, as some codices have it, "tormenting him," if, as Luke says, he "hurt him not"? Luke, however, gives the notice in full, thus: "And when the devil had thrown him in the midst, he came out of him, and "hurt him not."[5] Thus we are to understand that when Mark says, "tormenting him," he just refers to what Luke expresses in the sentence, "When he had thrown him in the midst." And when the latter appends the words, "and hurt him not," the meaning simply is, that the said tossing of the man's limbs and tormenting him did not debilitate him, as is often the case with the exit of devils, when, at times, some of

---

[1] Mark i. 1–21.　　[2] Mark iv. 31.

[3] The words, *Let us alone*, are omitted. [So the Greek text, according to the best MSS. — R.]

[4] Mark i. 22–39.　　[5] Luke iv. 35.

the members are even destroyed [1] in the process of removing the trouble.

CHAP. III. — OF THE QUESTION WHETHER MARK'S REPORTS OF THE REPEATED OCCASIONS ON WHICH THE NAME OF PETER WAS BROUGHT INTO PROMINENCE ARE NOT AT VARIANCE WITH THE STATEMENT WHICH JOHN HAS GIVEN US OF THE 'PARTICULAR TIME AT WHICH THE APOSTLE RECEIVED THAT NAME.

4. The same Mark continues as follows : "And there came a leper to Him, beseeching Him, and kneeling down to Him, and saying unto Him, If thou wilt, thou canst make me clean ; " and so on, down to where it is said, " And they cried out, saying, Thou art the Son of God : and He straightway charged them that they should not make Him known." [2]　Luke [3] also records something similar to the last passage which we have here adduced. But nothing emerges involving any discrepancy. Mark proceeds thus : " And He goeth up into a mountain, and calleth unto Him whom He would : and they came unto Him.　And He ordained twelve that they should be with Him, and that He might send them forth to preach ; and He gave them power to heal sicknesses, and to cast out devils.　And Simon He surnamed Peter ; " and so on, down to where it is said, " And he departed, and began to publish in Decapolis how great things Jesus had done : and all men did marvel." [4]　I am aware that I have spoken already of the names of the disciples when following the order of Matthew's narrative. [5]　Here, therefore, I repeat the caution, that no one should suppose Simon to have received the name Peter on this occasion for the first time, or fancy that Mark is here in any antagonism with John, who reports that disciple to have been addressed long before in these terms : " Thou shalt be called Cephas, which is, by interpretation, A stone." [6]　For John has there recorded the very words in which the Lord gave him that name. Mark, on the other hand, has introduced the matter in the form of a recapitulation in this passage, when he says, " And Simon He surnamed Peter."　For, as it was his intention to enumerate the names of the twelve apostles here, and it was necessary for him thus to mention Peter, he decided briefly to intimate the fact that the said name was not borne by that disciple all along, but was given him by the Lord, not, however, at the time with which Mark was immediately dealing, but on the occasion in connection with which John has introduced the very words employed by the Lord.　The other matters embraced within this paragraph, present nothing inconsistent with any of the other Gospels, and they have also been discussed previously.

CHAP. IV. — OF THE WORDS, " THE MORE HE CHARGED THEM TO TELL NO ONE, SO MUCH THE MORE A GREAT DEAL THEY PUBLISHED IT ; " AND OF THE QUESTION WHETHER THAT STATEMENT IS NOT INCONSISTENT WITH HIS PRESCIENCE, WHICH IS COMMENDED TO OUR NOTICE IN THE GOSPEL.

5. Mark continues thus : " And when Jesus was passed over again by ship unto the other side, much people gathered unto Him : and He was nigh unto the sea ; " and so on, down to where we read, " And the apostles gathered themselves together unto Jesus, and told Him all things, both what they had done, and what they had taught." [7]　This last portion Mark has in common with Luke, and there is no discrepancy between them.　The rest of the contents of this section we have already discussed.　Mark continues in these terms : " And He said unto them, Come ye apart into a desert place, and rest a while ; " and so on, down to the words, " But the more He charged them, so much the more a great deal they published it ; and were beyond measure astonished, saying, He hath done all things well : He maketh both the deaf to hear, and the dumb to speak." [8]　In all this there is nothing which presents the appearance of any want of harmony between Mark and Luke ; and the whole of the above we have already considered, when we were comparing these evangelists with Matthew.　At the same time, we must make sure that no one shall suppose that the last statement, which I have cited here from Mark's Gospel, is in antagonism with the entire body of the evangelists, who, in reporting most of His other deeds and words, make it plain that He knew what went on in men ; that is to say, that their thoughts and desires could not be concealed from Him.　Thus John puts it very clearly in the following passage : " But Jesus did not commit Himself unto them, because He knew all men, and needed not that any should testify of man ; for He knew what was in man." [9]　But what wonder is it that He should discern the present thoughts of men, if He announced beforehand to Peter the thought which he was to entertain in the future, [10] but which he certainly had not then, at the very time when he was boldly declaring himself ready to die for Him, or with Him ? [11]　This being the case, then, how can it fail to appear as if this knowledge and foreknowledge, which He possessed in so supreme a measure, is contradicted by Mark's statement, " He charged them that they should tell no man : but the more He charged them, so much the more a great deal they published it " ?　For if

---

[1] Reading *elisis*.　Various MSS. give *amputatis aut evulsis* = amputated or torn off.
[2] Mark i. 40–iii. 12.　　[3] Luke iv. 41.　　[4] Mark iii. 13–v. 20.
[5] See above, Book ii. chaps. 17 and 53.　　[6] John i. 42.

[7] Mark v. 21–vi. 30.　　　[8] Mark vi. 31–vii. 37.
[9] John ii. 24, 25.
[10] The text gives simply: *futuram Petro prænuntiavit*, to which *cogitationem* has to be supplied.　Some editions insert *negationem* = his future denial.
[11] Matt. xxvi. 33–35.

He, as one who held in His own knowledge all the intentions of men, both present and future, was aware that they would publish it all the more, the more He charged them not to publish it, what purpose could He have in giving them such a charge? Well, but may not the explanation be this, that he desired to give backward ones to understand how much more zealously and fervently they ought to preach on whom He lays the commission to preach, if even men who were interdicted were unable to keep silent?

CHAP. V. — OF THE STATEMENT WHICH JOHN MADE CONCERNING THE MAN WHO CAST OUT DEVILS ALTHOUGH HE DID NOT BELONG TO THE CIRCLE OF THE DISCIPLES; AND OF THE LORD'S REPLY, "FORBID THEM NOT, FOR HE THAT IS NOT AGAINST YOU IS ON YOUR PART;" AND OF THE QUESTION WHETHER THAT RESPONSE DOES NOT CONTRADICT THE OTHER SENTENCE, IN WHICH HE SAID, "HE THAT IS NOT WITH ME IS AGAINST ME."

6. Mark proceeds as follows: "In those days again,[1] the multitude being very great, and having nothing to eat;" and so on, down to the words, "John answered Him, saying, Master, we saw one casting out devils in Thy name, and he followeth not us; and we forbade him.[2] But Jesus said, Forbid him not; for there is no man which shall do a miracle in my name, that can lightly speak evil of me; for he that is not against you is on your side."[3] Luke relates this in similar terms, with this exception, that he does not insert the clause, "for there is no man which shall do a miracle in my name that can lightly speak evil of me." Consequently, there is nothing here to raise the question of any discrepancy between these two. We must see, however, whether this sentence must be supposed to stand in opposition to another of the Lord's sayings, namely, the one to this effect, "He that is not with me is against me; and he that gathereth not with me scattereth abroad."[4] For how was this man not against Him, who was not with Him, and of whom John reported that he did not unite with them in following Him, if he is against Him who is not with Him? Or if the man was against Him, how does He say to the disciples, "Forbid him not; for he that is not against you is on your side"? Will any one aver that it is of consequence to observe that here He says to the disciples, "He that is not against you is on your side;" whereas, in the other passage, He spoke of Himself in the terms,

"He that is not with me is against me"? That would make it appear, indeed, as if it were possible for one not to be with Him, although he was associated with those disciples of His who are, so to speak, His very members. Besides, how would the truth of such sayings as these stand then: "He that receiveth you receiveth me;"[5] and "Inasmuch as ye have done it unto one of the least of these my brethren, ye have done it unto me"?[6] Or is it possible for one not to be against Him, although he may be against His disciples? Nay; for what shall we make then of words like these: "He that despiseth you, despiseth me;"[7] and, "Inasmuch as ye did it not unto the least of mine, ye did it not unto me;"[8] and, "Saul, Saul, why persecutest thou me,"[9] — although it was His disciples that Saul was persecuting? But, in good truth, the sense intended to be conveyed is just this, that, so far as a man is not with Him, so far is he against Him; and again, that, so far as a man is not against Him, so far is he with Him. For example, take this very case of the individual who was working miracles in the name of Christ, and yet was not in the company of Christ's disciples: so far as this man was working miracles in His name, so far was he with them, and so far he was not against them.[10] But, inasmuch as they had prohibited the man from doing a thing in which, so far forth, he was really with them, the Lord said to them, "Forbid him not." For what they ought to have forbidden was what was outside their fellowship, so that they might bring him over to the unity of the Church, and not a thing like this, in which he was at one with them, that is to say, so far as he commended the name of their Master and Lord in the casting out of devils. And this is the principle on which the Catholic Church acts, not condemning common sacraments among heretics; for in these they are with us, and they are not against us. But she condemns and forbids division and separation, or any sentiment adverse to peace and truth. For therein they are against us, just because they are not with us in that, and, because, not gathering with us, they are consequently scattering.

CHAP. VI. — OF THE CIRCUMSTANCE THAT MARK HAS RECORDED MORE THAN LUKE AS SPOKEN BY THE LORD IN CONNECTION WITH THE CASE OF THIS MAN WHO WAS CASTING OUT DEVILS IN THE NAME OF CHRIST, ALTHOUGH HE WAS NOT FOLLOWING WITH THE DISCIPLES; AND OF THE QUESTION HOW THESE ADDITIONAL WORDS CAN BE SHOWN TO HAVE A REAL BEARING UPON

---

[1] *Iterum*, inserted. [The Greek text, according to the best mss., reads: "when there was again a great multitude." So Revised Version. Augustin's text is: "In those days again, when there was a great multitude." — R.]

[2] The words, "because he followeth not us," are omitted. [So the Vulgate and old Latin text; but the best Greek mss. omit the clause, "and he followeth not us," inserting the last clause, "because he followeth not us," as in Luke ix. 49. — R.]

[3] Mark viii 1–ix 39.   [4] Matt. xii. 30.

[5] Matt. x. 40.   [6] Matt. xxv. 40.   [7] Luke x. 16.
[8] Matt. xxv. 45.   [9] Acts ix. 4.
[10] [The correct reading in Luke ix. 50: "For he that is not against you is for you," gives the key to the meaning. See commentaries *in loco.* — R.]

WHAT CHRIST HAD IN VIEW IN FORBIDDING THE INDIVIDUAL TO BE INTERDICTED WHO WAS PERFORMING MIRACLES IN HIS NAME.

7. Mark proceeds with his narrative in these terms : " For whosoever shall give you a cup of water to drink in my name, because ye belong to Christ, verily I say unto you, he shall not lose his reward.   And whosoever shall offend one of these little ones that believe on me, it is better for him that a millstone were hanged about his neck, and he were cast into the sea.   And if thy hand offend thee, cut it off : it is better for thee to enter into life maimed, than having two hands to go into hell, into the fire that never shall be quenched ; where their worm dieth not, and the fire is not quenched." And so on, down to where it is said, " Have salt in yourselves, and have peace one with another." [1]   These words Mark represents to have been spoken by the Lord in the connection immediately following what He said in forbidding the man to be interdicted who was casting out devils in His name, and yet was not following Him along with the disciples.   In this section, too, he introduces some matters which are not found in any of the other evangelists, but also some which occur in Matthew as well, and some which we come across in like manner both in Matthew and in Luke. Those other evangelists, however, bring in these matters in different connections, and in another order of facts, and not at this particular point when the statement was made to Christ about the man who did not follow Him along with the disciples, and yet was casting out devils in His name.   My opinion, therefore, is, that the Lord did really utter sayings in this connection, according to Mark's attestation, of which he also delivered Himself on other occasions, and this for the simple reason, that they were sufficiently pertinent to this expression of His mind which he gave here, when He forbade the placing of any interdict upon the working of miracles in His name, even although that should be done by a man who did not follow Him along with His disciples.   For Mark presents the relation of the one passage to the other thus : " For he that is not against us is on our part ; for whosoever shall give you a cup of water to drink in my name, because ye belong to Christ, verily I say unto you, he shall not lose his reward." This makes it plain that even this man, whose case John had taken up, and thus had given occasion for the Lord to commence the discourse referred to, was not separating himself from the society of the disciples to any such effect as to scorn it like a heretic.   But his position was something parallel to the familiar one of men who, while not going the length yet of receiving the sacraments of Christ, nevertheless favour the Christian name so far as even to receive Christians, and accommodate themselves to them for this very reason, and none other, that they are Christians ; of which type of persons it is that He tells us that they do not lose their reward.   This does not mean, however, that they ought at once to think themselves quite safe and secure simply on account of this kindness which they cherish towards Christians, while at the same time they are neither cleansed by Christ's baptism, nor incorporated into the unity of His body.   But the import is, that they are now being guided by the mercy of God in such a way that they may also come to these higher things,[2] and so quit this present world in safety.   And such persons assuredly are more profitable [servants], even before they become associated with the number of Christians, than those individuals who, while already bearing the Christian name and partaking in the Christian sacraments, recommend courses which are only fitted to drag others, whom they may persuade to adopt them, along with themselves into eternal punishment.   These are the persons to whom He refers under the figure of the members of the body, and whom He commands to be cast out from the body, like an offending hand or eye ; that is to say, to be cut off from the fellowship of that unity, in order that they should seek rather to enter into life without such associates, than to go into hell in their company.   Moreover, they are separated from those from whom they separate themselves, just when no consent is yielded to their evil recommendations, that is to say, to the offences in which they indulge.   And if, indeed, they are discovered in the character of their perversity to all good men with whom they have any fellowship,[3] they are cut off completely from the fellowship of all, and also from participation in the divine sacraments. But if they are known in this character only to some, while their perversity is unknown to the majority, they must just be borne with, as the chaff is endured in the thrashing-floor previous to the winnowing ; that is to say, they must be dealt with in a manner which will neither involve any agreement with them in the fellowship of unrighteousness, nor lead to a forsaking of the society of the good on their account. This is what is done by those who have salt in themselves, and who have peace one with another.

CHAP. VII. — OF THE FACT THAT FROM THIS POINT ON TO THE LORD'S SUPPER, WITH WHICH ACT THE DISCUSSION OF ALL THE NARRATIVES OF THE FOUR EVANGELISTS CONJOINTLY

---

[1] Mark ix. 40-50.

[2] The text gives *ad ea.* Another reading is *ad eam* = that unity of His body.

[3] Reading *societas.*   Many MSS. give *notitia* = acquaintance.

8. Mark continues as follows : " And He arose
from thence, and cometh into the coasts of
Judæa by the farther side of Jordan : and the
people resort unto Him again ; and, as He was
wont, He taught them again ; " and so on, down
to where it is said, " For all they did cast in of
their abundance ; but she of her want did cast
in all that she had, even all her living." [1]   In
this entire context, all the above has been subjected to investigation already, with the view of
removing the appearance of any contrariety,
when we were comparing the other Gospels in
due order with Matthew. This narrative, however, of the poor widow who cast two mites into
the treasury, is reported only by two of them,
namely, Mark and Luke.[2] But their harmony
admits of no question.   And from this point
onwards to the Lord's Supper, which latter act
formed the starting-point for our discussion of
all the records of the four evangelists taken conjointly, Mark introduces nothing of a kind to
make it necessary for us to institute a special
comparison between it and any other statement,
or to conduct an inquiry with the view of dis-
pelling any appearance of discrepancy.

CHAP. VIII. — OF LUKE'S GOSPEL, AND SPECIALLY
OF THE HARMONY BETWEEN ITS COMMENCE-
MENT AND THE BEGINNING OF THE BOOK OF
THE ACTS OF THE APOSTLES.

9. Next in succession, therefore, let us now
go over the Gospel of Luke in regular order.
We shall omit, however, those passages which he
has in common with Matthew and Mark. For
all these have been already handled. Luke, then,
begins his narrative in the following fashion :
" Forasmuch as many have taken in hand to set
forth in order a declaration of these things which
have been fulfilled [3] among us, even as they delivered them unto us, which from the beginning
were eye-witnesses, and ministers of the word ;
it seemed good to me also, having had perfect
understanding of all things from the very first,
to write unto thee in order,[4] most excellent
Theophilus, that thou mightest know the certainty of those things, wherein thou hast been
instructed." [5] This beginning does not pertain
immediately to the narrative presented in the
Gospel. But it suggests to us to be cognizant
of the fact, that this same Luke is also the writer
of the other book which bears the name of the
Acts of the Apostles. Our ground for holding this

opinion is not merely the circumstance that the
name of Theophilus occurs there as well as here.
For it might quite well happen that there was
a second person with the name of Theophilus ;
and even if it was one and the same person that
was referred to in both cases, still another composition might have been addressed to him by a
different individual, just as the Gospel was written in his behoof by Luke. We base our view
of the identity of authorship, however, on the
fact that this second book commences in the
following strain : " The former treatise have I
made, O Theophilus, of all that Jesus began
both to do and teach, until the day in which
He,[6] through the Holy Ghost, gave commandment unto the apostles whom He chose to
preach the gospel." [7] This statement gives us
to understand that, previous to this, he had
written one of those four books of the gospel
which are held in the loftiest authority in the
Church. At the same time, when he tells us
that he had composed a treatise of all that Jesus
began both to do and teach until the day in
which He gave commandment to the apostles,
we are not to take this to mean that he actually
has given us a full account in his Gospel of all
that Jesus did and said when He lived with His
apostles on earth. For that would be contrary
to what John affirms when he says that there are
also many other things which Jesus did, the
which, if they should be written every one, the
world itself could not contain the books.[8] And
besides, it is the admitted fact that not a few
things have been narrated by the other evangelists, which Luke himself has not touched upon in
his history. The sense therefore is, that he wrote
a treatise of all these things, in so far as he made
a selection out of the whole mass of materials for
his narrative, and introduced those facts which he
judged fit and suitable for the satisfactory discharge of the responsible duty laid upon him.
Again, when he speaks of many who had " taken
in hand to set forth in order a declaration of those
things which have been fulfilled among us," he
seems to refer to certain parties who had not
been able to complete the task which they had
assumed. Hence he also says that it seemed
good to him also to " write carefully in order,
forasmuch as many have taken in hand," etc.
The allusion here, however, we ought to take to
be to those writers who have attained to no
authority in the Church, just because they were
utterly incompetent rightly to carry out what
they took in hand. Moreover, the author at
present before us has not confined himself to
the task of bringing down his narrative to the

---

1 Mark x. 1–xii. 44.   2 Luke xxi. 1–4.
3 Completæ sunt. [So Revised Version. — R.]
4 [Et mihi assecuto a principio omnibus (some MSS. have
omnia) diligenter ex ordine tibi scribere. Comp. Revised Version, and Augustin's explanation below. — R.]
5 Luke i. 1–4.

6 Usque in diem quo apostolis quos elegit, etc. Some editions
read quo apostolos elegit = on which He chose the apostles, giving
them commandment, etc.
7 Acts i. 1, 2.   8 John xxi. 25.

events of the Lord's resurrection and assumption ; neither has it been his aim simply to have a place commensurate in honour with his labours in the company of the four writers of the Gospel Scriptures. But he has also undertaken a record of what was done subsequently by the hands of the apostles ; and relating as many of those events as he believed to be needful and helpful to the edification of the faith of readers or hearers, he has given us a narrative so faithful, that his is the only book that has been reckoned worthy of acceptance in the Church as a history of the Acts of the Apostles ; while all these other writers who attempted, although deficient in the trustworthiness which was the first requisite, to compose an account of the doings and sayings of the apostles, have met with rejection. And, further, Mark and Luke certainly wrote at a time when it was quite possible to put them to the test not only by the Church of Christ, but also by the apostles themselves who were still alive in the flesh.

CHAP. IX. — OF THE QUESTION HOW IT CAN BE SHOWN THAT THE NARRATIVE OF THE HAUL OF FISHES WHICH LUKE HAS GIVEN US IS NOT TO BE IDENTIFIED WITH THE RECORD OF AN APPARENTLY SIMILAR INCIDENT WHICH JOHN HAS REPORTED SUBSEQUENTLY TO THE LORD'S RESURRECTION ; AND OF THE FACT THAT FROM THIS POINT ON TO THE LORD'S SUPPER, FROM WHICH EVENT ONWARDS TO THE END THE COMBINED ACCOUNTS OF ALL THE EVANGELISTS HAVE BEEN EXAMINED, NO DIFFICULTY CALLING FOR SPECIAL CONSIDERATION EMERGES IN THE GOSPEL OF LUKE ANY MORE THAN IN THAT OF MARK.

10. Luke, then, commences his Gospel in the following fashion : "There was, in the days of Herod the king of Judæa, a certain priest named Zacharias, of the course of Abia : and his wife was of the daughters of Aaron, and her name was Elisabeth ; " and so on, down to the passage where it is said, " Now when He had left speaking, He said unto Simon, Launch out into the deep, and let down your nets for a draught." [1] In this whole section, there is nothing to stir any question as to discrepancies. It is true that John appears to relate something resembling the last passage. But what he gives is really something widely different. I refer to what took place by the sea of Tiberias after the Lord's resurrection.[2] In that instance, not only is the particular time extremely different, but the circumstances themselves are of quite another character. For there the nets were cast on the right side, and a hundred and fifty and three fishes were caught. It is added, too, that they were great fishes. And the evangelist, therefore, has felt it necessary to state, that " for all there

were so many, yet was not the net broken," surely just because he had in view the previous case, which is recorded by Luke, and in connection with which the nets were broken [3] by reason of the multitude of fishes. As for the rest, Luke has not recounted things like those which John has narrated, except in relation to the Lord's passion and resurrection. And this whole section, which comes in between the Lord's Supper and the conclusion, has already been handled by us in a manner which has yielded, as the result of a comparison of the testimonies of all the evangelists conjointly, the demonstration of an entire absence of discrepancies between them.

CHAP. X. — OF THE EVANGELIST JOHN, AND THE DISTINCTION BETWEEN HIM AND THE OTHER THREE.

11. John remains, between whom and others there is left no comparison to be instituted. For, however the evangelists may each have reported some matters which are not recorded by the others, it will be hard to prove that any question involving real discrepancy arises out of these. Thus, too, it is a clearly admitted position that the first three — namely, Matthew, Mark, and Luke — have occupied themselves chiefly with the humanity of our Lord Jesus Christ, according to which He is both king and priest. And in this way, Mark, who seems to answer to the figure of the man in the well-known mystical symbol of the four living creatures,[4] either appears to be preferentially the companion of Matthew, as he narrates a larger number of matters in unison with him than with the rest, and therein acts in due harmony with the idea of the kingly character whose wont it is, as I have stated in the first book,[5] to be not unaccompanied by attendants ; or else, in accordance with the more probable account of the matter, he holds a course in conjunction with both [the other Synoptists]. For although he is at one with Matthew in the larger number of passages, he is nevertheless at one rather with Luke in some others. And this very fact shows him to stand related at once to the lion and to the steer, that is to say, to the kingly office which Matthew emphasizes, and to the sacerdotal which Luke introduces, wherein also Christ appears distinctively as man, as the figure which Mark sustains stands related to both these. On the other hand, Christ's divinity, in virtue of which He is equal to the Father, in accordance with which He is the Word, and God with God, and the Word that was made flesh in order to dwell among us,[6] in accordance with which also He and the Father are one,[7] has been taken specially

---

[1] Luke i. 5-v. 4.　　[2] John xxi. 1-11.

[3] [Rumpebantur, " were breaking," as in the Greek: comp. Revised Version. — R.]
[4] Apoc. iv. 6, 7.　　[5] See chap. iii.
[6] John i. 1, 14.　　[7] John x. 30.

in hand by John with a view to its recommendation to our minds. Like an eagle, he abides among Christ's sayings of the sublimer order, and in no way descends to earth but on rare occasions. In brief, although he declares plainly his own knowledge of the Lord's mother, he nevertheless neither unites with Matthew and Luke in recording His nativity, nor associates himself with all the three in relating His baptism; but all that he does there is simply to present the testimony delivered by John in a lofty and sublime fashion, and then, quitting the company of these others, he proceeds with Him to the marriage in Cana of Galilee. And there, although the evangelist himself mentions His mother by that very name, He nevertheless addresses her thus: "Woman, what have I to do with thee?"[1] In this, however, [it is to be understood that] He does not repel her of whom He received the flesh, but means to convey the conception of His divinity with special fitness at this time, when He is about to change the water into wine; which divinity, likewise, had made that woman, and had not itself been made in her.

12. Then, after noticing the few days spent in Capharnaum, the evangelist comes again to the temple, where he states that Jesus spoke of the temple of His body in these terms: "Destroy this temple, and in three days I will raise it up:"[2] in which declaration emphatic intimation is given not only that God was in that temple in the person of the Word that was made flesh, but also that He Himself raised the said flesh to life, in the veritable exercise of that prerogative which He has in His oneness with the Father, and according to which He does not act separately from Him; whereas it will perhaps be found that, in all other passages, the phrase which Scripture employs is one to the effect that God raised Him: neither is there any such expression found anywhere else as that, when God raised Christ, Christ also raised Himself, because He is one God with the Father; which is the import of the passage now before us, in which He says, "Destroy this temple, and in three days I will raise it up."

13. Then how great and how divine are the words reported to have been spoken with Nicodemus! From these the evangelist proceeds again to the testimony of John, and brings before our notice the fact, that the friend of the bridegroom cannot but rejoice because of the bridegroom's voice. In this statement He gives us to understand that the soul of man neither has light derivable from itself, nor can have blessing, except by participation in the unchangeable wisdom. Thereafter he carries us on to the case of the woman of Samaria, in connection with which mention is made of the water, whereof if a man drinks, he shall never thirst again. Once more, he brings us again to Cana of Galilee, where Jesus had made the water wine. In that narrative he tells us how He spoke to the nobleman, whose son was sick, in these terms: "Except ye see signs and wonders ye believe not:"[3] in which saying He aims at lifting the mind of the believer high above all things mutable, so that He would not have even the miracles themselves, which, however they may bear the impression of what is divine, are yet wrought in the instance of what is changeable in bodies, made objects of seeking on the part of the faithful.

14. Next he brings us back to Jerusalem, and tells the story of the healing of the man who had an infirmity of thirty-eight years' standing. What words are spoken on this occasion, and how ample is the discourse! Here we are met by the sentence, "The Jews sought to kill Him, because He not only broke the Sabbath, but said also that God was His Father, making Himself equal with God."[4] In this passage it is made sufficiently plain that He did not speak of God as His Father in the ordinary sense in which holy men are in the habit of using the phrase, but that He meant that He is His equal. For, a little before this, He had said to those who were impeaching Him with violating the Sabbath-day, "My Father worketh hitherto, and I work."[5] Then their fury flamed forth, not merely because He said that God was His Father, but because He wished it to be understood that He was equal with God, when He used the phrase, "My Father worketh hitherto, and I work." In which utterance He also shows it to be matter of course that, as the Father works, the Son should work also; because the Father does not work without the Son. And this is in accordance with what He states a little further on in the same passage, when these parties were incensed at His declaration, namely, "For what things soever He doeth, these also doeth the Son likewise."[6]

15. Then at length John descends to bear company with the other three, whose course is with the same Lord, but upon the earth, and joins them in recording the feeding of the five thousand men with the five loaves. In this narrative, however, he is the only one who mentions, that when the people wished to make Him a king, Jesus departed into a mountain Himself alone.[7] And in making that statement, his intention appears to me to have been just to communicate to the reasonable soul the truth, that Christ reigns over our mind and reason purely in a sphere in which He is exalted above

---

[1] John ii. 1-11.   [2] John ii. 12-22.

[3] John iv. 48.   [4] John v. 18.
[5] John v. 17.   [6] John v. 19.   [7] John vi. 15.

us, in which He has no community of nature with men, and in which He is verily by Himself alone, as He is the Father's only fellow. This, however, is a mystical truth, which escapes the cognizance of carnal men, whose life creeps upon the lower soil of this earth, just because it is so sublime a mystery. Hence Christ Himself also departs into the mountain from the men whose habit is to seek for His kingdom with earthly conceptions of it. Thus is it that He expresses Himself elsewhere to this effect, "My kingdom is not of this world."[1] And this, again, is something which is reported only by John, who soars high over earth in a kind of ethereal flight, and delights himself in the light of the Sun of righteousness. Then, on passing from the narrative connected with this mountain, and from the miracle of the five loaves, he still keeps company with the same three for a little while, until the notice of the crossing of the sea is reached, and the occasion on which Jesus walked upon the waters. But at this point he at once rises again to the region of the Lord's discourses, and relates those words, so grave, so lengthened, so sustainedly lofty and elevated, which had their occasion in the multiplying of the bread, when He addressed the multitudes to the following effect: "Verily, verily, I say unto you, ye seek me, not because ye saw the miracles, but because ye did eat of the loaves, and were filled. Labour not for the meat which perisheth, but for that meat which endureth unto everlasting life."[2] After which sayings, He continues to discourse in similar terms for a very long period, and in the most exalted strain. At that time, some fell away from the sublime teaching of such words, namely, those who walked no more with Him afterwards. But there were also those who did cleave to Him; and these were they who were able to receive the meaning of this saying, "It is the spirit that quickeneth, but the flesh profiteth nothing."[3] For surely it is true, that even through the flesh it is the spirit that profiteth,[4] and the spirit alone that profiteth; whereas the flesh without the spirit profiteth nothing.

16. Next we come to the passage where His brethren — that is to say, His relations according to the flesh — urge Him to go up to the feast-day, in order that He may have an opportunity of making Himself known to the multitude. And here, again, how supremely elevated is the tone of His reply! "My time is not yet come, but your time is alway ready. The world cannot hate you; but me it hateth, because I testify of it that the works thereof are evil."[5] So it is

the case, then, that "your time is alway ready," because ye desire that kind of day to which the prophet refers when he says, "But I have not laboured following Thee, O Lord; and the day of man I have not desired, Thou knowest:"[6] that is to say, to soar to the light of the Word, and to desire that day which Abraham desired to see, and which he did see, and was glad.[7] And again, how wonderful, how divine, how sublime are the words which John represents Him to have spoken after He had gone up to the temple, at the time of the feast! They are such as these: that where He was about to go, thither they could not come;[8] that they both knew Him, and knew whence He was;[9] that He who sent Him is true, whom they knew not,[9] which is much the same as if He had said, "Ye both know whence I am, and know not whence I am." And what else did He wish to be understood by such utterances, but that it was possible for Him to be known to them according to the flesh, in respect of lineage and country, but that, so far as regarded His divinity, He was unknown to them? On this occasion, too, when He spoke of the gift of the Holy Spirit, He showed them who He was, inasmuch as He could hold the power of bestowing that highest boon.

17. Again, how weighty are the things which this evangelist reports Jesus to have spoken, when He came back to the temple from Mount Olivet, and after the forgiveness which He extended to the adulteress, who had been brought before Him by His tempters, as one deserving to be stoned: on which occasion He wrote with His finger upon the ground, as if He would indicate that people of the character of these men would be written on earth, and not in heaven, as He also admonished His disciples to rejoice that their names were written in heaven![10] Or, it may be that He meant to convey the idea that it was by humbling Himself (which He expressed by bending down His head) that He wrought signs upon the earth; or, that the time was now come when His law should be written, not, as formerly, on the sterile stone, but on a soil which would yield fruit. Accordingly, after these incidents, He affirmed Himself to be the light of the world, and declared that he who followed Him would not walk in darkness, but would have the light of life. He said, also, that He was "the beginning which also discoursed to them."[11] By which designation He clearly distinguished Himself from the light which He made, and presented Himself as the Light by which all things have been made. Consequently, when He said that He was the light

---

[1] John xviii. 36. [2] John vi. 26, 27. [3] John vi. 63.
[4] The text gives: *et per carnem spiritus prodest.* Some editions read *et carni,* etc. = the spirit profiteth even the flesh. [The erroneous view of the term "flesh" leads to this explanation. It has already in this passage an ethical sense, which Augustin ignores. — R.]
[5] John vii. 6, 7.

[6] Jer. xvii. 16. [7] John viii. 56.
[8] John vii. 34. [9] John vii. 28.
[10] Luke x. 20.
[11] *Se esse principium quod et loqueretur eis,* as the rendering of the τὴν ἀρχὴν ὅ τι καὶ λαλῶ ὑμῖν in John viii. 25.

of the world, we are not to take the words to bear simply the sense intended when He addressed the disciples in similar terms, saying, "Ye are the light of the world." For they are compared only to the kindled light, which is not to be put beneath a bushel, but to be set upon a candlestick;[1] as He also says of John the Baptist, that "he was a burning and shining light."[2] But He is Himself the beginning, of whom it is likewise declared, that "of His fulness have all we received."[3] On the occasion presently under review, He asserted further that He, the Son, is the Truth, which will make us free, and without which no man will be free.[4]

18. Next, after telling the story of the giving of sight to the man who was blind from his birth, John tarries for a space over the copious discourse to which that incident gave occasion, on the subject of the sheep, and the shepherd, and the door, and the power of laying down His life and taking it again, wherein He gave token of the supreme might of His divinity. Thereafter, he relates how, at the time when the feast of the dedication was being celebrated in Jerusalem, the Jews said to Him, "How long dost thou make us to doubt? If thou be the Christ, tell us plainly."[5] And then he reports the sublime words which the Lord uttered when the opportunity thus arose for a discourse. It was on this occasion that He said, "I and my Father are one."[6] After this, again, he brings before us the raising of Lazarus from the dead: in connection with which miracle the Lord said, "I am the resurrection and the life : he that believeth on me, though he were dead, yet shall he live : and whosoever liveth and believeth in me shall never die."[7] In these words what do we recognise but the sublimity of the Godhead of Him, in fellowship with whom we shall live for ever? Once more, John joins Matthew and Mark in what is recorded about Bethany, where the scene took place with the precious ointment which was poured upon His feet and His head by Mary.[8] And then, on to the Lord's passion and resurrection, John keeps by the other three evangelists, but only in so far as his narrative engages itself with the same places.

19. Moreover, so far as regards the Lord's discourses, he does not cease to ascend to the sublimer and more extended utterances of which, from this point also, He delivered Himself. For he inserts a lofty address which the Lord spoke on the occasion when, through Philip and Andrew, the Gentiles expressed their desire to see Him, and which is introduced by none of the other evangelists. There, too, he reports the re-markable words which were spoken again on the subject of the light which enlightens and makes men the children of light.[9] Thereafter, in connection with the Supper itself, of which none of the evangelists has failed to give us some notice, how affluent and how lofty are those words of Jesus which John records, but which the others have passed over in silence ! I may instance not only His commendation of humility, when He washed the disciples' feet, but also that marvellously overpowering and pre-eminently copious discourse which the Lord delivered to the eleven who remained with Him after His betrayer had been indicated by the morsel of bread, and had gone out. It was in this discourse, over which John lingers long, that He said, "He that hath seen me, hath seen the Father also."[10] It was in it, too, that He expressed Himself so largely about the Holy Spirit, the Comforter, whom He was to send to them, and about His own glory, which He had with the Father before the world was, and about His making us one in Himself, even as He and the Father are one, — not that He and the Father and we should be one, but that we should be one as they are one. And many other things of a wonderfully sublime order did He utter in that connection. But who can fail to see that to discuss such themes in any manner that would be worthy of them, even if we were competent to do so, is at least not the task which we have undertaken in the present effort? For our object is to help those who are lovers of the Word of God and students of holy truth to understand that, in his Gospel, John was indeed an announcer and preacher of the same Christ, the true and truthful One, of whom the other three who have composed Gospels also testified, and to whom the rest of the apostles likewise bore witness, who, although they did not take in hand the construction of written narratives, did at least discharge the kindred service in officially preaching of Him : but that, at the same time, he was borne to far loftier heights in the doctrine of Christ from the very beginning of his book, and that it was but on rare occasions that he kept to the level pursued by the others. These occasions were the following in particular, namely : first by the Jordan, in reference to the testimony of John the Baptist ; secondly, on the other side of the sea of Tiberias, when the Lord fed the multitudes with the five loaves, and walked upon the waters ; thirdly, in Bethany, where He had the precious ointment poured over Him by the devotion of a woman of faith. And so he proceeds, until he meets them at the time of the Passion, which, as matter of course, he had to relate in conjunction with them. But, even in that section, and

---

1 Matt. v. 14, 15.   2 John v. 35.   3 John i. 16.
4 John viii. 36.   5 John x. 24.   6 John x. 30.
7 John xi. 25, 26.
8 John xii. 1–9 ; Matt. xxvi. 6–13 ; Mark xiv. 3–9.

9 John xii. 20–50.   10 John xiv. 9.

on the particular subject of the Lord's Supper, which has been left unnoticed by none of them, he has presented us with a much more affluent statement, as if he drew his materials directly from the treasure-store of that bosom of the Lord on which it was his wont to recline. Then, again, [John shows us how] He astonishes Pilate with words of a sublimer import, declaring that His kingdom is not of this world, and that He was born a King, and that He came into the world for this purpose, that He might bear witness to the truth.[1] [It is in this Gospel also that] He withdraws Himself[2] from Mary with some deep mystical intention after His resurrection, and says to her, "Touch me not; for I am not yet ascended to my Father."[3] It is here, too, that He imparts the Holy Spirit to the disciples by breathing on them[4] giving us thereby to understand that this Spirit who is consubstantial and co-eternal with the Trinity, should not be considered to be simply the Spirit of the Father, but should also be held to be the Spirit of the Son.

20. Finally, He here commits His sheep to the care of Peter, who loves Him, and thrice confesses that love, and then He states that He wills this very John so to tarry until He comes.[5] In which utterance, again, He seems to me to have conveyed in a profound and mystical way the fact that this[6] evangelical stewardship of John's, in which he is borne aloft into the most liquid light of the Word,[7] where it is possible to behold the equality and unchangeableness of the Trinity, and in which, above all, we see at what a distance from all others in respect of essential character that humanity stands by whose assumption it occurred that the Word was made flesh, cannot be clearly discerned and recognised until the Lord Himself comes. Consequently, it will tarry thus until He comes. At present it will tarry in the faith of believers, but hereafter it will be possible to contemplate it face to face,[8] when He, our Life, shall appear, and when we shall appear with Him in glory.[9] But if any one supposes that with man, living, as he still does, in this mortal life, it may be possible for a person to dispel and clear off every obscurity induced by corporeal and carnal fancies, and to attain to the serenest light of changeless truth, and to cleave constantly and unswervingly to that with a mind thoroughly estranged from the course of this present life, that man understands neither what he asks, nor who he is that put

such a supposition. Let such an individual rather accept the authority, at once lofty and free from all deceitfulness, which tells us that, as long as we are in the body, we are absent from the Lord, and that we walk by faith and not by sight.[10] And thus, with all perseverance keeping and guarding his faith and hope and charity, let him look forward to the sight which is promised, in accordance with that earnest which we have received of the Holy Ghost, who shall teach us all truth,[11] when God, who raised up Jesus Christ from the dead, shall also quicken our mortal bodies by His Spirit that dwelleth in us.[12] But before this body, which is dead by reason of sin, is quickened, it is without doubt corruptible, and presseth down the soul.[13] And if, in the body, man is ever helped to reach beyond the cloud with which the whole earth is covered,[14] — that is to say, beyond this carnal darkness with which the whole life of earth is covered, — it is simply as if he were touched with a rapid coruscation, only to sink swiftly into his natural infirmity, the desire surviving by which he may again be excited (to what is evil), and the purity being insufficient to establish him (in what is good). The more, however, any one can do this, the greater is he; while the less he can do so, the less is he. And if the mind of a man has as yet had no such experience — in which mind nevertheless Christ dwells by faith — he ought to strive earnestly to diminish the lusts of this world, and to make an end of them by the exercise of moral virtue, walking, as it were, in the company of these three evangelists with Christ the Mediator. And, with the joy of large hope, let him in faith hold Him who is alway the Son of God, but who, for our sakes, became the Son of man, in order that His eternal power and Godhead might be united with[15] our weakness and mortality, and, on the basis of what is ours, make a way for us in Himself and to Himself. That a man may be kept from sinning, he should be ruled by Christ the King. If he happens to sin, he may obtain remission from Christ, who is also priest. And thus, nurtured in the exercise of a good conversation and life, and borne out of the atmosphere of earth on the wings of a twofold love, as on a pair of strong pinions, so may he be enlightened by the same Christ, who is also the Word, the Word who was in the beginning, the Word who was with God, and the Word who was God; and although that will still be through a glass darkly, it will be a sublime kind of illumination far superior to every corporeal similitude. Wherefore, although it is the gifts of the active virtue

---

[1] John xviii. 36, 37.
[2] The text gives *vitans*. Many MSS. and editions read *visitans* = coming to Mary.
[3] John xx. 17.   [4] John xx. 22.   [5] John xxi. 23.
[6] Some MSS. insert *secretam* = secret.
[7] Reading, *lucem liquidissimam verbi sublimiter*. But various MSS. and editions give *verbi sublimitate fertur*, etc. = borne aloft in the sublimity of the word into the most liquid light.
[8] 1 Cor. xiii. 12.   [9] Col. iii. 4.

[10] 2 Cor. v. 6, 7.   [11] John xvi. 13.
[12] Rom. viii. 10, 11.   [13] Wisd. of Sol. ix. 13.
[14] Ecclus. xxiv. 3.
[15] *Contemperata* = attempered to.

that shine pre-eminent in the first three evangelists, while it is the gift of the contemplative virtue that discerns such subjects, nevertheless, this Gospel of John, in so far as it also is in part, will so tarry until that which is perfect comes.[1] And to one, indeed, is given by the Spirit the word of wisdom, to another the word of knowledge by the same Spirit.[2] One man regardeth the day to the Lord;[3] another receives a clearer draught from the breast of the Lord; another is caught up even to the third heaven, and hears unspeakable words.[4] But all, as long as they are in the body, are absent from the Lord.[5] And for all believers living in the good hope, whose names are written in the book of life, there is still in reserve that which is referred to in the words, "And I will love him,

and will manifest myself unto him."[6] Nevertheless, the greater the advance which a man may make in the apprehension and knowledge of this theme during the time of this absence from the Lord, all the more carefully should he guard against those devilish vices, pride and envy. Let him remember that this very Gospel of John, which urges us so pre-eminently to the contemplation of truth, gives a no less remarkable prominence to the inculcation of the sweet grace of charity. Let him also consider that most true and wholesome precept which is couched in the words, "The greater thou art, the more humble thyself in all."[7] For the evangelist who presents Christ to us in a far loftier strain of teaching than all the others, is also the one in whose narrative the Lord washes the disciples' feet.[8]

---

[1] 1 Cor. xiii. 12, 9, 10.   [2] 1 Cor. xii. 8.   [3] Rom. xiv. 6.
[4] 2 Cor. xii. 2–4.   [5] 2 Cor. v. 6.

[6] John xiv. 21.   [7] Ecclus. iii. 18.   [8] John xiii. 5.

ST. AUGUSTIN:

SERMONS ON SELECTED LESSONS OF THE NEW TESTAMENT

TRANSLATED BY

THE REV. R. G. MacMULLEN, M.A.

EDITED BY

PHILIP SCHAFF, D.D.

ADVERTISEMENT.

THE Sermons of St. Augustin, besides their other excellencies, furnish a beautiful picture of perhaps the deepest and most powerful mind of the Western Church adapting itself to the little ones of Christ. In them, he who has furnished the mould for all the most thoughtful minds for fourteen hundred years, is seen forming with loving tenderness the babes in Christ. Very touching is the child-like simplicity, with which he gradually leads them through what to them were difficulties, watching all the while whether he made himself clear to them, keeping up their attention, pleased at their understanding, dreading their approbation, and leading them off from himself to some practical result. Very touching the tenderness with which he at times reproves, the allowance which he makes for human infirmities and for those in secular life, if they will not make their infirmities their boast, or in allowed duties and indulgences forget God. But his very simplicity precludes the necessity of any preface. His Sermons explain themselves. They appear from a passage in the Commentary on the Psalms to have been often taken down in writing at the time by the more attentive sort of hearers (as were those of St. Chrysostom); Possidius states that this was done from the commencement of his presbyterate, and that "thence [1] through the body of Africa, excellent doctrine and the most sweet savour of Christ was diffused and made manifest, the Church of God beyond seas, when it heard thereof, partaking of the joy." Those on the New Testament have been now selected, both as furnishing a comment, and as a gradual introduction to what is found in a larger measure elsewhere, the spiritual interpretation of Holy Scripture. It will doubtless seem strange to some at first sight that the spiritual meaning of numbers, for instance, should be made a part of religious instruction. And yet, it might not require any great diffidence to think that St. Augustin knew better than any of us, the tendency and effects of his mode of teaching upon minds, which he evidently treated with such tender care, and that they who have entered into that system can estimate its value better than they who have not. It will appear also, probably, that a system which sees a meaning everywhere in Holy Scripture is more reverential than one which overlooks it; as, on the other hand, as a fact, the anti-mystical interpretation has both in ancient and modern times stood connected with a cold rationalism, and with heresy. This is, however, a large subject, upon which this does not seem the place to enter, since such interpretations are here only incidental and subordinate, and it is here intended only to give a practical warning. Those who close their eyes, of course, never see. The eye also requires to be insensibly familiarized with what, as new, is strange to it. But whoever will not set himself against what is in fact the received mode of interpretation of the Church, will be insensibly won by it, and will have his reward. The interpretations of St. Augustin were, as he himself often says, sought by his own prayers and the prayers of his people, and will, to those who receive them, open a rich variety of meaning and instruction. One might instance, of the most solemn sort, the analogy of the three dead, whom our Lord raised, with the three stages of sin, consent, act, and habit, as an affecting and impressive specimen of this mode of instruction, which has been adopted, in a manner, by the spiritual perception of the Western Church.

On his directly practical teaching, it will be borne in mind, that to him the Church is mainly indebted for the overthrow of Pelagianism, and the vindication of the doctrine of the free grace of God. When then he insists, as he does so frequently, on the value of good works and especially almsgiving, to which he seems to recur with such especial sympathy, it will not be hastily thought that so deep and consistent a thinker, and so imbued with Divine truth, was at variance with himself and with it, and we may in his teaching gain more constraining motives to encourage ourselves and others, if so one great stain of our times, the neglect of Christ's poor, may be mitigated or effaced. On the other hand, when he speaks of heresy, he speaks of what he had himself been; of the nothingness of this world's pleasures and applause, of what he had himself, when unbaptized, too miserably tasted; of Christ's power to save out of them, what he had himself felt; of the grace of God,

---

[1] *Vit.* c. 7.

what he had himself used; of the value of alms, as having himself given up what was his;[1] of humility, as showing it in the very language in which he praises it; of the joys of Heaven, and the love of God, as that for which he had abandoned freely and for ever all on earth, for which he was daily labouring, enduring, sighing.

It remains to say, that the text used is that of the Benedictines, in which their large resources in MSS. have been so excellently employed, and that the Editors are indebted for the translation to the Rev. R. G. Macmullen, M.A., Fellow of Corpus Christi College.

E. B. PUSEY.

CHRIST CHURCH, OXFORD, *Feast of St. Barnabas*, 1844.

---

[1] This he did immediately on his conversion. Possidius says, " He made no will, because as a poor man of God (*pauper Dei*) he had nothing whereof to make one" (c. ult.). The poor, Possidius calls his "*compauperes*," of whom he says "he was ever mindful, and supplied them out of the same sources as himself and all who lived with him [his clergy under monastic rule], — out of the returns of the possessions of the Church, or the oblations of the faithful" (c. 23). Possidius speaks (c. 4), how the report of " the continency and deep poverty of his monastery" won those separated from the Church.

CONTENTS OF SERMONS ON SELECTED LESSONS OF THE GOSPELS.

[The Scripture texts have been conformed to the Revised Version of 1881. — P.S.]

CONTENTS.

SERMONS ON SELECTED LESSONS OF THE NEW TESTAMENT.

SERMON I.

[LI. BENEDICTINE EDITION.]

OF THE AGREEMENT OF THE EVANGELISTS MAT-
THEW AND LUKE IN THE GENERATIONS OF THE
LORD.

1. MAY He, beloved, fulfil your expectation
who hath awakened it : for though I feel confident that what I have to say is not my own, but
God's, yet with far more reason do I say, what
the Apostle in his humility saith, "We have this
treasure in earthen vessels, that the excellency
of the power may be of God, and not of us."[1]
I do not doubt accordingly that you remember
my promise ; in Him I made it through whom
I now fulfil it, for both when I made the promise, did I ask of the Lord, and now when I fulfil
it, do I receive of Him. Now you will remember, beloved, that it was in the matins of the
festival of the Lord's Nativity, that I put off the
question which I had proposed for resolution,
because many came with us to the celebration
of the accustomed solemnities of that day to
whom the word of God is usually burdensome ;
but now I imagine that none have come here,
but they who desire to hear, and so I am not
speaking to hearts that are deaf, and to minds
that will disdain the word, but this your longing
expectation is a prayer for me. There is a
further consideration ; for the day of the public
shows[2] has dispersed many from hence, for
whose salvation I exhort you to share my great
anxiety, and do you with all earnestness of mind,
entreat God for those who are not yet intent
upon the spectacles of the truth, but are wholly
given up to the spectacles of the flesh ; for I
know and am well assured, that there are now
among you those who have this day despised
them, and have burst the bonds of their inveterate habits ; for men are changed both for the
better and the worse. By daily instances of this
kind are we alternately made joyful and sad ; we
joy over the reformed, are sad over the corrupted ; and therefore the Lord doth not say
that he who beginneth, shall be saved, "But he
that endureth unto the end shall be saved."[3]

2. Now what more marvellous, what more
magnificent thing could our Lord Jesus Christ,
the Son of God, and also the Son of man (for
this also He vouchsafed to be), grant to us, than
the gathering into His fold not only of the spectators of these foolish shows, but even some
of the actors in them ; for He hath combated[4]
unto salvation not only the lovers of the combats of men with beasts, but even the combatants themselves, for He also was made a spectacle
Himself. Hear how. He hath told us Himself, and foretold it before He was made a spectacle, and in the words of prophecy announced
beforehand what was to come to pass, as if it
were already done, saying in the Psalms, "They
pierced My hands and My feet, they told all My
bones."[5] Lo ! how He was made a spectacle,
for His bones to be told ! and this spectacle He
expresseth more plainly, "they observed and
looked upon Me." He was made a spectacle
and an object of derision, made a spectacle by
them who were to show Him no favour indeed
in that spectacle, but who were to be furious
against Him, just as at first He made His martyrs
spectacles ; as saith the Apostle, "We are made
a spectacle unto the world, and to angels, and
to men."[6] Now two sorts of men are spectators
of such spectacles ; the one, carnal, the other,
spiritual men. The carnal look on, as thinking
those martyrs who are thrown to the beasts, or
beheaded, or burnt in the flames, to be wretched
men, and they detest and abhor them ; but others look on, like the holy Angels, not regarding
the laceration of their bodies, but admiring the
unimpaired purity of their faith. A grand spectacle to the eyes of the heart doth a whole mind
in a mangled body exhibit ! When these things
are read of in the church, you behold them with
pleasure with these eyes of the heart, for if you
were to behold nothing, you would hear nothing ;
so you see you have not neglected the spectacles to-day, but have made a choice of spectacles. May God then be with you, and give
you grace with gentle persuasiveness to report
your spectacles to your friends, whom you have

---

[1] 2 Cor. iv. 7. [2] *Muneris.* [3] Matt. x. 22.
[4] *Ipsos venatores venatus est ad salutem.* [5] Ps. xxii. 16, 17.
[6] 1 Cor. iv. 9.

been pained to see this day running to the amphitheatre, and unwilling to come to the church; that so they too may begin to contemn those things, by the love of which themselves have become contemptible, and may, with you, love God, of whom none who love Him can ever be ashamed, for that they love Him who cannot be overcome: let them, as you do, love Christ, who by that very thing wherein He seemed to be overcome, overcame the whole world. For He hath overcome the whole world as we see, my brethren; He hath subjected all powers, He hath subjugated kings, not with the pride of soldiery, but by the ignominy of the Cross: not by the fury of the sword, but by hanging on the Wood, by suffering in the body, by working in the Spirit.[1] His body was lifted up on the Cross, and so He subdued souls to the Cross; and now what jewel in their diadem is more precious than the Cross of Christ on the foreheads of kings? In loving Him you will never be ashamed. Whereas from the amphitheatre how many return conquered, because those are conquered, for whom they are so madly interested! still more would they be conquered were they to conquer. For so would they be enslaved to the vain joy, to the exultation of a depraved desire, who are conquered by the very circumstance of running to these shows. For how many, my brethren, do you think have this day been in hesitation whether they would go here or there? And they who in this hesitation, turning their thoughts to Christ, have run to the church, have overcome, not any man, but the devil himself, him that hunteth[2] after the souls of the whole world. But they who in that hesitation have chosen rather to run to the amphitheatre, have assuredly been overcome by him whom the others overcame — overcame in Him who saith, "Be of good cheer, I have overcome the world."[3] For the Captain suffered Himself to be tried, only that He might teach His soldiers to fight.

3. That our Lord Jesus Christ might do this, He became the Son of man by being born of a woman. But now, would He have been any less a man, if He had not been born of the Virgin Mary" one may say. "He willed to be a man; well and good; He might have so been, and yet not be born of a woman; for neither did He make the first man whom He made, of a woman." Now see what answer I make to this. You say, Why did He choose to be born of a woman? I answer, Why should He avoid being born of a woman? Granted that I could not show that He chose to be born of a woman; do you show why He need have avoided it. But I have already said at other times, that if

He had avoided the womb of a woman, it might have betokened, as it were, that He could have contracted defilement from her; but by how much He was in His own substance more incapable of defilement, by so much less had He cause to fear the woman's womb, as though He could contract defilement from it. But by being born of a woman, He purposed to show to us some high mystery.[4] For of a truth, brethren, we grant too, that if the Lord had willed to become man without being born of a woman, it were easy to His sovereign Majesty. For as He could be born of a woman without a man, so could He also have been born without the woman. But this hath He shown us, that mankind of neither sex might despair of its salvation, for the human sexes are male and female. If therefore being a man, which it behoved Him assuredly to be, He had not been born of a woman, women might have despaired of themselves, as mindful of their first sin, because by a woman was the first man deceived, and would have thought that they had no hope at all in Christ. He came therefore as a man to make special choice of that sex, and was born of a woman to console the female sex, as though He would address them and say; "That ye may know that no creature of God is bad, but that[5] unregulated pleasure perverteth it, when in the beginning I made man, I made them male and female. I do not condemn the creature which I made. See I have been born a Man, and born of a woman; it is not then the creature which I made that I condemn, but the sins which I made not." Let each sex then at once see its honour, and confess its iniquity, and let them both hope for salvation. The poison to deceive man was presented him by woman, through woman let salvation for man's recovery be presented; so let the woman make amends for the sin by which she deceived the man, by giving birth to Christ. For the same reason again, women were the first who announced to the Apostles the Resurrection of God. The woman in Paradise announced death to her husband, and the women in the Church announced salvation to the men; the Apostles were to announce to the nations the Resurrection of Christ, the women announced it to the Apostles. Let no one then reproach Christ with His birth of a woman, by which sex the Deliverer could not be defiled, and to which it was in the purpose[6] of the Creator to do honour.[7]

4. But, say they, "how are we to believe that Christ was born of a woman?" I would answer, by the Gospel which hath been preached and is still preached to all the world. But these men, blind themselves, and aiming to blind

---

[1] *Spiritaliter.*   [2] *Venatorem.*   [3] John xvi. 33.   [4] *Sacramenti.*   [5] *Prava.*   [6] *Deberet.*   [7] *Commendare.*

others, seeing not what they ought to see, whilst they try to shake what ought to be believed, endeavour to obtrude a question on a matter which is now believed through all the earth. For they answer and say: "Do not think to overwhelm us with the authority of the whole world — let us look to Scripture itself, urge not arguments of mere [1] numbers against us, for the seduced multitude favours you." To this I answer, in the first place, "Does the seduced multitude favour me?" This multitude was once a scantling. Whence grew this multitude, which in this increase was announced so long before? For this which hath been seen to increase, is none other than the same which was seen beforehand. I need not have said, it was a scantling; once it was Abraham only. Consider, brethren; it was Abraham alone throughout all the world at that time; throughout the whole world, among all men, and all nations; Abraham alone to whom it was said, "In thy seed shall all nations be blessed;" [2] and what he alone believed of his own [3] single person, is exhibited as present now to many in the multitude of his seed. Then it was not seen, and was believed; now it is seen, and it is contested; and what was then said to one man, and was by that one believed, is disputed now by some few, when in many it is made good. He who made His disciples fishers of men, inclosed within His nets every kind of authority. If great numbers are to be believed, what more widely diffused over the whole world than the Church? If the rich are to be believed, let them consider how many rich He hath taken; if the poor, let them consider the thousands of poor; if nobles, almost all the nobility are within the Church; if kings, let them see all of them subjected to Christ; if the more eloquent, and wise, and learned, let them see how many orators, and scientific [4] men, and philosophers of this world, have been caught by those fishermen, to be drawn from the depth to salvation; let them think of Him who, coming down to heal by the example of His own humility that great evil of man's soul, pride, "chose the weak things of the world to confound the things which are mighty, and the foolish things of the world to confound the wise" (not the really wise, but who seemed so to be), "and chose the base things of the world, and things which are not, to bring to nought things that are." [5]

5. "Whatever you may choose to say," they say, "we find that in the place where we read that Christ was born, the Gospels disagree with one another, and two things which disagree cannot both be true;" for, says one, "when I have proved this disagreement, I may rightly disallow

belief in it, or, at least, do you who accept the belief in it, shew the agreement." And what disagreement, I ask, will you prove? "A plain one," says he, "which none can gainsay." With what security, brethren, do you hear all this, because ye are believers! Attend, dearly beloved, and see what wholesome advice the Apostle gives, who says, "As ye have therefore received Christ Jesus our Lord, so walk ye in Him, rooted and built up in Him, and established in the faith;" [6] for with this simple and assured faith ought we to abide stedfastly in Him, that He may Himself open to the faithful what is hidden in Him; for as the same Apostle saith, "In Him are hid all the treasures of wisdom and knowledge;" [7] and He does not hide them to refuse them, but to stir up desire for those hidden things. This is the advantage of their secrecy. Honour in Him then what as yet thou understandest not, and so much the more as the veils which thou seest are more in number: for the higher in honour any one is, the more veils are suspended in his palace. The veils make that which is kept secret honoured, and to those who honour it, the veils are lifted up; but as for those who mock at the veils, they are driven away from even approaching them. Because then we "turn unto Christ, the veil is taken away." [8]

6. They bring forward then their cavillings, [9] and say, "You allow that Matthew is an Evangelist." We answer: Yes indeed, with a godly confession, and a heart devout, in neither having any doubt at all, we answer plainly, Matthew is an Evangelist. "Do you believe him?" they say. Who will not answer, I do? How clear an assent doth that your godly murmur convey! So, brethren, you believe it in all assurance; you have no cause to blush for it. I am speaking to you, who was once deceived, when as in my early boyhood I chose to bring to the divine Scriptures a subtlety of criticising before the godly temper of one who was seeking truth: by my irregular [10] life I shut the gate of my Lord against myself: when I should have knocked for it to be opened, I went on so as to make it more closely shut, for I dared to search in pride for that which none but the humble can discover. How much more blessed now are you, with what sure confidence do you learn, and in what safety, who are still young ones in the nest of faith, and receive the spiritual food; whereas I, wretch that I was, as thinking myself fit to fly, left the nest, and fell down before I flew: but the Lord of mercy raised me up, that I might not be trodden down to death by passers by, and put me in the nest again; for those same things then troubled me, which now in quiet security I am

---

[1] *Populariter agere.*   [2] Gen. xxii. 18.   [3] *Singularitate.*
[4] *Periti.*   [5] 1 Cor. i. 27, 28.

[6] Col. ii. 6, 7.   [7] Col. ii. 3.   [8] 2 Cor. iii. 16.
[9] *Calumnias.*   [10] *Perversis moribus.*

proposing and explaining to you in the Name of the Lord.

7. As then I had begun to say, thus do they cavil. "Matthew," say they, "is an Evangelist, and you believe him?" Immediately that we acknowledge him to be an Evangelist, we necessarily believe him. Attend then to the generations of Christ, which Matthew has set down. "The book of the generation of Jesus Christ, the Son of David, the son of Abraham." [1] How the Son of David, and the Son of Abraham? He could not be shown to be so, but by the succession of generations; for certain it is that when the Lord was born of the Virgin Mary, neither Abraham nor David was in this world, and dost thou say that the same man is both the Son of David, and the Son of Abraham? Let us, as it were, say to Matthew, Prove thy word, for I am waiting for the succession of the generations of Christ. "Abraham begat Isaac; and Isaac begat Jacob; and Jacob begat Judas and his brethren; and Judas begat Phares and Zara of Thamar; and Phares begat Esrom; and Esrom begat Aram; and Aram begat Aminadab; and Aminadab begat Naasson; and Naasson begat Salmon; and Salmon begat Booz of Rachab; and Booz begat Obed of Ruth; and Obed begat Jesse; and Jesse begat David the king." [2] Now observe how from this point the genealogy is brought down from David to Christ, who is called the Son of Abraham, and the Son of David. "And David begat Solomon, of her that had been the wife of Urias; and Solomon begat Roboam; and Roboam begat Abia; and Abia begat Asa; and Asa begat Josaphat; and Josaphat begat Joram; and Joram begat Ozias; and Ozias begat Joatham; and Joatham begat Achaz; and Achaz begat Ezekias; and Ezekias begat Manasses; and Manasses begat Amon; and Amon begat Josias; and Josias begat Jechonias and his brethren, about the time they were carried away to Babylon; and after the carrying away into Babylon, Jechonias begat Salathiel; and Salathiel begat Zorobabel; and Zorobabel begat Abiud; and Abiud begat Eliakim; and Eliakim begat Azor; and Azor begat Sadoc; and Sadoc begat Achim; and Achim begat Eliud; and Eliud begat Eleazar; and Eleazar begat Matthan; and Matthan begat Jacob; and Jacob begat Joseph the husband of Mary, of whom was born Jesus, who is called Christ." Thus then by the order and succession of fathers and forefathers, Christ is found to be the Son of David, and the Son of Abraham.

8. Now upon this thus faithfully narrated, the first cavil they bring is, that the same Matthew goes on to say, "All the generations from Abraham to David are fourteen generations; and from David until the carrying away into Babylon are fourteen generations; and from the carrying away into Babylon unto Christ are fourteen generations." Then in order to tell us how Christ was born of the Virgin Mary, he went on and said, "Now the birth of Jesus Christ was on this wise;" [3] for by the line of the generations he had showed why Christ is called the Son of David, and the Son of Abraham. But now it needed to be shown how He was born and appeared among men: and so there follows immediately that narrative, by means of which we believe that our Lord Jesus Christ was not only born of the everlasting God, coeternal with Him who begat Him before all times, before all creation, by whom all things were made; but was also now born from the Holy Ghost, of the Virgin Mary, which we confess equally with the other; for you remember and know (for I am speaking to Catholics, to my brethren), that this is our faith, that this we profess and confess; for this faith thousands of martyrs have been slain in all the world.

9. This also which follows they like to laugh at, whose wish it is to destroy the authority of the Evangelical books, that they may show as it were that we have without any good reason believed what is said, "When as His mother Mary was espoused to Joseph, before they came together, she was found with Child of the Holy Ghost. Then Joseph her husband being a just man, and not willing to make her a public example, was minded to put her away privily;" [4] for because he knew that she was not with child by him, he thought that she was so to say [5] necessarily an adulteress. "Being a just man," as the Scripture saith, "and not willing to make her a public example," (that is, to divulge the matter, for so it is in many copies), "he was minded to put her away privily." The husband indeed was in trouble, but as being a just man he deals not severely; for so great justice is ascribed to this man, as that he neither wished to keep an adulterous wife, nor could bring himself [6] to punish and expose her. "He was minded to put her away privily," because he was not only unwilling to punish, but even to betray her; and mark his genuine justice; for he did not wish to spare her, because he had a desire to keep her; for many spare their adulterous wives through a carnal love, choosing to keep them even though adulterous, that they may enjoy them through a carnal desire. But this just man has no wish to keep her, and so does not love in any carnal sort; and yet he does not wish to punish her; and so in his mercy he spares her. How truly just a man is this! He would neither keep an adulteress, lest he should seem to spare her be-

---

[1] Matt. i. 1.　　　[2] Matt. i. 2–6.

[3] Matt. i. 7–18.　　[4] Matt. i. 19.　　[5] *Velut.*
[6] *Auderet.*

cause of an impure affection, and yet he would not punish or betray her. Deservedly indeed was he chosen for the witness of his wife's virginity: and so he who was in trouble through human infirmity, was assured by Divine authority.

10. For the Evangelist goes on to say, "While he thought on these things, behold, the angel of the Lord appeared unto him in sleep, saying, Joseph, fear not to take unto thee Mary thy wife; for That which is conceived in her is of the Holy Ghost.[1] And she shall bring forth a Son, and thou shalt call His name Jesus." Why Jesus? "for He shall save His people from their sins."[2] It is well known then, that "Jesus" in the Hebrew tongue is in Latin interpreted "Saviour," which we see from this very explanation of the name; for as if it had been asked, "Why Jesus?" he subjoined immediately as explaining the reason of the word, "for He shall save His people from their sins." This then we religiously believe, this most firmly hold fast, that Christ was born by the Holy Ghost of the Virgin Mary.

11. What then do our adversaries say? "If," says one, "I shall discover a lie, surely you will not then believe it all; and such I have discovered." Let us see: I will reckon up the generations; for by their slanderous cavillings they invite and bring us to this. Yes, if we live religiously, if we believe Christ, if we do not desire to fly out of the nest before the time, they only bring us to this — to the knowledge of mysteries. Mark then, holy brethren,[3] the usefulness of heretics; their usefulness, that is, in respect of the designs of God, who makes a good use even of those that are bad; whereas, as regards themselves, the fruit of their own designs is rendered to them, and not that good which God brings out of them. Just as in the case of Judas; what great good did he! By the Lord's Passion all nations are saved; but that the Lord might suffer, Judas betrayed Him. God then both delivers the nations by the Passion of His Son, and punishes Judas for his own wickedness. For the mysteries which lie hid in Scripture, no one who is content with the simplicity of the faith would curiously sift them, and therefore as no one would sift them, no one would discover them but for cavillers who force us. For when heretics cavil, the little ones are disturbed; when disturbed, they make search, and their search is, so to say, a beating of the head at the mother's breasts, that they may yield as much milk as is sufficient for these little ones. They search then, because they are troubled; but they who know and have learnt these things, because they have investigated them, and God

hath opened to their knocking, they in their turn open to those who are in trouble. And so it happens that heretics serve usefully for the discovery of the truth, whilst they cavil to seduce men into error. For with less carefulness would truth be sought out, if it had not lying adversaries; "For there must be also heresies among you," and as though we should enquire the cause, he immediately subjoined, "that they which are approved may be made manifest among you."[4]

12. What then is it that they say? "See; Matthew enumerates the generations, and says, that "from Abraham to David are fourteen generations, and from David until the carrying away into Babylon are fourteen generations, and from the carrying away into Babylon unto Christ are fourteen generations." Now three times fourteen make forty-two; yet they number them, and find them forty-one generations, and immediately they bring up their cavilling and their insulting mockery, and say, "What means it, when in the Gospel it is said that there are three times fourteen generations, yet when they are numbered all together, they are found to be not forty-two, but forty-one?" Doubtless there is a great mystery[5] here: and glad are we, and we give thanks unto the Lord, that by the occasion of cavillers we have discovered something which gives us in the discovery the more pleasure, in proportion to its obscurity when it was the object of search; for, as I have said before, we are exhibiting a spectacle to your minds. From Abraham then to David are fourteen generations: after that, the enumeration begins with Solomon, for David begat Solomon; the enumeration, I say, begins with Solomon, and reaches to Jechonias, during whose life the carrying away into Babylon took place; and so are there other fourteen generations, by reckoning in Solomon at the head of the second division, and Jechonias also, with whom that enumeration closes to fill up the number fourteen; and the third division begins with this same Jechonias.

13. Give attention, holy brethren, to this circumstance, at once mysterious and pleasant; for I confess to you the feeling[6] of my own heart, whereby I believe that when I have brought it forth, and you have got taste of it, you will give the same report of it. Attend then. In the third division, beginning from this Jechonias unto the Lord Jesus Christ, are found fourteen generations; for this Jechonias is reckoned twice, as the last of the former, and the first of the following division. "But why is Jechonias," one may say, "reckoned twice?" Nothing took place of old among the people of Israel, which was not a mysterious figure of things to come:

---

[1] Matt. i. 20.   [2] Matt. i. 21.   [3] *Sanctitas vestra.*   [4] 1 Cor. xi. 19.   [5] *Sacramentum.*   [6] *Gustatum.*

and indeed it is not without good reason that Jechonias is reckoned twice, because if there be a boundary between two fields, be it a stone, or any dividing wall, both he who is on the one side measures up to that same wall, and he who is on the other takes the beginning of his measurement again from the same. But why this was not done in the first connecting link of the divisions, when we number from Abraham to David fourteen generations, and begin to reckon the fourteen others, not from David over again, but from Solomon, a reason must be given which contains an important mystery.[1] Attend then. The carrying away into Babylon took place when Jechonias was appointed king in the room of his deceased father. The kingdom was taken from him, and another appointed in his room; still the carrying away unto the Gentiles took place during the lifetime of Jechonias, for no fault of Jechonias is mentioned for which he was deprived of the kingdom; but the sins rather of those who succeeded him are marked out. So then there follows the Captivity and the passing away into Babylon; and the wicked do not go alone, but the saints also go with them: for in that Captivity were the prophets Ezekiel and Daniel, and the Three Children who were cast into the flames, and so made famous. They all went according to the prophecy of the prophet Jeremiah.

14. Remember then, that Jechonias, rejected without any fault of his, ceased to reign, and passed over unto the Gentiles, when the carrying away unto Babylon took place. Now observe the figure hereby manifested beforehand, of things to come in the Lord Jesus Christ. For the Jews would not that our Lord Jesus Christ should reign over them, yet found they no fault in Him. He was rejected in His own person, and in that of His servants also, and so they passed over unto the Gentiles as into Babylon in a figure. For this also did Jeremiah prophesy, that the Lord commanded them to go into Babylon: and whatever other prophets told the people not to go into Babylon, them he reproved as false prophets.[2] Let those who read the Scriptures, remember this as we do; and let those who do not, give us credit. Jeremiah then on the part of God threatened those who would not go into Babylon, whereas to them who should go he promised rest there, and a sort of happiness in the cultivation of their vines, and planting of their gardens, and the abundance of their fruits. How then does the people of Israel, not now in figure but in verity, pass over unto Babylon? Whence came the Apostles? Were they not of the nation of the Jews? Whence came Paul himself? for he saith, "I also am an

Israelite, of the seed of Abraham, of the tribe of Benjamin."[3] Many of the Jews then believed in the Lord; from them were the Apostles chosen; of them were the more than five hundred brethren, to whom it was vouchsafed[4] to see the Lord after His resurrection;[5] of them were the hundred and twenty in the house,[6] when the Holy Ghost came down. But what saith the Apostle in the Acts of the Apostles, when the Jews refused the word of truth? "We were sent unto you, but seeing ye have rejected the word of God, lo! we turn unto the Gentiles."[7] The true passing over then into Babylon, which was then prefigured in the time of Jeremiah, took place in the spiritual dispensation of the time of the Lord's Incarnation. But what saith Jeremiah of these Babylonians, to those who were passing over to them? "For in their peace shall be your peace."[8] When Israel then passed over also into Babylon by Christ and the Apostles, that is, when the Gospel came unto the Gentiles, what saith the Apostle, as though by the mouth of Jeremiah of old? "I exhort therefore, that, first of all, supplications, prayers, intercessions, and giving of thanks be made for all men. For kings, and for all that are in authority; that we may lead a quiet and peaceable life in all godliness and honesty."[9] For they were not yet Christian kings, yet he prayed for them. Israel then praying in Babylon hath been heard; the prayers of the Church have been heard, and the kings have become Christian, and you see now fulfilled what was then spoken in figure; "In their peace shall be your peace," for they have received the peace of Christ, and have left off to persecute Christians, that now in the secure quiet of peace, the Churches might be built up, and peoples planted in the garden[10] of God, and that all nations might bring forth fruit in faith, and hope, and love, which is in Christ.

15. The carrying away into Babylon took place of old by Jechonias, who was not permitted to reign in the nation of the Jews, as a type of Christ, whom the Jews would not have reign over them. Israel passed over unto the Gentiles, that is, the preachers of the Gospel passed over unto the people of the Gentiles. What marvel then, that Jechonias is reckoned twice? for if he were a figure of Christ passing over from the Jews unto the Gentiles, consider only what Christ is between the Jews and Gentiles. Is He not that Corner-stone? In a corner-stone you see the end of one wall, and the beginning of another; up to that stone you measure one wall, and another from it; therefore the corner-stone which connects both walls is reckoned twice.

---

[1] Sacramentum.   [2] Jer. xxvii.

[3] Rom. xi. 1.   [4] Meruerunt.
[5] 1 Cor. xv. 6.   [6] Acts i. 15.   [7] Acts xiii. 46.
[8] Jer. xxix. 7.   [9] 1 Tim. ii. 1, 2.   [10] Agricultura.

Jechonias then as prefiguring the Lord was, as it were, a type of the corner-stone ; and as Jechonias was not permitted to reign over the Jews, but they went unto Babylon, so Christ, " the stone which the builders rejected, is made the head of the corner," [1] that the Gospel might reach unto the Gentiles. Hesitate not then to reckon the head of the corner twice, and you have at once the number written : and so there are fourteen in each of the three divisions, yet altogether the generations are not forty-two, but forty-one ; for as when the order of the stones runs in a straight line, they are all reckoned but once, but when there is a deviation from the straight line to make an angle, that stone at which the deviation begins must be reckoned twice, because it belongs at once to that line which is finished at it, and to that other line which begins from it ; so as long as the order of the generations continued in the Jewish people, it made no angle in the regular division of fourteen ; but when the line was turned that the people might pass over into Babylon, a sort of angle as it were was made at Jechonias, so that it was necessary to reckon him twice, as the type of that adorable Corner-stone.

16. They have another cavil. "The generations of Christ," say they, "are numbered through Joseph, and not through Mary." Attend awhile, holy brethren. "It ought not to be," they say, "through Joseph." And why not? Was not Joseph the husband of Mary? "No," they say. Who says so? For the Scripture saith by the authority of the Angel that he was her husband. "Fear not to take unto thee Mary thy wife, for That which is conceived in her is of the Holy Ghost." [2] Again, he was commanded to name the Child, though He was not born of his seed ; "She shall bring forth a Son, and thou shalt call His name Jesus." [3] Now the Scripture is intent on showing, that He was not born of Joseph's seed, when he is told in his trouble as to her being with child, "He is of the Holy Ghost ; " and yet his paternal authority is not taken from him, forasmuch as he is commanded to name the Child ; and again the Virgin Mary herself, who was well aware that it was not by him that she conceived Christ, yet calls him the father of Christ.

17. Consider when this was. When the Lord Jesus, as to His Human Nature, was twelve years old [4] (for as to His Divine Nature He is before all times, and without time), He tarried behind them in the temple, and disputed with the elders, and they wondered at His doctrine ; and His parents who were returning from Jerusalem sought Him among their company, among those, that is, who were journeying with them, and when they found Him not, they returned in trouble to Jerusalem, and found Him disputing in the temple with the elders, when He was, as I said, twelve years old. But what wonder? The Word of God is never silent, though it is not always heard. He is found then in the temple, and His mother saith to Him, "Why hast Thou thus dealt with us? Thy father and I have sought Thee sorrowing ; " and He said, "Wist ye not that I must be about My Father's service?" [5] This He said for that the Son of God was in the temple of God, for that temple was not Joseph's, but God's. See, says some one, "He did not allow that He was the Son of Joseph." Wait, brethren, with a little patience, because of the press of time, that it may be long enough for what I have to say. When Mary had said, "Thy father and I have sought Thee sorrowing," He answered, "Wist ye not that I must be about My Father's service?" for He would not be their Son in such a sense, as not to be understood to be also the Son of God. For the Son of God He was — ever the Son of God — Creator even of themselves who spake to Him ; but the Son of Man in time ; born of a Virgin without the operation of her husband, yet the Son of both parents. Whence prove we this? Already have we proved it by the words of Mary, "Thy father and I have sought Thee sorrowing."

18. Now in the first place for the instruction of the women, our sisters, such saintly modesty of the Virgin Mary must not be passed over, brethren. She had given birth to Christ — the Angel had come to her, and said, "Behold, thou shalt conceive in thy womb, and bring forth a Son, and shalt call His name Jesus. [6] He shall be great, and shall be called the Son of the Highest." [7] She [8] had been thought worthy to give birth to the Son of the Highest, yet was she most humble ; nor did she put herself before her husband, even in the order of naming him, so as to say, "I and Thy father," but she saith, "Thy father and I." She regarded not the high honour [9] of her womb, but the order of wedlock did she regard, for Christ the humble would not have taught His mother to be proud. "Thy father and I have sought Thee sorrowing." Thy father and I, she saith, "for the husband is the head of the woman." [10] How much less then ought other women to be proud ! for Mary herself also is called a woman, not from the loss of virginity, but by a form of expression peculiar to her country ; for of the Lord Jesus the Apostle also said, "made of a woman," [11] yet there is no interruption hence to the order and connection of our Creed [12] wherein we confess "that He was born of the Holy Ghost and the Virgin Mary." For as a vir-

[1] Ps. cxviii. 22.   [2] Matt. i. 20.   [3] Matt. i. 21.
[4] Luke ii. 42.
[5] Luke ii. 48, 49.   [6] Luke i. 31.   [7] Luke i. 32.
[8] *Meruerat.*   [9] *Dignitatem.*   [10] Ephes. v. 23.
[11] Gal. iv. 4.   [12] *Fidei.*

gin she conceived Him, as a virgin brought Him forth, and a virgin she continued ; but all females they called " women," [1] by a peculiarity of the Hebrew tongue.   Hear a most plain example of this.   The first woman whom God made, having taken her out of the side of a man, was called a woman before she " knew " her husband, which we are told was not till after they went out of Paradise, for the Scripture saith, " He made her a woman." [2]

19. The answer then of the Lord Jesus Christ, " I must be about My Father's service," does not in such sense declare God to be His Father, as to deny that Joseph was His father also ; And whence prove we this ?   By the Scripture, which saith on this wise, " And He said unto them, Wist ye not that I must be about My Father's service ; but they understood not what He spake to them : and when He went down with them, He came to Nazareth, and was subject to them." [3] It did not say, " He was subject to His mother," or was " subject to her," but " He was subject to them."   To whom was He subject? was it not to His parents?   It was to both His parents that He was subject, by the same condescension by which He was the Son of Man.   A little way back women received their precepts.   Now let children receive theirs — to obey their parents, and to be subject to them.   The world was subject unto Christ, and Christ was subject to His parents.

20. You see then, brethren, that He did not say, " I must needs be about My Father's service," in any such sense as that we should understand Him thereby to have said, " You are not My parents."   They were His parents in time, God was His Father eternally.   They were the parents of the Son of Man — " He," the Father of His Word, and Wisdom, and Power, by whom He made all things.   But if all things were made by that Wisdom, " which reacheth from one end to another mightily, and sweetly ordereth all things," [4] then were they also made by the Son of God to whom He Himself as Son of Man was afterwards to be subject ; and the Apostle says that He is the Son of David, " who was made of the seed of David according to the flesh." [5]   But yet the Lord Himself proposes a question to the Jews, which the Apostle solves in these very words ; for when he said, " who was made of the seed of David," he added, " according to the flesh," that it might be understood that He is not the Son of David according to His Divinity, but that the Son of God is David's Lord ; for thus in another place, when He is setting forth the [6] privileges of the

Jewish people, the Apostle saith, " Whose are the fathers, of whom as concerning the flesh Christ came, Who is over all, God blessed for ever." [7]   As, " according to the flesh," He is David's Son ; but as being " God over all, blessed for ever," He is David's Lord.   The Lord then saith to the Jews, " Whose Son say ye that Christ is ? "   They answered, " The Son of David." [8]   For this they knew, as they had learnt it easily from the preaching of the Prophets ; and in truth, He was of the seed of David, " but according to the flesh," by the Virgin Mary, who was espoused to Joseph.   When they answered then that Christ was David's Son, Jesus said to them, " How then doth David in spirit call Him Lord, saying, The Lord said unto my Lord, Sit Thou on My right hand, till I put Thine enemies under Thy feet.[9]   If David then in spirit call Him Lord, how is He his Son ? " [10] And the Jews could not answer Him.   So we have it in the Gospel.   He did not deny that He was David's Son, so that they could not understand that He was also David's Lord.   For they acknowledged in Christ that which He became in time, but they did not understand in Him what He was in all eternity.   Wherefore wishing to teach them His Divinity, He proposed a question touching His Humanity ; as though He would say, " You know that Christ is David's Son, answer Me, how He is also David's Lord ? " And that they might not say, " He is not David's Lord," He introduced the testimony of David himself.   And what doth he say?   He saith indeed the truth.   For you find God in the Psalms saying to David, " Of the fruit of thy body will I set upon thy seat." [11]   Here then He is the Son of David.   But how is He the Lord of David, who is David's Son?   " The Lord said unto my Lord, Sit Thou on My right hand." [9] Can you wonder that David's Son is his Lord, when you see that Mary was the mother of her Lord?   He is David's Lord then as being God. David's Lord, as being Lord of all ; and David's Son, as being the Son of Man.   At once Lord and Son.   David's Lord, " who, being in the form of God, thought it not robbery to be equal with God ; " [12] and David's Son, in that " He emptied Himself, taking the form of a servant." [13]

21. Joseph then was not the less His father, because he knew not the mother of our Lord, as though concupiscence and not conjugal affection constitutes the marriage bond.[14]   Attend, holy brethren ; Christ's Apostle was some time after this to say in the Church, " It remaineth that they that have wives be as though they had none." [15]   And we know many of our brethren

---

[1] אִשָּׁה *femina mulier omnis ætatis et conditionis, sive nupta est, sive non est.*   Gesenius, *Lex. Heb., vide exempla,* especially Gen. xxiv. 5 and Isa. iv. 1.   *Vid.* Serm. lii. 10.
[2] Gen. ii. 22.   [3] Luke ii. 49, 50, 51.   [4] Wisd. viii. 1.
[5] Rom. i. 3.   [6] *Commendaret.*

[7] Rom. ix. 5.   [8] Matt. xxii. 42.
[9] Ps. cx. 1.   [10] Matt. xxii. 43, 44, 45.
[11] Ps. cxxxii. 11.   [12] Phil. ii. 6.   [13] Phil. ii. 7.
[14] *Uxorem.*   [15] 1 Cor. vii. 29.

bringing forth fruit through grace, who for the Name of Christ practise an entire restraint by mutual consent, who yet suffer no restraint of true conjugal affection. Yea, the more the former is repressed, the more is the other strengthened and confirmed. Are they then not married people who thus live, not requiring from each other any carnal gratification, or exacting the satisfaction [1] of any bodily desire? And yet the wife is subject to the husband, because it is fitting that she should be, and so much the more in subjection is she, in proportion to her greater chastity; and the husband for his part loveth his wife truly, as it is written, "In honour and sanctification," [2] as a coheir of grace : as "Christ," saith the Apostle, "loved the Church." [3] If then this be a union, and a marriage; if it be not the less a marriage because nothing of that kind passes between them, which even with unmarried persons may take place, but then unlawfully; (O that all could live so, but many have not the power!) let them at least not separate those who have the power, and deny that the man is a husband or the woman a wife, because there is no fleshly intercourse, but only the union of hearts between them.

22. Hence, my brethren, understand the sense of Scripture concerning those our ancient fathers, whose sole design in their marriage was to have children by their wives. For those even who, according to the custom of their time and nation, had a plurality of wives, lived in such chastity with them, as not to approach their bed, but for the cause I have mentioned, thus treating them indeed with honour. But he who exceeds the limits which this rule prescribes for the fulfilment of this end of marriage, acts contrary to the very contract [4] by which he took his wife. The contract is read, read in the presence of all the attesting witnesses; and an express clause is there that they marry "for the procreation of children;" and this is called the marriage contract. [5] If it was not for this that wives were given and taken to wife, what father could without blushing give up his daughter to the lust of any man? But now, that the parents may not blush, and that they may give their daughters in honourable marriage, not to shame, [6] the contract is read out. And what is read from it? — the clause, "for the sake of the procreation of children." And when this is heard, the brow of the parent is cleared up and calmed. Let us consider again the feelings [7] of the husband who takes his wife. The husband himself would blush to receive her with any other view, if the father would blush with any other view to give her. Nevertheless, if they cannot contain (as I have said on other

occasions), let them require what is due, and let them not go to any others than those from whom it is due. Let both the woman and the man seek relief for their infirmity in themselves. Let not the husband go to any other woman, nor the woman to any other man, for from this adultery gets its name, as though it were "a going to another." [8] And if they exceed the bounds of the marriage contract, let them not at least exceed those of conjugal fidelity. Is it not a sin in married persons to exact from one another more than this design of the "procreation of children" renders necessary? It is doubtless a sin, though a venial one. The Apostle saith, "But I speak this of allowance," [9] when he was treating the matter thus. "Defraud ye not one the other, except it be with consent for a time, that ye may give yourselves to fasting and prayer; and come together again, that Satan tempt you not for your incontinency." [10] What does this mean? That you do not impose upon yourselves any thing beyond your strength, that you do not by your mutual continence fall into adultery. "That Satan tempt you not for your incontinency." And that he might not seem to enjoin what he only allowed (for it is one thing to give precepts to strength of virtue, and another to make allowance to infirmity), he immediately subjoined; "But this I speak of allowance, not of commandment. For I would that all men were even as I myself." As though he would say, I do not command you to do this; but I pardon you if you do.

23. So then, my brethren, give heed. Those famous men who marry wives only for the procreation of children, such as we read the Patriarchs to have been, and know it, by many proofs, by the clear and unequivocal testimony of the sacred books; whoever, I say, they are who marry wives for this purpose only, if the means could be given them of having children without intercourse with their wives, would they not with joy unspeakable embrace so great a blessing? would they not with great delight accept it? For there are two carnal operations by which mankind is preserved, to both of which the wise and holy descend as matter of duty, but the unwise rush headlong into them through lust; and these are very different things. Now what are these two things by which mankind is preserved? The first which is confined to ourselves and relates to taking nourishment (which cannot of course be taken without some gratification of the flesh), is eating and drinking; if you do not this you will die. By this one support then of eating and drinking does the race of man subsist, by a [11] law of its nature. But by this men are only supported as far as themselves are concerned; for they do

---

[1] *Debitum.*   [2] 1 Thess. iv. 4.   [3] Ephes. v. 25.
[4] *Tabulas.*   [5] *Tabulæ matrimoniales.*
[6] *Ut sint soceri non lenones.*   [7] *Frontem.*

[8] *Adulterium quasi ad alterum.*
[9] 1 Cor. vii. 6.   [10] 1 Cor. vii. 5.   [11] *Modo.*

not provide for any succession by eating and drinking, but by marrying wives. For so is the race of man preserved; first, by the means of life; but because whatever care they exercise they cannot of course live for ever, there is a second provision made, that those who are newly born may replace those who die. For the race of man is, as it is written, like the leaves on a tree, or an olive, that is, or a laurel, or some tree of this sort, which is never without foliage, yet whose leaves are not always the same.[1] For, as it is written, "it shooteth forth some, and casteth others," because those which sprout afresh replace the others as they fall, for the tree is ever casting its leaves, yet is ever clothed with leaves. So also the race of man feels not the loss of those who die day by day, because of the supply of those who are newly born; and thus the whole race of mankind is according to its own laws sustained, and as leaves are ever seen on the trees, so is the earth seen to be full of men. Whereas if they were only to die, and no fresh ones be born, the earth would be stripped of all its inhabitants, as certain trees are of all their leaves.

24. Seeing then that the human race subsists in such sort, as that those two supports, of which enough has now been said, are necessary to it, the wise, and understanding, and the faithful man descends to both as matter of duty, and does not fall into them through lust. But how many are there who rush greedily to their eating and drinking, and make their whole life to consist in them, as if they were the very reason for living. For whereas men really eat to live, they think that they live to eat. These will every wise man condemn, and holy Scripture especially, all gluttons, drunkards, gormandizers, "whose god is their belly."[2] Nothing but the lust of the flesh, and not the need of refreshment, carries them to the table. These then fall upon their meat and drink. But they who descend to them from the duty of maintaining life, do not live to eat, but eat to live. Accordingly, if the offer were made to these wise and temperate persons that they should live without food or drink, with what great joy would they embrace the boon! that now they might not even be forced to descend to that into which it had never been their custom to fall, but that they might be lifted up always in the Lord, and no necessity of repairing the wastings of their body might make them lay aside their fixed attention towards Him. How think ye that the holy Elias received the cruse of water, and the cake of bread, to satisfy him for forty days?[3] With great joy no doubt, because he eat and drank to live, and not to serve his lust. But try to bring this about, if you could, for a man who, like the beast in his stall, places

his whole blessedness and happiness in the table. He would hate your boon, and thrust it from him, and look upon it as a punishment. And so in that other duty of marriage, sensual men seek for wives only to satisfy their sensuality, and therefore at length are scarce contented even with their wives. And oh! I would that if they cannot or will not cure their sensuality, they would not suffer it to go beyond that limit which conjugal duty prescribes, I mean even that which is granted to infirmity. Nevertheless, if you were to say to such a man, "why do you marry?" he would answer perhaps for very shame, "for the sake of children." But if any one in whom he could have unhesitating credit were to say to him, "God is able to give, and yea, and will give you children without your having any intercourse with your wife;" he would assuredly be driven to confess that it was not for the sake of children that he was seeking for a wife. Let him then acknowledge his infirmity, and so receive that which he pretended to receive only as matter of duty.

25. It was thus those holy men of former times, those men of God sought and wished for children. For this one end — the procreation of children, was their intercourse and union with their wives. It is for this reason that they were allowed to have a plurality of wives. For if immoderateness in these desires could be well-pleasing to God, it would have been as much allowed at that time for one woman to have many husbands, as one husband many wives. Why then had all chaste women no more than one husband, but one man had many wives, except that for one man to have many wives is a means to the multiplication of a family, whereas a woman would not give birth to more children, how many soever more husbands she might have. Wherefore, brethren, if our fathers' union and intercourse with their wives, was for no other end but the procreation of children, it had been great matter of joy to them, if they could have had children without that intercourse, since for the sake of having them they descended to that intercourse only through duty, and did not rush into it through lust. So then was Joseph not a father because he had gotten a son without any lust of the flesh? God forbid that Christian chastity should entertain a thought, which even Jewish chastity entertained not! Love your wives then, but love them chastely. In your intercourse with them keep yourselves within the bounds necessary for the procreation of children. And inasmuch as you cannot otherwise have them, descend to it with regret. For this necessity is the punishment of that Adam from whom we are sprung. Let us not make a pride of our punishment. It is his punishment who because he was made mortal by sin, was condemned[4] to bring forth only a mortal

1 Ecclus. xiv. 18.   2 Phil. iii. 19.
3 1 Kings xix. 6.
                         4 Meruit.

posterity. This punishment God has not withdrawn, that man might remember from what state he is called away, and to what state he is called, and might seek for that union, in which there can be no corruption.

26. Among that people then, because it was necessary that there should be an abundant increase until Christ came, by the multiplication of that people in whom were to be prefigured all that was to be prefigured as instruction for the Church, it was a duty to marry wives, by means of whom that people in whom the Church should be foreshown might increase. But when the King of all nations Himself was born, then began the honour of virginity with the mother of the Lord, who had the privilege [1] of bearing a Son without any loss of her virgin purity. As that then was a true marriage, and a marriage free from all corruption, so why should not the husband chastely receive what his wife had chastely brought forth? For as she was a wife in chastity, so was he in chastity a husband; and as she was in chastity a mother, so was he in chastity a father. Whoso then says that he ought not to be called father, because he did not beget his Son in the usual [2] way, looks rather to the satisfaction of passion in the procreation of children, and not the natural feeling of affection. What others desire to fulfil in the flesh, he in a more excellent way fulfilled in the spirit. For thus they who adopt children, beget them by the heart in greater chastity, whom they cannot by the flesh beget. Consider, brethren, the laws of adoption; how a man comes to be the son of another, of whom he was not born, so that the choice of the person who adopts has more right in him than the nature of him who begets him has. Not only then must Joseph be a father, but in a most excellent manner a father. For men beget children of women also who are not their wives, and they are called natural children, and the children of the lawful marriage are placed above them. Now as to the manner of their birth, they are born alike; why then are the latter set above the other, but because the love of a wife, of whom children are born, is the more pure. The union of the sexes is not regarded in this case, for this is the same in both women. Where has the wife the pre-eminence but in her fidelity, her wedded love, her more true and pure affection? If then a man could have children by his wife without this intercourse, should he not have so much the more joy thereby, in proportion to the greater chastity of her whom he loves the most?

27. See too by this how it may happen, that one man may have not two sons only, but two fathers also. For by the mention of adoption, it may occur to your thoughts that so it may be. For it is said; A man can have two sons, but two fathers he cannot have. But the truth is, it is found that he can have two fathers also, if one have begotten him of his body, and another adopted him in love. If one man then can have two fathers, Joseph could have two fathers also; might be begotten by one, and adopted by another. And if this be so, what do their cavillings mean, who insist that Matthew has followed one set of generations, and Luke another? And in fact we find that so it is, for Matthew has given Jacob as the father of Joseph, and Luke Heli. Now it is true it might seem, as if one and the same man, whose son Joseph was, had two names. But inasmuch as the grandfathers, and all the other progenitors which they enumerate, are different, and in the very number of the generations, the one has more, and the other fewer, Joseph is plainly shown hereby to have had two fathers. Now having disposed of the cavil of this question, forasmuch as clear reason has shown that it may happen that he who has begotten a child may be one father, and he who has adopted him another: supposing two fathers, it is nothing strange if the grandfathers and the great grandfathers, and the rest in the line upwards which are enumerated, should be different as coming from different fathers.

28. And let not the law of adoption seem to you to be foreign to our Scriptures, and that, as if it were recognised [3] only in the practice of human laws, it cannot fall in with the authority of the divine books. For it is a thing established of old time, and frequently heard of in the Ecclesiastical books [4] — that not only the natural way of birth, but the free choice [5] of the will also, should give birth to a child. For women, if they had no children of their own, used to adopt children born of their husbands by their handmaids, and even oblige their husbands to give them children in this way; as Sarah, Rachel, and Leah.[6] And in doing this the husbands did not commit adultery, in that they obeyed their wives in that matter which had regard to conjugal duty, according to what the Apostle saith: "The wife hath not power of her own body, but the husband; and likewise also the husband hath not power of his own body, but the wife." [7] Moses too, who was born of a Hebrew mother and was exposed, was adopted by Pharaoh's daughter.[8] There were not then indeed the same forms of law as now, but the choice of the will was taken for the rule of law, as the Apostle saith also in another place, "The Gentiles which have not the law, do by nature the things contained in the law." [9] But if it is permitted to women to make

---

[1] *Meruit.*   [2] *Sic.*

[3] *Animadversum.*   [4] The Scriptures.   [5] *Gratia.*
[6] Gen. xvi. 2 and xxx.   [7] 1 Cor. vii. 4.   [8] Exod. ii. 10.
[9] Rom. ii. 14.

those their children to whom they have not given birth, why should it not be allowed men to do so too with those whom they have not begotten of their body, but of the love of adoption. For we read that the patriarch Jacob even, the father of so many children, made his grandchildren, the sons of Joseph, his own children, in these words : "These too shall be mine, and they shall receive the land with their brethren, and those which thou begettest after them shall be thine."[1] But it will be said, perhaps, that this word "adoption" is not found in the Holy Scriptures. As though it were of any importance by what name it is called, when the thing itself is there — for a woman to have a child to whom she has not given birth, or a man a child whom he has not begotten. And he may, without any opposition from me, refuse to call Joseph adopted, provided he grant that he may have been the son of a man of whose body he was not born. Yet the Apostle Paul does continually use this very word "adoption," and[2] that to express a great mystery. For though Scripture testifies that our Lord Jesus Christ is the only Son of God, it says, that the brethren and coheirs whom He hath vouchsafed to have, are made so by a kind of adoption through Divine grace. "When," saith he, "the fulness of time was come, God sent forth His Son, made of a woman, made under the law, to redeem them that were under the law, that we might receive the adoption of sons."[3] And in another place : "We groan within ourselves, waiting for the adoption, to wit, the redemption of our body."[4] And again, when he was speaking of the Jews, "I could wish that myself were accursed from Christ for my brethren, my kinsmen according to the flesh; who are Israelites, to whom pertaineth the adoption, and the glory, and the testaments, and the giving of the law; whose are the fathers, and of whom as concerning the flesh Christ came, Who is over all, God blessed for ever."[5] Where he shows, that the word "adoption," or at least the thing which it signifies, was of ancient use among the Jews, just as was the Testament and the giving of the Law, which he mentions together with it.

29. Added to this; there is another way peculiar to the Jews, in which a man might be the son of another of whom he was not born according to the flesh. For kinsmen used to marry the wives of their next of kin, who died without children, to raise up seed to him that was deceased.[6] So then he who was thus born was both his son of whom he was born, and his in whose line of succession he was born. All this has been said, lest any one, thinking it impossible for two fathers to be mentioned properly for one man,

should imagine that either of the Evangelists who have narrated the generations of the Lord are to be, by an impious calumny, charged so to say with a lie ; especially when we may see that we are warned against this by their very words. For Matthew, who is understood to make mention of that father of whom Joseph was born, enumerates the generations thus : "This one begat the other," so as to come to what he says at the end, "Jacob begat Joseph." But Luke — because he cannot properly be said to be begotten who is made a child either by adoption, or who is born in the succession of the deceased, of her who was his wife — did not say, "Heli begat Joseph," or "Joseph whom Heli begat," but "Who was the son of Heli," whether by adoption, or as being born of the next of kin in the succession of one deceased.[7]

30. Enough has now been said to show that the question, why the generations are reckoned through Joseph and not through Mary, ought not to perplex us ; for as she was a mother without carnal desire, so was he a father without any carnal intercourse. Let then the generations ascend and descend through him. And let us not exclude him from being a father, because he had none of this carnal desire. Let his greater purity only confirm rather his relationship of father, lest the holy Mary herself reproach us. For she would not put her own name before her husband ; but said, "Thy father and I have sought Thee sorrowing."[8] Let not then these perverse murmurers do that which the chaste spouse of Joseph did not. Let us reckon then through Joseph, because as he is in chastity a husband, so is he in chastity a father. And let us put the man before the woman, according to the order of nature and the law of God. For if we should cast him aside and leave her, he would say, and say with reason, "Why have you excluded me? Why do not the generations ascend and descend through me?" Shall we say to him, "Because thou didst not beget Him by the operation of thy flesh?" Surely he will answer, "And is it by the operation of the flesh that the Virgin bare Him? What the Holy

---

[1] Gen. xlviii. 5, 6.   [2] *In magno sacramento.*
[3] Gal. iv. 4, 5.   [4] Rom. viii. 23.   [5] Rom. ix. 3, etc.
[6] Deut. xxv. 5; Matt. xxii. 24.

[7] Of these two solutions, (1) that Joseph may have been the adopted son of Eli, or (2) the son of his wife, who, as the next of kin, married Jacob after his decease, the latter is stated by Africanus (Eus. *H. E.* i. 7) to be traditional and derived from kinsmen of the Lord's. It may be the more likely, in that the name of the wife of Matthan and Malchi (Estha) is also handed down, through whom, though half-blood, Heli and Jacob became, at all events, near kinsmen. Else in the Jerus. Talm. (ap. Lightfoot *ad loc.*) St. Mary is called the daughter of Heli, and her genealogy might be counted as his, to whom, according to the above statement, she was nearly related. The name Heli, indeed, is no way connected (as some have thought) with Eliachim, *i.q.* Joachim; but this name of the father of the Blessed Virgin is said by St. Augustin to have been taken by the Manichees from apocryphal books (comp. *Faust.* xxiii. 9), so neither is it any hindrance. St. Augustin remarks (*Quæst. Ev.* ii. 5) that any one possible explanation is sufficient, and yet that it would be rash to say that there were only the two that he had named. He treats it then as "madness" to ground any charge against the evangelists thereon; inasmuch as it can be solved, faith is indifferent to the "how," since God has not explained it.
[8] Luke ii. 48.

Spirit wrought, He wrought for both." "Being a just man,"[1] saith the Gospel. The husband then was just and the woman just. The Holy Spirit reposing in the justice of them both, gave to both a Son. In that sex which is by nature fitted to give birth, He wrought that birth which was for the husband also. And therefore doth the Angel bid them both give the Child a name, and hereby is the authority of both parents established. For when Zacharias was yet dumb, the mother gave a name to her new-born son. And when they who were present "made signs to his father what he would have him called, he took a writing-table and wrote"[2] the name which she had already pronounced. So to Mary too the Angel saith, "Behold, thou shalt conceive a Son, and shalt call His name Jesus."[3] And to Joseph also he saith, "Joseph, thou son of David, fear not to take unto thee Mary thy wife; for That which is conceived in her is of the Holy Ghost. And she shall bring forth a Son, and thou shalt call His name Jesus, for He shall save His people from their sins."[4] Again it is said, "And she brought forth a Son to him,"[5] by which he is established to be a father, not in the flesh indeed, but in love. Let us then acknowledge him to be a father, as in truth he is. For most advisedly and most wisely do the Evangelists reckon through him, whether Matthew in descending from Abraham down to Christ, or Luke in ascending from Christ through Abraham up to God. The one reckons in a descending, the other in an ascending order; but both through Joseph. And why? Because he is the father. How the father? Because he is the more undeniably[6] a father in proportion as he is more chastely so. He was thought, it is true, to be the father of our Lord Jesus Christ in another way: that is, as other parents are according to a fleshly birth, and not through the fruitfulness of a wholly spiritual love. For Luke said, "Who was supposed to be the father of Jesus."[7] Why supposed? Because men's thoughts and suppositions were directed to what is usually the case with men. The Lord then was not of the seed of Joseph, though He was supposed to be; yet nevertheless the Son of the Virgin Mary, who is also the Son of God, was born to Joseph, the fruit of his piety and love.

31. But why does St. Matthew reckon in a descending, and Luke in an ascending order? I pray you give attentive ear to what the Lord may help me to say on this matter; with your minds now at ease, and disembarrassed from all the perplexity of these cavillings. Matthew de-scends through his generations, to signify our Lord Jesus Christ descending to bear our sins, that in the seed of Abraham all nations might be blessed. Wherefore, he does not begin with Adam, for from him is the whole race of mankind. Nor with Noe, because from his family again, after the flood, descended the whole human race. Nor could the man Christ Jesus, as descended from Adam, from whom all men are descended, bear[8] upon the fulfilment of prophecy; nor, again, as descended from Noe, from whom also all men are descended; but only as descended from Abraham, who at that time was chosen, that all nations should be blessed in his seed, when the earth was now full of nations. But Luke reckons in an ascending order, and does not begin to enumerate the generations from the beginning of the account of our Lord's birth, but from that place, where he relates His Baptism by John. Now, as in the incarnation of the Lord, the sins of the human race are taken upon Him to be borne, so in the consecration of His Baptism are they taken on Him to be expiated. Accordingly, St. Matthew, as representing His descent to bear our sins, enumerates the generations in a descending order; but the other, as representing the expia-tion of sins, not His own, of course, but our sins, enumerates them in an ascending order. Again, St. Matthew descends through Solomon, by whose mother David sinned; St. Luke ascends through Nathan,[9] another son of the same David, through whom he was purged from his sin.[10] For we read, that Nathan was sent to him to reprove him, and that he might through repentance be healed. Both Evangelists meet together in David; the one in descending, the other in ascending; and from David to Abraham, or from Abraham to David, there is no difference in any one generation. And so Christ, both the Son of David and the Son of Abraham, comes up to God. For to God must we be brought back, when renewed in Baptism, from the aboli-tion of sins.

32. Now, in the generations which Matthew enumerates, the predominant[11] number is forty. For it is a custom of the Holy Scriptures, not to reckon what is over and above certain round numbers.[12] For thus it is said to be four hun-dred years, after which the people of Israel went out of Egypt, whereas it is four hundred and thirty.[13] And so here the one generation, which exceeds the fortieth, does not take away the predominance of that number. Now this num-ber signifies the life wherein we labour in this world, as long as we are absent from the Lord,

---

[1] Matt. i. 19.   [2] Luke i. 63.
[3] Luke i. 31.   [4] Matt. i. 20, 21.
[5] Luke ii 7.   There seems to be no trace of any such reading anywhere else.
[6] *Firmius.*   [7] Luke iii. 23.

[8] *Pertinere.*
[9] St. Augustin corrects this confusion of Nathan, the son of David, with the prophet Nathan, in his *Retract.* B. ii. c. 16.
[10] 2 Sam. xii. 1.   [11] *Eminet.*
[12] *Certos articulos numerorum.*   [13] Gen. xv. 13; Acts vii. 6.

during which the temporal dispensation of the preaching of the truth is necessary. For the number ten, by which the perfection of blessedness is signified, multiplied four times, because of the fourfold divisions of the seasons, and the fourfold divisions of the world, will make the number forty.[1] Wherefore Moses and Elias, and the Mediator Himself, our Lord Jesus Christ, fasted forty days, because in the time of this life, continence from the enticements of the body is necessary. Forty years also did the people wander in the wilderness.[2] Forty days the waters of the flood lasted.[3] Forty days after His resurrection did the Lord converse with the disciples, persuading them of the reality[4] of His risen body,[5] whereby He showed that in this life, " wherein we are absent from the Lord "[6] (which the number forty, as has been already said, mystically figures), we have need to celebrate the memory of the Lord's Body, which we do in the Church, till He come.[7] Forasmuch, then, as our Lord descended to this life, and " the Word was made flesh, that He might be delivered for our sins, and rise again for our justification,"[8] Matthew followed the number forty; so that the one generation which there exceeds that number, either does not hinder its predominance — just as those thirty years do not hinder the perfect number of four hundred — or that it even has this further meaning, that the Lord Himself, by the addition of whom the forty-one is made up, so descended to this life to bear our sins, as yet, by a peculiar and especial excellency, whereby He is in such sense man, as to be also God, to be found to be excepted from this life. For of Him only is that said, which never has been or shall be able to be said of any holy man, however perfected in wisdom and righteousness, " The Word was made Flesh."[9]

33. But Luke, who ascends up through the generations from the baptism of the Lord, makes up the number seventy-seven, beginning to ascend from our Lord Jesus Christ Himself through Joseph, and coming through Adam up to God. And that is, because by this number is signified the abolition of all sins, which takes place in Baptism. Not that the Lord Himself had any thing to be forgiven Him in baptism, but that by His humility He set forth its usefulness to us. And though that was only the baptism of John, yet there appeared in it to outward sense the Trinity of the Father, the Son, and the Holy Ghost ; and hereby was consecrated the Baptism of Christ Himself, whereby Christians were to be baptized. The Father in the voice which came from heaven, the Son in the person of the Mediator Himself, the Holy Ghost in the dove.[10]

34. Now, why the number seventy-seven should contain all sins which are remitted in Baptism, there occurs this probable reason, for that the number ten implies the perfection of all righteousness, and blessedness, when the creature denoted by seven[11] cleaves to the Trinity of the Creator ; whence also the Decalogue of the Law was consecrated in ten precepts. Now the "transgression" of the number ten is signified by the number eleven ; and sin is known to be transgression, when a man, in seeking something "more," exceeds the rule of justice. And hence the Apostle calls avarice "the root of all evils."[12] And to the soul which goes a-whoring from God, it is said, in the Person of the same Lord, " Thou wast in hope, if thou didst depart from Me, that thou wouldest have something more." Because the sinner then has in his transgression, that is, in his sin, regard to himself alone — in that he wishes to gratify himself by some private good of his own (whence they are blamed " who seek their own, not the things which are Jesus Christ's ; "[13] and charity is commended, " which seeketh not her own "[14]) ; therefore, this number eleven, by which transgression is signified, is multiplied, not ten times, but seven, and so makes up seventy-seven. For transgression looks[15] not to the Trinity of the Creator, but to the creature, that is, to the man himself, which creature the number seven denotes. Three, because of the soul, in which there[16] is a kind of image of the Trinity of the Creator (for it is in the soul that man has been made after the image of God) ; and four, because of the body. For the four elements[17] of which the body is made up are known by all. And if any one know them not, he may easily remember, that this body of the world, in which our bodies move along, has, so to say, four principal parts, which even Holy Scripture is constantly making mention of, East, and West, and North, and South. And forasmuch as sins are committed either by the mind, as in the will only, or by the works of the body also, and so visibly ; therefore the Prophet Amos continually introduces[18] God as threatening, and saying, " For three and four iniquities I will not turn away," that is, " I will not dissemble My wrath."[19] Three, because of the nature of the soul ; four, because of that of the body ; of which two, man consists.

35. So, then, seven times eleven, that is, as has been explained, the transgression of righteousness, which has regard only to the sinner himself, make up the number seventy-seven, in which it is signified, that all sins which are re-

[1] Deut. ix. 9; 1 Kings xix. 8; Matt. iv. 2.
[2] Num. xxxii. 13.   [3] Gen. vii. 4.   [4] *Veritatem.*
[5] Acts i. 3.   [6] 2 Cor. v. 6.   [7] 1 Cor. xi. 26.
[8] Rom. iv. 25.   [9] John i. 14.   [10] Matt. iii. 16.

[11] *Septenaria.*   [12] 1 Tim. vi. 10.
[13] Phil. ii. 21.   [14] 1 Cor. xiii. 5.   [15] *Pertinet.*
[16] *Vid.* Aug. *De Trin.* ix. 4, 5; xiv. c. 6–16, etc.; lib. xv. 40–43.
Ep. 169 (Ben.), 6.   *De Civ. Dei,* xi. 26 and 28.   *Conf.* xiii. 12 (11)
and note in Oxf. ed.
[17] *Primordia.*   [18] *Commemorat.*   [19] Amos i. 2, Sept.

mitted in Baptism are contained. And hence it is that Luke ascends up through seventy-seven generations unto God, as showing that man is reconciled unto God by the abolition of all sin. Hence the Lord Himself saith to Peter, who asked Him how oft he ought to forgive a brother, " I say not unto thee [1] seven times, but until seventy times and seven." [2]   Now, whatever else can be drawn out of these recesses and treasures of God's mysteries by those who are more diligent and more worthy than I, receive. Yet have I spoken according to my poor ability, as the Lord hath aided and given me power, and as I best could, considering also the little time I had. If any one of you be capable of anything further, let him knock at Him from whom I too receive what I am able to receive and speak. But, above all things, remember this ; not to be disturbed by the Scriptures, which you do not yet understand, nor be puffed up by what you do understand ; but what you do not understand, with submission [3] wait for, and what you do understand, hold fast with charity.

SERMON II.

[LII. BEN.]

OF THE WORDS OF ST. MATTHEW'S GOSPEL, CHAP. III. 13, " THEN JESUS COMETH FROM GALILEE TO THE JORDAN UNTO JOHN, TO BE BAPTIZED OF HIM." CONCERNING THE TRINITY.

1. THE lesson of the Gospel hath set before me a subject whereof to speak to you, beloved, as though by the Lord's command, and by His command in very deed. For my heart hath waited for an order as it were from Him to speak, that I might understand thereby that it is His wish that I should speak on that which He hath also willed should be read to you. Let your zeal and devotion then give ear, and before the Lord our God Himself aid ye my labour. For we behold and see as it were in a divine spectacle exhibited to us, the notice of our God in Trinity, conveyed [4] to us at the river Jordan. For when Jesus came and was baptized by John, the Lord by His servant (and this He did for an example of humility ; for He showeth that in this same humility is righteousness fulfilled, when as John said to Him, " I have need to be baptized of Thee, and comest Thou to me ? " [5] He answered, " Suffer it to be so now, that all righteousness may be fulfilled " [6]), when He was baptized then, the heavens were opened, and the Holy Spirit came down upon Him in the form of a Dove : and then a Voice from on high followed, " This is My beloved Son, in whom I am well pleased." [7] Here then we have the Trinity in a certain sort distin-guished. The Father in the Voice, — the Son in the Man, — the Holy Spirit in the Dove. It was only needful just to mention this, for most obvious is it to see. For the notice of the Trinity is here conveyed to us plainly and without leaving room for doubt or hesitation. For the Lord Christ Himself coming in the form of a servant to John, is doubtlessly the Son : for it cannot be said that it was the Father, or the Holy Spirit. " Jesus," it is said, " cometh ; " [8] that is, the Son of God. And who hath any doubt about the Dove ? or who saith, " What is the Dove ? " when the Gospel itself most plainly testifieth, " The Holy Spirit descended upon Him in the form of a dove." [9]   And in like manner as to that voice there can be no doubt that it is the Father's, when He saith, " Thou art My Son." [10]   Thus then we have the Trinity distinguished.

2. And if we consider the places, I say with confidence (though in fear I say it), that the Trinity is in a manner separable. When Jesus came to the river, He came from one place to another ; and the Dove descended from heaven to earth, from one place to another ; and the very Voice of the Father sounded neither from the earth, nor from the water, but from heaven ; these three are as it were separated in places, in offices, and in works. But one may say to me, " Show the Trinity to be inseparable rather. Remember that thou who art speaking art a Catholic, and to Catholics art thou speaking." For thus doth our faith teach, that is, the true, the right Catholic faith, gathered not by the opinion of private [11] judgment, but by the witness of the Scriptures, [12] not subject to the fluctuations of heretical rashness, but grounded on Apostolic truth : this we know, this we believe. This though we see it not with our eyes, nor as yet with the heart, so long as we are being purified by faith, yet by this faith we most rightly and most strenuously maintain — That the Father, Son, and Holy Spirit are a Trinity inseparable ; One God, not three Gods. But yet so One God, as that the Son is not the Father, and the Father is not the Son, and the Holy Spirit is neither the Father nor the Son, but the Spirit of the Father and of the Son. This ineffable Divinity, abiding ever in itself, making all things new, creating, creating anew, sending, recalling, judging, delivering, this Trinity, I say, we know to be at once ineffable and inseparable.

3. What am I then about? See : The Son came separately in the Man ; The Holy Spirit descended separately from heaven in the form of a Dove ; The Voice of the Father sounded separately out of heaven, " This is My Son." Where then is this inseparable Trinity ? God

---

[1] *Vide* Sermon xxxiii. (Bened. lxxxiii.).   [2] Matt. xviii. 22.
[3] *Honore.*   [4] *Commendari.*
[5] Matt. iii. 14.   [6] Matt. iii. 15.   [7] Matt. iii. 17.

[8] Matt. iii. 13.   [9] Matt. iii. 16.
[10] Matt. iii. 17 ; Mark i. 11.   [11] *Præsumptionis.*
[12] *Lectionis.*

hath made you attentive by my words. Pray for me, and open, as it were, the folds [1] of your hearts, and may He grant you wherewith your hearts so opened may be filled. Share my travail with me. For you see what I have undertaken; and not only what, but who I am that have undertaken it, and of what I wish to speak, and where and what my position is, even in that "body which is corruptible, and presseth down the soul, and the earthly habitation weigheth down the mind that museth upon many things." [2] When therefore I abstract my mind from the multiplicity of things, and gather it up into the One God, the inseparable Trinity, that so I may see something which I may say of it, think ye that in this "body which presseth down the soul," I shall be able to say (in order that I may speak to you something worthy of the subject), "O Lord, I have lifted up my soul unto Thee." [3] May He assist me, may He lift it up with me. For I am too infirm in respect of Him, and He in respect of me is too mighty.

4. Now this is a question which is often proposed by the most earnest brethren, and often has place in the conversation of the lovers of God's word; for this much knocking is wont to be made unto God, while men say, "Doeth the Father anything which the Son doeth not? or doeth the Son anything which the Father doeth not?" Let us first speak of the Father and the Son. And when He to Whom we say, "Be Thou my helper, leave me not," [4] shall have given good success to this essay of ours, then shall we understand how that the Holy Spirit also is in no way separated from the operation of the Father and the Son. As concerning the Father and the Son, then, brethren, give ear. Doeth the Father anything without the Son? We answer, No. Do you doubt it? For what doeth He without Him "by Whom all things were made? All things," saith the Scripture, "were made by Him." [5] And to inculcate it fully [6] upon the slow, and hard, and disputatious, it added, "And without Him was not anything made."

5. What then, brethren? "All things were made by Him." We understand then by this that the whole creation which was made by the Son, the Father made by His Word — God, by His Power and Wisdom. Shall we then say, "All things" indeed when they were created, "were made by Him," but now the Father doeth not all things by Him? God forbid! Be such a thought as this far from the hearts of believers; be it driven away from the mind of the devout; from the understanding of the godly! It cannot be that He created by Him, and doth not govern by Him. God forbid that what existeth should be governed without Him, when by Him it was made, that it might have existence! But let us show by the testimony of the same Scripture that not only were all things created and made by Him as we have quoted from the Gospel, "All things were made by Him, and without Him was nothing made," but that the things which were made are also governed and ordered by Him. You acknowledge Christ then to be the Power and Wisdom of God; acknowledge too what is said of Wisdom, "She reacheth from one end to another mightily, and sweetly doth she order all things." [7] Let us not then doubt that by Him are all things ruled, by whom all things were made. So then the Father doeth nothing without the Son, nor the Son without the Father.

6. But so a difficulty meets us, which we have undertaken to solve in the Name of the Lord, and by His will. If the Father doeth nothing without the Son, nor the Son without the Father, will it not follow, that we must say that the Father also was born of the Virgin Mary, the Father suffered under Pontius Pilate, the Father rose again and ascended into heaven? God forbid! We do not say this, because we do not believe it. "For I believed, therefore have I spoken: we also believe, and therefore speak." [8] What [9] is in the Creed? That the Son was born of a Virgin, not the Father. What is in the Creed? That the Son suffered under Pontius Pilate and was dead, not the Father. Have we forgotten, that some, misunderstanding this, are called "Patripassians," who say that the Father Himself was born of a woman, that the Father Himself suffered, that the Father is the same as the Son, that they are two names, not two things? And these hath the Church Catholic separated from the communion of saints, that they might not deceive any, but dispute in separation from her.

7. Let us then recall the difficulty of the question to your minds. One may say to me, "You have said that the Father doeth nothing without the Son, nor the Son without the Father, and testimonies you have adduced out of the Scriptures, that the Father doeth nothing without the Son, for that 'all things were made by Him;' and again, that that which was made is not governed without the Son, for that He is the Wisdom of the Father, 'reaching from one end to another mightily, and sweetly ordering all things.' And now you tell me, as if contradicting yourself, that the Son was born of a Virgin, and not the Father; the Son suffered, not the Father; the Son rose again, not the Father. See then, here I see the Son doing something

---

[1] *Aperientes sinum.* [2] Wisd. ix. 15. [3] Ps. lxxxvi. 4.
[4] Ps. xxvi. 9, Sept. (xxvii. English version).
[5] John i. 3. [6] *Satiate.*

[7] Wisd. viii. 1. [8] Ps. cxvi. 10.
[9] *Fide,* i.e. *Symb. fidei* (Ben.).

which the Father doeth not. Do you therefore either confess that the Son doeth something without the Father, or else that the Father also was born and suffered, and died and rose again. Say one or the other of these, choose one of the two." No : I will choose neither, I will say neither the one nor the other. I will neither say the Son doeth anything without the Father, for I should lie were I to say so ; nor that the Father was born, suffered, and died, and rose again, for I should equally lie were I to say this. " How then, saith he, will you disentangle yourself from these straits ? "

8. The proposing of the question pleases you. May God grant His aid, that its solution may please you too. See, what I am asking Him, that He would free both me and you. For in one faith do we stand in the Name of Christ ; and in one house do we live under one Lord, and in one body are we members under One Head, and by One Spirit are we quickened.[1] That the Lord then may set both me who speak, and you who hear, free from the straits of this most perplexing question, I say as follows : The Son indeed and not the Father was born of the Virgin Mary ; but this very birth of the Son, not of the Father, was the work both of the Father and the Son. The Father indeed suffered not, but the Son, yet the suffering of the Son was the work of the Father and the Son. The Father did not rise again, but the Son, yet the resurrection of the Son was the work of the Father and the Son. We seem then to be already quit of this question, but peradventure it is only by words of my own ; let us see whether it is not as well by words divine. It is my place then to prove by testimonies of the sacred books, that the birth, and passion, and resurrection of the Son were in such sort the works of the Father and the Son, that whereas it is the birth, and passion, and resurrection of the Son only, yet these three things which belong to the Son only, were wrought neither by the Father alone, nor by the Son alone, but by the Father and the Son. Let us prove each several point, you hear as judges ; the case has been already laid open ; now let the witnesses come forth. Let your judgment say to me, as is wont to be said to pleaders in a cause, " Establish what you promise." I will do so assuredly, with the Lord's assistance, and will cite the books of heavenly law. Ye have listened to me attentively while proposing the question, listen now with still more attention while I prove my point.

9. I must first teach you concerning the birth of Christ, how it is the work of the Father and the Son, though what the Father and the Son did work pertains only to the Son. I will quote

Paul ; one competently versed in the divine law. That Paul, I say, will I quote, who prescribes the laws of peace, not of litigation, for lawyers at this day also have a Paul who prescribes the laws of the courts,[2] not the Christian's laws. Let the holy Apostle show us then how the birth of the Son was the work of the Father. " But," saith he, " when the fulness of time was come, God sent forth His Son, made of a woman, made under the Law, to redeem them that were under the Law."[3] Thus have ye heard him, and because it is plain and express, have understood. See, the Father made the Son to be born of a Virgin. For " when the fulness of time was come, God sent His Son ; " the Father sent His Christ. How sent He Him? "made of a woman, made under the Law." The Father then made Him of a woman under the Law.

10. Doth this peradventure perplex you, that I said of a virgin, and Paul saith of a woman? Let not this perplex you ; let us not stop here, for I am not speaking to persons without instruction. The Scripture saith both, both " of a virgin," and " of a woman." Where saith it, " of a virgin? Behold, a virgin shall conceive, and bear a Son."[4] And " of a woman," as you have just heard ; here there is no contradiction. For the peculiarity of the Hebrew tongue gives[5] the name of " women " not to such as have lost their virgin estate, but to females generally. You have a plain passage in Genesis, when Eve herself was first made, " He made her a woman."[6] Scripture also in another place saith, that God ordered " the *women* " to be separated "which had not known man by lying with him."[7] This then ought now to be well established, and should not detain us, that so we may be able to explain, by the Lord's assistance, what will deservedly detain us.

11. We have then proved that the birth of the Son was the work of the Father ; now let us prove that it was the work of the Son also. Now what is the birth of the Son of the Virgin Mary? Surely it is His assumption of the form of a servant in the Virgin's womb. Is the birth of the Son ought else, but the taking of the form of a servant in the womb of the Virgin? Now hear how that this was the work of the Son also. " Who when He was in the form of God, thought it not robbery to be equal with God, but emptied Himself, taking upon Him the form of a servant."[8] " When the fulness of time was come, God sent forth His Son, made of a woman,"[9] who was " made [10] His Son of the seed of David according to the flesh."[11] In this then we see

[1] *Vegetamur.*

[2] *Litigatorum.*   [3] Gal. iv. 4, 5.   [4] Isa. vii. 14.
[5] *Vide* Serm. i. (li.) 18.   [6] Gen. ii. 22.
[7] Num. xxxi. 18; Judg. xxi. 11.
[8] Phil. ii 6, 7.   [9] Gal. iv. 4.
[10] *i e.* the term *made* belongs to His birth in the flesh, Who was begotten in eternity.
[11] Rom. i. 3.

that the birth of the Son was the work of the Father; but in that the Son Himself "emptied Himself, taking the form of a servant," we see that the birth of the Son was the work also of the Son Himself. This then has been proved; so let us pass on from this point, and receive ye with attention that which comes next in order.

12. Let us prove that the Passion also of the Son was the work of the Father and the Son. We may see[1] that the Passion of the Son is the work of the Father, since it is written, "Who spared not His own Son, but delivered Him up for us all;"[2] and that the Passion of the Son was His own work also, "Who loved me, and gave Himself for me."[3] The Father delivered up the Son, and the Son delivered up Himself. This Passion was wrought out for one, but by both. As therefore the birth, so the Passion, of Christ, was not the work of the Son without the Father, nor of the Father without the Son. The Father delivered up the Son, and the Son delivered up Himself. What did Judas in it, but his own sin? Let us then pass on from this point also, and come we to the resurrection.

13. Let us see the Son indeed, and not the Father, rising again, but both the Father and the Son working the resurrection of the Son. The resurrection of the Son is the work of the Father; for it is written, "Wherefore He exalted Him, and gave Him a name which is above every name."[4] The Father therefore raised the Son to life again, in exalting, and awakening Him from the dead. And did the Son also raise Himself? Assuredly He did. For He said of the temple, as the figure of His own body, "Destroy this temple, and in three days I will raise it again."[5] Lastly, as the laying down of life has reference to the Passion, so the taking it again has reference to the resurrection. Let us see then if the Son laid down His life indeed, and the Father restored His life to Him, and not He to Himself. For that the Father restored it is plain. For so saith the Psalm, "Raise Thou Me up, and I will requite them."[6] But why do ye wait for a proof from me that the Son also restored life to Himself? Let Him speak Himself; "I have power to lay down My life." I have not yet said what I promised. I have said, "to lay it down;" and you are crying out already, for you are flying past me. For well-instructed as ye are in the school of your heavenly teacher, as attentively listening to, and in pious affection rehearsing,[7] what is read, ye are not ignorant of what comes next. "I have power," saith He, "to lay down My life, and I have power to take it again. No man taketh it from Me, but I lay it down of Myself, and take it again."[8]

14. I have made good what I promised; I have established my propositions with, as I think, the strongest proofs and testimonies. Hold fast then what you have heard. I will recapitulate it briefly, and entrust it to be stored up in your minds as a thing, to my thinking, of the greatest usefulness. The Father was not born of the Virgin; yet this birth of the Son from the Virgin was the work both of the Father and the Son. The Father suffered not on the Cross; yet the Passion of the Son was the work both of Father and the Son. The Father rose not again from the dead; yet the resurrection of the Son was the work both of the Father and the Son. You see then a distinction of Persons, and an inseparableness of operation. Let us not say therefore that the Father doeth any thing without the Son, or the Son any thing without the Father. But perhaps you have a difficulty as to the miracles which Jesus did, lest peradventure He did some which the Father did not! Where then is that saying, "The Father who dwelleth in Me, He doeth the works?"[9] All that I have now said was plain; it needed to be barely mentioned; there was no necessity for much labour to make it understood, but only that care should be taken, that it might be brought to your remembrance.

15. I wish to say something further, and here I ask sincerely both for your more earnest attention, and your devotion to Godward. For none but bodies are held or contained in places suited to the nature[10] of bodies. The Divinity is beyond all such places: let no one seek for it as though it were in space. It is everywhere invisible and inseparably present; not in one part greater, and another smaller; but whole everywhere, and nowhere divided. Who can see? Who can comprehend this? Let us restrain ourselves: let us remember who we are, and of Whom we speak. Let this and that, or whatever appertains[11] to the nature of God, be with a pious faith embraced, with a holy respect entertained, and as far as is allowed us, as far as is possible for us, in an unspeakable sort understood. Let words be hushed: let the tongue be silent, let the heart be aroused, let the heart be lifted up thither. For it is not of such a nature as that it can ascend into the heart of man; but the heart of man must itself ascend to it. Let us consider the creatures ("for the invisible things of Him from the creation of the world are clearly seen, being understood by the things that are made"[12]), if haply in the things which God hath made, with which we have some familiarity of intercourse, we may find some resemblance, whereby we may prove that there are some three

1 *Faciat Pater passionem Filii.*
2 Rom. viii. 32. 3 Gal. ii. 20. 4 Phil. ii. 9.
5 John ii. 19. 6 Ps. xli. 10. 7 *Reddentes.*
8 John x. 18.

9 John xiv. 10. 10 *Corporalibus.*
11 *Quidquid est quod Deus est.*
12 Rom. i. 20.

things which may be exhibited [1] as three separably, yet whose operation is inseparable.

16. Come, brethren, give me your whole attention. But first of all consider what it is that I promise ; if haply I can find any resemblance in the creature, for the Creator is too high above us. And peradventure some one of us, whose mind the glare of truth hath, as it were, stricken with sparks of its brightness, can say those words, "I said in my ecstasy." — What saidst thou in thine ecstasy? — "I am cast away from the sight of Thine eyes." [2] For it seems to me as if he who said this had lifted up his soul unto God, and had been carried beyond himself, while they said daily unto him, "Where is thy God?" — had reached by a kind of spiritual contact to that unchangeable Light, and through the weakness [3] of his sight had been unable to endure it, and so had fallen back again into his own, as it were, sick and languid state, and had compared himself with that Light, and had felt that the eye of his mind could not yet be attempered to the light of God's wisdom. And because he had done this in ecstasy, hurried away from his bodily senses, and taken [4] up into God, when he was recalled in a manner from God to man, he said, "I said in my ecstasy." For I saw in ecstasy I know not what, which I could not long endure, and being restored to my mortal estate, [5] and the manifold thoughts of mortal things from the body which presseth down the soul, I said, what? "I am cast away from the sight of Thine eyes." Thou art far above, and I am far below. What then, brethren, shall we say of God? For if thou hast been able to comprehend what thou wouldest say, it is not God ; if thou hast been able to comprehend it, thou hast comprehended something else instead of God. If thou hast been able to comprehend Him as thou thinkest, by so thinking thou hast deceived thyself. This then is not God, if thou hast comprehended it ; but if it be God, thou hast not comprehended it. How therefore wouldest thou speak of that which thou canst not comprehend?

17. Let us see then, if haply we cannot find something in the creature whereby we may prove that some three things are exhibited [6] separately whose operation is yet inseparable. But whither shall we go? To the heaven, to dispute of the sun and moon and stars? To the earth, to dispute of shrubs, and trees, and animals which fill the earth? Or of the heaven and the earth itself, which contain all the things that are in heaven and earth? How long, O man, wilt thou roam over the creation? Return unto thyself, see, consider, examine thine own self. Thou art searching among the creatures for some three

things which are separately exhibited, whose operation is yet inseparable ; if then thou art searching for this among the creatures, search for it first in thine own self. For thou art not other than a creature. It is a resemblance thou art searching for. Wouldest thou search for it among the cattle? For of God it was thou wast speaking, when thou wast in search for this resemblance. Thou wast speaking of the Trinity of Majesty ineffable, and because thou didst fail in contemplating [7] the Divine Nature, and with becoming humility didst confess thine infirmity, thou didst come down to human nature ; there then pursue thine enquiry. Wilt thou make thy search among the cattle, in the sun, or the stars? What of these was made after the image and likeness of God? Thou mayest search in thine own self for something more familiar to thee, and more excellent than all these. For God made man after His own image and likeness. Search then in thine own self, if haply the image of the Trinity bear not some vestige of the Trinity. And what is this image? It is an image very different from its model ; yet different as it is, it is an image and a likeness notwithstanding, not indeed in the same way as the Son is the Image, being the Same Which the Father is. For an image is in one sort in a son, and in another in a mirror. There is great difference between them. Thine image in thy son is thine own self, for the son is by nature what thou art. In substance the same as thou, in person other than thou. Man then is not an image as the Only-begotten Son is, but made after a sort of image and likeness. Let him then search for something in himself, if so be he may find it, even for some three things which are exhibited [8] separately, whose operation is yet inseparable. I will search, and do ye search with me. I will not search in you, but do ye search in yourselves, and I in myself. Let us search in concert, and in concert discuss our common nature and substance.

18. See, O man, and consider whether what I am saying be true. Hast thou a body and flesh? I have, you say. For how am I in this place that I now occupy, and how do I move from place to place? How do I hear the words of one who is speaking, but by the ears of my body? How do I see the mouth of him who is speaking, but by the eyes of my body? It is plain then that thou hast a body, no need is there to trouble one's self about so plain a matter. Consider then another point, consider what it is that acts through this body. For thou hearest by means of the ear, but it is not the ear that hears. There is something else within which hears by means of the ear. Thou seest by means of the eye — examine this eye. What !

---

[1] *Proferantur.*　　　　[2] Ps. xxxi. 22, Sept.
[3] See Aug *Conf.* B. ix. ch. 23–26.　[4] *Subreptus.*
[5] *Membris.*　　　　　[6] *Demonstrari.*

[7] *Defecisti in divinis.*　　[8] *Pronuntientur.*

hast thou acknowledged the house, and paid no regard to him that inhabiteth it? Doth the eye see by itself? Is it not another that sees by means of the eye? I will not say, that the eye of a dead man, from whose body it is plain the inhabitant hath departed, sees not, but any man's eye who is only thinking of something else, sees not the form of the object that is before him. Look then into thine inner man. For there it is rather that the resemblance must be sought for of some three things which are exhibited separately, whose operation is yet inseparable. What then is in thy mind? Peradventure if I search, I find many things there, but there is something very nigh at hand, which is understood more easily. What then is in thy soul? Call it to mind, reflect upon it. For I do not require that credit should be given me in what I am about to say; if thou find it not in thyself, admit it not. Look inward then; but first let us see what had escaped me, whether man be not the image, not of the Son only, or of the Father only, but of the Father and the Son, and so consequently of course of the Holy Ghost also. The words in Genesis are, " Let Us make man after Our own image and likeness." [1] So then the Father doth not act without the Son, nor the Son without the Father. " Let Us make man after Our own image and likeness. Let us make," not, " I will make," or " Make thou," or " Let him make," but, " Let Us make after," not " thine image," or " mine," but, " after Our image."

19. I am asking, I am speaking remember of a distant [2] resemblance. So let no one say, See what he has compared to God! I have advertised you of this already, and by anticipation have both put you on your guard, and have guarded myself. The two are indeed very far removed from each other, as the lowest from the Highest, as the changeable from the Unchangeable, the created from the Creator, the human nature from the Divine. Lo! I apprise you of this at first, that no one may say ought against me, because there is so great a difference in the things whereof I am about to speak. Lest then while I am asking for your ears, ye should any of you be getting ready your teeth, remember I have undertaken merely to show, that there are some three things which are separately exhibited, whose operation is yet inseparable. How like or how unlike these things are to the Almighty Trinity is no concern of mine at present; but in the very creatures of the lowest order, and subject to change, we do find three things which may be separately exhibited, whose operation is yet inseparable. O carnal imagination! obstinate, unbelieving conscience! Why as con-

cerning that ineffable Majesty dost thou doubt as to that thing, which thou canst discover in thine own self? For I ask thee, O man, hast thou memory? If not, how hast thou retained what I have said? But perhaps thou hast forgotten already what I said but a little while ago. Yet these very words, " I said " — these two syllables, thou couldest not retain except by memory. For how shouldest thou know they were two, if as the second sounded, thou hadst forgotten the first? But why do I dwell longer on this? Why am I so urgent? Why do I so press conviction? For thou hast memory; it is plain. I am searching then for something else. Hast thou understanding? " I have," you will say. For hadst thou not memory, thou couldest not retain what I said; and hadst thou not understanding, thou couldest not comprehend what thou hast retained. Thou hast then this as well as the other. Thou recallest thine understanding unto that which thou dost retain within, and so thou seest it, and by seeing art fashioned into that state as to be said to know. But I am searching for a third thing. Memory thou hast, whereby to retain what is said; and understanding thou hast, whereby to understand what is retained; but as touching these two, I ask again of thee, Hast thou not with thy will retained and understood? Undoubtedly, with my will, you will say. So then thou hast will.

These are the three things which I promised I would bring home to your ears and minds. These three things are in thee, which thou canst number, but canst not separate. These three then, memory, understanding, and will — these three, I say, consider how they are separately exhibited,[3] yet is their operation inseparable.

20. The Lord will be my present help, and I see that He is present to help me; by your understanding what I say, I see that He is present to help me. For I perceive by these your voices how that you have understood me, and I surely trust that He will still assist us, that you may comprehend the whole. I promised to show you three things which are separately exhibited whose operation is yet inseparable. See then; I did not know what was in thy mind, and thou showedest me by saying, " Memory." This word, this sound, this expression came forth from thy mind to mine ears. For before that, thou hadst the silent idea of this memory, but thou didst not express it. It was in thee, but it had not yet come to me. But in order that that which was in thee might be passed on to me, thou didst express the very word, that is, " Memory." I heard it, I heard these three syllables in the word, " Memory." It is a noun, a word of three syllables, it sounded, and came

to my ear, and impressed[1] a certain idea on my mind. The sound has passed away, but the word whereby the idea was conveyed, and the idea itself, remains. But I ask, when thou didst pronounce this word, " Memory," thou seest certainly that it has reference to the memory only. For the other two things have their own proper names. For one is called " the understanding," and the other, " the will," not the " memory," but that one alone is called " memory." Nevertheless, whereby didst thou work in order to express this, in order to produce these three syllables? This word which has reference to the memory only, both memory was engaged in producing in thee, that thou mightest retain what thou saidst, and understanding, that thou mightest know what thou retainedst, and will, that thou mightest give expression to what thou knewest. Thanks be to the Lord our God! He hath helped us, both you and me. For I tell you the truth, beloved, that I undertook the examination and explanation of this subject with exceeding fear. For I was afraid lest haply I might gladden the spirit of the more enlarged in mind, and inflict on the slower capacities an afflictive weariness. But now I see both by the attention with which you have heard, and the quickness with which you have understood me, that you have not only caught what I have said, but that you have anticipated my words. Thanks be to the Lord!

21. See then, henceforth I speak in all security of that which you have already understood; I am inculcating no unknown lesson, but am only conveying to you by recapitulation what you have already received. Now, of these three things, one only has been yet named and expressed; " Memory " is the name of one only of those three, yet all the three concurred in producing the name of this single one of the three. The single word " memory " could not be expressed, but by the operation of the will, and the understanding, and the memory. The single word " understanding " could not be expressed, but by the operation of the memory, the will, and the understanding; and the single word " will " could not be expressed, but by the operation of the memory and the understanding and the will. What I promised, then, I think has been explained, that which I have pronounced separately, I conceived inseparably. The three together have produced each one of these, but yet this one which the three have produced has reference not to the three, but to one. The three together have produced the word " memory," but this word has reference to none but the memory only. The three together have produced the word " understanding," but it has

reference to none but the understanding only. The three together have produced the word " will," but it has reference to none but the will only. So the Trinity concurred in the formation of the Body of Christ, but it belongs to none but Christ only. The Trinity concurred in the formation of the Dove from heaven; but it belongs to none but the Holy Spirit only. The Trinity formed the Voice from heaven, but this Voice belongs to none but the Father only.

22. Let no one then say to me, no one with unfair cavils try to press upon my infirmity, saying, " Which then of these three, which you have shown to be in our mind or soul, which of them[2] answers to the Father, that is, so to say, to the likeness of the Father, which of them to that of the Son, and which of them to that of the Holy Ghost? " I cannot say — I cannot explain this. Let us leave somewhat to meditation and to silence. Enter into thine own self; separate thyself from all tumult. Look into thine inner self; see if thou have there some sweet retiring place of conscience, where there may be no noise, no disputation, no strife, or debatings; where there will be not a thought of dissensions, and obstinate contention. Be meek to hear the word, that so thou mayest understand. Perhaps thou mayest soon have to say, " Thou wilt make me hear of joy and gladness, and my bones shall rejoice;"[3] the bones, that is, which are *humbled*, not those that are lifted up.

23. It is enough, then, that I have shown that there are some three things which are exhibited separately, whose operation is yet inseparable. If thou hast discovered this in thine own self; if thou hast discovered it in man; if thou hast discovered it in a being[4] that walketh on the earth, and beareth about a frail " body, which weigheth down the soul;" believe that the Father, Son, and Holy Spirit may be exhibited separately, by certain visible symbols, by certain forms borrowed from the creatures, and still their operation be inseparable. This is enough. I do not say that " memory " is the Father, — the " understanding " the Son, — and " will " the Spirit; I do not say this; let men understand it how they will. I do not venture to say this. Let us reserve the greater truths for those who are capable of them: but, infirm as I am myself, I convey to the infirm only what is according to our powers. I do not say that these things are in any sort to be equalled with the Holy Trinity, to be squared after an analogy; that is, a kind of exact rule of comparison. This I do not say. But what do I say? See. I have discovered in thee three things, which are exhibited separately, whose operation is inseparable; and of these three, every single name is produced by the

---

[1] *Insinuavit.*

[2] *Pertinet.*
[3] Ps. l. 10, Sept. (li. 8, Englısh version).   [4] *Personâ.*

three together; yet does not this name belong to the three, but to some one of the three. Believe then in the Trinity, what thou canst not see, if in thyself thou hast heard, and seen, and retained it. For what is in thine own self thou canst know: but what is in Him who made thee, whatever it be, how canst thou know? And if thou shalt be ever able, thou art not able yet. And even when thou shalt be able, wilt thou be able so to know God, as He knoweth Himself? Let then this suffice you, beloved: I have said all I could; I have made good my promise as ye required. As to the rest which must be added, that your understanding may make advancement, this seek from the Lord.

SERMON III.

[LIII. BEN.]

ON THE WORDS OF THE GOSPEL, MATT. CHAP. V. 3 AND 8, "BLESSED ARE THE POOR IN SPIRIT:" ETC., BUT ESPECIALLY ON THAT, "BLESSED ARE THE PURE IN HEART: FOR THEY SHALL SEE GOD."

1. By the return of the commemoration of a holy virgin, who gave her testimony to Christ, and was found worthy[1] of a testimony from Christ, who was put to death openly, and crowned invisibly, I am reminded to speak to you, beloved, on that exhortation which the Lord hath just now uttered out of the Gospel,[2] assuring us that there are many sources of a blessed life, which there is not a man that does not wish for. There is not a man surely can be found, who does not wish to be blessed. But oh! if as men desire the reward, so they would not decline the work that leads to it! Who would not run with all alacrity, were it told him, "Thou shalt be blessed"? Let him then also give a glad and ready ear when it is said, "Blessed, if thou shalt do thus." Let not the contest be declined, if the reward be loved; and let the mind be enkindled to an eager execution of the work, by the setting forth of the reward. What we desire, and wish for, and seek, will be hereafter; but what we are ordered to do for the sake of that which will be hereafter, must be now. Begin now, then, to recall to mind the divine sayings, and the precepts and rewards of the Gospel. "Blessed are the poor in spirit, for theirs is the kingdom of heaven."[3] The kingdom of heaven shall be thine hereafter; be poor in spirit now. Wouldest thou that the kingdom of heaven should be thine hereafter? Look well to thyself whose thou art now. Be poor in spirit. You ask me, perhaps, "What is to be poor in spirit?" No one who is puffed up is poor in spirit; therefore he that is lowly is poor in spirit. The kingdom of heaven is exalted; but "he who humbleth himself shall be exalted."[4]

2. Mark what follows: "Blessed," saith He, "are the meek, for they shall inherit the earth."[5] Thou wishest to possess the earth now; take heed lest thou be possessed by it. If thou be meek, thou wilt possess it; if ungentle, thou wilt be possessed by it. And when thou hearest of the proposed reward, do not, in order that thou mayest possess the earth, unfold the lap of covetousness, whereby thou wouldest at present possess the earth, to the exclusion even of thy neighbour by whatever means; let no such imagination deceive thee. Then wilt thou truly possess the earth, when thou dost cleave to Him who made heaven and earth. For this is to be meek, not to resist thy God, that in that thou doest well He may be well-pleasing to thee, not thou to thyself; and in that thou sufferest ill justly, He may not be unpleasing to thee, but thou to thyself. For no small matter is it that thou shalt be well-pleasing to Him, when thou art displeased with thyself; whereas if thou art well-pleased with thine own self, thou wilt be displeasing to Him.

3. Attend to the third lesson, "Blessed are they that mourn, for they shall be comforted."[6] The work consisteth in mourning, the reward in consolation; for they who mourn in a carnal sort, what consolations have they? Miserable consolations, objects rather of fear. There the mourner is comforted by things which make him fear lest he have to mourn again. For instance, the death of a son causes the father sorrow, and the birth of a son joy. The one he has carried out to his burial, the other he has brought into the world; in the former is occasion of sadness, in the latter of fear: and so in neither is there consolation. That therefore will be the true consolation, wherein shall be given that which may not be lost, so that they may rejoice for their after consolation, who mourn that they are in[7] exile now.

4. Let us come to the fourth work and its reward, "Blessed are they that hunger and thirst after righteousness, for they shall be filled."[8] Dost thou desire to be filled? Whereby? If the flesh long for fulness, after digestion thou wilt suffer hunger again. So He saith, "Whosoever drinketh of this water shall thirst again."[9] If the remedy which is applied to a wound heal it, there is no more pain; but that which is applied against hunger, food that is, is so applied as to give relief only for a little while. For when the fulness is past, hunger returns. This remedy of fulness is applied day by day, yet the wound of weakness is not healed. Let us therefore "hunger and thirst after righteousness, that we may be

1 *Meruit.*
2 This portion of St. Matthew is the gospel during the whole octave of All Saints, as in our own Church on All Saints' Day; the corresponding portion of St. Luke is read in the Comm. Plur. Mart.
3 Matt. v. 3.

4 Luke xiv. 11 and xviii. 14.
5 Matt. v. 5 (4, Vulgate).　　6 Matt. v. 4 (5, Vulgate).
7 *Peregrinari.*　　8 Matt. v. 6.　　9 John iv. 13.

filled " with that righteousness after which we now hunger and thirst. For filled we shall be with that for which we hunger and thirst. Let our inner man then hunger and thirst, for it hath its own proper meat and drink. " I," saith He, "am the Bread which came down from heaven." [1] Here is the bread of the hungry ; long also for the drink of the thirsty, " For with Thee is the well of life." [2]

5. Mark what comes next : " Blessed are the merciful, for they shall obtain mercy." [3] Do this, and so shall it be done to thee ; deal so with others, that God may so deal with thee. For thou art at once in abundance and in want — in abundance of temporal things, in want of things eternal. The man whom thou hearest is a beggar, and thou art thyself God's beggar. Petition is made to thee, and thou makest thy petition. As thou hast dealt with thy petitioner, so shall God deal with His. Thou art at once full and empty ; fill the empty with thy fulness, that thy emptiness may be filled with the fulness of God.

6. Mark what comes next : " Blessed are the pure in heart, for they shall see God." [4] This is the end of our love ; an end whereby we are perfected, and not consumed. For there is an end of food, and an end of agarment ; of food when it is consumed by the eating ; of a garment when it is perfected in the weaving. Both the one and the other have an end ; but the one is an end of consumption, the other of perfection. Whatsoever we now do, whatsoever we now do well, whatsoever we now strive for, or are in laudable sort eager for, or blamelessly desire, when we come to the vision of God, we shall require no more. For what need he seek for, with whom God is present? or what shall suffice him, whom God sufficeth not? We wish to see God, we seek, we kindle with desire to see Him. Who doth not? But mark what is said : " Blessed are the pure in heart, for they shall see God." Provide thyself then with that whereby thou mayest see Him. For (to speak after the flesh) how with weak eyes desirest thou the rising of the sun? Let the eye be sound, and that light will be a rejoicing, if it be not sound, it will be but a torment. For it is not permitted with a heart impure to see that which is seen only by the pure heart. Thou wilt be repelled, driven back from it, and wilt not see it. For " blessed are the pure in heart, for they shall see God." How often already hath he enumerated the blessed, and the causes of their blessedness, and their works and recompenses, their merits and rewards ! But nowhere hath it been said, " They shall see God." " Blessed are the poor in spirit, for theirs is the kingdom of heaven." " Blessed are the meek, for they shall inherit the earth." " Blessed

are they that mourn, for they shall be comforted." " Blessed are they that hunger and thirst after righteousness, they shall be filled." " Blessed are the merciful, they shall obtain mercy." In none of these hath it been said, " They shall see God." When we come to the " pure in heart," there is the vision of God promised. And not without good cause ; for there, in the heart, are the eyes, by which God is seen. Speaking of these eyes, the Apostle Paul saith. " The eyes of your heart being enlightened." [5] At present then these eyes are enlightened, as is suitable to their infirmity, by faith ; hereafter as shall be suited to their strength, they shall be enlightened by sight. " For as long as we are in the body we are absent from the Lord ; For we walk by faith, not by sight." [6] Now as long as we are in this state of faith, what is said of us? " We see now through a glass darkly ; but then face to face." [7]

7. Let no thought be entertained here of a bodily face. For if enkindled by the desire of seeing God, thou hast made ready thy bodily face to see Him, thou wilt be looking also for such a face in God. But if now thy conceptions of God are at least so spiritual as not to imagine Him to be corporeal (of which [8] subject I treated yesterday at considerable length, if yet it was not in vain), if I have succeeded in breaking down in your heart, as in God's temple, that image of human form ; if the words in which the Apostle expresses his detestation of those, " who, professing themselves to be wise became fools, and changed the glory of the incorruptible God into an image made like unto corruptible man," [9] have entered deep into your minds, and taken possession of your inmost heart ; if ye do now detest and abhor such impiety, if ye keep clean for the Creator His own temple, if ye would that He should come and make His abode with you, " Think of the Lord with a good heart, and in simplicity of heart seek for Him." [10] Mark well who it is to whom ye say, if so be ye do say it, and say it in sincerity, " My heart said to Thee, I will seek Thy face." Let thine heart also say, and add, " Thy face, Lord, will I seek." [11] For so wilt thou seek it well, because thou seekest with thine heart. Scripture speaks of the " face of God, the arm of God, the hands of God, the feet of God, the seat of God," and His footstool ; but think not in all this of human members. If thou wouldest be a temple of truth, break down the idol of falsehood. The hand of God is His power. The face of God is the knowledge of God. The feet of God are His presence. The seat of God,

---

[1] John vi. 41.　　[2] Ps. xxxvi. 9.　　[3] Matt, v. 7.
[4] Matt. v. 8.

[5] Eph. i. 18.　　　　　　[6] 2 Cor. v. 6, 7.
[7] 1 Cor. xiii. 12.
[8] Probably the Sermon xxiii., on Ps. lxxiii. 23, *seu de visione Dei* (Ben.).
[9] Rom. i. 22, 23.　　　　[10] Wisd. i. 1.
[11] Ps. xxvi. 8, Sept. (xxvii. English version).

if thou art so minded, is thine own self. But perhaps thou wilt venture to deny that Christ is God! "Not so," you say. Dost thou grant this too, that "Christ is the power of God and the wisdom of God?"[1] "I grant it," you say. Hear then, "The soul of the righteous is the seat of wisdom."[2] "Yes." For where hath God His seat, but where He dwelleth? And where doth He dwell, but in His temple? "For the temple of God is holy, which temple ye are."[3] Take heed therefore how thou dost receive God. "God is a Spirit, and must be worshipped in spirit and in truth."[4] Let the ark of testimony enter now into thy heart, if thou art so minded, and let Dagon fall.[5] Now therefore give ear at once, and learn to long for God; learn to make ready that whereby thou mayest see God. "Blessed," saith He, "are the pure in heart, for they shall see God." Why dost thou make ready the eyes of the body? If He should be seen by them, that which should be so seen would be contained in space. But He who is wholly everywhere is not contained in space. Cleanse that whereby He may be seen.

8. Hear and understand, if haply through His help I shall be able to explain it; and may He help us to the understanding of all the above-named works and rewards, how suitable rewards are apportioned to their corresponding duties. For where is there anything said of a reward which does not suit, and harmonize with its work? Because the lowly seem as it were aliens from a kingdom, He saith, "Blessed are the poor in spirit, for theirs is the kingdom of heaven." Because meek men are easily despoiled of their land,[6] He saith, "Blessed are the meek, for they shall inherit the land."[7] Now the rest are plain at once; they are understood of themselves, and require no one to treat of them at length; they need only one to mention them. "Blessed are they that mourn." Now what mourner does not desire consolation? "They," saith He, "shall be comforted." "Blessed are they that hunger and thirst after righteousness." What hungry and thirsty man does not seek to be filled? "And they," saith He, "shall be filled." "Blessed are the merciful." What merciful man but wishes that a return should be rendered him by God of His own work, that it may be so done to him, as he doeth to the poor? "Blessed," saith He, "are the merciful, for they shall obtain mercy." How in each case hath every duty its appropriate reward: and nothing is introduced in the reward which doth not suit the precept! For the precept is, that thou be "poor in spirit;" the reward, that thou shalt have the "kingdom

of heaven." The precept is, that thou be "meek;" the reward, that thou shalt "possess the earth." The precept is, that thou "mourn;" the reward, that thou shalt be "comforted." The precept is, that thou "hunger and thirst after righteousness;" the reward, that thou shalt "be filled." The precept is, that thou be "merciful;" the reward, that thou shalt "obtain mercy." And so the precept is, that thou cleanse the heart; the reward, that thou shalt see God.

9. But do not so conceive of these precepts and rewards, as to think when thou dost hear, "Blessed are the pure in heart, for they shall see God," that the poor in spirit, or the meek, or they that mourn, or they who hunger and thirst after righteousness, or the merciful, will not see Him. Think not of those that are pure in heart, that they only will see Him, whilst the others will be excluded from the sight of Him. For all these several characters are the selfsame persons. They shall all see; but they shall not see in that they are poor in spirit, or meek, or in that they mourn, and hunger and thirst after righteousness, or are merciful, but in that they are pure in heart. Just as if bodily works were duly assigned to the several members of the body, and one were to say for example, Blessed are they who have feet, for they shall walk; blessed are they that have hands, for they shall work; blessed are they that have a voice, for they shall cry aloud; blessed are they who have a mouth and tongue, for they shall speak; blessed are they that have eyes, for they shall see. Even so our Lord arranging in their order the members as it were of the soul, hath taught what is proper to each. Humility qualifies[8] for the possession of the kingdom of heaven; meekness qualifies for possessing the earth; mourning for consolation; hunger and thirst after righteousness for being filled; mercy for the obtaining mercy; a pure heart for seeing God.

10. If then we desire to see God, whereby shall our eye be purified? For who would not care for, and diligently seek the means of purifying that eye whereby he may see Him whom he longeth after with an entire affection? The Divine record has expressly mentioned this when it says, "purifying their hearts by faith."[9] The faith of God then purifies the heart, the pure heart sees God. But because this faith is sometimes so defined by men who deceive themselves, as though it were enough only to believe (for some promise themselves even the sight of God and the kingdom of heaven, who believe and live evilly); against these, the Apostle James, incensed and indignant as it were with a

---

[1] 1 Cor. i. 24. [2] Wisd. i. [3] 1 Cor iii. 17.
[4] John iv. 24. [5] 1 Sam. v. 3. [6] *Terra.*
[7] *Terram.*

[8] *Apta est.* [9] Acts xv. 9.

holy [1] charity, saith in his Epistle, "Thou believest there is one God." Thou applaudest thyself for thy faith, for thou markest how that many ungodly men think there are gods many, and thou rejoicest in thyself because thou dost believe that there is but one God ; " Thou doest well : the devils also believe, and tremble." [2] Shall they also see God? They shall see Him who are pure in heart. But who can say that unclean spirits are pure in heart? And yet they also " believe and tremble."

11. Our faith then must be different from the faith of devils. For our faith purifies the heart ; but their faith makes them guilty. For they do wickedly, and therefore say they to the Lord, " What have we to do with Thee? " When thou hearest the devils say this, thinkest thou that they do not acknowledge Him? "We know," they say, " who Thou art : Thou art the Son of God." [3] This Peter says, and is commended ; the devil says it, and is condemned. Whence cometh this, but that though the words be the same, the heart is different? Let us then make a distinction in our faith, and not be content to believe. This is no such faith as purifieth the heart. " Purifying their hearts," it is said, " by faith." [4] But by what, and what kind of faith, save that which the Apostle Paul defines when he says, " Faith which worketh by love." [5] That faith distinguishes us from the faith of devils, and from the infamous and abandoned conduct of men. "Faith," he says. What faith? "That which worketh by love," and which hopeth for what God doth promise. Nothing is more exact or perfect than this definition. There are then in faith these three things. He in whom that faith is which worketh by love, must necessarily hope for that which God doth promise. Hope therefore is the associate of faith. For hope is necessary as long as we see not what we believe, lest perhaps through not seeing, and by despairing to see, we fail. That we see not, doth make us sad ; but that we hope we shall see, comforteth us. Hope then is here, and she is the associate of faith. And then charity also, by which we long, and strive to attain, and glow with desire, and hunger and thirst. This then is taken in also ; and so there will be faith, hope, and charity. For how shall there not be charity there, since charity is nothing else but love? And this faith is itself defined as that " which worketh by love." Take away faith, and all thou believest perisheth ; take away charity, and all that thou dost perisheth. For it is the province of faith to believe, of charity to do. For if thou believest without love, thou dost not apply thyself to good works ; or if thou dost, it is as a servant, not as a son, through fear of punishment,

not through love of righteousness. Therefore I say, that faith purifieth the heart, which worketh by love.

12. And what does this faith effect at present? What does it by so many testimonies of Scripture, by its manifold lessons, its various and plentiful exhortations, but make us "see now through a glass darkly, and hereafter face to face." But return not now in thought again to this thy bodily face. Think only of the face of the heart. Force, compel, press thine heart to think of things divine. Whatsoever occurs to thy mind that is like to a body, throw it off from thee. If thou canst not yet say, " It is this," yet at least say, " It is *not* this." For when wilt thou be able to say, " This is God"? Not even then, when thou shalt see Him ; for what thou shalt then see is ineffable. Thus the Apostle says, that he " was caught up into the third heaven, and heard ineffable words." [6] If the words are ineffable, what is He whose words they are? Therefore as thou dost think of God, perchance there is presented to thee the idea of some human figure of marvellous and exceeding greatness, and thou hast set it before the eyes of thy mind as something very great, and grand, and of vast extension. Still somewhere thou hast set bounds to it. If thou hast, it is not God. But if thou hast not set bounds to it, where can the face be? Thou art fancying to thyself some huge body, and in order to distinguish the members in it, thou must needs set bounds to it. For in no other way but by setting bounds to this large body, canst thou distinguish the members. But what art thou about, O foolish and carnal imagination ! Thou hast made a large bulky body, and so much the larger, as thou hast thought the more to honour God. Another adds one cubit to it, and makes it greater than before.

13. But " I have read," you will say. What hast thou read, who hast understood nothing? Yet tell me, what hast thou read? Let us not thrust back the babe in understanding with his play. Tell me, what hast thou read? " Heaven is My throne, and the earth is My footstool." [7] I hear thee ; I have read it also : but it may be that thou thinkest thyself to have the advantage, in that thou hast both read and believed. But I also believe what thou hast just said. Let us then believe it together. What do I say? Let us search it out together. Lo ! hold fast what thou hast so read and believed ; " Heaven is My throne (that is, " my seat," for " throne," [8] in Greek, is " seat," [9] in Latin), and the earth is My footstool." But hast thou not read these words as well, " Who has meted out the heaven with the palm of His hand?" [10] I conclude that

---

[1] *Spiritali.*   [2] Jas. ii. 19.   [3] Luke iv. 34; Matt. xvi. 16.   [6] 2 Cor. xii. 2–4.   [7] Isa. lxvi. 1.   [8] *Thronus.*
[4] Acts xv. 9.   [5] Gal. v. 6.   [9] *Sedes.*   [10] Isa. xl. 12.

thou hast read them; thou dost acknowledge them, and confess that thou believest them; for in that book we read both the one and the other, and believe both. But now think a while, and teach me. I make thee my teacher, and myself the little one. Teach me, I pray thee, "Who is He that sitteth on the palm of His hand?"

14. See, thou hast drawn the figure and lineaments of the members of God from a human body. And perhaps it has occurred to thee to think, that it is according to the body that we were made after the Image of God. I will admit this idea for a time to be considered, and canvassed, and examined, and by disputation to be thoroughly sifted. Now then, if it please thee, hear me; for I heard thee in what thou wast pleased to say. God sitteth in heaven, and meteth out the heaven with His palm. What! doth the same heaven become broad when it is God's seat, and narrow, when He meteth it out? Or is [1] God when sitting, limited to the measure of His palm? If this be so, God did not make us after His likeness, for the palm of our hand is much narrower than that part of the body whereon we sit. But if He be as broad in His palm as in His sitting, He hath made our members quite unlike His. There is no resemblance here. Let the Christian then blush to set up such an idol in his heart as this. Wherefore take heaven for all saints. For the earth also is spoken of all who are in the earth, " Let all the earth worship Thee." [2] If we may properly say with regard to those who dwell on the earth, " Let all the earth worship Thee," we may with the same propriety say also as to those who dwell in heaven, " Let all the heaven bear Thee." For even the Saints who dwell on earth, though in their body they tread the earth, in heart dwell in heaven. For it is not in vain that they are reminded to " lift up their hearts," [3] and when they are so reminded, they answer, "that they lift them up:" nor in vain is it said, " If ye then be risen with Christ, seek those things which are above, where Christ sitteth on the right hand of God. Set your affections on things above, not on things on the earth." [4] In so far therefore as they have their conversation there, they do bear God, and they are heaven; because they are the seat of God; and when they declare the words of God, "The heavens declare the glory of God." [5]

15. Return then with me to the face of the heart, and make *it* ready. That to which God speaketh is within. The ears, and eyes, and all the rest of the visible members, are either the dwelling place or the instrument of some thing within. It is the inner man where Christ doth dwell, now [6] by faith, and hereafter He will dwell in it, by the presence of His Divinity, when we shall have known "what is the length, and breadth, and depth, and height; when we shall have known also the love of Christ that surpasseth knowledge, that we may be filled with all the fulness of God." [7] Now then if thou wouldest enter into the meaning of these words, summon all thy powers [8] to comprehend the breadth, and length, and height, and depth. Wander not in the imagination of the thoughts through the spaces of the world, and the yet comprehensible extent of this so vast a body. Look for what I am speaking of in thine own self. The " breadth " is in good works; the " length " is in long-suffering and perseverance in well-doing; the " height " is in the expectation of rewards above, for which height's sake thou art bidden " to lift up thy heart." Do well, and persevere in well-doing, because of God's reward. Esteem earthly things as nothing, lest, when this earth shall be smitten with any scourge of that wise One, thou say that thou hast worshipped God in vain, hast done good works in vain, hast persevered in good works in vain. For by doing good works thou hadst as it were the " breadth," by persevering in them thou hadst as it were the " length ; " but by seeking earthly things thou hast not had the " height." Now observe the " depth ; " it is the grace of God in the secret dispensation of His will. " For who hath known the mind of the Lord? or who hath been His counsellor?" [9] and, "Thy judgments are as a great depth." [10]

16. This conversation of well-doing, of perseverance in well-doing, of hoping for rewards above, of the secret dispensation of the grace of God, in wisdom not in foolishness, nor yet in finding fault, because one man is after this manner and another after that; for " there is no iniquity with God ;" [11] apply this, I say, if you think good, also to the Cross of thy Lord. For it was not without a meaning [12] that He chose this kind of death, in whose power it was even either to die or not. Now if it was in His power to die or not, why was it not in His power also to die in this or the other manner! Not without a meaning then did He select the Cross, whereby to crucify thee to this world. For the " breadth " is the transverse beam in the cross where the hands are fastened, to signify good works. The " length " is in that part of the wood which reaches from this transverse beam to the ground. For there the body is crucified and in a manner stands, and this standing signifies perseverance.

---

[1] *An ipse Deus tantus est in sedendo quantus in palmo.*
[2] Ps. lxv. 4, Sept. (lxvi. English version).
[3] In the Communion Office.   [4] Col. iii. 1, 2.   [5] Ps. xix. 1.

[6] *Interim.*
[8] *Si tibi intellectus hic non displicet advoca te comprehendere.*
[9] Rom. xi. 34.
[11] 2 Chron. xix. 7; Rom. ix. 14.

[7] Eph. iii. 17, etc.
[10] Ps. xxxvi. 6.
[12] *Frustra.*

Now "the height" is in that part, which from the same transverse beam projects upward to the head, and hereby is signified the expectation of things above. And where is the "depth," but in that part which is fixed in the ground? For so is the dispensation of grace, hidden and in secret. It is not seen itself, but from thence is projected all that is seen. After this, when thou shalt have comprehended all these things, not in the mere understanding but in action also ("for a good understanding have all they that do hereafter),"[1] then if thou canst, stretch out thyself to attain to the knowledge of the "love of Christ which passeth knowledge." When thou hast attained to it, thou "wilt be filled with all the fulness of God." Then will be fulfilled the "face to face." Now thou wilt be filled with all the fulness of God, not as if God should be full of thee, but so that thou shalt be full of God. Seek there, if thou canst, for any bodily face. Away with such trifles from the eye of the mind. Let the child cast away his playthings, and learn to handle more serious matters. And in many things we are but children; and when we were more so than we are, we were borne with by our betters. "Follow peace with all men, and holiness, without which no man shall see God."[2] For by this is the heart purified; for that in it is that faith "which worketh by love." Hence, "Blessed are the pure in heart, for they shall see God."

SERMON IV.

[LIV. BEN.]

ON THAT THAT IS WRITTEN IN THE GOSPEL, MATT. V. 16, "EVEN SO LET YOUR LIGHT SHINE BEFORE MEN, THAT THEY MAY SEE YOUR GOOD WORKS, AND GLORIFY YOUR FATHER WHO IS IN HEAVEN:" AND CONTRARIWISE, CHAP. VI., "TAKE HEED THAT YE DO NOT YOUR RIGHTEOUSNESS BEFORE MEN, TO BE SEEN OF THEM."

1. IT is wont to perplex many persons, Dearly beloved, that our Lord Jesus Christ in His Evangelical Sermon, after He had first said, "Let your light so shine before men, that they may see your good works, and glorify your Father which is in heaven;"[3] said afterwards, "Take heed that ye do not your righteousness[4] before men to be seen of them."[5] For so the mind of him who is weak in understanding is disturbed, is desirous to obey both precepts, and distracted by diverse, and contradictory commandments. For a man can as little obey but one master, if he give contradictory orders, as he can serve two masters,[6] which the Saviour Himself hath testified in the same Sermon to be impossible. What then must the mind that is in this hesitation do,

when it thinks that it cannot, and yet is afraid not to obey? For if he set his good works in the light to be seen of men, that he may fulfil the command, "Let your light so shine before men, that they may see your good works, and glorify your Father which is in heaven;" he will think himself involved in guilt because he has done contrary to the other precept which says, "Take heed that ye do not your righteousness before men to be seen of them." And again, if fearing and avoiding this, he conceal his good works, he will think that he is not obeying Him who commands, saying, "Let your light shine before men, that they may see your good works."

2. But he who is of a right understanding, fulfils both, and will obey in both the Universal Lord of all, who would not condemn the slothful servant, if he commanded those things which could by no means be done. For give ear to "Paul, the servant of Jesus Christ, called to be an Apostle, separated unto the Gospel of God,"[7] both doing and teaching both duties. See how his "light shineth before men, that they may see his good works. We commend ourselves," saith he, "to every man's conscience in the sight of God."[8] And again, "For we provide things honest, not only in the sight of God, but also in the sight of men."[9] And again, "Please all men in all things, even as I please all men in all things."[10] See, on the other hand, how he takes heed, that he "do not his righteousness before men to be seen of them. Let every man," saith he, "prove his own work, and then shall he have glorying in himself, and not in another."[11] And again, "For our glorying is this, the testimony of our conscience."[12] And that, than which nothing is plainer, "If," saith he, "I yet pleased men, I should not be the servant of Christ."[13] But lest any of those who are perplexed about the precepts of our Lord Himself as contradictory, should much more raise a question against His Apostle and say, How sayest thou, "Please all men in all things, even as I also please all men in all things:" and yet also sayest, "If I yet pleased men, I should not be the servant of Christ"? May the Lord Himself be with us, who spake also in His servant and Apostle, and open to us His will, and give us the means of obeying it.

3. The very words of the Gospel carry with them their own explanation; nor do they shut the mouths of those who hunger, seeing they feed the hearts of them that knock. The intention of a man's heart, its direction and its aim, is what is to be regarded. For if he who wishes his good works to be seen of men, sets before men his own glory and advantage, and seeks for this in the sight of men, he does not fulfil either

---

[1] Ps. cxi. 10.　　[2] Heb. xii. 14.　　[3] Matt. v. 16.
[4] *Justitiam*, Vulgate.　　[5] Matt. vi. 1.　　[6] Matt. vi. 24.
[7] Rom i. 1.　　[8] 2 Cor. iv. 2.　　[9] 2 Cor. viii. 21.
[10] 1 Cor. x. 33.　　[11] Gal. vi. 4.　　[12] 2 Cor. i. 12.
[13] Gal. i. 10.

of those precepts which the Lord has given as touching this matter; because He has at once looked to "doing his righteousness before men to be seen of them;" and his light has not so shined before men that they should see his good works, and glorify His Father which is in heaven. It was himself he wished to be glorified, not God; he sought his own advantage, and loved not the Lord's will. Of such the Apostle says, "For all seek their own, not the things which are Jesus Christ's.[1] Accordingly, the sentence was not finished at the words, "Let your light so shine before men, that they may see your good works;" but there was immediately subjoined why this was to be done; "that they may glorify your Father which is in heaven;" that when a man who does good works is seen of men, he may have only the intention of the good work in his own conscience, but may have no intention of being known, save for the praise of God, for their advantage-sake to whom he is thus made known; for to them this advantage comes, that God who has given this power to man begins to be well-pleasing to them; and so they do not despair, but that the same power might be vouchsafed to themselves also if they would. And so He did not conclude the other precept, "Take heed that ye do not your righteousness before men," otherwise than in the words, "to be seen of them;" nor did He add in this case, "that they may glorify your Father which is in heaven," but rather, "otherwise ye have no reward of your Father which is in heaven." For by this He shows us, that they who are such, as He will not have His faithful ones to be, seek a reward in this very thing, that they are seen of men — that it is in this they place their good — in this that they delight the vanity of their heart — in this is their emptiness, and inflation, their swelling, and wasting away. For why was it not sufficient to say, "Take heed that ye do not your righteousness before men," but that he added, "that ye may be seen of them," except because there are some who do their "righteousness before men;" not that they may be seen of them, but that the works themselves may be seen; and the Father which is in heaven, who hath vouchsafed to endow with these gifts the ungodly whom He had justified, may be glorified?

4. They who are such, neither do they account their righteousness as their own, but His, by the faith of whom they live (whence also the Apostle says, "That I may win Christ, and be found in Him, not having mine own righteousness which is of the law, but that which is of the faith of Christ, the righteousness which is of God by faith;"[2] and in another place, "That we may be the righteousness of God in Him."[3] Whence

also he finds fault with the Jews in these words, "Being ignorant of God's righteousness, and wishing to establish their own righteousness, they have not submitted themselves to the righteousness of God"[4]). Whosoever then wish their good works to be so seen of men, that He may be glorified from whom they have received those things which are seen in them, and that thereby those very persons who see them, may through the dutifulness[5] of faith be provoked to imitate the good, their light shines truly before men, because there beams forth from them the light of charity; theirs is no mere empty fume of pride; and in the very act they take precautions, that they do not their righteousness before men to be seen of them, in that they do not reckon that righteousness as their own, nor do they therefore do it that they may be seen; but that He may be made known, who is praised in them that are justified, that so He may bring to pass in him that praises that which is praised in others, that is, that He may make him that praises to be himself the object of praise. Observe the Apostle too, how that when he had said, "Please all men in all things, as I also please all men in all things;"[6] he did not stop there, as if he had placed in that, namely, the pleasing men, the end of his intention; for else he would have said falsely, "If I yet pleased men, I should not be the servant of Christ;" but he subjoined immediately why it was that he pleased men; "Not seeking," saith he, "mine own profit, but the profit of many, that they may be saved."[6] So he at once did not please men for his own profit, lest he should not be "the servant of Christ;" and he did please men for their salvation's sake, that he might be a faithful Minister of Christ; because for him his own conscience in the sight of God was enough, and from him there shined forth in the sight of men something which they might imitate.

SERMON V.

[LV. BEN.]

ON THE WORDS OF THE GOSPEL, MATT. V. 22, "WHOSOEVER SHALL SAY TO HIS BROTHER, THOU FOOL, SHALL BE IN DANGER OF THE HELL OF FIRE."

1. THE section of the Holy Gospel which we just now heard when it was read, must have sorely alarmed us, if we have faith; but those who have not faith, it alarmed not. And because it does not alarm them, they are minded to continue in their false security, as knowing not how to divide and distinguish the proper times of security and fear. Let him then who is leading now that life which has an end, fear, that in

---

[1] Phil. ii. 21.　　[2] Phil. iii. 8, 9.　　[3] 2 Cor. v. 21.　　[4] Rom. x. 3.　　[5] *Pietate.*　　[6] 1 Cor. x. 33.

that life which is without end, he may have security. Therefore were we alarmed. For who would not fear Him who speaketh the truth, and saith, "Whosoever shall say to his brother, Thou fool, shall be in danger of hell fire." [1] Yet "the tongue can no man tame." [2] Man tames the wild beast, yet he tames not his tongue; he tames the lion, yet he bridles not his own speech; he tames all else, yet he tames not himself; he tames what he was afraid of, and what he ought to be afraid of, in order that he may tame himself, that he does not fear. But how is this? It is a true sentence, and came forth from an oracle of truth, "But the tongue can no man tame."

2. What shall we do then, my brethren? I see that I am speaking indeed to a large assembly, yet, seeing that we are one in Christ, let us take counsel as it were in secret. No stranger heareth us, we are all one, because we are all united in one.[3] What shall we do then? "Whosoever saith to his brother, Thou fool, shall be in danger of hell fire: But the tongue can no man tame." Shall all men go into hell fire? God forbid! "Lord, Thou art our refuge from generation to generation:" [4] Thy wrath is just: Thou sendest no man into hell unjustly. "Whither shall I go from Thy Spirit?" [5] and whither shall I flee from Thee, but to Thee? Let us then understand, Dearly beloved, that if no man can tame the tongue, we must have recourse to God, that He may tame it. For if thou shouldest wish to tame it, thou canst not, because thou art a man. "The tongue can no man tame." Observe a like instance to this in the case of those beasts which we do tame. The horse does not tame himself; the camel does not tame himself; the elephant does not tame himself; the viper does not tame himself; the lion does not tame himself; and so also man does not tame himself. But that the horse, and ox, and camel, and elephant, and lion, and viper, may be tamed, man is sought for. Therefore let God be sought to, that man may be tamed.

3. Therefore, "O Lord, art Thou become our refuge." To Thee do we betake ourselves, and with Thy help it will be well with us. For ill is it with us by ourselves. Because we have left Thee, Thou hast left us to ourselves. Be we then found in Thee, for in ourselves were we lost. "Lord, Thou art become our refuge." Why then, brethren, should we doubt that the Lord will make us gentle, if we give up ourselves to be tamed by him? Thou hast tamed the lion which thou madest not; shall not He tame thee, who made thee? For from whence didst thou get the power to tame such savage beasts? Art thou their equal in bodily strength? By

what power then hast thou been able to tame great beasts? The very beasts of burden, as they are called, are by their nature wild. For in their untamed state they are unserviceable. But because custom has never known them except as in the hands and under the bridle and power of men, dost thou imagine that they could have been born in this tame state? But now at all events mark the beasts which are unquestionably of savage kind. "The lion roareth, who doth not fear?" [6] And yet wherein is it that thou dost find thyself to be stronger than he? Not in strength of body, but in the interior reason of the mind. Thou art stronger than the lion, in that wherein thou wast made after the image of God. What! Shall the image of God tame a wild beast; and shall not God tame His own image?

4. In Him is our hope; let us submit ourselves to Him, and entreat His mercy. In Him let us place our hope, and until we are tamed, and tamed thoroughly, that is, are perfected, let us bear our Tamer. For oftentimes does our Tamer bring forth His scourge too. For if thou dost bring forth the whip to tame thy beasts, shall not God do so to tame His beasts (which we are), who of His beasts will make us His sons? Thou tamest thine horse; and what wilt thou give thy horse, when he shall have begun to carry thee gently, to bear thy discipline, to obey thy rule, to be thy faithful, useful [7] beast? How dost thou repay him, who wilt not so much as bury him when he is dead, but cast him forth to be torn by the birds of prey? Whereas when thou art tamed, God reserveth for thee an inheritance, which is God Himself, and though dead for a little time, He will raise thee to life again. He will restore to thee thy body, even to the full number of thy hairs; and will set thee with the Angels for ever, where thou wilt need no more His taming hand, but only to be possessed by His exceeding [8] mercy. For God will then be "all in all;" [9] neither will there be any unhappiness to exercise us, but happiness alone to feed us. Our God will be Himself our Shepherd; our God will be Himself our Cup; [10] our God will be Himself our glory; our God will be Himself our wealth. What multiplicity of things soever thou seekest here, He alone will be Himself all these things to thee.

5. Unto this hope is man tamed, and shall his Tamer then be deemed intolerable? Unto this hope is man tamed, and shall he murmur against his beneficent Tamer, if He chance to use the scourge? Ye have heard the exhortation of the Apostle, "If ye are without chasten-

---

[1] Matt. v. 22.   [2] Jas. iii. 8.   [3] *In unum.*
[4] Ps. lxxxix. 1, Sept. (xc. English version).   [5] Ps. cxxxix. 7.

[6] Amos iii. 8.
[7] There is a paranomasia here in the original, which it is not possible to preserve in the translation: "*Esse jumentum, hoc est adjumentum infirmitatis suæ.*"
[8] *Piissimo.*   [9] 1 Cor. xv. 28.   [10] *Potus.*

ing, ye are bastards, and not sons ;[1] for what son is he whom the father chasteneth not? Furthermore," he says, "we have had fathers of our flesh which corrected us, and we gave them reverence ; shall we not much rather be in subjection to the Father of spirits, and live?"[2] For what could thy father do for thee, that he corrected and chastised thee, brought out the scourge and beat thee? Could he make thee live for ever? What he could not do for himself, how should he do for thee? For some paltry sum of money which he had gathered together by usury and travail, did he discipline thee by the scourge, that the fruit of his labour when left to thee might not be squandered by thy evil living. Yes, he beats his son, as fearing lest his labours should be lost ; forasmuch as he left to thee what he could neither retain here, nor carry away. For he did not leave thee anything here which could be his own ; he went off, that so thou mightest come on. But thy God, thy Redeemer, thy Tamer, thy Chastiser, thy Father, instructeth thee. To what end? That thou mayest receive an inheritance, when thou shalt not have to carry thy father to his grave, but shalt have thy Father Himself for thine inheritance. Unto this hope art thou instructed, and dost thou murmur? and if any sad chance befall thee, dost thou (it may be) blaspheme? Whither wilt thou go from His Spirit? But now He letteth thee alone, and doth not scourge thee ; or He abandoneth thee in thy blaspheming ; shalt thou not experience His judgment? Is it not better that He should scourge thee and receive thee, than that He should spare thee and abandon thee?

6. Let us say then to the Lord our God, "Lord, Thou art become our refuge from generation to generation." In the first and second generations Thou art become our refuge. Thou wast our refuge, that we might be born, who before were not. Thou wast our refuge, that we might be born anew, who were evil. Thou wast a refuge to feed those that forsake Thee. Thou art a refuge to raise up and direct Thy children. "Thou art become our refuge." We will not go back from Thee, when Thou hast delivered us from all our evils, and filled us with Thine own good things. Thou givest good things now, Thou[3] dealest softly with us, that we be not wearied in the way ; Thou dost correct, and chastise, and smite, and direct us, that we may not wander from the way. Whether therefore Thou dealest softly with us, that we be not wearied in the way, or chastisest us, that we wander not from the way, "Thou art become our refuge, O Lord."

SERMON VI.

[LVI. BEN.]

ON THE LORD'S PRAYER IN ST. MATTHEW'S GOSPEL, CHAP. VI. 9, ETC. TO THE COMPETENTES.[4]

1. THE blessed Apostle, to show that those times when it should come to pass that all the nations should believe in Christ had been foretold by the Prophets, produced this testimony where it is written, "And it shall be, that whosoever shall call on the name of the Lord, shall be saved."[5] For before time the name of the Lord who made heaven and earth was called upon amongst the Israelites only ; the rest of the nations called upon dumb and deaf idols, by whom they were not heard, or by devils, by whom they were heard to their harm. "But when the fulness of time came," that was fulfilled which had been foretold, "And it shall be, that whosoever shall call upon the name of the Lord, shall be saved." Moreover, because the Jews, even those who believed in Christ, grudged the Gospel to the Gentiles, and said that the Gospel ought not to be preached to them who were not circumcised ; because against these the Apostle Paul alleged this testimony, "And it shall be, that whosoever shall call upon the Name of the Lord, shall be saved ; "[6] he immediately subjoined, to convince those who were unwilling that the Gospel should be preached to the Gentiles, the words, "But how shall they call upon Him, in whom they have not believed? or how shall they believe in Him of whom they have not heard? or how shall they hear without a preacher? or how shall they preach except they be sent?" Because then he said, "how shall they call upon Him in whom they have not believed?" ye have not first learnt the Lord's Prayer, and after that the Creed ; but first the Creed, where ye might know what to believe, and afterwards the Prayer, where ye might know whom to call upon. The Creed then has respect to the faith, the Lord's Prayer to prayer ; because it is he who believeth, that is heard when he calleth.

2. But many ask for what they ought not to ask, not knowing what is expedient for them. Two things therefore must he that prays beware of ; that he ask not what he ought not ; and that he ask not from whom he ought not. From the devil, from idols, from evil spirits,[7] must nothing be asked. From the Lord our God Jesus Christ, God the Father of Prophets, and Apostles, and

---

[1] Heb. xii. 8.   [2] Heb. xii. 7, 9.
[3] *Blandiris.*

[4] These were the last of the classes into which the catechumens were distributed, and were so called because they were now so far advanced as to "*seek* for baptism." See Serm. 216. 1 (*Ad competentes, quid enim aliud sunt competentes, quam simul petentes*) and Serm. 228. 1 (*Competentes dicebantur quoniam materna viscera, ut nascerentur, petendo pulsabant*). Bingham, *Antiqu.* B. x. ch. ii. sects. 5-12. See *Conf.* B. ix. 6 (14).
[5] Joel ii. 32.   [6] Rom. x. 13, etc.   [7] *Dæmonibus.*

Martyrs, from the Father of our Lord Jesus Christ, from God who made heaven and earth, the sea, and all things in them, from Him must we ask whatsoever we have to ask. But we must beware that we ask not of Him that which we ought not to ask. If because we ought to ask for life, thou ask it of dumb and deaf idols, what doth it profit thee? So if from God the Father, who is in heaven, thou dost wish for the death of thine enemies, what doth it profit thee? Hast thou not heard or read in the Psalm, in which the damnable end of the traitor Judas is foretold, how the prophecy spake of him, " Let his prayer be turned into sin? " [1] If then thou risest up, and prayest for evil on thine enemies, thy " prayer will be turned into sin."

3. You have read in the Holy Psalms, how that he who speaks in them imprecates, as it would seem, many curses upon his enemies. And surely, one may say, he who speaks in the Psalms is a righteous man; wherefore then does he so wish evil upon his enemies? He does not wish, but he foresees, it is a prophecy of one who is telling things to come, not a vow of malediction; for the prophets knew by the Spirit to whom evil was appointed to happen, and to whom good; and by prophecy they spake as if they wished for what they did foresee. But how canst thou know whether he for whom to-day thou art asking evil, may not to-morrow be a better man than thyself? But you will say, I know him to be a wicked man. Well: thou must know that thou art wicked too. Although it may be thou takest upon thyself to judge of another's heart what thou dost not know; but as for thine own self thou *knowest* that thou art wicked. Hearest thou not the Apostle saying, " Who was before a blasphemer, and a persecutor, and injurious: but I obtained mercy, because I did it ingorantly in unbelief? " [2] Now when the Apostle Paul persecuted the Christians, binding them wherever he found them, and drew them to the Chief Priests to be questioned and punished, what think ye, brethren, did the Church pray *against* him, or *for* him? Surely the Church of God which had learnt instruction from her Lord, who said as He hung upon the Cross, " Father, forgive them, for they know not what they do," [3] so prayed for Paul (or rather as yet Saul), that that might be wrought in him which was wrought. For in that he says, " But I was unknown by face to the churches of Judæa which are in Christ: only they heard that he who persecuted us in times past, now preacheth the faith which once he destroyed; and they magnified God in me; " [4] why did they magnify God, but because they asked this of God, before it came to pass?

4. Our Lord then first of all cut off " much speaking," that thou mightest not bring a multitude of words unto God, as though by thy many words thou wouldest teach Him. Therefore when thou prayest thou hast need of piety, not of wordiness. " For your Father knoweth what is needful for you, before ye ask Him." [5] Be ye loth then to use many words, for He knoweth what is needful for you. But lest peradventure any should say here, If He know what is needful for us, why should we use so much as a few words? why should we pray at all? He knoweth Himself; let Him then give what He knoweth to be needful for us. Yes, but it is His will that thou shouldest pray, that He may give to thy longings, that His gifts may not be lightly esteemed; seeing He hath Himself formed this longing desire in us. The words therefore which our Lord Jesus Christ hath taught us in His prayer, are the rule and standard of our desires. Thou mayest not ask for anything but what is written there.

5. " Do ye therefore say," saith he, " Our Father, which art in heaven." Where ye see ye have begun to have God for your Father. Ye will have Him, when ye are new born. Although even now before ye are born, ye have been conceived of His seed, as being on the eve of being brought forth in the font, the womb as it were of the Church. " Our Father, which art in heaven." Remember then, that ye have a Father in heaven. Remember that ye were born of your father Adam unto death, that ye are to be born anew of God the Father unto life. And what ye say, say in your hearts. Only let there be the earnest affection of prayer, and there will be the effectual [6] answer of Him who heareth prayer. " Hallowed be thy Name." Why dost thou ask, that God's Name may be hallowed? It *is* holy. Why then askest thou for that which is already holy? And then when thou dost ask that His Name may be hallowed, dost thou not as it were pray to Him for Him, and not for thyself? No. Understand it aright, and it is for thine own self thou askest. For this thou askest, that what is always in itself holy, may be hallowed in thee. What is " be hallowed?" " Be accounted holy," be not despised. So then you see, that the good thou dost wish, thou wishest for thine own self. For if thou despise the Name of God, for thyself it will be ill, and not for God.

6. " Thy kingdom come." [7] To whom do we speak? and will not God's kingdom come, if we ask it not. For of that kingdom do we speak which will be after the end of the world. For God hath a kingdom always; neither is He ever without a kingdom, whom the whole creation serveth. But what kingdom then dost

---

[1] Ps clx. 7.   [2] 1 Tim. i. 13.   [3] Luke xxiii. 34.
[4] Gal. i. 22, etc.

[5] Matt. vi. 8.   [6] *Exaudientis effectus.*
[7] Matt. vi. 10.

thou wish for? That of which it is written in the Gospel, "Come, ye blessed of My Father, receive the kingdom which is prepared for you from the beginning of the world."[1] Lo here is the kingdom whereof we say, "Thy kingdom come." We pray that it may come *in* us; we pray that we may be found in *it*. For come it certainly will; but what will it profit thee, if it shall find thee at the left hand? Therefore, here again it is for thine own self that thou wishest well; for thyself thou prayest. This it is that thou dost long for; this desire in thy prayer, that thou mayest so live, that thou mayest have a part in the kingdom of God, which is to be given to all saints. Therefore when thou dost say, "Thy kingdom come," thou dost pray for thyself, that thou mayest live well. Let us have part in Thy kingdom: let that come even to us, which is to come to Thy saints and righteous ones.

7. "Thy will be done."[2] What! if thou say not this, will not God do His will? Remember what thou hast repeated in the Creed, "I believe in God the Father Almighty." If He be Almighty, why prayest thou that His will may be done? What is this then, "Thy will be done"? May it be done in me, that I may not resist Thy will. Therefore here again it is for thyself thou prayest, and not for God. For the will of God will be done *in* thee, though it be not done *by* thee. For both in them to whom He shall say, "Come, ye blessed of My Father, receive the kingdom prepared for you from the beginning of the world;"[1] shall the will of God be done, that the saints and righteous may receive the kingdom; and in them to whom He shall say, "Depart ye into everlasting fire, prepared for the devil and his angels,"[3] shall the will of God be done, that the wicked may be condemned to everlasting fire. That His will may be done by thee is another thing. It is not then without a cause, but that it may be well with thee, that thou dost pray that His will may be done in thee. But whether it be well or ill with thee, it will still be done in thee: but O that it may be done by thee also. Why do I say then, "Thy will be done in heaven and in earth," and do not say, "Thy will be done by heaven and earth?" Because what is done by thee, He Himself doeth in thee. Never is anything done by thee which He Himself doeth not in thee. Sometimes, indeed, He doeth in thee what is not done by thee; but never is anything done by thee, if He do it not in thee.

8. But what is "in heaven and in earth," or, "as in heaven so in earth?" The Angels do Thy will; may we do it also. "Thy will be done as in heaven so in earth." The mind is heaven, the flesh is earth. When thou dost say

(if so be thou do say it) with the Apostle, "With my mind I serve the law of God, but with the flesh the law of sin;"[4] the will of God is done in heaven, but not yet in earth. But when the flesh shall be in harmony with the mind, and "death shall be swallowed up in victory,"[5] so that no carnal desires shall remain for the mind to be in conflict with, when strife in the earth shall have passed away, the war of the heart be over, and that be gone by which is spoken, "the flesh lusteth against the Spirit, and the Spirit against the flesh; for these are contrary the one to the other; so that ye cannot do the things that ye would;"[6] when this war, I say, shall be over, and all concupiscence shall have been changed into charity, nothing shall remain in the body to oppose the spirit, nothing to be tamed, nothing to be bridled, nothing to be trodden down; but the whole shall go on through concord unto righteousness, and the will of God will be done in heaven and in earth. "Thy will be done in heaven and in earth." We wish for perfection, when we pray for this. "Thy will be done as in heaven so in earth." In the Church the spiritual are heaven, the carnal are earth. So then, "Thy will be done as in heaven so in earth;" that as the spiritual do serve Thee, so the carnal being reformed may serve Thee also. "Thy will be done as in heaven so in earth." There is yet another very spiritual[7] meaning of it. For we are admonished to pray for our enemies. The Church is heaven, the enemies of the Church are earth. What then is, "Thy will be done as in heaven so in earth"? May our enemies believe, as we also believe in Thee! may they become friends, and end their enmities! They are earth, therefore are they against us; may they become heaven, and they will be with us.

9. "Give us this day our daily bread."[8] Now here it is manifest, that it is for ourselves we pray. When thou sayest, "Hallowed be Thy Name," it requires explanation how it is that it is for thyself thou prayest, not for God. When thou sayest, "Thy will be done;" here again is there need of explanation, lest thou think that thou art wishing well to God in this prayer, that His will may be done, and not rather that thou art praying for thyself. When thou sayest, "Thy kingdom come;" this again must be explained, lest thou think that thou art wishing well to God in this prayer that He may reign. But from this place and onwards to the end of the Prayer, it is plain that we are praying to God for our own selves. "When thou sayest, "Give us this day our daily bread," thou dost profess thyself to be God's beggar. But be not ashamed at this; how rich soever any man be on earth, he is still God's beggar. The beggar takes his stand

---

before the rich man's house; but the rich man himself stands before the door of the great rich One. Petition is made to him, and he maketh his petition. If he were not in need, he would not knock at the ears of God in prayer. And what doth the rich man need? I am bold to say, the rich man needeth even daily bread. For how is it that he hath abundance of all things? whence but because God hath given it him? What should he have, if God withdrew His hand? Have not many laid down to sleep in wealth, and risen up in beggary? And that he doth not want, is due to God's mercy, not to his own power.

10. But this bread, Dearly beloved, by which our body is filled, by which the flesh is recruited day by day; this bread, I say, God giveth not to those only who praise, but to those also who blaspheme Him; "Who maketh His sun to rise upon the evil and on the good, and sendeth rain upon the just and on the unjust."[1] Thou praisest Him, and He feedeth thee; thou dost blaspheme Him, He feedeth thee. He waiteth for thee to repent; but if thou wilt not change thyself, He will condemn thee. Because then both good and bad receive this bread from God, thinkest thou there is no other bread for which the children ask, of which the Lord said in the Gospel, "It is not meet to take the children's bread, and to cast it to dogs?"[2] Yes, surely there is. What then is that bread? and why is it called daily? Because this is necessary as the other; for without it we cannot live; without bread we cannot live. It is shamelessness to ask for wealth from God; it is no shamelessness to ask for daily bread. That which ministereth to pride is one thing, that which ministereth to life another. Nevertheless, because this bread which may be seen and handled, is given both to the good and bad; there is a daily bread, for which the children pray. That is the word of God, which is dealt out to us day by day. Our bread is daily bread; and by it live not our bodies, but our souls. It is necessary for us who are even now labourers in the vineyard, — it is our food, not our hire. For he that hires the labourer into the vineyard owes him two things; food, that he faint not, and his hire, wherewith he may rejoice. Our daily food then in this earth is the word of God, which is dealt out always in the Churches: our hire after labour is called eternal life. Again, if by this our daily bread thou understand what the faithful[3] receive, what ye shall receive, when ye have been bap-

tized, it is with good reason that we ask and say, "Give us this day our daily bread;" that we may live in such sort, as that we be not separated from the Holy Altar.

11. "And forgive us our debts, as we forgive our debtors."[4] Touching this petition again we need no explanation, that it is for ourselves that we pray. For we beg that our debts may be forgiven us. For debtors are we, not in money, but in sins. Thou art saying perchance at this moment, And you too. We answer, Yes, we too. What, ye Holy Bishops, are ye debtors? Yes, we are debtors too. What you! My Lord.[5] Be it far from thee, do not thyself this wrong. I do myself no wrong, but I say the truth; we are debtors: "If we say we have no sin, we deceive ourselves, and the truth is not in us."[6] We have been baptized, and yet are we debtors. Not that anything then remained, which was not remitted to us in Baptism, but because in our lives we are contracting ever what needs daily forgiveness. They who are baptized, and forthwith depart out of this life, come up from the font[7] without any debt; without any debt they leave the world. But they who are baptized and are still kept in this life, contract defilements by reason of their mortal frailty, by which though the ship be not sunk, yet have they need of recourse to the pump. For otherwise by little and little will that enter in by which the whole ship will be sunk. And to offer this prayer, is to have recourse to the pump. But we ought not only to pray, but to do alms also, because when the pump is used to prevent the ship from sinking, both the voices and hands are at work. Now we are at work with our voices, when we say, "Forgive us our debts, as we also forgive our debtors." And we are at work with our hands when we do this, "Break thy bread to the hungry, and bring the houseless poor into thine house.[8] Shut up alms in the heart of a poor[9] man, and it shall intercede for thee unto the Lord."[10]

12. Although therefore all our sins were forgiven in the "laver of regeneration," we should be driven into great straits, if there were not given to us the daily cleansing of the Holy Prayer. Alms and prayers purge away sins; only let not such sins be committed, for which we must necessarily be separated from our daily Bread; avoid we all such debts to which a severe and certain condemnation is due. Call not yourselves righteous, as though ye had no cause to say, "Forgive us our debts, as we also forgive

---

[1] Matt. v. 45.   [2] Matt. xv. 26.
[3] St. Augustin throughout these Sermons, as we see in other parts of his works, speaks with great reserve of the Holy Eucharist, as before those who were some of them unbaptized; *fideles* was the name of the baptized (Serm. 113. 2), — "*fidelibus dico eis quibus Christo Corpus erogamus dico;*" and in this sense it seems to be used in our Church Catechism: "The Body and Blood of Christ, which are verily and indeed taken and received *by the faithful* in the

Lord's Supper." This reserve of the ancient Church in itself implies the high doctrine of the Holy Eucharist; modern views have nothing to reserve.
[4] Matt. vi. 12.   [5] *Domine.*   [6] 1 John i. 8.
[7] *Ascendunt.*   [8] Isa. lviii. 7.
[9] The LXX. is, σύγκλεισον ἐλεημοσύνην ἐν τοῖς ταμείοις σου, καὶ αὕτη ἐξελεῖταί σε ἐκ πάσης κακώσεως.
[10] Ecclus. xxix. 12, Vulgate.

our debtors." Though ye abstain from idolatry, from the consolations [1] of astrologers, from the cures of enchanters, though ye abstain from the seductions of heretics, from the divisions of schismatics; though ye abstain from murders, from adulteries and fornications, from thefts and plunderings, from false witnessings, and all such other sins which I do not name, as have a ruinous consequence, for which it is necessary that the sinner be cut off from the altar, and be so bound in earth, as to be bound in heaven, to his great and deadly danger, unless again he be so loosed in earth, as to be loosed in heaven; yet after all these are excepted, still there is no want of occasions whereby a man may sin. A man sins in seeing with pleasure what he ought not to see. Yet who can hold in the quickness of the eye? For from this the eye is said to have received its very name, from its quickness.[2] Who can restrain the ear or eye? The eyes may be shut when thou wilt, and are shut in a moment, but the ears thou canst only with an effort close: thou must raise the hand and reach them, and if any one hold thy hand, they are kept open, nor canst thou close them against reviling, impure, or flattering, and seducing words. And when thou hearest any things thou oughtest not to hear, though thou do it not, dost thou not sin with the ear? for thou hearest something that is bad with pleasure? How great sins doth the deadly tongue commit! Yea, sometimes sins of such a nature, that a man is separated from the altar for them. To the tongue pertains the whole matter of blasphemies, and many idle words again are spoken, which are not convenient. But let the hand do nothing wrong, let the feet run not to any evil, nor the eye be directed to immodesty; let not the ear be open with pleasure to filthy talk; nor the tongue move to indecent speech; yet tell me, who can restrain the thoughts? How often do we pray, my brethren, and our thoughts are elsewhere, as though we forgot before whom we are standing, or before whom we are prostrating ourselves! If all these things be collected together against us, will they not therefore not overwhelm us, because they are small faults? What matter is it whether lead or sand overwhelm us? The lead is all one mass, the sand is small grains, but by their great number they overwhelm thee. So thy sins are small. Seest thou not how the rivers are filled, and the lands are wasted by small drops? They are small, but they are many.

13. Let us therefore say every day; and say it in sincerity of heart, and do what we say, "Forgive us our debts, as we also forgive our debtors." It is an engagement, a covenant, an agreement that we make with God. The Lord thy God saith to thee, Forgive, and I will forgive. Thou hast not forgiven; thou retainest thy sins against thyself, not I. I pray thee, my dearly beloved children, since I know what is expedient for you in the Lord's Prayer, and most of all in that sentence of it, "Forgive us our debts, as we also forgive our debtors;" hear me. Ye are about to be baptized, forgive everything; whatsoever any man have in his heart against any other, let him from his heart forgive it. So enter in, and be sure, that all your sins which ye have contracted, whether from your birth of your parents after Adam with original sin, for which sins' sake ye run with babes to the Saviour's grace, or whatever after sins ye have contracted in your lives, by word, or deed, or thought, all are forgiven; and you will go out of the water as from before the presence of your Lord, with the sure discharge of all debts.

14. Now because by reason of those daily sins of which I have spoken, it is necessary for you to say, in that [3] daily prayer of cleansing as it were, "Forgive us our debts, as we also forgive our debtors;" what will ye do? Ye have enemies. For who can live on this earth without them? Take heed to yourselves, love them. In no way can thine enemy so hurt thee by his violence, as thou dost hurt thyself if thou love him not. For he may injure thy estate, or flocks, or house, or thy man-servant, or thy maid-servant, or thy son, or thy wife; or at most, if such power be given him, thy body. But can he injure thy soul, as thou canst thyself? Reach forward, dearly beloved, I beseech you, to this perfection. But have I given you this power? He only hath given it to whom ye say, "Thy will be done as in heaven so in earth." Yet let it not seem impossible to you. I know, I have known by experience, that there are Christian men who do love their enemies. If it seem to you impossible, ye will not do it. Believe then first that it can be done, and pray that the will of God may be done in you. For what good can thy neighbour's ill do thee? If he had no ill, he would not even be thine enemy. Wish him well then, that he may end his ill, and he will be thine enemy no longer. For it is not the human nature in him that is at enmity with thee, but his sin. Is he therefore thine enemy, because he hath a soul and body? In this he is as thou art: thou hast a soul, and so hath he: thou hast a body, and so hath he. He is of the same substance as thou art; ye were made both out of the same earth, and quickened by the same Lord. In all this he is as thou art. Acknowledge in him then thy brother. The first pair, Adam and Eve, were our parents; the

---

[1] Constellationibus. (Bened.) Meliores notæ MSS. a consolationibus mathematicorum.
[2] Oculus a velocitate.

[3] Velut quotidiana mundatione istâ.

one our father, the other our mother ; and therefore we are brethren. But let us leave the consideration of our first origin. God is our Father, the Church our Mother, and therefore are we brethren. But you will say, my enemy is a heathen, a Jew, a heretic, of whom I spake some time ago on the words, " Thy will be done as in heaven so in earth." O Church, thy enemy is the heathen, the Jew, the heretic ; he is the *earth*. If thou art heaven, call on thy Father which is in heaven, and pray for thine enemies : for so was Saul an enemy of the Church ; thus was prayer made for him, and he became her friend. He not only ceased from being her persecutor, but he laboured to be her helper. And yet, to say the truth, prayer [1] was made against him ; but against his malice, not against his nature. So let thy prayer be against the malice of thine enemy, that it may die, and he may live. For if thine enemy were dead, thou hast lost it might seem an enemy, yet hast thou not found a friend. But if his malice die, thou hast at once lost an enemy and found a friend.

15. But still ye are saying, Who can do, who has ever done this ? May God bring it to effect in your hearts ! I know as well as you, there are but few who do it ; great men are they and spiritual who do so. Are all the faithful in the Church who approach the altar, and take the Body and Blood of Christ, are they all such? And yet they all say, " Forgive us our debts, as we also forgive our debtors." What, if God should answer them, " Why do ye ask me to do what I have promised, when ye do not what I have commanded ? " What have I promised? " To forgive your debts." What have I commanded ? " That ye also forgive your debtors." How can ye do this, if ye do not love your enemies ? What then must we do, brethren ? Is the flock of Christ reduced to such a scanty number ? If they only ought to say, " Forgive us our debts, as we also forgive our debtors," who love their enemies ; I know not what to do, I know not what to say. For must I say to you, If ye do not love your enemies, do not pray ; I dare not say so ; yea, pray rather that ye may love them. But must I say to you, If ye do not love your enemies, say not in the Lord's Prayer, " Forgive us our debts, as we also forgive our debtors "? Suppose that I were to say, Do not use these words. If ye do not, your debts are not forgiven ; and if ye do use them, and do not act thereafter, they are not forgiven. In order therefore that they may be forgiven, ye must both use the prayer, and do thereafter.

16. I see some ground on which I may comfort not some few only, but the multitude of Christians : and I know that ye are longing to hear it. Christ hath said, " Forgive, that ye may be forgiven." [2] And what do ye say in the Prayer which we have now been discussing? " Forgive us our debts, as we also forgive our debtors." So, Lord, forgive, as we forgive. This thou sayest, " O Father, which art in heaven, so forgive our debts, as we also forgive our debtors." For this ye ought to do, and if ye do it not, ye will perish. When your enemy asks pardon, at once forgive him. And is this much for you to do ? Though it were much for thee to love thine enemy when violent against thee, is it much to love a man who is a supplicant before thee ? What hast thou to say ? He was before violent, and then thou hatedst him. I had rather thou hadst not hated him even then : I had rather then when thou wert suffering from his violence, thou hadst remembered the Lord, saying, " Father, forgive them, for they know not what they do." [3] I would have then much wished that even at that time when thine enemy was violent against thee, thou hadst had regard to the Lord thy God speaking thus. But perhaps you will say, He did it, but then He did it as being the Lord, as the Christ, as the Son of God, as the Only-Begotten, as the Word made flesh. But what can I, an infirm and sinful man, do ? If thy Lord be too high an example for thee, turn thy thoughts upon thy fellow-servant. The holy Stephen was being stoned, and as they stoned him, on bended knees did he pray for his enemies, and say, " Lord, lay not this sin to their charge." [4] They were casting stones, not asking pardon, yet did he pray for them. I would thou wert like him ; reach forth. Why art thou for ever trailing thy heart along the earth ? Hear, " Lift up thy heart," reach forward, love thine enemies. If thou canst not love him in his violence, love him at least when he asks pardon. Love the man who saith to thee, " Brother, I have sinned, forgive me." If thou then forgive him not, I say not merely, that thou dost blot this prayer out of thine heart, but thou shalt be blotted thyself out of the book of God.

17. But if thou then at least forgive him, or let go hatred from thy heart, it is hatred from the heart I bid thee forego, and not proper discipline. What if one who asks my pardon, be one who ought to be chastised by me ! Do what thou wilt, for I suppose that thou dost love thy child even when thou dost chastise him. Thou regardest not his cries under the rod, because thou art reserving for him his inheritance. This I say then, that thou forego from thy heart all hatred, when thine enemy asks pardon of thee. But perhaps you will say, " he is playing false, he is pretending." O thou judge of

---

[1] *Vide* Sermon xl. (xc. Bened.) 9.   [2] Luke vi. 37.   [3] Luke xxiii. 34.   [4] Acts vii. 60.

another's heart, tell me thine own father's thoughts, tell me thine own thoughts yesterday. He asks and petitions for pardon; forgive, by all means forgive him. If thou wilt not forgive him, it is thyself thou dost hurt, not him, for he knows what he has to do. Thou art not willing to forgive thine own fellow-servant; he will go then to thy Lord, and say to Him, " Lord, I have prayed my fellow-servant to forgive me, and he would not; do Thou forgive me." Hath not the Lord power to release his servant's debts? So he, having obtained pardon from his Lord, returns loosed, whilst thou remainest bound. How bound? The time of prayer will come, the time must come for thee to say, " Forgive us our debts, as we also forgive our debtors;" and the Lord will answer thee, Thou wicked servant, when thou didst owe Me so great a debt, thou didst ask Me, and I forgave thee; "shouldest not thou also have had compassion on thy fellow-servant, even as I had pity on thee?"[1] These words are out of the Gospel, not of my own heart. But if on being asked, thou shalt forgive him who begs for pardon, then thou canst say this prayer. And if thou hast not as yet the strength to love him in his violence, still thou mayest offer this prayer, " Forgive us our debts, as we also forgive our debtors." Let us pass on to the rest.

18. " And lead us not into temptation. Forgive us our debts, as we also forgive our debtors,"[2] we say because of past sins, which we cannot undo, that they should not have been done. Thou canst labour not to do what thou hast done before, but how canst thou bring about, that that which thou hast done should not be done? As regards those things which have been done already, that sentence of the prayer is thy help, " Forgive us our debts, as we also forgive our debtors." As regards those into which thou mayest fall, what wilt thou do? " Lead us not into temptation, but deliver us from evil." " Lead us not into temptation, but deliver us from evil," that is, from temptation itself.

19. Now these three first petitions, " Hallowed be Thy Name, Thy kingdom come, Thy will be done as in heaven so in earth," these three regard the life eternal, for God's Name ought to be hallowed in us always, we ought to be in His kingdom always, we ought to do His will always. This will be to all eternity. But " daily bread " is necessary now. All the rest that we pray for from this article, regards the necessities of the present life. Daily bread is necessary in this life; the forgiveness of our debts is necessary in this life. For when we shall arrive at the other life, there will be an end of all debts. In

this life there is temptation, in this life the sailing is dangerous, in this life something is ever stealing its way in through the chinks of our frailties, which must be pumped out. But when we shall be made equal to the Angels of God; no more need to say and pray to God to forgive us our debts, when there will be none. Here then is the " daily bread;" here the prayer that our " debts may be forgiven;" here that we " enter not into temptation;" for in that life temptation does not enter; here that we may be " delivered from evil;" for in that life there will be no evil, but eternal and abiding good.

SERMON VII.

[LVII. BEN.]

AGAIN, ON MATT. VI.   ON THE LORD'S PRAYER.   TO THE COMPETENTES.

1. The order established for your edification requires that ye learn first what to believe, and afterwards what to ask. For so saith the Apostle, " Whosoever shall call upon the Name of the Lord, shall be saved."[3] This testimony blessed Paul cited out of the Prophet; for by the Prophet were those times foretold, when all men should call upon God; " Whosoever shall call upon the Name of the Lord, shall be saved." And he added, " How then shall they call on Him in whom they have not believed? And how shall they believe in Him of whom they have not heard? Or how shall they hear without a preacher? Or how shall they preach except they be sent?"[4] Therefore were preachers sent. They preached Christ. As they preached, the people heard, by hearing they believed, and by believing called upon Him. Because then it was most rightly and most truly said, " How shall they call on Him in whom they have not believed?" therefore have ye first learned what to believe: and to-day have learnt to call on Him in whom ye have believed.

2. The Son of God, our Lord Jesus Christ, hath taught us a Prayer; and though He be the Lord Himself, as ye have heard and repeated in the Creed, the Only Son of God, yet He would not be alone. He is the Only Son, and yet would not be alone; He hath vouchsafed to have brethren. For to whom doth He say, " Say, Our Father, which art in heaven?"[5] Whom did He wish us to call our Father, save His own Father? Did He grudge us this? Parents sometimes when they have gotten one, or two, or three children, fear to give birth to any more, lest they reduce the rest to beggary. But because the inheritance which He promiseth us is such as many may possess, and no one be straitened; therefore hath He called into His brotherhood the

---

[1] Matt. xviii. 32, 33.   [2] Matt. vi. 13.   [3] Joel ii. 32; Rom. x. 13.   [4] Rom. x. 14, 15.   [5] Matt. vi. 9.

peoples of the nations; and the Only Son hath numberless brethren; who say, "Our Father, which art in heaven." So said they who have been before us; and so shall say those who will come after us. See how many brethren the Only Son hath in His grace, sharing His inheritance with those for whom He suffered death. We had a father and mother on earth, that we might be born to labours and to death: but we have found other parents, God our Father, and the Church our Mother, by whom we are born unto life eternal. Let us then consider, beloved, whose children we have begun to be; and let us live so as becomes those who have such a Father. See, how that our Creator hath condescended to be our Father!

3. We have heard whom we ought to call upon, and with what hope of an eternal inheritance we have begun to have a Father in heaven; let us now hear what we must ask of Him. Of such a Father what shall we ask? Do we not ask rain of Him, to-day, and yesterday, and the day before? This is no great thing to have asked of such a Father, and yet ye see with what sighings, and with what great desire we ask for rain, when death is feared, when that is feared which none can escape. For sooner or later every man must die, and we groan, and pray, and travail in pain, and cry to God, that we may die a little later. How much more ought we to cry to Him, that we may come to that place where we shall never die!

4. Therefore is it said, "Hallowed be Thy Name." This we also ask of Him that his Name may be hallowed in us; for Holy is it always. And how is His Name hallowed in us, except while it makes us holy. For once we were not holy, and we are made holy by His Name; but He is always Holy, and His Name always Holy. It is for ourselves, not for God, that we pray. For we do not wish well to God, to whom no ill can ever happen. But we wish what is good for ourselves, that His Holy Name may be hallowed, that that which is always Holy, may be hallowed in us.

5. "Thy kingdom come."[1] Come it surely will, whether we ask or no. Indeed, God hath an eternal kingdom. For when did He not reign? When did He begin to reign? For His kingdom hath no beginning, neither shall it have any end. But that we may know that in this prayer also we pray for ourselves, and not for God (for we do not say, "Thy kingdom come," as though we were asking that God may reign); we shall be ourselves His kingdom, if believing in Him we make progress in this faith. All the faithful, redeemed by the Blood of His Only Son, will be His kingdom. And this His king-

dom will come, when the resurrection of the dead shall have taken place; for then He will come Himself. And when the dead are risen, He will divide them, as He Himself saith, "and He shall set some on the right hand, and some on the left."[2] To those who shall be on the right hand He will say, "Come, ye blessed of My Father, receive the kingdom." This is what we wish and pray for when we say, "Thy kingdom come;" that it may come to us. For if we shall be reprobates, that kingdom will come to others, but not to us. But if we shall be of that number, who belong to the members of His Only-begotten Son, His kingdom will come to us, and will not tarry. For are there as many ages yet remaining, as have already passed away? The Apostle John hath said, "My little children, it is the last hour."[3] But it is a long hour proportioned to this long day; and see how many years this last hour lasteth. But nevertheless, be ye as those who watch, and so sleep, and rise again, and reign. Let us watch now, let us sleep in death; at the end we shall rise again, and shall reign without end.

6. "Thy will be done as in heaven, so in earth."[1] The third thing we pray for is, that His will may be done as in heaven so in earth. And in this too we wish well for ourselves. For the will of God must necessarily be done. It is the will of God that the good should reign, and the wicked be damned. Is it possible that this will should not be done? But what good do we wish for ourselves, when we say, "Thy will be done as in heaven, so in earth"? Give ear. For this petition may be understood in many ways, and many things are to be in our thoughts in this petition, when we pray God, "Thy will be done as in heaven, so in earth." As Thy Angels offend Thee not, so may we also not offend Thee. Again, how is "Thy will be done, as in heaven, so in earth," understood? All the holy Patriarchs, all the Prophets, all the Apostles, all the spiritual are as it were God's heaven; and we in comparison of them are earth. "Thy will be done, as in heaven, so in earth;" as in them, so in us also. Again, "Thy will be done, as in heaven, so in earth;" the Church of God is heaven, His enemies are earth. So we wish well for our enemies, that they too may believe and become Christians, and so the will of God be done, as in heaven, so also in earth. Again, "Thy will be done, as in heaven, so in earth." Our spirit is heaven, and the flesh earth. As our spirit is renewed by believing, so may our flesh be renewed by rising again; and "the will of God be done, as in heaven, so in earth." Again, our mind whereby we see truth, and delight in this truth, is heaven; as, "I

---

[1] Matt. vi. 10.   [2] Matt. xxv. 33.   [3] 1 John ii. 18, Vulgate.

delight in the law of God, after the inward man."
What is the earth? "I see another law in my
members, warring against the law of my mind?" [1]
When this strife shall have passed away, and a
full concord brought about of the flesh and
spirit, the will of God will be done as in heaven,
so also in earth. When we repeat this petition,
let us think of all these things, and ask them all
of the Father. Now all these things which we
have mentioned, these three petitions, beloved,
have respect to the life eternal. For if the Name
of our God is sanctified in us, it will be for
eternity. If His kingdom come, where we shall
live for ever, it will be for eternity. If His will
be done as in heaven, so in earth, in all the ways
which I have explained, it will be for eternity.

7. There remain now the petitions for this life
of our pilgrimage ; therefore follows, " Give us
this day our daily bread." [2] Give us eternal
things, give us things temporal. Thou hast
promised a kingdom, deny us not the means of
subsistence. Thou wilt give everlasting glory
with Thyself hereafter, give us in this earth temporal support. Therefore is it "day by day,"
and "to-day," that is, in this present time. For
when this life shall have passed away, shall we
ask for daily bread then? For then it will not
be called, "day by day," but "to-day." Now
it is called, "day by day," when one day passes
away, and another day succeeds. Will it be
called, "day by day," when there will be one
eternal day? This petition for daily bread is
doubtless to be understood in two ways, both for
the necessary supply of our bodily food, and for
the necessities of our spiritual support. There
is a necessary supply of bodily food, for the
preservation of our daily life, without which we
cannot live. This is food and clothing, but the
whole is understood in a part. When we ask for
bread, we thereby understand all things. There
is a spiritual [3] food also which the faithful know,
which ye too will know, when ye shall receive it
at the altar of God. This also is "daily Bread,"
necessary only for this life. For shall we receive
the Eucharist when we shall have come to Christ
Himself, and begun to reign with Him for ever?
So then the Eucharist is our daily bread ; but let
us in such wise receive it, that we be not refreshed in our bodies only, but in our souls. For
the virtue which is apprehended there, is unity,
that gathered together into His body, and made
His members, we may be what we receive. Then
will it be indeed our daily bread. Again, what
I am handling before you now is "daily bread ;"
and the daily lessons which ye hear in church,
are daily bread, and the hymns ye hear and repeat are daily bread. For all these are necessary in our state of pilgrimage. But when we

shall have got to heaven, shall we hear the word, [4]
we who shall see the Word Himself, and hear
the Word Himself, and eat and drink Him as the
angels do now? Do the angels need books, and
interpreters, and readers? Surely not. They
read in seeing, for the Truth Itself they see, and
are abundantly satisfied from that fountain, from
which we obtain some few [5] drops. Therefore
has it been said touching our daily bread, that
this petition is necessary for us in this life.

8. " Forgive us our debts, as we forgive our
debtors." [6] Is this necessary except in this life?
For in the other we shall have no debts. For
what are debts, but sins? See, ye are on the
point of being baptized, then all your sins will
be blotted out, none whatever will remain.
Whatever evil ye have ever done, in deed, or
word, or desire, or thought, all will be blotted
out. And yet if in the life which is after Baptism there were security from sin, we should not
learn such a prayer as this, " Forgive us our
debts." Only let us by all means do what comes
next, " As we forgive our debtors." Do ye then
who are about to enter in to receive a plenary
and entire remission of your debts, do ye above
all things see that ye have nothing in your
hearts against any other, so as to come forth
from Baptism secure, as it were free and discharged of all debts, and then begin to purpose
to avenge yourselves on your enemies, who in
time past have done you wrong. Forgive, as
ye are forgiven. God can do no one wrong,
and yet He forgiveth who oweth nothing. How
then ought he to forgive, who is himself forgiven, when He forgiveth all, who oweth nothing
that can be forgiven Him?

9. " Lead us not into temptation, but deliver
us from evil." [7] Will this again be necessary in
the life to come? " Lead us not into temptation," will not be said, except where there can
be temptation. We read in the book of holy
Job, " Is not the life of man upon earth a temptation?" [8] What then do we pray for? Hear
what. The Apostle James saith, " Let no man
say when he is tempted, I am tempted of God." [9]
He spoke of those evil temptations, whereby
men are deceived, and brought under the yoke
of the devil. This is the kind of temptation he
spoke of. For there is another sort of temptation which is called a proving ; of this kind of
temptation it is written, " The Lord your God
tempteth (proveth) you to know whether ye
love Him." [10] What means " to know "? " To
make you know," for He knoweth already.
With that kind of temptation, whereby we are
deceived and seduced, God tempteth no man.
But undoubtedly in His deep and hidden judg-

---

[1] Rom. vii. 22, 23.   [2] Matt. vi. 11.
[3] See Sermon vi. (lvi. Bened.) 10 and note.

[4] Codex.   [5] Irroramur.   [6] Matt. vi. 12.
[7] Matt. vi. 13.   [8] Job vii. 1, Sept.; πειρατηρίον.
[9] Jas. i. 13.   [10] Deut. xiii. 3.

ment He abandons some. And when He hath abandoned them, the tempter finds his opportunity. For he finds in him no resistance against his power, but forthwith presents himself to him as his possessor, if God abandon him. Therefore that He may not abandon us, do we say, " Lead us not into temptation." " For every one is tempted," says the same Apostle James, " when he is drawn away of his own lust and enticed. Then lust, when it hath conceived, bringeth forth sin ; and sin, when it is finished, bringeth forth death." [1] What then has he hereby taught us ? To fight against our lusts. For ye are about to put away your sins in Holy Baptism ; but lusts will still remain, wherewith ye must fight after that ye are regenerate. For a conflict with your own selves still remains. Let no enemy from without be feared : conquer thine own self, and the whole world is conquered. What can any tempter from without, whether the devil or the devil's minister, do against thee ? Whosoever sets the hope of gain before thee to seduce thee, let him only find no covetousness in thee ; and what can he who would tempt thee by gain effect ? Whereas if covetousness be found in thee, thou takest fire at the sight of gain, and art taken by the bait of this corrupt food. [2] But if he find no covetousness in thee, the trap remains spread in vain. Or should the tempter set before thee some woman of surpassing beauty ; if chastity be within, iniquity from without is overcome. Therefore that he may not take thee with the bait of a strange woman's beauty, fight with thine own lust within ; thou hast no sensible perception of thine enemy, but of thine own concupiscence thou hast. Thou dost not see the devil, but the object that engageth thee thou dost see. Get the mastery then over that of which thou art sensible within. Fight valiantly, for He who hath regenerated thee is thy Judge ; He hath arranged the lists, He is making ready the crown. But because thou wilt without doubt be conquered, if thou have not Him to aid thee, if He abandon thee : therefore dost thou say in the prayer, " Lead us not into temptation." The Judge's wrath hath given over some to their own lusts ; and the Apostle says, " God gave them over to the lusts of their hearts." [3] How did He give them up ? Not by forcing, but by forsaking them.

10. " Deliver us from evil," may belong to the same sentence. Therefore, that thou mayest understand it to be all one sentence, it runs thus, " Lead us not into temptation, but deliver us from evil." Therefore he added " but," to show that all this belongs to one sentence, " Lead us not into temptation, but deliver us from evil." How is this ? I will propose them singly. " Lead us not into temptation, but deliver us from evil." By delivering us from evil, He leadeth us not into temptation ; by not leading us into temptation, He delivereth us from evil.

11. And truly it is a great temptation, dearly beloved, it is a great temptation in this life, when that in us is the subject of temptation, whereby we attain [4] pardon, if in any of our temptations we have fallen. It is a frightful temptation, when that is taken from us, whereby we may be healed from the wounds of other temptations. I know that ye have not yet understood me. Give me your attention, that ye may understand. Suppose avarice tempts a man, and he is conquered in any single temptation (for sometimes even a good wrestler and fighter may get roughly handled [5]) : avarice then has got the better of a man, good wrestler though he be, and he has done some avaricious act. Or there has been a passing lust ; it has not brought the man to fornication, nor reached unto adultery, for when this does take place, the man must at all events be kept back from the criminal act. But he " hath seen a woman to lust after her ; " [6] he has let his thoughts dwell on her with more pleasure than was right ; he has admitted the attack ; excellent combatant though he be, he has been wounded, but he has not consented to it ; he has beaten back the motion of his lust, has chastised it with the bitterness of grief, he has beaten it back ; and has prevailed. Still in the very fact that he had slipped, has he ground for saying, " Forgive us our debts." And so of all other temptations, it is a hard matter that in them all there should not be occasion for saying, " Forgive us our debts." What then is that frightful temptation which I have mentioned, that grievous, that tremendous temptation, which must be avoided with all our strength, with all our resolution ; what is it ? When we go about to avenge ourselves. Anger is kindled, and the man burns to be avenged. O frightful temptation ! Thou art losing that, whereby thou hadst to attain pardon for other faults. If thou hadst committed any sin as to other senses, and other lusts, hence mightest thou have had thy cure, in that thou mightest say, " Forgive us our debts, as we also forgive our debtors." But whoso instigateth thee to take vengeance, will lose for thee the power thou hadst to say, " As we also forgive our debtors." When that power is lost, all sins will be retained ; nothing at all is remitted.

12. Our Lord and Master, and Saviour, knowing this dangerous temptation in this life, when He taught us six or seven petitions in this Prayer, took none of them for Himself to treat of, and to commend to us with greater earnest-

---

[1] Jas. i. 14, 15.   [2] *Vitiosa esca laqueo.*
[3] Rom. i. 24, Vulgate.

[4] *Meremur.*   [5] *Vulneratur.*   [6] Matt. v. 28.

ness, than this one. Have we not said, "Our Father, which art in heaven;" and the rest which follows? Why after the conclusion of the Prayer, did He not enlarge upon it to us, either as to what He had laid down in the beginning, or concluded with at the end, or placed in the middle? For why said He not, if the Name of God be not hallowed in you, or if ye have no part in the kingdom of God, or if the will of God be not done in you, as in heaven, or if God guard you not, that ye enter not into temptation; why none of all these? but what saith He? "Verily I say unto you, that if ye forgive men their trespasses;"[1] in reference to that petition, "Forgive us our debts, as we also forgive our debtors." Having passed over all the other petitions which He taught us, this He taught us with an especial force. There was no need of insisting[2] so much upon those sins in which if a man offend, he may know the means whereby he may be cured: need of it there was, with regard to that sin in which if thou sin, there is no means whereby the rest can be cured. For this thou oughtest to be ever saying, "Forgive us our debts." What debts? There is no lack of them; for we are but men; I have talked somewhat more than I ought, have said something I ought not, have laughed more than I ought, have eaten more than I ought, have listened with pleasure to what I ought not, have drunk more than I ought, have seen with pleasure what I ought not, have thought with pleasure on what I ought not; "Forgive us our debts, as we also forgive our debtors." This if thou hast lost, thou art lost thyself.

13. Take heed, my brethren, my sons, sons of God, take heed, I beseech you, in that I am saying to you. Fight to the uttermost of your powers with your own hearts. And if ye shall see your anger making a stand against you, pray to God against it, that God may make thee conqueror of thyself, that God may make thee conqueror, I say, not of thine enemy without, but of thine own soul within. For He will give thee His present help, and will do it. He would rather that we ask this of Him, than rain. For ye see, beloved, how many petitions the Lord Christ hath taught us; and there is scarce found among them one which speaks of daily bread, that all our thoughts may be moulded after the life to come? For what can we fear that He will not give us, who hath promised and said, "Seek ye first the kingdom of God and His righteousness, and all these things shall be added unto you; for your Father knoweth that ye have need of these things before ye ask Him. Seek ye first the kingdom of God and His righteous-

ness, and all these things shall be added unto you."[3] For many have been tried even with hunger, and have been found gold, and have not been forsaken by God. They would have perished with hunger, if the daily inward bread were to leave their heart. After this let us chiefly hunger. For, "Blessed are they who hunger and thirst after righteousness, for they shall be filled."[4] But He can in mercy look upon our infirmity, and see us, as it is said, "Remember that we are dust."[5] He who from the dust made and quickened man, for that His work of clay's sake, gave His Only Son to death. Who can explain, who can worthily so much as conceive, how much He loveth us?

SERMON VIII.

[LVIII. BEN.]

AGAIN ON THE LORD'S PRAYER, MATT. VI. TO THE COMPETENTES.

1. You have just repeated the Creed, where in brief summary is contained the Faith. I have already before now told you what the Apostle Paul says, "How shall they call on Him in whom they have not believed?"[6] Because then you have both heard, and learnt, and repeated how you must believe in God; hear to-day how He must be called upon. The Son Himself, as you heard when the Gospel was read, taught His disciples and His faithful ones this Prayer. Good hope have we of obtaining our cause, when such an Advocate[7] hath dictated our suit. The Assessor of the Father, as you have confessed, who sitteth on the right hand of the Father; He is our Advocate who is to be our Judge. For from thence will He come to judge the quick and dead. Learn then this Prayer also which you will have to repeat in eight days time. But whosoever of you have not repeated the Creed well, have yet time enough, let them learn it; because on the Sabbath day[8] in the hearing of all who shall be present, you will have to repeat it: on the last[9] Sabbath day, when you will be here to be baptized. But in eight days from to-day will you have to repeat this Prayer, which you have heard to-day.

2. Of which the first clause is, "Our Father, which art in heaven."[10] We have found then a Father in heaven; let us take good heed how we live on earth. For he who hath found such a Father, ought so to live that he may be worthy to come to his inheritance. But we say all in common, "Our Father." How great a condescension! This the emperor says, and this says the beggar: this says the slave, and this his lord.

---

[1] Matt. vi. 14. [2] *Commendanda.*

[3] Matt. vi. 53. [4] Matt. v. 6.
[5] Ps. cii. 14, Sept. (ciii. English version). [6] Rom. x. 14.
[7] *Jurisperitus.* [8] Easter Eve.
[9] *i.e.* in Lent. [10] Matt. vi. 9.

They say all together, " Our Father, which art in heaven." Therefore do they understand that they are brethren, seeing they have one Father. Now let not the lord disdain to have his slave for a brother, seeing the Lord Christ has vouchsafed to have him for a brother.

3. " Hallowed be Thy Name, Thy kingdom come." [1] This hallowing of God's Name is that whereby we are made holy. For His Name is always Holy. We wish also for His kingdom to come ; come it will, though we wish it not ; but to wish and pray that His kingdom may come, is nothing else than to wish of Him, that He would make us worthy of His kingdom, lest haply, which God forbid, it should come, and not come to us. For to many that will never come, which nevertheless must come. For to them will it come, to whom it shall be said, " Come, ye blessed of My Father, receive the kingdom prepared for you from the foundation of the world." [2] But it will not come to them to whom it shall be said, " Depart from Me, ye cursed, into everlasting fire." [3] Therefore when we say, " Thy kingdom come," we pray that it may come to us. What is, " may come to us " ? May find us good. This we pray for then, that He would make us good ; for then to us will His kingdom come.

4. We go on, " Thy will be done as in heaven so in earth." [4] The Angels serve Thee in heaven, may we serve Thee in earth ! The Angels do not offend Thee in heaven, may we not offend Thee in earth ! As they do Thy will, so may we do it also ! And here what do we pray for, but that we may be good ? For when we do God's will (for He without doubt doeth His own will), then is His will done in us. And we may understand in another and a right sense these words, " Thy will be done as in heaven, so in earth." We receive the commandment of God, and it is well-pleasing to us, well-pleasing to our mind. " For we delight in the law of God after the inward man." [5] Then is His will done in heaven. For our spirit is compared to heaven, but to the earth our flesh. What then is " Thy will be done as in heaven, so in earth" ? That as Thy command is well-pleasing to our mind, so may our flesh consent thereto ; and so that strife be ended which is described by the Apostle, " for the flesh lusteth against the Spirit, and the Spirit against the flesh." [6] When the Spirit lusteth against the flesh, His will is even now done in heaven ; when the flesh lusteth not against the Spirit, His will is now done in earth. There will be harmony complete when He will ; be then the contest now, that there may be victory hereafter. Thus again, " Thy will be done as in heaven, so in earth," may be well understood, by making " heaven " to be the Church, because it is the

throne [7] of God ; and " earth " the unbelievers, to whom it is said, " Earth thou art, and unto earth shalt thou go." [8] When therefore we pray for our enemies, for the enemies of the Church, the enemies of the Christian name, we pray that His will may be done " as in heaven, so in earth," that is, as in Thy faithful ones, so in Thy blasphemers also, that they all may become " heaven."

5. There follows next, " Give us this day our daily bread." [9] It may be understood simply that we pour forth this prayer for daily sustenance, that we may have abundance : or if not that, that we may have no want. Now he said " daily," for as long as it is called " to-day." [10] Daily we live, and daily rise, and are daily fed, and daily hunger. May He then give us daily bread. Why did He not say " covering " too, for the support of our life is in meat and drink, our covering in raiment and lodging. Man should desire nothing more than these. Forasmuch as the Apostle saith, " We brought nothing into this world, neither can we carry anything out : having food and covering, [11] let us be therewith content." [12] Perish covetousness, and nature is rich. Therefore if this prayer have reference to our daily sustenance, since this is a good understanding of the words, " Give us this day our daily bread ; " let us not marvel, if under the name of bread other necessary things are also understood. As when Joseph invited his brethren, " These men," saith he, " will eat bread with me to-day." [13] Why, were they to eat bread only ? No, but in the mention of bread only, all the rest was understood. So when we pray for daily bread, we ask for whatever is necessary for us in earth for our bodies' sake. But what saith the Lord Jesus ? " Seek ye first the kingdom of God and His righteousness, and all these things shall be added unto you." [14] Again, this is a very good sense of, " Give us this day our daily bread," thy Eucharist, our daily food. For the faithful know what they receive, and good for them it is to receive that daily bread which is necessary for this time present. They pray then for themselves, that they may become good, that they may persevere in goodness, and faith, and a holy life. This do they wish, this they pray for ; for if they persevere not in this good life, they will be separated from that Bread. Therefore, " Give us this day our daily bread." What is this ? Let us live so, that we be not separated from Thy altar. Again, the Word of God which is laid open to us, and in a manner broken day by day, is " daily bread." And as our bodies hunger after that other, so do our souls after this bread. And so we both ask for this bread simply, and whatsoever is in this

---

[7] *Portat.*   [8] Gen. iii. 19, Sept.
[9] Matt. vi. 11.   [10] Heb. iii. 13.
[11] *Tegumentum ; σκεπάσματα.*   [12] 1 Tim. vi. 7, 8.
[13] Gen. xliii. 16, Sept.   [14] Matt. vi. 33.

[1] Matt. vi. 9, 10.   [2] Matt. xxv. 34.   [3] Matt. xxv. 41.
[4] Matt. vi. 10.   [5] Rom. vii. 22.   [6] Gal. v. 17.

life needful both for our souls and bodies, is included in " daily bread."

6. " Forgive us our debts," [1] we say, and we may well say so ; for we say the truth. For who is he that lives here in the flesh, and hath no debts? What man is there that lives so, that this prayer is not necessary for him? He may puff himself up, justify himself he cannot. It were well for him to imitate the Publican, and not swell as the Pharisee, " who went up into the temple," [2] and boasted of his deserts, and covered up his wounds. Whereas he who said, " Lord, be merciful to me a sinner," [3] knew wherefore he went up. This prayer the Lord Jesus, consider, my brethren, this prayer the Lord Jesus taught His disciples to offer, those great first Apostles of His, the leaders of our flock.[4] If the leaders of the flock then pray for the remission of their sins, what ought the lambs to do, of whom it is said, " Bring young rams unto the Lord"?[5] You knew then that you have repeated this in the Creed, because amongst the rest you have mentioned there " the remission of sins." There is one remission of sins which is given once for all ; another which is given day by day. There is one remission of sins which is given once for all in Holy Baptism ; another which is given as long as we live here in the Lord's Prayer. Wherefore we say, " Forgive us our debts."

7. And God has brought us into a covenant, and agreement, and a firm bond [6] with Him, in that we say, " as we also forgive our debtors." He who would say it effectually, " Forgive us our debts," must say truly, " as we also forgive our debtors." [1] If this which is last he either say not, or say deceitfully, the other which is first he says in vain. We say to you then especially who are approaching to Holy Baptism, from your hearts forgive everything. And ye faithful, who taking advantage of this occasion are listening to this prayer, and our exposition of it, do ye wholly and from your hearts forgive whatsoever ye have against any. Forgive it there where God seeth. For sometimes a man remitteth with the mouth, and in the heart retaineth ; he remitteth with the mouth for men's sake, and retaineth in the heart, as not fearing the eyes of God. But do ye remit entirely. Whatever ye have retained up to these holy days,[7] in these holy days at least remit. " The sun ought not to go down upon your wrath," [8] yet many suns have passed. Let then your wrath at length pass away also, now that we are celebrating the days of the great Sun, of that Sun of which Scripture saith, " Unto you shall the Sun of righteousness

arise with healing in His wings." [9] What is, " in His wings"? In His protection. Whence it is said in the Psalms, " Keep me under the shadow of Thy wings." [10] But as to others who in the day of judgment shall repent, but all too late, and who shall mourn, yet unavailingly, it hath been foretold by Wisdom what they shall then say as they repent and groan for anguish of spirit, " What hath pride profited us, or what good hath riches with our vaunting brought us? All these things are passed away like a shadow." And, " Therefore have we erred from the way of truth, and the light of righteousness hath not shined unto us, and the Sun of righteousness rose not upon us." [11] That Sun riseth upon the righteous only ; but this sun which we see, God " maketh," daily " to rise upon the good and evil." [12] The righteous attain to the seeing of that Sun ; and that Sun dwelleth now in our hearts by faith. If then thou art angry, let not this sun go down in thine heart upon thy wrath ; " Let not the sun go down upon thy wrath ; " lest haply thou be angry, and so the Sun of righteousness go down upon thee, and thou abide in darkness.

8. Now do not think that anger is nothing. " Mine eye was disordered because of anger," [13] saith the Prophet. Surely he whose eye is disordered cannot see the sun ; and if he should try to see it, it were pain, and no pleasure to him. And what is anger? The lust of vengeance. A man lusteth to be avenged, and Christ is not yet avenged, the holy martyrs are not yet avenged. Still doth the patience of God wait, that the enemies of Christ, the enemies of the martyrs, may be converted. And who are we, that we should seek for vengeance? If God should seek it at our hands, where should we abide? He who hath never in any matter done us harm, doth not wish to avenge Himself of us ; and do we seek to be avenged, who are almost daily offending God? Forgive therefore ; from the heart forgive. If thou art angry, yet sin not. " Be ye angry, and sin not." [14] Be ye angry as being but men, if so be ye are overcome by it ; yet sin not, so as to retain anger in your heart (for if ye do retain it, ye retain it against yourselves), lest ye enter not into that Light. Therefore forgive. What then is anger? The lust of vengeance. And what is hatred? Inveterate anger. If anger become inveterate, it is then called hatred. And this he seems to acknowledge, who when he had said, " Mine eye is disordered because of anger ; " added, " I have become inveterate among all mine enemies." [13] What was anger when it was

---

[1] Matt. vi. 12. [2] Luke xviii. 10, 11.
[3] Luke xviii. 13. [4] Arietes nostros.
[5] Ps. xxviii. 1, Sept. (xxix. English version).
[6] Chirographum.
[7] The Feast of Easter, the great season for baptizing. See Bingham, xi. 6, 7.
[8] Eph. iv. 26.

[9] Mal. iv. 2. [10] Ps. xvii. 8.
[11] Wisd. v. 8, 9, 6. [12] Matt. v. 45.
[13] Ps. vi. 8, Sept. (vi. 7, English version).
[14] Ps. iv. 5, Sept. (iv. 4, English version).

new, became hatred when it was turned into long continuance.[1] Anger is a "mote," hatred, a "beam." We sometimes find fault with one who is angry, yet we retain hatred in our own hearts; and so Christ saith to us, "Thou seest the mote in thy brother's eye, and seest not the beam in thine own eye."[2] How grew the mote into a beam? Because it was not at once plucked out. Because thou didst suffer the sun to rise and go down so often upon thy wrath, and madest it inveterate, because thou contractedst evil suspicions, and wateredst the mote, and by watering hast nourished it, and by nourishing it, hast made it a beam. Tremble then at least when it is said, "Whosoever hateth his brother is a murderer."[3] Thou hast not drawn the sword, nor inflicted any bodily wound, nor by any blow killed another; the thought only of hatred is in thy heart, and hereby art thou held to be a murderer, guilty art thou before the eyes of God. The other man is alive, and yet thou hast killed him. As far as thou art concerned, thou hast killed the man whom thou hatest. Reform then, and amend thyself. If scorpions or adders were in your houses, how would ye toil to purify them, that ye might be able to dwell in safety? Yet are ye angry, yea inveterate anger is in your hearts, and there grow so many hatreds, so many beams, so many scorpions, so many vipers, and will ye not then purify the house of God, your heart? Do then what is said, "As we also forgive our debtors;" and so say securely, "Forgive us our debts." For without debts in this earth ye cannot live; but those great crimes which it is your blessing to have been forgiven in Baptism, and from which we ought to be ever free, are of one sort, and of another are those daily sins, without which a man cannot live in this world, by reason of which this daily prayer with its covenant and agreement is necessary; that as we say with all cheerfulness, "Forgive us our debts;" so we may say with all truth, "As we also forgive our debtors." So much then have we said as touching past sins; what now for the future?

9. "Lead us not into temptation:"[4] forgive what we have done already, and grant that we may not commit any more sins. For whosoever is overcome by temptation, committeth sin. Thus the Apostle James saith, "Let no man say when he is tempted, he is tempted of God, for God cannot be tempted with evil, neither tempteth He any man. But every man is tempted, when he is drawn away of his own lust, and enticed. Then lust, when it hath conceived, bringeth forth sin: and sin, when it is finished, bringeth forth death."[5] Therefore that thou be not drawn away by thy lust; consent not to it. It hath no means

of conceiving, but by thee. Thou hast consented, hast as it were in thine heart admitted[6] her embrace. Lust has risen up, deny thyself to her, follow her not. It is a lust unlawful, impure, and shameful, it will alienate thee from God. Give it not then the embrace of thy consent, lest thou have to bewail the birth; for if thou consent, that is, when thou hast embraced her, she conceives, "and when lust hath conceived, it bringeth forth sin." Dost thou not yet fear? "Sin bringeth forth death;" at least, fear death. If thou fear not sin, yet fear that whereunto it leads. Sin is sweet; but death is bitter. This is the infelicity of men; that for which they sin, they leave here when they die, and the sin themselves they carry with them. Thou dost sin for money, it must be left here: or for a country seat; it must be left here: or for some woman's sake; she must be left here; and whatsoever it be for which thou dost sin, when thou shalt have closed thine eyes in death, thou must leave it here; yet the sin itself which thou committest, thou carriest with thee.

10. May sins then be forgiven; the past forgiven, and the future cease. But without them here below thou canst not live; be they either lesser sins, or small, or trivial. Yet let not even these small and trivial sins be despised. With little drops is the river filled. Let not even the lesser sins be despised. Through narrow chinks in the ship the water oozes in,[7] the hold keeps filling, and if it be disregarded the ship is sunk. But the sailors are not idle; their hands are active,[8] — active that the water may be drained off from day to day. So be thy hands active, that thou mayest pump from day to day. What is the meaning of "be thy hands active"? Let them give, do good works, so be thy hands engaged. "Break thy bread to the hungry, and bring the poor and houseless into thine house; if thou seest the naked, clothe him."[9] Do all thou canst, do it with the means thou canst command, do it cheerfully, and so put up thy prayer with confidence. It will have two wings, a double alms. What is "a double alms"? "Forgive, and ye shall be forgiven. Give, and it shall be given unto you."[10] The one alms is that which is done from the heart, when thou forgivest thy brother his sin. The other alms is that which is done out of thy substance, when thou dealest bread to the poor. Offer both, lest without either wing thy prayer remain motionless.

11. Therefore when we have said, "Lead us not into temptation," there follows, "But deliver us from evil." Now whoso wishes to be delivered from evil, bears witness that he is in evil. And thus saith the Apostle, "Redeeming

[1] Vetustatem.   [2] Matt. vii. 3.   [3] 1 John iii. 15.
[4] Matt. vi. 13.   [5] Jas. i. 13, etc.

[6] Concubuisti.   [7] Insudat aqua.   [8] Ambulant.
[9] Isa. lviii. 7, Sept.   [10] Luke vi. 37, 38.

the time, because the days are evil." [1]   But who is there " that wisheth for life, and loveth to see good days "? [2]   Seeing that all men in this flesh have only evil days ; who doth not wish it ?   Do thou what follows, " Keep thy tongue from evil, and thy lips that they speak no guile : depart from evil, and do good, seek peace, and ensue it ; " [3] and then thou hast got rid of evil days, and thy prayer, " deliver us from evil," is fulfilled.

12. Therefore the three first petitions, " Hallowed be Thy Name, Thy kingdom come, Thy will be done as in heaven, so in earth," are for eternity.   But the four following relate to this life, " Give us this day our daily bread."   Shall we ask day by day for daily bread, when we shall have come to that fulness of blessing ? " Forgive us our debts."   Shall we say this in that kingdom, when we shall have no debts ? " Lead us not into temptation."   Shall we be able to say this then, when there will be no temptation ?   "•Deliver us from evil."   Shall we say this, when there shall be nothing from which to be delivered ?   Therefore these four are necessary, because of our daily life, but the three first in reference to the life eternal.   But all things let us ask, with a view of attaining to that life, and let us pray here, that we be not separated from it.   Every day must this prayer be said by you, when you are baptized.   For the Lord's Prayer is said daily in the Church before the Altar of God, and the faithful hear it.   We have no fear therefore as to your not learning it carefully, because even if any of you should be unable to get it perfectly, he will learn it by hearing it day by day.

13. Therefore on the Saturday [4] when by the grace of God you will keep the Vigil, you will have to repeat not the Prayer, but the Creed. For if you do not know the Creed now, you will not hear that every day in the Church, and among the people.   But when you have learnt it, that you may not forget it, say it every day when you rise ; when you are preparing for sleep, rehearse your Creed, to the Lord rehearse it, remind yourselves of it, and be not weary of repeating it.   For repetition is useful, lest forgetfulness steal over you.   Do not say, " I said it yesterday, I have said it to-day, I say it every day, I know it perfectly well."   Call thy faith to mind, look into thyself, let thy Creed be as it were a mirror to thee.   Therein see thyself, whether thou dost believe all which thou professest to believe, and so rejoice day by day in thy faith.   Let it be thy wealth, let it be in a sort the daily clothing of thy soul.   Dost thou not always dress thyself when thou risest ?   So by the daily repetition of thy Creed dress thy soul, lest haply forgetfulness make it bare, and thou remain naked, and that take place which the Apostle saith, (may it be far from thee !) " If so be that being unclothed, [5] we shall not be found naked." [6] For we shall be clothed by our faith : and this faith is at once a garment and a breastplate ; a garment against shame, a breastplate against adversity.   But when we shall have arrived at that place where we shall reign, no need will there be to say the Creed.   We shall see God ; God Himself will be our vision ; the vision of God will be the reward of our present faith.

SERMON IX.

[LIX. BEN.]

AGAIN, ON THE LORD'S PRAYER, MATT. VI.   TO THE COMPETENTES.

1. You have rehearsed what you believe, hear now what you are to pray for.   Forasmuch as you would not be able to call on Him, in whom you should not first have believed ; as saith the Apostle, " How shall they call on Him, in whom they have not believed ? " [7]   Therefore have you first learned the Creed, where is a brief and sublime rule of your faith ; brief in the number of its words, sublime in the weight of its contents. [8] But the prayer which you receive to-day to be learned by heart, and to be repeated eight days hence, was dictated (as you heard when the Gospel was being read) by the Lord Himself to His disciples, and came from them unto us, since " their sound went into all the earth." [9]

2. Ye then who have found a Father in heaven, be loth to cleave to the things of earth.   For ye are about to say, " Our Father, which art in heaven." [10]   You have begun to belong to a great family.   Under this Father the lord and the slave are brethren ; under this Father the general and the common soldier are brethren ; under this Father the rich man and the poor are brethren. All Christian believers have divers fathers in earth, some noble, some obscure ; but they all call upon one Father which is in heaven.   If our Father be there, there is the inheritance prepared for us. But He is such a Father, that we can possess with Him what He giveth.   For He giveth an inheritance ; but He doth not leave it to us by dying. For He doth not depart Himself, but He abideth ever, that we may come to Him.   Seeing then we have heard of Whom we are to ask, let us

---

[5] The reading of D. F. G., some MSS. ap. Chrys. and Ambr. Ar. Pol. Vet. Lat. Tert. Paulin. Macar. ap. Mill. Auct. quæstt. V. T. St. Augustin's present text has elsewhere " *induti* " (see Sabat.) ; but the text of the Fathers is often involuntarily conformed to the Vulgate.
[6] 2 Cor. v. 3.   [7] Rom. x. 14.   [8] *Sententiarum.*
[9] Ps. xviii. 5, Sept. (xix. 4, English version).
[10] Matt. vi. 9.

---

[1] Eph. v. 16.   [2] Ps. xxxiv. 12.   [3] Ps. xxxiv. 13, 14.
[4] Easter Eve.   See Bingham, xxi. 1, 32.

know also what to ask for, lest haply we offend such a Father by asking amiss.

3. What then hath the Lord Jesus Christ taught us to ask of the Father which is in heaven? "Hallowed be Thy Name."[1] What kind of blessing is this that we ask of God, that His Name may be hallowed? The Name of God is always Holy; why then do we pray that it may be hallowed, except that we may be hallowed by it? We pray then that that which is Holy always, may be hallowed in us. The Name of God is hallowed in you when ye are baptized. Why will ye offer this prayer after ye have been baptized, but that that which ye shall then receive may abide ever in you?

4. Another petition follows, "Thy kingdom come."[2] God's kingdom will come, whether we ask it or not. Why then do we ask it, but that that which will come to all saints may also come to us; that God may count us also in the number of His saints, to whom His kingdom is to come?

5. We say in the third petition, "Thy will be done as in heaven, so in earth."[2] What is this? That as the Angels serve Thee in heaven, so we may serve Thee in earth. For His holy Angels obey Him; they do not offend Him; they do His commands through the love of Him. This we pray for then, that we too may do the commands of God in love. Again, these words are understood in another way, "Thy will be done as in heaven, so in earth." Heaven in us is the soul, earth in us is the body. What then is, "Thy will be done as in heaven, so in earth"? As we hear Thy precepts, so may our flesh consent unto us; lest, whilst flesh and spirit strive together, we be not able to fulfil the commands of God.

6. "Give us this day our daily bread,"[3] comes next in the Prayer. Whether we ask here of the Father support[4] necessary for the body, by "bread" signifying whatever is needful for us; or whether we understand that daily Bread, which ye are soon to receive from the Altar; well it is that we pray that He would give it us. For what is it we pray for, but that we may commit no evil, for which we should be separated from that holy Bread. And the word of God which is preached daily is daily bread. For because it is not bread for the body, it is not on that account not bread for the soul. But when this life shall have passed away, we shall neither seek that bread which hunger seeks; nor shall we have to receive the Sacrament of the Altar, because we shall be there with Christ, whose Body we do now receive; nor will those words which we are now speaking, need to be said to you, nor the sacred volume to

be read, when we shall see Him who is Himself the Word of God, by whom all things were made, by whom the Angels are fed, by whom the Angels are enlightened, by whom the Angels become wise; not requiring words of circuitous discourse; but drinking in the Only Word, filled with whom they burst forth[5] and never fail in praise. For, "Blessed," saith the Psalm, "are they who dwell in Thy house; they will be always praising Thee."[6]

7. Therefore in this present life, do we ask what comes next, "Forgive us our debts, as we also forgive our debtors."[7] In Baptism, all debts, that is, all sins, are entirely forgiven us. But because no one can live without sin here below, and if without any great crime which entails separation from the Altar, yet altogether without sins can no one live on this earth, and we can only receive the one Baptism once for all; in this Prayer we hear how we may day by day be washed, that our sins may day by day be forgiven us; but only if we do what follows, "As we also forgive our debtors." Accordingly, my Brethren, I advise you, who are in the grace of God my sons, yet my Brethren under that heavenly Father; I advise you, whenever any one offends and sins against you, and comes, and confesses, and asks your pardon, that ye do pardon him, and forthwith from the heart forgive him; lest ye keep off from your own selves that pardon, which comes from God. For if ye forgive not, neither will He forgive you. Therefore it is in this life that we make this petition, for that it is in this life that sins can be forgiven, where they can be done. But in the life to come they are not forgiven, because they are not done.

8. Next after this we pray, saying, "Lead us not into temptation, but deliver us from evil."[8] This also, that we be not led into temptation, it is necessary for us to ask in this life, because in this life there are temptations; and that "we may be delivered from evil," because there is evil here. And thus of all these seven petitions, three have respect to the life eternal, and four to the present life. "Hallowed be Thy name." This will be for ever. "Thy kingdom come." This kingdom will be for ever. "Thy will be done as in heaven, so in earth." This will be for ever. "Give us this day our daily bread." This will not be for ever. "Forgive us our debts." This will not be for ever. "Lead us not into temptation." This will not be for ever. "But deliver us from evil." This will not be for ever: but where there is temptation, and where there is evil, there is it necessary that we make this petition.

---

[1] Matt. vi. 9.　　[2] Matt. vi. 10.
[3] Matt. vi. 11.　　[4] Exhibitionem.
[5] Ructuant.　　[6] Ps. lxxxiv. 4.　　[7] Matt. vi. 12.
[8] Matt. vi. 13.

SERMON X.

[LX. BEN.]

ON THE WORDS OF THE GOSPEL, MATT. VI. 19,
"LAY NOT UP FOR YOURSELVES TREASURES UPON
EARTH," ETC. AN EXHORTATION TO ALMS-
DEEDS.

1. EVERY man who is in any trouble, and his own resources fail him, looks out for some prudent person from whom he may take counsel, and so know what to do. Let us suppose then the whole world to be as it were one single man. He seeks to escape evil, yet is slow in doing good; and as in this way tribulations thicken, and his own resources fail, whom can he find more prudent to receive counsel from than Christ? By all means, at least, let him find a better, and do what he will. But if he cannot find a better, let him come to Him whom he may find everywhere: let him consult, and take advice from Him, keep the good commandment, escape the great evil. For present temporal ills of which men are so sore afraid, under which they murmur exceedingly, and by their murmuring offend Him who is correcting them, so that they find not His saving Help;[1] present ills I say without a doubt are but passing; either they pass through us, or we pass through them; either they pass away whilst we live, or they are left behind us when we die. Now that is not in the matter of tribulation great, which in duration is short. Whosoever thou art that art thinking of to-morrow, thou dost not recall the remembrance of yesterday. When the day after to-morrow comes, this to-morrow also will be yesterday. But now if men are so disquieted with anxiety to escape temporal tribulations which pass, or rather fly over, what thought ought they to take that they may escape those which abide and endure without end?

2. A hard condition is the life of man. What else is it to be born, but to enter on a life of toil? Of our toil that is to be, the infant's very cry is witness. From this cup[2] of sorrow no one may be excused. The cup that Adam hath pledged, must be drunk. We were made, it is true, by the hands of Truth, but because of sin we were cast forth upon days of vanity. "We were made after the image of God,"[3] but we[4] disfigured it by sinful transgression. Therefore does the Psalm remind us how we were made, and to what a state we have come. For it says, "Though a man walk in the image[5] of God." See, what he was made. Whither hath he come? Hearken to what follows, "Yet will he be dis-

quieted in vain."[6] He walks in the image of truth, and will be disquieted in the counsel of vanity. Finally, see his disquiet, see it, and as it were in a glass, be displeased with thyself. "Though," he says, "man walk in the image of God," and therefore be something great, "yet will he be disquieted in vain;" and as though we might ask, How I pray thee, how is man disquieted in vain? "He heapeth up treasure," saith he, "and knoweth not for whom he doth gather it." See then, this man, that is the whole human race represented as one man, who is without resource in his own case, and hath lost counsel and wandered out of the way of a sound mind; "Heapeth up treasure, and knoweth not for whom he doth gather it." What is more mad, what more unhappy? But surely he is doing it for himself? Not so. Why not for himself? Because he must die, because the life of man is short, because the treasure lasts, but he who gathereth it, quickly passeth away. As pitying therefore the man who "walketh in the image of God," who confesseth things that are true, yet followeth after vain things, he saith, "He will be disquieted in vain." I grieve for him; "he heapeth up treasure, and knoweth not for whom he doth gather it." Doth he gather it for himself? No. Because the man dies whilst the treasure endures. For whom then? If thou hast any good counsel, give it to me. But counsel hast thou none to give me, and so thou hast none for thyself. Wherefore if we are both without it, let us both seek it, let us both receive it, and both consider the matter together. He is disquieted, he heapeth up treasure, he thinks, and toils, and is kept awake by anxiety. All day long art thou harassed by labour, all night agitated by fear. That thy coffer may be filled with money, thy soul is in a fever of anxiety.

3. I see it, I am grieved for thee; thou art disquieted, and as He who cannot deceive, assures us, "Thou art disquieted in vain." For thou art heaping up treasures: supposing that all thy undertakings succeed, to say nothing of losses, of so great perils and deaths in the prosecution of every several kind of gain (I speak not of deaths of the body, but of evil thoughts, for that gold may come in, uprightness[7] goeth out; that thou mayest be clothed outwardly, thou art made naked within), but to pass over these, and other such things in silence, to pass by all the things that are against thee, let us think only of the favourable circumstances. See, thou art laying up treasures, gains flow into thee from every quarter, and thy money runs like fountains; everywhere where want presseth, there doth abundance flow. Hast thou not heard, "If riches increase, set not your heart upon them?"[8] Lo,

---

[1] *Salvatorem.*
[2] *Convivio.* [3] Gen. i. 27. [4] *Detrivimus.*
[5] St. Ambrose, *ad loc.*, observes that *Dei* is not in the Greek, but explains "in imagine" in the same sense, as does St. Augustin, *ad loc.*, where he had not "*Dei.*" It seems a sort of gloss. It occurs in Cassiod. *Anon. de Trin.* ap. St. Ambrose.

[6] Ps. xxxviii. 7, Sept. (xxxix. 6, English version).
[7] *Fides.* [8] Ps. lxii. 10.

thou art getting, thou art disquieted, not fruit-lessly indeed, still in vain. "How," thou wilt ask, "am I disquieted in vain? I am filling my coffers, my walls will scarce hold what I get, how then am I disquieted in vain?" "Thou art heap-ing up treasure, and dost not know for whom thou gatherest it." Or if thou dost know, I pray thee tell me. I will listen to thee. For whom is it? If thou art not disquieted in vain, tell me for whom thou art heaping up thy treasure? "For myself," thou sayest. Dost thou dare say so, who must so soon die? "For my children." Dost thou dare say this of them who must so soon die? It is a great duty of natural affection[1] (it will be said) for a father to lay up for his sons; rather it is a great vanity, one who must soon die is laying up for those who must soon die also. If it is for thyself, why dost thou gather, seeing thou leavest all when thou diest. This is the case also with thy children; they will suc-ceed thee, but not to abide long. I say nothing about what sort of children they may be, whether haply debauchery may not waste what covetous-ness hath amassed. So another by dissoluteness[2] squanders what thou by much toil hast gathered together. But I pass over this. It may be they will be good children, they will not be dissolute, they will keep what thou hast left, will increase what thou hast kept, and will not dissipate what thou hast heaped together. Then will thy chil-dren be equally vain with thyself, if they do so, if in this they imitate thee their father. I would say to them what I said just now to thee. I would say to thy son, to him for whom thou art sav-ing I would say, " Thou art heaping up treasure, and knowest not for whom thou dost gather it." For as thou knewest not, so neither doth he know. If the vanity hath continued in him, hath the truth lost its power with respect to him?

4. I forbear to urge, that it may be even dur-ing thy life thou art but laying up for thieves. In one night may they come and find all ready the gathering of so many days and nights. It may be thou art laying up for a robber, or a highwayman. I will say no more on this, lest I call to mind and re-open the wound of past suf-ferings. How many things which an empty vanity hath heaped together, hath the cruelty of an enemy found ready to its hand. It is not my place to wish for this: but it is the concern of all to fear it. May God avert it! May His own scourges be sufficient. May He to whom we pray, spare us! But if He ask thee for whom are we laying by, what shall we answer? How then, O man, whosoever thou art, that are heaping up treasure in vain, how wilt thou answer me, as I handle this matter with thee, and with

thee seek counsel in a common cause? For thou didst speak and make answer, " I am lay-ing up for myself, for my children, for my pos-terity." I have said already how many grounds of fear there are, even as to those children them-selves. But I pass over the consideration, that thy children may so live as to be a curse[3] to thee, and as thine enemy would wish them; grant that they live as the father himself would have them. Yet how many have fallen into those mischances, I have declared, and reminded you of already. Thou didst shudder at them, though thou didst not amend thyself. For what hast thou to answer but this, " Perhaps it may not be so"? Well, I said so too; perhaps I say thou art but laying up for the thief, or robber, or highwayman. I did not say certainly, but perhaps. Where there is a perhaps, there is a perhaps-not; so then thou knowest not what will be, and therefore thou "art disquieted in vain." Thou seest now how truly spake the Truth, how vainly vanity is disquieted. Thou hast heard and at length learnt wisdom, because when thou sayest, " Perhaps it is for my chil-dren," but dost not dare to say, " I am sure that it is for my children," thou dost not in fact know for whom thou art gathering riches. So then, as I see, and have said already, thou art thyself without resource; thou findest nothing wherewith to answer me, nor can I to answer thee.

5. Let us both therefore seek and ask for counsel. We have opportunity of consulting not any wise man, but Wisdom Herself. Let us then both give ear to Jesus Christ, " to the Jews a stumbling stone, and to the Gentiles foolish-ness, but to them who are called, both Jews and Greeks, Christ the Power of God and the Wis-dom of God."[4] Why art thou preparing a strong defence for thy riches? Hear the Power of God, nothing is more strong than He. Why art thou preparing wise counsel[5] to protect thy riches? Hear the Wisdom of God, nothing is more Wise than He. Peradventure when I say what I have to say, thou wilt be offended, and so thou wilt be a Jew, " because to the Jews is Christ an offence." Or peradventure, when I have spoken, it will appear foolish to thee, and so wilt thou be a Gentile, " for to the Gentiles is Christ foolishness." Yet thou art a Christian, thou hast been called. " But to them who are called, both Jews and Greeks, Christ is the Power of God and the Wisdom of God." Be not sad then when I have said what I have to say; be not offended; mock not my folly, as you deem it, with an air of disdain.[6] Let us give ear. For what I am about to say, Christ hath said. If thou despise the herald, yet fear

---

1 *Pietas.*　　2 *Fluendo.*

3 *Pœnaliter.*
4 1 Cor. i. 23, 24.　5 *Argumenta.*　6 *Ore torto.*

the Judge. What shall I say then? The reader of the Gospel has but just now relieved me from this embarrassment. I will not read anything fresh, but will recall only to your recollection what has just been read. Thou wast seeking counsel, as failing in thine own resources; see then what the Fountain of right counsel saith, the Fountain from whose streams is no fear of poison, fill from It what thou mayest.

6. "Lay not up for yourselves treasures on earth, where moth and rust doth destroy, and where thieves break through and steal: But lay up for yourselves treasures in heaven, where no thief approacheth, nor moth corrupteth: For where your treasure is, there will your heart be also." [1] What more dost thou wait for? The thing is plain. The counsel is open, but evil desire lies hid; nay, not so, but what is worse, it too lies open. For plunder does not cease its ravages; avarice does not cease to defraud; maliciousness does not cease to swear falsely. And all for what? that treasure may be heaped together. To be laid up *where?* In the earth, and rightly indeed, *by* earth *for* earth. For to the man who sinned and who pledged us, as I have said, our cup of toil, was it said, "Earth thou art, and to earth shalt thou return." [2] With good reason is the treasure in earth, because the heart is there. Where then is that, "we lift them up unto the Lord?" Sorrow for your case, ye who have understood me; and if ye sorrow truly, amend yourselves. How long will ye be applauding and not doing? What ye have heard is true, nothing truer. Let that then which is true be done. One God we praise, yet we change not, that we may not in this very praise be disquieted in vain.

7. Therefore, "Lay not up for yourselves treasures on earth;" whether ye have found by experience how what is laid up in the earth is lost, or whether ye have not so experienced it, yet do ye too fear lest ye should do so. Let experience reform him whom words will not reform. One cannot rise up now, one cannot go out, but all together with one voice are crying, "Woe to us, the world is falling." [3] If it be falling, why dost thou not remove? If an architect were to tell thee, that thy house would soon fall, wouldest thou not remove before thou didst indulge in thy vain lamentations? The Builder of the world telleth thee the world will soon fall, and wilt thou not believe it? Hear the voice of Him who foretelleth it, hear the counsel of Him who giveth thee warning. The voice of prediction is, "Heaven and earth shall pass away." [4] The voice of warning is, "Lay not up for

yourselves treasure on earth." [5] If then thou dost believe God in His prediction; if thou despise not His warning, let what He says be done. He who has given thee such counsel doth not deceive thee. Thou shalt not lose what thou hast given away, but shalt follow what thou hast only sent before thee. Therefore my counsel is, "Give to the poor, and thou shalt have treasure in heaven." [6] Thou shalt not remain without treasure; but what thou hast on earth with anxiety, thou shalt possess in heaven free from care. Transport thy goods then. I am giving thee counsel for keeping, not for losing. "Thou shalt have," saith He, "treasure in heaven, and come, follow Me," that I may bring thee to thy treasure. This is not a wasting, but a saving. Why do men keep silence? Let them hear, and having at last by experience found what to fear, let them do that which will give them no cause of fear, let them transport their goods to heaven. Thou puttest wheat in the low ground; [7] and thy friend comes, who knows the nature of the corn and the land, and instructs thy unskilfulness, and says to thee, "What hast thou done?" Thou hast put the corn in the flat soil, in the lower land; the soil is moist; it will all rot, and thou wilt lose thy labour. Thou answerest, What then must I do? Remove it, he says, into the higher ground. Dost thou then give ear to a friend who gives thee counsel about thy corn, and despisest thou God who gives thee counsel about thine heart? Thou fearest to put thy corn in the low earth, and wilt thou lose thy heart in the earth? Behold the Lord thy God when He giveth thee counsel touching thine heart, saith, "Where thy treasure is, there will thy heart be also." [8] Lift up, saith He, thine heart to heaven, that it rot not in the earth. It is His counsel, who wisheth to preserve thy heart, not to destroy it.

8. If then this be so, what must be their repentance who have not done thereafter? How must they now reproach themselves! We might have had in heaven what we have now lost in earth. The enemy has broken up our house; but could he break heaven open? He has killed the servant who was set to guard; but could he kill the Lord who would have kept them, "where no thief approacheth, neither moth corrupteth." How many now are saying, "There we might have had, and hid our treasures safe, where after a little while we might have followed them securely. Why have we not hearkened to our Lord? Why have we despised the admonitions of the Father, and so have experienced the invasion of the enemy?" If then this be good counsel, let us not be slow in taking heed to it; and if what we have must be

---

[1] Matt. vi. 19-21.   [2] Gen. iii. 19, Sept.
[3] From this and the preceding sections it would appear as if this Sermon was written at a time of some great public trouble, probably when the barbarians were ravaging Africa.
[4] Matt. xxiv. 35.

[5] Matt. vi. 19.   [6] Matt. xix. 21.
[7] *In terra.*   [8] Matt. vi. 21.

transported, let us transfer it into that place, from whence we cannot lose it. What are the poor to whom we give, but our [1] carriers,[2] by whom we convey our goods from earth to heaven? Give then : thou art but giving to thy carrier, he carrieth what thou givest to heaven. How, sayest thou, does he carry it to heaven? For I see that he makes an end of it by eating. No doubt, he carries it, not by keeping it, but by making it his food. What? Hast thou forgotten, "Come, ye blessed of My Father, receive the kingdom ; for I was an hungred, and ye gave Me meat : " and, "Inasmuch as ye did it to one of the least of Mine, ye did it to Me." [3] If thou hast not despised the beggar that standeth before thee, consider to Whom what thou gavest him hath come. "Inasmuch," saith he, "as ye did it to one of the least of Mine, ye did it to Me." He hath received it, who gave thee wherewith to give. He hath received it, who in the end will give His Own Self to thee.

9. For this have I at divers times called to your remembrance, Beloved, and I confess to you it astonishes me much in the Scriptures of God, and I ought repeatedly to call your attention to it. I pray you to think of what our Lord Jesus Christ Himself saith, that at the end of the world, when He shall come to judgment, He will gather together all nations before Him, and will divide men into two parts ; that He will place some at His right hand, and others on His left ; and will say to those on the right hand, "Come, ye blessed of My Father, receive the kingdom prepared for you from the foundation of the world." But to those on the left, " Depart ye into everlasting fire, prepared for the devil and his angels." Search out the reasons either for so great a reward, or so great a punishment. "Receive the kingdom," and "Go into everlasting fire." Why shall the first receive the kingdom? "For I was an hungred, and ye gave Me meat." Why shall the other depart into everlasting fire? "For I was hungry, and ye gave Me no meat." What meaneth this, I ask? I see touching those who are to receive the kingdom, that they gave as good and faithful Christians, not despising the words of the Lord, and with sure trust hoping for the promises, they did accordingly ; because had they not done so, this very barrenness would not surely have accorded with their good life. For it may be they were chaste, no cheats, nor drunkards, and kept themselves from evil works. Yet if they had not added good works, they would have remained barren. For they would have kept, "Depart from evil," but they would not have kept, "and do good." [4] Notwithstanding, even to them He doth not say, "Come, receive the kingdom," for ye have lived in chastity ; ye have defrauded no man, ye have not oppressed any poor man, ye have invaded no one's landmark, ye have deceived no one by oath. He said not this, but, "Receive the kingdom, because I was an hungred, and ye gave Me meat." How excellent is this above all, when the Lord made no mention of the rest, but named this only ! And again to the others, " Depart ye into everlasting fire, prepared for the devil and his angels. How many things could He urge against the ungodly, were they to ask, "Why are we going into everlasting fire ! " Why? Do ye ask, ye adulterers, menslayers, cheats, sacrilegious blasphemers, unbelievers. Yet none of these did He name, but, "Because I was hungry, and ye gave Me no meat.

10. I see that you are surprised as I am. And indeed it is a marvellous thing. But I gather as best I can the reason of this thing so strange, and I will not conceal it from you. It is written, "As water quencheth fire, so alms quencheth sin." [5] Again it is written, "Shut up alms in the heart of a poor man, and it shall make supplication for thee before the Lord." [6] Again it is written, "Hear, O king, my counsel, and redeem thy sins by alms." [7] And many other testimonies of the Divine oracles are there, whereby it is shown that alms avail much to the quenching and effacing of sins. Wherefore to those whom He is about to condemn, yea, rather to those whom He is about to crown, He will impute alms only, as though He would say, "It were a hard matter for me not to find occasion to condemn you, were I to examine and weigh you accurately and with much exactness to scrutinize your deeds ; but, "Go into the kingdom, for I was hungry, and ye gave Me meat." Ye shall therefore go into the kingdom, not because ye have not sinned, but because ye have redeemed your sins by alms. And again to the others, "Go ye into everlasting fire, prepared for the devil and his angels." They too, guilty as they are, old in their sins, late in their fear for them, in what respect, when they turn their sins over in their mind, could they dare to say that they are undeservedly condemned, that this sentence is pronounced against them undeservedly by so righteous a Judge? In considering their consciences, and all the wounds of their souls, in what respect could they dare to say, We are unjustly condemned. Of whom it was said before in Wisdom, "Their own iniquities shall convince them to their face." [8] Without doubt they will see that they are justly condemned for their sins and wickednesses ; yet it will be as though He said to them, "It is not in conse-

---

[1] *Vide* Sermon 18. 4, and Sermon 38. 9.
[2] *Laturarii.*   [3] Matt. xxv. 34, etc.   [4] Ps. xxxiv. 14.

[5] Ecclus. iii. 30.   [6] Ecclus. xxix. 12, Vulgate.
[7] Dan. iv. 24, Sept. (iv. 27, English version).
[8] Wisd. iv. 20.

quence of this that ye think, but 'because I was hungry, and ye gave Me no meat.'" For if turning away from all these your deeds, and turning to Me, ye had redeemed all those crimes and sins by alms, those alms would now deliver you, and absolve you from the guilt of so great offences; for, "Blessed are the merciful, for to them shall be shown mercy." [1] But now go away into everlasting fire. "He shall have judgment without mercy, who hath showed no mercy." [2]

11. O that I may have induced you, my brethren, to give away your earthly bread, and to knock for the heavenly! The Lord is that Bread. He saith, "I am the Bread of life." [3] But how shall He give to thee, who givest not to him that is in need? One is in need before thee, and thou art in need before Another, and since thou art in need before Another, and another is in need before thee, that other is in need before him who is in need himself. For He before whom thou art in need, needeth nothing. Do then to others as thou wouldest have done to thee. For it is not in this case as with those friends who are wont to upbraid in a way one another with their kindnesses; as, "I did this for thee," and the other answers, "and I this for thee," that He wishes us to do Him some good office, because He has first done such an office for us. He is in want of nothing, and therefore is He the very Lord. I said unto the Lord, "Thou art my God, for Thou needest not my goods." [4] Notwithstanding though He be the Lord, and the Very Lord, and needeth not our goods, yet that we might do something even for Him, hath He vouchsafed to be hungry in His poor. "I was hungry," saith He, "and ye gave Me meat. Lord, when saw we Thee hungry? Forasmuch as ye did it to one of the least of Mine, ye did it to Me." [5] To be brief then, let men hear, and consider as they ought, how great a merit it is to have fed Christ when He hungereth, and how great a crime it is to have despised Christ when He hungereth.

12. Repentance for sins changes men, it is true, for the better; but it does not appear as if even it would profit ought, if it should be barren of works of mercy. This the Truth testifieth by the mouth of John, who said to them that came to him, "O generation of vipers, who hath warned you to flee from the wrath to come? Bring forth therefore fruits worthy of repentance; And say not we have Abraham to our father; for I say unto you, that God is able of these stones to raise up children unto Abraham. For now is the axe laid unto the root of the trees. Every tree therefore that bringeth not forth good

fruit shall be cut down, and cast into the fire." [6] Touching this fruit he said above, "Bring forth fruits worthy of repentance." Whoso then bringeth not forth these fruits, hath no cause to think that he shall attain [7] pardon for his sins by a barren repentance. Now what these fruits are, he showeth afterwards himself. For after these his words the multitude asked him, saying, "What shall we do then?" That is, what are these fruits, which thou exhortest us with such alarming force to bring forth? "But he answering said unto them, he that hath two coats, let him give to him that hath none; and he that hath meat, let him do likewise." My brethren, what is more plain, what more certain, or express than this? What other meaning then can that have which he said above, "Every tree that bringeth not forth good fruit, shall be cut down, and cast into the fire;" but that same which they on the left shall hear, "Go ye into everlasting fire, for I was hungry, and ye gave Me no meat." So then it is but a small matter to depart from sins, if thou shalt neglect to cure what is past, as it is written, "Son, thou hast sinned, do so no more." And that he might not think to be secure by this only, he saith, "And for thy former sins pray that they may be forgiven thee." [8] But what will it profit thee to pray for forgiveness, if thou shalt not make thyself meet to be heard, by not bringing forth fruits meet for repentance, that thou shouldest be cut down as a barren tree, and be cast into the fire? If then ye will be heard when ye pray for pardon of your sins, "Forgive, and it shall be forgiven you; Give, and it shall be given you." [9]

SERMON XI.

[LXI. BEN.]

ON THE WORDS OF THE GOSPEL, MATT. VII. 7, "ASK, AND IT SHALL BE GIVEN YOU;" ETC. AN EXHORTATION TO ALMS-DEEDS.

1. In the lesson of the Holy Gospel the Lord hath exhorted us to prayer. "Ask," saith He, "and it shall be given you; seek, and ye shall find; knock, and it shall be opened unto you. For every one that asketh receiveth, and he that seeketh findeth, and to him that knocketh it shall be opened. Or what man is there of you, whom if his son ask bread, will he give him a stone? Or if he ask a fish, will he give him a serpent? Or if he ask an egg, will he offer him a scorpion? [11] If ye then," saith He, "though ye be evil, know how to give good gifts unto your children, how much more shall your Father which is in heaven give good things to them that ask Him? [12] Though ye be evil," He saith, "ye know how to give good

---

[1] Matt. v. 7. [2] Jas. ii. 13. [3] John vi. 35.
[4] Ps. xv. 2, Sept. (xvi. 2, English version).
[5] Matt. xxv. 35, etc.
[6] Luke iii. 7, etc. [7] Mereri. [8] Ecclus. xxi. 1.
[9] Luke vi. 37, 38. [10] Matt. vii. 7-10. [11] Luke xi. 12.
[12] Matt. vii. 11.

gifts unto your children." A marvellous thing, Brethren! we are evil: yet have we a good Father. What is more evident? We have heard our proper name: "Though ye be evil, ye know how to give good gifts unto your children." And now see what kind of Father He showeth them, whom he called evil. "How much more shall your Father?" Father of whom? undoubtedly of the evil. And what kind of Father? "None is good but God only."[1]

2. For this cause have we who are evil a good Father, that we may not always continue evil. No evil man can make another man good. If no evil man can make another good, how can an evil man make himself good? He only can make of an evil man a good man, who is good eternally. "Heal me, and I shall be healed; save me, and I shall be saved."[2] Why then do those vain ones[3] say to me in words vain as themselves, "Thou canst save thyself if thou wilt"? "Heal me, O Lord, and I shall be healed." We were created good by The Good; for "God made man upright,"[4] but by our own free will, we became evil. We had power from being good to become evil, and we shall have power from being evil to become good. But it is He who is ever Good, who maketh the good out of the evil; for man by his own will had no power to heal himself. Thou dost not look out for a physician to wound thyself; but when thou hast wounded thyself, thou lookest out for one to cure thee. Good things then after the time present, temporal good things, such as are concerned with the body and flesh, we do know how to give to our children, even though we are evil. For even these are good things, who would doubt it? A fish, an egg, bread, fruit, wheat, the light we see, the air we breathe, all these are good; the very riches by which men are lifted up, and which make them loth to acknowledge other men to be their equals; by which, I say, men are lifted up rather in love of their dazzling clothing, than with any thought of their common nature, even these riches, I repeat, are good; but all these goods which I have now mentioned may be possessed by good and bad alike; and though they be good themselves, yet cannot they make their owners good.

3. A good then there is which maketh good, and a good there is whereby thou mayest do good. The Good which maketh good is God. For none can make man good, save He who is Good eternally. Therefore that thou mayest be good, call upon God. But there is another good whereby thou mayest do good, and that is, whatever thou mayest possess. There is gold, there is silver; they are good, not such as can make thee good, but whereby thou mayest do good. Thou hast gold and silver, and thou desirest more gold and silver. Thou both hast, and desirest to have; thou art at once full, and thirsty. This is a disease, not opulence. When men are in the dropsy,[5] they are full of water, and yet are always thirsty. They are full of water, and yet they thirst for water. How then canst thou take pleasure in opulence, who hast thereby this dropsical desire? Gold then thou hast, it is good; yet thou hast not whereby thou canst be made good, but whereby thou canst do good. Dost thou ask, What good can I do with gold? Hast thou not heard in the Psalm, "He hath dispersed abroad, he hath given to the poor, his righteousness remaineth for ever."[6] This is good, this is the good whereby thou art made good; righteousness. If thou have the good whereby thou art made good, do good with that good which cannot make thee good. Thou hast money, deal it out freely. By dealing it out freely, thou increasest righteousness. "For he hath dispersed abroad, hath distributed, hath given to the poor; his righteousness remaineth for ever." See what is diminished and what increased. Thy money is diminished, thy righteousness increased. That is diminished which thou must soon have lost, that diminished which thou must soon have left behind thee; that increased which thou shalt possess for ever.

4. It is then a secret of gainful dealing I am giving; learn so to trade. For thou dost commend the merchant who selleth lead and getteth gold, and wilt thou not commend the merchant, who layeth out money, and getteth righteousness? But thou wilt say, I do not lay out my money, because I have not righteousness. Let him who has righteousness lay his money out; I have not righteousness, so at least let me have my money. Dost thou not then wish to lay out thy money, because thou hast not righteousness? Yea, lay it out then rather that thou mayest have righteousness. For from whence shalt thou have righteousness but from God, the Fountain of righteousness? Therefore, if thou wilt have righteousness, be God's beggar, who just now out of the Gospel urged thee to ask, and seek, and knock. He knew His beggar, and lo the Householder, the mighty rich One, rich, to wit, in riches spiritual and eternal, exhorteth thee and saith, "Ask, seek, knock; he that asketh receiveth, he that seeketh findeth, to him that knocketh it shall be opened."[7] He exhorteth thee to ask, and will he refuse thee what thou askest?

5. Consider a similitude or comparison drawn from a contrary case (as of that unjust judge), which is an encouragement to us to prayer. "There was," saith the Lord, "in a city a cer-

---

[1] Luke xviii. 19.   [2] Jer. xvii. 14.   [3] Pelagians.
[4] Eccles. vii. 29.

[5] Morbo.   [6] Ps. cxii. 9.   [7] Matt. vii. 8.

tain judge, which feared not God, neither regarded man." [1] A certain widow importuned him daily, and said, " Avenge me." He would not for a long time ; but she ceased not to petition, and he did through her importunity what he would not of his own good will. [2] For thus by a contrary case hath He recommended us to pray.

6. Again, He saith, " A certain man to whom some guest had come, went to his friend, and began to knock and say, A guest is come to me, lend me three loaves." He answered, " I am already in bed, and my servants with me." The other does not leave off, but stands and presses his case, and knocks and begs as one friend of another. And what saith He? " I say unto you that he riseth, and not because of his friendship," but " because of the other's importunity he giveth him as many as he wanted. Not because of his friendship," though he is his friend, but "because of his importunity." [3] What is the meaning of " because of his importunity?" Because he did not leave off knocking ; because even when his request was refused, he did not turn away. He who was not willing to give, gave what was asked, because the other fainted not in asking. How much more then shall that Good One give who exhorteth us to ask, who is displeased if we ask not? But when at times He giveth somewhat slowly, it is that He is showing us the value of His good [4] things ; not that He refuses them. Things which have been long desired, are obtained with the greater pleasure, whereas those which are given quickly, are held cheap. Ask then, seek, be instant. By the very asking and seeking thou dost grow so as to contain the more. God is keeping in reserve for thee, what it is not His will to give thee quickly, that thou mayest learn for great things to long with great desire. Therefore " ought we always to pray, and not to faint." [5]

7. If then God hath made us His beggars by admonishing, and exhorting, and commanding us to ask, and seek, and knock, let us for our part pay regard to those who ask from us. We ask, and from whom do we ask? Who are we that ask? What do we ask? From whom, or who are we, or what is it that we ask? We ask of the Good God ; and we that ask are evil men ; but we ask for righteousness, whereby we may be good. We ask then for that which we may have for ever, wherewith when we shall be filled, we shall want no more. But in order that we may be filled, let us hunger and thirst ; hungering and thirsting, let us ask, and seek, and knock. " For blessed are they who hunger and thirst after righteousness." [6] Wherefore are they blessed? They do hunger and thirst, and are

they blessed? Is want ever a blessing? They are not blessed in that they hunger and thirst, but in that they will be filled. There will there be blessedness, in the fulness, not in the hunger. But hunger must go before the fulness, that no loathing attach to the bread.

8. We have said then, from whom it is that we ask, and who we are that ask, and what we ask. But we also are asked ourselves. For we are God's mendicants ; that He may acknowledge His mendicants, let us on our part acknowledge ours. But let us think in this case again, when anything is asked of us, who they are that ask, from whom they ask, and what they ask? Who then are they that ask? Men. From whom do they ask? From men. Who are they that ask? Mortals. From whom? From mortals. Who are they that ask? Frail beings. From whom? From frail beings. Who are they that ask? Wretches. And from whom? From wretches. Excepting in the matter of wealth, they that ask are as they of whom they ask. With what face canst thou ask before thy lord, who dost not acknowledge thine own equal? " I am not," he will say, " as he is," far be it from me to be such as he. It is thus that one clad in silk, and puffed up with pride, speaks of one who is wrapped in rags. But I ask you when you both are stripped. I ask you not as you are now when clothed, but as you were when you were first born. Both were naked, both weak, beginning a life of misery, and therefore beginning it with cries.

9. See then, recall, O rich man, to mind thy first beginnings ; see whether thou broughtest anything into the world. Now thou hast come indeed, and hast found so great abundance. But tell me, I pray thee, what didst thou bring hither? Tell me, or if thou art ashamed to say, hear the Apostle. " We brought nothing into this world." [7] He saith, " We brought nothing into this world." But perhaps because thou broughtest in nothing, but yet hast found much here, thou wilt take away something hence? This too, peradventure through love of riches, thou art afraid to confess. Hear this also, and let the Apostle who will not flatter, tell thee. " We brought nothing into this world," to wit when we were born ; " neither can we carry anything out," to wit when we shall depart out of the world. Thou broughtest in nothing, and thou shalt carry nothing away. Why then dost thou puff up thyself against the poor man? When infants first are born, let only the parents, servants, dependants, and the crowds of obsequious attendants, get out of the way ; and then let the wealthy children with their cries be recognised. Let the rich woman and the poor give birth together ; let them take no

---

[1] Luke xviii. 2.   [2] *Beneficio.*   [3] Luke xi. 5, etc.
[4] *Commendat.*   [5] Luke xviii. 1   [6] Matt. v. 6.   [7] 1 Tim. vi. 7.

notice of their children, let them go away for a little while ; then let them return, and recognise them if they can. See then, O rich man, "thou broughtest nothing into this world ; neither canst thou carry anything out." What I have said of them at their birth, I may say of them in death. If it be not so, when by any chance old sepulchres are broken up, let the bones of the rich be recognised if they can. Therefore, thou rich man, give ear to the Apostle, "We brought nothing into this world." Acknowledge it, true it is. "Neither can we carry anything out." Acknowledge it, this is true also.

10. What follows then? "Having food and covering, let us be therewith content ; for they who wish to be rich fall into temptation, and many and hurtful lusts, which drown men in destruction and perdition. For avarice is the root of all evil, which some following after, have erred from the faith."[1]   Now consider what they have abandoned. Grieved thou art that they have abandoned this, but see now in what they have entangled themselves. Hear ; "They have erred from the faith, and entangled themselves in many sorrows." But who? "They who wish to be rich." It is one thing to be rich, another to wish to become rich. He is rich, who is born of rich parents, and he is rich not because he wished it, but because many left him their inheritances. His[2] wealth I see, I make no question as to the pleasure he takes in it. In this Scripture it is covetousness that is condemned, not gold, or silver, or riches, but covetousness. For they who do not wish to become rich, or do not care about it, who do not burn with covetous desires, nor are inflamed by the fires of avarice, but who yet are rich, let them hear the Apostle (it has been read to-day), "Charge them that are rich in this world."[3]   Charge them what? Charge them before all things, not to be proud in their conceits, for there is nothing which riches do so much generate as pride. Each several fruit, each several grain of corn, each several tree, has its peculiar worm, and the worm of the apple is of one kind, and of the pear another, and of the bean another, and of the wheat another. The worm of riches is[4] pride.

11. "Charge therefore the rich of this world that they be not proud in their conceits." He hath shut out the abuse,[5] let him teach now the proper use. "That they be not proud in their conceits." But whence cometh the defence against pride? From that which follows : "Nor trust in the uncertainty of riches." They who trust not in the uncertainty of riches, are not proud in their conceits. If they be not proud in their conceits," let them fear. If they fear, they are not proud in their conceits. How many are they

who were rich yesterday, and are poor to-day? How many go to sleep rich, and through robbers coming and taking all away, wake up poor? Therefore "charge them not to trust in the uncertainty of riches, but in the Living God, who giveth us richly all things to enjoy," things temporal, and things eternal. But things eternal more for enjoyment, the things temporal for use. Things temporal as for travellers, things eternal as for inhabitants. Things temporal, whereby we may do good ; things eternal, whereby we may be made good. Therefore let the rich do this, "Let them not be proud in their conceits, nor trust in the uncertainty of riches, but in the Living God, who giveth us all things richly to enjoy." Let them do this. But what can they do with what they have? Hear what. "Let them be rich in good works, let them easily distribute."[6]   For they have wherewithal. Why then do they not do it? Poverty is a hard estate. But they may give easily, for they have the means. "Let them communicate," that is, let them acknowledge their fellow-mortals as their equals. "Let them communicate, let them lay up for themselves a good foundation against the time to come."[7] For, saith he, when I say, "Let them distribute easily, let them communicate," I have no wish to spoil, or strip them, or leave them empty. It is a painful lesson I teach ; I show them a place to put their goods, "let them lay up in store for themselves." For I have no wish that they should remain in poverty. "Let them lay up for themselves in store." I do not bid them lose their goods, but I show them whither to remove them. "Let them lay up in store for themselves a good foundation against the time to come, that they may hold on the true[8] life." The present then is a false life ; let them lay hold on the true life. "For it is vanity of vanities, and all is vanity. What so great abundance hath man in all his labour, wherewith he labour-eth under the sun?"[9]   Therefore the true life must be laid hold upon, our riches must be removed to the place of the true life, that we may find there what we give here. He maketh this exchange of our goods who also changeth ourselves.

12. Give then, my brethren, to the poor, "Having food and covering, let us be therewith content." The rich man has nothing from his riches, but what the poor man begs of him, food and covering. What more hast thou from all that thou possessest? Thou hast got food and necessary covering. Necessary I say, not useless, not superfluous. What more dost thou get from thy riches? Tell me. Assuredly all thou hast more will be superfluous. Let thy superfluities then be the poor man's necessaries. But

---

[1] 1 Tim. vi. 8-10. [2] *Video facultates non interrogo voluptates.*
[3] 1 Tim. vi. 17. [4] Sermon 35 (85, Bened.) 3. [5] *Vitium.*
[6] 1 Tim. vi. 18, Vulgate. [7] 1 Tim. vi. 19.
[8] *Veram*, Vulgate. [9] Eccles. i. 2, 3, Sept.

thou wilt say, I get costly banquets, I feed on costly meats. But the poor man, what does he feed on? On cheap food; the poor man feeds on cheap, and I, says he, on costly meats. Well, I ask you, when you both are filled, the costly enters into thee, but when it is once entered, what does it become? If we had but looking-glasses within us, should we not be put to shame for all the costly meat whereby thou hast been filled? The poor man hungers, and so does the rich; the poor man seeks to be filled, so does the rich. The poor man is filled with inexpensive, the rich with costly meats. Both are filled alike, the object [1] whither both wish to attain is one and the same, only the one reaches it by a short, the other by a circuitous way. But thou wilt say, I relish better my costly food. True, and it is hard for thee to be satisfied, dainty as thou art. Thou knowest not the relish of that which hunger seasons.[2] Not that I have said this to force the rich to feed on the meat and drink of the poor. Let the rich use what their infirmity has accustomed them to; but let them be sorry, that they are not able to do otherwise. For it would be better for them if they could. If then the poor man be not puffed up for his poverty, why shouldest thou for thine infirmity? Use then choice, and costly meats, because thou art so accustomed, because thou canst not do otherwise, because if thou dost change thy custom, thou art made ill. I grant thee this, make use of superfluities, but give to the poor necessaries; make use of costly meats, but give to the poor inexpensive food. He is looking to receive from thee, and thou art looking to receive from God; he is looking to the hand which was made as he was, and thou art looking to the hand that made thee, and made not thee only, but the poor man with thee. He set you both one and the same journey, this present life: you have found yourselves companions in it, you are walking one way: he is carrying nothing, thou art loaded excessively: he is carrying nothing with him, thou art carrying with thee more than thou dost need. Thou art loaded: give him of that thou hast; so shalt thou at once feed him, and lessen thine own burden.

13. Give then to the poor; I beg, I advise, I charge, I command you. Give to the poor whatever ye will. For I will not conceal from you, Beloved, why it is that I have deemed it necessary to deliver this discourse to you. As I am going to and from the Church, the poor importune me, and beg me to speak to you, that they may receive something of you. They have urged me to speak to you; and when they see that they receive nothing from you, they suppose that all my labour among you is in vain. Some-

thing also they expect from me. I give them all I can; but have I the means sufficient to supply all their necessities? Forasmuch then as I have not means sufficient to supply all their necessity, I am at least their ambassador to you. You have heard and applauded; God be thanked. You have received the seed, you have returned an answer. But these your commendations weigh me down rather, and expose me to danger. I bear them, and tremble whilst I bear them. Nevertheless, my brethren, these your commendations are but the tree's leaves; it is the fruit I am in quest of.

SERMON XII.
[LXII. BEN.]

ON THE WORDS OF THE GOSPEL, MATT. VIII. 8, "I AM NOT WORTHY THAT THOU SHOULDEST COME UNDER MY ROOF," ETC., AND OF THE WORDS OF THE APOSTLE, I COR. VIII. 10, "FOR IF A MAN SEE THEE WHO HAST KNOWLEDGE SITTING AT MEAT IN AN IDOL'S TEMPLE," ETC.

1. WE have heard, as the Gospel was being read, the praise of our faith as manifested in humility. For when the Lord Jesus promised that He would go to the Centurion's house to heal His servant, He answered, "I am not worthy that Thou shouldest come under my roof: but speak the word only, and he shall be healed."[3] By calling himself unworthy, he showed himself worthy for Christ to come not into his house, but into his heart. Nor would he have said this with so great faith and humility, had he not borne Him in his heart, of whose coming into his house he was afraid. For it were no great happiness for the Lord Jesus to enter into his house, and yet not to be in his heart. For this Master of humility both by word and example, sat down even in the house of a certain proud Pharisee, by name Simon;[4] and though He sat down in his house, there was no place in his heart, "where the Son of Man could lay His Head."[5]

2. For so, as we may understand from the words of the Lord Himself, did He call back from His discipleship a certain proud man, who of his own accord was desirous to go with Him. "Lord, I will follow Thee whithersoever Thou goest."[6] And the Lord seeing in his heart what was invisible, said, "Foxes have holes, and the birds of the air have nests, but the Son of Man hath not where to lay His Head."[7] That is, in thee, guile like the fox doth dwell, and pride as the birds of heaven. But the Son of Man simple as opposed to guile, lowly as opposed to pride, hath not where to lay His Head; and this very laying, not the raising up of the head, teaches

---

[1] *Possessio.*   [2] *Accendit.*

[3] Matt. viii. 8.   [4] Luke vii. 36.   [5] Luke ix. 58.
[6] Luke ix. 57.   [7] Matt. viii. 20.

humility. Therefore doth He call back this one who was desirous to go, and another who refused He draweth onward. For in the same place He saith to a certain man, " Follow Me." And he said, " I will follow Thee, Lord, but let me first go and bury my father." [1] His excuse was indeed a dutiful one : and therefore was he the more worthy to have his excuse removed, and his calling confirmed. What he wished to do was an act of dutifulness ; but the Master taught him what he ought to prefer. For He wished him to be a preacher of the living word, to make others live. But there were others by whom that first necessary office might be fulfilled. " Let the dead," He saith, " bury their dead." When unbelievers bury a dead body, the dead bury the dead. The body of the one hath lost its soul, the soul of the others hath lost God. For as the soul is the life of the body ; so is God the life of the soul. As the body expires when it loses the soul, so doth the soul expire when it loses God. The loss of God is the death of the soul : the loss of the soul the death of the body. The death of the body is necessary ; the death of the soul voluntary.

3. The Lord then sat down in the house of a certain proud Pharisee. He was in his house, as I have said, and was not in his heart. But into this centurion's house He entered not, yet He possessed his heart. Zacchæus again received the Lord both in house and heart.[2] Yet the centurion's faith is praised for its humility. For he said, " I am not worthy that Thou shouldest come under my roof ; " [3] and the Lord said, " Verily I say unto you, I have not found so great faith, no, not in Israel ; " [4] according to the flesh, that is. For he too was an Israelite undoubtedly according to the spirit. The Lord had come to fleshly Israel, that is, to the Jews, there to seek first for the lost sheep, among this people, and of this people also He had assumed His Body. " I have not found there so great faith," He saith. We can but measure the faith of men, as men can judge of it ; but He who saw the inward parts, He whom no man can deceive, gave His testimony to this man's heart, hearing words of lowliness, and pronouncing a sentence of healing.

4. But whence did he get confidence ? " I also," saith he, " am a man set under authority, having soldiers under me : and I say to this man, Go, and he goeth ; and to another, Come, and he cometh : and to my servant, Do this, and he doeth it." [5] I am an authority to certain who are placed under me, being myself placed under a certain authority above me. If then I a man under authority have the power of commanding, what power must Thou have, whom all powers serve ? Now this man was of the Gentiles, for he was a centurion. At that time the Jewish nation had soldiers of the Roman empire among them. There he was engaged in a military life, according to the extent of a centurion's authority, both under authority himself, and having authority over others ; as a subject obedient, ruling others who were under him. But the Lord (and mark this especially, Beloved, as need there is you should), though He was among the Jewish people only, even now announced beforehand that the Church should be in the whole world, for the establishment of which He would send Apostles ; Himself not seen, yet believed on by the Gentiles : by the Jews seen, and put to death. For as the Lord did not in body enter into this man's house, and still, though in body absent, yet present in majesty, healed his faith, and his house ; so the same Lord also was in body among the Jewish people only : among the other nations He was neither born of a Virgin, nor suffered, nor walked, nor endured His human sufferings, nor wrought His divine miracles. None of all this took place in the rest of the nations, and yet was that fulfilled which was spoken of Him, " A people whom I have not known, hath served Me." And how if it did not know Him ? " Hath obeyed Me by the hearing of the ear." [6] The Jewish nation knew, and crucified Him ; the whole world besides heard and believed.

5. This absence, so to say, of His body, and presence of His power among all nations, He signified also in the instance of that woman who had touched the edge of His garment, when He asketh, saying, " Who touched Me ? " [7] He asketh, as though He were absent ; as though present, He healeth. " The multitude," say the disciples, " press Thee, and sayest Thou, Who touched Me ? " For as if He were so walking as not to be touched by anybody at all, He said, " Who touched Me ? " And they answer, " The multitude press Thee." And the Lord would seem to say, I am asking for one who touched, not for one who pressed Me. In this case also is His Body now, that is, His Church. The faith of the few " touches " it, the throng of the many " press " it. For ye have heard, as being her children, that Christ's Body is the Church, and if ye will, ye yourselves are so. This the Apostle says in many places, " For His body's sake, which is the Church ; " [8] and again, " But ye are the body of Christ, and members in particular." [9] If then we are His body, what His body then suffered in the crowd, that doth His Church suffer now. It is pressed by many, touched by few. The flesh presses it, faith

---

[1] Luke ix. 59.   [2] Luke xix. 6.   [3] Matt. viii. 8.
[4] Matt. viii. 10.   [5] Matt. viii. 9.

[6] Ps. xvii. 44, 45, Sept. (xviii. 43, 44, English version).
[7] Luke viii. 45.   [8] Col. i. 24.   [9] 1 Cor. xii. 27.

touches it. Lift up therefore your eyes, I beseech you, ye who have wherewithal to see. For ye have before you something to see. Lift up the eyes of faith, touch but the extreme border of His garment, it will be sufficient for saving health.

6. See ye how that which ye have heard out of the Gospel was at that time to come is now present. Therefore, said He, on occasion of the commendation of the Centurion's faith, as in the flesh an alien, but of the household in heart, "Therefore I say unto you, Many shall come from the east and west." [1] Not all, but "many;" yet they shall "come from the East and West;" the whole world is denoted by these two parts. "Many shall come from the east and west, and shall sit down with Abraham, and Isaac, and Jacob, in the kingdom of heaven; but the children of the kingdom shall be cast out into outer darkness." "But the children of the kingdom," the Jews, namely. And how "the children of the kingdom"? Because they received the Law; to them the Prophets were sent, with them was the temple and the Priesthood; they celebrated the figures of all the things to come. Yet of what things they celebrated the figures, they acknowledged not the presence. And, "Therefore the children of the kingdom," He saith, "shall go into outer darkness, there shall be wailing and gnashing of teeth." And so we see the Jews reprobate, and Christians called from the East and West, to the heavenly banquet, to sit down with Abraham, and Isaac, and Jacob, where the bread is righteousness, and the [2] cup wisdom.

7. Consider then, brethren, for of these are ye; ye are of this people, even then foretold, and now exhibited.[3] Yes, verily, ye are of those who have been called from the East and West, to sit down in the kingdom of heaven, not in the temple of idols. Be ye then the Body of Christ, not the pressure of His Body. Ye have the border of His garment to touch, that ye may be healed of the issue of blood, that is, of carnal pleasures. Ye have, I say, the border of the garment to touch. Look upon the Apostles as the garment, by the texture of unity clinging closely to the sides of Christ. Among these Apostles was Paul, as it were the border, the least and last; as he saith himself, "I am the least of the Apostles." [4] In a garment the last and least thing is the border. The border is in appearance contemptible, yet is it touched with saving efficacy.[5] "Even to this hour we both hunger and thirst, and are naked and buffeted." [6] What state so low, so contemptible as this! Touch then, if thou art suffering from a bloody flux. There will go power out of Him

whose garment it is, and it will heal thee. The border was proposed to you just now to be touched, when out of the same Apostle there was read, "For if any one see him which hath knowledge sit at meat in an idol's temple, shall not the conscience of him who is weak, be emboldened to eat things offered to idols? And through thy knowledge shall thy weak brother perish, for whom Christ died!" [7] How think ye may men be deceived by idols, which they suppose are honoured by Christians? A man may say, "God knows my heart." Yes, but thy brother did not know thy heart. If thou art weak, beware of a still greater weakness; if thou art strong, have a care of thy brother's weakness. They who see what you do, are emboldened to do more, so as to desire not only to eat, but also to sacrifice there. And lo, "Through thy knowledge the weak brother perisheth." Hear then, my brother; if thou didst disregard the weak, wouldest thou disregard a brother also? Awake. What if so thou sin against Christ Himself? For attend to what thou canst not by any means disregard. "But," saith he, "when ye sin so against the brethren, and wound their weak conscience, ye sin against Christ." [8] Let them who disregard these words, go now, and sit at meat in the idol's temple; will they not be of those who press, and do not touch? And when they have been at meat in the idol's temple, let them come and fill the Church; not to receive saving health, but to make a pressure there.

8. But thou wilt say, I am afraid lest I offend those above me. By all means be afraid of offending them, and so thou wilt not offend God. For thou who art afraid lest thou offend those above thee, see whether there be not One above him whom thou art afraid of offending. By all means then be loth to offend those above thee. This is an established rule with thee. But then is it not plain, that he must on no account be offended, who is above all others? Run over now the list of those above thee. First are thy father and mother, if they are educating thee aright; if they are bringing thee up for Christ; they are to be heard in all things, they must be obeyed in every command; let them enjoin nothing against one above themselves, and so let them be obeyed. And who, thou wilt say, is above him who begat me? He who created thee. For man begets, but God creates. How it is that man begets, he does not know; and what he shall beget, he does not know. But He who saw thee that He might make thee, before that he whom He made existed, is surely above thy father. Thy country again should be above thy very parents; so that whereinsoever thy

---

[1] Matt. viii. 11.   [2] *Potus.*   [3] *Præsentato.*
[4] 1 Cor. xv. 9.   [5] *Salute.*   [6] 1 Cor. iv. 11.   [7] 1 Cor. viii. 10, 11.   [8] 1 Cor. viii. 12.

parents enjoin aught against thy country, they are not to be listened to. And whatsoever thy country enjoin against God, it is not to be listened to. For if thou wilt be healed, if after the issue of blood, if after twelve years' continuance in that disease, if after having spent thine all upon physicians, and not having received health, thou dost wish at length to be made whole ; O woman, whom I am addressing as a figure of the Church, thy father enjoineth thee this, and thy people that. But thy Lord saith to thee, " Forget thine own people, and thy father's house." [1] For what good ? for what advantage ? with what useful result ? " Because the King hath desired thy beauty." He hath desired what He made, since when deformed He loved thee, that He might make thee beautiful. For thee unbelieving, and deformed, He shed His Blood, and He made thee faithful and beauteous, He hath loved His own gifts in thee. For what didst thou bring to thy spouse ? What didst thou receive for dowry from thy former father, and former people ? Was it not the excesses [2] and the rags of sins ? Thy rags He cast away, thy robe impure [3] He tore asunder. He pitied thee that He might adorn thee. He adorned thee, that He might love thee.

9. What need of more, Brethren. Ye are Christians, and have heard, that " If ye sin against the brethren, and wound their weak conscience, ye sin against Christ." Do not disregard it, if ye would not be wiped out of the book of life. How long shall I go about to speak in bright and pleasing terms to you, what my grief forceth me to speak in some sort, and will not suffer me to keep secret ? Whosoever they are who are minded to disregard these things, and sin against Christ, let them only consider what they are doing. We wish the rest of the Heathen to be gathered in ; and ye are stones in their way : they have a wish to come ; they stumble, and so return. For they say in their hearts, Why should we leave the gods whom the very Christians worship as we do ? God forbid, thou wilt say, that I should worship the gods of the Gentiles. I know, I understand, I believe thee. But what account art thou making of the consciences of the weak which thou art wounding ? What account art thou making of their price, if thou disregard the purchase ? Consider for how great a price was the purchase made. " Through thy knowledge," saith the Apostle, " shall the weak brother perish ; " that knowledge which thou professest to have, in that thou knowest that an idol is nothing, and that in thy mind thou art thinking only of God, and so sittest down in the idol's temple. In this knowledge the weak brother perisheth. And lest thou shouldest pay no re-

gard to the weak brother, he added, " for whom Christ died." If thou wouldest disregard him, yet consider his Price, and weigh the whole world in the balance with the Blood of Christ. And lest thou shouldest still think that thou art sinning against a weak brother, and so esteem it after that he had heard that he was " Peter," a a trivial fault, and of small account, he saith, " Ye sin against Christ." For men are in the habit of saying, " I sin against man ; am I sinning against God ? " Deny then that Christ is God. Dost thou dare deny that Christ is God ? Hast thou learned this other doctrine, when thou didst sit at meat in the idol's temple ? The school of Christ doth not admit that doctrine. I ask ; Where learnedst thou that Christ is not God ? The Pagans are wont to say so. Seest thou what bad associations [4] do ? Seest thou, " that evil communications corrupt good manners ? " [5] There thou canst not speak of the Gospel, and thou dost hear others talking of idols. There thou losest the truth that Christ is God ; and what thou dost drink in there, thou vomitest out in the Church. It may be thou art bold enough to speak here ; bold enough to mutter among the crowds ; " Was not then Christ a man ? Was He not crucified ? " This hast thou learned of the Pagans. Thou hast lost thy soul's health, thou hast not touched the border. On this point then touch again the border, and receive health. As I taught thee to touch it in this that is written, " Whoso seeth a brother sit at meat in the idol's temple ; " [6] touch it also concerning the Divinity of Christ. The same border said of the Jews, " Whose are the fathers, and of whom as concerning the flesh Christ came, who is over all, God blessed for ever." [7] Behold, against Whom, even the Very God, thou dost sin, when thou sittest down with false gods.

10. It is no god, you will say ; because it is the tutelary genius of Carthage. As though if it were Mars or Mercury, it would be a god. But consider in what light it is esteemed by them ; not what it is in itself. For I know also as well as thou, that it is but a stone. If this " genius " be any ornament, let the citizens of Carthage live well ; and they themselves will be this " genius " of Carthage. But if the " genius " be a devil, ye have heard in that same Scripture, " The things which the Gentiles sacrifice, they sacrifice to devils, and not to God ; and I would not that ye should have fellowship with devils." [8] We know well that it is no God ; would that they knew it too ! but because of those weak ones who do not know it, their conscience ought not to be wounded. It is this that the Apostle warns us of. For that they regard that statue as something divine, and take it for a god, the altar is

---

[1] Ps. xlv. 10.   [2] *Luxurias*.   [3] *Cilicium*.

[4] *Mensæ*.   [5] 1 Cor. xv. 33.   [6] 1 Cor. viii. 10.   [7] Rom. ix. 5.   [8] 1 Cor. x. 20.

witness. What does the altar there, if it be not accounted a god? Let no one tell me; it is no deity, it is no God. I have said already, "Would that they only knew this, as we all do." But how they regard it, for what they take it, and what they do about it, that altar is witness. It is convincing against the intentions of all who worship there, grant that it may not be convincing also against those who sit at meat with them!

11. Yes, let not Christians press the Church, if the Pagans do. She is the Body of Christ. Were we not saying, that the Body of Christ was pressed, and not touched. He endured those who pressed Him; and was looking out for those who "touched" Him. And, Brethren, I would that if the Body of Christ be pressed by Pagans, by whom it is wont to be pressed; that at least Christians would not press the Body of Christ. Brethren, it is my business to speak to you, my business it is to speak to Christians; "For what have I to do to judge them that are without?"[1] the Apostle himself saith. Them we address in another way, as being weak. With them we must[2] deal softly, that they may hear the truth; in you the corruption must be cut out. If ye ask whereby the Pagans are to be gained over, whereby they are to be illuminated, and called to salvation; forsake their solemnities, forsake their trifling shows; and then if they do not consent to our truth, let them blush at their own scantiness.

12. If he who is over thee be a good man, he is thy nourisher; if a bad man, he is thy tempter. Receive the nourishment in the one case with gladness, and in the temptation show thyself approved. Be thou gold. Regard this world as the furnace of the goldsmith; in one narrow place are there things, gold, chaff, fire. To the two former the fire is applied, the chaff is burned, and the gold purified. A man has yielded to threats, and been led away to the idol's temple: Alas! I bewail the chaff; I see the ashes. Another has not yet yielded to threats nor terrors; has been brought before the judge, and stood firm in his confession, and has not bent down to the idol image: what does the flame with him? Does it not purify the gold? Stand fast then, Brethren, in the Lord; greater in power is He who hath called you. Be not afraid of the threats of the ungodly. Bear with your enemies; in them ye have those for whom ye may pray; let them by no means terrify you. This is saving health, draw out in this feast here from this source; here drink that wherewith ye may be satisfied, and not in those other feasts, that only whereby ye may be maddened. Stand fast in the Lord. Ye are silver, ye shall be gold. This similitude is not our own, it is out of Holy Scripture. Ye have read and heard, "As gold in the furnace hath He tried them, and received them as a burnt-offering."[3] See what ye shall be among the treasures of God. Be ye rich as touching God, not as if to make Him rich, but as to become rich from Him. Let Him replenish you; admit nought else into your heart.

13. Do we lift up ourselves unto pride, or tell you to be despisers against the powers ordained? Not so. Do ye again who are sick on this point, touch also that border of the garment? The Apostle himself saith, "Let every soul be subject unto the higher powers, for there is no power but of God, the powers that be are ordained of God. He then who resisteth the power, resisteth the ordinance of God."[4] But what if it enjoin what thou oughtest not to do? In this case by all means disregard the power through fear of Power. Consider these several grades of human powers. If the magistrate[5] enjoin anything, must it not be done? Yet if his order be in opposition to the Proconsul, thou dost not surely despise the power, but choosest to obey a greater power. Nor in this case ought the less to be angry, if the greater be preferred. Again, if the Proconsul himself enjoin anything, and the Emperor another thing, is there any doubt, that disregarding the former, we ought to obey the latter? So then if the Emperor enjoin one thing, and God another, what judge ye? Pay me tribute, submit thyself to my allegiance. Right, but not in an idol's temple. In an idol's temple He forbids it. Who forbids it? A greater Power. Pardon me then: thou threatenest a prison, He threateneth hell. Here must thou at once take to thee thy "faith as a shield, whereby thou mayest be able to quench all the fiery darts of the enemy."[6]

14. But one of these powers is plotting, and contriving evil designs against thee. Well: he is but sharpening the razor wherewith to shave the hair, but not to cut the head. Ye have but just now heard this that I have said in the Psalm, "Thou hast worked deceit like a sharp razor."[7] Why did He compare the deceit of a wicked man in power to a razor? Because it does not reach, save to our superfluous parts. As hairs on our body seem as it were superfluous, and are shaven off without any loss of the flesh; so whatsoever an angry man in power can take from thee, count only among thy superfluities. He takes away thy poverty; can he take away thy wealth? Thy poverty is thy wealth in thy heart. Thy superfluous things only hath he power to take away, these only hath he power to injure, even though he had license given him so far as to hurt the body. Yea even this life itself to those whose thoughts are of another life, this present life, I say, may be reckoned

---

[1] 1 Cor. v. 12.   [2] *Blandiendum.*

[3] Wisd. iii. 6.   [4] Rom. xiii. 1, 2.   [5] Curator.
[6] Eph. vi. 16.   [7] Ps. li. 4, Sept. (lii. 2, English version).

among the things superfluous. For so the Martyrs have despised it. They did not lose life, but they gained Life.

15. Be sure, Brethren, that enemies have no power against the faithful, except so far as it profiteth them to be tempted and proved. Of this be sure, Brethren, let no one say ought against it. Cast all your care upon the Lord, throw yourselves wholly and entirely upon Him. He will not withdraw Himself that ye should fall. He who created us, hath given us security touching our very hairs. "Verily I say unto you, even the hairs of your head are all numbered."[1] Our hairs are numbered by God; how much more is our conduct known to Him to whom our hairs are thus known? See then, how that God doth not disregard our least things. For if He disregarded them, He would not create them. For He verily both created our hairs, and still taketh count of them. But thou wilt say, though they are preserved at present, perhaps they will perish. On this point also hear His word, "Verily I say unto you, there shall not an hair of your head perish."[2] Why art thou afraid of man, O man, whose place is in the Bosom of God? Fall not out of His Bosom; whatsoever thou shalt suffer there, will avail to thy salvation, not to thy destruction. Martyrs have endured the tearing of their limbs, and shall Christians fear the injuries of Christian times? He who would do thee an injury now, can only do it in fear. He does not say openly, come to the idol-feast; he does not say openly, come to my altars, and banquet there. And if he should say so, and thou wast to refuse, let him make a complaint of it, let him bring it as an accusation and charge against thee: "He would not come to my altars, he would not come to my temple, where I worship." Let him say this. He does not dare; but in his guile he contrives another attack. Make ready thy hair; he is sharpening the razor; he is about to take off thy superfluous things, to shave what thou must soon leave behind thee. Let him take off what shall endure, if he can. This powerful enemy, what has he taken away? what great thing has he taken away? That which a thief or housebreaker could take: in his utmost rage, he can but take what a robber can. Even if he should have license given him to the slaying of the very body, what does he take away, but what the robber can take? I did him too much honour, when I said, "a robber." For be the robber who and what he may, he is a man. He takes from thee what a fever, or an adder, or a poisonous mushroom can take. Here lies the whole power of the rage of men, to do what a mushroom can! Men eat a poisonous mushroom, and they die. Lo! in what

frail estate is the life of man; which sooner or later thou must abandon; do not struggle then in such wise for it, as that thou shouldest be abandoned thyself.

16. Christ is our Life; think then of Christ. He came to suffer, but also to be glorified; to be despised, but to be exalted also; to die; but also to rise again. If the labour alarm thee, see its reward. Why dost thou wish to arrive by softness at that to which nothing but hard labour can lead? Now thou art afraid, lest thou shouldest lose thy money; because thou earnest thy money with great labour. If thou didst not attain to thy money, which thou must some time or other lose, at all events when thou diest, without labour, wouldest thou desire without labour to attain to the Life eternal? Let that be of higher value in thine eyes, to which after all thy labours thou shalt in such sort attain as never more to lose it. If this money, to which thou hast attained after all thy labours on such condition as that thou must some time lose it, be of high value with thee; how much more ought we to long after those things which are everlasting!

17. Give no credit to their words, neither be afraid of them. They say that we are enemies of their idols. May God so grant, and give all into our power, as He hath already given us that which we have broken down. For this I say, Beloved, that ye may not attempt to do it, when it is not lawfully in your power to do it; for it is the way of ill-regulated men, and the mad Circumcelliones,[3] both to be violent when they have no power, and to be ever eager in their wishes to die without a cause. Ye heard what we read to you, all of you who were present in the Mappalia.[4] "When the land shall have been given into your power (he saith first, "into your power," and so enjoined what was to be done); "then," saith he, "ye shall destroy their altars, and break in pieces their groves, and hew down all their images."[5] When we shall have got the power, do this. When the power has not been given us, we do not do it; when it is given, we do not neglect it. Many Pagans have these abominations on their own estates; do we go and break them in pieces? No, for our first efforts are that the idols in their hearts should be broken down. When they too are made Chris-

---

[1] Matt. x. 30.　　[2] Luke xxi. 18.

[3] By the Donatists called Agonistici (St. Augustin, *In Ps.* 133. 6), and by the Catholics Circilliones, or Circumcelliones, that is, Vagrants. *Circumcelliones dicti sunt, quia circum cellas vagantur, solent enim ire hac illac nusquam habentes pedes* (*In Ps.* 132. 3). They were of a very licentious and abandoned character, and in their fanaticism they would often commit suicide, to which the text may suppose to refer (*Lib. de Hæres.* c. 69; *Brev. Coll. cum Donat.* viii. [14]). They exercised extreme cruelty against the Catholics (*Cont. Cresc. Don.* lib. 3, xliii. [47], xlvi. [50]). Their form of salutation was *Deo laudes* (*Cont. lit. Petil.* lib. 2, lxv. [146]), which St. Augustin (*In Ps.* 133. 6) says was more feared than the roaring of a lion. For the time of their origin see *Opt.* lib. 3.

[4] A place where St. Cyprian's body was buried outside the walls of Carthage. Macrius in his *Hierolexicon* (ad verb) thinks it ought to be written *Mapalia*, i.e. *domus rurales*.

[5] Deut. vii. 1 and xii. 3.

tians themselves, they either invite us to so good a work, or anticipate us. At present we must pray for them, not be angry with them. If very painful feelings excite us, it is rather against Christians, it is against our brethren, who will enter into the Church in such a mind, as to have their body there, and their heart anywhere else. The whole ought to be within. If that which man seeth is within, why is that which God seeth without?

18. Now ye may know, Dearly Beloved, that these unite their murmurings with Heretics and with Jews. Heretics, Jews, and Heathens have made a unity against Unity. Because it has happened, that in some places the Jews have received chastisement because of their wickednesses; they charge and suspect us, or pretend, that we are always seeking the like treatment for them. Again, because it has happened that the heretics [1] in some places have suffered the penalty of the laws for the impiety and fury of their deeds of violence; they say immediately that we are seeking by every means some harm for their destruction. Again, because it has been resolved that laws should be passed against the Heathen, yea for them rather, if they were only wise. (For as when silly boys are playing with the mud, and dirtying their hands, the strict master comes, shakes the mud out of their hands, and holds out their book; so has it pleased God by the hands of princes His subjects to alarm their childish, foolish hearts, that they may throw away the dirt from their hands, and set about something useful. And what is this something useful with the hands, but, " Break thy bread to the hungry, and bring the houseless poor into thy house"?[2] But nevertheless these children escape from their master's sight, and return stealthily to their mud, and when they are discovered they hide their hands that they may not be seen.) Because then it has so pleased God, they think that we are looking out for the idols everywhere, and that we break them down in all places where we have discovered them. How so? Are there not places before our very eyes in which they are? Or are we indeed ignorant where they are? And yet we do not break them down, because God has not given them into our power. When does God give them into our power? When the masters of these things shall become Christians. The master of a certain place has just lately wished this to be done. If he had not

been minded to give the place itself to the Church, and only had given orders that there should be no idols on his property; I think that it ought to have been executed with the greatest devotion, that the soul of the absent Christian brother, who wishes on his land to return thanks to God, and would not that there should be anything there to God's dishonour, might be assisted by his fellow-Christians. Added to this, that in this case he gave the place itself to the Church. And shall there be idols in the Church's estate? Brethren, see then what it is that displeases the Heathens. It is but a little matter with them that we do not take them away from their estates, that we do not break them down: they would have them kept up even in our own places. We preach against idols, we take them away from the hearts of men; we are persecutors of idols; we openly profess it. Are we then to be the preservers of them? I do not touch them when I have not the power; I do not touch them when the lord of the property complains of it; but when he wishes it to be done, and gives thanks for it, I should incur guilt if I did it not.

SERMON XIII.

[LXIII. BEN.]

ON THE WORDS OF THE GOSPEL, MATT. VIII. 23, "AND WHEN HE WAS ENTERED INTO A BOAT," ETC.

1. By the Lord's blessing, I will address you upon the lesson of the Holy Gospel which has just been read, and take occasion thereby to exhort you, that against the tempest and waves of this world, faith sleep not in your hearts. " For the Lord Christ had not indeed death nor sleep in His power, and peradventure sleep overcame the Almighty One as He was sailing against His will?" If ye believe this, He is asleep in you; but if Christ be awake in you, your faith is awake. The Apostle saith, "that Christ may dwell in your hearts by faith." [3] This sleep then of Christ is a sign of a high mystery.[4] The sailors are the souls passing over the world in wood. That ship also was a figure of the Church. And all, individually indeed are temples of God, and his own heart is the vessel in which each sails; nor can he suffer shipwreck, if his thoughts are only good.

2. Thou hast heard an insult, it is the wind; thou art angry, it is a wave. When therefore the wind blows, and the wave swells, the ship is endangered, the heart is in jeopardy, the heart is tossed to and fro. When thou hast heard an insult, thou longest to be avenged; and, lo, avenged thou hast been, and so rejoicing in another's harm thou hast suffered shipwreck. And why is this? Because Christ is asleep in

---

[1] This refers doubtless to the laws against the Donatists. The Emperor Honorius issued an edict against them A.D. 405, and another A.D. 410, and A.D. 412, and again A.D. 414, on occasion of the death of Marcellinus, and to prevent any advantage which the Donatists might derive from his death. For he had been judge in the conference between the Catholics and Donatists, granted by the Emperor at the request of the deputies of the council of Carthage, four years before (Fleury, *H. E.* B xxii., cxxvi.): and to him had been entrusted the execution of the laws issued against the Donatists for the maintenance of the Catholic religion.
[2] Isa. lviii. 7.

[3] Eph. iii. 17.   [4] *Sacramenti*.

thee. What does this mean, Christ is asleep in thee? Thou hast forgotten Christ. Rouse Him up then, call Christ to mind, let Christ awake in thee, give heed to Him. What didst thou wish? To be avenged. Hast thou forgotten, that when He was being crucified, He said, "Father, forgive them, for they know not what they do?"[1] He who was asleep in thy heart did not wish to be avenged. Awake Him up then, call Him to remembrance. The remembrance of Him is His word; the remembrance of Him is His command. And then wilt thou say if Christ, awake in thee, What manner of man am I, who wish to be avenged! Who am I, who deal out threatenings against another man? I may die perhaps before I am avenged. And when at my last breath, inflamed with rage, and thirsting for vengeance, I shall depart out of this body, He will not receive me, who did not wish to be avenged; He will not receive me, who said, "Give, and it shall be given unto you; forgive, and it shall be forgiven you."[2] Therefore will I refrain myself from my wrath, and return to the repose of my heart. Christ hath commanded the sea, tranquillity is restored.

3. Now what I have said as to anger, hold fast as a rule in all your temptations. A temptation has sprung up; it is the wind; thou art disturbed; it is a wave. Awake up Christ then, let Him speak with thee. "Who is this, since the winds and the sea obey Him?"[3] Who is this, whom the sea obeyeth? "The sea is His, and He made it."[4] "All things were made by Him."[5] Imitate the winds then, and the sea rather; obey the Creator. At Christ's command the sea giveth ear; and art thou deaf? The sea heareth, and the wind ceaseth: and dost thou still blow on? What! I say, I do, I devise; what is all this, but to be blowing on, and to be unwilling to stop in obedience to the word of Christ? Let not the wave master you in this troubled state of your heart. Yet since we are but men, if the wind should drive us on, and stir up the affections of our souls, let us not despair; let us awake Christ, that we may sail on a tranquil sea, and so come to our country. "Let us[6] turn to the Lord," etc.

SERMON XIV.

[LXIV. BEN.]

ON THE WORDS OF THE GOSPEL, MATT. X. 16, "BEHOLD, I SEND YOU FORTH AS SHEEP IN THE MIDST OF WOLVES," ETC.

Delivered on a Festival of Martyrs.

1. WHEN the Holy Gospel was read, Brethren,

ye heard how our Lord Jesus Christ strengthened His Martyrs by His teaching, saying, "Behold, I send you forth as lambs in the midst of wolves."[7] Now consider, my Brethren, what he does. If but one wolf come among many sheep, be they ever so many thousands, they will all be put to confusion by one wolf in the midst of them: and though all may not be torn, yet all are frightened. What manner of design is this then, what manner of counsel, what manner of power, not to let in a wolf amongst the sheep, but to send the sheep against the wolves! "I send you," saith He, "as sheep in the midst of wolves;" not to the neighbourhood of wolves, but "in the midst of wolves." There was then at that time a herd of wolves, and but few sheep. For when the many wolves killed the few sheep, the wolves were changed and became sheep.

2. Let us hear then what advice He hath given, who hath promised the crown, but hath first appointed the combat; who is a spectator of the combatants, and assisteth them in their toil. What manner of conflict hath He prescribed? "Be ye," saith He, "wise as serpents, and simple as doves."[7] Whoso understandeth, and holdeth to this, may die in assurance[8] that he will not really die. For no one ought to die in this assurance, but he who knows that he shall in such sort die, as that death only shall die in him, and life be crowned.

3. Wherefore, Beloved, I must explain to you, though I have often spoken already on this subject, what it is to be "simple as doves, and wise as serpents." Now if the simplicity of doves be enjoined us, what hath the wisdom of the serpent to do in the simplicity of the dove? This in the dove I love, that she has no gall; this I fear in the serpent, that he has poison. But now do not fear the serpent altogether; something he has for thee to hate, and something for thee to imitate. For when the serpent is weighed down with age, and he feels the burden of his many years, he contracts and forces himself into a hole, and lays aside his old coat[9] of skin, that he may spring forth into new life. Imitate him in this, thou Christian, who dost hear Christ saying, "Enter ye in at the strait gate."[10] And the Apostle Paul saith to thee, "Put ye off the old man with his deeds, and put ye on the new man."[11] Thou hast then something to imitate in the serpent. Die not for the "old man," but for the truth. Whoso dies for any temporal good dies "for the old man." But when thou hast stripped thyself of

1 Luke xxiii. 34.   2 Luke vi. 37, 38.   3 Matt. viii. 27.
4 Ps xcv. 5.   5 John i 3.
6 For the full form, see end of Sermon xvii. (lxvii. Bened.).

7 Matt. x. 16.
8 *Securus.*
9 *Tunicam.*
10 Matt. vii. 13.
11 Col. iii. 9; Eph. iv. 22-24.

all " that old man," thou hast imitated the wisdom of the serpent. Imitate him in this again ; " keep thy head safe." And what does this mean, keep thy head safe? Keep Christ with thee. Have not some of you, it may be, observed, on occasions when you have wished to kill an adder, how to save his head, he will expose his whole body to the strokes of his assailant? He would not that that part of him should be struck, where he knows that his life resides. And our Life is Christ, for He hath said Himself, " I am the way, and the truth, and the life." [1] Here the Apostle also ; " The Head of the man is Christ." [2] Whoso then keepeth Christ in him, keepeth his head for his protection.

4. Now what need is there to commend to you in many words the simplicity of the dove? For the serpent's poison had need to be guarded against : there, there was a danger in imitation ; there, there was something to be feared ; but the dove may you imitate securely. Mark how the doves rejoice in society ; everywhere do they fly and feed together ; they do not love to be alone, they delight in communion, they preserve affection ; their cooings are the plaintive cries [3] of love, with kissings they beget their young. Yea even when doves, as we have often noticed, dispute about their holes, it is as it were but a peaceful strife. Do they separate, because of their contentions? Nay, still do they fly and feed together, and their very strife is peaceful. See this strife of doves, in what the Apostle saith, " If any man obey not our word by this epistle, mark that man, and have no company with him." Behold the strife ; but observe now how it is the strife of doves, not of wolves. He subjoined immediately, " Yet count him not as an enemy, but admonish him as a brother." [4] The dove loves even when she is in strife ; and the wolf even when he caresses, hates. Therefore having the simplicity of doves, and the wisdom of serpents, celebrate the solemnities of the Martyrs in sobriety of mind, [5] not [6] in bodily excess, sing lauds to God. For He who is the Martyrs' God, is our Lord God also, He it is who will crown us. If we shall have wrestled well, we shall be crowned by Him, who hath crowned already those whom we desire to imitate.

---

[1] John xiv. 6.
[2] 1 Cor. xi. 3.
[3] *Gemitibus amoris murmurant.*
[4] 2 Thess. iii. 14, 15.
[5] See, as to the excesses which prevailed at the festivals of the Martyrs, a letter of St. Augustin to Aurelius Bishop of Carthage and Primate of Africa (Ep. 22, al. 64), urging him to use his authority to suppress them. St. Ambrose had prohibited these feasts in the Church of Milan (Augustin, *Conf.* lib. 6. 2 [Am. edition, i. 90, note]). Aurelius succeeded in getting a canon (xxx.) made in the third Council of Carthage (A.D. 397), obliging the clergy to abstain from all such feasts in the Church, and as far as in them lay to restrain the people from the same practice (*Conc. Labbe,* t. 2, p. 1171; Bingham, B. xx. vii. § 10).
[6] *Ebrietate ventris.*

SERMON XV.

[LXV. BEN.]

ON THE WORDS OF THE GOSPEL, MATT. X. 28, " BE NOT AFRAID OF THEM THAT KILL THE BODY."

Delivered on a Festival of Martyrs.

1. THE Divine oracles which have just been read teach us in fearing not to fear, and in not fearing to fear. Ye observed when the Holy Gospel was being read, that our Lord God before He died for us, would have us to be firm ; and this by admonishing us " not " to fear, and withal to fear. For he said, " Fear not them which kill the body, but are not able to kill the soul." See where He advised us not to fear. See now where He advised us to fear. " But," saith he, " fear Him who hath power to destroy both body and soul in hell." [7] Let us fear therefore, that we may not fear. Fear seems to be allied to cowardice : seems to be the character of the weak, not the strong. But see what saith the Scripture, " The fear of the Lord is the hope of strength." [8] Let us then fear, that we may not fear ; that is, let us fear prudently, that we may not fear vainly. The holy Martyrs on the occasion of whose solemnity this lesson was read out of the Gospel, in fearing, feared not ; because in fearing God, they did not regard men.

2. For what need a man fear from man? And what is that whereby one man should cause another fear, since both of them are men? One threatens and says, " I will kill thee ; " and does not fear, lest after his threat he die before he have fulfilled it. " I will kill thee," he says. Who says it, and to whom? I hear two men, the one threatening, and the other alarmed : of whom the one is powerful, and the other weak, yet both are mortal. Why then does he so stretch out himself, he, in honour, a somewhat more inflated power, in body, equal weakness? Let him securely threaten death who does not fear death. But if he fear that whereby he causes fear ; let him think of himself, and compare himself with him whom he is threatening. Let him see in him whom he threateneth a likeness of condition, and so together with him let him seek like pity from the Lord. For he is but a man, and he threatens another man, a creature, another creature ; only the one puffed up under his Creator's eye, and the other fleeing for refuge to the same Creator.

3. Let the stout Martyr then, as he stands a man before another man, say ; " I do not fear, because I fear." Thou canst not do what thou art threatening, unless He will ; but what He threateneth, none can hinder Him from doing.

---

[7] Matt. x. 28.   [8] Prov. xiv. 26, Sept.

And then again, what dost thou threaten, and what canst thou do, if thou art permitted? Thy violence extends but to the flesh, the soul is safe from thee. Thou canst not kill what thou dost not see: visible thyself, thou threatenest that which is visible in me. But we have both an invisible Creator, whom we ought both to fear; who of that which was both visible and invisible created man. He made Him visible out of the earth, and with His Breath He breathed into Him an invisible Spirit. Therefore the invisible substance, that is, the soul, which has raised from the earth the earth as it lay, does not fear, when thou assaultest the earth. Thou canst strike the habitation, but canst thou strike him who dwells there? When the chain is broken, he escapes who before was bound, and he will now be crowned in secret. Why then dost thou threaten me, who canst do nothing to my soul? Through the desert of that to which thou canst do nothing, will that to which thy power extends rise again. For through the soul's desert, will the flesh also rise again; and will be restored to its inhabitant, now no more to fail, but to endure for ever. Behold (I am using the words of a Martyr), behold, I say, not even on account of my body do I fear thy threats. My body indeed is subject to thy power; but even the hairs of my head are numbered by my Creator. Why should I fear lest I lose my body, who cannot even lose a hair? How shall he not have a care of my body, to whom my meanest things are so well known? This body which may be wounded and slain will for a time be ashes, but it will be for ever immortal. But to whom shall this be? To whom shall the body be restored for life eternal, even though it have been slain, destroyed, and scattered to the winds? to whom shall it be so restored? To him who has not been afraid to lay down his own life, since he does not fear, lest his body should be slain.

4. For, Brethren, the soul is said to be immortal, and immortal it is according to a certain manner of its own: for it is a kind of life which is able to give life to the body by its presence. For by the soul doth the body live. This life cannot die, and therefore is the soul immortal. Why then said I according to a certain manner of its own? Hear why. Because there is a true immortality, an immortality which is an entire unchangeableness; of which the Apostle saith, speaking of God, "Who only hath immortality, dwelling in that light which no man may approach unto, whom no man hath seen, nor can see, to whom be honour and glory for ever and ever. Amen."[1] If then God only hath immortality, the soul must needs be mortal. See then why it was that I said that the soul is immortal after a certain manner of its own. For in fact it may also die. Understand this, Beloved, and there will remain no difficulty. I venture to say then that the soul can die, can be slain also. Yet it is undoubtedly immortal. See, I venture to say, it is at once immortal, and it may be slain; and therefore I said that there is a kind of immortality, an entire unchangeableness, that is, which God Only hath, of whom it is said, "Who Only hath immortality;" for if the soul cannot be slain, how did the Lord Himself say, when He would make us fear, "Fear Him who hath power to slay both body and soul in hell"?

5. Hitherto I have confirmed, not solved, the difficulty. I have proved that the soul can be slain. The Gospel cannot be gainsaid but by the ungodly soul. Lo, something occurs to me here, and comes into my mind to speak. Life cannot be gainsaid, but by a dead soul. The Gospel is life, impiety and infidelity are the death of the soul. See then, it can die, and yet it is immortal. How then is it immortal? Because there is always a sort of life which is never extinguished in it. And how does it die? Not in ceasing to be life, but by losing its life. For the soul is both life to something else, and it has its own proper life. Consider the order of the creatures. The soul is the life of the body: God is the life of the soul. As the life, that is the soul, is present with the body, that the body die not; so ought the life of the soul, that is God, to be with it that the soul die not. How does the body die? By the soul's leaving it. I say, by the soul's leaving the body dies; and it lies along a mere carcass, what was a little before a desirable, now a contemptible, object. There are in it still its several members, the eyes, and ears; but these are but the windows of the house, its inhabitant is gone. They who bewail the dead, cry in vain at the windows of the house; there is none within to hear. How many things does the fond affection of the mourner give utterance to, how many enumerate and call to mind; and with what a madness of sorrow, so to say, does he speak, as with one who was sensible of what was doing, when he is really speaking with one who is no longer there? He recounts his good qualities, and the tokens of his goodness towards himself. It was thou that didst give me this; and did this and that for me; it was thou who didst thus and thus dearly love me. But if thou wouldest only consider and understand, and restrain the madness of thy grief, he who once loved thee, is gone; in vain does the house receive thy knockings, in which thou canst not find a dweller.

6. Let us return to the subject I was speaking of a little while since. The body is dead.

---

[1] 1 Tim. vi. 16.

Why? Because its life, that is the soul, is gone. Again, the body is alive, and the man is impious, unbelieving, hard of belief, incorrigible; in this case whilst the body is alive, the soul by which the body lives is dead. For the soul is so excellent a thing, that it has power even though dead to give life to the body. So excellent a thing, I say, is the soul, so excellent a creature, that even though dead itself, it has power to quicken the body. For the soul of the impious, unbelieving, unregulated man is dead, and yet by it though dead the body lives. And therefore is it in the body; it sets on the hands to work, and the feet to walk; it directs the eye to see, it disposes the ears to hear, it discriminates tastes, avoids pains, seeks after pleasures. All these are tokens of the life of the body; but they are from the presence of the soul. If I were to ask a body whether it were alive; it would answer me, You see me walking, you see me working, you hear me talking, you perceive that I have certain aims and aversions, and do you not understand that the body is alive? By these works then of the soul which is placed within, I understand that the body is alive. I ask the soul also whether it is alive? It also has its proper works, by which it manifests its life. The feet walk. I understand by this that the body lives, but by the presence of the soul. I ask now, does the soul live? These feet walk. (To speak only of this one movement.) I am questioning both body and soul, as touching their life. The feet walk, I understand that the body lives. But whither do they walk? To adultery, it is said. Then is the soul dead. For so hath unerring Scripture said, "The widow who liveth in pleasure is dead." [1] Now since the difference is great between "pleasure" and adultery, how can the soul which is said to be dead in pleasure, live in adultery? It is surely dead. But it is dead even though it be not in this case. I hear a man speaking; the body then lives. For the tongue could not move itself in the mouth, and by its several motions give utterance to articulate sounds, were there not an inhabitant within; and a musician as it were to this instrument, to make use of his tongue. I understand it perfectly. Thus the body speaks; the body then lives. But I ask, is the soul alive also? Lo, the body speaks, and so is alive. But what does it speak? As I said concerning the feet; they walk, and so the body is alive, and I then asked, whither do they walk? that I might understand whether the soul was alive also. So also when I hear a man speak, I understand that the body is alive; I ask what does he speak, that I may know whether the soul is alive also. He speaks a lie. If so, then is the soul dead. How do we prove

this? Let us ask the truth itself, which saith, "The mouth that lieth, slayeth the soul." [2] I ask, why is the soul dead? I ask as I did just now, why is the body dead? Because the soul, its life, was gone. Why is the soul dead? Because God, its life, hath forsaken it.

7. After this brief examination then, know and hold for certain that the body is dead without the soul, and that the soul is dead without God. Every man without God hath a dead soul. Thou dost bewail the dead: bewail the sinner rather, bewail rather the ungodly man, bewail the unbeliever. It is written, "The mourning for the dead is seven days; for a fool and an ungodly man all the days of his life." [3] What! are there no bowels of Christian compassion in thee; that thou mournest for a body from which the soul is gone, and mournest not for the soul, from which God is departed? Let the Martyr remembering this make answer to him that threatens him, "Why dost thou force me to deny Christ?" Wouldest thou then force me to deny the truth? And if I will not, what wilt thou do? Thou wilt assault my body, that my soul shall depart from it; but this same soul of mine has its body only for the soul's sake. It is not so foolish or unwise. Thou wouldest wound my body; but wouldest thou, that through fear lest thou shouldest wound my body, and my soul should depart from it, I should wound mine own soul, and my God should depart from it? Fear not then, O Martyr, the sword of thy executioner; fear only thine own tongue, lest thou do execution upon thine own self, and slay, not thy body, but thy soul. Fear for thy soul, lest it die in hell-fire.

8. Therefore said the Lord, "Who hath power to slay both body and soul in hell-fire." How? when the ungodly shall be cast into hell-fire, will his body and his soul burn there? Everlasting punishment will be the death of the body; the absence of God will be the death of the soul. Wouldest thou know what the death of the soul is? Understand the Prophet who saith, "Let the ungodly be taken away, that he may not see the glory of the Lord." [4] Let the soul then fear its proper death, and not fear the death of its body. Because if it fear its own death, and so live in its God, by not offending and thrusting Him away from him, it will be found worthy [5] to receive its body again at the end; not unto everlasting punishment, as the ungodly, but unto life eternal, as the righteous. By fearing this death, and loving that life, did the Martyrs, in hope of the promises of God, and in contempt of the threats of persecutors, attain [6] themselves to be crowned with God, and have left to us the celebration of these solemnities.

[1] 1 Tim. v. 6.   [2] Wisd. i. 11.   [3] Ecclus. xxii. 12.   [4] Isa. xxvi. 10, Sept.   [5] *Merebitur.*   [6] *Meruerunt.*

SERMON XVI.

[LXVI. BEN.]

ON THE WORDS OF THE GOSPEL, MATT. XI. 2, "NOW WHEN JOHN HEARD IN THE PRISON THE WORKS OF THE CHRIST, HE SENT BY HIS DISCIPLES, AND SAID UNTO HIM, ART THOU HE THAT COMETH, OR LOOK WE FOR ANOTHER?" ETC.

1. THE lesson of the Holy Gospel has set before us a question touching John the Baptist. May the Lord assist me to resolve it to you, as He hath resolved it to us. John was commended, as ye have heard, by the testimony of Christ, and in such terms commended, as that there had not risen a greater among those who were born of women. But a greater than he had been born of a Virgin. How much greater? Let the herald himself declare, how great the difference is between himself and his Judge, whose herald he is. For John went before Christ both in his birth and preaching; but it was in obedience that he went before Him; not in preferring himself before Him. For so the whole train[1] of attendants walks before the judge; yet they who walk before, are really after him. How signal a testimony then did John give to Christ? Even to saying that he "was not worthy to loose the latchet of His shoes."[2] And what more? "Of His fulness," saith he, "have all we received."[3] He confessed that he was but a lamp lighted at His Light, and so he took refuge at His feet, lest venturing on high, he should be extinguished by the wind of pride. So great indeed was he, that he was taken for Christ; and if he had not himself testified that he was not He, the mistake would have continued, and he would have been reputed to be the Christ. What striking humility! Honour was proffered him by the people, and he himself refused it. Men were at fault in his greatness, and he humbled himself. He had no wish to increase by the words of men, seeing he had comprehended the Word of God.

2. This then did John say concerning Christ. And what said Christ of John? We have just now heard. "He began to say to the multitudes concerning John, What went ye out into the wilderness to see? A reed shaken with the wind?"[4] Surely not; for John was not "blown about by every wind of doctrine."[5] "But what went ye out for to see? A man clothed in soft raiment?"[6] No, for John was clothed in rough apparel; he had his raiment of camel's hair, not of down. "But what went ye out for to see? A Prophet? yea, and more than a Prophet."[7] Why "more than a Prophet"? The Prophets foretold that the Lord would come, whom they desired to see, and saw not; but to him was

vouchsafed what they sought. John saw the Lord; he saw Him, pointed his finger toward Him, and said, "Behold the Lamb of God, who taketh away the sins of the world;"[8] behold, here He is. Now had He come and was not acknowledged; and so a mistake was made also as to John himself. Behold then here is He whom the Patriarchs desired to see, whom the Prophets foretold, whom the Law prefigured. "Behold the Lamb of God, who taketh away the sins of the world." And he gave a goodly testimony to the Lord, and the Lord to him. "Among them that are born of women," saith the Lord, "there hath not risen a greater than John the Baptist: notwithstanding, he that is less in the kingdom of heaven is greater than he;"[9] less in time, but greater in majesty. This He said, meaning Himself to be understood. Now exceedingly great among men is John the Baptist, than whom among men Christ alone is greater. It may also[10] be thus stated and explained, "Among them that are born of women there hath not risen a greater than John the Baptist: notwithstanding, he that is the least in the kingdom of heaven is greater than he." Not in the sense that I have before explained it. "Notwithstanding, he that is the least in kingdom of heaven is greater than he;" the kingdom of heaven he meant where the Angels are; he then that is the least among the Angels, is greater than John. Thus He set forth to us the excellence[11] of that kingdom which we should long for; set before us a city, of which we should desire to be citizens. What sort of citizens are there? how great are they! Whoso is the least there, is greater than John. Than what John? "Than whom there hath not risen a greater among them that are born of women."

3. Thus have we heard the true and good record both of John concerning Christ, and of Christ concerning John. What then is the meaning of this; that John sent his disciples to Him when He was shut up in prison, on the eve of being put to death, and said to them, "Go, say to Him, Art Thou He that should come, or do we look for another?"[12] Is this then all that praise? That praise is it turned to doubting? What sayest thou, John. To Whom art thou speaking? What sayest thou? Thou speakest to thy Judge, thyself the herald. Thou stretchedst out the finger, and pointedst Him out; thou saidst, "Behold the Lamb of God, behold Him who taketh away the sins of the world." Thou saidst, "Of His fulness have we all received." Thou saidst, "I am not worthy to unloose the latchet of His shoes." And dost

---

[1] *Officium*.
[2] John i. 27.
[3] John i. 16.
[4] Matt. xi. 7.
[5] Eph. iv. 14.
[6] Matt. xi. 8.
[7] Matt. xi. 9.

[8] John i. 29.
[9] Matt. xi. 11.
[10] He gives these two interpretations of this passage; again *Cont. adv. leg.* and *Prop.* ii. 5 (20).
[11] *Commendavit*.
[12] Matt. xi. 3.

thou now say, "Art Thou He that should come, or do we look for another?" Is not this the same Christ? And who art thou? Art thou not His forerunner? Art thou not he of whom it was foretold, "Behold, I send my messenger before Thy face, who shall prepare Thy way before thee?"[1] How dost thou prepare the way, and thou art thyself straying from the way? So then the disciples of John came; and the Lord said to them, "Go, tell John, the blind see, the deaf hear, the lame walk, the lepers are cleansed, the poor have the Gospel preached to them; and blessed is he whosoever shall not be offended in Me."[2] Do not suspect that John was offended in Christ. And yet his words do sound so; "Art Thou He that should come?" Ask my works; "The blind see, the deaf hear, the lame walk, the lepers are cleansed, the dead are raised, the poor have the Gospel preached to them;" and dost thou ask whether I am He? My works, saith He, are My words. "Go, show him again. And as they departed." Lest haply any one should say, John was good at first, and the Spirit of God forsook him; therefore after their departure, he spake these words; after their departure whom John had sent, Christ commended John.[2]

4. What is the meaning then of this obscure question? May that Sun shine upon us, from which that lamp derived its flame. And so the resolution of it is altogether plain. John had separate disciples of his own; not as in separation from Christ, but prepared as a witness to him. For meet it was that such an one should give his testimony to Christ, who was himself also gathering disciples, and who might have been envious of Him, for that he could not see Him. Therefore because John's disciples highly esteemed their master, they heard from John his record concerning Christ, and marvelled; and as he was about to die, it was his wish that they should be confirmed by him. For no doubt they were saying among themselves; Such great things doth he say of Him, but none such of himself. "Go then, ask Him;" not because I doubt, but that ye may be instructed. "Go, ask Him," hear from Himself what I am in the habit of telling you; ye have heard the herald, be confirmed by the Judge. "Go, ask Him, Art Thou He that should come, or do we look for another?" They went accordingly and asked; not for John's sake, but for their own. And for their sakes did Christ say, "The blind see, the lame walk, the deaf hear, the lepers are cleansed, the dead are raised, the poor have the Gospel preached to them." Ye see Me, acknowledge Me then; ye see the works, acknowledge the Doer. "And blessed is he whosoever shall not

be offended in Me." But it is of you I speak, not of John. For that we might know that He spake not this of John, as they departed, "He began to speak to the multitudes concerning John;" the True, the Truth Himself, proclaimed his true praises.

5. I think this question has been sufficiently explained. Let it suffice then to have prolonged my address thus far. Now keep the poor in mind. Give, ye who have not given hitherto; believe me, ye will not lose it. Yes, truly, that only it seems ye lose, which ye do not carry to the circus.[3] Now must we render unto the poor the offerings of such of you as have offered anything, and the amount which we have is much less than your usual offerings. Shake off this sloth. I am become a beggar for beggars; what is that to me? I would be a beggar for beggars, that ye may be reckoned among the number of children.

SERMON XVII.

[LXVII. BEN.]

ON THE WORDS OF THE GOSPEL, MATT. XI. 25, "I THANK THEE, O FATHER, LORD OF HEAVEN AND EARTH, THAT THOU DIDST HIDE THESE THINGS FROM THE WISE AND UNDERSTANDING," ETC.

1. WHEN the Holy Gospel was being read, we heard that the Lord Jesus exulted in Spirit, and said, "I confess to Thee, O Father, Lord of heaven and earth, for that Thou hast hid these things from the wise and prudent, and hast revealed them unto babes."[4] Thus much to begin[5] with, we find before we pass on further, if we consider the words of the Lord with due attention, with diligence, and above all with piety, that we ought not invariably to understand when we read of "confession" in the Scriptures, the confession[6] of a sinner. Now especial need there was of saying this, and of reminding you, Beloved, of this, because as soon as this word was uttered by the reader's voice, there followed upon it the sound of the beating of your breasts, when ye had heard, I mean, what the Lord said, "I confess to Thee, O Father." At the uttering of these words, "I confess," ye beat your breasts. Now what means this beating of the breast, but to show that which lies hid within the breast, and to chastise by the visible beating the secret sin? And why did ye this, but because ye heard, "I confess to Thee, O Father." Ye heard the words "I confess," but ye did not consider, who it is that confesses. But consider now. If Christ, from whom all sin is far removed, said, "I confess:" confession does not belong to the sinner only, but sometimes to him also that praiseth God. We confess then, whether

in praising God, or accusing ourselves. In either case it is a godly confession, either when thou blamest thyself, who art not without sin, or when thou praisest Him who can have no sin.

2. But if we consider it well : thine own blame is His praise. For why is it that thou dost now confess in accusing thyself for thy sin? in accusing thyself why dost thou confess? but because thou art become alive from the dead? for the Scripture saith, " Confession perisheth from the dead, as from one that is not." [1] If confession perisheth from the dead, he who confesseth must be alive ; and if he confesseth sin he hath undoubtedly risen again from death. Now if he that confesseth sin hath risen again from the dead, who hath raised him? No dead man can raise himself. He only was able to raise Himself, who though His Body was dead, was not dead. For He raised up that which was dead. He raised up Himself, who in Himself was alive, but in His Body that was to be raised was dead. For not the Father only, of whom it was said by the Apostle, " Wherefore God also hath exalted Him," [2] raised the Son, but the Lord also raised Himself, that is, His Body. Whence He said, " Destroy this temple, and in three days I will raise it again." [3] But the sinner is dead, especially he whom the load of sinful habit presseth down, who is buried as it were like Lazarus. For he was not merely dead, he was buried also. [4] Whosoever then is oppressed by the load of evil habit, of a wicked life, of earthly lusts, I mean, so that that in his case is true which is piteously described in a certain Psalm, " The fool hath said in his heart, There is no God," [5] he is such an one, of whom it is said, " Confession perisheth from the dead, as from one that is not." And who shall raise him up, but He who when the stone was removed, cried out, and said, " Lazarus, come forth?" [6] Now what is to " come forth," but to bring forth what was hidden? He then who confesseth " cometh forth." " Come forth " he could not were he not alive ; he could not be alive, had he not been raised again. And therefore in confession the accusing of one's self, is the praise of God.

3. Now one may say, what profit then is the Church, if he that confesseth comes forth, at once raised to life again by the voice of the Lord? What profit to Him that confesseth, is the Church, to which the Lord said, " Whatsoever ye shall bind on earth, shall be bound in heaven." [7] Consider this very case of Lazarus : he comes forth, but with his bands. He was alive already through confession, but he did not yet walk free, entangled as he was in his bands. What then doth the Church to which it was said,

" Whatsoever ye shall loose, shall be loosed ;" but what [8] the Lord said forthwith to His disciples, " Loose him, and let him go "? [9]

4. Whether then we accuse ourselves, or directly praise God, in both ways do we praise God. If with a pious intention we accuse ourselves, by so doing we praise God. When we praise God directly, we do as it were celebrate His Holiness, who is without sin : but when we accuse ourselves, we give Him glory, by whom we have risen again. This if thou shalt do, the enemy will find none occasion whereby to [10] overreach thee before the judge. For when thou shalt be thine own accuser, and the Lord thy Deliverer, what shall he be but a mere calumniator? With good reason hath the Christian hereby provided protection for himself against his enemies, not those that may be seen, flesh and blood, to be pitied, rather than to be feared, but against those against whom the Apostle exhorts us to arm ourselves : " We wrestle not against flesh and blood ;" [11] that is, against men whom ye see raging against you. They are but vessels, which another uses, they are but instruments which another handles. " The devil," saith the Scripture, " entered into the heart of Judas, that he should betray the Lord." [12] One may say then, what have I done? Hear the Apostle, " Give not place to the devil." [13] Thou hast given him place by an evil will : he entered, and possessed, and now uses thee. He had not possessed thee, hadst thou not given him place.

5. Therefore doth he warn and say, " We wrestle not against flesh and blood, but against principalities and powers." Any one might suppose this meant against the kings of the earth, against the powers of this world. How so? are they not flesh and blood? And once for all it is said, " not against flesh and blood." Turn thy attention from all men. What enemies then remain? " Against principalities and powers of spiritual wickedness, the rulers of the world." [14] It might seem as though he gave the devil and his angels more than they have. It is so, he has called them the " rulers of the world." But to prevent misunderstanding, he explains what this world is, of which they are the rulers. " The rulers of the world, of this darkness." What is, " of the world, of this darkness?" The world is full of those who love it, and of unbelievers, over whom he is ruler. This the Apostle calls darkness. This darkness the devil and his angels are the rulers of. This is not the natural, and unchangeable darkness : this darkness changes, and becomes light ; it believes, and by believing is enlightened. When this takes place in it, it will hear the words, " For ye were sometimes

[1] Ecclus. xvii. 28, Sept. [2] Phil. ii. 9. [3] John ii. 19.
[4] John xi. 17. [5] Ps. xiv. 1. [6] John xi. 43.
[7] Matt. xvi. 19 and xviii. 18.

[8] Vid. Serm. 48 (98, Bened.) 6. [9] John xi. 44.
[10] Circumveniat. [11] Eph. vi. 12. [12] John xiii. 2.
[13] Eph. iv. 27. [14] Vulgate.

darkness, but now are ye light in the Lord." [1] For when ye were darkness, ye were not in the Lord : again, when ye are light, ye are light not in yourselves, but in the Lord. "For what hast thou which thou hast not received?" [2] Inasmuch then as they are invisible enemies, by invisible means must they be subdued. A visible enemy indeed thou mayest overcome by blows ; thy invisible enemy thou conquerest by belief. A man is a visible enemy ; to strike a blow is visible also. The devil is an invisible enemy ; to believe is invisible also. Against invisible enemies then there is an invisible fight.

6. From these enemies how can any man say that he is safe? For this I had begun to speak of, but I thought it necessary to treat of these enemies at some little length. But now that we know our enemies, let us see to our defence against them. "In praising I will call upon the Lord, so shall I be safe from mine enemies." [3] Thou seest what thou hast to do. "In praising call ;" that is, "in praising the Lord, call." For thou wilt not be safe from thine enemies, if thou praise thyself. "In praising call upon the Lord, and thou shalt be safe from thine enemies." For what doth the Lord Himself say? "The sacrifice of praise shall glorify Me, and there is the way, in which I will show him My salvation." [4] Where is the way? In the sacrifice of praise. Let not your foot then wander out of this way. Keep in the way ; depart not from it ; from the praise of the Lord depart not a foot, nay, not a nail's breadth. For if thou wilt deviate from this way, and praise thyself instead of the Lord, thou wilt not be safe from thine enemies ; for it is said of them, "They have laid stumbling-blocks for me by the way." [5] Therefore in whatever measure thou thinkest that thou hast good of thine own self, thou hast deviated from the praise of God. Why dost thou marvel then, if thine enemy seduce thee, when thou art thine own seducer? Hear the Apostle, "For if a man think himself to be something when he is nothing, he seduceth himself." [6]

7. Give heed then to the Lord confessing ; "I confess to Thee, O Father, Lord of heaven and earth." I confess to Thee, that is, I praise Thee. I praise Thee, not I accuse myself. Now as far as the taking of very [7] man is concerned, all is grace, singular and perfect grace. What merit had that man [8] who is Christ, if thou take away

the grace, even that so pre-eminent grace, whereby it behoved that there should be One Christ, and that He whom we acknowledge should be He? Take away this grace, and what is Christ but a mere man? what but the same as thou art thyself? He took a Soul, He took a Body, He took a perfect Man ; He uniteth him to Himself, the Lord maketh one Person with the servant. What pre-eminent grace is this ! Christ in heaven, Christ on earth ; Christ at once both in heaven and earth ; not two Christs, but the same Christ, both in heaven and earth. Christ with the Father, Christ in the Virgin's womb ; Christ on the Cross, Christ succouring some souls in hell ; and on the self-same day Christ in paradise with the robber who confessed. And how did the robber attain [9] to this blessedness, but because he held on that way, in which "He showeth His salvation"? That way, from which let not thy foot wander. For in that he accused himself, he praised God, and made his own life blessed. He looked in hope [10] for this from the Lord, and said to Him, "Lord, remember me when Thou comest into Thy kingdom." [11] For he considered his own wicked deeds, and thought it much, if mercy should be shown him even at the last. But the Lord immediately after He had said, "Remember me"—when? "when Thou comest into Thy kingdom," saith, "Verily I say unto thee, To-day shalt thou be with Me in paradise." Mercy offered at once, what misery deferred.

8. Hear then the Lord confessing ; "I confess to Thee, O Father, Lord of heaven and earth." [12] What do I confess? Wherein do I praise thee? For this confession, as I have said before, signifieth praise. "Because Thou hast hid these things from the wise and prudent, and hast revealed them unto babes." What is this, Brethren? Understand by that which is opposed to them. "Thou hast hid these things," saith he, "from the wise and prudent ;" and he did not say, thou hast revealed them to the foolish and imprudent, but "Thou hast hid these things" indeed "from the wise and prudent, and hast revealed them unto babes." To these wise and

[1] Eph. v. 8.
[2] 1 Cor. iv. 7.   [3] Ps. xvii. 4, Sept. (xviii. 3, English version).
[4] Ps. xlix. 23, Sept. (l. English version).
[5] Ps. cxxxix. 6, Sept. (cxl. 5, English version).
[6] Gal. vi. 3, Vulg.   [7] *Ipsius.*
[8] It was the doctrine of Paul of Samosata, that the man Christ was exalted to be the Son of God (προκοπῇ, from Luke ii. 52), as if by merit. Origen seems to hold the same, at least as regards the (supposed) pre-existent soul of Christ (*vid.* Huet. *Origen,* ii. 3, § 6; *vid.* however De la Rue's note): and the Arians, at least implicitly (Socr. *Hist.* i. 6, Athan. *Orat. contr. Arian,* i. 35, iii. 51; and

Leporius, *Cassian. Incarn.* i. 3, 4). The same heresy was imputed to the Nestorians (but falsely according to Garner, in *Mar. Merc.* pt. i. p. 431), and thereby connected them with the Pelagians, as if unassisted human nature could merit grace. The Church on the other hand, proceeding from Rom i. 4, taught that the human nature which became the manhood of the Word was predestined to be such by grace before its creation, and became such in the moment of creation. St. Athanasius touches on this subject against the Arians (*Orat.* i. 46); St. Augustin enlarges on it against the Pelagians (*De Prædest. Sanct.* 23, 30; *De Corrept. et Grat.* 30); St. Cyril, against the Nestorians (*Contra Nest.* iii. p. 83); Vigilius, against the Monophysites (*Contra Eutych.* v. B. P. t. 4, p. 528, ed. 1624). When St. Augustin says "that man," he is speaking of our Lord's human nature as abstracted from that Divine Person in whom it actually existed, and not as if it ever existed as a separate hypostasis. This use of "homo" and ἄνθρωπος is very frequent with the Fathers; what is more startling is the expression "homo *ille*," yet *vid.* also Augustin, *De Præd. Sanct.* 30; Alcuin, *De Trin.* iii. 1; Agobard, *Cont. Felic.* B. P. t. 9, p. 1194. However, this point is a subject of debate among theologians (*vid.* Petav. *De Incarn.* xi. fin.).
[9] *Meruit.*   [10] *Præsumpsit.*   [11] Luke xxiii. 42.
[12] Matt. xi. 25.

prudent, who are really objects of derision, to the arrogant who in false pretence are great, yet in truth are only swollen up, he opposed not the foolish, nor the imprudent, but babes. Who are babes? The humble. Therefore "Thou hast hidden these things from the wise and prudent." Under the name of the wise and prudent, He hath Himself explained that the proud are understood, when He said, "Thou hast revealed them unto babes." Therefore from those who are not babes Thou hast hidden them. What is from those who are not babes? From those who are not humble. And who are they but the proud? O way of the Lord! Either there was none, or it lay hid, that it might be revealed to us. Why did the Lord exult? "Because it was revealed unto babes." We must be little babes; for if we would wish to be great, "wise and prudent" as it were, it is not revealed unto us. Who are these great ones? The wise and prudent. "Professing themselves to be wise, they became fools." [1] Here then thou hast a remedy suggested from its opposite. For if by "professing thyself wise, thou art become a fool; profess thyself a fool, and thou wilt be wise." But profess it in truth, profess it from the heart, for it is really so as thou professest. If thou profess it, do not profess it before men, and forbear to profess it before God. As to thyself, and all that is thine, thou art altogether dark. For what else is it to be a fool, but to be dark in heart? He saith of them at last, " Professing themselves to be wise, they became fools." Before they professed this, what do we find? "And their foolish heart was darkened." [2] Acknowledge then that thou art not to thyself a light. At best thou art but an eye, thou art not the light. And what good is even an open and a sound eye, if the light be wanting? Acknowledge therefore that of thine own self thou art no light to thyself; and cry out as it is written, "Thou, Lord, wilt light my candle : Thou wilt enlighten, O Lord, my darkness with Thy Light." [3] For myself I was all darkness; but Thou art the Light that scattereth the darkness, and enlighteneth me; of myself I am no light to myself, yea I have no portion of light but in Thee.

9. So John also, the friend of the Bridegroom, was thought to be the Christ, was thought to be the Light. "He was not that Light, but that he might bear witness of the Light." [4] But what was the Light? It was the true Light. What is the true Light? "That which lighteneth every man." If that be the true Light which lighteneth every man, then it lightened John also, who professed and confessed rightly, "Of His fulness have all we received." [5] See if he said ought else, but "Thou, O Lord, shalt lighten my can-

dle." Finally, being now enlightened, He gave His testimony. For the benefit of the blind the lamp gave witness to the Day. See how that He is a lamp ; " Ye sent," He said, " unto John, and ye were willing for a season to rejoice in his light ; he was a burning and a shining lamp." [6] He, the lamp, that is, a thing enlightened, was lighted that it might shine. That which can be lighted can be extinguished also. Now that it may not be extinguished, let it not expose itself to the wind of pride. Therefore, " I confess to Thee, O Father, Lord of heaven and earth, because Thou hast hid these things from the wise and prudent," from those who thought themselves to be light, and were darkness ; and who because they were darkness, and thought themselves to be light, could not even be enlightened. But they who were darkness, and confessed that they were darkness, were little babes, not great ; were humble, not proud. Rightly therefore did they say, "O Lord, Thou wilt lighten my candle." They knew themselves, they praised the Lord. They did not stray from the way of salvation ; " They in praise called upon the Lord, and they were saved from their enemies." [7]

10. Turning then to the Lord our God, the Father Almighty, in purity of heart, let us render unto Him, as our frailty best can, our highest and abundant thanks, with our whole mind praying His singular goodness, that in His good pleasure He would vouchsafe to hear our prayers, that by His Power He would drive out the enemy from our deeds and thoughts, would enlarge our faith, direct our minds, grant us spiritual thoughts, and bring us safe to His endless blessedness, through His Son Jesus Christ. Amen.

SERMON XVIII.

[LXVIII. BEN.]

AGAIN ON THE WORDS OF THE GOSPEL, MATT. XI. 25, "I THANK THEE, O FATHER, LORD OF HEAVEN AND EARTH," ETC.

1. WE have heard the Son of God saying, " I confess to Thee, O Father, Lord of heaven and earth." What doth he confess to Him? Wherein doth he praise Him? " Because Thou hast hid these things from the wise and prudent, and hast revealed them unto babes." [8] Who are the " wise and prudent " ? Who the " babes " ? What hath He hid from the wise and prudent, and revealed unto babes? By the " wise and prudent," He signifieth those of whom St. Paul speaks ; " Where is the wise? where is the scribe? where is the disputer of this world? Hath not God made foolish the wisdom of this

---

world?"[1]   Yet perhaps thou still askest who they are. They are they peradventure who in their much disputation concerning God, have spoken falsely of Him; who, puffed up by their own doctrines, could in no wise find out and know God, and who for the God whose substance is incomprehensible and invisible, have thought the air and sky to be God, or the sun to be God, or anything which holds high place[2] among the creatures to be God. For observing the grandeur and beauty and powers of the creatures, they rested in them, and found not the Creator.

2. These men does the Book of wisdom reprove, where it is said, "For if they were able to know so much as to aim at the world, how did they not sooner find out the Lord thereof?"[3] They are accused as wasting their time and their busy disputes in investigating and measuring as it were the creature; they sought out the courses of the stars, the intervals of the planets, the movements[4] of the heavenly bodies, so as to arrive by certain[5] calculations to that degree of knowledge as to foretell the eclipses of the sun and moon; and that as they had foretold, so should the event be according to the day and hour, and to the portion of the bodies which should be eclipsed. Great industry, great activity of mind. But in these things they sought after the Creator, who was not far off from them, and they found Him not. Whom if they could have found, they might have had within them. With the best reason then, and very rightly were they accused, who could investigate the numbers of the stars, and their varied movements, and know and foretell the eclipses of the luminaries: rightly accused, I say, in that they found not Him by whom these had been created and ordained, because they neglected to seek Him.   But be not thou much disquieted, if thou art ignorant of the courses of the stars, and the proportions[6] of the celestial and terrestrial bodies. Behold the fair beauty of the world, and praise its Creator's counsel. Behold what He has made, and love Him who made it: be this thy greatest care. Love Him who made it; for He made thee also after His own image, that thou mightest love Him.

3. If then it is strange that those things of which Christ said, "Thou hast hid these things from the wise and prudent," were hidden from such wise men as these, who, occupied wholly about the creatures, chose to seek the Creator carelessly, and could not find Him; still more strange is it that there should even be found some "wise and prudent" men who were able to know Him. "For the wrath of God is revealed from heaven against all ungodliness, and unrighteousness of men who hold the truth in

unrighteousness."[7]   Perhaps thou dost ask, what truth do they hold in unrighteousness? "Because that which may be known of God is manifest among them." How is it manifest? He goes on to say, "For God hath manifested it to them."[8] Dost thou still enquire how He manifested it to them to whom He gave not the law? How? "For the invisible things of Him from the creation of the world are clearly seen, being understood by the things that are made."[9] There were then some such, not as Moses the servant of God, not as many Prophets who had an insight into and knowledge of these things, and were aided by the Spirit of God, which they drew in by faith, and drank with the throat[10] of godliness, and poured[11] forth again by the mouth of the interior man. Not such as these were they; but far unlike them, who by means of this visible creation were able to attain to the understanding of the Creator, and to say of these things which God hath made;[12] Behold what things He hath made, He governeth and containeth also. He who hath made them, Himself filleth what He hath made with His own presence. Thus much they were enabled to say. For these Paul also made mention of in the Acts of the Apostles, where, when he had said of God, "For in Him we live and move and have our being"[13] (forasmuch as he was speaking to the Athenians among whom those learned men had existed); he subjoined immediately; "As certain also of your own have said." Now it was no trivial thing they said; "That in Him we live and move and have our being."

4. In what then were they unlike the others? why were they blamed? why rightly accused? Hear the words of the Apostle which I had begun to quote; "The wrath of God," saith he, "is revealed from heaven against all ungodliness" (even of those, namely, who had not received the law); "against all ungodliness and unrighteousness of men, who hold the truth in unrighteousness." What truth? "Because that which may be known of God is manifest in them." By whose manifestation of it? "For God hath manifested it to them." How? "For the invisible things of Him from the creation of the world are clearly seen, being understood by the things that are made, even His Eternal Power and Godhead." Why did He manifest it? "That they might be without excuse." Wherein then are they to be blamed? "Because that when they knew God, they glorified Him not as God."

5. What mean these words, "Glorified Him not as God?" They did not give Him thanks.

[1] 1 Cor. i. 20.   [2] *Sublimiter eminet.*   [3] Wisd. xiii. 9.
[4] *Itinera.*   [5] Vid. *Conf.* v. 3 (4).   [6] *Numeros.*
[7] Rom. i. 18.   [8] Rom. i. 19.   [9] Rom. i. 20.
[10] *Faucibus.*   [11] *Ructuaverunt.*
[12] Vid. *Conf.* vii. 9 (13-15).   [13] Acts xvii. 28.

Is this then to glorify God ; to give God thanks?
Yes, verily. For what can be worse, if having
been created after the image of God, and having
come to know God, thou shalt not be thankful to
Him? This surely, this is to glorify God, to give
God thanks. The faithful know where and when
it is said, "Let us give thanks unto our Lord
God." But who gives thanks to God, save he
who "lifts up his heart unto the Lord?" Therefore are they blameable and without excuse,
"Because when they knew God, they glorified
Him not as God, nor gave Him thanks. But"—
what? "But they became vain in their imaginations." Whence did they become vain, but
because they were proud? Thus smoke vanishes
away by rising up aloft, and a flame burns the
more brightly and strongly in proportion as it is
kept [1] low ; "They became vain in their imaginations, and their foolish heart was darkened."
So smoke, though it rise higher than the flame,
is dark.

6. Finally, mark what follows, and see the
point on which the whole matter depends.
"For professing themselves to be wise, they
became fools." For arrogating to themselves
what God had given, God took away what He
had given. Therefore from the proud He hid
Himself, who conveyed the knowledge of Himself only to those who through the creature
sought diligently after the Creator. Well then
did our Lord say, "Thou hast hid these things
from the wise and prudent ; " whether from those
who in their manifold disputations, and most
busy search, have reached to the full investigation of the creature, but knew nothing of the
Creator, or from them who when they knew
God, glorified Him not as God, nor gave Him
thanks, and who could not see perfectly or
healthfully because they were proud. "Therefore Thou hast hid these things from the wise and
prudent, and hast revealed them unto babes."
What babes? To the lowly. Say on whom
doth My Spirit rest? "Upon him that is lowly
and quiet, and who trembleth at My words." [2]
At these words Peter trembled ; Plato trembled
not. Let the fisherman hold fast what that most
famous philosopher has lost. "Thou hast hid
these things from the wise and prudent, and
hast revealed them unto babes." Thou hast
hid them from the proud, and revealed them to
the humble. What things are these? For when
He said this, He did not intend the heaven
and earth, or point them out as it were with His
hand as He spake. For these who does not
see? The good see them, the bad see them ;
for He "maketh His sun to rise on the evil and
the good." [3] What then are these things? "All
things are delivered unto Me of My Father." [4]

SERMON XIX.

[LXIX. BEN.]

ON THE WORDS OF THE GOSPEL, MATT. XIX. 28,
"COME UNTO ME, ALL YE THAT LABOUR AND
ARE HEAVY LADEN," ETC.

1. WE heard in the Gospel that the Lord,
rejoicing greatly in Spirit, said unto God the
Father, "I confess to Thee, O Father, Lord of
heaven and earth, because Thou hast hid these
things from the wise and prudent, and hast
revealed them unto babes. Even so, Father :
for so it seemed good in Thy sight. All things
are delivered unto Me of My Father : and no
man knoweth the Son, but the Father ; neither
knoweth any man the Father, save the Son, and
he to whomsoever the Son will reveal Him." [5] I
have labour in talking, you in hearing : let us then
both give ear to Him who goes on to say, "Come
unto Me, all ye that labour." [6] For why do we
labour all, except that we are mortal men, frail
creatures and infirm, bearing about vessels of
clay which crowd and straiten one another. But
if these vessels of flesh are straitened, let the
open [7] expanse of charity be enlarged. What
then does He mean by, "Come unto Me, all ye
that labour," but that ye may labour no more?
In a word, His promise is clear enough ; forasmuch as He called those who were in labour,
they might perchance enquire, for what profit
they were called : "and," saith He, "I will refresh you."

2. "Take My yoke upon you, and learn of
Me ; " [8] not to raise the fabric of the world,
not to create all things visible and invisible, not
in the world so created to work miracles and
raise the dead ; but, " that I am meek and lowly
in heart." Thou wishest to be great, begin from
the least. Thou art thinking to construct some
mighty fabric in height ; first think of the foundation of humility. And how great soever a mass
of building one may wish and design to place
above it, the greater the building is to be, the
deeper does he dig his foundation. The building in the course of its erection, rises up on high,
but he who digs its foundation, must first go
down very low. So then you see even a building is low before it is high, and the top is raised
only after humiliation.

3. What is the top in the erection of that
building which we are constructing? Whither
will the highest point of this building reach? I
say at once, even to the Vision of God. Ye see
how high, how great a thing it is to see God.
Whoso longeth after it, understands both what I
say and what he hears. The Vision of God is
promised to us, of the very God, the Supreme
God. For this is good, to see Him who seeth.

---

[1] *Humilius apprehendendo.*   [2] Isa. lxvi. 2.
[3] Matt. v. 45.   [4] Matt. xi. 27.

[5] Matt. xi. 25-27.   [6] Matt. xi. 28.
[7] *Spatia.*   [8] Matt. xi. 29.

For they who worship false gods, see them easily; but they see them "who have eyes and see not." But to us is promised the Vision of the Living and the Seeing God, that we may desire eagerly to see that God of whom Scripture saith, "He that planted the ear, shall he not hear? He that formed the eye, doth he not consider?"[1] Doth He then not hear, who hath made for thee that whereby thou hearest? and doth not He see, who hath created that whereby thou seest? Well therefore in the foregoing words of this very Psalm doth He say, "Understand therefore ye unwise among the people, and ye fools at length be wise."[2] For many men commit evil deeds whilst they think they are not seen by God. And it is difficult indeed for them to believe that He *cannot* see them; but they think that He *will* not. Few are found of such great impiety, that that should be fulfilled in them which is written, "The fool hath said in his heart, There is no God."[3] This is but the madness of a few. For as great piety belongs but to the few, no less also does great impiety. But the multitude of men speak thus: What! is God thinking now upon this, that He should know what I am doing in my house, and does God care for what I may choose to do upon my bed? Who says this? "Understand, ye unwise among the people, and ye fools at length be wise." Because as being a man, it is a labour for thee to know all that takes place in thy house, and for all the doings and words of thy servants to reach thee; thinkest thou that it is a like labour for God to observe thee, who did not labour to create thee? Doth not He fix His eye upon thee, who made thine eye? Thou wast not, and He created thee and gave thee being; and doth not He care for thee now that thou art, who "calleth those things which be not as though they were"?[4] Do not then promise thyself this. Whether thou wilt or no, He seeth thee, and there is no place whither thou canst hide thyself from His eyes. "For if thou goest up into heaven, He is there; if thou goest down into hell, He is there also."[5] Great is thy labour, whilst unwilling to depart from evil deeds: yet wishest not to be seen by God. Hard labour truly! Daily art thou wishing to do evil, and dost thou suspect that thou art not seen? Hear the Scripture which saith, "He that planted the ear, shall He not hear? He that formed the eye, doth not He consider?" Where canst thou hide thy evil deeds from the eyes of God? If thou wilt not depart from them, thy labour is great indeed.

4. Hear Him then who saith, "Come unto Me, all ye that labour." Thou canst not end thy labour by flying. Dost thou choose to fly from Him, and not rather to Him? Find out then whither thou canst escape, and so fly. But if thou canst not fly from Him, for that He is everywhere present; fly (it is quite nigh[6]) to God, who is present where thou art standing. Fly. Lo in thy flight thou hast passed the heavens, He is there; thou hast descended into hell, He is there; whatever deserts of the earth thou shalt choose, there is He, who hath said, "I fill heaven and earth."[7] If then He fills heaven and earth, and there is no place whither thou canst fly from Him; cease this thy labour, and fly to His presence, lest thou feel His coming. Take courage from the [8] hope that thou shalt by well-living see Him, by whom even in thy evil living thou art seen. For in evil living thou canst be seen, thou canst not see; but by well-living thou art both seen and seest. For with how much more tender nearness[9] will He who crowneth the worthy look on thee, who in His pity saw thee that He might call thee when unworthy? Nathanael said to the Lord whom as yet he did not know, "Whence knewest thou me?" The Lord said unto him, "When thou wast under the fig-tree I saw thee."[10] Christ saw thee in thine own shade; and will He not see thee in His Light? For what is, "When thou wast under the fig-tree I saw thee"? What does it mean? Call to mind the original sin of Adam, in whom we all die. When he first sinned, he made himself aprons of fig-leaves,[11] signifying by these leaves the irritations of lust to which he had been reduced by sinning. Hence are we born; in this condition are we born; born in sinful flesh, which "the likeness of sinful flesh" alone can cure. Therefore "God sent His own Son in the likeness of sinful flesh."[12] He came of this flesh, but He came not as other men. For the Virgin conceived Him not by lust, but by faith. He came into the Virgin, who was before the Virgin. He made choice of her whom He created, He created her whom He designed to choose. He brought to the Virgin fruitfulness: He took not away her unimpaired purity. He then who came to thee without the irritation of the leaves of the fig-tree, "when thou wast under the fig-tree," saw thee. Make ready then to see Him in His height of glory,[13] by whom in His pity thou wast seen. But because the top is high, think of the foundation. What foundation? dost thou say? "Learn of Him, for He is meek and lowly in heart." Dig this foundation of lowliness deep in thee, and so wilt thou attain to the crowning top of charity. "Turning to the Lord," etc.

---

[1] Ps. xciii. 9, Sept. (xciv. English version).
[2] Ps. xciii. 8, Sept. (xciv. English version).
[3] Ps. xiv. 1.　　[4] Rom. iv. 17.　　[5] Ps. cxxxix. 8.

[6] De proximo.
[7] Jer. xxiii. 24.　　[8] Præsume.
[9] Familiarius.
[10] John i. 48.
[11] Gen. iii. 7.　　[12] Rom. viii. 3.
[13] Sublimiter.

SERMON XX.

[LXX. BEN.]

AGAIN ON THE WORDS OF THE GOSPEL, MATT. XI.
28, "COME UNTO ME, ALL YE THAT LABOUR
AND ARE HEAVY LADEN, AND I WILL GIVE YOU
REST," ETC.

1. IT seems strange to some, Brethren, when
they hear the Lord say, "Come unto Me, all ye
that labour and are heavy laden, and I will refresh you. Take my yoke upon you and learn
of Me, for I am meek and lowly in heart, and ye
shall find rest unto your souls. For My yoke is
easy and My burden is light." [1]   And they consider that they who have fearlessly bowed their
necks to this yoke, and have with much submission taken this burden upon their shoulders, are
tossed about and exercised by so great difficulties in the world, that they seem not to be
called from labour to rest, but from rest to labour rather ; since the Apostle also saith, "All
who will live godly in Christ Jesus, shall suffer
persecution." [2]   So one will say, "How is the
yoke easy, and the burden light," when to bear
this yoke and burden is nothing else, but to live
godly in Christ? And how is it said, "Come
unto Me, all ye that labour and are heavy laden,
and I will refresh you"? and not rather said,
"Come ye who are at ease and idle, that ye
may labour." For so he found those men idle
and at ease, whom he hired into the vineyard,[3]
that they might bear the heat of the day. And
we hear the Apostle under that easy yoke and
light burden say, "In all things approving ourselves as the ministers of God, in much patience,
in afflictions, in necessities, in distresses, in
stripes," [4] etc., and in another place of the same
Epistle, "Of the Jews five times received I
forty stripes save one.   Thrice was I beaten with
rods, once was I stoned, thrice have I suffered
shipwreck, a night and a day have I been in the
deep : " [5] and the rest of the perils, which may
be enumerated indeed, but endured they cannot be but by the help of the Holy Spirit.

2. All these grievous and heavy trials which
he mentioned, did he very frequently and abundantly sustain ; but in very deed the Holy Spirit
was with him in the wasting of the outward
man, to renew the inner man from day to day,
and by the taste of spiritual rest in the affluence
of the delights of God to soften down by the
hope of future blessedness all present hardships,
and to alleviate all heavy trials.   Lo, how sweet
a yoke of Christ did he bear, and how light a
burden ; so that he could say that all those hard
and grievous sufferings at the recital of which as
just above every hearer shudders, were a "light
tribulation ; " as he beheld with the inward eyes,

the eyes of faith, at how great a price of things
temporal must be purchased the life to come,
the escape from the everlasting pains of the
ungodly, the full enjoyment, free from all anxiety,
of the eternal happiness of the righteous.   Men
suffer themselves to be cut and burnt, that the
pains not of eternity, but of some more lasting
sore than usual, may be bought off at the price
of severer pain.   For a languid and uncertain
period of a very short repose, and that too at the
end of life, the soldier is worn down by all the
hard trials of war, restless it may be for more
years in his labours, than he will have to enjoy
his rest in ease.   To what storms and tempests,
to what a fearful and tremendous raging of sky
and sea, do the busy merchantmen expose
themselves, that they may acquire riches incon-
stant as the wind, and full of perils and tempests,
greater even than those by which they were acquired !   What heats, and colds, what perils,
from horses, from ditches, from precipices, from
rivers, from wild beasts, do huntsmen undergo,
what pain of hunger and thirst, what straitened
allowances of the cheapest and meanest meat and
drink, that they may catch a beast ! and sometimes after all, the flesh of the beast for which they
endure all this is of no use for the table.   And
although a boar or a stag be caught, it is more
sweet to the hunter's mind because it has been
caught, than it is to the eater's palate because it
is dressed.   By what sharp corrections of almost
daily stripes is the tender age of boys brought
under !   By what great pains even of watching
and abstinence in the schools are they exercised,
not to learn true wisdom, but for the sake of
riches, and the honours of an empty show, that
they may learn arithmetic,[6] and other literature,
and the deceits of eloquence !

3. Now in all these instances, they who do
not love these things feel them as great severi-
ties ; whereas they who love them endure the
same, it is true, but they do not seem to feel
them severe.   For love makes all, the hardest
and most distressing things, altogether easy, and
almost nothing.   How much more surely then
and easily will charity do with a view to true
blessedness, that which mere desire does as it
can, with a view to what is but misery?   How
easily is any temporal adversity endured, if it be
that eternal punishment may be avoided, and
eternal rest procured !   Not without good reason
did that vessel of election say with exceeding
joy, "The sufferings of this present time are not
worthy to be compared with the glory which
shall be revealed in us." [7]   See then how it is that
that "yoke is easy, and that burden light." And
if it be strait to the few who choose it, yet is
it easy to all who love it.   The Psalmist saith,

---

[1] Matt. xi. 28-30.   [2] 2 Tim. iii. 12.   [3] Matt. xx. 4.
[4] 2 Cor. vi. 4.   [5] 2 Cor. xi. 24, etc.

[6] *Numeros.*   [7] Rom. viii. 18.

" Because of the words of Thy lips I have kept hard ways." [1] But the things which are hard to those who labour, lose their roughness [2] to those same men when they love. Wherefore it has been so arranged by the dispensation of the Divine goodness, that to " the inner man who is renewed from day to day," [3] placed no longer under the Law but under Grace, and freed from the burdens of numberless observances which were indeed a heavy yoke, but meetly imposed on a stubborn neck, every grievous trouble which that prince who is cast forth could inflict from without on the outward man, should through the easiness of a simple faith, and a good hope, and a holy charity, become light through the joy within. For to a good will nothing is so easy, as this good will to itself, and this is enough for God. How much soever therefore this world may rage, most truly did the angels exclaim when the Lord was born in the flesh, " Glory to God in the highest, and on earth peace to men of good will ; " [4] because " His yoke," who was then born, " is easy, and His burden light." And as the Apostle saith, " God is faithful, who will not suffer us to be tempted above that we are able to bear ; but will with the temptation also make a way to escape, that we may be able to bear it." [5]

SERMON XXI.

[LXXI. BEN.]

ON THE WORDS OF THE GOSPEL, MATT. XII. 32, " WHOSOEVER SHALL SPEAK A WORD AGAINST THE HOLY SPIRIT, IT SHALL NOT BE FORGIVEN HIM, NEITHER IN THIS WORLD, NOR IN THAT WHICH IS TO COME." OR, " ON THE BLASPHEMY AGAINST THE HOLY GHOST."

1. THERE has been a great question raised touching the late lesson of the Gospel, to the solution of which I am unequal by any power of mine own ; but " our sufficiency is of God," [6] to whatever degree we are capable of receiving His aid. First then consider the magnitude of the question ; that when ye see the weight of it laid upon my shoulders, ye may pray in aid of my labours, and in the assistance which is vouchsafed to me, may find edification for your own souls. When " one possessed with a devil was brought to the Lord, blind and dumb, and He had healed him so that he could speak and see, and all the people were amazed and said, Is not this the Son of David? the Pharisees hearing it said, This fellow doth not cast out devils but by Beelzebub the prince of the devils. But Jesus knew their thoughts, and said unto them, Every

kingdom divided against itself shall be brought to desolation. and every city or house divided against itself shall not stand. And if Satan cast out Satan, he is divided against himself; how shall then his kingdom stand ? " [7] In these words He wished it to be understood from their own confession, that, through their not believing in Him they had chosen to belong to the kingdom of the devil, which as being divided against itself could accordingly not stand. Let then the Pharisees make choice of which they will. If Satan cannot cast out Satan, they can find nothing to say against the Lord ; but if he can, then let them much more look to themselves, and depart out of his kingdom, which as being divided against itself cannot stand.

2. But now that they may not think that it is the prince of the devils in whom the Lord Jesus Christ casteth out devils, let them attend to what follows ; " And if I," He saith, " by Beelzebub cast out devils, by whom do your children cast them out? Therefore shall they be your judges." [8] He spoke this undoubtedly of his disciples, the " children " of that people ; who as being the disciples of the Lord Jesus Christ were well conscious that they had learnt no evil arts from their Good Master, that through the prince of the devils they should cast out devils. " Therefore," He saith, " shall they be your judges." They, He saith, the base and contemptible things of this world, in whom none of this artificial malice, but the holy simplicity of My power [9] is seen ; they shall be My witnesses, they shall be your judges. Then He subjoins, " But if I by the Spirit of God cast out devils, then the kingdom of God is come unto you." [10] What is this? " If I by the Spirit of God cast out devils," He saith, and your children, to whom I have given no hurtful and deceitful doctrine but a simple faith, can in no other way cast them out ; no doubt the kingdom of God is come unto you ; whereby the kingdom of the devil is subverted, and ye also are subverted with it.

3. And after that He had said, " By whom do your children cast them out? " to show that in them it was His grace, not their own desert ; He saith, " Or else how can one enter into a strong man's house and spoil his goods, except He first bind the strong man, and then He will spoil his house? " [11] Your children, saith He, who either have already believed in Me, or who shall yet believe, and cast out devils, not through the prince of the devils, but through the simplicity of holiness, who assuredly either once were, or still are what ye are also, sinners and ungodly ; and so in the house of the devil, and the vessels of the devil, how could they be rescued from him whom he held so firmly through the iniquity

---

[1] Ps. xvi. 4, Sept. (xvii. English version).   [2] *Mitescunt.*
[3] 2 Cor. iv. 16.   [4] Luke ii. 14.   [5] 1 Cor. x. 13.
[6] 2 Cor. iii. 5.

[7] Matt. xii. 22–26.   [8] Matt. xii. 27.   [9] *Virtutis.*
[10] Matt. xii. 28.   [11] Matt. xii. 29.

which reigned over them, unless he were bound by the chains of My justice, that I might take away from him his vessels which once were vessels of wrath, and make them vessels of mercy? This it is which the blessed Apostle also says when he rebukes the proud, and those who boast as it were of their own deserts, " For who maketh thee to differ?" [1] That is, who maketh thee to differ from the mass of perdition derived from Adam and from the vessels of wrath. And that no man might say, " My own righteousness," he says, " What hast thou, that thou didst not receive?" And on this point he says of himself also, " We also once were by nature the children of wrath, even as others." [2] So then he himself was a vessel in the house of that strong one, strong in evil, when he was a persecutor of the Church, a " blasphemer, injurious, living in malice and envy," as he confesses. But He who bound the strong one, took away from him this vessel of perdition, and made it a vessel of election.

4. Afterwards, that the unbelievers and ungodly, the enemies of the Christian name, might not suppose by reason of the divers heresies and schisms of those who under the Christian name gather together flocks of lost sheep, that the kingdom of Christ also is divided against itself, He next adds, " He that is not with Me is against Me, and he that gathereth not with Me, scattereth abroad." [3] He does not say, he who is under the outward profession [4] of My Name; or the form of My Sacrament; but " he who is not with Me is against Me." Nor doth He say, he who gathereth not under the outward profession of My Name; but " he who gathereth not with Me, scattereth abroad." Christ's kingdom then is not divided against itself; but men try to divide that which was bought with the price of the Blood of Christ. " For the Lord knoweth them that are His. And, let every one that nameth the Name of Christ depart from iniquity." [5] For if he depart not from iniquity, he belongeth not to the kingdom of Christ, even though he name the Name of Christ. To give then some illustrations for example's sake, the spirit of covetousness, and the spirit of luxuriousness, because the one heaps together, and the other lavishes, are divided against themselves; yet they belong both to the kingdom of the devil. Among idolaters the spirit of Juno and the spirit of Hercules are divided against themselves; and both belong to the kingdom of the devil. The heathen Christ's enemy, and the Jew Christ's enemy, are divided against themselves; and both belong to the kingdom of the devil. Arianus and Photinianus both are heretics, and both are divided against themselves. The Donatist and Maxim-

ianist [6] both are heretics, and both divided against themselves. All men's vices and errors that are contrary to each other are divided against themselves, and all belong to the kingdom of the devil; therefore his kingdom shall not stand. But the righteous and the ungodly, the believer and the unbeliever, the Catholic and the heretic, are indeed divided against themselves, but they do not belong all to the kingdom of Christ. "The Lord knoweth them that are His." Let no one flatter himself upon a mere name. If he would that the Name of the Lord should profit him, let "him that calleth upon the Name of the Lord depart from iniquity."

5. But these words of the Gospel, though they had some obscurity, which I think by the Lord's assistance I have explained, were yet not so difficult, as that which follows would seem to be. " Wherefore I say unto you, all manner of sin and blasphemy shall be forgiven unto men, but the blasphemy against the Spirit shall not be forgiven unto men. And whosoever speaketh a word against the Son of Man, it shall be forgiven him; but whosoever speaketh against the Holy Ghost, it shall not be forgiven him, neither in this world, neither in the world to come." [7] What then will become of those whom the Church desires to gain? When they have been reformed and come into the Church from whatsoever error, is the hope in the remission of all sins that is promised them a false hope? For who is not convicted of having spoken a word against the Holy Ghost, before he became a Christian or a Catholic? In the first place, are not they who are called Pagans, the worshippers of many and false gods, and the adorers of idols, forasmuch as they say that the Lord Christ wrought miracles by magical arts, are not they like these who said that He cast out devils through the prince of the devils? And again, when day by day they blaspheme our sanctification, what else blaspheme they but the Holy Ghost? What? Do not the Jews — they who spoke concerning our Lord what gave occasion to this very discourse — do they not even to the present day speak a word against the Holy Ghost, by denying that He is now in Christians, just as the others denied Him to be

[6] Maximianus, Deacon of the Church of Carthage, of the faction of Donatus, took offence at Primianus Bishop of Carthage, who had excommunicated him, and induced certain of the Donatist bishops to call Primianus to account; and when he would not acknowledge their authority, he was, as Cæcilianus had been, condemned in his absence. Primianus was restored by others of the Donatist bishops to communion, and Maximianus, together with twelve bishops who had assisted at his ordination as bishop, was condemned (Augustin, *De Gest. Emerit. Donat.* 9, etc., *Lib. ad. Bonif.*; Ep. 185(al. 56) 17). The rest were restored to communion on their submission. The Maximianists were afterwards condemned by a Council of three hundred and ten bishops at the Council of Vagaia, A.D. 394 (Ep. 108 (255) 6, and 141 (al. 152) 6). St. Augustin frequently urges the separation of the Maximianists from the Donatists as condemnatory on their own principles of their own schism against the Catholic Church.

[7] Matt. xii. 31, 32.

[1] 1 Cor. iv. 7. [2] Eph. ii. 3. [3] Matt. xii. 30.
[4] *Voce.* [5] 2 Tim. ii. 19.

in Christ? For not even did they revile the Holy Ghost, by asserting either that He existed not, or that though He existed, yet that He was not God, but a creature; or that He had no power to cast out devils; they did not speak thus unworthily, or anything like it, of the Holy Ghost. For the Sadducees indeed denied the Holy Ghost; but the Pharisees maintained His existence against their heresy,[1] but they denied that He was in the Lord Jesus Christ, who they thought cast out devils through the prince of the devils, whereas He did cast them out through the Holy Ghost. And hence, both Jews and whatsoever heretics there are who confess the Holy Ghost, but deny that He is in the Body of Christ, which is His One Only Church, none other than the One Catholic Church, are without doubt like the Pharisees who at that time although they confessed the existence of the Holy Ghost, yet denied that He was in Christ, whose works in casting out devils they attributed to the prince of devils. I say nothing of the fact that some heretics either boldly maintain that the Holy Ghost is not the Creator but a creature, as the Arians, and Eunomians, and Macedonians, or so entirely deny His existence, as to deny that God is Trinity, but assert that He is God the Father only, and that He is sometimes called the Son, and sometimes the Holy Ghost; as the Sabellians, whom some call Patripassians, because they hold that the Father suffered; and forasmuch as they deny that He has any Son, without doubt they deny His Holy Spirit also. The Photinians again who say that the Father only is God, and the Son a mere man, deny altogether that there is any third Person of the Holy Ghost.

6. It is plain then that the Holy Ghost is blasphemed both by Pagans, and by Jews, and by heretics. Are they then to be left, and accounted without all hope, since the sentence is fixed, "Whosoever speaketh a word against the Holy Ghost it shall not be forgiven him, neither in this world, neither in the world to come"? and are they only to be deemed free from the guilt of this most grievous sin who are Catholics from infancy? For all those who have believed the word of God, that they might become Catholics, came surely into the grace and peace of Christ, either from among the Pagans, or Jews, or heretics: and if there be no pardon for them for the word which they have spoken against the Holy Ghost, in vain do we promise and preach to men, to turn to God, and receive peace and remission of sins, whether in Baptism or in the Church. For it is not said, "It shall not be forgiven him except in baptism;" but, "it shall not be forgiven, neither in this world, neither in the world to come."

7. Some think that they only sin against the Holy Ghost, who having been washed in the laver of regeneration in the Church, and having received the Holy Spirit, as though unthankful for so great a gift of the Saviour, have plunged themselves afterwards into any deadly sin; as adultery, or murder, or an absolute apostasy,[2] either altogether from the Christian name, or from the Catholic Church. But how this sense of it may be proved, I know not; since the place of repentance is not denied in the Church to any sins whatever; and the Apostle says that heretics themselves are to be reproved to this end, "If God peradventure will give them repentance to the acknowledging of the truth; And that they may recover themselves out of the snare of the devil, who are taken captive by him at his will."[3] For what is the advantage of amendment without any hope of forgiveness? Finally, The Lord did not say, "the baptized[4] Catholic who shall speak a word against the Holy Ghost;" but "he who," that is whosoever speaketh, be he who he may, "it shall not be forgiven him, neither in this world, neither in the world to come." Whether then he be a heathen, or a Jew, or a Christian, or a heretic from among Jews or Christians, or whatsoever other title of error he have, it is not said, this man, or that man; but "whosoever speaketh a word against the Holy Ghost," that is who blasphemeth the Holy Ghost, "it shall not be forgiven him, neither in this world, neither in the world to come." But moreover if every error contrary to truth, and inimical to Christian peace, as we have shown before, "speaketh a word against the Holy Ghost;" and yet the Church doth not cease to reform and gather out of every error those who shall receive remission of sins, and the Holy Ghost Himself, whom they have blasphemed; I think I have discovered an important secret for the clearing up this so great a question. Let us seek then from the Lord the light of explanation.

8. Lift up then, Brethren, lift up unto me your ears, and your hearts unto the Lord. I tell you, my Beloved; perhaps there is not in all holy Scripture found a more important or more difficult question. Wherefore (that I may make you a confession about myself), I have always in my discourses to the people avoided the difficulty and embarrassment of this question; not because I had no ideas of any sort on the subject, for in a matter of such great importance, I would not be negligent in "asking," and "seeking," and "knocking;" but because I did not think I could do justice[5] to that understanding of it which was in some degree opened to me, by words suggested at the moment.

---

[1] Acts xxiii. 8.

[2] *Ipsa discessio.*   [3] 2 Tim. ii. 25, 26.   [4] *Fidelis.*
[5] *Sufficere.*

But as I listened to to-day's lesson, upon which it was my duty to discourse to you, as the Gospel was being read, there was such a beating at my heart, that I believed that it was God's will that you should hear something on the subject by my ministry.

9. First then, I pray you to consider and understand that the Lord did not say, "No blasphemy of the Spirit shall be forgiven," or, "whosoever speaketh any word whatsoever against the Holy Ghost, it shall not be forgiven him;" but "whosoever speaketh a word;"[1] for had he said the former, there would have remained to us no subject of disputation at all. Since if no blasphemy, and no word which is spoken against the Holy Ghost, shall be forgiven unto men; the Church could not gain any one out of all the classes of ungodly sinners who gainsay the gift of Christ, and the sanctification of the Church, whether Jews, or heathens, or heretics of whatsoever sort, and some even of little[2] knowledge in the Catholic Church itself. But God forbid that the Lord should say this: God forbid, I say, that the Truth should say that every blasphemy and every word which should be spoken against the Holy Ghost, hath no forgiveness neither in this world, neither in the world to come.

10. His will indeed was to exercise us by the difficulty of the question, not to deceive us by a false decision. Wherefore there is no necessity for any one to think, that every blasphemy or every word which is spoken against the Holy Ghost hath no remission; but necessary it plainly is, that there should be some certain blasphemy, and some word which if it be spoken against the Holy Ghost can never attain[3] to pardon and forgiveness. For if we take it to mean "every word," who then can be saved? But if again we think there is no such "word," we contradict the Saviour. There is then without doubt some certain blasphemy and some word which if it be spoken against the Holy Ghost, shall not be forgiven. Now what this word is, it is the Lord's will we should enquire; and therefore He hath not expressed it. His will, I say, was that it should be enquired into, not denied. For the style of the Scriptures is often such, that when anything is so expressed as not to be limited either to a universal or particular signification, it is not necessary that it should be understood universally, and not particularly. This proposition then would be expressed in its whole extent, that is, universally, if it were said, "All blasphemy[4] of the Spirit shall not be for-

given;" or, "Whosoever speaketh any word whatsoever against the Holy Ghost, it shall not be forgiven him, neither in this world, neither in the world to come." But it would be expressed partially, that is, particularly, if it were said, "Some certain blasphemy of the Spirit shall not be forgiven." But because this proposition is laid down neither in a universal, nor a particular form (for it is not said, "Every blasphemy;" or some certain blasphemy of the Spirit; but only indefinitely, "blasphemy of the Spirit shall not be forgiven;" neither is it said, "Whosoever speaketh any word whatever," or "whosoever speaketh some certain word," but indefinitely, "whosoever speaketh a word"), there is no necessity that we should understand "every blasphemy and every word;" but necessary it plainly is that the Lord designed some kind of blasphemy, and some word to be understood; though He would not express it, that, if we should receive any right understanding of it by asking, and seeking, and knocking, we might not entertain a low esteem of it.

11. In order to seeing this more plainly, consider that which the same Lord also saith of the Jews, "If I had not come and spoken to them, they had not had sin."[5] For this again was not said with any such meaning, as if He intended it to be understood that the Jews would have been without any sin at all, if He had not come and spoken to them. For indeed He found them full of and laden with sins. Wherefore He saith, "Come unto Me, all ye that labour and are heavy laden."[6] Laden! with what, but with the burdens of sins and transgressions of the Law? "For the Law entered that sin might abound."[7] Since then He saith Himself in another place, "I came not to call the righteous, but sinners to repentance;"[8] how would "they not have had sin if He had not come"? if it be not that this proposition being expressed neither universally, nor particularly, but indefinitely, does not constrain us to understand it of all sin? But certainly unless we understand that there was some sin which they would not have had if Christ had not come and spoken unto them, we must say that the proposition was false, which God forbid. He doth not say then, "If I had not come and spoken unto them, they had had no sin;" lest the Truth should lie. Nor again did He say definitely, "If I had not come and spoken unto them, they had not had some certain sin;" lest our devout earnestness[9] should not be exercised. For in the full abundance of the Holy Scriptures we feed upon the plain parts, we are exercised by the obscure: by the one, hunger is driven away, and daintiness[10] by the other. Seeing then that it is not

---

[1] This *word* must be supplied from the former clause in the verse, "Whosoever speaketh a word against the Son of Man" (Matt. xii. 32). It does not occur in the second clause of the verse in any of the versions.

[2] *Imperitorum.*

[3] *Mereatur.*   [4] ἡ τοῦ Πνεύματος βλασφημια.

[5] John xv. 22.   [6] Matt. xi. 28.   [7] Rom v. 20.
[8] Matt. ix. 13.   [9] *Studium.*   [10] *Fastidium.*

said, "they had had no sin," we need not be disturbed, though we acknowledge that the Jews would have been sinners, even if the Lord had not come. But yet because it is said, " If I had not come, they had not had sin ; " it must needs be that they contracted, though not all, yet some sin which they had not before, from the coming of the Lord. And this verily is that sin, that they believed not in Him who was present with and spake to them, and that counting Him as an enemy because He spake the truth, they put Him besides to death. This sin so great and terrible it is clear they had not had if He had not come and spoken to them. As then when we hear the words, " They had not had sin ; " we do not understand all, but some, sin ; so when we hear in to-day's lesson, " Blasphemy of the Spirit shall not be forgiven ; " we understand not all, but a certain kind of blasphemy ; and when we hear, " Whosoever speaketh a word against the Holy Ghost, it shall not be forgiven him ; " we ought not to understand every, but some certain word.

12. For in that He saith also in this very text, " But blasphemy of the Spirit shall not be forgiven ; " surely we must needs understand not blasphemy of every spirit, but the Holy Spirit. And though He had not expressed this anywhere else more plainly, who could be so silly as to understand it in any other way? According to the same rule of speech is this expression also understood, " Except a man be born of water and of the Spirit." [1] For He doth not say in that place, and of the Holy Spirit ; yet this is understood. Nor because He said of water and of the Spirit, is any one forced to understand it of every spirit. Wherefore when you hear, " But the blasphemy of the Spirit shall not be forgiven ; " as you must not understand it of every spirit, so not of every blasphemy against the Spirit.

13. I see that you are now wishing to hear, since it is not every blasphemy of the Spirit, what that blasphemy is which shall not be forgiven, and what that word is, since it is not every word which if it shall be spoken against the Holy Ghost, shall not be forgiven neither in this world, neither in the world to come. And for my part I should be willing to tell you at once, what you are so very intently waiting to hear ; but bear for a while the delay which a more careful diligence requires, till by the Lord's assistance I shall unfold the whole meaning of the passage before us. Now the other two Evangelists, Mark and Luke, when they spake of the same thing, did not say " blasphemy " or " a word," that we might understand it not of every blasphemy, but of some sort of blasphemy ; not every word, but some certain word. What then

did they say? In Mark it is thus written, " Verily I say unto you, all sins shall be forgiven unto the sons of men, and blasphemies, wherewithsoever they shall blaspheme. But he that shall blaspheme against the Holy Ghost, hath never forgiveness, but shall be held guilty of an eternal offence." [2] In Luke it is thus : " And whosoever shall speak a word against the Son of Man, it shall be forgiven him ; but unto him that blasphemeth against the Holy Ghost, it shall not be forgiven." [3] Is there any departure from the truth of the same proposition because of some diversity in the expression? For indeed there is no other reason why the Evangelists do not relate the same things in the same way, but that we may learn thereby to prefer things to words, not words to things, and to seek for nothing else in the speaker, but for his intention, to convey which only the words are used. For what real difference is there whether it is said, " Blasphemy of the Spirit shall not be forgiven ; " or " he that blasphemeth against the Holy Ghost, it shall not be forgiven him." Except perhaps that the same thing is declared more plainly in this last than in the other form ; and so one Evangelist does not overthrow, but explains the other. Now " blasphemy of the Spirit " is an unevident [4] expression ; because it is not directly said *what* spirit ; for every spirit is not the Holy Spirit. Thus it might be called " blasphemy of the spirit," when a man blasphemes with the spirit ; as that may be called " prayer of the spirit," when one prays with the spirit. Whence the Apostle says, " I will pray with the spirit, and I will pray with the understanding also." [5] But when it is said, " he that shall blaspheme against the Holy Ghost," these ambiguities are removed. So the expression, " hath never forgiveness, but shall be held guilty of an eternal offence ; " what is it, but what according to Matthew is expressed, " it shall not be forgiven him, neither in this world, neither in the world to come"? The very same idea is expressed in different words and different forms of speech. And what is in Matthew, " Whosoever speaketh a word against the Holy Ghost," that we might not understand it of anything but blasphemy, others have more clearly expressed, " He that shall blaspheme against the Holy Ghost." Yet the same thing is said by all ; nor did any one of them depart from the intention of the Speaker, for the sake of understanding which only are words spoken, and written, and read, and heard.

14. But one may say, See I have admitted and understood that where the word " blasphemy " is used, and neither all, nor some certain blasphemy expressed, it may be understood

---

[1] John iii. 5.

[2] Mark iii. 28, 29. *Reus æterni peccati,* ἁμαρτήματος (for κρίσεως). So also Cyprian, Ep. xvi.
[3] Luke xii. 10.   [4] *Clause dictum.*   [5] 1 Cor. xiv. 15.

either of all, or of some certain blasphemy, but not necessarily of all; but again if it be not understood of some, that that which is said would be untrue: so again if it is not said every or some certain word, it is not necessary that every word should be understood, but unless some word be understood, in no way can what is said be true. But when we read, "He that shall blaspheme," how can I understand any certain blasphemy, when the word "blasphemy" is not used, or any certain word, when the word "word" is not used, but it seems to be said as it were generally, "He that shall blaspheme." To this objection [1] I reply thus. If it were said in this passage also, "He that shall blaspheme with any kind of blasphemy whatever against the Holy Ghost," there would be no reason why we should think that some particular blasphemy was to be sought for, when we ought rather to understand all blasphemy; but because all blasphemy could not be meant, lest the hope of forgiveness in case of their amendment should be taken away from heathens, and Jews, and heretics, and all kinds of men, who by their divers errors and contradictions blaspheme against the Holy Ghost; it remains without a doubt, that in the passage where it is written, "He that shall blaspheme against the Holy Ghost hath never forgiveness," he must be meant, not who hath in any way whatever blasphemed; but he who hath blasphemed in such a particular way, that he can never be pardoned.

15. For as in that it is said, "God tempteth no man," [2] it is not to be understood that God tempteth no man with any kind, but only not with some certain kind of temptation; lest that be false, which is written, "The Lord your God tempteth you;" [3] and lest we deny that Christ is God, or say that the Gospel is false, when we read that He asked His disciple "tempting him; but He Himself knew what He would do." [4] For there is a temptation which induces to sin, with which "God tempteth no man," and there is a temptation which only proves our faith, with which even God vouchsafes to tempt. So when we hear, "He that shall blaspheme against the Holy Ghost," we must not take it of every kind of blasphemy, as neither in the other place, of every kind of temptation.

16. So again when we hear, "He that believeth and is baptized shall be saved;" [5] we do not of course understand it of one who believes in such a way "as the devils believe and tremble;" [6] nor of those who receive baptism in such sort as Simon Magus,[7] who though he could be baptized, could not be saved. As then when He said, "He that believeth and is baptized shall be saved,"

He had not in his view all who believe and are baptized, but some only; those, to wit, who are settled in that faith, which, according to the Apostle's distinction, "worketh by love:" [8] so when he said, "He that shall blaspheme against the Holy Ghost hath never forgiveness," he did not intend every kind, but a specific sin of blasphemy against the Holy Ghost, by which whosoever shall be bound, he shall never by any remission be loosed.

17. That expression also of His, "He that eateth My Flesh and drinketh My Blood dwelleth in Me, and I in him," [9] how must we understand? Can we include in these words those even of whom the Apostle says, "that they eat and drink judgment to themselves;" [10] when they eat this flesh and drink this blood? What! did Judas the impious seller and betrayer of his Master [11] (though, as Luke the Evangelist declares more plainly, he ate and drank with the rest of His disciples this first Sacrament of His body and blood, consecrated [12] by the Lord's hands), did he "dwell in Christ and Christ in him"? Do so many, in fine, who either in hypocrisy eat that flesh and drink that blood, or who after they have eaten and drunk become apostate, do they "dwell in Christ or Christ in them"? Yet assuredly there is a certain manner of eating that Flesh and drinking that Blood, in which whosoever eateth and drinketh, "he dwelleth in Christ and Christ in him." As then he doth not "dwell in Christ and Christ in him," who "eateth the Flesh and drinketh the Blood of Christ" in any manner whatsoever, but only in some certain manner, to which He doubtless had regard when He spake these words. So in this expression also, "He that shall blaspheme against the Holy Ghost hath never forgiveness," he is not guilty of this unpardonable sin, who shall blaspheme in any way whatever, but in that particular way, which it is His will, who uttered this true and terrible sentence, that we should seek out and understand.

18. Now as to what that mode, or immoderateness [13] rather, of blasphemy is, what that particular blasphemy, and what that word against the Holy Ghost, the order of my discourse requires me to say what I think, and not to put off any longer your expectation which has been so long but so necessarily deferred. Ye know, Dearly beloved, that in that invisible and incorruptible Trinity, which our faith and the Church Catholic maintains and preaches, God the Father is not the Father of the Holy Spirit, but of the Son; and that God the Son is not the Son of the Holy Spirit, but of the Father; but that God the Holy Spirit is the Spirit not of

[1] *Contradictioni.*   [2] Jas i. 13.   [3] Deut. xiii. 3.
[4] John vi 5, 6.   [5] Mark xvi. 16.   [6] Jas ii. 19.
[7] Acts viii. 13.

[8] Gal. v. 6.   [9] John vi. 56.   [10] 1 Cor. xi. 29.
[11] Luke xxii 21   [12] *Confectum.*
[13] *Blasphemandi modus, vel potius immoderatio.*

the Father only, or of the Son only, but of the Father and the Son. And that this Trinity, although the [1] Property and particular [2] Subsistence [3] of each person is preserved, is yet, because of the undivided and inseparable Essence or Nature of Eternity,[4] Truth, and Goodness, not three Gods but One God. And by this means, according to our capacity, and as far as it is granted us to see these things "through a glass darkly," especially being such as we now are, there is conveyed to [5] us the idea of Origination [6] in the Father, Nativity in the Son, and the Communion of the Father and the Son in the Holy Spirit, and in the Three Equality. By That then which is the Bond of communion [7] between the Father and the Son, it is Their pleasure that we should have communion both among ourselves and with Them, and to gather us together in one by that same Gift, which One They both have, that is, by the Holy Spirit, at once God and the Gift of God. For in This are we reconciled to the Divinity, and take delight in It. For what would the knowledge of whatever good we know profit us, unless we also loved it? But as it is by the truth that we learn, so is it by charity that we love, that so we may attain also to a fuller knowledge, and enjoy in blessedness what we know. "Love moreover is shed abroad in our hearts by the Holy Ghost which is given unto us." [8] And because it is through sin that we are alienated from the possession of true good, "Love covereth a multitude of sins." [9] So then the Father is Himself the True Origin [10] to the Son, who is the Truth, and the Son is the Truth, originating [11] from the True Father, and the Holy Spirit is Goodness, shed abroad [12] from the Good Father and the Good Son; but in all Three the Divinity is equal, and the Unity Inseparable.

19. First then in order to our receiving eternal life which shall be given at the last, there comes to us a gift from God's goodness from the beginning of our faith, to wit, the remission of sins. For while they remain, there remains in some sort enmity against God, and alienation from Him, which comes from what is evil in us; since Scripture does not speak falsely, which says, "Your sins separate between you and God." [13] He does not then bestow on us His good things, except He take away our evil things. And the former increase in proportion as the latter are diminished; nor will the one

be perfected, till the other be brought to an end. But now that the Lord Jesus forgives sins by the Holy Ghost, just as by the Holy Ghost He casts out devils, may be understood by this, that after His Resurrection from the dead, when He had said to His disciples, "Receive ye the Holy Ghost," He immediately subjoined, "Whosesoever sins ye remit, they shall be remitted unto them, and whosesoever sins ye retain, they shall be retained." [14] For that regeneration also, in which there is a remission of all past sins, is wrought by the Holy Ghost, as the Lord saith, "Except a man be born of water and of the Spirit, he cannot enter into the kingdom of God." [15] But it is one thing to be born of the Spirit, another to be nourished by the Spirit; just as it is one thing to be born of the flesh, which happens when the mother is delivered of her child; another to be nourished by the flesh, which happens when she gives suck to her infant, who turns himself that he may drink with pleasure thither whence he was born, to have life; that he may receive the support of life from thence, whence he received the beginning of his birth. We must believe then that the first blessing of God's goodness in the Holy Ghost is the remission of sins. Whence the preaching of John the Baptist, who was sent as the forerunner of the Lord, also begins with it. For thus it is written, "In those days came John the Baptist preaching in the wilderness of Judæa, saying, Repent ye, for the kingdom of heaven is at hand." [16] Hence too the beginning of our Lord's preaching, as we read, "From that time Jesus began to preach and to say, Repent, for the kingdom of heaven is at hand." [17] Now John, amongst the other things which he spake to those who came to be baptized by him, said, "I indeed baptize you with water unto repentance; but He that cometh after me is mightier than I, whose shoes I am not worthy to bear; He shall baptize you with the Holy Ghost and with fire." [18] The Lord also said, "John truly baptized with water, but ye shall be baptized with the Holy Ghost not many days hence," [19] even at Pentecost. Now as to John's expression, "with fire," though tribulation also might be understood, which believers were to suffer for the name of Christ; yet may we reasonably think that the same Holy Spirit is signified also under the name of "fire." [20] Wherefore when He came it is said, "And there appeared unto them cloven tongues like as of fire, and it sat upon each of them." [21] Hence also the Lord Himself said, "I am come to send fire on the earth." [22] Hence also the Apostle saith, "Fervent in the spirit;" [23] for from

---

[1] *Proprietate.*   [2] *Substantia.*
[3] See note on the word Hypostasis in the Nicene Anathema, St. Ath. *Treatises against Arianism*, part 1, p. 66, Oxford translation.
[4] *Conf.* lib. vii. x. (16).   [5] *Insinuatur.*
[6] *Auctoritas;* St. Augustin, *C. Maxim.* iii. 14, guards the word against any idea of inequality; see Pet. *De Trin.* v. and 5. 11-13, who observes that the Greeks have no *word* exactly corresponding, although ἀρχή, αἴτιον, are equivalent.
[7] *Commune.*   [8] Rom. v. 5.   [9] 1 Pet. iv. 8.
[10] *Origo.*   [11] *Orta.*   [12] *Effusa.*
[13] Isa. lix. 2.

[14] John xx. 22, 23.   [15] John iii 5.   [16] Matt. iii. 1, 2.
[17] Matt. iv. 17.   [18] Matt. iii. 11.   [19] Acts i. 5.
[20] See note g on Tert. *De Bapt.* c. 10, p. 268, Oxford translation.
[21] Acts ii. 3.   [22] Luke xii. 49.   [23] Rom. xii. 11.

Him comes the fervour of love. "For it is shed abroad in our hearts by the Holy Ghost which is given unto us."[1] And the contrary to this fervour is what the Lord said, "The love of many shall wax cold."[2] Now perfect love is the perfect gift of the Holy Spirit. But the first "gift" is that which is concerned with the remission of sins; by which blessing "we are delivered from the power of darkness;"[3] and the prince of this world,[4] who worketh in the children of disobedience"[5] by no other power than the fellowship and the bond of sin, is "cast out" by our faith. For by the Holy Spirit, by whom the people of God are gathered together into one, is the unclean spirit who is divided against himself cast out.

20. Against this gratuitous gift, against this grace of God, does the impenitent heart speak. This impenitence then is "the blasphemy of the Spirit, which shall not be forgiven, neither in this world, neither in the world to come." For against the Holy Spirit, by whom they whose sins are all forgiven are baptized, and whom the Church hath received, that "whosoever sins she remits, they may be remitted," does he speak, whether in the thought only, or also in the tongue, a very heinous and exceedingly ungodly word, who "when the patience of God leadeth him to repentance, after his hardness and impenitent heart treasureth up unto himself wrath against the day of wrath, and revelation of the righteous judgment of God, who will render to every man according to his deeds."[6] This impenitence then, for so by some one general name may we call both this blasphemy and the word against the Holy Ghost which hath no forgiveness for ever; this impenitence, I say, against which both the herald and the Judge cried out, saying, "Repent ye, for the kingdom of heaven is at hand;"[7] against which the Lord first opened the mouth of the Gospel preaching, and against which He foretold that the same Gospel was to be preached in all the world, when He said to His disciples after His resurrection from the dead, "it behoved Christ to suffer, and to rise from the dead the third day, and that repentance and remission of sins should be preached in His Name among all nations, beginning at Jerusalem:"[8] this impenitence, in one word, hath no forgiveness "neither in this world, nor in the world to come;" for that repentance only obtaineth forgiveness in this world, that it may have its effect in the world to come.

21. But this impenitence or impenitent heart may not be pronounced[9] upon, as long as a man

lives in the flesh. For we are not to despair of any so long as "the patience of God leadeth the ungodly to repentance," and doth not hurry him out of this life; "God, who willeth not the death of a sinner, but that he should return from his ways and live."[10] He is a heathen to-day; but how knowest thou whether he may not be a Christian to-morrow? He is a heretic to-day; but what if to-morrow he follow the Catholic truth? He is a schismatic to-day; but what if to-morrow he embrace Catholic peace? What if they, whom thou observest now in any kind of error that can be, and whom thou condemnest as in most desperate case, what if before they end this life, they repent and find the true life in that which is to come? Wherefore, Brethren, let also what the Apostle says urge you to this. "Judge nothing before the time."[11] For this blasphemy of the Spirit, for which there is no forgiveness (which I have understood to be not every kind of blasphemy, but a particular sort, and that as I have said or discovered, or even as I think clearly shown to be the case, the persevering hardness of an impenitent heart), cannot be taken hold of in any one, I repeat it, as long as he is still in this life.

22. And let it not seem absurd, that whereas a man who perseveres in hardened impenitence even to the end of this life, speaks long and much against this grace of the Holy Spirit; yet the Gospel has called this so long contradiction of an impenitent heart, as though it were something of short duration, "a word," saying, "Whosoever speaketh a word against the Son of Man, it shall be forgiven him; but whosoever speaketh against the Holy Ghost, it shall not be forgiven him, neither in this world, neither in the world to come." For though this blasphemy be long continued, and made up of, and drawn out at length in very many words, yet it is the manner of Scripture to call even many words "a word." For no prophet ever spoke one word only; yet we read, "the *word* which came to such and such a prophet." And the Apostle says, "Let the elders be counted worthy of double honour, especially they who labour in the word and doctrine."[12] He does not say, "in words," but, "in the word." And St. James, "Be ye doers of the word, and not hearers only."[13] He again does not say, "of the words," but, "of the word;" although so many words out of the Holy Scriptures are read, and spoken, and heard in the Church at her celebrations and solemnities. As therefore, how long a time soever any of us have laboured in preaching the Gospel, he is not called a preacher of the words, but of the word; and how long time soever any of you may have attentively and

---

[1] Rom. v. 5. [2] Matt. xxiv. 12. [3] Col. i. 13.
[4] John xii. 31. [5] Eph. ii. 2. [6] Rom. ii. 4-6.
[7] Matt. iii. 2 and iv. 17. [8] Luke xxiv. 46, 47.
[9] *Judicari.*

[10] Ezek. xviii. 23. [11] 1 Cor. iv. 5. [12] 1 Tim. v. 17.
[13] Jas. i. 22.

diligently listened to our preaching, he is called a most earnest " hearer " not of the words, but " of the word ; " so after the style of the Scripture and the custom of the Church, whoso throughout His whole life in the flesh, to whatever length it may be extended, shall have spoken no matter how many words, whether by mouth, or the thought only with an impenitent heart, against that remission of sins which is granted in the Church, he speaks " a word " against the Holy Ghost.

23. Therefore not only every word spoken against the Son of Man, but, in fact, every sin and blasphemy shall be forgiven unto men ; because where there is not this sin of an impenitent heart against the Holy Ghost, by whom sins are remitted in the Church, all other sins are forgiven. But how shall that sin be forgiven, which hinders the forgiveness of other sins also? All sins then are forgiven to them in whom is not this sin, which shall never be forgiven ; but to him in whom it is, since this sin is never forgiven, neither are other sins forgiven ; because the remission of all is hindered by the bond of this one. It is not then that " whosoever speaketh a word against the Son of Man shall be forgiven," but " whoso speaketh against the Holy Ghost shall not be forgiven," for that in the Trinity the Holy Ghost is greater than the Son, which no heretic even has ever maintained ; but since whosoever he be that resisteth the truth and blasphemeth the Truth, which is Christ, even after such a manifestation of Himself among men, as that the Word who is the Son of Man and very Christ, " became flesh and dwelt among us ; " if he have not also spoken that word of the impenitent heart against the Holy Ghost, of whom it is said, " Except a man be born of water and of the Spirit ; "[1] and again, " Receive ye the Holy Ghost ; whosesoever sins ye remit they are remitted unto them ; "[2] that is, if he shall repent, he shall thereby receive the gift of the remission of all his sins, and of this also, that he " hath spoken a word against the Son of Man," because to the sin of ignorance, or obstinacy, or blasphemy of whatever kind, he hath not added the sin of impenitence against the gift of God, and the grace of regeneration or reconciliation, which is conferred in the Church by the Holy Spirit.

24. Wherefore, neither must we imagine, as some do, that the word which is spoken against the Son of Man is forgiven, but that which is spoken against the Holy Ghost is not forgiven, because Christ became the Son of Man by reason of His assuming flesh, in which respect the Holy Ghost of course is greater, who in His Own Substance is equal to the Father and the Only-begotten Son according to His Divinity, according to which also the Only-begotten Son Himself is equal to the Father and the Holy Spirit. For if this were the reason, surely nothing would have been said of any other kind of blasphemy, that that only might appear capable of forgiveness, which is spoken against the Son of Man, regarded only as man. But forasmuch as it is first said, " All manner of sin and blasphemy shall be forgiven unto men ; "[3] which in another Evangelist is also thus expressed, " All sins shall be forgiven unto the sons of men, and blasphemies wherewithsoever they shall blaspheme ; "[4] without doubt, that blasphemy also which is spoken against the Father is included in that general expression ; and yet that alone is laid down as unpardonable, which is spoken against the Holy Ghost. What ! did the Father also take the form of a servant, that in this respect the Holy Ghost should be greater than He? No surely : but after the universal mention of all sins and of all blasphemy, He wished to express more prominently the blasphemy which is spoken against the Son of Man for this reason, because although men should be even bound in that sin which He mentioned when He said, " If I had not come and spoken to them, they had not had sin : "[5] which sin also in the Gospel according to John He shows to be a very grievous one, when He says of the Holy Spirit Himself, when He promised that He would send Him, " He shall reprove the world of sin, and of righteousness, and of judgment : of sin, because they believed not on Me : "[6] yet if that hardness of the impenitent heart have not spoken a word against the Holy Ghost, even this which is spoken against the Son of Man shall be forgiven.

25. Here perhaps some one may ask, " whether the Holy Ghost only forgiveth sins, and not the Father and the Son also?" I answer, Both the Father and the Son forgive them. For the Son Himself saith of the Father, " If ye forgive men their trespasses, your heavenly Father will also forgive you."[7] And we say to Him in the Lord's Prayer, " Our Father, which art in heaven."[8] And amongst the other petitions we ask this, saying, " Forgive us our debts."[9] And again of Himself He saith, " That ye may know that the Son of Man hath power on earth to forgive sins."[10] " If then," you will say, " The Father, the Son, and the Holy Spirit forgive sins, why is that impenitence which shall never be forgiven, said to relate only to the blasphemy of the Spirit, as though he who should be bound in this sin of impenitence should seem to resist the gift of the Holy Spirit, because by that gift is wrought the remission of sins?" Now on

---

[1] John iii. 5.   [2] John xx. 22, 23.

[3] Matt. xii. 31.   [4] Mark iii. 28.   [5] John xv. 22.
[6] John xvi. 8, 9.   [7] Matt. vi. 14.   [8] Matt. vi. 9.
[9] Matt. vi. 12.   [10] Matt. ix. 6.

this point, I will also ask, Whether Christ only cast out devils, or the Father and the Holy Spirit also? For if Christ only, what means His saying, "The Father that dwelleth in Me, He doeth the works." [1] For so it is said, "He doeth the works," as if the Son doeth them not, but the Father who dwelleth in the Son. Why then in another place doth He say, "My Father worketh hitherto, and I work." [2] And a little after, "For what things soever He doeth, these also doeth the Son likewise." [3] But when in another place He says, "If I had not done amongst them the works which none other man did," [4] He speaks as if He did them alone. Now if these things are so expressed, as that nevertheless the works of the Father and the Son are inseparable, what must we believe of the Holy Spirit, but that He also worketh equally with them? For in that very place, from which this question arose which we are discussing, when the Son was casting out devils, He yet said, "If I in the Holy Spirit cast out devils, then the kingdom of God is come unto you." [5]

26. And here perhaps one may say, "That the Holy Spirit is rather given by the Father and the Son, than that He worketh anything by His own will, and that this is the scope of the words, "In the Holy Spirit I cast out devils," because not the Spirit Himself, but Christ in the Spirit, did it; so that the expression, "I cast out in the Holy Spirit," might be understood as if it were said, "I cast out by the Holy Spirit." For this is the usual style of the Scriptures, "They killed in the sword," that is, by the sword. They "burnt in the fire," [6] that is, by the fire. "And Joshua took knives of flints, in which to circumcise," that is, by which to circumcise, "the children of Israel." [7] But let those who on this account take from the Holy Spirit His proper power, look to that which we read to have been spoken by the Lord, "The Spirit bloweth where It listeth." [8] And as to what the Apostle says, "But all these worketh that one and the self-same Spirit, dividing to every man severally as He will;" [9] it might be feared, lest one imagine that the Father and the Son do not work them: whereas amongst these works he has expressly mentioned both the "gifts of healings," and the "workings of miracles," in which surely is included also the driving out of devils. But when he adds the words, "Dividing to every man severally as He will;" does he not clearly show also the Power of the Holy Spirit, yet as plainly inseparable from the Father and the Son? If then these things are so expressed, as that notwithstanding the operation of the

Trinity is understood to be inseparable : so that when the operation of the Father is spoken of, it is understood that He does not exercise it without the Son, and the Holy Spirit ; and when the operation of the Son is spoken of, it is not without the Father and the Holy Spirit ; and when the operation of the Holy Spirit is spoken of, it is not without the Father and the Son ; it is sufficiently clear to those who have a sound faith, or who even understand as they best can, both that the words, "He doeth the works," [1] are spoken of the Father, in that from Him is also [10] the first principle of the works, from whom is the existence of the Persons who co-operate in working : for that both the Son is born of Him, and the Holy Spirit proceedeth from Him, as the First Beginning, of whom the Son is born, and with whom He hath one Spirit in common ; and again that when the Lord said, "If I had not done among them the works which none other did," [4] He did not speak in reference to the Father and the Spirit, as that They did not co-operate with Him in those works ; but to men by whom we read of many miracles having been done, but by none such miracles as the Son did. And what the Apostle says of the Holy Spirit, "But all these worketh that one and the self-same Spirit, dividing to every man severally as He will," is not said, because the Father and the Son do not co-operate with Him ; but because in these works there are not many spirits, but One Spirit, and in His divers operations He is not diverse from Himself.

27. "And yet it is not without cause, but with reason and with truth said, that the Father, and not the Son and the Holy Spirit, said, "Thou art My beloved Son, in whom I am well pleased." [12] Nevertheless, we do not deny that the Son and the Holy Spirit co-operated in working this miracle of the voice sounding from heaven, though we know that it belongs to the Person of the Father only. For though the Son bearing flesh, was there conversing with men on earth, He was not the less on that account in the Bosom of the Father also as the Only-Begotten Word, when that Voice came out of the cloud ; nor could it be either wisely and through the Spirit [13] believed, that God the Father separated the operation of these audible and passing words from the co-operation of His Wisdom and His Spirit. In the same way when we say most rightly, that not the Father, nor the Holy Spirit, but the Son walked upon the sea, who only had that flesh and those feet which rested on the waves ; [14] yet who would deny that the Father and the Holy Spirit co-operated in the work of so

---

[1] John xiv. 10.   [2] John v. 17.   [3] John v. 19.
[4] John xv. 24.   [5] Matt. xii. 28.
[6] Ps. lxxiii. 7, Sept. (lxxiv. 7, English version).
[7] Josh. v. 3.   [8] John iii. 8.   [9] 1 Cor. xii. 11.

[10] *Origo.*   [11] Serm. ii. (lii. Bened.) 8–13 (iv.).
[12] Matt. xvii. 5; Luke iii. 22.   [13] *Spiritualiter.*
[14] Matt. xiv. 25.

great a miracle? For so again we say most truly that the Son only took this our flesh, not the Father, nor the Holy Spirit, and yet he hath no true wisdom who denies that the Father, or the Holy Spirit co-operated in the work of His Incarnation which belongeth only to the Son. So also we say that neither the Father, nor the Son, but the Holy Spirit only appeared both in the "form of a dove," [1] and in "tongues as it were of fire;" [2] and gave to those to whom He came the power to tell in many and various tongues "the wonderful works of God;" and yet from this miracle which regards the Holy Spirit only, we cannot separate the co-operation of the Father and the Only-Begotten Word. So also the Whole Trinity work the works of each several Person in the Trinity, the Two co-operating in the work of the Other, through a perfect harmony of operation in the Three, and not through any deficiency of the power to work effectually in One. And since this is so, hence it is that the Lord Jesus cast out devils in the Holy Spirit. Not that He was not able to accomplish this alone, or that He assumed that aid as being insufficient for this work; but it was meet that the spirit who is divided against himself should be driven out by that Spirit, which the Father and the Son who are not divided in themselves have in common.

28. And thus sins, because they are not forgiven out of the Church, must be forgiven by that Spirit, by whom the Church is gathered together into one. In fact, if any one out of the Church repent him of his sins, and for this so great sin whereby he is an alien from the Church of God, has an heart impenitent, what doth that other repentance profit him? seeing by this alone he speaketh a word against the Holy Ghost, whereby he is alienated from the Church, which hath received this gift, that in her remission of sins should be given in the Holy Ghost? Which remission though it be the work of the Whole Trinity, is yet understood specially to belong to the Holy Spirit. For He is the Spirit of the adoption of sons, "in whom we cry Abba, Father;" [3] that we may be able to say to Him, "Forgive us our debts." [4] And, "Hereby we know," as the Apostle John says, "that Christ dwelleth in us, by His Spirit which He hath given us." [5] "The Spirit Itself beareth witness with our spirit that we are the children of God." [6] For to Him appertains the fellowship, by which we are made the one body of the One only Son of God. Whence it is written, "If there be therefore any consolation in Christ, if any comfort of love, if any fellowship of the Spirit." [7] With a view to this fellowship they to whom

He first came spake with the tongues of all nations. Because as by tongues the fellowship of mankind is more closely united; so it behoved that this fellowship of the sons of God and members of Christ which was to be among all nations should be signified by the tongues of all nations; that as at that time he was known to have received the Holy Ghost, who spake with the tongues of all nations; so now he should acknowledge that he has received the Holy Ghost, who is held by the bond of the peace of the Church, which is spread throughout all nations. Whence the Apostle says, "Endeavouring to keep the unity of the Spirit in the bond of peace." [8]

29. Now that He is the Spirit of the Father, the Son Himself saith, "He proceedeth from the Father." [9] And in another place, "For it is not ye that speak, but the Spirit of your Father which speaketh in you." [10] And that He is the Spirit of the Son also the Apostle saith, "God hath sent the Spirit of His Son into your hearts, crying, Abba Father;" [11] that is, making you cry. For it is we that cry; but in Him, that is, by His shedding abroad love in our hearts, without which whoso crieth, crieth in vain. Whence he says again, "If any man have not the Spirit of Christ, he is none of His." [12] To which Person then in the Trinity could the communion of this fellowship peculiarly appertain, but to that Spirit which is common to the Father and the Son?

30. That they who have separated from the Church have not this Spirit, the Apostle Jude has declared most plainly, saying, "Who separate themselves, natural, having not the Spirit." [13] Whence the Apostle Paul reproving those even in the Church itself, who by the names of men, though having a place in her unity, were raising a kind of schism, says amongst other things, "But the natural man perceiveth not the things of the Spirit of God, for they are foolishness unto him, neither can he know them, because they are spiritually discerned." [14] This shows his meaning, "doth not perceive," that is, doth not receive the word of knowledge. These as having a place in the Church, he speaks of as babes, not yet spiritual, but still carnal, and such as are to be fed with milk, not with meat. "Even," he says, "as unto babes in Christ, have I given you milk and not meat; for hitherto ye were not able to bear it, neither yet now are ye able." [15] When we say, "not yet," we must not despair, if that which is "not yet" tends to be. For he says, "ye are yet carnal." And showing how it is that they are carnal, he says, "For whereas there is among you envying, and strife, and divisions, are ye not carnal, and walk as men?" And again more plainly, "For while one saith, I

---

1 Matt. iii. 16.   2 Acts ii. 3.   3 Rom. viii. 15.
4 Matt. vi. 12.   5 1 John iii. 24.   6 Rom. viii. 16.
7 Phil. ii. 1.

8 Eph. iv. 3.   9 John xv. 26.   10 Matt. x. 20.
11 Gal. iv. 6.   12 Rom. viii. 9.   13 Jude 19.
14 1 Cor. ii. 14.   15 1 Cor. iii. 1, 2, 3, Vulgate.

am of Paul, and another, I of Apollos, are ye not carnal? Who then is Paul, and who is Apollos, but ministers by whom ye believed?"[1] These then, that is, Paul and Apollos, agreed together in the unity of the Spirit and the bond of peace; and yet because the Corinthians began to divide them among themselves, and "to be puffed up for one against another," they are said to be men — carnal and natural men, not able to receive the things of the Spirit of God; and yet because they are not separated from the Church, they are called "babes in Christ;" for indeed he desired that they should be either Angels, or even Gods, whom he reproved because they were men, that is, in those contentions, "They savoured not the things which be of God, but the things which be of men."[2] But of those who are separated from the Church it is not merely said, "perceiving not the things of the Spirit of God," lest it should be referred to the perception of knowledge; but it is said, "Having not the Spirit." For it does not follow, that he who hath it, should also by knowledge perceive what he hath.

31. The "babes" then "in Christ" who have yet place in the Church, who are still natural and carnal, and cannot "perceive," that is, understand and know what they have, have this Spirit. For how could they be babes in Christ except they were born anew of the Holy Spirit? Nor ought it to seem any wonder that one may have something, and yet not know what he hath. For to say nothing of the Divinity of the Almighty, and the Unity of the Unchangeable Trinity, who can easily perceive by knowledge what the soul is; and yet who is there that hath not a soul? Finally, that we may know most certainly that "babes in Christ," who do not "perceive the things of the Spirit of God," have notwithstanding the Spirit of God; let us look how the Apostle Paul, when a little while after he is rebuking them, saith, "Know ye not that ye are the temples of God, and the Spirit of God dwelleth in you?"[3] This surely he would in no wise say to those who are separated from the Church, who are described as "having not the Spirit."

32. But neither can he be said to be in the Church, and to belong to that fellowship of the Spirit, who is mixed up with Christ's sheep by a bodily intercourse only in deceitfulness of heart. For the "Holy Spirit of discipline will flee deceit."[4] Wherefore whosoever are baptized in the congregations or separations rather[5] of schismatics or heretics, although they have not been born again of the Spirit, like as it were to Ishmael, who was Abraham's son after the flesh; not like Isaac, who was his son after the Spirit,[6] because by promise; yet when they come to the Catholic Church, and are joined to the fellowship of the Spirit which without the Church they beyond doubt had not, the washing of the flesh is not repeated in their case. For "this form of godliness" was not wanting to them even when they were without; but there is added to them "the Unity of the Spirit in the bond of peace," which cannot be given but within. Before they were Catholics indeed, they were as they of whom the Apostle says, "Having a form of godliness, but denying the power thereof."[7] For the visible form of the branch may exist even when separated from the vine; but the invisible life of the root cannot be had, but in the vine. Wherefore the bodily sacraments, which even they who are separated from the Unity of Christ's Body bear and celebrate, may give "the form of godliness;" but the invisible and spiritual power of godliness cannot in any wise be in them, just as sensation does not accompany a man's limb, when it is amputated from the body.

33. And since this is so, remission of sins, seeing it is not given but by the Holy Spirit, can only be given in that Church which hath the Holy Spirit. For this is the effect of the remission of sins, that the prince of sin, the spirit who is divided against himself, should no more reign in us, and that being delivered from the power of the unclean spirit, we should thenceforward be made the temple of the Holy Spirit, and receive Him, by whom we are cleansed through receiving pardon, to dwell in us, to work, increase, and perfect righteousness. For at His first coming, when they who had received Him spake with the tongues of all nations, and the Apostle Peter addressed those who were present in amazement, they were pricked in heart, and said to Peter and to the rest of the Apostles, "Men and brethren, what shall we do?" show us. "And Peter said to them, Repent, and be baptized every one of you in the Name of Jesus Christ for the remission of sins, and ye shall receive the gift of the Holy Ghost."[8] In the Church truly in which was the Holy Ghost, were both brought to pass, that is, both the remission of sins, and the receiving of this gift. And therefore was it "In the Name of Jesus Christ;" because when He promised the same Holy Ghost; He said, "Whom the Father will send in My Name."[9] For the Spirit dwelleth in no man without the Father and the Son; as neither doth the Son without the Father and the Holy Spirit, nor the Father without them. Their indwelling is inseparable, as their operation is inseparable; but sometimes they manifest them-

---

[1] 1 Cor. iii. 4, 5.   [2] Matt. xvi. 23.
[3] 1 Cor. iii. 16.   [4] Wisd. i. 5.
[5] *Congregationibus vel potius segregationibus.*

[6] Gal. iv. 29.   [7] 2 Tim. iii. 5.   [8] Acts ii. 37, 38.
[9] John xiv. 26.

selves separately by symbols [1] borrowed from the creatures, not in their own substance; just as they are pronounced separately by the voice in syllables which occupy separately their own spaces, and yet they are not separated from each other by any intervals, or moments of time. For they never can be pronounced together, whereas they can never exist, except together. But as I have already said, and not once only, the remission of sins, whereby the kingdom of the spirit which is divided against himself is overthrown and driven out, and the fellowship of the unity of the Church of God, out of which this remission of sins is not, are regarded as the peculiar work of the Holy Spirit, with the co-operation doubtless of the Father and the Son, because the Holy Spirit is Himself in some sort the fellowship of the Father and the Son. For the Father is not possessed [2] as Father by the Son and the Holy Spirit in common; because He is not the Father of Both. And the Son is not possessed as Son by the Father and the Holy Spirit in common; because He is not the Son of Both. But the Holy Spirit is possessed as the Spirit by the Father and the Son in common, because He is the One Spirit of Both.

34. Whosoever therefore shall be guilty of impenitence against the Spirit, in whom the unity and fellowship of the communion of the Church is gathered together, shall never have forgiveness; because he has stopped the source of forgiveness against himself, and deservedly shall he be condemned with the spirit, which is divided against himself, who is himself also divided against the Holy Spirit which is not divided against Himself. And of this the very testimonies of the Gospel warn us, would we with good attention search them. For according to Luke the Lord does not say, "That he who blasphemeth against the Holy Ghost shall not be forgiven:" in that place where He is answering those who said that He cast out devils by the prince of the devils. Whence it would seem that this was not said once only by the Lord; but we must not carelessly pass over the consideration of the occasion on which this last also was spoken. For He was speaking of those who should have confessed or denied Him before men, when He said, "Also I say unto you, Whosoever shall confess Me before men, him shall the Son of Man also confess before the Angels of God. But he that denieth Me before men, shall be denied before the angels of God." [3] And lest from this the salvation of the Apostle Peter should be despaired of, he immediately subjoined, "And whosoever shall speak a word against the Son of Man, it shall be forgiven him; but unto him that blasphemeth against the Holy

Ghost, it shall not be forgiven; [4] blasphemeth," that is, with that blasphemy of an impenitent heart, by which resistance is made to remission of sins which is granted in the Church by the Holy Ghost. And this blasphemy Peter had not, who presently repented, when "he wept bitterly," [5] and who after he had overcome the spirit who is divided against himself, and who had desired to "have him to harass him," [6] and against whom the "Lord prayed for him that his faith might not fail," even received the Very Holy Spirit whom he resisted not, that not only his sin might be forgiven him, but that through him remission of sins might be preached and dispensed.

35. And in the narrative of the two other Evangelists, the occasion of speaking out this sentence of the blasphemy of the Spirit arose from the mention of the unclean spirit, who is divided against himself. For it had been said of the Lord, that "He cast out devils by the prince of the devils." In that place the Lord says, that "by the Holy Spirit He casteth out devils," that so the spirit who is not divided against Himself may overcome and cast out him who is divided against himself; but that that man would abide in his perdition, who refuses through impenitence to pass over into His peace, who is not divided against Himself. For thus runs the narrative of Mark; "Verily I say unto you, All sins shall be forgiven unto the sons of men, and blasphemies wherewith soever they shall blaspheme; but he that shall blaspheme against the Holy Ghost hath never forgiveness, but shall be held guilty of an eternal offence." [7] When he had delivered these words of the Lord, he then subjoined his own, saying, "Because they said He hath an unclean spirit;" [8] that He might show that the cause of His saying this arose hence, because they had said that "He cast out devils by Beelzebub the prince of the devils." Not that this was a blasphemy which shall not be forgiven, forasmuch as even this shall be forgiven, if a right repentance follow it; but because, as I have said, there arose hence a cause for that sentence to be delivered by the Lord, since mention had been made of the unclean spirit whom the Lord shows to be divided against himself, because of the Holy Spirit who is not only not divided against Himself, but who also makes those whom He gathers together undivided, by forgiving those sins which are divided against themselves, and by inhabiting those who are cleansed, that it may be with them, as it is written in the Acts of the Apostles, "The multitude of them that believed were of one heart and of one soul." [9] And this gift of

---

[1] Significationes.   [2] Habetur.   [3] Luke xii. 8, 9.

[4] Luke xii. 10.   [5] Matt. xxvi. 75.
[6] Luke xxii. 31.   [7] Mark iii. 28, 29.
[8] Mark iii. 30.   [9] Acts iv. 32.

forgiveness none resists, but he who has the hardness of an impenitent heart. For in another place also the Jews said of the Lord that He had a devil,[1] yet He spake nothing there of the blasphemy of the Holy Spirit; because they did not so bring forward the mention of the unclean spirit as that he could be shown out of their own mouths to be divided against himself, as Beelzebub, by whom they said that devils could be cast out.

36. But in this passage according to Matthew, the Lord far more plainly explained what he intended to be understood here; namely, that he it is who speaks a word against the Holy Ghost, who with an impenitent heart resists the Unity of the Church, where in the Holy Spirit is given the remission of sins. For this spirit they have not, as has been said already, who even though they bear and handle[2] the sacraments of Christ, are separated from His congregation. For when He spoke of the division of Satan against Satan, and how that He Himself cast out devils by the Holy Spirit, that Spirit, namely, which is not, as the other, divided against Himself; lest any one should think because of those who gather together their irregular assemblies[3] under the Name of Christ, but without His fold, that the kingdom of Christ also was divided against itself, He immediately added, "He that is not with Me is against Me, and he that gathereth not with Me scattereth abroad,"[4] that He might show that they did not belong to Him who by gathering "without" wished not to "gather" but "to scatter abroad." And afterwards He subjoined, "Wherefore I say unto you, All manner of sin and blasphemy shall be forgiven unto men; but the blasphemy of the Spirit shall not be forgiven."[5] What is this "wherefore?" Shall the blasphemy of the Spirit only not be forgiven, because "he who is not with Christ is against Him, and he who gathereth not with Him scattereth abroad?" Even so, doubtless. For he that gathereth not with Him, howsoever he may gather under His name, hath not the Holy Ghost.

37. Thus then hath He altogether forced us to understand that the remission of no sin nor blasphemy can be effected anywhere else, save in the gathering together of Christ, which scattereth not abroad. For it is gathered together in the Holy Spirit, which is not as that unclean spirit, divided against Himself. And therefore all congregations, or dispersions rather, which call themselves Churches of Christ, and are divided against themselves and contrary one to the other, and hostile to the congregation of Unity, which is His True Church, do not therefore belong to His congregation, because they seem to have His Name. But they might belong to it, if the Holy Spirit in whom this congregation is joined together, were divided against Himself. But because this is not so ("for he that is not with Christ is against Him, and he that gathereth not with Him scattereth abroad"); therefore all manner of sin and all blasphemy shall be forgiven unto men in this congregation, which Christ gathereth together in the Holy Spirit, who is not divided against Himself. But that blasphemy of the Spirit Himself, whereby in an impenitent heart resistance is made to this so great gift of God even to the end of this present life, shall not be forgiven. For though a man so oppose himself to the truth, as to resist God speaking, not in the Prophets, but in His Only Son (since for our sakes He was pleased that He should be the Son of Man, that He might speak to us in Him), yet shall he be forgiven when in repentance he shall have recourse to the goodness of God, who forasmuch as He "willeth not the death of the wicked, but rather that he should turn from his way and live,"[6] hath given the Holy Spirit to His Church, that whosoever forgiveth sins in the Spirit, they should be forgiven. But whoso stands out as an enemy to this gift, so as not in repentance to seek it, but by impenitence to gainsay it, his sin becomes unpardonable; not sin of any one specific kind, but the contempt, or even opposing of the remission of sins itself. And so a word is spoken against the Holy Spirit, when men never come from the dispersion to the congregation which has received the Holy Spirit for the remission of sins. Unto which congregation if any come without hypocrisy, though it be through the ministry of a wicked clergyman, a reprobate and a hypocrite, so he be a Catholic minister, he shall receive remission of sins in this Holy Spirit. For such is the working of this Spirit in the Holy Church, even in this present time, when the corn[7] is as it were being threshed with the chaff, that he despises no man's sincere confession, and is deceived by no man's false pretences, and so flies from the reprobate, as yet by their ministry to gather together those that are approved.[8] One refuge then there is against unpardonable blasphemy, that we take heed of an impenitent heart; and that it be not thought that repentance can avail ought, unless the Church be kept to, in which remission of sins is given, and the fellowship of the Spirit is preserved in the bond of peace.

38. I have through the mercy and assistance of the Lord handled, as I best was able, this most difficult question, if indeed I have been able to do it in any measure. Nevertheless, whatever I have not been able to apprehend in the difficul-

---

[1] John vii. 20 and viii. 48.   [2] *Portantes et tractantes.*
[3] *Conventicula.*   [4] Matt. xii. 30.   [5] Matt. xii. 31.

[6] Ezek. xxxiii. 11.   [7] *Area.*   [8] *Probos.*

ties of it, let it not be imputed to the truth itself, which is a healthful exercise to the godly, even when it is hidden, but to my infirmity, who either could not see what others might have understood, or could not explain what I did understand. But for that which perhaps I have been able to discover by force of meditation, and to develop in words, to Him must the thanks be given, from whom I have sought, from whom I have asked, unto whom I have knocked, that I might have wherewithal to be nourished myself in meditation, and to minister to you in speaking.

SERMON XXII.

[LXXII. BEN.]

ON THE WORDS OF THE GOSPEL, MATT. XII. 33, "EITHER MAKE THE TREE GOOD, AND ITS FRUIT GOOD," ETC.

1. THE Lord Jesus hath admonished us, that we be good trees, and that so we may be able to bear good fruits. For He saith, "Either make the tree good, and his fruit good, or else make the tree corrupt, and his fruit corrupt, for the tree is known by his fruit." [1] When He says, "Make the tree good, and his fruit good;" this of course is not an admonition, but a wholesome precept, to which obedience is necessary. But when He saith, "Make the tree corrupt, and his fruit corrupt;" this is not a precept that thou shouldest do it; but an admonition, that thou shouldest beware of it. For He spoke against those, who thought that although they were evil, they could speak good things or have good works. This the Lord Jesus saith is impossible. For the man himself must first be changed, in order that his works may be changed. For if a man abide in his evil state, he cannot have good works; if he abide in his good state, he cannot have evil works.

2. But who was found good by the Lord, since "Christ died for the ungodly"? [2] He found them all corrupt trees, but to those who "believed in His Name, He gave power to become the sons of God." [3] Whosoever then now is a good man, that is, a good tree, was found corrupt, and made good. And if when He came He had chosen to root up the corrupt trees, what tree would have remained which did not deserve to be rooted up? But He came first to impart [4] mercy, that He might afterwards exercise judgment, to whom it is said, "I will sing unto Thee, O Lord, of mercy and judgment." [5] He gave then remission of sins to those who believed in Him, He would not even take account with them of past reckonings. [6] He gave remission of sins,

He made them good trees. He delayed the ax, He gave [7] security.

3. Of this ax does John speak, saying, "Now is the ax laid unto the root of the trees; every tree which bringeth not forth good fruit shall be hewn down, and cast into the fire." [8] With this ax does the Householder in the Gospel threaten, saying, "Behold these three years I come to this tree, and find no fruit on it." Now I must clear [9] the ground; wherefore let it be cut down. And the husbandman intercedes, saying, "Lord, let it alone this year also, till I shall dig about it and dung it; and if it bear fruit, well; and if not, then Thou shalt come and cut it down." [10] So the Lord hath visited mankind as it were three years, that is, at three several times. The first time was before the Law; the second under the Law; the third is now, which is the time of grace. For if He did not visit mankind before the Law, whence was Abel, and Enoch, and Noe, and Abraham, and Isaac, and Jacob, whose Lord He was pleased to be called? And He to whom all nations belonged, as though He were the God of three men only, said, "I am the God of Abraham, and Isaac, and Jacob." [11] But if He did not visit under the Law, He would not have given the Law itself. After the Law, came the very Master of the house in person; He suffered, and died, and rose again; He gave the Holy Spirit, He made the Gospel to be preached throughout all the world, and yet a certain tree remained unfruitful. Still is there a certain portion of mankind, which doth not yet amend itself. The husbandman intercedes; the Apostle prays for the people; "I bow my knees," he saith, "unto the Father for you, that being rooted and grounded in love, ye may be able to comprehend with all saints what is the breadth, and length, and depth, and height; and to know the love of Christ which passeth knowledge, that ye might be filled with all the fulness of God." [12] By bowing the knees, he intercedes with the Master of the house for us, that we be not rooted up. Therefore since He must necessarily come, let us take care that He find us fruitful. The digging about the tree is the lowliness of the penitent. For every ditch is low. The dunging it, is the filthy [13] robe [14] of repentance. For what is more filthy than dung; yet if well used, what more profitable?

4. Let each one then be a good tree; let him not suppose that he can bear good fruit, if he remain a corrupt tree. There will be no good fruit, but from the good tree. Change the heart, and the work will be changed. Root out desire, plant in charity. "For as desire is the root of

---

[1] Matt. xii. 33. [2] Rom. v. 6. [3] John i. 12.
[4] Prærogare. [5] Ps. ci. 1. [6] Chartis.
[7] Distulit securim, dedit securitatem.
[8] Matt. iii. 10. [9] Evacuare. [10] Luke xiii. 7, etc.
[11] Exod. iii. 15. [12] Eph. iii. 14, 17-19.
[13] Sordes pœnitentiæ.
[14] Bingh. Antiq. xviii. c. 2, § 2.

all evil," [1] so is charity the root of all good. Why then do men fret and contend one with another, saying, " What is good?" O that thou knewest what good is ! What thou dost wish to have is not very good ; this is good which thou dost not wish to be. For thou dost wish to have health of body ; it is good indeed ; yet thou canst not think that to be any great good, which the wicked have as well. Thou dost wish to have gold and silver ; I grant that these also are good things, but then only if thou make a good use of them ; and a good use of them thou wilt not make, if thou art evil thyself. And hence gold and silver are to the evil evil ; to the good are good, not because gold and silver make them good ; but because they find them good, they are turned to a good use. Again, thou dost wish to have honour, it is good ; but this too only if thou make a good use of it. To how many has honour been the occasion of destruction ! And again, to how many has honour been the instrument [2] of good works !

5. Let us then, if we can, make a distinction as to these goods ; for it is of good trees that we are speaking. And here there is nothing, which every one ought so much to think of, as to turn his eyes upon himself, to learn in himself, examine himself, inspect himself, search into himself, and find out himself ; and kill what is displeasing ; and long for and plant in that which is well-pleasing (to God). For when a man finds himself so empty of better goods, why is he greedy of external goods? And what profit is there in a coffer full of goods, with an empty conscience? Thou wishest to have good things, and dost thou not then wish to be good thyself? Seest thou not that thou oughtest rather to blush for thy good things, if thy house is full of good things, and thou its owner art evil? For what is there, tell me, thou wouldest wish to have that is bad. Not any one thing I am sure ; neither wife ; nor son ; nor daughter ; nor manservant ; nor maidservant ; nor country seat ; nor a coat ; nay nor a shoe ; [3] and yet thou art willing to have a bad life. I pray thee prefer thy way of life to thy shoes. All things which encompass thy sight, as being of elegance and beauty, are highly prized by thee ; and art thou so lightly esteemed by thyself, and so devoid of beauty? If the good things of which thine house is full, which thou hast longed to possess, and feared to lose, could make answer to thee, would they not cry out to thee, As thou wishest to have us good, so do we also wish to have a good owner? And now in speechless accents do they address thy Lord against thee : " Lo ! thou hast given him so many good things, and he himself is evil. What profit is there to him

in that he hath, when he hath not Him who hath given him all ! "

6. One then who has been admonished, and it may be moved to compunction by these words, may ask what is good? what is the nature of good? and whence it comes? Well is it that thou hast understood that it is thy duty to ask this. I will answer thy enquiries, and will say, " That is good which thou canst not lose against thy will." For gold thou mayest lose even against thy will ; and so thou canst a house ; and honours, and even the health of the body ; but the good whereby thou art truly good, thou dost neither receive against thy will, nor against thy will dost lose it. I enquire then, " What is the nature of this good?" One of the Psalms teaches us an important matter, perchance it is even this that we are seeking for. For it says, " O ye sons of men, how long will ye be heavy in heart?" [4] How long will that tree be in its three [5] years fruitlessness? " O ye sons of men, how long will ye be heavy in heart?" What is " heavy in heart"? " Why do ye love vanity, and seek after leasing?" And then it goes on to say what we must really seek after ; "Know ye that the Lord hath magnified His Holy One?" [6] Now Christ hath come, now hath He been magnified, now hath He risen again, and ascended into heaven, now is His Name preached through the world : " How long will ye be heavy in heart?" Let the times past suffice ; now that that Holy One hath been magnified, " How long will ye be heavy in heart?" After the three years, what remains but the ax? " How long will ye be heavy in heart? Why do ye love vanity, and seek after leasing?" Vain, useless, frivolous,[7] fleeting things are these still sought after, now that Christ the Holy One hath been so magnified? Truth now is crying aloud, and is vanity still sought after? " How long will ye be heavy in heart?"

7. With good reason is this world severely scourged ; for the world hath known now its Master's words. " And the servant," He saith, " that knew not his Master's will, and did commit things worthy of stripes, shall be beaten with few stripes." [8] Why? That he may seek after his Master's will. The servant then who knew not His will, this was the world, before " He magnified His Holy One ; " it was " the servant who knew not his Master's will," and therefore " shall be beaten with few stripes." But the servant who now knoweth his Master's will, that is now, since the Godhead " sanctified His Holy One," and " doeth not His will, shall be beaten with many stripes." What marvel then, if the world be now much beaten? " It is the servant which knew his Master's will, and did commit things

---

1 1 Tim. vi. 10. *Cupiditas*, Vulgate.
2 *Ministerium*.   3 Vide Serm. ccxxxii. (vii.) 8.

4 Ps. iv. 3, Sept. (iv. 2, English version).   5 *Triennio*.
6 Ps. iv. 4.   7 *Pompatica*.   8 Luke xii. 48.

worthy of stripes." Let him then not refuse to be beaten with many stripes; since if in unrighteousness he will not hear his teacher, in righteousness must he feel his avenger. At least, let him not murmur against Him that chasteneth him, when he sees that he is worthy of stripes, that so he may attain[1] mercy; through Christ our Lord, who liveth and reigneth, with God the Father and the Holy Spirit, for ever and ever. Amen.

SERMON XXIII.

[LXXIII. BEN.]

ON THE WORDS OF THE GOSPEL, MATT. XIII. 19, ETC., WHERE THE LORD JESUS EXPLAINETH THE PARABLES OF THE SOWER.

1. BOTH yesterday and to-day ye have heard the parables of the sower, in the words of our Lord Jesus Christ. Do ye who were present yesterday, recollect to-day. Yesterday we read of that sower, who when he scattered seed, "some fell by the way side,"[2] which the birds picked up; "some in stony places," which dried up from the heat; "some among thorns, which were choked," and could not bring forth fruit; and "other some into good ground, and it brought forth fruit, a hundred, sixty, thirty fold." But to-day the Lord hath again spoken another parable of the sower, "who sowed good seed in his field. While men slept the enemy came, and sowed tares upon it."[3] As long as it was only in the blade, it did not appear; but when the fruit of the good seed began to appear, "then appeared the tares also." The servants of the householder were offended, when they saw a quantity of tares among the good wheat, and wished to root them out, but they were not suffered to do so; but it was said to them, "Let both grow together until the harvest."[4] Now the Lord Jesus Christ explained this parable also; and said that He was the sower of the good seed, and He showed how that the enemy who sowed the tares was the devil; the time of harvest, the end of the world; His field, the whole world. And what saith He? "In the time of harvest I will say to the reapers, Gather ye together first the tares, to burn them, but gather the wheat into My barn." Why are ye so hasty, He says, ye servants full of zeal? Ye see tares among the wheat, ye see evil Christians among the good; and ye wish to root up the evil ones; be quiet, it is not the time of harvest. That time will come, may it only find you wheat! Why do ye vex yourselves? Why bear impatiently the mixture of the evil with the good? In the field they may be with you, but they will not be so in the barn.

2. Now ye know that those three places mentioned yesterday where the seed did not grow, "the way side," "the stony ground," and "the thorny places," are the same as these "tares." They received only a different name under a different similitude. For when similitudes are used, or the literal meaning of a term is not expressed, not the truth but a similitude of the truth is conveyed by them. I see that but few have understood my meaning; yet it is for the benefit of all that I speak. In things visible, a way side is a way side, stony ground is stony ground, thorny places are thorny places; they are simply what they are, because the names are used in their literal sense. But in parables and similitudes one thing may be called by many names; therefore there is nothing inconsistent in my telling you that that "way side," that "stony ground," those "thorny places," are bad Christians, and that they too are the "tares." Is not Christ called "the Lamb"? Is not Christ "the Lion" too? Among wild beasts, and cattle, a lamb is simply a lamb, and a lion, a lion: but Christ is both. The first are respectively what they are in propriety of expression; the Latter both together in a figurative sense.[5] Nay much more; besides this it may happen that under a figure, things very different from one another may be called by one and the same name. For what is so different as Christ and the devil? yet both Christ and the devil are called "a lion." Christ is called "a lion:" "The Lion hath prevailed of the tribe of Judah;"[6] and the devil is called a lion: "Know ye not that your adversary the Devil walketh about as a roaring lion, seeking whom he may devour?"[7] Both the one and the other then is a lion; the one a lion by reason of His strength; the other for his savageness; the one a lion for His "prevailing;" the other for his injuring. The devil again is a serpent, "that old serpent;"[8] are we commanded then to imitate the devil, when our Shepherd told us, "Be ye wise as serpents, and simple as doves"?[9]

3. Accordingly I yesterday addressed "the way side," I addressed the "stony ground," I addressed the "thorny places;" and I said, Be ye changed whilst ye may: turn up with the plough the hard ground, cast the stones out of the field, pluck up the thorns out of it. Be loth to retain that hard heart, from which the word of God may quickly pass away and be lost. Be loth to have that lightness of soil, where the root of charity can take no deep hold. Be loth to choke the good seed which is sown in you by my labours, with the lusts and the cares of this world. For it is the Lord who sows; and we are only His labourers. But be ye the "good

---

[1] *Mereatur.*   [2] Matt. xiii. 3–8.   [3] Matt. xiii. 24, 25.
[4] Matt. xiii. 30.

[5] *Per similitudinem.*   [6] Rev. v. 5.   [7] 1 Pet. v. 8.
[8] Rev. xii. 9.   [9] Matt. x. 16.

ground." I said yesterday, and I say again to-day to all, Let one bring forth "a hundred, another sixty, another thirty fold." In one the fruit is more, in another less; but all will have a place in the barn. Yesterday I said all this, to-day I am addressing the tares; but the sheep themselves are the tares. O evil Christians, O ye, who in filling only press the Church by your evil lives; amend yourselves before the harvest come. "Say not, I have sinned, and what hath befallen me?"[1] God hath not lost His power; but He is requiring repentance from thee. I say this to the evil, who yet are Christians; I say this to the tares. For they are in the field; and it may so be, that they who to-day are tares, may to-morrow be wheat. And so I will address the wheat also.

4. O ye Christians, whose lives are good, ye sigh and groan as being few among many, few among very many. The winter will pass away, the summer will come; lo! the harvest will soon be here. The angels will come who can make the separation, and who cannot make mistakes. We in this time present are like those servants, of whom it was said, "Wilt Thou that we go and gather them up?"[2] for we were wishing, if it might be so, that no evil ones should remain among the good. But it has been told us, "Let both grow together until the harvest."[3] Why? For ye are such as may be deceived. Hear finally; "Lest while ye gather up the tares, ye root up also the wheat with them."[4] What good are ye doing? Will ye by your eagerness make a waste of My harvest? The reapers will come, and who the reapers are He hath explained, "And the reapers are the angels."[5] We are but men, the reapers are the angels. We too indeed, if we finish our course, shall be equal to the angels of God; but now when we chafe against the wicked, we are as yet but men. And we ought now to give ear to the words, "Wherefore let him that thinketh he standeth, take heed lest he fall."[6] For do ye think, my Brethren, that these tares we read of do not get up into this[7] seat?[8] Think ye that they are all below, and none above up here? God grant we may not be so. "But with me it is a very small thing that I should be judged of you."[9] I tell you of a truth, my Beloved, even in these high seats there is both wheat, and tares, and among the laity there is wheat, and tares. Let the good tolerate the bad; let the bad change themselves, and imitate the good. Let us all, if it may be so, attain to God; let us all through His mercy escape the evil of this world. Let us seek after

good days, for we are now in evil days; but in the evil days let us not blaspheme, that so we may be able to arrive at the good days.

SERMON XXIV.

[LXXIV. BEN.]

ON THE WORDS OF THE GOSPEL, MATT. XIII. 52, "THEREFORE EVERY SCRIBE WHO HATH BEEN MADE A DISCIPLE TO THE KINGDOM OF HEAVEN," ETC.

1. THE lesson of the Gospel reminds me to seek out, and to explain to you, Beloved, as the Lord shall give me power, who is "that Scribe instructed in the kingdom of God, who is "like unto an householder bringing out of his treasure things new and old."[10] For here the lesson ended. "What are the new and old things of an instructed Scribe?" Now it is well known who they were, whom the ancients, after the custom of our Scriptures, called Scribes, those, namely, who professed the knowledge of the Law. For such were called Scribes among the Jewish people, not such as are so called now in the service[11] of judges, or the custom of states. For we must not enter school to no purpose, but we must know in what signification to take the words of Scripture; lest when anything is mentioned out of it, which is usually understood in another secular use of the term, the hearer mistake it, and by thinking of its customary meaning, understand not what he has heard. The Scribes then were they who professed the knowledge of the Law, and to them belonged both the keeping and the studying, as well as also the transcribing and the expounding, of the books of the Law.

2. Such were they whom our Lord Jesus Christ rebukes, because they have the keys of the kingdom of heaven, and "would neither enter in themselves, nor suffer others to enter in;"[12] in these words finding fault with the Pharisees and Scribes, the teachers of the law of the Jews. Of whom in another place He says, "Whatsoever they say, do, but do not ye after their works, for they say and do not."[13] Why is it said to you, "For they say and do not?" but that there are some of whom what the Apostle says, is clearly exemplified, "Thou that preachest a man should not steal, dost thou steal? Thou that sayest a man should not commit adultery, dost thou commit adultery? Thou that abhorrest idols, dost thou commit sacrilege? Thou that makest thy boast of the Law, through breaking the Law dishonourest thou God? For the name of God is blasphemed among the Gentiles through you."[14] It is surely plain that the Lord speaks of these, "For they say and do not." They then are

---

1 Ecclus v. 4.   2 Matt. xiii. 28.   3 Matt. xiii. 30.
4 Matt. xiii. 29.   5 Matt. xiii. 39.   6 1 Cor. x. 12.
7 Apsidas.
8 Apsis the higher semicircular or arched part of the chancel, where the bishop had his throne with the presbyters. See Bing. Antiq. B. viii. c. vi. §§ 9, 10.
9 1 Cor. iv. 3.

10 Matt. xiii. 52.   11 Officiis.   12 Luke xi. 52.
13 Matt. xxiii. 3.   14 Rom. ii. 21, etc.

Scribes, but not "instructed in the kingdom of God."

3. Peradventure some of you may say, "And how can a bad man speak what is good, when it is written, in the words of the Lord Himself, 'A good man out of the good treasure of his heart bringeth forth good things, and an evil man out of the evil treasure of his heart bringeth forth evil things. Ye hypocrites, how can ye being evil speak good things?'"[1] In the one place He says, "How can ye being evil speak good things?" in the other He says, "What they say, do, but do ye not after their works. For they say, and do not." If " they say and do not," they are evil; if they are evil, they cannot "speak good things;" how then are we to do what we hear from them, when we cannot hear from them what is good? Now take heed, Holy and Beloved,[2] how this question may be solved. Whatever an evil man brings forth from himself, is evil; whatever an evil man brings forth out of his own heart, is evil; for there is the evil treasure. But whatever a good man brings forth out of his heart, is good; for there is the good treasure. Whence then did those evil men bring forth good things? " Because they sat in Moses' seat."[3] Had He not first said, "They sit in Moses' seat;" He would never have enjoined that evil men should be heard. For what they brought forth out of the evil treasure of their own heart, was one thing; another what they gave utterance to out of the seat of Moses, the criers so to say of the judge. What the crier says, will never be attributed to him if he speak in the presence of the judge. What the crier says in his own house is one thing, what the crier says as hearing it from the judge is another. For whether he will or no, the crier must proclaim the sentence[4] of punishment even of his own friend. And so whether he will or no, must he proclaim the sentence of the acquittal even of his own enemy. Suppose him to speak from his heart; he acquits his friend, and punishes his enemy. Suppose him to speak from the judge's chair; he punishes his friend, and acquits his enemy. So with the Scribes; suppose them to speak out of their own heart; thou wilt hear, "Let us eat and drink, for to-morrow we shall die."[5] Suppose them to speak from Moses' seat; thou wilt hear, "Thou shalt not kill, Thou shalt not commit adultery, Thou shalt not steal, Thou shalt not bear false witness. Honour thy father and mother; thou shalt love thy neighbour as thyself."[6] Do then this which the official seat[7] proclaims by the mouth of the Scribes; not that which their heart utters. For so embracing both judgments of the Lord, thou wilt not be

obedient in the one, and guilty of disobedience in the other; but wilt understand that both agree together, and wilt regard both that as true, "that a good man out of the good treasure of his heart bringeth forth good things, and an evil man out of the evil treasure bringeth forth evil things;" and that other also, that those Scribes did not speak good things out of the evil treasure of their heart, but that they were able to speak good things out of the treasure of Moses' seat.

4. So then those words of the Lord will not disturb you, when He says, "Every tree is known by his own fruit. Do men gather grapes of thorns, and figs of thistles?"[8] The Scribes and Pharisees of the Jews therefore were thorns and thistles, and notwithstanding, "what they say do, but do ye not after their works." So then the grape is gathered from thorns, and the fig from thistles, as He has given thee to understand according to the method I have just laid down. For so sometimes in the vineyard's thorny hedge, the vines get entangled, and clusters of grapes hang from the brambles. Thou hadst no sooner heard the name of thorns, than thou wert on the point of disregarding the grape. But seek for the root of the thorns, and thou wilt see where to find it. Follow too the root of the hanging cluster, and thou wilt see where to find it. So understand that the one refers to the Pharisee's heart, the other to Moses' seat.

5. But why were they such as they were? "Because," says St. Paul, "the vail is upon their heart. And they do not see that the old things are passed away, and all things are become new."[9] Hence it is that they were such, and all others who even now are like them. Why are they old things? Because they have been a long while published. Why new? Because they relate to the kingdom of God. How the vail then is taken away, the Apostle himself tells us. "But when thou shalt turn to the Lord, the vail shall be taken away."[10] So then the Jew who does not turn to the Lord, does not carry on his mind's eye to the end. Just as at that time the children of Israel in this figure did not carry on the gaze of their eyes "to the end,"[11] that is, to the face of Moses. For the shining face of Moses contained a figure of the truth; the vail was interposed because the children of Israel could not yet behold the glory of his countenance. "Which figure is done away."[12] For so said the Apostle; "which is done away." Why done away? Because when the emperor comes, the images of him are taken away. The image is looked upon, when the emperor is not present; but where he is, whose image it is, there the image is removed. There were then

---

[1] Matt. xii. 35, 34.   [2] *Sanctitas Vestra.*
[3] Matt. xxiii. 2.   [4] *Vocem.*   [5] Isa. xxii. 13.
[6] Exod. xx. 12, etc.   [7] *Cathedra.*

[8] Luke vi. 44; Matt. vii. 16.   [9] 2 Cor. iii. 15, v. 17.
[10] 2 Cor. iii. 16.   [11] 2 Cor. iii. 13.   εἰς τὸ τέλος.
[12] τοῦ καταργουμένου. *Quod evacuatur.*

images borne before Him, before that our Emperor the Lord Jesus Christ came. When the images were taken away, the glory of the Emperor's presence is seen. Therefore, "When any one turneth to the Lord, the vail is taken away." For the voice of Moses sounded through the vail, but the face of Moses was not seen. And so now the voice of Christ sounds to the Jews by the voice of the old Scriptures : they hear their voice, but they see not the face of Him that speaketh. Would they then that the vail should be taken away? " Let them turn to the Lord." For then the old things are not taken away, but laid up in a treasury, that the Scribe may henceforth be " instructed in the kingdom of God, bringing forth out of his treasure " not " new things " only, nor " old things " only. For if he bring forth " new things " only or " old things " only ; he is not " a scribe instructed in the kingdom of God, bringing forth out of his treasure things new and old." If he say and do them not ; he brings forth from the official seat, not from the treasure of his heart. And (we speak the truth, Holy Brethren) what things are brought out of the old, are illustrated by the new. Therefore do " we turn to the Lord, that the vail may be taken away."

SERMON XXV.

[LXXV. BEN.]

ON THE WORDS OF THE GOSPEL, MATT. XIV. 24, " BUT THE BOAT WAS NOW IN THE MIDST OF THE SEA, DISTRESSED BY THE WAVES."

1. THE lesson of the Gospel which we have just heard is a lesson of humility to us all, that we may see and know where we are, and whither we must tend and hasten. For that ship which carries the disciples, which was tossed in the waves by a contrary wind, is not without its meaning. Nor without a meaning [1] did the Lord after He had left the multitudes, go up into a mountain to pray alone ; and then coming to His disciples found them in danger, walking on the sea, and getting up into the ship strengthened them, and appeased the waves. But what marvel if He can appease all things who created all? Nevertheless after He was come up into the ship, they who were being borne in her, came saying, " Of a truth Thou art the Son of God." [2] But before this plain discovery of Himself [3] they were troubled, saying, " It is a phantom. [4] But He coming up into the ship took away the fluctuation of mind from their hearts, when they were now more endangered in their souls by doubting, than before in their bodies by the waves.

2. Yet in all this that the Lord did, He instructs us as to the nature of our life here. In this world there is not a man who is not a stranger ; though all do not desire to return to their own country. Now by this very journey we are exposed to waves and tempests ; but we must needs be at least in the ship. For if there be perils in the ship, without the ship there is certain destruction. For whatever strength of arm he may have who swims in the open sea, yet in time he is carried away and sunk, mastered by the greatness of its waves. Need then there is that we be in the ship, that is, that we be carried in the wood, that we may be able to cross this sea. Now this Wood in which our weakness is carried is the Cross of the Lord, by which we are signed, and delivered from the dangerous tempests [5] of this world. We are exposed to the violence of the waves ; but He who helpeth us is God.

3. For in that when the Lord had left the multitudes, " He went up alone into a mountain to pray ; " [6] that mountain signifies the height of heaven. For having left the multitudes, the Lord after His Resurrection ascended Alone into heaven, and " there," as the Apostle says, " He maketh intercession for us." [7] There is some meaning then in His " leaving the multitudes, and going up into a mountain to pray Alone." For He Alone is as yet the First-begotten from the dead, after the resurrection of His Body, unto the right hand of the Father, the High Priest and Advocate of our prayers. The Head of the Church is above, that the rest of the members may follow at the end. If then " He maketh intercession for us," above the height of all creatures, as it were on the mountain top, " He prayeth Alone."

4. Meanwhile the ship which carries the disciples, that is, the Church, is tossed and shaken by the tempests of temptation ; and the contrary wind, that is, the devil her adversary, rests not, and strives to hinder her from arriving at rest. But greater is " He who maketh intercession for us." For in this our tossing to and fro in which we toil, He giveth us confidence in coming to us, and strengthening us ; only let us not in our trouble throw ourselves out of the ship, and cast ourselves into the sea. For though the ship be in trouble, still it *is* the ship. She alone carrieth the disciples, and receiveth Christ. There is danger, it is true, in the sea ; but without her there is instant perishing. Keep thyself therefore in the ship, and pray to God. For when all counsels fail, when even the rudder is unserviceable, and the very spreading of the sails is rather dangerous than useful, when all human help and strength is gone, there remains only for the sailors the earnest cry of entreaty,

---

[1] *Causa.*   [2] Matt. xiv. 33.   [3] *Evidentiam.*
[4] φάντασμα. Matt. xiv. 26.

[5] *Submersionibus.*   [6] Matt. xiv. 23.   [7] Rom. viii. 34.

and pouring out of prayer to God. He then who grants to sailors to reach the haven, shall He so forsake His own Church, as not to bring it on to rest?

5. Yet, Brethren, this exceeding trouble is not in this ship, save only in the absence of the Lord. What! can he who is in the Church, have his Lord absent from him? When has he his Lord absent from him? When he is overcome by any lust. For as we find it said in a certain place in a figure,[1] " Let not the sun go down upon your wrath : neither give place to the devil : "[2] and this is understood not of this visible sun which holds as it were the zenith of glory among the rest of the visible creation, and which can be seen equally by us and by the beasts ; but of that Light which none but the pure hearts of the faithful see ; as it is written, "That was the true Light, which lighteneth every man that cometh into the world."[3] For this light of the visible sun " lighteneth " even the minutest and smallest animals. Righteousness then and wisdom is that true light, which the mind ceases to see, when it is overcome by the disordering of anger as by a cloud ; and then, as it were, the sun goes down upon a man's wrath. So also in this ship, when Christ is absent, every one is shaken by his own storms, and iniquities, and evil desires. For, for example, the law tells thee, "Thou shalt not bear false witness." If thou observe the truth of witness, thou hast light in the soul ; but if overcome by the desire of filthy lucre, thou hast determined in thy mind to speak false witness, thou wilt at once begin through Christ's absence to be troubled by the tempest, thou wilt be tossed to and fro by the waves of thy covetousness, thou wilt be endangered by the violent storm of thy lusts, and as it were through Christ's absence be well nigh sunk.

6. What cause of fear is there, lest the ship be diverted from her course, and take a backward direction ; which happens when, abandoning the hope of heavenly rewards, desire turneth the helm, and a man is turned to those things which are seen and pass away ! For whosoever is disturbed by the temptations of lusts, and nevertheless still looks into those things which are within, is not so utterly in a desperate state, if he beg pardon for his faults, and exert himself to overcome and surmount the fury of the raging sea. But he who is so turned aside from what he was, as to say in his heart, "God does not see me ; for He does not think of me, nor care whether I sin ; " he hath turned the helm, borne away by the storm, and driven back to the point he came from. For there are many thoughts in the hearts of men ; and when Christ is absent, the ship is tossed by the waves of this world, and by tempests manifold.

7. Now the fourth watch of the night, is the end of the night ; for each watch consists of three hours. It signifies then, that now in the end of the world the Lord is come to help, and is seen to walk upon the waters. For though this ship be tossed about by the storms of temptations, yet she sees her Glorified God walking above all the swellings of the sea ; that is, above all the principalities of this world. For before it was said by an expression suited to the time of His Passion,[4] when according to the flesh He showed forth an example of humility, that the waves of the sea vainly raged[5] against Him, to which He yielded voluntarily for our sakes, that that prophecy, "I am come into the depths of the sea, and the floods overflow Me,"[6] might be fulfilled. For He did not repel the false witnesses, nor the savage shout of those that said, "Let Him be crucified." He did not by His power repress the savage hearts and words of those furious men, but in patience endured them all. They did unto Him whatsoever they listed ; because He "became obedient to death, even the death of the Cross."[7] But after that He was risen from the dead, that He might pray alone for His disciples placed in the Church as in a ship, and borne on in the faith of His Cross, as in wood, and in peril through this world's temptations as through the waves of the sea ; His Name began to be honoured even in this world in which He was despised, accused, and slain ; that He who in the dispensation of His suffering in the flesh, "had come into the depths of the sea, and the floods had overwhelmed Him," might now through the glory of His Name tread upon the necks of the proud as on the foaming waters. Just as we now see the Lord walking as it were upon the sea, under whose feet we behold the whole madness of this world subjected.

8. But to the perils of tempests are added also the errors of heretics ; and there are not wanting those who so try the minds of them that are in the ship, as to say that Christ[8] was not born of a Virgin, nor had a real body, but seemed to the eyes what He was not. And these opinions of heretics have sprung up now, when the Name of Christ is already glorified throughout all nations ; when Christ, that is, is as it were now walking on the sea. The disciples in their trial said, "It is a phantom."[9] But He giveth us strength against these pestilent opinions by His own voice, " Be of good cheer, it is I ; be not afraid."[10] For men in vain fear have conceived these opinions

---

[1] *In sacramento.*   [2] Eph. iv. 26, 27.   [3] John i. 9.

[4] *Ex voce passionis ejus.*   [5] *Evanuerunt.*
[6] Ps. lxix. 2.   [7] Phil. ii. 8.
[8] Manichees, *Conf.* B. v. 9 (16), 10 (20) ; B. ix. 3 (6).
[9] Matt. xiv. 26.   [10] Matt. xiv. 27.

concerning Christ, looking at his Honour and Majesty ; and they think that He could not be so born, who hath deserved to be so Glorified, fearing Him as it were "walking on the sea." For by this action the excellency of His honour is figured ; and so they think that He was a phantom. But when he saith, "It is I ;" what else doth He say but that there is nothing in Him which does not really exist? Accordingly if He showeth His flesh, it is flesh ; if bones, they are bones ; if scars, they are scars. For "there was not in Him yea and nay, but in Him was yea,"[1] as the Apostle says. Hence that expression, "Be of good cheer, it is I ; be not afraid." That is, do not so stand in awe of My Majesty, as to wish to take away the reality of My Being from Me. Though I walk upon the sea, though I have under My feet the elation and the pride of this world, as the raging waves, yet have I appeared as very Man, yet does My Gospel proclaim the very truth concerning Me, that I was born of a Virgin, that I am the Word made flesh ; that I said truly, "Handle Me, and see, for a spirit hath not bones as ye see Me have,"[2] that they were true impresses of My wounds which the hands of the doubting Apostle handled. And therefore "It is I ; be not afraid."

9. But this, that the disciples thought He was a phantom, does not represent these only, does not designate them only who deny that the Lord had human flesh, and who sometimes by their blind perverseness disturb even those who are in the ship ; but those also who think that the Lord has in anything spoken falsely, and who do not believe that the things which He has threatened the ungodly will come to pass. As though He were partly true, and partly false, appearing like a phantom in His words, as though He were something which is "yea and nay." But they who understand His voice aright, who saith, "It is I ; be not afraid ;" believe at once all the words of the Lord, so that as they hope for the rewards He promises, so do they fear the punishments He threatens. For as that is true which He will say to those who are set on the right hand, "Come, ye blessed of My Father, receive the kingdom prepared for you from the foundation of the world ;"[3] so is that true, which they on the left hand will hear, "Depart ye into everlasting fire, prepared for the devil and his Angels."[4] For this very opinion, by which men think that Christ's threatenings against the unrighteous and the abandoned are not true, has arisen from this, that they see many nations and multitudes innumerable subject to His Name ; so that hence Christ appears to them to be a phantom, because He walked upon the sea ; that is, He seems to speak falsely in His threats of punishment, be-

cause, as it were, He cannot destroy such numberless people who are subject to His Name and honour. But let them hear Him, saying, "It is I ;" let them not therefore "be afraid," who believing Christ to be true in all things, not only seek after what He hath promised, but avoid also what He hath threatened ; because though He walk upon the sea, that is, though all the nations of men in this world are subject unto Him ; yet is He no phantom, and therefore He doth not speak falsely, when He saith, "Not every one that saith unto Me, Lord, Lord, shall enter into the kingdom of heaven."[5]

10. What then does Peter's daring to come to Him on the waters also signify? For Peter generally stands for a figure of the Church. What else then do we think is meant by, "Lord, if it be Thou, bid me come unto Thee on the water ;"[6] but, Lord, if Thou art true, and in nothing speakest falsely, let Thy Church also be glorified in this world, because prophecy hath proclaimed this concerning Thee. Let her walk then on the waters, and so let her come to Thee, to whom it is said, "The rich among the people shall entreat Thy favour."[7] But since to the Lord the praise of men is no temptation, but men are ofttimes in the Church disordered by human praises and honours, and well nigh sunk by them ; therefore did Peter tremble in the sea, terrified at the great violence of the storm. For who does not fear those words, "They who call thee blessed cause thee to err, and disturb the ways of thy feet?"[8] And because the soul hath much wrestling against the eager desire of human praise, good is it in such peril to betake one's self to prayer and earnest entreaty : lest haply he who is charmed with praise, be overwhelmed and sunk by blame. Let Peter cry out as he totters in the water, and say, "Lord, save me." For the Lord will reach forth His hand, and though He chide, saying, "O thou of little faith, wherefore didst thou doubt?" wherefore didst thou not look straight forward upon Him to whom thou wast making thy way, and glory only in the Lord? Nevertheless He will snatch him from the waves, and will not suffer Him to perish, who confesses his own infirmity, and begs His help. But when they had received the Lord into the ship, and their faith was strengthened and all doubt removed, and the tempests of the sea assuaged, so that they were come to a firm and secure landing, they all worship Him, saying, "Of a truth Thou art the Son of God." For this is that everlasting joy, where Truth made manifest, and the Word of God, and the Wisdom by which all things were made, and the exceeding height of His Mercy, are both known and loved.

---

[1] 2 Cor. i. 19.   [2] Luke xxiv. 39.   [3] Matt. xxv. 34.
[4] Matt. xxv. 41.

[5] Matt. vii. 21.   [6] Matt. xiv. 28.
[7] Ps. xlv. 12.   [8] Isa. iii. 12, Vulgate.

SERMON XXVI.

[LXXVI. BEN.]

AGAIN ON MATT. XIV. 25 : OF THE LORD WALK-
ING ON THE WAVES OF THE SEA, AND OF PETER
TOTTERING.

1. THE Gospel which has just been read touching the Lord Christ, who walked on the waters
of the sea ;[1] and the Apostle Peter, who as he
was walking, tottered through fear, and sinking
in distrust, rose again by confession, gives us to
understand that the sea is the present world, and
the Apostle Peter the type of the One Church.
For Peter in the order of Apostles first, and in
the love of Christ most forward, answers oftentimes alone for all the rest. Again, when the
Lord Jesus Christ asked, whom men said that
He was, and when the disciples gave the various
opinions of men, and the Lord asked again and
said, " But whom say ye that I am?" Peter
answered, "Thou art the Christ, the Son of the
living God." One for many gave the answer,
Unity in many. Then said the Lord to Him,
" Blessed art thou, Simon Barjonas : for flesh
and blood hath not revealed it unto thee, but My
Father which is in heaven."[2] Then He added,
"and I say unto thee." As if He had said,
" Because thou hast said unto Me, 'Thou art the
Christ the Son of the living God ;' I also say
unto thee, 'Thou art Peter.'" For before he
was called Simon. Now this name of Peter was
given him by the Lord, and that in a figure, that
he should signify the Church. For seeing that
Christ is the rock (Petra), Peter is the Christian
people. For the rock (Petra) is the original
name. Therefore Peter is so called[3] from the
rock ; not the rock from Peter ; as Christ is not
called Christ from the Christian, but the Christian from Christ. " Therefore," he saith, "Thou
art Peter ; and upon this Rock" which thou hast
confessed, upon this Rock which thou hast acknowledged, saying, " Thou art the Christ, the
Son of the living God, will I build My Church ; "
that is upon Myself, the Son of the living God,
" will I build My Church." I will build thee
upon Myself, not Myself upon thee.

2. For men who wished to be built upon men,
said, " I am of Paul ; and I of Apollos ; and I
of Cephas,"[4] who is Peter. But others who
did not wish to be built upon Peter, but upon
the Rock, said, " But I am of Christ." And when
the Apostle Paul ascertained that he was chosen,
and Christ despised, he said, " Is Christ divided?
was Paul crucified for you? or were ye baptized
in the name of Paul?"[5] And, as not in the
name of Paul, so neither in the name of Peter ;
but in the name of Christ : that Peter might be
built upon the Rock, not the Rock upon Peter.

3. This same Peter therefore who had been
by the Rock pronounced " blessed," bearing the
figure of the Church, holding the chief place in
the Apostleship,[6] a very little while after that he
had heard that he was " blessed," a very little
while after that he had heard that he was " Peter," a very little while after that he had heard
that he was to be " built upon the Rock," displeased the Lord when He had heard of His
future Passion, for He had foretold His disciples that it was soon to be. He feared lest
he should by death, lose Him whom he had
confessed as the fountain of life. He was troubled,
and said, " Be it far from Thee, Lord : this shall
not be to Thee."[7] Spare Thyself, O God, I
am not willing that Thou shouldest die. Peter
said to Christ, I am not willing that Thou
shouldest die ; but Christ far better said, I am
willing to die for thee. And then He forthwith
rebuked him, whom He had a little before
commended ; and calleth him Satan, whom
he had pronounced " blessed." " Get thee behind Me, Satan," he saith, " thou art an offence
unto Me : for thou savourest not the things that
be of God, but those that be of men."[8] What
would He have us do in our present state, who
thus findeth fault because we are men? Would
you know what He would have us do? Give
ear to the Psalm ; " I have said, Ye are gods,
and ye are all the children of the Most High."
But by savouring the things of men ; " ye shall
die like men."[9] The very same Peter a little
while before blessed, afterwards Satan, in one
moment, within a few words ! Thou wonderest at the difference of the names, mark the
difference of the reasons of them. Why wonderest thou that he who was a little before
blessed, is afterwards Satan? Mark the reason
wherefore he is blessed. " Because flesh and
blood hath not revealed it unto thee, but My
Father which is in heaven."[10] Therefore blessed,
because flesh and blood hath not revealed it
unto thee. For if flesh and blood revealed this
to thee, it were of thine own ; but because flesh
and blood hath not revealed it unto thee, but
My Father which is in heaven, it is of Mine,
not of thine own. Why of Mine? " Because
all things that the Father hath are Mine."[11] So
then thou hast heard the cause, why he is
" blessed," and why he is " Peter." But why was
he that which we shudder at, and are loth to
repeat, why, but because it was of thine own?
" For thou savourest not the things which be
of God, but those that be of men."

4. Let us, looking at ourselves in this member

---

[1] Matt. xiv. 25.   [2] Matt. xvi. 17, etc.
[3] Vide Sermon cclxx. 2, and ccxcv. 1.
[4] 1 Cor. i. 12.   [5] 1 Cor. i. 13.

[6] *Apostolatus principatum.*
[7] Matt. xvi. 22.   [8] Matt. xvi. 23.   [9] Ps. lxxxii. 6, 7.
[10] Matt. xvi. 17.   [11] John xvi. 15.

of the Church, distinguish what is of God, and what of ourselves. For then we shall not totter, then shall we be founded on the Rock, shall be fixed and firm against the winds, and storms, and streams, the temptations, I mean, of this present world. Yet see this Peter, who was then our figure; now he trusts, and now he totters; now he confesses the Undying, and now he fears lest He should die. Wherefore? because the Church of Christ hath both strong and weak ones; and cannot be without either strong or weak; whence the Apostle Paul says, " Now we that are strong ought to bear the infirmities of the weak." [1] In that Peter said, " Thou art the Christ, the Son of the living God," he represents the strong: but in that he totters, and would not that Christ should suffer, in fearing death for Him, and not acknowledging the Life, he represents the weak ones of the Church. In that one Apostle then, that is, Peter, in the order of Apostles first and chiefest, in whom the Church was figured, both sorts were to be represented, that is, both the strong and weak; because the Church doth not exist without them both.

5. And hence also is that which was just now read, " Lord, if it be Thou, bid me come unto Thee on the water." [2] For I cannot do this in myself, but in Thee. He acknowledged what he had of himself, and what of Him, by whose will he believed that he could do that, which no human weakness could do. Therefore, " if it be Thou, bid me; " because when thou biddest, it will be done. What I cannot do by taking it upon myself,[3] Thou canst do by bidding me. And the Lord said " Come." [4] And without any doubting, at the word of Him who bade him, at the presence of Him who sustained, at the presence of Him who guided him, without any delay, Peter leaped down into the water, and began to walk. He was able to do what the Lord was doing, not in himself, but in the Lord. " For ye were sometimes darkness, but now are ye light in the Lord." [5] What no one can do in Paul, no one in Peter, no one in any other of the Apostles, this can he do in the Lord. Therefore well said Paul by a wholesome despising of himself, and commending of Him; " Was Paul crucified for you, or were ye baptized in the name of Paul?" [6] So then, ye are not *in* me, but together *with* me; not under me, but under Him.

6. Therefore Peter walked on the water by the bidding of the Lord, knowing that he could not have this power of himself. By faith he had strength to do what human weakness could not do. These are the strong ones of the Church. Mark this, hear, understand, and act accordingly. For we must not deal with the strong on any other

principle [7] than this, that so they should become weak; but thus we must deal with the weak, that they may become strong. But the presuming on their own strength keeps many back from strength. No one will have strength from God, but he who feels himself weak of himself. " God setteth apart a spontaneous rain for His inheritance." [8] Why do you, who know what I was about to say, anticipate me? Let your quickness be moderated, that the slowness of the rest may follow. This I said, and I say it again; hear it, receive it, and act on this principle. No one is made strong by God, but he who feels himself weak of his own self. And therefore a " spontaneous rain," as the Psalm says, " spontaneous; " not of our deserts, but " spontaneous." " A spontaneous rain " therefore " God setteth apart for his inheritance; " for " it was weak; but Thou hast perfected it." Because Thou " hast set apart for it a spontaneous rain," not looking to men's deserts, but to Thine own grace and mercy. This inheritance then was weakened, and acknowledged its own weakness in itself, that it might be strong in Thee. It would not be strengthened, if it were not weak, that by Thee it might be " perfected " in Thee.

7. See Paul a small portion of this inheritance, see him in weakness, who said, " I am not meet to be called an Apostle, because I persecuted the Church of God." Why then art thou an Apostle? " By the grace of God I am what I am. I am not meet, but by the grace of God I am what I am." Paul was " weak," but Thou hast " perfected " him. But now because by " the grace of God he is what he is," look what follows; " And His grace in me was not in vain, but I laboured more abundantly than they all." [9] Take heed lest thou lose by presumption what thou hast attained [10] through weakness. This is well, very well; that " I am not meet to be called an Apostle. By His grace I am what I am, and His grace in me was not in vain: " all most excellent. But, " I laboured more abundantly than they all; " thou hast begun, it would seem, to ascribe to thyself what a little before thou hadst given to God. Attend and follow on; " Yet not I, but the grace of God with me." Well! thou weak one; thou shalt be exalted in exceeding strength, seeing thou art not unthankful. Thou art the very same Paul, little in thyself; and great in the Lord. Thou art he who didst thrice beseech the Lord, that " the thorn of the flesh, the messenger of Satan, by whom thou wast buffeted, might be taken away from thee." [11] And what was said to thee? what didst thou hear when thou madest this petition? " My grace is sufficient for thee: for My strength is

---

[1] Rom. xv. 1. [2] Matt. xiv. 28. [3] *Præsumendo.*
[4] Matt. xiv. 29. [5] Eph. v. 8.
[6] 1 Cor. i. 13.

[7] *Alibi.* [8] Ps. lxvii. 10, Sept. (lxviii. 9, English version).
[9] 1 Cor. xv. 9, etc. [10] *Meruisti.*
[11] 2 Cor. xii. 7, 8.

made perfect in weakness." [1] For he was "weak," but Thou didst "perfect" him.

8. So Peter also said, " Bid me come unto Thee on the water." I who dare this am but a man, but it is no man whom I beseech. Let the God-man bid, that man may be able to do what man cannot do. "Come," said He. And He went down, and began to walk on the water ; and Peter was able, because the Rock had bidden him. Lo, what Peter was in the Lord ; what was he in himself? "When he saw the wind boisterous, he was afraid ; and beginning to sink, he cried out, Lord, I perish, save me." When he [2] looked for strength from the Lord, he had strength from the Lord ; as a man he tottered, but he returned to the Lord. " If I said, my foot hath slipped " [3] (they are the words of a Psalm, the notes of a holy song ; and if we acknowledge them they are our words too ; yea, if we will, they are ours also). " If I said my foot hath slipped." How slipped, except because it was mine own. And what follows? " Thy mercy, Lord, helped me." Not mine own strength, but Thy mercy. For will God forsake him as he totters, whom He heard when calling upon Him? Where then is that, " Who hath called upon God, and hath been forsaken by Him?" [4] where again is that, " Whosoever shall call on the Name of the Lord, shall be delivered." [5] Immediately reaching forth the help of His right hand, He lifted him up as he was sinking, and rebuked his distrust ; " O thou of little faith, wherefore didst thou doubt?" Once thou didst trust in Me, hast thou now doubted of Me?

9. Well, brethren, my sermon must be ended. Consider the world to be the sea ; the wind is boisterous, and there is a mighty tempest. Each man's peculiar lust is his tempest. Thou dost love God ; thou walkest upon the sea, and under thy feet is the swelling of the world. Thou dost love the world, it will swallow thee up. It skilleth only how to devour its lovers, not to carry them. But when thy heart is tossed about by lust, in order that thou mayest get the better of thy lust, call upon the Divinity of Christ. Think ye that the wind is then contrary, when there is this life's adversity? For so when there are wars, when there is tumult, when there is famine, when there is pestilence, when even to every individual man his private calamity arriveth, then the wind is thought to be contrary, then it is thought that God must be called upon. But when the world wears her smile of temporal happiness, it is as if there were no contrary wind. But do not ask upon this matter the tranquil state of the times : ask only your own lust. See if there be tranquillity within thee : see if there be no inner wind which overturns thee ; see to this. There needs great virtue to struggle with happiness, lest this very happiness allure, corrupt, and overthrow thee. There needs, I say, great virtue to struggle with happiness, and great happiness not to be overcome by happiness. Learn then to tread upon the world ; remember to trust in Christ. And " if thy foot have slipped ; " if thou totter, if some things there are which thou canst not overcome, if thou begin to sink, say, " Lord, I perish, save me." Say, " I perish," that thou perish not. For He only can deliver thee from the death of the body, who died in the body for thee. Let us turn to the Lord, etc.

SERMON XXVII.

[LXXVII. BEN.]

ON THE WORDS OF THE GOSPEL, MATT. XV. 21, "JESUS WENT OUT THENCE, AND WITHDREW INTO THE PARTS OF TYRE AND SIDON. AND BEHOLD, A CANAANITISH WOMAN," ETC.

1. THIS woman of Canaan, who has just now been brought before us in the lesson of the Gospel, shows us an example of humility, and the way of godliness ; shows us how to rise from humility unto exaltation. Now she was, as it appears, not of the people of Israel, of whom came the Patriarchs, and Prophets, and the parents of the Lord Jesus Christ according to the flesh ; of whom the Virgin Mary herself was, who was the Mother of Christ. This woman then was not of this people ; but of the Gentiles. For, as we have heard, the Lord " departed into the coasts of Tyre and Sidon, and behold, a woman of Canaan came out of the same coasts," [6] and with the greatest earnestness begged of Him the mercy to heal her daughter, " who was grievously vexed with a devil." Tyre and Sidon were not cities of the people of Israel, but of the Gentiles ; though they bordered on that people. So then, as being eager to obtain mercy she cried out, and boldly knocked ; and He made as though He heard her not, [7] not to the end that mercy might be refused her, but that her desire might be enkindled ; and not only that her desire might be enkindled, but that, as I have said before, her humility might be set forth. Therefore did she cry, while the Lord was as though He heard her not, but was ordering in silence what He was about to do. The disciples besought the Lord for her, and said, " Send her away ; for she crieth after us." And He said, " I am not sent, but unto the lost sheep of the house of Israel." [8]

2. Here arises a question out of these words ; " If He was not sent but unto the lost sheep

---

[1] 2 Cor. xii. 9.　　　　　[2] Præsumsit de Domino.
[3] Ps xciv. 18.　　　　　　[4] Ecclus. ii. 10, Sept.
[5] Joel ii. 32.

[6] Matt. xv. 21, etc.　　　[7] Dissimulabatur ab ea.
[8] Matt. xv. 23, 24.

of the house of Israel, how came we from among the Gentiles into Christ's fold? What is the meaning of the so deep economy [1] of this mystery, that whereas the Lord knew the purpose of His coming — that He might have a Church in all nations, He said that 'He was not sent, but unto the lost sheep of the house of Israel'?" We understand then by this that it behoved Him to manifest His Bodily presence, His Birth, the exhibition of His miracles, and the power of His Resurrection, among that people : that so it had been ordained, so set forth from the beginning, so predicted, and so fulfilled ; that Christ Jesus was to come to the nation of the Jews, to be seen and slain, and to gain from among them those whom He foreknew. For that people was not wholly condemned, but sifted. There was among them a great quantity of chaff, but there was also the hidden worth [2] of the grain ; there was among them that which was to be burnt, there was among them also that wherewith the barn was to be filled. For whence came the Apostles? whence came Peter? whence the rest?

3. Whence was Paul himself, who was first called Saul? That is, first proud, afterwards humble? For when he was Saul, his name was derived from Saül : now Saül was a proud king ; and in his reign he persecuted the humble David.[3] So when he who was afterwards Paul,[4] was Saul, he was proud, at that time a persecutor of the innocent, at that time a waster of the Church. For he had received letters from the chief priests (burning as he was with zeal for the synagogue, and persecuting the Christian name), that he might ‚show up whatever Christians he should find, to be punished.[5] While he is on his way, while he is breathing out slaughter, while he is thirsting for blood, he is thrown to the ground by the voice of Christ from heaven the persecutor, he is raised up the preacher. In him was fulfilled that which is written in the Prophet, " I will wound and I will heal." [6] For that only in man doth God wound, which lifteth itself up against God. He is no unkind [7] physician who opens the swelling, who cuts, or cauterizes the corrupted part. He gives pain, it is true ; but he only gives pain, that he may bring the patient on to health. He gives pain ; but if he did not, he would do no good. Christ then by one word laid Saul low, and raised up Paul ; that is, He laid low the proud, and raised up the humble. For what was the reason of his change of name, that whereas he was afore called Saul, he chose afterwards to be called Paul ; but that he acknowledged in himself that the name of Saul when he was a persecutor, had been a name of pride? He chose therefore a humble name ; to

be called Paul, that is, the least. For Paul is, "the least." Paul is nothing else but little. And now glorying in this name, and giving us a lesson [8] of humility, he says, " I am the least of the Apostles." [9] Whence then, whence was he, but of the people of the Jews? Of them were the other Apostles, of them was Paul, of them were they whom the same Paul mentions, as having seen the Lord after His resurrection. For he says, " That He was seen of above five hundred brethren at once ; of whom the greater part remain unto this present, but some are fallen asleep." [10]

4. Of this people too, of the people of the Jews, were they, who when Peter was speaking, setting forth the Passion, and Resurrection, and Divinity of Christ (after that the Holy Ghost had been received, when all they on whom the Holy Ghost had come, spake with the tongues of all nations), being pricked in spirit as they heard him, sought counsel for their salvation, understanding as they did that they were guilty of the Blood of Christ ; because they had crucified, and slain Him, in whose name though slain by them they saw such great miracles wrought ; and saw the presence of the Holy Ghost. And so seeking counsel they received for answer ; " Repent, and be baptized every one of you, in the name of our Lord Jesus Christ, and your sins shall be forgiven you." [11] Who should despair of the forgiveness of his sins, when the crime of killing Christ was forgiven to those who were guilty of it? They were converted from among this people of the Jews ; were converted, and baptized. They came to the Lord's table, and in faith drank that Blood, which in their fury they had shed. Now in what sort they were converted, how decidedly,[12] and how perfectly, the Acts of the Apostles show. " For they sold all that they possessed, and laid the prices of their things at the Apostles' feet ; and distribution was made unto every man according as he had need ; and no man said that ought was his own, but they had all things common." [13] And, " They were," as it is written, " of one heart and of one soul." Lo here are the sheep of whom He said, " I am not 'sent but unto the lost sheep of the house of Israel." For to them He exhibited His Presence, for them in the midst of their violence against Him He prayed as He was being crucified, " Father, forgive them, for they know not what they do." [14] The Physician understood how those frenzied men were in their madness putting the Physician to death, and in putting their Physician to death, though they knew it not, were preparing a medicine for themselves. For by the Lord so put to death are all

[1] *Dispensatio.*
[2] *Dignitas.*
[3] 1 Sam. xviii. 29.   [4] 1 Cor. i. 1.   [5] Acts ix. 1, etc.
[6] Deut. xxxii. 39.   [7] *Impius.*
[8] *Commendans.*   [9] 1 Cor. xv. 9.   [10] 1 Cor. xv. 6.
[11] Acts ii. 38.   [12] *Planè.*   [13] Acts iv. 32, etc.
[14] Luke xxiii. 34.

we cured, by His Blood redeemed, by the Bread of His Body delivered from famine. This Presence then did Christ exhibit to the Jews. And so He said, "I am not sent, but unto the lost sheep of the house of Israel;" that to them He might exhibit the Presence of His body; not that He might disregard, and pass over the sheep which He had among the Gentiles.

5. For to the Gentiles He went not Himself, but sent His disciples. And in this was fulfilled what the Prophet said; "A people whom I have not known hath served Me." See how deep, how clear, how express the prophecy is; "a people whom I have not known," that is, to whom I have not exhibited My Presence, "hath served Me." How? It goes on to say, "By the hearing of the ear they have obeyed Me:"[1] that is, they have believed, not by seeing, but by hearing. Therefore have the Gentiles the greater praise. For the others saw and slew Him; the Gentiles heard and believed. Now it was to call and gather together the Gentiles, that that might be fulfilled which we have just now chanted, "Gather us from among the Gentiles, that we may confess to Thy Name, and glory in Thy praise,"[2] that the Apostle Paul was sent. He, the least, made great, not by himself, but by Him whom he once persecuted, was sent to the Gentiles,[3] from a robber become a shepherd, from a wolf a sheep. He, the least Apostle, was sent to the Gentiles, and laboured much among the Gentiles, and through him the Gentiles believed. His Epistles are the witnesses.

6. Of this you have a very sacred figure in the Gospel also. A daughter of a ruler of the synagogue was really dead, and her father besought the Lord, that He would go to her; he had left her sick, and in extreme danger.[4] The Lord set out to visit and heal the sick; in the mean time it was announced that she was dead, and it was told the father; "Thy daughter is dead, trouble not the Master." But the Lord who knew that He could raise the dead, did not deprive the despairing father of hope, and said to him, "Fear not: only believe." So he set out to the maiden; and in the way a certain woman, who had suffered from an issue of blood, and in her lengthened illness had spent to no purpose all that she had upon physicians, pressed herself in, how she could, amongst the crowds. When she touched the border of His garment, she was made whole. And the Lord said, "Who touched Me?" The disciples who knew not what had taken place, and saw that He was thronged by the multitudes, and that He was troubling Himself about one single woman who had touched Him gently, answered in astonishment, "The multitudes press Thee, and sayest Thou, Who touched Me?' And He said, Somebody hath touched Me? for the other press, she hath touched. The many[5] then rudely[6] press the Body of Christ, few touch it healthfully. "Somebody," saith He, "hath touched Me, for I perceive that virtue is gone out of Me. And when the woman saw that she was not hid, she fell down at His feet," and confessed what had taken place. After this He set out again, and arrived whither He was going, and raised to life the young daughter of the ruler of the synagogue who was found to be dead.

7. This was a literal fact, and was fulfilled as it is related; but nevertheless these very things which were done by the Lord had some further signification, being (if we may so say) a sort of visible and significative words. And this is especially plain, in that place where He sought fruit on the tree out of season, and because He found none, dried up the tree by His curse.[7] Unless this action be regarded as a figure, there is no good meaning in it; first to have sought fruit on that tree when it was not the season for fruit on any tree; and then even if it were now the time of fruit, what fault in the tree was it to have none? But because it signified, that He seeketh not for leaves only, but for fruit also, that is, not for the words only, but for the deeds of men, by drying up that tree whereon he found only leaves, he signified their punishment who can speak good things, but will not do them. And so it is in this place also. For surely there is a mystery in it. He who foreknoweth all things saith, "Who touched Me?" The Creator maketh Himself like one who is ignorant; and He asketh, who not only knew this, but who even foreknew all other things. Doubtless there is something which Christ would speak to us in this significant mystery.

8. That daughter of the ruler of the synagogue was a figure of the people of the Jews, for whose sake Christ had come, who said, "I am not sent but unto the lost sheep of the house of Israel." But the woman who suffered from the issue of blood, figured the Church from among the Gentiles, to which Christ was not sent in His bodily presence. He was going to the former, He was intent on her recovery; meanwhile the latter runs to meet Him, touches His border as though He knew it not; that is, she is healed by Him who is in some sense absent. He saith, "Who touched Me?" as though He would say; I do not know this people; "A people whom I have not known hath served Me. Some one hath touched Me. For I perceive that virtue is gone out of Me;" that is, that My Gospel hath gone out and filled the whole world. Now it is the border that is touched, a small and outside[8] part of the gar-

---

[1] Ps. xvii 44, 45 (xviii. 43, 44, English version).

[2] Ps cvi 47.   [3] Acts ix. 15.   [4] Luke viii. 41, etc.

[5] Serm. xii. (lxii.) 5 (4).   [6] Molesti.

[7] Mark xi. 13, etc.   [8] Extrema.

ment. Consider the Apostles as it were the garment of Christ. Among them Paul was the border; that is, the last and least. For he said of himself that he was both; "I am the least of the Apostles." [1] For he was called after them all, he believed after them all, he healed more than they all. The Lord was not sent but "unto the lost sheep of the house of Israel." But because a "people whom He had not known, was also to serve Him, and to obey Him in the hearing of the ear," He made mention of them too when He was among the others. For the same Lord said in a certain place, "Other sheep I have which are not of this fold; them also I must bring, that there may be one fold and one shepherd." [2]

9. Of these was this woman; therefore she was not refused, but only put off. "I am not sent," saith He, "but unto the lost sheep of the house of Israel." And she was instant in her cries : she persevered, she knocked, as if she had already heard, "Ask, and receive; seek, and thou shalt find; knock, and it shall be opened unto thee." She kept on, she knocked. For so the Lord when He spake these words, "Ask, and ye shall receive; seek, and ye shall find; knock, and it shall be opened unto you;" [3] had also said before, "Give not that which is holy unto the dogs, neither cast ye your pearls before swine, lest they trample them under their feet, and turn again and rend you;" [4] that is, lest after despising your pearls, they should even ill use you.[5] Cast not therefore before them what they despise.

10. And how distinguish we (as might be answered) who are "swine," and who are "dogs"? This has been shown in the case of this woman. For He only answered to her entreaties, "It is not meet to take the children's bread, and to cast it to dogs." [6] Thou art a dog, thou art one of the Gentiles, thou worshippest idols. But for dogs what is so proper [7] as to lick stones? "It is not" therefore "meet to take the children's bread, and to cast it to dogs." Had she retired after these words, she had gone away as she had come, a dog; but by knocking she was made of a dog one of human kind.[8] For she persevered in asking, and from that reproach as it were she manifested her humility, and obtained mercy. For she was not excited, nor incensed, because she was called a dog, as she asked the blessing, and prayed for mercy, but she said, "Truth, Lord;" [9] "Thou hast called me a dog, and truly a dog I am, I acknowledge my name : it is the Truth that speaks : but I ought not on that account to be refused this blessing. Verily I am a dog; 'yet the dogs

eat of the crumbs which fall from their masters' table.' It is but a moderate and a small blessing I desire; I do not press to the table, I only seek for the crumbs."

11. See, Brethren, how the value of humility is set before us! The Lord had called her a dog; and she did not say, "I am not," but she said, "I am." And because she acknowledged herself to be a dog, immediately the Lord said, "Woman, great is thy faith; be it unto thee even as thou hast asked." [10] Thou hast acknowledged thyself to be a dog, I now acknowledge thee to be of human kind. "O woman, great is thy faith;" thou hast asked, and sought, and knocked; receive, find, be it opened unto thee. See, Brethren, how in this woman who was a Canaanite, that is, who came from among the Gentiles, and was a type, that is a figure, of the Church, the grace of humility has been eminently set before us. For the Jewish nation, to the end that it might be deprived of the grace of the Gospel, was puffed up with pride, because to them it had been vouchsafed [11] to receive the Law, because out of this nation the Patriarchs had proceeded, the Prophets had sprung, Moses, the servant of God, had done the great miracles in Egypt which we have heard of in the Psalm,[12] had led the people through the Red Sea, when the waters retired, and had received the Law, which he gave to this people. This was that whereupon the Jewish nation was lifted up, and through this very pride it happened that they were not willing to humble themselves to Christ the author of humility, and the restrainer of proud swelling, to God the Physician, who, being God, for this cause became Man, that man might know himself to be but man. O mighty remedy! If this remedy cure not pride, I know not what can cure it. He is God, and is made Man; He lays aside His Divinity, that is, in a manner sequestrates,[13] hides, that is, what was His Own, and appears only in that He had taken to Him. Being God He is made man : and man will not acknowledge himself to be man, that is, will not acknowledge himself to be mortal, will not acknowledge himself to be frail, will not acknowledge himself to be a sinner, will not acknowledge himself to be sick, that so at least as sick he may seek the physician; but what is more perilous still, he fancies himself in sound health.

12. So then for this reason that people did not come to Him, that is by reason of pride; and the natural branches are said to be broken off from the olive tree, that is from that people founded [14] by the Patriarchs; in other words, the Jews are for their punishment justly barren through the spirit of pride; and the wild olive is grafted into that olive tree. The wild olive tree

---

[1] 1 Cor. xv. 9. [2] John x. 16. [3] Matt. vii. 7.
[4] Matt. vii. 6. [5] *Molesti.* [6] Matt. xv. 26.
[7] *Familiare.* [8] *Homo.* [9] Matt. xv. 27.

[10] Matt. xv. 28. [11] *Meruisset.* [12] Ps. cvi.
[13] *Sequestrat.* [14] *Creato.*

is the people of the Gentiles. So says the Apostle, "that the wild olive tree is grafted into the good olive tree, but the natural branches are broken off." [1] Because of pride they were broken off: and the wild olive tree grafted in because of humility. This humility did the woman show forth when she said, "Truth, Lord," "I am a dog, I desire only the crumbs." In this humility also did the Centurion please Him; who when he desired that his servant might be healed by the Lord, and the Lord said, "I will come and heal him," answered, "Lord, I am not worthy that Thou shouldest come under my roof, but speak the word only, and my servant shall be healed. I am not worthy that Thou shouldest come under my roof." [2] He did not receive Him into his house, but he had received Him already in his heart. The more humble, the more capacious, and the more full. For the hills drive back the water, but the valleys are filled by it. And what then, what said the Lord to those who followed Him after that he had said, " I am not worthy that Thou shouldest come under my roof"? "Verily I say unto you, I have not fouud so great faith, no, not in Israel;" that is, in that people to whom I came, "I have not found so great faith." And whence great? Great from being the least, that is, great from humility. "I have not found so great faith;" like a grain of mustard seed, which by how much smaller it is, by so much the more burning is it. Therefore did the Lord at once graft the wild olive into the good olive tree. He did it then when He said, "Verily I say unto you, I have not found so great faith, no, not in Israel."

13. Lastly, mark what follows. "Therefore," — that is, because "I have not found so great faith in Israel," that is, so great humility with faith, — "Therefore I say unto you, that many shall come from the east and west, and shall sit down with Abraham and Isaac and Jacob in the kingdom of heaven." [3] "Shall sit," that is, "shall rest." For we must not form notions of carnal banquets there, or desire any such thing in that kingdom, as to change not vices for virtues, but only to make an exchange of vices. For it is one thing to desire the kingdom of heaven for the sake of wisdom and life eternal; another, for the sake of earthly felicity, as though there we should have it in more abundant and greater measure. If thou think to be rich in that kingdom, thou dost not cut off, but only changest desire; and yet rich thou wilt really be, and in none other place but there wilt thou be rich; for here thy want gathers together the abundance of things. Why have rich men much? Because they want much. A greater want heaps together as it were greater means; there want itself shall

die. Then thou shalt be truly rich, when thou shalt be in want of nothing. For now thou art not surely rich, and an Angel poor, who has not horses, and carriages, and servants. Why? Because he does not want any of these: because in proportion to his greater strength, is his want the less. Therefore there there are riches, and the true riches. Figure not to yourselves then banquets of this earth in that place. For the banquets of this world are daily medicines; they are necessary for a kind of sickness we have, wherewith we are born. This sickness every one is sensible of, when the hour for refreshment is passed. Wouldest thou see how great a sickness this is, that as an acute fever would be fatal in seven days? Do not fancy thyself then to be in health. Immortality will be health. For this present is only one long sickness. Because thou dost support thy disease by daily medicines; thou fanciest thyself in health; take away the medicines, and then see what thou canst do.

14. For from the moment we are born, we must needs be dying. This disease must needs bring us to death. This indeed physicians say when they examine their patients. For instance, "This man has the dropsy, he is dying; this disease cannot be cured. This man has the leprosy: [4] this disease too cannot be cured. He is in a consumption. Who can cure this? He must needs die, he must perish." See, the physician has now pronounced that he is in a consumption; that he cannot but die; and yet sometimes the dropsical patient does not die of his disease, and the leprous does not die of his, nor the consumptive patient of his; but now it is absolutely necessary that every one who is born should die of this. He dies of it, he cannot do otherwise. This the physician and the unskilled both pronounce upon; and though he die somewhat more slowly, does he on that account not die? Where then is there true health, except where there is true immortality? But if it be true immortality, and no corruption, no wasting, what need will there be there of nourishment? Therefore, when you hear it said, "They shall sit down with Abraham, Isaac, and Jacob;" [3] get not your body, but your soul in order. There shalt thou be filled; and this inner [5] man has its proper food. In relation to it is it said, "Blessed are they which do hunger and thirst after righteousness, for they shall be filled." [6] And so truly filled shall they be that they shall hunger no more.

15. Therefore did the Lord graff in at once the wild olive tree, when He said, "Many shall come from the east and west, and shall sit down with Abraham, and Isaac, and Jacob, in the kingdom of heaven;" that is, they shall be

[1] Rom. xi. 17, etc.   [2] Matt. viii. 7, etc.   [4] Elephantiosus.   [5] Interior venter.
[3] Matt. viii. 11.   [6] Matt. v. 6.

grafted into the good olive tree. For Abraham, and Isaac, and Jacob, are the roots of this olive tree; "but the children of the kingdom," that is, the unbelieving Jews, "shall go away into outer darkness." The "natural branches shall be broken off," that the "wild olive tree may be grafted in." Now why did the natural branches deserve to be cut off, except for pride? why the wild olive tree to be grafted in, except for humility? Whence also that woman said, "Truth, Lord, yet the dogs eat of the crumbs which fall from their masters' table." [1] And thereupon she hears, "O woman, great is thy faith." [2] And so again that centurion, "I am not worthy that Thou shouldest come under my roof." [3] "Verily I say unto you, I have not found so great faith, no, not in Israel." [4] Let us then learn, or let us hold fast, humility. If we have it not yet, let us learn it; if we have it, let us not lose it. If we have it not yet, let us have it, that we may be grafted in; if we have it already, let us hold it fast, that we may not be cut off.

SERMON XXVIII.

[LXXVIII. BEN.]

ON THE WORDS OF THE GOSPEL, MATT. XVII. 1, "AFTER SIX DAYS JESUS TAKETH WITH HIM PETER, AND JAMES, AND JOHN HIS BROTHER," ETC.

1. WE must now look into and treat of that vision which the Lord showed on the mount. For it is this of which He had said, "Verily I say unto you, there be some standing here which shall not taste of death till they see the Son of Man in His Kingdom." [5] Then began the passage which has just been read. "When He had said this, after six days He took three disciples, Peter, and James, and John, and went up into a mountain." [6] These three were those "some," of whom He had said, "There be some here which shall not taste of death, till they see the Son of Man in His kingdom." There is no small difficulty here. For that mount was not the whole extent of His kingdom. [7] What is a mountain to Him who possesseth the heavens? Which we not only read He doth, but in some sort see it with the eyes of the heart. He calleth that His kingdom, which in many places He calleth the "kingdom of heaven." Now the kingdom of heaven is the kingdom of the saints. "For the heavens declare the glory of God." [8] And of these heavens it is immediately said in the Psalm, "There is no speech nor language where their voice is not heard. Their sound is gone out through all the earth, and their words unto the end of the world." [9] Whose words, but of

the heavens? And of the Apostles, and all faithful preachers of the word of God. These heavens therefore shall reign together with Him who made the heavens. Now consider what was done, that this might be made manifest.

2. The Lord Jesus Himself shone bright as the sun; His raiment became white as the snow; and Moses and Elias talked with Him. [10] Jesus Himself indeed shone as the sun, signifying that "He is the light which lighteth every man that cometh into the world." [11] What this sun is to the eyes of the flesh, that is He to the eyes of the heart; and what that is to the flesh of men, that is He to their hearts. Now His raiment is His Church. For if the raiment be not held together by him who puts it on, it will fall off. Of this raiment, Paul was as it were a sort of last border. For he says himself, "I am the least of the Apostles." [12] And in another place, "I am the last of the Apostles." Now in a garment the border is the last and least part. Wherefore as that woman which suffered from an issue of blood, when she had touched the Lord's border was made whole, [13] so the Church which came from out of the Gentiles, was made whole by the preaching of Paul. What wonder if the Church is signified by white raiment, when you hear the Prophet Isaiah saying, "Though your sins be as scarlet, I will make them white as snow"? [14] Moses and Elias, that is, the Law and the Prophets, what avail they, except they converse with the Lord? Except they give witness to the Lord, who would read the Law or the Prophets? Mark how briefly the Apostle expresses this; "For by the Law is the knowledge of sin; but now the righteousness of God without the Law is manifested:" behold the sun; "being witnessed by the Law and the Prophets," [15] behold the shining of the Sun.

3. Peter sees this, and as a man savouring the things of men says, "Lord, it is good for us to be here." [16] He had been wearied with the multitude, he had found now the mountain's solitude; there he had Christ the Bread of the soul. What! should he depart thence again to travail and pains, possessed of a holy love to Godward, and thereby of a good conversation? He wished well for himself; and so he added, "If Thou wilt, let us make here three tabernacles; one for Thee, and one for Moses, and one for Elias." To this the Lord made no answer; but notwithstanding Peter was answered. "For while he yet spake, a bright cloud came, and overshadowed them." [17] He desired three tabernacles; the heavenly answer showed him that we have One, which human judgment desired to divide. Christ, the Word of God, the Word of

---

[1] Matt. xv. 27. [2] Matt. xv. 28. [3] Matt. viii. 8.
[4] Matt. viii. 10. [5] Matt. xvi. 28.
[6] Matt. xvii. 1; Luke ix. 28.
[7] *Regnum comprehensum.* [8] Ps. xix. 1.
[9] Ps. xix. 3, 4.

[10] Matt. xvii. 2, 3. [11] John i. 9. [12] 1 Cor. xv. 9.
[13] Mark v. 34. [14] Isa. i. 18. [15] Rom. iii. 20, 21.
[16] Matt. xvii. 4. [17] Matt. xvii. 5.

God in the Law, the Word in the Prophets. Why, Peter, dost thou seek to divide them? It were more fitting for thee to join them. Thou seekest three; understand that they are but One.

4. As the cloud then overshadowed them, and in a way made one tabernacle for them, "a voice also sounded out of the cloud, which said, This is My beloved Son." Moses was there; Elias was there; yet it was not said, "These are My beloved sons." For the Only Son is one thing; adopted sons another. He was singled out [1] in whom the Law and the prophets glorified. "This is My beloved Son, in whom I am well pleased; hear Him!" Because ye have heard Him in the Prophets, and ye have heard Him in the Law. And where have ye not heard Him? "When they heard this, they fell" to the earth. See then in the Church is exhibited to us the Kingdom of God. Here is the Lord, here the Law and the Prophets; but the Lord as the Lord; the Law in Moses, Prophecy in Elias; only they as servants and as ministers. They as vessels; He as the fountain: Moses and the Prophets spake, and wrote; but when they poured out, they were filled from Him.

5. But the Lord stretched out His hand, and raised them as they lay. And then "they saw no man, save Jesus only." [2] What does this mean? When the Apostle was being read, you heard, "For now we see through a glass darkly, but then face to face." [3] And "tongues shall cease," when that which we now hope for and believe shall come. In then that they fell to the earth, they signified that we die, for it was said to the flesh, "Earth thou art, and unto earth shalt thou return." [4] But when the Lord raised them up, He signified the resurrection. After the resurrection, what is the Law to thee? what Prophecy? Therefore neither Moses nor Elias is seen. He only remaineth to thee, "Who in the beginning was the Word, and the Word was with God, and the Word was God." [5] He remaineth to thee, "that God may be all in all." Moses will be there; but now no more the Law. We shall see Elias there too; but now no more the Prophet. For the Law and the Prophets have only given witness to Christ, that it behoved Him to suffer, and to rise again from the dead the third day, and to enter into His glory. And in this glory is fulfilled what He hath promised to them that love Him, "He that loveth Me shall be loved of My Father, and I will love him." [6] And as if it were said, What wilt Thou give him, seeing Thou wilt love him? "And I will manifest Myself unto him." Great gift! great promise! God doth not reserve for thee as a reward anything of His own, but Himself. O thou covetous one; why doth not what

Christ promiseth suffice thee? Thou dost seem to thyself to be rich; yet if thou have not God, what hast thou? Another is poor, yet if he hath God, what hath he not?

6. Come down, Peter: thou wast desiring to rest on the mount; come down, "preach the word, be instant in season, out of season, reprove, rebuke, exhort with all longsuffering and doctrine." [7] Endure, labour hard, bear thy measure of torture; that thou mayest possess what is meant by the white raiment of the Lord, through the brightness and the beauty of an upright labouring in charity. For when the Apostle was being read we heard in praise of charity, "She seeketh not her own.[8] She seeketh not her own;" since she gives what she possesses. In another place there is more danger in the expression, if you do not understand it right. For the Apostle, charging the faithful members of Christ after this rule of charity, says, " Let no man seek his own, but another's." [9] For on hearing this, covetousness is ready with its deceits, that in a matter of business under pretence of seeking another's, it may defraud a man, and so, "seek not his own, but another's." But let covetousness restrain itself, let justice come forth; so let us hear and understand. It is to charity that it is said, "Let no man seek his own, but another's." Now, O thou covetous one, if thou wilt still resist, and twist the precept rather to this point, that thou shouldest covet what is another's; then lose what is thine own. But as I know thee well, thou dost wish to have both thine own and another's. Thou wilt commit fraud that thou mayest have what is another's; submit then to robbery that thou mayest lose thine own. Thou dost not wish to seek thine own, but then thou takest away what is another's. Now this if thou do, thou doest not well. Hear and listen, thou covetous one: the Apostle explains to thee in another place more clearly this that he said, " Let no man seek his own, but another's." He says of himself, " Not seeking mine own profit, but the profit of many, that they may be saved." [10] This Peter understood not yet when he desired to live on the mount with Christ. He was reserving this for thee, Peter, after death. But now He saith Himself, " Come down, to labour in the earth; in the earth to serve, to be despised, and crucified in the earth. The Life came down, that He might be slain; the Bread came down, that He might hunger; the Way came down, that He might be wearied in the way; the Fountain came down, that He might thirst; and dost thou refuse to labour? 'Seek not thine own.' Have charity, preach the truth; so shalt thou come to eternity, where thou shalt find security."

---

[1] *Commendabatur.*   [2] Matt. xvii. 7, 8.   [3] 1 Cor. xiii. 12.   [7] 2 Tim. iv. 2.   [8] 1 Cor. xiii. 5.   [9] 1 Cor. x. 24.
[4] Gen. iii. 19, Sept.   [5] John i 1.   [6] John xiv. 21.   [10] 1 Cor. x. 33.

SERMON XXIX.

[LXXIX. BEN.]

AGAIN ON THE WORDS OF THE GOSPEL, MATT. XVII., WHERE JESUS SHOWED HIMSELF ON THE MOUNT TO HIS THREE DISCIPLES.

1. WE heard when the Holy Gospel was being read of the great vision on the mount, in which Jesus showed Himself to the three disciples, Peter, James, and John. "His face did shine as the sun:" this is a figure of the shining of the Gospel. "His raiment was white as the snow:" [1] this is a figure of the purity of the Church, to which it was said by the Prophet, "Though your sins be as scarlet, I will make them white as snow." [2] Elias and Moses were talking with Him; because the grace of the Gospel receives witness from the Law and the Prophets. The Law is represented in Moses, the Prophets in Elias; to speak briefly. For there are the mercies of God vouchsafed through a holy Martyr to be rehearsed. Let us give ear. Peter desired three tabernacles to be made, one for Moses, one for Elias, and one for Christ. The solitude of the mountain had charms for him; he had been wearied with the tumult of the world's business. But why sought he three tabernacles, but because he knew not as yet the unity of the Law, and of Prophecy, and of the Gospel? Lastly, he was corrected by the cloud, "While he yet spake, behold, a bright cloud overshadowed them." Lo, the cloud hath made one tabernacle; wherefore didst thou seek for three? "And a voice came out of the cloud, This is My beloved Son, in whom I am well pleased, hear ye Him." [3] Elias speaketh; but "hear Him;" Moses speaketh; but "hear Him." The Prophets speak, the Law speaketh; but "hear Him," who is the voice of the Law, and the tongue of the Prophets. He spake in them, and when He vouchsafed so to do, He appeared in His own person. "Hear ye Him:" let us then hear Him. When the Gospel spake, think it was the cloud: from thence hath the voice sounded out to us. Let us hear Him; that is, let us do what He saith, let us hope for what He hath promised.

SERMON XXX.

[LXXX. BEN.]

ON THE WORDS OF THE GOSPEL, MATT. XVII. 19, "WHY COULD NOT WE CAST IT OUT"? ETC., AND ON PRAYER.

1. OUR Lord Jesus Christ reproved unbelief even in His own disciples, as we heard just now when the Gospel was being read. For when they had said, "Why could not we cast him out?"

He answered, "Because of your unbelief." [4] If the Apostles were unbelievers, who is a believer? What must the lambs do, if the rams totter? Yet the mercy of the Lord did not disdain them in their unbelief; but reproved, nourished, perfected, crowned them. For they themselves, as mindful of their own weakness, said to Him, as we read in a certain place in the Gospel, "Lord, increase our faith. [5] Lord," say they, "increase our faith." The knowing that they had a deficiency, was the first advantage; a greater happiness still, to know who it was of whom they were asking. "Lord," say they, "increase our faith." See, if they did not bring their hearts as it were to the fountain, and knocked that that might be opened to them, out of which they might fill them. For He would that men should knock at Him, not that He might repel those that knock, but that He might exercise those who long.

2. For do you think, Brethren, that God doth not know what is needful for you? He knoweth and preventeth our desires, who knoweth our want. And so when He taught His disciples to pray, and warned them not to use many words in prayer, He saith, "Use not many words; for your Father knoweth what things ye have need of before ye ask Him." [6] Now the Lord saith something different from this. What is this? Because He misliked that we should use many words in prayer, He said to us, "When ye pray, use not many words; for your Father knoweth what things ye have need of before ye ask Him." If our "Father knoweth what things we have need of before we ask Him," why do we use even few words? What is the use of prayer at all, if "our Father knoweth" already "what things we have need of"? He saith to one, Do not make thy prayer to Me at great length; for I know what is needful for thee. If so, Lord, why should I so much as pray at all? Thou wouldest not that I should use long prayers, yea rather Thou dost even bid me to use near none at all. And then what meaneth that precept in another place? For He who saith, "Use not many words in prayer," saith in another place, "Ask, and it shall be given you." [7] And that thou mightest not think that this first precept to ask was given cursorily, He added, "Seek, and ye shall find." And that thou mightest not think that this too was cursorily given, see what He added further, see with what He finished. "Knock, and it shall be opened unto you:" see what He added. He would have thee ask that thou mayest receive, and seek that thou mayest find, and knock that thou mayest enter in. Seeing then that our Father knoweth already what is needful for us, how and

---

[1] Matt. xvii. 2.   [2] Isa. i. 18.   [3] Matt. xvii. 5.   [4] Matt. xvii. 19, 20.   [5] Luke xvii. 5.   [6] Matt. vi. 7, 8.   [7] Matt. vii. 7.

why do we ask? why seek? why knock? why weary ourselves in asking, and seeking, and knocking, to instruct Him who knoweth already? And in another place the words of the Lord are, "Men ought always to pray, and not to faint."[1] If men "ought always to pray," how doth He say, "Use not many words"? How can I always pray, if I so quickly make an end? Here Thou biddest me to finish quickly; there "always to pray and not to faint:" what doth this mean? Now that thou mayest understand this, "ask, seek, knock." For for this cause is it closed, not to shut thee out, but to exercise thee. Therefore, brethren, ought we to exhort to prayer, both ourselves and you. For other hope have we none amid the manifold evils of this present world, than to knock in prayer, to believe and to maintain the belief firm in the heart, that thy Father only doth not give thee what He knoweth is not expedient for thee. For thou knowest what thou dost desire; He knoweth what is good for thee. Imagine thyself under a physician, and in weak health, as is the very truth; for all this life of ours is a weakness; and a long life is nothing else but a prolonged weakness. Imagine thyself then to be sick under the physician's hand. Thou hast a desire to ask thy physician leave to drink a draught of fresh wine. Thou art not prohibited from asking, for it may chance to do thee no harm, or even good to receive it. Do not then hesitate to ask; ask, hesitate not; but if thou receive not, do not take it to heart. Now if thou wouldest act thus in the hands of a man, the physician of the body, how much more in the hands of God, who is the Physician, the Creator, and Restorer, both of thy body and soul?

3. Wherefore, see how the Lord in this passage exhorted His disciples to prayer, when He said, "Ye could not cast out this devil because of your unbelief."[2] For then exhorting them to prayer He ended thus; "this kind is not cast out but by prayer and fasting." If a man must pray, to cast out devils from another, how much more to cast out his own covetousness? how much more to cast out his own drunkenness? how much more to cast out his own luxuriousness? how much more to cast out his own uncleanness? How many things in a man are there, which if they are persevered in, allow of no admission into the kingdom of heaven! Consider, Brethren, how a physician is entreated for the preservation of temporal health, how, if any one is desperately ill, is he ashamed or slow to throw himself at a man's feet? to bathe in tears the footsteps of any very able chief physician? And what if the physician say to him, "Thou canst not else be cured, except I bind thee, and use the fire and knife"? He will answer, "Do what thou wilt, only cure me." With what eagerness does he long for the health of a few days, fleeting as a vapour, that for it he is content to be bound, and submit to the fire, and knife, and to be watched, that he neither eat nor drink what, or when, he pleases! All this he will endure, that he may die a little later; and yet he will not endure ever so little, that he may never die. If God, who is the Heavenly Physician over us, saith to thee, "Wilt thou be cured?" what wouldest thou say but "Yes." Or it may be thou wouldest not say so, because thou fanciest thyself to be in health, that is, because thou art more grievously sick.

4. For if we suppose two sick persons, one who implores the physician with tears, the other, who in his sickness with infatuation derides him; he will hold out hope to the one that weeps, and will deplore the case of the other that laughs. Why? but because the sounder in health he thinks himself, the more dangerous his sickness is! This was the case with the Jews. Christ came to them that were sick; He found them all sick. Let no one then flatter himself on his healthful state, lest the physician give him up.[3] He found all sick; it is the Apostle's judgment, "For all have sinned, and come short of the glory of God."[4] Though He found them all sick, yet were there two sorts of sick folk. The one came to the Physician, clave to Christ, heard, honoured, followed Him, were converted. He received all without disdaining any, for to heal them, who healed of free favour, who cured by Almighty power. When then He received them, and joined them to Himself to be healed, they rejoiced. But there was another sort of sick, who had already become infatuated through the sickness of iniquity, and did not know themselves to be sick; they mocked Him, because He received the sick, and said to His disciples, "Lo, what manner of man is your Master, who eateth with publicans and sinners." And He who knew what and who they were answered them, "They that be whole need not a physician, but they that are sick." And He showed them who the "whole" were, and who the "sick." "I am not come," He saith, "to call the righteous, but sinners."[5] If sinners, He would say, do not come to Me, wherefore am I come? for whose sake am I come? If all are whole, wherefore hath so great a Physician come down from heaven? why hath He prepared for us a medicine not out of His stores,[6] but of His own blood? That sort of sick then who had a milder sickness, who felt themselves to be sick, clave to the Physician, that they might be healed. But they whose sickness was

---

[1] Luke xviii. 1.   [2] Matt. xvii. 19, 20.
[3] *Renuntiet ad illum.*   [4] Rom. iii. 23.
[5] Matt. ix. 11, etc.   [6] *Armario suo.*

more dangerous mocked the Physician, and abused the sick. Whither did their frenzy proceed at last? To seize the Physician, bind, scourge, crown Him with thorns, hang Him upon a Tree, kill Him on the Cross! Why dost thou marvel? The sick slew the Physician; but the Physician by being slain healed the frantic patient.

5. For first, not forgetting on the Cross His own character,[1] and manifesting forth His patience to us, and giving us an example of love to our enemies; as He saw them raging round Him, who had known their disease, seeing He was the Physician, who had known the frenzy by which they had become infatuated, He said at once to the Father, "Father, forgive them; for they know not what they do."[2] Now suppose ye that those Jews were not malignant, cruel, bloody, turbulent, and enemies of the Son of God? Suppose ye that that cry, "Father, forgive them, for they know not what they do," was ineffectual and in vain? He saw them all, but He knew amongst them those that should one day be His. In a word, He died, because it was so expedient, that by His Death He might kill death. God died, that an exchange might be effected by a kind of heavenly contract, that man might not see death. For Christ is God, but He died not in that Nature in which He is God. For the same Person is God and man; for God and man is one Christ. The human nature[3] was assumed, that we might be changed for the better; He did not degrade the Divine[4] Nature down to the lower. For He assumed that which He was not, He did not lose that which He was. Forasmuch then as He is both God and man, being pleased that we should live by that which was His, He died in that which was ours. For He had nothing Himself, whereby He could die; nor had we anything whereby we could live. For what was He who had nothing whereby He could die? "In the beginning was the Word, and the Word was with God, and the Word was God."[5] If thou seek for anything in God whereby He may die, thou wilt not find it. But we all die, who are flesh; men bearing about sinful flesh. Seek out for that whereby sin may live; it hath it not. So then neither could He have death in that which was His own, nor we life in that which was our own; but we have life from that which is His, He death from what is ours. What an exchange! What hath He given, and what received? Men who trade enter into commercial intercourse for exchange of things. For ancient commerce was only an exchange of things. A man gave what he had, and received what he had not. For example, he had wheat, but had no barley; another had barley, but no wheat;

the former gave the wheat which he had, and received the barley which he had not. How[6] simple it was that the larger quantity should make up for the cheaper sort! So then another man gives barley, to receive wheat; lastly, another gives lead, to receive silver, only he gives much lead against a little silver; another gives wool, to receive a ready-made garment. And who can enumerate all these exchanges? But no one gives life to receive death. Not in vain then was the voice of the Physician as He hung upon the tree. For in order that He might die for us because the Word could not die, "The Word was made flesh, and dwelt among us."[7] He hung upon the Cross, but in the flesh. There was the meanness,[8] which the Jews despised; there the dearness,[9] by which the Jews were delivered. For for them was it said, "Father, forgive them, for they know not what they do."[2] And that voice was not in vain. He died, was buried, rose again, having passed forty days with His disciples, He ascended into heaven, He sent the Holy Ghost on them, who waited for the promise. They were filled with the Holy Ghost, whom they had received, and began to speak with the tongues of all nations. Then the Jews who were present, amazed that unlearned and ignorant men, whom they had known as brought up among them with one tongue, should in the Name of Christ speak in all tongues, were in astonishment, and learnt from Peter's words whence this gift came. He gave it, who hung upon the tree. He gave it, who was derided as He hung upon the tree, that from His seat in heaven He might give the Holy Spirit. They of whom He had said, "Father, forgive them, for they know not what they do," heard, believed. They believed, were baptized, and their conversion was effected. What conversion? In faith they drank the Blood of Christ, which in fury they had shed.

6. Therefore, to finish this discourse with that with which we began it, let us pray, and let us rely on God; let us live as He enjoineth; and when we totter in this life, let us call upon Him as the disciples called, saying, "Lord, increase our faith."[10] Peter both put his trust in Him, and tottered; but notwithstanding he was not disregarded and left to sink, but was lifted up and raised. For his trust whence was it? Not from anything of his own; but from what was the Lord's. How? "Lord, if it be Thou, bid me come unto Thee on the water." For on the water was the Lord walking. "If it be Thou, bid me come unto Thee on the water." For I know that if it be Thou, Thou biddest, and it is done. "And He saith, Come." He went down at His bidding, but in his own weakness he was afraid. Never-

---

[1] *Personam suam.* [2] Luke xxiii. 34. [3] *Homo.*
[4] *Deum.* [5] John i. 1.
[6] *Quanti erat.* [7] John i. 14. [8] *Vilitas.*
[9] *Caritas.* [10] Luke xvii. 5.

theless when he was afraid, he cried out, "Lord, save me." Then the Lord took him by the hand, and said, "O thou of little faith, wherefore didst thou doubt?"[1] He first invited him, He delivered him, as he tottered, and stumbled; that it might be fulfilled which was said in the Psalm, "If I said my foot hath slipped, Thy mercy, O Lord, aided me."[2]

7. There are then two kinds of blessings, temporal and eternal. Temporal blessings are health, substance, honour, friends, a home, children, a wife, and the other things of this life in which we are sojourners. Put we up then in the hostelry of this life as travellers passing on, and not as owners intending to remain. But eternal blessings are, first, eternal life itself, the incorruption and immortality of body and soul, the society of Angels, the heavenly city, glory[3] unfailing, Father and father-land, the former without death, the latter without a foe. These blessings let us desire with all eagerness, let us ask with all perseverance, not with length of words, but with the witness of groans. Longing desire prayeth always, though the tongue be silent. If thou art ever longing, thou art ever praying. When sleepeth prayer? When desire groweth cold. So then let us beg for these eternal blessings with all eager desire, let us seek for those good things with an entire earnestness, let us ask for those good things with all assurance. For those good things do profit him that hath them, they cannot harm him. But those other temporal good things sometimes profit, and sometimes harm. Poverty hath profited many, and wealth hath harmed many; a private life hath profited many, and exalted honour hath harmed many. And again, money hath profited some, honourable distinction hath profited some; profited them who use them well; but from those who use them ill, the not withdrawing them hath harmed them more. And so, Brethren, let us ask for those temporal blessings too, but in moderation, being sure that if we do receive them, He giveth them, who knoweth what is expedient for us. Thou hast asked, and what thou hast asked, hath not been given thee? Trust thy Father, who would give it thee, were it expedient for thee. Lo! judge in this case by thine own self. For such as thy son who knows not the ways of men is in regard to thee, such in regard to the Lord art thou thyself, who knowest not the things of God. Lo, thy son cries a whole day before thee, that thou wouldest give him a knife, or a sword; thou dost refuse to give it him, thou wilt not give it, thou disregardest his tears, lest thou shouldest have to bewail his death. Let him cry, and beat himself, or throw himself upon the

ground, that thou mayest set him on horseback; thou wilt not do it, because he does not know how to govern the horse, he may throw and kill him. To whom thou refusest a part, thou art reserving the whole. But that he may grow up, and possess the whole in safety, thou givest him not that little thing which is full of peril to him.

8. And so, Brethren, we say, pray as much as ye are able. Evils abound, and God hath willed that evils should abound. Would that evil men did not abound, and then evils would not abound. Bad times! troublesome times! this men are saying. Let our lives be good; and the times are good. We make our times; such as we are, such are the times. But what can we do? We cannot, it may be, convert the mass of men to a good life. But let the few who do give ear live well; let the few who live well endure the many who live ill. They are the corn, they are in the floor; in the floor they can have the chaff with them, they will not have them in the barn. Let them endure what they would not, that they may come to what they would. Wherefore are we sad, and blame we God? Evils abound in the world, in order that the world may not engage our love. Great men, faithful saints were they who have despised the world with all its attractions;[4] we are not able to despise it even disfigured as it is. The world is evil, lo, it is evil, and yet it is loved as though it were good. But what is this evil world? For the heavens and the earth, and the waters, and the things that are therein, the fish, and birds, and trees, are not evil. All these are good: but it is evil men who make this evil world. Yet as we cannot be without evil men, let us, as I have said, whilst we live pour out our groans before the Lord our God, and endure the evils, that we may attain to the things that are good. Let us not find fault with the Master of the household; for He is loving to us. He beareth us, and not we him. He knoweth how to govern what He made; do what He hath bidden, and hope for what He hath promised.

SERMON XXXI.

[LXXXI. BEN.]

ON THE WORDS OF THE GOSPEL, MATT. XVIII. 7, WHERE WE ARE ADMONISHED TO BEWARE OF THE OFFENCES OF THE WORLD.

1. The divine lessons, which we have just heard as they were being read, warn us to gather in a stock of virtues, to fortify a Christian heart, against the offences which were predicted to come, and this from the mercy of the Lord. "For what is man," saith Scripture, "saving that

---

[1] Matt. xiv. 28, etc.   [2] Ps. xciv. 18.   [3] Dignitas.   [4] Speciosum.

Thou art mindful of him?"[1] "Woe unto the world because of offences,"[2] saith the Lord; the Truth says so; He alarmeth and warneth us, He would not have us to be off our guard; for surely He would not make us desperate. Against this "woe," against this evil, that is, which is to be feared, and dreaded, and guarded against, Scripture counsels, and exhorts, and instructs us in that place, where it is said, "Great praise have they who love Thy law, and nothing is an offence to them."[3] He hath shown us an enemy to be guarded against, but He hath not omitted to show us also a wall of defence. Thou wast thinking, as thou heardest, "Woe unto the world because of offences," whither thou mightest go beyond the world, that thou mightest not be exposed to offences. Therefore to avoid offences, whither wilt thou go beyond the world, unless thou fly to Him who made the world? And how shall we be able to fly to Him who made the world, unless we give ear to His law which is preached everywhere? And to give ear to it is but a small matter, unless we love it. For divine Scripture in making thee secure against offences doth not say, "Great peace have they who" hear "Thy law. For not the hearers of the law are just before God.[4] But" because "the doers of the law shall be justified," and, "faith worketh by love:"[5] it saith, "Great peace have they who love Thy law, and nothing is an offence to them." To this sentiment also agrees the passage which we have chanted in course; "But the meek shall inherit the earth, and shall delight themselves in the abundance of peace."[6] Because, "great peace have they who love Thy law." For these "meek" ones are they who "love the law of God." For, "Blessed is the man whom Thou chastenest, O Lord, and teachest him out of Thy law, that Thou mayest give him rest from the days of adversity, until the pit be digged for the sinner."[7] How diverse seem those words of Scripture, yet into one meaning do they so flow and meet together, that whatsoever out of that most rich fountain thou canst hear, so that thou acquiesce therein, and art in loving harmony with the truth, thou wilt be at once filled with peace; glowing with love, and fortified against offences.

2. It is our place then to see, or seek, or learn, how we must be "meek;" and we are guided by that which I have just brought forward out of the Scriptures, to find what we are in quest of. Be attentive then, Beloved, for a little while; it is a weighty matter that is in hand, that we may be meek; a necessary thing in the adversities of life. But it is not the adverse circumstances of this life which are called offences;

but mark what "offences" are. A man, for instance, under some hard necessity is weighed down by a press of trouble. That he is weighed down with a press of trouble, is no offence. By such pressure were even Martyrs pressed, but not oppressed. Of an offence beware, but of a press of trouble not so much. The last presseth thee, an offence oppresseth thee. What then is the difference between the two? In the press of trouble thou didst make ready to maintain patience, to hold fast constancy, not to abandon faith, not to consent to sin. This if thou maintain, or shall have maintained, the trouble that presseth thee shall not be thy fall; but that press of trouble shall avail to the same end as in the oil press, not to destroy the olive, but to extract the oil. In a word, if in this trouble that presseth thee thou ascribe praise unto God, how useful will the press be to thee, whereby such oil is pressed out! Under such a press the Apostles sat in chains, and in that press they sang a hymn to God. What precious oil was this that was pressed and forced out! Beneath a heavy press did Job sit on the dunghill, without resource, without help, without substance, without children; full, but of worms only, as far, that is, as concerned the outward man, but because he too was full of God within, he praised God, and that press was no "offence" to him. Where then was the "offence"? When his wife came to him and said, "Speak a word against God, and die."[8] When all had been taken from him by the devil, an Eve was reserved for the exercised sufferer, not to console but to tempt her husband. See then where the offence was. She exaggerated his miseries, and her miseries too with his, and began to persuade him to blaspheme. But he who was "meek," because "God had taught him out of His law, and given him rest from the days of adversity;" had "great peace" in his heart as "loving the law of God, and nothing was an offence to him." She was an offence, but not to him. In a word, behold the meek man, behold one taught in the law of God, the eternal law of God I mean. For that law on tables was not yet given to the Jews in the time of Job, but in the hearts of the godly there remained still the eternal law, from which that which was given to the people was copied. Because then by the law of God he had "rest given him from the days of adversity," and "had great peace as loving the law of God," behold how "meek" he is, and what he answers. Learn hereby what I propose to enquire; who are the meek. "Thou speakest," he says, "as one of the foolish women speaketh. If we have received good from the hand of the Lord, shall we not bear the evil?"[9]

[1] Ps. viii. 4.   [2] Matt. xviii. 7.   [3] Ps. cxix. 165.
[4] Rom. ii. 13.   [5] Gal. v. 6.   [6] Ps. xxxvii. 11.
[7] Ps. xciv. 12, 13.

[8] Job ii. 9, Sept.   [9] Job ii. 10, Sept.

3. We have heard by an example who the meek are: let us, if we can, define them in words. The meek are they, to whom in all their good deeds, in all the things they do well, nothing is pleasing but God; to whom in all the evils they suffer, God is not displeasing. Now, Brethren, attend to this rule, to this pattern; let us stretch ourselves out to it, let us seek for increase, that we may fill it. For what does it profit, that we plant, and water, except God shall give the increase? "For neither is he that planteth anything, neither he that watereth; but God that giveth the increase." [1] Give ear, whosoever thou art, that wouldest be "meek," who wouldest have "rest from the days of adversity, who lovest the law of God," that there may be "no offence unto thee," and that thou mayest "have great peace," that thou mayest "possess the earth, and delight in the multitude of peace;" give ear, whosoever thou art that wouldest be "meek." Whatsoever good thou doest, be not pleased with thyself. "For God resisteth the proud, but giveth grace unto the humble." [2] So then whatever good thou doest, let nought but God be pleasing to thee; whatever evil thou sufferest, let not God be displeasing to thee. What needest thou more? Do this, and thou shalt live. The days of adversity shall not overwhelm thee; thou shalt escape that which is said, "Woe unto the world because of offences." For to what world is there woe because of offences, but to that of which it is said, "And the world knew Him not?" [3] Not to that world of which it is said, "God was in Christ reconciling the world unto Himself." [4] There is an evil world, and there is a good world; the evil world, are all the evil men in this world; and the good world, all the good in this world. As we observe frequently with a field. This field is full: of what? Of wheat. Yet we say also, and say truly too, This field is full of chaff. So with a tree, it is full of fruit. Another says, it is full of leaves. And both he who says it is full of fruit, says true; and he who says it is full of leaves, says true. Neither has the full display of leaves taken away the room for the fruit, nor the full display of the fruit driven off the abundance of leaves. It is full of both; but the one the wind searcheth out, the other the husbandman gathereth in. So therefore when thou dost hear, "Woe unto the world because of offences," be not afraid; "love the law of God, nothing shall be an offence to thee."

4. But thy wife comes to thee advising thee to some evil thing. Thou dost love her as a wife should be loved; she is one of thy members. "But if thine eye offend thee, if thine hand offend thee, if thy foot offend thee," thou hast just heard the Gospel, "cut them off, and cast them from thee." [5] Whosoever he be that is dear to thee, whosoever he be that is held in high estimation by thee, let him be so long of high esteem with thee, so long thy beloved member, as he shall not begin to offend thee, that is, to advise thee to any evil. Hear now how that this is the meaning of "offence." I have brought forward the example of Job and his wife; but there the word "offence" did not occur. Hear the Gospel: when the Lord prophesied of His Passion, Peter began to persuade Him not to suffer. "Get thee behind Me, Satan, thou art an offence to Me." [6] Here undoubtedly the Lord who hath given thee an example of life, hath taught thee both what an "offence" is, and how an offence is to be avoided. Him to whom He had a little while before said, "Blessed art thou, Simon Bar-jona;" [7] He had shown to be His member. But when he begins to be an offence, He cuts off the member; only He restored the member, and put it into its place again. He then will be an "offence" to thee, who shall begin to persuade thee to any evil thing. And here, Beloved, take heed; this takes place for the most part not through any evil will, but through a mistaken good will. Thy friend who loves thee, and is loved by thee again, thy father, thy brother, thy child, thy wife, sees thee in an evil case, and would have thee do what is evil. What do I mean by "sees thee in an evil case"? Sees thee in some press of trouble. This pressure it may be thou art suffering for righteousness' sake; art suffering it because thou wilt not give false witness. I would speak merely by way of illustration. Examples abound; for "woe to the world, because of offences." See, for instance, some powerful person, to cover his rapine and plunder, asks of you the service of a false witness. You refuse: refuse the false oath, lest thou shouldest deny Him that is true. That I may not dwell long on this, he is angry, he is powerful, he oppresses thee: a friend comes who would not have thee in this press of trouble, in this evil case; "I pray thee, do what is told thee; what great matter is it?" And then perhaps as Satan with the Lord, "It is written of Thee, He shall give His Angels charge concerning Thee, that Thou dash not Thy foot against a stone." [8] Perhaps too this friend of thine, because he sees thou art a Christian, wishes to persuade thee out of the Law to do what he thinks you ought to do. "Do what the other tells." "What? Do what the other wishes." "But it is a lie, it is false." "Well, have you not read, 'All men are liars'?" [9] Now is he an

[1] 1 Cor. iii. 7.　　[2] Jas. iv. 6.　　[3] John i. 10.
[4] 2 Cor. v. 19.
[5] Matt. xviii. 8, 9.　　[6] Matt. xvi. 23.　　[7] Matt. xvi. 17.
[8] Matt. iv. 6.　　[9] Ps. cxvi. 11.

"offence." He is a friend, what will you do? He is an eye, he is a hand : " Cut it off, and cast it from thee." What is, " cut it off, and cast it from thee "? Consent not to him. For members in our body make up unity by consent, by consent they live, by consent are joined together one with the other. Where there is dissent, there is disease, or a sore. He is then one of thy members; thou wilt love him. But he is an offence to thee ; " Cut him off, and cast him from thee." Consent not to him; drive him off from thine ears, it may be he will return amended.

5. And how wilt thou do this that I say, " Cut him off, and cast him from thee," and so, it may be, amend him? answer me, how thou art going to do it? He wished to persuade thee out of the Law to tell a lie. For he said, " speak." And perhaps he did not dare to say, "speak a lie ;" but thus, " speak what the other wishes." Thou sayest, " But it is a lie." And he to excuse it, says, " All men are liars." Then do thou, my brother, say against this, " The mouth that lieth slayeth the soul." [1] Mark, it is no light thing thou hast heard, " The mouth that lieth slayeth the soul." What can that powerful enemy, who oppresseth me, do to me, that thou pitiest me, and my condition, and wouldest not have me be in this evil case; whereas thou wouldest that I should be evil? What can that powerful man do to me, and what can he oppress? The flesh. He can oppress thy body, thou wilt say : I grant he may oppress it to destruction.[2] Still how much more mildly does he deal with me, than I should with myself were I to lie ! He kills my flesh ; I kill my soul. He in his power and anger slays the body; " the mouth that lieth slayeth the soul." He slays the body ; and die it must, though it should not be slain ; but the soul which iniquity slayeth not, the truth receiveth for ever. Preserve then what thou canst preserve ; and let that perish which must perish sometime or other. Thou hast given an answer then, but thou hast not solved the " All men are liars." Make answer to him to this too, that he may not fancy that he has said anything to persuade to lying, in bringing a testimony out of the Law ; so urging thee out of the Law against the Law. For it is written in the Law, " Thou shalt not bear false witness ; " [3] and it is written in the Law, " All men are liars." Recur then to that which I just lately suggested, when I defined in words as best I could the " meek " man. He is " meek " to whom in all things that he does well, nothing but God is pleasing, and in all the evils which he suffers, God is not displeasing. Make answer then to him who says, Lie, for it is written, " All men are liars : " I will not lie, for it is

written, " The mouth that lieth slayeth the soul." I will not lie, because it is written, " Thou shalt destroy them that speak lying." [4] I will not lie, because it is written, " Thou shalt not bear false witness." Though he whom I displease by the truth harass my body with oppressions, I will give ear to my Lord, " Fear not them which kill the body." [5]

6. " How then are all men liars? What ! Thou art not a man, I suppose ? " Answer quickly and truly. " And O that I may not be a man, that so I may not be a liar." For see ; " God looked down from heaven upon the children of men, to see if there were any that did understand, and seek after God. They are all gone out of the way, they are all together become unprofitable : there is none that doeth good, no not even one." [6] Why ? Because they wished to be sons of men. But in order that he might deliver them from these iniquities, cure, heal, change, the sons of men ; " he gave them power to become the sons of God." [7] What marvel then ! Ye were men, if we were the sons of men ; ye were all men, and were liars, for, " All men are liars." The grace of God came to you, and " gave you power to become the sons of God." Hear the voice of My Father saying, " I have said, Ye are gods ; and ye are all the children of the Most High." [8] Since then they are men, and the sons of men, if they are not the children of the Most High, they are liars, for, " all men are liars." If they are the sons of God, if they have been redeemed by the Saviour's grace, if purchased with His precious Blood, if born again of water and of the Spirit, if predestinated to the inheritance of heaven, then indeed are they children of God. And so thereby are gods. What then would a lie have to do with thee ? For Adam was a mere man, Christ, man and God ; God, the Creator of all creation. Adam a mere man, the Man Christ, the Mediator with God, the Only Son of the Father, the God-man. Lo, thou, O man, art far from God, and God is far above man ; between them the God-man placed Himself. Acknowledge Christ, and by Him as Man ascend up to God.

7. Being then now reformed, and, if my words have been so blessed, " meek," let us " hold fast our profession without wavering." Let us love the law of God, that we may escape that which is written, " Woe unto the world because of offences." Now I would say a few words about " offences," of which the world is full, and how it is that offences thicken, pressing troubles abound. The world [9] is laid waste, the winepress is trodden. Ah ! Christians, heavenly shoot, ye strangers on the earth, who seek a city in heaven, who long to be associated with the holy Angels ; under-

---

[1] Wisd. i. 11.
[2] *Corpus, dicis tu, premit : dico ego, perimit.* [3] Deut. v. 20.
[4] Ps. v. 6. [5] Matt. x. 28. [6] Ps. xiv. 2, 3.
[7] John i. 12. [8] Ps. lxxxii. 6.
[9] By the inundation of the Goths, Serm. lv. (cv. Ben.).

stand that ye have come here on this condition only, that ye should soon depart. Ye are passing on through the world, endeavouring to reach Him who created it. Let not the lovers of the world, who wish to remain in the world, and yet, whether they will or no, are compelled to move from it; let them not disturb you, let them not deceive nor seduce you. These pressing troubles are not offences. Be ye righteous, and they will be only exercises. Tribulation comes; it will be as ye choose it, either an exercise, or a condemnation. Such as it shall find you to be, will it be. Tribulation is a fire; does it find thee gold? it takes away the filth: does it find thee chaff? it turns it into ashes. The pressing troubles then which abound are not " offences." But what are " offences"? Those expressions, those words in which we are thus addressed. " See what Christian times bring about;" lo, these are the true offences. For this is said to thee, to this end, that if thou love the world, thou mayest blaspheme Christ. And this he saith to thee who is thy friend, and counsellor; and so " thine eye." This he saith to thee who ministereth to thee, and shareth thy labours, and so " thine hand." This he saith to thee it may be who supporteth thee, who lifteth thee up from a low earthly state; and so " thy foot." Cast them all aside, cut them off, throw them all away from thee; consent not unto them. Answer such men, as he who was advised to give false witness answered. So do thou answer too say to the man who saith to thee, " See, it is in Christian times that there are such pressing troubles; that the whole world is laid waste;" answer him, " And this Christ foretold me, before it came to pass."

8. For wherefore art thou disturbed? Thine heart is disturbed by the pressing troubles of the world, as that ship was, in which Christ was asleep. Lo! what is the cause, stout-hearted man, that thy heart is disturbed? That ship in which Christ is asleep,[1] is the heart in which faith is asleep. For what new thing, what new thing, I ask, is told thee, Christian? " In Christian times is the world laid waste, the world is failing." Did not thy Lord tell thee, the world shall be laid waste? Did not thy Lord tell thee, the world shall fail? Why when the promise was made, didst thou believe, and art disturbed now, when it is being completed? So then the tempest beats furiously against thine heart; beware of shipwreck, awake up Christ. The Apostle says, "that Christ may dwell in your hearts by faith."[2] Christ dwelleth in thee by faith. Present faith, is Christ present; waking faith, is Christ awake; slumbering[3] faith, is Christ asleep. Arise and stir thyself; say, " Lord, we perish." See what the Heathen say to us; and what is

worse, what evil Christians say! Awake up, O Lord, we perish. Let thy faith awake, and Christ begins to speak to thee. " 'Why art thou troubled?' I told thee beforehand of all these things. I foretold them, that when evils came, thou mightest hope for good things, that thou mightest not faint in the evil." Wonderest thou that the world is failing? Wonder that the world is grown old. It is as a man who is born, and grows up, and waxes old. There are many complaints in old age; the cough, the rheum, the weakness of the eyes, fretfulness, and weariness. So then as when a man is old; he is full of complaints; so is the world old; and is full of troubles. Is it a little thing that God hath done for thee, in that in the world's old age, He hath sent Christ unto thee, that He may renew thee then, when all is failing? Dost thou not know that He notified this in the seed of Abraham? " The seed of Abraham," says the Apostle, " which is Christ. He saith not, And to seeds, as of many; but as of One, And to thy seed, which is Christ."[4] Therefore was there a son born to Abraham in his old age, because in the old age of this world was Christ to come. He came when all things were growing old, and made them new. As a made, created, perishing thing, the world was now declining to its fall. It could not but be that it should abound in troubles; He came both to console thee in the midst of present troubles, and to promise thee everlasting rest. Choose not then to cleave to this aged world, and to be unwilling to grow young in Christ, who telleth thee, " The world is perishing, the world is waxing old, the world is failing; is distressed by the heavy breathing of old age. But do not fear, " Thy youth shall be renewed as the eagle's."[5]

9. See, they say, in Christian times it is that Rome perishes. Perhaps Rome is not perishing; perhaps she is only scourged, not utterly destroyed; perhaps she is chastened, not brought to nought. It may be so; Rome will not perish, if the Romans do not perish. And perish they will not if they praise God; perish they will if they blaspheme Him. For what is Rome, but the Romans? For the question is not of her wood and stones, of her lofty insulated[6] palaces, and all her spacious walls. All this was made only on this condition that it should fall some other day. When man built it, he laid stone on stone; and when man destroyed it, he removed stone from stone. Man made it, man destroyed it. Is any injury done to Rome, because it is said, " She is falling"? No, not to Rome, but to her builder perhaps. Do we then its builder any injury, because we say, Rome is falling, which Romulus built?

---

[1] Matt. viii. 24.   [2] Eph. iii. 17.   [3] *Oblita.*   [4] Gal. iii. 16.   [5] Ps. ciii. 5.   [6] *Insulis.*

This world itself will be burnt with fire, which God built. But neither does what man has made fall to ruin, except when God wills it; nor what God has made, except when He wills. For if the work of man fall not without God's will, how can God's work fall by the will of man? Yet God both made the world that was one day to fall for thee; and therefore made He thee as one who was one day to die. Man himself, the city's ornament, man himself, the city's inhabitant, ruler, governor, comes on this condition that he may die, entered into the world on this condition that he may pass away; "Heaven and earth shall pass away:"[1] what wonder then if some time or other there should be an end of a single city? And yet peradventure the city's end is not come now; yet some time or other come it will. But why does Rome perish amid the sacrifices of Christians? Why was her mother Troy burnt amid the sacrifices of Heathens? The gods in whom the Romans have placed all their hope, yea the Roman gods in whom the Heathen Romans placed their hope, removed from the flames of Troy to found Rome. These very gods of Rome were originally the gods of Troy. Troy was burnt, and Æneas took the fugitive gods; yea rather himself a fugitive he took away these senseless gods. For they could be carried by the fugitive; but they could not flee away themselves. And coming with these gods into Italy, with these false gods, he founded Rome. It is too long to go through the whole story; yet would I briefly mention what their own writings contain. An author of theirs well known to all speaks thus; "As I have received the account, the Trojans who under the guidance of Æneas were wandering about as fugitives without any settled abode, originally built and inhabited Rome."[2] So they had their gods with them, they builded Rome in Latium, and there they placed the gods to be worshipped, which before were worshipped in Troy. Juno is introduced by their poet, incensed against Æneas and the fugitive Trojans, saying,

"A race of wandering slaves abhorred by me,
    With prosperous passage cuts the Tuscan sea,
    To fruitful Italy their course they steer,
    And for their vanquished gods, design new temples
      there."[3]

Now when these vanquished gods were carried into Italy, was it as a protecting deity, or[4] as a presage[5] of their future fall? "Love" therefore "the law of God, and nothing shall be an offence to you." We pray you, we beseech you,

we exhort you; be meek, sympathize with the suffering, bear the weak; and on this occasion of the concourse of so many strangers, and needy, and suffering people, let your hospitality and your good works abound. Let but Christians do what Christ enjoineth, and so will the Heathen blaspheme only to their own hurt.

SERMON XXXII.

[LXXXII. BEN.]

ON THE WORDS OF THE GOSPEL, MATT. XVIII. 15, "IF THY BROTHER SIN AGAINST THEE, GO, SHEW HIM HIS FAULT BETWEEN THEE AND HIM ALONE;" AND OF THE WORDS OF SOLOMON, HE THAT WINKETH WITH THE EYES DECEITFULLY, HEAPETH SORROW UPON MEN; BUT HE THAT REPROVETH OPENLY, MAKETH PEACE.

1. OUR Lord warns us not to neglect one another's sins, not by searching out what to find fault with, but by looking out for what to amend. For He said that his eye is sharp to cast out a mote out of his brother's eye, who has not a beam in his own eye. Now what this means, I will briefly convey to you, Beloved. A mote in the eye is anger; a beam in the eye is hatred. When therefore one who has hatred finds fault with one who is angry, he wishes to take a mote out of his brother's eye, but is hindered by the beam which he carries in his own eye. A mote is the beginning of a beam. For a beam in the course of its growth, is first a mote. By watering the mote, you bring it to a beam; by nourishing anger with evil suspicions, you bring it on to hatred.

2. Now there is a great difference between the sin of one who is angry, and the cruelty of one who holds another in hatred. For even with our children are we angry; but who is ever found to hate his children? Among the very cattle too, the cow in a sort of weariness will sometimes in anger drive away her sucking calf; but anon she embraces it with all the affection of a mother. She is in a way disgusted with it, when she butts at it; yet when she misses it, she will seek after it. Nor do we discipline our children otherwise, than with a degree of anger and indignation; yet we should not discipline them at all, but in love to them. So far then is every one who is angry from hating; that sometimes one would be rather convicted of hating, if he were not angry. For suppose a child wishes to play in some river's stream, by whose force he would be like to perish; if you see this, and patiently suffer it, this would be hating; your patient suffering him, is his death. How far better is it to be angry and correct him, than by not being angry to suffer him to perish! Above all things then is hatred to be avoided,

---

[1] Matt. xxiv. 35.   [2] Sallust in *Catil.* 6.   [3] *Æn.* i. 71, 2.
[4] *De Civit. Dei*, lib. i. c. 3. *Immo vero victos deos tanquam præsides ac defensores colere, quid est aliud quam tenere non numina bona sed omina mala?*
[5] *Numen erat*, an omen.

and the beam to be cast out of the eye. Great is the difference indeed between one's exceeding due limits in some words through anger, which he afterwards wipes off by repenting of it; and the keeping an insidious purpose shut up in the heart. Great, lastly, the difference between these words of Scripture, "Mine eye is disordered because of anger."[1] Whereas of the other it is said, "Whosoever hateth his brother is a murderer."[2] Great is the difference between an eye disordered, and clean put out. A mote disorders, a beam puts clean out.

3. In order then that we may be able well to do and to fulfil what we have been admonished of to-day, let us first persuade ourselves to this, above all things to have no hate. For when there is no beam in thine own eye, thou seest rightly whatever may be in thy brother's eye; and art uneasy, till thou cast out of thy brother's eye what thou seest to hurt it. The light that is in thee, doth not allow thee to neglect thy brother's light. Whereas if thou hate, and wouldest correct him, how dost thou improve his light, when thou hast lost thine own light? For the same Scripture, where it is written, "Whosoever hateth his brother is a murderer," hath expressly told us this also. "He that hateth his brother is in darkness even until now."[3] Hatred then is darkness. Now it cannot but be, that he who hateth another, should first injure himself. For him he endeavours to hurt outwardly, he lays himself waste inwardly. Now in proportion as our soul is of more value than our body, so much the more ought we to provide for it, that it be not hurt. But he that hateth another, doth hurt his own soul. And what would he do to him whom he hateth? What would he do? He takes away his money, can he take his faith away? he wounds his good fame, can he wound his conscience? Whatever injury he does, is but external; now observe what his injury to himself is? For he who hateth another is an enemy to himself within. But because he is not sensible of what harm he is doing to himself, he is violent against another, and that the more dangerously, that he is not sensible of the evil he is doing to himself; because by this very violence he has lost the power of perception. Thou art violent against thine enemy; by this violence of thine he is spoiled, and thou art wicked. Great is the difference between the two. He hath lost his money, thou thine innocence. Ask which hath suffered the heavier loss? He hath lost a thing that was sure to perish, and thou art become one who must now perish thyself.

4. Therefore ought we to rebuke in love; not with any eager desire to injure, but with an earnest care to amend. If we be so minded, most excellently do we practise that which we have been recommended to-day; "If thy brother shall sin against thee, rebuke him between thee and him alone."[4] Why dost thou rebuke him? Because thou art grieved, that he should have sinned against thee? God forbid. If from love of thyself thou do it, thou doest nothing. If from love to him thou do it, thou doest excellently. In fact, observe in these words themselves, for the love of whom thou oughtest to do it, whether of thyself or him. "If he shall hear thee, thou hast gained thy brother." Do it for his sake then, that thou mayest "gain" him. If by so doing thou "gain" him, hadst thou not done it, he would have been lost. How is it then that most men disregard these sins, and say, "What great thing have I done? I have only sinned against man." Disregard them not. Thou hast sinned against man; but wouldest thou know that in sinning against man thou art lost. If he, against whom thou hast sinned, have "rebuked thee between thee and him alone," and thou hast listened to him, he hath "gained" thee. What can "hath gained thee," mean; but that thou hadst been lost, if he had not gained thee. For if thou wouldest not have been lost, how hath he gained thee? Let no man then disregard it, when he sins against a brother. For the Apostle saith in a certain place, "But when ye sin so against the brethren, and wound their weak conscience, ye sin against Christ;"[5] for this reason, because we have been all made members of Christ. How dost thou not sin against Christ, who sinnest against a member of Christ?

5. Let no one therefore say, "I have not sinned against God, but against a brother. I have sinned against a man, it is a trifling sin, or no sin at all." It may be, thou sayest it is a trifling sin, because it is soon cured. Thou hast sinned against a brother; give him satisfaction, and thou art made whole. Thou didst a deadly thing quickly, but quickly too hast thou found a remedy. Who of us, my Brethren, can hope for the kingdom of heaven, when the Gospel says, "Whosoever shall say to his brother, Thou fool, shall be in danger of hell fire?"[6] Exceeding terror! but behold in the same place the remedy: "If thou bring thy gift to the altar, and there rememberest that thy brother hath ought against thee, leave there thy gift before the altar."[7] God is not angry that thou deferrest to lay thy gift upon the Altar. It is thee that God seeketh more than thy gift. For if thou come with a gift to thy God, bearing an evil mind against thy brother, He will answer thee, "Thou art lost, what hast thou brought Me? Thou bringest thy gift, and thou art thyself no

---

[1] Ps vi. 8, Sept. (7, English version).   [2] 1 John iii. 15.
[3] 1 John ii. 9.

[4] Matt. xviii. 15.   [5] 1 Cor. viii. 12.   [6] Matt. v. 22.
[7] Matt. v. 23, 24.

proper gift for God. Christ seeketh him whom He hath redeemed with His Blood, more than what thou hast found in thy barn." So then, "Leave there thy gift before the altar, and go thy way, first be reconciled to thy brother, and so thou shalt come and offer thy gift." Lo that "danger of hell fire," how quickly dissolved it is ! When thou wast not yet reconciled, thou wast "in danger of hell fire ; " once reconciled, thou offerest thy gift before the altar in all security.

6. But men are easy and ready enough to inflict injuries, and hard to seek for reconciliation. Ask pardon, says one, of him whom thou hast offended, of him whom thou hast injured. He answers, " I will not so humble myself." But now if thou despise thy brother, at least give ear to thy God. " He that humbleth himself shall be exalted." [1] Wilt thou refuse to humble thyself, who hast already fallen? Great is the difference between one who humbleth himself, and one who lieth on the ground. Already dost thou lie on the ground, and wilt thou then not humble thyself? Thou mightest well say, I will not descend ; if thou hadst first been unwilling to fall.

7. This then ought one to do who hath done an injury. And he who hath suffered one, what ought he to do? What we have heard to-day, " If thy brother shall sin against thee, rebuke him between thee and him alone." [2] If thou shalt neglect this, thou art worse than he. He hath done an injury, and by doing an injury, hath stricken himself with a grievous wound ; wilt thou disregard thy brother's wound? Wilt thou see him perishing, or already lost, and disregard his case? Thou art worse in keeping silence, than he in his reviling. Therefore when any one sins against us, let us take great care, not for ourselves, for it is a glorious thing to forget injuries ; only forget thine own injury, not thy brother's wound. Therefore " rebuke him between thee and him alone," intent upon his amendment, but sparing his shame. For it may be that through shamefacedness he will begin to defend his sin, and so thou wilt make him whom thou desirest to amend, still worse. " Rebuke him " therefore " between him and thee alone. If he shall hear thee, thou hast gained thy brother ; " because he would have been lost, hadst thou not done it. But " if he will not hear thee," that is, if he will defend his sin as if it were a just action, " take with thee one or two more, that in the mouth of two or three witnesses every word may be established ; and if he will not hear them, refer it to the Church ; but if he will not hear the Church, let him be unto thee as an heathen man and a publican." [3] Reckon him no more amongst the number of thy brethren. But yet neither is his salvation on that account to be neglected. For the very heathen,

that is, the Gentiles and Pagans, we donot reckon among the number of brethren ; but yet are we ever seeking their salvation. This then have we heard the Lord so advising, and with such great carefulness enjoining, that He even added this immediately, "Verily I say unto you, Whatsoever ye shall bind on earth, shall be bound in heaven ; and whatsoever ye shall loose on earth, shall be loosed in heaven." [4] Thou hast begun to hold thy brother for a publican ; " thou bindest him on earth ; " but see that thou bind him justly. For unjust bonds justice doth burst asunder. But when thou hast corrected, and been "reconciled to thy brother," thou hast "loosed him on earth." And when "thou shalt have loosed him on earth, he shall be loosed in heaven also." Thus thou doest a great thing, not for thyself, but for him ; for a great injury had he done, not to thee, but to himself.

8. But since this is so, what is that which Solomon says, and which we heard first to-day out of another lesson, " He that winketh with the eyes deceitfully, heapeth sorrow upon men ; but he that reproveth openly, maketh peace "? [5] If then "he that reproveth openly, maketh peace ; " how "rebuke him between him and thee alone"? We must fear, lest the divine precepts should be contrary to one another. But no : let us understand that there is the most perfect agreement in them, let us not follow the conceits of certain vain ones,[6] who in their error think that the two Testaments in the Old and New Books are contrary to each other ; that so we should think that there is any contradiction here, because one is in the book of Solomon, and the other in the Gospel. For if any one unskilful in, and a reviler of the divine Scriptures, were to say, " See where the two Testaments contradict each other. The Lord saith, 'Rebuke him between him and thee alone.' Solomon saith, 'He that reproveth openly maketh peace.'" Doth not the Lord then know what He hath commanded? Solomon would have the sinners' hard forehead bruised : Christ spareth his shame who blushes for his sins. For in the one place it is written, " He that reproveth openly maketh peace ; " but in the other, " Rebuke him between him and thee alone ; " not " openly," but apart and secretly. But wouldest thou know, whosoever thou art that thinkest such things, that the two Testaments are not opposed to each other, because the first of these passages is found in the book of Solomon, and the other in the Gospel? Hear the Apostle. And surely the Apostle is a Minister of the New Testament. Hear the Apostle Paul then, charging Timothy, and saying, "Them that sin rebuke before all, that others also may fear." [7] So then not the book of

---

[1] Luke xiv. 11.   [2] Matt. xviii. 15.   [3] Matt. xviii. 16, 17.

[4] Matt. xviii. 18.   [5] Prov. x. 10, Sept.   [6] The Manichees.
[7] 1 Tim. v. 20.

Solomon, but an Epistle of Paul the Apostle seems to be at issue with the Gospel. Let us then without any[1] prejudice to his honour lay aside Solomon for a while; let us hear the Lord Christ and His servant Paul. What sayest Thou, O Lord? "If thy brother sin against thee, rebuke him between him and thee alone." What sayest thou, O Apostle? "Them that sin rebuke before all, that others also may fear." What are we about? Are we listening to this controversy as judges? That be far from us. Yea, rather as those whose place is under the Judge, let us knock, that we may obtain, that it be opened to us; let us fly beneath the wings of our Lord God. For He did not speak in contradiction to His Apostle, seeing that He Himself spoke "in" him also, as he says, "Would ye receive a proof of Christ, who speaketh in me?"[2] Christ in the Gospel, Christ in the Apostle: Christ therefore spake both; one by His own Mouth, the other by the mouth of His herald. For when the herald pronounces anything from the tribunal, it is not written in the records, "the herald said it;" but he is written as having said it, who commanded the herald what to say.

9. Let us then so give ear to these two precepts, Brethren, as that we may understand them, and let us settle ourselves in peace between them both. Let us but be in agreement with our own heart, and Holy Scripture will in no part disagree with itself. It is entirely true, both precepts are true; but we must make a distinction, that sometimes the one, sometimes the other must be done; that sometimes a brother must be "reproved between him and thee alone," sometimes a brother "must be reproved before all, that others also may fear." If we do sometimes the one, and sometimes the other, we shall hold fast the harmony of the Scriptures, and shall not err in fulfilling and obeying them. But a man will say to me, "When am I to do this one, and when the other? lest I 'reprove between me and him alone,' when I ought to 'reprove before all;' or 'reprove before all,' when I ought to reprove in secret."

10. You will soon see, Beloved, what we ought to do, and when; only I would we may not be slow to practise it. Attend and see: "If thy brother sin against thee, rebuke him between him and thee alone." Why? Because it is against thee that he hath sinned. What is that, "hath sinned against thee"? Thou knowest that he hath sinned. For because it was secret when he sinned against thee, seek for secrecy, when thou dost correct his sin. For if thou only know that he hath sinned against thee, and thou wouldest "rebuke him before all," thou art not a reprover, but

a betrayer. Consider how that "just man" Joseph spared his wife with such exceeding kindness, in so great a crime as he had suspected her of, before he knew by whom she had conceived; because he perceived that she was with child, and he knew that he had not come in unto her. There remained then an unavoidable[3] suspicion of adultery, and yet because he only had perceived, he only knew it, what does the Gospel say of him? "Then Joseph being a just man, and not willing to make her a public example."[4] The husband's grief sought no revenge; he wished to profit, not to punish the sinner. "And not willing to make her a public example, he was minded to put her away privily." But while he thought on these things, "behold, the Angel of the Lord appeared unto him,"[5] in sleep; and told him how it was, that she had not defiled her husband's bed, but that she had conceived of the Holy Ghost the Lord of them both. Thy brother then hath sinned against thee; if thou alone know it, then hath he really sinned against thee alone. For if in the hearing of many he hath done thee an injury, he hath sinned against them also whom he hath made witnesses of his iniquity. For I tell you, my dearly beloved Brethren, what you can yourselves recognise in your own case. When any one does my brother an injury in my hearing, God forbid that I should think that injury unconnected with myself. Certainly he has done it to me also; yea to me the rather, to whom he thought what he did was pleasing. Therefore those sins are to be reproved before all, which are committed before all; they are to be reproved with more secrecy, which are committed more secretly. Distinguish times, and Scripture is in harmony with itself.

11. So let us act; and so must we act not only when the sin is committed against ourselves, but when the sin is so committed by any one as that it is unknown by the other. In secret ought we to rebuke, in secret to reprove him; lest if we would reprove him publicly, we should betray the man. We wish to rebuke and reform him; but what if his enemy is looking out to hear something that he may punish? For example, a Bishop knows of some one who has killed another, and no one else knows of him. I wish to reprove him publicly; but thou art seeking to prosecute him.[6] Decidedly then I will neither betray him, nor neglect him; I will reprove him in secret; I will set the judgment of God before his eyes; I will alarm his bloodstained conscience; I will persuade him to repentance. With this charity ought we to be endued. And hence men sometimes find fault with us, as if we do not reprove; or they think

---

that we know what we do not know, or that we hush up what we know. And it may be that what thou knowest, I know also; but I will not reprove in thy presence; because I wish to cure, not to act informer. There are men who commit adultery in their own houses, they sin in secret, sometimes they are discovered to us by their own wives, generally through jealousy, sometimes as seeking their husband's salvation; in such cases we do not betray them openly, but reprove them in secret. Where the evil has happened, there let the evil die. Yet do we not neglect that wound; above all things showing the man who is in such a sinful state, and bears such a wounded conscience, that that is a deadly wound which they who suffer from, sometimes by an unaccountable perverseness despise; and seek out testimonies in their favour, I know not whence, null certainly and void, saying, " God careth not for sins of the flesh." [1] Where is that then which we have heard to-day, "Whoremongers and adulterers God will judge"?[2] Lo! whosoever thou art that labourest under such a disease attend. Hear what God saith; not what thine own mind, in indulgence to thine own sins, may say, or what thy friend, thine enemy rather and his own too, bound in the same bond of iniquity with thee may say. Hear then what the Apostle saith; " Marriage is honourable in all, and the bed undefiled. But whoremongers and adulterers God will judge."

12. Come then, Brother, be reformed. Thou art afraid lest thine enemy should prosecute thee; and art thou not afraid lest God should judge thee? Where is thy faith? Fear whilst there is the time for fear. Far off indeed is the day of judgment; but every man's last day cannot be far off; for life is short. And since this shortness is ever uncertain, thou knowest not when thy last day may be. Reform thyself today, because of to-morrow. Let the reproof in secret be of service to thee now. For I am speaking openly, yet do I reprove in secret. I knock at the ears of all; but I accost [3] the consciences of some. If I were to say, "Thou adulterer, reform thyself;" perhaps in the first place I might say what I had no knowledge of; perhaps suspect on a rash hearsay report. I do not then say, "Thou adulterer, reform thyself;" but " whosoever thou art among this people who art an adulterer, reform thyself." So the reproof is public; the reformation secret. This I know, that whoso feareth, will reform himself.

13. Let no one say in his heart, "God careth not for sins of the flesh." "Know ye not," saith the Apostle, " that ye are the temple of God, and the Spirit of God dwelleth in you? If any man defile the temple of God, him will God

destroy."[4] " Let no man deceive himself." But perhaps a man will say, " My soul is the temple of God, not my body," and will add this testimony also, " All flesh is as grass, and all the glory of man as the flower of grass." [5] Unhappy interpretation! conceit meet for punishment! The flesh is called grass, because it dies; but take thou heed that that which dies for a time, rise not again with guilt. Wouldest thou ascertain a plain judgment on this point also? " Know ye not," says the same Apostle, " that your body is the temple of the Holy Ghost which is in you, which ye have of God?"[6] Do not then any longer disregard sins of the body; seeing that your " bodies are the temples of the Holy Ghost which is in you, which ye have of God." If thou didst disregard a sin of the body, wilt thou disregard a sin which thou committest against a temple? Thy very body is a temple of the Spirit of God within thee. Now take heed what thou doest with the temple of God. If thou wert to choose to commit adultery in the Church within these walls, what wickedness could be greater? But now thou art thyself the temple of God. In thy going out, in thy coming in, as thou abidest in thy house, as thou risest up, in all thou art a temple. Take heed then what thou doest, take heed that thou offend not the Indweller of the temple, lest He forsake thee, and thou fall into ruins. " Know ye not," he says, " that your bodies" (and this the Apostle spake touching fornication, that they might not think lightly of sins of the body) " are the temples of the Holy Ghost which is in you, which ye have of God, and ye are not your own?" For " ye have been bought with a great [7] price." If thou think so lightly of thine own body, have some consideration for thy price.

14. I know, and as I do every one knows, who has used a little more than ordinary consideration, that no man who has any fear of God omits to reform himself in obedience to His words, but he who thinks that he has longer time to live. This it is which kills so many, while they are saying, "To-morrow, To-morrow;" and suddenly the door is shut. He remains outside with the raven's croak,[8] because he had not the moaning of the dove. " To-morrow, To-morrow;" is the raven's croak. Moan plaintively as the dove, and beat thy breast; but whilst thou art inflicting blows on thy breast, be the better for the beating; lest thou seem not to beat thy conscience, but rather with blows to harden it, and make an evil conscience more unyielding instead of better. Moan with no fruitless moaning. For it may be thou art saying to thyself, "God hath promised me forgiveness, whenever I reform myself I am

1 *Vide* Serm. ccxxiv. (2).   2 Heb. xiii. 4.   3 *Convenio.*

4 1 Cor. iii. 16, 17.   5 1 Pet. i. 24.   6 1 Cor. vi. 19.
7 Vulgate.
8 Serm. ccxxiii. 4. *Enarr. in Ps.* cii. 16.

secure ; I read the divine Scripture, " In the day that the wicked man turneth away from his wickedness, and doeth that which is lawful and right, I will forget all his iniquities." [1] I am secure then, whenever I reform myself, God will give me pardon for my evil deeds." What can I say to this? Shall I lift up my voice against God? Shall I say to God, Do not give him pardon? Shall I say, This is not written, God hath not promised this? If I should say ought of this, I should say falsely. Thou speakest well and truly ; God hath promised pardon on thy amendment, I cannot deny it ; but tell me, I pray thee ; see, I consent, I grant, I acknowledge that God hath promised thee pardon, but who hath promised thee a to-morrow? Where thou dost read to me that thou shalt receive pardon, if thou reform thyself ; there read to me how long thou hast to live. Thou dost confess, " I cannot read it there." Thou knowest not then how long thou hast to live. Reform thyself, and so be always ready. Be not afraid of the last day, as a thief, who will break up thy house as thou sleepest ; but awake and reform thyself to-day. Why dost thou put it off till to-morrow? If thy life is to be a long one, let it be both long and good. No one puts off a good dinner, because it is to be a long one, and dost thou wish to have a long evil life? Surely if it is to be long, it will be all the better if it be good ; if it is to be short, it is well that its good be as long as possible.[2] But men neglect their life to such a degree, as that they are unwilling to have anything bad except it. You buy a farm, and you look out for a good one ; you wish to marry a wife, you choose a good one ; you wish for the birth of children, and you long for good ones ; you bargain for shoes, and you do not wish for bad ones ; and yet a bad life you [3] do love. How hath thy life offended thee, that thou art willing to have it only bad ; that amid all thy good things thou shouldest thyself alone be evil?

15. So then, my Brethren, if I should wish to reprove any of you individually in secret, perhaps he would listen to me. I reprove many of you now in public ; all praise me ; may some give attentive heed to me ! I have no love for him who praises me with his voice, and with his heart despises me. For when thou dost praise, and not reform thyself, thou art a witness against thyself. If thou art evil, and thou art pleased with what I say, be displeased with thyself ; because if thou art displeased with thyself as being evil, when thou dost reform, thou wilt be well pleased with thyself, which if I mistake not I said the day before yesterday. In all my words I set a mirror before you. Nor are they my

words, but I speak at the bidding of the Lord, by whose terrors I refrain from keeping silence. For who would not rather choose to keep silence, and not to give account for you? But now I have undertaken the burden, and I cannot, and I ought not to shake it off my shoulders. When the Epistle to the Hebrews was being read, my Brethren, ye heard, " Obey them that have the rule over you, and submit yourselves : for they watch for your souls, as they that must give account, that they may do it with joy, and not with grief ; for that is unprofitable for you." [4] When do we it with joy? When we see man making progress in the words of God. When does the labourer in the field work with joy? When he looks at the tree, and sees the fruit ; when he looks at the crop, and sees the prospect of abundance of corn in the floor ; when he sees that he has not laboured in vain, has not bowed his back, and bruised his hands, and endured the cold and heat in vain. This is what he says, " That they may do it with joy, and not with grief ; for that is unprofitable for you." Did he say, " unprofitable for them "? No. He said, " unprofitable for you." For when those who are set over you are saddened at your evil deeds, it is profitable for them ; their very sadness is profitable for them ; but it is unprofitable for you. But we do not wish that anything should be profitable for us, which for you is unprofitable. Let us then, Brethren, do good together in the Lord's field ; that at the reward we may rejoice together.

SERMON XXXIII.

[LXXXIII. BEN.]

ON THE WORDS OF THE GOSPEL, MATT. XVII. 21, " HOW OFT SHALL MY BROTHER SIN AGAINST ME," ETC.

1. YESTERDAY the holy Gospel warned us not to neglect the sins of our brethren : " But if thy brother shall sin against thee, rebuke him between him and thee alone. If he shall hear thee, thou hast gained thy brother. But if he shall refuse to hear thee, take with thee two or three more ; that in the mouth of two or three witnesses, every word may be established. And if he shall neglect to hear them too, tell it to the Church. But if he shall neglect to hear the Church, let him be unto thee as an heathen man and a publican." [5] To-day also the section which follows, and which we heard when it was read, relates to the same subject. For when the Lord Jesus had said this to Peter, he went on to ask his Master, how often he should forgive a brother who had sinned against him ; and he enquired whether seven times would be enough. " The Lord answered him, Not only seven times, but seventy times seven." [6]

[1] Ezek. xviii. 21, 22.
[2] Bene factum est, ut bona produceretur.
[3] Serm. xxii. (lxxii. Ben.) 5 (iv.).

[4] Heb. xiii. 17.   [5] Matt. xviii. 15-17.   [6] Matt. xviii. 22.

Then he added a parable very full of terror : That the "kingdom of heaven is like unto an house-holder, which took account with his servants ; among whom he found one that owed ten thousand talents. And when he commanded all that he had, and all his family, and himself to be sold, and the debt to be paid, he fell down at his lord's feet," [1] and prayed for delay, and obtained [2] entire remission. For as we have heard, " His lord was moved with compassion, and forgave him all the debt." Then that man free from his debt, but a bondslave of iniquity, after he had gone out from the presence of his lord, found in his turn a debtor of his own, who owed him, not ten thousand talents, the sum· which had been remitted to him, but a hundred denarii ; and " he began to drag him by the throat, and say, Pay me that thou owest." [3] Then he besought his fellow-servant as he had done his lord ; but he did not find his fellow-servant such a man as the other had found his lord. He not only would not forgive him the debt ; but he did not even grant him a delay. He hurried him along with great violence [4] to make him pay, he who had been but just now set free from his debt to his lord. His fellow-servants were displeased ; and " went and told their lord what was done ; " and the lord summoned his servant to his presence, and said to him, " O thou wicked servant, when thou didst owe me so great a debt, in pity to thee I forgave thee all. Shouldest not thou also have had compassion on thy fellow-servant, even as I had pity on thee ? " [5] And he commanded that all which he had forgiven him should be paid.

2. It is then for our instruction that He put forth this parable, and by this warning He would save us from perishing. " So," said He, " shall My heavenly Father do also unto you, if ye from your hearts forgive not every one his brother their trespasses." [6] Lo, Brethren, the thing is plain, useful is the admonition, and a wholesome obedience is by all means due, that what hath been bidden may be fulfilled. For every man is at once God's debtor, and hath also some brother a debtor to himself. For who is there who is not God's debtor, but he in whom there can be found no sin ? And who is there who hath not a brother his debtor, but he against whom no one hath sinned ? Think you that any one among mankind can be found, who is not himself bounden to his brother by some sin ? So then every man is a debtor, yet having himself his own debtors too. The righteous God therefore appointeth a rule for thee toward thy debtor, which He also will observe with His. For two works of mercy are there, which deliver us, which the Lord hath Himself briefly laid

down in the Gospel : " Forgive, and ye shall be forgiven : give, and it shall be given unto you." [7] " Forgive, and ye shall be forgiven," relates to pardoning. " Give, and it shall be given unto you," relates to doing kindnesses. As to what He saith of pardoning, thou both wishest thy sin to be pardoned thee, and thou hast another whom thou mayest pardon. Again, as to the doing kindnesses ; a beggar asks of thee, and thou art God's beggar. For we are all when we pray God's beggars ; we stand, yea rather we fall prostrate before the door of the Great House-holder, we groan in supplication wishing to receive something ; and this something is God Himself. What does the beggar ask of thee ? Bread. And what dost thou ask of God, but Christ, who saith, " I am the living Bread which came down from heaven "? [8] Would you be forgiven ? Forgive. " Forgive, and it shall be forgiven you." Would you receive ? " Give, and it shall be given unto you."

3. But now hear what in so plain a precept may cause a difficulty. In this question of forgiveness when pardon is asked, and it is due from him who should grant it, it may be a difficulty to us as it was to Peter. " How often ought I to forgive ? Is up to seven times sufficient ? " " It is not sufficient," saith the Lord, " I say not unto thee, Until seven times ; but, Until seventy times seven." [9] Now reckon up how often thy brother hath sinned against thee. If thou canst reach the seventy-eighth fault, so as to get beyond the seventy times seven, then set about revenge. Is this then what He really means, and is it really so, that if he shall sin " seventy times seven," thou shouldest forgive him ; but if he shall sin seventy times and eight, it should then be lawful for thee not to forgive ? Nay I am bold to say, that if he should even sin seventy-eight times, thou must forgive. Yea, as I have said, if he shall sin seventy-eight times, forgive. And if he sin a hundred times, forgive. And why need I say, so and so often ? In one word,[10] as often as he shall sin, forgive him. Have I then taken upon me to overpass the measure of my Lord ? He fixed the limit of forgiveness in the number seventy-seven ; shall I presume to overleap this limit ? It is not so, I have not presumed to go at all beyond. I have heard the Lord Himself speaking in His Apostle, where there is no measure or number fixed. For He says, " Forgiving one another, if any man have a quarrel against any, as God in Christ hath forgiven you." [11] Here you have the rule. If Christ have forgiven thee thy sins " seventy times and seven " only, if He have pardoned up to this point, and refused to pardon

---

[1] Matt. xviii. 23–26.   [2] *Meruit.*   [3] Matt. xviii. 28.
[4] *Contortum.*   [5] Matt. xviii. 31–33.
[6] Matt. xviii 35.

[7] Luke vi. 37, 38.   [8] John vi. 51.   [9] Matt. xviii. 21, 22.
[10] *Vid.* Serm. lxiv. (cxiv. Ben.) 1.
[11] Col. iii. 13; Eph. iv. 32.

beyond it; then do thou also fix this limit, and be loth to forgive beyond it. But if Christ hath found thousands of sins upon sins, and hath yet forgiven all; withdraw not then thy mercy, but ask the forgiveness of that large number. For it was not without a meaning that the Lord said "seventy times seven;" forasmuch as there is no trespass whatever which thou oughtest not to forgive. See this servant in the parable, who being a debtor was found to have a debtor, owed ten thousand talents. And I suppose that ten thousand talents are at least ten thousand sins. For I will not say how but one talent will include all sins. But how much did the other servant owe him? He owed a hundred denarii. Now is not this more than "seventy and seven"? And yet the Lord was wroth, because he did not forgive him. For not only is a hundred more than "seventy-seven;" but a hundred denarii perhaps are a thousand "asses." But what was this to ten thousand talents?

4. And so let us be ready to forgive all the trespasses which are committed against us, if we desire to be forgiven. For if we consider our sins, and reckon up what we do in deed, what by the eye, what by the ear, what by thought, what by numberless movements; I know not whether we so much as sleep without a talent. And therefore do we daily beg, daily knock at the ears of God by prayer, daily prostrate ourselves and say, "Forgive us our debts, as we forgive our debtors."[1] What debts of thine? All, or a certain part? Thou wilt answer, All. So then do thou with thy debtor. This then is the rule thou layest down, this the condition thou speakest of; this the covenant and agreement thou dost mention when thou prayest, saying, "Forgive us, as we forgive our debtors."

5. What then, Brethren, is the meaning of "seventy times seven"? Hear, for it is a great mystery, a wonderful sacrament. When the Lord was baptized, the Evangelist St. Luke has in that place commemorated His generations in the regular order, series, and line in which they had come down to that generation in which Christ was born. Matthew begins at Abraham,[2] and comes down to Joseph in a descending order; but Luke begins to reckon in an ascending order. Why does the one reckon in a descending, and the other in an ascending order? Because Matthew set forth the generation of Christ by which He came down to us; and so he began to reckon when Christ was born in a descending order.[3] Whereas, because Luke begins to reckon when Christ was baptized; in this is the beginning of ascension, he begins to reckon in an ascending order, and in his reckoning he has completed seventy-seven genera-

tions.[4] With whom did he begin his reckoning? Observe with whom? He began to reckon from Christ up to Adam himself, who was the first sinner, and who begat us with the bond of sin. He reckoned up to Adam, and so there are reckoned seventy-seven generations; that is, from Christ up to Adam and from Adam up to Christ are the aforesaid seventy-seven generations. So then if no generation was omitted, there is no exemption of any trespass which ought not to be forgiven. For therefore did he reckon up his seventy-seven generations, which number the Lord mentioned as to the forgiveness of sins; since he begins to reckon from the baptism, wherein all sins are remitted.

6. And, Brethren, observe in this a yet greater mystery.[5] In the number seventy-seven is a mystery of the remission of sins. So many are the generations found to be from Christ to Adam. Now then, ask with somewhat more careful diligence for the secret meaning of this number, and enquire into its hidden meaning; with more careful diligence knock, that it may be opened unto thee. Righteousness consists in the observance of the Law of God: true. For the Law is set forth in ten precepts. Therefore it was that the servant in the parable "owed ten thousand talents." This is that memorable Decalogue written by the finger of God, and delivered to the people by Moses, the servant of God. He "owed" then "ten thousand talents;" which signifies all sins, with reference to the number of the Law. And the other "owed a hundred denarii;" derived equally from the same number. For a hundred times a hundred make ten thousand; and ten times ten make a hundred. And the one "owed ten thousand talents," and the other ten times ten denarii. For there was no departure from the number[6] of the law, and in both numbers you will find every kind of sin included. Both are debtors, and both implore and beg for pardon; but the wicked, ungrateful servant would not repay what he had received, would not grant the mercy which had been undeservedly accorded to him.

7. Consider then, Brethren; every man begins from Baptism; he goes out free, the "ten thousand talents" are forgiven him; and when he goes out, he will soon find some fellow-servant his debtor. Let him note then, what sin itself is;[7] for the number eleven is the transgression of the law. For the law is ten, sin eleven. For the law is denoted by ten, sin by eleven. Why is sin denoted by eleven? Because to get to eleven, there is the transgression of the ten.[8] But the due limit is fixed in the law; and the transgression of it is sin. Now when you have

---

[1] Matt. vi. 12.   [2] Matt. i. 1.
[3] *Vid.* Serm. i. (li. Ben.) 31-5 (xxi.-iv.).
[4] Luke iii. 23, etc.   [5] *Sacramentum.*
[6] *Legitimo numero.*   [7] *Observes ergo ipsum peccatum.*
[8] *Vid.* Serm. i. (li. Ben.) 34 (xxiii.).

passed beyond the ten, you come to eleven. This high mystery was figured out when the tabernacle was commanded to be built. There are many things mentioned there in number, which are a great mystery.[1] Among the rest, curtains of haircloth were ordered to be made, not ten, but eleven;[2] because by haircloth is signified the confession of sins. Now what do you require more? Would you know how that all sins are contained in this number "seventy-seven"? Seven then is usually put for a whole; because in seven days the revolution of time is completed, and when the seventh is ended, it returns to the first again, that the same revolution may be continued. In such revolutions whole ages pass away : yet there is no departure from the number seven. For He spoke of all sins, when He said "seventy times seven;" for multiply that eleven seven times, and it makes seventy-seven. Therefore would He have all sins forgiven, for He marked them out by the number "seventy-seven." Let no one then retain against himself by refusing to forgive, lest it be retained against him, when he prayeth. For God saith, "Forgive, and thou shalt be forgiven." For I have forgiven thee first ; do thou at least forgive after that. For if thou wilt not forgive, I will call thee back, and put upon thee again all that I had remitted to thee. For the Truth doth not speak falsely ; Christ neither deceiveth, nor is deceived, and He hath said at the close of the parable, "So likewise shall your Father which is in heaven do unto you."[3] Thou findest a Father, imitate thy Father. For if thou wilt not imitate Him, thou art devising[4] to be disinherited. "So likewise" then "shall My heavenly Father do also unto you, if ye from your hearts forgive not every one his brother their trespasses." Say not with the tongue, "I forgive," and put off to forgive in the heart ; for by His threat of vengeance God showeth thee thy punishment. God knoweth where thou speakest. Man can hear thy voice ; God looketh into thy conscience. If thou sayest, I forgive ; forgive. Better is it that thou shouldest be violent in words, and forgive in the heart, than in words be soft, and in the heart relentless.

8. Now then unruly boys will beg, and take it[5] hard to be beat, taking exception against[6] us when we wish to chastise them after this fashion. "I have sinned, but forgive me." Well, I have forgiven, and he sins again. "Forgive me," he cries, and I have forgiven him. He sins a third time. "Forgive me," he cries, and a third time I have forgiven him. Now then the fourth time let him be beat. And he will say, "What ! have I tired you out to seventy-seven times?" Now

if by such exceptions the severity of discipline sleep, upon the suppression of discipline wickedness will rage with impunity. What then is to be done? Let us reprove with words, and if need be with scourges ; but let us withal forgive the sin, and cast away the remembrance of it from the heart. For therefore did the Lord add, "from your hearts," that though through affection discipline be exercised, gentleness might not depart out of the heart. For what is so kind and gentle as the surgeon with his knife? He that is to be cut cries, yet cut he is ; he that is to be cauterized cries, but cauterized he is. This is not cruelty ; on no account let that surgeon's treatment be called cruelty. Cruel he is against the wounded part that the patient may be cured ; for if the wound be softly dealt with, the man is lost. Thus then would I advise, my Brethren, that we love our brethren, howsoever they may have sinned against us ; that we let not affection toward them depart out of our hearts, and that when need is, we exercise discipline toward them ; lest by the relaxation of discipline, wickedness increase, and we begin to be accused on God's behalf, for it has been read to us, "Them that sin rebuke before all, that others also may fear."[7] Certainly, if one, as is the only true way, distinguishes the times, and so solves the question, all is true. If the sin be in secret, rebuke it in secret. If the sin be public and open, rebuke it publicly that the sinner may be reformed ; and "that others also may fear."

SERMON XXXIV.

[LXXXIV. BEN.]

ON THE WORDS OF THE GOSPEL, MATT. XIX. 17, "IF THOU WOULDEST ENTER INTO LIFE, KEEP THE COMMANDMENTS."

1. THE Lord said to a certain young man, "If thou wilt enter into life, keep the commandments."[8] He did not say, "If thou wilt enter into life eternal," but "If thou wilt enter into life ;" laying down that as life, which is to be life eternal. Let us first then set forth the value of the love of this life. For even this present life, under whatever circumstances, is loved ; and men fear and dread to end it of whatever kind it be ; however full of trouble and misery. Hence may we see, hence consider, how the life eternal should be loved ; when this life so miserable, and which must sometime come to an end, is loved so much. Consider, Brethren, how greatly should that life be loved, where thou wilt never end life. Thou dost love, it seems, this present life, where thou dost labour so much, hastest to and fro, art busy, sufferest fatigue ; yea scarcely to be enumerated are the necessities

---

[1] *In magno sacramento.*
[2] Exod. xxvi. 7. *Cilicina*: τριχίνας, Sept.
[3] Matt. xviii. 35.
[4] *Disponis.*   [5] *Nolunt.*   [6] *Præscribunt.*
[7] 1 Tim. v. 20.   [8] Matt. xix. 17.

of this miserable life; sowing, ploughing, clearing the ground, sailing, grinding, cooking, weaving; and after all these things thou hast to end thy life. See the evils thou dost suffer in this miserable life, which thou lovest; and dost thou think that thou shalt always live, and never die? Temples, stones, marbles, joined so strongly together with iron and lead, fall into ruin for all their strength; and does a man suppose that he shall never die? Learn then, Brethren, to seek for eternal life, where you will not endure all this, but will reign with God for ever. "For he who wisheth life," as the Prophet says, "loveth to see good days." [1] For in evil days death is rather wished for than life. Do we not hear and see men when they are involved in some tribulations and distresses, in law-suits or sicknesses and they see that they are in travail, do we not hear them saying nothing else but, "O God, send me death, hasten my days"? Yet when sickness comes, they run about, and physicians are fetched, and money and rewards are promised. Death himself says to thee, "Lo, here I am, whom but a little while ago thou wert asking of the Lord, why wouldest thou fly from me now? I have found thee to be a self-deceiver, and a lover of this miserable life."

2. But as concerning these days which we are passing now, the Apostle says, "Redeeming the time, because the days are evil." [2] Are not these days indeed evil which we spend in this corruptible flesh, in or under so heavy a load of the corruptible body, amid so great temptations, amid so great difficulties, where there is but false pleasure, no security of joy, a tormenting fear, a greedy covetousness, a withering sadness? Lo, what evil days! yet no one is willing to end these same evil days, and hence men earnestly pray God that they may live long. Yet what is it to live long, but to be long tormented? What is it to live long, but to add evil days to evil days? When boys are growing up, it is as if days are being added to them; whereas they do not know that they are being diminished; and their very reckoning is false. For as we grow up, the number of our days rather diminishes than increases. Appoint for any man at his birth, for instance, eighty years; every day he lives, he diminishes somewhat of that sum. Yet silly men rejoice at the oft-recurring birthdays, both of themselves and their children. O sensible man! If the wine in thy bottle is diminished, thou art sad; days art thou losing, and art thou glad? These days then are evil; and so much the more evil, in that they are loved. This world is so alluring, that no one is willing to finish a life of sorrow. For the true, the blessed life is this, when we shall rise again, and reign with Christ. For the ungodly too shall rise again, but to go into the fire. Life then is there none but that which is blessed. And blessed life there can be none but that which is eternal, where are "good days;" and those not many days, but one day. They are called "days" after the custom of this life. That day knows no rising, it knows no setting. To that day there succeeds no to-morrow; because no yesterday precedes it. This day, or these days, and this life, this true life, have we in promise. It is then the reward of a certain work. So if we love the reward, let us not fail in the work; and so shall we reign with Christ for ever.

SERMON XXXV.

[LXXXV. BEN.]

ON THE WORDS OF THE GOSPEL, MATT. XIX. 17, "IF THOU WOULDEST ENTER INTO LIFE, KEEP THE COMMANDMENTS."

1. THE Gospel lesson which has now sounded in our ears, Brethren, requires rather an attentive hearer and a doer, than an expositor. What is more clear than this light, "If thou wilt enter into life, keep the commandments"? [3] What then have I to say but, "If thou wilt enter into life, keep the commandments"? Who is there that does not wish for life? and yet who is there that does wish to keep the commandments? If thou dost not wish to keep the commandments, why seekest thou after life? If thou art slow to the work, why dost thou hasten to the reward? The rich young man in the Gospel said that he had kept the commandments: then he heard the greater precepts, "If thou wilt be perfect, one thing is lacking to thee, go sell all that thou hast, and give to the poor;" thou shalt not lose them, but "thou shalt have treasure in heaven; and come and follow Me." [4] For what shall it profit thee, if thou shalt do all the rest, and yet not follow Me?" But as ye have heard, "he went away" sad and "sorrowful; for he had great riches." What he heard, have we heard also. The Gospel is Christ's voice. He sitteth in heaven; but He doth not cease to speak on earth. Let us not be deaf, for He is crying out. Let us not be dead; for He is thundering. If thou wilt not do the greater things, do at least the less. If the burden of the greater be too much for thee, at least take up the less. Why art thou slow to both? why settest thyself against both? The greater are, "Sell all that thou hast, and give to the poor, and follow Me." The less are, "Thou shalt do no murder, Thou shalt not commit adultery, Thou shalt not steal, Thou shalt not bear false witness. Honour thy father and thy mother; and, Thou shalt love thy neigh-

---

[1] Ps. xxxiv. 12, Vulgate.   [2] Eph. v. 16.   [3] Matt. xix. 17.   [4] Matt. xix. 21.

bour as thyself." [1]   These do; why do I call to thee, to sell thy possessions, from whom I cannot gain, that thou wouldest keep from plundering what is another's? Thou hast heard, "Thou shalt not steal;" yet thou dost plunder. Before the eyes of so great a Judge, I find thee not a thief only, but a plunderer. Spare thyself, have pity on thyself. This life yet allows thee respite, do not refuse correction. Yesterday thou wast a thief; be not so to-day too. Or if peradventure thou hast been so to-day already, be not so to-morrow. Put a stop sometime to thy evil doing, and so require good for a reward. Thou wouldest have good things, and wouldest not be good; thy life is a contradiction to thy desires. If to have a good country-seat, is a great good: how great an evil must it be to have an evil soul!

2. The rich man "went away sorrowful;" and the Lord said, "How hardly shall he that hath riches enter into the kingdom of heaven!" [2] And by putting forth a comparison He showed the difficulty to be such that it was absolutely impossible. For every impossible thing is difficult; but not every difficult thing is impossible. As to how difficult it is, take heed to the comparison; "Verily I say unto you, It is easier for a camel to go through the eye of a needle, than for a rich man to enter into the kingdom of God." [3] A camel to go through the eye of a needle! If He had said a gnat, it would be impossible. And then when His disciples heard it, they were grieved and said, "If this be so, who then can be saved?" [4] What rich man? Give ear then to Christ, ye poor, I am speaking to the people of God. Ye are more of you poor than rich, do ye then at least receive what I say, yet give heed. Whosoever of you boast of your poverty, beware of pride, lest the humble rich surpass you; beware of impiety, lest the pious rich surpass you; beware of drunkenness, lest the sober rich surpass you. Do not glory of your poverty, if they must not glory of their riches.

3. And let the rich give ear, if indeed they are rich; let them give ear to the Apostle, "Charge the rich of this world," [5] for there are who are the rich of another world. The poor are the rich of another world. The Apostles are the rich of another world, who said, "As having nothing, and yet possessing all things." [6] So that ye may know of what poor he is speaking he added, "of this world." Let the "rich" then "of this world" give ear to the Apostle, "Charge," he says, "the rich of this world, that they be not proud in their conceits." The first worm of riches is pride. [7] A consuming moth, which gnaws the whole, and reduces it even to dust. "Charge them," therefore, "not to be proud in their conceits, nor to trust in the uncertainty of riches" (they are the Apostle's words), "but in the living God." A thief may take away thy gold; who can take away thy God? What hath the rich man, if he hath not God? What hath the poor man not, if he have God? Therefore he says, "Nor to trust in riches, but in the living God, who giveth us all things richly to enjoy;" with which all things He giveth also Himself.

4. If then they ought not to "trust in riches," not to confide in them, "but in the living God;" what are they to do with their riches? Hear what: "Let them be rich in good works." [8] What does this mean? Explain, O Apostle. For many are loth to understand what they are loth to practise. Explain, O Apostle; give none occasion to evil works by the obscurity of thy words. Tell us what thou dost mean by, "let them be rich in good works." Let them hear and understand; let them not be suffered to excuse themselves; but rather let them begin to accuse themselves, and to say what we have just heard in the Psalm, "For I acknowledge my sin." [9] Tell us what this is, "let them be rich in good works. Let them easily distribute." And what is "let them easily distribute"? What! is this too not understood? "Let them easily distribute, let them communicate." Thou hast, another hath not: communicate, that God may communicate to thee. Communicate here, and thou shalt communicate there. Communicate thy bread here, and thou shalt receive Bread there. What bread here? That which thou dost gather with sweat and toil, according to the curse upon the first man. What Bread there? Even Him who said, "I am the Living Bread which came down from heaven." [10] Here thou art rich, but thou art poor there. Gold thou hast, but thou hast not yet the Presence of Christ. Lay out what thou hast, that thou mayest receive what thou hast not. "Let them be rich in good works, let them easily distribute, let them communicate." [11]

5. Must they then lose all they have? He said, "Let them communicate," not "Let them give the whole." Let them keep for themselves as much as is sufficient for them, let them keep more than is sufficient. Let us give a certain portion of it. What portion? A tenth? [12] The Scribes and Pharisees gave tithes for whom Christ had not yet shed His Blood. The Scribes and Pharisees gave tithes; lest haply thou shouldest think thou art doing any great thing in breaking thy bread to the poor; and this is scarcely a thousandth part of thy means.

[1] Matt. xix. 18, 19.   [2] Matt. xix. 23.   [3] Matt. xix. 24.
[4] Matt. xix. 25.   [5] 1 Tim. vi. 17.   [6] 2 Cor. vi. 10.
[7] Serm. xi. (lxi. Ben.) 10 (ix.).

[8] 1 Tim. vi. 18.   [9] Ps. li. 3.   [10] John vi. 51.
[11] Vulgate.   [12] Luke xviii. 12.

And yet I am not finding fault with this; do even this. So hungry and thirsty am I, that I am glad even of these crumbs. But yet I cannot keep back what He who died for us said whilst He was alive. "Except your righteousness exceed the righteousness of the Scribes and Pharisees, ye shall in no case enter into the kingdom of heaven." [1] He does not deal softly with us; for He is a physician, He cuts to the quick. "Except your righteousness exceed the righteousness of the Scribes and Pharisees, ye shall in no case enter into the kingdom of heaven." The Scribes and Pharisees gave the tenth. How is it with you? Ask yourselves. Consider what you do, and with what means you do it; how much you give, how much you leave for yourselves; what you spend on mercy, what you reserve for luxury. So then, "Let them distribute easily, let them communicate, let them lay up in store for themselves a good foundation against the time to come, that they may hold on eternal life."

6. I have admonished the rich; now hear, ye poor. Ye rich, lay out your money; ye poor, refrain from plundering. Ye rich, distribute your means; ye poor, bridle your desires. Hear, ye poor, this same Apostle; "Godliness with sufficiency is a great getting." [2] Getting is the acquiring of gain. The world is yours in common with the rich; ye have not a house in common with the rich, but ye have the heaven in common, the light in common. Seek only for a sufficiency, seek for what is enough, and do not wish for more. All the rest is a weight, rather than a help; a burden, rather than an honour. "Godliness with sufficiency is great gain." First is Godliness. Godliness is the worship of God. "Godliness with sufficiency. For we brought nothing into this world." [3] Didst thou bring anything hither? Nay, not even did ye rich bring anything. Ye found all here, ye were born naked as the poor. In both alike is the same bodily infirmity; the same infant crying, the witness of our misery. "For we brought nothing into this world" (he is speaking to the poor), "neither can we carry anything out. And having food and covering, let us be therewith content." [4] "For they who wish to be rich." "Who wish to be," not who are. For they who are so, well and good. They have heard their lesson, that they be "rich in good works, that they distribute easily, that they communicate." They have heard already. Do ye now hear who are not yet rich. "They who wish to be rich, fall into temptation and a snare, and into many hurtful and foolish lusts." Do ye not fear? Hear what follows; "which drown men in destruction and perdition." [5] Dost thou not now fear? "for avarice is the root of all

evil"? [6] Avarice is the wishing to be rich, not the being rich already. This is avarice. Dost thou not fear to be "drowned in destruction and perdition"? Dost thou not fear "avarice the root of all evil"? Thou pluckest up out of thy field the root of thorns, and wilt thou not pluck up out of thy heart the root of evil desires? Thou cleansest thy field from which thy body gets its fruit, and wilt thou not cleanse thy heart where thy God indwelleth? "For avarice is the root of all evil, which while some coveted after, they have erred from the faith, and entangled themselves in many sorrows."

7. Ye have now heard what ye must do, ye have heard what ye must fear, ye have heard how the kingdom of heaven may be purchased, ye have heard by what the kingdom of heaven may be hindered. Be ye all of one mind in obeying the word of God. God made both the rich and poor. Scripture says, "The rich and the poor meet together, the Lord is the Maker of them both." [7] The rich and the poor meet together. In what way, except in this present life? The rich and the poor are born alike. Ye meet one another as ye walk on the way together. Do not thou oppress, nor thou defraud. The one hath need, the other hath plenty. But "the Lord is the Maker of them both." By him who hath, He helpeth him that needeth; by him who hath not, He proveth him that hath. We have heard, we have spoken; let us fear, let us take heed, let us pray, let us attain.

SERMON XXXVI.

[LXXXVI. BEN.]

ON THE WORDS OF THE GOSPEL, MATT. XIX. 21, "GO, SELL THAT THOU HAST, AND GIVE TO THE POOR," ETC.

1. THE Gospel by the present lesson has reminded me to speak to you, Beloved, of the heavenly treasure. For our God hath not, as unbelieving covetous men suppose, wished us to lose what we have: if what hath been enjoined us be properly understood, and piously believed, and devoutly received; He hath not enjoined us to lose, but rather shown a place where we may lay up. For no man can help thinking of his treasure, and following his riches in a kind of journeying of the heart. If then they are buried in the earth, his heart will seek the lowest earth; but if they are reserved in heaven, his heart [8] will be above. If Christians therefore have the will to do what they know that they also make open profession of (not that all who hear know this; [9] and I would that they who have known it, knew it not in vain); if then they have the

---

[1] Matt. v. 20. [2] 1 Tim. vi. 6. [3] 1 Tim. vi. 7.
[4] 1 Tim. vi. 8. [5] 1 Tim. vi. 9.

[6] 1 Tim. vi. 10. [7] Prov. xxii. 2. [8] *Sursum cor.*
[9] But communicants only, as alone hearing the words in the Office.

will to "lift up the heart" above, let them lay up there, what they love; and though yet in the flesh on earth, let them dwell with Christ in heart; and as her Head went before the Church, so let the heart of the Christian go before him. As the members are to go where Christ the Head hath gone before, so shall each man at his rising again go where his heart hath now gone before. Let us go hence then by that part of us which we may; our whole man will follow whither one part of us is gone before. Our earthly house must fall to ruin; our heavenly house is eternal. Let us move our goods beforehand, whither we are ourselves getting ready to come.

2. We have just heard a certain rich man seeking counsel from the "Good Master" as to the means of obtaining eternal life. Great was the thing he loved, and of little value was that he was unwilling to renounce. And so in perverseness of heart, on hearing Him whom he had but now called "Good Master," through the overpowering love of what was valueless, he lost the possession of what was of great price. If he had not wished to obtain eternal life, he would not have asked counsel how to obtain eternal life. How is it then, Brethren, that he rejected the words of Him whom he had called "Good Master," drawn out for him as they were from the doctrine of the faith? What? Is He a Good Master before He teacheth, and when He hath taught, a bad one? Before He taught, He was called "Good." He did not hear what he wished, but he did hear what was proper for him; he had come with longing, but he went away in sadness. What if He had told him, "Lose what thou hast"? when he went away sad, because it was said, "Keep what thou hast securely." "Go," saith He, "sell all that thou hast, and give to the poor."[1] Art thou afraid, it may be, lest thou shouldest lose it. See what follows; "And thou shalt have treasure in heaven." Before now it may be thou hast set some young slave to guard thy treasures; thy God will be the guardian of thy gold. He who gave them on earth, will Himself keep them in heaven. Perhaps he would not have hesitated to commit what he had to Christ, and was only sad because it was told him, "Give to the poor;" as though he would say in his heart, "Hadst Thou said, Give it to Me, I will keep it in heaven for thee; I would not hesitate to give it to my Lord, the 'Good Master;' but now thou hast said, 'Give to the poor.'"

3. Let no one fear to lay out upon the poor, let no one think that he is the receiver whose hand he sees. He receives it Who bade thee give it. And this I say not out of mine own heart, or by any human conjecture; hear Him

Himself, who at once exhorteth thee, and giveth thee a title of security. "I was an hungred," saith He, "and ye gave Me meat." And when after the enumeration of all their kind offices, they answered, "When saw we Thee an hungred?" He answered, "Inasmuch as ye have done it unto one of the least of these of Mine, ye have done it unto Me."[2] It is the poor man who begs, but He that is Rich receives. Thou givest to one who will make away with it, He receiveth it Who will restore it. Nor will He restore only what He receiveth; He is pleased to borrow upon interest, He promiseth more than thou hast given. Give the rein now to thy avarice, imagine thyself an usurer. If thou wert an usurer indeed, thou wouldest be rebuked by the Church, confuted by the word of God, all thy brethren would execrate thee, as a cruel usurer, desiring to wring gain from other's tears. But now be an usurer, no one will hinder thee. Thou art willing to lend to a poor man, who whenever he may repay thee will do it with grief; but lend now to a debtor who is well able to pay, and who even exhorteth thee to receive what he promiseth.

4. Give to God, and press God for payment.[3] Yea rather give to God, and thou wilt be pressed to receive payment. On earth indeed thou hadst to seek thy debtor; and he sought too, but only to find where he might hide himself from thy face. Thou hadst gone to the judge, and said, "Bid that my debtor be summoned;" and he on hearing this gets away, and cares not even to wish thee well,[4] though to him perhaps in his need thou hadst given wealth by thy loan. Thou hast one then on whom thou mayest well lay out thy money. Give to Christ; He will of His own accord press thee to receive, whilst thou wilt even wonder that He hath received ought of thee. For to them who are placed on His right hand He will first say, "Come, ye blessed of My Father." "Come" whither? "Receive the kingdom prepared for you from the foundation of the world." For what? "For I was an hungred, and ye gave Me meat; I was thirsty, and ye gave Me drink; I was a stranger, and ye took Me in; naked, and ye clothed Me; I was sick and in prison, and ye visited Me." And they will say, "Lord, when saw we Thee?"[5] What doth this mean? The debtor presses to pay,[6] and the creditors make excuses. But the trusty debtor will not let them suffer loss thereby. "Do ye hesitate to receive? I have received, and are ye ignorant of it?" and He makes answer how He has received; "Inasmuch as ye have done it unto one of the least of these of

---

[1] Matt. xix. 21.

[2] Matt. xxv. 40.   [3] Conveni Deum.
[4] Nec salutare te quærit, cui forte egenti salutem commodando præstiteras?
[5] Matt. xxv. 34, etc.   [6] Convenit.

Mine, ye have done it unto Me." "I received it not by Myself; but by Mine. What was given to them came to Me; be secure, ye have not lost it. Ye looked to those who were little able to pay on earth; ye have One who is well able to pay in heaven. I," He saith, "have received, I will repay."

5. And what have I received, and what do I repay? "'I was an hungred,' He saith, 'and ye gave Me meat;' and the rest. I received earth, I will give heaven; I received temporal things, I will restore eternal; I received bread, I will give life." Yea, we may even say thus, "I have received bread, I will give Bread; I have received drink, I will give Drink; I have received houseroom, I will give a House; I was visited in sickness, I will give Health; I was visited in prison, I will give Liberty. The bread which ye gave to My poor is consumed; the Bread which I will give both recruiteth[1] the failing and doth not fail." May He then give us Bread, He who is the living Bread which came down from heaven. When He shall give Bread, He will give Himself. For what didst thou intend when thou didst lend on usury? To give money, and to receive money; but to give a smaller sum, and to receive a larger. "I," saith God, "will give thee an exchange for the better for all that thou hast given Me. For if thou wert to give a pound of silver, and to receive a pound of gold, with how great joy wouldest thou be possessed? Examine and question avarice. "I have given a pound of silver, I receive a pound of gold!" What proportion is there between silver and gold! Much more then, what proportion is there between earth and heaven! And thy silver and gold thou wert to leave here below; whereas thou wilt not abide thyself for ever here. "And I will give thee something else, and I will give thee something more, and I will give thee something better; I will give thee even that which will last for ever." So then, Brethren, be our avarice restrained, that another, which is holy, may be enkindled. Evil altogether is her counsel, who hinders you from doing good. Ye are willing to serve an evil mistress, not owning a Good Lord. And sometimes two mistresses occupy the heart, and tear the slave asunder who deserves to be in slavery to such a double yoke.

6. Yes, sometimes two opposing mistresses have possession of a man, avarice and luxuriousness. Avarice says, "Keep;" luxuriousness says, "Spend." Under two mistresses bidding and exacting diverse things what canst thou do? They have both their mode of address. And when thou dost begin to be unwilling to obey them, and to take a step towards thy liberty; because they have no power to command, they use caresses. And their caresses are more to be guarded against than their commands. What says avarice? "Keep for thyself, keep for thy children. If thou shouldest be in want, no one will give to thee. Live not for the time present only; consult for the future." On the other hand is luxuriousness. Live whilst thou mayest. Do good to thine own soul. Die thou must, and thou knowest not when; thou knowest not to whom thou shalt leave what thou hast, or who shall possess it. Thou art taking the bread out of thine own mouth, and perhaps after thy death thine heir will not so much as place a cup of wine upon thy tomb; or if so be he place a cup, he will drink himself drunk with it, not a drop[2] will come down to thee. Do well therefore to thine own soul, when and whilst thou canst." Thus avarice did enjoin one thing; "Keep for thyself, consult for the future." Luxuriousness another, "Do well to thine own soul."

7. But O free man, called unto liberty, be weary, be weary of thy servitude to such mistresses as these. Acknowledge thy Redeemer, thy Deliverer. Serve Him, He enjoineth easier things, He enjoineth not things contrary one to another. I am bold further to say; avarice and luxuriousness did enjoin upon thee contrary things, so that thou couldest not obey them both; and one said, "Keep for thyself, and consult for the future;" the other said, "Spend freely, do well to thine own soul." Now let thy Lord and thy Redeemer come forth, and He shall say the same, and yet no contrary things. If thou wilt not, His house hath no need of an unwilling servant. Consider thy Redeemer, consider thy Ransom. He came to redeem thee, He shed His Blood. Dear He held thee whom He purchased at so dear a price. Thou dost acknowledge Him who bought thee, consider from what He redeemeth thee. I say nothing of the other sins which lord it proudly over thee; for thou wast serving innumerable masters. I speak only of these two, luxuriousness and avarice, giving thee contrary injunctions, hurrying thee into different things. Deliver thyself from them, come to thy God. If thou wast the servant of iniquity, be now the servant of righteousness. The words which they spake to thee, and the contrary injunctions they gave thee, the very same thou hearest now from thy Lord, yet are His injunctions not contrary. He doth not take away their words, but he taketh away their power. What did avarice say to thee? "Keep for thyself, consult for the future." The word is not changed, but the man is changed. Now, if thou wilt,

---

[1] *Et reficit et non deficit.*

[2] See, on the custom of festivals at the funeral of the dead, St. Augustin, Ep. 22 (al. 64) to Aurelius Bishop of Carthage and Primate of Africa, calling for their abolition. He gives an account of his having abolished them at Hippo, where he was only a Priest, in the 29th (167) Letter, to his friend Alypius Bishop of Thagaste. See also *Conf.* vi. 2.

compare the counsellors. The one is avarice, the other righteousness.

8. Examine these contrary injunctions. "Keep for thyself," says avarice. Suppose thou art willing to obey her, ask her where thou art to keep? Some well-defended place she will show thee, walled chamber, or iron chest. Well, use all precautions; yet peradventure some thief in the house will burst open the secret places; and whilst thou art taking precautions for thy money, thou wilt be in fear of thy life. It may be whilst thou art keeping up thy store, he whose mind is set to plunder them, has it even in his thoughts to kill thee. Lastly, even though by various precautions thou shouldest defend thy treasure and thy clothes against thieves; defend them still against the rust and moth. What canst thou do then? Here is no enemy without to take away thy goods, but one within consuming them.

9. No good counsel then has avarice given. See she has enjoined thee to keep, yet has not found a place where thou mayest keep. Let her give also her next advice, "Consult for the future." For what future? for a few and those uncertain days. She says, "Consult for the future," to a man who, it may be, will not live even till to-morrow. But suppose him to live as long as avarice thinks he will, not as long as she can prove, or assure him, or have any confidence about, but suppose him to live as long as she thinks, that he grow old and so come to his end: when he is even now bent double with old age, and leaning on his stick for support, still is he seeking gain, and hears avarice saying still, "Consult for the future." For what future? When he is even at his last breath she speaks. She says, "for thy children's sake." Would that at least we did not find the old men who had no children avaricious. Yet to these even, to such as these even, who cannot even excuse their iniquity by any empty [1] show of natural affection, she ceases not to say, "Consult for the future." But it may be that these will soon blush for themselves; so let us look to those who have children, whether they are certain that their children will possess what they shall leave? Let them observe in their lifetime the children of other men, some losing what they had by the unjust violence of others, others by their own wickedness consuming what they possessed; and they remain in poor estate, who were the children of rich men. Cease then to be the home-born slaves of avarice. But a man will say, "My children will possess this." It is uncertain; I do not say, it is false, but at best, it is uncertain. But now suppose it to be certain, what dost thou wish to leave them? What thou hast gotten for thyself. Assuredly what thou hast gotten was

not left thee, yet thou hast it. If thou hast been able to get possession of what was not left to thee, then will they also be able to get what thou shalt not leave to them.

10. Thus have the counsels of avarice been refuted; but now let the Lord say the same words, now let righteousness speak: the words will be the same, but not the same the meaning. "Keep for thyself," saith the Lord, "consult for the future." Now ask Him, "Where shall I keep?" "Thou shalt have treasure in heaven, where no thief approacheth, nor moth corrupteth." [2] Against what an enduring future shalt thou keep it! "Come, ye blessed of My Father, receive the kingdom prepared for you from the foundation of the world." [3] And of how many days this kingdom is, the end of the passage shows. For after He had said of those on the left hand, "So these shall go away into everlasting burning;" of those on the right hand He saith, "but the righteous into life eternal." [4] This is "consulting for the future." A future which has no future beyond it. Those days without an end are called both "days," and "a day." For one when he was speaking of those days, saith, "That I may dwell in the house of the Lord for length of days." [5] And they are called a day, "This day have I begotten thee." [6] Now those days are one day; because there is no time, in it; that day is neither preceded by a yesterday, nor succeeded by a to-morrow. So then let us "consult for *the* future:" the words indeed which avarice said to thee are not different in terms from this, yet by them is avarice overthrown.

11. One thing may yet be said, "But what am I to do about my children?" Hear on this point also the counsel of thy Lord. If thy Lord should say to thee, "The thoughts of them concern Me more who did create, than thee who didst beget them," [7] peradventure thou couldest have nothing to say. Yet thou wilt look upon that rich man who went away sorrowful, and was rebuked in the Gospel, and wilt say to thyself perhaps, "That rich man did evil in not selling all and giving to the poor, because he had no children; but I have children; I have those for whom I should be keeping something. In this weakness too the Lord is ready to advise with thee. I would be bold to speak through His mercy; I would be bold to say something, not of mine own imagining, but of His pity. Keep then for thy children too, but hear me. Suppose (such is man's condition) any one should lose one of his children; mark, Brethren, mark how that avarice has no excuse, either as respects this world or the world to come. Such, I say, is man's condition; for

---

[1] *Imagine.*

[2] Matt. xix. 21; Luke xii. 33.
[3] Matt. xxv. 34. [4] Matt. xxv 46. [5] Ps. xxiii. 6.
[6] Ps. ii. 7. [7] *Vide* Serm. ix. 20, 21 (Ben.).

it is not that I wish it, but we see instances. Some Christian child has been lost: thou hast lost a Christian child; not that thou hast indeed lost him, but hast sent him before thee. For he is not gone [1] quite away, but gone before. Ask thine own faith: surely thou too wilt go thither presently, where he hath gone before. It is but a short question I ask, which yet I suppose no one will answer. Does thy son live? Ask thy faith. If he live then, why is his portion seized upon by his brothers? But thou wilt say, What, will he return and possess it? Let it then be sent to him whither he is gone before; he cannot come to his goods, his goods can go to him. Consider only with Whom he is. If any son were serving at the Court, and became the Emperor's friend, and were to say to thee, "Sell my portion, which is there, and send it to me;" wouldest thou find what to answer him? Well, thy son is now with the Emperor of all emperors, with the King of all kings, with the Lord of all lords; send to Him. I do not say thy son is in need himself; but his Lord with whom he is, is in need upon the earth. He vouchsafes to receive here, what He gives in heaven. Do what some avaricious men are wont to do, make out a conveyance,[2] bestow upon those who are in pilgrimage, what thou mayest receive in thine own country.

12. But now I am not speaking at all of thyself, but of thy child. Thou art hesitating to give what is thine own, yea, rather art hesitating to restore what is another's; surely thou art hereby convicted, that it was not for thy children that thou wast laying up. See, thou dost not give to thy children, seeing thou wilt even take away from thy children. From this child at all events wilt thou take away. Why is he unworthy to receive his part, because he is living with One worthier than all? There would be reason in it, if he with whom thy son is living, were unwilling to receive it. Rich shalt thou now be for thine house, but that the house of God. So far it is then from me to say to thee, "Give what thou hast;" that I am saying to thee, "Pay that thou owest." But thou wilt say, "His brothers will have it." O evil maxim, which may teach thy children to wish for their brother's death. If they shall be enriched by the property of their deceased brother, take heed how they may watch for [3] one another in thine house. What then wilt thou do? Wilt thou divide his patrimony, and so give lessons of parricide?

13. But I am unwilling to speak of the loss of a child, lest I seem to threaten calamities, which do befall men. Let us speak in some more happy and auspicious tone. I do not say then, thou wilt have one less; reckon rather that thou hast one more. Give Christ a place

with thy children, be thy Lord added to thy family; be thy Creator added to thy offspring, be thy Brother added to the number of thy children. For though there is so great a distance, yet hath He condescended to be a Brother. And though He be the Father's Only Son, He hath vouchsafed to have coheirs. Lo, how bountifully hath He given! why wilt thou give in such barren sort? Thou hast two children; reckon Him a third: thou hast three, let Him be reckoned as a fourth: thou hast five, let Him be called a sixth; thou hast ten, let Him be the eleventh. I will say no more; keep the place of one child for thy Lord. For what thou shalt give to thy Lord, will profit both thee and thy children; whereas, what thou dost keep for thy children wrongly, will hurt both thee and them. Now thou wilt give one portion, which thou hast reckoned as one child's portion. Reckon that thou hast got one child more.

14. What great demand is this, my Brethren? I give you counsel only; do I use violence?[4] As saith the Apostle, "This I speak for your own profit, not that I may cast a snare upon you."[5] I imagine, Brethren, that it is a light and easy thought for a father of children to suppose that he has one child more, and thereby to procure such an inheritance as thou mayest possess for ever, both thou and thy children. Avarice can say nothing against it. Ye have cried out in acclamation at these words. Turn your words rather against her; let her not overcome you; let her not have greater power in your hearts, than your Redeemer. Let her not have greater power in your hearts, than He who exhorteth us to "lift up our hearts." And so now let us dismiss her.

15. What says luxuriousness? What? "Do well to thine own soul." See also the Lord says the same, "Do well to thine own soul." What luxuriousness was saying to thee, the same saith Righteousness to thee. But consider here again in what sense the words are used. If thou wouldest do well to thine own soul, consider that rich man who wished to do well to his soul, after the counsel of luxuriousness and avarice. His "ground brought forth plentifully, and he had no room where to bestow his fruits; and he said, What shall I do?" I have no room where to bestow my fruits; I have found out what to do; "I will pull down my" old "barns, and build new," and will fill them, "and say to my soul, Thou hast much goods; take thy pleasure." Hear the counsel against luxuriousness; "Thou fool, this night thy soul shall be required of thee; and whose shall those things be which thou hast provided?"[6] And whither must that soul which shall be required of him go? This night it shall be required, and shall go he knows not whither.

[1] *Neque enim ille decessit sed præcessit.*
[2] *Fac trajectitium.*   [3] *Attendant.*
[4] *Guttur ligo.*   [5] 1 Cor. vii. 35.   [6] Luke xii. 16, etc.

16. Consider that other luxurious, proud, rich man. He "feasted sumptuously every day, and was clothed in purple and fine linen;" and "the poor man laid at his gate full of sores, and desired" in vain "the crumbs from the rich man's table;"[1] he fed the dogs with his sores, but he was not fed by the rich man. They both died; one of them was buried; of the other what is said? "He was carried by the Angels into Abraham's bosom." The rich man sees the poor man; yea rather it is now the poor man sees the rich; he longs for a drop of water on his tongue from his finger, from him who once longed for a crumb from his table. Indeed their lot was changed. The dead rich man asks for this in vain: O let not us who are alive hear it in vain. For he wished to return again to the world,[2] and was not permitted; he wished one of the dead to be sent to his brethren, neither was this granted him. But what was said to him? "They have Moses and the Prophets;" and he said, "They will not hear except one go from the dead." Abraham said to him, "If they hear not Moses and the Prophets, neither will they believe though one go from the dead."

17. What luxuriousness then said in a perverted sense concerning the giving of alms, and procuring rest for our souls against the time to come, that so we may "do well to our souls," Moses also and the Prophets have spoken. Let us give ear while we are alive. Because there he will desire in vain to hear, who has despised these words when he heard them here. Are we expecting that one should rise even from the dead, and tell us to do well to our own souls? It has been done already: thy father hath not risen again, but thy Lord hath risen. Hear Him, and accept good counsel. Spare not thy treasures, spend as freely as thou canst. This was the voice of luxuriousness: it has become the Lord's Voice. Spend as freely as thou canst, do well to thy soul, lest this night thy soul be required. Here then ye have in Christ's Name a discourse as I think on the duty of almsgiving. This your voice now applauding, is then only well-pleasing to the Lord, if He see withal your hands active in works of mercy.

SERMON XXXVII.

[LXXXVII. BEN.]

DELIVERED ON THE LORD'S DAY, ON THAT WHICH IS WRITTEN IN THE GOSPEL, MATT. XX. 1, "THE KINGDOM OF HEAVEN IS LIKE UNTO A MAN THAT WAS A HOUSEHOLDER, WHO WENT OUT EARLY IN THE MORNING TO HIRE LABOURERS INTO HIS VINEYARD."

1. YE have heard out of the Holy Gospel a parable well suited to the present season, concerning the labourers in the vineyard. For now is the time of the material[3] vintage. Now there is also a spiritual vintage, wherein God rejoiceth in the fruit of His vineyard. For we cultivate God, and God cultivateth us.[4] But we do not so cultivate God as to make Him any better thereby. For our cultivation is the labour of the heart, not of the hands.[5] He cultivateth us as the husbandman doth his field. In then that He cultivateth us, He maketh us better; because so doth the husbandman make his field better by cultivating it, and the very fruit He seeketh in us is, that we may cultivate Him. The culture He exerciseth on us is, that He ceaseth not to root out by His Word the evil seeds from our hearts, to open our heart, as it were, by the plough of His Word, to plant the seed of His precepts, to wait for the fruit of piety. For when we have so received that culture into our heart, as to cultivate Him well, we are not ungrateful to our Husbandman, but render the fruit wherein He rejoiceth. And our fruit doth not make Him the richer, but us the happier.

2. See then; hear how, as I have said, "God cultivateth us." For that we cultivate God, there is no need to be proved to you. For all men have this on their tongue, that men cultivate God, but the hearer feels a kind of awe, when he hears that God cultivates man; because it is not after the ordinary usage of men to say, that God cultivateth men, but that men cultivate God. We ought therefore to prove to you, that God also doth cultivate men; lest perchance we be thought to have spoken a word contrary to sound doctrine,[6] and men dispute in their heart against us, and as not knowing our meaning, find fault with us. I have determined therefore to show you, that God doth also cultivate us; but as I have said already, as a field, that He may make us better. Thus the Lord saith in the Gospel, "I am the Vine, ye are the branches, My Father is the Husbandman."[7] What doth the Husbandman do? I ask you who are husbandmen. I suppose he cultivates his field. If then God the Father be a Husbandman, He hath a field; and His field He cultivateth, and from it He expecteth fruit.

3. Again, He "planted a vineyard," as the Lord Jesus Christ Himself saith, "and let it out to husbandmen, who should render Him the fruit in the proper season. And He sent His servants to them to ask for the hire of the vineyard. But they treated them despitefully, and killed some,"[8] and contemptuously refused to render the fruits. "He sent others also," they suffered the like treatment. And then the House-

---

[1] Luke xvi. 19, etc. [2] *Superos.*

[3] *Corporalis.*
[4] *Colit nos Deus et colimus Deum.* Conf. B. xiii. 1.
[5] *Colimus enim eum adorando non arando.*
[6] *Indisciplinatum.* [7] John xv. 1, 5.
[8] Matt. xxi. 33, etc.

holder, the Cultivator of His field, and the Planter, and Letter out of His vineyard, said; "I will send Mine Only Son, it may be they will at least reverence Him." And so He saith, "He sent His Own Son also. They said among themselves, This is the heir, come, let us kill Him, and the inheritance shall be ours. And they killed Him, and cast Him out of the vineyard. When the Lord of the vineyard cometh, what will He do to those wicked husbandmen? They answered, He will miserably destroy those wicked men, and will let out His vineyard unto other husbandmen, which shall render Him the fruits in their seasons." The vineyard was planted when the law was given in the hearts of the Jews. The Prophets were sent, seeking fruit, even their good life: the Prophets were treated despitefully by them, and were killed. Christ also was sent, the Only Son of the Householder; and they killed Him who was the Heir, and so lost the inheritance. Their evil counsel turned out contrary to their designs. They killed Him that they might possess the inheritance; and because they killed Him, they lost it.

4. Ye have just heard too the parable out of the Holy Gospel; that "the kingdom of heaven is like unto a householder, which went out to hire labourers into His vineyard. He went out in the morning," and hired those whom he found, and agreed with them for a denarius as their hire. He "went out again at the third hour, and found others," and brought them to the labour of the vineyard. "And the sixth and ninth hour he did likewise. He went out also at the eleventh hour," near the end of the day, "and found some idle and standing still, and he said to them, Why stand ye here?" Why do ye not work in the vineyard? They answered, "Because no man hath hired us." "Go ye also," said He, "and whatsoever is right I will give you."[1] His pleasure was to fix their hire at a denarius. How could they who had only to work one hour dare hope for a denarius? Yet they congratulated themselves in the hope that they should receive something. So then these were brought in even for one hour. At the end of the day he ordered the hire to be paid to all, from the last to the first. Then he began to pay at those who had come in at the eleventh hour, and he commanded a denarius to be given them. When they who had come at the first hour saw that the others had received a denarius, which he had agreed for with themselves, "they hoped that they should have received more:" and when their turn came, they also received a denarius. "They murmured against the good man of the house, saying, Behold, thou hast made us who have borne the burning and heat of the day, equal and like to those who have laboured but one hour in the vineyard." And "the good man," returning a most just answer to one of them, said, "Friend, I do thee no wrong;" that is, "I have not defrauded thee, I have paid thee what I agreed for with thee. "I have done thee no wrong," for I have paid thee what I agreed for. To this other it is my will not to render a payment, but to bestow a gift. "Is it not lawful for me to do what I will with mine own? Is thine eye evil, because I am good?" If I had taken from any one what did not belong to me, rightly I might be blamed, as fraudulent and unjust: if I had not paid any one his due, rightly might I be blamed as fraudulent, and as withholding what belonged to another; but when I pay what is due, and give besides to whom I will, neither can he to whom I owed find fault, and he to whom I gave ought to rejoice the more." They had nothing to answer; and all were made equal; "and the last became first, and the first last;" by equality[2] of treatment, not by inverting their order. For what is the meaning of, "the last were first, and the first last"? That both the first and last received the same.

5. How is it that he began to pay at the last? Are not all, as we read, to receive together? For we read in another place of the Gospel, that He will say to those whom He shall set on the right hand, "Come, ye blessed of My Father, receive the kingdom prepared for you from the beginning of the world."[3] If all then are to receive together, how do we understand in this place, that they received first who began to work at the eleventh hour, and they last who were hired at the first hour? If I shall be able so to speak, as to reach your understanding, God be thanked. For to Him ought ye to render thanks, who distributeth to you by me; for nought of my own do I distribute. If ye ask me, for example, which of the two has received first, he who has received after one hour, or he who after twelve hours; every man would answer that he who has received after one hour, has received before him who received after twelve hours. So then though they all received at the same hour, yet because some received after one hour, others after twelve hours, they who received after so short a time are said to have received first. The first righteous men, as Abel, and Noe, called as it were at the first hour, will receive together with us the blessedness of the resurrection. Other righteous men after them, Abraham, Isaac, Jacob, and all of their age, called as it were at the third hour, will receive together with us the blessedness of the resurrection. Other righteous

---

[1] Matt. xx. 1, etc.   [2] Æquando non præposterando.   [3] Matt. xxv. 34.

men, as Moses, and Aaron, and whosoever with them were called as it were at the sixth hour, will receive together with us the blessedness of the resurrection. After them the Holy Prophets, called as it were at the ninth hour, will receive together with us the same blessedness. In the end of the world all Christians, called as it were at the eleventh hour, will receive with the rest the blessedness of that resurrection. All will receive together; but consider those first men, after how long a time do they receive it? If then those first receive after a long time, we after a short time; though we all receive together, yet we seem to have received first, because our hire will not tarry long in coming.

6. In that hire then shall we be all equal, and the first as the last, and the last as the first; because that denarius is life eternal, and in the life eternal all will be equal. For although through diversity of attainments [1] the saints will shine, some more, some less; yet as to this respect, the gift of eternal life, it will be equal to all. For that will not be longer to one, and shorter to another, which is alike everlasting; that which hath no end will have no end either for thee or me. After one sort in that life will be wedded chastity, after another virgin purity; in one sort there will be the fruit of good works, in another sort the crown of martyrdom. [2] One in one sort, and another in another; yet in respect to the living for ever, this man will not live more than that, nor that than this. For alike without end will they live, though each shall live in his own brightness: and the denarius in the parable is that life eternal. Let not him then who has received after a long time murmur against him who has received after a short time. To the first, it is a payment; to the other, a free gift; yet the same thing is given alike to both.

7. There is also something like this in this present life, and besides that solution of the parable, by which they who were called at the first hour are understood of Abel and the righteous men of his age, and they at the third, of Abraham and the righteous men of his age, and they at the sixth, of Moses and Aaron and the righteous men of their age, and they at the eleventh, as in the end of the world, of all Christians; besides this solution of the parable, the parable may be seen to have an explanation in respect even of this present life. For they are as it were called at the first hour, who begin to be Christians fresh from their mother's womb; boys are called as it were at the third, young men at the sixth, they who are verging toward old age, at the ninth hour, and they who are called as if at the eleventh hour, are they who are altogether decrepit; yet all these are to receive the one and the same denarius of eternal life.

8. But, Brethren, hearken ye and understand, lest any put off to come into the vineyard, because he is sure, that, come when he will, he shall receive this denarius. And sure indeed he is that the denarius is promised him; but this is no injunction to put off. For did they who were hired into the vineyard, when the householder came out to them to hire whom he might find, at the third hour for instance, and did hire them, did they say to him, "Wait, we are not going thither till the sixth hour"? or they whom he found at the sixth hour, did they say, "We are not going till the ninth hour"? or they whom he found at the ninth hour, did they say, "We are not going till the eleventh? For he will give to all alike; why should we fatigue ourselves more than we need?" What He was to give, and what He was to do, was in the secret of His own counsel: do thou come when thou art called. For an equal reward is promised to all; but as to this appointed hour of working, there is an important question. For if, for instance, they who are called at the sixth hour, at that age of life that is, in which as in the full heat of noon, is felt the glow of manhood's years; if they, called thus in manhood, were to say, "Wait, for we have heard in the Gospel that all are to receive the same reward, we will come at the eleventh hour, when we shall have grown old, and shall still receive the same. Why should we add to our labour?" it would be answered them thus, "Art not thou willing to labour now, who dost not know whether thou shalt live to old age? Thou art called at the sixth hour; come. The Householder hath it is true promised thee a denarius, if thou come at the eleventh hour, but whether thou shalt live even to the seventh, no one hath promised thee. I say not to the eleventh, but even to the seventh hour. Why then dost thou put off him that calleth thee, certain as thou art of the reward, but uncertain of the day? Take heed then lest peradventure what he is to give thee by promise, thou take from thyself by delay." Now if this may rightly be said of infants as belonging to the first hour, if it may be rightly said of boys as belonging to the third, if it may be rightly said of men in the vigour of life, as in the full-day heat of the sixth hour; how much more rightly may it be said of the decrepit? Lo, already is it the eleventh hour, and dost thou yet stand still, and art thou yet slow to come?

9. But perhaps the Householder hath not gone out to call thee? If he hath not gone out, what mean our addresses to you? For we are servants of his household, we are sent to hire labourers. Why standest thou still then? Thou hast now ended the number of thy years; hasten after the denarius. For this is the "going out" of the Householder, the making himself known; foras-

---

[1] *Meritorum.* [2] *Passionis.*

much as he that is in the house is hidden, he is not seen by those who are without; but when he "goeth out" of the house, he is seen by those without. So Christ is in secret, as long as He is not known and acknowledged; but when He is acknowledged, He hath gone out to hire labourers. For now He hath come forth from a hidden place, to be known of men: everywhere Christ is known, Christ is preached; all places whatsoever under the heaven proclaim aloud the glory of Christ. He was in a manner the object of derision and contempt among the Jews, He appeared in low estate and was despised. For He hid His Majesty, and manifested His infirmity. That in Him which was manifested was despised, and that which was hidden was not known. "For had they known it, they would not have crucified the Lord of glory." [1] But is He still to be despised now that He sitteth in heaven, if He were despised when He was hanging on the tree? They who crucified Him wagged their head, and standing before His Cross, as though they had attained the fruit of their cruel rage, they said in mockery, "If He be the Son of God, let Him come down from the Cross. He saved others, Himself He cannot save." [2] He came not down, because He lay hid. For with far greater ease could He have come down from the Cross, who had power to rise again from the grave. He showed forth an example of patience for our instruction. He delayed His power, and was not acknowledged. For He had not then gone out to hire labourers, He had not made Himself known. On the third day He rose again, He showed Himself to His disciples, ascended into heaven, and sent the Holy Ghost on the fiftieth day after the resurrection, the tenth after the ascension. The Holy Ghost who was sent filled all who were in one room, one hundred and twenty men. [3] They "were filled with the Holy Ghost, and began to speak with the tongues of all nations;" [4] now was the calling manifest, now He went out to hire. For now the power of truth began to be made known to all. For then even one man having received the Holy Ghost, spake by himself with the tongues of all nations. But now in the Church oneness itself, as one man speaks in the tongues of all nations. For what tongue has not the Christian religion reached? to what limits does it not extend? Now is there no one "who hideth himself from the heat thereof;" [5] and delay is still ventured by him who stands still at the eleventh hour.

10. It is plain then, my Brethren, it is plain to all, do ye hold it fast, and be sure of it, that whensoever any one turns himself to the faith of our Lord Jesus Christ, from a useless [6] or abandoned way of life, all that is past is forgiven him, and as though all his debts were cancelled, a new account is entered into with him. All is entirely forgiven. Let no one be anxious in the thought that there remains anything which is not forgiven him. But on the other hand, let no one rest in a perverse security. For these two things are the death of souls, despair, and perverse hope. For as a good and right hope saveth, so doth a perverse hope deceive. First, consider how despair deceiveth. There are men, who when they begin to reflect on the evils they have done, think they cannot be forgiven; and whilst they think they cannot be forgiven, forthwith they give up their souls to ruin, and perish through despair, saying in their thoughts, "Now there is no hope for us; for such great sins as we have committed cannot be remitted or pardoned us; why then should we not satisfy our lusts? Let us at least fill up the pleasure of the time present, seeing we have no reward in that which is to come. Let us do what we list, though it be not lawful; that we may at least have a temporal enjoyment, because we cannot [7] attain to the receiving an eternal." In saying such things they perish through despair, either before they believe at all, or when Christians already, they have fallen by evil living into any sins and wickednesses. The Lord of the vineyard goeth forth to them, and by the Prophet Ezekial knocketh, and calleth to them in their despair, and as they turn their backs to Him that calleth them. "In whatsoever day a man shall turn from his most wicked way, I will forget all his iniquities." [8] If they hear and believe this voice, they are recovered from despair, and rise up again from that very deep and bottomless gulf, wherein they had been sunk.

11. But these must fear, lest they fall into another gulf, and they die through a perverse hope, who could not die through despair. For they change their thoughts, which are far different indeed from what they were before, but not less pernicious, and begin again to say in their hearts, "If in whatever day I turn from my most evil way, the merciful God, as He truly promiseth by the Prophet, will forget all my iniquities, why should I turn to-day and not to-morrow? Let this day pass as yesterday, in excess of guilty pleasure, in the full flow of licentiousness, let it wallow in deadly delights; to-morrow I shall 'turn myself,' and there will be an end to it." One may answer thee, An end of what? Of mine iniquities, thou wilt say. Well, rejoice indeed, that to-morrow there will be an end of thine iniquities. But what if before to-morrow thine own end shall be? So then thou dost well indeed to rejoice that

God hath promised thee forgiveness for thine iniquities, if thou art converted; but no one has promised thee to-morrow. Or if perchance some astrologer hath promised it, it is a far different thing from God's promise. Many have these astrologers deceived, in that they have promised themselves advantages, and have found only losses. Therefore for the sake of these again whose hope is wrong, doth the House-holder go forth. As He went forth to those who had despaired wrongly, and were lost in their despair, and called them back to hope; so doth He go forth to these also who would perish through an evil hope; and by another book He saith to them, "Make no tarrying to turn to the Lord."[1] As He had said to the others, "In whatsoever day a man shall turn from his most wicked way, I will forget all his iniquities," and took despair away from them, because they had now given up their soul to perdition, despairing of forgiveness by any means; so doth He go forth to these also who have a mind to perish through hope and delay; and speaketh to them, and chideth them, "Make no tarrying to turn to the Lord, and put not off from day to day; for suddenly shall the wrath of the Lord come forth, and in the day of vengeance He will destroy thee." Therefore put not off, shut not against thyself what now is open. Lo, the Giver of for-giveness openeth the door to thee; why dost thôu delay? Thou oughtest to rejoice, were He to open after ever so long a time to thy knock-ing; thou hast not knocked, yet doth He open, and dost thou remain outside? Put not off then. Scripture saith in a certain place, as touching works of mercy, "Say not, Go, and come again, and to-morrow I will give;[2] when thou canst do the kindness at once; for thou knowest not what may happen on the morrow." Here then is a precept of not putting off being merciful to another, and wilt thou by putting off be cruel against thine own self? Thou oughtest not to put off to give bread, and wilt thou put off to receive forgiveness? If thou dost not put off in showing pity towards another, "pity thine own soul also in pleasing God."[3] Give alms to thine own soul also. Nay I do not say, give to it, but thrust not back His Hand that would give to thee.

12. But men continually injure themselves ex-ceedingly in their fear to offend others. For good friends have much influence for good, and evil friends for evil. Therefore it was not the Lord's will to choose first senators, but fisher-men, to teach us for our own salvation to disre-gard the friendship of the powerful. O signal mercy of the Creator! For He knew that had He chosen the senator, he would say, "My rank has been chosen." If He had first made choice of the rich man, he would say, "My wealth has been chosen." If He had first made choice of an emperor, he would say, "My power has been chosen." If the orator he would say, "My elo-quence has been chosen." If of the philosopher, he would say, "My wisdom has been chosen." Meanwhile He says, let these proud ones be put off awhile, they swell too much. Now there is much difference between substantial size and swelling; both indeed are large, but both are not alike sound. Let them then, He says, be put off, these proud ones, they must be cured by some-thing solid. First give Me, He says, this fisher-man. "Come, thou poor one, follow Me; thou hast nothing, thou knowest nothing, follow Me. Thou poor and ignorant[4] one, follow Me. There is nothing in thee to inspire awe, but there is much in thee to be filled." To so copious a fountain an empty vessel should be brought. So the fisherman left his nets, the fisherman received grace, and became a divine orator. See what the Lord did, of whom the Apostle says, "God hath chosen the weak things of the world to confound the things which are mighty, and base things of the world hath God chosen, yea and things which are not, as if they were, that those things which are may be brought to nought."[5] And so now the fishermen's words are read, and the necks of orators are brought down. Let all empty winds then be taken away, let the smoke be taken away which vanishes as it mounts; let them be utterly despised when the question is of this salvation.

13. If any one in a city had some bodily sickness, and there was in that place some very skilful physician who was an enemy to the sick man's powerful friends; if any one, I say, in a city were labouring under some dangerous bodily sickness; and there was in the same city a very skilful physician, an enemy as I said, of the sick man's powerful friends, and they were to say to their friend, "Do not call him in, he knows nothing;" and they were to say this, not from any judgment of their mind, but through dislike of him; would he not for his own safety's sake remove from him the groundless assertions[6] of his powerful friends, and with whatever offence to them, in order that he might live but a few days longer, call that physician in, whom com-mon report had given out as most skilful to drive away the disease of his body? Well, the whole race of mankind is sick, not with diseases of the body, but with sin. There lies one great patient from East to West throughout the world. To cure this great patient came the Almighty Physician down. He humbled Himself even to mortal flesh, as it were to the sick man's bed.

[1] Ecclus. v. 7. [2] Prov. iii. 28.
[3] Ecclus. xxx. 23, Vulgate.

[4] *Idiota.* [5] 1 Cor. i. 27, 28. [6] *Fabulas.*

Precepts of health He gives, and is despised; they who do observe them are delivered. He is despised, when powerful friends say, " He knows nothing." If He knew nothing, His power would not fill the nations. If He knew nothing, He would not have been, before He was with us. If He knew nothing, He would not have sent the Prophets before Him. Are not those things which were foretold of old, fulfilled now? Does not this Physician prove the power of His art by the accomplishment of His promises? Are not deadly errors overturned throughout the whole world; and by the threshing of the world lusts subdued? Let no one say, " The world was better aforetime than now; ever since that Physician began to exercise His art, many dreadful things we witness here." Marvel not at this? Before that any were in course of healing, the Physician's residence [1] seemed clean of blood; but now rather as seeing what thou dost, shake off all vain delights, and come to the Physician, it is the time of healing, not of pleasure.

14. Let us then think, Brethren, of being cured. If we do not yet know the Physician, yet let us not like frenzied men be violent against Him, or as men in a lethargy turn away from Him. For many through this violence have perished, and many have perished through sleep. The frenzied are they who are made mad for want of sleep. The lethargic are they who are weighed down by excessive sleep. Men are to be found of both these kinds. Against this Physician it is the will of some to be violent, and forasmuch as He is Himself sitting in heaven, they persecute His faithful ones on earth. Yet even such as these He cureth. Many of them having been converted from enemies have become friends, from persecutors have become preachers. Such as these were the Jews, whom, though violent as men in frenzy against Him while He was here, He healed, and prayed for them as He hung upon the Cross. For He said, " Father, forgive them, for they know not what they do." [2] Yet many of them when their fury was calmed, their frenzy as it were got under, came to know God, and Christ. When the Holy Ghost was sent after the Ascension, they were converted to Him whom they crucified, and as believers drunk in the Sacrament His Blood, which in their violence they shed.

15. Of this we have examples. Saul persecuted the members of Jesus Christ, who is now sitting in heaven; grievously did he persecute them in his frenzy, in the loss of his reason, in the transport of his madness. But He with one word, calling to him out of heaven, " Saul, Saul, why persecutest thou Me?" [3] struck down the frantic one, raised him up whole, killed the persecutor, quickened the preacher. And so again many lethargic ones are healed. For to such are they like, who are not violent against Christ, nor malicious against Christians, but who in their delay are only dull and heavy with drowsy words, are slow to open their eyes to the light, and are annoyed with those who would arouse them. " Get away from me," says the heavy, lethargic man, " I pray thee, get away from me." Why? " I wish to sleep." But you will die in consequence. He through love of sleep will answer, " I wish to die." And Love from above calls out, " I do not wish it." Often does the son exhibit this loving affection to an aged father, though he must needs die in a few days; and is now in extreme old age. If he sees that he is lethargic, and knows from the physician that he is oppressed with a lethargic complaint, who tells him, " Arouse your father, do not let him sleep, if you would save his life"! Then will the son come to the old man, and beat, and squeeze, or pinch, or prick him, or give him any uneasiness, and all through his dutiful affection to him; and will not allow him to die at once, die though he soon must from very age; and if his life is thus saved, the son rejoices that he has now to live some few days more with him who must soon depart to make way for him. With how much greater affection then ought we to be importunate [4] with our friends, with whom we may live not a few days in this world, but in God's presence for ever! Let them then love us, and do what they hear us say, and worship Him, whom we also worship, that they may receive what we also hope for. " Let us turn to the Lord," etc.

SERMON XXXVIII.

[LXXXVIII. BEN.]

ON THE WORDS OF THE GOSPEL, MATT. XX. 30, ABOUT THE TWO BLIND MEN SITTING BY THE WAY SIDE, AND CRYING OUT, " LORD, HAVE MERCY ON US, THOU SON OF DAVID."

1. YE know, Holy Brethren, full well as we do, that our Lord and Saviour Jesus Christ is the Physician of our eternal health; and that to this end He took the weakness of our nature, that our weakness might not last for ever. For He assumed a mortal body, wherein to kill death. And, " though He was crucified through weakness," as the Apostle saith, " yet He liveth by the power of God." [5] They are the words too of the same Apostle; " He dieth no more, and death shall have no more dominion over Him." [6] These things, I say, are well known to your faith. And there is also this which follows from it, that we should know that all the miracles which He

---

[1] Statio.   [2] Luke xxiii. 34.   [3] Acts ix. 4.   [4] Molesti.   [5] 2 Cor. xiii. 4.   [6] Rom. vi. 9.

did on the body, avail to our instruction, that we may from them perceive that which is not to pass away, nor to have any end. He restored to the blind those eyes which death was sure sometime to close; He raised Lazarus to life who was to die again. And whatever He did for the health of bodies, He did it not to this end that they should be for ever; whereas at the last He will give eternal health even to the body itself. But because those things which were not seen, were not believed; by means of these temporal things which were seen, He built up faith in those things which were not seen.

2. Let no one then, Brethren, say that our Lord Jesus Christ doeth not those things now, and on this account prefer the former to the present ages of the Church. In a certain place indeed the same Lord prefers those who " do not see, and yet believe," [1] to them who see and therefore believe. For even at that time so irresolute was the infirmity of His disciples, that they thought that He whom they saw to have risen again must be handled, in order that they might believe. It was not enough for their eyes that they had seen Him, unless their hands also were applied to His limbs, and the scars of His recent wounds were touched; that that disciple who was in doubt, might cry out suddenly when he had touched and recognised the scars, " My Lord and my God." [2] The scars manifested Him who had healed all wounds in others. Could not the Lord have risen again without the scars? Yes, but He knew the wounds which were in the hearts of His disciples, and to heal them He had preserved the scars on His own Body. And what said the Lord to him who now confessed and said, " My Lord and my God "? " Because thou hast seen," He said, " thou hast believed; blessed are they who do not see, and yet believe." Of whom spake He, Brethren, but of us? Not that He spake only of us, but of those also who shall come after us. For after a little while when He had departed from the sight of men, that faith might be established in their hearts, whosoever believed, believed, though they saw Him not, and great has been the merit of their faith; for the procuring of which faith they brought only the movement of a pious heart, and not the touching of their hands.

3. These things then the Lord did to invite us to the faith. This faith reigneth now in the Church, which is spread throughout the whole world. And now He worketh greater cures, on account of which He disdained not then to exhibit those lesser ones. For as the soul is better than the body, so is the saving health of the soul better than the health of the body. The blind body doth not now open its eyes by a

miracle of the Lord, but the blinded heart openeth its eyes to the word of the Lord. The mortal corpse doth not now rise again, but the soul doth rise again which lay dead in a living body. The deaf ears of the body are not now opened; but how many have the ears of their heart closed, which yet fly open at the penetrating word of God, so that they believe who did not believe, and they live well, who did live evilly, and they obey, who did not obey; and we say, " Such a man is become a believer; " and we wonder when we hear of them whom once we had known as hardened. Why then dost thou marvel at one who now believes, who is living innocently, and serving God; but because thou dost behold him seeing, whom thou hadst known to be blind; dost behold him living, whom thou hadst known to be dead; dost behold him hearing, whom thou hadst known to be deaf? For consider that there are who are dead in another than the ordinary sense, of whom the Lord spake to a certain man who delayed to follow the Lord, because he wished to bury his father; " Let the dead," said He, " bury their dead." [3] Surely these dead buriers are not dead in body; for if this were so, they could not bury dead bodies. Yet doth he call them dead; where, but in the soul within? For as we may often see in a household, itself sound and well, the master of the same house lying dead; so in a sound body do many carry a dead soul within; and these the Apostle arouses thus, " Awake, thou that sleepest, and arise from the dead, and Christ shall give thee light." [4] It is the Same who giveth light to the blind, that awakeneth the dead. For it is with His voice that the cry is made by the Apostle to the dead, " Awake, thou that sleepest." And the blind will be enlightened with light, when he shall have risen again. And how many deaf men did the Lord see before His eyes, when He said, " He that hath ears to hear, let him hear." [5] For who was standing before Him without his bodily ears? What other ears then did He seek for, but those of the inner man?

4. Again, what eyes did He look for when He spake to those who saw indeed, but who saw only with the eyes of the flesh? For when Philip said to Him, " Lord, show us the Father, and it sufficeth us ; " [6] he understood indeed that if the Father were shown him, it might well suffice him; but how would the Father suffice him whom He that was equal to the Father sufficed not? And why did He not suffice? Because He was not seen. And why was He not seen? Because the eye whereby He might be seen was not yet whole. For this, namely, that the Lord was seen in the flesh with the out-

ward eyes, not only the disciples who honoured Him saw, but also the Jews who crucified Him. He then who wished to be seen in another way, sought for other eyes. And therefore it was that to him who said, "Show us the Father, and it sufficeth us;" He answered, "Have I been so long time with you; and yet hast thou not known Me, Philip? He who hath seen Me, hath seen the Father also." [1] And that He might in the mean while heal the eyes of faith, he has first of all instructions given him regarding faith, that so he might attain to sight. And lest Philip should think that he was to conceive of God under the same form in which he then saw the Lord Jesus Christ in the body, he immediately subjoined; "Believest thou not that I am in the Father, and the Father in Me?" [2] He had already said, "He who hath seen Me, hath seen the Father also." But Philip's eye was not yet sound enough to see the Father, nor consequently to see the Son who is Himself Coequal with the Father. And so Jesus Christ took in hand to cure, and with the medicines and salve of faith to strengthen the eyes of his mind, which as yet were weak and unable to behold so great a light, and He said, "Believest thou not that I am in the Father, and the Father in Me?" Let not him then who cannot yet see what the Lord will one day show him, seek first to see what he is to believe; but let him first believe that the eye by which he is to see may be healed. For it was only the form of the servant which was exhibited to the eyes of servants; because if "He who thought it not robbery to be equal with God," [3] could have been now seen as equal with God by those whom He wished to be healed, He would not have needed to "empty Himself, and to take the form of a servant." But because there was no way whereby God could be seen, but whereby man could be seen, there was; therefore He who was God was made man, that that which was seen might heal that whereby He was not seen. For He saith Himself in another place, "Blessed are the pure in heart, for they shall see God." [4] Philip might of course have answered and said, "Lord, lo, I see Thee; is the Father such as I see Thee to be? forasmuch as Thou hast said, 'He who hath seen Me, hath seen the Father also'?" But before Philip answered thus, or perhaps before he so much as thought it, when the Lord had said, "He who hath seen Me, hath seen the Father also;" He immediately added, "Believest thou not that I am in the Father, and the Father in Me?" For with that eye he could not yet see either the Father, or the Son who is equal with the Father; but that his eye might be healed for seeing, he was to be anointed unto

believing. So then before thou seest what thou canst not now see, believe what as yet thou seest not. "Walk by faith," that thou mayest attain to sight. Sight will not gladden him in his home whom faith consoleth not by the way. For so says the Apostle, "As long as we are in the body, we are in pilgrimage from the Lord." [5] And he subjoins immediately why we are still "in pilgrimage," though we have now believed; "For we walk by faith," He says, "not by sight."

5. Our whole business then, Brethren, in this life is to heal this eye of the heart whereby God may be seen. To this end are celebrated the Holy Mysteries; to this end is preached the word of God; to this end are the moral exhortations of the Church, those, that is, that relate to the correction of manners, to the amendment of carnal lusts, to the renouncing the world, not in word only, but in a change of life: to this end is directed the whole aim of the Divine and Holy Scriptures, that that inner man may be purged of that which hinders us from the sight of God. For as the eye which is formed to see this temporal light, a light though heavenly, yet corporeal, and manifest, not to men only, but even to the meanest animals (for for this the eye is formed, to see this light); if anything be thrown or fall into it, whereby it is disordered, is shut out from this light; and though it encompass the eye with its presence, yet the eye turns itself away from, and is absent from it; and through its disordered condition is not only rendered absent from the light which is present, but the light to see which it was formed, is even painful to it. So the eye of the heart too when it is disordered and wounded turns away from the light of righteousness, and dares not and cannot contemplate it.

6. And what is it that disorders the eye of the heart? Evil desire, covetousness, injustice, worldly concupiscence, these disorder, close, blind the eye of the heart. And yet when the eye of the body is out of order, how is the physician sought out, what an absence of all delay to open and cleanse it, that that may be healed whereby this outward light is seen! There is running to and fro, no one is still, no one loiters, if even the smallest straw fall into the eye. And God it must be allowed made the sun which we desire to see with sound eyes. Much brighter assuredly is He who made it; nor is the light with which the eye of the mind is concerned of this kind at all. That light is eternal Wisdom. God made thee, O man, after His own image. Would He give thee wherewithal to see the sun which He made, and not give thee wherewithal to see Him who made thee, when He made thee after His own image? He

hath given thee this also; both hath He given thee. But much thou dost love these outward eyes, and despisest much that interior eye; it thou dost carry about bruised and wounded. Yea, it would be a punishment to thee, if thy Maker should wish to manifest Himself unto thee; it would be a punishment to thine eye, before that it is cured and healed. For so Adam in paradise sinned, and hid himself from the face of God. As long then as he had the sound heart of a pure conscience, he rejoiced at the presence of God; when that eye was wounded by sin, he began to dread the Divine light, he fled back into the darkness, and the thick covert of the trees, flying from the truth, and anxious for the shade.

7. Therefore, my Brethren, since we too are born of him, and as the Apostle says, "In Adam all die;"[1] for we were all at first two persons; if we were loth to obey the physician, that we might not be sick; let us obey Him now, that we may be delivered from sickness. The physician gave us precepts, when we were whole; He gave us precepts that we might not need a physician. "They that are whole," He saith, "need not a physician, but they that are sick."[2] When whole we despised these precepts, and by experience have felt how to our own destruction we despised His precepts. Now we are sick, we are in distress, we are on the bed of weakness; yet let us not despair. For because we could not come to the Physician, He hath vouchsafed to come Himself to us. Though despised by man when he was whole, He did not despise him when he was stricken. He did not leave off to give other precepts to the weak, who would not keep the first precepts, that he might not be weak; as though He would say, "Assuredly thou hast by experience felt that I spake the truth when I said, Touch not this. Be healed then now at length, and recover the life thou hast lost. Lo, I am bearing thine infirmity; drink thou the bitter cup. For thou hast of thine own self made those my so sweet precepts which were given to thee when whole, so toilsome. They were despised and so thy distress began; cured thou canst not be, except thou drink the bitter cup, the cup of temptations, wherein this life abounds, the cup of tribulation, anguish, and sufferings. Drink then," He says, "drink, that thou mayest live." And that the sick man may not make answer, "I cannot, I cannot bear it, I will not drink;" the Physician, all whole though he be, drinketh first, that the sick man may not hesitate to drink. For what bitterness is there in this cup, which He hath not drunk? If it be contumely; He heard it first when He drove out the devils, "He hath a devil, and by Beelze-

bub He casteth out devils."[3] Whereupon in order to comfort the sick, He saith, "If they have called the Master of the house Beelzebub, how much more shall they call them of His household?"[4] If pains are this bitter cup, He was bound and scourged and crucified. If death be this bitter cup, He died also. If infirmity shrink with horror from any particular kind of death, none was at that time more ignominious than the death of the cross. For it was not in vain that the Apostle, when setting forth His obedience, added, "Made obedient unto death, even the death of the cross."[5]

8. But because He designed to honour His faithful ones at the end of the world, He hath first honoured the cross in this world; in such wise that the princes of the earth who believe in Him have prohibited any criminal from being crucified; and that cross which the Jewish persecutors with great mockery prepared for the Lord, even kings His servants at this day bear with great confidence on their foreheads. Only the shameful nature of the death which our Lord vouchsafed to undergo for us is not now so apparent, Who, as the Apostle says, "was made a curse for us."[6] And when as He hung, the blindness of the Jews mocked Him, surely He could have come down from the Cross, who if He had not so willed, had not been on the Cross; but it was a greater thing to rise from the grave than to come down from the Cross. Our Lord then in doing these Divine, and in suffering these human things, instructs us by His Bodily miracles and Bodily patience, that we may believe, and be made whole to behold those things invisible which the eye of the body hath no knowledge of. With this intent then He cured these blind men of whom the account has just now been read in the Gospel. And consider what instruction He has by their cure conveyed to the man who is sick within.

9. Consider the issue of the thing, and the order of the circumstances. Those two blind men sitting by the way side cried out as the Lord passed by, that He would have mercy upon them. But they were restrained from crying out by the multitude which was with the Lord. Now do not suppose that this circumstance is left without a mysterious meaning. But they overcame the crowd who kept them back by the great perseverance of their cry, that their voice might reach the Lord's ears; as though He had not already anticipated their thoughts. So then the two blind men cried out that they might be heard by the Lord, and could not be restrained by the multitudes. The Lord "was passing by," and they cried out. The Lord "stood still," and they were healed. For "the Lord Jesus

---

[1] 1 Cor. xv. 22.   [2] Matt. ix. 12.

[3] Mark iii. 22.   [4] Matt. x. 25.   [5] Phil. ii. 8.
[6] Gal. iii. 13.

stood still, and called them, and said, What will ye that I shall do unto you? They say unto Him, That our eyes may be opened." [1] The Lord did according to their faith, He recovered their eyes. If we have now understood by the sick, the deaf, the dead, the sick, and deaf, and dead, within; let us look out in this place also for the blind within. The eyes of the heart are clossd; "Jesus passeth by" that we may cry out. What is, "Jesus passeth by"? Jesus is doing things which last but for a time. What is "Jesus passeth by"? Jesus doeth things which pass by. Mark and see how many things of His have "passed by." He was born of the Virgin Mary; is He being born always? As an infant was He suckled; is He suckled always? He ran through the successive ages of life unto man's full estate; doth He grow in body always? Boyhood succeeded to infancy, to boyhood youth, to youth man's full stature in several passing successions. Even the very miracles which He did are "passed by," they are read and believed. For because these miracles are written that so they might be read, they "passed by" when they were being done. In a word, not to dwell long on this, He was Crucified: is He hanging on the Cross always? He was Buried, He Rose again, He Ascended into heaven; "now He dieth no more, death shall no more have dominion over Him." [2] And His Divinity abideth ever, yea, the Immortality of His Body now shall never fail. But nevertheless all those things which were wrought by Him in time have "passed by;" and they are written to be read, and they are preached to be believed. In all these things then, "Jesus passeth by."

10. And what are "the two blind men by the way side," but the two people to cure whom Jesus came? Let us show those two people in the Holy Scriptures. It is written in the Gospel, "Other sheep I have which are not of this fold; them also must I bring, that there may be one fold and One Shepherd." [3] Who then are the two people? One the people of the Jews, and the other of the Gentiles. "I am not sent," He saith, "but unto the lost sheep of the house of Israel." [4] To whom did He say this? To the disciples; when that woman of Canaan who confessed herself to be a dog, cried out that she might be found worthy of the crumbs from the master's [5] table. And because she was found worthy, now were the two people to whom He had come made manifest: the Jewish people, to wit, of whom He said, "I am not sent but unto the lost sheep of the house of Israel;" and the people of the Gentiles, whose type this woman exhibited whom He had first rejected, saying, "It is not meet to cast the children's bread to

the dogs;" and to whom when she said, "Truth, Lord, yet the dogs eat of the crumbs which fall from their master's table;" He answered, "O woman, great is thy faith, be it unto thee even as thou wilt." [6] For of this people also was that centurion of whom the same Lord saith, "Verily I say unto you, I have not found so great faith, no, not in Israel." Because he had said, "I am not worthy that Thou shouldest come under my roof, but speak the word only, and my servant shall be healed." [7] So then the Lord even before His Passion and Glorification pointed out two people, the one to whom He had come because of the promises to the Fathers; and the other whom for His mercy's sake He did not reject; that it might be fulfilled which had been promised to Abraham, "In thy seed shall all nations be blessed." [8] Wherefore also the Apostle after the Lord's Resurrection and Ascension, when He was despised by the Jews, went to the Gentiles. Not that he was silent however towards the Churches which consisted of Jewish believers; "I was unknown," he says, "by face unto the Churches of Judæa which were in Christ. But they heard only that he which persecuted us in times past, now preacheth the faith which once he destroyed, and they glorified God in me." [9] So again Christ is called the "Corner Stone who made both one." [10] For a corner joins two walls which come from different sides together. And what was so different as the circumcision and uncircumcision, having one wall from Judæa, the other from the Gentiles? But they are joined together by the corner stone. "For the stone which the builders rejected, the same is become the head of the corner." [11] There is no corner in a building, except when two walls coming from different directions meet together, and are joined in a kind of unity. The "two blind men" then crying out unto the Lord were these two walls according to the figure.

11. Attend now, dearly Beloved. The Lord was "passing by," and the blind men "cried out." What is "was passing by"? As we have already said, He was doing works which "passed by." Now upon [12] these passing works is our faith built up. For we believe on the Son of God, not only in that He is the word of God, by whom all things were made; for if He had always continued "in the form of God, equal with God," and had not "emptied Himself in taking the form of a servant," the blind men would not even have perceived Him, that they might be able to cry out. But when He wrought passing works, that is, "when He humbled Himself, having become obedient unto death, even the death of the cross," the "two blind men cried

---

[1] Matt. xx. 32, 33.　　[2] Rom. vi. 9.　　[3] John x. 16.
[4] Matt. xv. 24.　　[5] Mereretur.

[6] Matt. xv. 26–28.　　[7] Matt. viii. 10, 8.　　[8] Gen. xxii. 18.
[9] Gal. i. 22-24.　　[10] Eph. ii. 14, 20.　　[11] Ps. cxviii. 22.
[12] Secundum.

out, Have mercy on us, thou Son of David." For this very thing that He David's Lord and Creator, willed also to be David's Son, He wrought in time, He wrought "passing by."

12. Now what is it, Brethren, "to cry out" unto Christ, but to [1] correspond to the grace of Christ by good works? This I say, Brethren, lest haply we cry aloud with our voices, and in our lives be dumb. Who is he that crieth out to Christ, that his inward blindness may be driven away by Christ as He is "passing by," that is, as He is dispensing to us those temporal sacraments, whereby we are instructed to receive the things which are eternal? Who is he that crieth out unto Christ? Whoso despiseth the world, crieth out unto Christ. Whoso despiseth the pleasures of the world, crieth out unto Christ. Whoso saith not with his tongue, but with his life, "The world is crucified unto me, and I unto the world," [2] crieth out unto Christ. Whoso "disperseth abroad and giveth to the poor, that his righteousness may endure for ever," [3] crieth out unto Christ. For let him that hears, and is not deaf to the sound, "sell that ye have, and give to the poor; provide yourselves bags which wax not old, a treasure in the heavens that faileth not; " [4] let him as he hears the sound as it were of Christ's footsteps "passing by," cry out in response to this in his blindness, that is, let him do these things. Let his voice be in his actions. Let him begin to despise the world, to distribute to the poor his goods, to esteem as nothing worth what other men love, let him disregard injuries, not seek to be avenged, let him give his "cheek to the smiter," let him pray for his enemies; if any "one have taken away his goods," let "him not ask for them again;" [5] if he "have taken anything from any man, let him restore fourfold." [6]

13. When he shall begin to do all this, all his kinsmen, relations, and friends will be in commotion. They who love this world, will oppose him. What madness this! you are too extreme: [7] what! are not other men Christians? This is folly, this is madness. And other such like things do the multitude cry out to prevent the blind from crying out. The multitude rebuked them as they cried out; but did not overcome their cries. Let them who wish to be healed understand what they have to do. Jesus is now also "passing by;" let them who are by the way side cry out. These are they "who know God with their lips, but their heart is far from Him." [8] These are by the way side, to whom as blinded [9] in heart Jesus gives His precepts. For when those passing things which Jesus did are re-

counted, Jesus is always represented to us as "passing by." For even unto the end of the world there will not be wanting "blind men sitting by the way side." Need then there is that they who sit by the way side should cry out. The multitude that was with the Lord would repress the crying of those who were seeking for recovery. Brethren, do ye see my meaning? For I know not how to speak, but still less do I know how to be silent. I will speak then, and speak plainly. For I fear "Jesus passing by" and "Jesus standing still;" and therefore I cannot keep silence. Evil and lukewarm Christians hinder good Christians who are truly earnest, [10] and wish to do the commandments of God which are written in the Gospel. This multitude which is with the Lord hinders those who are crying out, hinders those that is who are doing well, that they may not by perseverance be healed. But let them cry out, and not faint; let them not be led away as if by the authority of numbers; let them not imitate those who became Christians before them, who live evil lives themselves, and are jealous of the good deeds of others. Let them not say, "Let us live as these so many live." Why not rather as the Gospel ordains? Why dost thou wish to live according to the remonstrances of the multitude who would hinder thee, and not after the steps of the Lord, "who passeth by"? They will mock, and abuse, and call thee back; do thou cry out till thou reach the ears of Jesus. For they who shall persevere in doing such things as Christ hath enjoined, and regard not the multitudes that hinder them, nor think much of their appearing to follow Christ, that is of their being called Christians; but who love the light which Christ is about to restore to them, more than they fear the uproar of those who are hindering them; they shall on no account be separated from Him, and Jesus will "stand still," and make them whole.

14. For how are our eyes made whole? That as by faith we perceive Christ "passing by" in the temporal economy, [11] so we may attain to the knowledge of Him as "standing still" in His unchangeable Eternity. For then is the eye made whole when the knowledge of Christ's Divinity is attained. Let your love apprehend this; attend ye to the great mystery [12] which I am to speak of. All the things which were done by our Lord Jesus Christ in time, graft faith in us. We believe on the Son of God, not on the Word only, "by which all things were made;" but on this very Word, "made flesh that He might dwell among us," who was born of the Virgin Mary, and the rest which the Faith contains, and which are represented to us that Christ

---

[1] Congruere. [2] Gal. vi. 14. [3] Ps. cxii. 9.
[4] Luke xii. 33. [5] Luke vi. 30. [6] Luke xix. 8.
[7] Nimius. [8] Isa. xxix. 13; Matt. xv. 8.
[9] Obtritis.

[10] Studiosos. [11] Dispensatione. [12] Sacramentum.

might "pass by," and that the blind, hearing His footsteps as He "passeth by," might by their works "cry out," by their life exemplifying the profession of their faith. But now in order that they who cry out may be made whole, "Jesus standeth still." For he saw Jesus now "standing still," who says, "Though we have known Christ after the flesh, yet now henceforth know we Him no more."[1] For he saw Christ's Divinity as far as in this life is possible. There is then in Christ the Divinity and the Humanity. The Divinity "standeth still," the Humanity "passeth by." What means, The Divinity "standeth still"? It changeth not, is not shaken, doth not depart away. For He did not so come to us, as to depart from the Father; nor did He so ascend as to change His place. When He assumed Flesh, it changed place; but God assuming Flesh, seeing He is not in place, doth not change His place. Let us then be touched by Christ "standing still," and so our eyes be made whole. But whose eyes? The eyes of those who "cry out" when He is "passing by;" that is, who do good works through that faith, which hath been dispensed in time, to instruct us in our infancy.

15. Now what thing more precious can we have than the eye made whole? They rejoice who see this created light which shines from heaven, or even that which is given out from a lamp. And how wretched do they seem, who cannot see this light? But wherefore do I speak, and talk of all these things, but to exhort you all to "cry out," when Jesus "passeth by." I hold up this light which perhaps ye do not see as an object of love to you, Holy Brethren. Believe, whilst as yet ye see not; and "cry out" that ye may see. How great is thought to be the unhappiness of men, who do not see this bodily light? Does any one become blind; immediately it is said; "God is angry with him, he has committed some wicked deed." So said Tobias' wife to her husband. He cried out because of the kid, lest it had come of theft; he did not like to hear the sound of any stolen thing in his house; and she, maintaining what she had done, reproached her husband; and when he said, "Restore it if it be stolen;" she answered insultingly, "Where are thy righteous deeds?"[2] How great was her blindness who maintained the theft; and how clear a light he saw, who commanded the stolen thing to be restored! She rejoiced outwardly in the light of the sun; he inwardly in the light of Righteousness. Which of them was in the better light?

16. It is to the love of this light that I would exhort you, Beloved; that ye would cry out by your works, when the Lord "passeth by;" let

the voice of faith sound out, that "Jesus standing still," that is, the Unchangeable, Abiding Wisdom of God, and the Majesty of the Word of God, "by which all things were made," may open your eyes. The same Tobias in giving advice to his son, instructed him to this, to cry out; that is, he instructed him to good works. He told him to give to the poor, charged him to give alms to the needy, and taught him, saying, "My son, alms suffereth not to come into darkness."[3] The blind gave counsel for receiving and gaining light. "Alms," saith he, "suffereth not to come into darkness." Had his son in astonishment answered him, "What then, father, hast thou not given alms, that thou now speakest to me in blindness; art not thou in darkness, and yet thou dost say to me, "Alms suffereth not to come into darkness." But no, he knew well what the light was, concerning which he gave his son instruction, he knew well what he saw in the inner man. The son held out his hand to his father, to enable him to walk on earth; and the father to the son, to enable him to dwell in heaven.

17. To be brief; that I may conclude this Sermon, Brethren, with a matter which touches me very nearly, and gives me much pain, see what crowds there are which "rebuke the blind as they cry out." But let them not deter you, whosoever among this crowd desire to be healed; for there are many Christians in name, and in works ungodly; let them not deter you from good works. Cry out amid the crowds that are restraining you, and calling you back, and insulting you, whose lives are evil. For not only by their voices, but by evil works, do wicked Christians repress the good. A good Christian has no wish to attend the public shows. In this very thing, that he bridles his desire of going to the theatre, he cries out after Christ, cries out to be healed. Others run together thither, but perhaps they are heathens or Jews? Ah! indeed, if Christians went not to the theatres, there would be so few people there, that they would go away for very shame. So then Christians run thither also, bearing the Holy Name only to their condemnation. Cry out then by abstaining from going, by repressing in thy heart this worldly[4] concupiscence; hold on with a strong and persevering cry unto the ears of the Saviour, that Jesus may "stand still" and heal thee. Cry out amidst the very crowds, despair not of reaching the ears of the Lord. For the blind men in the Gospel did not cry out in that quarter, where no crowd was, that so they might be heard in that direction, where there was no impediment from persons hindering them. Amidst the very crowds they cried out; and yet the

Lord heard them. And so also do ye even amidst sinners, and sensual men, amidst the lovers of the vanities of the world, there cry out that the Lord may heal you. Go not to another quarter to cry out unto the Lord, go not to heretics, and cry out unto Him there. Consider, Brethren, how in that crowd which was hindering them from crying out, even there were they who cried out made whole.

18. For observe this too, Holy Brethren, what it is to persevere in crying out. I will speak of what many as well as myself have experienced in Christ's name ; for the Church does not cease to give birth to such as these. When any Christian has begun to live well, to be fervent in good works, and to despise the world ; in this newness of his life he is exposed to the animadversions and contradictions of cold Christians. But if he persevere, and get the better of them by his endurance, and faint not in good works ; those very same persons who before hindered will now respect him.[1] For they rebuke, and hinder, and withstand him so long as they have any hope that he will yield to them. But if they shall be overcome by their perseverance who make progress, they turn round and begin to say, "He is a great man, a holy man, happy he to whom God hath given such grace." Now do they honour him, they congratulate and bless and laud him ; just as that multitude did which was with the Lord. They first hindered the blind men that they might not cry out ; but when they continued to cry so as to attain to be heard, and to obtain the Lord's mercy, that same multitude now says, "Jesus calleth you." And they who a little before "rebuked them that they should hold their peace," use now the voice of exhortation. Now he only is not called by the Lord, who is not in labour in this world. But who is there in this life who is not in labour through his sins and iniquities? But if all labour, it is said to all, "Come unto Me, all ye that labour."[2] Now if this is said to all, why ascribest thou thy miscarriage[3] to Him that so inviteth thee? Come. His house is not too narrow for thee ; the kingdom of God is possessed equally by all, and wholly by each one ; it is not diminished by the increasing number of those who possess it, because it is not divided. And that which is possessed by many with one heart, is whole and entire for each one.

19. Yet in the mysterious sense of this passage, Brethren, we recognise what is expressed most plainly in other places of the sacred books, that there are within the Church both good and bad, as I often express it, wheat and chaff. Let no one leave the floor before the time, let him bear with the chaff in the time of threshing, let

him bear with it in the floor. For in the barn he will have none of it to bear with. The Winnower will come, who shall divide the bad from the good. There will then be a bodily separation too, which a spiritual separation now precedes. In heart be always separated from the bad, in body be united with them for a time, only with caution. Yet be not negligent in correcting those who belong to you, who in any way appertain to your charge, by admonition, or instruction, by exhortation, or by threats. Do it, in whatsoever way ye can. And because ye find in Scripture and in the examples of Saints, whether of those who lived before or after the coming of the Lord in this life, that the bad do not defile the good in unity with them, do not on this account become slow in the correction of the bad. In two ways the bad will not defile thee ; if thou consent not to him, and if thou reprove him ; this is, not to communicate with him, not to consent to him. For there is a communication, when an agreement either of the will or of the approbation is joined to his deed. This the Apostle teaches us, when he says, "Have no communication with the unfruitful works of darkness."[4] And because it was a small matter not to consent, if negligence in correction accompanied it, he says, "But rather reprove them." See how he comprehended both at once, "Have no communication, but rather reprove them." What is, "Have no communication"? Do not consent to them, do not praise them, do not approve them. What is, "But rather reprove them"? Find fault with, rebuke, repress them.

20. But then in the correction and repressing of other men's sins, one must take heed, that in rebuking another he do not lift up himself ; and that sentence of the Apostle must be thought of, "Wherefore let him that thinketh he standeth, take heed lest he fall."[5] Let the voice of chiding sound outwardly in tones of terror, let the spirit of love and gentleness be maintained within. "If a man be overtaken in a fault," as the same Apostle says, "ye which are spiritual restore such an one in the spirit of meekness ; considering thyself, lest thou also be tempted. Bear ye one another's burdens, and so shall ye fulfil the law of Christ."[6] And again in another place, "The servant of the Lord must not strive, but be gentle unto all men, apt to teach, patient, in meekness instructing those that oppose themselves ; if God peradventure will give them repentance to the acknowledging of the truth ; and that they may recover themselves out of the snare of the devil, who are held captive by him at his will."[7] So then be neither consenting to

---

[1] Obsequentur. [2] Matt. xi. 28. [3] Culpam.

[4] Eph. v. 11. [5] 1 Cor. x. 12. [6] Gal. vi. 1, 2.
[7] 2 Tim. ii. 24, etc.

evil, so as to approve of it ; nor negligent so as not to reprove it ; nor proud so as to reprove it in a tone of insult.

21. But whoso forsaketh unity, violateth charity ; and whosoever violateth charity, how great gifts soever he have, he is nothing. "If he speak with the tongues of men and of angels ; if he knew all mysteries, if he have all faith, so as to remove mountains, if he distribute all his goods to the poor, if he give his body to be burned, and have not charity ; it is nothing ; it profiteth him nothing."[1] He possesseth all things to no useful end, who hath not that one thing by which he may use all these things well. So then let us embrace charity, "studying to keep the unity of the Spirit in the bond of peace."[2] Let not those seduce us who understand the Scriptures in a carnal manner, and who in making a bodily separation, are separated themselves by a spiritual sacrilege from the good corn of the Church which is spread over the whole world. For throughout the whole world hath the good seed been sown. That good Sower, the Son of Man, hath scattered the good seed not in Africa only, but everywhere. But the enemy hath sown tares upon it. Yet what saith the Householder? "Let both grow together until the harvest."[3] Grow where? In the field, of course. What is the field? Is it Africa? No ! What is it then? Let us not interpret it ourselves, let the Lord speak ; let us not suffer any one to make his guess at his own pleasure. For the disciples said to the Master, "Declare unto us the parable of the tares." And the Lord declared it : "The good seed," said He, "are the children of the Kingdom. But the tares are the children of the wicked one." Who sowed them? "The enemy that sowed them," said He, "is the devil." What is the field? "The field," said He, "is this world." What is the harvest? "The harvest," said He, "is the end of the world." Who are the reapers? "The reapers," said He, "are the Angels " Is Africa the world? Is this present time the harvest? Is Donatus the reaper? Look then for the harvest throughout the whole world, throughout the whole world "grow unto the harvest," throughout the whole world bear with the tares even until the harvest. Let not perverse men seduce you, that chaff so light, which flies out of the floor before the coming of the Winnower ; let them not seduce you. Hold them fast even to this single parable of the tares, and suffer them not to speak of anything else. This man, one will say, surrendered[4] the Scriptures ; no, not so : but this other man

surrendered them. Whosoever it might be who has surrendered them, has their faithlessness made void the faithfulness of God? What is "the faithfulness of God"? That which He promised to Abraham, saying, "In thy seed shall all nations be blessed."[5] What is the faithfulness of God? "Let both grow together until the harvest." Grow where? Throughout the field. What is throughout the field? Throughout the world.

22. Here they say ; "It is true both kinds did once grow throughout the world, but the good wheat is diminished, and confined to this our country, and our small communion."[6] But the Lord doth not allow thee to interpret as thou wilt. He who explaineth this parable Himself, shutteth thy mouth, thy sacrilegious, profane, and ungodly mouth, that is counter to thine own interests, while thou runnest counter to the testator, even as he calleth thee to the inheritance. How doth He shut thy mouth? by saying, "Let both grow until the harvest."[7] If the harvest hath come already, let us believe that the wheat has been diminished. Though not even then shall it be diminished, but gathered up into the barn. For so He saith, "Gather ye together first the tares, and bind them in bundles to burn them, but gather the wheat into My barn." If then they grow until the harvest, and after the harvest are gathered in, how are they diminished, thou wicked, thou ungodly one? I grant that in comparison with the tares and chaff the wheat is less in quantity ; still "both grow together until the harvest." For "when iniquity aboundeth, the love of many waxeth cold ; "[8] the tares and the chaff multiply. But because throughout the whole world wheat cannot be wanting, which "by enduring unto the end shall be saved, both grow together until the harvest." And if because of the abundance of the wicked it is said, "When the Son of Man cometh, thinkest thou, shall He find faith on the earth?"[9] and by this denomination are signified all those who by transgression of the law imitate him to whom it was said, "Earth thou art, and unto earth shalt thou return ; "[10] yet because of the abundance of the good also, and because of him to whom it was said, "Thy seed shall be as the stars of heaven, and as the sand of the sea ; "[11] is that also written, "Many shall come from the East and West, and shall sit down with Abraham, and Isaac, in the kingdom of God."[12] "Both " then "grow together until the harvest," and both the tares or chaff have their passages in the Scriptures, and the wheat theirs. And they who do not understand

---

[1] 1 Cor. xiii. 1–3.   [2] Eph. iv. 3.   [3] Matt. xiii. 24, etc.
[4] The occasion of the Donatist schism was a charge brought against Cecilianus, Bishop of Carthage, and Felix, Bishop of Aptunga, who had ordained him, of being traditors, that is, of having surrendered such copies of the Holy Scriptures as they had in their possession in times of persecution.

[5] Gen. xxvi. 4.   [6] Paucitatem.
[7] Matt. xiii. 30.   [8] Matt. xxiv. 12.
[9] Luke xviii. 8, Vulgate.   [10] Gen iii. 19, Sept.
[11] Gen. xv. 5 and xxii. 17.   [12] Matt. viii. 11.

them, confound them and are themselves confounded; and in their blind desire they make such an uproar, that they will not be silenced even by the clear manifestation of the truth.

23. See, they say, the Prophet says, "Depart ye, go ye out from thence, and touch no unclean thing;"[1] how then for peace sake should we bear with the wicked, from whom we are commanded to "go out and depart that we touch not the unclean thing"? We understand that "departure" spiritually, they corporally. For I also cry out with the Prophet (for however mean a vessel I am, God maketh use of me to minister to you); I also cry out and say to you, "Depart ye, go ye out from thence, and touch not the unclean thing;" but with the touch of the heart, not of the body. For what is it to "touch the unclean thing," but to consent to sin. And what is it to "go out from thence," but to do what appertaineth to the rebuking of the wicked, as far as can be done, according to each one's grade and condition,[2] with the maintenance of peace? Thou art displeased at a man's sin, thou hast not "touched the unclean thing." Thou hast reproved, rebuked, admonished him, hast administered, if the case required it, a suitable discipline, and such as doth not violate unity; then thou hast "gone out from thence." Now consider the actions of the Saints, lest perhaps this should seem to be an interpretation of my own. As Saints have understood these words, so surely ought they to be understood. "Go ye out from them," says the Prophet. I will first maintain this meaning of the words from their customary use, and will afterwards show that that meaning is not my own. It often happens that men are accused; and when they are accused they defend themselves, and when the accused defends himself with good reason and justice, the hearers say, "He has got out of this." Got out; whither has he gone? He abides still in the place where he was, yet has he "got out of this." How has he got out of it? By the good account he has rendered, and by his most satisfactory defence. This is what the holy Apostles did when they "shook off the dust from their feet"[3] against those who did not receive the message of peace which was sent to them. That watchman, "got out from thence," to whom it was said, "I have made thee a watchman unto the house of Israel."[4] For it was told him, "If thou warn the wicked, and he turn not from his wickedness, nor from his way, that wicked one shall die in his iniquity, and thou shalt deliver thy soul."[5] This if he do, he "goes out from

him," not by a bodily separation, but by the defence of his own work. For he did what it was his duty to do; though the other, whose duty it was to obey, obeyed not. This then is that, "Go ye out from thence."

24. So cried Moses and Isaiah, Jeremiah and Ezekiel. Let us see then if they acted thus, if they left the people of God, and betook themselves to other nations. How many and vehement rebukes did Jeremiah utter against the sinners, and wicked ones of his people. Yet he lived amongst them, he entered into the same temple with them, celebrated the same mysteries;[6] he lived in that congregation of wicked men, but by his crying out "he went out from them." This is "to go out from them;" this is not "to touch the unclean thing," the not consenting to them in will, and the not sparing them in word. What shall I say of Jeremiah, of Isaiah, of Daniel, and Ezekiel, and the rest of the prophets, who did not retire from the wicked people, lest they should desert the good who were mingled with that people, among whom themselves were able to be such as they were? When Moses himself, Brethren, was receiving the law in the mount, the people below made an idol.[7] The people of God, the people who had been led through the waves of the Red Sea which gave way to them, and overwhelmed their enemies who followed after, after so many signs and miracles displayed in plagues upon the Egyptians even unto death, and for "their" protection unto deliverance, yet demanded an idol by force, made an idol, adored an idol, sacrificed unto an idol. God showeth His servant what the people had done, and saith that He will destroy them from before His Face. Moses maketh intercession for them as he was about to return to this people; yet had he a good opportunity of retiring and "going out from them," as these persons understand it, that he might "not touch the unclean thing," might not live among them; but he did not so. And that he might not seem to have acted thus from necessity rather than from love, God offered him another people; so that He might destroy these: "I will make of thee," He said, "a great nation."[8] But he did not accept it; he cleaveth to the sinners, he prayeth for the sinners. And how does he pray? O signal proof of love, my Brethren! How does he pray? Mark that, as it were, mother's fondness, of which I have often spoken. When God threatened the sacrilegious people, Moses' tender heart trembled, and on their behalf he opposed himself to the wrath of God. "Lord," he says, "if Thou wilt forgive their sin, forgive; but if not, blot me out of Thy book

[1] Isa. lii. 11.
[2] Persona.
[3] Luke x. 11.
[4] Ezek. iii. 17.
[5] Ezek. iii. 19.

[6] Sacramenta.
[7] Exod. xxxii.
[8] Exod. xxxii. 10.

which Thou hast written." [1]   With what a father's and mother's [2] fondness, yet with what assurance said he this, as he considered at once the justice and the mercy of God ; that in that He is just, He would not destroy the righteous man ; and that in that He is merciful, He would pardon the sinners.

25. It is now surely plain to your discernment,[3] in what manner all such testimonies of the Scriptures are to be received ; so that when Scripture says, that we must depart from the wicked, we are bid to understand this in no other sense, but that we depart in heart ; lest by the separation from the good, we commit a greater evil than we shrink from in the union of the wicked, as these Donatists have done. But if they were truly good, and so had reproved the wicked, and not rather being themselves wicked, had defamed [4] the good, they would for peace sake bear with any, be they who they might, seeing they have received the Maximianists [5] as sound, whom they condemned before as lost. Undoubtedly the Prophet has said plainly, " Depart ye, go ye out from thence, and touch not the unclean thing." But that I may understand what he said, I pay attention to what he did. By his own deeds he explains his words. He said, " Depart ye." To whom did he say so ? To the righteous of course. From whom did he bid them depart? From sinners and wicked men of course. I ask then, did he depart from such himself? I find that he did not. So then he understood it in another sense. For surely he would be the first to do what he enjoined. He departed from them in heart, he rebuked and reproved them. By keeping himself from consenting to them, he " did not touch the unclean thing ; " but by rebuking them he " went out " free in the sight of God ; and to him God neither imputeth his own sins, because he sinned not ; nor the sins of others, because he approved them not ; nor negligence, because he kept not silence ; nor pride, because he continued in unity. So then, my Brethren, how many soever ye have among you, who are still weighed down by the love of the world, covetous, or perjured persons, adulterers, spectacle hunters, consulters of astrologers, of fanatics, of soothsayers, of augurs and diviners, drunkards, sensualists, whatever there is of bad that ye know ye have among you ; show your disapprobation of it all as far as ye are able, that ye may in heart " depart ; " and reprove them, that ye may " go out from them ; " and consent not to them, that " ye touch not the unclean thing."

---

[1] Exod. xxxii. 32.
[2] Visceribus.
[3] Prudentia.
[4] By their false accusations against Cecilian of being a traditor, of which they were themselves convicted. Ep. 43 (162), etc. Aug. Serm. cxiv. (clxiv. Ben.).
[5] See Serm. xxi. (lxxi. Ben.) 4 (ii.), note.

SERMON XXXIX.

[LXXXIX. BEN.]

ON THE WORDS OF THE GOSPEL, MATT. XXI. 19, WHERE JESUS DRIED UP THE FIG-TREE ; AND ON THE WORDS, LUKE XXIV. 28, WHERE HE MADE A PRETENCE AS THOUGH HE WOULD GO FURTHER.

1. THE lesson of the Holy Gospel which has just been read, has given us an alarming warning, lest we have leaves only, and have no fruit. That is, in few words, lest words be present and deeds be wanting. Very terrible ! Who does not fear when in this lesson he sees with the eyes of the heart the withered tree, withered at that word being spoken to it, " Let no fruit grow on thee henceforward for ever"? [6] Let the fear work amendment, and the amendment bring forth fruit. For without doubt, the Lord Christ foresaw that a certain tree would deservedly become withered, because it would have leaves, and would have no fruit. That tree is the synagogue, not that which was called, but that which was reprobate. For out of it also was called the people of God, who in sincerity and truth waited in the Prophets for the salvation of God, Jesus Christ. And forasmuch as it waited in faith, it was thought worthy [7] to know Him when He was present. For out of it came the Apostles, out of it came the whole multitude of those who went before the ass of the Lord, and said, " Hosanna to the Son of David, blessed is He that cometh in the Name of the Lord." [8] There was a great company then of believing Jews, a great company of those who believed in Christ before He shed His Blood for them. For it was not in vain that the Lord Himself had come to none " but to the lost sheep of the house of Israel." [9] But in others, after He was crucified, and was now exalted into heaven, He found the fruit of repentance ; and these He did not make to wither, but cultivated them in His field, and watered them with His word. Of this number were those four thousand Jews who believed, after that the disciples and those who were with them, filled with the Holy Ghost, spake with the tongues of all nations,[10] and in that diversity of tongues announced in a way beforehand, that the Church should be throughout all nations. They believed at that time, and " they were the lost sheep of the house of Israel ; " but because " the Son of Man had come to seek and to save that which was lost," [11] He found these also. But they lay hid here and there among thorns, as though wasted and dispersed by the wolves ; and because they lay hid among thorns, He did not come to find them, save when torn by the

---

[6] Matt. xxi. 19.   [7] Meruit.   [8] Matt. xxi. 9.
[9] Matt. xv. 24.   [10] Acts ii. 4.   [11] Luke xix. 10.

thorns of His Passion; yet come He did, He found, He redeemed them. They had slain, not Him so much, as themselves. They were saved by Him who was slain for them. For, as the Apostles spake, they were pricked;[1] they were pricked in conscience, who had pricked Him with the spear; and being pricked they sought for counsel, received it when it was given, repented, found grace, and believing drunk that Blood which in their fury they had shed. But they who have remained in this bad and barren race, even unto this day, and shall remain unto the end, were figured in that tree. You come to them at this day, and find with them all the writings of the Prophets. But these are but leaves; Christ is an hungred, and He seeketh for fruit; but findeth no fruit among them, because He doth not find Himself among them. For He hath no fruit, who hath not Christ. And he hath not Christ, who holdeth not to Christ's unity, who hath not charity. And so by this chain he hath no fruit who hath not charity. Hear the Apostle, "Now the fruit of the Spirit is charity;" so setting forth the praise of this cluster, that is, of this fruit; "The fruit of the Spirit," he says, "is charity,[2] joy, peace, longsuffering." Do not wonder at what follows, when charity leads the way.

2. Accordingly, when the disciples marvelled at the withering of the tree, He set forth to them the value of faith, and said to them, "If ye have faith, and doubt not;"[3] that is, if in all things ye have trust in God; and do not say, "God can do this, this He cannot do;" but rely on the omnipotence of the Almighty; "ye shall not only do this, but also if ye shall say to this mountain, Be thou removed, and be thou cast into the sea, it shall be done. And all things whatsoever ye shall ask in prayer, believing, ye shall receive."[4] Now we read that miracles were wrought by the disciples, yea rather by the Lord through the disciples; for, "without Me," He says, "ye can do nothing."[5] The Lord could do many things without the disciples, but the disciples nothing without the Lord. He who could make[6] even the disciples themselves, was not certainly assisted by them to make them. We read then of the Apostles' miracles, but we nowhere read of a tree being withered by them, nor of a mountain removed into the sea. Let us enquire therefore where this was done. For the words of the Lord could not be without effect. If ye are thinking of "trees" and "mountains" in their ordinary and familiar sense, it has not been done. But if ye think of that tree of which He spake, and of that mountain of the Lord of which the Prophet said, "In the last days the mountain of the Lord's house shall be manifest;"[7] if ye think of it, and understand it thus, it has been done, and done by the Apostles. The tree is the Jewish nation, but I say again, that part of it which was reprobate, not that which was called; that tree which we have spoken of is the Jewish nation. The mountain, as the prophetic testimony hath taught us, is the Lord Himself. The withered tree is the Jewish nation reft of the honour of Christ; the sea is this world with all the nations. Now see the Apostles speaking to this tree which was about to be withered away, and casting the mountain into the sea. In the Acts of the Apostles they speak to the Jews who gainsay and resist the word of truth, that is, who have leaves and have no fruit, and they say to them, "It was necessary that the word of God should first have been spoken to you: but seeing ye have put it from you" (for ye use the words of the Prophets, yet do not acknowledge Him whom the Prophets foretold, that is, ye have leaves only), "lo, we turn to the Gentiles." For this also was foretold by the Prophets; "Behold, I have given Thee for a light of the Gentiles, that Thou mayest be My salvation unto the end of the earth."[8] See then, the tree hath withered away; and Christ hath been removed unto the Gentiles, the mountain into the sea. For how should not the tree wither away which is planted in that vineyard, of which it was said, "I will command my clouds that they rain no rain upon it"?[9]

3. Now that in order to convey this truth the Lord acted prophetically, I mean that, as concerning this tree, it was not His will merely to exhibit a miracle, but that by the miracle He conveyed the intimation of something to come, there are many things which teach and persuade us, yea even against our wills force us to believe. In the first place, what fault in the tree was it that it had no fruit, when even if it had no fruit at the proper season, that is, the season of its fruit, it would not assuredly be any fault in the tree; for the tree as being without sense and reason could not be to blame. But to this is added, that as we read it in the narrative of the other Evangelist who expressly mentions this, "it was not the time for that fruit."[10] For that was the time when the fig-tree shoots forth its tender leaves, which come, we know, before the fruit; and this we prove, because the day of the Lord's Passion was at hand, and we know at what time He suffered; and if we did not know it, we ought of course to give credit to the Evangelist who says, "The time of figs was not yet." So then if it was only a miracle

---

[1] Acts ii. 37.   [2] Gal. v. 22.
[3] Matt. xxi. 21.   [4] Matt. xxi. 22.   [5] John xv. 5.
[6] The meaning of "*facio*" as "to *do*," and "to make," cannot be expressed in our language.

[7] Isa. ii. 2.   [8] Acts xiii. 46, etc.; Isa. xlix. 6.
[9] Isa. v. 6.   [10] Mark xi. 13.

that was to have been set forth, and not something to be prophetically figured, it would have been much more worthy of the clemency and mercy of the Lord, to have made green again any tree He might find withered; as He healed the sick, as He cleansed the lepers, as He raised the dead. But then contrariwise, as though against the ordinary rule of His clemency, He found a green tree, not yet bearing fruit out of its proper season, but still not refusing the hope of fruit to its dresser, and He withered it away; as though He would say to us, "I have no delight in the withering away of this tree, but thus I would convey to you, that I have not designed to do this without any cause for it, but only because I desired thereby to convey to you a lesson you might the more regard. It is not this tree that I have cursed, it is not on a tree without sense that I have inflicted punishment, but I have made thee fear, whosoever thou art that dost consider the matter, that thou mightest not despise Christ when He is an hungered, that thou mightest love rather to be enriched with fruit, than to be overshadowed by leaves."

4. This one thing is that which the Lord intimates that He designed to signify by what He did. What else is there? He cometh to the tree being hungry, and seeketh fruit. Did He not know that it was not the time for it? What the cultivator of the tree knew, did not its Creator know? He seeketh on the tree then for fruit which it had not yet. Doth He really seek for it, or rather make a pretence of seeking it? For if He really sought it, He was mistaken. But this be far from Him, to be mistaken! He made then a pretence of seeking it. Fearing to allow this, that he maketh a pretence, thou dost confess that He was mistaken. Again, thou dost turn away from the idea of His being mistaken, and so run into that of His making a pretence. We are parched up between the two. If we are parched, let us beg for rain, that we may grow green, lest in saying anything unworthy of the Lord, we rather wither away. The Evangelist indeed says, "He came to the tree, and found no fruit on it."[1] "He found none," would not be said of Him, unless He had either really sought for it, or made a pretence of seeking, though He knew that there was none there. Wherefore we do not hesitate, let us by no means say that Christ was mistaken. What then? shall we say He made a pretence? Shall we say this? How shall we get out of this difficulty? Let us say what, if the Evangelist had not said of the Lord in another place, we should not of ourselves dare to say. Let us say what the Evangelist has written, and when we have said, let us understand it. But in order that we

may understand it, let us first believe. For, "unless ye believe," says the Prophet, "ye shall not understand."[2] The Lord Christ after His Resurrection, was walking in the way with two of His disciples, by whom He was not yet recognised, and with whom He joined company as a third traveller. They came to the place whither they were going, and the Evangelist says, "But He made a pretence as though He would have gone further."[3] But they kept Him, saying, in the spirit of a courteous kindness,[4] that it was already drawing toward evening, and praying Him to tarry there with them; being received and entertained by them, He breaketh Bread, and is known of them in blessing and breaking of the Bread. So then, let us not now fear to say, that He made a pretence of seeking, if He made a pretence of going further. But here there arises another question. Yesterday[5] I insisted[6] at some length on the truth which is in the Apostles; how then do we find any "pretence" in the Lord Himself? Therefore, Brethren, I must tell you, and teach you according to my poor abilities, which the Lord giveth me for your benefit, and must convey to you what ye may hold as a rule[7] in the interpretation of all Scripture. Everything that is said or done is to be understood either in its literal signification, or else it signifies something figuratively; or at least contains both of these at once, both its own literal interpretation,[8] and a figurative signification also. Thus I have set forth three things, examples of them must now be given; and from whence, but from the Holy Scriptures? It is said in its literal acceptation, that the Lord suffered, that He rose again, and ascended into heaven; that we shall rise again at the end of the world, that we shall reign with Him for ever, if we do not despise Him. Take all this as spoken literally, and look not out for figures; as it is expressed, so it really is. And so also with divers actions. The Apostle went up to Jerusalem to see Peter, the Apostle actually did this, it actually took place, it was an action peculiar to himself. It is a fact which he tells you; a simple fact according to its literal meaning. "The stone which the builders refused, is become the Head of the corner,"[9] is spoken in a figure. If we take "the stone" literally, what "stone did the builders refuse, which became the Head of the corner"? If we take "the stone" literally, of what corner is this "stone" become the Head? If we admit that it was figuratively expressed, and take it figuratively,

---

[1] Matt. xxi. 19.

[2] Isa. vii. 9, Sept.   [3] Luke xxiv. 28.
[4] *More humanitatis.*
[5] Probably in that Sermon which is marked as next before this in Posidonius' Catalogue, ch. 9, namely, "From the Epistle to the Galatians, where Paul reproved Peter." Ben. ed. note.
[6] *Commendavimus.*   [7] *Regulariter.*   [8] *Cognitionem.*
[9] Matt. xxi. 42; Ps. cxviii. 22.

the Corner-stone is Christ: the head of the corner, is the Head of the Church. Why is the Church the Corner? Because she has called the Jews from one side, and the Gentiles from another, and these two walls as it were coming from different quarters, and meeting together in one, she has bound together by the grace of her peace. For, "He is our peace, who hath made both one." [1]

5. Ye have heard instances of a literal expression, and a literal action, and of a figurative expression; ye are waiting for an instance of a figurative action. There are many such, but meanwhile, as is suggested by this mention of the corner-stone, when Jacob anointed the stone which he had placed at his head as he slept, and in his sleep saw a mysterious [2] dream, ladders rising from the earth to heaven, and Angels ascending and descending, and the Lord standing upon the ladder,[3] he understood what it was designed to figure, and took the stone for a figure of Christ, to prove to us thereby that he was no stranger to the understanding of that vision and revelation. Do not wonder then that he anointed it, for Christ received His Name from "the anointing." Now this Jacob was said in the Scripture to be "a man without guile." [4] And this Jacob ye know was called Israel. Accordingly in the Gospel, when the Lord saw Nathanael, He said, "Behold an Israelite indeed, in whom is no guile." And that Israelite not yet knowing who it was that talked with him, answered, "Whence knewest Thou me?" And the Lord said to him, "When thou wast under the fig-tree I saw thee;" [5] as though he would say, When thou wast in the shadow of sin, I predestinated thee. And Nathanael, because he remembered that he had been under the fig-tree, where the Lord was not, acknowledged His Divinity, and answered, "Thou art the Son of God, Thou art the King of Israel." He who had been under the fig-tree was not made a withered fig-tree; he acknowledged Christ. And the Lord said unto him, "Because I said, When thou wast under the fig-tree I saw thee, believest thou? thou shalt see greater things than these." What are these "greater things"? "Verily I say unto you" (for he "is an Israelite in whom is no guile;" remember Jacob in whom was no guile; and recollect of what he is speaking, the stone at his head, the vision in his sleep, the ladder from earth to heaven, the Angels ascending and descending; and so see what it is that the Lord would say to "the Israelite without guile"); "Verily I say unto you, Ye shall see heaven opened" (hear, thou guileless Nathanael, what guileless Jacob saw); "ye shall see heaven opened, and Angels ascend-

ing and descending" (unto whom?) "unto the Son of Man." Therefore was He, as the Son of Man, anointed on the head; for "the head of the woman is the man, and the head of the man is Christ." [6] Now observe, He did not say, "ascending from the Son of Man, and descending to the Son of Man," as if He were only above; but "ascending and descending unto the Son of Man." Hear the Son of Man crying out from above, "Saul, Saul." Hear the Son of Man from below, "Why persecutest thou Me?" [7]

6. Ye have heard an instance of a literal expression, as "that we shall rise again;" of a literal action, as that, according as it is said, "Paul went up to Jerusalem to see Peter." [8] "The stone which the builders refused," is a figurative expression; "the anointed stone" which was at Jacob's head, is a figurative action. There is now due to your expectation an example made out of both together, something which is at once a literal fact, and which also signifies something else figured by it. "We know that Abraham had two sons, the one by a bondmaid, the other by a free-woman;" [9] this was literally a fact, not only a story, but a fact; are ye looking for that which was figured in it? "These are the two Testaments." That then which is spoken figuratively, is a sort of fiction. But since it has some real event represented by it, and the very figure itself has its ground of truth, it escapes all imputation of falsehood. "The sower went out to sow his seed; and as he sowed, some fell by the way side, some fell upon stony places, some fell among thorns, and some fell upon good ground." [10] Who went out "to sow," or when went he out, or upon what "thorns," or "stones," or "way side," or in what field did he sow? If we receive this as a fictitious story, we understand it in a figurative sense; it is fictitious. For if any sower really went out, and did cast the seed in these different places, as we have heard, it were no fiction, and so no falsehood. But now though it be a fiction, yet it is no falsehood. Why? Because the fiction has some further signification, it deceives thee not. It requires only one to understand it, and does not lead any one into error. And thus Christ wishing to convey this lesson to us, sought for fruit, and hereby set forth to us a figurative, and no deceiving fiction; a fiction therefore worthy of praise, not of blame; not one by the examination of which we might run into what was false; but by the diligent investigation of which we might discover what is true.

7. I see that one may say, Explain to me; what did that signify, that "He made a pretence of going further"? For if it had no further

[1] Eph. ii. 14.   [2] *Magnum*.   [3] Gen. xxviii. 11, etc.
[4] Gen. xxv. 27.   [5] John i. 47, etc.
[6] 1 Cor. xi. 3.   [7] Acts ix. 4.   [8] Gal. i. 18.
[9] Gal. iv. 22.   [10] Matt. xiii. 3, etc.

meaning, it is a deceit, a lie. We must then according to our rules of exposition, and distinctions, tell you what this "pretence of going further," signified; "He made a pretence of going further," and is kept back from going further. In so far then as the Lord Christ being as they supposed absent in respect of His Bodily presence, was thought to be really absent, He will as it were "go further." But hold Him fast by faith, hold Him fast at the breaking of Bread. What shall I say more? Have ye recognised Him? If so, then have ye found Christ. I must not speak [1] any longer on this Sacrament. They who put off the knowledge of this Sacrament, Christ goeth further from them. Let them then hold It fast, let them not let Him go; let them invite Him to their home, and so they are invited to heaven.

SERMON XL.

[XC. BEN.]

ON THE WORDS OF THE GOSPEL, MATT. XXII. 2, ETC., ABOUT THE MARRIAGE OF THE KING'S SON; AGAINST THE DONATISTS, ON CHARITY. DELIVERED AT CARTHAGE IN THE RESTITUTA.[2]

1. ALL the faithful [3] know the marriage of the king's son, and his feast, and the spreading [4] of the Lord's Table is open to them all [5] who will. But it is of importance to each one to see how he approaches, even when he is not forbidden to approach It. For the Holy Scriptures teach us that there are two feasts of the Lord; one to which the good and evil come, the other to which the evil come not. So then the feast, of which we have just now heard when the Gospel was being read, has both good and evil guests. All who excused themselves from this feast are evil; but not all those who entered in are good. You therefore who are the good guests at this feast do I address, who have in your minds the words, "He that eateth and drinketh unworthily, eateth and drinketh judgment to himself." [6] All you who are such do I address, that ye look not for the good without, that ye bear with the evil within.

2. I do not doubt that ye wish to hear, Beloved, who they are of whom I have spoken in my address, that they should not look for the good without, and should bear with the evil within. If all within are evil, whom do I address? If all within are good, whom did I advise them to bear with being evil? Let me first then with the Lord's assistance get out of this difficulty as best I can. If you consider good perfectly and strictly [7] speaking, none is good but God Alone.

Ye have the Lord saying most plainly, "Why callest thou Me good? there is none Good but One, that is, God." [8] How then can that marriage feast have good and bad guests, if "none is good but God Alone"? In the first place ye ought to know, that after a certain sort we are all evil. Yes, doubtless after a certain sort are we all evil; but after no sort are we all good. For can we compare ourselves with the Apostles, to whom the Lord Himself said, "If ye then being evil know how to give good gifts unto your children?" [9] If we consider the Scriptures, there was but one evil one among the twelve Apostles, with reference to whom the Lord said in a certain place, "And ye are clean, but not all." [10] But yet in addressing them all together, He said, "If ye being evil." Peter heard this, John heard this, Andrew heard this, all the rest of the eleven Apostles heard it. What did they hear? "If ye being evil know how to give good gifts unto your children; how much more shall your Father which is in heaven give good things to them that ask Him?" When they heard that they were evil, they were in despair; but when they heard that God in heaven was their Father, they revived. "Ye being evil;" what then is due to the evil, but punishment? "How much more shall your Father which is in heaven?" What is due to children but reward. In the name of "evil" is the dread of punishment; in the name of "children" is the hope of heirs.

3. According to a certain respect then they were evil, who after another respect were good. For to them to whom it is said, "Ye being evil know how to give good gifts unto your children;" is added immediately, "How much more shall your Father which is in heaven?" He is then the Father of the evil, but not of those who are to be left so; because He is the Physician of them who are to be cured. According to a certain sort then they were evil. And yet those guests of the Householder at the King's marriage, were not I suppose of that number of whom it was said, "they invited good and bad," [11] that they should be reckoned among the number of the bad, who we have heard were shut out in his person who was found not to have a wedding garment. According to a certain respect, I repeat they were bad, who yet were good; and according to a certain respect they were good, who yet were bad. Hear John according to what respect they were bad: "If we say that we have no sin, we deceive ourselves, and the truth is not in us." [12] Behold after what respect they were bad: because they had sin. According to what respect were they good? "If we confess our sins, He is faithful and just to forgive us our sins, and to cleanse us from all unrighteousness." [13] If

[1] See Serm. vi. (lvi. Ben.) 10 (vi.) note.
[2] The great Church in Carthage where the bodies of the Martyrs Sts. Perpetua and Felicitas lay. See Ben. ed. in Sermon xix. note.
[3] *Baptized fideles.*   [4] *Apparatus.*   [5] *Voluntati omnium.*
[6] 1 Cor. xi. 29.   [7] *Liquido.*

[8] Matt. xix. 17.   [9] Matt. vii. 11.   [10] John xiii. 10.
[11] Matt. xxii. 10.   [12] 1 John i. 8.   [13] 1 John i. 9.

then we should say, on the principle of this interpretation which ye have now heard me bring, as I think, out of the sacred Scriptures, viz. that the same men are both after a certain manner good, and after a certain manner bad; if we should wish to receive according to this sense the words, "they invited good and bad," the same persons, that is, at once good and bad; if we should wish so to receive them, we are not permitted so to do, by reason of that one who was found "not having a wedding garment," and who was not merely "cast forth," so as to be deprived of that feast, but so as to be condemned in the punishment of everlasting darkness.

4. But one will say, What of one man? what strange, what great matter is it, if one among the crowd "not having a wedding garment" crept in unperceived to the servants of the Householder? Could it be said because of that one, "they invited good and bad"? Attend therefore, my Brethren, and understand. That one man represented one class; for they were many. Here some diligent hearer may answer me, and say, "I have no wish for you to tell me your guesses; I wish to have it proved to me that that one represented many."[1] By the Lord's present help, I will prove it clearly; nor will I search far, that I may be able to prove it. God will assist me in His own words in this place, and will furnish you by my ministry with a plain proof of it. "The Master of the house came in to see the guests."[2] See, my Brethren, the servants' business was only to invite and bring in the good and bad; see that it is not said, that the servants took notice of the guests, and found among them a man which had not on a wedding garment, and spoke to him. This is not written. The Master of the house saw him, the Master of the house discovered, the Master of the house inspected, the Master of the house separated him out. It was not right to pass over this. But I have undertaken to establish another point, how that that one signifies many. "The Master of the house" then "came in to see the guests, and He found there a man which had not on a wedding garment. And He saith unto him, Friend, how camest thou in hither, not having a wedding garment? And he was speechless."[3] For He who questioned him was One, to whom he could give no feigned reply. The garment that was looked for is in the heart, not on the body; for had it been put on externally, it could not have been concealed even from the servants. Where that wedding garment must be put on, hear in the words, "Let thy priests be clothed with righteousness."[4] Of that garment the Apostle speaks,[5] "If so be that we shall be found clothed,

and not naked."[6] Therefore was he discovered by the Lord, who escaped the notice of the servants. Being questioned, he is speechless: he is bound, cast out, and condemned one by many. I have said, Lord, that Thou teachest us that in this Thou dost give warning to all. Recollect then with me, my Brethren, the words which ye have heard, and ye will at once discover, at once determine, that that one was many. True it was one man whom the Lord questioned, to one He said, "Friend, how camest thou in hither?" It was one who was speechless, and of that same one was it said, "Bind him hand and foot, and cast him into outer darkness; there shall be weeping and gnashing of teeth."[7] Why? "For many are called, but few chosen."[8] How can any one gainsay this manifestation of the truth? "Cast him," He saith, "into outer darkness." "Him," that one man assuredly, of whom the Lord saith, "for many are called, but few chosen." So then it is the few who are not cast out. He was it is true but one man "who had not the wedding garment. Cast him out." But why is he cast out? "For many are called, but few chosen." Leave alone the few, cast out the many. It is true, that man was but one. Yet undoubtedly that one not only was many, but those many in numbers far surpassed the number of the good. For the good are many also; but in comparison of the bad, they are few. In the crop there is much wheat; compare it with the chaff, and the grains of corn are few. The same persons considered in themselves are many, in comparison with the bad are few. How do we prove that in themselves they are many? "Many shall come from the East and from the West." Whither shall they come? To that feast, into which both good and bad enter. But speaking of another feast, He subjoined, "and shall sit down with Abraham, and Isaac, and Jacob in the kingdom of heaven."[9] That is the feast to which the bad shall not approach. Be that feast which now is, received worthily, that we may attain to the other. The same then are many, who are also few; in themselves many; in comparison with the bad few. Therefore what saith the Lord? He found one, and said, "Let the many be cast out, the few remain." For to say, "many are called, but few chosen," is nothing else than to show plainly who in this present feast are accounted to be such, as to be brought to that other feast, where no bad men shall come.

5. What is it then? I would not that ye all who approach the Lord's Table which is in this life, should be with the many who are to be shut out, but with the few who are to be reserved. And how shall ye be able to attain to this? Take "the wedding garment." Ye will say, "Explain

---

, [1] Serm. xlv. (xcv. Ben.) 6.   [2] Matt. xxii. 11.
[3] Matt xxii. 12   [4] Ps. cxxxii. 9.
[5] See note, Serm. viii. (lviii. Ben.) 13 (xi.).

[6] 2 Cor. v. 3.   [7] Matt. xxii. 13.   [8] Matt. xxii. 14.
[9] Matt. viii. 11.

this 'wedding garment' to us." Without a doubt, that is the garment which none but the good have, who are to be left at the feast, reserved unto that other feast to which no bad man approaches, who are to be brought safely thither by the grace of the Lord ; these have " the wedding garment." Let us then, my Brethren, seek for those among the faithful who have something which bad men have not, and this will be " the wedding garment." If we speak of sacraments, ye see how that these are common to the bad and good. Is it Baptism? Without Baptism it is true no one attaineth to God ; but not every one that hath Baptism attaineth to Him. I cannot therefore understand Baptism, the Sacrament itself that is, to be " the wedding garment ; " for this garment I see in the good, I see in the bad. Peradventure it is the Altar, or That which is received at the Altar. But no ; we see that many eat, and " eat and drink judgment to themselves." What is it then? Is it fasting? The wicked fast also. Is it running together to the Church? The wicked run thither also. Lastly, is it miracles? Not only do the good and bad perform them, but sometimes the good perform them not. See, among the ancient people Pharaoh's magicians wrought miracles, the Israelites did not ; among the Israelites, Moses only and Aaron wrought them ; the rest did not, but saw, and feared, and believed.[1] Were the magicians of Pharaoh who did miracles, better men than the people of Israel who could not do them, and yet that people were the people of God. In the Church itself, hear the Apostle, " Are all prophets? Have all the gifts of healing? Do all speak with tongues?"[2]

6. What is that " wedding garment " then? This is the wedding garment : " Now the end of the commandment," says the Apostle, " is charity out of a pure heart, and of a good conscience, and of faith unfeigned."[3] This is " the wedding garment." Not charity of any kind whatever ; for very often they who are partakers together of an evil conscience seem to love one another. They who commit robberies together, who love the hurtful arts of sorceries, and the stage together, who join together in the shout of the chariot race, or the wild beast fight ; these very often love one another ; but in these there is no " charity out of a pure heart, and of a good conscience, and of faith unfeigned. The wedding garment " is such charity as this. " Though I speak with the tongues of men and of Angels, and have not charity, I am become as sounding brass, and a tinkling cymbal."[4] Tongues have come in alone, and it is said to them, " How came ye in hither not having a wedding garment?" " Though," said he, " I have the gift

of prophecy, and understand all mysteries, and all knowledge, and though I have all faith, so that I could remove mountains, and have not charity, I am nothing." See, these are the miracles of men who very often have not " the wedding garment." " Though," he says, " I have all these, and have not Christ, I am nothing." Is then " the gift of prophecy " nothing? is then " the knowledge of mysteries "[5] nothing? It is not that these are nothing ; but " I," if I have them, " and have not charity, am nothing." How many good things profit nothing without this one good thing ! If then I have not charity, though I bestow alms freely upon the poor, though I have come to the confession of Christ's Name even unto blood and fire, these things may be done even through the love of glory, and so are vain. Because then they may be done even from the love of glory, and so be vain, and not through the rich charity of a godly affection, he names them all also in express terms, and do thou give ear to them ; " though I distribute all my goods for the use of the poor, and though I give my body to be burned, and have not charity, it profiteth me nothing."[6] This then is " the wedding garment." Question yourselves ; if ye have it, ye may be without fear in the Feast of the Lord. In one and the same man there exist two things, charity and desire. Let charity be born in thee, if it be yet unborn, and if it be born, be it nourished, fostered, increased. But as to that desire, though in this life it cannot be utterly extinguished ; " for if we say that we have no sin we deceive ourselves, and the truth is not in us ; "[7] but in so far as desire is in us, so far we are not without sin : let charity increase, desire decrease ; that the one, that is, charity, may one day be perfected, and desire be consumed. Put on " the wedding garment : " you I address, who as yet have it not. Ye are already within, already do ye approach to the Feast, and still have ye not yet the garment to do honour to the Bridegroom ; " Ye are yet seeking your own things, not the things which are Jesus Christ's."[8] For " the wedding garment " is taken in honour of the union, the union, that is, of the Bridegroom to the Bride. Ye know the Bridegroom ; it is Christ. Ye know the Bride ; it is the Church. Pay honour[9] to the Bride, pay honour to the Bridegroom. If ye pay due honour to them both, ye will be their children. Therefore in this make progress. Love the Lord, and so learn to love yourselves ; that when by loving the Lord ye shall have loved yourselves, ye may securely love your neighbour as yourselves. For when I find a man that does not love himself, how shall I commit his neighbour whom he should love as himself to him? And who is

---

[1] Exod. vii.   [2] 1 Cor. xii. 29, etc.   [3] 1 Tim. i. 5.
[4] 1 Cor. xiii. 1.

[5] *Sacramentorum.*   [6] 1 Cor. xiii. 3.   [7] 1 John i. 8.
[8] Phil. ii. 21.   [9] *Deferte.*

there, you will say, who does not love himself ? Who is there? See, " He that loveth iniquity hateth his own soul." [1] Does he love himself, who loves his body, and hates his soul to his own hurt, to the hurt of both his body and soul? And who loves his own soul? He that loveth God with all his heart and with all his mind. To such an one I would at once entrust his neighbour. " Love your neighbour as yourselves."

7. One may say, " Who is my neighbour?" Every man is your neighbour. Had we not all the same two parents? Animals of every species are neighbours one to the other, the dove to the dove, the leopard to the leopard, the asp to the asp, the sheep to the sheep, and is not man neighbour to man? Call to mind the ordering of the creation. God spake, the waters brought forth swimming creatures, great whales, fish, birds, and such like things. Did all the birds come of one bird? Did all vultures come of one vulture? Did all doves come of one dove? Did all snakes come of one snake? or all gilt-heads of one gilt-head?[2] or all sheep of one sheep? No, the earth assuredly brought forth all these kinds together. But when it came to man, the earth did not bring forth man. One father was made for us ; not even two, father and mother : one father, I say, was made for us, not even two, father and mother ; but out of the one father came the one mother ; the one father came from none, but was made by God, and the one mother came out of him. Mark then the nature of our race : we flowed out of one fountain ; and because that one was turned to bitterness, we all became from a good, a wild olive tree. And so grace came also. One begat us unto sin and death, yet as one race, yet as neighbours one to another, yet as not merely like, but related to each other. There came *One* against *one;* against the one who scattered, One who gathereth. Thus against the one who slayeth, is the One who maketh alive. " For as in Adam all die, even so in Christ shall all be made alive." [3] Now as whosoever is born of the first, dieth ; so whosoever believeth in Christ is made alive. Provided, that is, that he have " the wedding garment," and be invited as one who is to remain, and not to be cast out.

8. So then, my Brethren, have charity. I have explained it to be this garment, this " wedding garment." Faith is praised, it is plain, it is praised : but what kind of faith this is, the Apostle distinguishes. For certain who boasted of faith, and had not a good conversation, the Apostle James rebukes and says, " Thou believest there is one God, thou doest well ; the devils also believe and tremble." [4] Call to mind with me whereupon Peter was praised, whereupon

called blessed. Was it because he said, " Thou art the Christ, the Son of the living God "? [5] He who pronounced Him blessed, regarded not the sound of the words, but the affection of the heart. For would ye know that Peter's blessedness lay not in these words? The devils also said the same. " We know Thee who Thou art, the Son of God." [6] Peter confessed Him to be " the Son of God ; " the devils confessed Him to be " the Son of God." " Distinguish, my lord, distinguish between the two." I do make a plain distinction. Peter spake in love, the devils from fear. And again Peter says, " I am with Thee, even unto death." [7] The devils say, " What have we to do with Thee ?" So then thou who art come to the feast, glory not of faith only. Distinguish well the nature of this faith ; and then in thee is recognised " the wedding garment." Let the Apostle make the distinction, let him teach us ; " neither circumcision availeth anything, nor uncircumcision, but faith." [8] Tell us, what faith? do not even the devils believe and tremble? I will tell thee, he says, and listen, I will now draw the distinction, " But faith which worketh by love." What faith, then, and of what kind? " That which worketh by love." " Though I have all knowledge," he says, " and all faith, so that I could remove mountains, and have not charity, I am nothing." Have faith with love ; for love without faith ye cannot have. This I warn, this I exhort, this in the name of the Lord I teach you, Beloved, that ye have faith with love ; for ye may possibly have faith without love. I do not exhort you to have faith, but love. For ye cannot have love without faith ; the love I mean of God and your neighbour ; whence can it come without faith? How doth he love God, who doth not believe on God? How doth the fool love God, " who saith in his heart, there is no God "? [9] Possible it is that ye may believe that Christ hath come and not love Christ. But it is not possible that ye should love Christ, and yet say that Christ hath not come.

9. So then, have faith with love. This is the " wedding garment." Ye who love Christ, love one another, love your friends, love your enemies. Let not this be hard to you. What then do ye lose thereby, when ye gain so much? What? dost thou ask of God as some great favour, that thine enemy may die? This is not " the wedding garment." Turn thy thoughts to the Bridegroom Himself hanging upon the Cross for thee, and praying to His Father for His enemies ; " Father," saith He, " forgive them, for they know not what they do." [10] Thou hast seen the Bridegroom speaking thus; see too

---

[1] Ps. x. 5, Sept. (xi. 5, English version).   [2] *Aurata.*
[3] 1 Cor. xv. 22.   [4] Jas. ii. 19.

[5] Matt. xvi. 16.   [6] Matt. viii. 29; Mark i. 24.
[7] Matt. xxvi. 35.   [8] Gal. v. 6.   [9] Ps. liii. 1.
[10] Luke xxiii. 34.

the friend of the Bridegroom, a guest "with the wedding garment." Look at the blessed Stephen, how he rebukes the Jews as though in rage and resentment, "Ye stiffnecked and uncircumcised in heart and ears, ye have resisted the Holy Ghost. Which of the Prophets have not your fathers killed?"[1] Thou hast heard how severe he is with his tongue. And at[2] once thou art prepared to speak against any one; and I would it were against him who offendeth God, and not who offendeth thee. One offendeth God, and thou dost not rebuke him; he offendeth thee, and thou criest out; where is that "wedding garment"? Ye have heard therefore how Stephen was severe; now hear how he loved. He offended those whom he was rebuking, and was stoned by them. And as he was being overwhelmed and bruised to death by the hands of his furious persecutors on every side, and the blows of the stones, he first said, "Lord Jesus Christ, receive my spirit."[3] Then after he had prayed for himself standing, he bent the knee for them who were stoning him, and said, "Lord, lay not this sin to their charge; let me die in my body, but let not these die in their souls. And when he had said this, he fell asleep."[4] After these words he added no more; he spake them and departed; his last prayer was for his enemies. Learn ye hereby to have "the wedding garment." So do thou too bend the knee, and beat thy forehead against the ground, and as thou art about to approach the Table of the Lord, the Feast of the Holy Scriptures, do not say, "O that mine enemy might die! Lord, if I have deserved ought of Thee, slay mine enemy." Because if so be that thou sayest so, dost thou not fear lest He should answer thee, "If I should choose to slay thine enemy, I should first slay thee. What! dost thou glory because thou hast now come invited hither? Think only what thou wast but a little while ago. Hast thou not blasphemed Me? hast thou not derided Me? didst thou not wish to wipe out My Name from off the earth? Yet now thou dost applaud thyself because thou hast come invited hither! If I had slain thee when thou wast Mine enemy, how could I have made thee My friend? Why, by thy wicked prayers dost thou teach Me to do, what I did not in thine own case?" Yea rather God saith to thee, "Let me teach thee to imitate Me. When I was hanging on the Cross, I said, 'Forgive them, for they know not what they do.'[5] This lesson I taught My brave soldier. Be thou My recruit against the devil. In no other way wilt thou fight at all unconquerably, unless thou dost pray for thine enemies. Yet by all means ask this, yea ask this very thing,

ask that thou mayest persecute thine enemy; but ask it with discernment; distinguish well what thou askest. See, a man is thine enemy; answer me, what is it in him which is at enmity with thee? Is it in this, that he is a man, that he is at enmity with thee? No. What then? That he is evil. In that he is a man, in that he is that I made him, he is not at enmity with thee." He saith to thee, "I did not make man evil; he became evil by disobedience, who obeyed the devil[6] rather than God. What he has made himself, is at enmity with thee; in that he is evil, he is thine enemy; not in that he is a man. For I hear the word "man," and "evil;" the one is the name of nature, the other of sin; the sin I cure; and the nature I preserve." And so thy God saith to thee, "See, I do avenge thee, I do slay thine enemy; I take away that which makes him evil, I preserve that which constitutes him a man: now if I shall have made him a good man, have I not slain thine enemy, and made him thy friend?" So ask on what thou art asking, not that the men may perish, but that these their enmities may perish. For if thou pray for this, that the man may die; it is the prayer of one wicked man against another; and when thou dost say, "Slay the wicked one," God answereth thee, "Which of you?"

10. Extend your love then, and limit it not to your wives and children. Such love is found even in beasts and sparrows. Ye know the sparrows and the swallows how they love their mates, how together they hatch their eggs, and nourish their young together, by a sort of free[7] and natural kindliness, and with no thought of a return. For the sparrow does not say, "I will nourish my young, that when I am grown old, they may feed me." He has no such thought; he loves and feeds them, for the love of them; displays the affection of a parent, and looks for no return. And so, I know, I am sure, do ye love your children. "For the children ought not to lay up for the parents, but the parents for the children."[8] Yea upon this plea it is that many of you excuse your covetousness, that ye are getting for your children, and are laying by for them.[9] But I say, extend your love, let this love grow; for to love wives and children, is not yet that "wedding garment." Have faith to Godward. First love God. Extend yourselves out to God; and whomsoever ye shall be able, draw on to God. There is thine enemy: let him be drawn to God. There is a son, a wife, a servant; let them be all drawn to God. There is a stranger; let him be drawn to God. There is an enemy; let him be drawn to God. Draw,

---

[1] Acts vii. 51, 52.   [2] *Adhuc.*   [3] Acts vii. 59.
[4] Acts vii. 60.   [5] Luke xxiii. 34.

[6] *Zabulo;* Lactant. *De Mort. Pers.* 16.
[7] *Grata.*   [8] 2 Cor. xii. 14.
[9] *Vid.* Serm. xxxvi. (lxxxvi. Ben.) 11 (ix., x.).

draw on thine enemy; by drawing him on he shall cease to be thine enemy. So let charity be advanced, so be it nourished, that being nourished it may be perfected; so be "the wedding garment" put on; so be the image of God, after which we were created, by this our advancing, engraven anew in us. For by sin was it bruised, and worn away. How is it bruised? how worn away? When it is rubbed against the earth? And what is, "When it is rubbed against the earth"? When it is worn by earthly lusts. For "though man[1] walketh in this image, yet is he disquieted in vain."[2] Truth is looked for in God's image, not vanity. By the love of the truth then be that image, after which we were created, engraven anew, and His Own tribute rendered to our Cæsar. For so ye have heard from the Lord's answer, when the Jews tempted Him, as He said, "Why tempt ye Me, ye hypocrites; show Me the tribute money,"[3] that is, the impress and superscription of the image. Show me what ye pay, what ye get ready, what is exacted of you. And "they showed Him a denarius;" and "He asked whose image and superscription it had." They answered, "Cæsar's." So Cæsar looks for his own image. It is not Cæsar's will that what he ordered to be made should be lost to him, and it is not surely God's will that what He hath made should be lost to Him. Cæsar, my Brethren, did not make the money; the masters of the mint[4] make it; the workmen have their orders, he issues his commands to his ministers. His image was stamped upon the money; on the money was Cæsar's image. And yet he requires what others have stamped; he puts it in his treasures; he will not have it refused him. Christ's coin is man. In him is Christ's image, in him Christ's Name, Christ's gifts, Christ's rules of duty.[5]

SERMON XLI.

[XCI. BEN.]

ON THE WORDS OF THE GOSPEL, MATT. XXII. 42, WHERE THE LORD ASKS THE JEWS WHOSE SON THEY SAID DAVID WAS.

1. WHEN the Jews were asked (as we have just now heard out of the Gospel when it was being read), how our Lord Jesus Christ, whom David himself called his Lord was David's Son, they were not able to answer. For what they saw in the Lord, that they knew. For He appeared to them as the Son of man; but as the Son of God He was hidden. Hence it was, that they believed that He could be overcome, and that they derided Him as He hung upon the Tree, saying, "If He be the Son of God, let Him come down from the Cross, and we will believe on Him."[6] They saw one part of what He was, they knew not the other. "For had they known Him, they would not have crucified the Lord of glory."[7] Yet they knew that the Christ was to be the Son of David. For even now they hope that He will come. They know not that He is come already, but this their ignorance is voluntary. For even if they did not acknowledge Him on the tree, they ought not to have failed to acknowledge Him on His Throne. For in whose Name are all nations called and blessed, but in His whom they think not to have been the Christ? For this Son of David, that is, "of the seed of David according to the flesh," is the Son of Abraham. Now if it was said to Abraham, "In thy seed shall all nations be blessed;"[8] and they see now that in our Christ are all nations blessed, why wait they for what is already come, and fear not that which is yet to come? for our Lord Jesus Christ, making use of a prophetic testimony to assert His authority, called Himself "the Stone." Yea such a stone, "that whosoever shall stumble against it shall be shaken; but on whomsoever it shall fall, it shall grind him to powder."[9] For when this stone is stumbled against, it lieth low; by lying low, it "shaketh" him that stumbleth against it; being lifted on high, by its coming down it "grindeth" the proud "to powder." Already therefore are the Jews "shaken" by that stumbling; it yet remains that by His Glorious Advent they should be "ground to powder" also, unless peradventure whilst they are yet alive, they acknowledge Him that they die not. For God is patient, and inviteth them day by day to the Faith.

2. But when the Jews could not answer the Lord proposing a question, and asking "whose Son they said Christ was;" and they answered, "the Son of David;"[10] He goes on with the further question put to them, "How then doth David in spirit call Him Lord, saying, The Lord said unto my Lord, Sit thou on My right hand till I make Thine enemies My footstool. If David then," He saith, "in spirit call Him Lord, how is He his Son?"[11] He did not say, "He is not his Son, but how is He his son?" When he saith "How," it is a word not of negation, but of enquiry; as though He should say to them, "Ye say well indeed that Christ is David's Son, but David himself doth call Him Lord; whom he then calleth Lord, how is He his Son?" Had the Jews been instructed in the Christian faith, which we hold; had they not closed their hearts against the Gospel, had they wished to

---

[1] Serm. x. (lx. Ben.) 2, etc.
[2] Ps. xxxviii. 7, Sept. (xxxix. 6, English version).
[3] Matt. xxii. 18, 19.   [4] *Monetarii.*   [5] *Officia.*

[6] Matt. xxvii. 42.   [7] 1 Cor. ii. 8.   [8] Gen. xxii. 18.
[9] Ps. cxviii. 22; Luke xx. 17, 18.   [10] Matt. xxii. 42.
[11] Matt. xxii. 43-45.

have spiritual life in them, they would, as instructed in the faith of the Church, have made answer to this question and said, " Because in the beginning was the Word, and the Word was with God, and the Word was God : "¹ see how He is David's Lord. But because "The Word was made flesh, and dwelt among us ; "² see how He is David's Son. But as being ignorant, they were silent, nor when they shut their mouths did they open their ears, that what they could not answer when questioned, they might after instruction know.

3. But seeing that is a great thing to know the mystery how He is David's Son and David's Lord : how one Person is both Man and God ; how in the form of Man He is less than the Father, in the form of God equal with the Father ; how again He saith, on the one hand, "The Father is greater than I ; "³ and on the other, " I and My Father are one ; "⁴ seeing this is a great mystery,⁵ our conduct must be fashioned, that it may be comprehended. For to the unworthy is it closed up, it is opened to those who are meet for it. It is not with stones, or clubs, or the fist, or the heel, that we knock unto the Lord. It is the life which knocks, it is to the life that it is opened. The seeking is with the heart, the asking is with the heart, the knocking is with the heart, the opening is to the heart. Now that heart which asks rightly, and knocks and seeks rightly, must be godly. Must first love God for His Own sake (for this is godliness) ; and not propose to itself any reward which it looks for from Him other than God Himself. For than Him is there nothing better. And what precious thing can he ask of God, in whose sight God Himself is lightly esteemed? He giveth earth, and thou rejoicest, thou lover of the earth, who art thyself become earth. If when He giveth earthly goods, thou dost rejoice, how much more oughtest thou to rejoice when He giveth thee Himself, who made heaven and earth? So then God must be loved for His own sake. For the Devil not knowing what was passing in the heart of holy Job, brought this as a great charge against him, saying, " Doth Job worship God for His Own sake."⁶

4. So then if the adversary brought this charge, we ought to fear lest it be brought against us. For with a very slanderous accuser have we to deal. If he seek to invent what is not, how much more will he seek to object what really is. Nevertheless let us rejoice, that ours is such a Judge, as cannot be deceived by our accuser. For if we had a man for our judge, the enemy might invent for him what he would. For none is more subtle in invention than the devil. For he it is who at this time also invents all false accusations against the saints. He knows his accusations can have no avail with God, and so He scatters them among men. Yet what does this profit him, seeing the Apostle says, " Our glorying is this, the testimony of our conscience?"⁷ Yet think ye that he does not invent these false charges with aught of subtlety? Yes, well he knows what evil he shall work thereby, if the watchfulness of faith resist him not. For for this reason scatters he his evil charges against the good, that the weak may think that there are no good, and so may give themselves up to be hurried along, and made a prey of by their lusts, whilst they say within themselves, " For who is there that keeps the commandments of God, or who is there that preserves chastity?" and whilst he thinks that no one does, he himself becomes that no one. This then is the devil's art. But such a man was Job, that he could not invent any such charge against him ; for his life was too well known and manifest. But because he had great riches, he brought that against him, which if it had any existence, might lie in the heart, and not appear in the conduct. He worshipped God, he gave alms ; and with what heart he did this none knew, no not the Devil himself; but God had known. God giveth His testimony to His own servant ; the Devil calumniates the servant of God. He is allowed to be tried, Job is proved, the Devil is confounded. Job is found to worship God for His Own sake, to love Him for His Own sake ; not because He gave him ought, but because He did not take away Himself. For he said, "The Lord gave, the Lord hath taken away ; as it seemed good to the Lord, so is it done, blessed be the Name of the Lord."⁸ The fire of temptation approached him ; but it found him gold, not stubble ; it cleared away the dross from it, but did not reduce it to ashes.

5. Because then, in order to understand the mystery⁵ of God, how Christ is both man and God, the heart must be cleansed : and it is cleansed by a good conversation, by a pure life,⁹ by chastity, and sanctity, and love, and by " faith, which worketh by love "¹⁰ (now all this that I am speaking of, is, as it were, the tree which hath its root in the heart ; for it is only from the root of the heart that actions proceed ; in which if thou plant desire, thorns spring forth ; if thou plant charity, good fruit) : the Lord, after that question which He had proposed to the Jews, when they were not able to answer it, immediately went on to speak of good actions, that He might show why they were unworthy to understand what He asked them. For when those proud and wretched men were not able to answer, they ought of course to have said, " we do not know ; Master, tell us." But no : they

---

¹ John i. 1.   ² John i. 14.   ³ John xiv. 28.
⁴ John x. 30.   ⁵ Sacramentum.   ⁶ Job i. 9. Gratis.

⁷ 2 Cor. i. 12.   ⁸ Job i. 21, Sept.   ⁹ Vita.
¹⁰ Gal. v. 6.

were speechless at the proposing of the question, and they opened not their mouth to seek instruction. And so the Lord in reference to their pride said immediately, " Beware of the Scribes which love the chief seats in the synagogues, and the first rooms at feasts." [1] Not because they hold them, but because they love them. For in these words he accused their heart. Now none can accuse the heart, but He who can inspect it. For meet it is that to the servant of God, who holds some post of honour in the Church, the first place should be assigned ; because if it were not given him, it were evil for him who refuses to give it ; but yet it is no good to him to whom it is given. It is meet and right then that in the congregation of Christians their Prelates [2] should sit in eminent place, that by their very seat they may be distinguished, and that their office may be duly marked ; yet not so that they should be puffed up for their seat ; but that they should esteem it a burden, for which they are to render an account. But who knows whether they love this, or do not love it? This is a matter of the heart, it can have no other judge but God. Now the Lord Himself warned His disciples, that they should not fall into this leaven ; as He calls it in another place, " Beware ye of the leaven of the Pharisees and of the Sadducees." [3] And when they supposed that He said this to them because they had brought no bread ; He answered them, " Have ye forgotten how many thousands were filled with the five loaves? Then understood they," it is said, " that He called their doctrine leaven." [4] For these present temporal good things they loved, but they neither feared the evil things eternal, nor loved the good things eternal. And so their hearts being closed, they could not understand what the Lord asked them.

6. But what then has the Church of God to do, that it may be able to understand what it has first obtained [5] grace to believe? It must make the mind capacious for receiving what shall be given it. And that this may be done, that the mind, that is, may be capacious, our Lord God suspends His promises, He has not taken them away. Therefore does He suspend them, that we may stretch out ourselves ; and therefore do we stretch ourselves out, that we may grow ; and therefore do we grow, that we may reach them. Behold the Apostle Paul stretching himself out unto these suspended promises : " Not as though I had already attained, either were already perfect. Brethren, I count not myself to have apprehended : but this one thing I do ; forgetting those things which are behind, and stretching forth unto those things which are before, I press earnestly toward the mark for the prize of the high calling of God in Christ Jesus." [6] He was running on the earth ; the prize hung suspended from heaven. He ran then on the earth ; but in spirit he ascended. Behold him thus stretching himself out, behold him hanging forth after the suspended prize. " I press on," he says, " for the prize of the high calling of God in Christ Jesus."

7. We must journey on then, yet for this no need of anointing the feet, or looking out for beasts, or providing a vessel. Run with the heart's affection, journey on with love, ascend by charity. Why seekest thou for the way? Cleave unto Christ, who by Descending and Ascending hath made Himself the Way. Dost thou wish to ascend? Hold fast to Him that ascendeth. For by thine own self thou canst not rise. " For no man hath ascended up to heaven, but He that came down from heaven, even the Son of Man which is in heaven." [7] If no one ascendeth but He that descended, that is, the Son of Man, our Lord Jesus, dost thou wish to ascend also? Be then a member of Him who Only hath ascended. For He the Head, with all the members, is but One Man. And since no one can ascend, but he who in His Body is made a member of Him ; that is fulfilled, " that no man hath ascended, but He that descended." For thou canst not say, " Lo, why hath Peter, for instance, ascended, why hath Paul ascended, why have the Apostles ascended, if no one hath ascended, but He that descended?" The answer to this is, " What do Peter, and Paul, and the rest of the Apostles, and all the faithful, what do they hear from the Apostle? ' Now ye are the Body of Christ, and members in particular.' [8] If then the Body of Christ and His members belong to One, do not thou make two of them. For He left ' father and mother, and clave to his wife, that two might be one flesh.' [9] He left His Father, in that here He did not show Himself as equal with the Father ; but ' emptied Himself, taking the form of a servant.' [10] He left His mother also, the synagogue of which He was born after the flesh. He clave to His Wife, that is, to His Church. Now in the place where Christ Himself brought forward this testimony, He showed that the marriage bond might not be dissolved : ' Have ye not read,' said He, ' that God which made them at the beginning, made them male and female ; and said, They twain shall be in one flesh? What therefore God hath joined together, let not man put asunder.' [11] And what is the meaning of ' They twain shall be in one flesh'? He goes on to say ; ' Wherefore they are no more twain but one flesh.' Thus ' no man hath ascended, but He that descended.' " [7]

8. For that ye may know, that the Bridegroom

---

[1] Matt. xxiii. 6; Mark xii. 39. [2] *Prepositi plebis.*
[3] Matt. xvi. 6. [4] Matt. xvi. 9, 12.
[5] *Meruit.*

[6] Phil. iii. 12, etc. [7] John iii. 13. [8] 1 Cor. xii. 27.
[9] Eph. v. 31. [10] Phil. ii. 7. [11] Matt. xix. 4, etc.

and the Bride are One according to the Flesh of Christ, not according to His Divinity (for according to His Divinity we cannot be what He is; seeing that He is the Creator, we the creature; He the Maker, we His work; He the Framer, we framed by Him; but in order that we might be one with Him in Him, He vouchsafed to be our Head, by taking of us flesh wherein to die for us); that ye may know then that this whole is One Christ, He said by Isaiah, "He hath bound a mitre on me as a bridegroom, and clothed me with ornaments as a bride."[1] He is then at once the Bridegroom and the Bride. That is, the Bridegroom in Himself as the Head, the Bride in the body. "For they twain," saith He, "shall be in one flesh; so now they are no more twain, but one flesh."

9. Seeing then that we are of His members, in order that we may understand this mystery as I have said, Brethren, let us live holily, let us love God for His Own sake. Now He who showeth to us while in our pilgrimage the form of a servant, reserveth for those that reach their country the form of God. With the form of a servant hath He laid down the way, with the form of God He hath prepared the home. Seeing then that it is a hard matter for us to comprehend this, but no hard matter to believe it; for Isaiah says, "Unless ye believe ye shall not understand;"[2] let us "walk by faith as long as we are in pilgrimage from the Lord, till we come to sight where we shall see face to face."[3] As walking by faith, let us do good works. In these good works, let there be a free love of God for His Own sake, and an active[4] love of our neighbour. For we have nothing we can do for God; but because we have something we may do for our neighbour, we shall by our good offices to the needy, gain His favour who is the source of all abundance.[5] Let every one then do what he can for others; let him freely bestow upon the needy of his superfluity. One has money; let him feed the poor, let him clothe the naked, let him build a church, let him do with his money all the good he can. Another has good counsel; let him guide his neighbour, let him by the light of holiness drive away the darkness of doubting. Another has learning; let him draw out of this store of the Lord, let him minister food to his fellow-servants, strengthen the faithful, recall the wandering, seek the lost, do all the good he can. Something there is, which even the poor may deal out to one another; let one lend feet to the lame, another give his own eyes to guide the blind; another visit the sick, another bury the dead. These are things which all may do, so that in a word it would be hard to find one who has not some means of doing good to others. And last of all comes that important duty which the Apostle speaks of; "Bear ye one another's burdens, and so shall ye fulfil the law of Christ."[6]

SERMON XLII.

[XCII. BEN.]

ON THE SAME WORDS OF THE GOSPEL, MATT. XXII. 42.

1. THE question which was proposed to the Jews, Christians ought to solve. For the Lord Jesus Christ, who proposed it to the Jews, did not solve it Himself, to the Jews, I mean, He did not, but to us He hath solved it. I will put you in remembrance, Beloved, and ye will find that He hath solved it. But first consider the knot of the question. He asked the Jews what they "thought of Christ, whose Son He was to be;" for they too look for the Christ. They read of Him in the Prophets, they expected Him to come, when He was come they killed Him; for where they read that Christ would come, there did they read that they should kill Christ. But His future coming they hoped for in the Prophets; for they did not see their future crime. He therefore so questioned them about the Christ, not as if about One who was unknown to them, or whose Name they had never heard, or whose coming they had never hoped for. For they err in that even yet they hope for Him. And we indeed hope for Him too; but we hope for Him as One who is to come as Judge, not to be judged. For the Holy Prophets prophesied both, that He should come first to be judged unrighteously, that He should come afterwards to judge with righteousness. "What think ye," then, saith he, "of Christ? whose Son is He? They answered Him, The Son of David."[7] And this was entirely according to the Scriptures. But He said, "How then doth David in spirit call Him Lord, saying, The Lord said unto My Lord, Sit Thou on My right hand, till I make Thine enemies Thy footstool. If David then in spirit call Him Lord, how is He his Son?"[8]

2. Here then is need of a caution, lest Christ be thought to have denied that He was the Son of David. He did not deny that He was the Son of David, but He enquired the way. "Ye have said that Christ is the Son of David, I do not deny it; but David calls Him Lord; tell me how is He his Son, who is also his Lord; tell me how?" They did not tell Him, but were silent. Let us then tell by the explanation of Christ Himself. Where? By His Apostle. But first, whereby do we prove that Christ hath Himself explained it? The Apostle says, "Would ye receive a proof of Christ who

---

speaketh in me?"[1] So then in the Apostle hath He vouchsafed to solve this question. In the first place, what said Christ speaking by the Apostle to Timothy? "Remember that Jesus Christ of the seed of David was raised from the dead according to my Gospel."[2] See, Christ is the Son of David. How is He also David's Lord? Tell us, O Apostle: "who being in the form of God, thought it not robbery to be equal with God." Acknowledge David's Lord. If thou acknowledge David's Lord, our Lord, the Lord of heaven and earth, the Lord of the Angels, equal with God, in the form of God, how is He David's Son? Mark what follows. The Apostle shows thee David's Lord by saying, "Who being in the form of God, thought it not robbery to be equal with God." And how is He David's Son? "But He emptied Himself, taking the form of a servant, being made in the likeness of men; and being found in fashion as a man, He humbled Himself, having become obedient unto death, even the death of the cross. Wherefore God also hath highly exalted Him."[3] Christ "of the seed of David," the Son of David, rose again because "He emptied Himself." How did He "empty Himself"? By taking that which He was not, not by losing that which He was. He "emptied Himself," He "humbled himself." Though He was God, He appeared as man. He was despised as He walked on earth, He who made the heaven. He was despised as though a mere man, as though of no power. Yea, not despised only, but slain moreover. He was that stone that lay on the ground, the Jews stumbled against it, and were shaken. And what doth He Himself say? "Whosoever shall fall on this stone shall be shaken, but on whomsoever it shall fall, it shall grind him to powder."[4] First, He lay low, and they stumbled against Him; He shall come from above, and He will "grind" them that have been shaken "to powder."

3. Thus have ye heard that Christ is both David's Son, and David's Lord: David's Lord always, David's Son in time: David's Lord, born of the substance of His Father, David's Son, born of the Virgin Mary, conceived by the Holy Ghost. Let us hold fast both. The one of them will be our eternal habitation, the other is our deliverance from our present exile. For unless our Lord Jesus Christ had vouchsafed to become man, man had perished. He was made that which He made, that what He made might not perish. Very Man, Very God; God and man whole Christ. This is the Catholic faith. Whoso denieth that Christ is God is a Photinian;[5]

whoso denieth that Christ is man is a Manichæan.[6] Whoso confesseth that Christ is God equal with the Father and very man, that He truly suffered, truly shed His blood (for the Truth would not have set us free, if He had given a false price for us); whoso confesseth both, is a Catholic. He hath the country, he hath the way. He hath the country, "In the beginning was the Word;"[7] He hath the country, "Being in the form of God, He thought it not robbery to be equal with God."[8] He hath the way, "The Word was made flesh;"[9] He hath the way, "He emptied Himself, taking the form of a servant."[10] He is the home whither we are going, He is the way whereby we go. Let us by Him go unto Him, and we shall not go astray.

SERMON XLIII.

[XCIII. BEN.]

ON THE WORDS OF THE GOSPEL, MATT. XXV. I, "THEN SHALL THE KINGDOM OF HEAVEN BE LIKENED UNTO TEN VIRGINS."

1. YE who were present yesterday remember my promise; which with the Lord's assistance is to be made good to-day, not to you only, but to the many others also who have come together. It is no easy question, who the ten virgins are, of whom five are wise, and five foolish. Nevertheless, according to the context of this passage which I have wished should be read again to you to-day, Beloved, I do not think, as far as the Lord vouchsafes to give me understanding, that this parable or similitude relates to those women only who by a peculiar and more excellent sanctity are called Virgins in the Church, whom by a more usual term we are wont also to call, "The Religious;"[11] but if I mistake not this parable relates to the whole Church.[12] But though we should understand it of those only who are called "the Religious," are they but ten? God forbid that so great a company of virgins should be reduced to so small a number! But perhaps one may say, "But what if though they be so many in outward profession, yet in truth they are so few, that scarce ten can be found!" It is not so. For if he had meant that the good virgins only should be understood by the ten, He would not have represented five foolish ones among them. For if this is the number of the virgins which are called, why are the doors of the great house shut against five?

2. So then let us understand, dearly Beloved, that this parable relates to us all, that is, to

---

[1] 2 Cor. xiii. 3.   [2] 2 Tim. ii. 8.
[3] Phil. ii. 6, etc.   [4] Matt. xxi. 44.
[5] Vinc. Lirinens. *Commonit.* xii.; *Conf.* vii. 26 (xx.), Oxf. transl. and note *f.*

[6] *Conf.* v. 16 (ix), 20 (x.), 25 (xix.), vii. 25 (xix.), Oxf. trans. and note *A*, p. 325. *De Dono Perseverant.* c. 67 (xxiv.), Serm. lxvi. (cxvi. Ben) 1–5 (i.–iv.), Epist. 236 (al. 74) 2.
[7] John i. 1.   [8] Phil. ii. 6.   [9] John i. 14.
[10] Phil. ii. 7.   [11] *Sancti moniales.*
[12] Bing. *Antiq.* B. vii. c. iv. sect. 8.

the whole Church together, not to the Clergy [1] only of whom we spoke yesterday; nor to the laity only; but generally to all. Why then are the Virgins five and five? These five and five virgins are all Christian souls together. But that I may tell you what by the Lord's inspiration I think, it is not souls of every sort, but such souls as have the Catholic faith, and seem to have good works in the Church of God; and yet even of them, "five are wise, and five are foolish." First then let us see why they are called "five," and why "virgins," and then let us consider the rest. Every soul in the body is therefore denoted [2] by the number five, because it makes use of five senses. For there is nothing of which we have perception by the body, but by the five folded gate, either by the sight, or the hearing, or the smelling, or the tasting, or the touching. Whoso then abstaineth from unlawful seeing, unlawful hearing, unlawful smelling, unlawful tasting, and unlawful touching, by reason of his uncorruptness [3] hath gotten the name of virgin.

3. But if it be good to abstain from the unlawful excitements of the senses, and on that account every Christian soul has gotten the name of virgin; why are five admitted and five rejected? They are both virgins, and yet are rejected. It is not enough that they are virgins; and that they have lamps. They are virgins, by reason of abstinence from unlawful indulgence of the senses; they have lamps, by reason of good works. Of which good works the Lord saith, "Let your works shine before men, that they may see your good works, and glorify your Father which is in heaven." [4] Again He saith to His disciples, "Let your loins be girded and your lamps burning." [5] In the "girded loins" is virginity; in the "burning lamps" good works.

4. The title of virginity is not usually applied to married persons: yet even in them there is a virginity of faith, which produces wedded chastity. For that you may know, Holy Brethren, that every one, every soul, as touching the soul, and that uncorruptness of faith by which abstinence from things unlawful is practised, and by which good works are done, is not unsuitably called "a virgin;" the whole Church which consists of virgins, and boys, and married men and married women, is by one name called a Virgin. Whence prove we this? Hear the Apostle saying, not to the religious women only but to the whole Church together; "I have espoused you to One Husband, that I may present you as a chaste virgin to Christ." [6] And because the devil, the corrupter of this virginity, is to be guarded against, after the Apostle had said, "I have espoused you to one husband, that I may present you as a chaste virgin to Christ;"

he subjoined, "But I fear, lest as the serpent beguiled Eve through his subtilty, so your minds should be corrupted from the simplicity that is in Christ." [7] Few have virginity in the body; in the heart all ought to have it. If then abstinence from what is unlawful be good, whereby it has received the name of virginity, and good works are praiseworthy, which are signified by the lamps; why are five admitted and five rejected? If there be a virgin, and one who carries lamps, who yet is not admitted; where shall he see himself, who neither preserveth a virginity from things unlawful, and who not wishing to have good works walketh in darkness?

5. Of these then, my Brethren, yea, of these let us the rather treat. He who will not see what is evil, he who will not hear what is evil, he that turneth away his smell from the unlawful fumes, and his taste from the unlawful food of the sacrifices, he who refuseth the embrace of another man's wife, breaketh his bread to the hungry, bringeth the stranger into his house, clotheth the naked, reconcileth the litigious, visiteth the sick, burieth the dead; he surely is a virgin, surely he hath lamps. What seek we more? Something yet I seek. What seekest thou yet, one will say? Something yet I seek; the Holy Gospel hath set me on the search. It hath said that even of these, virgins, and carrying lamps, some are wise and some foolish. By what do we see this? By what make the distinction? By the oil. Some great, some exceedingly great thing doth this oil signify. Thinkest thou that it is not charity? This we say as searching out what it is; we hazard no precipitate judgment. I will tell you why charity seems to be signified by the oil. The Apostle says, "I show unto you a way above the rest." [8] Though I speak with the tongues of men and of Angels, and have not charity, I am become as sounding brass, or a tinkling cymbal." [9] This, that is "charity," is "that way above the rest," which is with good reason signified by the oil. For oil swims above all liquids. Pour in water, and pour in oil upon it, the oil will swim above. Pour in oil, pour in water upon it, the oil will swim above. If you keep the usual order, it will be uppermost; [10] if you change the order, it will be uppermost. "Charity never falleth." [11]

6. What is it then, Brethren? Let us treat now of the five wise and the five foolish virgins. They wished to go to meet the Bridegroom. What is the meaning of "to go and meet the Bridegroom"? To go with the heart, to be waiting for his coming. But he tarried. "While he tarries, they all slept." What is "all"? Both the foolish and the wise, "all slumbered and slept." Think we is this sleep good? What

---

[1] Præpositos. [2] Censetur. [3] Integritatem.
[4] Matt. v. 16. [5] Luke xii. 35. [6] 2 Cor. xi. 2.

[7] 2 Cor. xi. 3. [8] Supereminentiorem. 1 Cor. xii. 31.
[9] 1 Cor. xiii. 1. [10] Vincit. [11] 1 Cor. xiii. 8. Cadit.

is this sleep? Is it that at the tarrying of the Bridegroom, "because iniquity aboundeth, the love of many waxeth cold"? Are we to understand this sleep so? I like it not. I will tell you why. Because among them are the wise virgins; and certainly when the Lord said, "Because iniquity shall abound, the love of many shall wax cold;" He went on to say, "But he that shall endure unto the end, the same shall be saved."[1] Where would ye have those wise virgins be? Are they not among those that "shall endure unto the end"? They would not be admitted within at all, Brethren, for any other reason, than because they have "endured unto the end." No coldness of love then crept over them, in them love did not wax cold; but preserves its glow even unto the end. And because it glows even unto the end, therefore are the gates of the Bridegroom opened to them; therefore are they told to enter in, as that excellent servant, "Enter thou into the joy of thy Lord."[2] What then is the meaning of they "all slept"?[3] There is another sleep which no one escapes. Remember ye not the Apostle saying, "But I would not have you to be ignorant, brethren, concerning them which are asleep,"[4] that is, concerning them which are dead? For why are they called "they which are asleep," but because they are in their own day? Therefore "they all slept." Thinkest thou that because one is wise, he has not therefore to die? Be the virgin foolish, or be she wise, all suffer equally the sleep of death.

7. But men continually say to themselves, "Lo, the day of judgment is coming now, so many evils are happening, so many tribulations thicken; behold all things which the Prophets have spoken, are well-nigh fulfilled; the day of judgment is already at hand." They who speak thus, and speak in faith, go out as it were with such thoughts to "meet the Bridegroom." But, lo! war upon war, tribulation upon tribulation, earthquake upon earthquake, famine upon famine, nation against nation, and still the Bridegroom comes not yet. Whilst then He is expected to come, all they who are saying, "Lo, He is coming, and the Day of Judgment will find us here," fall asleep. Whilst they are saying this, they fall asleep. Let each one then have an eye to this his sleep, and persevere even unto his sleep in love; let sleep find him so waiting. For suppose that he has fallen asleep. "Will not He who falls asleep afterwards rise again?"[5] Therefore "they all slept;" both of the wise and the foolish virgins in the parable, it is said, "they all slept."

8. "Lo, at midnight there was a cry made."[6]

What is, "at midnight"? When there is no expectation, no belief at all of it. Night is put for ignorance. A man makes as it were a calculation with himself: "Lo, so many years have passed since Adam, and the six thousand years are being completed, and then immediately according to the computation of certain expositors, the Day of Judgment will come;" yet these calculations come and pass away, and still the coming of the Bridegroom is delayed, and the virgins who had gone to meet him sleep. And, lo, when He is not looked for, when men are saying, "The six thousand years were waited for, and, lo, they are gone by, how then shall we know when He will come?" He will come at midnight. What is, "will come at midnight"? Will come when thou art not aware. Why will He come when thou art not aware of it? Hear the Lord Himself, "It is not for you to know the times or the seasons which the Lord hath put in His own power."[7] "The day of the Lord," says the Apostle, "will come as a thief in the night."[8] Therefore watch thou by night that thou be not surprised by the thief. For the sleep of death — will ye, or nill ye — it will come.

9. "But when that cry was made at midnight." What cry was this, but that of which the Apostle says, "In the twinkling of an eye, at the last trump"? "For the trumpet shall sound, and the dead shall be raised incorruptible, and we shall be changed"?[9] And so when the cry was made at midnight, "Behold, the Bridegroom cometh;" what follows? "Then all those virgins arose." What is, "they" all arose? "The hour will come," said the Lord Himself, "when all that are in the graves shall hear His voice, and shall come forth."[10] Therefore at the last trumpet they all arose. "Now those wise virgins had brought oil with them in their vessels; but the foolish brought no oil with them."[11] What is the meaning of "brought no oil with them in their vessels"? What is "in their vessels"? In their hearts. Whence the Apostle says, "Our glorying is this, the testimony of our conscience."[12] There is the oil, the precious oil; this oil is of the gift of God. Men can put oil into their vessels, but they cannot create the olive. See, I have oil; but didst thou create the oil? It is of the gift of God. Thou hast oil. Carry it with thee. What is "carry it with thee"? Have it within, there please thou God.

10. For, lo, those "foolish virgins, who brought no oil with them," wish to please men by that abstinence of theirs whereby they are called virgins, and by their good works, when they seem to carry lamps. And if they wish to please men, and on that account do all these praiseworthy

[1] Matt. xxiv. 12, 13. [2] Matt. xxv. 21. [3] Matt. xxv. 5.
[4] 1 Thess. iv. 13. [5] Ps. xl. 9, Sept. (xli. 8, English version).
[6] Matt. xxv. 6.

[7] Acts i. 7. [8] 1 Thess. v. 2 [9] 1 Cor. xv. 52.
[10] John v. 28, 29. [11] Matt. xxv. 4, 3. [12] 2 Cor. i. 12.

works, they do not carry oil with them. Do you then carry it with thee, carry it within where God seeth; there carry the testimony of thy conscience. For he who walks to gain the testimony of another, does not carry oil with him. If thou abstain from things unlawful, and doest good works to be praised of men; there is no oil within. And so when men begin to leave off their praises, the lamps fail. Observe then, Beloved, before those virgins slept, it is not said that their lamps were extinguished. The lamps of the wise virgins burned with an inward oil, with the assurance of a good conscience, with an inner glory, with an inmost charity. Yet the lamps of the foolish virgins burned also. Why burnt they then? Because there was yet no want of the praises of men. But after that they arose, that is in the resurrection from the dead, they began to trim their lamps, that is, began to prepare to render unto God an account of their works. And because there is then no one to praise, every man is wholly employed in his own cause, there is no one then who is not thinking of himself, therefore were there none to sell them oil; so their lamps began to fail, and the foolish betook themselves to the five wise, "give us of your oil, for our lamps are going out." [1] They sought for what they had been wont to seek for, to shine that is with others' oil, to walk after others' praises. "Give us of your oil, for our lamps are going out."

11. But they say, "Not so, lest there be not enough for us and you, but go ye rather to them that sell, and buy for yourselves." [2] This was not the answer of those who give advice, but of those who mock. And why mock they? Because they were wise, because wisdom was in them. For they were not wise by ought of their own; but that wisdom was in them, of which it is written in a certain book, she shall say to those that despised her, when they have fallen upon the evils which she threatened them; "I will laugh over your destruction." [3] What wonder then is it, that the wise mock the foolish virgins? And what is this mocking?

12. "Go ye to them that sell, and buy for yourselves:" [2] ye who never were wont to live well, but because men praised you, who sold you oil. What means this, "sold you oil"? "Sold praises." Who sell praises, but flatterers? How much better had it been for you not to have acquiesced in flatterers, and to have carried oil within, and for a good conscience-sake to have done all good works; then might ye say, "The righteous shall correct me in mercy, and reprove me, but the oil of the sinner shall not fatten [4] my head." [5] Rather, he says, let the righteous correct me, let the righteous reprove me, let the righteous buffet me, let the righteous correct me, than the "oil of the sinner fatten mine head." What is the oil of the sinner, but the blandishments of the flatterer?

13. "Go ye" then "to them that sell," this have ye been accustomed to do. But we will not give to you. Why? "Lest there be not enough for us and you." What is, "lest there be not enough"? This was not spoken in any lack of hope, but in a sober and godly humility. For though the good man have a good conscience; how knows he, how He may judge who is deceived by no one? He hath a good conscience, no sins conceived in the heart solicit [6] him, yet, though his conscience be good, because of the daily sins of human life, he saith to God, "forgive us our debts;" seeing he hath done what comes next, "as we also forgive our debtors." [7] He hath broken his bread to the hungry from the heart, from the heart hath clothed the naked; out of that inward oil he hath done good works, and yet in that judgment even his good conscience trembleth.

14. See then what this, "Give us oil," is. They were told "Go ye rather to them that sell." In that ye have been used to live upon the praises of men, ye do not carry oil with you; but we can give you none; "lest there be not enough for us and you." For scarcely do we judge of ourselves, how much less can we judge of you? What is "scarcely do we judge of ourselves"? Because, "When the righteous King sitteth on the throne, who will glory that his heart is pure?" [8] It may be thou dost not discover anything in thine own conscience; but He who seeth better, whose Divine glance penetrateth into deeper things, discovereth it may be something, He seeth it may be something, He discovereth something. How much better mayest thou say to Him, "Enter not into judgment with Thy servant"? [9] Yea, how much better, "Forgive us our debts"? Because it shall be also said to thee because of those torches, because of those lamps; "I was hungry, and ye gave Me meat." What then? did not the foolish virgins do so too? Yea, but they did it not before Him. How then did they do it? As the Lord forbiddeth, who said, "Take heed that ye do not your righteousness before men to be seen of them, otherwise ye have no reward of your Father which is in heaven: and when ye pray, be not as the hypocrites, for they love to pray, standing in the streets, that they may be seen of men. Verily I say unto you, they have received their reward." [10] They have bought oil, they have given the price; they have bought

1 Matt. xxv. 8.   2 Matt. xxv. 9.   3 Prov. i. 26.
4 Impinguabit.
5 Ps. cxl 5, Sept. (cxli English version).

6 Titillant.   7 Matt vi. 12.   8 Prov. xx. 8, 9, Sept.
9 Ps. cxliii. 2.   10 Matt. vi. 1, etc.

it, they have not been defrauded of men's praises, they have sought men's praises, and have had them. These praises of men aid them not in the judgment day. But the other virgins, how have they done? "Let your works shine before men, that they may see your good works, and glorify your Father which is in heaven." [1] He did not say, "may glorify you." For thou hast no oil of thine own self. Boast thyself and say, I have it; but from Him, "for what hast thou that thou hast not received?" [2] So then in this way acted the one, and in that the other.

15. Now it is no wonder, that "while they are going to buy," while they are seeking for persons by whom to be praised, and find none; while they are seeking for persons by whom to be comforted, and find none; that the door is opened, that "the Bridegroom cometh," [3] and the Bride, the Church, glorified then with Christ, that the several members may be gathered together into their whole. "And they went in with Him into the marriage, and the door was shut." Then the foolish virgins came afterwards; but had they bought any oil, or found any from whom they might buy it? Therefore they found the doors shut; they began to knock, but too late.

16. It is said, and it is true, and no deceiving saying, "Knock, and it shall be opened unto you;" [4] but now when it is the time of mercy, not when it is the time of judgment. For these times cannot be confounded, since the Church sings to her Lord of "mercy and judgment." [5] It is the time of mercy; repent. Canst thou repent in the time of judgment? Thou wilt be then as those virgins, against whom the door was shut. "Lord, Lord, open to us." What! did they not repent, that they had brought no oil with them? Yes, but what profiteth them their late repentance, when the true wisdom mocked them? Therefore "the door was shut." And what was said to them? "I know you not." Did not He know them, who knoweth all things? What then is, "I know you not?" [6] I refuse, I reject you. In my art I do not acknowledge you, my art knoweth not vice; now this is a marvellous thing, it doth not know vice, and it judgeth vice. It doth not know it in the practice of it; it judgeth by reproving it. Thus then, "I know you not."

17. The five wise virgins came, and "went in." How many are ye, my Brethren, in the profession of Christ's Name! let there be among you the five wise, but be not five such persons only. Let there be among you the five wise, belonging to this wisdom of the number five. For the hour will come, and come when we know not. It will come at midnight, Watch ye. Thus did the Gospel close; "Watch, for ye know neither the day nor the hour." [7] But if we are all to sleep, how shall we watch? Watch with the heart, watch with faith, watch with hope, watch with charity, watch with good works; and then, when thou shalt sleep in thy body, the time will come that thou shalt rise. And when thou shalt have risen, make ready the lamps. Then shall they go out no more, then shall they be renewed [8] with the inner oil of conscience; then shall that Bridegroom fold thee in His spiritual [9] embrace, then shall He bring thee into His House where thou shalt never sleep, where thy lamp can never be extinguished. But at present we are in labour, and our lamps flicker [10] amid the winds and temptations of this life; but only let our flame burn strongly, that the wind of temptation may increase the fire, rather than put it out.

SERMON XLIV.

[XCIV. BEN.]

ON THE WORDS OF THE GOSPEL, MATT. XXV. 24, ETC., WHERE THE SLOTHFUL SERVANT WHO WOULD NOT PUT OUT THE TALENT HE HAD RECEIVED, IS CONDEMNED.

1. My lords, my brethren, and fellowbishops have deigned to visit us and gladden us by their presence; but I know not why they are unwilling to assist me, when wearied. I have said this to you, Beloved, in their hearing, that your hearing may in a manner intercede for me with them, that when I ask them they also may discourse unto you in their turn. Let them dispense what they have received, let them vouchsafe to work rather than excuse themselves. Be pleased, however, to hear from me, fatigued though I be and have difficulty in speaking, a few words only. For we have besides a record of God's mercies vouchsafed through a holy Martyr, which we must give willing audience to altogether. [11] What is it then? what shall I say unto you? Ye have heard in the Gospel both the due recompense [12] of the good servants, and the punishment of the bad. And the whole wickedness of that servant who was reprobate and severely condemned, was that he would not put out his money to use. He kept the entire sum he had received; but the Lord looked for profit from it. God is coveteous with regard to our salvation. If he who did not put out to use is so condemned, what must they look for who lose what they have received? We then are the dispensers, we put out, ye receive. We look for profit; do ye live well. For this is the profit

---

[1] Matt. v. 16.   [2] 1 Cor. iv. 7.   [3] Matt. xxv. 10.
[4] Matt. vii. 7.   [5] Ps. ci. 1.   [6] Matt. xxv. 12.
[7] Matt. xxv. 13.   [8] *Vegetentur.*   [9] *Incorporeis.*
[10] *Fluctuant.*   [11] *Vid.* Serm. xxix. (lxxix. Ben.).
[12] *Meritum.*

in our dealings with you. But do not think that this office of putting out to use does not belong to you also. Ye cannot execute it indeed from this elevated seat, but ye can wherever ye chance to be. Wherever Christ is attacked, defend Him; answer murmurers, rebuke blasphemers, from their fellowship keep yourselves apart. So do ye put out to use, if ye make gain of any. Discharge our office in your own houses. A bishop is called from hence, because he superintends, because he takes care and attends to others. To every man then, if he is the head of his own house, ought the office of the Episcopate to belong, to take care how his household believe, that none of them fall into heresy, neither wife, nor son, nor daughter, nor even his slave, because he has been bought at so great a price. The Apostolic teaching has set the master over the slave, and put the slave under the master;[1] nevertheless Christ gave the same price for both. Do not neglect then the least of those belonging to you, look after the salvation of all your household with all vigilance. This if ye do, ye put out to use; ye will not be slothful servants, ye will not have to fear so horrible a condemnation.

SERMON XLV.

[XCV. BEN.]

ON THE WORDS OF THE GOSPEL, MARK VIII. 5, ETC., WHERE THE MIRACLE OF THE SEVEN LOAVES IS RELATED.

1. IN expounding to you the Holy Scriptures, I as it were break bread for you. Do ye in hunger receive it, and break[2] forth with a fulness of phrase from the heart; and ye who are rich in your banquet, be not meagre in good works and deeds. What I deal out to you is not mine own. What ye eat, I eat; what ye live upon, I live upon. We have in heaven a common store-house; for from thence comes the Word of God.

2. The "seven loaves"[3] signify the sevenfold operation of the Holy Spirit; the "four thousand men," the Church established on the four Gospels; "the seven baskets of fragments," the perfection of the Church. For by this number very constantly is perfection figured. For whence is that which is said, "seven times in a day will I praise thee"?[4] Does a man sin who does not praise the Lord so often? What then is "seven times will I praise," but "I will never cease from praise"? For he who says "seven times," signifies all time. Whence in this world there are continual revolutions of seven days. What then is "seven times in a day will I praise Thee," but what is said in

another place, "His praise shall always be in my mouth"?[5] With reference to this perfection, John writes to seven Churches. The Apocalypse is a book of St. John the Evangelist; and he writes "to seven Churches."[6] Be ye hungered;[7] own ye these baskets. For those fragments were not lost; but seeing that ye too belong to the Church, they have surely profited you. In that I explain this to you, I minister to Christ; and when ye hear peaceably, ye "sit down."[3] I in my body sit, but in my heart I am standing, and ministering to you in anxiety; lest peradventure, not the food, but the vessel offend any of you. Ye know the feast of God, ye have often heard it, that it is for the heart, not for the belly.

3. Of a truth four thousand men were filled by seven loaves; what is more wonderful than this! Yet even this were not enough, had not seven baskets also been filled with the fragments that remained. O great mysteries! they were works, and the works spake. If thou understand these doings, they are words. And ye too belong to the four thousand, because ye live under the fourfold Gospel. To this number the children and women did not belong. For so it is said, "And they that did eat were four thousand men, excepting women and children."[8] As though the void of understanding, and the effeminate were without number. Yet let even these eat. Let them eat: it may be the children will grow, and will be children no more; it may be the effeminate will be amended, and become chaste. Let them eat; we dispense, we deal out to them. But who these are, God inspecteth His feast, and if they do not amend themselves, He who knew how to invite them thither, knoweth also how to separate them from the rest.

4. Ye know it, dearly Beloved; call to mind the parable of the Gospel, how that the Lord came in to inspect the guests at a certain feast of His. The Master of the house who had invited them, as it is written, "found there a man which had not on a wedding garment."[9] For to the marriage had that Bridegroom invited them who is "fair in beauty above the children of men." That Bridegroom became deformed because of His deformed spouse, that he might make her fair. How did the Fair One become deformed? If I do not prove it, I am blaspheming. The testimony of his fair beauty the Prophet gives me, who saith, "Thou art fair in beauty above the children of men."[10] The testimony of his deformity another Prophet gives me, who saith, "We saw Him, and He had no grace, nor beauty; but His countenance was

---

[1] Eph. vi. 5; Tit. ii. 9.   [2] *Saginam laudis eructuate.*
[3] Mark viii. 6.   [4] Ps. cxix. 164.

[5] Ps. xxxiv. 1.   [6] Rev. i. 4.
[7] *Voraces,* Edd. ant.; *veraces,* B. from 1 Ms. 2da manu.
[8] Matt. xv. 38.   [9] Matt. xxii. 11.
[10] Ps. xliv. 3 (xlv. 2, English version).

marred, and His whole look [1] deformed." [2] O Prophet, who saidst, "Thou art fair in beauty above the children of men ; " thou art contradicted ; another Prophet cometh out against thee, and saith, "Thou speakest falsely. We have seen Him. What is this that thou sayest, 'Thou art fair in beauty above the children of men? We have seen Him, and He had no grace nor beauty.'" Are then these two Prophets at disagreement in the Corner-stone of peace? Both spake of Christ, both spake of the Corner-stone. In the corner the walls unite. If they do not unite, it is not a building, but a ruin. No, the Prophets agree, let us not leave them in strife. Yea, rather let us understand their peace ; for they know not how to strive. O Prophet, who saidst, "Thou art fair in beauty above the children of men ; " where didst thou see Him? Answer me, answer where didst thou see Him? "Being in the form of God, He thought it not robbery to be equal with God." [3] There I saw Him. Dost thou doubt that He who is "equal with God" is "fair in beauty above the children of men "? Thou hast answered ; now let him answer who said, "We saw Him, and He had no grace, nor beauty." Thou hast said so ; tell us where didst thou see Him? He begins from the other's words ; where the other ended, there he begins. Where did he end? "Who being in the form of God, thought it not robbery to be equal with God." Lo, where he saw Him who was "fair in beauty above the children of men ; " do thou tell us, where thou sawest that "He had no grace nor beauty. But He emptied Himself, taking the form of a servant, being made in the likeness of men, and found in fashion as a man." [4] Of His deformity he still further says ; "He humbled Himself, having become obedient unto death, even the death of the cross." Lo, where I saw Him. Therefore are they both in peaceful concord, both are at peace together. What is more "fair" than God? What more "deformed " than the Crucified?

5. So then this Bridegroom, "fair in beauty above the children of men," became deformed that He might make His Spouse fair to whom it is said, "O thou beauteous among women," [5] of whom it is said, "Who is this that cometh up, whitened " [6] with the brightness of light, not the colouring of falsehood ! He then who called them to the wedding, found a man who had not a wedding garment, and He said unto him,

"Friend, how camest thou in hither, not having a wedding garment? And he was speechless." For he found not what to answer. And the Master of the house Who had invited him said, "Bind him hands and feet, and cast him into outer darkness ; there shall be weeping and gnashing of teeth." [7] For so small a fault, so great a punishment? For great it is. It is called a small fault not to have "the wedding garment ; " small, but only by those who do not understand. How would He have been so incensed, how would He have so judged, to cast him, on account of the wedding garment which he had not, "bound hands and feet into outer darkness, where was weeping and gnashing of teeth," unless it had been a very grievous fault, not to have "the wedding garment "? I say this ; seeing ye have been invited through me ; for though He invited you, He invited you by my ministry. Ye are all at the feast, have the wedding garment. I will explain what it is, that ye may all have it, and if any one now hears me who has it not, let him, before the Master of the house comes and inspects His guests, be changed for the better, let him receive "the wedding garment," and so sit down in all assurance.

6. For in truth, dearly Beloved, he who was cast forth from the feast, does not signify one man ; far from it. They are many. And the Lord Himself who put forth this parable, the Bridegroom Himself, who calleth together to the feast, and quickeneth whom He calleth, He hath Himself explained to us, that that man does not denote one man, but many, there, in that very place, in the same parable. I do not go far for this, I find the explanation there, there I break the bread, and set it before you to be eaten. For He said, when he who had not "the wedding garment was cast out thence into outer darkness," He said and added immediately, "for many are called, but few chosen." [8] Thou hast cast forth one man from hence, and Thou sayest, "for many are called, but few chosen." Without doubt the chosen are not cast forth ; and they were the few guests who remained ; and the "many " were represented in that one, because that one who hath not "the wedding garment " is the body of the wicked.

7. What is "the wedding garment " ? Let us search for it in the Holy Scriptures. What is "the wedding garment"? Without doubt it is something which the bad and good have not in common ; let us discover this, and we shall discover "the wedding garment." Among the gifts of God, what have not the good and bad in common? [9] That we are men and not beasts, is a gift of God ; but this is common to good

---

[1] *Positio.* [2] Isa. liii. 2, Sept. [3] Phil. ii. 6.
[4] Phil. ii. 7, 8. [5] Cant. i. 8.
[6] Cant. viii. 5, Sept. *Dealbata,* "not as women whiten themselves, who would appear what they are not; not as a whitened wall, — not thus whitened, but enlightened, because not of itself white. — Grace came illumining and whitening; first thou wert black, but hast been made white by His grace. For ye were darkness, but now are ye light in the Lord." St. Aug. *In Ps.* 103, s. 1, § 6.

[7] Matt. xxii. 12, etc. [8] Matt. xxii. 14.
[9] *Vid.* Serm. xl. (xc. Ben.) 5, etc.

and bad. That the light from heaven rises upon us, that the rain descends from the cloud, the fountains flow, the fields yield their fruit; these are gifts, but common to the good and bad. Let us go to the marriage feast, let us leave the others without, who being called come not. Let us consider the guests themselves, that is, Christians. Baptism is a gift of God, the good and bad have it. The Sacraments of the Altar the good and bad receive together. Saul prophesied for all his wickedness, and in his rage against a holy and most righteous man, even while he was persecuting him, he prophesied. Are the good only said to believe? "The devils also believe and tremble." [1] What shall I do? I have sifted all, and have not yet come to "the wedding garment." I have unfolded my envelopings, I have considered all, or almost all, and have not yet come to that garment. The Apostle Paul in a certain place has brought me a great collection [2] of excellent things; he has laid them open before me, and I have said to him, "Show me, if so be thou hast found among them that 'wedding garment.'" He begins to unfold them one by one, and to say, "Though I speak with the tongues of men and of Angels, though I have all knowledge, and the gift of prophecy, and all faith, so that I could remove mountains; though I distribute all my goods to the poor, and give my body to be burned." [3] Precious garments! nevertheless, there is not yet here that "wedding garment." Now bring out to us "the wedding garment." Why dost thou keep us in suspense, O Apostle? Peradventure prophecy is a gift of God which both good and bad have not. "If," says He, "I have not charity, nothing profiteth me." See "the wedding garment;" put it on, ye guests, that ye may sit down securely. Do not say; "we are too poor to have that garment." Clothe others, and ye are clothed yourselves. It is winter, clothe the naked. Christ is naked; and He will give you that "wedding garment" whosoever have it not. Run to Him, beseech Him; He knoweth how to sanctify His faithful ones, He knoweth how to clothe His naked ones. That ye may be able as having "the wedding garment" to be free from the fear of the outer darkness, and the binding of your members and hands and feet; let not your works fail. If they fail, with hands bound what canst thou do? with feet bound, whither wilt thou fly? Keep then that "wedding garment," put it on, and so sit down in security, when He comes to inspect. The Day of Judgment will come; He is now giving a long space, let him who erewhile was naked now be clothed.

SERMON XLVI.

[XCVI. BEN.]

ON THE WORDS OF THE GOSPEL, MARK VIII. 34, "IF ANY MAN WOULD COME AFTER ME, LET HIM DENY HIMSELF," ETC. AND ON THE WORDS 1 JOHN II. 15, "IF ANY MAN LOVE THE WORLD, THE LOVE OF THE FATHER IS NOT IN HIM."

1. HARD and grievous does that appear which the Lord hath enjoined, that "whosoever will come after Him, must deny himself." [4] But what He enjoineth is not hard or grievous, who aideth us that what He enjoineth may be done. For both is that true which is said to Him in the Psalm, "Because of the words of Thy lips I have kept hard ways." [5] And that is true which He said Himself, "My yoke is easy, and My burden is light." [6] For whatsoever is hard in what is enjoined us, charity makes easy. We know what great things love itself can do. Very often is this love even abominable and impure; but how great hardships have men suffered, what indignities and intolerable things have they endured, to attain to the object of their love? whether it be a lover of money who is called covetous; or a lover of honour, who is called ambitious; or a lover of beautiful women, who is called voluptuous. And who could enumerate all sorts of loves? Yet consider what labour all lovers undergo, and are not conscious of their labours; and then does any such one most feel labour, when he is hindered from labour. Since then the majority of men are such as their loves are, and that there ought to be no other care for the regulation of our lives, than the choice of that which we ought to love; why dost thou wonder, if he who loves Christ, and who wishes to follow Christ, for the love of Him denies himself? For if by loving himself man is lost, surely by denying himself he is found.

2. The first destruction of man, was the love of himself. For if he had not loved himself, if he had preferred God to himself, he would have been willing to be ever subject unto God; and would not have been turned to the neglect of His will, and the doing his own will. For this is to love one's self, to wish to do one's own will. Prefer to this God's will; learn to love thyself by not loving thyself. For that ye may know that it is a vice to love one's self, the Apostle speaks thus, "For men shall be lovers of their own selves." [7] And can he who loves himself have any sure trust in himself? No; for he begins to love himself by forsaking God, and is driven away from himself to love those things

---

[1] Jas. ii. 19.
[2] *Involucrum*
[3] 1 Cor. xiii. 1, etc

[4] Mark viii. 34.   [5] Ps. xvi. 4, Sept. (xvii. English version).
[6] Matt. xi. 30.   [7] 2 Tim iii. 2.

which are beyond himself; to such a degree that when the aforesaid Apostle had said, " Men shall be lovers of their own selves," he subjoined immediately, "lovers of money." Already thou seest that thou art without. Thou hast begun to love thyself: stand in thyself if thou canst. Why goest thou without? Hast thou, as being rich in money, become a lover of money? Thou hast begun to love what is without thee, thou hast lost thyself. When a man's love then goes even away from himself to those things which are without, he begins to share the vanity of his vain desires, and prodigal as it were to spend his strength. He is dissipated, exhausted, without resource or strength, he feeds swine; and wearied with this office of feeding swine, he at last remembers what he was, and says, " How many hired servants of my Father's are eating bread, and I here perish with hunger ! " [1] But when the son in the parable says this, what is said of him, who had squandered all he had on harlots, who wished to have in his own power what was being well kept for him with his father; he wished to have it at his own disposal, he squandered all, he was reduced to indigence : what is said of him? " And when he returned to himself." If " he returned to himself," he had gone away from himself. Because he had fallen from himself, had gone away from himself, he returns first to himself, that he may return to that state from which he had fallen away by falling from himself. For as by falling away from himself, he remained in himself; so by returning to himself, he ought not to remain in himself, lest he again go away from himself. Returning then to himself, that he might not remain in himself, what did he say? " I will arise and go to my Father."[2] See, whence he had fallen away from himself, he had fallen away from his Father; he had fallen away from himself, he had gone away from himself to those things which are without. He returns to himself, and goes to his Father, where he may keep himself in all security. If then he had gone away from himself, let him also in returning to himself, from whom he had gone away, that he may " go to his Father," deny himself. What is " deny himself"? Let him not trust in himself, let him feel that he is a man, and have respect to the words of the prophet, " Cursed is every one that putteth his hope in man." [3] Let him withdraw himself from himself, but not towards things below. Let him withdraw himself from himself, that he may cleave unto God. Whatever of good he has, let him commit to Him by whom he was made ; whatever of evil he has, he has made it for himself. The evil that is in him God made not ; let him destroy what himself has done, who has been thereby undone. " Let him deny himself,"

He saith, " and take up his cross, and follow Me."

3. And whither must the Lord be followed? Whither He is gone, we know; but a very few days since we celebrated the solemn memorial of it. For He has risen again, and ascended into heaven ; thither must He be followed. Undoubtedly we must not despair of it, because He hath Himself promised us, not because man can do anything. Heaven was far away from us, before that our Head had gone into heaven. But now why should we despair, if we are members of that Head? Thither then must He be followed. And who would be unwilling to follow Him to such an abode? Especially seeing that we are in so great travail on earth with fears and pains. Who would be unwilling to follow Christ thither, where is supreme felicity, supreme peace, perpetual security? Good is it to follow Him thither : but we must see by what way we are to follow. For the Lord Jesus did not say the words we are engaged in, when He had now risen from the dead. He had not yet suffered, He had still to come to the Cross, had to come to His dishonouring, to the outrages, the scourging, the thorns, the wounds, the mockeries, the insults, Death. Rough as it were is the way ; it makes thee to be slow; thou hast no mind to follow. But follow on. Rough is the way which man has made for himself, but what Christ hath trodden in His passage is worn smooth. For who would not wish to go to exaltation? Elevation is pleasing to all ; but humility is the step to it. Why dost thou put out thy foot beyond thee? Thou hast a mind to fall, not to ascend. Begin by the step, and so thou hast ascended. This step of humility those two disciples were loth to have an eye to, who said, " Lord, bid that one of us may sit at Thy right hand, and the other at the left in Thy kingdom." [4] They sought for exaltation, they did not see the step. But the Lord showed them the step. For what did He answer them? " Ye who seek the hill of exaltation, can ye drink the cup of humiliation?" And therefore He does not say simply, " Let him deny himself, and follow Me " howsoever : but He said more, " Let him take up his cross, and follow Me."

4. What is, " Let him take up his cross "? Let him bear whatever trouble he has ; so let him follow Me. For when he shall begin to follow Me in conformity to My life and precepts, he will have many to contradict him, he will have many to hinder him, he will have many to dissuade him, and that from among those who are even as it were Christ's companions. They who hindered the blind men from crying out were walking with Christ.[5] Whether therefore they be

---

[1] Luke xv. 17.   [2] Luke xv. 18.   [3] Jer. xvii. 5.

[4] Mark x. 37.
[5] *Vid.* Serm. xxxviii. (lxxxviii. Ben.) 13 (xiv). Matt. xx. 31.

threats or caresses, or whatsoever hindrances there be, if thou wish to follow, turn them into thy cross, bear it, carry it, do not give way beneath it. There seems to be an exhortation to martyrdom in these words of the Lord. If there be persecution, ought not all things to be despised in consideration of Christ? The world is loved; but let Him be preferred by whom the world was made. Great is the world; but greater is He by whom the world was made. Fair is the world; but fairer is He by whom the world was made. Sweet is the world; but sweeter is He by whom the world was made. Evil is the world; and good is He by whom the world was made. How shall I be able to explain and unravel what I have said? May God help me? For what have I said? what have ye applauded? See, it is but a question, and yet ye have already applauded. How is the world evil, if He by whom the world was made is good? Did not God make all things, "and behold they were very good"? Does not Scripture at each several work of creation testify that God made it good, by saying, "And God saw that it was good," and at the end summed them all up together thus how that God had made them, "And behold they were very good"?[1]

5. How then is the world evil, and He good by whom the world was made? How? "Since the world was made by Him, and the world knew Him not."[2] The world was made by Him, the heaven and earth and all things that are in them: "the world knew Him not," the lovers of the world; the lovers of the world and the despisers of God; this "world knew Him not." So then the world is evil, because they are evil who prefer the world to God. And He is good who made the world, the heaven, and earth, and sea, and themselves who love the world. For this only, that they love the world and do not love God, He made not in them. But themselves, all that appertains to their nature He made; what appertains to guiltiness, He made not. This is that I said a little while ago, "Let man efface what he has made, and so will he be well-pleasing to Him who made Him."

6. For there is among men themselves a good world also; but one that has been made good from being evil. For the whole world if you take the word "world" for men, putting aside (what we call the world) the heaven and earth and all things that in them are; if you take the world for men, the whole world did he who first sinned make evil. The whole mass was corrupted in the root. God made man good; so runs the Scripture, "God made man upright; and men themselves found out many cogitations."[3] Run from these "many" to One, gather up thy

scattered things into one: flow on together, fence thyself in, abide with One; go not to many things. There is blessedness. But we have flowed away, have gone on to perdition: we were all born with sin, and to that sin wherein we were born have we too added by our evil living, and the whole world has become evil. But Christ came, and He chose that which He made, not what He found; for He found all evil, and by His grace He made them good. And so was made another "world;" and the "world" now persecutes the "world."

7. What is the "world" which persecutes? That of which it is said to us, "Love not the world, neither the things that are in the world. If any man love the world, the love of the Father is not in him. For all that is in the world, is the lust of the flesh, and the lust of the eyes, and the pride of life, which is not of the Father, but of the world. And the world passeth away, and the lust thereof: but he that doeth the will of God abideth for ever,"[4] even as God abideth for ever. Lo! I have spoken of two "worlds," the "world" which persecutes, and that which it persecutes. What is the "world" which persecutes? "All that is the world, the lust of the flesh, and the lust of the eyes, and the pride of life, which is not of the Father, but of the world;" and "the world passeth away." Lo, this is the "world" which persecutes. What is the "world" which it persecutes? "He that doeth the will of God abideth for ever," even as God abideth for ever.

8. But see, that which persecutes is called the "world;" let us prove whether that also which suffers persecution is called "the world." What! Art thou deaf to the voice of Christ who speaketh, or rather to Holy Scripture which testifieth, "God was in Christ reconciling the world unto Himself."[5] "If the world hate you, know ye that it first hated Me."[6] See, the "world" hates. What does it hate but the "world"? What "world"? "God was in Christ reconciling the world unto Himself." The condemned "world" persecutes; the reconciled "world" suffers persecution. The condemned "world" is all that is without the Church; the reconciled "world" is the Church. For He says, "The Son of Man came not to judge the world, but that the world through Him may be saved."[7]

9. Now in this world, holy, good, reconciled, saved, or rather to be saved, and now saved in hope, "for we are saved in hope;"[8] in this world, I say, that is in the Church which wholly follows Christ, He hath said as of universal application, "Whosoever will follow Me, let him deny himself." For it is not that the virgins ought to give ear to this, and the married women

---

[1] Gen. i. [2] John i. 10.
[3] Eccles. vii. 30, Sept. (vii. 29, English version).
[4] 1 John ii. 15, etc. [5] 2 Cor. v. 19. [6] John xv. 18.
[7] John iii. 17. [8] Rom. viii. 24.

ought not; or that the widows ought, and the women who still have their husbands ought not; or that monks ought, and the married men ought not; or that the clergy ought, and the laymen ought not: but let the whole Church, the whole body, all the members, distinguished and distributed throughout their several offices, follow Christ. Let the whole Church follow Him, that only Church, let the dove follow Him, let the spouse follow Him, let her who has been redeemed and endowed with the Bridegroom's blood, follow Him. There virgin purity hath its place; there widowed continence hath its place; married chastity there hath its place; but adultery hath no place of its own there; and no place there hath lasciviousness, unlawful and meet for punishment. But let these several members which have their place there, in their kind and place and measure, "follow Christ;" let them "deny themselves;" that is, let them presume nothing of themselves: let them "take up their cross," that is, let them in the world endure for Christ's sake whatever the world may bring upon them. Let them love Him, who Alone doth not deceive, who Alone is not deceived, Alone deceiveth not; let them love Him, for that is true which He doth promise. But because He doth not give at once, faith wavers. Hold on, persevere, endure, bear delay and thou hast borne the cross.

10. Let not the virgin say, "I shall alone be there." For Mary shall not be there alone, but the widow Anna shall be there also. Let not the woman which hath an husband say, "The widow will be there, not I;" for it is not that Anna will be there, and Susanna not be there. But by all means let them who would be there prove themselves hereby, that they who have here a lower place envy not, but love in others the better place. For, for instance, my Brethren, that ye may understand me; one man has chosen a married life, another a life of continence; if he who has chosen the married life, has adulterous lusts, he has "looked back;" he has lusted after that which is unlawful. He too who would wish afterwards to return from continence to a married life, has "looked back;" he has chosen what is in itself lawful, yet he has "looked back." Is marriage then to be condemned? No. Marriage is not to be condemned; but see whither he had come who has chosen it. He had already got before it. When he was living as a young man in voluptuousness, marriage was before him; he was making his way towards it; but when he had chosen continence, marriage was behind him. "Remember," saith the Lord, "Lot's wife." [1] Lot's wife, by looking behind, remained motionless. To what-

ever point then any one has been able to reach, let him fear to "look back" from thence; and let him walk in the way, let him "follow Christ." "Forgetting those things which are behind, and stretching forth unto those things which are before, let him by an earnest inward intention press on toward the prize of the calling of God in Christ Jesus." [2] Let those that are married regard the unmarried as above themselves; let them acknowledge that they are better; let them in them love what themselves have not; and let them in them love Christ.

SERMON XLVII.

[XCVII. BEN.]

ON THE WORDS OF THE GOSPEL, MARK XIII. 32, "BUT OF THAT DAY OR THAT HOUR KNOWETH NO ONE, NOT EVEN THE ANGELS IN HEAVEN, NEITHER THE SON, BUT THE FATHER.

1. THE advice, Brethren, which ye have just heard Scripture give, when it tells us to watch for the last day, every one should think of as concerning his own last day; lest haply when ye judge or think the last day of the world to be far distant, ye slumber with respect to your own last day. Ye have heard what Jesus said concerning the last day of this world, "That neither the Angels of heaven, nor the Son knew it, but the Father." [3] Where indeed there is a great difficulty, lest understanding this in a carnal way, we think that the Father knoweth anything which the Son knoweth not. For indeed when He said, "the Father knoweth it;" He said this because in the Father the Son also knoweth it. For what is there in a day which was not made by the Word, by whom the day was made? Let no one then search out for the last Day, when it is to be; but let us watch all by our good lives, lest the last day of any one of us find us unprepared, and such as any one shall depart hence on his last day, such he be found in the last day of the world. Nothing will then assist thee which thou shalt not have done here. His own works will succour, or his own works will overwhelm every one.

2. And how have we in the Psalm sung unto the Lord, "Lord, have mercy on me, for man hath trodden me down"? [4] He is called a man who lives after the manner of men. For it is said to them who live after God, "Ye are gods, and ye are all the children of the Most High." [5] But to the reprobate, who were called to be the sons of God, and who wished rather to be men, that is, to live after the manner of men, he says, "But ye shall die like men, and fall as one of

[1] Luke xvii. 32.

[2] Phil. iii. 13, 14. [3] Mark xiii. 32.
[4] Ps. lv. 2, Sept. (lvi. 1, English version).
[5] Ps. lxxxii. 6.

the princes."[1] For that man is mortal, ought to avail for his instruction, not for boasting. Whereupon does a worm that is to die on the morrow boast himself? I speak to your love, Brethren ; proud mortals ought to be made blush by the devil. For he, though proud, is yet immortal ; he is a spirit, though a malignant one. The last day is kept in store for him at the end as his punishment ; nevertheless he is not subject to the death to which we are subject. But man heard the sentence, " Thou shalt surely die."[2] Let him make a good use of his punishment. What is that I have said, " Let him make a good use of his punishment"? Let him not by that from which he received his punishment fall into pride ; let him acknowledge that he is mortal, and let it break down his elation. Let him hear it said to him, " Why is earth and ashes proud?"[3]　　Even if the devil is proud, he is not " earth and ashes." Therefore was it said, " But ye shall die like men, and shall fall as one of the princes."[1] Ye do not consider that ye are mortals, and ye are proud as the devil. Let man then make a good use of his punishment, Brethren ; let him make a good use of his evil, that he may make advancement to his good. Who does not know, that the necessity of our dying is a punishment ; and the more grievous, that we know not when? The punishment is certain, the hour uncertain ; and of that punishment alone are we certain in the ordinary course of human affairs.

3. All else of ours, both good and evil, is uncertain ; death alone is certain. What is this that I say? A child is conceived, perhaps it will be born, perhaps it will be an untimely birth. So it is uncertain : Perhaps he will grow up, perhaps he will not grow up ; perhaps he will grow old, perhaps he will not grow old ; perhaps he will be rich, perhaps poor ; perhaps he will be distinguished, perhaps abased ; perhaps he will have children, perhaps he will not ; perhaps he will marry, perhaps not ; and so on, whatever else among good things you may name. Now look too at the evils of life : Perhaps he will have sickness, perhaps he will have not ; perhaps he will be stung by a serpent, perhaps not ; perhaps he will be devoured by a wild beast, perhaps he will not. And so look at all evils ; everywhere is there a " perhaps it will be," and " perhaps it will not." But canst thou say, " Perhaps he will die," and " perhaps he will not die"?[4] As when medical men examine an illness, and ascertain that it is fatal, they make this announcement ; " He will die, he will not get over this." So from the moment of a man's birth, it may be said, " He will not get over this." When he is born he begins to be ailing. When he dies, he

ends indeed this ailment : but he knows not whether he does not fall into a worse. The rich man in the Gospel had ended his voluptuous ailment, he came to a tormenting one. But the poor man ended his ailment, and arrived at perfect health.[5] But he made choice in this life of what he was to have hereafter ; and what he reaped there, he sowed here. Therefore while we live we ought to watch, and to make choice of that which we may possess in the world to come.

4. Let us not love the world. It overwhelms its lovers, it conducts them to no good. We must rather labour in it that it seduce us not, than fear lest it should fall. Lo, the world falleth ; the Christian standeth firm ; because Christ doth not fall. For wherefore saith the Lord, " Rejoice, for that I have overcome the world"?[6] We might answer Him if we pleased, "'Rejoice,' yes do Thou rejoice. If Thou 'hast overcome,' do thou rejoice. Why should we?" Why doth He say to us, " Rejoice ;" but ·because it is for us that He hath overcome, for us hath fought? For wherein fought He? In that He took man's nature upon Him. Take away His birth of a virgin, take away that He emptied Himself, " taking the form of a servant, being made in the likeness of men, and found in fashion as a man ;"[7] take away this, and where is the combat, where the contest? where the trial? where the victory, which no battle has preceded? " In the beginning was the Word, and the Word was with God, and the Word was God. All things were made by Him, and without Him was nothing made."[8] Could the Jews have crucified this Word? Could those impious men have mocked this Word? Could this Word have been buffeted? Could this Word have been crowned with thorns? But that He might suffer all this, " the Word was made flesh ;"[9] and after He had suffered all this, by rising again He " overcame." So then He hath " overcome " for us, to whom He hath shown the assurance of His resurrection. Thou sayest then to God, " Have mercy upon me, O Lord, for man hath trodden me down."[10] Do not " tread down " thyself, and man will not overcome thee. For, lo, some powerful man alarms thee. By what does he alarm thee? " I will spoil thee, will condemn, will torture, will kill thee." And thou criest, " Have mercy upon me, O Lord, for man hath trodden me down." If thou say the truth, and mark thyself well, one dead " treads thee down," because thou art afraid of the threats of a man ; and man " treads thee down," because thou wouldest not be afraid, unless thou wert a man. What is the remedy then? O man, cleave to God, by whom thou

---

[1] Ps. lxxxii. 7.　　[2] Gen. ii. 17.　　[3] Ecclus. x. 9.
[4] Vid. Serm. xxvii. (lxxvii. Ben.) 14 (x.).

[5] Luke xvi. 22.　　[6] John xvi. 33.　　[7] Phil. ii. 7.
[8] John i. 1, 3.　　[9] John i. 14.
[10] Ps. lv. 2, Sept. (lvi. 1, English version).

wast made a man ; cleave fast to Him, put thy affiance in Him, call upon Him, let Him be thy strength. Say to Him, " In Thee, O Lord, is my strength." And then thou shalt sing at the threatenings of men ; and what thou shalt sing hereafter, the Lord Himself telleth thee, " I will hope in God, I will not fear what man can do unto me." [1]

SERMON XLVIII.

[XCVIII. BEN.]

ON THE WORDS OF THE GOSPEL, LUKE VII. 2, ETC. ; ON THE THREE DEAD PERSONS WHOM THE LORD RAISED.

1. THE miracles of our Lord and Saviour Jesus Christ make indeed an impression on all who hear of, and believe them ; but on different men in different ways. For some amazed at His miracles done on the bodies of men, have no knowledge to discern the greater ; whereas some admire the more ample fulfilment in the souls of men at the present time of those things which they hear of as having been wrought on their bodies. The Lord Himself saith, " For as the Father raiseth up the dead, and quickeneth them ; even so the Son quickeneth whom He will." [2] Not of course that the Son " quickeneth " some, the Father others ; but the Father and the Son " quicken " the same ; for the Father doeth all things by the Son. Let no one then who is a Christian doubt, that even at the present time the dead are raised. Now all men have eyes, wherewith they can see the dead rise again in such sort, as the son of that widow rose, of whom we have just read out of the Gospel ; [3] but those eyes wherewith men see the dead in heart rise again, all men have not, save those who have risen already in heart themselves. It is a greater miracle to raise again one who is to live for ever, than to raise one who must die again.

2. The widowed mother rejoiced at the raising again of that young man ; of men raised again in spirit day by day does Mother Church rejoice. He indeed was dead in the body, but they in soul. His visible death was bewailed visibly ; their death invisible was neither enquired into nor perceived. He sought them out who had known them to be dead ; He Alone knew them to be dead, who was able to make them alive. For if the Lord had not come to raise the dead, the Apostle would not have said, " Rise, thou that sleepest, and arise from the dead, and Christ shall give thee light." [4] You hear of one asleep in the words, " Rise, thou that sleepest ; " but understand it of one dead when you hear, " And

arise from the dead." Thus they who are even dead in the body [5] are often said to be asleep. And certainly they all are but asleep, in respect of Him who is able to awaken them. For in respect of thee, a dead man is dead indeed, seeing he will not awake, beat or prick or tear him as thou wilt. But in respect of Christ, he was but asleep to whom it was said, " Arise," [6] and he arose forthwith. No one can as easily awaken another in bed, as Christ can in the tomb.

3. Now we find that three dead persons were raised by the Lord " visibly," thousands " invisibly." Nay, who knows even how many dead He raised visibly? For all the things that He did are not written. John tells us this, " Many other things Jesus did, the which if they should be written, I suppose that the whole world could not contain the books." [7] So then there were without doubt many others raised : but it is not without a meaning that the three are expressly recorded. For our Lord Jesus Christ would that those things which He did on the body should be also spiritually understood. For He did not merely do miracles for the miracles' sake ; but in order that the things which He did should inspire wonder in those who saw them, and convey truth to them who understand. As he who sees letters in an excellently written manuscript, and knows not how to read, praises indeed the transcriber's [8] hand, and admires the beauty of the characters ; [9] but what those characters mean or signify he does not know ; and by the sight of his eyes he is a praiser of the work, but in his mind has no comprehension of it ; whereas another man both praises the work, and is capable of understanding it ; such an one, I mean, who is not only able to see what is common to all, but who can read also ; which he who has never learned cannot. So they who saw Christ's miracles, and understood not what they meant, and what they in a manner conveyed to those who had understanding, wondered only at the miracles themselves ; whereas others both wondered at the miracles, and attained to the meaning of them. Such ought we to be in the school of Christ. For he who says that Christ only worked miracles, for the miracles' sake, may say too that He was ignorant that it was not the time for fruit, when He sought figs upon the fig-tree. [10] For it was not the time for that fruit, as the Evangelist testifies ; and yet being hungry He sought for fruit upon the tree. Did not Christ know, what any peasant knew? What the dresser of the tree knew, did not the tree's Creator know? So then when being hungry He sought fruit on the tree, He signified that He was

---

[1] Ps. lvi. 11.   [2] John v. 21.   [3] Luke vii. 12.
[4] Eph. v. 14.

[5] Visibiliter.   [6] Luke vii. 14.   [7] John xxi. 25.
[8] Antiquarii.   [9] Apicum.
[10] Vid. Serm. xxxix. (lxxxix. Ben.). Mark xi. 13.

hungry, and seeking after something else than this; and He found that tree without fruit, but full of leaves, and He cursed it, and it withered away. What had the tree done in not bearing fruit? What fault of the tree was its fruitlessness? No; but there are those who through their own will are not able to yield fruit. And barrenness is "their" fault, whose fruitfulness is their will. The Jews then who had the words of the Law, and had not the deeds, were full of leaves, and bare no fruit. This have I said to persuade you, that our Lord Jesus Christ performed miracles with this view, that by those miracles He might signify something further, that besides that they were wonderful and great, and divine in themselves, we might learn also something from them.

4. Let us then see what He would have us learn in those three dead persons whom He raised. He raised again the dead daughter of the ruler of the synagogue, for whom when she was sick petition was made to Him, that He would deliver her from her sickness. And as He is going, it is announced that she is dead; and as though He would now be only wearying Himself in vain, word was brought to her father, "Thy daughter is dead, why weariest thou the Master any further?"[1] But He went on, and said to the father of the damsel, "Be not afraid, only believe."[2] He comes to the house, and finds the customary funeral obsequies already prepared, and He says to them, "Weep not, for the damsel is not dead, but sleepeth."[3] He spake the truth; she was asleep; asleep, that is, in respect of Him, by whom she could be awakened. So awakening her, He restored her alive to her parents. So again He awakened that young man, the widow's son,[4] by whose case I have been now reminded to speak with you, Beloved, on this subject, as He Himself shall vouchsafe to give me power. Ye have just heard how he was awakened. The Lord "came nigh to the city; and behold there was a dead man being carried out" already beyond the gate. Moved with compassion, for that the mother, a widow and bereaved of her only son, was weeping, He did what ye have heard, saying, "Young man, I say unto thee, Arise. He that was dead arose, and began to speak, and He restored him to his mother."[5] He awakened Lazarus likewise from the tomb. And in that case when the disciples with whom He was speaking knew that he was sick, He said (now "Jesus loved him"), "Our friend Lazarus sleepeth." They thinking of the sick man's healthful sleep; say, "Lord, if he sleep he is well." "Then said Jesus," speaking now more plainly, I tell you, "our friend Lazarus is dead."[6] And

in both He said the truth; "He is dead in respect of you, he is asleep in respect of Me."

5. These three kinds of dead persons, are three kinds of sinners whom even at this day Christ doth raise. For that dead daughter of the ruler of the synagogue was within in the house, she had not yet been carried out from the secresy of its walls into public view. There within was she raised, and restored alive to her parents. But the second was not now indeed in the house, but still not yet in the tomb, he had been carried out of the walls, but not committed to the ground. He who raised the dead maiden who was not yet carried out, raised this dead man who was now carried out, but not yet buried. There remained a third case, that He should raise one who was also buried; and this He did in Lazarus. There are then those who have sin inwardly in the heart, but have it not yet in overt act. A man, for instance, is disturbed by any lust. For the Lord Himself saith, "Whosoever looketh on a woman to lust after her, hath committed adultery with her already in his heart."[7] He has not yet in body approached her, but in heart he has consented; he has one dead within, he has not yet carried him out. And as it often happens, as we know, as men daily experience in themselves, when they hear the word of God, as it were the Lord saying, "Arise;" the consent unto sin is condemned, they breathe again unto saving health and righteousness. The dead man in the house arises, the heart revives in the secret of the thoughts. This resurrection of a dead soul takes place within, in the retirement of the conscience, as it were within the walls of the house. Others after consent proceed to overt act, carrying out the dead as it were, that that which was concealed in secret, may appear in public. Are these now, who have advanced to the outward act, past hope? Was it not said to the young man in the Gospel also, "I say unto thee, Arise"? Was he not also restored to his mother? So then he too who has committed the open act, if haply admonished and aroused by the word of truth, he rise again at the Voice of Christ, is restored alive. Go so far he could, perish for ever he could not. But they who by doing what is evil, involve themselves even in evil habit, so that this very habit of evil suffers them not to see that it is evil, become defenders of their evil deeds; are angry when they are found fault with; to such a degree, that the men of Sodom of old said to the righteous man who reproved their abominable design, "Thou art come to sojourn, not to give laws."[8] So powerful in that place was the habit of abominable filthiness, that profligacy now passed for right-

---

[1] Mark v. 35.　　[2] Mark v. 36.　　[3] Mark v. 39.
[4] Luke vii. 12.　　[5] Luke vii. 14, 15.　　[6] John xi. 11, etc.　　|　　[7] Matt. v. 28.　　[8] Gen. xix. 9.

eousness, and the hinderer of it was found fault with rather than the doer. Such as these pressed down by a malignant habit, are as it were buried. Yea, what shall I say, Brethren? In such sort buried, as was said of Lazarus, " By this time he stinketh."[1] That heap placed upon the grave, is this stubborn force of habit, whereby the soul is pressed down, and is not suffered either to rise, or breathe again.

6. Now it was said, " He hath been dead four days."[1] So in truth the soul arrives at that habit, of which I am speaking by a kind of four-fold progress. For there is first the provocation as it were of pleasure in the heart, secondly consent, thirdly the overt act, fourthly the habit. For there are those who so entirely throw off things unlawful from their thoughts, as not even to feel any pleasure in them. There are those who do feel the pleasure, and do not consent to them ; death is not yet perfected, but in a certain sort begun. To the feeling of pleasure is added consent ; now at once is that condemnation incurred. After the consent, progress is made unto the open act ; the act changes into a habit ; and a sort of desperate condition is produced, so as that it may be said, " He hath been dead four days, by this time he stinketh." Therefore, the Lord came, to whom of course all things were easy ; yet He found in that case as it were a kind of difficulty. He " groaned "[2] in the spirit, He showed that there is need of much and loud remonstrance to raise up those who have grown hard by habit. Yet at the voice of the Lord's cry, the bands of necessity were burst asunder. The powers of hell trembled, and Lazarus is restored alive. For the Lord delivers even from evil habits those who " have been dead four days ; " for this man in the Gospel, " who had been dead four days," was asleep only in respect of Christ whose will it was to raise him again. But what said He? Observe the manner of his arising again. He came forth from the tomb alive, but he could not walk. And the Lord said to the disciples ; " Loose him, and let him go."[3] " He " raised him from death, " they " loosed him from his bonds. Observe how there is something which appertaineth to the special Majesty of God who raiseth up. A man involved in an evil habit is rebuked by the word of truth. How many are rebuked, and give no ear ! Who is it then who deals within with him who does give ear? Who breathes life into him within? Who is it who drives away the unseen death, gives the life unseen? After rebukes, after remonstrances, are not men left alone to their own thoughts, do they not begin to turn over in their minds how evil a life they are living, with how very bad a habit they are

weighed down? Then displeased with themselves, they determine to change their life. Such have risen again ; they to whom what they have been is displeasing have revived : but though reviving, they are not able to walk. These are the bands of their guilt. Need then there is, that whoso has returned to life should be loosed, and let go. This office hath He given to the disciples to whom He said, " Whatsoever ye shall bind on earth, shall be bound in heaven also."[4]

7. Let us then, dearly Beloved, in such wise hear these things, that they who are alive may live ; they who are dead may live again. Whether it be that as yet the sin has been conceived in the heart, and not come forth into open act ; let the thought be repented of, and corrected, let the dead within the house of conscience arise. Or whether he has actually committed what he thought of ; let not even thus his case be despaired of. The dead within has not arisen, let him arise when " he is carried out." Let him repent him of his deed, let him at once return to life ; let him not go to the depth of the grave, let him not receive the load of habit upon him. But peradventure I am now speaking to one who is already pressed down by this hard stone of his own habit, who is already laden with the weight of custom, who " has been in the grave four days already, and who stinketh." Yet let not even him despair ; he is dead in the depth below, but Christ is exalted on high. He knows how by His cry to burst asunder the burdens of earth, He knows how to restore life within by Himself, and to deliver him to the disciples to be loosed. Let even such as these repent. For when Lazarus had been raised again after the four days, no foul smell remained in him when he was alive. So then let them who are alive, still live ; and let them who are dead, whosoever they be, in which kind soever of these three deaths they find themselves, see to it that they rise again at once with all speed.

SERMON XLIX.

[XCIX. BEN.]

ON THE WORDS OF THE GOSPEL, LUKE VII. 37, " AND BEHOLD, A WOMAN WHO WAS IN THE CITY, A SINNER," ETC. ON THE REMISSION OF SINS, AGAINST THE DONATISTS.

1. SINCE I believe that it is the will of God that I should speak to you on the subject whereof we are now reminded by the words of the Lord out of the Holy Scriptures, I will by His assistance deliver to you, Beloved, a Sermon touching the remission of sins. For when the Gospel was being read, ye gave most earnest heed, and the story was reported, and represented

---

[1] John xi. 39.   [2] John xi. 38.   [3] John xi. 44.   [4] Matt. xviii. 18.

before the eyes of your heart. For ye saw, not with the body, but with the mind, the Lord Jesus Christ "sitting at meat in the Pharisee's house," [1] and when invited by him, not disdaining to go. Ye saw too a "woman" famous in the city, famous indeed in ill fame, "who was a sinner," without invitation force her way into the feast, where her Physician was at meat, and with an holy shamelessness seek for health. She forced her way then, as it were unseasonably as regarded the feast, but seasonably as regarded her expected blessing; for she well knew under how severe a disease she was labouring, and she knew that He to whom she had come was able to make her whole; she approached then, not to the Head of the Lord, but to His Feet; and she who had walked long in evil, sought now the steps of Uprightness. First she shed tears, the heart's blood; and washed the Lord's Feet with the duty of confession. She wiped them with her hair, she kissed, she anointed them: she spake by her silence; she uttered not a word, but she manifested her devotion.

2. So then because she touched the Lord, in watering, kissing, washing, anointing His feet; the Pharisee who had invited the Lord Jesus Christ, seeing He was of that kind of proud men of whom the Prophet Isaiah says, "Who say, Depart far from me, touch me not, for I am clean;" [2] thought that the Lord did not know the woman. This he was thinking with himself, and saying in his heart, "This man if He were a prophet, would have known what woman this is that" hath approached His feet. He supposed that He did not know her, because He repelled her not, because He did not forbid her to approach Him, because He suffered Himself to be touched by her, sinner as she was. For whence knew he, that He did not know her? But what if He did know, O thou Pharisee, inviter and yet derider of the Lord! Thou dost feed the Lord, yet by whom thou art to be fed thyself, thou dost not understand. Whereby knowest thou, that the Lord did not know what that woman had been, save because she was permitted to approach Him, save because by His sufferance she kissed His Feet, save because she washed, save because she anointed them? For these things a woman unclean ought not to be permitted to do with the Feet that are clean? So then had such a woman approached that Pharisee's feet, he would have been sure to say what Isaiah says of such; "Depart from me, touch me not, for I am clean." But she approached the Lord in her uncleanness, that she might return clean: she approached sick, that she might return whole: she approached Him confessing, that she might return professing Him.

3. For the Lord heard the thoughts of the Pharisee. Let now the Pharisee understand even by this, whether He was not able to see her sins, who could hear his thoughts. So then He put forth to the man a parable concerning two men, who owed to the same creditor. For He was desirous to heal the Pharisee also, that He might not eat bread at his house for nought; He hungered after him who was feeding Him, He wished to reform him, to slay, to eat him, to pass him over into His Own Body; just as to that woman of Samaria, He said, "I thirst." What is, "I thirst"? I long for thy faith. Therefore are the words of the Lord in this parable [3] spoken; and there is this double object in them, both that that inviter might be cured together with those who ate at the table with Him, who alike saw the Lord Jesus Christ, and were alike ignorant of Him, and that that woman might have the assurance her confession merited, and not be pricked any more with the stings of her conscience. "One," said He, "owed five hundred denarii, and the other fifty; He forgave them both: which loved him most?" He to whom the parable was proposed answered, what of course common reason obliged him to answer. "I suppose, Lord, he to whom he forgave most. Then turning to the woman he said unto Simon, Seest thou this woman? I entered into thine house, thou gavest Me no water for My feet: she hath washed My feet with tears, and wiped them with her hairs. Thou gavest Me no kiss: this woman since the time she came in, hath not ceased to kiss My feet. My head with oil thou didst not anoint: but this woman hath anointed My feet with ointment. Therefore I say, her many sins are forgiven her, for she loved much. But to whom little is forgiven, the same loveth little." [4]

4. Here arises a difficulty which must in real truth be resolved, and which requires your fixed attention, Beloved, lest haply my words may not be equal to the removing and clearing of the whole obscurity of it by reason of the stress of time; especially as this flesh of mine exhausted by its heat, now longs to be recruited, and demanding its due, and clogging the eagerness of the soul gives proof of that which is said, "The spirit indeed is willing, but the flesh is weak." [5] Cause there is for fear, yea great cause for fear, lest by these words of the Lord, there steal over the minds of those who understand them not aright, who indulge their fleshly lusts, and are loth to be brought away from them into liberty, that sentiment which, even as the Apostles preached, sprung up in the tongues of slanderous men, of whom the Apostle Paul says, "And as some affirm that we say, Let us do evil

---

[1] Luke vii. 36.   [2] Isa. lxv. 5, Sept.   [3] John iv. 7.   [4] Luke vii. 41, etc.   [5] Matt. xxvi. 41.

that good may come." [1] For a man may say, "If 'he to whom little is forgiven, loveth little ;' and he to whom more is forgiven, loveth more ; and it is better to love more, than to love less ; it is right that we should sin much, and owe much which we may desire to be forgiven us, that so we may love Him the more who forgiveth us our large debts. For that woman in the Gospel who was a sinner, in the same proportion as she owed more, loved the more Him who forgave her her debts, as the Lord Himself saith, ' Her many sins are forgiven her, for she loved much.' Now why did she love much, but because she owed much ? And afterwards He added and subjoined, ' But to whom little is forgiven, the same loveth little.' Is it not better," he may say, " that much should be forgiven me, than less, that thereupon I may love my Lord the more "? Ye see no doubt the great depth of this difficulty ; ye see it, I am sure. Ye see too my stress of time ; yes, this also do ye see and feel.

5. Accept then a few words. If I shall not do justice to the magnitude of the question, lay up for a time [2] what I shall say at present, and hold me a debtor for some future time. Suppose now two men, that by the clearer force of examples ye may think upon what I have proposed to you. One of them is full of sins, has lived most wickedly for a length of time ; the other of them has committed but few sins ; they come both to grace, are both baptized, they enter debtors, they go out free ; more has been forgiven to one, less to the other. I ask, how much does each love? If I shall find that he loves most, to whom the most sins have been forgiven, it is to his greater advantage that he has sinned much, his much iniquity was to his greater advantage, that so his love might not be lukewarm. I ask the other how much he loves, I find less ; for if I find that he too loves, as much as the other, to whom much has been forgiven, how shall I make answer to the words of the Lord, how shall that be true which the Truth hath said, " To whom little is forgiven, the same loveth little "? " See," a man says, " but little has been forgiven me, I have not sinned much ; yet I love as much as he, to whom much has been forgiven." Dost thou speak truth, or Christ? Has thy lie been forgiven thee to this end, that thou shouldest fix the charge of lying on Him who forgave thee? If little has been forgiven thee, thou lovest little. For if but little has been forgiven thee, and thou lovest very much, thou contradictest Him who said, " To whom little is forgiven, the same loveth little." Therefore I give the more credit to Him, who knoweth thee better than thou dost know thyself. If thou dost suppose that but little hath

been forgiven thee, it is certain that thou lovest but little. " What then," says he, " ought I to do? Ought I to commit many sins, that there may be many which He shall be able to forgive me, that I may be able to love more?" It presses me sore, but may the Lord, who hath proposed this saying of truth to us, deliver me out of this strait.

6. This was spoken on account of that Pharisee who thought that he had either no sins, or but few. Now unless he had had some love, he would not have invited the Lord. But how little was it ! He gave Him no kiss, not so much as water for His Feet, much less tears ; he did not honour Him with any of those offices of respect, with which that woman did, who well knew what need she had of being cured, and by whom she might be cured. O Pharisee, therefore dost thou love but little, because thou dost fondly think that but little is forgiven thee ; not because little really is forgiven thee, but because thou thinkest that that which is forgiven is but little. " What then?" he says ; " Am I who have never committed murder, to be reckoned a murderer? Am I who have never been guilty of adultery, to be punished for adultery? Or are these things to be forgiven me, which I have never committed?" See : once more suppose two persons, and let us speak to them. One comes with supplication, a sinner covered over with thorns as a hedgehog, and timid exceedingly as a hare. But the rock is the hedgehog's and the hare's refuge. [3] He comes then to the Rock, he finds refuge, he receives succour. The other has not committed many sins ; what shall we do for him that he may love much? what shall we persuade him? Shall we go against the words of the Lord, " To whom little is forgiven, the same loveth little "? Yes, most truly so, to whom little is really forgiven. But O thou who sayest that thou hast not committed many sins : why hast thou not? by whose guidance? God be thanked, that by your movement and voice ye have made signs that ye have understood me. Now then, as I think, the difficulty has been solved. The one has committed many sins, and so is made a debtor for many ; the other through God's guidance has committed but few. To Him to whom the one ascribes what He hath forgiven, does the other also ascribe what he hath not committed. Thou hast not been an adulterer in that past life of thine, which was full of ignorance, when as yet thou wast not enlightened, as yet discerned not good and evil, as yet believed not on Him, who was guiding thee though thou didst not know Him. Thus doth thy God speak to thee : " I was guiding thee for Myself, I was keeping thee for Myself. That thou mightest

---

[1] Rom. iii. 8.   [2] *Interim.*   [3] Ps. ciii. 18, χοιρογρυλλίοις, Sept. (civ. English version).

not commit adultery, no enticers were near thee ; that no enticers were near thee, was My doing. Place and time were wanting ; that they were wanting again, was My doing. Or enticers were nigh thee, and neither place nor time was wanting ; that thou mightest not consent, it was I who alarmed thee. Acknowledge then His grace, to whom thou also owest it, that thou hast not committed the sin. The other owes me what was done, and thou hast seen forgiven him ; and thou owest to me what thou hast not done." For there is no sin which one man commits, which another man may not commit also, if He be wanting as a Director, by whom man was made.

7. Now then seeing I have resolved this profound difficulty, as best I could in so short a space of time (or if I have not resolved it yet, let me be held, as I have already said, a debtor for the rest) ; let us now rather consider briefly that question of the remission of sins. Christ was supposed to be but a man both by him who invited Him, and by them who sat as guests at the table with Him. But that woman who was a sinner had seen something more than this in the Lord. For why did she all those things, but that her sins might be forgiven her ? She knew then that He was able to forgive sins ; and they knew that no man was able to forgive them. And we must believe that they all, they who were at the table, that is, and that woman who approached to the Feet of the Lord, all knew that no man could forgive sins. Forasmuch then as they all knew this ; she who believed that He could forgive sins, understood Him to be more than man. So when He had said to the woman, " Thy sins are forgiven thee ; " they immediately said, " Who is this that forgiveth sins also ? " Who is this, whom the woman who was a sinner already knew ? Thou who sittest at the table as if in sound health, knowest not thy Physician ; because it may be through a stronger fever thou hast even lost thy reason. For thus the frantic patient as he laughs is bewailed by those who are in health. Nevertheless, ye do well to know, and hold fast that truth ; yea, hold it fast, that no man is able to forgive sins. This woman who believed that she could be forgiven by Christ, believed Christ not to be man only, but God also. " Who," say they, " is this that forgiveth sins also ? " And the Lord did not tell them as they said, " Who is this ? " " It is the Son of God, the Word of God ; " He did not tell them this, but suffering them to abide for a while still in their former opinion, He really solved the question which had excited them. For He who saw them at the table, heard their thoughts, and turning to the woman, He said, " Thy faith hath made thee whole." Let these who say, " Who is this that forgiveth sins also ? " who think me

to be but a man, think me but a man. For thee " thy faith hath made thee whole."

8. The Good Physician not only cured the sick then present, but provided also for them who were to be hereafter. There were to be men in after times, who should say, " It is I [1] who forgive sins, I who justify, I who sanctify, I who cure whomsoever I baptize." Of this number are they who say, " Touch me not." [2] Yes, so thoroughly are they of this number, that lately, in our conference,[3] as ye may read in the records of it, when a place was offered them by the commissary,[4] that they should sit with us, they thought it right to answer, " It is told us in Scripture with such not to sit," lest of course by the contact of the seats, our contagion (as they think) should reach to them. See if this is not, " Touch me not, for I am clean." But on another day, when I had a better opportunity, I represented to them this most wretched vanity, when there was a question concerning the Church, how that the evil in it do not contaminate the good : I answered them, because they would not on this account sit with us, and said that they had been so advised by the Scripture of God, seeing forsooth that it is written, " I have not sat in the council of vanity ; " [5] I said, " If ye will not sit with us, because it is written, ' I have not sat in the council of vanity ; ' why have ye entered this place with us, since it is written in the following words, ' And with them that do iniquity I will not enter in '? " So then in that they say, " Touch me not, for I am clean," they are like to that Pharisee, who had invited the Lord, and who thought that He did not know the woman, simply because He did not hinder her from touching His Feet. But in another respect the Pharisee was better, because whereas he supposed Christ to be but a man, he did not believe that by a man sins could be forgiven. There was shown then a better understanding in Jews than heretics. What said the Jews ? " ' Who is this that forgiveth sins also ? ' Does any man dare to usurp this to himself ? " What on the other hand says the heretic ? " It is I who forgive, I cleanse, I sanctify." Let not me, but Christ, answer him : " O man, when I was thought by the Jews to be but a man, I gave forgiveness of sins to faith. (It is not I, but Christ who answereth thee.) And thou, O heretic, mere man as thou art, dost say, " Come,

---

[1] The Donatists, holding the validity of Baptism to depend on the holiness of the minister, made it, in fact, man's act, man's gift. St. Augustin answers, Baptism is Christ's, not man's, and that " as His, it availeth equally to whom, however unequal they through whom, it is given." Ep. 93, *ad Vinc. Don* § 47. See other passages, Tract. 67, on Holy Baptism, p. 192 sqq.
[2] Isa. lxv. 5.
[3] The Collatio Carthag. of which part of the acts remain. See also St. Augustin, *Brev. Coll. c. Don.* and *Ad Don. post Collat.* In it the Donatists being entirely confuted by St. Augustin, larger numbers than before joined the Church. Poss. *Vit.* c. 13.
[4] *Cognitore.* Marcellinus, see Serm. xiii. (lxiii. Ben) 18 (xii.) note.   [5] Ps. xxvi. 4, Sept.

O woman, I will make thee whole." Whereas when I was thought to be but a man, I said, "Go, woman, thy faith hath made thee whole."

9. They answer, "knowing not," as the Apostle says, "either what they speak, or whereof they affirm:"[1] they answer and say, "If men do not forgive sins, then that is false which Christ saith, 'Whatsoever ye shall loose on earth, shall be loosed in heaven also.'"[2] But thou dost not know why this is said, and in what sense this is said. The Lord was about to give to men the Holy Spirit, and He wished it to be understood that sins are forgiven to His faithful by His Holy Spirit, and not by men's deserts. For what art thou, O man, but an invalid who hast need of healing. Wouldest thou make thyself my physician? Together with me, seek the Physician. For that the Lord might show this more plainly, that sins are forgiven by the Holy Spirit, which He hath given to His faithful ones, and not by men's deserts, after He had risen from the dead, He saith in a certain place, "Receive ye the Holy Ghost;"[3] and when He had said, "Receive ye the Holy Ghost," He subjoined immediately, "Whosesoever sins ye remit, they are remitted unto them;"[4] that is, the Spirit remits them, not ye. Now the Spirit is God. God therefore remits, not ye. But what are ye in regard to the Spirit? "Know ye not that ye are the temple of God, and the Spirit of God dwelleth in you?"[5] And again, "Know ye not that your bodies are the temples of the Holy Ghost which is in you, which ye have of God?"[6] So then God dwelleth in His holy temple, that is in His holy faithful ones, in His Church; by them doth He remit sins; because they are living temples.

10. But He who remitteth by man, can also remit even without man. For He who is able to give by another, hath no less the power to give by Himself. To some He gave by the ministry of John. By whom did He give to John himself? With good reason, as God wished to show this, and to attest this truth, when certain in Samaria had had the Gospel preached to them,[7] and had been baptized, and baptized by Philip the Evangelist, one of the seven deacons that were first chosen, they did not receive the Holy Ghost, though they had been baptized. Tidings were brought to the disciples who were at Jerusalem, and they came to Samaria,[8] in order that they who had been baptized, might by imposition of their hands receive the Holy Ghost. And so it was; "They came and laid their hands on them, and they received the Holy Ghost."[9] For the Holy Ghost was at that time given in such sort, that He even visibly showed Himself to have been given. For they who received Him spake with tongues of all nations; to signify that the Church among the nations was to speak in the tongues of all. So then they received the Holy Ghost, and He appeared evidently to be in them. Which when Simon saw, supposing that this power was of men, he wished it might be his also. What he thought to be of men, he wished to buy of men. "How much money," says he, "will ye take of me, that by imposition of my hands the Holy Ghost may be given?" Then Peter says to him with execration, "Thou hast neither part nor lot in this faith. For thou hast thought that the gift of God may be purchased with money. Thy money perish with thee;"[10] and the rest which he spake in the same place suitably to the occasion.

11. Now why I have wished to bring this subject before you, give heed, Dearly Beloved. It was meet that God should first show that He worketh by the ministry of men; but afterwards by Himself, lest men should think, as Simon thought, that it was man's gift, and not God's. Though the disciples themselves knew this well already. For there were one hundred and twenty[11] men collected together, when without the imposition of any hand the Holy Ghost came upon them. For who had laid hands on them at that time? And yet He came, and filled them first. After that offence of Simon, what did God do? See Him teaching, not by words but by things. That same Philip, who had baptized the men, and the Holy Ghost had not come upon them, unless the Apostles had met together and laid their hands upon them, baptized the officer, that is, the eunuch of queen Candace, who had worshipped in Jerusalem, and returning thence was reading in his chariot Isaiah the Prophet,[12] and understood it not. Philip being admonished went up to his chariot, explained the Scripture, unfolded the faith, preached Christ.[13] The eunuch believed on Christ, and said when they came unto a certain water, "See water, who doth hinder me to be baptized? Philip said to him, Dost thou believe on Jesus Christ? He answered, I believe that Jesus Christ is the Son of God. Immediately he went down with him into the water."[14] When the mystery and sacrament of Baptism had been accomplished, that the gift of the Holy Ghost might not be thought to be of men, there was no waiting, as in the other case, for the Apostles to come, but the Holy Ghost[15] came forthwith. Thus was Simon's thought destroyed, lest in such a thought he might have followers.

---

[10] Acts viii. 19–21.   [11] Acts i. 15.   [12] Acts viii. 28.
[13] Acts viii. 29.   [14] Acts viii. 36, etc.
[15] St. Augustin probably conceives of the presence of the Holy Ghost, which "caught away Philip," as sanctifying the Eunuch. "He went on his way rejoicing," his Baptism being perfected. St. Augustin is followed by the Gloss Ord.

---

[1] 1 Tim. i. 7.   [2] Matt. xviii. 18.   [3] John xx. 22.
[4] John xx. 23.   [5] 1 Cor. iii. 16.   [6] 1 Cor. vi. 19.
[7] Acts viii. 5.   [8] Acts viii. 14.   [9] Acts viii. 17.

12. Again, another more wonderful example. Peter came to Cornelius the centurion,[1] to a Gentile man, uncircumcised : he began to preach Christ Jesus both to him, and to those who were with him. "While Peter was yet speaking,"[2] I do not say, when as yet he had not laid on his hands, but when he had not even yet baptized them, and when they who were with Peter were in doubt whether the uncircumcised ought to be baptized (for there had arisen an offence between the Jews who believed, and those who had been brought to the faith from among the Gentiles, between the Jews, that is, and the Christians who were baptized though uncircumcised), that God might take away this question, "while Peter was speaking, the Holy Ghost came," filled Cornelius, filled them who were with him. And by this very attestation of so great a thing, as it were a loud voice came to Peter, "Why dost thou doubt of water? Already I am here."

13. So then let every soul which is to be delivered from her manifold wickedness by the grace of the Lord, to be cleansed as it were in the Church from her filthy prostitution, believe with all assurance, approach the Feet of the Lord, seek His Footsteps, confess in pouring out tears upon them, and wipe them with her hair. The Feet of the Lord are the preachers of the Gospel. The woman's hair is all superfluous possessions. Let her wipe the Feet with her hair, yea by all means wipe them, let her do works of mercy ; and when she has wiped them, let her kiss them, let her receive peace, that she may have love. She has approached to such an one, has been baptized by such an one as the Apostle Paul : from him let her hear, "Be ye followers of me, even as I also am of Christ."[3] But she has been baptized by another, by one "who seeks his own things, not the things which are Jesus Christ's : "[4] let her hear from the Lord, "Do what they say, but do not what they do."[5] So let her assurance be in Him, whether she meet with a good Evangelist, or with one who acts not as he speaks. For she hears from the Lord with firm assurance, "O woman, go thy way, thy faith hath made thee whole."

SERMON L.

[c. ben.]

ON THE WORDS OF THE GOSPEL, LUKE IX. 57, ETC., WHERE THE CASE OF THE THREE PERSONS IS TREATED OF, OF WHOM ONE SAID, "I WILL FOLLOW THEE WHITHERSOEVER THOU GOEST," AND WAS DISALLOWED : ANOTHER DID NOT DARE TO OFFER HIMSELF, AND WAS AROUSED ; THE THIRD WISHED TO DELAY, AND WAS BLAMED.

1. GIVE ye ear to that which the Lord hath given me to speak on the lesson of the Gospel. For we have read, that the Lord Jesus acted differently, when one man offered himself to follow Him, and was disallowed ; another did not dare this, and was aroused ; a third put off, and was blamed. For the words, "Lord, I will follow Thee whithersoever Thou goest,"[6] what is so prompt, what so active, what so ready, and what so fitly disposed to so great a good, as this "following the Lord whithersoever He should go"? Thou wonderest at this, saying, "How is this, that one so ready found no favour with the Good Master and Lord Jesus Christ, though He was inviting disciples to give them the kingdom of Heaven?" But inasmuch as He was such a Master as could see beforehand things to come, we understand, Brethren, that this man, if he had followed Christ, would have been sure to "seek his own things, not the things which are Jesus Christ's."[4] For He hath said Himself, "Not every one that saith unto Me, Lord, Lord, shall enter into the kingdom of heaven."[7] And of such was this man, nor did he know himself so well as the Physician knew him. For if he saw himself to be a dissembler now, if he had known himself at this time to be full of duplicity and guile, then he did not know with Whom he was speaking. For He it is of whom the Evangelist says, "He had no need that any one should testify to Him of man, for He Himself knew what was in man."[8] What then did He answer? "Foxes have holes, and the birds of the air have nests, but the Son of Man hath not where to lay His Head."[9] But where hath He not? In thy faith. For in thy heart foxes have holes, thou art full of guile ; in thy heart birds of the air have nests ; thou art lifted up. Full of guile and self-elation as thou art, thou shalt not follow Me. How can a guileful man follow Simplicity?

2. And then forthwith to another who was silent, and said nothing, and promised nothing, He saith, "Follow Me!" As much evil as He saw in the other, so much good saw He in this man. "Follow Me,"[10] Thou sayest to one who hath no wish for it. Lo, here is a man quite ready, "I will follow Thee whithersoever Thou goest ;" and yet Thou sayest to another who hath no such wish, "Follow thou Me." "The first," saith He, "I decline, because I see in him holes, I see nests." "But then why dost Thou press this other, whom Thou dost challenge to follow Thee, and he makes excuses? Lo, Thou dost even force him, and he doth not come ; Thou dost exhort him, and he doth not follow. For what doth he say? 'I will go first to bury my father.'" The faith of his heart showed itself to the Lord ; but his dutiful affec-

---

1 Acts x. 25.   2 Acts x. 44.   3 1 Cor. iv. 16, xi. 1.
4 Phil. ii. 21.   5 Matt. xxiii. 3.

6 Luke ix. 57.   7 Matt vii 21.   8 John ii. 25.
9 Luke ix. 58.   10 Luke ix. 59.

tion made him delay. But the Lord Christ when He is preparing men for the Gospel, will have no excuse from this carnal and temporal affection interfere. It is true that both the law of God prescribes these duties, and the Lord Himself reproves the Jews, because they destroyed this very commandment of God. And the Apostle Paul has in his Epistle laid it down, and said, "This is the first commandment with promise." What? "Honour thy father and thy mother."[1] God of a surety spake it. This young man then wished to obey God, and to bury his father; but it is place, and time, and circumstance, which is in this case to give way to place, and time, and circumstance. A father must be honoured, but God must be obeyed. He that begat us must be loved, but He that created us must be preferred. "I am calling thee," saith He, "to My Gospel; I have need of thee for another work: this is a greater work than that which thou wishest to be doing. 'Let the dead bury their dead.'[2] Thy father is dead: there are other dead men to bury the dead." Who are the dead who bury the dead? Can a dead man be buried by dead men? How can they lay him out, if they are dead? How can they carry him, if they are dead? How can they bewail him, if they are dead? Yet they do lay him out, and carry, and bewail him, and they are dead; because they are unbelievers. That which is written in the Song of Songs is a lesson to us, when the Church says, "Set in order love in me."[3] What is, "Set in order love in me"? Make the proper degrees, and render to each what is his due. Do not put what should come before, below that which should come after it. Love your parents, but prefer God to them. Mark the mother of the Maccabees, "'My sons, I know not how ye appeared in my womb.'[4] Conceive you I could, give you birth I could; but 'form you I could not:' hear Him therefore, prefer Him to me: trouble not yourselves, that I must remain here without you." Thus she commanded them, and they followed her. What this mother taught her children, did the Lord Jesus Christ teach him to whom He said, "Follow Me."

3. See now how another disciple presented himself, to whom no one said anything: he said, "Lord, I will follow Thee, but I will first go to bid them farewell which are at my house."[5] I suppose this is his meaning, "Let me tell my friends, lest haply they seek me as usual." And the Lord said, "No man putting his hand on the plough, and looking back, is fit for the kingdom of God."[6] The East calls thee, and thou art looking toward the west. In this lesson we learn this, that the Lord chooses whom He will.

But He chooses them, as the Apostle says, both according to His Own grace, and according to their righteousness. For such are the words of the Apostle; "Attend," he says, "to what Elias saith: Lord, they have killed Thy Prophets, they have overthrown Thine altars, and I am left alone, and they seek my life. But what saith the answer of God to him? I have reserved to Myself seven thousand men, who have not bowed the knee before Baal."[7] Thou thinkest that thou art the only servant who is working faithfully: there are others too who fear Me, and they not few. For I have "seven thousand" there. And then he added, "Even so then at this present time also." For some Jews believed, though the most were reprobate; like him who carried holes for foxes in his heart. "Even so then," saith he, "at this present time also, there is a remnant saved through the election of grace:" that is, there is the same Christ even now, as then, who also then said to that Elias, "I have reserved to Myself." What is, "I have reserved to Myself"? I have chosen them, because I saw their hearts that they trusted in Me, and not in themselves, nor in Baal. They are not changed, they are as they were made by Me. And thou who art speaking, except thou hadst placed thy trust in Me, where wouldest thou be? Except thou wert replenished by My grace, wouldest not thou too be bowing the knee before Baal? But thou art replenished by My grace; because thou hast not put thy trust at all in thine own strength, but wholly in My grace. Do not therefore glory in this, as to suppose thou hast no fellow-servants in thy service; there are others whom I have chosen, as I have chosen thee, those, namely, who put their trust in Me; as the Apostle says, "Even now also a remnant is saved through the election of grace."

4. Beware, O Christian, beware of pride. For though thou art a follower of the saints, ascribe it always wholly to grace; for that there should be any "remnant" in thee, the grace of God hath brought to pass, not thine own deserts. For the Prophet Isaiah again having this remnant in view, had said already, "Except the Lord of Hosts had left us a seed, we should have become as Sodom, and should have been like unto Gomorrah."[8] "So then," says the Apostle, "at this present time also a remnant is saved through the election of grace. But if by grace," says he, "then is it no more of works" (that is, "be now no more lifted up upon thine own deserts"); "otherwise grace is no more grace."[9] For if thou dost build [10] on thine own work; then is a reward rendered unto thee, not grace freely bestowed. But if it be grace, it is gratuitously given. I ask thee then, O sinner, "Dost thou be-

---

1 Eph. vi 2.   2 Luke ix. 60.   3 Cant. ii. 4, Sept.   7 Rom. xi. 3, etc.   8 Isa. i. 9.   9 Rom. xi. 5, 6.
4 2 Macc. vii. 22.   5 Luke ix. 61.   6 Luke ix. 62.   10 *Præsumis*.

lieve in Christ?" Thou sayest, "I do believe." "What dost thou believe? That all thy sins may be forgiven thee freely through Him?" Then hast thou what thou hast believed. O grace gratuitously given! And thou, righteous man, what dost thou believe, that thou canst not keep thy righteousness without God? That thou art righteous then, impute it wholly to His mercy; but that thou art a sinner, ascribe it to thine own iniquity. Be thou thine own accuser, and He will be thy gracious Deliverer. For every crime, wickedness, or sin comes of our own negligence, and all virtue and holiness come of God's gracious goodness. "Let us turn to the Lord."

SERMON LI.

[CI. BEN.]

ON THE WORDS OF THE GOSPEL, LUKE X. 2, "THE HARVEST TRULY IS PLENTEOUS," ETC.

1. By the lesson of the Gospel which has just been read, we are reminded to search what that harvest is of which the Lord says, "The harvest truly is great, but the labourers are few. Pray ye the Lord of the harvest, that He would send forth labourers into His harvest."[1] Then to His twelve disciples, whom He also named Apostles, He added other seventy-two, and sent them all, as appears from His words, to the harvest then ready. What then was that harvest? For that harvest was not among these Gentiles, among whom there had been nothing sown. It remains therefore that we understand that this harvest was among the people of the Jews. It was to that harvest that the Lord of the harvest came, to that harvest He sent reapers; but to the Gentiles He sent not reapers, but sowers. Understand we then that it was harvest among the people of the Jews, sowing time among the peoples of the Gentiles. For out of that harvest were the Apostles chosen, where now that the harvest was, the corn was already ripe; for there had the Prophets sown. Delightful it is to take a view of God's husbandry, and to feel delight in His gifts, and the labourers in His field. For in this husbandry did he labour, who said, "I laboured more than they all."[2] But the strength to labour was given him by the Lord of the harvest. Therefore he added, "Yet it is not I, but the grace of God which is with me." For that he was employed in this husbandry he clearly enough shows, where he says, "I have planted, Apollos watered."[3] But this Apostle, from Saul, becoming Paul, that is, from being proud, the least of all (for the name of Saul is derived from Saül; but Paul is little; whence in a way interpreting his own name, he says, "I am the least

of the Apostles ")[4]: this Paul I say, the little, and the least, sent unto the Gentiles, says that he was sent particularly to the Gentiles. He himself so writes, we read, believe, preach it. He then in his Epistle to the Galatians says, that having been now called by the Lord Jesus, he came to Jerusalem, and "communicated the Gospel"[5] unto the Apostles, that their right hands were given to him, the sign of harmony, the sign of agreement, that what they had learnt from him differed in no respect from them. Afterwards he says that it was agreed between him and them, that he should go to the Gentiles, and they unto the circumcision, he as a sower, they as reapers. So also with good reason, though they knew it not, did the Athenians give him his name. For as they heard the word from him, they said, "Who is this sower of words?"[6]

2. Attend then and be it your delight with me to take a view of the husbandry of God and the two harvests in it, the one already past, the other yet to come; the one already past among the people of the Jews, the one yet to come among the peoples of the Gentiles. Let us prove this; and whereby, but by the Scripture of God, the Lord of the harvest? See we have it said there in this present lesson, "The harvest is great, but the labourers are few. Pray ye the Lord of the harvest, that He would send forth labourers into His harvest."[1] But because in that harvest there were to be gainsaying and persecuting Jews, He says, "Behold, I send you forth as lambs among wolves."[7] Let us show something clearer still touching this harvest in the Gospel according to John, where the Lord sat as He was wearied at the well, great mysteries[8] indeed were transacted, but the time is too short to treat of them all. But give ye ear to that which relates to the present subject. For we have undertaken to show a harvest among the people, among whom the Prophets preached; for therefore were they sowers, that the Apostles might be reapers. A woman of Samaria talks with the Lord Jesus, and when the Lord among other things had told her how God ought to be worshipped, she says, "We know that Messias cometh who is called Christ, and He will teach us all things. And the Lord saith to her, I that speak with thee am He."[9] Believe what thou hearest; why dost thou make search for what thou seest? "I that speak with thee am He." But as to what she had said, "We know that the Messias will come," whom Moses and the Prophets have announced, "who is called Christ." The harvest was already in the ear. When it had yet to grow it had

---

[1] Luke x. 2.   [2] 1 Cor. xv. 10.   [3] 1 Cor. iii. 6.

[4] 1 Cor. xv. 9.   [5] Gal. ii. 1, etc.
[6] Acts xvii. 18   σπερμολόγος.   [7] Luke x. 3.
[8] *Sacramenta.*   [9] John iv. 25, 26.

received the Prophets as sowers, now that it was come to ripeness it waited for the Apostles as reapers. Presently as she heard this she believed and left her water-pot, and ran in haste, and began to announce the Lord. The disciples at that time had gone to buy bread; who on their return found the Lord talking with the woman, and they marvelled. Yet did they not dare to say to Him, "What or why talkest Thou with her?"[1] They had astonishment in themselves, they repressed their boldness in their heart. To this Samaritan woman then the Name of Christ was nothing new, she was already waiting for His coming, already did she believe that He would come. Whence had she believed it, if Moses had not sown? But hear this more expressly noted. The Lord then said to His disciples, "Ye say that the summer is yet far distant, lift up your eyes, and see the fields white already to harvest."[2] And then He adds, "Others have laboured, and ye are entered into their labours."[3] Abraham laboured, Isaac, Jacob, Moses, the Prophets laboured in sowing; at the Lord's coming the harvest was found ripe. The reapers sent with the scythe of the Gospel, carried the sheaves into the Lord's floor, where Stephen was to be threshed.

3. But here comes in that Paul, and he is sent to the Gentiles. And this he does not conceal in setting forth the grace, which he had specially and peculiarly received. For he says in his Scriptures, that he was sent to preach the Gospel where Christ had not been named.[4] But because that first harvest was past already, and all the Jews who remained are no harvest, let us consider that harvest which we ourselves are. For it has been sown by Apostles and Prophets. The Lord Himself sowed it. For He was in the Apostles, seeing that Christ also Himself reaped it. For they are nothing without Him; He is perfect without them. For He saith Himself to them, "For without Me, ye can do nothing."[5] What then doth Christ from henceforth sowing among the Gentiles say? "A sower went out to sow."[6] "There" are reapers "sent out" to reap, "here" an unwearied sower "went out" to sow. For what fear did it cause him, that "some seed fell on the way side, and some on rocky places, and some among thorns"? If he had been afraid of these unmanageable[7] grounds, he would never have got to the good ground. What is it to us, what affair of ours is it to be disputing now of the Jews, and talking of the chaff? this only concerns us, that we be not "the way side," nor "the rock," nor "the thorns," but "the good ground." Be our heart well-prepared, that from it may come the "thir-

ty," or the "sixty fold," or the thousand, and the "hundred fold;" some more, some less; but all is wheat. Let it not be "the way side," where the enemy as a bird may take away the seed trodden down by the passers by. Let it not be "the rock," where the shallow soil makes it spring up immediately, so that it cannot bear the sun. Let it not be the "thorns," the lusts of this world, the anxieties of an ill-ordered[8] life. For what is worse than that anxiety of life, which doth not suffer one to attain unto Life? What more miserable, than by caring for life, to lose Life? What more unhappy, than by fearing death, to fall into death? Let the thorns be rooted up, the field prepared, the seeds put in, let them grow unto the harvest, let the barn be longed for, not the fire feared.

4. My place accordingly it is, whom with all my unworthiness the Lord hath appointed to be a labourer in His field, to say these things to you, to sow, to plant, to water, yea to dig round about some trees, and to apply the basket of[9] dung; belongeth it to me to do these things faithfully; to you to receive them faithfully; to the Lord to aid me in my labour, and you in your belief, all of us labouring, but in Him overcoming the world. What then belongs to your place I have already said; now I wish to say what belongs to ours. But peradventure it seems to some of you, that it is something superfluous which I have declared that I wish to say, and speaking within themselves they are saying in thought, "O that he would now let us go! He has said already what belongs to our place, as to that which belongs to his, what is that to us?" I think it is better that in a reciprocal and mutual love, we should belong to you. Ye are now indeed of one family, we of the same family are dispensers, it is true, but we all belong to one Lord. Nor what I give, do I give of mine own; but of His from whom I also receive. For if I should give of mine own, I shall give a lie. "For he that speaketh a lie, speaketh of his own."[10] So then ye ought to give ear to that which belongs to the duty of the dispenser, whether it be that ye may have joy in yourselves, if ye find yourselves to be such, or whether it be that ye may be even in this very thing instructed. For how many are there among this people who shall some day be dispensers! I too was once where ye now are; and I who am seen now to be measuring out to my fellowservants their food from this higher place, a few years since in a lower place was receiving food with my fellowservants. I am speaking now a Bishop to laymen; but I know that in speaking to them I

---

[1] John iv. 27.   [2] John iv 35.   [3] John iv. 38.
[4] Rom. xv. 20.   [5] John xv. 5.   [6] Luke viii. 5.
[7] Difficiles.

[8] Vitiosæ.
[9] i.e. to appoint the exercises of penance: see Sermon lx. (cx. Ben) (i.).
[10] John viii. 44.

am speaking to many who will some day be bishops also.

5. Let us see then how we must understand what the Lord enjoined on them whom He sent to preach the Gospel, and let us consider in our mind this prepared harvest. "Carry," He saith, "neither purse, nor scrip, nor shoes; and salute no man by the way. And into whatsoever house ye enter, say, Peace be to this house. If the Son of peace be there, your peace shall rest upon it; if not, it shall return to you again." [1] If it hath "rested," hath the other lost it? This be far from the mind of Saints! So then this is not to be taken in a carnal sense; and hence it may be neither are the "purse," nor "shoes," nor "scrip;" nor above all that, where if we take it simply without examination, pride seems to be enjoined us, that we "salute no man by the way."

6. Let us give heed to our Lord, our True Example and Succour. Let us prove that He is our Succour; "Without Me ye can do nothing." [2] Let us prove that He is our Example; "Christ," says Peter, "suffered for us, leaving us an example that we should follow His steps." [3] Our Lord Himself had bags in the way, and these bags He entrusted to Judas. It is true He suffered from the thief; but I as desiring to learn of my Lord say, "O Lord, Thou didst suffer from the thief, whence hadst Thou that of which he could take away? Me, a wretched and infirm man Thou hast admonished not even to carry a purse; Thou didst carry bags, and hadst that in which Thou couldest suffer from the thief. If Thou hadst not carried them, neither could he have found anything to take away." What remains, but that he here saith to me, "Understand what that thou hearest, 'Carry no purse,' means? What is a purse? Money shut up, that is, concealed wisdom. What is, 'Carry no purse? Be not wise within your own selves only. [4] Receive ye the Holy Ghost.' It should be a fountain in thee, not a purse; from whence distribution is made to others, not where it is itself shut in." And the scrip is the same as the purse.

7. What are "the shoes"? The shoes which we use, are the skins of dead beasts, the coverings of our feet. By this then are we bidden to renounce dead works. This Moses was admonished of in a figure, when the Lord speaking to him said, "Loose thy shoes from off thy feet; for the place wherein thou standest is holy ground." [5] What ground is so holy as the Church of God? In it therefore let us stand, let us loose our shoes, let us, that is, renounce dead works. For as touching these shoes, wherewith we walk, the same my Lord again assures me. For if He had not been shod Himself, John

would not have said of Him, "I am not worthy to unloose the latchet of His shoes." [6] Be there obedience then, let not a haughty severity steal over us. "I," says one, "fulfil the Gospel, because I walk with naked feet." Well, thou canst do it, I cannot. But let us both keep that which we both receive together. How? Let us glow with charity, let us love one another; and so it shall be, that I will love your strength, and thou shalt bear my weakness.

8. But what thinkest thou, who dost not choose to understand in what sense these words are used, and who art forced by thy [7] perverse interpretation to slander even the Lord Himself as to the "bags" and "shoes;" what thinkest thou? Does it please thee then, that as we meet our friends in the way, we should neither pay them our salutations if they are our betters, nor return the salutations of our inferiors? What, dost thou fulfil the Gospel, because thou art saluted, and art silent? But thus thou wilt not be like to the traveller going on the way, but to the mile-stone pointing out the way. Let us then lay aside this coarse [8] interpretation, and understand aright the words of the Lord, "and salute no man by the way." For it is not without a cause that we are enjoined this, nor would He mislike us to do what He enjoined. What then is, "Salute no man by the way"? It might indeed be even simply taken thus, that He has commanded us to do what He enjoins with all speed; and that His words "Salute no man by the way," are as though He had said, "Put all other things by, till ye accomplish what has been enjoined you;" according to that style of speaking by which expressions are wont to be exaggerated in the custom of conversation. Nor need we go far; in the same discourse a little while afterwards He says, "And thou, Capernaum, which art exalted to heaven, shalt be thrust down to hell." [9] What is, "exalted to heaven"? Did the walls of that city touch the clouds, or reach to the stars? But what is, "exalted to heaven"? Thou seemest thyself to be surpassing happy, surpassing powerful, thou art exceeding proud. As then for the sake of exaggeration this was said, "Thou art exalted unto heaven," to that city, which was not exalted, nor rose up unto heaven; so to express haste hyperbolically was it said, "So run, so do what I have enjoined you, that travellers by the way may not in the least retard you; but disregarding all things else, hasten to the end set before you."

9. But there is another more recondite meaning in these words which it is not difficult to understand, which respects more particularly myself and all dispensers, and you too who are hearers. He that salutes, wishes salvation. [10] For

---

[1] Luke x. 4–6. [2] John xv. 5. [3] 1 Pet. ii. 21.
[4] Rom. xii. 16. [5] Exod. iii. 5.

[6] Luke iii. 16. [7] *Praviter.* [8] *Stoliditatem.*
[9] Luke x. 15. [10] *Salutem.*

so the ancients in their letters wrote thus, "Such a one sends salvation to another." Salutation derives its name from this salvation. What then is, "Salute no man by the way"? They who "salute by the way," do so "by occasion." I see that ye have quickly understood me, yet for all that I must not finish yet. For ye have not all understood so quickly. I have seen that some understand by their voice, I see more asking for something further by their silence. But seeing that we are talking of the way, let us walk as it were in the way: ye quick ones, wait for the slow, and walk evenly. What then did I say, He "who salutes by the way," salutes only by occasion? He was not going to him whom he salutes. He was about one thing, another came in his way; he was seeking one thing, he found across his path some other thing to do. What then is it to "salute by occasion"? "By occasion" to announce salvation. Now what else is it to announce salvation, but to preach the Gospel? If then thou dost preach, do it by love, and not "by occasion." There are men then, who though "they seek their own things," yet preach no other Gospel; of whom the Apostle says with sighing, "For all seek their own, not the things which are Jesus Christ's."[1] And these "saluted," that is announced salvation, they preached the Gospel; but they sought some other thing, and therefore they saluted only "by occasion." And what is this? If thou art such an one, whosoever thou art, thou doest it; nay not all of you who do it are such, but it may be that some of you who do it are. But if thou art such, it is not that thou doest it, but it is done by thee.

10. For such as these did the Apostle suffer; yet did he not enjoin them so to be. And these do something, or something is done by them; they seek something else, yet they preach the word. Care not what the preacher seeks after; be it thy will to hold fast what he preaches; but let his intention be no concern of thine. Hear the word of salvation from his mouth, from his mouth hold fast this salvation. Be not thou the judge of his heart. If thou seest that he is seeking after other things, what is that to thee? Hear Him who is Salvation;[2] "What they say, do."[3] He has given thee assurance who hath said, "What they say, do." Do they evil? "Do not what they do." Do they good. They do not "salute by the way," they do not preach the Gospel by occasion; "be ye followers of them, even as they also are of Christ."[4] A good man preaches to thee; pluck the grape from the vine. A bad man preaches to thee, pluck the grape as it hangs in the hedge. The cluster has grown on the vine-branch entangled among the thorns,

but it has not grown from the thorns. By all means when thou seest any such thing as this and art hungry, be careful as thou pluckest it, lest when thou puttest forth thy hand to the grape, thou be torn by the thorns. This is what I say; in such wise hear what is good, as that thou imitate not the evil of the character. Let him preach "by occasion," salute by the way; it will injure him because he has not given ear to the precept of Christ, "Salute no man by the way;" it will not injure thee, who, whether thou dost hear of salvation[2] from a passer by, or from one who comes direct to thee, dost hold fast that salvation. Hear the Apostle, who as I have said already gives us to understand this. "What then?" "So that in every way, whether by occasion or in truth, Christ is preached; and herein I do rejoice, yea, and will rejoice. For I know that this shall turn to my salvation through your prayer."[5]

11. Let then such as these, the Apostles of Christ, the preachers of the Gospel, who "salute not by the way," that is, who do not seek or do any other thing, but who in genuine charity preach the Gospel, let them come into the house, and say, "Peace to this house." They speak not with the mouth only; they pour out that of which they are full; they preach peace, and they have peace. They are not as those of whom it was said, "Peace, Peace, and there is no peace."[6] What is, "Peace, Peace, and there is no peace"? They preach it, but they have it not; they praise it and they love it not; they say, and do not. But yet do thou receive the peace, "whether by occasion or in truth Christ be preached." Whoso then is full of peace, and salutes, saying, "Peace to this house, if the son of peace be there, his peace shall rest upon him; if not," for peradventure there is no one of peace there, yet he who saluted has lost nothing, "it shall return," says he, "to you again." It shall return to thee, though it never departed from thee. For this He would mean to say, It profiteth thee that thou hast declared it, it hath not profited him at all who hath not received it; thou hast not lost thy reward, because he hath remained empty; it is rendered thee for thy good will, it is rendered thee for the charity which thou hast bestowed, He will render it to thee who hath given thee assurance of it by that Angelic voice, "Peace on earth to men of good will."[7]

SERMON LII.

[CII. BEN.]

ON THE WORDS OF THE GOSPEL, LUKE X. 16, "HE THAT REJECTETH YOU REJECTETH ME."

1. WHAT our Lord Jesus Christ at that time

---

[1] Phil. ii. 21.　[2] *Salutem.*　[3] Matt. xxiii. 3.
[4] 1 Cor. iv. 16, xi. 1; Sermon xxiv. (lxxiv. Ben.) 4.

[5] Phil. i. 18, 19. προφάσει; *per occasionem*, Vulgate.
[6] Jer. viii. 11.　[7] Luke ii. 14, Vulg.

spake to His disciples was put in writing, and prepared for us to hear. And so we have heard His words. For what profit would it be to us, if He were seen, and were not heard? And now it is no hurt, that He is not seen, and yet is heard. He saith then, " He that despiseth you, despiseth Me." [1] If to the Apostles only He said, " He that despiseth you, despiseth Me ; " do ye despise us. But if His word reach to us, and He hath called us, and set us in their place, see that ye despise not us, lest the wrong ye shall do unto us reach to Him. For if ye fear not us, fear Him who said, " He that despiseth you, despiseth Me." But why do we, who are unwilling to be despised by you, speak to you, except that we may have joy of your good conversation? Let your good works be the solace of our perils. Live well, that ye may not die ill.

2. And in these words which I have spoken, " Live well, that ye may not die ill," do not think of those who it may be have lived evilly, and have died in their beds ; and the pomp of their funeral has been displayed, and they have been laid in costly coffins, in sepulchres prepared with exceeding beauty and labour ; nor because each one of you perhaps is saying, " I should wish so to die," do ye think that it is a vain thing I have chosen to say ; when I said that I would that ye should live well, that ye may not die ill? On the other hand, the case of some one, it may be, occurs to you, who has both lived well, and according to the opinion of men has died ill ; perhaps he has died from the fall of a house, has died by shipwreck, has died by wild beasts ; and each carnal man is saying in his heart, " What good is it to live well? See this man has so lived, and in this wise has he died." " Return therefore to your heart ; " and if ye are faithful ones, ye will find Christ there ; He speaketh to you there. For I cry aloud, but He in silence giveth more instruction. I speak by the sound of words ; He speaketh within by the fear of the thoughts. May He then engraft my word in your heart ; for I have taken upon me to say, " Live well, that ye may not die ill." See, for faith is in your hearts, and Christ dwelleth there, and it is His place to teach what I desire to give utterance to.

3. Remember that rich and that poor man in the Gospel ; " the rich man clothed in purple and fine linen," and crammed with daily feastings ; and the poor man " lying before " the rich man's gate, hungry, and looking for " the crumbs from his table, full of sores, licked " by " dogs." [2] Remember, I say ; and whence do ye remember, but because Christ is there in your hearts? Tell me, what have ye asked Him within, and what hath He answered. For he goes on to say, " It

came to pass that that poor man died, and was carried by the Angels into Abraham's bosom. The rich man also died, and was buried in hell. And being in torments he lifted up his eyes, and saw Lazarus resting in Abraham's bosom. Then he cried, saying, Father Abraham, have mercy on me, and send Lazarus that he may dip his finger in water, and drop it on my tongue, for I am tormented in this flame." [3] Proud in the world,[4] in hell a beggar ! For that poor man did attain to his crumbs ; but the other attained not to the drop of water. Of these two then, tell me, which died well, and which died ill? Do not ask the eyes, return to the heart. For if ye ask the eyes, they will answer you falsely. For vastly splendid, and disguised with much worldly show, are the honours which could be paid to that rich man in his death. What crowds of mourning slaves and handmaids might there be ! what pompous train of dependants ! what splendid funeral obsequies ! what costliness of burial ! I suppose he was overwhelmed with spices. What shall we say then, Brethren, that he died well, or died ill? If ye ask the eyes, he died very well ; if ye enquire of your inner Master, he died most ill.

4. If then those haughty men who keep their own goods to themselves, and bestow none of them upon the poor, die in this way ; how do they die who plunder the goods of others? Therefore have I said with true reason, " Live well, that ye die not ill," that ye die not as that rich man died. Nothing proves an evil death, but the time after death. On the other hand, look at that poor man ; not with the eyes, for so ye will err ; let faith look at him, let the heart see him. Set him before your eyes lying on the ground, " full of sores, and the dogs" coming and " licking his sores." Now when ye recall him before your eyes in this guise, immediately ye loathe him, ye turn your face away, and stop your nostrils : see then with the eyes of the heart. " He died, and was carried by the Angels into Abraham's bosom." The rich man's family was seen bewailing him ; the Angels were not seen rejoicing. What then did Abraham answer the rich man? " Son, remember that thou in thy lifetime receivedst good things." [5] Thou thoughtest nothing good, but what thou hadst in this life. Thou hast received them ; but those days are past ; and thou hast lost the whole ; and thou hast remained behind to be tormented in hell."

5. Opportune then was it, Brethren, that those words should be spoken to you. Have respect unto the poor, whether lying on the ground, or walking ; have respect unto the poor, do good

---

[1] Luke x. 16.　　[2] Luke xvi. 19, etc.　　[3] Luke xvi. 22–24.　　[4] *Temporis.*　　[5] Luke xvi. 25.

works. Ye who are wont so to do, do it still; and ye who are not wont to do so, do it now. Let the number of those who do good works increase; since the number of the faithful increases also. Ye do not yet see how great is the good ye do; for so the husbandman also sees not the crop when he sows, but he trusts the ground. Wherefore dost thou not trust God? Our harvest will come. Think, that we are busy in travail now, are working in travail now, but sure to receive, as it is written, "They went on and wept as they cast their seed; but they shall surely come with exultation, bringing their sheaves with them." [1]

SERMON LIII.

[CIII. BEN.]

ON THE WORDS OF THE GOSPEL, LUKE X. 38, "AND A CERTAIN WOMAN NAMED MARTHA RECEIVED HIM INTO HER HOUSE," ETC.

1. THE words of our Lord Jesus Christ which have just been read out of the Gospel, give us to understand, that there is some one thing for which we must be making, when we toil amid the manifold engagements of this life. Now we make for this as being yet in pilgrimage, and not in our abiding place; as yet in the way, not yet in our country; as yet in longing, not yet in enjoyment. Yet let us make for it, and that without sloth and without intermission, that we may some time be able to reach it.

2. Martha and Mary were two sisters, true kinswomen both, not only in blood, but in religion also; both clave to the Lord, both with one heart served the Lord when He was present in the flesh. Martha received Him, as strangers are usually received. Yet it was the handmaid received her Lord, the sick her Saviour, the creature her Creator. And she received Him to be fed in the body, herself to be fed in spirit. For the Lord was pleased to "take on Him the form of a servant," [2] and "having taken the form of a servant" in it to be fed by servants, by reason of His condescension, not His condition. For this truly was condescension, to allow Himself to be fed by others. He had a body, wherein He might hunger indeed and thirst; but do ye not know that when He hungered in the wilderness Angels ministered to Him? [3] So then, in that He was pleased to be fed, He showed favour to them that fed Him. And what marvel is this, seeing He showed this same favour to the widow as touching the Holy Elias, whom He had before fed by the ministry of a raven? [4] Did He fail in His power of feeding him, when He sent him to the widow? By no means. He did not fail in His power of feeding him, when

He sent him to the widow; but He designed to bless the religious widow, by means of her pious office paid to His servant. Thus then was the Lord received as a guest, "who came unto His own, and His own received Him not: but as many as received Him, to them gave He power to become the sons of God:" [5] adopting servants, and making them brethren; redeeming captives, and making them co-heirs. Yet let none of you, as perhaps may be the case, say, "O blessed they who obtained the grace [6] to receive Christ into their own house!" Do not grieve, do not murmur, that thou wert born in times when thou seest the Lord no more in the flesh; He has not taken this blessedness from thee. "Forasmuch," says He, "as ye have done it unto the least of Mine, ye have done it unto Me." [7]

3. These few words, as the shortness of the time allowed me, would I speak concerning the Lord who was pleased to be fed in the flesh, while He feedeth in the spirit: let us now come to the subject which I have proposed concerning unity. Martha, who was arranging and preparing to feed the Lord, was occupied about much serving. Mary her sister chose rather to be fed by the Lord. She in a manner deserted her sister who was toiling about much serving, and she sat herself at the Lord's feet, and in stillness heard His word. Her most faithful ear had heard already; "Be still, and see that I am the Lord." [8] Martha was troubled, Mary was feasting; the one was arranging many things, the other had her eyes upon the One. Both occupations were good; but yet as to which was the better, what shall we say? We have One whom we may ask, let us give ear together. Which was the better, we heard now when the lesson was read, and let us hear again as I repeat it. Martha appeals to her Guest, lays the request of her pious complaints before the Judge, that her sister had deserted her, and neglected to assist her when she was so busied in her serving. Without any answer from Mary, yet in her presence, the Lord gives judgment. Mary preferred as in repose to commit her cause to the Judge, and had no mind to busy herself in making answer. For if she were to be getting ready words to answer, she must remit her earnest attention to hear. Therefore the Lord answered, who was in no difficulty for words, in that He was the Word. What then did He say? "Martha, Martha." [9] The repetition of the name is a token of love, or perhaps of exciting attention; she is named twice, that she might give the more attentive heed. "Martha, Martha," hear: "Thou art occupied about many things: but one thing is needful;" [10] for so

---

[1] Ps. cxxv. 6, Sept. (cxxvi. English version).
[2] Phil. ii. 7.   [3] Matt. iv. 11.   [4] 1 Kings xvii. 6.

[5] John i. 11, 12.   [6] Meruerunt.   [7] Matt. xxv. 40.
[8] Ps. xlvi. 10.   [9] Luke x. 41.   [10] Luke x. 42.

meaneth *unum opus est*, not "one work," that is, one single work, but one is needful, is expedient, is necessary, which one thing Mary had chosen.[1]

4. Consider, Brethren, this "one thing," and see if even in multitude itself anything pleases, but "this oneness." See how great a number, through God's mercy, ye are: who could bear you, if ye did not mind "one thing"? Whence in this many is this quiet? Give oneness, and it is a people; take oneness away, and it is a crowd. For what is a crowd, but a disordered multitude? But give ear to the Apostle: "Now I beseech you, brethren." He was speaking to a multitude; but he wished to make them all "one." "Now I beseech you, brethren, that ye all speak the same thing, and that there be no schisms among you; but that ye be perfected in the same mind, and in the same knowledge."[2] And in another place, "That ye be of one mind, thinking one thing, doing nothing through strife or vainglory."[3] And the Lord prays to the Father touching them that are His: "that they may be one even as We are One."[4] And in the Acts of the Apostles; "And the multitude of them that believed were of one soul, and of one heart."[5] Therefore, "Magnify the Lord with me, and let us exalt His Name in one together."[6] For one thing is necessary, that celestial[7] Oneness, the Oneness in which the Father, and the Son, and Holy Spirit are One. See how the praise of Unity is commended to us. Undoubtedly our God is Trinity. The Father is not the Son, the Son is not the Father, the Holy Spirit is neither the Father, nor the Son, but the Spirit of both; and yet these Three are not Three Gods, nor Three Almighties; but One God, Almighty, the whole Trinity is one God; because One thing is necessary. To this one thing nothing brings us, except being many we have one heart.

5. Good are ministrations done to the poor, and especially the due services and the religious offices done to the saints of God. For they are a payment, not a gift, as the Apostle says, "If we have sown unto you spiritual things, is it a great thing if we shall reap your carnal things?"[8] Good are they, we exhort you to them, yea by the word of the Lord we build you up, "be not slow to entertain" the saints. Sometimes, they who were not aware of it, by entertaining those whom they knew not, have entertained angels.[9] These things are good; yet better is that thing which Mary hath chosen. For the one thing hath manifold trouble from necessity; the other hath sweetness from charity. A man wishes when

he is serving, to meet with something; and sometimes he is not able: that which is lacking is sought for, that which is at hand is got ready; and the mind is distracted. For if Martha had been sufficient for these things, she would not have demanded her sister's help. These things are manifold, are diverse, because they are carnal, because they are temporal; good though they be, they are transitory. But what said the Lord to Martha? "Mary hath chosen that better part." Not thou a bad, but she a better. Hear, how better; "which shall not be taken away from her."[10] Some time or other, the burden of these necessary duties shall be taken from thee: the sweetness of truth is everlasting. "That which she hath chosen shall not be taken away from her." It is not taken away, but yet it is increased. In this life, that is, is it increased, in the other life it will be perfected, never shall it be "taken away."

6. Yea, Martha, blessed in thy good serving, even thou (with thy leave would I say it) seekest this reward for all thy labour — quiet. Now thou art occupied about much serving, thou hast pleasure in feeding bodies which are mortal, though they be the bodies of Saints; but when thou shalt have got to that country, wilt thou find there any stranger whom thou mayest receive into thine house? wilt thou find the hungry, to whom thou mayest break thy bread? or the thirsty, to whom thou mayest hold out thy cup? the sick whom thou mayest visit? the litigious, whom thou mayest set at one? the dead, whom thou mayest bury? None of all these will be there, but what will be there? What Mary hath chosen; there shall we be fed, and shall not feed others. Therefore there will that be in fulness and perfection which Mary hath chosen here; from that rich table, from the word of the Lord did she gather up some crumbs. For would ye know what will be there? The Lord Himself saith of His servants: "Verily I say unto you, that He will make them to sit down to meat, and will pass by[11] and serve them."[12] What is "to sit down to meat," but to "be still"? What is, "to sit down to meat," but to rest? What is, "He will pass by and serve them"? First, He passeth by, and so serveth. And where? In that heavenly Banquet, of which he saith, "Verily I say unto you, Many shall come from the East and West, and shall sit down with Abraham, and Isaac, and Jacob, in the kingdom of heaven.[13] There will the Lord feed us, but first He passeth on from hence. For (as ye should know) the Pasch is by interpretation Passing-over. The Lord came, He did divine things, He suffered human things. Is He still spit upon? Is He still struck with

---

[1] St. Augustin is explaining the words *unum opus est*, which in themselves might mean, "there is one work," or as in the text.
[2] 1 Cor. i. 10.   [3] Phil. ii. 2, 3.   [4] John xvii. 22.
[5] Acts iv. 32.   [6] Ps. xxxiv. 3.   [7] *Supernum.*
[8] 1 Cor. ix. 11.   [9] Heb. xiii. 2.

[10] Luke x. 42.   [11] παρελθων; *transiens*, Vulgate.
[12] Luke xii. 37.   [13] Matt. viii. 11.

the palm of the hand? Is He still crowned with thorns? Is He still scourged? Is He still crucified? Is He still wounded with a spear? "He hath passed by." And so too the Gospel tells us, when He kept the Paschal feast with His disciples. What says the Gospel? "But when the hour was come that Jesus should pass out of this world unto the Father."[1] Therefore did He pass,[2] that He might feed us; let us follow, that we may be fed.

SERMON LIV.

[CIV. BEN.]

AGAIN, ON THE WORDS OF THE GOSPEL, LUKE X. 38, ETC., ABOUT MARTHA AND MARY.

1. WHEN the holy Gospel was being read, we heard that the Lord was received by a religious woman into her house, and her name was Martha. And while she was occupied in the care of serving, her sister Mary was sitting at the Lord's Feet, and hearing His Word. The one was busy, the other was still; one was giving out, the other was being filled. Yet Martha, all busy as she was in that occupation and toil of serving, appealed to the Lord, and complained of her sister, that she did not help her in her labour. But the Lord answered Martha for Mary; and He became her Advocate, who had been appealed to as Judge. "Martha," He saith, "thou art occupied about many things, when one thing is necessary. Mary hath chosen the better part, which shall not be taken from her."[3] For we have heard both the appeal of the appellant, and the sentence of the Judge. Which sentence answered the appellant, defended the other's cause. For Mary was intent on the sweetness of the Lord's word. Martha was intent, how she might feed the Lord; Mary intent how she might be fed by the Lord. By Martha a feast was being prepared for the Lord, in whose feast Mary was even now delighting herself. As Mary then was listening with sweet pleasure to His most sweet word, and was feeding with the most earnest affection, when the Lord was appealed to by her sister, how, think we, did she fear, lest the Lord should say to her, "Rise and help thy sister"? For by a wondrous sweetness was she held; a sweetness of the mind which is doubtless greater than that of the senses.[4] She was excused, she sat in greater confidence. And how excused? Let us consider, examine, investigate it thoroughly as we can, that we may be fed also.

2. For what, do we imagine that Martha's serving was blamed, whom the cares of hospitality had engaged, who had received the Lord Himself into her house? How could she be

rightly blamed, who was gladdened by so great a guest? If this be true, let men give over their ministrations to the needy; let them choose for themselves "the better part, which shall not be taken from" them; let them give themselves[5] wholly to the word, let them long after the sweetness of doctrine; be occupied about the saving knowledge; let it be no care to them, what stranger is in the street, who there is that wants bread, or clothing, or to be visited, to be redeemed, to be buried; let works of mercy cease, earnest heed be given to knowledge only. If this be "the better part," why do not all do this, when we have the Lord Himself for our defender in this behalf? For we do not fear in this matter, lest we should offend His justice, when we have the support of His judgment.

3. And yet it is not so; but as the Lord spake so it is. It is not as thou understandest; but it is as thou oughtest to understand it. So mark; "Thou art occupied about many things, when one thing is needful. Mary hath chosen the better part." Thou hast not chosen a bad part; but she a better. And how better? Because thou art "about many things," she about "one thing." One is preferred to many. For one does not come from many, but many from one.

The things which were made, are many, He who made them is One. The heaven, the earth, the sea, and all things that in them are, how many are they! Who could enumerate them? who conceive their vast number? Who made all these? God made them all. Behold, "they are very good."[6] Very good are the things He made; how much better is He who made them! Let us consider then our "occupations about many things." Much serving is necessary for the refreshment of our bodies. Wherefore is this? Because we hunger, and thirst. Mercy is necessary for the miserable. Thou breakest bread to the hungry; because thou hast found an hungry man; take hunger away; to whom dost thou break bread? Take houseless wandering[7] away; to whom dost thou show hospitality? Take nakedness away; to whom dost thou furnish clothes? Let there be no sickness; whom dost thou visit? No captivity; whom dost thou redeem? No quarrelling; whom dost thou reconcile? No death; whom dost thou bury? In that world to come, these evils will not be; therefore these services will not be either. Well then did Martha, as touching the bodily — what shall I call it, want, or will, of the Lord? — minister to His mortal flesh. But who was He in that mortal flesh? "In the beginning was the Word, and the Word was with God, and the Word was God:"[8] see what Mary was listening to! "The Word was made flesh, and dwelt

[1] John xiii. 1. [2] μεταβῇ; transeat, Vulgate.
[3] Luke x. 41, 42. [4] Ventris.
[5] Vacent. [6] Gen. i. 31. [7] Peregrinationem.
[8] John i. 1.

among us : "[1] see to whom Martha was ministering ! Therefore "hath Mary chosen the better part, which shall not be taken from her." For she chose that which shall abide for ever ; " it shall not be taken from her." She wished to be occupied about " one thing." She understood already, " But it is good for me to cleave to the Lord."[2] She sat at the feet of our Head. The more lowlily she sat, the more amply did she receive. For the water flows together to the low hollows of the valley, runs down from the risings of the hill. The Lord then did not blame Martha's work, but distinguished between their services. " Thou art occupied about many things ; yet one thing is needful." Already hath Mary chosen this for herself. The labour of manifoldness passeth away, and the love of unity abideth. Therefore what she hath chosen, "shall not be taken from her." But from thee, that which thou hast chosen (of course this follows, of course this is understood) from thee, that which thou hast chosen shall be taken away. But to thy blessedness shall it be taken away, that that which is better may be given. For labour shall be taken away from thee, that rest may be given. Thou art still on the sea, she is already in port.

4. Ye see then, dearly Beloved, and, as I suppose, ye understand already, that in these two women, who were both well pleasing to the Lord, both objects of His love, both disciples ; ye see, I say (and an important thing it is which whosoever understand, understand hereby, a thing which, even those of you who do not understand ought to give ear to, and to know), that in these two women the two lives are figured, the life present, and the life to come, the life of labour, and the life of quiet, the life of sorrow, and the life of blessedness, the life temporal, and the life eternal. These are the two lives : do ye think of them more fully. What this life contains, I speak not of a life of evil, or iniquity, or wickedness, or luxuriousness, or ungodliness ; but of labour, and full of sorrows, by fears subdued, by temptations disquieted : even this harmless life I mean, such as was suitable for Martha : this life I say, examine as best ye can ; and as I have said, think of it more fully than I speak. But a wicked life was far from that house, and was neither with Martha nor with Mary; and if it ever had been, it fled at the Lord's entrance. There remained then in that house, which had received the Lord, in the two women the two lives, both harmless, both praiseworthy ; the one of labour, the other of ease ; neither vicious, neither slothful. Both harmless, both, I say, praiseworthy : but one of labour, the other of ease : neither vicious, which the

life of labour must beware of ; neither slothful, which the life of ease must beware of. There were then in that house these two lives, and Himself, the Fountain of life. In Martha was the image of things present, in Mary of things to come. What Martha was doing, that we are now ; what Mary was doing, that we hope for. Let us do the first well, that we may have the second fully. For what of it have we now? How far have we it? As long as we are here, how much of it is there that we have ? For in some measure are we employed in it now, and ye too when removed from business, and laying aside domestic cares, ye meet together, stand, listen. In so far as ye do this, ye are like Mary. And with greater facility do ye do that which Mary doeth, than I who have to distribute. Yet if I say ought, it is Christ's ; therefore doth it feed you, because it is Christ's. For the Bread is common to us all, of which I too live as well as you. " But now we live, if ye, Brethren, stand fast in the Lord."[3] I would not that ye should stand fast in us, but in the Lord. " For neither is he that planteth anything, neither he that watereth ; but God that giveth the increase."[4]

SERMON LV.

[CV. BEN.]

ON THE WORDS OF THE GOSPEL, LUKE XI. 5, "WHICH OF YOU SHALL HAVE A FRIEND, AND SHALL GO UNTO HIM AT MIDNIGHT," ETC.

1. WE have heard our Lord, the Heavenly Master, and most faithful Counsellor exhorting us, who at once exhorteth us to ask, and giveth when we ask. We have heard Him in the Gospel exhorting us to ask instantly, and to knock even after the likeness of intrusive importunity. For He has set before us, for the sake of example, " If any of you had a friend, and were to ask of him at night for three loaves,[5] when a friend out of his way had come to him, and he had nothing to set before him ; and he were to answer that he was now at rest, and his servants with him, and that he must not be disturbed by his entreaties ; but the other were to be instant and persevering in knocking, and not being alarmed in modesty to depart, but compelled by necessity to continue on ; that he would rise, though not for friendship's sake, at least for the other's importunity, and would give him as many as he wished." And how many did he wish? He wished for no more than three. To this parable then, the Lord adjoined an exhortation, and urged us earnestly to ask, seek, knock, till we receive what we ask, and seek, and knock for, making use of an example from a contrary

---

[1] John i. 14.   [2] Ps lxxiii. 28.   [3] 1 Thess. iii. 8.   [4] 1 Cor. iii. 7.   [5] Luke xi. 5.

case ; as of that "judge who neither feared God, nor regarded man," [1] and yet when a certain widow besought him day by day, overcome by her importunity, he gave her that which he could not in kindness give her, against his will.   But our Lord Jesus Christ, who is in the midst of us a Petitioner, with God a Giver, would not surely exhort us so strongly to ask, if He were not willing to give.   Let then the slothfulness of men be put to shame ; He is more willing to give, than we to receive ; He is more willing to show mercy, than we to be delivered from misery ; and doubtless if we shall not be delivered, we shall abide in misery.   For the exhortation He giveth us, He giveth only for our own sakes.

2. Let us awake, and believe Him who exhorteth us, obey Him who promiseth us, and rejoice in Him who giveth unto us.   For peradventure, some time or other some friend out of his way has come to us too, and we have found nothing to set before him ; and under the experience of this necessity, we have received both for ourselves and him.   For it cannot be, but that some one of us hath fallen in with a friend who asked him something, which he could not answer ; and then he has discovered that he has it not, when he is pressed to give it.   A friend has come to thee " out of the way," out, that is, of the life of this world, in which all men are passing along as strangers, and no one abides here as possessor ; but to every man it is said, " Thou hast been refreshed, pass on, go on thy way, give place to the next comer." [2]   Or perhaps from an evil " way," that is, from an evil life, some friend of thine wearied out, and not finding the truth, by the hearing and perceiving of which he may be made happy, but exhausted amid all the lust and poverty of the world, comes to thee, as to a Christian, and says, " Give me an account of this, make me a Christian."   And he asks what it may be thou didst not know through the simplicity of thy faith ; and so thou hast not whereby to recruit him in his hunger, and reminded thus discoverest thine own indigence ; and when thou wishest to teach thou art forced to learn ; and whilst thou dost blush before him who asked thee, as not finding in thyself what he was seeking for, thou art compelled to seek, that thou mayest be thought worthy [3] to find.

3. And where shouldest thou seek.   Where but in the books of the Lord ?   Peradventure what he has asked is contained in the book, but it is obscure.   Perhaps the Apostle has declared it in some Epistle : declared it in such wise, that thou canst read, but canst not understand it : thou art not permitted to pass on.   For the interrogator urges thee ; Paul himself, or Peter, or any of the Prophets thou art not allowed to ask.

For this family is now at rest with their Lord, and intense is the ignorance of this life, that is, it is midnight, and thy hungry friend is urgent upon thee.   A simple faith haply sufficed thee, him it suffices not.   Is he then to be abandoned ?   Is he to be cast out of thy house ?   Therefore unto the Lord Himself, unto Him with whom the family is at rest, knock by prayer, ask, be instant.   He will not, as that friend in the parable, arise and give thee as overcome by importunity.   He wisheth to give ; thou for thy knocking hast not yet received ; knock on ; He wisheth to give.   And what He wisheth to give, He deferreth, that thou mayest long the more for it when deferred, lest if given quickly it should be lightly esteemed.

4. But when thou hast gotten the three loaves, that is, to feed on and understand the Trinity, thou hast that whereby thou mayest both live thyself, and feed others.   Now thou needest not fear the stranger who comes out of his way to thee, but by taking him in mayest make him a citizen of the household : nor needest thou fear lest thou come to the end of it.   That Bread will not come to an end, but it will put an end to thine indigence.   It is Bread, God the Father, and it is Bread, God the Son, and it is Bread, God the Holy Ghost.   The Father Eternal, the Son Coeternal with Him, and the Holy Ghost Coeternal.   The Father Unchangeable, the Son Unchangeable, the Holy Ghost Unchangeable.   The Father Creator, and the Son, and the Holy Ghost.   The Father the Shepherd and the Giver of life, and the Son, and the Holy Ghost.   The Father the Food and Bread eternal, and the Son, and the Holy Ghost.   Learn, and teach ; live thyself, and feed others.   God who giveth to thee, giveth thee nothing better than Himself.   O thou greedy one, what else wast thou seeking for ?   Or if thou seek for aught else, what will suffice thee whom God doth suffice not ?

5. But necessary it is that thou have charity, that thou have faith, that thou have hope ; that that which is given may be sweet unto thee.   And these same, faith, hope, charity, are three.   And these too are gifts of God.   For faith we have received from Him ; " As God," saith he, " hath distributed to every one the measure of faith." [4]   And hope we have received from Him, to whom it is said, " Wherein Thou hast caused me to hope." [5]   And charity we have received from Him, of whom it is said, " The charity of God is shed abroad in our hearts by the Holy Ghost, which hath been given to us." [6]   Now these three are likewise in some measure different ; but all gifts of God.   For " there abide these three, faith, hope, charity ; but the greatest

---

[1] Luke xviii 2.   [2] Ecclus. xxix. 27.   [3] *Mereāris.*   [4] Rom. xii. 3.   [5] Ps. cxix. 49.   [6] Rom. v. 5.

of these is charity." [1]   In those loaves it is not said that any one loaf was greater than the others ; but simply that three loaves were asked for, and were given.

6. See other three things : "Who is there of you, whom if his son ask a loaf, will he give him a stone ? Or who is there of you of whom if his son ask a fish, will he give him a serpent? or if he ask an egg, will he offer him a scorpion? If ye then, being evil, know how to give good gifts unto your children, how much more shall your Father which is in heaven give good things to them that ask him !" [2]   Let us then again consider these three things, if haply there be not here those three, " faith, hope, charity ; but the greatest of these is charity." Set down then these three things, a loaf, a fish, an egg ; the greatest of these is a loaf. Therefore in these three things do we well understand charity by " the loaf." On which account He has opposed a stone to a loaf; because hardness is contrary to charity. By " a fish " we understand faith. A certain holy man has said, and we are glad to say it too ; " The ' good fish ' is a godly faith." It lives amidst the waves, and is not broken or dissolved by the waves. Amidst the temptations and tempests of this world, liveth godly faith ; the world rages, yet it is uninjured. Observe only that that serpent is contrary to faith. For My faith is she betrothed to whom it is said in the Song of Songs, " Come from Lebanon, My spouse, coming and passing over to Me from the beginning of faith." [3]   Therefore betrothed too, because faith is the beginning of betrothal. For something is promised by the bridegroom, and by this plighted faith is he held bound. Now to the fish the Lord opposed the serpent, to faith the devil. Wherefore to this betrothed one does the Apostle say, "I have betrothed you to One Husband, to present you a chaste virgin to Christ." And, " I fear lest as the serpent beguiled Eve through his subtilty, so your minds also should be corrupted from the purity which is in Christ ; " [4] that is, which is in the faith of Christ. For he says, "That Christ may dwell in your hearts by faith." [5] Therefore let not the devil corrupt our faith, let him not devour the fish.

7. There remains hope, which, as I think, is compared to an egg. For hope has not yet arrived at attainment ; and an egg is something, but not yet the chicken. So then quadrupeds give birth to young ones, but birds to the hope of young. Hope therefore exhorts us to this, to despise things present, to wait for things to come ; " forgetting those things which are behind," let us, with the Apostle, " reach forth unto

those things which are before." [6]   For so he says ; " But one thing I do, forgetting those things which are behind, reaching forth unto those things which are before, I follow on earnestly unto the prize of the high calling of God in Christ Jesus." Nothing then is so hostile to hope, as to " look back," to place hope, that is, in those things which flit by and pass away ; but in those things should we place it, which are not yet given, but which sometime will be given, and will never pass away. But when the world is deluged by trials,[7] as it were the sulphureous rain of Sodom, the example of Lot's wife must be feared. For she " looked behind ; " [8] and in the spot where she looked behind, there did she remain. She was turned into salt, that she might season the wise by her example. Of this hope the Apostle Paul speaketh thus ; " For we are saved in hope ; but hope that is seen is not hope ; for what a man seeth, why doth he yet hope for : but if we hope for that we see not, then do we with patience wait for it. For what a man seeth, why doth he yet hope for." [9]   It is an egg, and not as yet the chicken. And it is covered with a shell ; it is not seen because it is covered ; let it be with patience waited for ; let it feel the warmth, that it may come to life. Press on, " reach forth unto the things which are before, forget the past. For the things which are seen, are temporal. Not looking back," says he, " at the things which are seen, but at the things which are not seen. For the things which are seen are temporal ; but the things which are not seen are eternal." [10]   Unto those things which are not seen then extend thy hope, wait, endure. Look not back. Fear " the scorpion " for thine " egg." See how he wounds with the tail, which he has behind him. Let not then the " scorpion " crush thine " egg," let not this world crush thy hope (so to say) with its poison, therefore against thee, because behind. How loudly does the world talk to thee, what an uproar does it make behind thy back, that thou mayest look back ! that is, that thou mayest place thy hope in present things (and yet not even present, for they cannot be called present which have no fixedness), and mayest turn thy mind away from that which Christ hath promised, and not yet given, but who, seeing He is faithful, will give it, and mayest be content to look for rest in a perishing world.

8. For for this cause does God mingle bitternesses with the felicities of earth, that another felicity may be sought, in whose sweetness there is no deceit ; yet by these very bitternesses does the world endeavour to turn thee away from thy longing pursuit after the things " which are be-

---

[1] 1 Cor. xiii. 13.   [2] Luke xi. 11–13.
[3] Cant. iv. 8, Sept. See on St. Cyprian, Ep. p. 278, note *n*.
[4] 2 Cor. xi. 2, 3.   [5] Eph. iii. 17.

[6] Phil. iii. 13.
[7] As by the irruption of the barbarian tribes.
[8] Gen. xix. 26.   [9] Rom. viii. 24, 25.   [10] 2 Cor. iv. 18.

fore," and to turn thee back. For these bitternesses, for these tribulations dost thou murmur and say, "See, all things are perishing in Christian times." What complaint is this! God hath not promised me that these things shall not perish; Christ hath not promised me this. The Eternal hath promised things eternal: if I believe, from a mortal, I shall be made eternal. What noise is this, O world[1] impure! what murmuring is this! Why art thou trying to turn me back? Perishing as thou art, thou wishest to detain me; what wouldest thou do, if thou hadst any permanence? Whom wouldest thou not beguile by thy sweetness, if with all thy bitternesses thou dost impose thy false nourishment[2] upon us? For me, if I have hope, if I hold fast my hope, my "egg" has not been wounded by the "scorpion." "I will bless the Lord at all times, His praise shall be ever in my mouth."[3] Be the world prosperous, or be the world turned upside down; "I will bless the Lord," who made the world. Yes, verily, I will bless Him. Be it well with me according to the flesh, or be it ill according to the flesh, "I will bless the Lord at all times, His praise shall be ever in my mouth." For if I bless when it is well, and blaspheme when it is ill with me; I have received the "scorpion's" sting, being pricked "I have looked back;" which be far from us. "The Lord gave, the Lord hath taken away: it is done, as the Lord pleased; blessed be the name of the Lord."[4]

9. The city which has given us birth according to the flesh still abideth, God be thanked. O that it may receive a spiritual birth, and together with us pass over unto eternity! If the city which has given us birth according to the flesh abide not, yet that which has given us birth according to the Spirit abides for ever. "The Lord doth build up Jerusalem."[5] Has He by sleeping brought His building to ruin, or by not keeping it, let the enemy into it? "Except the Lord keep the city, he that keepeth it waketh but in vain."[6] And what "city"? "He that keepeth Israel shall neither slumber nor sleep."[7] What is Israel, but the seed of Abraham? What the seed of Abraham, but Christ? "And to thy seed," he says, "which is Christ."[8] And to us what says he? "But ye are Christ's, therefore Abraham's seed, heirs according to the promise."[9] "In thy seed," saith He, "shall all nations be blessed."[10] The holy city, the faithful city, the city on earth a sojourner, hath its foundation in heaven. O faithful one, do not corrupt thy hope, do not lose thy charity, "gird up thy loins," light, and hold out thy lamps before thee; "wait for the Lord, when He will return from the wedding."[11] Why art thou alarmed, because the kingdoms of the earth are perishing? Therefore hath a heavenly kingdom been promised thee, that thou mightest not perish with the kingdoms of the earth. For it was foretold, foretold distinctly, that they should perish. For we cannot deny that it was foretold. Thy Lord for whom thou art waiting, hath told thee, "Nation shall rise up against nation, and kingdom against kingdom."[12] The kingdoms of the earth have their changes; He will come of whom it is said, "and of His kingdom there shall be no end."[13]

10. They who have promised this to earthly kingdoms have not been guided by truth, but have lied through flattery. A certain poet of theirs has introduced Jupiter speaking, and he says of the Romans;

> To them no bounds of empire I assign,
> Nor term of years to their immortal line.[14]

Most certainly truth makes no such answer. This empire which thou hast given "without term of years," is it on earth, or in heaven? On earth assuredly. And even if it were in heaven, yet "heaven and earth shall pass away."[15] Those things shall pass away which God hath Himself made; how much more rapidly shall that pass away which Romulus founded! Perhaps if we had a mind to press Virgil on this point, and tauntingly to ask him why he said it; he would take us aside privately, and say to us, "I know this as well as you, but what could I do who was selling words to the Romans, if by this kind of flattery I did not promise something which was false? And yet even in this very instance I have been cautious, when I said, 'I assigned to them an empire without term of years,' I introduced their Jupiter to say it. I did not utter this falsehood in my own person, but put upon Jupiter the character of untruthfulness: as the god was false, the poet was false. For would ye know that I well knew the truth of it? In another place, when I did not introduce this stone, called Jupiter, but spoke in my own person, I said,

> 'Th' impending ruin of the Roman state.'[16]

See how I spoke of the impending ruin of the state. I spoke of its impending ruin. I did not suppress it." When he spoke in truth he was not silent as to its ruin; when in flattery, he promised that it should abide for ever.

11. Let us not then faint, my Brethren: an end there will be to all earthly kingdoms. If that end be now, God knoweth. For peradventure it is not yet, and we, through some infirmity, or mercifulness, or misery, are wishing that it may

---

[1] *Munde immunde.*   [2] *Alimenta mentiris.*   [3] Ps. xxxiv. 1.
[4] Job i. 21, Sept.   [5] Ps. cxlvii. 2.   [6] Ps. cxxvii. 1.
[7] Ps. cxxi. 4.   [8] Gal. iii. 16.   [9] Gal. iii. 29.
[10] Gen. xii. 3 and xxii. 18.

[11] Luke xii. 35, 36.   [12] Mark xiii. 8.   [13] Luke i. 33.
[14] Virg. *Æneid,* i. 282-283 (Dryden).   [15] Luke xxi. 33.
[16] *Georg.* ii. 489.

not be yet; nevertheless will it not therefore some day be? Fix your hope in God, desire the things eternal, wait for the things eternal. Ye are Christians, Brethren, we are all Christians. Christ did not come down into the flesh that [1] we might live softly; let us endure rather than love the things present; manifest is the harm of adversity, deceitful is the soft blandishment of prosperity. Fear the sea, even when it is a calm. On no account let us hear in vain, "Let us lift up our hearts." Why place we our hearts in the earth, when we see that the earth is being turned upside down? We cannot but exhort you, that ye may have something to say and answer in defence of your hope against the deriders and blasphemers of the Christian name. Let no one by his murmuring turn you back from waiting for the things to come. All who by reason of these adversities blaspheme our Christ, are the "scorpion's" tail. Let us put our egg under the wings of that Hen of the Gospel, which crieth out to that false and abandoned city, "O Jerusalem, Jerusalem, how often would I have gathered thy children together, even as a hen her chickens, and thou wouldest not!" [2] Let it not be said to us, "How often would I, and thou wouldest not!" For that hen is the Divine Wisdom; but I assumed flesh to accommodate Itself to its chickens. See the hen with feathers bristling, with wings hanging down, with voice broken, and tremulous, and faint, and languid, accommodating herself to her little ones. Our egg then, that is, our hope, let us place beneath the wings of this Hen.

12. Ye have noticed, it may be, how a hen will tear a scorpion in pieces. O then that the Hen of the Gospel would tear in pieces and devour these blasphemers, creeping out of their holes, and inflicting hurtful stings, would pass them over into Her Body, and turn them into an egg. Let them not be angry; we seem to be excited; but we do not return curses for curses. "We are cursed, and we bless, being defamed, we entreat." [3] But "let him not speak of Rome, it is said of me: O that he would hold his tongue about Rome;" as though I were insulting it, and not rather entreating the Lord for it, and exhorting you all, unworthy as I am. Be it far from me to insult it! The Lord avert this from my heart, and from the grief of my conscience. Have we not had many brethren there? have we not still? Does not a large portion of the pilgrim city Jerusalem live there? has it not endured there temporal afflictions? but it has not lost the things eternal. What can I say then, when I speak of Rome, but that that is false, which they say of our Christ, that He is Rome's destroyer, and that the gods of wood

and stone were her defenders? Add what is more costly, "gods of brass." Add what is costlier still, "of silver and gold:" the "idols of the nations are silver and gold." [4] He did not say, "stone;" he did not say, "wood;" he did not say, "clay;" but, what they value highly, "silver and gold." Yet these silver and golden idols "have eyes, and see not." [5] The gods of gold, of wood, are as regards their costliness unequal; but as to "having eyes, and seeing not," they are equal. See to what sort of guardians learned men have entrusted Rome, to those "who have eyes, and see not." Or if they were able to preserve Rome, why did they first perish themselves? They say; "Rome perished at the same time." Nevertheless they perished. "No," they say, "they did not perish themselves, but their statues." Well, how then could they keep your houses, who were not able to keep their own statues? Alexandria once lost such gods as these. Constantinople some time since, ever since it was made a grand city, for it was made so by a Christian Emperor, lost its false gods; and yet it has increased, and still increases, and remains. And remain it will, as long as God pleases. For we do not to this city either promise an eternal duration because we say this. Carthage remains now in its possession of the Name of Christ, yet once on a time its goddess Cælestis [6] was overthrown; because celestial she was not, but terrestrial.

13. And that which they say is not true, that immediately on losing her gods Rome has been taken [7] and ruined. It is not true at all; their images were overthrown before; and even so were the Goths with Rhadagaisus [8] conquered. Remember, my Brethren, remember; it is no long time since, but a few years, call it to mind. When all the images in the city of Rome had been overthrown, Rhadagaisus king of the Goths came with a large army, much more numerous than that of Alaric was. Rhadagaisus was a Pagan; he sacrificed to Jupiter every day. Everywhere it was announced, that Rhadagaisus did not cease from sacrificing. Then said they all, "Lo, we do not sacrifice, he does sacrifice, we, who are not allowed to sacrifice must be conquered by him who does sacrifice." But God making proof that not even temporal deliverance, nor the preservation of these earthly kingdoms, consist in these sacrifices, Rhadagaisus, by the Lord's help, was marvellously overcome. Afterwards came other Goths who did not sacrifice, they came, who though they were not Catholics in the Christian faith, were yet

---

[1] *Ad delicias.*   [2] Matt. xxiii. 37.   [3] 1 Cor. iv. 12, 13.

[4] Ps. cxv. 4.   [5] Ps. cxv. 5.
[6] Tutelary goddess of Carthage. *De Civit. Dei,* ii. 4 and 26; Ps. 62, § 7, 98, § 14. Tert. *Apol.* i. 12, 24.
[7] By Alaric, Gibbon, vol. 4, 109, etc.
[8] King of the Goths, who invaded Italy, A.D. 406, four years before the taking of Rome by Alaric, 410, Gibbon, *Rom. Emp.* vol. 4, 31-38.

hostile and opposed to idols, and they took Rome ; they conquered those who put their trust in idols, who were still seeking after the idols they had lost, and desiring still to sacrifice to the lost gods. And amongst them too were some of our brethren, and these were afflicted also : but they had learnt to say, "I will bless the Lord at all times."[1] They were involved in the afflictions of their earthly kingdom : but they lost not the kingdom of heaven ; yea, rather, they were made the better for obtaining it through the exercise of tribulations. And if they did not in their tribulations blaspheme, they came out as sound vessels from the furnace, and were filled with the blessing of the Lord. Whereas those blasphemers, who follow and long after earthly things, who place their hope in earthly things, when these they have lost, whether they will or no, what shall they retain? where shall they abide? Nothing without, nothing within ; an empty coffer, an emptier conscience. Where is their rest? where their salvation? where their hope? Let them then come, let them give over blaspheming, let them learn to adore ; let the scorpions with their stings be devoured by the Hen, let them be turned into His body who makes them pass over into it ; let them on earth be exercised, in heaven be crowned.

SERMON LVI.

[CVI. BEN.]

ON THE WORDS OF THE GOSPEL, LUKE XI. 39, "NOW DO YE PHARISEES CLEANSE THE OUTSIDE OF THE CUP AND THE PLATTER," ETC.

1. YE have heard the holy Gospel, how the Lord Jesus in that which He said to the Pharisees, conveyed doubtless a lesson to His own disciples, that they should not think that righteousness consists in the cleansing of the body. For every day did the Pharisees wash themselves in water before they dined ; as if a daily washing could be a cleansing of the heart. Then He showed what sort of persons they were. He told them who saw them ; for He saw not their faces only but their inward parts. For that ye may know this, that Pharisee, to whom Christ made answer, thought within himself, he uttered nothing aloud, yet the Lord heard him. For within himself he blamed the Lord Christ, because He had so come to his feast without having washed. He was thinking, the Lord heard, therefore He answered. What then did He answer? "Now do ye Pharisees wash the outside of the platter ; but within ye are full of guile and ravening."[2] What! is this to come to a feast! how did He not spare the man by whom He had been invited? Yea rather by rebuking He did spare

him, that being reformed He might spare him in the judgment. And what is it that He showeth to us? That Baptism also which is conferred once for all, cleanses by faith. Now faith is within, not without. Wherefore it is said and read in the Acts of the Apostles, "Cleansing their hearts by faith."[3] And the Apostle Peter thus speaks in his Epistle ; "So too hath He given you a similitude from Noah's ark, how that eight souls were saved by water." And then he added, "So also in a like figure will baptism save us, not the putting away of the filth of the flesh, but the answer of a good conscience."[4] "This answer of a good conscience" did the Pharisees despise, and washed "that which was without ;" within they continued full of pollution.

2. And what did He say to them after this? "But rather give alms, and behold all things are clean unto you."[5] See the praise of alms, do, and prove it. But mark awhile ; this was said to the Pharisees. These Pharisees were Jews, the choice men as it were of the Jews. For those of most consideration and learning were then called Pharisees. They had not been washed by Christ's Baptism ; they had not yet believed on Christ, the Only-begotten Son of God, who walked among them, yet was not acknowledged by them. How then doth He say to them, "Give alms, and behold all things are clean unto you"? If the Pharisees had paid heed to Him, and given alms, at once according to His word "all things would have been clean to them ;" what need then was there for them to believe on Him? But if they could not be cleansed, except by believing on Him, who "cleanseth the heart by faith ;" what means, "Give alms, and behold all things are clean unto you"? Let us carefully consider this, and peradventure He Himself explains it.

3. When He had spoken thus, doubtless they thought that they did give alms. And how did they give them? They tithed all they had, they took away a tenth of all their produce, and gave it. It is no easy matter to find a Christian who doth as much. See what the Jews did. Not wheat only, but wine, and oil ; nor this only, but even the most trifling things, cummin, rue, mint, and anise,[6] in obedience to God's precept, they tithed all ; put aside, that is, a tenth part, and gave alms of it. I suppose then that they recalled this to mind, and thought that the Lord Christ was speaking to no purpose, as if to those who did not give alms ; whereas they knew their own doings, how that they tithed, and gave alms of the minutest and most trifling of their produce. They mocked Him within themselves as He spake thus, as if to men who did not give alms. The Lord knowing this, immediately subjoined,

---

[1] Ps. xxxiv. 1.   [2] Luke xi. 39.   [3] Acts xv. 9.   [4] 1 Pet. iii. 20, 21.   [5] Luke xi. 41.   [6] Matt. xxiii. 23.

"But woe unto you, Scribes and Pharisees, who tithe mint, and cummin, and rue, and all herbs." [1] That ye may know, I am aware of your alms. Doubtless these tithes are your alms; yea even the minutest and most trifling of your fruits do ye tithe; "Yet ye leave the weightier matters of the law, judgment and charity." Mark. Ye have "left judgment and charity," and ye tithe herbs. This is not to do alms. "These," saith He, "ought ye to do, and not to leave the other undone." Do what? "Judgment and charity, justice and mercy;" and "not to leave the other undone." Do these; but give the preference to the others.

4. If this be so, why did He say to them, "Do alms, and behold all things are clean unto you"? What is, "Do alms"? Do mercy. What is, "Do mercy"? If thou understand, begin with thine own self. For how shouldest thou be merciful to another, if thou art cruel to thyself? "Give alms, and all things are clean unto you." Do true alms. What is alms? Mercy. Hear the Scripture; "Have mercy on thine own soul, pleasing God." [2] Do alms, "Have mercy on thine own soul, pleasing God." Thine own soul is a beggar before thee, return to thy conscience. Whosoever thou art, who art living in wickedness or unbelief, return to thy conscience; and there thou findest thy soul in beggary, thou findest it needy, thou findest it poor, thou findest it in sorrow, nay perhaps thou dost not find it in need, but dumb through its neediness. For if it beg, it "hungereth after righteousness." Now when thou findest thy soul in such a state (all this is within, in thy heart), first do alms, give it bread. What bread? If the Pharisee had asked this question, the Lord would have said to him, "Give alms to thine own soul." For this He did say to him; but he did not understand it, when He enumerated to them the alms which they were used to do, and which they thought were unknown to Christ; and He saith to them, "I know that ye do this, 'ye tithe mint and anise, cummin and rue;' but I am speaking of other alms; ye despise 'judgment and charity.' In judgment and charity give alms to thine own soul." What is "in judgment"? Look back, and discover thyself; mislike thyself, pronounce judgment against thyself. And what is charity? "Love the Lord God with all thy heart, and with all thy soul, and with all thy mind; love thy neighbour as thyself:" [3] and thou hast done alms first to thine own soul, within thy conscience. Whereas if thou neglect this alms, give what thou wilt, give how much thou wilt; reserve of thy goods not a tenth, but a half; give nine parts, and leave but one for thine own self: thou doest nothing, when thou doest not alms to thine own

soul, and art poor in thyself. Let thy soul have its food, that it perish not by famine. Give her bread. What bread, thou wilt say? He speaketh with thee Himself. If thou wouldest hear, and understand, and believe the Lord, He would say to thee Himself, "I am the Living Bread which came down from heaven." [4] Wouldest thou not first give this Bread to thine own soul, and do alms unto it? If then thou believest, thou oughtest so to do, that thou mayest first feed thine own soul. Believe in Christ, and the things which are within shall be cleansed; and what is without shall be clean also. "Let us turn to the Lord," etc.

SERMON LVII.

[CVII. BEN.]

ON THE WORDS OF THE GOSPEL, LUKE XII. 15, "AND HE SAID UNTO THEM, TAKE HEED, AND KEEP YOURSELVES FROM ALL COVETOUSNESS." [5]

1. I DOUBT not but that ye who fear God, do hear His word with awe, and execute it with cheerfulness; that what He hath promised, ye may at present hope for, hereafter receive. We have just now heard the Lord Christ Jesus, the Son of God, giving us a precept. The Truth, who neither deceiveth, nor is deceived, hath given us a precept; let us hear, fear, beware. What is this precept then: "I say unto you, Beware of all covetousness"? [6] What is, "of all covetousness"? What is, "of all"? Why did He add, "of all"? For He might have spoken thus, "Beware of covetousness." It suited Him to add, "of all;" and to say, "Beware of all covetousness."

2. Why He said this, the occasion as it were out of which these words arose, is shown to us in the holy Gospel. A certain man appealed to Him against his brother, who had taken away all his patrimony, and gave not back his proper portion to his brother. Ye see then how good a case this appellant had. For he was not seeking to take by violence another's, but was seeking only for his own which had been left him by his parents; these was he demanding back by his appeal to the judgment of the Lord. He had an unrighteous brother; but against an unrighteous brother had he found a righteous Judge. Ought he then in so good a cause to lose that opportunity? Or who would say to his brother, "Restore to thy brother his portion," if Christ would not say it? Would that judge be likely to say it, whom perhaps his richer and extortionate brother might corrupt by a bribe? Forlorn then as he was, and despoiled of his father's

---

[1] Luke xi 42.　　[2] Ecclus. xxx. 23, Vulgate.
[3] Matt. xxii. 37, etc.

[4] John vi. 41.
[5] πάσης, for τῆς, πλεονεξίας — A. B. D. K. L. M. Q. X., etc., Verss. ap. Scholz. Griesbach regards it as the more probable reading. [Tischendorf, Westcott and Hort read πάσης with ℵ and B.]
[6] Luke xii. 15.

goods, when he had found such and so great a Judge he goes up to Him, he appeals to, he beseeches Him, he lays his cause before Him in few words. For what occasion was there to set forth his cause at length, when he was speaking to Him who could even see the heart? "Master," he says, "speak to my brother, that he divide the inheritance with me."[1] The Lord did not say to him, "Let thy brother come." No, He neither sent for him to be present, nor in his presence did He say to him who had appealed to Him, "Prove what thou wast saying." He asked for half an inheritance, he asked for half an inheritance on earth; the Lord offered him a whole inheritance in heaven. The Lord gave more than asked for.

3. "Speak to my brother, that he divide the inheritance with me." Just case, short case. But let us hear Him who at once gives judgment and instruction. "Man," He saith. "O man;" for seeing thou valuest this inheritance so highly, what art thou but a man? He wished to make him something more than man. What more did He wish to make him, from whom He wished to take covetousness away? What more did He wish to make him? I will tell you, "I have said, Ye are gods, and all of you are children of the Most High."[2] Lo, what He wished to make him, to reckon him that hath no covetousness among the "gods." "Man, who made Me a divider among you?"[3] So the Apostle Paul His servant, when he said, "I beseech you, brethren, that ye all speak the same thing, and that there be no schisms among you,"[4] was unwilling to be a divider. And afterwards he thus admonished them who were running after his name, and dividing Christ: "Every one of you saith, I am of Paul, and I of Apollos, and I of Cephas, and I of Christ. Is Christ divided? Was Paul crucified for you? or were ye baptized in the name of Paul?"[5] Judge then, how wicked are those men, who would have Him to be divided, who would not be a divider. "Who," saith He, "hath made Me a divider among you?"

4. Thou hast petitioned for a kindness; hear counsel. "I say unto you, Beware of all covetousness."[6] "Perhaps," he would say, "thou wouldest call him covetous and greedy, if he were seeking another's goods; but I say, seek not even thine own greedily or covetously." This is "Of all, beware of all covetousness." A heavy burden this! If by any chance this burden be imposed on them that are weak; let Him be sought unto, that He who imposes it, may vouchsafe to give us strength. For it is not a thing to be lightly regarded, my Brethren, when our Lord, our Redeemer, our Saviour, who

died for us, who gave His Own Blood as our ransom, to redeem us, our Advocate and Judge; it is no light matter when He saith, "Beware." He knoweth well how great the evil is; we know it not, let us believe Him. "Beware," saith He. Wherefore? of what? "of all covetousness." I am but keeping what is mine own, I am not taking away another's; "Beware of all covetousness." Not only is he covetous, who plunders the goods of others; but he is covetous too, who greedily keeps his own. But if he is so blamed who greedily keeps his own; how is he condemned who plunders what is another's! "Beware," He saith, "of all covetousness: For a man's life consisteth not in the abundance of the things which he possesseth." He that stores up great abundance, how much does he take therefrom to live? When he has taken it, and in a way separated in thought sufficient to live upon from it, let him consider for whom the rest remains; lest haply when thou keepest wherewith to live, thou art gathering only wherewith to die. Behold Christ, behold truth, behold severity. "Beware," saith truth: "Beware," saith severity. If thou love not the truth, fear severity. "A man's life consisteth not in the abundance of the things which he possesseth." Believe Him, He doth not deceive thee. On the other hand, thou sayest, "Yea, 'a man's life' does 'consist in the abundance of the things which he possesses.'" He doth not deceive thee; thou deceivest thyself.

5. Out of this occasion then, when that appellant was seeking his own portion, not desiring to plunder another's, arose that sentence of the Lord, wherein He said not, "Beware of covetousness;" but added, "of all covetousness." Nor was this all: He giveth another example of a certain rich man, "whose ground had turned out well."[7] "There was," He saith, "a certain rich man, whose ground had turned[8] out well." What is, "had turned out well"? The ground which he possessed had brought forth a great produce. How great? So that he could not find where to bestow it: suddenly, through his abundance he became straitened — this old covetous man. For how many years had already passed away, and yet those barns had been enough? So great then was the produce, that the accustomed places were not sufficient. And the wretched man sought counsel, not as to how he should lay the additional produce out, but how he should store it up; and in thinking he discovered an expedient. He seemed as it were wise in his own eyes, by the discovery of this expedient. Knowingly did he think of it, wisely hit upon it. What was this he wisely hit upon? "I will destroy," he says,

---

[1] Luke xii. 13.   [2] Ps. lxxii. 6.   [3] Luke xii. 14.
[4] 1 Cor. i. 10.   [5] 1 Cor. i. 12, 13.   [6] Luke xii. 15.   [7] Luke xii. 16.   [8] *Successerat.*

"my" old "barns, and will build new ones greater, and will fill them; and I will say to my soul." What wilt thou say to thy soul? "Soul, thou hast much goods laid up for many years, take thine ease, eat, drink, be merry."[1] This did the wise discoverer of this expedient say to his soul.

6. "And God," who doth not disdain to speak even with fools, "said unto him."[2] Some of you may peradventure say, And how did God speak with a fool? O, my Brethren, with how many fools does He speak here, when the Gospel is read! When it is read, are not they who hear and do not, fools? What then did the Lord say? For he, I repeat, thought himself wise by the discovery of his expedient. "Thou fool," He saith; "Thou fool," who seemest wise unto thyself; "Thou fool," who hast said to thy soul, "Thou hast much goods laid up for many years: to-day is thy soul required of thee!" Thy soul to which thou hast said, "Thou hast much goods," to-day is "required," and hath no good at all. Let it then despise these goods, and be herself good, that when she is "required," she may depart in assured hope. For what is more perverse[3] than a man[4] who wishes to have "much goods," and does not wish to be good himself? Unworthy art thou to have them, who dost not wish to be what thou dost wish to have. For dost thou wish to have a bad country house? No indeed, but a good one. Or a bad wife? No, but a good one. Or a bad hood?[5] Or even a bad shoe? And why a bad soul only? He did not in this place say to this fool who was thinking on vain things, building barns, and who had no regard to the wants[6] of the poor; He did not say to him, "To-day shall thy soul be hurried away to hell:" He said no such thing as this, but "is required of thee." "I do not tell thee whither thy soul shall go; yet hence, where thou art laying up for it such store of things, must it depart, whether thou wilt or no." Lo, "thou fool," thou hast thought to fill thy new and greater barns, as if there was nothing to be done with what thou hast.

7. But peradventure he was not yet a Christian. Let us hear then, Brethren, to whom as believers the Gospel is read, by whom He who spake these things, is worshipped, whose mark is borne by us on our forehead, and is held in the heart. For of very great concernment is it where a man hath the mark of Christ, whether in the forehead, or both in the forehead and the heart. Ye have heard to-day the words of the holy prophet Ezekiel, how that before God sent one to destroy the ungodly people, He first sent one to mark them, and said to him, "Go and set a mark upon the foreheads of the men that sigh and moan for the sins of my people that are done in the midst of them."[7] He did not say, "which[8] are done without them;" but "in the midst of them." Yet they "sigh and moan;" and therefore are they "marked on the forehead:" in the forehead of the inner man, not the outer. For there is a forehead in the face, there is a forehead in the conscience. So it happens that when the inner forehead is stricken, the outer grows red; either red with shame, or pale with fear. So then there is a forehead of the inner man. There were they "marked" that they might not be destroyed; because though they did not correct the sins which were "done in the midst of them," yet they sorrowed for them, and by that very sorrow separated themselves; and though separated in God's sight, they were mixed with them in the eyes of men. They are "marked" secretly, are not hurt openly. Afterwards the Destroyer is sent, and to him it is said, "Go, lay waste, spare neither young nor old, male nor female, but come not near those who have the mark on their forehead."[9] How great security is granted to you, my Brethren, who among this people are sighing, and moaning for the iniquities which are being done in the midst of you, and who do them not!

8. But that ye may not commit iniquities, "beware of all covetousness." I will tell you in its full extent, what is "of all covetousness." In matter of lust he is covetous, whom his own wife suffices not. And idolatry itself is called covetousness; because again in matter of divine worship[10] he is covetous, whom the one and true God suffices not. What but the covetous soul makes for itself many gods? What but the covetous soul makes to itself false[11] martyrs? "Beware of all covetousness." Lo, thou lovest thine own goods, and dost boast thyself in that thou seekest not the goods of others; see what evil thou doest in not hearing Christ, who saith, "Beware of all covetousness." See thou dost love thine own goods, thou dost not take away the goods of others; thou hast the fruits of thy labour, they are justly thine; thou hast been left an heir, some one whose good graces thou hast attained has given it to thee; thou hast been on the sea, and in its perils, hast committed no fraud, hast sworn no lie, hast acquired what it hath pleased God thou shouldest; and thou art keeping it greedily as in a good conscience, because thou dost not possess it from evil sources, and dost not seek what is another's. Yet if thou give not heed to Him who hath said, "Beware of all

1 Luke xii. 18, 19.   2 Luke xii. 20.   3 Iniquius.
4 Vid. Serm. xxii. (lxxii. Ben.) 4 (iii.); xxxii. (lxxxii. Ben.) 14 (xi.); xxxv. (lxxxv. Ben.).
5 Casulam.   6 Ventres.

7 Ezek. ix. 4.   8 Against the Donatists.
9 Ezek. ix. 6.   10 Divinitate.
11 In allusion to the Circumcelliones amongst the Donatists. See ab. p. 305, note.

covetousness," hear how great evils thou wilt be ready to do for thine own goods' sake. Lo, for example, it hath chanced to thee to be made a judge. Thou wilt not be corrupted, because thou dost not seek the goods of others; no one giveth thee a bribe and says, "Give judgment against my adversary." This be far from thee, a man, who seekest not the things of others, how couldest thou be persuaded to do this? Yet see what evil thou wilt be ready to do for thine own goods' sake. Peradventure he that wishes thee to judge evilly, and pronounce sentence for him against his adversary is a powerful man, and able to bring up false accusation against thee, that thou mayest lose what thou hast. Thou dost reflect, and think upon his power, think of thine own goods thou art keeping, which thou dost love: not which thou hast possessed, but in whose power[1] rather thou art thyself unhappily fixed. This thy bird-lime, by reason of which thou hast not the wings of virtue free, thou dost look to; and thou sayest within thine own self, "I am offending this man, he has much influence in the world; he will suggest evil accusations against me, and I shall be outlawed,[2] and lose all I have." Thus thou wilt give unrighteous judgment, not when thou seekest another's, but when thou keepest thine own.

9. Give me a man who has given ear to Christ, give me a man who has heard with fear, "Beware of all covetousness;" and let him not say to me, "I am a poor man, a plebeian of mean estate, one of the common people, how can I hope ever to be a judge? I am in no fear of this temptation, the peril of which thou hast placed before mine eyes." Yet lo, even this poor man I will tell what he ought to fear. Some rich and powerful person calls thee to give false witness for him. What wilt thou be doing now? Tell me. Thou hast a good little property of thine own; thou hast laboured for it, hast acquired, and kept it. That person requires of thee; "Give false witness for me, and I will give thee so and so much." Thou who seekest not the things of others, sayest, "That be far from me: I do not seek for what it has not pleased God to give me, I will not receive it; depart from me." "Hast thou no wish to receive what I give? I will take away what thou hast already." See now prove thyself, question now thine own self. Why dost thou look at me? Look inward on thine own self, look at thine own self within, examine thine own self within; sit down before thine own self, and summon thine own self before thee, and stretch thyself upon the rack of God's commandment, and torment thyself with His fear, and deal not softly with thyself; answer thine

own self. Lo, if any one were to threaten thee with this, what wouldest thou do? "I will take away from thee what with so great labour thou hast acquired, if thou wilt not give false witness for me." Give him that; "Beware of all covetousness." "O my servant," He will say to thee, "whom I have redeemed and made free, whom from a servant I have adopted to be a brother, whom I have set as a member in My Body, give ear to Me: He may take away what thou hast acquired, Me he shall not take away from thee. Art thou keeping thine own goods, that thou mayest not perish? What, have I not said unto thee, 'Beware of all covetousness'?"

10. Lo, thou art in confusion, tossed to and fro; thy heart as a ship is shaken about by tempests. Christ is asleep: awake Him, that sleepeth, and thou shalt be exposed no more to the raging of the storm. Awake Him, who was pleased to have nothing here, and thou hast all, who came even to the Cross for thee, whose "Bones" as He was naked and hanging "were numbered" by them that mocked Him; and "beware of all covetousness." Covetousness of money is not all; "beware of covetousness" of life. A dreadful covetousness, covetousness much to be feared. Sometimes a man will despise what he has, and say, "I will not give false witness; I will not. You tell me, I will take away what thou hast. Take away what I have; you do not take away what I have within. For he was not left a poor man, who said, 'The Lord gave, the Lord hath taken away; it is done as it pleased the Lord; blessed' therefore 'be the Name of the Lord. Naked came I out of my mother's womb, naked shall I return to the earth.'[3] Naked outwardly, well-clothed within. Naked as regards these rags, these corruptible rags outwardly, clothed within. With what? 'Let thy priests be clothed with righteousness.'"[4] But what if he say to thee, when thou hast despised the things which thou possessest, what if he say to thee, "I will kill thee"? If thou have given ear to Christ, answer him, "Wilt Thou kill me? Better that thou shouldest kill my body, than that I by a false tongue should kill my soul! What canst thou do to me? Thou wilt kill my body; my soul will depart at liberty, to receive again at the end of the world even this very body she hath despised. What canst thou do to me then? Whereas if I should give false witness for thee, with my tongue do I kill myself; and not in my body do I kill myself; 'For the mouth that lieth killeth the soul.'"[5] But peradventure thou dost not say so. And why dost thou not say so? Thou wishest to live; thou wishest to live longer than God hath appointed for thee? Dost

---

[1] *Quibus male inhæsisti.*   [2] *Proscribor.*   [3] Job i. 21.   [4] Ps. cxxxii. 9.   [5] Wisd. i. 11.

thou then " beware of all covetousness "?   So long was it God's will that thou shouldest live, till this person came to thee.   It may be that he will kill thee, to make a martyr of thee. Entertain then no undue desire of life ; and so thou wilt not have an eternity of death.   Ye see how that that covetousness everywhere, when we wish for more than is necessary, causes us to sin.   Beware we of all covetousness, if we would enjoy eternal wisdom.

SERMON LVIII.

[CVIII. BEN.]

ON THE WORDS OF THE GOSPEL, LUKE XII. 35, " LET YOUR LOINS BE GIRDED ABOUT, AND YOUR LAMPS BURNING ; AND BE YE YOURSELVES LIKE," ETC.   AND ON THE WORDS OF THE 34TH PSALM, V. 12, " WHAT MAN IS HE THAT DESIR-ETH LIFE," ETC.

1. OUR Lord Jesus Christ both came to men, and went away from men, and is to come to men.   And yet He was here when He came, nor did He depart when He went away, and He is to come to them to whom He said, " Lo, I am with you, even unto the end of the world." [1] According to the " form of a servant " then, which He took for our sakes, was He born at a certain time, and was slain, and rose again, and now " dieth no more, neither shall death have any more dominion over Him ; " [2] but according to His Divinity, wherein He was equal to the Father, was He already in this world, and " the world was made by Him, and the world knew Him not." [3]   On this point ye have just heard the Gospel, what admonition it has given us, putting us on our guard, and wishing us to be unencumbered and prepared to await the end ; that after these last [4] things, which are to be feared in this world, that rest may succeed which hath no end.   Blessed are they who shall be partakers of it.   For then shall they be in se-curity, who are not in security now ; and again then shall they fear, who will not fear now. Unto this waiting, and for this hope's sake, have we been made Christians.   Is not our hope not of this world?   Let us then not love the world. From the love of this world have we been called away, that we may hope for and love another. In this world ought we to abstain from all un-lawful desires, to have, that is, " our loins girded ; " and to be fervent and to shine in good works, that is, to have " our lights burning." For the Lord Himself said to His disciples in another place of the Gospel, " No man lighteth

a candle and putteth it under a bushel, but on a candlestick, that it may give light unto all that are in the house." [5]   And to show of what He was speaking, He subjoined and said, " Let your light so shine before men, that they may see your good works, and glorify your Father which is in heaven." [6]

2. Therefore He would that " our loins should be girded, and our lights burning." [7]   What is, " our loins girded "?   " Depart from evil." [8] What is to " burn "?   What is to have our " lights burning "?   It is this, " And do good." What is that which He said afterwards, " And ye yourselves like unto men that wait for their Lord, when He will return from the wedding : " [9] ex-cept that which follows in that Psalm, " Seek after peace, and ensue it "? [8]   These three things, that is, " abstaining from evil, and doing good," and the hope of everlasting reward, are re-corded in the Acts of the Apostles, where it is written, that Paul taught them of " temperance and righteousness," [10] and the hope of eternal life.   To temperance belongs, " let your loins be girded."   To righteousness, " and your lights burning."   To the hope of eternal life, the waiting for the Lord.   So then, " depart from evil," this is temperance, these are the loins girded : " and do good," this is righteousness, these are the " lights burning ; "   " seek peace, and ensue it," this is the waiting for the world to come : therefore, " Be ye like unto men that wait for their Lord, when He will come from the wedding."

3. Having then these precepts and promises, why seek we on earth for " good days," where we cannot find them?   For I know that ye do seek them, when ye are either sick, or in any of the tribulations, which in this world abound. For when life draws towards its close, the old man is full of complaints, and with no joys. Amid all the tribulations by which mankind is worn away, men seek for nothing but " good days," and wish for a long life, which here they cannot have.   For even a man's long life is narrowed within so short a span to the wide ex-tent of all ages, as if it were but one drop to the whole sea.   What then is man's life, even that which is called a long one?   They call that a long life, which even in this world's course is short ; and as I have said, groans abound even unto the decrepitude of old age.   This at the most is but brief, and of short duration ; and yet how eagerly is it sought by men, with how great diligence, with how great toil, with how great carefulness, with how great watchfulness, with how great labour do men seek to live here for a long time, and to grow old.   And yet this very living long, what is it but running to the

1 Matt. xxviii. 20.   2 Rom. vi. 9.   3 John i. 10.
4 The troubles through the incursions of the barbarian tribes, as heralds of the end.   See St. Cyprian, *Ad Demetr.* 2, p. 201, Oxf. tr.; *De Mort.* v. 2, p. 216, 7.

5 Matt. v. 15.   6 Matt. v. 16.   7 Luke xii. 35.
8 Ps. xxxiv. 14.   9 Luke xii. 36.   10 Acts xxiv. 25.

end? Thou hadst yesterday, and thou dost wish also to have to-morrow. But when this day and to-morrow are passed, thou hast them not. Therefore thou dost wish for the day to break, that that may draw near to thee whither thou hast no wish to come. Thou makest some annual festival with thy friends, and hearest it there said to thee by thy well-wishers, "Mayest thou live many years," thou dost wish that what they have said, may come to pass. What? Dost thou wish that years and years may come, and the end of these years come not? Thy wishes are contrary to one another; thou dost wish to walk on, and dost not wish to reach the end.

4. But if, as I have said, there is so great care in men, as to desire with daily, great and perpetual labours, to die somewhat later: with how great cause ought they to strive, that they may never die? Of this, no one will think. Day by day "good days" are sought for in this world, where they are not found; yet no one wishes so to live, that he may arrive there where they are found. Therefore the same Scripture admonishes us, and says, "Who is the man that wisheth for life, and loveth to see good days?"[1] Scripture so asked the question, as that It knew well what answer would be given It; knowing that all men would "seek for life and good days." In accordance with their desire It asked the question, as if the answer would be given It from the heart of all, " I wish it ; " It said thus, " Who is the man that wisheth for life, and loveth to see good days?" Just as even at this very hour in which I am speaking to you, when ye heard me say, "Who is the man that wisheth for life, and loveth to see good days?" ye all answered in your heart, "I." For so do I too, who am speaking with you, "wish for life and good days ; " what ye seek, that do I seek also.

5. Just as if gold were necessary for us all, and we all, I as well as you, were wishing to get at the gold, and there was some anywhere in a field of yours, in a place subject to your power, and I were to see you searching for it, and were to say to you, "What are ye searching for?" ye were to answer me, "Gold." And I were to say to you, "Ye are searching for gold, and I am searching for gold too : what ye are searching for, I am searching for ; but ye are .not searching for it where we can find it. Listen to me then, where we can find it; I am not taking it away from you, I am showing you the spot ; " yea, let us all follow Him, who knows where what we are seeking for, is. So now too seeing that ye desire "life and good days," we cannot say to you, " Do not desire ' life and good days ; ' " but this we say, " Do not seek for ' life and good days ' here in this world, where ' good days '

cannot be." Is not this life itself like unto death? Now these days here hasten and pass away : for to-day has shut out yesterday ; to-morrow only rises that it may shut out to-day. These days themselves have no abiding ; wherefore wouldest thou abide with them? Your desire then whereby ye wish for " life and good days," I not only do not repress, but I even more strongly inflame. By all means " seek " for " life, seek for good days ; " but let them be sought there, where they can be found.

6. For would ye with me hear His counsel, who knoweth where " good days " and where " life " is? Hear it not from me, but together with me. For One says to us, " Come, ye children, hearken unto Me." And let us run together, and stand, and prick up our ears, and with our hearts understand the Father, who hath said, " Come, ye children, hearken unto Me, I will teach you the fear of the Lord." [2] And then follows what he would teach us, and to what end the fear of the Lord is useful. " Who is the man that wisheth life, and loveth to see good days?" We all answer, "We wish it." Let us listen then to what follows, " Refrain thy tongue from evil, and thy lips that they speak no guile." [3] Now say, " I wish it." Just now when I said, " Who is the man that wisheth for life, and loveth to see good days?" we all answered, " I." Come then, let some one now answer " I." So then, " Refrain thy tongue from evil, and thy lips that they speak no guile." Now say, " I." Wouldest thou then have " good days " and " life," and wouldest thou not " refrain thy tongue from evil, and thy lips that they speak no guile "? Alert to the reward, slow to the work ! And to whom if he does not work is the reward rendered? I would that in thy house thou wouldest render the reward even to him that does work ! For to him that works not, I am sure thou dost not render it. And why? Because thou owest nothing to him that does not work ! And God hath a reward proposed. What reward? " Life and good days," which life we all desire, and unto which days we all strive to come. The promised reward He will give us. What reward? " Life and good days." And what are "good days"? Life without end, rest without labour.

7. Great is the reward He hath set before us : in so great a reward as is set before us, let us see what He hath commanded us. For enkindled by the reward of so great a promise, and by the love of the reward, let us make ready at once our strength, our sides, our arms, to do His bidding. Is it as if He were to command us to carry heavy burdens, to dig something it may be, or to raise up some machine? No, no such

---

[1] Ps. xxxiv. 12.   [2] Ps. xxxiv. 11.   [3] Ps. xxxiv. 13.

laborious thing hath He enjoined thee, but hath enjoined thee only to "refrain" that member which amongst all thy members thou dost move so quickly. "Refrain thy tongue from evil." It is no labour to erect a building, and is it a labour to hold in the tongue? "Refrain thy tongue from evil." Speak no lie, speak no revilings, speak no slanders, speak no false witnesses, speak no blasphemies. "Refrain thy tongue from evil." See how angry thou art, if any one speaks evil of thee. As thou art angry with another, when he speaks evil of thee; so be thou angry with thyself, when thou speakest evil of another. "Let thy lips speak no guile." What is in thine heart within, be that spoken out. Let not thy breast conceal one thing, and thy tongue utter another. "Depart from evil, and do good." For how should I say, "Clothe the naked," to him who up to this time would strip him that is clothed? For he that oppresses his fellow-citizen, how can he take in the stranger? So then in proper order, first "depart from evil," and "do good;" first "gird up thy loins," and then "light the lamp." And when thou hast done this, wait in assured hope for "life and good days." "Seek peace, and ensue it;" and then with a good face wilt thou say unto the Lord, "I have done what Thou hast bidden, render me what Thou hast promised."

SERMON LIX.

[CIX. BEN.]

ON THE WORDS OF THE GOSPEL, LUKE XII. 56, 58, "YE KNOW HOW TO INTERPRET THE FACE OF THE EARTH AND THE HEAVEN," ETC.; AND OF THE WORDS, "FOR AS THOU ART GOING WITH THINE ADVERSARY BEFORE THE MAGISTRATE, ON THE WAY GIVE DILIGENCE TO BE QUIT OF HIM," ETC.

1. WE have heard the Gospel, and in it the Lord reproving those who knew how to discern the face of the sky, and know not how to discover the time of faith, the kingdom of heaven which is at hand. Now this He said to the Jews; but His words reach even unto us. Now the Lord Jesus Christ Himself began the preaching of His Gospel in this way; "Repent ye, for the kingdom of heaven is at hand."[1] In like manner too John the Baptist and His forerunner began thus; "Repent ye, for the kingdom of heaven is at hand."[2] And now the Lord rebuketh those who would not repent, when "the kingdom of heaven was at hand." "The kingdom of heaven," as He saith Himself, "will not come with observation."[3] And again He saith, "The kingdom of heaven is within you."[4] Let every one then wisely receive the admonitions of the Master,[5] that he may not lose the season

of the mercy of the Saviour, which is now being dealt out, as long as the human race is spared. For to this end is man spared, that he may be converted, and that he may not be to be condemned. God only knoweth when the end of the world shall come: nevertheless now is the time of faith. Whether the end of the world shall find any of us here, I know not; and perhaps it will not find us. Our time is very near to each one of us, seeing we are mortal. We walk in the midst of chances. If we were made of glass, we should have to fear chances less than we have. What is more fragile than a vessel of glass? And yet it is kept, and lasts for ages. For though the chances of a fall are feared for the vessel of glass, yet there is no fear of fever or old age for it. We then are more fragile and more infirm; because all the chances which are incessant in human things, we doubtless through our frailness are in daily dread of; and if these chances come not, yet time goes on; a man avoids this stroke, can he avoid his end? he avoids accidents which happen from without, can that which is born within be driven away? Again, now the entrails engender worms, now some other disease attacks on a sudden; lastly, let a man be spared ever so long, at last when old age comes, there is no way of putting off that.

2. Wherefore let us give ear to the Lord, let us do within ourselves what He hath enjoined. Let us see who that adversary is, of whom He hath put us in fear, saying, "If thou goest with thine adversary to the magistrate, give diligence in the way to be delivered from him; lest haply he deliver thee to the magistrate, and the magistrate to the officer, and thou be cast into prison, from whence thou shalt not come out, till thou payest the very last farthing."[6] Who is this "adversary"? If the devil; we have been delivered from him already. What a price was given for us that we might be redeemed from him! Of which the Apostle says, speaking of this our redemption, "Who hath delivered us from the power of darkness, and hath translated us into the kingdom of the Son of his love."[7] We have been redeemed, we have renounced the devil; how shall we "give diligence to be delivered from him," that he make us not, as sinners, his captives again? But this is not the "adversary" of whom the Lord gives us warning. For in another place another Evangelist has so expressed it, that if we join both expressions together, and compare both expressions of the two Evangelists with each other, we shall soon understand who this adversary is. For see, what did Luke say here? "When thou goest with thine adversary to the magistrate, give diligence in the way to be delivered from him."[8]

---

[1] Matt. iv. 17.　　[2] Matt. iii. 2.　　[3] Luke xvii. 20.
[4] Luke xvii. 21.　　[5] Præceptoris.

[6] Luke xii. 58, 59.　　[7] Col. i. 13.　　[8] Luke xii. 58.

But the other Evangelist has expressed this same thing thus : " Agree with thine adversary quickly, whiles thou art in the way with him." All the rest is alike : " Lest haply the adversary deliver thee to the judge, and the judge deliver thee to the officer, and thou be cast into prison." [1] Both Evangelists have explained this alike. One said, " Give diligence in the way to be delivered from him ; " the other said, " Agree with him." For thou wilt not be able to " be delivered from him," unless thou " agree with him." Wouldest thou " be delivered from him? Agree with him." But what? is it the devil with whom the Christian ought to " agree " ?

3. Let us then seek out this " adversary," with whom we ought to " agree, lest he deliver us to the judge, and the judge to the officer ; " let us seek him out, " and agree with him." If thou sin, the word of God is thine adversary.[2] For example, it is a delight to thee perchance to be drunken ; it says to thee, " Do it not." It is a delight to thee to frequent the spectacles, and such triflings ; it says to thee, " Do it not." It is a delight to thee to commit adultery ; the word of God saith to thee, " Do it not." In what sins soever thou wouldest do thine own will, it saith to thee, " Do it not." It is the adversary of thy will, till it become the author of thy salvation. O how goodly, how useful an " adversary " ! It does not seek our will, but our advantage. It is our " adversary," as long as we are our own adversaries. As long as thou art thine own enemy, thou hast the word of God thine enemy ; be thine own friend, and thou art in agreement with it. " Thou shalt do no murder ; " give ear, and thou hast " agreed " with it. " Thou shalt not steal ; " give ear, and thou hast " agreed " with it. " Thou shalt not commit adultery ; " give ear, and thou hast " agreed " with it. " Thou shalt not give false witness ; " give ear, and thou hast " agreed " with it. " Thou shalt not covet thy neighbour's wife ; " give ear, and thou hast agreed with it. " Thou shalt not covet thy neighbour's goods ; " [3] give ear, and thou hast " agreed " with it. In all these things thou hast agreed with this " thine adversary," and what hast thou lost to thyself? Not only hast thou lost nothing ; but thou hast even found thyself, who hadst been lost. " The way," is this life ; if we shall " agree with the adversary," if we shall come to terms with him ; when " the way " is ended, we shall not fear the " judge, the officer, the prison."

4. When is " the way " ended? It is not ended at the same hour to all. Each several man hath his hour when he shall end his " way." This life is called " the way ; " when thou hast ended this life, thou hast ended " the way."

We are going on, and the very living is advancing. Unless peradventure ye imagine that time advances, and we stand still ! It cannot be. As time advances, we too advance ; and years do not come to us, but rather go away. Greatly are men mistaken when they say, " This boy has little good sense yet, but years will come on him, and he will be wise." Consider what thou sayest. " Will come on him," thou hast said ; " I will show that they go away," whereas thou sayest, " they come on." And hear how easily I prove it. Let us suppose that we have known the number of his years from his birth ; for instance (that we may wish him well) he has to live fourscore years, he is to arrive at old age. Write down fourscore years. One year he has lived ; how many hast thou in the total? how many hast thou down? Fourscore ! Deduct one. He has lived ten ; seventy remain. He has lived twenty ; sixty remain. Yet surely, it will be said, they did come ; what can this mean? Our years come that they may depart ; they come, I say that they may go. For they do not come, that they may abide with us, but as they pass through us, they wear us out, and make us less and less strong. Such is " the way " into which we have come. What then have we to do with that " adversary," that is, with the word of God? " Agree with him." For thou knowest not when " the way " may be ended. When " the way " is ended, there remain " the judge," and " the officer," and " the prison." But if thou maintain a good will to " thine adversary," and " agree with him ; " instead of a " judge," shalt thou find a father, instead of a cruel " officer," an Angel taking thee away into Abraham's bosom, instead of a " prison," paradise. How rapidly hast thou changed all things " in the way," because thou hast " agreed with thine adversary " !

SERMON LX.

[CX. BEN.]

ON THE WORDS OF THE GOSPEL, LUKE XIII. 6, WHERE WE ARE TOLD OF THE FIG-TREE, WHICH BARE NO FRUIT FOR THREE YEARS ; AND OF THE WOMAN WHICH WAS IN AN INFIRMITY EIGHTEEN YEARS ; AND ON THE WORDS OF THE NINTH PSALM, V. 19, " ARISE, O LORD ; LET NOT MAN PREVAIL : LET THE NATIONS BE JUDGED IN THY SIGHT."

1. TOUCHING " the fig-tree " which had its three years' trial, and bare no fruit, and " the woman which was in an infirmity eighteen years," hearken to what the Lord may grant me to say. The fig-tree is the human race. And the three years are the three times ; one before the Law, the second under the Law, the third under grace. Now there is nothing unsuitable in understanding

---

[1] Matt. v. 25.   [2] Serm. ix. 3. *De decem chordis.*
[3] Exod. xx. 13, etc.

by "the fig-tree" the human race. For when the first man sinned, he covered his nakedness with fig-leaves;[1] covered those members, from which we derive our birth. For what before his sin should have been his glory, after sin became his shame. So before that, "they were naked, and were not ashamed."[2] For they had no reason to blush, when no sin had gone before; nor could they blush for their Creator's works, because they had not yet mingled any evil work of their own with the good works of their Creator. For they had not yet eaten of the tree of knowledge of good and evil, of which they had been forbidden to eat. After then that they had eaten and sinned, the human race sprang from them; that is, man from man, debtor from debtor, mortal from mortal, sinner from sinner. In this "tree" then he entitles those, who through the whole range of time would not bear fruit; and for this cause the axe was hanging over the unfruitful tree. The gardener intercedes for it, punishment is deferred, that help may be administered. Now the gardener who intercedes, is every saint who within the Church prays for those who are without the Church. And what does he pray? "Lord, let it alone this year also;" that is, in this time of grace, spare the sinners, spare the unbelievers, spare the barren, spare the unfruitful. "I will dig about it, and put a basket of dung about it; if it bear fruit, well; but if not, thou shalt come and cut it down."[3] "Thou shalt come:" When? Thou shalt come in judgment, when Thou shalt come to judge the quick and dead. Meanwhile they are spared. But what is the "digging"? What is the "digging about it," but the teaching lowliness and repentance? For a ditch is low ground. The basket of dung understand in its good effects. It is filthy, but it produces fruit. The gardener's filth is the sinner's sorrows. They who repent, repent in filthy robes; if, that is, they understand aright, and repent in truth. To this tree then is it said, "Repent ye, for the kingdom of heaven is at hand."[4]

2. What is that "woman who was in an infirmity eighteen years"? In six days God finished His works. Three times six are eighteen. What the "three years" then in "the tree" signified, that do the "eighteen years" in this woman. She was bent down, she could not look up; because in vain did she hear, "Up with your hearts." But the Lord made her straight. There is hope then, for the children, that is, even until the day of judgment come. Man ascribes much to himself. Yet what is man? A righteous man is something great. But yet a righteous man is righteous only by the grace of God. "For what

is man, save that thou art mindful of him?"[5] Wouldest thou see what man is? "All men are liars."[6] We have chanted, "Arise, Lord; let not man prevail."[7] What is, "let not man prevail"? Were not the Apostles men? Were not Martyrs men? The Lord Jesus Himself, without ceasing to be God, vouchsafed to be Man. What then is, "Arise, Lord; let not man prevail"? If "all men are liars; arise," Truth, "let not" falsehood "prevail." If man then would be anything good, it must not be of anything of his own. For if he should wish to be anything of his own he will be "a liar." If he would wish to be true, he must be so of that which is from God, not of anything of his own.

3. Therefore, "Arise, Lord; let not man prevail." So much did lying prevail before the flood, that after the flood only eight men remained.[8] By them the earth was again replenished with lying men, and out of them was elected the people of God. Many miracles were wrought, divine benefits imparted. They were brought right through to the land of promise, delivered from Egyptian bondage: Prophets were raised up among them, they received the temple, they received the priesthood, they received the anointing, they received the Law. Yet of this very people was it said afterwards, "The strange children have lied unto me."[9] At last He was sent who had been promised afore by the Prophets. "Let not man prevail," even the more, because that God was made Man. But even He, though He did divine works, was despised, though He showed forth so many acts of mercy, He was apprehended, He was scourged, He was hanged. Thus far "did man prevail," to apprehend the Son of God, to scourge the Son of God, to crown the Son of God with thorns, to hang the Son of God upon the tree. So far "did man prevail:" how far, but up to the time that having been taken down from the tree, He was laid in the sepulchre? If He had remained there, man would have "prevailed" indeed. But this prophecy addresses the very Lord Jesus Himself, saying, "Arise, Lord, let not man prevail." O Lord, Thou hast vouchsafed to come in the flesh, the Word made Flesh. The Word above us, the Flesh among us, the Word-flesh[10] between God and Man: Thou didst choose a virgin to be born from according to the flesh, when Thou wast to be conceived, Thou didst find a Virgin; when Thou wast born, Thou didst leave a Virgin. But Thou wast not acknowledged; Thou wast seen, and yet wast hidden. Infirmity was seen, Power was hidden. All this was done, that Thou mightest shed that Blood, which is our Price.

---

[1] Gen. iii. 7.   [2] Gen. ii. 25.   [3] Luke xiii. 8, 9.
[4] Matt. iii. 2.

[5] Ps. viii. 4.   [6] Ps. cxvi. 11.   [7] Ps. ix. 19.
[8] 1 Pet. iii. 20.
[9] Ps. xvii. 45, Sept. (cxliv. 11).
[10] *Conf.* B. x. 67-70 (42, 43).

Thou didst so great miracles, didst give health to the weaknesses of the sick, didst show forth many acts of mercy, and receivedst evil for good. They mocked Thee, Thou didst hang upon the tree; the ungodly wagged their heads before Thee, and said, "If Thou be the Son of God, come down from the cross."[1] Hadst Thou then lost Thy power, or rather wast Thou showing forth Thy Patience? and yet they mocked Thee, and yet they derided Thee, yet, when Thou wast slain, they went away as if victorious. Lo, Thou art laid in the sepulchre: "Arise, Lord, let not man prevail." "Let not" the ungodly enemy "prevail, let not" the blind Jew "prevail." For when Thou wert crucified, the Jew in his blindness seemed to himself to have "prevailed." "Arise, Lord, let not man prevail." It is done, yea, it is done. And now what remains, but that "the nations be judged in thy sight"? For He hath risen again, as ye know, and ascended into heaven; and from thence He shall come to judge the quick and the dead.

4. Ah! unfruitful tree, mock not, because thou art yet spared; the axe is delayed, be not[2] thou secure; He will come and thou shalt be cut down. Believe that He will come. All these things which now ye see, once were not. Once the Christian people were not over the whole world. It was read of in prophecy, not seen in the earth; now it is both read and seen. Thus was the Church herself completed. It was not said to her, "See, O daughter, and hear;" but, "Hear and see."[3] Hear the predictions, see the completions. As then, my beloved Brethren, Christ had once not been born of a Virgin, but His birth was promised, and He was born; He had once not done His miracles, they were promised, and He did them: He had not yet suffered, it was promised, and so it came to pass: He had not risen again, it was foretold, and so fulfilled: His Name was not throughout the world, it was foretold, and so fulfilled: the idols were not destroyed and broken down, it was foretold, and so fulfilled: heretics had not assailed the Church, it was foretold, and so fulfilled. So also the Day of Judgment is not yet, but seeing it hath been foretold, it shall be fulfilled. Can it be that He who in so many things hath shown Himself true, should be false touching the Day of Judgment? He hath given us a bond[4] of His promises. For God hath made Himself a debtor, not by owing ought, that is, not by borrowing; but by promising. We cannot therefore say to Him, "Give back what Thou hast received." Since "who hath first given to Him, and it shall be recompensed unto him again?"[5]

We cannot say to Him, "Give what Thou hast received;" but we say without [6]scruple, "Give what Thou hast promised."

5. For hence it is that we are bold to say, day by day, "Thy kingdom come;"[7] that when His kingdom comes, we too may reign with Him. Which hath been promised to us in these words; "Then will I say unto them, Come, ye blessed of My Father, receive the kingdom prepared for you from the beginning of the world."[8] But assuredly only if we shall have done what follows in that place. "For I was an hungred, and ye gave Me meat," etc. He made these promises to our fathers; but He hath given us a security,[9] for us too to read. If He who hath vouchsafed to give us this security, were to make a reckoning with us and say, "Read my debts, the debts, that is, of my promises, and reckon up what I have already paid, and reckon also what I still owe; see how many I have paid already; and what I owe is but little; will ye for that little that remains, think Me an untrustworthy promiser?" What should we have to answer against this most evident truth? Let him then who is barren repent, and bear "fruit worthy of repentance." He that is bent down, who looks only on the earth, rejoices in earthly happiness, who thinks this the only happy life, where he may be happy, and who believes no other can be; whosoever he be that is so bent down, let him be made straight; if he cannot by himself, let him call upon God. For was that woman made straight by herself? Woe had it been for her, if He had not stretched out His Hand.

SERMON LXI.

[CXI. BEN.]

ON THE WORDS OF THE GOSPEL, LUKE XIII. 21 AND 23, WHERE THE KINGDOM OF GOD IS SAID TO BE "LIKE UNTO LEAVEN, WHICH A WOMAN TOOK AND HID IN THREE MEASURES OF MEAL;" AND OF THAT WHICH IS WRITTEN IN THE SAME CHAPTER, "LORD, ARE THEY FEW THAT ARE SAVED?"

1. "THE three measures of meal"[10] of which the Lord spake, is the human race. Recollect the deluge; three only remained, from whom the rest were to be re-peopled. Noë had three sons, by them was repaired the human race. That holy "woman who hid the leaven," is Wisdom. Lo, the whole world crieth out in the Church of God, "I know that the Lord is great."[11] Yet doubtless there are but few who are saved. Ye remember a question which was lately set before us out of the Gospel, "Lord," it was said, "are there few that be saved?"[12] What said the Lord

---

[1] Matt. xxvii. 40.
[2] A paranomasia not to be preserved in the original, *dilata est securis, noli esse secura.*
[3] Ps. xliv. 11, Sept. (xlv. 10, English version).
[4] *Chirographum.*   [5] Rom. xi. 35.

[6] *Planè.*   [7] Matt. vi. 10.   [8] Matt. xxv. 34.
[9] *Cautionem.*   [10] Luke xiii. 21.   [11] Ps. cxxxv. 5.
[12] Luke xiii. 23.

to this? He did not say, "Not few, but many are they who are saved." He did not say this. But what said He, when He had heard, "Are there few that be saved? Strive to enter by the strait gate."[1] When thou hearest then, "Are there few that be saved?" the Lord confirmed what He heard. Through the "strait gate" but "few" can "enter." In another place He saith Himself, "Strait and narrow is the way which leadeth unto life, and few there be that go thereby: but broad and spacious is the way that leadeth to destruction, and many there be which walk thereby."[2] Why rejoice we in great numbers? Give ear to me, ye "few." I know that ye are "many," who hear me, yet but "few" of you hear to obey. I see the floor, I look for the corn. And hardly is the corn seen, when the floor is being threshed; but the time is coming, that it shall be winnowed. But few then are saved in comparison of the many that shall perish. For these same "few" will constitute in themselves a great mass. When the Winnower shall come with His fan in His Hand, "He will cleanse His floor, and lay up the wheat into the garner; but the chaff He will burn with unquenchable fire."[3] Let not the chaff scoff at the wheat; in this He speaketh truth, and deceiveth no one. Be ye then in yourselves among many a many, few though ye be in comparison of a certain many. So large a mass is to come out of this floor, as to fill the garner of heaven. For the Lord Christ would not contradict Himself, who hath said, "Many there are who enter in by the narrow gate, many who go to ruin through the wide gate;" contradict Himself, who hath in another place said, "Many shall come from the East and West."[4] "Many" then are the "few;" both "few" and "many." Are the "few" one sort, and the "many" another? No. But the "few" are themselves the "many;" "few" in comparison of the lost, "many" in the society of the Angels. Hearken, dearly Beloved. The Apocalypse hath this written; "After this I beheld of all languages, and nations, and tribes, a great multitude, which no man can number, coming with white robes and palms."[5] This is the mass of the saints. With how much clearer voice will the floor say, when it has been fanned, separated from the crowd of ungodly, and evil, and false Christians, when those who "press" and do not "touch" (for a certain woman in the Gospel "touched," the crowd "pressed" Christ), shall have been severed unto everlasting fire; when all they then, who are to be damned shall have been separated off, with how great assurance will the purified mass, standing at the Right Hand, fearing now for itself the admixture of no evil men, nor the loss of any of the good,

now about to reign with Christ, say, "I know that the Lord is great"![6]

2. If then, my Brethren (I am speaking to the corn), if they acknowledge what I say, predestined unto life eternal, let them speak by their works, not by their voices. I am constrained to speak to you, what I ought not. For I ought to find in you matter of praise, not to seek subjects for admonition. Yet see I will say but a few words, I will not dwell upon it. Acknowledge the duty of hospitality, thereby some have attained unto God. Thou takest in some stranger, whose companion in the way thou thyself also art; for strangers are we all. He is a Christian who, even in his own house and in his own country, acknowledges himself to be a stranger. For our country is above, there we shall not be strangers. For every one here below, even in his own house, is a stranger. If he be not a stranger, let him not pass on from hence. If pass on he must, he is a stranger. Let him not deceive himself, a stranger he is; whether he will or not, he is a stranger. And he leaves that house to his children, one stranger to other strangers. Why? If thou wert at an inn, wouldest thou not depart when another comes? The same thou doest even in thine own house. Thy father left a place to thee, thou wilt some day leave it to thy children. Neither dost thou abide here, as one who is to abide always, nor to those who are so to abide, wilt thou leave it. If we are all passing away, let us do something which cannot pass away, that when we shall have passed away, and have come thither whence we may not pass away, we may find our good works there. Christ is the keeper, why dost thou fear lest thou shouldest lose what thou spendest on the poor? "Let us turn to the Lord," etc.

And after the Sermon.

I suggest to you, Beloved, what ye know already. To-morrow breaks the anniversary day of the venerable[7] lord Aurelius' ordination; he asks and admonishes you, dear Brethren, by my humble ministry, that ye would be so good[8] as to meet together with all devotion at the basilica of Faustus. Thanks be to God.

SERMON LXII.

[CXII. BEN.]

ON THE WORDS OF THE GOSPEL, LUKE XIV. 16, "A CERTAIN MAN MADE A GREAT SUPPER," ETC.

Delivered in the basilica Restituta.[9]

1. Holy lessons have been set forth before us, to which we should both give ear, and upon which by the Lord's help I would deliver some

---

[1] Luke xiii. 24.   [2] Matt. vii. 13, 14.   [3] Luke iii. 17.
[4] Matt. viii. 11.   [5] Rev. vii. 9.
[6] Ps. cxxxv. 5.   [7] Senis.   [8] Dignemini.
[9] See Serm. xl. (xc. Ben.).

observations. In the Apostolic lesson thanks are rendered unto the Lord for the faith of the Gentiles, of course, because it was His work. In the Psalm we have said, "O God of hosts, turn us, and show us Thy Face, and we shall be saved." [1] In the Gospel we have been called to a supper; yea, rather others have been called, we not called, but led; not only led, but even forced. For so have we heard, that "a certain Man made a great supper." [2] Who is this Man, but, "the Mediator between God and men, the Man Christ Jesus"? [3] He sent that those who had been invited might come, for the hour was now come, that they should come. Who are they who had been invited, but those who had been called by the Prophets who were sent before? When? Of old, ever since the Prophets were sent, they invited to Christ's supper. They were sent then to the people of Israel. Often were they sent, often did they call men, to come at the hour of supper. But they received those who invited them, refused the supper. What means "they received those who invited them, refused the supper"? They read the Prophets and killed Christ. But when they killed Him, then though they knew it not, they prepared a Supper for us. When the Supper was now prepared, when Christ had been offered up, when the Supper of the Lord, which the faithful know, had been set forth after the resurrection of Christ, and established by His Hands and Mouth, were the Apostles sent to them, to whom the Prophets had been sent before. "Come ye to the supper."

2. They who would not come made excuses. And how did they excuse themselves? There were three excuses: "One said, I have bought a farm,[4] and I go to see it; have me excused. Another said, I have bought five pairs of oxen, and I go to prove them; I pray thee have me excused. A third said, I have married a wife, have me excused; I cannot come." [5] Do we suppose that these are not the excuses, which hinder all men, who decline to come to this supper? Let us look into them, discuss, find them out; but only that we may beware. In the purchase of the farm, the spirit of domination is marked out; therefore pride is rebuked. For men are delighted to have a farm, to hold, to possess it, to have men in it under them, to have dominion. An evil vice, the first vice. For the first man wished to have dominion, in that he would not that any should have dominion over him. What is to have dominion, but to take pleasure in one's own power? There is a greater power, let us submit ourselves to it, that we may be able to be safe. "I have bought a farm, have me excused." Having discovered pride, he would not come.

3. "Another said, I have bought five pairs of oxen." Would it not have been enough, "I have bought oxen"? Something beyond doubt there is, which by its very obscurity challenges us to seek out, and understand; and in that it is shut, He exhorteth us to knock. The five pairs of oxen are the senses of this body. There are numbered five senses of this body, as is known to all; and they who, it may be, do not consider it, will doubtless perceive it on being reminded of it. There are then found to be five senses of this body. In the eyes is the sight, the hearing in the ears, the smell in the nose, the taste in the mouth, the touch in all the members. We have perception of white and black, and things coloured in whatever way, light and dark, by the sight. Harsh and musical sounds, we have perception of by the hearing. Of sweet and offensive smells, we have perception by the smell. Of things sweet and bitter by the taste. Of things hard and soft, smooth and rough, warm and cold, heavy and light, by the touch. They are five, and they are pairs. Now that they are pairs, is seen most easily in the case of the three first senses. There are two eyes, two ears, two nostrils; see three pairs. In the mouth, that is in the sense of taste, a certain doubling is found, because nothing affects the taste, unless it is touched by the tongue and the palate. The pleasure of the flesh which pertains to the touch, has this doubling in a less obvious way. For there is both an outer and an inner touch. And so it too is double. Why are they called pairs of oxen? Because by these senses of the body, earthly things are sought for. For oxen turn up the earth. So there are men far off from faith, given up to earthly things, occupied in the things of the flesh; who will not believe anything but what they attain to by the five senses of their body. In those five senses do they lay down for themselves the rules of their whole will. "I will not believe," says one, "anything but what I see. See, here is what I know, and am sure of. Such a thing is white, or black, or round, or square, or coloured so and so; this I know, am sensible of, have a hold of; nature itself teaches it me. I am not forced to believe what you cannot show me. Or it is a voice: I perceive that it is a voice; it sings well, it sings ill, it is sweet, it is harsh. I know, I know this, it has come to me. There is a good or a bad smell: I know, I perceive it. This is sweet, this is bitter; this is salt, this insipid. I know not what you would tell me more. By the touch I know what is hard, what is soft; what is smooth, what is rough; what is warm, and what cold. What more would you show me?"

4. By such an impediment was our Apostle Thomas held back, who as to the Lord Christ, the resurrection that is of Christ, would not

---

[1] Ps. lxxx. 7.   [2] Luke xiv. 16.   [3] 1 Tim. ii. 5.
[4] *Villam*, Vulgate.   [5] Luke xiv. 18-20.

believe even his own eyes only. "Unless," says he, "I put my fingers into the places of the nails and wounds, and unless I put my hand into His side, I will not believe." [1] And the Lord who could have risen again without any vestige of a wound, kept the scars, that they might be touched by the doubting Apostle, and the wounds of his heart be healed. And yet as designing to call to His supper others, against the excuse of "the five pairs of oxen," He said, "Blessed they who do not see, and believe." [2] We, my Brethren, who have been called to this supper, have not been kept back by "these five pairs." For we have not in this age desired to see the Face of the Lord's Body, nor have we longed to hear the Voice proceeding out of the mouth of that Body; we have not sought in Him for any passing [3] odour. A certain "woman anointed Him with most costly ointment," that "house was filled with the odour;" [4] but we were not there; lo, we did not smell, yet we believe. He gave to the disciples the Supper consecrated by His Own Hands; but we did not sit down at that Feast, and yet we daily eat this same Supper by faith. And do not think it strange that in that supper which He gave with His Own Hand, one was present without faith: the faith that appeared afterwards was more than a compensation for that faithlessness then. Paul was not there who believed, Judas was there who betrayed. How many now too in this same Supper, though they saw not then that table, nor beheld with their eyes, nor tasted with their mouths, the bread which the Lord took in His Hands, yet because it is the same as is now prepared, how many now also in this same Supper, "eat and drink judgment to themselves"? [5]

5. But whence arose an occasion, so to say, to the Lord, to speak of this supper? One of them that sat at meat with Him (for He was at a feast, whither He had been invited), had said, "Blessed are they who eat bread in the kingdom of God." [6] He sighed as though after distant things, and the Bread Himself was sitting down before him. Who is the Bread of the kingdom of God, but He who saith, "I am the Living Bread which came down from heaven"? [7] Do not get thy mouth ready, but thine heart. On this occasion it was that the parable of this supper was set forth. Lo, we believe in Christ, we receive Him with faith. In receiving Him we know what to think of. We receive but little, and we are nourished in heart. It is not then what is seen, but what is believed, that feeds us. Therefore we too have not sought for that outward sense; nor have we said, "Let them believe who have seen with their eyes, and handled

with their hands the Lord Himself after His resurrection, if what is said be true; we do not touch Him, why should we believe?" If we were to entertain such thoughts, we should be kept back from the supper by those "five pairs of oxen." That ye may know, Brethren, that not the gratification of these five senses, which softens and ministers pleasure, but a kind of curiosity was denoted, He did not say, "'I have bought five pairs of oxen,' and I go to feed them;" but, "I go to prove them." He who wishes to "prove" by "the pairs of oxen," does not wish to be in doubt, just as St. Thomas by these "pairs" did not wish to be in doubt. "Let me see, let me touch, let me put in my fingers." "'Behold,' saith the Lord, 'put in thy fingers along My Side, and be not unbelieving.' [8] For thy sake have I been slain; at the place which thou wishest to touch, have I shed My Blood, that I might redeem thee; and dost thou still doubt of Me, unless thou touch Me? Behold, this too I grant; behold, this too I show thee; touch, and believe; find out the place of My wound, heal the wound of thy doubting."

6. "The third said, I have married a wife." This is the pleasure of the flesh, which is a hindrance to many: and I would that it were so only without, and not within! There are men who say, "There is no happiness for a man, if he have not the pleasures of the flesh." These are they whom the Apostle censures, saying, "'Let us eat and drink, for to-morrow we shall die.' [9] Who hath risen to this life from the other? Who hath ever told us what goes on there? We take away with us, what in the time present makes our happiness." He that speaks thus, "has married a wife," attaches himself to the flesh, places his delight in the pleasures of the flesh, excuses himself from the supper; let him look well to it that he die not by an inward famine. Attend to John, the holy Apostle and Evangelist; "Love not the world, neither the things that are in the world." [10] O ye who come to the Supper of the Lord, "Love not the world, neither the things that are in the world." He did not say, "Have not;" but, "Love not." Thou hast had, possessed, loved. The love of earthly things, is the bird-lime of the spirit's wings. Lo, thou hast desired, thou hast stuck fast. "Who will give thee wings as of a dove?" [11] When wilt thou fly, whither thou mayest in deed, seeing thou hast perversely wished to rest here, where thou hast to thy hurt stuck fast? "Love not the world," is the divine trumpet. By the voice of this trumpet unceasingly is it proclaimed to the compass of the earth, and to the whole world, "Love not the world, neither the things that are in the world.

---

[1] John xx. 25. [2] John xx. 29. [3] *Temporalem.*
[4] John xii. 3. [5] 1 Cor. xi. 29. [6] Luke xiv. 15.
[7] John vi. 51.

[8] John xx. 27. [9] 1 Cor. xv. 32. [10] 1 John ii. 15.
[11] Ps. liv. 7, Sept. (lv. 6, English version).

Whosoever loveth the world, the love of the Father is not in him. For all that is in the world, is the lust of the flesh, and the lust of the eyes, and the ambition of life." [1] He begins at the last with which the Gospel ends. He begins at that, at which the Gospel made an end. "The lust of the flesh, I have married a wife. The lust of the eyes, I have bought five pairs of oxen. The ambition of life, I have bought a farm."

7. Now these senses are denoted by the mention of the eyes only, the whole by a part, because the pre-eminence in the five senses belongs to the eyes. Wherefore though sight belongs peculiarly to the eyes, we are accustomed to use the word "seeing" through all the five senses. How? In the first place, in relation to the eyes themselves we say; "See how white it is, look and see how white it is:" this has relation to the eyes. Hear and see how musical it is! Could we say conversely, "Hear and see how white it is"? This expression, "see," runs through all the senses; whereas the distinguishing expression [2] of the other senses does not in its turn run through it. "Mark and see how musical; smell and see how agreeable it is; taste and see how sweet it is; touch and see how soft it is." And yet surely since they are senses, we should rather say thus; "Hear and be sensible how musical it is; smell and be sensible how agreeable it is; taste and be sensible how sweet it is; touch and be sensible how hot it is; handle and be sensible how smooth it is; handle and be sensible how soft it is." But we say none of these. For thus the Lord Himself after His resurrection, when He appeared to His disciples, and when though they saw Him they still wavered in faith, supposing that they saw a spirit, said, "Why do ye doubt, and why do thoughts arise in your hearts? See My Hands and My Feet." It is not enough to say, "See;" He saith, "Touch, and handle, and see." [3] "Look and see, handle and see; with the eyes alone see, and see by all the senses." Because He was looking for the inner sense of faith, He offered Himself to the outward senses of the body. We have made no attainment [4] in the Lord by these outward senses, we have heard with our ears, have believed with our heart; and this hearing not from His mouth, but from the mouth of His preachers, from their mouths who were already at the supper, and who by the pouring forth of what they there drunk in invited us.

8. Let us away then with vain and evil excuses, and come we to the supper by which we may be made fat within. Let not the puffing up of pride keep us back, let it not lift us up, nor unlawful curiosity scare us, and turn us away from

God; let not the pleasure of the flesh hinder us from the pleasure of the heart. Let us come, and be filled. And who came but the beggars, the "maimed," the "halt," the "blind"? But there came not thither the rich, and the whole, who walked, as they thought, well, and saw acutely; who had great confidence in themselves, and were therefore in the more desperate case, in proportion as they were more proud. Let the beggars come, for He inviteth them, "who, though He was rich, for our sakes became poor, that we beggars through His poverty might be enriched." [5] Let the maimed come, "for they that are whole need not a physician, but they that are in evil case." [6] Let the halt come who may say to Him, "Set in order my steps in Thy paths." [7] Let the blind come who may say, "Enlighten mine eyes, that I may never sleep in death." [8] Such as these came at the hour, when those who had been first invited, had been rejected for their own excuses: they came at the hour, they entered in from the streets and lanes of the city. And the servant "who had been sent," brought answer, "Lord, it is done as Thou hast commanded, and yet there is room." "Go out," saith He, "into the highways and hedges, and compel those whom thou shalt find to come in." [9] Whom thou shalt find wait not till they choose to come, compel them to come in. I have prepared a great supper, a great house, I cannot suffer any place to be vacant in it. The Gentiles came from the streets and lanes: let the heretics come from the hedges, here they shall find peace. For those who make hedges, their object is to make divisions. Let them be drawn away from the hedges, let them be plucked up from among the thorns. They have stuck fast in the hedges, they are unwilling to be compelled. [10] Let us come in, they say, of our own good will. This is not the Lord's order, "Compel them," saith he, "to come in." Let compulsion be found outside, the will will arise within.

SERMON LXIII.

[CXIII. BEN.]

ON THE WORDS OF THE GOSPEL, LUKE XVI. 9, "MAKE TO YOURSELVES FRIENDS BY MEANS OF THE MAMMON OF UNRIGHTEOUSNESS," ETC.

1. OUR duty is to give to others the admonitions we have received ourselves. The recent lesson of the Gospel has admonished us to make friends of the mammon of iniquity, that they too may "receive" those who do so "into everlasting habitations." But who are they that shall have

---

[1] 1 John ii. 15, 16, Vulgate. [2] *Proprietas.*
[3] Luke xxiv. 38, 39. [4] *Carpsimus.*

[5] 2 Cor. viii. 9. [6] Matt. ix. 12, Vulgate. [7] Ps. xvii. 5.
[8] Ps. xiii. 3. [9] Luke xiv. 22, 23.
[10] This alludes to the laws made against the Donatists by the Christian Emperors. See St. Augustin's Epis. 195, and especially § 24.

everlasting habitations, but the Saints of God? And who are they who are to be received by them into everlasting habitations, but they who serve their need, and minister cheerfully to their necessities? Accordingly let us remember, that in the last judgment the Lord will say to those who shall stand on His right hand, " I was an hungred, and ye gave Me meat ; " and the rest which ye know. And upon their enquiring when they had afforded these good offices to Him, He answered, " When ye did it to one of the least of Mine, ye did it unto Me." [1] These least are they who receive into everlasting habitations. This He said to them on the right hand, because they did so : and the contrary He said to them on the left, because they would not. But what have they on the right hand who did so, received, or rather, what are they to receive? " Come," says He, " ye blessed of My Father, possess the kingdom prepared for you from the foundation of the world. For I was an hungred, and ye gave Me meat. When ye did it to one of the least of Mine, ye did it unto Me." [2] Who then are these least ones of Christ? They are those who have left all they had, and followed Him, and have distributed whatever they had to the poor ; that unencumbered and without any worldly fetter they might serve God, and might lift their shoulders free from the burdens of the world, and winged as it were aloft. These are the least. And why the least? Because lowly, because not puffed up, not proud. Yet weigh them in the scales, these least ones, and thou wilt find them a heavy weight.

2. But what means it, that He says they are " friends of the mammon of iniquity "? What is " the mammon of iniquity "? First, what is " mammon "? For it is not a Latin word. It is a Hebrew word, and cognate to the Punic language. For these languages are allied to one another by a kind of nearness of signification. What the Punics call mammon, is called in Latin, " lucre " [3] What the Hebrews call mammon, is called in Latin, " riches." That we may express the whole then in Latin, our Lord Jesus Christ says this, " Make to yourselves friends of the riches of iniquity." Some, by a bad understanding of this, plunder the goods of others, and bestow some of that upon the poor, and so think that they do what is enjoined them. For they say, " To plunder the goods of others, is the mammon of iniquity ; to spend some of it, especially on the poor saints, this is to make friends with the mammon of iniquity. This understanding of it must be corrected, yea, must be utterly effaced from the tablets of your heart. I would not that ye should so understand it. Give alms of your righteous labours : give out of that which

ye possess rightfully. For ye cannot corrupt Christ your Judge, that He should not hear you together with the poor, from whom ye take away. For if thou wert to despoil any one who was weak, thyself being stronger and of greater power, and he were to come with thee to the judge, any man you please on this earth, who had any power of judging, and he were to wish to plead his cause with thee ; if thou wert to give anything of the spoil and plunder of that poor man to the judge, that he might pronounce judgment in thy favour ; would that judge please even thee ? True, he has pronounced judgment in thy favour, and yet so great is the force of justice, that he would displease even thee. Do not then represent God to thyself as such an one as this. Do not set up such an idol in the temple of thine heart. Thy God is not such as thou oughtest not to be thyself. If thou wouldest not judge so, but wouldest judge justly ; even so thy God is better than thou : He is not inferior to thee : He is more just, He is the fountain of justice. Whatsoever good thou hast done, thou hast gotten from Him ; and whatsoever good thou hast given vent to,[4] thou hast drunk in from Him. Dost thou praise the vessel, because it hath something from Him, and blame the fountain? Do not give alms out of usury and increase. I am speaking to the faithful, am speaking to those to whom we distribute the body of Christ. Be in fear and amend yourselves : that I may not have hereafter to say, Thou doest so, and thou too doest so. Yet I trow, that if I should do so, ye ought not to be angry with me, but with yourselves, that ye may amend yourselves. For this is the meaning of the expression in the Psalm, " Be ye angry, and sin not." [5] I would have you be angry, but only that ye may not sin. Now in order that ye may not sin, with whom ought ye to be angry but with yourselves? For what is a penitent man, but a man who is angry with himself ? That he may obtain pardon, he exacts punishment from himself ; and so with good right says to God, " Turn Thine eyes from my sins, for I acknowledge my sin." [6] If thou acknowledgest it, then He will pardon it. Ye then who have done so wrongly, do so no more : it is not lawful.

3. But if ye have done so already, and have such money in your possession, and have filled your coffers thereby, and were heaping up treasure by these means : what ye have comes of evil, now then add not evil to it, and make to yourselves friends of the mammon of iniquity. Had Zacchæus what he had from good sources? [7] Read and see. He was the chief of the publicans, that is, he was one to whom the public taxes were paid in : by this he had his wealth.

---

[1] Matt. xxv. 35, etc.　　[2] Matt. xxv. 40.　　[3] *Lucrum.*

[4] *Eructuasti.*　　[5] Ps. iv. 4, Sept.　　[6] Ps. li. 9.
[7] Luke xix. 2, etc.

He had oppressed many, had taken from many, and so had heaped much together. Christ entered into his house, and salvation came upon his house ; for so said the Lord Himself, "This day is salvation come to this house."[1] Now mark the method of this salvation. First he was longing to see the Lord, because he was little in stature : but when the crowd hindered him, he got up into a sycamore tree, and saw Him as He passed by. But Jesus saw him, and said, "Zacchæus, come down, I must abide at thy house." Thou art hanging there, but I will not keep thee in suspense. I will not, that is, put thee off. Thou didst wish to see Me as I passed by, to-day shalt thou find Me dwelling at thy house. So the Lord went in unto him, and he, filled with joy, said, "The half of my goods I give to the poor." Lo, how swiftly he runs, who runs to make friends of the mammon of iniquity. And lest he should be held guilty on any other account, he said, "If I have taken anything from any man, I" will "restore fourfold." He inflicted sentence of condemnation on himself, that he might not incur damnation. So then, ye who have anything from evil sources, do good therewith. Ye who have not, wish not to acquire by evil means. Be thou good thyself, who doest good with what is evilly acquired : and when with this evil thou beginnest to do any good, do not remain evil thyself. Thy money is being converted to good, and dost thou thyself continue evil ?

4. There is indeed another way of understanding it ; and I will not withhold it too. The mammon of iniquity is all the riches of this world, from whatever source they come. For howsoever they be heaped together, they are the mammon of iniquity, that is, the riches of iniquity. What is, "they are the riches of iniquity"? It is money which iniquity calls by the name of riches. For if we seek for the true riches, they are different from these. In these Job abounded, naked as he was, when he had a heart full to Godward, and poured out praises like most costly gems to his God, when he had lost all he had.[2] And from what treasure did he this, if he had nothing? These then are the true riches. But the other sort are called riches by iniquity. Thou dost possess these riches. I blame it not : an inheritance has come to thee, thy father was rich, and he left it to thee. Or thou hast honestly acquired them : thou hast a house full of the fruit of just labour ; I blame it not. Yet even thus do not call them riches. For if thou dost call them riches, thou wilt love them : and if thou love them, thou wilt perish with them. Lose, that thou be not lost : give, that thou mayest gain : sow, that thou mayest reap. Call

not these riches, for "the true" they are not. They are full of poverty, and liable ever to accidents. What sort of riches are those, for whose sake thou art afraid of the robber, for whose sake thou art afraid of thine own servant, lest he should kill thee, and take them away, and fly? If they were true riches, they would give thee security.

5. So then those are the true riches, which when we have them, we cannot lose. And lest haply thou shouldest fear a thief because of them, they will be there where none can take them away. Hear thy Lord, "Lay up for yourselves treasures in heaven, where no thief approacheth."[3] Then will they be riches, when thou hast removed them hence. As long as they are in the earth, they are not riches. But the world calls them riches, iniquity calls them so. God calls them therefore the mammon of iniquity, because iniquity calls them riches. Hear the Psalm, "O Lord, deliver me out of the hand of strange children, whose mouth hath spoken vanity, and their right hand is a right hand of iniquity. Whose sons are as new plants, firmly rooted from their youth. Their daughters decked out, adorned round about after the similitude of a temple. Their storehouses full, flowing out from this into that. Their oxen fat, their sheep fruitful, multiplying in their goings forth. There is no breach of wall, nor going forth, no crying out in their streets."[4] Lo, what sort of happiness the Psalmist has described : but hear what is the case with them whom he has set forth as children of iniquity. "Whose mouth hath spoken vanity, and their right hand is a right hand of iniquity." Thus has he set them forth, and said that their happiness is only upon the earth. And what did he add? "They are happy the people that hath these things." But who called them so? "Strange children," aliens from the race, and belonging not to the seed of Abraham : they "called the people happy that hath these things." Who called them so? "They whose mouth hath spoken vanity." It is a vain thing then to call them happy who have these things. And yet they are called so by them, "whose mouth hath spoken vanity." By them the "mammon of iniquity" of the Gospel is called riches.

6. But what sayest thou? Seeing that these "strange children" that they "whose mouth hath spoken vanity," have "called the people happy that hath these things," what sayest thou? These are false riches, show me the true. Thou findest fault with these, show me what thou praisest. Thou wishest me to despise these, show me what to prefer. Let the Psalmist

---

[1] Luke xix. 9. [2] Job i. 21. [3] Matt. vi. 20; Luke xii. 33. [4] Ps. cxliv. 11, etc., Sept.

speak himself. For he who said, "they called the people happy that hath these things," gives us such an answer, as if we had said to him, that is, to the Psalmist[1] himself, "Lo, this thou hast taken away from us, and nothing hast thou given us: lo, these, lo, these we despise; whereby shall we live, whereby shall we be happy? For they who have spoken, they will undertake to answer[2] for themselves. For they have 'called' men 'who have' riches 'happy.' But what sayest thou?" As if he had been thus questioned, he makes answer and says, They call the rich happy: but I say, "Happy are the people whose is the Lord their God." Thus then thou hast heard of the true riches, make friends of the mammon of iniquity, and thou shalt be "a happy people, whose is the Lord their God." At times we go along the way, and see very pleasant and productive estates, and we say, "Whose estate is that?" We are told, "such a man's;" and we say, "Happy man!" We "speak vanity." Happy he whose is that house, happy he whose that estate, happy he whose that flock, happy he whose that servant, happy he whose is that household. Take away vanity if Thou wouldest hear the truth. "Happy he whose is the Lord" his "God." For not he who has that estate is happy: but he whose is that "God." But in order to declare most plainly the happiness of possessions, thou sayest that thy estate has made thee happy. And why? Because thou livest by it. For when thou dost highly praise thine estate, thou sayest thus, "It finds me food, I live by it." Consider whereby thou dost really live. He by whom thou livest, is He to whom thou sayest, "With Thee is the fountain of life."[3] "Happy is the people whose God is the Lord." O Lord my God, O Lord our God, make us happy by Thee, that we may come unto Thee. We wish not to be happy from gold, or silver, or land, from these earthly, and most vain, and transitory goods of this perishable life. Let not "our mouth speak vanity." Make us happy by Thee, seeing that we shall never lose Thee. When we shall once have gotten Thee, we shall neither lose Thee, nor be lost ourselves. Make us happy by Thee, because "Happy is the people whose is the Lord their God." Nor will God be angry if we shall say of Him, He is our estate. For we read, that "the Lord is the portion of my inheritance."[4] Grand thing, Brethren, we are both His inheritance, and He is ours, seeing that we both cultivate His service,[5] and He cultivateth us.[6] It is no derogation[7] to His honour that He cultivateth us. Because if we cultivate Him as our God, He cultivateth us as His field. And, (that ye may know that He doth cultivate us) hear Him whom He hath sent to us: "I," saith He, "am the vine, ye are the branches, My Father is the Husbandman."[8] Therefore He doth cultivate us. But if we yield fruit, He prepares for us His garner. But if under the attention of so great a hand we will be barren, and for good fruit[9] bring forth thorns, I am loth to say what follows.[10] Let us make an end with a theme of joy. "Let us turn then to the Lord," etc.

SERMON LXIV.

[CXIV. BEN.]

ON THE WORDS OF THE GOSPEL, LUKE XVII. 3, "IF THY BROTHER SIN, REBUKE HIM," ETC., TOUCHING THE REMISSION OF SINS.

Delivered at the Table of St. Cyprian, in the presence of Count Boniface.

1. THE Holy Gospel which we heard just now as it was being read, has admonished touching the remission of sins. And on this subject must ye be admonished now by my discourse. For we are ministers of the word, not our own word, but the word of our God and Lord, whom no one serves without glory, whom no one despises without punishment. He then the Lord our God, who abiding with the Father made us, and having been made for us, re-made us, He the Lord our God Jesus Christ Himself says to us what we have heard just now in the Gospel. "If," He saith, "thy brother shall sin against thee, rebuke him, and if he shall repent, forgive him; and if he shall sin against thee seven times in a day, and shall come and say, I repent, forgive him."[11] He would not have "seven times in a day" otherwise understood than "as often as may be," lest haply he sin eight times, and thou be unwilling to forgive. What then is "seven times"? Always, as often as he shall sin and repent. For this, "Seven times in a day will I praise thee,"[12] is the same as in another Psalm, "His praise shall always be in my mouth."[13] And there is the strongest reason why seven times should be put for that which is always: for the whole course of time revolves in a circle of seven coming and returning days.

2. Whosoever then thou art that hast thy thoughts on Christ, and desirest to receive what He hath promised, be not slow to do that which He hath enjoined. Now what hath He promised? "Eternal life." And what hath He enjoined? That pardon be given to thy brother. As if He had said to thee, "Do thou, O man, give pardon to a man, that I, who am God, may

---

[1] *Psalmo.*   [2] *Recipient.*   [3] Ps. xxxvi. 9.
[4] Ps. xvi. 5.   [5] *Colimus.*
[6] *Colit. Quia et colimus eum, et colit nos. Vide* Serm. xlvii., **xxix.**, xxvii., ii.; *Conf.* B. xiii. 1.
[7] *Injuria.*

[8] John xv. 1.   [9] *Frumento.*   [10] See John xv. 2 and 6.
[11] Luke xvii. 4.   [12] Ps. cxix. 164.   [13] Ps. xxxiv. 1.

come unto thee." But that I may pass over, or rather pass by for a while, those more exalted divine promises in which our Creator engages to make us equal with His Angels, that we may with Him, and in Him, and by Him, live without end; not to speak of this just now, dost thou not wish to receive of thy God this very thing, which thou art commanded to give thy brother? This very thing, I say, which thou art commanded to give thy brother, dost thou not wish to receive from thy Lord? Tell me if thou wishest it not; and so give it not. What is this, but that thou shouldest forgive him that asks thee, if thou require to be forgiven? But if thou have nothing to be forgiven thee, I dare to say, be unwilling to forgive. Though I ought not even to say this. Though thou have nothing to be forgiven thee, forgive.

3. Thou art just on the point of saying to me, " But I am not God, I am a man, a sinner." God be thanked that thou dost confess thou hast sins. Forgive then, that they may be forgiven thee. Yet the Lord Himself our God exhorteth us to imitate Him. In the first place God Himself, Christ, exhorteth us, of whom the Apostle Peter said, " Christ hath suffered for us, leaving you an example that ye should follow His steps, who did no sin, neither was guile found in His mouth."[1] He then verily had no sin, yet did He die for our sins, and shed His Blood for the remission of sins. He took upon Him for our sakes what was not His due, that He might deliver us from what was due to us. Death was not due to Him, nor life to us. Why? Because we were sinners. Death was not due to Him, nor life to us; He received what was not due to Him, He gave what was not due to us. But since we are speaking of the remission of sins, lest ye should think it too high a thing to imitate Christ, hear the Apostle saying, " Forgiving one another, even as God in Christ hath forgiven you."[2] " Be ye therefore imitators of God." They are the Apostle's words, not mine. Is it indeed a proud thing to imitate God? Hear the Apostle, " Be ye imitators of God as dearly beloved children."[3] Thou art called a child: if thou refuse to imitate Him, why seekest thou His inheritance?

4. This would I say even if thou hadst no sin which thou mightest desire to be forgiven thee. But as it is, whosoever thou art, thou art a man; though thou be righteous, thou art a man; be thou layman, or monk, or clerk, or Bishop, or Apostle, thou art a man. Hear the Apostle's voice, " If we shall say that we have no sin, we deceive ourselves."[4] He, that famous John, and an Evangelist, he whom the Lord Christ loved beyond all the rest, who lay on His breast, he says, " If we shall say." He did not say, " If ye shall say that ye have no sin," but " if we shall say that we have no sin, we deceive ourselves, and the truth is not in us." He joined himself in the guilt, that he might be joined in the pardon also. " If we shall say." Consider who it is that says, " If we shall say that we have no sin, we deceive ourselves, and the truth is not in us. But if we shall confess our sins, He is faithful and just to forgive us our sins, and to cleanse us from all iniquity."[5] How does He cleanse? By forgiving, not as though He found nothing to punish, but as finding something to forgive. So then, Brethren, if we have sins, let us forgive them that ask us. Let us not retain enmities in our heart against another. For the retaining of enmities more than anything corrupts this heart of ours.

5. I would then that thou shouldest forgive, seeing that I find thee asking forgiveness. Thou art asked, forgive: thou art asked, and thou wilt ask thyself; thou art asked, forgive; thou wilt ask to be forgiven; for, lo, the time of prayer will come: I have thee fast in the words thou wilt have to speak. Thou wilt say, " Our Father, which art in heaven." For thou wilt not be in the number of children, if thou shalt not say, " Our Father." So then thou wilt say, " Our Father, which art in heaven." Follow on; " Hallowed be Thy Name." Say on, " Thy kingdom come." Follow still on, " Thy will be done, as in heaven, so in earth." See what thou addest next, " Give us this day our daily bread."[6] Where are thy riches? So thou art a beggar. Nevertheless in the mean while (it is the point I am speaking of), say what is next after, " Give us this day our daily bread." Say what follows this: " Forgive us our debts." Now thou hast come to my words, " Forgive us our debts." By what right? by what covenant? on what condition? on what express stipulation? " As we also forgive our debtors." It is but a small thing that thou dost not forgive; yea thou dost more, thou liest unto God. The condition is laid down, the law fixed. " Forgive as I forgive." Therefore He does not forgive, unless thou forgivest. " Forgive as I forgive." Thou wishest to be forgiven when thou askest, forgive him that asks of thee. He that is skilled in heaven's laws[7] has dictated these prayers: He does not deceive thee; ask according to the tenor of His heavenly voice: say, " Forgive us, as we also forgive," and do what thou sayest. He that lies in his prayers, loses the benefit he seeks: he that lies in his prayers, both loses his cause, and finds his punishment. And if any one lies to the emperor, he is convicted of his lie at his coming: but when thou liest in prayer, thou by thy

---

[1] 1 Pet. ii. 21, 22. [2] Col. iii. 13; Eph. iv. 32.
[3] Eph. v. 1. [4] 1 John i. 8.

[5] 1 John i. 9. [6] Matt. vi. 9, etc. [7] *Jurisperitus.*

very prayer art convicted. For God does not seek for witness as regards thee to convict thee. He who dictated the prayers to thee, is thine Advocate : if thou liest, He is a witness against thee : if thou dost not amend thyself, He will be thy Judge. So then both say it, and do. For if thou say it not, thou wilt not obtain making thy requests contrary to the law ; but if thou say it and do it not, thou wilt be further guilty of lying. There is no means of evading that verse, save by fulfilling what we say. Can we blot this verse out of our prayer? Would ye that that clause, " Forgive us our debts," should be there, and that we should blot out what follows, " As we also forgive our debtors "? Thou shalt not blot it out, lest thou be first blotted out thyself. So then in this prayer thou sayest, " Give," and thou sayest, " Forgive : " that thou mayest receive what thou hast not, and may be forgiven what thou hast done amiss. So then thou wishest to receive, give ; thou wishest to be forgiven, forgive. It is a brief summary. Hear Christ Himself in another place, " Forgive, and ye shall be forgiven." What will ye forgive? What others have sinned against you. What shall ye be forgiven? What ye have sinned yourselves. " Forgive." " Give, and there shall be given you what ye desire," [1] eternal life. Support the temporal life of the poor man, sustain the poor man's present life, and for this so small and earthly seed ye shall receive for harvest life eternal. Amen.

SERMON LXV.

[CXV. BEN.]

ON THE WORDS OF THE GOSPEL, LUKE XVIII. I, " THEY OUGHT ALWAYS TO PRAY, AND NOT TO FAINT," ETC. AND ON THE TWO WHO WENT UP INTO THE TEMPLE TO PRAY : AND OF THE LITTLE CHILDREN WHO WERE PRESENTED UNTO CHRIST.

1. THE lesson of the Holy Gospel builds us up unto the duty of praying and believing, and of not putting our trust in ourselves, but in the Lord. What greater encouragement to prayer than the parable which is proposed to us of the unjust judge? For an unjust judge, who feared not God, nor regarded man, yet gave ear to a widow who besought him, overcome by her importunity, not inclined thereto by kindness.[2] If he then heard her prayer, who hated to be asked, how must He hear who exhorts us to ask? When therefore by this comparison from a contrary case the Lord had taught that " men ought always to pray and not to faint," [3] He added and said, " Nevertheless, when the Son of Man shall come, thinkest thou that He shall find faith on the earth?" [4]

If faith fail, prayer perishes. For who prays for that which he does not believe? Whence also the blessed Apostle, when he exhorted to prayer, said, " Whosoever shall call upon the Name of the Lord, shall be saved." [5] And in order to show that faith is the fountain of prayer, he went on and said, " How then shall they call on Him in whom they have not believed?" [6] So then that we may pray, let us believe ; and that this same faith whereby we pray fail not, let us pray. Faith pours out prayer, and the pouring out of prayer obtains the strengthening of faith. Faith, I say, pours out prayer, the pouring out of prayer obtains strengthening even for faith itself. For that faith might not fail in temptations, therefore did the Lord say, " Watch and pray, lest ye enter into temptation." [7] " Watch," He saith, " and pray, lest ye enter into temptation." What is to " enter into temptation," but to depart from faith? For so far temptation advances as faith gives way : and so far temptation gives way, as faith advances. For that you may know, Beloved, more plainly, that the Lord said, " Watch and pray, lest ye enter into temptation," as touching faith lest it should fail and perish ; He said in the same place of the Gospel, " This night hath Satan desired to sift [8] you as wheat, and I have prayed for thee, Peter, that thy faith fail not." [9] He that defendeth prayeth, and shall not he pray who is in peril? For in the words of the Lord, " when the Son of Man shall come, thinkest thou that He shall find faith on the earth?" He spoke of that faith, which is perfect. For it is scarce found on the earth. Lo ! this Church of God is full : and who would come hither, if there were no faith? But who would not remove mountains, if there were full faith? Look at the very Apostles : they would not have left all they had, have trodden under foot this world's hope, and followed the Lord, if they had not had great faith ; and yet if they had had full faith, they would not have said to the Lord, " Increase our faith." [10] See again, that man confessing both of himself (behold faith, yet not full faith), who when he had presented to the Lord his son to be cured of an evil spirit, and was asked whether he believed, answered and said, " Lord, I believe, help Thou mine unbelief." [11] " Lord," says he, " I believe," I believe ; therefore there was faith. But " help Thou mine unbelief," therefore there was not full faith.

2. But inasmuch as faith belongs not to the proud, but to the humble, " He spake this parable unto certain who seemed to themselves to be righteous, and despised others. Two men went up into the temple to pray, the one a

---

[1] Luke vi. 37, 38. [2] *Pietate.* [3] Luke xviii. 1.
[4] Luke xviii. 8, Vulgate.
[5] Rom. x. 13. [6] Rom. x. 14. [7] Luke xxii. 46.
[8] *Vexare.* [9] Luke xxii. 31, 32. [10] Luke xvii. 5.
[11] Mark ix. 24.

Pharisee, and the other a publican. The Pharisee said, God, I thank Thee that I am not as the rest of men." [1]   He might at least have said, " as many men." What does, " as the rest of men," mean, but all except himself? " I," he says, " am just, the rest are sinners." " I am not as the rest of men, unjust, extortioners, adulterers." And, lo, from thy neighbour, the publican, thou takest occasion of greater pride. " As," he says, " this publican." " I," he says, " am alone, he is of the rest." " I am not," says he, " such as he is, through my righteous deeds, whereby I have no unrighteousness." " I fast twice in the week, I give tithes of all that I possess." [2]   In all his words seek out for any one thing that he asked of God, and thou wilt find nothing. He went up to pray : he had no mind to pray to God, but to laud himself. Nay, it is but a small part of it, that he prayed not to God, but lauded himself. More than this he even mocked him that did pray. " But the Publican stood afar off ; " [3] and yet he was in deed near to God. The consciousness of his heart kept him off, piety brought him close. " But the Publican stood afar off : " yet the Lord regarded him near. " For the Lord is high, yet hath He respect unto the lowly." [4] But " those that are high " as was this Pharisee, " He knoweth afar off." " The high " indeed " God knoweth afar off," but He doth not pardon them. Hear still more the humility of the Publican. It is but a small matter that he stood afar off ; " he did not even lift up his eyes unto heaven." He looked not, that he might be looked upon. He did not dare to look upwards, his conscience pressed him down : but hope lifted him up. Hear again, " he smote his breast." He punished himself : wherefore the Lord spared him for his confession. " He smote his breast, saying, Lord, be merciful to me a sinner." See who he is that prays. Why dost thou marvel that God should pardon, when he acknowledges his own sin ? Thus thou hast heard the case [5] of the Pharisee and Publican ; now hear the sentence ; thou hast heard the proud accuser, thou hast heard the humble criminal ; hear now the Judge. " Verily I say unto you." The Truth saith, God saith, the Judge saith it. " Verily I say unto you, That Publican went down from the temple justified rather than that Pharisee." [6] Tell us, Lord, the cause. Lo ! I see that the publican goes down from the temple justified rather than the Pharisee. I ask why? Dost thou ask why? Hear why. " Because every one that exalteth himself shall be abased, and he that humbleth himself shall be exalted." [6] Thou hast heard the sentence, beware of its evil

cause. In other words, thou hast heard the sentence, beware of pride.

3. Let now those ungodly babblers, whosoever they be, who presume on their own strength, let them hear and see these things : let them hear who say, God made me a man, I make myself just. O thou who art worse and more detestable than the Pharisee ! The Pharisee in the Gospel did indeed call himself just, but yet he gave thanks to God for it. He called himself just, but yet he gave God thanks. " I thank Thee, O God, that I am not as the rest of men." " I thank Thee, O God. He gives God thanks, that he is not as the rest of men : and yet he is blamed as being proud and puffed up ; not in that he gave God thanks, but in that he desired as it were no more to be added unto him. " I thank thee that I am not as the rest of men, unjust." So then thou art just ; so then thou askest for nothing ; so then thou art full already ; so then the life of man is not a trial upon earth ; [7] so then thou art full already ; so then thou aboundest already, so then thou hast no ground for saying, " Forgive us our debts ! " What must his case be then who impiously impugns grace, if he is blamed who give thanks proudly ?

4. And, lo, after the case had been stated, and the sentence pronounced, little children also came forth, yea, rather, are carried and presented to be touched. To be touched by whom, but the Physician ? Surely, it will be said, they must be whole. To whom are the infants presented to be touched ? To whom ? To the Saviour. If to the Saviour, they are brought to be saved. To whom, but to Him " who came to seek and to save what was lost." [8] How were they lost ? As far as concerns them personally, I see that they are without fault, I am seeking for their guiltiness. Whence is it ? I listen to the Apostle, " By one man sin entered into the world. By one man," he says, " sin entered into the world, and death by sin, and so death passed upon all men by him in whom all sinned." [9] Let then the little children come, let them come : let the Lord be heard. " Suffer little children to come unto Me." [10] Let the little ones come, let the sick come to the Physician, the lost to their Redeemer : let them come, let no man hinder them. In the branch they have not yet committed any evil, but they are ruined in their root. " Let the Lord bless the small with the great." [11] Let the Physician touch both small and great. The cause of the little ones we commend to their elders. Speak ye for them who are mute, pray for them who weep. If ye are not their elders to no purpose, be ye their guardians : defend them who are not able yet to manage their own cause. Common is the loss, let the finding be common :

[1] Luke xviii. 9-11.   [2] Luke xviii. 12.   [3] Luke xviii. 13.
[4] Ps. cxxxviii. 6.   [5] *Controversiam.*
[6] Luke xviii. 14.

[7] Job vii. 1, Sept.   [8] Luke xix. 10.   [9] Rom. v. 12.
[10] Luke xviii. 16.   [11] Ps. cxv. 13.

we were lost all together, together be we found in Christ. Uneven is the desert, but common is the grace. They have no evil but what they have drawn from the source : they have no evil but what they have derived from the first original. Let not them keep them off from salvation, who to what they have so derived have added much more evil. The elder in age is the elder in iniquity too. But the grace of God effaces what thou hast derived, effaces too what thou hast added. For, "where sin abounded, grace hath superabounded."[1]

SERMON LXVI.

[CXVI. BEN.]

ON THE WORDS OF THE GOSPEL, LUKE XXIV. 36, "HE HIMSELF STOOD IN THE MIDST OF THEM, AND SAITH UNTO THEM, PEACE BE UNTO YOU," ETC.

1. THE Lord appeared to His disciples after His resurrection, as ye have heard, and saluted them, saying, "Peace be unto you."[2] This is peace indeed, and the salutation of salvation : for the very word salutation has received its name from salvation.[3] And what can be better than that Salvation Itself should salute man? For Christ is our Salvation. He is our Salvation, who was wounded for us, and fixed by nails to the tree, and being taken down from the tree, was laid in the sepulchre. And from the sepulchre He arose, with His wounds healed, His scars kept. For this He judged expedient for His disciples, that His scars should be kept, whereby the wounds of their hearts might be healed. What wounds? The wounds of unbelief. For He appeared to their eyes, exhibiting real flesh, and they thought they saw a spirit. It is no light wound, this wound of the heart. Yea, they have made a malignant heresy who have abided in this wound. But do we suppose that the disciples had not been wounded, because they were so quickly healed? Only, Beloved, suppose, if they had continued in this wound, to think that the Body which had been buried, could not rise again, but that a spirit in the image of a body, deceived the eyes of men : if they had continued in this belief, yea, rather in this unbelief, not their wounds, but their death would have had to be bewailed.

2. But what said the Lord Jesus? "Why are ye troubled, and why do thoughts ascend into your hearts?"[4] If thoughts ascend into your heart, the thoughts come from the earth. But it is good for a man, not that a thought should ascend into his heart, but that his heart should itself ascend upwards, where the Apostle would have

believers place their hearts, to whom he said, "If ye be risen with Christ, mind those things which are above, where Christ is sitting at the right hand of God. Seek those things which are above, not the things which are upon the earth. For ye are dead, and your life is hid with Christ in God. When Christ your life shall appear, then shall ye also appear with Him in glory."[5] In what glory? The glory of the resurrection. In what glory? Hear the Apostle saying of this body, "It is sown in dishonour, it shall rise in glory."[6] This glory the Apostles were unwilling to assign to their Master, their Christ, their Lord : they did not believe that His Body could rise from the sepulchre : they thought Him to be a Spirit, though they saw His flesh, and they believed not their very eyes. Yet we believe them who preach but do not show Him. Lo, they believed not Christ who showed Himself to them. Malignant wound ! Let the remedies for these scars come forth. "Why are ye troubled, and why do thoughts ascend into your hearts? See My hands and My feet," where I was fixed with the nails. "Handle and see." But ye see, and yet do not see. "Handle and see." What? "That a spirit hath not flesh and bones, as ye see me have. When He had thus spoken," so it is written, "He showed them His hands and His feet."[7]

3. "And while they were yet in hesitation, and wondered for joy."[8] Now there was joy already, and yet hesitation continued. For a thing incredible had taken place, yet taken place it had. Is it at this day a thing incredible, that the Body of the Lord rose again from the sepulchre? The whole cleansed world[9] has believed it ; whoso has not believed it, has remained in his uncleanness. Yet at that time it was incredible : and persuasion was addressed not to the eyes only, but to the hands also, that by the bodily senses faith might descend into their heart, and that faith so descending into their heart might be preached throughout the world to them who neither saw nor touched, and yet without doubting believed. "Have ye," saith He, "anything to eat?" How much doeth the good Builder still to build up the edifice of faith? He did not hunger, yet He asked to eat. And He ate by an act of His power, not through necessity. So then let the disciples acknowledge the verity of His body, which the world has acknowledged at their preaching.

4. If haply there be any heretics who still in their hearts maintain that Christ exhibited Himself to sight, but that Christ's was not very flesh ; let them now lay aside that error, and let the

---

[1] Rom. v. 20.　　[2] Luke xxiv. 36.　　[3] Salutatio a salute.
[4] Luke xxiv. 38.

[5] Col. iii. 1, etc.　　[6] 1 Cor. xv. 43.　　[7] Luke xxiv. 38-40.
[8] Luke xxiv. 41.
[9] Totus hoc credidit mundus, qui non credidit remansit immundus.

Gospel persuade them. We do but blame them for entertaining this conceit: He will damn them if they shall persevere in it. Who art thou who dost not believe that a body laid in the sepulchre could rise again? If thou art a Manichee, who dost not believe that He was crucified either, because thou dost not believe that He was even born, thou declarest that all that He showed was false. He showed what was false, and dost thou speak the truth? Thou dost not lie with thy mouth, and did He lie in His body? Lo thou dost suppose that He appeared unto the eyes of men what He really was not, that He was a spirit, not flesh. Hear Him: He loves thee, let Him not condemn thee. Hear Him speaking: lo, He speaks to thee, thou unhappy one, He speaks to thee, "Why art thou troubled, and why do thoughts ascend into thine heart?" "See," saith He, "My hands and My feet. Handle and see, because a spirit hath not flesh and bones as ye see Me have." This spake the Truth, and did He deceive? It was a body then, it was flesh; that which had been buried, appeared. Let doubting perish, and meet praise ensue.

5. He showed Himself then to the disciples. What is "Himself"? The Head of His Church. The Church was foreseen by Him as in time to be throughout the world, by the disciples it was not yet seen. He showed the Head, He promised the Body. For what did He add next? "These are the words which I spake to you, while I was yet with you." [1] What is this, "While I was yet with you"? Was He not with them then when He was speaking to them? What is, "when I was yet with you"? was with you as mortal, which now I am not. I was with you when I had yet to die. What is, "with you"? With you who were to die, Myself to die. Now I am no more with you: for I am with those who are to die, Myself to die no more for ever. This then is what I said to you. What? "That all things must be fulfilled which are written in the Law, and in the Prophets, and in the Psalms concerning Me." [1] I told you that all things must be fulfilled. "Then opened He their understanding." [2] Come then, O Lord, employ Thy keys, open, that we may understand. Lo, Thou dost tell all things, and yet are not believed. Thou art thought to be a spirit, art touched, art rudely handled, [3] and yet they who touch Thee hesitate. Thou dost admonish them out of the Scriptures, and yet they understand Thee not. Their hearts are closed, open, and enter in. He did so. "Then opened He their understanding." Open, O Lord, yea, open the heart of him who is in doubt concerning Christ. Open "his" understanding who believes that Christ was a phantom. "Then opened He their under-

standing, that they might understand the Scriptures."

6. And "He said unto them." What? "That thus it behoved. That thus it is written, and thus it behoved." What? "That Christ should suffer, and rise from the dead the third day." [4] And this they saw, they saw Him suffering, they saw Him hanging, they saw Him with them alive after His resurrection. What then did they not see? The Body, that is, the Church. Him they saw, her they saw not. They saw the Bridegroom, the Bride yet lay hid. Let him promise her too. "Thus it is written, and thus it behoved Christ to suffer, and to rise from the dead the third day." This is the Bridegroom, what of the Bride? "And that repentance and remission of sins should be preached in His Name among all nations, beginning at Jerusalem." [5] This the disciples did not yet see: they did not yet see the Church throughout all nations, beginning at Jerusalem. They saw the Head, and they believed the Head touching the Body. By this which they saw, they believed that which they saw not. We too are like to them: we see something which they saw not, and something we do not see which they did see. What do we see, which they saw not? The Church throughout all nations. What do we not see, which they saw? Christ present in the flesh. As they saw Him, and believed concerning the Body, so do we see the Body; let us believe concerning the Head. Let what we have respectively seen help us. The sight of Christ helped them to believe the future Church: the sight of the Church helps us to believe that Christ has risen. Their faith was made complete, and ours is made complete also. Their faith was made complete from the sight of the Head, ours is made complete by the sight of the Body. Christ was made known to them "wholly," and to us is He so made known: but He was not seen "wholly" by them, nor by us has He been "wholly" seen. By them the Head was seen, the Body believed. By us the Body has been seen, the Head believed. Yet to none is Christ lacking: in all He is complete, though to this day His Body remains imperfect. The Apostles believed; through them many of the inhabitants of Jerusalem believed; Judæa believed. Samaria believed. Let the members be added on, the building added on to the foundation. "For no other foundation can any man lay," says the Apostle, "than that which is laid, which is Christ Jesus." [6] Let the Jews rage madly, and be filled with jealousy: Stephen be stoned, Saul keep the raiment of them who stone him, Saul, one day to be the Apostle Paul. [7] Let Stephen be killed, the Church of Jerusalem dispersed in confusion: out of it go forth burning brands, and

---

[1] Luke xxiv. 44. [2] Luke xxiv. 45.
[3] *Ulsaris.*

[4] Luke xxiv. 46. [5] Luke xxiv. 47. [6] 1 Cor. iii. 11.
[7] Acts vii. 58.

spread themselves and spread their flame. For in the Church of Jerusalem, as it were burning brands were set on fire by the Holy Spirit, when they had all one soul, and one heart to God-ward.[1] When Stephen was stoned, that pile suffered persecution : the brands were dispersed, and the world was set on fire.

7. And then intent on his furious schemes, that Saul received letters from the chief of the priests, and began his journey in his cruel rage, breathing out slaughter, thirsting for blood, to drag bound and to hurry off to punishment whomsoever he could, and from every quarter that he could, and to satiate himself with the shedding of their blood. But where was God, where was Christ, where He that had crowned Stephen? Where, but in heaven? Let Him now look on Saul, and mock him in his fury, and call from heaven, "'Saul, Saul, why persecutest thou Me?'[2] I am in heaven, and thou in earth, and yet thou persecutest Me. Thou dost not touch the body, but my members thou art treading down. Yet what art thou doing? What art thou gaining? 'It is hard for thee to kick against the pricks.' Kick as thou wilt, thou only distressest thyself. Lay aside thy fury then, recover soundness. Lay aside evil counsel, seek after good succour." By that voice he was struck to the earth. Who was struck to the earth? The persecutor. Lo, by that one word was he overcome. After what wast thou going, after what was thy fury carrying thee? Those whom thou wast seeking out, now thou followest ; whom thou wast persecuting, now for them thou sufferest persecution. He rises up the preacher, who was struck to the earth, the persecutor. He heard the Lord's voice. He was blinded, but in the body only, that he might be enlightened in heart. He was brought to Ananias, catechised on sundry points, baptized, and so came forth an Apostle. Speak then, preach, preach Christ, spread His doctrine, O thou goodly leader of the flock,[3] but lately a wolf. See him, mark him, who once was raging. "But for me, God forbid that I should glory, save in the Cross of our Lord Jesus Christ, by whom the world has been crucified to me and I to the world."[4] Spread the Gospel : scatter with thy mouth what thou hast conceived in thine heart. Let the nations hear, let the nations believe ; let the nations multiply, let the Lord's empurpled spouse spring forth from the blood of Martyrs. And from her how many have come already, how many members have cleaved to the Head, and cleave to Him still and believe ! They were baptized, and others shall be baptized, and after them shall others come. Then I say, at the end of the world shall the stones be joined to the foundation, living stones, holy stones, that at the end the whole edifice may be built by that Church, yea by this very Church which now sings the new song, while the house is in building. For so the Psalm itself says, " When the house was in building after the captivity ; " and what says it, " Sing unto the Lord a new song, sing unto the Lord all the earth."[5] How great a house is this ! But when does it sing the new song? When it is in building. When is it dedicated? At the end of the world. Its foundation has been already dedicated, because He hath ascended into heaven, and dieth no more. When we too shall have risen to die no more, then shall we be dedicated.

SERMON LXVII.

[CXVII. BEN.]

ON THE WORDS OF THE GOSPEL, JOHN I. 1, " IN THE BEGINNING WAS THE WORD, AND THE WORD WAS WITH GOD, AND THE WORD WAS GOD," ETC. AGAINST THE ARIANS.

1. THE section of the Gospel which has been read, most dearly beloved brethren, looketh for the pure eye of the heart. For from John's Gospel we have understood our Lord Jesus Christ according to His Divinity for the creating of the whole creation, and according to His Humanity for the recovery of the creature fallen. Now in this same Gospel we find what sort and how great a man was John, that from the dignity of the dispenser it may be understood of how great a price is the Word which could be announced by such a man ; yea, rather how without price is That which surpasseth all things. For any purchasable thing is either equal to the price, or it is below it, or it exceeds it. When any one procures a thing for as much as it is worth, the price is equal to the thing which is procured ; when for less, it is below it ; when for more, it exceeds it. But to the Word of God nothing can either be equalled, or to exchange can anything be below It, or above It. For all things can be below the Word of God, for that " all things were made by Him ; "[6] yet are they not in such wise below, as if they were the price of the Word, that any one should give something to receive That. Yet if we may say so, and if any principle or custom of speaking admit this expression, the price for procuring the Word, is the procurer himself, who will have given himself for himself to This Word. Accordingly when we buy anything we look out for something to give, that for the price we give we may have the thing we wish to buy. And that which we give is without us ; and if it was with us before, what we give becomes without us, that that which we procure may be with us. What-

---

[1] Acts iv. 32.   [2] Acts ix. 4.   [3] *Aries.*
[4] Gal. vi. 14.

[5] Ps. xcv. 1, Sept. (xcvi. 1, English version).   [6] John i. 3.

ever price the purchaser may find it, it must needs be such as that he gives what he has, and receives what he has not; yet so that he from whom the price goes himself remains, and that for which he gives the price is added to him. But whoso would procure this Word, whoso would have it, let him not seek for anything without himself to give, let him give himself. And when he shall have done this, he doth not lose himself, as he loseth the price when he buys anything.

2. The Word of God then is set forth before all men; let them who can, procure It, and they can who have a godly will. For in That Word is peace; and "peace on earth is to men of good will." [1] So then whoso will procure it, let him give himself. This is as it were the price of the Word, if so it may in any way be said, when he that giveth doth not lose himself, and gaineth the Word for which he giveth himself, and gaineth himself too in the Word to whom he giveth himself. And what giveth he to the Word? Not ought that is any other's than His, for whom he giveth himself; but what by the Same Word was made, that is given back to Him to be remade; "All things were made by Him." If all things, then of course man too. If the heaven, and earth, and sea, and all things that are therein, if the whole creation; of course more manifestly he, who being made after the image of God by the Word was made man.

3. I am not now, brethren, discussing how the words, "In the beginning was the Word, and the Word was with God, and the Word was God," [2] can be understood. After an ineffable sort it may be understood; it cannot by the words of man be made to be understood. I am treating of the Word of God, and telling you why It is not understood. I am not now speaking to make It understood, but I tell you what hinders It from being understood. For He is a certain Form, a Form not formed, but the Form of all things formed; a Form unchangeable, without failure, without decay, without time, without place, surpassing all things, being in all things, as at once a kind of foundation in which they are, and a Head-stone under which they are. If you say that all things are in Him, you lie not. For This Word is called the Wisdom of God; and we have it written, "In Wisdom hast Thou made all things." [3] Lo, then in Him are all things: and yet in that He is God, under Him are all things. I am showing how incomprehensible is what has been read; yet it has been read, not that it should be comprehended by man, but that man should sorrow that he comprehends it not, and find out whereby he is

hindered from comprehending, and remove those hindrances, and, himself changed from worse to better, aspire after the perception of the unchangeable Word. For the Word doth not advance or increase by the addition of those who know It; but is Entire, if thou abide; Entire, if thou depart; Entire, when thou dost return; abiding in Itself, and renewing all things. It is then the Form of all things, the Form unfashioned, without time, as I have said, and without space. For whatsoever is contained in space, is circumscribed. Every form is circumscribed by bounds; it hath limits wherefrom and whereunto it reaches. Again, what is contained in place, and has extension in a sort of bulk and space, is less in its parts than in the whole. God grant that ye may understand.

4. Now from the bodies which are day by day before our eyes, which we see, which we touch, among which we live, we are able to judge how that every body hath a form in space. Now everything which occupies a certain space, is less in its parts than in its whole. The arm, for instance, is a part of the human body; of course the arm is less than the whole body. And if the arm be less, it occupies a smaller space. So again the head, in that it is a part of the body, is contained in less space, and is less than the whole body of which it is the head. So all things which are in space, are less in their several parts than in the whole. Let us entertain no such idea, no such thought concerning That Word. Let us not form our conceptions of spiritual things from the suggestion of the flesh. That Word, That God, is not less in part than in the whole.

5. But thou art not able to conceive of any such thing. Such ignorance is more pious than presumptuous knowledge. For we are speaking of God. It is said, "And the Word was God." [2] We are speaking of God; what marvel, if thou do not comprehend? For if thou comprehend, He is not God. Be there a pious confession of ignorance, rather than a rash profession of knowledge. To reach to God in any measure by the mind, is a great blessedness; but to comprehend Him, is altogether impossible. God is an object for the mind, He is to be understood; a body is for the eyes, it is to be seen. But thinkest thou that thou comprehendest a body by the eye? Thou canst not at all. For whatever thou lookest at, thou dost not see the whole. If thou seest a man's face, thou dost not see his back at the time thou seest the face; and when thou seest the back, thou dost not at that time see the face. Thou dost not then so see, as to comprehend; but when thou seest another part which thou hadst not seen before, unless memory aid thee to remember that thou hast seen that

---

[1] Luke ii. 14.   [2] John i. 1.   [3] Ps. civ. 24.

from which thou dost withdraw, thou couldest never say that thou hadst comprehended anything even on the surface. Thou handlest what thou seest, turnest it about on this side and that, or thyself dost go round it to see the whole. In one view then thou canst not see the whole. And as long as thou turnest it about to see it, thou art but seeing the parts; and by putting together that thou hast seen the other parts, thou dost fancy that thou seest the whole. But this must not be understood as the sight of the eyes, but the activity of the memory. What then can be said, Brethren, of that Word? Lo, of the bodies which are before our eyes we say they cannot comprehend them by a glance; what eye of the heart then comprehendeth God? Enough that it reach to Him if the eye be pure. But if it reach, it reacheth by a sort of incorporeal and spiritual touch, yet it doth not comprehend; and that, only if it be pure. And a man is made blessed by touching with the heart That which ever abideth Blessed; and that is this Very Everlasting Blessedness, and that Everlasting Life, whereby man is made to live; that Perfect Wisdom, whereby man is made wise; that Everlasting Light, whereby man becomes enlightened. And see how by this touch thou art made what thou wast not, thou dost not make that thou touchest be what it was not before. I repeat it, there grows no increase to God from them that know Him, but to them that know Him, from the knowledge of God. Let us not suppose, dearly beloved Brethren, that we confer any benefit on God, because I have said that we give Him in a manner a price. For we do not give Him aught whereby He can be increased, Who when thou fallest away, is Entire, and when thou returnest, abideth Entire, ready to make Himself seen that He may bless those who turn to Him, and punish those with blindness who turn away. For by this blindness, as the beginning of punishment, doth He first execute vengeance on the soul that turns away from Him. For whoso turns away from the True Light, that is from God, is at once made blind. He is not yet sensible of his punishment, but he hath it already.

6. Accordingly, dearly beloved brethren, let us understand that the Word of God is incorporeally, inviolably, unchangeably, without temporal nativity, yet born of God. Do we think that we can any how persuade certain unbelievers that that is not inconsistent with the truth, which is said by us according to the Catholic faith, which is contrary to the Arians, by whom the Church of God hath been often tried, forasmuch as carnal men receive with greater ease what they have been accustomed to see? For some have dared to say, "The Father is greater than the Son, and precedes Him in time;" that is,

the Father is greater than the Son, and the Son is less than the Father, and is preceded by the Father in time. And they argue thus; "If He was born, of course the Father was before His Son was born to Him." Attend; may He be with me, whilst your prayers assist me, and with godly heed desire to receive what He may give, what He may suggest to me; may He be with me, that I may be able in some sort to explain what I have begun. Yet, brethren, I tell you before I begin, if I shall not be able to explain it, do not suppose that it is the failure of the proof, but of the man. Accordingly I exhort and entreat you to pray; that the mercy of God may be with me, and make the matter be so explained by me, as is meet for you to hear, and for me to speak. They then say thus; "If He be the Son of God, He was born." This we confess. For He would not be a Son, if He were not born. It is plain, the faith admits it, the Catholic Church approves it, it is truth. They then go on; "If the Son was born to the Father, the Father was before the Son was born to Him." This the faith rejects, Catholic ears reject it, it is anathematized, whoso entertains this conceit is without, he belongs not to the fellowship and society of the saints. Then says he, "Give me an explanation, how the Son could be born to the Father, and yet be coeval with Him of whom He was born?"

7. And what can we do, brethren, when we are conveying lessons of spiritual things to carnal men; even if so be we ourselves too are not carnal, when we intimate these spiritual truths to carnal men, to men accustomed to the idea of earthly nativities, and seeing the order of these creatures, where succession and departure separates off in age them that beget and them that are begotten? For after the father the son is born, to succeed the father, who in time of course must die. This do we find in men, this in other animals, that the parents are first, the children after them in time. Through this custom of observation they desire to transfer carnal things to spiritual, and by their intentness on carnal things are more easily led into error. For it is not the reason of the hearers which follows those who preach such things, but custom which even entangles themselves, that they do preach such things. And what shall we do? Shall we keep silence? Would that we might! For perchance by silence something might be thought of worthy of the unspeakable subject. For whatsoever cannot be spoken, is unspeakable. Now God is unspeakable. For if the Apostle Paul saith, that he "was caught up even unto the third heaven, and that he heard unspeakable words;"[1] how much more unspeakable is He,

_____
[1] 2 Cor. xii. 4.

who showed such things, which could not be spoken by him to whom they were shown? So then, brethren, it were better if we could keep silence, and say, "This the faith contains; so we believe; thou art not able to receive it, thou art but a babe; thou must patiently endure till thy wings be grown, lest when thou wouldest fly without wings, it should not be the free [1] course of liberty, but the fall of temerity." What do they say against this? "O if he had anything to say, he would say it to me. This is the mere excuse of one who is at fault. He is overcome by the truth, who does not choose to answer." He to whom this is said, if he make no answer, though he be not conquered in himself, is yet conquered in the wavering brethren. For the weak brethren hear it, and they think that there is really nothing to be said; and perhaps they think right that there is nothing to be said, yet not that there is nothing to be felt. For a man can express nothing which he cannot also feel; but he may feel something which he cannot express.

8. Nevertheless, saving the unspeakableness of that Sovereign Majesty, lest when we shall have produced certain similitudes against them, any one should think that we have by them arrived at that which cannot be expressed or conceived by babes (and if it can be at all even by the more advanced, it can only be in part, only in a riddle, only "through a glass;" but not as yet, "face to face"[2]), let us too produce certain similitudes against them, whereby they may be refuted, not "it" comprehended. For when we say that it may very possibly happen, that it may be understood, that He may both be born, and yet Coeternal with Him of whom He was born, in order to refute this, and prove it as it were to be false, they bring forth similitudes against us. From whence? From the creatures, and they say to us, "Every man of course was before he begat a son, he is greater in age than his son; and so a horse was before he begat his foal, and a sheep, and the other animals." Thus do they bring similitudes from the creatures.

9. What! must we labour too, that we may find resemblances of those things which we are establishing? And what if I should not find any, might I not rightly say, "The Nativity of the Creator hath, it may be, no resemblance of itself among the creatures? For as far as He surpasseth the things which are here, in that He is there, so far doth He surpass the things which are born here, in that He was born there. All things here have their being from God; and yet what is to be compared with God? So all things which are born here, are born by His agency. And so perhaps there is no resemblance of His Nativity found, as there is none found whether of His Substance, Unchangeableness, Divinity, Majesty. For what can be found here like these? If then it chance that no resemblance of His Nativity either be found, am I therefore overwhelmed, because I have not found resemblances to the Creator of all things, when desiring to find in the creature what is like the Creator?"

10. And in very truth, Brethren, I am not likely to discover any temporal resemblances which I can compare to eternity. But as to those which thou hast discovered, what are they? What hast thou discovered? That a father is greater in time than his son; and therefore thou wouldest have the Son of God to be less in time than the Eternal Father, because thou hast found that a son is less than a father born in time. Find me an eternal father here, and thou hast found a resemblance. Thou findest a son less than a father in time, a temporal son less than a temporal father. Hast thou found me a temporal son younger than an eternal father? Seeing then that in Eternity is stability, but in time variety; in Eternity all things stand still, in time one thing comes, another succeeds; thou canst find a son of lesser age succeeding his father in the variety of time, for that he himself succeeded to his father also, not a son born in time to a father eternal. How then, Brethren, can we find in the creature aught coeternal, when in the creature we find nothing eternal? Do thou find an eternal father in the creature, and I will find a coeternal son. But if thou find not an eternal father, and the one surpasses the other in time; it is sufficient, that for a resemblance I find something coeval. For what is coeternal is one thing, what is coeval another. Every day we call them coeval who have the same measure of times; the one is not preceded by the other in time, yet they both whom we call coeval once began to "be." Now if I shall be able to discover something which is born coeval with that of which it is born; if two coeval things can be discovered, that which begets, and that which is begotten; we discover in this case things coeval, let us understand in the other things coeternal. If here I shall find that a thing begotten hath begun to be ever since that which begets began to be, we may understand at least that the Son of God did not begin to be, ever since He that begat Him did not begin to be. Lo, brethren, perhaps we may discover something in the creature, which is born of something else, and which yet began to be at the same time as that of which it is born began to be. In the latter case, the one began to be when the other began to be; in the former the one did not begin to be, ever since the other began not to be. The first then is coeval, the second coeternal.

11. I suppose that your holiness has understood already what I am saying, that temporal

[1] *Aura.*   [2] 1 Cor. xiii. 12.

things cannot be compared to eternal; but that by some slight and small resemblance, things coeval may be with things coeternal. Let us find accordingly two coeval things; and let us get our hints as to these resemblances from the Scriptures. We read in the Scriptures of Wisdom, "For she is the Brightness of the Everlasting Light." Again we read, "The unspotted Mirror of the Majesty of God."[1] Wisdom Herself is called, "The Brightness of the Everlasting Light," is called, "The Image of the Father;" from hence let us take a resemblance, that we may find two coeval things, from which we may understand things coeternal. O thou Arian, if I shall find that something that begets does not precede in time that which it begat, that a thing begotten is not less in time than that of which it is begotten; it is but just that thou concede to me, that these coeternals may be found in the Creator, when coevals can be found in the creature. I think that this indeed occurs already to some brethren. For some anticipated me as soon as I said, "For She is the Brightness of the Everlasting Light." For the fire throws out light, light is thrown out from the fire. If we ask which comes from which, every day when we light a candle are we reminded of some invisible and indescribable thing, that the candle as it were of our understanding may be lighted in this night of the world. Observe him who lights a candle. While the candle is not lighted, there is as yet no fire, nor any brightness which proceedeth from the fire. But I ask, saying, "Does the brightness come from the fire, or the fire from the brightness?" Every soul answers me (for it has pleased God to sow the beginnings of understanding and wisdom in every soul); every soul answers me, and no one doubts, that that brightness comes from the fire, not the fire from the brightness. Let us then look at the fire as the father of that brightness; for I have said before that we are looking for things coeval, not coeternal. If I desire to light a candle, there is as yet no fire there, nor yet that brightness; but immediately that I have lighted it, together with the fire comes forth the brightness also. Give me then here a fire without brightness, and I believe you that the Father ever was without the Son.

12. Attend; The matter has been explained by me as so great a matter could be, by the Lord helping the earnestness of your prayers, and the preparation of your heart, ye have taken in as much as ye were able to receive. Yet these things are ineffable. Do not suppose that anything worthy of the subject has been spoken, if it only be for that things carnal are compared with coeternal, things temporal with things abiding ever, things subject to extinction to things immortal. But inasmuch as the Son is said also to be the Image of the Father, let us take from this too a sort of resemblance, though in things very different, as I have said before. The image of a man looking into a glass is thrown out from the glass. But this cannot assist us for the clearing of that which we are endeavouring in some sort to explain. For it is said to me, "A man who looks into a glass of course, 'was' already, and was born before that. The image came out only as soon as he looked at himself. For a man who looks in a glass, 'was' before he came to the glass." What then shall we find, from which we may be able to draw out such a resemblance, as we did from the fire and the brightness? Let us find one from a very little thing. You know without any difficulty how water often throws out the images of bodies. I mean, when any one is passing, or standing still along the water, he sees his own image there. Let us suppose then something born on the water's side, as a shrub, or an herb, is it not born together with its image? As soon as ever it begins to be, its image begins to be with it, it does not precede in its birth its own image; it cannot be showed to me that anything is born upon the water's side, and that its image has appeared afterwards, whereas it first appeared without its image; but it is born together with its image; and yet the image comes from it, not it from the image. It is born then together with its image, and the shrub and its image begin to be together. Dost thou not confess that the image is begotten of that shrub, not the shrub of the image? So then thou dost confess that the image is from that shrub. Accordingly that which begets and that which is begotten began to "be" together. Therefore they are coeval. If the shrub had been always, the image from the shrub would have been always too. Now that which has its being from something else, is of course born of it. It is possible then that one that begets might always be, and always be together with that which was born of him. For here it was that we were in perplexity and trouble, how the Eternal Nativity might be understood. So then the Son of God is so called on this principle, that there is the Father also, that He hath One from whom He derives His Being; not on this, that the Father is first in time, and the Son after. The Father always was, the Son always from the Father. And because whatever "is" from another thing, is born, therefore the Son was always born. The Father always was, the image from Him always was; as that image of the shrub was born of the shrub, and if the shrub had always been, the image would also have always been born from the shrub. Thou couldest not find things begotten coeternal with the eter-

nal begetters, but thou hast found things born coeval with those that begat them in time. I understand the Son coeternal with the Eternal who begat Him. For what with regard to things of time is coeval, with regard to things eternal is coeternal.

13. Here there is somewhat for you to consider, Brethren,[1] as a protection against blasphemies. For it is constantly said, " See thou hast produced certain resemblances; but the brightness which is thrown out from the fire, shines less brilliantly than the fire itself, and the image of the shrub has less proper[2] subsistence, than that shrub of which it is the image. These instances have a resemblance, but they have not a thorough equality : wherefore they do not seem to be of the same substance." What then shall we say, if any one say, ".The Father then is to the Son, such as the brightness is to the fire, and the image to the shrub "? See I have understood the Father to be eternal; and the Son to be coeternal with Him ; nevertheless say we that He is as the brightness which is thrown out from and is less brilliant than the fire, or as the image which is reflected from and has less real existence than the shrub? No, but there is a thorough equality. " I do not believe it," he will say, " because thou hast not discovered a resemblance." Well then, believe the Apostle, because he was able to see what I have said. For he says, " He thought it not robbery to be equal with God."[3] Equality is[4] perfect likeness in every way. And what said he? " Not robbery." Why? Because that is robbery which belongs to another.

14. Yet from these two comparisons, these two kinds, we may perhaps find in the creature a resemblance whereby we may understand how the Son is both coeternal with the Father, and in no respect less than He. But this we cannot find in one kind of resemblances singly : let us join both kinds together. How both kinds? One, of which they themselves give instances of resemblances, and the other, of which we gave. For they gave instances of resemblances from those things which are born in time, and are preceded in time by them of whom they are born, as man of man. He that is born first is greater in time ; but yet man and man, that is of the same substance. For man begets a man, and a horse a horse, and a sheep a sheep. These beget after the same substance, but not after the same time. They are diverse in time, but not in nature diverse. What then do we praise here in this nativity? The equality of nature surely. But what is wanting? The equality of time. Let us retain the one thing which is praised here, that is, the equality of

nature. But in the other kind of resemblances, which we gave from the brightness of the fire and the image of the shrub, you find not an equality of nature, you do find an equality of time. What do we praise here? Equality of time. What is wanting? Equality of nature. Join the things which you praise together. For in the creatures there is wanting something which you praise, in the Creator nothing can be wanting : because what you find in the creature, came forth from the Hand of the Creator. What then is there in things coeval? Must not that be given to God which you praise herein? But what is wanting must not be attributed to that Sovereign Majesty, in the which there is no defect. See I offer to you things begetting coeval with things begotten : in these you praise the equality of time, but find fault with the inequality[5] of nature. What you find fault with, do not attribute to God ; what you praise, attribute to Him ; so from this kind of resemblances you attribute to Him instead of a cotemporaneousness a coeternity, that the Son may be coeternal with Him of whom He was born. But from the other kind of resemblances, which itself too is a creature of God, and ought to praise the Creator, what do you praise in them? Equality of nature. You had before assigned coeternity by reason of the first distinction ; by reason of this last, assign equality ; and the nativity of the same substance is complete. For what is more mad, my brethren, than that I should praise the creature in anything which does not exist in the Creator? In man I praise equality of nature, shall I not believe it in Him who made man? That which is born of man is man ; shall not that which is born of God, be That which He is of whom He was born? Converse have I none with works which God hath not made. Let then all the works of the Creator praise Him. I find in the one case a cotemporaneousness, I get at the knowledge of a coeternity in the other. In the first I find an equality of nature, I understand an equality of substance in the other. In this then that is " wholly," which in the other case is found in the several parts, and several things. It is then " wholly" here altogether, and not only what is in the creature ; I find it wholly here, but as being in the Creator, in so much higher a way, in that the one is visible, the Other Invisible ; the one temporal, the Other Eternal ; the one changeable, the Other Unchangeable ; the one corruptible, the Other Incorruptible. Lastly, in the case of men themselves, what we find, man and man, are two men ; here the Father and the Son are One God.

15. I render unspeakable thanks to our Lord

---

[1] *Propter.*   [2] *Proprietatem.*   [3] Phil. ii. 6.
[4] *Conjungitur.*   [5] *Disparilitatem.*

God, that He hath vouchsafed, at your prayers, to deliver my infirmity from this most perplexed and difficult place. Yet above all things remember this, that the Creator transcends indescribably whatever we could gather from the creature, whether by the bodily senses, or the thought of the mind. But wouldest thou with the mind reach Him? Purify thy mind, purify thine heart. Make clean the eye whereby That, whatever It be, may be reached. For "blessed are the clean in heart, for they shall see God." [1] But whilst the heart was not cleansed, what could be provided and granted more mercifully by Him, than that That Word of whom we have spoken so great and so many things, and yet have spoken nothing worthy of Him; that That Word, "by whom all things were made," should become that which we are, that we might be able to attain to That which we are not? For we are not God; but with the mind or the interior eye of the heart we can see God. Our eyes dulled by sins, blinded, enfeebled by infirmity, desire to see; but we are in hope, not yet in possession. We are the children of God. This saith John, who says, "In the beginning was the Word, and the Word was with God, and the Word was God;" [2] he who lay on the Lord's Breast, who drew in these secrets from the Bosom of His Heart; he says, "Dearly beloved, we are the children of God, and it doth not yet appear what we shall be; we know that, when He shall appear, we shall be like Him, for we shall see Him as He is." [3] This is promised us.

16. But in order that we may attain, if we cannot yet see God the Word, let us hear the Word made Flesh; seeing we are carnal, let us hear the Word Incarnate. For for this cause came He, for this cause took upon Him our infirmity, that thou mightest be able to receive the strong words of a God bearing thy weakness. And He is truly called "milk." For He giveth milk to infants, that He may give the meat of wisdom to them of riper years. Suck then now with patience, that thou mayest be fed to thy heart's most [4] eager wish. For how is even the milk, wherewith infants are suckled, made? Was it not solid meat on the table? But the infant is not strong enough to eat the meat which is on the table; what does the mother do? She turns the meat [5] into the substance of her flesh, and makes milk of it. Makes for us what we may be able to take. So the Word was made Flesh, that we little ones, who were indeed as infants with respect to food, might be nourished by milk. But there is this difference; that when the mother makes the food turned into flesh milk, the food is turned into milk; whereas the Word abiding Itself unchangeably assumed Flesh,

that there might be, as it were, a tissue of the two. What He is, He did not corrupt or change, that in thy fashion, He might speak to thee, not transformed and turned into man. For abiding unalterable, unchangeable, and altogether inviolable, He became what thou art in respect of thee, what He is in Himself in respect of the Father.

17. For what doth He say Himself to the infirm, to the end that recovering that sight, they may be able in some measure to reach the Word by whom all things were made? "Come unto Me, all ye that labour and are heavy laden, and I will refresh you. Take My yoke upon you, and learn of Me, that I am meek and lowly in heart." [6] What doth the Master, the Son of God, the Wisdom of God, by whom all things were made, proclaim? He calleth the human race, and saith, "Come unto Me, all ye that labour, and learn of Me." Thou wast thinking haply that the Wisdom of God would say, "Learn how I have made the heavens and the stars; how all things also were numbered in Me before they were made, how by virtue of unchangeable principles [7] your very hairs were numbered." Didst thou think that Wisdom would say these things, and such as these? No. But first that. "That I am meek and lowly in heart." Lo, see here what ye can comprehend, brethren; it is surely a little thing. We are making our way to great things, let us receive the little things, and we shall be great. Wouldest thou comprehend the height of God? First comprehend the lowliness of God. Condescend to be humble for thine own sake, seeing that God condescended to be humble for thy sake too; for it was not for His own. Comprehend then the lowliness of Christ, learn to be humble, be loth to be proud. Confess thine infirmity, lie patiently before the Physician; when thou shalt have comprehended His lowliness, thou risest with Him; not as though He should rise Himself in that He is the Word; but thou rather, that He may be more and more comprehended by thee. At first thou didst understand falteringly and hesitatingly; afterwards thou wilt understand more surely and more clearly. He doth not increase, but thou makest progress, and He seemeth as it were to rise with thee. So it is, brethren. Believe the commandments of God, and do them, and He will give you the strength of understanding. Do not put the last first, [8] and, as it were, prefer knowledge to the commandments of God; lest ye be only the lower, and none the more firmly rooted. Consider a tree; first it strikes downwards, that it may grow up on high; fixes its root low in the ground, that it may extend its top to heaven.

---

[1] Matt. v. 8.   [2] John i. 1.   [3] 1 John iii. 2.
[4] *Avidè.*   [5] *Incarnat.*

[6] Matt. xi. 28, 29.   [7] *Rationum.*   [8] *Præsumatis.*

Does it make an effort to grow except from humiliation? And wouldest thou without charity comprehend these transcendent matters, shoot toward the heaven without a root? This were a ruin, not a growing. With "Christ" then "dwelling in your hearts by faith, be ye rooted and grounded in charity, that ye may be filled with all the fulness of God."[1]

SERMON LXVIII.

[CXVIII. BEN.]

ON THE SAME WORDS OF THE GOSPEL, JOHN I., "IN THE BEGINNING WAS THE WORD," ETC.

1. ALL ye who are looking for a man's many words, understand the One Word of God, "In the beginning was the Word."[2] Now, "In the beginning God made the heaven and the earth."[3] But, "The Word was," since we have heard, "In the beginning God made." Acknowledge we in Him the Creator; for Creator is He who made; and the creature what He made. For no creature which was made "was," as God the Word "was," by whom it was made, always. Now when we heard "The Word was," with whom was It? We understand the Father who did not make nor create the Same Word, but begat Him. For, "In the beginning God made the heaven and the earth." Whereby made He them? "The Word was, and the Word was with God;"[2] but what kind of Word? Did it sound and so pass away? Was it a mere thought, and motion[4] of the mind? No. Was it suggested by memory, and uttered? No. What kind of Word then? Why dost thou look for many words from me? "The Word was God." When we hear, "The Word was God," we do not make a second God; but we understand the Son. For the Word is the Son of God. Lo, the Son, and What but God? For "The Word was God." What the Father? God of course. If the Father is God and the Son God, do we make two Gods? God forbid. The Father is God, the Son God; but the Father and the Son One God. For the Only Son of God was not made, but born. "In the beginning God made the heaven and the earth;" but the Word was of the Father. Was the Word therefore made by the Father? No. "All things were made by Him."[5] If by Him all things were made, was He too made by Himself? Do not imagine that He by whom thou hearest all things were made was Himself made among all things. For if He were made Himself, all things were not made by Him, but Himself was made among the rest. You say, "He was made;" what, by Himself? Who can make

himself? If then He was made, how by Him were all things made? See, Himself too was made, as you say, not I, for that He was begotten, I do not deny. If then you say that He was made, I ask by what, by whom? By Himself? Then He "was," before He was made, that He might make Himself. But if all things were made by Him, understand that He was not Himself made. If thou art not able to understand, believe, that thou mayest understand. Faith goes before; understanding follows after; since the Prophet says, "Unless ye believe, ye shall not understand.[6] The Word was." Look not for time in Him, by whom times were made. "The Word was." But you say, "There was a time that the Word was not." You say falsely; nowhere do you read this. But I do read for you, "In the beginning was the Word." What look you for before the beginning? But if you should be able to find anything before the beginning, this will be the beginning. He is mad who looks for anything before the beginning. What then doth he say was before the beginning? "In the beginning was the Word."

2. But you will say, "The Father both 'was,' and was before the Word." What are you looking for? "In the beginning was the Word." What you find, understand; seek not for what you are not able to find. Nothing is before the beginning. "In the beginning was the Word." The Son is the Brightness of the Father. Of the Wisdom of the Father, which is the Son, it is said, "For He is the brightness of the Everlasting Light."[7] Are you seeking for a Son without a Father? Give me a light without brightness. If there was a time when the Son was not, the Father was a light obscure. For how was He not an obscure Light, if It had no brightness? So then the Father always, the Son always. If the Father always, the Son always. Do you ask of me, whether the Son were born? I answer, "born." For He would not be a Son if not born. So when I say, the Son always was, I say in fact was always born. And who understands, "Was always born"? Give me an eternal fire, and I will give thee an eternal brightness. We bless God who hath given to us the holy Scriptures. Be ye not blind in the brightness of the light. Brightness is engendered of the Light, and yet the Brightness is Coeternal with the Light that engenders It. The Light always, its Brightness always. It begat Its Own Brightness; but was it ever without Its Brightness? Let God be allowed to beget an eternal Son. I pray you hear of whom we are speaking; hear, mark, believe, understand. Of God are we speaking. We confess

---

[1] Eph. iii. 17 and 19.   [2] John i. 1.   [3] Gen. i. 1.
[4] *Volvebatur.*   [5] John i. 3.
[6] Isa. vii. 9, Sept.   [7] Wisd. vii. 26.

and believe the Son coeternal with the Father. But you will say, "When a man begets a Son, he that begets is the elder, and he that is begotten the younger." It is true ; in the case of men, he that begets is the elder, and he that is begotten, the younger, and he arrives in time to his father's strength. But why, save that whilst the one grows, the other grows old? Let the father stand still a while, and in his growing the son will follow on him, and you will see him equal. But see, I give you whereby to understand this. Fire engenders a coeval brightness. Among men you only find sons younger, fathers older ; you do not find them coeval : but as I have said, I show you brightness coeval with its parent fire. For fire begets brightness, yet is it never without brightness. Since then you see that the brightness is coeval with its fire, suffer God to beget a Coeternal Son. Whoso understandeth, let him rejoice : but whoso understandeth not, let him believe. For the word of the Prophet cannot be disannulled ; "Unless ye believe, ye shall not understand." [1]

SERMON LXIX.

[CXIX. BEN.]

ON THE SAME WORDS, JOHN I. "IN THE BEGINNING WAS THE WORD," ETC.

1. THAT our Lord Jesus Christ in seeking lost man was made Man, our preaching has never withholden, and your faith has ever retained ; and moreover, that this our Lord, who for our sakes was made Man, was always God with the Father, and always will be, yea rather always Is ; for where there is no succession of time, there is no "hath been" and "will be." For that of which it is said, "it hath been," is now no more ; that of which it is said, "it will be," is not yet ; but He always is, because He truly "is," that is, is unchangeable. For the Gospel lesson has just now taught us a high and divine mystery. For this beginning of the Gospel St. John poured forth,[2] for that he drank it in from the Lord's Breast. For ye remember, that it has been very lately read to you, how that this St. John the Evangelist lay in the Lord's Bosom.[3] And wishing to explain this clearly, he says, "On the Lord's Breast ;"[4] that we might understand what he meant, by "in the Lord's bosom." For what, think we, did he drink in who was lying on the Lord's Breast? Nay, let us not think, but drink ;[5] for we too have just now heard what we may drink in.

2. "In the beginning was the Word, and the Word was with God, and the Word was God."[6] O glorious preaching ! O[7] the result of the full feast of the Lord's Breast ! "In the beginning was the Word." Why seekest thou for what was before It? "In the beginning was the Word." If the Word had been made (for made indeed that was not by which all things were made) ; if the Word had been made, the Scripture would have said, "In the beginning God made the Word ;" as it is said in Genesis, "In the beginning God made the heaven and the earth."[8] God then did not in the beginning make the Word ; because, "In the beginning was the Word." This Word which was in the beginning, where was It? Follow on, "And the Word was with God." But from our daily hearing the words of men we are wont to think lightly of this name of "Word." In this case do not think lightly of the Name of "Word ;" "The Word was God. The same," that is the Word, "was in the beginning with God. All things were made by Him, and without Him was nothing made."

3. Extend your hearts, help the poverty of my words. What I shall be able to express, give ear to ; on what I shall not be able to express, meditate. Who can comprehend the abiding Word? All our words sound, and pass away. Who can comprehend the abiding Word, save He who abideth in Him? Wouldest thou comprehend the abiding Word? Do not follow the current of the flesh. For this flesh is indeed a current ; for it has none abiding. As it were from a kind of secret fount of nature men are born, they live, they die ; or whence they come, or whither they go, we know not. It is a hidden water, till it issue from its source ; it flows on, and is seen in its course ; and again it is hidden in the sea. Let us despise this stream flowing on, running, disappearing, let us despise it. "All flesh is grass, and all the glory of flesh is as the flower of grass. The grass withereth, the flower falleth away." Wouldest thou endure? "But the word of the Lord endureth for ever."[9]

4. But in order to succour us, "The Word was made Flesh, and dwelt among us."[10] What is, "The Word was made Flesh"? The gold became grass. It became grass for to be burned ; the grass was burned, but the gold remained ; in the grass It perisheth not, yea, It changed the grass. How did It change it? It raised it up, quickened it, lifted it up to heaven, and placed it at the right Hand of the Father. But that it might be said, "And the Word was made Flesh, and dwelt among us," let us recollect awhile what went before. "He came unto His Own, and His Own received Him not. But as many as received Him, to them gave He power to become the sons of God." "To become,"

---

[1] Isa. vii. 9, Sept.　[2] *Ructuavit.*　[3] John xiii. 23.
[4] John xiii. 25.　[5] *Non putemus sed potemus.*
[6] John i. 1.　[7] *Saginam Dominici pectoris eructuare.*

[8] Gen. i. 1.　[9] Isa. xl. 6, 7, Sept.; 1 Pet. i. 24, 25.
[10] John i. 14.

for they "were" not ; but He "was" Himself in the beginning. "He gave them" then "power to become the sons of God, to them that believe in His Name ; who were born not of blood, nor of the will of the flesh, nor of the will of man, but of God." [1] Lo, born they are, in whatever age of the flesh they may be ; ye see infants ; see and rejoice. Lo, they are born ; but they are born of God. Their mother's womb is the water of baptism.

5. Let no man in poorness of soul entertain this conceit, and turn over such most beggarly thoughts in his mind, and say to himself, "How 'in the beginning was the Word, and the Word was with God, and the Word was God : all things were made by Him ;' and lo, 'the Word was made flesh, and dwelt among us?'" Hear why it was done. "To those" we know "who believed on Him He hath given power to become the sons of God." Let not those then to whom He hath given power to become the sons of God, think it impossible to become the sons of God. "The Word was made flesh, and dwelt among us." Do not imagine that it is too great a thing for you to become the sons of God ; for your sakes He became the Son of man, who was the Son of God. If He was made, that He might be less, who was more ; can He not bring it to pass, that of that less which we were, we may be something more? He descended to us, and shall not we ascend to Him? For us He accepted our death, and shall He not give us His Life? For thee He suffered thy evil things, and shall He not give thee His good things?

6. "But how," one will say, "can it be, that the Word of God, by whom the world is governed, by whom all things both were, and are created, should contract Himself into the womb of a Virgin ; should abandon the world, and leave the Angels, and be shut up in one woman's womb?" Thou skillest not to conceive of things divine. The Word of God (I am speaking to thee, O man, I am speaking to thee of the omnipotence of the Word of God) could surely do all, seeing that the Word of God is omnipotent, at once remain with the Father, and come to us ; at once in the flesh come forth to us, and lay concealed in Him. For He would not the less have been, if He had not been born of flesh. He "was" before His own flesh ; He created His Own mother. He chose her in whom He should be conceived, He created her of whom He should be created. Why marvellest thou? It is God of whom I am speaking to thee : "The Word was God."

7. I am treating of the Word, and perchance the word of men may furnish somewhat like ; though very unequal, far distant, in no way comparable, yet something which may convey a hint to you by way of resemblance. Lo, the word which I am speaking to you, I have had previously in my heart : it came forth to thee, yet it has not departed from me ; that began to be in thee, which was not in thee ; it continued with me when it went forth to thee. As then my word was brought forth to thy sense, yet did not depart from my heart ; so That Word came forth to our senses, yet departed not from His Father. My word was with me, and it came forth into a voice : the Word of God was with the Father, and came forth into Flesh. But can I do with my voice that which He could do with His Flesh? For I am not master [2] of my voice as it flies ; He is not only master of His Flesh, that It should be born, live, act ; but even when dead He raised It up, and exalted unto the Father the Vehicle as it were in which He came forth to us. You may call the Flesh of Christ a Garment, you may call It a Vehicle, and as perchance Himself vouchsafed to teach us, you may call It His Beast ; for on this beast He raised him who had been wounded by robbers ; [3] lastly, as He said Himself more expressly, you may call It a Temple ; This Temple knows death no more, Its seat is at the right Hand of the Father : in This Temple shall He come to judge the quick and dead. What He hath by precept taught, He hath by example manifested. What He hath in His own Flesh shown, that oughtest thou to hope for in thy flesh. This is faith ; hold fast what as yet thou seest not. Need there is, that by believing thou abide firm in that thou seest not ; lest when thou shalt see, thou be put to shame.

SERMON LXX.

[CXX. BEN.]

ON THE SAME WORDS OF JOHN I., "IN THE BEGINNING WAS THE WORD," ETC.

1. THE beginning of John's Gospel, "In the beginning was the Word." [4] Thus he begins, this he saw, and transcending the whole creation, mountains, air, the heavens, the stars, Thrones, Dominions, Principalities, Powers, all Angels, and Archangels, transcending all ; he saw the Word in the beginning, and drank It in. He saw above every creature, he drank in from the Lord's breast. For this same St. John the Evangelist is he whom Jesus specially loved ; insomuch that he lay on His Breast at supper. There was this secret, that therefrom might be drunk in, what in the Gospel was to be poured forth. Happy they who hear and understand. Of the next degree of blessedness are they who though they understand not, believe. For how great a

---

[1] John i. 11-14.   [2] *Tenere.*   [3] Luke x. 30.   [4] John i. 1.

thing it is to see This Word of God, who can explain in human words?

2. Lift up your hearts, my Brethren, lift them up as best ye can; whatsoever occurs to you from the idea of any body whatsoever, reject. If the Word of God occurs to you under the idea of the light of this sun, expand, extend it how you will, set no bounds in your thought to that light; it is nothing to the Word of God. Whatsoever of this sort the mind conceives, is less in one part than in the whole. Of the Word conceive as Whole everywhere. Understand ye what I say; because of my stress of time I am limiting myself as much as I can for your sakes. Understand ye what I say. Lo, this light from heaven, which is called by the name of the sun, when it comes forth, it enlightens the earth, unfolds the day, develops forms, distinguishes colours. Great blessing it is, great gift of God to all mortal men; let His works magnify Him. If the sun is so beauteous, what more beauteous than the sun's Maker? And yet look, Brethren; lo, he pours his rays through the whole earth; penetrates open places, the closed resist him; he sends his light through windows, can he also through a wall? To the Word of God all is open, from the Word of God nothing is hid. Observe another difference, how far from the Creator is the creature, especially the bodily creature. When the sun is in the East, it is not in the West. Its light indeed shed from that vast body reaches even to the West; but itself is not there. When it begins to set, then it will be there. When it rises, it is in the East; when it sets, it is in the West. By these operations of his, it has given name to those quarters. Because it is in the East when it rises at the East, it has made it be called the Rising Sun; because it is at the West when it sets at the West, it has made it be called the Setting Sun. At night it is nowhere seen. Is the Word of God so? When It is in the East, is It not in the West; or when It is in the West, is It not in the East? or does It ever leave the earth, and go under or behind the earth? It is Whole everywhere. Who can in words explain this? Who see it? By what means of proof shall I establish to you what I say? I am speaking as a man, it is to men I speak; I am speaking as one weak, to men weaker am I speaking. And yet, my brethren, I am bold to say that I do in some sort see what I am saying to you, though "through a glass," or "darkly," I do in some sort understand even within my heart a word touching this thing. But it seeks to go forth to you, and finds no meet vehicle. The vehicle of the word is the sound of the voice. What I am saying within mine own self I seek to say to you, and words fail. For I wish to speak of the Word of God. How great a Word,

what kind of Word? "All things were made by Him."[1] See the works, and stand in awe of the Worker. "All things were made by Him."

3. Return with me, O human infirmity, return, I say. Let us comprehend these human things if we can. We are men, I who speak, am a man, and to men I speak, and utter the sound of my voice. I convey the sound of my voice to men's ears, and by the sound of my voice I somehow through the ear lay up understanding also in the heart. Let us then speak on this point what and how we can, let us comprehend it. But if we have not ability to comprehend even this, in respect of the Other what are we? Lo, ye are listening to me; I am speaking a word. If any one goes out from us, and is asked outside what is being done here, he answers, "The Bishop is speaking a word." I am speaking a word of the Word. But what a word, of what a Word? A mortal word, of the Word Immortal; a changeable word, of the Word Unchangeable; a passing word of the Word Eternal. Nevertheless, consider my word. For I have told you already, the Word of God is Whole everywhere. See, I am speaking a word to you; what I say reaches to all. Now that what I am saying might come to you all, did ye divide what I say? If I were to feed you, to wish to fill not your minds, but your bodies, and to set loaves before you to be satisfied therewith; would ye not divide my loaves among you? Could my loaves come to every one of you? If they came to one only, the rest would have none. But now see, I am speaking, and ye all receive. Nay, not only all receive, but all receive it whole. It comes whole to all, to each whole. O the marvels of my word! What then is the Word of God? Hear again. I have spoken; what I have spoken, has gone forth to you, and has not gone away from me. It has reached to you, and has not been separated from me. Before I spake, I had it, and ye had not; I spake, and ye began to have, and I lost nothing. O the marvel of my word! What then is the Word of God? From little things form conjectures of things great. Consider earthly things, laud the heavenly. I am a creature, ye are creatures; and such great miracles are done with my word in my heart, in my mouth, in my voice, in your ears, in your hearts. What then is the Creator? O Lord, hear us. Make us, for that Thou hast made us. Make us good, for that Thou hast made us enlightened men. These white-robed, enlightened ones hear Thy word by me. For enlightened by Thy grace they stand before Thee. "This is the day which the Lord hath made."[2] Only let them labour, let them pray

[1] John i. 3. [2] Ps. cxviii. 24.

for this, that when these days shall have gone by, they may not become darkness, who have been made the light of the wonders and the blessings of God.

SERMON LXXI.

[CXXI. BEN.]

ON THE WORDS OF THE GOSPEL, JOHN I. 10, " THE WORLD WAS MADE THROUGH HIM," ETC.

1. By the Lord "was the world made, and the world knew Him not." [1] What world was made by Him, what world knew Him not? For it is not the same world that was made by Him, which knew Him not. What is the world that was made by Him? The heaven and earth. How did not the heaven know Him, when at His Passion the sun was darkened? How did not the earth know Him, when as He hung upon the Cross, it quaked? But "the world knew Him not," whose Prince he is, of whom it is said, "Behold, the prince of this world cometh, and findeth nothing in me." [2] Wicked men are called the world; unbelieving men are called the world. They have gotten their name from that they love. By the love of God we are made gods; so by the love of the world, we are called the world. But "God was in Christ reconciling the world unto Himself." [3] "The world" then "knew Him not." What? "all men?"

2. "He came unto His Own, and His Own received Him not." [4] All things are His, but they are called His Own, from among whom His mother was, among whom He had taken Flesh, to whom He had sent before the heralds of His advent, to whom He had given the law, whom He had delivered from the Egyptian bondage, whose father Abraham according to the flesh He elected. For He said truth, "Before Abraham was, I am." [5] He did not say, "Before Abraham was," or "before Abraham was made, I was made." For "in the beginning the Word was," not, "was made." So then "He came unto His Own," He came to the Jews. "And His Own received Him not."

3. "But as many as received Him." [6] For of course the Apostles were there, who "received Him." There were they who carried branches before His beast. They went before and followed after, and spread their garments, and cried with a loud voice, "Hosanna to the Son of David, Blessed is He That cometh in the Name of the Lord." [7] Then said the Pharisees unto Him, "Restrain the children, that they cry not out so unto Thee." And He said, "If these shall

hold their peace, the stones will cry out." [8] Us He saw when He spake these words ; " If these shall hold their peace, the stones will cry out." Who are stones, but they who worship stones? If the Jewish children shall hold their peace, the elder and the younger Gentiles shall cry out. Who are the stones, but they of whom speaketh that very John, who came "to bear witness of the Light"? [9] For when he saw these self-same Jews priding themselves on their birth from Abraham, he said to them, "O generation of vipers." [10] They called themselves the children of Abraham; and he addressed them, "O generation of vipers." Did he do Abraham wrong? God forbid! He gave them a name from their character. For that if they were the children of Abraham, they would imitate Abraham; as He too telleth them who say to Him, "We be free, and were never in bondage to any man; we have Abraham for our father." And He said, "If ye were Abraham's children, ye would do the deeds of Abraham. Ye wish to kill Me, because I tell you the truth. This did not Abraham." [11] Ye were of his stock, but ye are a degenerate stock. So then what said John? "O generation of vipers, who hath warned you to flee from the wrath to come?" Because they came to be baptized with the baptism of John unto repentance. "Who hath warned you to flee from the wrath to come? Bring forth therefore fruits worthy of repentance. And say not in your hearts, We have Abraham to our father. For God is able of these stones to raise up children unto Abraham." [12] For God is able of these stones which he saw in the Spirit; to them he spake; he foresaw us; "For God is able of these stones to raise up children unto Abraham." Of what stones? "If these shall hold their peace, the stones will cry out." Ye have just now heard, and cried out. It is fulfilled, "The stones shall cry out." For from among the Gentiles we came, in our forefathers we worshipped stones. Therefore are we called dogs too. Call to mind what that woman heard who cried out after the Lord, for she was a Canaanitish woman, a worshipper of idols, the handmaid of devils. What said Jesus to her? "It is not good to take the children's bread, and to cast it to dogs." [13] Have ye never noticed, how dogs will lick the greasy stones? So are all the worshippers of images. But grace has come to you. "But as many as received Him, to them gave He power to become the sons of God." See ye have here some just now born: to them hath He "given power to become the sons of God." To whom hath He given it? "To them that believe in His Name."

4. And how do they become the sons of God?

---

[1] John i. 10.   [2] John xiv. 30.   [3] 2 Cor. v. 19.
[4] John i. 11.   [5] John viii. 58.   [6] John i. 12.
[7] Matt. xxi. 9.

[8] Luke xix. 39, 40.   [9] John i. 8.   [10] Matt. iii. 7.
[11] John viii. 39, 40.   [12] Luke iii. 7, 8.
[13] Matt. xv. 26.

"Who were born, not of blood, nor of the will of man, nor of the will of the flesh, but of God." [1] Having received power to become the sons of God, they are born of God. Mark then: They are born of God, "not of blood," like their first birth, like that wretched birth, issuing out of wretchedness. But they who are born of God, what *were* they? whereby were they first born? Of blood; of the joint blood of the male and female, of the carnal union of male and female, from this were they born. From whence now? They are born of God. The first birth of the male and female; the second birth of God and the Church.

5. Lo, they are born of God; whereby is it brought to pass that they should be born of God, who were first born of men? Whereby is it brought to pass, whereby? "And the Word was made Flesh, that It might dwell among us." [2] Wondrous exchange; He made Flesh, they spirit. What is this? What condescension is here, my brethren! Lift up your minds to the hope and comprehension of better things. Give not yourselves up to worldly desires. "Ye have been bought with a Price;" [3] for your sakes the Word was made Flesh; for your sakes He who was the Son of God, was made the Son of man: that ye who were the sons of men, might be made sons of God. What was He, what was He made? What were ye, what were ye made? He was the Son of God. What was He made? The Son of man. Ye were the sons of men. What were ye made? The sons of God. He shared with us our evil things, to give us His good things. But even in that He was made the Son of man, He is different much from us. We are the sons of men by the lust of the flesh; He the Son of man by the faith of a virgin. The mother of any other man whatever conceives by a carnal union; and every one is born of human parents, his father and his mother. But Christ was born of the Holy Ghost, and the Virgin Mary. He came to us, but from Himself departed not far; yea from Himself as God He departed never; but added what He was to our nature. For He came to that which He was not, He did not lose what He was. He was made the Son of man; but did not cease to be the Son of God. Hereby the Mediator, in the middle. What is, "in the middle"? Neither up above, nor down below. How neither up above, nor down below? Not above, since He is Flesh; not below, since He is not a sinner. But yet in so far as He is God, above always. For He did not so come to us, as to leave the Father. From us He went, and did not leave us; to us will He come again, and will not leave Him.

SERMON LXXII.

[CXXII. BEN.]

ON THE WORDS OF THE GOSPEL, JOHN I. 48, "WHEN THOU WAST UNDER THE FIG TREE, I SAW THEE," ETC.

1. WHAT we have heard said by the Lord Jesus Christ to Nathanael, if we understand it aright, does not concern him only. For our Lord Jesus saw the whole human race under the fig-tree. For in this place it is understood that by the fig-tree He signified sin. Not that it always signifies this, but as I have said in this place, in that fitness of significancy, in which ye know that the first man, when he sinned, covered himself with fig leaves. For with these leaves they covered their nakedness when they blushed for their sin; [4] and what God had made them for members, they made for themselves occasions of shame. For they had no need to blush for the work of God; but the cause of sin preceded shame. If iniquity had not gone before, nakedness would never have been put to the blush. For "they were naked, and were not ashamed." [5] For they had committed nothing to be ashamed for. But why have I said all this? That we may understand that by the fig-tree sin is signified. What then is, "when thou wast under the fig-tree, I saw thee"? [6] When thou wast under sin, I saw thee. And Nathanael looking back upon what had occurred, remembered that he had been under a fig-tree, where Christ was not. He was not there, that is, by His Bodily Presence; but by His knowledge in the Spirit where is He not? And because he knew that he was under the fig-tree alone, where the Lord Christ was not; when He said to him, "When thou wast under the fig-tree, I saw thee;" he both acknowledged the Divinity in Him, and cried out, "Thou art the King of Israel." [7]

2. The Lord said, "Because I said unto thee, I saw thee when thou wast under the fig-tree, marvellest thou? thou shalt see greater things than these." [8] What are these greater things? And He said, "Ye shall see heaven open, and the Angels of God ascending and descending upon the Son of Man." [9] Let us call to mind the old story written in the sacred Book. I mean in Genesis. [10] When Jacob slept at a certain place, he put a stone at his head; and in his sleep he saw a ladder reaching from earth even unto heaven; and the Lord was resting upon it; and Angels were ascending and descending by it. This did Jacob see. A man's dream would not have been recorded, had not some great mystery been figured in it, had not some great prophecy been to be understood in that vision. Accord-

---

[1] John i. 13.   [2] John i. 14.   [3] 1 Cor. vi. 20.

[4] Gen. iii. 7.   [5] Gen. ii. 25.   [6] John i. 48.
[7] John i. 49.   [8] John i. 50.   [9] John i. 51.
[10] Gen. xxviii. 11.

ingly, Jacob himself, because he understood what he had seen, placed a stone there, and anointed it with oil. Now ye recognise the anointing; recognise The Anointed also. For He is "the Stone which the builders rejected; He was made the Head of the corner."[1] He is the Stone of which Himself said, "Whosoever shall stumble against This Stone shall be shaken; but on whomsoever That Stone shall fall, It will crush him."[2] It is stumbled against as It lies on the earth; but It will fall on him, when He shall come from on high to judge the quick and dead. Woe to the Jews, for that when Christ lay low in His humility, they stumbled against Him. "This Man," say they, "is not of God, because He breaketh the sabbath day."[3] "If He be the Son of God, let Him come down from the cross."[4] Madman, the Stone lies on the ground, and so thou deridest It. But since thou dost deride It, thou art blind; since thou art blind, thou stumblest; since thou stumblest, thou art shaken; since thou hast been shaken by It as It now lies on the ground, hereafter shalt thou be crushed by It as It falls from above. Therefore Jacob anointed the stone. Did he make an idol of it? He showed[5] a meaning in it, but did not adore it. Now then give ear, attend to this Nathanael, by the occasion of whom the Lord Jesus hath been pleased to explain to us Jacob's vision.

3. Ye that are well instructed in the school of Christ, know that this Jacob is Israel too. They are two names; for they are one man. His first name Jacob, which is by interpretation supplanter, he received when he was born. For when those twins were born, his brother Esau was born first; and the hand of the younger was found on the elder's foot.[6] He held his brother's foot who preceded him in his birth, and himself came after. And because of this occurrence, because he held his brother's heel,[7] he was called Jacob, that is, Supplanter. And afterwards, when he was returning from Mesopotamia, the Angel wrestled with him in the way.[8] What comparison can there be between an Angel's and a man's strength? Therefore it is a mystery, a sacrament, a prophecy, a figure; let us therefore understand it. For consider the manner of the struggle too. While he wrestleth, Jacob prevailed against the Angel. Some high meaning is here. And when the man had prevailed against the Angel, he kept hold of Him; yes, the man kept hold of Him whom he had conquered. And said to Him, "I will not let Thee go, except Thou bless me."[9] When the conqueror was blessed by the Conquered, Christ was figured. So then that Angel, who is understood to be the Lord Jesus, saith to Jacob, "Thou shalt not be any more

called Jacob, but Israel shall thy name be,"[10] which is by interpretation, "Seeing God." After this He touched the sinew of his thigh, the broad part, that is, of the thigh, and it dried up; and Jacob became lame. Such was He who was conquered. So great power had this Conquered One, as to touch the thigh, and make lame. It was then with His Own will that He was conquered. For He "had power to lay down" His strength, "and He had power to take It up."[11] He is not angry at being conquered, for He is not angry at being crucified. For He even blessed him, saying, "Thou shalt not be called Jacob, but Israel." Then the "supplanter" was made "the seer of God." And He touched, as I have said, his thigh, and made him lame. Observe in Jacob the people of the Jews, those thousands who followed and went before the Lord's beast, who in concert with the Apostles worshipped the Lord, and cried out, "Hosanna to the Son of David, Blessed is He that cometh in the Name of the Lord."[12] Behold Jacob blessed. He has continued lame until now in them who are at this day Jews. For the broad part of the thigh signifies the multitude of increase. Of whom the Psalm, when it prophesied that the Nations should believe, speaketh, saying, "A people whom I have not known, hath served Me; by the hearing of the ear it hath obeyed Me."[13] I was not there, and I was heard; here I was, and I was killed. "A people whom I have not known, hath served Me; by the hearing of the ear it hath obeyed Me." Therefore, "faith cometh by hearing, and hearing by the word of Christ."[14] And it goes on, "The strange children have lied unto Me;" concerning the Jews. "The strange children have lied unto Me, the strange children have faded away and have halted from their paths." I have pointed out Jacob to you, Jacob blessed and Jacob lame.

4. But as arising out of this occasion, this must not be passed over, which may haply of itself perplex some of you; with what design is it, that when this Jacob's grandfather Abraham's name was changed (for he too was first called Abram, and God changed his name, and said, "Thou shalt not be called Abram, but Abraham"[15]); from that time he was not called Abram. Search in the Scriptures, and you will see that before he received another name, he was called only Abram; after he received it, he was called only Abraham. But this Jacob, when he received another name, heard the same words, "Thou shalt not be called Jacob, but Israel shalt thou be called."[16] Search the Scriptures, and see how that he was always called both, both

---

[1] Ps. cxviii. 22.   [2] Matt. xxi. 44.   [3] John ix. 16.
[4] Matt. xxvii. 40.   [5] *Significavit.*   [6] Gen. xxv. 25, 26.
[7] *Plantam.*   [8] Gen. xxxii. 24.   [9] Gen. xxxii. 26.

[10] Gen. xxxv. 10.   [11] John x. 18.   [12] Matt. xxi. 9.
[13] Ps. xvii. 43, 44, Sept. (xviii. 43, 44, English version).
[14] Rom. x. 17.   [15] Gen. xvii. 5.
[16] Gen. xxxii. 28, xxxv. 10.

Jacob and Israel. Abram after he had received another name, was called only Abraham. Jacob after he had received another name, was called both Jacob and Israel. The name of Abraham was to be developed in this world; for here he was made the father of many nations, whence he received his name. But the name of Israel relates to another world, where we shall see God. Therefore the people of God, the Christian people in this present time, is both Jacob and Israel, Jacob in fact, Israel in hope. For the younger people is called the Supplanter of its brother the elder people. What! have we supplanted the Jews? No, but we are said to be their supplanters, for that for our sakes they were supplanted. If they had not been blinded, Christ would not have been crucified; His precious Blood would not have been shed; if that Blood had not been shed, the world would not have been redeemed. Because then their blindness hath profited us, therefore hath the elder brother been supplanted by the younger, and the younger is called the Supplanter. But how long shall this be?

5. The time will come, the end of the world will come, and all Israel shall believe; not they who now are, but their children who shall then be. For these present walking in their own ways, will go to their own place, will pass on to everlasting damnation. But when they shall have been made all one people, that shall come to pass which we sing, "I shall be satisfied when Thy glory shall be manifested."[1] When the promise which is made to us, that we "see face to face," shall come. "Now we see through a glass darkly," and "in part;"[2] but when both people, now purified, now raised again, now crowned, now changed into an immortal form, and into everlasting incorruption, shall see God face to face, and Jacob shall be no more, but there shall be Israel only; then shall the Lord see him in the person of this holy Nathanael, and shall say, "Behold an Israelite indeed, in whom is no guile."[3] When thou dost hear, "Behold an Israelite indeed;" let Israel come into thy mind; when Israel shall come into thy mind, let his dream come into thy mind, in which he saw a ladder from earth even to heaven, the Lord standing upon it, the Angels of God ascending and descending. This dream did Jacob see. But after this he was called Israel; that is, some little time after as he came from Mesopotamia, and on his journey. If then Jacob saw the ladder, and he is also called Israel; and this Nathanael is an "Israelite indeed, in whom is no guile;" therefore when he wondered because the Lord said to him, "I saw thee under the fig-tree;"[4] did He say to him, "Thou shalt see greater things than these."[5] And so He announced to

him Jacob's dream. To whom did He announce it? To him whom He called "an Israelite, in whom was no guile." As if He had said, "His dream, by whose name I have called thee, shall be manifested in thee; make no haste to wonder, "thou shalt see greater things than these. Ye shall see heaven open, and the Angels of God ascending and descending unto the Son of Man."[6] See what Jacob saw; see why Jacob anointed the stone with oil; see why Jacob prophetically signified and prefigured the Anointed One. For that action was a prophecy.

6. Now I know what you are waiting for; I understand what you would hear from me. This too will I briefly declare, as the Lord enableth me; "ascending and descending unto the Son of Man." How — if they descend to Him, He is here; if they ascend to Him, He is above. But if they ascend to Him, and descend to Him, He is at once above and here. It cannot any way possibly be, that they should ascend to Him, and descend to Him, unless He be both there whither they ascend, and here whither they descend — How do we prove that He is both there, and that He is here? Let Paul, who was first Saul, answer us. He found it by experience, when he was first a persecutor, and afterwards became a preacher; first Jacob, afterwards Israel; who was himself too "of the stock of Israel, of the tribe of Benjamin."[7] In him let us see Christ above, Christ below. First, the very Voice of the Lord from heaven shows this; "Saul, Saul, why persecutest thou me?"[8] What! had Paul ascended into heaven? Had Paul so much as cast a stone into heaven? He was persecuting the Christians, binding them, haling them to be put to death, searching them out in every place where they lay hid, when they were found on no consideration sparing them. To whom the Lord Christ saith, "Saul, Saul." Whence crieth He? From heaven. Therefore He is above. "Why persecutest thou Me?" Therefore He is below. Thus have I explained all, though briefly, yet as well as I could to you, Beloved. I have ministered to you according to my duty, and now for your duty, do ye think upon the poor. Let us turn to the Lord, etc.

SERMON LXXIII.

[CXXIII. BEN.]

ON THE WORDS OF THE GOSPEL, JOHN II. 2, "AND JESUS ALSO WAS BIDDEN, AND HIS DISCIPLES, TO THE MARRIAGE."

1. YE know, Brethren, for ye have learnt it as believing in Christ, and continually too do we by our ministry impress it upon you, that the humility of Christ is the medicine of man's

---

1 Ps. xvi. 15, Sept. (xvii. 15, English version).   2 1 Cor. xiii. 12.
3 John i. 47.   4 John i. 48.   5 John i. 50.
6 John i. 51.   7 Phil. iii. 5.   8 Acts ix. 4.

swollen pride. For man would not have perished, had he not been swollen up through pride. For " pride," as saith the Scripture, " is the beginning of all sin." [1] Against the beginning of sin, the beginning of righteousness is necessary. If then pride be the beginning of all sin, whereby should the swelling of pride be cured, had not God vouchsafed to humble Himself? Let man blush to be proud, seeing that God hath humbled Himself. For when man is told to humble himself, he disdains it ; and when men are injured, it is pride that makes them wish to be avenged. Forasmuch as they disdain to humble themselves, they wish to be avenged ; as if another's punishment could be any profit to any man. One who has been hurt and suffered wrong wishes to be avenged ; he seeks his own remedy from another's punishment, and gains a great torment. The Lord Christ therefore vouchsafed to humble Himself in all things, showing us the way ; if we but think meet to walk thereby.

2. Among His other acts, lo, the Virgin's Son comes to the marriage ; who being with the Father instituted marriage. As the first woman, by whom came sin, was made of a man without a woman ; so the Man by whom sin was done away, was made of a woman without a man. By the first we fell, by the other we rise. And what did He at this marriage? Of water He made wine. What greater sign of power? He who had power to do such things, vouchsafed to be in need. He who made of water wine, could also have of stones made bread. The power was the same ; but then the devil tempted Him, therefore Christ did it not. For ye know that when the Lord Christ was tempted, the devil suggested this to Him. For He was an hungred, since this too He vouchsafed to be, since this too made part of His Humiliation. The Bread was hungry, as the Way fainted, as saving Health was wounded, as the Life died. When then He was an hungred as ye know, the tempter said to Him, " If Thou be the Son of God, command that these stones be made bread." [2] And He made answer to the tempter, teaching thee to answer the tempter. For to this end does the general fight, that the soldiers may learn. What answer did He make? " Man doth not live by bread alone, but by every word of God." [3] And He did not make bread of the stones, who of course could as easily have done it, as He made of water wine. For it is an exercise of the same power to make bread of stone ; but He did it not, that He might despise the tempter's will. For no otherwise is the tempter overcome, but by being despised. And when He had overcome the devil's temptation, " Angels came and ministered to Him." [4] He

then who had so great power, why did He not do the one, and do the other? Read, yea, recollect what thou hast just heard, when He did this, when, that is, He made of the water wine ; what did the Evangelist add? " And His disciples believed on Him." [5] Would the devil on the other occasion have believed on Him?

3. He then who could do so great things, was hungry, and athirst, was wearied, slept, was apprehended, beaten, crucified, slain. This is the way ; walk by humility, that thou mayest come to eternity. Christ-God is the Country whither we go ; Christ-Man is the Way whereby we go. To Him we go, by Him we go ; why fear we lest we go astray? He departed not from the Father ; and came to us. He sucked the breasts, and He contained the world. He lay in the manger, and He fed the Angels. God and Man, the same God who is Man, the same Man who is God. But not God in that wherein He is Man. God, in that He is the Word ; Man, in that the Word was made Flesh ; by at once continuing to be God, and by assuming man's Flesh ; by adding what He was not, not losing what He was. Therefore henceforward, having now suffered in this His humiliation, dead, and buried, He has now risen again, and ascended into heaven, there He is, and sitteth at the right Hand of the Father : and here He is needy in His poor. Yesterday too I set this forth to your Affection by occasion of what He said to Nathanael, " Thou shalt see a greater thing than this. For I say unto you, Ye shall see Heaven open, and the Angels of God ascending and descending unto the Son of Man." [6] We searched out what this meant, and spake at some length ; must we recapitulate the same to-day? Let those who were present remember ; yet I will briefly run over it.

4. He would not say, " ascending unto the Son of Man," unless He were above ; He would not say, " descending unto the Son of Man," unless He were also below. He is at once above, and below ; above in Himself, below in His ; above with the Father, below in us. Whence also was that Voice to Saül, " Saul, Saul, why persecutest thou Me?" [7] He would not say, " Saul, Saul," unless that He was above. But Saul was not persecuting Him above. He then who was above would not have said, " Why persecutest thou me ? " unless He were below also. Fear Christ above ; recognise Him below. Have Christ above bestowing His bounty, recognise Him here in need. Here He is poor, there He is rich. That Christ is poor here, He tells us Himself for me, " I was an hungred, I was thirsty, I was naked, I was a stranger, I was in prison." [8] And to some He said, " Ye have

---

[1] Ecclus. x. 13.   [2] Matt. iv. 3.   [3] Matt. iv. 4.
[4] Matt. iv. 11.

[5] John ii. 11.   [6] John i. 50, 51.   [7] Acts ix. 4.
[8] Matt. xxv. 35, etc.

ministered unto Me," and to some He said, "Ye have not ministered unto Me." Lo, we have proved Christ poor; that Christ is Rich, who knows not? And even here it was a property of these riches to turn the water into wine. If he who has wine is rich, how rich is He who maketh wine? So then Christ is rich and poor; as God, rich; as Man, poor. Yea rich too now as Very Man He hath ascended into heaven, sitteth at the right Hand of the Father; yet still He is poor and hungry here, thirsty, and naked.

5. What art thou? Rich, or poor? Many tell me, I am poor; and they tell the truth. I recognise some poor having something, and some having want. But some have much gold and silver. O that they would acknowledge themselves poor! Poor they will acknowledge themselves, if they acknowledge the poor about them. For how is it? How much soever thou hast, thou rich man whosoever thou art, thou art God's beggar. The hour of prayer comes, and there I prove thee. Thou makest thy petition. How art thou not poor, who makest thy petition? I say more, Thou makest petition for bread. Wilt thou not have to say, "Give us our daily bread"?[1] Thou, who askest for daily bread, art thou poor, or rich? And yet Christ saith to thee, "Give Me of that which I have given thee. For what didst thou bring here, when thou camest hither? All things that I created, thyself created hast found here; nothing didst thou bring, nothing shalt thou take away. Why wilt thou not give Me of Mine Own? For thou art full, and the poor man is empty. Look at your first origin; naked were ye both born. Thou too then wast born naked. Great store hast thou found here; didst thou bring ought with thee? I ask for Mine Own; give, and I will repay. Thou hast found Me a bountiful giver, make Me at once thy debtor. It is not enough to say, 'Thou hast found Me a bountiful giver, make Me at once thy debtor;' let Me regard thee as lending upon interest. Thou givest me but little, I will repay more. Thou givest me earthly things, I will repay heavenly. Thou givest me temporal things, I will restore eternal. I will restore thee to thyself, when I shall have restored thee unto Me."

SERMON LXXIV.

[CXXIV. BEN.]

ON THE WORDS OF THE GOSPEL, JOHN V. 2, "NOW THERE IS IN JERUSALEM BY THE SHEEP *GATE* A POOL," ETC.

1. THE lesson of the Gospel has just sounded in our ears, and made us intent to know what is the meaning of what has been read. This, I suppose, is looked for from me, this I promise, by the Lord's assistance, to explain as well as I can. For without doubt it is not without a meaning, that those miracles were done, and something they figured out to us bearing on eternal saving[2] health. For the health of the body which was restored to this man, of how long duration was it? "For what is your life?" saith Holy Scripture; "it is a vapour that appeareth for a little time, and then vanisheth away."[3] Therefore in that health was restored to this man's body for a time, some enduringness was restored to a vapour. So then this is not to be valued much; "Vain is the health of man."[4] And, brethren, recollect that Prophetical and Evangelical testimony, for it is read in the Gospel; "All flesh is grass, and all the glory of flesh as the flower of grass; the grass withereth, the flower falleth away, the Word of the Lord endureth for ever."[5] The Word of the Lord communicateth glory even to the grass, and no transitory glory; for even to flesh He giveth immortality.

2. But first passeth away the tribulation of this life, out of which He giveth us help, to whom we have said, "Give us help from tribulation."[4] And all this life is indeed a tribulation to the understanding. For there are two tormentors of the soul, torturing it not at once, but alternating their tortures. These two tormentors' names are, Fear and Sorrow. When it is well with thee, thou art in fear; when it is ill, thou art in sorrow. This world's prosperity, whom doth it not deceive, its adversity not break? In this grass, and in the days of grass, the surer way must be kept to, the Word of God. For when it had been said, "All flesh is grass, and all the glory of flesh as the flower of grass, the grass withereth, the flower falleth away;" as though we should ask, "What hope has grass? what stability the flower of grass?" it is said, "but the Word of the Lord endureth for ever." And whence, you will say, is that Word to me? "The Word was made Flesh, and dwelt among us."[6] For the Word of the Lord saith to thee, "Do not reject My promise, for I have not rejected thy grass." This then that the Word of the Lord hath granted to us, that we might hold to Him, that we might not pass away with the flower of grass; this, I say, that He hath granted to us, that the Word should be made Flesh, taking Flesh, not changed into flesh, abiding, and assuming, abiding what He was, assuming what He was not; this, I say, that He hath granted to us, that pool also signifies.[7]

---

[1] Matt. vi. 11.

[2] Throughout this chapter there is the double meaning in the original of *salus* for "health" and "salvation."
[3] Jas. iv. 14.　　　　　　　　　[4] Ps. lx. 11.
[5] Isa. xl. 6, 7; Jas. i. 10; 1 Pet. i. 24, 25.
[6] John i. 14.　　　　　　　　　[7] John v.

3. I am speaking briefly. That water was the Jewish people; the five porches were the Law. For Moses wrote five books. Therefore was the water enclosed by five porches as that people was held in by the Law. The troubling of the water is the Lord's Passion among that people. He who descended was healed, and only one; for this is unity. Whosoever are offended at the Passion of Christ are proud; they will not descend, they are not healed. And, say they, "Am I to believe that God was Incarnate, that God was born of a woman, that God was crucified, scourged, dead, wounded, buried?" Be it far from me to believe this of God, it is unworthy of Him. Let the heart speak, not the neck. To the proud the humiliation of the Lord seems unworthy of Him, therefore is saving health from such far off. Lift not thyself up; if thou wouldest be made whole, descend. Well might piety be alarmed, if Christ in the flesh subject to change were only spoken of. But now the truth sets forth to thee, Christ Unchangeable in His Nature as the Word. For, "In the beginning was the Word, and the Word was with God;" not a word to sound, and so pass away; for "the Word was God." [1] So then thy God endureth unchangeable. O true piety; thy God endureth, fear not; He doth not perish, and through Him, thou too dost not perish. He endureth, He is born of a woman, but in the Flesh. The Word made even His Mother. He who was before He was made, made her in whom He was to be made Himself. He was an infant, but in the Flesh. He sucked, He grew, He took nourishment, He ran through the several stages of life, He came to man's estate, but in the Flesh. He was wearied, and He slept, but in the Flesh. He suffered hunger and thirst, but in the Flesh. He was apprehended, bound, scourged, assailed with railings, crucified finally, and killed, but in the Flesh. Why art thou alarmed? "The Word of the Lord endureth for ever." Whoso rejecteth this humiliation of God, doth not wish for healing from the deadly swelling of pride.

4. So then by His Flesh did the Lord Jesus Christ grant hope to our flesh. For He took on Him what we knew well in this earth, what aboundeth here, to be born, and to die. To be born and to die, abounded here; to rise again and to live for ever, was not here. Poor earthly merchandize found He here, He brought here strange and heavenly. If thou art alarmed at death, love the resurrection. He hath given thee help out of tribulation; for vain thy health had ever been. Let us acknowledge therefore and love the saving health in this world strange, that is, health everlasting, and live we in this world

as strangers. Let us think that we are but passing away, so shall we be sinning less. Let us rather give thanks to our Lord God, that He hath been pleased that the last day of this life should be both near and uncertain. From the earliest infancy even to decrepit old age, it is but a short span. If Adam had died to-day, what would it have profited him, that he had lived so long? What "long time" is there in that in which there is an end? No one recalleth yesterday; to-day is pressed on by to-morrow, that it may pass away. In this little span let us live well, that we may go whence we may not pass away. And now even as we are talking, we are indeed passing away. Our words run on, and the hours fly by; so does our age, so our actions, so our honours, so our misery, so our happiness here below. All passeth away, but let us not be alarmed; "The Word of God endureth for ever." Let us turn to the Lord, etc.

SERMON LXXV.

[CXXV. BEN.]

AGAIN IN JOHN V. 2, ETC., ON THE FIVE PORCHES, WHERE LAY A GREAT MULTITUDE OF IMPOTENT FOLK, AND OF THE POOL OF SILOA.

1. SUBJECTS strange neither to your ears nor hearts are now repeated: yet do they revive the affections of the hearer, and by repetition in some sort renew us: nor is it wearisome to hear what is well known already, for the words of the Lord are always sweet. The exposition of the sacred Scriptures is as the sacred Scriptures themselves: though they be well known, yet are they read to impress the remembrance of them. And so the exposition of them, though it be well known, is nevertheless to be repeated, that they who have forgotten it may be reminded, or they who chanced not to hear it may hear; and that with those who do retain what they are used to hear, it may by the repetition be brought to pass that they shall not be able to forget it. For I remember that I have already spoken to you, Beloved, on this lesson of the Gospel. Yet to repeat the same explanation to you is not wearisome, even as it was not wearisome to repeat the same Lesson to you. The Apostle Paul saith in a certain Epistle, "To write the same things to you, to me indeed is not wearisome, but for you it is necessary." [2] So too with myself to say the same things to you, to me is not wearisome, but for you it is safe.

2. The five porches in which the infirm folk lay signify the Law, which was first given to the Jews and to the people of Israel by Moses the servant of God. For this Moses the minister of the Law wrote five books. In relation therefore

---

[1] John i. 1.

[2] Phil. iii. 1, Vulgate.

to the number of the books which he wrote, the five porches figured the Law. But because the Law was not given to heal the infirm, but to discover and to manifest them; for so saith the Apostle, "For if there had been a law given which could have given life, verily righteousness should have been by the Law; But the Scripture hath concluded all under sin, that the promise by faith of Jesus Christ might be given to them that believe;"[1] therefore in those porches the sick folk lay, but were not cured. For what saith he? "If there had been a law given which could have given life." Therefore those porches which figured the Law could not cure the sick. Some one will say to me, "Why then was it given?" The Apostle Paul hath himself explained: "Scripture," saith he, "hath concluded all under sin, that the promise by faith of Jesus Christ might be given to them that believe." For these folk who were sick, thought themselves to be whole. They received the Law, which they were not able to fulfil; they learnt in what disease they were, and they implored the Physician's aid; they wished to be cured because they came to know they were in distress, which they would not have known if they had not been unable to fulfil the Law which had been given. For man thought himself innocent, and from this very pride of false innocence became more mad. To tame this pride then and to lay it bare, the Law was given; not to deliver the sick, but to convince the proud. Attend then, Beloved; to this end was the Law given, to discover diseases, not to take them away. And so then those sick folk who might have been sick in their own houses with greater privacy, if those five porches had not existed, were in those porches set forth to the eyes of all men, but were not by the porches cured. The Law therefore was useful to discover sins, because that man being made more abundantly guilty by the transgression of the Law, might, having tamed his pride, implore the help of Him That pitieth. Attend to the Apostle; "The Law entered that sin might abound; but where sin abounded, grace hath much more abounded."[2] What is, "The Law entered that sin might abound"? As in another place he saith, "For where there is no law, there is no transgression."[3] Man may be called a sinner before the Law, a transgressor he cannot. But when he hath sinned, after that he hath received the Law, he is found not only a sinner, but a transgressor. Forasmuch then as to sin is added transgression, therefore "hath sin abounded." And when sin abounds, human pride learns at length to submit itself, and to confess to God, and to say, "I am weak." To say to those words of the Psalm which none but the humbled soul

saith, "I said, Lord, be merciful unto me; heal my soul, for I have sinned against thee."[4] Let the weak soul then say this that is at least convinced by transgression, and not cured, but manifested by the Law. Hear too Paul himself showing thee, both that the Law is good, and yet that nothing but the grace of Christ delivereth from sin. For the Law can prohibit and command; apply the medicine, that that which doth not allow a man to fulfil the Law, may be cured, it cannot, but grace only doeth that. For the Apostle saith, "For I delight in the Law of God after the inner man."[5] That is, I see now that what the Law blames is evil, and what the Law commands is good. "For I delight in the Law of God after the inner man. I see another law in my members resisting the law of my mind, and bringing me into captivity in the law of sin." This derived from the punishment of sin, from the propagation of death, from the condemnation of Adam, "resists the law of the mind, and brings it into captivity in the law of sin which is in the members." He was convinced; he received the Law, that he might be convinced: see now what profit it was to him that he was convinced. Hear the following words, "Wretched man that I am, who shall deliver me from the body of this death? The grace of God through Jesus Christ our Lord."[6]

3. Give heed then. Those five porches were significative of the Law, bearing the sick, not healing them; discovering, not curing them. But who did cure the sick? He that descended into the pool. And when did the sick man descend into the pool? When the Angel gave the sign by the moving of the water. For thus was that pool sanctified, for that the Angel came down and moved the water. Men saw the water; and from the motion of the troubled water they understood the presence of the Angel. If any one then went down, he was cured. Why then was not that sick man cured? Let us consider his own words; "I have no man," he says, "when the water is moved, to put me into the pool, but while I am coming, another steppeth down."[7] Couldest not thou then step down afterwards, if another step down before thee? Here it is shown us, that only one was cured at the moving of the water. Whosoever stepped down first, he alone was cured: but whoever stepped down afterwards, at that moving of the water was not cured, but waited till it was moved again. What then does this mystery[8] mean? For it is not without a meaning. Attend, Beloved. Waters are put in the Apocalypse for a figure of peoples. For when in the Apocalypse John saw many waters, he asked what it meant, and it was told him that they

---

[1] Gal. iii. 21, 22.   [2] Rom. v. 20.   [3] Rom. iv. 15.

[4] Ps. xli. 4.   [5] Rom. vii. 22.   [6] Rom. vii. 24, 25, Vulgate.
[7] John v. 7.   [8] *Sacramentum.*

were peoples.[1] The water then of the pool signified the people of the Jews. For as that people was held in by the five books of Moses in the Law, so that water too was enclosed by five porches. When was the water troubled? When the people of the Jews was troubled. And when was the people of the Jews troubled, but when the Lord Jesus Christ came? The Lord's Passion was the troubling of the water. For the Jews were troubled when the Lord suffered. See, what was just now read had relation to this troubling. "The Jews wished to kill Him, not only because He did these things on the sabbaths, but because He called Himself the Son of God, making Himself equal with God."[2] For Christ called Himself the Son after one manner, in another was it said to men, "I said, Ye are Gods, and ye are all children of the Most High."[3] For if He had made Himself the Son of God in such sort as any man whatever may be called the son of God (for by the grace of God men are called sons of God); the Jews would not have been enraged. But because they understand Him to call Himself the Son of God in another way, according to that, "In the beginning was the Word, and the Word was with God, and the Word was God;"[4] and according to what the Apostle saith, "Who being in the form of God, thought it not robbery to be equal with God;"[5] they saw a man, and they were enraged, because He made Himself equal with God. But He well knew that He was equal, but Wherein they saw not. For that which they saw they wished to crucify; by That which they saw not, they were judged. What did the Jews see? What the Apostles also saw, when Philip said, "Show us the Father, and it sufficeth us."[6] But what did the Jews not see? What not even the Apostles saw, when the Lord answered, "Have I been so long time with you, and yet have ye not known Me? He that seeth Me, seeth the Father also."[7] Because then the Jews were not able to see This in Him, they held Him for a proud and ungodly man, making Himself equal with God. Here was a troubling, the water was troubled, the Angel had come. For the Lord is called also the "Angel of the Great Counsel,"[8] in that He is the messenger of the Father's will. For Angel in Greek is in Latin "messenger." So you have the Lord saying that He announces to us the kingdom of Heaven. He then had come, the "Angel of the Great Counsel," but the Lord of all the Angels. "Angel" on this account, because He took Flesh; the "Lord of Angels," in that by "Him all things were made, and without Him was nothing made."[9] For

if all things, Angels too. And therefore Himself was not made, because by Him all things were made. Now what was made, was not made without the operation of the Word. But the flesh which became the mother of Christ, could not have been born, if it had not been created by the Word, which was afterwards born of it.

4. The Jews then were troubled. What is this? "Why doeth He these things on the sabbath days?" And especially at those words of the Lord, "My Father worketh hitherto, and I work."[10] Their carnal understanding of this, that God rested on the seventh day from all His works,[11] "troubled them." For this is written in Genesis, and most excellently written it is, and on the best reasons. But they thinking that God as it were rested from fatigue on the seventh day after all, and that He therefore blessed it, because on it He was refreshed from His weariness, did not in their foolishness understand, that He who made all things by the Word, could not be wearied. Let them read, and tell me how could God be wearied, who said, "Let it be made, and it was made." To-day if a man could so do, as God did, how would he be wearied? He said, "Let there be light, and the light was made." Again, "Let there be a firmament, and it was made:"[12] if indeed He said, and it was not done, He was wearied. In another place briefly, "He spake, and they were made; He commanded, and they were created."[13] He then who worketh thus, how doth He labour? But if He labour not, how doth He rest? But in that sabbath, in which it is said that God rested from all His works, in the Rest of God our rest was signified; because the sabbath of this world shall be, when the six ages shall have passed away. The six days as it were of the world are passing away. One day hath passed away, from Adam unto Noë; another from the deluge unto Abraham; the third from Abraham unto David; the fourth from David unto the carrying away into Babylon; the fifth from the carrying away into Babylon unto the advent of our Lord Jesus Christ. Now the sixth day is in passing. We are in the sixth age, in the sixth day. Let us then be reformed after the image of God, because that on the sixth day man was made after the image of God.[14] What formation did then, let reformation do in us, and what creation did there, let creating-anew do in us. After this day in which we now are, after this age, the rest which is promised to the saints and prefigured in those days, shall come. Because in very truth too, after all things which He made in the world, He hath made nothing new in creation afterwards. The creatures themselves

---

[1] Rev. xvii. 15.   [2] John v. 18.   [3] Ps. lxxxii. 6.
[4] John i. 1.   [5] Phil. ii. 6.   [6] John xiv. 8.
[7] John xiv. 9.   [8] Isa. ix. 6, Sept.   [9] John i. 3.

[10] John v. 17.   [11] Gen. ii. 2.   [12] Gen. i. 3, 6, 7.
[13] Ps. xxxii. 9, Sept. (xxxiii. 9, English version).
[14] Gen. i. 27.

shall be transformed and changed. For since the creatures were fashioned, nothing more has been added. But nevertheless, if He who made did not rule the world, what is made would fall to ruin: He cannot but administer that which He hath made. Because then nothing hath been added to the creation, He is said to have rested from all His works; but because He doth not cease to govern what He made, rightly did the Lord say, "My Father worketh even hitherto." Attend, Beloved. He finished, He is said to have rested; for He finished His works, and hath added no more. He governeth what He hath made; therefore He doth not cease to work. But with the same facility that He made, with the same doth He govern. For do not suppose, brethren, that when He created He did not labour, and that He laboureth in that He governeth: as in a ship, they labour who build the ship, and they who manage it labour too; for they are men. For with the same facility wherewith "He spake and they were made," with the same facility and judgment doth He govern all things by the Word.

5. Let us not, because human affairs seem to be in disorder, fancy that there is no governance of human affairs. For all men are ordered in their proper places; but to every man it seems as though they have no order. Do thou only look to what thou wouldest wish to be; for as thou shalt wish to be, the Master[1] knoweth where to place thee. Look at a painter. Before him are placed various colours, and he knows where to set each colour on. Questionless the sinner hath chosen to be the black colour; does not then the Artist[1] know where to place him? How many parts does the painter finish off with the colour of black? how many ornaments does he make of it? With it he makes the hair, the beard, the eye-brows; he makes the face of white only. Look then to that which thou wouldest wish to be; take no care where He may order thee who cannot err, He knoweth where to place thee. For so we see it happen by the common laws of the world. Some man, for instance, has chosen to be a house-breaker: the law of the judge knows that he has acted contrary to the law: the law of the judge knows where to place him; and orders him most properly. He indeed has lived evilly; but not evilly has the law ordered him. From a house-breaker he will be sentenced to the mines; from the labour of such how great works are constructed? That condemned man's punishment is the city's ornament. So then God knoweth where to place thee. Do not think that thou art disturbing the counsel of God, if thou art minded to be disorderly. Doth not He who knew how to create, know how to

order thee? Good were it for thee to strive for this, to be set in a good place. What was said of Judas by the Apostle? "He went unto his own place."[2] By the operation of course of Divine Providence, because by an evil will he chose to be evil, but God did not by ordering evil make it. But because that evil man himself chose to be a sinner, he did what he would, and suffered what he would not. In that he did what he would, his sin is discovered; in that he suffered what he would not, the order of God is praised.

6. Wherefore have I said all this? That ye, brethren, may understand what was most excellently said by the Lord Jesus Christ, " My Father worketh even hitherto." In that He doth not abandon the creature which He made. And He said, "As He worketh, so do I also work." In this He at once signified that He was equal with God. " My Father," saith He, "worketh hitherto, and I work." Their carnal sense touching the rest[3] was troubled. For they thought that the Lord being wearied rested, that He should work no more. They hear, " My Father worketh even hitherto:" they are troubled. "And I work:"[4] He hath made Himself equal with God: they are troubled. But be not alarmed. The water is troubled, now the sick man is to be cured. What meaneth this? Therefore are they troubled, that the Lord may suffer. The Lord doth suffer, the precious Blood is shed, the sinner is redeemed, grace is given to the sinner, to him that saith, "Wretched man that I am, who shall deliver me from the body of this death? The grace of God, through Jesus Christ our Lord."[5] But how is he cured? If he step down. For that pool was so made, that men should go down, and not come up to it. For there might be pools of such a kind, so constructed, that men must go up to them. But why was this made in such a way that men must go down to it? Because the Lord's Passion searches for the humble. Let the humble go down, let him not be proud, if he wishes to be cured. But why was it but " one "? Because the Church is only One throughout the world, unity is saved. When then one is made whole, unity is signified. By one understand unity. Depart not then from unity, if thou wouldest not be without a part in this saving[6] cure.

7. What then does it mean that the man was in infirmity thirty-eight years? I know, brethren, that I have spoken of this already; but even those who read forget, how much more they who hear but seldom? Attend therefore for a little while, Beloved. In[7] the number forty, the accomplishment of righteousness is

---

[1] Artifex.

[2] Acts i. 25.　　[3] Sabbato.　　[4] John v. 17.
[5] Rom. vii. 24, 25, Vulg.　　[6] Salute.
[7] Serm. i. (li. Ben.) 32 (xxii.).

figured. The accomplishment of righteousness, in that we live here in labour, in toil, in self-restraint, in fastings, in watchings, in tribulations; this is the exercise of righteousness, to bear this present time, and to fast as it were from this world; not from the food of the body, which we do but seldom; but from the love of the world, which we ought to do always. He then fulfils the law who abstains from this world. For he cannot love that which is eternal, unless he shall cease to love that which is temporal. Consider a man's love: think of it as, so to say, the hand of the soul. If it is holding anything, it cannot hold anything else. But that it may be able to hold what is given to it, it must leave go what it holds already. This I say, see how expressly I say it; "Whoso loveth the world cannot love God; he hath his hand engaged." God saith to him, "Hold what I give." He will not leave go what he was holding; he cannot receive what is offered. Have I said a man should not possess ought? If he is able, if perfection require this of him, let him not possess. If hindered by any necessity he is not able, let him possess, not be possessed; let him hold, not be held; let him be the lord of his possessions, not the slave; as saith the Apostle "However, brethren, the time is short; it remaineth that both they that have wives, be as though they had not; and they who buy, as though they possessed not; and they who rejoice, as though they rejoiced not; and they who weep, as though they wept not; and they who use this world, as though they used [1] it not; for the fashion of this world passeth away. I would have you be without carefulness." [2] What is, "Do not love what thou dost possess in this world"? Let it not hold thine hand fast, by which God must be held. Let not thy love be engaged, whereby thou canst make thy way to God, and cleave to Him who created thee.

8. Thou wilt say and make answer to me, "Yea, God knows that I possess innocently what I have." Temptation proves thee. There is a troubling of thy possessions, and thou dost blaspheme. It is but lately we were in such a case. There is a troubling of thy possessions, and thou art not found what thou wast, and dost show that there is one thing in thy mouth to-day, and another in thy mouth yesterday. And I would that thou wouldest only defend thine own even with vehemence; [3] and not try to usurp with audacity another's; and what is worse, to escape reprehension, maintain that what is another's is thine own. But why need I say more? This I advise, this I say, Brethren, and as a brother advise; God bids, and I admonish because I am admonished. He alarmeth me, who doth not

allow me to keep silence. He exacteth of me what He hath given. For He hath given it to be laid out, not to be kept up. And if I should keep it and hide it, He saith to me, "Thou wicked and slothful servant, wherefore gavest thou not My money to the exchangers, that at My coming I might require it with usury?" [4] And what will it profit me that I have lost nothing of that which I received? That is not enough for my Lord, He is covetous; but God's covetousness is our salvation. He is covetous, He looketh for His own money, He gathereth in His Own image. "Thou shouldest have given," saith He, "the money to the exchangers, that at My coming I might require it with usury." And if by any chance forgetfulness should make me fail of admonishing you, the temptations and tribulations at least which we are suffering, would be an admonition to you. Ye have heard at least the word of God. Blessed be the Lord and His glory. For ye are here gathered together, and are hanging on the word of God's minister. Turn not your attention to our flesh, by which the word is given out to you; for hungry men regard not the meanness of the dish, but the preciousness of the food. God is proving you. Ye are gathered together, ye praise the word of God; temptation will prove in what manner ye hear it: ye will have the active business of life whereby your true character will be shown. For so he who to-day is shouting with railings, was yesterday a ready listener. Therefore I forewarn; therefore I tell you, therefore I do not withhold it, my Brethren, that the time of questioning will come. For the Lord maketh question of the righteous and of the ungodly. This you know ye have sung, this have we sung together; "The Lord maketh question of the righteous and the ungodly." And what follows? "But he that loveth iniquity, hateth his own soul." [5] And in another place, "Into the thoughts of the ungodly there shall be questioning made." [6] God doth not make question of thee there, where I question thee. I question thy tongue, God questioneth thy thoughts. For He knoweth how thou dost hear, and He knoweth how to require, Who ordereth me to give. He hath wished me to be a dispenser, the requiring He hath reserved to Himself. To admonish, to teach, to rebuke, is ours; but to save, and to crown, or to condemn, and to cast into hell, is not ours; "But the Judge shall deliver to the officer, and the officer to the prison. Verily I say unto thee, thou shalt not go out thence, till thou payest the last farthing." [7]

9. Let us then return to our subject. The perfection of righteousness is shown by the number forty. What is it to fulfil the number

---

[1] Vulgate. [2] 1 Cor. vii. 29-32. [3] *Clamore.*

[4] Luke xix. 22, 23. [5] Ps. x. 5, Sept. (xi. 5, English version).
[6] Wisd. i. 9. [7] Matt. v. 25, 26.

forty? To restrain one's self from the love of this world. Restraint from temporal things, that they be not loved to our destruction, is, as it were, fasting from this world. Therefore the Lord fasted forty days, and Moses, and Elias. He then who gave His servants the power to fast forty days, could He not fast eighty or a hundred? Why then did He not will to fast more than He had given His servants to do, but because in this number forty is the mystery of fasting, the restraint from this world? What is this to say? What the Apostle says; "The world is crucified to me, and I to the world."[1] He then fulfils the number forty. And what doth the Lord show? That because Moses did this, this Elias, this Christ, that this both the Law, and the Prophets, and the Gospel, teach; that thou mayest not think that there is one thing in the Law, another in the Prophets, another in the Gospel. All Scripture teacheth thee nothing else, but restraint from the love of the world, that thy love may speed on to God. As a figure that the Law teaches this, Moses fasted forty days. As a figure that the Prophets teach it, Elias fasted forty days. As a figure that the Gospel teaches it, the Lord fasted forty days. And therefore in the mount too these three appeared, the Lord in the middle, Moses and Elias at the sides. Wherefore? Because the Gospel itself receives testimony from the Law and the Prophets.[2] But why in the number forty is the perfection of righteousness? In the Psalter it is said, "O God, I will sing a new song unto Thee, upon a psaltery of ten strings will I sing praises unto Thee."[3] Which signifies the ten precepts of the Law, which the Lord came not to destroy, but to fulfil. And the Law itself throughout the whole world, it is evident, hath four quarters, the East, and West, South, and North, as the Scripture saith. And hence the vessel which bare all the emblematic animals, which was exhibited to Peter, when he was told, "Kill and eat,"[4] that it might be shown that the Gentiles should believe and enter into the body of the Church, just as what we eat entereth into our body, and which was let down from heaven by four corners (these are the four quarters of the world), showed that the whole world should believe. Therefore in the number forty is restraint from the world. This is the fulfilling of the Law: now the fulfilling of the Law is charity. And therefore before the Pasch we fast forty days. For this time before the Pasch is the sign of this our toilsome life, wherein, in toils, and cares, and continence, we fulfil the Law. But afterwards we celebrate the Pasch, that is, the days of the Lord's resurrection signifying our own resurrection. Therefore fifty days are cele-

brated; because the reward of the denarius is added to the forty, and it becomes fifty. Why is the reward a denarius? Have ye not read, how that they who were hired into the vineyard, whether at the first, or sixth, or the last hour, could only receive the denarius?[5] When to our righteousness shall be added its reward, we shall be in the number fifty. Yea, and then shall we have none other occupation, save to praise God. And therefore throughout those days we say, "Halleluiah." For Halleluiah is the praise of God. In this frail estate of mortality, in this fortieth number here, as though before the resurrection, let us groan in prayers, that we may sing praises then. Now is the time of longing, then will be the time of embracing and enjoying. Let us not faint in the time of forty, that we may joy in the time of fifty.

10. Now who is he that fulfilleth the Law, but he that hath charity? Ask the Apostle, "Charity is the fulfilling of the Law.[6] For all the Law is fulfilled in one word, in that which is written, Thou shalt love thy neighbour as thyself."[7] But the commandment of charity is twofold; "Thou shalt love the Lord thy God with all thy heart, and with all thy soul, and with all thy mind. This is the great commandment. The other is like it; Thou shalt love thy neighbour as thyself." They are the words of the Lord in the Gospel: "On these two commandments hang all the Law and the Prophets."[8] Without this twofold love the Law cannot be fulfilled. As long as the Law is not fulfilled, there is infirmity. Therefore he had two short, who was infirm thirty and eight years. What means, "had two short"? He did not fulfil these two commandments. What doth it profit that the rest is fulfilled, if those are not fulfilled? Hast thou thirty-eight? If thou have not those two, the rest will profit thee nothing. Thou hast two short, without which the rest avail not, if thou have not the two commandments which conduct unto salvation. "If I speak with the tongues of men and angels, and have not charity, I am become as sounding brass, or a tinkling cymbal. And if I know all mysteries, and all knowledge, and if I have all faith, so that I could remove mountains, and have not charity, I am nothing. And if I distribute all my substance, and if I give my body to be burned, and have not charity, it profiteth me nothing."[9] They are the Apostle's words. All those things therefore which he mentioned are as it were the thirty-eight years; but because charity was not there, there was infirmity. From that infirmity who then shall make whole, but He who came to give charity? "A new commandment I give unto you, that ye love one another."[10] And because He came to

[1] Gal. vi. 14.   [2] Rom. iii. 21.   [3] Ps. cxliv. 9.
[4] Acts x. 13.

[5] Matt. xx. 2.   [6] Rom. xiii. 10.   [7] Gal. v. 14.
[8] Matt. xxii. 37-40.   [9] 1 Cor. xiii. 1-3.   [10] John xiii. 34.

give charity, and charity fulfilleth the Law, with good reason said He, " I came not to destroy the Law, but to fulfil." [1] He cured the sick man, and told him to carry his couch, and go unto his house.[2] And so too He said to the sick of the palsy whom He cured.[3] What is it to carry our couch? The pleasure of our flesh. Where we lie in infirmity, is as it were our bed. But they who are cured master [4] and carry it, are not by this flesh mastered. So then, thou whole one, master the frailness of thy flesh, that in the sign of the forty days' fast from this world, thou mayest fulfil the number forty, for that He hath made that sick man whole, " Who came not to destroy the Law, but to fulfil."

11. Having heard this, direct your heart to Godward. Do not deceive yourselves. Ask yourselves then when it is well with you in the world; then ask yourselves, whether ye love the world, or whether ye love it not; learn to let it go before ye are let go yourselves. What is to let it go? Not heartily to love it. Whilst there is yet something with thee which thou must one day lose, and either in life or death let it go, it cannot be with thee always; whilst I say it is yet with thee, loosen thy love; be prepared for the will of God, hang upon God. Hold thee fast to Him, whom thou canst not lose against thy will, that if it chance thee to lose these temporal things, thou mayest say, " The Lord gave, the Lord hath taken away, as it hath pleased the Lord, so is it done, blessed be the Name of the Lord." [5] But if it chance, and God so wills it, that the things thou hast be with thee even to the last: for thy detachment from this life thou receivest the denarius, the fifty, and the perfection of blessedness cometh to pass in thee, when thou shalt sing Halleluiah. Having these things which I have now brought forward in your memory, may they avail to overthrowing your love of the world. Evil is its friendship, deceitful, it makes a man the enemy of God. Soon, in one single temptation, a man offendeth God, and becometh His enemy. Nay not then becometh His enemy; but is then discovered to have been His enemy. For when he was loving and praising Him, he was an enemy; but he neither knew it himself, nor did others. Temptation came, the pulse is touched, and the fever discovered. So then, brethren, the love of the world, and the friendship of the world, make men the enemies of God. And it does not make good what it promises, it is a liar, and deceiveth. Therefore men never cease hoping in this world, and who attains to all he hopes for? But whereunto soever he attains, what he has attained to is forthwith disesteemed by him. Other things begin to be desired, other fond things are hoped for; and when they

come, whatsoever it is that comes to thee, is disesteemed. Hold thee fast then to God, for He can never be of light esteem, for nothing is more beautiful than He. For for this cause are these things disesteemed, because they cannot stand, because they are not what He is. For nought, O soul, sufficeth thee, save He who created thee. Whatsoever else thou apprehendest is wretched; for He Alone can suffice thee who made thee after His Own likeness. Thus it was expressly said, " Lord, show us the Father, and it sufficeth us." [6] There only can there be security; and where security can be, there in a certain sort will be insatiable satiety. For thou wilt neither be so satiated, as to wish to depart; nor will anything be wanting, as though thou couldest suffer want.

SERMON LXXVI.

[CXXVI. BEN.]

ON THE WORDS OF THE GOSPEL, JOHN V. 19, " THE SON CAN DO NOTHING OF HIMSELF, BUT WHAT HE SEETH THE FATHER DOING."

1. THE mysteries and secrets of the kingdom of God first seek for believing men, that they may make them understanding. For faith is understanding's step; and understanding faith's attainment.[7] This the Prophet expressly says to all who prematurely and in undue order look for understanding, and neglect faith. For he says, " Unless ye believe, ye shall not understand." [8] Faith itself then also hath a certain light of its own in the Scriptures, in Prophecy, in the Gospel, in the Lessons of the Apostles. For all these things which are read to us in this present time, are lights in a dark place, that we may be nourished up unto the day. The Apostle Peter says, " We have a more sure word of prophecy, whereunto ye do well that ye take heed, as unto a light in a dark place, until the day dawn, and the daystar arise in your hearts." [9]

2. Ye see then, Brethren, how exceedingly unregulated and disordered in their haste are they who like immature conceptions seek an untimely birth before the birth; who say to us, " Why dost thou bid me believe what I do not see? Let me see something that I may believe. Thou biddest me believe whilst yet I see not; I wish to see, and by seeing to believe, not by hearing." Let the Prophet speak. " Unless ye believe, ye shall not understand." Thou wishest to ascend, and dost forget the steps. Surely, out of all order. O man, if I could show thee already what thou mightest see, I should not exhort thee to believe.

3. Faith [10] then, as it has been elsewhere de-

---

[1] Matt. v. 17. [2] John v. 8, 9. [3] Mark ii. 9.
[4] *Continent.* [5] Job i. 21, Sept.
[6] John xiv. 8. [7] *Meritum.*
[8] Isa. vii. 9, Sept. [9] 2 Pet. i. 19.
[10] *Substantia; ὑπόστασις.*

fined, is " the firm support of those who hope,[1] the evidence of things which are not seen."[2] If they are not seen, how are they evidenced to be? What! Whence are these things which thou seest, but from That which thou seest not? To be sure thou dost see somewhat that thou mayest believe somewhat, and from that thou seest, mayest believe what thou seest not. Be not ungrateful to Him who hath made thee see, whereby thou mayest be able to believe what as yet thou canst not see. God hath given thee eyes in the body, reason in the heart; arouse the reason of the heart, wake up the interior inhabitant of thine interior eyes, let it take to its windows, examine the creature of God. For there is one within who sees by the eyes. For when thy thoughts within thee are on any other subject, and the inhabitant within is turned away, the things which are before thine eyes thou seest not. For to no purpose are the windows open, when he who looks through them is away. It is not then the eyes that see, but some one sees by the eyes; awake him, arouse him. For this hath not been denied thee; God hath made thee a rational animal, set thee over the cattle, formed thee after His Own image. Oughtest thou to use them as the cattle do; only to see what to add to thy belly, not to thy soul? Stir up, I say, the eye of reason, use thine eyes as a man should, consider the heaven and earth, the ornaments of the heaven, the fruitfulness of the earth, the flight of the birds, the swimming of the fish, the virtue[3] of the seeds, the order of the seasons; consider the works, and seek for the Author; take a view of what thou seest, and seek Him whom thou seest not. Believe on Him whom thou seest not, because of these things which thou seest. And lest thou think that it is with mine own words that I have exhorted thee; hear the Apostle saying, " For the invisible things of God from the creation of the world are clearly seen by those things which are made."[4]

4. These things thou disregardedst, nor didst look upon them as a man, but as an irrational animal. The Prophet cried out to thee, and cried in vain. "Be ye not like to horse and mule, which have no understanding."[5] These things I say thou didst see, and disregard. God's daily miracles were disesteemed, not for their easiness, but their constant repetition. For what is more difficult to understand than a man's birth, that one who was in existence should by dying depart into darkness,[6] and that one who was not, by being born should come forth to light?[7] What so marvellous, what so difficult to comprehend? But with God easy to be done. Marvel

at these things, awake; at His unusual works, thou canst wonder, are they greater than those which thou art accustomed to see? Men wondered that our Lord God Jesus Christ filled so many thousands with five loaves;[8] and they do not wonder that through a few grains the whole earth is filled with crops. When the water was made wine,[9] men saw it, and were amazed; what else takes place with the rain along the root of the vine? He did the one, He does the other; the one that thou mayest be fed, the other that thou mayest wonder. But both are wonderful, for both are the works of God. Man sees unusual things, and wonders; whence is the man himself who wonders? where was he? whence came he forth? whence the fashion of his body? whence the distinction of his limbs? whence that beautiful form? from what beginnings? what contemptible beginnings? And he wonders at other things, when he the wonderer is himself a great wonder. Whence then are these things which thou seest but from Him whom thou seest not? But as I had begun to say, because these things were disesteemed by thee, He came Himself to do unusual things, that in these usual ones too thou mightest acknowledge thy Creator.[10] He came to Whom it is said, " Renew signs."[11] To Whom it is said, "Show forth Thy marvellous mercies."[12] For dispensing them He ever was; He dispensed them, and no one marvelled. Therefore came He a Little one to the little, He came a Physician to the sick, who was able to come when He would, to return when He would, to do whatsoever He would, to judge as He would. And this, His will, is very righteousness; yea what He willeth, I say, is very righteousness. For that is not unrighteous which He willeth, nor can that be right which He willeth not. He came to raise the dead, men marvelling that He restored a man to the light who was in light already, He who day by day bringeth forth to the light those who were not.

5. These things He did, yet was He despised by the many, who considered not so much what great things He did, as how small He was; as though they said within themselves, "These are divine things, but He is a man." Two things then thou seest, divine works, and a man. If divine works cannot be wrought but by God, take heed lest in This Man God lie concealed. Attend, I say, to what thou seest, believe what thou seest not. He hath not abandoned thee, who hath called thee to believe; though He enjoin thee to believe that which thou canst not see: yet hath He not given thee up to see nothing whereby thou mayest be able to believe what thou dost not see. Is the creation itself a small

---

[1] *Sperantium*, as St. Augustin uniformly reads, Tract. 79 and 95, in *Joh. de pecc. mer.* ii. 31. St. Ambrose and St. Jerome have the pass.
[2] Heb. xi. 1.   [3] *Vim.*   [4] Rom. i. 20.
[5] Ps. xxxii. 9.   [6] *Secreta.*   [7] *Publica.*

[8] Matt. xiv. 21.   [9] John ii 9.   [10] *Artificem.*
[11] Ecclus. vi. 37.
[12] Ps. xvi. 7, Sept. (xvii. 7, English version).

sign, a small indication of the Creator? He also came, He did miracles. Thou couldest not see God, a man thou couldest; so God was made Man, that in One thou mightest have both what to see, and what to believe. "In the beginning was the Word, and the Word was with God, and the Word was God." [1] Thus thou hearest, and as yet seest not. Lo, He comes, lo, He is born, lo, He comes forth of a woman, who made man and woman. He who made man and woman was not made by man and woman. For thou wouldest peradventure have been likely to despise Him for being born, the manner of His birth canst thou not despise; for He ever was before that He was born. Lo, I say, He took a Body, He was clothed in Flesh, He came forth from the womb. [2] Dost thou now see? seest thou now, I say? I ask as to the Flesh, but I point out as to That Flesh; something thou seest, and something thou seest not. Lo, in this very Birth, there are at once two things, one which thou mayest see, and another thou mayest not see; but so that by this which thou seest, thou mayest believe that which thou seest not. Thou hadst begun to despise, because thou seest Him who was born; believe what thou dost not see, that He was born of a virgin. "How trifling a person," says one, "is he who was born!" But how great is He who was of a virgin born! And He who was born of a virgin brought thee a temporal miracle; He was not born of a father, of any man, I mean, His father, yet was He born of the flesh. But let it not seem impossible to thee, that He was born by His mother only, Who made man before father and mother.

6. He brought thee then a temporal miracle, that thou mayest seek and admire Him who is Eternal. For He "who came forth as a Bridegroom out of His chamber," [3] that is, out of the virgin's womb, where the holy nuptials were celebrated of the Word and the Flesh: He brought, I say, a temporal miracle; but He is Himself eternal, He is coeternal with the Father, He it is, who "In the beginning was the Word, and the Word was with God, and the Word was God." [1] He did for thee whereby thou mightest be cured, that thou mightest be able to see what thou didst not see. What thou despisest in Christ, is not yet the contemplation of him that is made whole, but the medicine of the sick. Do not hasten to the vision of the whole. The Angels see, the Angels rejoice, the Angels feed Thereon and live; Whereon they feed faileth not, nor is their food minished. In the thrones

of glory, in the regions of the heavens, in the parts which are above the heavens, the Word is seen by the Angels, and is their Joy; is their Food, and endureth. But in order that man might eat Angel's Bread, the Lord of Angels became Man. This is our Salvation, the Medicine of the infirm, the Food of the whole.

7. And He spake to men, and said what ye have now heard, "The Son can do nothing of Himself, but what He seeth the Father do." [4] Is there now any one, think we, that understandeth this? Is there any one, think we, in whom the eye-salve of the flesh hath now its effect to the discerning in any fashion the brightness of the Divinity? He hath spoken, let us speak too; He, because the Word; we, because of the Word. And why speak we, howsoever we do it, of the Word? Because we were made by the Word after the likeness of the Word. As far then as we are capable of, as far as we can be partakers of that ineffableness, let us also speak, and let us not be contradicted. For our faith hath gone before, so that we may say, "I believed, therefore have I spoken." [5] I speak then that which I believe; whether or no I also see, or howsoever I see; He seeth rather; ye cannot see it. But when I shall have spoken, whether he who sees what I speak of, believe that I see too what I have spoken of, or whether he believe it not, what is that to me? Let him only really [6] see, and let him believe what he will of me.

8. "The Son can do nothing of Himself, but what He seeth the Father do." Here rises up an error of the Arians; but it rises up that it may fall; because it is not humbled, that it may rise. What is it which hath set thee [7] off? Thou wouldest say that the Son is less than the Father. For thou hast heard, "The Son can do nothing of Himself, but what He seeth the Father do." From this thou wouldest have the Son called less; it is this I know, I know it is this hath set thee off; believe that He is not less, thou canst not as yet see it, believe, this is what I was saying a little while ago. "But how," you will say, "am I to believe against His own words"? He saith Himself, "The Son can do nothing of Himself, but what He seeth the Father do." Attend too to that which follows; "For what things soever the Father doeth, the same also doeth the Son likewise;" He did not say, "such things," Beloved, consider a while, that ye cause not confusion [8] to yourselves. There is need of a tranquil heart, a godly and devout faith, a religious earnest attention; attend, not to me the poor vessel, but to Him who putteth the bread in the vessel. Attend then a while. For in all that I have said above in exhorting

[1] John i. 1.
[2] The punctuation of the reprint of the Ben. has been followed, " *Jamne vides jam, inquam, vides? carnem interrogo, sed carnem ostendo.*" The Ben. pointed, "*vides carnem,*" but noted *Locus mendosus.* The meaning may be, "It is of His Birth in the Flesh that I enquire, but I point out the mode of that Birth, *i.e.* of a Virgin."
[3] Ps. xix. 5.

[4] John v. 19.   [5] Ps. cxvi. 10.   [6] *Sinceriter.*
[7] *Movit.*   [8] *Strepitum.*

you to faith, that the mind imbued with faith may be capable of understanding, all that has been said has had a pleasing, glad, and easy sound, has cheered your minds, ye have followed it, ye have understood what I said. But what I am now about to say I hope there are some who will understand; yet I fear that all will not understand. And seeing that God hath by the lesson of the Gospel proposed to us a subject to speak upon, and we cannot avoid that which the Master hath proposed; I fear lest haply they who will not understand, who perhaps will be the greater number, should think that I have spoken to them in vain; but yet because of those who will understand, I do not speak in vain. Let him who understandeth rejoice, let him who doth not understand bear it patiently; what he doth not understand, let him bear, and that he may understand, let him bear delay.

9. He doth not say then, "What things soever the Father doeth, such doeth the Son:" as if the Father doeth some things, and the Son others. For it did seem as though He had meant this when He said above, "The Son doeth nothing of Himself, but what He seeth the Father do." Mark; He did not there either say, "But what He heareth the Father enjoin;" but, "what He seeth the Father do." If then we consult the carnal understanding, or sense rather, He hath set before Him as it were two workmen,[1] the Father and the Son, the Father working without seeing any, the Son working from seeing the Father. This is still a carnal view. Nevertheless, in order to understand those things which are higher, let us not decline these lower and mean things. First, let us set something before our eyes in this way; let us suppose there are two workmen, father and son. The father has made a chest, which the son could not make, unless he saw the father making it: he keeps his mind on the chest which the father has made, and makes another chest like it, not the same. I put off for a while the words which follow, and now I ask the Arian; "Dost thou understand it in the sense of this supposition? Hath the Father done something, which when the Son saw Him do, He too hath done something like it? For do the words by which thou art perplexed seem to have this meaning?" Now He doth not say, "The Son can do nothing of Himself, but what He heareth the Father enjoin." But He saith, "The Son can do nothing of Himself, but what He seeth the Father do." See, if thou understand it thus; the Father hath done something, and the Son attendeth that He may see what He Himself too hath to do; and that, some other thing like that which the Father had done. This which the Father hath done,

by whom hath He done it? If not by the Son, if not by the Word, thou hast incurred the charge of blasphemy against the Gospel. "For all things were made by Him."[2] So then what the Father had done, He had done by the Word; if by the Word He had done it, He had done it by the Son. Who then is that other who attends, that He may do some other thing which he seeth the Father do? Ye have not been wont to say that the Father hath two sons: there is One, One Only-Begotten of Him. But through His mercy, Alone as regards His Divinity and not Alone as regards the inheritance. The Father hath made coheirs with His Only Son; not begotten them like Him of His Own Substance, but adopted them by Him out of His Own family. For "we have been called," as Holy Scripture testifieth, "into the adoption of sons."[3]

10. What then sayest thou? It is the Only Son Himself That speaketh; the Only-Begotten Son speaketh in the Gospel: the Word Himself hath given us the words, we have heard Himself saying, "The Son can do nothing of Himself, but what He seeth the Father do." Now then the Father doeth that the Son may see what to do; and nevertheless the Father doeth nothing but by the Son. Assuredly thou art confused, thou heretic, assuredly thou art confused; but thy confusion is as from taking helebore, that thou mayest be cured. Even now thou canst not find thine own self, thou dost even thyself condemn thine own judgment and thy carnal view, I think. Put behind thee the eyes of the flesh, raise up what eyes thou hast in thine heart, behold things divine. They are men's words it is true thou hearest, and by a man, by the Evangelist, by the Gospel thou hearest men's words, as a man; but it is of the Word of God thou hearest, that thou mayest hear what is human, come to know what is Divine. The Master hath given trouble, that He might instruct; hath sown a difficulty,[4] that He might excite an earnest attention. "The Son can do nothing of Himself, but what He seeth the Father do." It might follow[5] that He should say, "For what things soever the Father doeth, the like doeth the Son." This He doth not say; but, "What things soever the Father doeth, the same doeth the Son likewise." The Father doeth not some things, the Son other things; because all things that the Father doeth, He doeth by the Son. The Son raised Lazarus; did not the Father raise him?[6] The Son gave sight to the blind man; did not the Father give him sight?[7] The Father by the Son in the Holy Ghost. It is the Trinity; but the Operation of

---

[1] Artifices.

[2] John i. 3.   [3] Eph. i. 5.   [4] Quæstionem.
[5] Consequens.   [6] John xi.   [7] John ix.

the Trinity is One, the Majesty One, the Eternity One, the Coeternity One, and the Works the Same. The Father doth not create some men, the Son others, the Holy Ghost others; the Father and the Son and the Holy Ghost create one and the same man; and the Father and the Son and the Holy Ghost, One God, createth him.

11. You observe a Plurality of Persons, but acknowledge the Unity of the Divinity. For because of the Plurality of Persons it was said, "Let Us make man after Our image and likeness." He did not say, "I will make man, and do Thou attend when I am making him, that Thou too mayest be able to make another." "Let Us make," He saith; I hear the Plurality; "after Our image;"[1] again I hear the Plurality. Where then is the Singularity of the Divinity? Read what follows, "And God made man."[2] It is said, "Let Us make man;" and it is not said, "The Gods made man." The Unity is understood in that it was said, "God made man."

12. Where then is that carnal view?[3] Be it confounded, hidden, brought to nought; let the Word of God speak to us. Even now as godly men, as believing already, as already imbued with faith, and having gotten some attainment[4] of understanding, turn we to the Word Himself, to the Fountain of light, and let us say together, "O Lord, the Father doeth ever the same things as Thou; for that whatsoever the Father doeth, by Thee He doeth it. We have heard that Thou art the Word in the beginning;[5] we have not seen, but believed. There too have we heard what follows, that 'all things were made by Thee.'[6] All things then that the Father doeth, He doeth by Thee. Therefore Thou doest the same things as the Father. Why then didst Thou wish to say, 'The Son can do nothing of Himself'? For I see a certain equality in Thee with the Father, in that I hear, 'What things soever the Father doeth, the same doeth the Son;' I recognise an equality, hereby I understand, and comprehend as far as I am able, 'I and My Father are One.'[7] What meaneth it, that Thou canst do nothing, but what Thou seest the Father do? What meaneth this?"

13. Peradventure He would say to me, yea say to us all: "Now as to this that I have said, 'The Son can do nothing, but what He seeth the Father do;' My 'Seeing' how dost thou understand? My 'Seeing,' what is it? Put aside for a while the form of the servant which He took for thy sake. For in that servant's form our Lord had eyes and ears in the Flesh, and

that human form was the same figure of a Body, such as we bear, the same outlines of members. That Flesh had come from Adam: but He was not as Adam. So then the Lord walking whether on the earth or in the sea, as it pleased Him, as He would, for whatever He would, He could; looked at what He would; He fixed His eyes, He saw; He turned away His eyes, and did not see; who followed was behind Him, whoso could be seen, before Him; with the eyes of His Body, He saw only what was before Him. But from His Divinity nothing was hid. Put aside, put aside, I say, for a while the form of the servant, look at the Form of God in which He was before the world was made; in which He was equal to the Father; hereby receive and understand what He saith to thee, 'Who being in the form of God, thought it not robbery to be equal with God.'[8] There see Him if thou canst, that thou mayest be able to see what His 'Seeing' is." "In the beginning was the Word." How doth the Word see? Hath the Word eyes, or are our eyes found in Him, the eyes not of the flesh, but the eyes of godly hearts? For, "Blessed are the pure in heart, for they shall see God."[9]

14. Christ thou seest Man and God; He doth manifest to thee the Man, God He reserveth for thee. Now see how He reserveth God for thee, who doth manifest Himself to thee as Man. "Whoso loveth Me," saith He, "keepeth My commandments; whoso loveth Me shall be loved of My Father, and I will love him."[10] And as if it were asked, "What wilt Thou give to him whom Thou lovest?" "And I will manifest Myself," saith He, "to him." What meaneth this, Brethren? He whom they saw already, promised that He would manifest Himself to them. To whom? Those by whom He was seen, or those also by whom He was not seen? Thus speaking to a certain Apostle, who asked to see the Father, that it might suffice him, and said, "Show us the Father, and it sufficeth us"[11]—Then He standing before this servant's eyes, in the form of a servant, reserving for his eyes when[12] deified[13] the Form of God, saith to him, "Have I been so long time with you, and have ye not known Me? He that seeth Me, seeth the Father also." Thou askest to see the Father; see Me, thou seest Me, and dost not see Me. Thou seest what for thee I have assumed, thou dost not see What I have reserved for thee. Give ear to My commandments, purify thine eyes. "For whoso loveth

---

[8] Phil. ii. 6.
[9] Matt. v. 8.
[10] John xiv. 21.
[11] John xiv. 8.
[12] *Deificati.*
[13] *Vid.* St. Athanasius, *Treatise against Arians*, Oxford edit. Nicene Def. ch. iii. 12, § 14, and Disc. 1, ch. xi. § 39, p. 336, and note c. *Vide* St. Augustin, *Ps.* 49, § 2.

---

[1] Gen. i. 26.   [2] Gen. i. 27.   [3] *Intentio.*
[4] *Merito.*   [5] John i. 1.   [6] John i. 3.
[7] John x. 30.

Me, keepeth My commandments, and I will love him." To him as keeping My commandments, and by My commandments made whole, will I manifest Myself.

15. If then, Brethren, we are not able to see what the "Seeing" of the Word is, whither are we going? what Vision it may be with too great haste are we requiring? why are we wishing to have shown us what we are not able to see? These things accordingly are spoken of which we desire to see, not as what we are able already to comprehend. For if thou seest the "Seeing" of the Word, peradventure in that thou seest the "Seeing" of the Word, thou wilt see the Word Himself; that the Word may not be one thing, the "Seeing" of the Word another, lest there be Therein anything joined, and coupled, and double, and compacted. For It is something Simple, of a Simplicity ineffable. Not as with a man, the man is one thing, the man's seeing another. For sometimes a man's seeing is extinguished, and the man remains. This it is of which I said that I was about to say something which all would not be able to understand; the Lord even grant that some may have understood. My Brethren, to this end doth He exhort us, that we may see, that the "Seeing" of the Word is beyond our powers; for they are small; be they nourished, perfected. Whereby? By the commandments. What commandments? "He that loveth Me, keepeth My commandments."[1] What commandments? For already do we wish to increase, to be strengthened, perfected, that we may see the "Seeing" of the Word. Tell us, Lord, now what commandments? "A new commandment I give unto you, that ye love one another."[2] This charity then, Brethren, let us draw from the plentifulness of the Fountain, let us receive it; be nourished by it. Receive thou[3] that whereby thou mayest be able to receive. Let charity give thee birth, let charity nourish thee; charity bring thee to perfection, charity strengthen thee; that thou mayest see this "Seeing" of the Word, that the Word is not one thing and His "Seeing" another, but that the "Seeing" of the Word is the Very Word Himself; and so perhaps thou wilt soon understand that that which is said, "The Son can do nothing of Himself, but what He seeth the Father do," is as if He had said, "The Son would not be, if He had not been born of the Father." Let this suffice, Brethren; I know that I have said that which perhaps, if meditated upon, may develop itself to many, which oftentimes when expressed in words may chance to be obscured.[4]

---

[1] John xiv. 21.
[2] John xiii. 34.
[3] *Cape per quod sis capax.*
[4] See Tract. 18 and 20 in *Joh.*

SERMON LXXVII.

[CXXVII. BEN.]

ON THE WORDS OF THE GOSPEL, JOHN V. 25, "VERILY, VERILY, I SAY UNTO YOU, THE HOUR COMETH, AND NOW IS, WHEN THE DEAD SHALL HEAR THE VOICE OF THE SON OF GOD; AND THEY THAT HEAR SHALL LIVE," ETC.; AND ON THE WORDS OF THE APOSTLE, "THINGS WHICH EYE SAW NOT," ETC., 1 COR. II. 9.

1. OUR hope, Brethren, is not of this present time, nor of this world, nor in that happiness whereby men are blinded that forget God. This ought we above all things to know, and in a Christian heart hold fast, that we were not made Christians for the good things of the present time, but for something else which God at once promiseth, and man doth not yet comprehend. For of this good it is said, "That eye hath not seen, nor ear heard, neither hath it entered into the heart of man, what things God hath prepared for them that love Him."[5] Because then this good, so great, so excellent, so ineffable, fell not in with man's understanding, it required God's promise. For what hath been promised him, man blind of heart doth not now comprehend; nor can it be shown to him at present, what he will one day be to whom the promise is given. For so an infant child, if he could understand the words of one speaking, when himself could neither speak, nor walk, nor do anything, but feeble as we see he is, unable to stand,[6] requiring the assistance of others, were able only to understand him who should speak to him and tell him, "Lo, as thou seest me walking, working, speaking, after a few years thou shalt be as I am;" as he considered himself and the other, though he would see what was promised; yet considering his own feebleness, would not believe, and yet he would see what was promised. But with us infants, as it were, lying in this flesh and feebleness, that which is promised is at once great and is not seen; and so faith is aroused whereby we believe that we do not see, that we may attain[7] to see what we believe. Whosoever derideth this faith, so as to think that he is not to believe in that he doth not see; when that shall come which he believed not, is put to shame: being confounded is separated, being separated, is condemned. But whoso shall have believed, is put aside at the right hand, and shall stand with great confidence and joy among those to whom it shall be said, "Come, blessed of My Father, receive the kingdom which hath been prepared for you from the beginning of the world."[8] But the Lord made an end when He spake these words, thus, "These shall go into

---

[5] 1 Cor. ii. 9.   [6] *Jacentem.*   [7] *Mereamur.*
[8] Matt. xxv. 34.

everlasting burning, but the righteous into life eternal." [1] This is the life eternal which is promised us.

2. Because men love to live on this earth, life is promised them; and because they exceedingly fear to die, eternal life is promised them. What dost thou love? To live. This shalt thou have. What dost thou fear? To die. Thou shalt not suffer it. This seemed to be enough for human infirmity, that it should be said, "Thou shalt have eternal life." This the mind of man can comprehend, by its present condition it can in some sort comprehend what is to be. But by the imperfection of its present condition how far can it comprehend it? Because he lives, and does not wish to die; he loves eternal life, he wishes to live always, never to die. But they who shall be tormented in punishments, have even a wish to die, and cannot. It is no great thing then to live long, or to live for ever; but to live blessedly is a great thing. Let us love eternal life, and hereby may we know how greatly we ought to labour for eternal life, when we see men who love the present life, which lasts but for a time and must be brought to an end, labour so for it, that when the fear of death comes, they will do whatever they can, not to put away, but to put off death. How does a man labour, when death threatens, by flight, by concealment, by giving all he has, and redeeming himself, by toil, by endurance of torments and uneasinesses, by calling in physicians, and whatever else a man can do? See, how that after exhausting all his labour and his means, he is but able to contrive to live a little longer; to live always, he is not able. If then men strive with so great labour, with so great efforts, so great a cost, such earnestness, such watchfulness, such carefulness, that they may live a little longer; how should they strive that they may live for ever? And if they are called wise, who by all means strive to put off death, and live a few days, that they lose not a few days: how foolish are they who so live as to lose the day eternal!

3. This then only can be promised us, that this gift of God may in whatever measure be sweet to us, from this which we have at present; seeing that it is of His gift we have it, that we live, that we are in health. When then eternal life is promised, let us set before our eyes a life of such a kind, as to remove from it everything unpleasant which we suffer here. For it is easier for us to find what is not there, than what is there. Lo, here we live; we shall live there also. Here we are in health when we are not sick, and there is no pain in the body; there we shall be in health also. And when it is well with us in

this life, we suffer no scourge; we shall suffer none there also. Suppose then a man here below living, in sound health, suffering no scourge; if any one were to grant him that he should be for ever so, and that this good estate should never cease, how greatly would he rejoice? how greatly be transported? how would he not contain himself in joy without pain, without torment, without end of life? If God had promised us this only, which I have mentioned, which I have just now in such words as I was able, described and set forth; at what a price ought it to be purchased if it were to be sold, how great a sum ought to be given to buy it? Would all that thou hadst suffice, even though thou shouldest possess the whole world? And yet it is to be sold; buy it if thou wilt. And be not much disquieted for a thing so great, because of the largeness of the price. Its price is no more than what thou hast. Now to procure any great and precious thing, thou wouldest get ready gold, or silver, or money, or any increase of cattle, or fruits, which might be produced in thy possessions, to buy this I know not what great and excellent thing, whereby to live in this earth happily. Buy this too, if thou wilt. Do not look for what thou hast, but for what thou art. The price of this thing is thyself. Its price is what thou art thyself. Give thine own self, and thou shalt have it. Why art thou troubled? why disquieted? What? Art thou going to seek for thine own self, or to buy thyself? Lo, give thine own self as thou art, such as thou art to that thing, and thou shalt have it. But you will say, "I am wicked, and perhaps it will not accept me." By giving thyself to it, thou wilt be good. The giving thyself to this faith and promise, this is to be good. And when thou shalt be good, thou wilt be the price of this thing; and shalt have, not only what I have mentioned, health, safety, life, and life without end; thou shalt not only have this, I will take away other things yet. There shall there be no weariness, and sleeping; there shall there be no hunger, and thirst; there shall there be no growing, and growing old; because there shall be no birth either where the numbers remain entire. The number that is there is entire; nor is there any need for it to be increased, seeing there is no chance of diminution there. Lo, how many things have I taken away, and I have not yet said what shall be there. Lo, already there is life, and safety; no scourge, no hunger, no thirst, no failing, none of these; and yet I have not said, "what eye hath not seen, nor ear heard, nor hath ascended into the heart of man." For if I have said it, it is false that is written, "Eye hath not seen, nor ear heard, neither hath it ascended into the heart of man." For whence should it ascend into my heart, that I should say "that which hath not ascended into

[1] Matt. xxv. 46.

the heart of man"? It is believed, and not seen; not only not seen, but not even expressed. How then is it believed, if it is not expressed? Who believes what he doth not hear? But if he hear it that he may believe, it is expressed; if expressed, it is thought of; if thought of and expressed, then it entereth into the ears of men. And because it would not be expressed if it were not thought of, it hath ascended also into the heart of man. Lo, already the mere proposing of so great a thing disturbs us, that we cannot put it forth clearly in words. Who then can explain the thing itself?

4. Let us attend to the Gospel; just now the Lord was speaking, and let us do what He said. "He that believeth in Me," saith He, "passeth from death unto life, and cometh not into judgment. Verily I say unto you, that the hour shall come, and now is, when the dead shall hear the Voice of the Son of God, and they that hear shall live. For as the Father hath life in Himself, so hath He given to the Son to have life in Himself." [1] By begetting Him He gave it; in that He begat, He gave it. For the Son is of the Father, not the Father of the Son; but the Father is the Father of the Son, and the Son is the Son of the Father. I say the Son is begotten of the Father, not the Father of the Son; and the Son was always, always therefore begotten. Who can comprehend this "always begotten"? For when any man hears of one begotten, it occurs to him; "Therefore there was a time, when he who was begotten was not." What say we then? Not so; there was no time before the Son, for that "all things were made by Him." [2] If all things were made by Him, times also were made by Him; how could times be before the Son, by whom times were made? Take away then all times, the Son was with the Father always. If the Son were with the Father always, and yet the Son, He was begotten always; if begotten always, He who was begotten was always with Him That begat Him.

5. You will say, "This have I never seen, one begetting, and always with him whom he begat; but he that begat came first, and he that was begotten followed in time." You say well, "I have never seen this;" for this appertains to "that which eye hath not seen." Do you ask how it may be expressed? It cannot be expressed; "For the ear hath not heard, neither hath it ascended unto the heart of man." Be it believed and adored, when we believe, we adore; when we adore, we grow; when we grow, we comprehend. For as yet whilst we are in this flesh, as long as we are absent from the Lord, we are, with respect to the Holy Angels who see these things, infants to be suckled by faith, here-

after to be fed by sight. For so saith the Apostle, "As long as we are in the body we are absent from the Lord. For we walk by faith, not by sight." [3] We shall some day come to sight, which is thus promised us by John in his Epistle; "Dearly beloved, we are the sons of God, and it hath not yet appeared what we shall be." [4] We are the sons of God now by grace, by faith, by the Sacrament, by the Blood of Christ, by the redemption of the Saviour; "We are the sons of God, and it hath not yet appeared what we shall be. We know that when He shall appear, we shall be like Him, for we shall see Him as He is."

6. Lo, unto the comprehending of what are we being nourished up; lo, unto the embracing and the feeding on what are we being nourished up; yet so as that that which is fed on is not diminished, and he that feedeth is supported. For now food supports us by eating it; but the food which is eaten, is diminished; but when we shall begin to feed on Righteousness, to feed on Wisdom, to feed on that Food Immortal, we are at once supported, and That Food is not diminished. For if the eye knows how to feed on light, and yet doth not diminish the light; for the light will be no less because it is seen by more; it feeds the eyes of more, and yet is as great as it was before: both they are fed, and it is not diminished; if God hath granted this to the light which He hath made for the eyes of the flesh, what is He Himself, the Light for the eyes of the heart? If then any choice [5] food were praised to thee, on which thou wast to dine, thou wouldest prepare the stomach; God is praised to thee, prepare the heart.

7. Behold what thy Lord saith to thee: "The hour shall come," saith He, "and now is." "The hour shall come," yea, that very hour, "now is, when"—what? "when the dead shall hear the Voice of the Son of God, and they that shall hear shall live." They then that shall not hear, shall not live. What is, "They that shall hear"? They that shall obey. What is, "They that shall hear"? They that shall believe and obey, they shall live. So then before they believed and obeyed, they lay dead; they walked, and were dead. What availed it to them, that they walked, being dead? And yet if any among them were to die a bodily death, they would run, get ready the grave, wrap him up, carry him out, bury him, the dead, the dead; of whom it is said, "Let the dead bury their dead." [6] Such dead as these are in such wise raised by the Word of God, as to live in faith. They who were dead in unbelief, are aroused by the Word. Of this hour said the Lord, "The hour shall come, and now is." For with His Own Word did He raise

---

[1] John v. 24–26. [2] John i. 3. [3] 2 Cor. v. 6, 7. [4] 1 John iii. 2. [5] Magnus.
[6] Matt. viii. 22.

them that were dead in unbelief; of whom the Apostle says, "Arise thou that sleepest, and rise up from the dead, and Christ shall give thee light." [1] This is the resurrection of hearts, this is the resurrection of the inner man, this is the resurrection of the soul.

8. But this is not the only resurrection, there remains a resurrection of the body also. Whoso riseth again in soul, riseth again in body to his blessedness. For in soul all do not rise again; in body all are to rise again. In soul, I say, all do not rise again; but they that believe and obey; for, "They that shall hear shall live." But as the Apostle says, "All men have not faith." [2] If then all men have not faith, all men do not rise again in soul. When thy hour of the resurrection of the body shall come, all shall rise again; be they good or bad, all shall rise again. But whoso first riseth again in soul, to his blessedness riseth again in body; whoso doth not first rise again in soul, riseth again in body to his curse. Whoso riseth again in soul, riseth again in body unto life; whoso riseth not again in soul, riseth again in body unto punishment. Seeing then that the Lord hath impressed upon us this resurrection of souls, unto which we ought all to hasten, and to labour that we may live therein, and living persevere even unto the end, it remained for Him to impress upon us the resurrection of bodies also, which is to be at the end of the world. Now hear how He hath impressed this too.

9. When He had said, "Verily I say unto you, The hour shall come, and now is, when the dead," that is, the unbelievers, "shall hear the Voice of the Son of God," that is, the Gospel, "and they that shall hear," that is, that shall obey, "shall live," that is, shall be justified, and shall be unbelievers no longer; when, I say, He had said this, forasmuch as He saw that we had need to be instructed as to the resurrection of the flesh also, and were not to be left thus, He went on and said, "For as the Father hath life in Himself, so hath He given to the Son to have life in Himself." This refers to the resurrection of souls, to the quickening of souls. Then He added, "And hath given Him power to execute judgment also, because He is the Son of Man." This Son of God, is Son of Man. For if the Son of God had continued the Son of God, and had not been made the Son of Man, He would not have delivered the sons of men. He who had made man, was Himself made that which He made, that what He made might not perish. But He was in such wise made the Son of Man, as to continue the Son of God. For He was made Man by assuming that which He was not, not by losing That

which He was; continuing God, He was made Man. He took thee, He was not consumed in thee. As such then came He to us, the Son of God, and Son of Man, the Maker and the Made, the Creator and the Created; the Creator of His mother, Created of His mother; such came He to us. In respect of His being the Son of God, He saith, "The hour shall come, and now is, when the dead shall hear the Voice of the Son of God." He did not say, "Of the Son of Man;" for He was impressing the truth, wherein He is equal to the Father. "And they that shall hear shall live. For as the Father hath life in Himself, so hath He given to the Son to have life in Himself;" not by participation, but "in Himself." For we have not life in ourselves, but in our God. But He, the Father, hath life in Himself; and He begat such a Son as should have life in Himself; not be made a partaker of life, but Himself be Life, of which life we should be partakers; that is, should have life in Himself, and Himself be Life. But that He should be made the Son of Man, He took from us. Son of God in Himself; that He should be the Son of Man, He took from us. Son of God of That which is His Own, Son of Man of ours. That which is the less, took He from us; That which is the more, gave He to us. For thus He died in that He is the Son of Man, not in that He is the Son of God. Yet the Son of God died; but He died in respect to the flesh, not in respect to "the Word which was made flesh, and dwelt among us." [3] So then in that He died, He died of that which was ours; in that we live, we live of That which is His. He could not die of That which was His own, nor could we live of that which is our own. As God then, as the Only-Begotten, as equal with Him who begat Him, did the Lord Jesus impress this upon us, that if we hear, we shall live.

10. But, saith He, "He hath given Him power to execute judgment also, because He is the Son of Man." So then that Form is to come to judgment. The Form of Man is to come to judgment; therefore He said, "He hath given Him power to execute judgment also, because He is the Son of Man." The Judge here shall be the Son of Man; here shall That Form judge which was judged. Hear and understand: the Prophet had said this already, "They shall look on Him whom they pierced." [4] That Very Form shall they see which they smote with a spear. He shall sit as Judge, Who stood at the judge's seat. He shall condemn the real criminals, Who was made a criminal falsely. He shall come Himself, That Form shall come. This you find in the Gospel too; when before the eyes of His disciples He was going into

---

[1] Eph. v. 14. [2] 2 Thess. iii. 2. [3] John i. 14. [4] Zech. xii. 10; John xix. 37.

heaven, they stood and looked on, and the Angelic voice spake, " Ye men of Galilee, why stand ye," etc. " This Jesus shall come in like manner as ye see Him going into heaven." [1] What is, " shall come in like manner "? Shall come in this Very Form. For " He hath given Him power to execute judgment, because He is the Son of Man." Now see on what principle this was behoveful and right, that they who were to be judged might see the Judge. For they who were to be judged were both good and bad. " But blessed are the pure in heart, for they shall see God." [2] It remained that in the Judgment the Form of the servant should be manifested both to good and bad, the Form of God be reserved for the good alone.

11. For what is it that the good are to receive? Behold I am now expressing that which I did not express a little above; and yet in expressing I do not express it. For I said that there we shall be in sound health, shall be safe, shall be living, shall be without scourges, without hunger and thirst, without failing, without loss of our eyes. All this I said; but what we shall have more, I said not. We shall see God. Now this will be so great, yea so great a thing will it be, that in comparison of it, all the rest is nothing. I said that we shall be living, that we shall be safe and sound, that we shall suffer no hunger and thirst, that we shall not fall into weariness, that sleep will not oppress us. All this, what is it to that happiness, whereby we shall see God? Because then God cannot be now manifested as He is, whom nevertheless we shall see; therefore, " what eye hath not seen, nor ear heard," [3] this the good shall see, this shall the godly see, this the merciful shall see, this shall the faithful see, this shall they see who shall have a good lot in the resurrection of the body, for that they have had a good obedience in the resurrection of the heart.

12. Shall then the wicked man see God too? of whom Isaiah saith, " Let the ungodly be taken away, that he see not the Glory of God." [4] Both the ungodly and the godly then shall see that Form; and when the sentence, " Let the ungodly be taken away that he see not the Glory of God," shall have been pronounced; it remains that as to the godly and the good, that be fulfilled which the Lord Himself promised, when He was here in the flesh, and seen not by the good only, but by the evil also. He spake amongst the good and evil, and was seen of all, as God, hidden, as Man, manifested; as God ruling men, as Man appearing among men : He spake, I say, among them, and said, " Whoso loveth Me, keepeth My commandments ; and he that loveth Me, shall be loved of My Father, and I will love him." [5]

And as if it were said to Him, And what wilt Thou give him? And " I will," He saith, " manifest Myself to him." When did He say this? When He was seen by men. When did He say this? When He was seen even by them, by whom He was not loved. How then was He to manifest Himself to them that loved Him, save in Such a Form, as they who loved Him then saw not? Therefore, seeing that the Form of God was being reserved, the Form of man manifested ; by the Form of man, speaking to men, conspicuous and visible, He manifested Himself to all, both good and bad, He reserved Himself for them that loved Him.

13. When is He to manifest Himself to them that love Him? After the resurrection of the body, when " the ungodly shall be taken away that he see not the Glory of God." For then " when He shall appear, we shall be like Him ; for we shall see Him as He is." [6] This is life eternal. For all that we said before is nothing to that life. That we live, what is it? That we are in health, what is it? That we shall see God, is a great thing. This is life eternal; this Himself hath said, " But this is life eternal, that they may know Thee the Only True God, and Jesus Christ whom Thou hast sent." [7] This is life eternal, that they may know, see, comprehend, acquaint themselves with what they had believed, may perceive that which they were not yet able to comprehend. Then may the mind see what " eye hath not seen, nor ear heard, neither hath it ascended into the heart of man ; " this shall be said to them at the end, " Come, ye blessed of My Father, receive the kingdom which hath been prepared for you from the beginning of the world." [8] Those wicked ones then shall go into everlasting burning. But the righteous, whither? Into life eternal? What is life eternal? " This is life eternal, that they may know Thee, the Only True God, and Jesus Christ, whom Thou hast sent."

14. Speaking then of the future resurrection of the body, and not leaving us thus, He saith, " He hath given Him power to execute judgment also, because He is the Son of Man. Marvel not at this, for the hour shall come." He did not add in this place, " and now is ; " because this hour shall be hereafter, because this hour shall be at the end of the world, because this shall be the last hour, shall be at the last trump. " Marvel not at this," because I have said, " He hath given Him power to execute judgment also, because He is the Son of Man. Marvel not." For this reason have I said this, because it behoves Him as Man to be judged by men. And what men shall He judge? Those whom He finds alive? Not only those, but

---

[1] Acts i. 11.   [2] Matt. v. 8.   [3] 1 Cor. ii. 9.
[4] Isa. xxvi. 10, Sept.   [5] John xiv. 21.   [6] 1 John iii. 2.   [7] John xvii. 3.   [8] Matt. xxv. 34.

what? "The hour shall come, when they that are in the graves."[1] How did He express those that are dead in the flesh? "They who are in the graves," whose corpses lie buried, whose ashes are covered up, whose bones are dispersed, whose flesh is flesh no more, and yet is entire to God. "The hour shall come, when all that are in the graves shall hear His Voice, and shall come forth." Be they good or bad, they shall hear the Voice, and shall come forth. All the bands of the grave[2] shall be burst asunder; all that was lost, yea rather was thought to be lost, shall be restored. For if God made man who was not, can He not re-fashion that which was?

15. I suppose when it is said, "God shall raise the dead again," no incredible thing is said; for it is of God, not of man, that it is said. It is a great thing which shall be done, yea, an incredible thing that shall be done. But let it not be incredible, for see, who It is That doeth it. He it is said shall raise thee, Who created thee. Thou wast not, and thou art; and once made, shalt thou not be? God forbid thou shouldest think so! God did something more marvellous when He made that which was not; and nevertheless He did make that which was not; and shall it be disbelieved that He is able to re-fashion that which was, by those very persons whom He made what they were not? Is this the return we make to God, we who were not, and were made? Is this the return we make Him, that we will not believe that He is able to raise again what He hath made? Is this the return which His creature renders Him? "Have I therefore," God saith to thee, "made thee, O man, before thou wast, that thou shouldest not believe Me, that thou shalt be what thou wast, who hast been able to be what thou wast not?" But you will say, "Lo, what I see in the tomb, is dust, ashes, bones; and shall this receive life again, skin, substance, flesh, and rise again? what? these ashes, these bones, which I see in the tomb?" Well. At least thou seest ashes, thou seest bones in the tomb; in thy mother's womb there was nothing. This thou seest, ashes at least there are, and bones; before that thou wast, there was neither ashes, nor bones; and yet thou wast made, when thou wast not at all; and dost thou not believe that these bones (for in whatever state, of whatever kind they are, yet they *are*), shall receive the form again which they had, when thou hast received what thou hadst not? Believe; for if thou shalt believe this, then shall thy soul be raised up. And thy soul shall be raised up "now;" "The hour shall come, and now is;" then to thy blessing shall thy flesh rise again, "when the hour shall come, that all that are in the graves shall hear His

Voice, and shall come forth." For thou must not at once rejoice, because thou dost hear "and come forth;" hear what follows, "They that have done good unto the resurrection of life; but they that have done evil unto the resurrection of damnation."[3] Turning to the Lord, etc.

SERMON LXXVIII.

[CXXVIII. BEN.]

ON THE WORDS OF THE GOSPEL, JOHN V. 31, "IF I BEAR WITNESS OF MYSELF," ETC.; AND ON THE WORDS OF THE APOSTLE, GAL. V. 16, "WALK BY THE SPIRIT, AND YE SHALL NOT FULFIL THE LUST OF THE FLESH. FOR THE FLESH LUSTETH," ETC.

1. WE have heard the words of the holy Gospel; and this that the Lord Jesus saith, "If I bear witness of Myself, My witness is not true,"[4] may perplex some. How then is not the witness of the Truth true? Is it not Himself who hath said, "I am the Way, and the Truth, and the Life"?[5] Whom then are we to believe, if we must not believe the Truth? For of a surety he is minded to believe nothing but falsehood, who does not choose to believe the truth. So then this was spoken on their principles, that you should understand it thus, and gather this meaning from these words; "If I bear witness of Myself, My witness is not true," that is, as ye think. For He knew well that His Own witness of Himself was true; but for the sake of the weak, and hard of belief, and without understanding, the Sun looked out for lamps. For their weakness of sight could not bear the dazzling brightness of the Sun.

2. Therefore was John sought for to bear witness to the Truth; and ye have heard what He said; "Ye came unto John; he was a burning and a shining lamp, and ye were willing for a season to rejoice in his light."[6] This lamp was prepared for their confusion, for of this was it said so long time before in the Psalms, "I have prepared a lamp for Mine Anointed."[7] What! a lamp for the Sun! "His enemies will I clothe with confusion: but upon Himself shall my sanctification flourish."[8] And hence they were in a certain place confounded by means of this very John, when the Jews said to the Lord, "By what authority doest Thou these things? Tell us." To whom He answered, "Do ye tell Me too, The baptism of John, was it from heaven, or of men?" They heard, and held their peace. For they thought at once with themselves. "If we shall say, Of men: the people will stone us; for they hold John as a prophet. If we shall say, From heaven; He will say to

---

[1] John v. 28. [2] *Inferorum.*

[3] John v. 29. [4] John v. 31. [5] John xiv. 6.
[6] John v. 33, 35. [7] Ps. cxxxii. 17. [8] Ps. cxxxii. 18, Sept.

us, Why then have ye not believed him?"[1] For John bare witness to Christ. So straitened in their hearts by their own questions, and taken in their own snares, they answered, "We do not know." What else could the voice of darkness be? It is right indeed for a man when he does not know, to say, "I know not." But when he does know, and says, "I know not;" he is a witness against himself. Now they knew well John's excellency, and that his baptism was from heaven; but they were unwilling to acquiesce in Him to whom John bare witness. But when they said, "We do not know;" Jesus answered them. "Neither will I tell you by what authority I do these things." And they were confounded; and so was fulfilled, "I have prepared a lamp for Mine Anointed, His enemies will I clothe with confusion."

3. Are not Martyrs witnesses of Christ, and do they not bear witness to the truth? But if we think more carefully, when those Martyrs bear witness, He beareth witness to Himself. For He dwelleth in the Martyrs, that they may bear witness to the truth. Hear one of the Martyrs, even the Apostle Paul; "Would ye receive a proof of Christ, who speaketh in Me?"[2] When John then beareth witness, Christ, who dwelleth in John, beareth witness to Himself. Let Peter bear witness, let Paul bear witness, let the rest of the Apostles bear witness, let Stephen bear witness, it is He who dwelleth in them all that beareth witness to Himself. For He without them is God, they without Him, what are they?

4. Of Him it is said, "He ascended up on high, He led captivity captive, He gave gifts unto men."[3] What is, "He led captivity captive"? He conquered death. What is, "He led captivity captive"? The devil was the author of death, and the devil was himself by the Death of Christ led captive. "He ascended up on high." What do we know higher than heaven? Visibly and before the eyes of His disciples He ascended into heaven. This we know, this we believe, this we confess. "He gave gifts unto men." What gifts? The Holy Spirit. He who giveth such a Gift, what is He Himself? For great is God's mercy; He giveth a Gift equal to Himself; for His Gift is the Holy Spirit, and the Whole Trinity, Father and Son and Holy Spirit, is One God. What hath the Holy Spirit brought us? Hear the Apostle; "The love of God," saith he, "hath been shed abroad in our hearts."[4] Whence, thou beggar, hath the love of God been shed abroad in thine heart? How, or wherein hath the love of God been shed abroad in the heart of man? "We have," saith he, "this treasure in earthen vessels." Why in earthen vessels? "That the

excellency of the power may be of God?"[5] Finally, when he had said, "The love of God hath been shed abroad in our hearts;" that no man might think that he hath this love of God of himself, he added immediately, "By the Holy Spirit, who hath been given to us." Therefore, that thou mayest love God, let God dwell in thee, and love Himself in thee, that is, to His love let Him move thee, enkindle, enlighten, arouse thee.

5. For in this body of ours there is a struggle; as long as we live, we are in combat; as long as we are in combat, we are in peril; but, "in all these things we are conquerors through Him who loved us."[6] Our combat ye heard of just now when the Apostle was being read. "All the law," saith he, "is fulfilled in one word, even in this, Thou shalt love thy neighbour as thyself."[7] This love is from the Holy Spirit. "Thou shalt love thy neigbour as thyself." First see, if thou knowest yet how to love thyself; and then will I commit to thee the neighbour whom thou art to love as thyself. But if thou dost not yet know how to love thyself; I fear lest thou shouldest deceive thy neighbour as thyself. For if thou lovest iniquity, thou dost not love thyself. The Psalm is witness; "But whoso loveth iniquity, hateth his own soul."[8] Now if thou hate thine own soul, what doth it profit thee that thou dost love thy flesh? If thou hate thine own soul, and lovest thy flesh, thy flesh shall rise again; but only that thy soul may be tormented. Therefore the soul must first be loved, which is to be subdued unto God, that this service may maintain its due order, the soul to God, the flesh to the soul. Wouldest thou that thy flesh should serve thy soul? Let thy soul serve God. Thou oughtest to be ruled, that thou mayest be able to rule. For so perilous is this struggle, that if thy Ruler forsake thee, ruin must ensue.

6. What struggle? "But if ye bite and devour one another, take heed that ye be not consumed one of another. But I say, Walk in the Spirit."[9] I am quoting the words of the Apostle, which have been just read out of his Epistle. "But I say, Walk in the Spirit, and ye shall not fulfil the lusts of the flesh." "But I say, Walk in the Spirit, and the lusts of the flesh," he did not say, "Ye shall not have;" nor did he say, "Ye shall not do;" but, "Ye shall not fulfil." Now what this is, with the Lord's assistance, I will declare as I shall be able; give attention, that ye may understand, if ye are walking in the Spirit. "But I say, Walk in the Spirit, and ye shall not fulfil the lusts of the flesh." Let him follow on; if haply anything, as this which is here obscure, may be understood more easily by the sequel of his words. For I said, that it was not without a

---

[1] Luke xx. 2, etc.　　[2] 2 Cor. xiii. 3, Vulgate.
[3] Ps. lxviii. 18; Eph. iv. 8.　　[4] Rom. v. 5.
[5] 2 Cor. iv. 7.　　[6] Rom. viii. 37.　　[7] Gal. v. 14.
[8] Ps. x. 5, Sept. (xi. 5, English version).　　[9] Gal. v. 15, 16.

meaning that the Apostle would not say, "Ye shall not have the lusts of the flesh;" nor again would even say, "Ye shall not do the lusts of the flesh;" but said, "Ye shall not fulfil the lusts of the flesh." He hath set forth this struggle before us. In this battle are we occupied, if we are in God's service.[1] What then follows? "For the flesh lusteth against the spirit, and the spirit against the flesh. For these are contrary the one to the other, so that ye do not the things that ye would."[2] This, if it be not understood, is with exceeding peril heard. And therefore anxious as I am lest men by an evil interpretation should perish, I have undertaken with the Lord's assistance to explain these words to your affection. We have leisure enough, we have begun early in the morning, the hour of dinner does not press; on this day, the sabbath that is, they that hunger after the word of God are wont especially to meet together. Hear and attend, I will speak with what carefulness I can.

7. What then is that which I said, "Is heard with peril if it be not understood"? Many overcome by carnal and damnable lusts, commit all sorts of crimes and impurities, and wallow in such abominable uncleanness, as it is a shame even to mention; and say to themselves these words of the Apostle. See what the Apostle has said, "So that ye cannot do the things that ye would."[2] I would not do them, I am forced, I am compelled, I am overcome, "I do the things that I would not,"[3] as the Apostle says. "The flesh lusteth against the Spirit, and the Spirit against the flesh, so that ye cannot do the things that ye would." You see with what peril this is heard, if it be not understood. You see how it concerns the pastor's office, to open the closed fountains, and to minister to the thirsty sheep the pure, harmless water.

8. Be not willing then to be overcome when thou fightest. See what kind of war, what kind of battle, what kind of strife he hath set forth, within, within thine own self. "The flesh lusteth against the Spirit." If the Spirit lust not also against the flesh, commit adultery. But if the Spirit lust against the flesh, I see a struggle, I do not see a victory, it is a contest. "The flesh lusteth against the Spirit." Adultery has its pleasure. I confess that it has its pleasure. But, "The Spirit lusteth against the flesh:" Chastity too has its pleasure. Therefore let the Spirit overcome the flesh; or by all means not be overcome by the flesh. Adultery seeks the darkness, chastity desires the light. As thou wouldest wish to appear to others, so live; as thou wouldest wish to appear to men, even when beyond the eyes of men so live; for He who

made thee, even in the darkness seeth thee. Why is chastity praised publicly by all? Why do not even adulterers praise adultery? "Whoso" then "seeketh the truth, cometh to the light."[4] But adultery has its pleasure. Be it contradicted, resisted, opposed. For it is not so that thou hast nothing wherewith to fight. Thy God is in thee, the good Spirit hath been given to thee. And notwithstanding this flesh of ours is permitted to lust against the spirit by evil suggestions and real[5] delights. Be that secured which the Apostle saith, "Let not sin reign in your mortal body."[6] He did not say, "Let it not be there." It is there already. And this is called sin, because it has befallen us through the wages[7] of sin. For in Paradise the flesh did not lust against the spirit, nor was there this struggle there, where was peace only; but after the transgression, after that man was loth to serve God, and was given up to himself; yet not so given up to himself as that he could so much as possess himself; but possessed by him, by whom deceived; the flesh began to lust against the Spirit. Now it is in the good that it lusteth against the Spirit; for in the bad it has nothing to lust against. For there doth it lust against the Spirit, where the Spirit is.

9. For when he says, "The flesh lusteth against the Spirit, and the Spirit against the flesh;" do not suppose that so much hath been attributed to the spirit of man. It is the Spirit of God who fighteth in thee against thyself, against that which in thee is against thee. For thou wouldest not stand to Godward; thou didst fall, wast broken; as a vessel when it falls from a man's hand to the ground, wast thou broken. And because thou wast broken, therefore art thou turned against thyself; therefore art thou contrary to thine own self. Let there be nought in thee contrary to thyself, and thou shalt stand in thine integrity. For that thou mayest know that this office appertaineth to the Holy Spirit; the Apostle saith in another place, "For if ye live after the flesh, ye shall die; but if ye through the Spirit do mortify the deeds of the flesh, ye shall live."[8] From these words man was at once uplifting himself, as though by his own spirit he were able to mortify the deeds of the flesh. "If ye live after the flesh, ye shall die; but if through the Spirit ye do mortify the deeds of the flesh, ye shall live." Explain to us, Apostle, through what spirit? For man also hath a spirit appertaining to his proper nature, whereby he is man. For man consists of body and spirit. And of this spirit of man it is said, "No man knoweth the things of a man, save the spirit of man which is in him."[9] I see then that man himself hath

---

[1] *Deo militamus.*   [2] Gal. v 17.
[3] Rom. vii. 19.

[4] John iii. 21.   [5] *Genuinis.*   [6] Rom. vi. 12.
[7] *Merito.*   [8] Rom. viii. 13.   [9] 1 Cor. ii. 11.

his own spirit appertaining to his proper nature, and I hear thee saying, "But if through the Spirit ye do mortify the deeds of the flesh, ye shall live." I ask, through what spirit; my own, or God's? For I hear thy words, and am still perplexed by this ambiguity. For when the word "spirit" is used, it is used sometimes of the spirit of a man, and of cattle, as it is written, that "all flesh which had in itself the spirit of life, died by the flood." [1] And so the word spirit is spoken of cattle, and spoken of man too. Sometimes even the wind is called spirit; as it is in the Psalm, "Fire, hail, snow, frost, the spirit of the tempest." [2] For as much then as the word "spirit" is used in many ways, by what spirit, O Apostle, hast thou said that the deeds of the flesh are to be mortified; by mine own, or by the Spirit of God? Hear what follows, and understand. The difficulty is removed by the following words. For when he had said, "But if through the Spirit ye mortify the deeds of the flesh, ye shall live;" [3] he added immediately, "For as many as are acted [4] upon by the Spirit of God, they are the sons of God." Thou dost act, if thou art acted upon, and actest well, if thou art acted upon by the Good. So then when he said to thee, "If through the Spirit ye mortify the deeds of the flesh, ye shall live;" and it was doubtful with thee of what spirit he had spoken, in the words following understand the Master, acknowledge the Redeemer. For That Redeemer hath given thee the Spirit Whereby thou mayest mortify the deeds of the flesh. "For as many as are acted upon by the Spirit of God, they are the sons of God." They are not the sons of God if they are not acted upon by the Spirit of God. But if they are acted upon by the Spirit of God, they fight; because they have a mighty Helper. For God doth not look on at our combattings as the people do at the gladiators. [5] The people may favour the gladiator, help him they cannot when he is in peril.

10. So then here to; "The flesh lusteth against the Spirit, and the Spirit against the flesh." And what means, "So that ye cannot do the things that ye would"? For here is the peril with one who understands it amiss. Be it now my office to explain it, howsoever incompetent. "So that ye cannot do the things that ye would." Attend, ye holy ones, whosoever ye are that are fighting. To them that are battling do I speak. They who are fighting, understand; he that is not fighting, understands me not. Yea, he that is fighting, I will not say understands me, but anticipates me. What is the chaste man's wish? That no lust should rise up in his members at all opposed to chastity. He wisheth for peace, but as yet he

hath it not. For when we shall have come to that state, where there shall rise up no lust at all to be opposed, there will be no enemy for us to struggle with; nor is victory a matter for expectation there, for that there is triumphing over the now vanquished foe. Hear of this victory, in the Apostle's own words; "This corruptible must put on incorruption, and this mortal must put on immortality. Now when this corruptible shall have put on incorruption, and this mortal shall have put on immortality; then shall be brought to pass the saying that is written, Death is swallowed up in victory." Hear the voices of them that triumph; "O death, where is thy contention? O death, where is thy sting?" [6] Thou hast smitten, thou hast wounded, thou hast thrown down; but He hath been wounded for me who made me. O death, death, He who made me hath been wounded for me, and by His Death hath overcome thee. And then in triumph shall they say, "O death, where is thy contention? O death, where is thy sting?"

11. But now, when "the flesh lusteth against the Spirit, and the Spirit against the flesh," is the contention of death; we do not what we would. Why? Because we would that there should be no lusts, but we cannot hinder it. Whether we will or not, we have them; whether we will or not, they solicit, [7] they allure, they sting, they disturb us, they will be rising. They are repressed, not yet extinguished. How long does the flesh lust against the Spirit, and the Spirit against the flesh? Will it be so, even when the man is dead? God forbid! Thou puttest off the flesh, how then shalt thou draw the lusts of the flesh along with thee? Nay, if thou hast fought well, thou shalt be received into rest. And from this rest, thou passest to be crowned, not condemned; that thou mayest after it be brought to the Kingdom. As long then as we live here, my brethren, so it is; so is it with us even who have grown old in this warfare, less mighty enemies it is true we have, but yet we have them. Our enemies are in a measure wearied out even now by age; but nevertheless, wearied though they be, they do not cease to harass by such excitements as they can the quiet of old age. Sharper is the fight of the young; we know it well, we have passed through it: "The flesh" then "lusteth against the Spirit, and the Spirit against the flesh; so that ye cannot do the things that ye would." For what would ye, O holy men, and good warriors, and brave soldiers of Christ? what would ye? That there should be no evil lusts at all. But ye cannot help it. Sustain [8] the war, hope for triumph. For now in the meanwhile ye must fight. "The flesh lusteth against the Spirit, and

---

[1] Gen. vi. 17 and vii. 22.
[2] Ps. cxlvii. 8, Sept. (cxlviii. 8, English version).
[3] Rom. viii. 13. [4] *Aguntur.* [5] *Venatores.*
[6] 1 Cor. xv. 53, etc. [7] *Titillant.* [8] *Exercete.*

the Spirit against the flesh; so that ye cannot do the things that ye would;" that is, that there should be no lusts of the flesh at all.

12. But do what ye are able; what the Apostle himself says in another place, which I had already begun to repeat; "Let not sin reign in your mortal body, to obey the desires thereof."[1] Lo, what I would not; evil desires arise; but obey them not. Arm thyself, assume the weapons of war. The precepts of God are thy arms. If thou listen to me as thou shouldest, thou art armed even by that which I am speaking. "'Let not sin,' he says, 'reign in your mortal body.' For as long as ye bear a mortal body, sin doth fight against you; but let it not reign." What is, "Let it not reign"? That is, "to obey the desires thereof." If ye begin to obey, it reigns. And what is it to obey, but to "yield your members as instruments of iniquity unto sin"? Nothing more excellent than this teacher. What wouldest thou that I should yet explain to thee? Do what thou hast heard. Yield not thy members instruments of iniquity unto sin. God hath given thee power by His Spirit to restrain thy members. Lust riseth up, restrain thy members; what can it do now that it hath risen? Restrain thou thy members; yield not thy members instruments of iniquity unto sin; arm not thine adversary against thyself. Restrain thy feet, that they go not after unlawful things. Lust hath risen up, restrain thy members; restrain thine hands from all wickedness; restrain the eyes, that they wander not astray; restrain the ears, that they hear not the words of lust with pleasure; restrain the whole body, restrain the sides, restrain its highest and lowest parts. What can lust do? How to rise up, it knoweth. How to conquer, it knoweth not. By rising up constantly without effect, it learns not even to rise.

13. Let us then return to the words, which I had set forth out of the Apostle as obscure, and we shall now see them to be plain. For this I had set forth, that the Apostle did not say, "Walk in the Spirit, and ye shall not have the lusts of the flesh;" because we must necessarily have them. Why then did he not say, "Ye shall not do the lusts of the flesh"? Because we do them; for we do lust. The very lusting, is doing. But the Apostle says, "Now it is no more I that do it, but sin that dwelleth in me."[2] What then hast thou to beware of? This doubtless, that thou fulfil them not. A damnable lust hath risen up, it hath risen, made its suggestion; let it not be heard. It burneth, and is not quieted, and thou wouldest that it should not burn. Where then is, "So that ye cannot do the things that ye would"? Do not give it

thy members. Let it burn without effect, and it will spend itself. In thee then these lusts are done. It must be confessed, they are done. And therefore he said, "Ye shall not fulfil." Let them not then be fulfilled. Thou hast determined to do, thou hast fulfilled. For thou hast fulfilled it, if thou determinest upon committing adultery, and dost not commit it, because no place hath been found, because no opportunity is given, because, it may be, she for whom thou seemest to be disturbed is chaste; lo, now she is chaste, and thou art an adulterer. Why? Because thou hast fulfilled lusts. What is, "hast fulfilled"? Hast determined in thy mind upon committing adultery. If now, which God forbid, thy members too have wrought, thou hast fallen down headlong into death.

14. Christ raised up the daughter of the ruler of the synagogue who was dead in the house.[3] She was in the house, she had not yet been carried out. So is the man who hath determined on some wickedness in his heart; he is dead, but he lies within. But if he has come as far as to the action of the members, he has been carried out of the house. But the Lord raised also the young man, the widow's son, when he was being carried out dead beyond the gate of the city.[4] So then I venture to say, Thou hast determined in thine heart, if thou call thyself back from thy deed, thou wilt be cured before thou put it into action. For if thou repent in thine heart, that thou hast determined on some bad and wicked and abominable and damnable thing; there where thou wast lying dead, within, so within hast thou arisen. But if thou have fulfilled, now hast thou been carried out; but thou hast One to say to thee, "Young man, I say unto thee, Arise." Even though thou have perpetrated it, repent thee, return at once, come not to the sepulchre. But even here I find a third one dead, who was brought even to the sepulchre. He has now upon him the weight of habit, a mass of earth presses him down exceedingly. For he has been practised much in unclean deeds, and is weighed down exceedingly by his immoderate[5] habit. Here too Christ crieth, "Lazarus, come forth."[6] For a man of very evil habit "now stinketh." With good reason did Christ in that case cry out; and not cry out only, but with a loud Voice cried out. For at Christ's Cry even such as these, dead though they be, buried though they be, stinking though they be, yet even these shall rise again, they shall rise again. For of none that lieth dead need we despair under such a Raiser up. Turn we to the Lord, etc.

---

[3] Mark v. 35. *Vid*. Serm. xlviii. (Ben. xcviii.).
[4] Luke vii. 12, etc.
[5] *Nimiâ*.
[6] John xi. 43.

[1] Rom. vi. 12.   [2] Rom. vii. 17.

SERMON LXXIX.

[CXXIX. BEN.]

ON THE WORDS OF THE GOSPEL, JOHN V. 39,
"YE SEARCH THE SCRIPTURES, BECAUSE YE
THINK THAT IN THEM YE HAVE ETERNAL LIFE,"
ETC. AGAINST THE DONATISTS.

1. GIVE heed, Beloved, to the lesson of the
Gospel which has just sounded in our ears, whilst
I speak a few words as God shall vouchsafe to
me. The Lord Jesus was speaking to the Jews,
and said to them, "Search the Scriptures, in
which ye think ye have eternal life, they testify
of me."[1] Then a little after He said, "I am
come in My Father's Name, and ye have not
received Me; if another shall come in his own
name, him ye will receive."[2] Then a little after;
"How can ye believe, who look for glory one
from another, and seek not the glory which is
of God only?"[3] At last He saith, "I do not
accuse you to the Father; there is one that
accuseth you, Moses, in whom ye trust. For
had ye believed Moses, ye would haply believe
Me also, for he wrote of Me. But seeing ye
believe not his words, how can ye believe Me?"[4]
At these sayings which have been set before us
from divine[5] inspiration, out of the reader's
mouth, but by the Saviour's ministry, give ear to
a few words, not to be estimated by their number, but to be duly weighed.

2. For all these things it is easy to understand
as touching the Jews. But we must beware, lest,
when we give too much attention to them, we
withdraw our eyes from ourselves. For the
Lord was speaking to His disciples; and assuredly what He spake to them, He spake to us
too their posterity. Nor to them only does what
He said, "Lo, I am with you alway even unto
the end of the world,"[6] apply, but even to all
Christians that should be after them, and succeed them even unto the end of the world.
Speaking then to them He said, "Beware of the
leaven of the Pharisees."[7] They at that time
thought that the Lord had said this, because they
had brought no bread; they did not understand
that "Beware of the leaven of the Pharisees"
meant, "beware of the doctrine of the Pharisees."
What was the doctrine of the Pharisees, but that
which ye have now heard? "Seeking glory one
of another, looking for glory one from another,
and not seeking the glory which is of God only."
Of these the Apostle Paul thus speaks; "I bear
them record that they have a zeal of God, but
not according to knowledge."[8] "They have," he
says, "a zeal of God;" I know it, I am sure of
it; I was once among them, I was such as they.
"They have," he says, "a zeal of God, but not

according to knowledge." What is this, O
Apostle, "not according to knowledge"? Explain to us what the knowledge is thou dost set
forth, which thou dost grieve is not in them, and
wouldest should be in us? He went on and
subjoined and developed what he had set forth
closed. What is, "They have a zeal of God, but
not according to knowledge? For they being
ignorant of God's righteousness, and wishing to
establish their own, have not submitted themselves unto the righteousness of God."[9] To be
ignorant then of God's righteousness, and to
wish to establish one's own, this is to "look for
glory one from another, and not to seek the glory
which is of God only." This is the leaven of
the Pharisees. Of this the Lord bids beware.
If it is servants that He bids, and the Lord that
bids, let us beware; lest we hear, "Why say ye
to Me, Lord, Lord, and do not the things which
I say?"[10]

3. Let us then leave a while the Jews to whom
the Lord was then speaking. They are without,
they will not listen to us, they hate the Gospel
itself, they procured false witness against the
Lord, that they might condemn Him when alive;
other witness they bought with money against
Him when dead. When we say to them,
"Believe on Jesus," they answer us, "Are we to
believe on a dead man?" But when we add,
"But He rose again;" they answer, "Not" at
all;" His disciples stole Him away from the
sepulchre. The Jewish buyers love falsehood
and despise the truth of the Lord, the Redeemer.
What thou art saying, O Jew, thy parents bought
for money; and this which they bought hath
continued in thee. Give heed rather to Him
That bought thee, not to him who bought a lie
for thee.

4. But as I have said, let us leave these, and
attend rather to these our brethren, with whom
we have to do. For Christ is the Head of the
Body. The Head is in Heaven, the Body is on
earth; the Head is the Lord, the Body His
Church. But ye remember it is said, "They
shall be two in one flesh." "This is a great mystery,"[12] says the Apostle, "but I speak in Christ
and in the Church."[13] If then they are two in one
flesh, they are two in one voice. Our Head the
Lord Christ spake to the Jews these things which
we heard, when the Gospel was being read, The
Head to His enemies; let the Body too, that is,
the Church, speak to its enemies. Ye know to
whom it should speak. What has it to say? It
is not of myself that I have said, that the voice is
one; because the flesh is one, the voice is one.
Let us then say this to them; I am speaking
with the voice of the Church. "O Brethren,
dispersed children, wandering sheep, branches

---

[1] John v. 39. [2] John v. 43. [3] John v. 44.
[4] John v. 45-47. [5] Divinitus. [6] Matt. xxviii. 20.
[7] Matt. xvi. 6. [8] Rom. x. 2.

[9] Rom. x. 3. [10] Matt. vii. 21; Luke vi. 46. [11] Absit.
[12] Sacramentum. [13] Eph. v. 31, 32.

cut off, why do ye calumniate me? Why do ye not acknowledge me? " Search the Scriptures, in which ye think ye have eternal life, they testify of me ; " to the Jews our Head saith, what the Body saith to you ; " Ye shall seek me, and shall not find me." [1] Why? Because ye do not " search the Scriptures, which testify of me."

5. A testimony for the Head ; " To Abraham and his seed were the promises made. He saith not, And to seeds, as of many, but as of one, And to thy seed, which is Christ." [2] A testimony for the body unto Abraham, which the Apostle hath brought forward. " To Abraham were the promises made. As I live, saith the Lord, I swear by Myself, because thou hast obeyed My Voice, and hast not spared thine own beloved son for Me, that in blessing I will bless thee, and in multiplying I will multiply thy seed as the stars of heaven, and as the sand of the sea, and in thy seed shall all nations of the earth be blessed." [3] Thou hast here a testimony for the Head, and one for the Body. Hear another, short, and almost in one sentence including a testimony for the Head and for the Body. The Psalm was speaking of the Resurrection of Christ ; " Be Thou exalted, O God, above the heavens." [4] And immediately for the Body ; " And Thy glory above all the earth." Hear a testimony for the Head ; " They digged My Hands and My Feet, they numbered all My Bones ; and they looked and stared upon Me ; they divided My garments among them, and cast lots upon My vesture." [5] Hear immediately a testimony for the Body, a few words after, " All the ends of the world shall remember themselves and be turned unto the Lord, and all the kindreds of the nations shall worship in His sight ; for the kingdom is the Lord's, and He shall have dominion over the nations." [6] Hear for the Head ; And " He is as a bridegroom coming forth out of His bride-chamber." [7] And in this same Psalm hear for the Body ; " Their sound went out into all the earth, and their words unto the ends of the world." [8]

6. These passages are for the Jews, and for these of our own brethren. Why so? Because these Scriptures of the Old Testament both the Jews receive, and these our brethren receive. But Christ Himself, whom the others do not receive, let us see if these last receive. Let Him speak Himself, speak both for Himself who is the Head, and for His Body which is the Church ; for so in us the head speaks for the body. Hear for the Head ; He was risen from the dead, He found the disciples hesitating, doubting, not believing for joy ; He " opened their understand-

ing that they might understand the Scriptures, and said to them, Thus it is written, and thus it behoved Christ to suffer, and to rise again from the dead the third day." Thus for the Head ; let Him speak for the Body too ; " And that repentance and remission of sins should be preached in His Name throughout all nations, beginning at Jerusalem." [9] Let the Church then speak to her enemies, let her speak. She does speak clearly, she is not silent : only let them give ear. Brethren, ye have heard the testimonies, now acknowledge me. " Search the Scriptures, in which ye hope ye have eternal life : they testify of me." What I have said is not of mine own, but of my Lord's ; and notwithstanding, ye still turn away, still turn your backs. " How can ye believe me, who look for glory one from another, and seek not the glory which is of God only? For being ignorant of God's righteousness, ye have a zeal of God, but not according to knowledge. For being ignorant of God's righteousness, and wishing to establish your own, ye have not submitted yourselves to the righteousness of God." [10] What else is it to be ignorant of God's righteousness, and to wish to establish your own, but to say, " It is I who sanctify, it is I who justify ; what I may have given is holy "? Leave to God what is God's ; recognise, O man, what is man's. Thou art ignorant of God's righteousness, and wishest to establish thine own. Thou dost wish to justify me ; it is enough for thee that thou be justified with me.

7. It is said of Antichrist, and all understand of him what the Lord said, " I am come in My Father's Name, and ye have not received Me ; if another shall come in his own name, him ye will receive." [11] But let us hear John too ; " Ye have heard that Antichrist cometh, and even now are there many Antichrists." [12] What is it in Antichrist that we are in horror of, but that he is to honour his own name, and to despise the Name of the Lord? What else doeth he that saith, " It is I that justify "? We answer him, " I came to Christ, not with my feet, but with my heart I came ; where I heard the Gospel, there did I believe, there was I baptized ; because I believed on Christ, I believed on God." Yet says he, " Thou art not clean." " Why? " " Because I was not there." " Tell me why am not I cleansed, a man who was baptized in Jerusalem, who was baptized, for instance, among the Ephesians, to whom an Epistle you read was written, and whose peace you despise? Lo, to the Ephesians the Apostle wrote ; a Church was founded, and remains even to this day ; yea, remains in greater fruitfulness, remains in greater numbers, holds fast that which it received of the Apostle, ' If any man preach ought to you than

---

[1] John vii. 36. [2] Gal. iii. 16. [3] Gen. xxii. 16, etc.
[4] Ps. lvii. 11.
[5] Ps. xxi. 17-19, Sept. (xxii. 16-18, English version).
[6] Ps. xxi. 28, 29, Sept. (xxii. 27, 28, English version).
[7] Ps. xix. 5. [8] Ps. xix. 4.

[9] Luke xxiv. 45-47. [10] Rom. x. 2, 3. [11] John v. 43.
[12] 1 John ii. 18.

that ye have received, let him be accursed.'[1] What now? what dost thou say to me? Am I not clean? There was I baptized, am I not clean?" "No, even thou art not." "Why?" "Because I was not there." "But He who is everywhere was there. He who is everywhere was there, in whose Name I believed. Thou coming I know not whence, yea, rather not coming, but wishing that I should come to thee, fixed in this place, sayest to me, 'Thou wast not baptized duly, seeing I was not there.' Consider who was there. What was said to John? 'Upon whom thou shalt see the Spirit descending like a dove, this is He which baptizeth.'[2] Him hast thou seeking for thee; nay, for that thou hast grudged me who was baptized by Him, thou hast lost Him rather."

8. Understand then, my Brethren, our language and theirs, and look which ye would choose. This is what we say; "Be we holy, God knoweth it; be we unrighteous, this again He knoweth better; place not your hope in us, whatsoever we be. If we be good, do as is written, 'Be ye imitators of me, as I also am of Christ.'[3] But if we be bad, not even thus are ye abandoned, not even thus have ye remained without counsel: give ear to Him, saying, 'Do what they say; but do not what they do.'"[4] Whereas they on the contrary say, "If we were not good, ye were lost." Lo, here is "another that shall come in his own name." Shall my life then depend on thee, and my salvation be tied up in thee? Have I so forgotten my foundation? Was not Christ the Rock?[5] Is it not that he that buildeth upon the rock, neither the wind nor the floods overthrow him?[6] Come then, if thou wilt, with me upon the Rock, and do not wish to be to me for the rock.

9. Let the Church then say those last words also, "If ye had believed Moses, ye would believe me also; for he wrote of me;"[7] for that I am His body of whom he wrote. And of the Church did Moses write. For I have quoted the words of Moses "In thy seed shall all nations of the earth be blessed."[8] Moses wrote this in the first book. If ye believed Moses, ye would also believe Christ. Because ye despise Moses' words, it must needs be that ye despise the words of Christ. "They have" there, saith He, "Moses and the Prophets, let them hear them. Nay, father Abraham, but if one went unto them from the dead," him they will hear. "And He said, If they hear not Moses and the Prophets, neither will they believe, if one rise again from the dead."[9] This was said of the Jews: was it therefore not said of heretics? He had risen from the dead, who said, "It behoved Christ to

suffer, and to rise again from the dead the third day." This I believe. I believe it, he says. Dost thou believe? Wherefore believest thou not what follows? In that thou believest, "It behoved Christ to suffer, and to rise again from the dead the third day;" this was spoken of the Head; believe also that which follows concerning the Church, "That repentance and remission of sins should be preached throughout all nations."[10] Wherefore dost thou believe as touching the Head, and believest not as touching the Body? What hath the Church done to thee, that thou wouldest so to say behead her? Thou wouldest take away the Church's Head, and believe the Head, leave the Body as it were a lifeless trunk. It is all to no purpose that thou dost caress the Head, like any devoted servant. He that would take off the head, doth his best to kill both the head and the body. They are ashamed to deny Christ, yet are they not ashamed to deny Christ's words. Christ neither we nor ye have seen with our eyes. The Jews saw, and slew Him. We have not seen Him, and believe; His words are with us. Compare yourselves with the Jews: they despised Him hanging upon the Tree, ye despise Him sitting in heaven; at their suggestion Christ's title was set[11] up, by your setting[12] yourselves up, Christ's Baptism is effaced. But what remains, Brethren, but that we pray even for the proud, that we pray even for the puffed up, who so extol themselves? Let us say to God on their behalf, "Let them know that the Lord is Thy Name; and" not "that" men, but "Thou Only art the Most High over all the earth."[13] Let us turn to the Lord, etc.

SERMON LXXX.

[CXXX. BEN.]

ON THE WORDS OF THE GOSPEL, JOHN VI. 9, WHERE THE MIRACLE OF THE FIVE LOAVES AND THE TWO FISHES IS RELATED.

1. IT was a great miracle that was wrought, dearly beloved, for five thousand men to be filled with five loaves and two fishes, and the remnants of the fragments to fill twelve baskets. A great miracle: but we shall not wonder much at what was done, if we give heed to Him That did it. He multiplied the five loaves in the hands of them that brake them, who multiplieth the seeds that grow in the earth, so as that a few grains are sown, and whole barns are filled. But, because he doth this every year, no one marvels. Not the inconsiderableness[14] of what is done, but its constancy takes away admiration of it. But when the Lord did these things, He

1 Gal. i 9.   2 John i. 33.   3 1 Cor. iv. 16, xi. 1.
4 Matt. xxiii. 3.   5 1 Cor. x. 4.   6 Matt. vii. 25.
7 John v. 46.   8 Gen. xxii. 18.   9 Luke xvi. 29-31.

10 Luke xxiv. 46, etc.   11 *Stetit.*   12 *Stantibus.*
13 Ps. lxxxii. 19, Sept. (lxxxiii. 18, English version).
14 *Vilitas.*

spake to them that had understanding, not by words only, but even by the miracles themselves. The five loaves signified the five books of Moses' Law. The old Law is barley compared to the Gospel wheat. In those books are great mysteries concerning Christ contained. Whence He saith Himself, "If ye had believed Moses, ye would believe Me also; for he wrote of Me."[1] But as in barley the marrow is hid under the chaff, so in the veil of the mysteries of the Law is Christ hidden. As those mysteries of the Law are developed and unfolded; so too those loaves increased when they were broken. And in this that I have explained to you, I have broken bread unto you. The five thousand men signify the people ordered under the five books of the Law. The twelve baskets are the twelve Apostles, who themselves too were filled with the fragments of the Law. The two fishes are either the two precepts of the love of God and our neighbour, or the two people of the circumcision and uncircumcision, or those two sacred personages of the king and the priest. As these things are explained, they are broken; when they are understood, they are eaten.

2. Let us turn to Him who did these things. He is Himself "The Bread which came down from heaven;"[2] but Bread which refresheth the failing, and doth not fail; Bread which can be tasted,[3] cannot be wasted. This Bread did the manna also figure. Wherefore it is said, "He gave them the Bread of heaven, man ate Angels' Bread."[4] Who is the Bread of heaven, but Christ? But in order that man might eat Angels' Bread, the Lord of Angels was made Man. For if He had not been made Man, we should not have His Flesh; if we had not His Flesh, we should not eat the Bread of the Altar. Let us hasten to the inheritance, seeing we have hereby received a great earnest of it. My brethren, let us long for the life of Christ, seeing we hold as an earnest the Death of Christ. How shall He not give us His good things, who hath suffered our evil things? In this our earth, in this evil world, what abounds, but to be born, to labour, and to die? Examine thoroughly man's estate, convict me if I lie: consider all men whether they are in this world for any other end than to be born, to labour, and to die? This is the merchandize of our country: these things here abound. To such merchandize did that Merchantman descend. And forasmuch as every merchant gives and receives; gives what he has, and receives what he has not; when he procures anything, he gives money, and receives what he buys: so Christ too in this His traffic gave and received. But what received He? That which aboundeth here, to be born, to labour, and to die. And what did He give? To be born again, to rise again, and to reign for ever. O Good Merchant, buy us. Why should I say buy us, when we ought to give Thee thanks that Thou hast bought us? Thou dost deal out our Price to us, we drink Thy Blood; so dost thou deal out to us our Price. And we read the Gospel, our title[5] deed. We are Thy servants, we are Thy creatures: Thou hast made us, Thou hast redeemed us. Any one can buy his servant, create him he cannot; but the Lord hath both created and redeemed His servants; created them, that they might be; redeemed them, that they might not be captives ever. For we fell into the hands of the prince of this world, who seduced Adam, and made him his servant, and began to possess us as his slaves. But the Redeemer came, and the seducer was overcome. And what did our Redeemer to him who held us captive? For our ransom he held out His Cross as a trap; he placed in It as a bait His Blood. He indeed had power to shed His Blood, he did not attain[6] to drink it. And in that he shed the Blood of Him who was no debtor, he was commanded to render up the debtors; he shed the Blood of the Innocent, he was commanded to withdraw from the guilty. He verily shed His Blood to this end, that He might wipe out our sins. That then whereby he held us fast was effaced by the Redeemer's Blood. For he only held us fast by the bonds of our own sins. They were the captive's chains. He came, He bound the strong one with the bonds of His Passion; He entered into his house,[7] into the hearts, that is, of those where he did dwell, and took away his vessels. We are his vessels. He had filled them with his own bitterness. This bitterness too he pledged to our Redeemer in the gall. He had filled us then as his vessels; but our Lord spoiling his vessels, and making them His Own, poured out the bitterness, filled them with sweetness.

3. Let us then love Him, for He is sweet. "Taste and see that the Lord is sweet."[8] He is to be feared, but to be loved still more. He is Man and God; the One Christ is Man and God; as one man is soul and body: but God and Man are not two Persons. In Christ indeed there are two substances, God and Man; but one Person, that the Trinity may remain, and that there be not a quaternity introduced by the addition of the human[9] nature. How then can it be that God should not have mercy upon us, for whose sake God was made Man? Much is that which He hath done already; more

---

[1] John v. 46.   [2] John vi. 41.
[3] *Qui sumi potest, consumi non potest*
[4] Ps. lxxvii. 24, 25, Sept. (lxxviii. English version).

[5] *Instrumentum.*   [6] *Meruit.*   [7] Matt. xii. 29.
[8] Ps. xxxiii. 8, Vulgate (xxxiv. 8, English version).
[9] *Homine. Vid.* Serm. xvii. (lxvii. Ben.) 7 (iv.), note.

wonderful is that which He hath done, than what He hath promised; and by that which He hath done, ought we to believe what He hath promised. For that which He hath done, we should scarcely believe, unless we also saw it. Where do we see it? In the peoples that believe, in the multitude that has been brought unto Him. For that hath been fulfilled which was promised to Abraham;[1] and from these things which we see, we believe what we do not see. Abraham was one single man, and to him was it said, "In thy seed shall all nations be blessed." If he had looked to himself, when would he have believed? He was one single man, and was now old; and he had a barren wife, and one who was so far advanced in age, that she could not conceive, even though she had not been barren. There was nothing at all from which any hope could be drawn. But he looked to Him That gave the promise, and believed what he did not see. Lo, what he believed, we see. Therefore from these things which we see, we ought to believe what we see not. He begat Isaac, we saw it not; and Isaac begat Jacob, and this we did not see; and Jacob begat twelve sons, and them we saw not; and his twelve sons begat the people of Israel; this great people we see. I have now begun to mention those things which we do see. Of the people of Israel was born the Virgin Mary, and she gave birth to Christ; and, lo, in Christ all nations are blessed. What more true? more certain? more plain? Together with me, long after the world to come, ye who have been gathered together out of the nations. In this world hath God fulfilled His promise concerning the seed of Abraham. How shall He not give us His eternal promises, whom He hath made to be Abraham's seed? For this the Apostle saith; "But if ye be Christ's" (they are the Apostle's words), "then are ye Abraham's seed."[2]

4. We have begun to be some great thing; let no man despise himself: we were once nothing; but we are something. We have said unto the Lord, "Remember that we are dust;"[3] but out of the dust He made man, and to dust He gave life, and in Christ our Lord hath He already brought this same dust to the Kingdom of Heaven. For from this dust took He flesh, from this took earth, and hath raised earth to heaven, He who made heaven and earth. If then these two new things, not yet done, were set before us, and it were asked of us, "Which is the most wonderful, that He who is God should be made Man, or he who is man should be made a man of God? which is the more wonderful? which the more difficult?" What hath Christ promised

us? That which as yet we see not; that is, that we should be His men, and reign with Him, and never die? This is so to say with difficulty believed, that a man once born should arrive at that life, where he shall never die. This is what we believe with a heart well cleansed,[4] cleansed, I mean, of the world's dust; that this dust close not up our eye of faith. This it is that we are bid believe, that after we have been dead, we shall be even with our dead bodies in life, where we shall never die. Wonderful it is; but more wonderful is that which Christ hath done. For which is the more incredible, that man should live for ever, or that God should ever die? That men should receive life from God is the more credible; that God should receive death from men I suppose is the more incredible. Yet this hath been brought to pass already: let us then believe that which is to be. If that which is the more incredible hath been brought to pass, shall He not give us that which is the more credible? For God hath power to make of men Angels, who hath made of earthy and filthy spawn,[5] men. What shall we be? Angels. What have we been? I am ashamed to call it to mind; I am forced to consider it, yet I blush to tell it. What have we been? Whence did God make men? What were we before we were at all? We were nothing. When we were in our mother's wombs, what were we? It is enough that ye remember. Withdraw your minds from the whence ye were made, and think of what ye are. Ye live; but so do herbs and trees live. Ye have sensation, and so have cattle sensation. Ye are men, ye have got beyond the cattle, ye are superior to the cattle; for that ye understand how great things He hath done for you. Ye have life, ye have sensation, ye have understanding, ye are men. Now to this benefit what can be compared? Ye are Christians. For if we had not received this, what would it profit us, that we were men! So then we are Christians, we belong to Christ. For all the world's rage, it doth not break us; because we belong to Christ. For all the world's caresses, it doth not seduce us; we belong to Christ.

5. A great Patron have we found, Brethren. Ye know that men depend[6] much upon their patrons. A dependent of a man in power will make answer to any one who threatens him, "Thou canst do nothing to me, as long as my lord's head is safe." How much more boldly and surely may we say, "Thou canst do nothing to us, whilst our Head is safe." Forasmuch as our Patron is our Head. Whosoever depend upon any man as patron, are his dependents; we are the members of our Patron. Let Him bear us in Himself, and let no man tear us away from Him. Since what labours soever we shall have endured

[1] Gen. xii. 3.   [2] Gal. iii. 29.
[3] Ps. cii. 14, Sept. (ciii. English version).

[4] *Excusso.*   [5] *Semina.*   [6] *Tendunt se.*

in this world, all that passeth away, is nothing. The good things shall come which shall not pass away; by labours we arrive at them. But when we have arrived, no one teareth us away from them. The gates of Jerusalem are shut; they receive the bolts too, that to that city it may be said, "Praise the Lord, O Jerusalem, praise thy God, O Sion. For He hath strengthened the bolts of thy gates; He hath blessed thy children within thee. Who hath made thy borders peace." [1] When the gates are shut, and the bolts drawn, no friend goeth out, no enemy entereth in. There shall we have true and assured security, if here we shall not have abandoned the truth.

SERMON LXXXI.

[CXXXI. BEN.]

ON THE WORDS OF THE GOSPEL, JOHN VI. 53, "EXCEPT YE EAT THE FLESH," ETC., AND ON THE WORDS OF THE APOSTLES. AND THE PSALMS. AGAINST THE PELAGIANS.

Delivered at the Table of the Martyr St. Cyprian, the 9th of the Calends of October, — 23 Sept., on the Lord's day.

1. WE have heard the True Master, the Divine Redeemer, the human Saviour, commending to us our Ransom, His Blood. For He spake to us of His Body and Blood; He called His Body Meat, His Blood Drink. The faithful recognise the Sacrament of the faithful. But the hearers what else do they but hear? When therefore commending such Meat and such Drink He said, "Except ye shall eat My Flesh and drink My Blood, ye shall have no life in you;" [2] (and this that He said concerning life, who else said it but the Life Itself? But that man shall have death, not life, who shall think that the Life is false), His disciples were offended, not all of them indeed, but very many, saying within themselves, "This is an hard saying, who can hear it?" [3] But when the Lord knew this in Himself, and heard the murmurings of their thought, He answered them, thinking though uttering nothing, that they might understand that they were heard, and might cease to entertain such thoughts. What then did He answer? "Doth this offend you?" "What then if ye shall see the Son of Man ascend up where He was before?" [4] What meaneth this? "Doth this offend you?" "Do ye imagine that I am about to make divisions of this My Body which ye see; and to cut up My Members, and give them to you? 'What then if ye shall see the Son of Man ascend up where He was before?'" Assuredly, He who could ascend Whole could not be consumed. So then He both gave us of His Body and Blood a healthful refreshment, and briefly solved so great a question as to His Own Entireness. Let them then who eat, eat on, and them that drink, drink; let them hunger and thirst; eat Life, drink Life. That eating, is to be refreshed; but thou art in such wise refreshed, as that that whereby thou art refreshed, faileth not. That drinking, what is it but to live? Eat Life, drink Life; thou shalt have life, and the Life is Entire. But then this shall be, that is, the Body and the Blood of Christ shall be each man's Life; if what is taken in the Sacrament visibly is in the truth itself eaten spiritually, drunk spiritually. For we have heard the Lord Himself saying, "It is the Spirit That quickeneth, but the flesh profiteth nothing. The words that I have spoken unto you, are Spirit and Life. But there are some of you," saith He, "that believe not." [5] Such were they who said, "This is a hard saying, who can hear it?" It is hard, but only to the hard; that is, it is incredible, but only to the incredulous.

2. But in order to teach us that this very believing is matter of gift, not of desert, He saith, "As I have said unto you, no man cometh unto Me, except it were given him of My Father." [6] Now as to where the Lord said this, if we call to mind the foregoing words of the Gospel, we shall find that He had said, "No man cometh unto Me, except the Father which hath sent Me draw him." [7] He did not say *lead*, but *draw*. This violence is done to the heart, not the body. Why then dost thou marvel? Believe, and thou comest; love, and thou art drawn. Do not suppose here any rough and uneasy violence; it is gentle, it is sweet; it is the very sweetness that draweth thee. Is not a sheep drawn, when fresh grass is shown to it in its hunger? Yet I imagine that it is not bodily driven on, but fast bound by desire. In such wise do thou come too to Christ; do not conceive of long journeyings; where thou believest, there thou comest. For unto Him, who is everywhere we come by love, not by sailing. But forasmuch as even in this kind of voyage, waves and tempest of divers temptations abound; believe on the Crucified; that thy faith may be able to ascend the Wood. Thou shalt not sink, but shalt be borne upon the Wood. Thus, even thus, amid the waves of this world did he sail, who said, "But God forbid that I should glory, save in the Cross of our Lord Jesus Christ." [8]

3. But wonderful it is, that when Christ Crucified is preached, two hear, one despiseth, the other ascendeth. Let him that despiseth, impute it to himself; let not him that ascendeth, arrogate it to himself. For he hath heard from the True Master; "No man cometh unto Me, except

---

[1] Ps. cxlvii. 12-14.   [2] John vi. 53.   [3] John vi. 60.
[4] John vi. 61, 62.

[5] John vi. 63, 64.   [6] John vi. 65.   [7] John vi. 44.
[8] Gal. vi. 14.

it were given unto him of My Father." Let him joy, that it hath been given; let him render thanks to Him who giveth it, with a humble, not an arrogant heart; lest what he hath attained [1] through humility, he lose through pride. For even they who are already walking in this way of righteousness, if they attribute it to themselves, and to their own strength, perish out of it. And therefore Holy Scripture teaching us humility saith by the Apostle, "Work out your own salvation with fear and trembling." [2] And lest hereupon they should attribute ought to themselves, because he said, "Work," he subjoined immediately, "For it is God who worketh in you both to will and to do of His good pleasure." [3] "It is God who worketh in you;" therefore "with fear and trembling," make a valley, receive the rain. Low grounds are filled, high grounds are dried up. Grace is rain. Why dost thou marvel then, if "God resist the proud, and giveth grace unto the lowly"? [4] Therefore, "with fear and trembling;" that is, with humility. "Be not high-minded, but fear." [5] Fear that thou mayest be filled; be not high-minded, lest thou be dried up.

4. But you will say, "I am walking in this way already; once there was need for me to learn, there was need for me to know by the teaching of the law what I had to do: now I have the free choice of the will; who shall withdraw me from this way?" If thou read carefully, thou wilt find that a certain man began to uplift himself, on a certain abundance of his, which he had nevertheless received; but that the Lord in mercy, to teach him humility, took away what He had given; and he was on a sudden reduced to poverty, and confessing the mercy of God in his recollection, he said, "In my abundance I said, I shall never be moved." [6] "In my abundance I said." But I said it, I who am a man said it; "All men are liars, I said." [7] Therefore, "in my abundance I said;" so great was the abundance, that I dared to say, "I shall never be moved." What next? "O Lord, in Thy favour Thou gavest strength to my beauty." But "Thou turnedst away Thy Face from me, and I was troubled." [8] "Thou hast shown me," saith he, "that that wherein I did abound, was of Thee. Thou hast shown me Whence I should seek, to Whom attribute what I had received, to Whom I ought to render thanks, to Whom I should run in my thirst, Whereby be filled, and with Whom keep that whereby I should be filled. 'For my strength will I keep to Thee;' [9] whereby I am by Thy bounty filled, through Thy safe keeping I will not lose.

'My strength will I keep to Thee.' That Thou mightest show me this, 'Thou turnedst away Thy Face from me, and I was troubled.' 'Troubled,' because dried up; dried up, because exalted. Say then thou dry and parched one, that thou mayest be filled again; 'My soul is as earth without water unto Thee.' [10] Say, 'My soul is as earth without water unto Thee.' For Thou hast said, not the Lord, 'I shall never be moved.' Thou hast said it, presuming on thine own strength; but it was not of thyself, and thou didst think as if it were."

5. What then doth the Lord say? "Serve ye the Lord in fear, and rejoice unto Him with trembling." [11] So the Apostle too, "Work out your own salvation with fear and trembling. For it is God who worketh in you." Therefore rejoice with trembling: "Lest at any time the Lord be angry." I see that you anticipate me by your crying out. For you know what I am about to say, you anticipate it by crying out. And whence have ye this, but that He taught you to whom ye have by believing come? This then He saith; hear what ye know already; I am not teaching, but in preaching am calling to your remembrance; nay, I am neither teaching, seeing that ye know already, nor calling to remembrance, seeing that ye remember, but let us say all together what together with us ye retain. "Embrace discipline, and rejoice," but, "with trembling," [12] that, humble ye may ever hold fast that which ye have received. "Lest at any time the Lord be angry;" with the proud of course, attributing to themselves what they have, not rendering thanks to Him, from whom they have. "Lest at any time the Lord be angry, and ye perish from the righteous way." Did he say, "Lest at any time the Lord be angry, and ye come not into the righteous way"? Did he say, "Lest the Lord be angry, and He bring you not to the righteous way"? or "admit you not into the righteous way? Ye are walking in it already, be not proud, lest ye even perish from it. 'And ye perish,' saith he, 'from the righteous way.'" "When His wrath shall be kindled in a short time" [13] against you. At no distant time. As soon as thou art proud, thou losest at once what thou hadst received. As though man terrified by all this were to say, "What shall I do then?" It follows, "Blessed are all they that trust in Him:" not in themselves, but in Him. "By grace are we saved, not of ourselves, but it is the gift of God." [14]

6. Peradventure ye are saying, "What does he mean, that he is so often saying this? A second and a third time he says it; and scarcely ever speaks, but when he says it." Would that I may not say it in vain! For men there are

---

1 *Meruit.* 2 Phil. ii. 12. 3 Phil. ii. 13.
4 Jas. iv. 6. 5 Rom. xi. 20.
6 Ps. xxix. 6, Sept. (xxx. English version). 7 Ps. cxvi. 11.
8 Ps. xxix. 8, Sept (xxx. 7, English version).
9 Ps. lviii. 10, Sept. (lix. 9, English version).

10 Ps. cxlii. 6, Sept. (cxliii. English version). 11 Ps. ii. 11, Sept
12 Ps. ii. 12, Sept. 13 Ps. ii. 13, Sept. 14 Eph. ii. 8.

unthankful to grace, attributing much to poor and disabled nature. True it is, when man was created he received great power of free-will; but he lost it by sin. He fell into death, became infirm, was left in the way by the robbers half dead; the Samaritan, which is by interpretation keeper, passing by lifted him up on his own beast;[1] he is still being brought to the inn. Why is he lifted up? He is still in process of curing. "But," he will say, "it is enough for me that in baptism I received remission of all sins." Because iniquity was blotted out, was therefore infirmity brought to an end? "I received," says he, "remission of all sins." It is quite true. All sins were blotted out in the Sacrament of Baptism, all entirely, of words, deeds, thoughts, all were blotted out. But this is the "oil and wine" which was poured in by the way. Ye remember, beloved Brethren, that man who was wounded by the robbers, and half dead by the way, how he was strengthened, by receiving oil and wine for his wounds. His error indeed was already pardoned, and yet his weakness is in process of healing in the inn. The inn, if ye recognise it, is the Church. In the time present, an inn, because in life we are passing by: it will be a home, whence we shall never remove, when we shall have got in perfect health unto the kingdom of heaven. Meanwhile receive we gladly our treatment in the inn, and weak as we still are, glory we not of sound health: lest through our pride we gain nothing else, but never for all our treatment to be cured.

7. "Bless the Lord, O my soul."[2] Say, yea say to thy soul, "Thou art still in this life, still bearest about a frail flesh, still "doth the corruptible body press down the soul;"[3] still after the entireness of remission hast thou received the remedy of prayer; for still, whilst thy weaknesses are being healed, dost thou say, "Forgive us our debts."[4] Say then to thy soul, thou lowly valley, not an exalted hill; say to thy soul, "Bless the Lord, O my soul, and forget not all His benefits."[5] What benefits? Tell them, enumerate them, render thanks. What benefits? "Who forgiveth all thine iniquities."[6] This took place in baptism. What takes place now? "Who healeth all thy weaknesses." This takes place now; I acknowledge. But as long as I am here, "the corruptible body presseth down the soul." Say then also that which comes next, "Who redeemeth thy life from corruption."[7] After redemption from corruption, what remaineth? "When this corruptible shall have put on incorruption, and this mortal shall have put on immortality, then shall be brought to pass the saying that is written, Death is swallowed up in

victory. Where, O death, is thy contention?" There rightly, "O death, where is thy sting?"[8] Thou seekest its place, and findest it not. What is "the sting of death"? What is, "O death, where is thy sting?" Where is sin? Thou seekest, and it is nowhere. For "the sting of death is sin." They are the Apostle's words, not mine. Then shall it be said, "O death, where is thy sting?" Sin shall nowhere be, neither to surprise thee, nor to assault thee, nor to inflame[9] thy conscience. Then it shall not be said, "Forgive us our debts." But what shall be said? "O Lord our God, give us peace: for Thou hast rendered all things unto us."[10]

8. Finally, after the redemption from all corruption, what remaineth but the crown of righteousness? This at least remaineth, but even in it, or under it, let not the head be swollen that it may receive the crown. Hear, mark well the Psalm, how that crown will not have a swollen head. After he had said, "Who redeemeth thy life from corruption;" he saith, "Who crowneth thee." Here thou wert ready at once to say, "'Crowneth thee,' is an acknowledgment of my merits, my own excellence hath done it; it is the payment of a debt, not a gift." Give ear rather to the Psalm. For it is thou again that sayest this; and "all men are liars."[11] Hear what God saith; "Who crowneth thee with mercy and pity." Of His mercy He crowneth thee, of His pity He crowneth thee. For thou hadst no worthiness that He should call thee, and being called should justify thee, being justified glorify thee. "The remnant is saved by the election of grace. But if by grace, then is it no more of works; otherwise grace is no more grace. For to him that worketh, the reward shall not be reckoned according to grace, but according to debt."[12] The Apostle saith, "Not according to grace, but according to debt." But "thee He crowneth with pity and mercy;" and if thy own merits have gone before, God saith to thee, "Examine well thy merits, and thou shalt see that they are My gifts."

9. This then is the righteousness of God. As it is called, "The Lord's salvation,"[13] not whereby the Lord is saved, but which He giveth to them whom He saveth; so too the grace of God through Jesus Christ our Lord is called the righteousness of God, not as that whereby the Lord is righteous, but whereby He justifieth those whom of ungodly He maketh righteous. But some, as the Jews in former times, both wish to be called Christians, and still ignorant of God's righteousness, desire to establish their own, even in our own times, in the times of open grace, the times of the full revelation of grace

---

[1] Luke x. 30, etc.   [2] Ps. ciii. 1.   [3] Wisd. ix. 15.
[4] Matt. vi. 12.   [5] Ps. ciii. 2.   [6] Ps. ciii. 3.
[7] Ps. ciii. 4.

[8] 1 Cor. xv. 54, 55.   [9] *Titillet.*   [10] Isa. xxvi. 12, Sept.
[11] Ps. cxvi. 11.   [12] Rom. xi. 5, 6, iv. 4.
[13] Ps. iii. 9, Sept. (iii. 8, English version).

which before was hidden; in the times of grace now manifested in the floor, which once lay hid in the fleece. I see that a few have understood me, that more have not understood, whom I will by no means defraud by keeping silence. Gideon, one of the righteous men of old, asked for a sign from the Lord, and said, "I pray, Lord, that this fleece which I put in the floor be bedewed,[1] and that the floor be dry."[2] And it was so; the fleece was bedewed, the whole floor was dry. In the morning he wrung out the fleece in a basin; forasmuch as to the humble is grace given; and in a basin, ye know what the Lord did to His disciples. Again, he asked for another sign; "O Lord, I would," saith he, "that the fleece be dry, the floor bedewed." And it was so. Call to mind the time of the Old Testament, grace was hidden in a cloud, as the rain in the fleece. Mark now the time of the New Testament, consider well the nation of the Jews, thou wilt find it as a dry fleece; whereas the whole world, like that floor, is full of grace, not hidden, but manifested. Wherefore we are forced exceedingly to bewail our brethren, who strive not against hidden, but against open and manifested grace. There is allowance for the Jews. What shall we say of Christians? Wherefore are ye enemies to the grace of Christ? Why rely ye on yourselves? Why unthankful? For why did Christ come? Was not nature here before? Was not nature here, which ye only deceive by your excessive praise? Was not the Law here? But the Apostle says, "If righteousness come by the Law, then Christ is dead in vain."[3] What the Apostle says of the Law, that say we of nature to these men. "If righteousness come by nature, then Christ is dead in vain."

10. What then was said of the Jews, the same altogether do we see in these men now. "They have a zeal of God: I bear them record that they have a zeal of God, but not according to knowledge."[4] What is. "not according to knowledge"? "For being ignorant of God's righteousness, and wishing to establish their own, they have not submitted themselves unto the righteousness of God."[5] My Brethren, share with me in my sorrow. When ye find such as these, do not hide them; be there no such misdirected[6] mercy in you; by all means, when ye find such, hide them not. Convince the gainsayers, and those who resist, bring to us. For already have two[7] councils on this question been sent to the Apostolic see; and rescripts also have come from thence. The question has been brought to an issue; would that their error may sometime

be brought to an issue too! Therefore do we advise that they may take heed, we teach that they may be instructed, we pray that they may be changed. Let us turn to the Lord, etc.

SERMON LXXXII.

[CXXXII. BEN.]

ON THE WORDS OF THE GOSPEL, JOHN VI. 55, "FOR MY FLESH IS MEAT INDEED, AND MY BLOOD IS DRINK INDEED. HE THAT EATETH MY FLESH," ETC.

1. As we heard when the Holy Gospel was being read, the Lord Jesus Christ exhorted us by the promise of eternal life to eat His Flesh and drink His Blood. Ye that heard these words, have not all as yet understood them. For those of you who have been baptized and the faithful do know what He meant. But those among you who are yet called Catechumens, or Hearers, could be hearers, when it was being read, could they be understanders too? Accordingly our discourse is directed to both. Let them who already eat the Flesh of the Lord and drink His Blood, think What it is they eat and drink, lest, as the Apostle says, "They eat and drink judgment to themselves."[8] But they who do not yet eat and drink, let them hasten when invited to such a Banquet. Throughout these days the teachers feed you, Christ daily feedeth you, That His Table is ever ordered before you. What is the reason, O Hearers, that ye see the Table, and come not to the Banquet? And peradventure, just now when the Gospel was being read, ye said in your hearts, "We are thinking what it is that He saith, 'My Flesh is meat indeed, and My Blood is drink indeed.'[9] How is the Flesh of the Lord eaten, and the Blood of the Lord drunk? We are thinking what He saith." Who hath closed it against thee, that thou dost not know this? There is a veil over it; but if thou wilt, the veil shall be taken away. Come to the profession,[10] and thou hast resolved the difficulty. For what the Lord Jesus said, the faithful know well already. But thou art called a Catechumen, art called a Hearer, and art deaf. For the ears of the body thou hast open, seeing that thou hearest the words which were spoken; but the ears of the heart thou hast still closed, seeing thou understandest not what was spoken. I plead,[11] I do not discuss it. Lo, Easter[12] is at hand, give in thy name for baptism. If the festivity arouse thee not, let the very curiosity induce thee: that thou mayest know the meaning of, "Whoso eateth My Flesh and drinketh My Blood dwelleth in Me, and I in him."[13] That thou mayest know

---

[1] *Compluatur.*   [2] Judg. vi. 37.   [3] Gal. ii. 21.
[4] Rom. x. 2.   [5] Rom. x. 3.   [6] *Perversa.*
[7] Of Carthage and Milevis which are among the Epistles of St. Augustin, 175, 176. And the rescripts of the Roman Pontiff, Innocent (A.D. 417), in the Epistles 181, 182. Ben. ed. note.

[8] 1 Cor. xi. 29.   [9] John vi. 55.   [10] Baptismal profession
[11] *Disputo non dissero.*   [12] *Pascha.*
[13] John vi. 56.

with me what is meant, " Knock, and it shall be opened unto thee : " [1] and as I say to thee, " Knock, and it shall be opened unto thee," so do I too knock, open thou to me. When I speak aloud to the ears, I knock at the breast.

2. But if the Catechumens, my Brethren, are to be exhorted not to delay to approach to this so great grace of regeneration ; what great care ought we to have in building up the faithful, that their approaching may profit them, and that they eat and drink not such a Banquet unto their own judgment? Now that they may not eat and drink unto judgment, let them live well. Be ye exhorters, not by words, but by your conduct ; that they who have not been baptized, may in such wise hasten to follow you, that they perish not by imitating you. Do ye who are married keep the fidelity of the marriage-bed with your wives. Render what you require. As a husband thou requirest chastity from thy wife ; give her an example, not words. Thou art the head, look where thou goest. For thou oughtest to go where it may not be dangerous for her to fol- low : yea, thou oughtest to walk thyself where thou wouldest have her follow. Thou requirest strength from the weaker sex ; the lust of the flesh ye have both of you : let him that is the stronger, be the first to conquer. And yet, which is to be lamented, many men are conquered by the women. Women preserve chastity, which men will not preserve ; and in that they preserve it not, would wish to appear men : as though he was in sex the stronger, only that the enemy might more easily subdue him. There is a struggle, a war, a combat. The man is stronger than the woman, the " man is the head of the woman." [2] The woman combats and overcomes ; dost thou succumb to the enemy? The body stands firm, and does the head lie low? But those of you who have not yet wives, and who yet already approach to the Lord's Table, and eat the Flesh of Christ, and drink His Blood, if ye are about to marry, keep yourselves for your wives. As ye would have them come to you, such ought they also to find you. What young man is there who would not wish to marry a chaste wife? And if he were about to espouse a virgin, who would not desire she should be unpolluted? Thou lookest for one unpolluted, be unpolluted thyself. Thou lookest for one pure, be not thyself impure. For it is not that she is able, and thou art not able. If it were not possible, then could not she be so. But seeing that she can, let this teach thee, that it is possible. And that she may have this power, God is her ruler. But thou wilt have greater glory if thou shalt do it. Why greater glory? The vigilance of parents is a check to her, the

very modesty of the weaker sex is a bridle to her ; lastly, she is in fear of the laws of which thou art not afraid. Therefore it is then that thou wilt have greater glory if thou shalt do it ; be- cause if thou do it, thou fearest God. She has many things to fear besides God, thou fearest God alone. But He whom thou fearest is greater than all. He is to be feared in public, He in secret. Thou goest out, thou art seen ; thou goest in, thou art seen ; the lamp is lighted, He seeth thee ; the lamp is extinguished, He seeth thee ; thou enterest into thy closet, He seeth thee ; in the retirement [3] of thine own heart, He seeth thee. Fear Him, Him whose care it is to see thee ; and even by this fear be chaste. Or if thou wilt sin, seek for some place where He may not see thee, and do what thou wouldest.

3. But ye who have taken the vow already, chasten your bodies more strictly, and suffer not yourselves to loosen the reins of concupiscence even after those things which are permitted ; that ye may not only turn away from an unlawful connection, [4] but may despise even a lawful look. Remember, in whichever sex ye are, whether men or women, that ye are leading on earth the life of Angels : " For the Angels are neither given in marriage, nor marry." [5] This shall we be, when we shall have risen again. How much better are ye, who before death begin to be what men will be after the resurrection ! Keep your proper degrees, for God keepeth for you your honours. The resurrection of the dead is com- pared to the stars that are set in heaven. " For star differeth from star in glory," as the Apostle says ; " so also is the resurrection of the dead." [6] For after one manner virginity shall shine there, after another shall wedded chas- tity shine there, after another shall holy widow- hood shine there. They shall shine diversely, but all shall be there. The brilliancy unequal, the heaven the same.

4. With your thoughts then on your degrees, and keeping your professions, approach ye to the Flesh of the Lord, approach to the Blood of the Lord. Whoso knoweth himself to be other- wise, let him not approach. Be moved to com- punction rather by my words. For they who know that they are keeping for their wives, what from their wives they require, they who know that they are in every way keeping continence, if this they have vowed to God, feel joy at my words ; but they who hear me say, " Whosoever of you are not keeping chastity, approach not to that Bread," are saddened. And I should have no wish to say this ; but what can I do? Shall I fear man, so as to suppress the truth? What, if those servants do not fear the Lord,

---

shall I therefore too not fear? as if I do not know that it is said, "'Thou wicked and slothful servant,'[1] thou shouldest dispense, and I require." Lo, I have dispensed, O Lord my God; lo, in Thy Sight, and in the sight of Thy Holy Angels, and of this Thy people, I have laid out Thy money; for I am afraid of Thy judgment. I have dispensed, do Thou require. Though I should not say it, Thou wouldest do it. Therefore I rather say, I have dispensed, do Thou convert, do Thou spare. Make them chaste who have been unchaste, that in Thy Sight we may rejoice together when the judgment shall come, both he who hath dispensed and he to whom it hath been dispensed. Doth this please you? May it do so! Whosoever of you are unchaste, amend yourselves, whilst ye are alive. For I have power to speak the word of God, but to deliver the unchaste, who persevere in wickedness, from the judgment and condemnation of God, have I no power.

SERMON LXXXIII.

[CXXXIII. BEN.]

ON THE WORDS OF THE GOSPEL OF JOHN VII. 6, ETC., WHERE JESUS SAID THAT HE WAS NOT GOING UP UNTO THE FEAST, AND NOTWITHSTANDING WENT UP.

1. I PURPOSE by the Lord's assistance to treat of this section[2] of the Gospel which has just been read; nor is there a little difficulty here, lest the truth be endangered, and falsehood glory. Not that either the truth can perish, nor falsehood triumph. Now hearken for a while what difficulty this lesson has; and being made attentive by the propounding of the difficulty, pray that I may be sufficient for its solution. "The Jews' feast of tabernacles was at hand;"[3] these it seems are the days which they observe even to this day, when they build huts.[4] For this solemnity of theirs is called from the building of tabernacles; since σκηνὴ means a "tabernacle," σκηνοπηγία is the building of a tabernacle. These days were kept as feast days among the Jews; and it was called one feast day, not because it was over in one day, but because it was kept up by a continued festivity; just as the feast day of the Passover, and the feast day of unleavened bread, and notwithstanding, as is manifest, that feast is kept throughout many days. This anniversary then was at hand in Judæa, the Lord Jesus was in Galilee, where He had also been brought up, where too He had relations and kinsfolk, whom Scripture calls "His brethren." "His brethren, therefore," as we have heard it read, "said unto

Him, Pass from hence, and go into Judæa; that Thy disciples also may see Thy works that Thou doest. For no man doeth anything in secret, and himself seeketh to be known openly. If Thou do these things, manifest Thyself to the world."[5] Then the Evangelist subjoins, "For neither did His brethren believe in Him."[6] If then they did not believe in Him, the words they threw out were of envy. "Jesus answered them, My time is not yet come; but your time is alway ready. The world cannot hate you; but Me it hateth, because I testify of it that the works thereof are evil. Go ye up to this feast day. I go[7] not up to this feast day, for My time is not yet accomplished."[8] Then follows the Evangelist; "When He had said these words, He Himself stayed in Galilee. But when His brethren were gone up, then went He also up to the feast day, not openly, but as it were in secret."[9] Thus far is the extent of the difficulty, all the rest is clear.

2. What then is the difficulty? what makes the perplexity? what is in peril? Lest the Lord, yea, to speak more plainly, lest the Truth Itself should be thought to have lied. For if we would have it thought that He lied, the weak will receive an authority for lying. We have heard say that He lied. For those who think that He lied, speak thus, "He said that He should not go up to the feast day, and He went up." In the first place then, let us, as far as in the press of time we can, see whether he does lie, who says a thing and does it not. For example, I have told a friend, "I will see you to-morrow;" some greater necessity occurs to hinder me; I have not on that account spoken falsely. For when I made the promise, I meant what I said. But when some greater matter occurred, which hindered the accomplishment[10] of my promise, I had no design to lie, but I was not able to fulfil the promise. Lo, to my thinking I have used no labour to persuade you, but have merely suggested to your good sense,[11] that he who promises something, and doeth it not, does not lie, if, that he do it not, something has occurred to hinder the fulfilment of his promise, not to be any proof of falsehood.

3. But some one who hears me will say, "Canst thou then say this of Christ, that He either was not able to fulfil what He would, or that He did not know things to come?" Thou doest well, good is thy suggestion, right thy hint; but, O man, share with me my anxiety. Dare we to say that He lies, Who we do not dare to say is weak in power? I for my part, to the

---

[1] Matt. xxv. 26.　　[2] Capitulo.　　[3] John vii. 2.
[4] Casas.

[5] John vii. 3, 4.　　[6] John vii. 5.
[7] In the Greek it is οὔπω, nondum, and so in some Latin copies (Ben. note); Griesbach and Scholz place οὐκ in the text, as having the authority of the mss. D, K, most Verss., and the Fathers.
[8] John vii. 6-8.　　[9] John vii. 9, 10.　　[10] Fidem.
[11] Prudentiam.

best of my thinking, as far as according to my infirmity I am able to judge, would choose that a man should be deceived in any matter rather than lie in any. For to be deceived is the portion of infirmity, to lie of iniquity. "Thou hatest, O Lord," saith he, "all them that work iniquity." [1] And immediately after, "Thou shalt destroy all them that speak a lie." [2] Either "iniquity" and "a lie" are upon a level; or, "Thou shalt destroy," is more than "Thou hatest." For he who is held in hatred, is not immediately punished by destruction. But let that question be, whether there be ever a necessity to lie; for I am not now discussing that; it is a dark question, and has many lappings; [3] I have not time to cut them, and to come to the quick. [4] Therefore let the treatment of it be deferred to some other time; for peradventure it will be cured by the Divine assistance without any words of mine. But attend and distinguish between what I have deferred, and what I wish to treat of to-day. Whether on any occasion one may lie, this difficult and most obscure question I defer. But whether Christ lied, whether the Truth spake anything false, this, being reminded of it by the Gospel lesson, have I undertaken to-day.

4. Now what the difference is between being deceived, and lying, I will briefly state. He is deceived who thinks what he says to be true, and therefore says it, because he thinks it true. Now if this which he that is deceived says, were true, he would not be deceived; if it were not only true, but he also knew it to be true, he would not lie. He is deceived then, in that it is false, and he thinks it true; but he only says it because he thinks it true. The error lies in human infirmity, not in the soundness of the conscience. But whosoever thinks it to be false, and asserts it as true, he lies. See, my Brethren, draw the distinction, ye who have been brought up in the Church, instructed in the Lord's Scriptures, not uninformed, nor simple, [5] nor ignorant [6] men. For there are among you men learned and erudite, and not indifferently instructed in all kinds of literature; and with those of you who have not learnt that literature which is called liberal, it is more that ye have been nourished up in the word of God. If I labour in explaining what I mean, do ye aid me both by the attention of your hearing, and the thoughtfulness [7] of your meditations. Nor will ye aid, unless ye are aided. Wherefore pray we mutually for one another, and look equally for our common Succour. He is deceived, who whereas what he says is false, thinks it to be true; but he lies, who thinks a thing to be false, and gives it

out as true, whether it be true or false. Observe what I have added, "whether it be true or false;" yet he who thinks it to be false, and asserts it as true, lies; he aims to deceive. For what good is it to him, that it is true? He all the while thinks it false, and says it as if it were true. What he says is true in itself, it is in itself true; with regard to him it is false, his conscience does not hold that which he is saying; he thinks in himself one thing to be true, he gives out another for truth. His is a double heart, not single; he does not bring out that which he has in it. The double heart has long since been condemned. "With deceitful lips in a heart and a heart have they spoken evil things." [8] Had it been enough to say, "in the heart have they spoken evil things," where is the "deceitful lips"? [9] What is deceit? When one thing is done, another pretended. Deceitful lips are not a single heart; and because not a single heart, therefore "in a heart and a heart;" therefore "in a heart" twice, because the heart is double.

5. How then think we of the Lord Jesus Christ, that He lied? If it is a less evil to be deceived than to lie, dare we to say that He lies who we dare not to say is deceived? But He is neither deceived, nor doth He lie; but in very deed as it is written (for of Him is it understood, of Him ought it to be understood), "Nothing false is said unto the King, and nothing false shall proceed out of His mouth." If by King here he meant any man, let us prefer Christ the King, to a man-king. But if, which is the truer understanding of it, it is Christ of whom he spake, if I say, as is the truer understanding of it, it is Christ of whom he spake (for to Him indeed nothing false is said, in that He is not deceived; from His Mouth nothing false proceedeth, in that He doth not lie); let us look how we are to understand the section of the Gospel, and let us not make the [10] pitfall of a lie, as it were, on heavenly authority. But it is most absurd to be seeking to explain the truth, and to prepare a place for a lie. What art thou teaching me, I ask thee, who art explaining this text to me, what wouldest thou teach me? I do not know whether you would dare to say, "Falsehood." For if you should dare to say this, I turn away mine ears, and fasten them up with thorns, that if you should try to force your way, I might through their very pricking make away without the explanation of the Gospel. Tell me what thou wouldest wish to teach me, and thou hast resolved the difficulty. Tell me, I pray thee; lo, here I am; mine ears are open, my heart is ready, teach me. But I ask, what? I will not travel through many things. What art thou going to teach me? Whatsoever learning thou art

---

[1] Ps. v. 5. [2] Ps. v. 6. [3] Sinus.
[4] Vivum. [5] Rustici. [6] Idiotæ.
[7] Prudentia.

[8] Ecclus. ii. 14, Vulgate (ii. 12, English version). [9] Ps. xii. 2.
[10] Voraginem.

about to bring forward, whatsoever strength to show in disputation, tell me this one thing only, one of two things I ask; art thou going to teach me truth or falsehood? What do we suppose he will answer lest one depart; lest while he is open-mouthed and making an effort to bring out his words, I forthwith leave him: what will he promise but truth? I am listening, standing, expecting, most earnestly expecting. See here, he who promised that he will teach me truth, insinuates falsehood concerning Christ. How then shall he teach truth, who would say that Christ is false? If Christ is false, can I hope that thou wilt tell me the truth?

6. Consider again. What does he say? Hath Christ spoken falsely? Where, I ask thee? "Where He says, 'I go not up to the feast day;' and went up." For my part, I should wish thoroughly to examine this place, if so be we may see that Christ did not speak falsely. Yea rather, seeing that I have no doubt that Christ did not speak falsely, I will either thoroughly examine this passage and understand it, or, not understanding it, I will defer it. Yet that Christ spoke falsely will I never say. Grant that I have not understood it; I will depart in my ignorance. For better is it with piety to be ignorant, than with madness to pronounce judgment. Notwithstanding we are trying to examine, if so be by His assistance, who is the Truth, we may find something, and be found something ourselves, and this something will not be in the Truth a lie. For if in searching I find a lie, I find not a something but a nothing. Let us then look where it is thou sayest that Christ lied. He will say, "In that He said, 'I go not up to this feast,' and went up." Whence dost thou know that He said so? What if I were to say, nay, not I, but any one, for God forbid that I should say it; what if another were to say, "Christ did not say this;" whereby dost thou refute him, whereby wilt thou prove it? Thou wouldest open the book, find the passage, point it out to the man, yea with great confidence force the book upon him if he resisted, "Hold it, mark, read, it is the Gospel you have in your hands." But why, I ask thee, why dost thou so rudely accost[1] this feeble one? Do not be so eager; speak more composedly, more tranquilly. See, it is the Gospel I have in my hands; and what is there in it? He answers: "The Gospel declares that Christ said what thou deniest." And wilt thou believe that Christ said it, because the Gospel declares it? "Decidedly for that reason," says he. I marvel exceedingly how thou shouldest say that Christ lieth, and the Gospel doth not lie. But lest haply when I speak of the Gospel, thou shouldest think of the book itself, and im-

agine the parchment and ink to be the Gospel, see what the Greek word means; Gospel is "a good messenger," or "a good message." The messenger then doth not lie, and doth He who sent him, lie? This messenger, the Evangelist to wit, to give his name also, this John who wrote this, did he lie concerning Christ, or say the truth? Choose which you will, I am ready to hear you on either side. If he spake falsely, you have no means of proving that Christ spake those words. If he said the truth, truth cannot flow from the fountain of falsehood. Who is the Fountain? Christ: let John be the stream. The stream comes to me, and you say to me, "Drink securely;" yea, whereas you alarm me as to the Fountain Himself, whereas you tell me there is falsehood in the Fountain, you say to me, "Drink securely." What do I drink? What said John, that Christ spake falsely? Whence came John? From Christ. Is he who came from Him, to tell me truth, when He from whom he came lied? I have read in the Gospel plainly, "John lay on the Lord's Breast;"[2] but I conclude that he drank in truth. What saw he as he lay on the Lord's Breast? What drank he in? what, but that which he poured forth? "In the beginning was the Word, and the Word was with God, and the Word was God. The Same was in the beginning with God. All things were made by Him, and without Him was nothing made. That which was made in Him was life, and the Life was the Light of men; And the Light shineth in darkness, and the darkness comprehended It not;"[3] nevertheless It shineth, and though I chance to have some obscurity, and cannot thoroughly comprehend It, still It shineth. "There was a man sent from God, whose name was John; he came to bear witness of the Light, that all men through him might believe. He was not the Light:" who? John: who? John the Baptist. For of him saith John the Evangelist, "He was not the Light;" of whom the Lord saith, "He was a burning, and a shining lamp."[4] But a lamp can be lighted, and extinguished. What then? whence drawest thou the distinction? of what place art thou enquiring? He to whom the lamp bare witness, "was the True Light."[5] Where John added, "the True," there art thou looking out for a lie. But hear still the same Evangelist John pouring forth what he had drunk in; "And we beheld," saith he, "His glory." What did he behold? what glory beheld he? "The glory as of the Only-Begotten of the Father, full of grace and truth."[6] See then, see, if we ought not haply to restrain weak or rash disputings, and to presume nothing false of the truth, to give to the Lord what is His due; let us give glory to the Fountain, that we may fill ourselves

---

[1] Conturbas.

[2] John xiii. 23. [3] John i. 1, etc. [4] John v. 35.
[5] John i. 9. [6] John i. 14.

securely. "Now God is true, but every man a liar."[1] What is this? God is full; every man is empty; if he will be filled, let him come to Him That is full. "Come unto Him, and be enlightened."[2] Moreover, if man is empty, in that he is a liar, and he seeks to be filled, and with haste and eagerness runs to the fountain, he wishes to be filled, he is empty. But thou sayest, "Beware of the fountain, there is falsehood there." What else sayest thou, but "there is poison there"?

7. "You have already," he says, "said all, already have you checked, already chastened me. But tell me how He did not speak falsely who said, 'I go not up,' and went up?" I will tell you, if I can; but think it no little matter, that if I have not established you in the truth, I have yet kept you back from rashness. I will nevertheless tell you, what I imagine you know even already, if you remember the words which I have set forth to you. The words themselves solve the difficulty. That feast was kept for many days. On this, that is this present feast day, saith He, this day, that is when they hoped, He went not up; but when He Himself resolved to go. Now mark what follows, "When He had said these words, He Himself stayed in Galilee." So then He did not go up on that feast day. For His brethren wished that He should go first; therefore had they said, "Pass from hence into Judæa." They did not say, "Let us pass," as though they would be His companions; or, "Follow us into Judæa," as though they would go first; but as though they would send Him before them. He wished that they should go before; He avoided this snare, impressing His infirmity as Man, hiding the Divinity; this He avoided, as when He fled into Egypt.[3] For this was no effect of want of power, but even of truth, that He might give an example of caution; that no servant of His might say, "I do not fly, because it is disgraceful;" when haply it might be expedient to fly. As He was going to say to His disciples, "When they have persecuted you in this city, flee ye into another;"[4] He gave them Himself this example. For He was apprehended, when He willed; He was born, when He willed. That they might not anticipate Him then, and announce that He was coming, and plots be prepared; He said, "I go not up to this feast day."[5] He said, "I go not up," that He might be hid; He added "this," that He might not lie. Something He expressed,[6] something He suppressed, something He repressed; yet said He nothing false, for "nothing false proceedeth out of His Mouth." Finally, after He had said these words,

"When His brethren were gone up;"[7] the Gospel declares it, attend, read what you have objected to me; see if the passage itself do not solve the difficulty, see if I have taken from anywhere else what to say. This then the Lord was waiting for, that they should go up first, that they might not announce beforehand that He was coming, "When His brethren were gone up, then went He also up to the feast day, not openly, but as it were in secret." What is, "as it were in secret"? He acts there as if in secret. What is, "as it were in secret"? Because neither was this really in secret. For He did not really make an effort to be concealed, who had it in His Own power when He would be taken. But in that concealment, as I have said, He gave His weak disciples, who had not the power to prevent being taken when they would not, an example of being on their guard against the snares of enemies. For He went up afterwards even openly, and taught them in the temple; and some said, "'Lo, this is He; lo, He is teaching.' Certainly our rulers said that they wished to apprehend Him: 'Lo, He speaketh openly, and no one layeth hands on Him.'"[8]

8. But now if we turn our attention to ourselves, if we think of His Body, how that we are even He. For if we were not He, "Forasmuch as ye have done it unto one of the least of Mine, ye have done it unto Me,"[9] would not be true. If we were not He, "Saul, Saul, why persecutest thou Me?"[10] would not be true. So then we are He, in that we are His members, in that we are His Body, in that He is our Head, in that Whole Christ is both Head and Body.[11] Peradventure then He foresaw us that we were not to keep the feast days of the Jews, and this is, "I go not up to this feast day." See neither Christ nor the Evangelist lied; of the which two if one must needs choose one, the Evangelist would pardon me, I would by no means put him that is true before the Truth Himself; I would not prefer him that was sent to Him by whom he was sent. But God be thanked, in my judgment what was obscure has been laid open. Your piety will aid me before God. Behold, I have, as I was best able, resolved the question, both concerning Christ and the Evangelist. Hold fast the truth with me as men who love it, embrace charity without contention.

SERMON LXXXIV.

[CXXXIV. BEN.]

ON THE WORDS OF THE GOSPEL, JOHN VIII. 31, "IF YE ABIDE IN MY WORD, *THEN* ARE YE TRULY MY DISCIPLES," ETC.

1. YE know well, Beloved, that we all have

---

[1] Rom. iii. 4.
[2] Ps. xxxiii. 6, Sept. (xxxiv. 5, English version).
[3] Matt. ii. 14.   [4] Matt. x. 23.   [5] John vii. 8.
[6] *Aliquid intulit, aliquid abstulit, aliquid distulit.*

[7] John vii. 10.   [8] John vii. 25, 26.   [9] Matt. xxv. 40.
[10] Acts ix. 4.   [11] Eph. i. 22, 23; 1 Cor. xii. 12.

One Master, and are fellow disciples under Him. Nor are we your masters, because we speak to you from this higher spot; but He is the Master of all, who dwelleth in us all. He just now spake to us all in the Gospel, and said to us, what I also am saying to you; but He saith it of us, as well of us as of you. "If ye shall continue in My word," not of course in my word who am now speaking to you; but in His who spake just now out of the Gospel. "If ye shall continue in My word," saith He, "ye are My disciples indeed."[1] To be a disciple, it is not enough to come, but to continue. He doth not therefore say, "If ye shall hear My word;" or, "If ye shall come to My word;" or, "If ye shall praise My word;" but observe what He said, "If ye shall continue in My word, ye are My disciples indeed, and ye shall know the truth, and the truth shall free you."[2] What shall we say, Brethren? To continue in the word of God, is it toilsome, or is it not? If it be toilsome, look at the great reward; if it be not toilsome, thou receivest the reward for nought. Continue we then in Him who continueth in us. We, if we continue not in Him, fall; but He if He continue not in us, hath not on that account lost an habitation. For He skilleth to continue in Himself, who never leaveth Himself. But for man, God forbid that he should continue in himself who hath lost himself. So then we continue in Him through indigence; He continueth in us through mercy.

2. Now then seeing it hath been set forth what we ought to do, let us see what we are to receive. For He hath appointed a work, and promised a reward. What is the work? "If ye shall continue in Me." A short work; short in description, great in execution. "If ye shall continue." What is, "If ye shall continue"? "If ye shall build on the Rock."[3] O how great a thing is this, Brethren, to build on the Rock, how great is it! "The floods came, the winds blew, the rain descended, and beat upon that house, and it fell not; for it was founded upon a rock."[4] What then is to continue in the word of God, but not to yield to any temptations? The reward, what is it? "Ye shall know the truth, and the truth shall free you." Bear with me, for ye perceive that my voice is feeble;[5] assist me by your calm[6] attention. Glorious reward! "Ye shall know the truth." Here one may haply say, "And what doth it profit me to know the truth?" "And the truth shall free you." If the truth have no charms for you, let freedom have its charms. In the usage of the Latin tongue, the expression, "to be free," is used in two senses; and chiefly we are accustomed to hear this word in this sense, that whosoever is free may be understood to escape some danger, to be rid of some embarrassment. But the proper signification of "to be free," is "to be made free;" just as "to be saved," is "to be made safe;" "to be healed," is, "to be made whole;" so "to be freed," is "to be made free." Therefore I said, "If the truth have no charms for you, let freedom have its charms." This is expressed more evidently in the Greek language, nor can it be there understood in any other sense. And that ye may know that in no other sense can it be understood; when the Lord spake, the Jews answered, "We were never in bondage to any man; how sayest thou the Truth shall free you?"[7] That is, "the Truth shall make you free," how sayest thou to us, who were never in bondage to any man? "How," say they, "dost Thou promise them freedom, who as Thou seest never bare the hard yoke of bondage?"

3. They heard what they ought; but they did not what they ought. What did they hear? Because I said, "The truth shall free you;" ye turned your thoughts upon yourselves, that ye are not in bondage to man, and ye said, "We were never in bondage to any man. Every one," Jew and Greek, rich and poor, the man in authority and private station, the emperor and the beggar, "Every one that committeth sin is the servant of sin."[8] "Every one," saith He, "that committeth sin is the servant of sin." If men but acknowledge their bondage, they will see from whence they may obtain freedom. Some free-born man has been taken captive by the barbarians, from a free man is made a slave; another hears, and pities him, considers how that he has money, becomes his ransomer, goes to the barbarians, gives money, ransoms the man. And he has indeed restored freedom, if he have taken away iniquity. But what man has ever taken away iniquity from another man? He who was in bondage with the barbarians, has been redeemed by his ransomer; and great difference there is between the ransomer and the ransomed; yet haply are they fellow-slaves under the lordship of iniquity. I ask him that was ransomed, "Hast thou sin?" "I have," he says. I ask the ransomer, "Hast thou sin?" "I have," he says. So then neither do thou boast thyself that thou hast been ransomed, nor thou uplift thyself that thou art his ransomer; but fly both of you to the True Deliverer. It is but a small part of it, that they who are under sin, are called servants; they are even called dead; what a man is afraid of captivity bringing upon him, iniquity has brought on him already. For what? because they seem to be alive, was He then mistaken who said, "Let the dead bury their dead"?[9] So

[1] John viii. 31. [2] John viii. 32. [3] Matt. vii. 24.
[4] Matt. vii. 25. [5] Obtusam. [6] Tranquillitate. [7] John viii. 33. [8] John viii. 34. [9] Matt. viii. 22.

then all under sin are dead, dead servants, dead in their service, servants in their death.

4. Who then freeth from death and from bondage, save He, who is " Free among the dead "?[1] Who is " Free among the dead," save He who among sinners is without sin? " Lo, the prince of the world cometh," saith our Redeemer Himself, our Deliverer, " Lo, the prince of the world cometh, and shall find nothing in Me."[2] He holds fast those whom he hath deceived, whom he hath seduced, whom he hath persuaded to sin and death; " in Me shall he find nothing." Come, Lord, Redeemer come, come; let the captive acknowledge thee, him that leadeth captive flee thee; be Thou my Deliverer. Lost as I was, He hath found me in Whom the devil findeth nothing that cometh of the flesh. The prince of this world findeth in Him Flesh, he findeth it; but what kind of Flesh? A mortal Flesh, which he can seize, which he can crucify, which he can kill. Thou art mistaken, O deceiver, the Redeemer is not deceived; thou art mistaken. Thou seest in the Lord a mortal Flesh, it is not flesh of sin, it is the likeness of flesh of sin. " For God sent His Son in the likeness of flesh of sin." True Flesh, mortal Flesh; but not flesh of sin. " For God sent His Son in the likeness of flesh of sin, that by sin He might condemn sin in the Flesh."[3] " For God sent His Son in the likeness of flesh of sin;" in Flesh, but not in flesh of sin; but " in the likeness of flesh of sin." For what purpose? " That by sin," of which assuredly there was none in Him, " He might condemn sin in the flesh; that the righteousness of the Law might be fulfilled in us, who walk not after the flesh, but after the Spirit."[4]

5. If then it was " the likeness of flesh of sin," not flesh of sin, how, " That by sin He might condemn sin in the flesh"? So a likeness is wont to receive the name of that thing of which it is a likeness. The word man is used for a real man; but if you show a man painted on the wall, and enquire what it is, it is answered, " A man." So then Flesh having the likeness of flesh of sin, that it might be a sacrifice for sin, is called " sin." The same Apostle says in another place, " He made Him to be sin for us, who knew no sin."[5] " Him who knew no sin:" Who is He who knew no sin, but He That said, " Behold the prince of the world cometh, and shall find nothing in me?"[2] Him who knew no sin, made He sin for us;" even Christ Himself, who knew no sin, God made sin for us. What does this mean, Brethren? If it were said, " He made sin upon Him," or, " He made Him to have sin;" it would seem intolerable; how do we tolerate what is said, " He made Him sin," that Christ

Himself should be sin? They who are acquainted with the Scriptures of the Old Testament recognise what I am saying. For it is not an expression once used, but repeatedly, very constantly, sacrifices for sins are called " sins." A goat, for instance, was offered for sin, a ram, anything; the victim itself which was offered for sin was called " sin." A sacrifice for sin then was called " sin;" so that in one place the Law says, " That the Priests are to lay their hands upon the sin."[6] " Him" then, " who knew no sin, He made sin for us;" that is, " He was made a sacrifice for sin." Sin was offered, and sin was cancelled. The Blood of the Redeemer was shed, and the debtor's bond was cancelled. This is the " Blood, That was shed for many for the remission of sins."[7]

6. What meaneth this then thy senseless exultation, O thou that didst hold me captive, for that my Deliverer had mortal Flesh? See, if He had sin; if thou hast found anything of thine in Him, hold Him fast. " The Word was made Flesh."[8] The Word is the Creator, the Flesh His creature. What is there here of thine, O enemy? And the Word is God, and His Human[9] Soul is His creature, and His Human Flesh His creature, and the Mortal Flesh of God is His creature. Seek for sin here. But what art thou seeking? The Truth saith, " The prince of this world shall come, and shall find nothing in Me."[2] He did not therefore not find Flesh, but nothing of his own, that is, no sin. Thou didst deceive the innocent, thou madest them guilty. Thou didst slay the Innocent; thou destroyedst Him from whom thou hadst nothing due, render back what thou didst hold fast. Why then didst thou exult for a short hour, because thou didst find in Christ mortal Flesh? It was thy trap: whereupon thou didst rejoice, thereby hast thou been taken. Wherein thou didst exult that thou hadst found something, therein thou sorrowest now that thou hast lost what thou didst possess. Therefore, brethren, let us who believe in Christ, continue in His word. For if we shall continue in His word, we are His disciples indeed. For not those twelve only, but all we who continue in His word are His disciples indeed. And " we shall know the Truth, and the Truth shall free us;" that is, Christ the Son of God who hath said, " I am the Truth,"[10] shall make you free, that is, shall free you, not from barbarians, but from the devil; not from the captivity of the body, but from the iniquity of the soul. It is He Only who freeth in such wise. Let no one call himself free, lest he remain a slave. Our soul shall not remain in bondage, for that day by day our debts are forgiven.

---

[1] Ps. lxxxviii. 5.   [2] John xiv. 30.   [3] Rom. viii. 3.
[4] Rom. viii. 4.   [5] 2 Cor. v. 21.

[6] Lev. iv. 29, Sept.   [7] Matt. xxvi. 28.
[8] John i. 14.   [9] *Hominis.*
[10] John xiv. 6.

SERMON LXXXV.

[CXXXV. BEN.]

ON THE WORDS OF THE GOSPEL, JOHN IX. 4 AND
31, "WE MUST WORK THE WORKS OF HIM THAT
SENT ME," ETC. AGAINST THE ARIANS. AND OF
THAT WHICH THE MAN WHO WAS BORN BLIND
AND RECEIVED HIS SIGHT SAID, "WE KNOW THAT
GOD HEARETH NOT SINNERS."

1. THE Lord Jesus, as we heard when the
Holy Gospel was being read, opened the eyes of
a man who was born blind. Brethren, if we consider our hereditary punishment, the whole world
is blind. And therefore came Christ the Enlightener, because the devil had been the Blinder.
He made all men to be born blind, who seduced
the first man. Let them run to the Enlightener,
let them run, believe, receive the clay made
of the spittle. The Word is as it were the spittle,
the Flesh is the earth. Let them wash the face
in the pool of Siloa. Now it was the Evangelist's
place to explain to us what Siloa means, and he
said, "which is by interpretation, Sent."[1] Who
is This That is Sent, but He who in this very
Lesson said, "I am come to do the works of
Him That sent Me."[2] Lo, Siloa, wash the face,
be baptized, that ye may be enlightened, and
that ye who before saw not, may see.

2. Lo, first open your eyes to that which is
said; "I am come," saith He, "to do the works
of Him That sent Me." Now here at once
stands forth the Arian, and says, "Here you see
that Christ did not His Own works, but the
Father's who sent Him." Would he say this, if
he saw, that is, if he had washed his face in Him
who was sent, as it were in Siloa? What then
dost thou say? "Lo," says he, "Himself said it."
What said He? "I am come to do the works
of Him That sent Me." Are they not then His
Own? No. What then is that which the Siloa
Himself saith, the Sent Himself, the Son Himself, the Only Son Himself, whom thou complain-
est of as degenerate? What is that He saith,
"All things that the Father hath are Mine."[3]
You say that He did the works of Another, in
that He said, "I must do the works of Him That
sent Me." I say that the Father had the things
of another: I am speaking according to your
[4] principles. Why would you object to me that
Christ said, "I am come to do His works," as
if, "not Mine own but 'His That sent Me'"?

3. I ask Thee, O Lord Christ, resolve the
difficulty, put an end to the contention. "All
things," saith He, "that the Father hath are
Mine." Are they then not the Father's, if they
are Thine? For He doth not say, "All things
that the Father hath He hath given unto Me;"

although, if He had said even this, He would
have shown His equality. But the difficulty is
that He said, "All things that the Father hath
are Mine." If you understand it aright, All
things that the Father hath, are the Son's; all
things that the Son hath, are the Father's. Hear
Him in another place; "All Mine are Thine,
and Thine are Mine."[5] The question is finished,
as to the things which the Father and the Son
have: they have them with one consent, do not
thou introduce [6] dissension. What He calleth
the works of the Father, are His Own works;
for, "Thine too are Mine," for He speaketh of
the works of That Father, to whom He said,
"All Mine are Thine, and Thine are Mine."
So then, My works are Thine, and Thy works
are Mine. "For what things soever the Father
doeth;"[7] Himself hath said, the Lord hath said,
the Only-Begotten hath said, the Son hath
said, the Truth hath said. What hath He said?
"What things soever the Father doeth, these
also doeth the Son in like manner." Signal
expression! signal truth! signal equality. "All
things that the Father doeth, these doeth the
Son also." Were it enough to say, "All things
that the Father doeth, these doeth the Son also"?
It is not enough; I add, "in like manner." Why
do I add, "in like manner"? Because they
who do not understand, and who walk with eyes
not yet open, are wont to say, "The Father
doeth them by way of command, the Son of
obedience, therefore not in like manner." But
if in like manner, as the One, so the Other; so
what things the One, the same the Other.

4. "But," says he, "the Father commands,
that the Son may execute." Carnal indeed is
thy conceit, but without prejudice to the truth,
I grant it to you. Lo, the Father commands,
the Son obeys; is the Son therefore not of the
same Nature, because the One commands, and
the Other obeys? Give me two men, father
and son; they are two men: he that commands
is a man; he that obeys is a man; he that commands and he that obeys have one and the same
nature. Does not he that commands, beget a
son of his own nature? Does he who obeys,
by obeying lose his nature? Now take for the
present, as you thus take two men, the Father
commanding, the Son obeying, yet God and God.
But the first two together are two men, the Latter
together is but One God; this is a divine miracle. Meanwhile if you would that with you I
acknowledge the obedience, do you first with
me acknowledge the Nature. The Father begat That which Himself is. If the Father begat
ought else than what Himself is, He did not
beget a true Son. The Father saith to the Son,
"From the womb before the day-star, I begat

---

[1] John ix. 7.   [2] John ix. 4.   [3] John xvi. 15.
[4] Cor.

[5] John xvii. 10.   [6] Litigare.   [7] John v. 19.

Thee." [1] What is, "before the day-star"? By the day-star times are signified. So then before times, before all that is called "before;" before all that is not, or before all that is. For the Gospel does not say, "In the beginning God made the Word;" as it is said, "In the beginning God made the Heaven and the earth;" [2] or, "In the beginning was the Word born;" or, "In the beginning God begat the Word." But what says it? "He was, He was, He was." You hear, "He was;" believe. "In the beginning was the Word, and the Word was with God, and the Word was God." [3] So often do ye hear, "Was:" seek not for time, for that He always "was." He then who always was, and was always with the Son, for that God is able to beget without time; He said to the Son, "From the womb before the day-star I begat Thee." What is from the womb? Had God a womb? Shall we imagine that God was fashioned with bodily members? God forbid! And why said He, "From the womb," but that it might be understood that He begat Him of His Own Substance? So then from the womb came forth That which Himself was who begat. For if He who begat was one thing, and another came forth out of the womb; it were a monster, not a Son.

5. Therefore let the Son do the works of Him That sent Him, and the Father also do the works of the Son. "At all events," you say, "the Father wills, the Son executes." Lo, I show, that the Son willeth, and the Father executeth. Do you say, "where dost thou show this?" I show it at once. "Father, I will." [4] Now here if I had a mind to cavil, lo, the Son commandeth, and the Father executeth. What wilt Thou? "That where I am, they may be also with Me." We have escaped, there shall we be, where He is; there shall we be, we have escaped. Who can undo the "I Will" of the Almighty? You hear the will of His power, hear now the power of His will. "As the Father," saith He, "raiseth up the dead and quickeneth them; even so the Son quickeneth whom He will." [5] "Whom He will." Say not, The Son quickeneth them, whom the Father commandeth Him to quicken. "He quickeneth whom He will." So then whom the Father will, and whom Himself will: because where there is One Power, there is One Will. Let us then in a heart blind no more hold fast that the Nature of the Father and the Son is One and the Same; because the Father is very Father, the Son is very Son. What He is, That did He beget: because the Begotten was not degenerate.

6. There is a something in the words of that man who was blind, which may cause perplexity, and peradventure make many who understand them not aright despair. For he said amongst the rest of his words, the same man whose eyes were opened, "We know that God heareth not sinners." [6] What shall we do, if God heareth not sinners? Dare we pray to God if He heareth not sinners? Give me one who may pray: lo, here is One to hear. Give me one who may pray, sift thoroughly the human race from the imperfect to the perfect. Mount up from the spring to the summer; for this we have just chanted. "Thou hast made summer and spring;" [7] that is, "Those who are already spiritual, and those who are still carnal hast Thou made;" for so the Son Himself saith, "Thine Eyes have seen My imperfect being." [8] That which is imperfect in My Body, Thine Eyes have seen. And what then? Have they who are imperfect hope? Undoubtedly they have. Hear what follows; "And in Thy Book shall all be written." But perhaps, Brethren, the spiritual pray and are heard, because they are not sinners? What then must the carnal do? What must they do? Shall they perish? Shall they not pray to God? God forbid! Give me that publican in the Gospel. Come, thou publican, stand forth, show thy hope, that the weak may not lose hope. For behold the publican went up with the Pharisee to pray, and with face cast down upon the ground, standing afar off, beating his breast, he said, "Lord, be merciful to me a sinner. [9] And he went down justified rather than the Pharisee." Said he true or false, who said, "Be merciful to me a sinner"? If he said true, he was a sinner; yet was he heard and justified. What then is that, that thou whose eyes the Lord opened, didst say, "We know that God heareth not sinners"? [10] Lo, God doth hear sinners. But wash thou thy inferior face, let that be done in thy heart, which hath been done in thy face; and thou wilt see that God doth hear sinners. The imagination of thine heart hath deceived thee. There is still something for Him to do to thee. We see that this man was cast out of the synagogue; Jesus heard of it, came to him, and said to him, "Dost thou believe on the Son of God?" And He said, "Who is He, Lord, that I should believe on Him?" [11] He saw, and did not see; he saw with the eyes, but as yet with the heart he saw not. The Lord said to him, "Thou both seest Him," that is, with the eyes; "and He that talketh with thee is He.

[1] Ps. cix. 3, Sept. (cx English version).   [2] Gen. i. 1.
[3] John i. 1.   [4] John xvii. 24.   [5] John v. 21.

[6] John ix. 31.
[7] Ps. lxxiii. 17, Sept. (lxxiv. English version).
[8] Ps. cxxxviii. 16, Sept. (cxxxix. English version).
[9] Luke xviii. 13.
[10] Theoph. and Euthym. understand this not thus absolutely, but that God does not hear sinners so as to enable them to work miracles, the miracle being allowed; St. Hilary applies it to those who continue in sin, and whose prayer is not truly prayer, "prayer being not the profession of words, but of faith." *In Ps.* lii § 13.
[11] John ix. 35, 36.

He then fell down, and worshipped Him."[1] Then washed he the face of his heart.

7. Apply yourselves then earnestly to prayer, ye sinners: confess your sins, pray that they may be blotted out, pray that they may be diminished, pray that as ye increase, they may decrease : yet do not despair, and sinners though ye be, pray. For who hath not sinned? Begin with the priests. To the priests it is said, " First offer sacrifices for your own sins, and so for the people."[2] The sacrifices convicted the priests ; that if any one should call himself righteous and without sin, it might be answered him, " I look not at what thou sayest, but at what thou offerest ; thine own victim convicteth thee. Wherefore dost thou offer for thine own sins, if thou have no sins? Dost thou in thy sacrifice lie unto God?" But peradventure the priests of the ancient people were sinners ; of the new people are not sinners. Of a truth, Brethren, for that God hath so willed, I am His priest ; I am a sinner ; with you do I beat the breast, with you I ask for pardon, with you I hope that God will be merciful. But peradventure the Holy Apostles, those first and highest leaders[3] of the flock, shepherds, members of The Shepherd, these peradventure had no sin. Yes, indeed, even they had, they had indeed ; they are not angry at this, for they confess it. I should not dare. First hear the Lord Himself saying to the Apostles, " In this manner pray ye."[4] As those other priests were convicted by the sacrifices, so these by prayer. And amongst the other things which He commanded them to pray for, He appointed this also, " Forgive us our debts, as we also forgive our debtors."[5] What do the Apostles say? Every day they pray for their debts to be forgiven them. They come in debtors, they go out absolved, and return debtors to prayer. This life is not without sin, that as often as prayer is made, so often should sins be forgiven.

8. But what shall I say? Peradventure when they learnt the prayer, they were still weak. Some one, perhaps, will say this. When the Lord Jesus taught them that prayer, they were yet babes, weak, carnal ; they were not yet spiritual, who have no sin. What then, Brethren? When they became spiritual, did they cease to pray? Then Christ ought to have said, " Pray in such wise now ; " and to have given them, when spiritual, another prayer. It is one and the same. He who gave it is One and the Same ; use it then in prayer in the Church. But we will take away all controversy, when you say the Holy Apostles were spiritual, up to the time of the Lord's Passion they were carnal ; this you must say. And indeed, the truth is, as He was hanging, they were in alarm, and the

Apostles then despaired when the robber believed. Peter dared to follow, when the Lord was led to suffering, he dared to follow, who came to the house, and was wearied in the palace, and stood at the fire, and was cold ; he stood at the fire, he was frozen with a chilling fear. Being questioned by the maid-servant, he denied Christ once ; being questioned a second time, he denied Him ; being questioned a third time, he denied Him.[6] God be thanked, that the questioning ceased ; if the questioning had not ceased, long would the denial have been repeated. So then after He rose again, then He confirmed them, then did they become spiritual. Had they at that time then no sin? The Apostles spiritual, wrote spiritual epistles, they sent them to the Churches ; " they had no sin." This you say. I do not believe you, I ask themselves. Tell us, O holy Apostles, after the Lord rose again, and confirmed you with the Holy Ghost sent from heaven ; did ye cease to have sin? Tell us, I pray you. Let us hear, that sinners may not despair, that they may not leave off to pray to God, because they are not without sin. Tell us. One of them saith. And who? He whom the Lord loved the most, and who lay on the Lord's Breast,[7] and drank in the mysteries of the kingdom of heaven which he was to pour forth again. Him I ask ; " Have ye sin or not?" He maketh answer and saith, " If we shall say that we have no sin, we deceive ourselves, and the truth is not in us."[8] Now it is the same John who said, " In the beginning was the Word, and the Word was with God, and the Word was God."[9] See ye what heights he had passed, that he could reach to the Word ! Such an one, and so great, who like an eagle soared above the clouds, who in the serene clearness of his mind saw, " In the beginning was the Word ; " he hath said, " If we shall say that we have no sin, we deceive ourselves, and the truth is not in us. But if we shall confess our sins, He is faithful and just to forgive us our sins, and to cleanse us from all unrighteousness."[10] Therefore pray ye.

SERMON LXXXVI.

[CXXXVI. BEN.]

ON THE SAME LESSON OF THE GOSPEL, JOHN IX., ON THE GIVING SIGHT TO THE MAN THAT WAS BORN BLIND.

1. WE have heard the lesson of the Holy Gospel which we are in the habit of hearing ; but it is a good thing to be reminded : good to refresh the memory from the lethargy of forgetfulness. And in fact this very old lesson has

---

[1] John ix. 37, 38.　[2] Lev. xvi.; Heb. vii. 27.
[3] *Arietes.*　[4] Matt. vi. 9.　[5] Matt. vi. 12.

[6] Matt. xxvi. 69, etc.　[7] John xiii. 23.　[8] 1 John i. 8.
[9] John i. 1.　[10] 1 John i. 9.

given us as much pleasure as if it were new. Christ gave sight to one blind from his birth; why do we marvel? Christ is the Saviour; by an act of mercy He made up that which He had not given in the womb. Now when He gave that man no eyes, it was no mistake of His surely; but a delay with a view to a miracle. You are saying, it may be, "Whence knowest thou this?" From Himself I have heard it; He just now said it; we heard it all together. For when His disciples asked Him, and said, "Lord, who did sin, this man or his parents, that he was born blind?" [1] What answer He made, ye, as I did, heard. "Neither hath this man sinned, nor his parents, but that the works of God should be made manifest in him." [2] Lo then wherefore it was that He delayed when He gave him no eyes. He did not give what He could give, He did not give what He knew He should give, when need was. Yet do not suppose, Brethren, that this man's parents had no sin, or that he himself had not, when he was born, contracted original sin, for the remission of which sin infants are baptized unto remission of sins. But that blindness was not because of his parents' sin, nor because of his own sin; "but that the works of God should be made manifest in him." For we all when we were born contracted original sin: and yet we were not born blind. However enquire carefully, And we were born blind. For who was not born blind? blind, that is, in heart. But the Lord Jesus, for that He had created both, cured both.

2. With the eyes of faith ye have seen this man blind, ye have seen him too of blind seeing; but ye have heard him erring. Wherein this blind man erred, I will tell you; first, in that he thought Christ a prophet, and knew not that He was the Son of God. And then we have heard an answer of His entirely false; for he said, "We know that God heareth not sinners." [3] If God heareth not sinners, what hope have we? If God heareth not sinners, why do we pray, and publish the record of our sin by the beating of the breast? Where again is that Publican, who went up with the Pharisee into the temple,[4] and while the Pharisee was boasting, parading [5] his own merits, he standing afar off, and with his eyes fastened on the ground, and beating his breast, was confessing his sins? And this man, who confessed his sins, went down from the temple justified rather than the other Pharisee. Assuredly then God doth hear sinners. But he who spake these words had not yet washed the face of the heart in Siloa. The sacrament had gone before on his eyes; but in the heart had not been yet effected the blessing

of the grace. When did this blind man wash the face of his heart? When the Lord admitted him into Himself after he had been cast out by the Jews. For He found him, and said to him as we have heard; "Dost thou believe on the Son of God?" And he, "Who is He, Lord, that I may believe on Him?" [6] With the eyes, it is true, he saw already; did he see already in the heart? No, not yet. Wait; he will see presently. Jesus answered him, "I that speak with thee am He." [7] Did he doubt? No, forthwith he washed his face. For he was speaking with That Siloa, "which is by interpretation, Sent." [8] Who is the Sent, but Christ? Who often bare witness, saying, "I do the will of My Father That sent Me." [9] He then was Himself the Siloa. The man approached blind in heart, he heard, believed, adored; washed the face, saw.

3. But they who cast him out continued blind, forasmuch as they cavilled at the Lord, that it was the sabbath when He made clay of the spittle, and anointed the eyes of the blind man. For when the Lord cured with a word, the Jews openly cavilled. For He did no work on the sabbath day, when He spake, and it was done. It was a manifest cavil; they cavilled at Him merely commanding, they cavilled at Him speaking; as if they did not themselves speak all the sabbath day. I might say that they do not speak not only on the sabbath, but on no day, forasmuch as they have kept back from the praises of the True God. Nevertheless, as I have said, brethren, it was a manifest cavil. The Lord said to a certain man, "Stretch forth thine hand;" [10] he was made whole, and they cavilled for that He healed on the sabbath day. What did He do? what work did He do? what burden did He bear? But in this instance, the spitting on the ground, the making clay, and anointing the man's eyes, is doing some work. Let no one doubt it, it was doing a work. The Lord did break the sabbath; but was not therefore guilty. What is that I have said, "He brake the sabbath"? He, the Light had come, He was removing the shadows. For the sabbath was enjoined by the Lord God, enjoined by Christ Himself, who was with the Father, when that Law was given; it was enjoined by Him, but in shadow of what was to come. "Let no man therefore judge you in meat, or in drink, or in respect of an holy day, or of the new moon, or of the sabbath days, which are a shadow of things to come." [11] He had now come whose coming these things announced. Why do the shadows delight us? Open your eyes, ye Jews; the Sun is present. "We know." [12] What do

---

[1] John ix. 2.   [2] John ix. 3.   [3] John ix. 31.
[4] Luke xviii. 10.   [5] *Ventilante*.

[6] John ix. 35, 36.   [7] John ix. 37.
[8] John ix. 7.   [9] John iv. 34, v. 30, vi. 38.
[10] Matt. xii. 13.   [11] Col. ii. 16, 17.   [12] John ix. 24.

ye know, ye blind in heart? what know ye? "That this man is not of God, because he thus breaketh the sabbath day."[1] The sabbath, unhappy men, this very sabbath did Christ ordain,[2] who ye say is not of God. Ye observe the sabbath in a carnal manner, ye have not the spittle of Christ. In this earth of the sabbath look also for the spittle of Christ, and ye will understand that by the sabbath Christ was prophesied. But ye, because ye have not the spittle of Christ in the earth upon your eyes, ye have not come unto Siloa, and have not washed the face, and have continued blind, blind to the good of this blind man, yea now no longer blind either in body or heart. He received clay with the spittle, his eyes were anointed, he came to Siloa, he washed his face, he believed on Christ, he saw, he continued not in that exceedingly fearful judgment; "For judgment I came into this world, that they which see not may see, and that they which see may be made blind."[3]

4. Exceeding alarm ! "That they which see not may see:" Good. It is a Saviour's office, a profession of healing power, "That they which see not may see." But what, Lord, is that Thou hast added, "That they which see may be made blind"? If we understand, it is most true, most righteous. Yet what is, "They which see"? They are the Jews. Do they then see? According to their own words, they see; according to the truth, they do not see. What then is, "they see"? They think they see, they believe they see. For they believed they did see, when they maintained the Law against Christ. "We know;" therefore they see. What is "We know," but we see? What is, "this Man is not of God, because He thus breaketh the sabbath day"? They see; they read what the Law said. For it was enjoined that whosoever should break the sabbath day, should be stoned.[4] Therefore said they that He was not of God; but though seeing, they were blind to this, that for judgment He came into the world who is to be the Judge of quick and dead; why came He? "That they which see not may see:" that they who confess that they do not see, may be enlightened. "And that they which see may be made blind;" that is, that they who confess not their own blindness, may be the more hardened. And, in fact, "That they which see may be made blind," has been fulfilled; the defenders of the Law, Doctors[5] of the Law, the teachers of the Law, the understanders of the Law, crucified the Author of the Law. O blindness, this is that which "in part hath happened to Israel."[6] That Christ might be crucified, and the fulness of the Gentiles might come in, "blindness in part hath happened to Israel." What is, "that they which see not may see"? That the fulness of the Gentiles might come in, "blindness in part hath happened to Israel." The whole world lay in blindness ; but He came, "that they which see not may see, and that they which see may be made blind." He was disowned by the Jews, He was crucified by the Jews ; of His Blood He made an eye-salve for the blind. They who boasted that they saw the light, being more hardened, being made blind, crucified the Light. What great blindness? They killed the Light, but the Light Crucified enlightened the blind.

5. Hear one seeing, who once was blind. Behold, against what a cross they have miserably stumbled, who would not confess their blindness to the Physician ! The Law had continued with them. What serveth the Law without grace? Unhappy men, what can the Law do without grace? What doeth the earth without the spittle of Christ? What doeth the Law without grace, but make them more guilty? Why? Because hearers of the Law and not doers, and hereby sinners, transgressors. The son of the hostess of the man of God was dead, and his staff was sent by his servant, and laid upon his face,[7] but he did not revive. What doeth the Law without grace? What saith the Apostle, now seeing, now of blind, enlightened? "For if there had been a Law given which could give life, verily righteousness should have been by the Law."[8] Take heed ; let us answer and say ; what is this that he hath said? "If there had been a Law given which could give life, verily righteousness should have been by the Law." If it could not give life, why was it given? He went on and added, "But the Scripture hath concluded all under sin, that the promise by the faith of Jesus Christ might be given to them that believe."[9] That the promise of illumination, the promise of love by the faith of Jesus Christ might be given to them that believe, that Scripture, that is the Law, hath concluded all under sin. What is, "hath concluded all under sin"? "I had not known concupiscence, except the Law had said, Thou shalt not lust."[10] What is, "hath concluded all under sin"? Hath made the sinner a transgressor also. For it could not heal the sinner. "It hath concluded all under sin;" but with what hope? The hope of grace, the hope of mercy. Thou hast received the Law: thou didst wish to keep it, thou wast not able ; thou hast fallen from pride, hast seen thy weakness. Run to the Physician, wash the face. Long for Christ, confess Christ, believe on Christ ; the Spirit is added to the letter, and thou wilt be saved. For if thou take away the Spirit from the letter, "the letter killeth ;" if

---

[1] John ix. 16.　　[2] *Prædicavit.*　　[3] John ix. 39.
[4] Num. xv. 36.　　[5] *Tractatores.*
[6] Rom. xi. 25.

[7] 2 Kings iv. 29.　　[8] Gal. iii. 21.
[9] Gal. iii. 22.　　[10] Rom. vii. 7.

it kill, where is hope? "But the Spirit giveth life."[1]

6. Let then Gehazi, Elisha's servant, receive the staff, as Moses the servant of God received the Law. Let him receive the staff, receive it, run, go before, anticipate him, lay the staff upon the face of the dead child. And so it was; he did receive it, he ran, he laid the staff upon the face of the dead child. But to what purpose? what serveth the staff? "If there had been a Law given which could give life," the boy might have been raised to life by the staff; but seeing that "the Scripture hath concluded all under sin," he still lies dead. But why hath it concluded all under sin? "That the promise by the faith of Jesus Christ might be given to them that believe." Let then Elisha come, who sent the staff by the servant to prove that he was dead; let him come himself, come in his own person, himself enter into the woman's house, go up to the child, find him dead, conform himself to the members of the dead child, himself not dead, but living. For this he did; he laid his face upon his face, his eyes upon his eyes, his hands upon his hands, his feet upon his feet, he straitened, he contracted himself, being great, he made himself little. He contracted himself; so to say, he lessened himself. "For being in the Form of God, He emptied Himself, taking the form of a servant."[2] What is He conformed Himself, alive to the dead? Do ye ask, what this is? Hear the Apostle; "God sent His Son."[3] What is, he conformed himself to the dead? Let him tell this, let him go on and declare it again; "In the likeness of flesh of sin." This is to conform Himself Alive to the dead; to come to us in the likeness of flesh of sin, not in the flesh of sin. Man lay dead in a flesh of sin, the likeness of flesh of sin conformed Himself to him. For He died who had not wherefore to die. He died, Alone "Free among the dead;" forasmuch as the whole flesh of men was indeed a flesh of sin. And how should it rise again, had not He who had no sin, conforming Himself to the dead, come in the likeness of flesh of sin? O Lord Jesus, who hast suffered for us, not for Thyself, who hadst no guilt, and didst endure its punishment, that thou mightest dissolve at once the guilt and punishment.

SERMON LXXXVII.

[CXXXVII. BEN.]

THE TENTH CHAPTER OF THE GOSPEL OF JOHN. OF THE SHEPHERD, AND THE HIRELING, AND THE THIEF.

1. YOUR faith, dearly beloved, is not ignorant, and I know that ye have so learnt by the teach-ing of that Master from heaven, in whom ye have placed your hope, that our Lord Jesus Christ, who hath now suffered for us and risen again, is the Head of the Church, and the Church is His Body, and that in His Body the unity of the members and the bond of charity is, as it were, its sound health. But whosoever groweth cold in charity, is become enfeebled in the Body of Christ. But He who hath already exalted our Head, is able also to make even the feeble members whole; provided, that is, that they be not cut off by excessive impiety, but adhere to the Body until they be made whole. For whatsoever yet adhereth to the body, is not beyond hope of healing; whereas that which hath been cut off, can neither be in process of curing, nor be healed. Since then He is the Head of the Church, and the Church is His Body, Whole Christ is both the Head and the Body. He hath already risen again. We have therefore the Head in heaven. Our Head interceadeth for us. Our Head without sin and without death, now propitiateth God for our sins; that we too at the end rising again, and changed into heavenly glory, may follow our Head. For where the Head is, there are the rest of the members also. But whilst we are here, we are members; let us not despair, for we shall follow our Head.

2. For consider, Brethren, the love of this our Head. He is now in heaven, yet doth He suffer here, as long as His Church suffereth here. Here Christ is hungered, here He is athirst, is naked, is a stranger, is sick, is in prison. For whatsoever His Body suffereth here, He hath said that Himself suffereth; and at the end, severing off this His Body to the right hand, and severing the rest by whom He is now trodden under foot to the left, He will say to those on the right hand, "Come, ye blessed of My Father, receive the kingdom which hath been prepared for you from the beginning of the world." For what deservings? "For I was an hungred, and ye gave Me meat;" and so He goes over the rest, as if He had Himself received; to such a degree that they, not understanding it, make answer and say, "Lord, when saw we Thee an hungred, a stranger, and in prison?" And He saith to them, "Forasmuch as ye have done it to one of the least of Mine, ye have done it unto Me."[4] So also in our own body, the head is above, the feet are on the earth; yet in any crowding and throng of men, when any one treads on your foot, does not the head say, "You are treading upon me?" No one has trodden on your head, or on your tongue; it is above, in safety, no harm has happened unto it; and yet because by the bond of charity there is unity from the head even to the feet, the tongue does

---

[1] 2 Cor. iii. 6.   [2] Phil. ii. 6.   [3] Rom. viii. 3.   [4] Matt. xxv. 34, etc.

not separate itself therefrom, but says, "You are treading upon me;" when no one has touched it. As then the tongue, which no one has touched, says, "You are treading upon me;" so Christ, the Head, which no one treadeth on, said, "I was an hungred, and ye gave Me meat." And to them who did not so, He said, "I was an hungred, and ye gave Me no meat." And how did He finish? Thus; "These shall go into everlasting burning, but the righteous into life eternal."

3. When our Lord then was speaking on this occasion, He said, that He is "the Shepherd," He said also that He is "the Door." You find them both in that place, both "I am the Door," and "I am the Shepherd."¹ In the Head He is the Door, the Shepherd in the Body. For He saith to Peter, in whom singly He formeth the Church; "Peter, lovest thou Me?" He answered, "Lord, I do love Thee." "Feed My sheep." And a third time, 'Peter, lovest thou Me?"² "Peter was grieved because He asked him the third time;" as though He who saw the conscience of the denier, saw not the confessor's faith. He had known him always, had known him even when Peter had not known himself. For he did not know himself at that time when he said, " I will be with Thee even unto death;"³ and how infirm he was he knew not. Just as it constantly happens in fact to invalids, that the sick man knows not what is going on within him, but the physician knows; when yet the former is suffering from the very sickness, and the physician is not. The physician can better tell what is going on in another, than he who is sick what is going on in himself. Peter then was at that time the invalid, and the Lord the Physician. The former declared that he had strength, when he had not; but the Lord touching the pulse of his heart, declared that he should deny Him thrice. And so it came to pass, as the Physician foretold, not as the sick presumed. Therefore, after His resurrection the Lord questioned him, not as being ignorant with what a heart he would confess the love of Christ, but that he might by a threefold confession of love, efface the threefold denial of fear.

4. Therefore doth the Lord require this of Peter, "Peter, lovest thou Me?" As though, "What wilt thou give Me, what wilt thou do for Me, seeing that thou lovest Me?" What was Peter to do for his Lord risen again, and going into heaven, and sitting on the right hand of the Father? As if He had said, "This shalt thou give Me, this shalt thou do for Me, if thou lovest Me, feed My sheep; enter in by the Door, not go up by another way." Ye heard when the Gospel was being read, "He that entereth in by

Door, is the shepherd; but he that goeth up another way, is a thief and a robber; and he seeketh to disperse, and to scatter, and to spoil."⁴ Who is he that entereth in by the Door? He that entereth in by Christ. Who is he? He who imitateth the Passion of Christ, who acknowledgeth the Humility of Christ; that whereas God was made Man for us, man may acknowledge himself to be, not God, but man. For whoso wisheth to appear God, when he is man, doth not imitate Him, who, being God, was made Man. But to thee it is not said, Be anything less than thou art; but acknowledge what thou art. Acknowledge thyself feeble, acknowledge thyself man, acknowledge thyself a sinner; acknowledge that it is He That justifieth, acknowledge that thou art full of stains. Let the stain of thine heart appear in thy confession, and thou shalt belong to Christ's flock. For the confession of sins invites the physician's healing; as in sickness, he that says, "I am well," seeketh not the physician. Did not the Pharisee and the Publican go up to the temple?⁵ The one boasted of his sound estate, the other showed his wounds to the Physician. For the Pharisee said, "I thank Thee, O God, that I am not as this publican."⁶ He gloried over the other. So then if that publican had been whole, the Pharisee would have grudged it him; for that he would not have had any one over whom to extol himself. In what state then had he come, who had this envious spirit? Surely he was not whole; and whereas he called himself whole, he went not down cured. But the other casting his eyes down to the ground, and not daring to lift them up unto heaven, smote his breast, saying, "God be merciful to me a sinner."⁷ And what saith the Lord? "Verily I say unto you, that the publican went down from the temple justified rather than the Pharisee. For every one that exalteth himself shall be abased, and he that humbleth himself shall be exalted."⁸ They then who exalt themselves, would go up into the sheepfold by another way; but they who humble themselves, enter in by the Door into the sheepfold. Therefore said He of the one, "he entereth in;" of the other, "he goeth up." He that goeth up, you see, who seeks exaltation, does not enter in, but falls. Whereas he that abases himself, that he may enter in by the Door, falls not, but is the shepherd.

5. But the Lord mentioned three characters,⁹ and our duty is to search them out in the Gospel, that of the shepherd, the hireling, and the thief. I suppose you took notice when the lesson was being read, that He marked out the shepherd, the hireling, and the thief. "The Shepherd,"

---

¹ John x. 7, 11.   ² John xxi 15, etc.   ³ Luke xxii. 33.

⁴ John x. 1, etc.   ⁵ Luke xviii. 10.   ⁶ Luke xviii. 11.
⁷ Luke xviii. 13.   ⁸ Luke xviii. 14.   ⁹ *Personas.*

said He, "layeth down His life for the sheep,"[1] and entereth in by the door.[2] The thief and the robber, said He, go up by another way.[3] "The hireling," He said, if he seeth a wolf or even a thief, "fleeth; because he careth not for the sheep;"[4] for he is an hireling, not a shepherd. The one entereth in by the door, because he is the shepherd; the second goeth up another way, because he is a thief; the third seeing them who wish to spoil the sheep feareth and fleeth, because he is an hireling, because he careth not for the sheep; for he is an hireling. If we shall find these three characters, ye have found, holy brethren, both those whom ye should love, and those whom ye should tolerate, and those of whom ye must beware. The Shepherd is to be loved, the hireling is to be tolerated, of the robber must we beware. There are men in the Church of whom the Apostle speaks, who preach the Gospel by occasion, seeking of men their own advantage, whether of money, or of honour, or human praise.[5] They preach the Gospel, wishing to receive rewards in whatsoever way they can, and seek not so much his salvation to whom they preach, as their own advantage. But he who heareth the word of salvation from him who hath not salvation, if he believe Him whom he preacheth, and put not his hope in him, by whom salvation is preached to him; he that preacheth shall have loss; he to whom he preacheth shall have gain.

6. You have the Lord saying of the Pharisees, "They sit in Moses' seat."[6] The Lord did not mean them only; as if He would send those who should believe on Christ to the school of the Jews, that they might learn there wherein is the way to the kingdom of heaven. Did not the Lord come for this end, that He might establish a Church, and separate those Jews who had a good faith, and a good hope, and a good love, as wheat from the chaff, and might make them one wall of the circumcision, to which should be joined another wall from the uncircumcision of the Gentiles, of which two walls coming from different directions, Himself should be the Corner-Stone? Did not the same Lord therefore say of these two people who were to be one, "And other sheep I have, which are not of this fold"? Now He was speaking to the Jews; "Them also," said He, "must I bring, that there may be one fold, and One Shepherd."[7] Therefore there were two ships[8] out of which He had called His disciples. They figured these two people, when they let down their nets, and took up so great a draught[9] and so large a number of fishes, that the nets were almost broken. "And they laded," it is said, "both

the ships." The two ships figured the One Church, but made out of two peoples, joined together in Christ, though coming from different parts. Of this too the two wives, who had one husband Jacob, Leah and Rachel, are a figure.[10] Of these two, the two blind men also are a figure, who sat by the way side, to whom the Lord gave sight.[11] And if ye pay attention to the Scriptures, ye will find the two Churches, which are not two but One, figured out in many places. For to this end the Corner-Stone serveth, for to make of two One. To this end serveth That Shepherd, for to make of two flocks One. So then the Lord who was to teach the Church, and to have a school of His Own beyond the Jews, as we see at present, would He be likely to send those who believe on Him unto the Jews, to learn? But under the name of the Scribes and Pharisees He intimated that there would be some in His Church who would say and not do; but, in the person of Moses He designated Himself. For Moses represented Him, and for this reason did he put a vail before him, when he was speaking to the people; because as long as they were in the law given up to carnal joys and pleasures, and looking for an earthly kingdom, a vail was put upon their face, that they should not see Christ in the Scriptures. For when the vail was taken away, after that the Lord had suffered, the secrets of the temple were discovered. Accordingly when He was hanging on the Cross, the vail of the temple was rent from the top even to the bottom;[12] and the Apostle Paul says expressly, "But when thou shalt turn to Christ, the vail shall be taken away."[13] Whereas with him who turneth not to Christ, though he read the law of Moses, the vail is laid upon his heart, as the Apostle says. When the Lord then would signify beforehand that there would be some such in His Church, what did He say? "The Scribes and Pharisees sit in Moses' seat. What they say, do; but do not what they do."[14]

7. When wicked clerics hear this which is said against them, they would pervert it. For I have heard that some do wish to pervert this sentence. Would they not, if they might, efface it from the Gospel? But because they cannot efface it, they go about to pervert it. But the grace and mercy of the Lord is present, and allows them not to do so; for He hath hedged round all His declarations[15] with His truth, and in such wise balanced them; that if any one would wish to cut off anything from them, or to introduce anything by a bad reading or interpretation, any right hearted man may join to the Scripture what has been cut off from the Scripture, and read what went above or below, and he will find the sense which the other wished to interpret wrongly. What

---

[1] John x. 11. [2] John x. 2. [3] John x 1.
[4] John x. 12, 13. [5] Phil. i. 18, ii. 21. [6] Matt. xxiii. 2.
[7] John x. 16. [8] Luke v. 2. [9] Vim.

[10] Gen xxix. 23, 28. [11] Matt. xx. 30. [12] Matt. xxvii. 51,
[13] 2 Cor. iii. 16. [14] Matt. xxiii. 2, 3. [15] Sententias.

then, think ye, do they say of whom it is said, "Do what they say"? That it is (and in truth it is so) addressed to laymen. For what does the layman who wishes to live well say to himself, when he takes notice of a wicked cleric? "The Lord said, 'What they say, do; what they do, do not.' Let me walk in the way of the Lord, not follow this man's conversation. Let me hear from him not his words, but God's. I will follow God, let him follow his own lust. For if I should wish to defend myself in such wise before God as to say, 'Lord, I saw that thy cleric living evilly, and therefore I lived evilly;' would He not say to me, 'Thou wicked servant, hadst thou not heard from Me, "What they say, do, but what they do, do not"?' But a wicked layman, an unbeliever, who belongs not to Christ's flock, who belongs not to Christ's wheat, who as chaff is only borne with in the floor, what does he say to himself when the word of God begins to reprove him? "Away; why talkest thou to me? The very Bishops and Clergy do not do it, and dost thou force me to do it?" Thus he seeks for himself not a patron for his bad cause, but a companion for punishment. For will that wicked one whosoever he be that he has chosen to imitate, will he ever defend him in the day of judgment? For as with all whom the devil seduces, he seduces them not to be partakers of a kingdom, but of his damnation; so all who follow the wicked, seek companions for themselves to hell, not protection unto the kingdom of heaven.

8. How then do they pervert this declaration, when it is said to them in their wicked lives, "With good reason was it said by the Lord, 'What they say, do; what they do, do not'"? "It was well said," say they. "For it was said to you, that ye should do what we say; but that ye should not do what we do. For we offer sacrifice, you may not." See the cunning craftiness of these men; what shall I call them? hirelings. For if they were shepherds, they would not say such things. Therefore the Lord, that He might shut their mouths, went on, and said, "They sit in Moses' seat; what they say, do; but what they do, do not; for they say, and do not."[1] What is it then, Brethren? If He had spoken of offering sacrifice; would He have said, "For they say, and do not"? For they do offer[2] sacrifice, they do offer unto God. What is it that they say, and do not? Hear what follows; "For they bind heavy burdens, and grievous to be borne, and lay them on men's shoulders, and they themselves will not touch them with one of their fingers."[3] So openly did He rebuke, describe, and point them out. But those men when they thus wish to pervert the passage, show plainly that they seek nothing in the Church but their own advantage; and that they have not read the Gospel; for had they known but this very page, and read the whole, they would never have dared to say this.

9. But attend to a more clear proof that the Church hath such as these. Lest any one should say to us, "He spake entirely of the Pharisees, He spake of the Scribes, He spake of the Jews; for the Church hath none such." Who then are they of whom the Lord saith, "Not every one that saith unto Me, Lord, Lord, shall enter into the kingdom of heaven"?[4] And He added, "Many shall say to Me in that day, Lord, Lord, have we not prophesied in Thy Name, and in Thy Name done many mighty[5] works,[6] and in Thy Name have eaten and drunken?" What! do the Jews do these things in Christ's name? Assuredly it is manifest, that He speaks of them who have the Name of Christ. But what follows? "Then will I say to them, I never knew you; depart from Me, all ye that work iniquity."[7] Hear the Apostle sighing concerning such as these. He says that some preach the Gospel "through charity," others "by occasion;" of whom he says, "They do not preach the Gospel rightly."[8] A right thing, but themselves not right. What they preach is right; but they who preach it are not right. Why is he not right? Because he seeketh something else in the Church, seeketh not God. If he sought God, he would be chaste; for the soul hath in God her lawful husband. Whosoever seeketh from God ought besides God, doth not seek God chastely. Consider, Brethren; if a wife love her husband because he is rich, she is not chaste. For she loves not her husband, but her husband's gold. Whereas if she love her husband, she loves him both in nakedness and poverty. For if she love him because he is rich; what if (as human chances are) he be [9]outlawed, and all on a sudden be reduced to need? She gives him up, mayhap; because what she loved was not her husband, but his property. But if she love her husband indeed, she loves him even more when poor; for that she loves with pity too.

10. And yet, Brethren, our God never can be poor. He is rich, He made all things, heaven and earth, the sea and Angels. In the heaven, whatsoever we see, whatsoever we see not, He made it. But notwithstanding, we ought not to love these riches, but Him who made them. For He hath promised thee nothing but Himself. Find anything more precious, and He will give thee this. Beauteous is the earth, the heaven, and the Angels; but more beauteous is He who made them. They then who preach God, as loving God; who preach God, for God's

---

sake, feed the sheep, and are no hirelings. This chastity did our Lord Jesus Christ require of the soul, when He said to Peter, " Peter, lovest thou Me " ? [1] What is " Lovest thou Me " ? Art thou chaste? Is not thine heart adulterous? Dost thou seek not thine own things in the Church, but Mine? If then thou be such an one, and lovest Me, " feed My sheep." For thou shalt be no hireling, but thou shalt be a shepherd.

11. But they did not preach chastely, concerning whom the Apostle sighs. But what doth he say? " What then? Notwithstanding every way, whether by occasion or in truth, Christ is preached." [2] He suffers then that hirelings there should be. The shepherd preacheth Christ in truth, the hireling by occasion preacheth Christ, seeking something else. Notwithstanding, both the one and the other preacheth Christ. Hear the voice of the shepherd Paul ; " Whether by occasion or in truth, Christ is preached." Himself a shepherd, he was pleased to have the hireling. For they act where they are able, they are useful as far as they are able. But when the Apostle for other uses sought for those whose ways the weak ones might imitate ; he saith, " I have sent unto you Timotheus, who shall bring you into remembrance of my ways." [3] And what doth he say? " I have sent unto you a shepherd, to bring you into remembrance of my ways ; " that is, who himself also walketh as I walk. And in sending this shepherd, what doth he say? " For I have no one so likeminded, who with sincere affection is anxious for you." Were there not many with him? But what follows? " For all seek their own, not the things which are Jesus Christ's ; " [4] that is, " I have wished to send unto you a shepherd ; for there are many hirelings ; but it were not meet for an hireling to be sent." An hireling is sent for the transaction of other affairs and business ; but for those which Paul then desired, a shepherd was necessary. And he scarcely found one shepherd among many hirelings ; for the shepherds are few, the hirelings many. But what is said of the hirelings? " Verily I say unto you, they have received their reward." [5] Of the shepherd, what saith the Apostle? " But whosoever shall cleanse himself from such as these shall be a vessel unto honour, sanctified, and useful to the Lord, prepared always unto every good work." [6] Not unto certain things prepared, and unto certain not prepared, but " unto every good work prepared." So much have I said, concerning the shepherds.

12. But we will now speak of the hirelings. " The hireling when he seeth the wolf lying in wait for the sheep, fleeth." This the Lord said. Why? · " Because he careth not for the sheep." [7] So long then is the hireling of use, as he seeth not the wolf coming, as he seeth not the thief and the robber ; but when he seeth them, he fleeth. And who is there of the hirelings, who fleeth not from the Church, when he seeth the wolf and the robber? And wolves and robbers abound. They are they who go up by another way. Who are these who go up? They who of Donatus' way [8] wish to make havoc of Christ's sheep, they go up by another way. They do not enter in by Christ, because they are not humble. Because they are proud, they go up. What is, " they go up " ? They are lifted up. Whereby do they go up? By another way : whence they wish to be named from their way. They who are not in unity are of another way, and by this way they go up, that is, are lifted up, and wish to spoil the sheep. Now mark how they go up. " It is we," they say, " who sanctify, we justify, we make righteous." See whither they have got up. " But he that exalteth himself, shall be abased." [9] Our Lord God is able to abase them. Now the wolf is the devil, he lieth in wait to deceive, and they that follow him ; for it is said that " they are clothed indeed with the skins of sheep, but inwardly they are ravening wolves." [10] If the hireling observe any one indulging in wicked talking, or in sentiments to the deadly hurt of his soul, or doing ought that is abominable and unclean, and notwithstanding that he seems to bear a character of some importance in the Church (from which if he hopes for advantage he is an hireling) ; says nothing, and when he sees the man perishing in his sin, sees the wolf following him, sees his throat dragged by his teeth to punishment ; says not to him, " Thou sinnest ; " does not chide him, lest he lose his own advantage. This I say is, " When he seeth the wolf, he fleeth ; " he does not say to him, " Thou art doing wickedly." This is no flight of the body, but of the soul. He whom thou seest standing still in body flies in heart, when he sees a sinner, and does not say to him, " Thou sinnest ; " yea when he even is in concert with him.

13. My Brethren, does ever either Presbyter or Bishop come up here, and say anything from this higher place, but that the property of others must not be plundered, that there must be no fraud committed, no wickedness done? They cannot say ought else who sit in Moses' seat, [11] and it is it that speaks by them, not they themselves. What then is, " Do men gather grapes of thorns, or figs of thistles ? " and, " Every tree is known by his fruit " ? [12] Can a Pharisee speak good things? A Pharisee is a thorn ; how from

[1] John xxi. 16.   [2] Phil i. 18.   [3] 1 Cor. iv. 17.
[4] Phil. ii. 20, etc.   [5] Matt. vi. 2.   [6] 2 Tim. ii. 21.

[7] John x. 12, 13.   [8] *Parte.*   [9] Luke xiv. 11.
[10] Matt. vii. 15.   [11] Matt. xxiii. 2.   [12] Matt. vii. 16, xii 33.

a thorn do I gather grapes? Because Thou, Lord, hast said, "What they say, do; but what they do, do not."¹ Dost Thou bid me gather grapes of thorns when Thou sayest, "Do men gather grapes of thorns"? The Lord answereth thee, "I have not bidden thee gather grapes of thorns: but look, mark well, if haply, as is often the case, the vine when it trails all along upon the ground, be not entangled in thorns." For we sometimes find this, my Brethren, a vine planted over sedge, how it has there a thorny hedge, and throws out its branches, and entangles them in the thorny hedge, and the grape hangs among the thorns; and he that sees it plucks the grape, yet not from the thorns, but from the vine which is entangled in the thorns. In like manner then the Pharisees are thorny; but by sitting in Moses' seat, the vine wraps them round, and grapes, that is, good words, good precepts, hang from them. Do thou pick the grape, the thorn will not prick thee, when thou readest, "What they say, do; but what they do, do not." But the thorn will prick thee, if thou do what they do. So then that thou mayest gather the grape, and not be caught in the thorns, "What they say, do; but what they do, do not." Their deeds are the thorns, their words are the grapes, but from the vine, that is, from Moses' seat.

14. These then flee, when they see the wolf, when they see the robber. Now this it was that I had begun to say, that from this higher place they can say nothing, but, "Do well," "do not forswear yourselves," "defraud not," "cheat not any." But sometimes men's lives are so bad, that counsel is asked of a Bishop on the taking away of another man's estate, and from him is such counsel sought. It has sometimes happened to ourselves, we speak from experience: for we should not have believed it. Many men require from us evil counsels, counsels of lying, of fraud; thinking that they please us thereby. But by the Name of Christ, if what we are saying is pleasing to the Lord, no such man has tempted us, and found what he wished in us. For with the good pleasure of Him who hath called us, we are shepherds, not hirelings. But as saith the Apostle, "But with me it is a very small thing that I should be judged of you, or of man's day; yea, I judge not even mine own self. For I am conscious of nothing by myself, but I am not hereby justified. But He That judgeth me is the Lord."² My conscience is not therefore good, because ye praise it. For how praise ye what ye do not see? Let Him praise, who seeth; yea let Him correct, if He seeth ought there which offendeth His Eyes. For I too do not say that I am perfectly whole;

but I beat my breast, and say to God, "Be merciful, that I sin not." Yet I do think, for I speak in His Presence, that I seek nothing from you, but your salvation; and constantly do I groan over the sins of my brethren, and I suffer distress,³ and am tormented in mind, and often do I reprove them; yea, I never cease reproving them. All who remember what I say are witnesses, how often my brethren who sin have been reproved, and earnestly reproved, by me.

15. I am now treating of my counsel with you, holy Brethren. In Christ's Name ye are the people of God, ye are a Catholic people, ye are members of Christ; ye are not divided from unity. Ye are in communion with the members of the Apostles, ye are in communion with the memories of the Holy Martyrs, who are spread over the whole world, and ye belong to my cure, that I may render a good account of you. Now my whole account, what it is ye know. "Lord, Thou knowest that I have spoken, Thou knowest that I have not kept silence, Thou knowest in what spirit I have spoken, Thou knowest that I have wept before Thee, when I spake, and was not heard." This I imagine is my whole account. For the Holy Spirit by the prophet Ezekiel hath given me sure hope. Ye know this passage concerning the watchman; "O son of man," saith He, "I have set thee a watchman unto the house of Israel; if when I say unto the wicked, O wicked man, thou shalt die the death, thou dost not speak;" that is (for I speak to thee that thou mayest speak), "if thou dost not announce it, and the sword," that is, what I have threatened on the sinner, "come, and take him away; that wicked man indeed shall die in his iniquity; but his blood will I require at the watchman's hand."⁴ Why? Because he did not speak. "But if the watchman see the sword coming, and blow the trumpet," that he may fly, and he look not to himself, that is, amend not himself, that it find him not in the punishment which God threateneth, and "the sword shall come and take any one away; that wicked man indeed shall die in his iniquity; but thou," saith He, "hast delivered thine own soul." And in that place of the Gospel, what else saith He to the servant? when he said, "Lord, I knew Thee to be a" difficult⁵ or "hard Man, in that Thou reapest where Thou hast not sowed, and gatherest where Thou hast not strawed; and I was afraid, and went and hid Thy talent in the earth, lo, Thou hast that is Thine." And He said, "'Thou wicked and slothful servant,' because thou knewest Me to be a difficult and hard Man, to reap where I have not sown, and to gather where I have not strawed, My very covetousness ought the more to teach thee, that I look for profit from My money. 'Thou oughtest

---

therefore to have given My money to the exchangers, and at My coming I should have required Mine own with usury.'"[1] Did He say, "Thou oughtest to give, and require"? It is we then, Brethren, who give, He will come to require. Pray ye, that He may find us prepared.

SERMON LXXXVIII.

[CXXXVIII. BEN.]

ON THE WORDS OF THE GOSPEL, JOHN X. 14, "I AM THE GOOD SHEPHERD," ETC. AGAINST THE DONATISTS.

1. WE have heard the Lord Jesus setting forth to us the office of a good shepherd. And herein He hath doubtless given us to know, as we may understand it, that there are good shepherds. And yet that the multitude of shepherds might not be understood in a wrong sense; He saith, "I am the good Shepherd."[2] And wherein He is the good Shepherd, He showeth in the words following; "The good Shepherd," saith He, "layeth down His life for the sheep. But he that is an hireling, and not the shepherd, seeth the wolf coming, and fleeth; because he careth not for the sheep, for he is an hireling.[3] Christ then is the good Shepherd. What was Peter? was he not a good shepherd? Did not he too lay down his life for the sheep? What was Paul? what the rest of the Apostles? what the blessed Bishops, Martyrs, who followed close upon their times? What again our holy Cyprian? Were they not all good shepherds, not hirelings, of whom it is said, "Verily I say unto you, they have received their reward"?[4] All these then were good shepherds, not simply for that they shed their blood, but that they shed it for the sheep. For not in pride, but in charity they shed it.

2. For even among the heretics, they who for their iniquities and errors have suffered any trouble, vaunt themselves in the name of martyrdom, that with this fair covering disguised[5] they may plunder the more easily, for wolves they are. Now if ye would know in what rank they are to be held, hear that good shepherd, the Apostle Paul, that not all who even give up their bodies in suffering to the flames, are to be accounted to have shed their blood for the sheep, but rather against the sheep. "If," saith he, "I speak with the tongues of men, and angels, but have not charity, I am become as sounding brass, or a tinkling cymbal. If I should know all mysteries, and have all prophecy, and all faith, so that I could remove mountains, but have not charity, I am nothing."[6] Now a great thing truly is this faith that removes mountains. They

are indeed all great things; but if I have them without charity, saith he, not they, but I am nothing. But up to this point he hath not touched them, who glory in sufferings under the false name of martyrdom. Hear how he toucheth, yea rather pierceth them through and through. "If I should distribute," saith he, "all my goods to the poor, and deliver my body to be burned." Now here they are. But mark what follows; "but have not charity, it profiteth me nothing." Lo, they have come to suffering, come even to the shedding of blood, yea come to the burning of the body; and yet it profiteth them nothing, because charity is lacking. Add charity, they all profit; take charity away, all the rest profit nothing.

3. What a good is this charity, Brethren! What more precious? what yieldeth greater light? or strength? or profit? or security? Many are the gifts of God, which even the wicked have, who shall say, "Lord, we have prophesied in Thy Name, in Thy Name have cast out devils, in Thy Name done many mighty works."[7] And He will not answer, "Ye have not done them." For in the Presence of so great a Judge, they will not dare to lie or boast of things they have not done. But for that they had not charity, He answereth them all, "I know you not." Now how can he have so much as the smallest charity, who when even[8] convicted, loves not unity? It was then as impressing on good shepherds this unity, that our Lord was unwilling to mention many shepherds. For it is not, as I have said already, that Peter was not a good shepherd, and Paul, the rest of the Apostles, and the holy Bishops who were after them, and blessed Cyprian. All these were good shepherds; and notwithstanding to good shepherds, He commended not good shepherds, but a good Shepherd. "I," saith He, "am the good Shepherd."

4. Let us question the Lord with such little understanding as we have, and in most humble discourse hold converse with so great a Master. What sayest Thou, O Lord, Thou good Shepherd? For Thou art the good Shepherd, who art also the good Lamb; at once Pastor and Pasturage, at once Lamb and Lion. What sayest Thou? Let us give ear and aid us, that we may understand. "I," saith He, "am the good Shepherd." What is Peter? is he either not a shepherd, or a bad one? Let us see, if he be not a shepherd. "Lovest thou Me?"[9] Thou saidst to Him Lord, "Lovest thou Me?" And he answered, "I do love Thee." And Thou to him, "Feed My sheep." Thou, Thou, Lord,

---

[1] Matt. xxv. 24, etc.; Luke xix. 21, etc.
[2] John x. 11.   [3] John x. 12, 13   [4] Matt. vi. 2, 4.
[5] *Dealbati.*   [6] 1 Cor. xiii. 1, etc.

[7] Matt. vii. 22.
[8] Referring it would seem to the conference held but a little while before this with the Donatist party at Carthage.
[9] John xxi. 15.

by Thine Own questioning, by the strong assurance of Thine Own words, madest of the lover a shepherd. He is a shepherd then to whom Thou didst commit Thy sheep to be fed. Thou didst Thyself entrust them, he is a shepherd. Let us now see whether he be not a good one. This we find by the very question, and his answer. Thou didst ask, whether he loved Thee; he answered, "I do love Thee." Thou sawest his heart, that he answered truth. Is he not then good, who loveth so great a Good? Whence that answer drawn from his inmost heart? Wherefore was this Peter, who had Thine eyes in his heart for witnesses, sad because Thou askedst him not once only, but a second and a third time, that by a threefold confession of love, he might efface the threefold sin of denial; wherefore, I say, being sad that he was asked repeatedly by Him who knew what He was asking, and had given what He heard; wherefore being sad, did he return such an answer, "Lord, Thou knowest all things, Thyself knowest that I love Thee"? What! in making such a confession, such a profession rather, would he lie? In truth then, he made answer of his love to Thee, and from his inmost heart he gave utterance to a lover's words. Now Thou hast said, "A good man out of the good treasure of the heart bringeth forth good things."[1] So then he is both a shepherd, and a good shepherd; nothing it is true to the power and goodness of the Shepherd of shepherds; but nevertheless even he is both a shepherd, and a good one; and all other such are good shepherds.

5. What means it then, that to good shepherds Thou dost set forth One Only Shepherd, but that in One Shepherd Thou teachest unity? and the Lord Himself explains this more clearly by my ministry, putting you, beloved, in remembrance by this Gospel, and saying, "Hear ye what I have set forth, I have said, 'I am the good Shepherd;' because all the rest, all the good shepherds, are My members." One Head, One Body, One Christ. So then both the Shepherd of shepherds, and the shepherds of the Shepherd, and the sheep with their shepherds under The Shepherd. What is all this, but what the Apostle says? "For as the body is one, and hath many members, and all the members of the body, being many, are one body; so also is Christ."[2] Therefore if Christ be even so, with good reason doth Christ in Himself containing all good shepherds, set forth One, saying, "'I am the good Shepherd.' 'I am,' I Alone am, all the rest with Me are one in unity. Whoso feedeth without Me, feedeth against Me. 'He that gathereth not with Me, scattereth.'"[3] Hear then this unity more forcibly set forth; "Other

sheep," saith He, "I have which are not of this fold."[4] For He was speaking to the first fold of the stock of the fleshly Israel. But there were others of the stock of the faith of this Israel, and they were yet without, were among the Gentiles, predestinated, not yet gathered in. These He knew who had predestinated them: He knew, who had come to redeem them with the shedding of His Own Blood. He saw them who did not yet see Him; He knew them who yet believed not on Him. "Other sheep," saith He, "I have which are not of this fold;" because they are not of the stock of the flesh of Israel. But nevertheless they shall not be outside of this fold, "for them also I must bring, that there may be One Fold, and One Shepherd."

6. With good reason then to This Shepherd of shepherds, doth His Beloved, His Spouse, His Fair One, but by Him made fair, before by sin deformed, beautiful afterward through pardon and grace, speak in her love and ardour after Him, and say to Him, "Where feedest Thou?"[5] And observe how, by what transport this spiritual love is here animated. And far better are they by this transport delighted, who have tasted ought of the sweetness of this love. They hear this properly, who love Christ. For in them, and of them, doth the Church sing this in the Song of Songs; who love Christ, as it seemed without beauty, yet the Only Beautiful One. "For we saw Him," it is said, "and He had neither beauty nor comeliness."[6] Such He appeared on the Cross, such when crowned with thorns did He exhibit Himself, disfigured, and without comeliness, as if He had lost His power, as if not the Son of God. Such seemed He to the blind. For it is in the person of the Jews that Isaiah said this, "We saw Him, and He had no beauty nor comeliness." When it was said, "If He be the Son of God, let Him come down from the Cross. He saved others, Himself He cannot save."[7] And smiting Him on the head with a reed, they said, "Prophesy unto us, thou Christ, who smote Thee?"[8] Because "He had neither beauty nor comeliness." As such did ye Jews see Him. For "blindness hath happened in part to Israel, until the fulness of the Gentiles enter in,"[9] until the other sheep come. Because then blindness hath happened, therefore did ye see the Comely One without comeliness. "For had ye known Him, ye would never have crucified the Lord of Glory."[10] But ye did it, because ye knew Him not. And yet He who as though without beauty bare with you, all Beauteous as He was, prayed for you; "Father," saith He, "forgive them, for they know not what they do."[11] For if He were without comeliness, how is it that

---

[1] Matt. xii. 35.   [2] 1 Cor. xii. 12.   [3] Matt. xii. 30.

[4] John x. 16.   [5] Cant. i. 7.   [6] Isa. liii. 2, Sept.
[7] Mark xv. 31.   [8] Matt. xxvi. 68.   [9] Rom. xi. 25.
[10] 1 Cor. ii. 8.   [11] Luke xxiii. 34.

she loveth Him, who saith, "Tell me, O Thou whom my soul loveth" ? [1] How is it that she loveth Him? how is it that she burneth for Him? how is it that she feareth so much to stray from Him? How is it that she hath so great delight in Him, that her only punishment is to be without Him? What would there be for which He should be loved, if He were not beautiful? But how could she love Him so, if He appeared to her as He did to those blind men persecuting Him, and knowing not what they do? As what then did she love Him? As "comely in form above the sons of men. Comely in form above the sons of men, grace is poured abroad in Thy Lips." [2] So then from these Thy Lips, "Tell me, O Thou whom my soul loveth. Tell me," says she, "O Thou whom," not my flesh, but, "my soul loveth. Tell me where Thou feedest, where Thou liest down in the midday; lest haply I light, as one veiled, upon the flocks of Thy companions." [3]

7. It seems obscure, obscure it is; for it is a mystery of the sacred marriage bed. For she says, "The King hath brought me into His chamber." [4] Of such a chamber is this a mystery. But ye who are not as profane kept off from this chamber, hear ye what ye are, and say with her, if with her ye love (and ye do love with her, if ye are in her); say all, and yet let one say, for unity saith; "Tell me, O Thou whom my soul loveth. For they had one soul to Godward, and one heart. [5] Tell me where Thou feedest, where Thou liest down in the midday?" What does the midday [6] signify? "Great heat, and great brightness." So then, "make known to me who are Thy wise ones," fervent in spirit, and brilliant in doctrine. "Make known to me Thy Right Hand, and men learned in heart, in wisdom." [7] To them may I cleave in Thy Body, to them be united, with them enjoy Thee. Tell me then, "tell me, where Thou feedest, where Thou liest down in the midday;" lest I fall upon them who say other things of Thee, entertain other sentiments of Thee; believe other things of Thee, preach other things of Thee; and have their own flocks, and are Thy companions; for that they live of Thy table, and handle the sacraments of Thy table. For companions are so called, because they eat together, [8] messmates as it were. Such are reproved in the Psalm; "For if Mine enemy had spoken great things against Me, I would surely have hidden Myself from him; and if he that hated Me had spoken great things against Me, I would surely

have hidden Myself from him; but thou a man of one mind with Me, My guide, and My familiar, who didst take sweet meats together with Me, in the house of God we walked with consent." [9] Why then now against the house of the Lord with dissent, but that "they have gone out from us, but they were not of us?" [10] Therefore, "O Thou whom my soul loveth," that I may not fall upon such, Thy companions, but companions such as Samson's were, who kept not faith with their friend, but wished to corrupt his wife. [11] Therefore, that I may not fall upon such as these, "that I may not light upon them," that is, fall upon them, "as one that is veiled," as one that is concealed, that is, and obscure, not as established upon the mountain. "Tell me" then, "O thou whom my soul loveth, where Thou feedest, where Thou liest down in the midday;" who are the wise and faithful in whom Thou dost specially rest, lest by chance as in blindness I fall upon the flocks, not Thy flocks, but the flocks of Thy companions. For thou didst not say to Peter, "Feed thy sheep," but, "Feed My sheep." [12]

8. Let then the "good Shepherd," and, "the Comely in form above the sons of men," make answer to this beloved one; make answer to her whom He hath made beautiful from among the children of men. Hear ye what He answereth, and understand, beware of that wherewith He alarmeth, love that which He adviseth. What doth He answer? How free from soft caresses, yea, to her caresses He returneth severity! He is sharp that He may bind her closely, that He may keep her. "If thou know not thyself," saith He, "O thou fair one among women:" [13] for however fair others may be by the gifts of thy Spouse, they are heresies, fair in outward ornament, not within: [14] fair are they without, and outwardly they shine, they disguise themselves by the name of righteousness; "but all the beauty of the King's daughter is within." [15] "If" then "thou know not thyself;" that thou art one, that thou art throughout all nations, that thou art chaste, that thou oughtest not to corrupt thyself with the disordered converse of evil companions. "If thou know not thyself," that in uprightness, "he hath espoused thee to Me, to present you a chaste Virgin to Christ;" [16] and that in uprightness thou shouldest present thine own self to Me, lest by evil converse, "as the serpent beguiled Eve through his subtilty, so your minds too should be corrupted from my purity." [17] "If," I say, "thou know not thyself" to be such, "go thy way; go thy way." For to others I shall say, "Enter thou into the joy of

---

[1] Cant. i. 7.   [2] Ps. xlv. 2.   [3] Cant. i. 7, Sept.
[4] Cant. i. 4.   [5] Acts iv. 32.
[6] It is not possible in English to preserve the same translation for the word *meridies*, which occurs throughout this passage in the two senses of the *noon* or *midday*, and the *South*.
[7] Ps. lxxxix. 12, Sept (xc. English version).
[8] *Sodales enim dicti sunt, quod simul edant, quasi simul edales.*

[9] Ps. liv. 13, etc., Sept. (lv. 12-14, English version).
[10] 1 John ii. 19.   [11] Judg. xiv.   [12] John xxi. 17.
[13] Cant. viii. Sept.   [14] *Visceribus.*   [15] Ps. xlv. 13.
[16] 2 Cor. xi. 2.   [17] 2 Cor. xi. 3.

thy Lord." [1]   To thee I shall not say, " Enter in ; " but, " Go thy way ; " that thou mayest be among those, who "went out from us." "Go thy way." That is, "if thou know not thyself," then, " go thy way." But if thou know thyself, enter in. But, "if thou know not thyself, go thy way by the footsteps of the flocks, and feed thy kids in the tents of the shepherds. Go thy way by the footsteps," not "of the Flock," but, "of the flocks, and feed," not as Peter, " My sheep," but, " thy kids ; in the tents," not "of the Shepherd," but, "of the shepherds ; " not of unity, but of dissension ; not established there, where there is One flock and One Shepherd. The beloved one was confirmed, edified, made stronger, prepared to die for her Spouse and to live with her Spouse.

9. These words which I have quoted out of the Holy Song of Songs, of a kind of bridal song of the Bridegroom and the Bride (for it is a spiritual wedding, wherein we must live in great purity, for Christ hath granted to the Church in spirit that which His Mother had in body, to be at once a Mother and a Virgin) ; these words, I say, the Donatists accommodate to their own perverted sense in a very different meaning. And how I will not conceal from you, and what ye may answer them, I will, by the Lord's help, as well as I shall be able, briefly recommend. When then we begin to press them with the light of the Church's unity spread over the whole world, and demand of them to show us any testimony out of the Scriptures, where God hath foretold that the Church should be in Africa, as if all the rest of the nations were lost ; they are in the habit of taking this testimony in their mouths, and saying ; " Africa is under the midday sun ; the Church then " they say, " asking the Lord where He feedeth, where He lieth down ; He answereth, ' Under the midday sun ; ' " as if the voice of her who put the question, were, " Tell me, O Thou whom my soul loveth, where Thou feedest, where Thou liest down ; " and the Voice of Him who answereth, were, " Under the midday sun ; " that is, in Africa. If then it be the Church which asketh, and the Lord maketh answer where he feedeth, in Africa, because the Church was in Africa ; then she who asketh was not in Africa. "Tell me," she saith, " O Thou whom my soul loveth, where Thou feedest, where Thou liest down ; " and He maketh answer to some Church out of Africa, " Under the midday sun," in Africa I lie down, in Africa I feed, as if it were, " I do not feed in thee." I repeat, if she who asketh is the Church, which no one disputes, which not even themselves gainsay ; and they hear something about Africa ; then she who

asketh is out of Africa ; and because it is the Church, the Church is out of Africa.

10. But see, I admit that Africa is under the midday sun ; although Egypt is rather under the meridian, under the midday sun than Africa. Now after what fashion This Shepherd is there in Egypt, they who know, will acknowledge ; and for them that know not, let them enquire how large a flock He gathereth there, how great a multitude He hath of holy men and women who utterly despise the world. That flock hath so increased, that it hath expelled superstitions even thence. To pass over how it hath in its increase banished thence the whole superstition of idols, which had been firmly fixed there ; I admit what you say, O evil companions ; I admit it altogether, I agree that Africa is in the South, and that Africa is signified in that which is said, " Where feedest Thou, where dost Thou lie down under the midday sun ? " But do ye too equally observe how that up to this point these are the words of the Bride, and not yet of the Bridegroom. Hitherto it is the Bride that saith, " Tell me, O Thou whom my soul loveth, where Thou feedest, where Thou dost lie down in the midday, lest by chance I light, as one veiled." O thou deaf, and blind one, if in the " midday " thou seest Africa, why in her that is "veiled" dost thou not see the Bride ? "Tell me," she said, " O Thou whom my soul loveth." Without doubt she addresses her Spouse, when she says, " whom " [in the masculine [2]] " my soul loveth." Just as if it were said, " Tell me, O thou whom " [in the feminine [3]] " my soul loveth ; " we should understand that the Bridegroom spake these words to His Bride ; so when you hear, " Tell me, O thou whom " (in the masculine) "my soul loveth, where Thou feedest, where Thou liest down ; " add to this, to her words belongs also what follows, " In the midday." I am asking, " where Thou feedest in the midday, lest by chance I light as one veiled upon the flocks of Thy companions." I consent entirely, I admit what you understand of Africa ; it is signified by, " the midday." But then as you understand it, the Church of Christ beyond the sea is addressing her Spouse, in fear of falling into the African error, " O Thou whom my soul loveth, tell me," teach me. For I hear that " in the midday," that is in Africa, there are two parties, yea rather many schisms.[4] " Tell me," then, " where Thou feedest," what sheep belong to Thee, what fold Thou biddest me love there, whereunto ought I to unite myself. " Lest by chance I light as one veiled." For they mock me as if I were concealed, they mock me as destroyed, as though I existed nowhere else. " Lest," then, " as one veiled," as if concealed,

" I light upon the flocks," that is, upon the congregations of the heretics, " thy companions ; " the Donatists, the Maximinianists, the Rogatists, and all the other pests who gather without, and who therefore scatter; "Tell me," I pray Thee, if I must seek my Shepherd there, that I fall not into the gulf of re-baptizing. I exhort you, I beseech you by the sanctity of such nuptials, love this Church, be ye in this holy Church, be ye this Church; love the good Shepherd, the Spouse so fair, who deceiveth no one, who desireth no one to perish. Pray too for the scattered sheep; that they too may come, that they too may acknowledge Him, that they too may love Him; that there may be One Flock and One Shepherd. Let us turn to the Lord, etc.

SERMON LXXXIX.

[CXXXIX. BEN.]

ON THE WORDS OF THE GOSPEL, JOHN X. 30, " I AND THE FATHER ARE ONE."

1. YE have heard what the Lord God, Jesus Christ, the Only Son of God, born of God the Father without any mother, and born of a Virgin mother without any human father, said, " I and My Father are One." [1] Receive ye this, believe it in such wise that ye may attain [2] to understand it. For faith ought to go before understanding, that understanding may be the reward of faith. For the Prophet hath said most expressly, " Unless ye believe, ye shall not understand." [3] What then is simply preached is to be believed; what is with exactness discussed, is to be understood. At first then [4] to imbue your minds with faith we preach to you Christ, the Only Son of God the Father. Why is added, " The Only Son "? Because He whose Only Son He is, hath many sons by grace. All the rest then, all saints are sons of God by grace, He Alone by Nature. They who are sons of God by grace are not What the Father is. And no saint hath ever dared to say, what that Only Son saith, " I and My Father are One." Is He not then our Father too? If He be not our Father, how say we when we pray, " Our Father, which art in heaven "? [5] But we are sons whom He hath made sons by His Own will, not begotten as sons of His Own Nature. And in truth He hath begotten us too, but as it is said, as adopted ones, begotten by the favour of His adoption, not by Nature. And this too are we called, for that " God hath called us into the adoption of sons ; " [6] we are though adopted, men. He is called the Only Son, the Only Begotten, in that He is That which the Father is; but we are men, The Father is God. In then that He is

That which the Father is ; He said, and said truly, " I and My Father are One." What is, " are One "? Are of one Nature. What is, " are One "? Are of one Substance.

2. Peradventure, ye but imperfectly understand what " of one Substance " is. Take we pains that ye may understand it ; may God assist both me who speak, and you that hear ; me, that I may speak such things as are true and fit for you ; and you, that before and above all things ye may believe ; and then that ye may understand as best ye can. What then is " of One Substance "? Let me make use of similitudes to you, that what is imperfectly understood may be made clear by example. As, suppose, God is gold. His Son is gold also. If similitudes ought not to be given for heavenly things from things earthly, how is it written, " Now the Rock was Christ "? [7] So then, Whatsoever the Father is, This is the Son also ; as I have said, for example, " The Father is gold, the Son is gold." For he who says, " The Son is not of the Very Substance which the Father is ; " what else says he but, " The Father is gold, the Son is silver "? If the Father be gold, and the Son silver ; the Only Son hath degenerated from the Father. A man begets a man ; of what substance the father is who begets, of the same substance is the Son who is begotten. What is, " of the same substance "? The one is a man, and the other is a man ; the one hath a soul ; so hath the other a soul ; the one hath a body, so hath the other a body ; what one is, that is the other.

3. But the Arian heresy makes answer, and says. What says it to me? " Mark what thou hast said "? What have I said? " That the Son of a man may be compared to the Son of God." Certainly he may be compared ; but not as you suppose, in strictness of expression ; [8] but for a similitude. But tell me now what you would make of this. " Do you not see," says he, " that the father who begets is greater [9] in age, and the son who is begotten less? How then say ye? tell me ; how then say ye, that the Father and the Son, God and Christ, are equal ; when ye see that when a man begets a son, the son is less, and the father greater? " Thou wise one, in eternity thou art looking for times ; where there are no times, thou art looking for differences of age ! When the father is greater in age, and the son less, both are in time ; the one groweth, for that the other groweth old. For by nature, the man, the father, did not beget one less, by nature, as I said, but by age. Wouldest thou know, how that by nature he did not beget one less? Wait, let him grow, and he will be equal to his father. For a little boy even by growing attains to his father's full size. Whereas

---

[1] John x. 30.   [2] Mereamini.   [3] Isa. vii. 9, Sept.
[4] He seems to be addressing the Catechumens (Bened. note).
[5] Matt. vi. 9.   [6] Eph. i. 5.

[7] 1 Cor. x. 4.   [8] Ad proprietatem.   [9] Major.

you assert that the Son of God is in such wise born less, as never to grow, and by growing even to attain to His Father's size. Now then a man's son born of a man, is born in a better condition than the Son of God. How? Because the former grows, and attains to his father's size. But Christ, if it is as ye say, is in such wise born less, as that He must ever remain less, and no growth of years at least is to be looked for here. Thus then you say that there is a diversity in nature. But why say you so, but because you will not believe the Son to be of the Same Substance which the Father is? Finally, first acknowledge that He is of the Same Substance, and so call Him less. Consider the case of a man, he is a man. What is his substance? He is a man. What is he whom he begets? He is less, but he is a man. The age is unequal, the nature equal. Do you then say too, "What the Father is, That is the Son, but the Son is less"? Say so, make a step forward, say, "of the Same Substance, only less;" and you will get to His being equal. For it is not a little step you take, it is not a little approach you make to the truth, of acknowledging Him equal, if you shall acknowledge Him to be of the Same Substance, though less. "But He is not of the Same Substance," this you say. So then in that you say this, here is gold and silver; what you say is as if a man were to beget a horse. For a man is of one substance, a horse of another. If then the Son is of another substance than the Father, the Father hath begotten a monster. For when a creature, that is a woman, gives birth to anything that is not a man, it is called a monster. But that it be not a monster, he that is born is that which he is that begat him, that is, a man and a man, a horse and a horse, a dove and a dove, a sparrow and a sparrow.

4. To His creatures hath He given to beget that which they are. To His creatures, to mortal, earthly creatures, hath God given, hath granted to beget that which they are; and thinkest thou that He hath not been able to reserve this for Himself, He who is before all ages? Should He who hath no beginning of time, beget a son, different from That which Himself is, beget a degenerate son? Hear ye how great a blasphemy it is to say, that the Only Son of God is of another substance. Most certainly if He is so, He is degenerate. If you should say to any child of man, "Thou art degenerate," how great an offence is it! And yet in what sense is any child of man said to be degenerate? As, for example, his father is brave, he is a poltroon and a coward. If any one sees him, and would rebuke him, as he thinks of his brave father, what does he say to him? "Get thee hence, thou degenerate one!" What is "degenerate one"? "Thy father was a brave man, and thou

tremblest through fear." He to whom this is said, is degenerate by some fault, by nature he is equal. What is, "by nature he is equal"? He is a man, which his father also is. But the one brave, the other a coward; the one bold, the other timid; yet both men. By some fault then he is degenerate, not by nature. But when you say, that the Only Son, the One Son of the Father, is degenerate, you say nought else, but that He is not What the Father is; and you do not say, that having been already born, He has become degenerate; but He was begotten so. Who can endure this blasphemy? If they could in any sort whatever see this blasphemy, they would fly from it, and become catholics.

5. But what shall I say, Brethren? Let us not be angry with them; but pray we for them, that God would give them understanding; for peradventure they were born so. [1] What is, were born so? They receive what they hold from their parents. They prefer their birth to the truth. Let them become what they are not, that they may be able to keep what they are; that is, let them become catholics, that they may keep their nature as men; that the creation of God in them perish not, let the grace of God be added to them. For they imagine that by their outrage of the Son they honour the Father. When you say to him, "Thou blasphemest;" he answers, "Why do I blaspheme?" "In that thou sayest that the Son is not what the Father is." And he answers me, "Yea, it is thou who blasphemest." Why? "Because thou wouldest make the Son equal to the Father." "I do wish to make the Son equal with the Father, but is this to make a stranger equal? The Father rejoiceth when I equal with Him His Only Son; He rejoiceth because He is not envious. And because God is not envious of His Only Son, therefore did He beget Him Such as He is Himself. Thou doest wrong both to the Son, and to the Father Himself, for whose honour thou wouldest do outrage to the Son. For in truth for this reason dost thou say that the Son is not of the Same Substance, lest thou shouldest do wrong to His Father. I will soon show thee, that thou doest wrong to both." "How?" saith he. "If I say to any man's son, Thou art degenerate, thou art not like thy father; degenerate, thou art not what thy father is. The son hears it, and is angry, and says, 'Was I then born degenerate?' The father hears it, and is more angry still. And in his anger what says he? 'Have I then begotten a degenerate son? If I then be one thing, and I have begotten another, I have begotten a monster.' What is it then, that whereas thou wishest to pay honour to the One by doing outrage to

---
[1] Arians.

the Other, thou doest outrage to Both? Thou offendest the Son, but thou wilt not propitiate the Father. When thou honourest the Father by outraging the Son, thou offendest both the Son and the Father. From whom wilt thou fly? to whom wilt thou fly? When the Father is angry with thee, dost thou fly to the Son? What doth He say to thee? 'To whom dost thou fly, to Me, whom thou hast made degenerate?' When the Son is offended, dost thou run to the Father? He too saith to thee; 'To whom dost thou fly, to Me who, thou hast said, have begotten a degenerate Son?'" Let this suffice for you; hold it fast, commit it to memory, inscribe it in your faith. But that ye may understand it, pour out your prayers to God, the Father and the Son, who are One.

SERMON XC.

[CXL. BEN.]

ON THE WORDS OF THE GOSPEL, JOHN XII. 44, "HE THAT BELIEVETH ON ME, BELIEVETH NOT ON ME, BUT ON HIM THAT SENT ME." AGAINST A CERTAIN EXPRESSION OF MAXIMINUS, A BISHOP OF THE ARIANS, WHO SPREAD HIS BLASPHEMY IN AFRICA WHERE HE WAS WITH THE COUNT SEGISVULT.

1. WHAT is it, Brethren, which we have heard the Lord saying, "He that believeth on Me, believeth not on Me, but on Him that sent Me"?[1] It is good for us to believe on Christ, especially seeing that He hath also Himself expressly said this which ye have now heard, that is, that "He had come a Light into the world, and whosoever believeth on Him shall not walk in darkness, but shall have the light of life."[2] Good then it is to believe on Christ; and a great evil is it not to believe on Christ. But because Christ the Son is, Whatsoever He is, of the Father, but the Father is not of the Son, but is the Father of the Son; He recommends to us indeed faith in Himself, but refers the honour to His Original.[3]

2. For hold this fast as a firm and settled truth, if ye would continue Catholics, that God the Father begat God the Son without time, and made Him of a Virgin in time. The first nativity exceedeth times; the second nativity enlighteneth times. Yet both nativities are marvellous; the one without a mother, the other without a father. When God begat the Son, He begat Him of Himself, not of a mother; when the Mother gave birth to her Son, she gave Him birth as a Virgin, not by man. He was born of the Father without a beginning; He was born

of a mother, as to-day,[4] at an appointed beginning. Born of the Father He made us; born of a mother He re-made us. He was born of the Father, that we might be; He was born of a mother, that we might not be lost. But the Father begat Him equal to Himself, and All Whatsoever the Son is, He hath of the Father. But What God the Father is, He hath not of the Son. Accordingly we say that the Father is God, of none; the Son, God of God. Wherefore all that the Son doeth marvellously, all that He saith truly, He attributeth to Him of whom He is; yet can He not be ought else than He of whom He is. Adam was made a man; he had power to become something other than he was made. For he was made righteous, and he had power to become unrighteous. But the Only-Begotten Son of God, What He is, This cannot be changed; He cannot be changed into anything else, cannot be diminished, What He was He cannot but be, He cannot but be equal to the Father. But undoubtedly He who gave all things to the Son by His Birth, gave it to One not needing ought; without doubt this very equality too with the Father, the Father gave to the Son. How did the Father give It? did He beget Him less, and add to Him to complete His Form, that He might make Him equal? If He had done this, He would have given it to one in need. But I have told you already what ye ought most firmly to hold fast, that is, that All That the Son is, the Father gave Him, gave Him, that is, by His Birth, not as in need of ought. If He gave it to Him by His Birth, and not as in need, then doubtless He both gave Him equality, and in giving Him equality, begat Him equal. And although the One be One Person, and the Other Another; yet is not the One one thing, and the Other another; but What the One is, That the Other also. He who is the One, is not the Other; but What the One, That too the Other.

3. "He Who sent Me," saith He, ye have heard it; "He Who sent Me," saith He, "He gave Me a commandment what I should say, and what I should speak; and I know that His commandment is life everlasting."[5] It is John's Gospel, hold it fast. "He Who sent Me, He gave Me a commandment what I should say, and what I should speak; and I know that His commandment is life everlasting." O that He would grant me to say what I wish! For my poverty and His abundance straiteneth me. "He," saith He, "gave Me a commandment, what I should say, and what I should speak; and I know that His commandment is life everlast-

---

[1] John xii. 44.   [2] John xii. 46; John viii. 12.
[3] *Authorem.*

[4] The Bened. conjecture that the word "*hodie*" here and at the end was added in order to adapt this Sermon to be preached on Christmas Day.
[5] John xii. 49, 50.

ing." Search in the Epistle of this John the Evangelist for what he hath said of Christ. " Let us believe," he says, " His True Son Jesus Christ. This is the True God and Everlasting Life." [1] What is, "The True God, and Everlasting Life"? The True Son of God is "the True God, and Everlasting Life." Why did He say, "On His True Son"? Because God hath many sons, therefore was He to be distinguished, by adding that He was the True Son. Not by simply saying that He is the Son; but by adding, as I have said, that He is the True Son; therefore He was to be distinguished, because of the many sons which God hath. For we are sons by grace, He by Nature. We made by the Father through Him; He Himself That Which the Father is; are we too That Which God is?

4. But some man coming across us, knowing not what he is saying, says, "For this reason was it said, ' I and My Father are One ;' [2] for that They have with One Another an agreement of will, not because the Nature of the Son is the Very Same as the Nature of the Father. For the Apostles too (now this is what he said,[3] not I), for the Apostles too are one with the Father and the Son." Horrible blasphemy! "And the Apostles," says he, "are one with the Father and the Son, in that they obey the will of the Father and the Son." Has he dared to say this? Let Paul then say, "I and God are one." Let Peter say it, let every one of the Prophets say, "I and God are one." They do not say it; God forbid they should. They know that they are a different nature, a nature that needeth to be saved; they know that they are a different nature, a nature that needeth to be enlightened. No one says, "I and God are one." Whatsoever progress he may make, howsoever he may surpass others in holiness, with how great eminence soever of virtue he may excel, he never saith, "I and God are one;" for if he have excellence, and therefore saith it; by saying it, he loseth what he had.

5. Believe then that the Son is equal with the Father; but yet that the Son is of the Father; but the Father not of the Son. The Original is with the Father, equality with the Son. For if He be not equal, He is not a true Son. For what are we saying, Brethren? If He is not equal, He is less; if He is less, I ask the nature that needeth to be saved, in its misbelief, " how is He born less?" Answer, Doth He as being less grow or not? If He groweth, then the Father groweth old. but if He will ever be what He was born; if He was born less, He will continue less; with this His loss He will be perfect; born perfect with this loss of the Father's Form, He is never to attain to the Father's Form. Thus do ye ungodly assail [4] the Son; thus do ye heretics blaspheme the Son. What then saith the Catholic faith? The Son is God, of God the Father; God the Father, not God of the Son. But God the Son equal with the Father, Born equal; not Born less, not made equal, but Born equal. What the Father is, That is He also who was born. Was the Father ever without the Son? God forbid ! Take away your "ever," where there is no time. The Father always, the Son always. The Father without beginning of time, the Son without beginning of time; the Father never before the Son, the Father never without the Son. But yet because the Son is God of God the Father, and the Father God, but not of God the Son; let not the honouring of the Son in the Father displease us. For the honouring of the Son giveth honour to the Father, it diminisheth not His Own Divinity.

6. Because then I was speaking of what I had brought forward, " And I knew," saith He, " that His commandment is everlasting life." [5]   Mark, Brethren, what I am saying; " I know that His commandment is everlasting life."   And we read in the same John concerning Christ, " He is The True God and Everlasting Life." [1] If the Father's commandment is " everlasting Life," and Christ the Son Himself is " everlasting Life ;" the Son is Himself the Father's Commandment.   For how is not That the Father's Commandment, which is the Father's Word?   Or if you take the commandment given to the Son by the Father in a carnal sense, as if the Father said to the Son, " I command Thee this, I wish Thee to do that ;" in what words spake He to the Only Word? When He gave commandment to the Word, did He look for words?   That the Father's Commandment then is " Life everlasting," and that the Son Himself is " Life everlasting," believe ye and receive, believe and understand, for the Prophet saith, " Unless ye believe ye shall not understand." [6]   Do ye not comprehend?   Be enlarged.   Hear the Apostle : " Be ye enlarged, bear not the yoke with unbelievers." [7]   They who will not believe this before they comprehend, are unbelievers.   And because they have determined to be unbelievers, they will remain in their ignorance.   Let them believe then that they may understand.   Most certainly the Father's Commandment is " everlasting Life."   Therefore the Father's Commandment is the Very Son who was born this day; a Commandment not given in time, but a Commandment Born.   The Gospel of John exercises our minds, refines [8] and uncarnalizes them, that of God we may think not

---

[1] 1 John v. 20.   [2] John x. 30.
[3] Maximinus in his Conference with St. Augustin, and St. Augustin in his Answer, B. ii. cont. Maxim. ch. 22.

[4] *Addicitis.*   [5] John xii. 50.   [6] Isa. vii. 9, Sept.
[7] 2 Cor. vi. 13, 14.   [8] *Limat.*

after a carnal but a spiritual manner. Let so much then, Brethren, suffice you; lest in length of disputation, the sleep of forgetfulness steal over you.

SERMON XCI.

[CXLI. BEN.]

ON THE WORDS OF THE GOSPEL, JOHN XIV. 6, "I AM THE WAY, AND THE TRUTH, AND THE LIFE."

1. AMONGST other things, when the Holy Gospel was being read, ye heard what the Lord Jesus said, "I am the Way, and the Truth, and the Life." [1] Truth and life doth every man desire; but not every man doth find the way. That God is a certain Life Eternal, Unchangeable, Intelligible, Intelligent, Wise, Making wise, some philosophers even of this world have seen. The fixed, settled, unwavering truth, wherein are all the principles [2] of all things created, they saw indeed, but afar off; they saw, but amid the error in which they were placed; and therefore what way to attain to that so great, and ineffable, and beatific a possession they found not. For that even they saw (as far as can be seen by man) the Creator by means of the creature, the Worker by His work, the Framer of the world by the world, the Apostle Paul is witness, whom Christians ought surely to believe. For he said when he was speaking of such; "The wrath of God is revealed from heaven against all ungodliness." [3] These are, as ye recognise, the words of the Apostle Paul; "The wrath of God is revealed from heaven against all ungodliness, and unrighteousness of men; who detain the truth in unrighteousness." Did he say that they do not detain truth? No: but, "They detained the truth in unrighteousness." What they detain, is good; but wherein they detain it, is bad. "They detain the truth in unrighteousness."

2. Now it occurred to him that it might be said to him, "Whence do these ungodly men detain the truth? Hath God spoken to any one of them? Have they received the Law as the people of the Israelites by Moses? Whence then do they detain the truth, though it be even in this unrighteousness?" Hear what follows, and he shows. "Because that which can be known of God," he says, "is manifest in them; for God hath manifested it unto them." [4] Manifested it unto them to whom He hath not given the Law? Hear how He hath manifested it. "For the invisible things of Him are clearly seen, being understood by the things that are made." [5] Ask the world, the beauty of the heaven, the brilliancy and ordering of the stars, the sun, that sufficeth for the day, the moon, the solace of the

night; ask the earth fruitful in herbs, and trees, full of animals, adorned with men; ask the sea, with how great and what kind of fishes filled; ask the air, with how great birds stocked; [6] ask all things, and see if they do not as if it were by a language [7] of their own make answer to thee, "God made us." These things have illustrious philosophers sought out, and by the art have come to know the Artificer. What then? Why is the wrath of God revealed against this ungodliness? "Because they detain the truth in unrighteousness?" Let him come, let him show how. For how they came to know Him, he hath said already. "The invisible things of Him," that is God, "are clearly seen, being understood by the things that are made; His eternal Power also and Godhead; so that they are without excuse. Because that when they knew God, they glorified Him not as God, neither were thankful; but became vain in their imaginations, and their foolish heart was darkened." [8] They are the Apostle's words, not mine: "And their foolish heart was darkened; for professing themselves to be wise, they became fools." [9] What by curious search they found, by pride they lost. "Professing themselves to be wise," attributing, that is, the gift of God to themselves, "they became fools." They are the Apostle's words, I say; "Professing themselves to be wise, they became fools."

3. Show, prove their foolishness. Show, O Apostle, and as thou hast shown us whereby they were able to attain to the knowledge of God, for that "the invisible things of Him are clearly seen, being understood by those things that are made;" so now show how, "professing themselves to be wise, they became fools." Hear; Because "they changed," he says, "the glory of the incorruptible God into the likeness of the image of a corruptible man, and of birds, and of four-footed beasts, and of creeping things." [10] For of figures of these animals, the Pagans made themselves gods. Thou hast found out God, and thou worshippest an idol. Thou hast found out the truth, and this very truth dost thou detain in unrighteousness. And what by the works of God thou hast come to know, by the works of man thou losest. Thou hast considered the universe, [11] hast collected the order of the heaven, the earth, the sea, and all the elements; thou wilt not take heed to this, that the world is the work of God, an idol is the work of a carpenter. If the carpenter as he has given the figure, could also give a heart, the carpenter would be worshipped by his own idol. For, O man, as God is thy Framer, so the idol's framer is a man. Who is thy God? He That made thee. Who is the carpenter's god? He That made him.

---

[1] John xiv. 6.   [2] *Rationes.*   [3] Rom. i. 18.   [6] *Viget.*   [7] *Sensu.*   [8] Rom. i. 21.
[4] Rom. i. 19.   [5] Rom. i. 20.   [9] Rom. i. 22.   [10] Rom. i. 23.   [11] *Totum.*

Who is the idol's god? He that made it. If then the idol had a heart, would he not worship the carpenter who made it? See in what unrighteousness they detained the truth, and found not the way that leadeth to that possession which they saw.

4. But Christ, for that He is with the Father, the Truth, and Life, the Word of God, of whom it is said, "The Life was the Light of men;"[1] for that I say He is with the Father, the Truth, and Life, and we had no way whereby to go to the Truth, the Son of God, who is ever in the Father the Truth and Life, by assuming man's nature became the Way. Walk by Him as Man, and thou comest to God. By Him thou goest, to Him thou goest. Look not out for any way whereby to come to Him, besides Himself. For if He had not vouchsafed to be the Way, we should have always gone astray. He then became the Way Whereby thou shouldest come; I do not say to thee, seek the Way. The Way Itself hath come to thee, arise and walk. Walk, with the life,[2] not with the feet. For many walk well with the feet, and with their lives walk ill. For sometimes even those who walk well, run outside the way. Thus you will find men living well, and not Christians. They run well; but they run not in the way. The more they run, the more they go astray; because they are out of the Way. But if such men as these come to the Way, and hold on the Way, O how great is their security, because they both walk well, and do not go astray! But if they do not hold on the Way, however well they walk, alas! how are they to be bewailed! For better is it to halt in the way, than to walk on stoutly outside the way. Let this suffice for you, Beloved. Turn we to the Lord, etc.

SERMON XCII.

[CXLII. BEN.]

ON THE SAME WORDS OF THE GOSPEL, JOHN XIV. 6, "I AM THE WAY," ETC.

1. THE divine lessons raise us up, that we be not broken by despair; and terrify us again, that we be not tossed to and fro by pride. But to hold the middle, the true, the strait way, as it were between the left hand of despair, and the right hand of presumption, would be most difficult for us, had not Christ said, "I am the Way, and the Truth, and the Life."[3] As if He had said, "By what way wouldest thou go? 'I am the Way.' Whither wouldest thou go? 'I am the Truth.' Where wouldest thou abide? 'I am the Life.'" Let us then walk with all assurance in the Way; but let us fear snares by the way side. The enemy does not dare to lay his

snares in the way; because Christ is the Way; but most certainly by the way side he ceases not to do so. Whence too it is said in the Psalm, "They have laid stumblingblocks for me by the way side."[4] And another Scripture saith, "Remember that thou walkest in the midst of snares."[5] These snares among which we walk are not in the way; but yet they are "by the way side." What fearest thou, what art thou alarmed at, so thou walk in the Way? Fear then, if thou forsake the Way. For for this reason is the enemy even permitted to lay snares by the way side, lest through the security of exultation the Way be forsaken, and ye fall into the snares.

2. Christ Humbled is the Way; Christ the Truth and the Life, Christ Highly Exalted and God. If thou walk in the Humbled, thou shalt attain to the Exalted. If infirm as thou art, thou despise not the Humbled, thou shalt abide exceeding strong in the Exalted. For what cause was there of Christ's Humiliation, save thine infirmity? For solely and irremediably did thine infirmity press thee in, and this circumstance it was that made so great a Physician come to thee. For if thy sickness had been even such, that thou couldest have gone to the Physician, this infirmity might have seemed endurable. But because thou couldest not go to Him, He came to thee. He came teaching humility, whereby we might return; for that pride allowed us not to return to life; yea had even made us depart from life. For the heart of man being lifted up against God, and neglecting in its sound state His saving precepts, the soul fell away into infirmity; let her in her infirmity learn to hear Him whom in her strength she despised. Let her hear Him that she may rise, whom she despised, that she might fall. Let her at length, taught by experience, give ear to what she had no mind, when taught by precept, to obtain. For her misery hath taught her, how evil a thing it is to go a whoring from the Lord. For to fall away from that Simple and Singular Good, into this multitude of pleasures, into the love of the world, and earthly corruption, is to go a whoring from the Lord. And He hath addressed her as in a sense a harlot, to warn her to return: very often by the Prophets doth He reproach her as a harlot, but yet not despaired of, for that He who reproacheth the harlot hath in His Hands the cleansing of the harlot too.

3. For He doth not so reproach as to insult her; but He would bring her to confusion of face to heal her. Vehement are the exclamations of Scripture, nor doth it deal softly by flattery with those whom it would by healing

---

[1] John i. 4.   [2] *Moribus.*   [3] John xiv. 6.

[4] Ps. cxxxix. 6, Sept. (cxl. 5, English version).
[5] Ecclus. ix. 13.

recover. "Ye adulterers, know ye not that the friend of this world is constituted the enemy of God?"[1] The love of the world maketh the soul adulterous, the love of the Framer of the world maketh the soul chaste; but unless she blush for her corruption, she hath no desire to return to that chaste embrace. Be she confounded that she may return, who was vaunting herself that she should not return. It was pride then that hindered the soul's return. But whoso reproacheth doth not cause the sin, but showeth the sin. What the soul was loth to see, is placed before her eyes; and what she desired to have behind her back, is brought before her face. See thyself in thyself. "Why seest thou the mote in thy brother's eye, but perceivest not the beam in thine own eye?"[2] The soul which went away from herself, is recalled to herself. As she had gone away from herself, so went she away from her Lord. For she had respect to herself, and pleased herself, and became enamoured of her own power. She withdrew from him, and abode not in herself; and from her own self she is repelled, and from herself shut out, and she falleth away unto things without her. She loves the world, loves the things of time, loves earthly things; who if she but loved herself to the neglect of Him by whom she was made, would at once be less, at once fail by loving that which is less. For she is less than God; yea less by far, and by so much less as the thing made is less than the Maker. It was God then That ought to have been loved, yea in such wise ought God to be loved, that if it might be so, we should forget ourselves. What then is this change? The soul hath forgotten herself, but by loving the world; let her now forget herself, but by loving the world's Maker. Driven away even from herself, I say, she hath in a manner lost herself, and hath not skilled to see her own actions, she justifies her iniquities; she is puffed up, and prides herself in insolence, in voluptuousness, in honours, in posts of authority, in riches, in the power of vanity. She is reproved, rebuked, is shown to herself, mislikes herself, confesses her deformity, longs for her first beauty, and she who went away in profusion returns in confusion.[3]

4. Seemeth he to pray against her, or for her, who says, "Fill their faces with shame"? It seems to be an adversary, it seems an enemy. Hear what follows, and see whether a friend can offer this prayer. "Fill," says he, "their faces with shame, and they shall seek Thy Name, O Lord."[4] Did he hate them whose faces he desired to be filled with shame? See how he loves them whom he would have seek

the Name of the Lord. Does he love only, or hate only? or does he both hate, and love? Yea, he both hates, and loves. He hates what is thine, he loves thee. What is, "He hates what is thine, he loves thee"? He hates what thou hast made, he loves what God hath made. For what are thine own things but sins? And what art thou but what God made thee, a man after His Own image and likeness? Thou dost neglect what thou wast made, love what thou hast made. Thou dost love thine own works without thee, dost neglect the work of God within thee. Deservedly dost thou go away, deservedly fall off, yea, deservedly even from thine own self depart; deservedly hear the words, "A spirit that goeth and returneth not."[5] Hear rather Him That calleth and saith, "Turn ye unto Me, and I will turn unto you."[6] For God doth not really turn away, and turn again; Abiding the Same He rebuketh, Unchangeable He rebuketh. He hath turned away, in that thou hast turned thyself away. Thou hast fallen from Him, He hath not fallen away from thee.[7] Hear Him then saying to thee, "Turn ye unto Me, and I will turn unto you." For this is, "I turn unto you, in that ye turn unto Me." He followeth on the back of him that flieth, He enlighteneth the face of him that returneth. For whither wilt thou fly in flying from God? Whither wilt thou fly in flying from Him who is contained in no place, and is nowhere absent? He That delivereth him that turneth to him, punisheth him that turneth away. Thou hast a Judge by flying; have a Father by returning.

5. But he had been swollen up by pride, and by this swelling could not return by the strait way. He who became the Way, crieth out, "Enter ye in by the strait gate."[8] He tries to enter in, the swelling impedes him; and his trying is so much the more hurtful, in proportion as the swelling is a greater impediment. For the straitness irritates[9] his swelling; and being irritated he will swell the more; and swelling more, when will he enter in? So then let him bring down the swelling. And how? Let him take the medicine of humility; let him against the swelling drink the bitter but wholesome cup; drink the cup of humility. Why doth he squeeze himself? The bulk, not for its size, but for its swelling, doth not allow him. For size hath solidity, swelling inflation. Let not him that is swollen fancy himself of great size; that he may be great, and substantial,[10] and solid, let him bring down his swelling. Let him not long after these present things, let him not glory in this pomp of things failing and corruptible; let him hearken to Him who said, "Enter in by the strait gate," saying also,

---

[1] Jas. iv. 4.   [2] Matt. vii. 3.
[3] *Quæ ibat effusa redit confusa.*
[4] Ps. lxxxii. 17, Sept. (lxxxiii. 16, English version).

[5] Ps. lxxvii. 39, Sept. (lxxviii. English version).
[6] Zech. i. 3.   [7] Tract. 2 in *Evang. Joan.* n. 8.
[8] Matt. vii. 13.   [9] *Vexat.*   [10] *Certus.*

"I am the Way." [1] For as if some swollen one had asked, "How shall I enter in?" He saith, "'I am the Way.' Enter in by Me; Thou walkest only by Me, to enter in by the door." For as He said, "I am the Way;" so also, "I am the Door." [2] Why seekest thou whereby to return, whither to return, whereby to enter in? Lest thou shouldest in any respect go astray, He became all for thee. Therefore in brief He saith, "Be humble, be meek." Let us hear Him saying this most plainly, that thou mayest see whereby is the way, what is the way, whither is the way. Whither wouldest thou come? But peradventure in covetousness thou wouldest possess all things. "All things are delivered unto Me of My Father," [3] saith He. It may be thou wilt say, "They were delivered to Christ: but are they to me?" Hear the Apostle speak; hear, as I said some time ago, lest thou be broken by despair; hear how thou wert loved when thou hadst nothing to be loved for, hear how thou wert loved when unsightly, deformed, before there was ought in thee which was meet to be loved. Thou wast first loved, that thou mightest be made meet to be loved. For Christ, as the Apostle says, "died for the ungodly." [4] What! will you say that the ungodly deserved to be loved? I ask, what did the ungodly deserve? To be damned. Here you will answer, Yet, "Christ died for the ungodly." Lo, what was done for thee when ungodly; what is reserved for thee now godly? "Christ died for the ungodly." Thou didst desire to possess all things; desire it not through covetousness, seek it through piety, seek it through humility. For if thou seek thus, thou shalt possess. For thou shalt have Him by whom all things were made, and with Him shalt possess all things.

6. I do not say this as though the result of reasoning. Hear the Apostle himself saying, "He that spared not His Own Son, but delivered Him up for us all; how hath He also not with Him given us all things?" [5] Lo, covetous one, thou hast all things. All things that thou lovest, despise, that thou be not kept back from Christ, and hold to Him in whom thou mayest possess all things. The Physician Himself then needing no such medicine, yet that He might encourage the sick, drank what He had no need of; addressing him as it were refusing it, and raising him up in his fear, He drank first. "The Cup," saith He, "which I shall drink of;" [6] "I who have nothing in Me to be cured by that Cup, am yet to drink it, that thou who needest to drink it, may not disdain to drink." Now consider, Brethren, ought the human race to be any longer sick after having received such a medicine? God hath been now Humbled, and is man still

proud? Let him hear, let him learn. "All things," saith He, "have been delivered unto Me of My Father." [3] If thou desirest all things, thou shalt have them with Me; if thou desirest the Father, by Me and in Me thou shalt have Him. "No man knoweth the Father but the Son." Do not despair; come to the Son. Hear what follows, "And he to whom the Son will reveal Him." Thou saidst, "I am not able. Thou callest me through a strait way; I am not able to enter in by a strait way." "Come," saith He, "unto Me, all ye that labour and are heavy laden." Your burden is your swelling. "Come unto Me, all ye that labour and are heavy laden, and I will refresh you. Take My yoke upon you, and learn of Me." [7]

7. The Master of the Angels crieth out, the Word of God, by whom all reasonable souls are without failing fed, the Food That refresheth, and abideth Entire, crieth out and saith, "Learn of Me." Let the people hear Him, saying, "Learn of Me." Let them make answer, "What do we learn of Thee?" For we must be going to hear I know not what from the Great Artificer, when He saith, "Learn of Me." Who is it that saith, "Learn of Me"? He who formed the earth, who divided the sea and the dry land, who created the fowls, who created the animals of the earth, who created all things that swim, who set the stars in the heaven, who distinguished the day and the night, who established the firmament, who separated the light from the darkness, He it is who saith, "Learn of Me." Is He haply about to tell us this, that we should do these things with Him? Who can do this? God Only doeth them. "Fear not," He saith, "I am not laying any burden on thee. 'Learn of Me,' this which for thy sake I was made. 'Learn of Me,'" saith He, "not to form the creature which by Me was made. Neither do I tell you indeed, to learn those things which I have granted to some, to whom I would, not to all, to raise the dead, to give sight to the blind, to open the ears of the deaf; nor to wish as for some great thing to learn these things of Me." The disciples returned with joy and exultation, saying, "Lo, even the devils are subject unto us through Thy Name." [8] And the Lord said to them, "In this rejoice not, that the devils are subject unto you; rejoice rather, because your names are written in heaven." [9] To whom He would, He gave the power to cast out devils, to whom He would, He gave the power to raise the dead. Such miracles were done even before the Incarnation of the Lord; the dead were raised, lepers were cleansed; [10] we read of these things. And who did them then, but He who in after time was the Man-Christ after David,

---

[1] John xiv. 6. [2] John x. 7. [3] Matt. xi. 27. [4] Rom. v. 6. [5] Rom. viii. 32. [6] Matt. xx. 22.

[7] Matt. xi. 28, 29. [8] Luke x. 17. [9] Luke x. 20. [10] 2 Kings iv. and v.

but God-Christ before Abraham? He gave the power for all these things, He did them Himself by men; yet gave He not that power to all. Ought they to whom He gave it not to despair, and say that they have no part in Him because they have not been thought [1] worthy to receive these gifts? In the body are divers members: this member can do one thing, that another. God hath compacted the body together, He hath not given to the ear to see, nor to the eye to hear, nor to the forehead to smell, nor to the hand to taste; He hath not given them these functions; but to all the members hath He given soundness, hath given union, hath given unity, hath by His Spirit quickened and united all alike. And so here He hath not given to some to raise the dead, to others He hath not given the power of disputation; yet to all what hath He given? "Learn of Me, that I am meek and lowly in heart." Forasmuch as we have heard Him say, "I am meek and lowly in heart;" here, my Brethren, is our whole remedy, "Learn of Me, that I am meek and lowly in heart." What doth it profit a man if he do miracles, and is proud, is not meek and lowly in heart? Will he not be reckoned in the number of those who shall come at the last day, and say, "Have we not prophesied in Thy Name, and in Thy Name have done many mighty works?" [2] But what shall they hear? "I know you not, Depart from Me, all ye that work iniquity." [3]

8. What then doth it profit us to learn? "That I am meek," saith He, "and lowly in heart." He engrafteth charity, and that most genuine charity, without confusion, without inflation, without elation, without deceit; this doth He engraft, who saith, "Learn of Me, that I am meek and lowly in heart." How can one proud and puffed up have any genuine [4] charity? He must needs be envious. And mayhap one who is envious, loves, and we are mistaken? God forbid that any one should be so mistaken, as to say that an envious man hath charity. And so what saith the Apostle? "Charity envieth not." Why doth it not envy? "It is not puffed up;" [5] he immediately annexed the cause for which he took away envying from charity. Because it is not puffed up, it envieth not. It is true, he said first, "Charity envieth not;" but as though thou didst ask, "Why doth it not envy?" he added, "It is not puffed up." If then it envieth because it is puffed up; if it be not puffed up, it envieth not. If charity is not puffed up, and therefore envieth not; then doth He engraft charity who saith, "Learn of Me, that I am meek and lowly in heart." [6]

9. Let any man have then what he will, let him boast himself of what he will. "If I speak with the tongues of men and of Angels, but have not charity, I am become as sounding brass, or a tinkling cymbal." What is more sublime than the gift of divers tongues? It is "brass," it is "a tinkling cymbal," if thou take charity away. Hear other gifts; "If I should know all mysteries." [7] What more excellent? what more magnificent? Hear yet another; "If I should have all prophecy, and all faith, so that I could remove mountains, but have not charity, I am nothing." [8] He comes to still greater things, Brethren. What else has he said? "If I should distribute all my goods to the poor." What more perfect thing can be done? When indeed the Lord commanded the rich man this for perfection's sake, saying, "If thou wilt be perfect, go, sell all that thou hast, and give to the poor." [9] Was he then at once perfect, because he sold all his goods and gave them to the poor? No; and therefore He added, "And come, follow Me." "Sell all," saith He, "give to the poor, and come, follow Me." "Why should I follow Thee? Now that I have sold all, and distributed to the poor, am I not perfect? What need is there that I should follow Thee?" "Follow Me," that thou mayest learn that "I am meek and lowly in heart." For what? can any man sell all he hath, and give to the poor, who is not yet meek, not yet lowly in heart? Assuredly he can. "For if I should distribute all my goods to the poor." And hear still further. For some, who had left all they had, and had already followed the Lord, but not yet followed Him perfectly (for to follow Him perfectly is to imitate Him), could not bear the trial of suffering. Peter, Brethren, was already one of those who had left all and followed the Lord. For as that rich man went away in sadness, when the disciples being troubled, asked how then any one could be perfect, and the Lord consoled them, they said to the Lord, "Behold, we have forsaken all, and followed Thee; what shall we have therefore?" [10] And the Lord told them what He would give them here, what He would reserve for them hereafter. Now Peter was already of the number of those who had so done. But when it came to the crisis [11] of suffering, at the voice of a maid-servant he denied Him thrice with whom he had promised that he was ready to die.

10. Take good heed then, Beloved: "Go," saith He, "sell all that thou hast, give to the poor, and thou shalt have treasure in heaven, and come, follow Me." Peter is perfect, now that the Lord sitteth in heaven at the right Hand of the Father, then did he attain perfection and maturity. For when he followed the Lord to His Passion, he was not perfect; but

---

[1] *Meruerunt.*   [2] Matt. vii. 22.   [3] Matt. vii. 23.
[4] *Sincerissimam.*   [5] 1 Cor. xiii. 4.   [6] Matt. xi. 29.

[7] *Sacramenta.*   [8] 1 Cor. xiii. 1, etc.   [9] Matt. xix. 21.
[10] Matt. xix. 27.   [11] *Articulum.*

when there began to be no one on earth for him to follow, then was he perfected. But thou truly hast always One before thee to follow; the Lord hath set up an example on earth, when He left the Gospel with thee, in the Gospel He is with thee. For He did not speak falsely when He said, "Lo, I am with you alway, even unto the end of the world."[1] Therefore follow the Lord. What is, "Follow the Lord"? Imitate the Lord. What is, "Imitate the Lord"? "Learn of Me, that I am meek and lowly in heart." Because if I should distribute all my goods to the poor, and give up my body to be burned, but not have charity, it profiteth me nothing. To this charity then I exhort your Charity; now I should not exhort to charity, but with some charity. I exhort then that what is commenced may be filled up; and pray that what is begun may be perfected. And I beg that ye would offer this prayer for me, that what I advise may be perfected in me also. For we are all now imperfect, and there shall we be perfected, where all things are perfect. The Apostle Paul says, "Brethren, I do not reckon myself to have apprehended."[2] He says, "Not that I have already attained, either am already perfect."[3] And shall any man dare to vaunt himself on perfection? Yea rather let us acknowledge our imperfection, that we may attain[4] perfection.

SERMON XCIII.

[CXLIII. BEN.]

ON THE WORDS OF THE GOSPEL, JOHN XVI. 7, "I TELL YOU THE TRUTH; IT IS EXPEDIENT FOR YOU THAT I GO AWAY," ETC.

1. THE medicine for all the wounds of the soul, and the one propitiation for the offences of men, is to believe on Christ; nor can any one be cleansed at all, whether from original sin which he derived from Adam,[5] in whom all men have sinned, and become by nature children of wrath; or from the sins which they have themselves added, by not resisting the concupiscence of the flesh, but by following and serving it in unclean and injurious deeds: unless by faith they are united and compacted into His Body, who was conceived without any enticement of the flesh and deadly pleasure, and whom His Mother nourished in her womb without sin, and "Who did no sin, neither was deceit found in His Mouth."[6] They verily who believe on Him, become the children of God; because they are born of God by the grace of adoption, which is by the faith of Jesus Christ our Lord. Wherefore, dearly Beloved, it is with good reason that the same Lord and our Saviour mentions this

one sin only, of which the Holy Ghost convinces the world, that it believeth not on Him. "I tell you the truth," He saith, "It is expedient for you that I go away. For if I go not away, the Comforter will not come unto you; but if I depart, I will send Him unto you. And when He shall come, He will convince the world of sin, and of righteousness, and of judgment. Of sin, because they believe not on Me. Of righteousness, because I go to the Father, and ye shall see Me no more. Of judgment, because the prince of this world is already judged."[7]

2. Of this one only sin then He would have the world to be convinced, that they believe not on Him; to wit, because by believing on Him all sins are loosed, He would have this one imputed by which the rest are bound. And because by believing they are born of God, and become children of God; "For," saith he, "to them gave He power to become the sons of God, to them that believe on Him."[8] Whoso then believeth on the Son of God, in so far as he adhereth to Him, and becometh himself also by adoption a son and heir of God, and a joint-heir with Christ, in so far he sinneth not. Whence John saith, "Whosoever is born of God sinneth not."[9] And therefore the sin of which the world is convinced is this, that they believe not on Him. This is the sin of which He also saith, "If I had not come, they had not had sin."[10] For what! had they not innumerable other sins? But by His coming this one sin was added to them that believed not, by which the rest should be retained. Whereas in them that believe, because this one was wanting, it was brought to pass that all should be remitted to them that believe. Nor is it with any other view that the Apostle Paul saith, "All have sinned, and have need of the glory of God;"[11] that, "whosoever believeth on Him, should not be confounded;"[12] as the Psalm also saith, "Come ye unto Him, and be enlightened, and your faces shall not be confounded."[13] Whoso then glorieth in himself shall be confounded; for he shall not be found without sins. Accordingly he only shall not be confounded who glorieth in the Lord. "For all have sinned, and have need of the glory of God." And so when he was speaking of the infidelity of the Jews, he did not say, "For if some of them have sinned, shall their sin make the faith of God of none effect?" For how should he say, "If some of them have sinned;" when he said himself, "For all have sinned"? But he said, "If some of them believed not, shall their unbelief make the faith of God of none effect?"[14] That he might

---

[1] Matt. xxviii. 20.　　[2] Phil. iii. 13.　　[3] Phil. iii. 12.
[4] *Mereamur.*　　[5] Ps. li. 5.　　[6] 1 Pet. ii. 22.

[7] John xvi. 7–11.　　[8] John i. 12.　　[9] 1 John iii. 9.
[10] John xv. 22.　　[11] Rom. iii. 23.　　[12] Rom. ix. 33.
[13] Ps. xxxiii. 6, Sept. (xxxiv. 5, English version).
[14] Rom. iii. 3.

point out more expressly this sin, by which alone the door is closed against the rest that they by the grace of God should not be remitted. Of which one sin by the coming of the Holy Ghost, that is by the gift of His grace, which is granted to the faithful, the world is convinced, in the Lord's words, "Of sin, because they believed not on Me."

3. Now there would be no great merit and glorious blessedness in believing, if the Lord had always appeared in His Risen Body to the eyes of men. The Holy Ghost then hath brought this great gift to them that should believe, that Him whom they should not see with the eyes of flesh, they might with a mind sobered from carnal desires, and inebriated with spiritual longings, sigh after. Whence it was that when that disciple who had said that he would not believe, unless he touched with the hands His Scars, after he had handled the Lord's Body, cried out as though awaking from sleep, "My Lord and my God;" the Lord said to him, "Because thou hast seen Me, thou hast believed; blessed are they that have not seen, and yet have believed."[1] This blessedness hath the Holy Ghost, the Comforter, brought to us, that the form of a servant which He took from the Virgin's womb, being removed from the eyes of flesh, the purified eye of the mind might be directed to This Form of God, in which He continued equal with the Father, even when He vouchsafed to appear in the Flesh; so as that with the Same Spirit filled the Apostle might say, "Though we have known Christ after the flesh; yet now we know Him so no longer."[2] Because even the Flesh of Christ he knew not after the flesh, but after the Spirit, who, not by touching in curiosity, but in believing assured, acknowledgeth the power of His Resurrection; not saying in his heart, "Who hath ascended into heaven? that is, to bring Christ down; or, Who hath descended into the deep? that is, to bring back Christ from the dead." "But," saith he, "the word is nigh thee, in thy mouth, that Jesus is the Lord; and if thou shalt believe in thine heart that God hath raised Him from the dead, thou shalt be saved. For with the heart man believeth unto righteousness, and with the mouth confession is made unto salvation."[3] These, Brethren, are the words of the Apostle, pouring them forth with the holy inebriation of the Holy Ghost Himself.

4. Forasmuch then as we could in no way have had this blessedness by which we see not and yet believe, unless we received it of the Holy Ghost; it is with good reason said, "It is expedient for you that I go away. For if I go not away, the Comforter will not come unto you;

but if I depart, I will send Him unto you."[4] By His Divinity indeed He is with us always; but unless He had in Body gone away from us, we had always seen His Body after the flesh, and never believed after a spiritual sort; by the which belief justified and blessed we might attain[5] with cleansed hearts to contemplate the Very Word, God with God, "by whom all things were made," and "who was made Flesh, that He might dwell among us." And if not with the contact of the hand, but "with the heart man believeth unto righteousness;" with good reason is the world, which will not believe save what it sees, convinced of our righteousness. Now that we might have that righteousness of faith of which the unbelieving world should be convinced, therefore said the Lord, "Of righteousness, because I go to the Father, and ye shall see Me no more." As if He had said, "This shall be your righteousness, that ye believe on Me, the Mediator, of whom ye shall be most fully assured that He is risen again and gone to the Father, though ye see Him not after the Flesh; that by Him reconciled, ye may be able to see God after the Spirit." Whence He saith to the woman who represents the Church, when she fell at His Feet after His Resurrection, "Touch Me not, for I am not yet ascended to the Father."[6] Which expression is understood mystically, thus. "Believe not in Me after a carnal manner by means of bodily contact; but thou shalt believe after a spiritual manner; that is, with a spiritual faith shalt touch Me, when I shall have ascended to the Father." For, "blessed are they who do not see, and believe." And this is the righteousness of faith, of which the world, which hath it not, is convinced of us who are not without it; for "the just liveth by faith."[7] Whether it be then that as rising again in Him, and in Him coming to the Father, we are invisibly and in justification perfected; or that as not seeing and yet believing we live by faith, for that "the just liveth by faith;" with these meanings said He, "Of righteousness, because I go to the Father, and ye shall see Me no more."

5. Nor let the world excuse itself by this, that it is hindered by the devil from believing on Christ. For to believers the prince of the world is cast out,[8] that he work no more in the hearts of men whom Christ hath begun to possess by faith; as he worketh in the children of unbelief,[9] whom he is constantly stirring up to tempt and disturb the righteous. For because he is cast out, who once had dominion interiorly he wageth war exteriorly. Although then by means of his persecutions, "the Lord doth direct the meek in judgment;"[10] nevertheless in this very fact of

---

[1] John xx. 29.   [2] 2 Cor. v. 16.   [3] Rom. x. 6, etc.

[4] John xvi. 7.   [5] *Mereremur*.   [6] John xx. 17.
[7] Hab. ii. 4; Rom. i. 17.   [8] John xii. 31.
[9] Eph. ii. 2.   [10] Ps. xxv. 9.

his being cast out, is he "judged already." And of this "judgment" is the world convinced; for in vain doth he who will not believe on Christ complain of the devil whom, judged, that is, cast out, and for the exercising of us allowed to attack us from without, not only men, but even women, and boys, and girls, Martyrs have overcome. Now in whom have they overcome, but in Him on whom they have believed, and whom seeing not, they loved, and by whose dominion in their hearts they have got rid of a most oppressive [1] lord. And all this by grace, by the gift, that is, of the Holy Ghost. Rightly then doth the Same Spirit convince the world, both of "sin," because it believeth not on Christ; "and of righteousness," because they who have had the will have believed, though Him on whom they believed they saw not; and by His Resurrection have hoped that themselves also should be in the resurrection perfected; "and of judgment," because if they had had the will to believe, they could be hindered by none, "for that the prince of this world hath been judged already."

SERMON XCIV.

[cxliv. ben.]

ON THE SAME WORDS OF THE GOSPEL, JOHN XVI. 8, "HE WILL CONVICT THE WORLD IN RESPECT OF SIN, AND OF RIGHTEOUSNESS, AND OF JUDGEMENT."

1. WHEN our Lord and Saviour Jesus Christ was speaking at length of the coming of the Holy Ghost, He said among the rest, "He shall convince the world of sin, and of righteousness, and of judgment." [2] Nor when He had said this, did He pass on to another subject; but vouchsafed to convey a somewhat more explicit notice of this same truth. "Of sin," said He, "because they believed not on Me. Of righteousness, because I go to the Father. Of judgment, because the prince of this world hath been judged already." [3] There arises therefore within us a desire of understanding, why as if it were men's only sin, not to believe on Christ, He said it of this alone, that the Holy Ghost should convince the world; but if it is plain that besides this unbelief there are manifold other sins of men, why of this alone should the Holy Ghost convince the world? Is it because all sins are by unbelief retained, by faith remitted; that therefore God imputeth this one above all the rest, by which it comes to pass that the rest are not loosed, so long as proud man believes not in an Humbled God? For so it is written; "God resisteth the proud, but giveth grace unto the humble." [4] Now this grace of God is a gift of God. But the greatest gift is the Holy Ghost

Himself; and therefore is it called grace. For forasmuch "as all had sinned, and needed the glory of God; because by one man sin entered into the world, and death by his sin in whom all have sinned;" [5] therefore is it grace because given gratuitously. And therefore is it given gratuitously, because it is not rendered as a reward after a strict scrutiny of deserts, but given as a gift after the pardon of sins.

2. Therefore of sin are unbelievers, that is, the lovers of the world, convinced; for they are signified by the name of the world. For when it is said, "He will convince the world of sin;" it is of none other sin than that they have not believed on Christ. For if this sin exist not, no sins will remain, because when the just man lives by faith, all are loosed. Now the difference is great as to whether one believe that Jesus is Christ, or whether he believe on Christ. For that Jesus is Christ even the devils believed, and yet the devils believed not on Christ. For he believeth on Christ, who both hopeth in Christ and loveth Christ. For if he have faith without hope and love, he believeth that Christ is, but he doth not believe on Christ. Whoso then believeth on Christ, by believing on Christ, Christ cometh unto him, and in a manner uniteth Himself to him, and he is made a member in His Body. Which cannot be, but by the accession of hope and love.

3. What mean again His words, "Of righteousness, because I go to the Father"? And first must we enquire, if the world is convinced of sin, why it is also of righteousness? For who can rightly be convinced of righteousness? Is it indeed that the world is convinced of its own sin, but of Christ's righteousness? I do not see what else can be understood; since He saith, "Of sin, because they believed not on Me. Of righteousness, because I go to the Father." They believed not, He goeth to the Father. Their sin therefore, and His righteousness. But why would He name righteousness in this only, that He goeth to the Father? Is it not righteousness also that He came hither from the Father? Or is that rather mercy, that He came from the Father to us, and righteousness, that He goeth to the Father?

4. So, Brethren, I think it expedient, that in so profound a depth of Scripture, in words, wherein peradventure there lies some hidden truth which may in due season be laid open, we should as it were together enquire faithfully, that we may attain [6] to find healthfully. Why then doth He call this righteousness, in that He goeth to the Father, and not also in that He came from the Father? Is it that in that it is mercy that He came, therefore it is righteousness that

---

[1] *Pessimo.*
[2] John xvi. 8.
[3] John xvi. 9-11.
[4] Prov. iii. 34; Jas. iv. 6.
[5] Rom. iii. 23, v. 12.
[6] *Mereamur.*

He goeth? that so in our own case too we may learn that righteousness cannot be fulfilled in us, if we are slow to give a place first [1] to mercy, "not seeking our own things, but the things of others also." Which advice when the Apostle had given, he immediately joined to it the example of our Lord Himself; "Doing nothing," saith he, "through strife or vain glory; but in lowliness of mind, each esteeming the other better than themselves. Not looking every man on his own things, but also on the things of others." Then he added immediately, "Let this mind be in each of you which was also in Christ Jesus, who, being in the Form of God, thought it not robbery to be equal with God; but emptied Himself, taking the form of a servant, being made in the likeness of men, and found in fashion as a man; He humbled Himself, having become obedient even unto death, yea the death of the cross." [2] This is the mercy whereby He came from the Father. What then is the righteousness whereby He goeth to the Father? He goes on and says; "Wherefore God also hath exalted Him, and given Him a Name which is above every name; that at the Name of Jesus every knee should bow, of things in heaven, and things in earth, and things under the earth, and that every tongue should confess that the Lord Jesus Christ is in the Glory of God the Father." This is the righteousness whereby He goeth to the Father.

5. But if He Alone goeth to the Father, what doth it profit us? Why is the world convinced by the Holy Ghost of this righteousness? And yet if He did not Alone go to the Father, He would not say in another place, "No man hath ascended up to heaven, but He That descended from heaven, the Son of man who is in heaven." [3] But the Apostle Paul also says, "For our conversation is in heaven." [4] And why is this? Because he also says, "If ye be risen with Christ, seek the things which are above, where Christ sitteth on the right hand of God. Mind the things which are above, not those which are upon the earth. For ye are dead, and your life is hid with Christ in God." [5] How then is He Alone? Is He therefore Alone because Christ with all His members is One, as the Head with His Body? Now what is His Body, but the Church? As the same teacher says, "Now ye are the Body of Christ, and members in particular." [6] Forasmuch then as we have fallen, and He descended for our sakes, what is, "No man hath ascended, but He That descended;" but that no man hath ascended, except as made one with Him, and as a member fastened into His Body who descended? And thus He saith to His disciples, "Without Me ye can do

nothing." [7] For in one way is He One with the Father, and in another one with us. He is One with the Father, in that the Substance of the Father and the Son is One; He is One with the Father, in that, "Being in the Form of God, He thought it not robbery to be equal with God." But He was made One with us, in that "He emptied Himself, taking the form of a servant;" He was made one with us, according to the seed of Abraham, "in whom all nations shall be blessed." Which place when the Apostle had brought forward, he said, "He saith not, And to seeds, as of many; but as of one, And to thy Seed, which is Christ." [8] And for that we too belong to that which is Christ, by our incorporation together, and coherence to That Head, It is One Christ. And also for that he says to us too, "Therefore are ye Abraham's seed, heirs according to the promise." [9] For if the seed of Abraham be One, and That One Seed of Abraham can only be understood of Christ; but this seed of Abraham we also are; therefore This Whole, that is, the Head and the Body, is One Christ.

6. And therefore we ought not to deem ourselves separated from that righteousness, which the Lord Himself makes mention of, saying, "Of righteousness, because I go to the Father." For we too have risen with Christ, and we are with Christ our Head, now for a while [10] by faith and hope; but our hope will be completed in the last resurrection of the dead. But when our hope shall be completed, then shall our justification be completed also. And the Lord who was to complete it showed us in His Own Flesh (that is, in our Head), Wherein He rose again and ascended to the Father, what we ought to hope for. For that thus it is written, "He was delivered for our sins, and rose again for our justification." [11] The world then is convinced "of sin" in those who believe not on Christ; "and of righteousness," in those who rise again in the members of Christ. Whence it is said, "That we may be the righteousness of God in him." [12] For if not in Him, in no way righteousness. But if in Him, He goeth with us Whole to the Father, and this perfect righteousness will be fulfilled in us. And therefore "of judgment" too is the world convinced, "because the prince of this world hath been judged already;" that is, the devil, the prince of the unrighteous, who in heart inhabit only in this world which they love, and therefore are called "the world;" as our conversation is in heaven, if we have risen again with Christ. Therefore as Christ together with us, that is His Body, is One; so the devil with all the ungodly whose head he is, with as it were his own body, is one.

---

[1] *Prærogare.*　[2] Phil. ii. 3, etc.　[3] John iii. 13.
[4] Phil. iii. 20.　[5] Col. iii. 1–3.　[6] 1 Cor. xii. 27.

[7] John xv. 5.　[8] Gal. iii. 16.　[9] Gal. iii. 29.
[10] *Interim.*　[11] Rom. iv. 25.　[12] 2 Cor. v. 21.

Wherefore as we are not separated from the righteousness, of which the Lord said, "Because I go to the Father;" so the ungodly are not separated from that judgment, of which He said, "Because the prince of this world hath been judged already."

SERMON XCV.

[CXLV. BEN.]

ON THE WORDS OF THE GOSPEL, JOHN XVI. 24, "HITHERTO HAVE YE ASKED NOTHING IN MY NAME;" AND ON THE WORDS OF LUKE X. 17, "LORD, EVEN THE DEMONS ARE SUBJECT UNTO US IN THY NAME."

1. WHEN the Holy Gospel was being read, we heard what in truth ought at once to put every earnest soul in motion to seek, not to faint. For whoso is not moved, is not changed. But there is a dangerous movement, of which it is written, "Suffer not my feet to be moved." [1] But there is another movement of him who seeketh, knocketh, asketh. What then has been read we have all heard; but I suppose we have not all understood. It makes mention of that which together with me ye should seek, with me ask, for the receiving of which ye should with me knock. For as I hope the grace of the Lord will be with us, that whereas I wish to minister to you, I too may be thought [2] worthy to receive. What is it, I pray you, that we have just heard that the Lord said to His disciples? "Hitherto have ye asked nothing in My Name." [3] Is He not speaking to those disciples, who, after He had sent them, having given them power to preach the Gospel, and to do mighty works, returned with joy, and said to Him, "Lord, even the devils are subject unto us through Thy Name"? [4] Ye recognise, ye recollect this which I have quoted from the Gospel, which in every passage and every sentence speaketh truth, nowhere false, nowhere deceiveth. How then is it true, "Hitherto have ye asked nothing in My Name"? and, "Lord, even the devils are subject unto us through Thy name"? Of a surety this puts the mind in motion to ascertain the secret of this difficulty. Therefore ask we, seek, knock. Be there in us faithful godliness, not a restlessness of the flesh, but a submission of the mind, that He who seeth us knocking may open unto us.

2. What the Lord then may give to be ministered unto you, do ye with earnest attention, that is, with hunger, receive; and when I shall have spoken it, ye will doubtless with sound taste [5] approve what is placed before you out of the Lord's store. The Lord Jesus knew whereby the soul of man, that is, the rational mind, made after the image of God, could be satisfied: only, that is, by Himself. This He knew, and knew that it was as yet without that fulness. He knew that He was manifest, and He knew that He was hidden. He knew what in Him was exhibited, what concealed. He knew all this. "How great," says the Psalm, "is the multitude of Thy sweetness, O Lord, which Thou hast hidden to them that fear Thee; which Thou hast wrought for them that hope in Thee!" [6] "Thy sweetness" both great and manifold "hast Thou hidden to them that fear Thee." If thou hidest it to them that fear Thee, to whom dost Thou open it? "Thou hast wrought it for them that hope in Thee." A twofold question has arisen, but either is solved by the other. If any one inquires after the other, what is this, "Thou hast hidden it to them that fear Thee; wrought it for them that hope in Thee"? Are they that fear, and they that hope, different? Do not the very same who fear God, hope in God? Who hopeth on Him who doth not fear Him? Who in a godly sort feareth Him, and hath not hope in Him? Let this then first be solved. Somewhat would I say concerning those who hope and those who fear.

3. The Law hath fear, Grace hope. But what difference is there between the Law and Grace, since the Giver both of the Law and Grace is One? The Law alarmeth him who relieth on himself, Grace assisteth him who trusteth in God. The Law, I say, alarmeth; do not make light of this because it is brief; weigh it well, and it is considerable. Look well at what I have said, take what we minister, prove wherefrom we take it. The Law alarmeth him who relieth on himself, Grace assisteth him who trusteth in God. What saith the Law? Many things: and who can enumerate them? I bring forward one small and short precept from it which the Apostle hath brought forward, a very small one; let us see who is sufficient [7] for it. "Thou shalt not lust." [8] What is this, Brethren? We have heard the Law; if there be no grace, thou hast heard thy punishment. Why dost thou boast to me whosoever thou art that hearing this dost rely upon thyself, why dost thou boast to me of innocence? Why dost thou flatter thyself thereupon? Thou canst say, "I have not plundered the goods of others;" I hear, I believe, perhaps I even see it, thou dost not plunder the goods of others. Thou hast heard, "Thou shalt not lust." "I do not go in to another man's wife;" this again I hear, believe, see. Thou hast heard, "Thou shalt not lust." Why dost thou inspect thyself all round without, and dost not inspect within? Look in, and thou wilt see

---

[1] Ps. lxvi. 9.   [2] *Merear.*   [3] John xvi. 24.
[4] Luke x. 17.   [5] *Faucibus.*

[6] Ps. xxx. 20, Sept. (xxxi. 19, English version).
[7] *Supportat.*   [8] Rom. vii. 7.

another law in thy members   Look in, why dost thou pass over thyself?   Descend into thine own self.   Thou wilt " see another law in thy members resisting the law of thy mind, and bringing thee into captivity in the law of sin which is in thy members." [1]   With good reason then is the sweetness of God hidden to thee.   The law placed in thy members, resisting the law of thy mind, bringeth thee into captivity.   Of that sweetness which to thee is hidden, the holy Angels drink ; thou canst not drink and taste that sweetness, captive as thou art.   " Thou hadst not known concupiscence, unless the Law had said, Thou shalt not lust."   Thou heardest, fearedst, didst try to fight, couldest not overcome.   For " sin taking occasion by the commandment wrought death."   Surely ye recognise them, they are the Apostle's words.   " Sin taking occasion by the commandment, wrought in me all manner of concupiscence." [2]   Why didst thou vaunt thyself in thy pride?   Lo, with thine own arms hath the enemy conquered thee.   Thou verily didst look for a commandment as a defence : and, lo, by the commandment the enemy hath found an occasion of entering in.   " For sin taking occasion by the commandment," he saith, " deceived me, and by it slew me." [3]   What means what I said, " With thine own arms hath the enemy conquered thee " ?   Hear the same Apostle going on, and saying ; " Wherefore the Law indeed is holy, and the commandment holy, and just, and good." [4]   Make answer now to the revilers [5] of the Law : make answer on the Apostle's authority, " The commandment is holy, the Law holy, the commandment just and good.   Was then that which is good, made death unto me?   God forbid !   But sin that it might appear sin, by that which is good wrought death in me." [6]   Why is this but because on receiving the commandment thou didst fear, not love?   Thou fearedst punishment, thou didst not love righteousness.   Whoso feareth punishment, wisheth, if it were possible, to do what pleaseth him, and not to have what he feareth.   God forbiddeth adultery, thou hast coveted another's wife, thou dost not go in unto her, thou dost not do so, opportunity is given thee, thou hast time, a favourable place is open, witnesses are absent, yet thou dost not do it, wherefore?   Because thou fearest the punishment.   But no one will know it.   Will not God know it?   So it is clear, because God knoweth what thou art about to do, thou doest it not ; but here thou fearest the threatenings of God, not lovest His commandments.   Why dost thou not do it?   Because if thou do, thou wilt be cast into hell fire.   It is the fire thou fearest.   O if thou didst love

chastity, thou wouldest not do it, even though thou mightest be altogether unpunished.   If God were to say to thee, " Lo, do it, I will not condemn thee, I will not condemn thee to hell fire, but I will withhold My Face from thee."   If thou did it not because of this threat, it would be from the love of God that thou didst not do it, not from the fear of judgment.   But thou wouldest do it, perhaps I mean thou wouldest do so ; for it is not my place to judge.   If thou do it not on this principle because thou abhorrest the contamination of adultery, because thou lovest His precepts, that thou mayest obtain [7] His promises, and not because thou fearest His condemnation, it is the grace which maketh saints that aideth thee ; it is all of grace, ascribe it not to thine own self, attribute it not to thine own strength.   Thou actest from delight in it, well ; thou actest in charity, well ; I assent, I agree.   Charity worketh by thee, when thou actest with thy will.   At once dost thou taste sweetness, if thou hope on the Lord.

4. But whence hast thou this charity, if yet thou hast it?   for I am afraid lest even yet it is through fear thou doest it not, and lest thou seem great in thine own eyes.   Now if it is through charity that thou doest it not, thou art truly great.   Hast thou charity?   " I have," you say.   Whence?   " From myself."   Far art thou from sweetness, if thou hast it from thine own self.   Thou wilt love thine own self, because thou wilt love that from which thou hast it.   But I will convict thee that thou hast it not.   For in that thou dost think that thou hast so great a thing from thine own self, by that very fact I do not believe thou hast it.   For if thou hadst, thou wouldest know from whence thou hadst it.   Hast thou charity from thyself, as if it were some light, some little thing?   " If thou shouldest speak with the tongues of men and Angels, but have not charity, thou wouldest be a sounding brass and a tinkling cymbal.   If thou shouldest know all mysteries, and have all knowledge, and all prophecy, and all faith so that thou couldest remove mountains, but not have charity," these things could not profit thee.   " If thou shouldest distribute all thy goods to the poor, and deliver up thy body to be burned, but not have charity, thou wouldest be nothing." [8]   How great is this charity, which if it be wanting, all things profit nothing !   Compare it not to thy faith, not to thy knowledge, not to thy gift of tongues, [8] to lesser things, to the eye of thy body, the hand, the foot, the belly, to any one lowest member compare charity, are these least things to be in any way compared to charity?   So then the eye and nose thou hast from God, and hast thou charity from thine own self?   If thou hast given

---

[1] Rom. vii. 23.   [2] Rom. vii. 8, 13.   [3] Rom. vii. 11.
[4] Rom. vii. 12.   [5] The Manichæans.
[6] Rom. vii. 13.

[7] *Exigas.*   [8] 1 Cor. xiii. 1, etc.   [9] *Linguæ tuæ.*

thyself charity which surpasseth all things, thou hast made God of light account with thee. What more can God give thee? Whatever He may have given, is less. Charity which thou hast given thyself, surpasseth all things. But if thou hast it, thou hast not given it to thyself. " For what hast thou which thou hast not received?" [1] Who gave to me, who gave to thee? God. Acknowledge Him in His gifts, that thou feel not His condemnation. By believing the Scriptures, God hath given thee charity, a great boon, charity, which surpasseth all things. God gave it thee, " because the charity of God hath been shed abroad in our hearts;" by thine own self, perhaps? God forbid; " by the Holy Ghost, who hath been given us." [2]

5. Return with me to that captive, return with me to my proposition. "The Law alarmeth him that relieth on himself, grace assisteth him who trusteth in God." For look at that captive. " He seeth another law in his members resisting the law of his mind, and leading him captive in the law of sin, which is in his members." [3] Lo, he is bound, lo, he is dragged along, lo, he is led captive, lo, he is subjected. What hath that profited him, " Thou shalt not lust"? He hath heard, " Thou shalt not lust;" that he might know his enemy, not that he might overcome him. " For he had not known concupiscence," that is, his enemy, "unless the Law had said, Thou shalt not lust." [4] Now thou hast seen the enemy, fight, deliver thyself, make good thy liberty, let the suggestions of pleasure be kept down, unlawful delight be utterly destroyed. Arm thyself, thou hast the Law, march on, conquer if thou canst. For what good is it that through the little portion of God's grace thou hast already, thou " delightest in the Law of God after the inward man? But thou seest another law in thy members resisting the law of thy mind;" not " resisting" yet powerless for aught, but " leading thee captive in the law of sin." Behold, whence to thee who fearest that " plentifulness of sweetness is hidden!" to him that feareth it "is hidden," how is it " wrought" out for him that " trusteth"? [5] Cry out under thine enemy, for that thou hast an assailant, thou hast an Helper too, who looketh upon thee as thou fightest, who helpeth thee in difficulty; but only if He find thee " trusting;" for the proud He hateth. What then wilt thou cry under this enemy? "Wretched man that I am!" [6] Ye see it already, for ye have cried out. Be this your cry, when haply thou art distressed under the enemy, say ye, in your inmost heart say, in sound faith say, " Wretched man that I am!" Wretched

that I am! " Therefore wretched," because " I." "Wretched man that I am," both because " I," and because " man." For " he is disquieted in vain." [7] For though " man walketh in the Image;" [8] yet, " wretched man that I am, who shall deliver me from the body of this death?" Wilt thou thyself? where is thy strength, where is thy confidence? Of a surety thou both criest out, and art silent; silent, that is, from extolling thyself, not from calling upon God. Be silent, and cry out. For God Himself too is both silent, and crieth aloud; He is silent from judgment, He is not silent from precept; so be thou too silent from elation, not from invocation; lest God say to thee, " I have been silent, shall I be silent always?" [9] Cry out therefore, "O wretched man that I am!" Acknowledge thyself conquered, put thine own strength to shame, and say, " Wretched man that I am, who shall deliver me from the body of this death?" What did I say above? The Law alarmeth him that relieth upon himself. Behold, man relied upon himself, he attempted to fight, he could not get the better, he was conquered, prostrated, subjugated, led captive. He learnt to rely upon God, and it remaineth that him whom the Law alarmed while he relied upon himself, grace should assist now that he trusteth in God. In this confidence he saith, " Who shall deliver me from the body of this death? The grace of God by Jesus Christ our Lord." [10] Now see the sweetness, taste it, relish it; hear the Psalm, " Taste and see that the Lord is sweet." [11] He hath become sweet to thee, for that He hath delivered thee. Thou wast bitter to thine own self, when thou didst rely upon thyself. Drink sweetness, receive the earnest of so great abundance.

6. The disciples then of the Lord Jesus Christ while yet under the Law had to be cleansed still, to be nourished still, to be corrected still, to be directed still. For they still had concupiscence; whereas the Law saith, " Thou shalt not lust." [12] Without offence to those holy rams, the leaders of the flock, without offence to them I would say it, for I say the truth: the Gospel relates, that they contended which of them should be the greatest, and whilst the Lord was yet on earth, they were agitated by a dissension about preeminence. [13] Whence was this, but from the old leaven? whence, but from the law in the members, resisting the law of the mind? They sought for eminence; yea, they desired it; they thought which should be the greatest; therefore is their pride put to shame by a little child. [14] Jesus calleth unto him the age of humility to tame the swelling desire. With good reason then when

---

[1] 1 Cor. iv. 7.   [2] Rom. v. 5.   [3] Rom. vii. 23.
[4] Rom. vii. 7.
[5] Ps. xxx. 20, Sept. (xxxi. 19, English version).
[6] Rom. vii. 24.

[7] Ps. xxxviii. 7 (xxxix. 6, English version).
[8] *i.e.* of God. Vid. *Enarrat. in Ps.* xxxviii.
[9] Isa. xlii. 14, Sept.
[10] Rom. vii. 24, 25, Vulgate.   [11] Ps. xxxiv. 8, Vulgate.
[12] Exod. xx. 17.   [13] Luke xxii. 24.   [14] Matt. xviii. 2.

they returned too, and said, "Lord, behold even the devils are subject unto us through Thy Name." (It was for a nothing that they rejoiced; of what importance was it compared to that which God promised?) The Lord, the Good Master, quieting fear, and building up a firm support, said to them, "In this rejoice not that the devils are subject unto you." Why so? Because "many will come in My Name, saying, Behold, in Thy Name we have cast out devils; and I will say to them, I know you not. In this rejoice not, but rejoice because your names are written in heaven." [1] Ye cannot yet be there, yet notwithstanding ye are already written there. Therefore "rejoice." So that place again, "Hitherto have ye asked nothing in My Name." [2] For what ye have asked, in comparison with that which I am willing to give, is nothing. For what have ye asked in My Name? . That the devils should be subject unto you? " In this rejoice not," that is, what ye have asked is nothing; for if it were anything, He would bid them rejoice. So then it was not absolutely nothing, but that it was little in comparison of that greatness of God's rewards. For the Apostle Paul was not really not anything; and yet in comparison of God, "Neither is he that planteth anything, neither he that watereth." [3] And so I say to you, and I say to myself, both to myself and you I say, when we ask in Christ's Name for these temporal things. For ye have asked undoubtedly. For who doth not ask? One asketh for health, if he is sick; another asketh for deliverance, if he is in prison; another asketh for the port, if he is tossed about at sea; another asketh for victory, if he is in conflict with an enemy; and in the Name of Christ he asketh all, and what he asketh is nothing. What then must be asked for? "Ask in My Name." [2] And He said not what, but by the very words we understand what we ought to ask. "Ask, and ye shall receive, that your joy may be full. Ask, and ye shall receive, in My Name." But what? Not nothing; but what? "That your joy may be full;" that is, ask what may suffice you. For when thou askest for temporal things, thou askest for nothing. "Whoso shall drink of this water, shall thirst again." [4] He letteth down the watering pot of desire into the well, he taketh up whereof to drink, only that he may thirst again. "Ask, that your joy may be full;" that is, that ye may be satisfied, not feel delight only for a time. Ask what may suffice you; speak Philip's language, "Lord, show us the Father, and it sufficeth us." [5] The Lord saith to you, "Have I been so long time with you, and have ye not known Me? Philip, he that seeth Me, seeth the

Father also." [6] Render then thanks to Christ, made weak for you that are weak, and make ready your desires [7] for Christ's Divinity, to be satisfied therewith. Turn we to the Lord, etc.

SERMON XCVI.

[CXLVI. BEN.]

ON THE WORDS OF THE GOSPEL, JOHN XXI. 16, "SIMON, *SON* OF JOHN, LOVEST THOU ME?" ETC.

1. YE have observed, beloved, that in to-day's lesson it was said by the Lord to Peter in a question, "Lovest thou Me?" To whom he answered, "Thou knowest, Lord, that I love thee." This was done a second, and a third time; and at each several reply, the Lord said, "Feed My lambs." [8] To Peter did Christ commend His lambs to be fed, who fed even Peter himself. For what could Peter do for the Lord, especially now that He had an Immortal Body, and was about to ascend into heaven? As though He had said to him, "'Lovest thou Me?' Herein show that thou lovest Me, 'Feed my sheep.'" So then, Brethren, do ye with obedience hear that ye are Christ's sheep; seeing that we on our part with fear hear, "Feed My sheep"? If we feed with fear, and fear for the sheep; these sheep how ought they to fear for themselves? Let then carefulness be our portion, obedience yours; pastoral watchfulness our portion, the humility of the flock yours. Although we too who seem to speak to you from a higher place, are with fear beneath your feet; forasmuch as we know how perilous an account must be rendered of this as it were exalted seat. Wherefore, dearly beloved, Catholic plants, Members of Christ, think What a Head ye have! Children of God, think What a Father ye have found. Christians, think What an Inheritance is promised you. Not such as on earth cannot be possessed by children, save when their parents are dead. For no one on earth possesses a father's inheritance, save when he is dead. But we whilst our Father liveth shall possess what He shall give; for that our Father cannot die. I add more, I say more, and say the truth; our Father will Himself be our Inheritance.

2. Live consistently, especially ye candidates of Christ, recently baptized, just regenerated, as I have admonished you before, so say I now, and give expression to my solicitude; for the present lesson of the Gospel hath forced upon me a greater fear: take heed to yourselves, do not imitate evil Christians. Say not I will do this, for many of the faithful do it. This is not to procure a defence for the soul; but to look out for companions unto hell. Grow ye in this floor of the Lord; herein ye will find good men to

---

[1] Luke x. 20; Matt. vii. 22.   [2] John xvi. 24.
[3] 1 Cor. iii. 7.   [4] John iv. 13.
[5] John xiv. 8.

[6] John xiv. 9, Vulgate.   [7] *Fauces.*   [8] John xxi. 15.

please you, if ye yourselves are good. For are ye our private property? Heretics and schismatics have made their own private property out of what they have stolen from the Lord, and would feed, not Christ's flocks, but their own against Christ. It is true indeed, they place His title on these their spoils, that their robberies may be as it were maintained by the title of His Power. What doeth Christ when such as these are converted, who have received the title of His Baptism out of the Church? He casteth out the spoiler, He doth not efface the title, and taketh possession of the house; because He hath found His title there. What need is there that He should change His Own Name? Do they take heed to what the Lord said to Peter, "Feed My lambs, feed My sheep"? Did He say to him, "Feed thy lambs;" or, "Feed thy sheep"? But for them who are shut out, what said He in the Song of Songs, unto the Church? The Spouse speaking to the Bride, saith, "If thou know not thyself, O thou fair one among women, go forth."[1] As though He said, "I do not cast thee out, 'go forth, if thou know not thyself, O thou fair one among women,' if thou know not thyself in the mirror of divine Scripture, if thou give not heed, O thou fair woman, to the mirror which with no false lustre deceiveth thee; if thou know not that of thee it is said, 'Thy glory shall be above all earth;'[2] that of thee it is said, 'I will give thee nations for thine inheritance, and the limits of the earth for thy possession;'[3] and other innumerable testimonies which set forth the Catholic Church. If then thou know not these, thou hast no part in Me, thou canst not make thyself My heir. 'Go forth then in the footsteps of the flocks,' not in the fellowship of the flock; and feed thy goats, not as it was said to Peter, 'My sheep.'" To Peter it was said, "My sheep;" to schismatics it is said, "thy goats." In the one place "sheep," in the other "goats;" in the one place "Mine," in the other "thine." Recollect the right Hand and the left of our Judge; recollect where the goats shall stand, and where the sheep;[4] and it will be plain to you where is the right hand, where the left, the white and the black, the lightsome, and the darksome, the fair and the deformed, that which is about to receive the kingdom, and that which is to find everlasting punishment.

SERMON XCVII.

[CXLVII. BEN.]

ON THE SAME WORDS OF THE GOSPEL OF JOHN XXI. 15, "SIMON, *SON* OF JOHN, LOVEST THOU ME MORE THAN THESE?" ETC.

1. YE remember that the Apostle Peter, the first of all the Apostles, was disturbed at the Lord's Passion. Of his own self disturbed, but by Christ renewed. For he was first a bold presumer, and became afterwards a timid denier. He had promised that he would die for the Lord, when the Lord was first to die for him. When he said then, "I will be with Thee even unto death," and "I will lay down my life for Thee;" the Lord answered him, "Wilt thou lay down thy life for Me? Verily I say unto thee, Before the cock crow, thou shalt deny Me thrice."[5] They came to the hour; and because that Christ was God, and Peter a man, the Scripture was fulfilled, "I said in my panic, Every man is a liar."[6] And the Apostle says, "For God is true, and every man a liar."[7] Christ true, Peter a liar.

2. But what now? The Lord asketh him as ye heard when the Gospel was being read, and saith to him, "Simon, son of John, lovest thou Me more than these?" He answered and said, "Yea, Lord, Thou knowest that I love Thee."[8] And again the Lord asked this question, and a third time He asked it. And when he asserted in reply his love, He commended to him the flock. For each several time the Lord Jesus said to Peter, as he said, "I love thee;" "Feed My lambs," feed My "little sheep." In this one Peter was figured the unity of all pastors, of good pastors, that is, who know that they feed Christ's sheep for Christ, not for themselves. Was Peter at this time a liar, or did he answer untruly that he loved the Lord? He made this answer truly; for he made answer of that which he saw in his own heart. Whereas when he said, "I will lay down my life for Thee," he would presume on future strength. Now every man knows it may be what sort of man he is at the time when he is speaking; what he shall be on the morrow, who knows? So then Peter turned back his eyes to his own heart, when he was asked by the Lord, and in confidence made answer of what he saw there: "'Yea, Lord, Thou knowest that I love Thee.' What I tell Thee, Thou knowest; what I see here in my heart, Thou seest also." Nevertheless, he did not venture to say what the Lord had asked. For the Lord had not simply said, "Lovest Thou me?" but had added, "Lovest thou Me more than these?" that is, "Lovest thou Me more than these here do?" He was speaking of the other disciples; Peter could not say ought but, "I love Thee;" he did not venture to say, "more than these." He would not be a liar a second time. It were enough for him to bear testimony to his own heart; it was no duty of his to be judge of the heart of others.

---

[1] Cant. i. 8, Sept.　　[2] Ps. lvii. 11.　　[3] Ps. ii. 8.
[4] Matt. xxv. 33.

[5] Matt. xxvi. 34; Luke xxii. 33; John xiii. 37, 38.
[6] Ps. cxvi. 11.　　[7] Rom. iii. 4.
[8] John xxi. 15.

3. Peter then was true ; or rather was Christ true in Peter? Now when the Lord Jesus Christ would, He abandoned Peter, and Peter was found a man ; but when it so pleased the Lord Jesus Christ, He filled Peter, and Peter was found true. The Rock (Petra) made Peter true, for the Rock was Christ. And what did He announce to him, when he answered a third time that he loved Christ, and a third time the Lord commended His little sheep to Peter? He announced to him beforehand his suffering. "When thou wast young," saith He, "thou girdedst thyself, and wentest whither thou wouldest ; but when thou shalt be old, thou shalt stretch forth thine hands, and another shall gird thee, and carry thee whither thou wouldest not."[1] The Evangelist hath explained to us Christ's meaning. "This spake He," saith he, "signifying by what death he should glorify God ; "[2] that is that he was crucified for Christ ; for this is, "Thou shalt stretch forth thine hands." Where now is that denier? Then after this the Lord Christ said, "Follow Me." Not in the same sense as before, when he called the disciples. For then too He said, "Follow Me ; " but then to instruction, now to a crown. Was he not afraid to be put to death when he denied Christ? He was afraid to suffer that which Christ suffered. But now he must be afraid no more. For he saw Him now Alive in the Flesh, whom he had seen hanging on the Tree. By His Resurrection Christ took away the fear of death ; and forasmuch as He had taken away the fear of death, with good reason did He enquire of Peter's love. Fear had thrice denied, love thrice confessed. The [3] threefoldness of denial, the forsaking of the Truth ; the threefoldness of confession, the testimony of love.

---

[1] John xxi. 18. [2] John xxi. 19. [3] *Trinitas.*

INDEXES.

OUR LORD'S SERMON ON THE MOUNT.

INDEX OF SUBJECTS.

OUR LORD'S SERMON ON THE MOUNT.

INDEX OF TEXTS.

[Texts followed by a star are commented upon at length.]

THE HARMONY OF THE GOSPELS.

INDEX OF SUBJECTS.

THE HARMONY OF THE GOSPELS.

INDEX OF TEXTS.

SERMONS ON SELECTED LESSONS OF THE GOSPELS.

INDEX OF SUBJECTS.

Abraham, called only so, after change of name, because name related to earthly promises — not so name of Israel, 471; wondrous things promised to, and fulfilled, 500; and in us his seed, 500; believed without sight, 500.

Absolution, analogy between, and loosing grave-clothes of Lazarus, 311, 415; Church has power of, 325, 326.

Adoption, a sonship higher than that of nature, 255; frequently mentioned in Holy Scripture, 255, 256; the term of ancient use among the Jews, 256; "raising up seed to brother," 256; used by St. Paul to express the mystery of our adoption in Christ, 256.

Adversary, to be agreed with and delivered from, 442; not so Satan, 442, the Law our, so long as we our own, 443; must agree with, by obedience, and so made no longer adversary, 443.

Affliction, blessing to Christians, curse to the worldly as having no hope beyond world, 435.

Africa, Church not confined to, 526 sq. See *Donatists*.

Ages, the six, of the world, 477.

Alaric, 434.

Alms, with Lord's Prayer a remedy against daily sins after Baptism, 277; not to be given of usury and oppressive gains, but of our righteous labours, 450; giving and forgiving make double, 287; good works without, will not avail in Day of Judgment, 293; value given to, in Day of Judgment, marvellous, 293; should be given freely, as being all of us of one family, 297, 298; blind Tobias guides his son to attain inward light by, 384; to be given first in deeds of mercy to our own souls, 435, 436.

Analogies, earthly, partial from their very nature, 463; Holy Scripture justifies use of, in things relating to God, not to explain accurately, but to illustrate, 527.

Angels, holy celibates lead life of, 505.

Anger, the lust of vengeance, 286; if indulged in, becomes hatred and murder, 286, 357; great difference between, and hatred, 358; may have love in it, 357.

Antichrist cometh in his own name, 497.

Apostles, the "children" of the Jews who cast out devils, and are their judges, 318; witnesses of Christ, 318; reaped among the Jews, sowed among the Gentiles, 422; our Lord sowed and reaped in, as being in, 423; precepts given to, on receiving their commission, not to be understood carnally, 424; spiritual meaning of purse and shoes forbidden to, 424; of not saluting by the way enjoined on, 424, 425; saw The Head, and through Him believed The Body (the Church) not yet seen, 457; this the opposite to our state, 457; burning brands filled with fire from Holy Spirit, not to be put out by persecution, themselves set fire to world, 458; had need of pardon themselves, as sinners, 514; contention of, for pre-eminence, part of old leaven of law, 542.

Apostolic See, two Councils on Pelagian heresy sent to, and rescripts sent back from, 504.

Apsis, 335 (note).

Arians, say Holy Ghost a creature, 320; errors of, carnal, from desire of seeing things, 460, from pride, 483; irreverence of, 512.

Avarice. See *Covetousness*.

Babylon, carrying into, type of the passing of the Apostles to the Gentiles, 250.

Banquets, of the world, for the weakness of our bodies, 346; cf God, for the heart, not belly, 406.

Baptism, the laver of regeneration, 277; especial time of solemnizing, last Sabbath in Lent (Easter Eve), 284; first gift of Spirit in,

remission of sins, 324; all sin forgiven in, 278, 282, 286, 289, 417, 503; infirmity still remains after, 283, 503; the inward washing cleansing the soul through faith with alms, 435; the womb of the New Birth, 467; removes veil from Lord's Supper, 504; opens eyes of blind, 512; figured in the parable of the good Samaritan, 503; question whether he who hath sinned little or much, before, loves the more, 417; cleanses not through merits of minister, but by grace of Holy Spirit, 419, 420.

Barley, figure of the Law, as opposed to wheat (the Gospel), 498. See *Wheat*.

Beatitudes, the: each duty in, has its own reward, 268; the members of the soul, which all together make it in proportion, 268.

Bethesda, pool of, the Jews, five porches, the Law (five books of Moses), the troubling of, Christ's Passion, descending of one to, typical of unity, 475, 476, 477; going down to, of humility, 478.

Beware, how awful a word from our Lord, 437.

Birth, new, glory of, contrasted with misery of first, 469; natural, where different from, 470; where like that of Christ, 470.

Bishop, origin of name of, 406; the master of a family its, 406.

Blasphemy, unpardonable, refuge against, 331. See *Spirit, Holy*.

Blessed, the: commemoration of, 266; leads to thoughts of the course of blessedness, 266; a course of contest here, but reward hereafter, 266.

Blessedness, to touch with heart The Blessed One, 459 sq.

Blessings, temporal, to be sought with moderation, eternal, with longing and perseverance, 352.

Blind, the two, by way side, figures of Jews and Gentiles, 382.

Blindness, the punishment of those

SERMONS ON SELECTED LESSONS OF THE GOSPELS.

INDEX OF TEXTS.